"For once, with this intense, engrossing, and indeed brilliant work, we have a biography that justifies its length. Seldom have the history of an artist, the development of his imagination, the fevers of his soul been more grandly yet intimately described."
—*Interview*

"Richly satisfying . . . one is awestruck that so much creativity flowed from such self-destructive havoc."
—*Houston Chronicle*

"A huge page-turner . . . sensational."
—*Wilson Library Journal*

"The most thoroughly detailed biographical portrait ever of a U.S. artist. It's as imposing as a history book, as entertaining as a novel and as close as the reader may ever come to sharing the breadth—and sensing the madness—of artistic genius and the genesis of a masterpiece."
—*USA Today*

"Clearly the definitive work."   —*Financial Times* (London)

"The authors of this huge biography have probably come as close as anyone can to solving the enigmas of Jackson Pollock's psyche."
—*Boston Sunday Globe*

"In the hands of Naifeh and Smith, the world of twentieth-century American art comes sparklingly alive."
—*Charleston Evening Post*

"Controversial . . . a blockbuster biography with mass appeal."
—*Smart*

"Comprehensive, crammed with facts, details and anecdotes gathered over seven years of exhaustive research, including interviews with the painter Lee Krasner, who was Pollock's wife; the art critic Clement Greenberg; many of Pollock's friends, and surviving members of the Pollock family."
—*New York Times Book Review*

JACKSON

POLLOCK

An American Saga

BY STEVEN NAIFEH
AND GREGORY WHITE SMITH

HarperPerennial

A Division of HarperCollins*Publishers*

We would like to acknowledge
the special assistance of

Paul Brach
Giovanni Favretti
David Peretz
Carol Southern
S. Frederick Starr

This book was originally published in 1989 by Clarkson N. Potter, Inc. It is here reprinted by arrangement with Clarkson N. Potter, Inc.

First HarperPerennial edition published 1991.

LIBRARY OF CONGRESS CATALOG CARD NUMBER 90-55511

ISBN 0-06-097367-6

91 92 93 94 95 MPC 10 9 8 7 6 5 4 3 2 1

For our parents

William and Kathryn Smith
and
George and Marion Naifeh

CONTENTS

A color insert appears between pages 504 and 505.

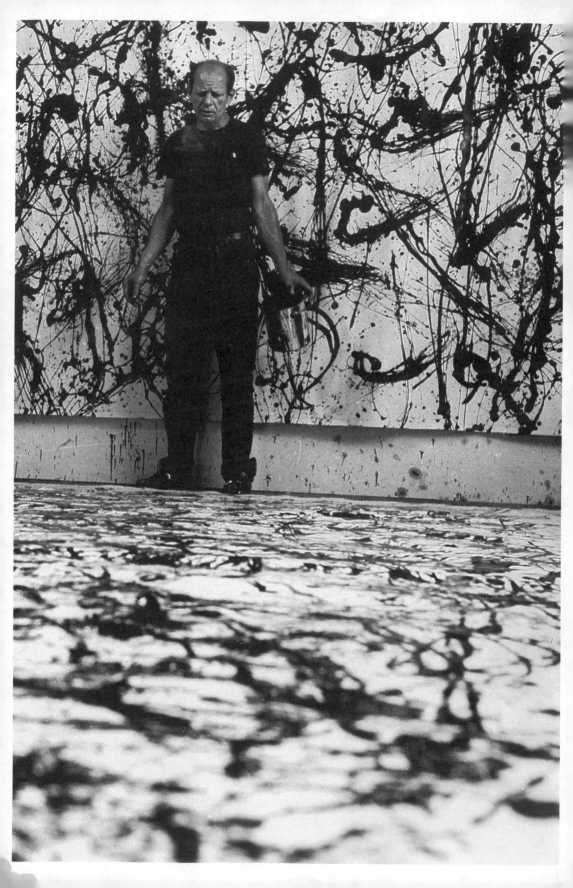

PROLOGUE

DEMONS

" I 'm going to kill myself."

Tony Smith recognized Jackson Pollock's whiskey voice. The late night call was not unusual for Jackson. Even talk of suicide had the air of ritual about it. Yet there was something in Pollock's voice that Smith hadn't heard before, a harder edge that alarmed him. With his ample Irish charm he tried to calm the distant voice, but Pollock was inconsolable. "Hold on," Smith finally said. "I'll be out." He put down the phone and drove off into the night in the middle of an early spring downpour. It would be hours before he could reach Pollock's house at the eastern end of Long Island—hours in which, knowing Jackson, anything could happen.

It was March 1952, only two years after Pollock's breakthrough 1949 show at the Betty Parsons Gallery gave the emerging avant-garde art world its first bright, bumptious triumph; only a little more than a year after the vast, luminous landscapes of *Autumn Rhythm* and *Lavender Mist* dazzled and confounded the critics; only five years after Clement Greenberg pronounced him "the most powerful painter in contemporary America"; only two and a half years after *Life* magazine thrust him into the spotlight of America's celebrity-mad postwar media, making him, virtually overnight, American art's first "star."

As the drive through the darkness and the downpour stretched into its fourth hour, Tony Smith must have wondered, as many others had, what strange, reverse alchemy could have transformed so much acclamation into such self-destructive agony.

Smith knew that Pollock was drinking again. After two enormously productive and relatively dry years—even in the driest seasons he kept cooking sherry buried in the backyard—Jackson had gone back to the bottle. He had always been, in Greenberg's phrase, "an alcoholic *in excelsis*," but drinking itself was never the problem. Even when it began with beer in the morning and ended with bourbon at night; even when its roots reached back to junior high school, or further, to an alcoholic father; even when his life dissolved, as it had several times over the last twenty years, into a series of drunken binges punctuated by hospitalization, drinking alone could not explain what was happening to Pollock. It couldn't explain the long, plaintive discussions about suicide with friends. "It's a way out," he told Roger Wilcox one day, to which Wilcox replied, "How the hell do you know? You may get yourself into worse trouble."

Drinking alone couldn't explain why, just a few months earlier, Pollock's new Cadillac convertible—bought as a boast of success—had skidded off a dry road and wrapped itself around a tree. Jackson walked away unhurt, but those who knew him, like Tony Smith, knew that he would try again—and not because of alcohol. There was something behind the drinking that was pushing at Jackson from within, tormenting him, even trying to kill him. Jackson Pollock had demons inside. Everyone could see that. But no one knew where they came from or what they wanted.

There were no streetlights along rural Fireplace Road, but Smith knew well to turn at the second drive on the right after passing Ashawagh Hall and Old Stone Highway. In the turbulent darkness, the house was invisible until his headlights swept the driveway, illuminating on the right the old farmhouse, ghostly pale behind a veil of rain, and on the left the barn that Jackson had converted into a studio. The storm had blown down the electrical lines; there were no lights on inside, just a faint, yellowish glow in the studio windows.

Whatever anxieties weighed on Smith during the five-hour trip, he could not have been prepared for the scene inside. Illuminated only by candlelight, Jackson stood in the middle of the studio clutching a knife and hurling obscenities. "I was afraid," Smith later admitted, "because Pollock, even in his last years, was very strong. He could have done me in with a swipe of the knife." Despite the liquor and the rage, Jackson looked surprisingly lean and fit. On the advice of a self-promoting "organic healer" on Park Avenue, he had been bathing in a solution of rock salt and drinking an emulsion of guano and ground beets in order to establish "a proper balance of gold and silver in his urine." This grueling, expensive regimen was supposed to cure his craving for alcohol, but it turned out to be just the latest in a series of failed attempts to quiet the clamorous voices in his head. According to Reuben Kadish, one of his closest friends, "He liked to put himself in the hands of people that he thought could control his life and straighten it out for him."

But they never could. The studio reeked of liquor.

Jackson's leathery face was deeply creased across the forehead and around the mouth. A soft fuzz covered the prominent crown of his head, where, years before, there had been a bumper crop of thick blond hair. Even without it, he was a handsome man—never more so than on the rare occasions when he smiled and showed his dimples. Like many others in the art world, women and men, Smith felt a physical attraction to Pollock. Part of that attraction, however, was the knowledge that beneath the boyish dimples and the tragi-comic drunken antics lurked this towering, inexplicable rage.

In the house, Pollock's wife, Lee Krasner, cowered behind the bed. Since her childhood in Brooklyn, Lee had been terrified by storms of all kinds. She had spent the last seven hours sitting in darkness and fear as her husband stormed through the house, brandishing the knife—at himself, at her—roaring curses at the world. She had done what she always did when Jackson drank too much and the rage came out: tried to become invisible; slipped away to a distant corner and waited for the storm to pass. She knew better than to confront him. Eventually, he would fall down from exhaustion or from drink or both and she would come to him, cradle his head as she had seen his mother do, and shoulder his weight to bed.

This time, however, the storm showed no sign of abating.

Tony Smith knew both Jackson Pollocks: the shy, sober one, given to depre-cating himself, saying in a soft voice, "I can't do anything but paint" or "the pictures just come to me"; and the drunken one, the one Clement Greenberg said "behaved like a six-year-old, demanding to be the center of attention." Smith had often gone drinking with Pollock and almost as often seen him drunk—playful drunk, dangerous drunk, depressed drunk. But even he, unlike Lee, had never seen this rage.

"What the fuck are you doing here?" Jackson roared.

The demons demanded concealment. As a teenager, Pollock had written his brothers, "People have always frightened and bored me consequently I have been within my own shell." At parties, he would stare wordlessly into his drink, feeling "stripped of his skin," he said, by the unreturned glances of those around him. A friend described him as a "pained, painful person," who, when he did speak, spaced his words out like poles along a desert road, with "awk-ward, long silences" strung between them. According to Roger Wilcox, Jackson needed to work up his courage with two or three beers before he could even set foot in a bar.

At other times, Pollock hid behind a facade of barroom bluster and macho posturing. By the age of thirty, he had perfected the "ugly-touch, Hemingway" persona out of which legends later grew: drinking, risk-taking, fast driving, foul talking, quick hitting, easy fucking, and no apologies. But always underneath there was a shy, sensitive boy yearning to be liked: a boy who, despite having been raised in a family of men, had turned first to his mother, Stella, for support and a sense of identity; a boy who preferred the company of neighborhood girls and their games of "house"; a boy estranged from his father, unable to pass his brothers' tests of manhood, and traumatized throughout his life by anxiety and dread over his own ambiguous sexual urges.

Pollock's efforts at concealment met with uncanny success. In an effort so thorough that it seems almost consciously designed to frustrate later chroni-clers, he left no journals, only a score of letters and a scattering of postcards and business-related notes. He veiled his thoughts and emotions not only from posterity but also from the numerous analysts and doctors who attempted to pry their way into his private world. On those rare occasions when he tried to make contact, the telephone, with its anonymity and evanescence, proved the perfect confessional. His late night phone calls, like the one to Smith, were legendary. As he sat with his head bowed and his broad shoulders hunched over the phone as if to climb inside it, his low voice would open out on great green stretches of conversation.

He was capable of sweetness and generosity as well as rage and insularity. In the midst of persistent—although often overstated—poverty, he lent other artists money, he helped friends remodel their houses, painted a bike for one neighbor's child, taught another to use a bow and arrow. He could defuse barroom brawls with his notoriously beguiling smile or the "renowned twinkle in his eye," with a few disarming words or a well-aimed apology.

Like his rage, however, his sweetness was always followed by regret, a feeling that he had given away too much, and he would draw back into the hard-shelled, cowboy persona that was Jackson Pollock to the world. His life was a give and take, giving a small piece of himself—often inadvertently—then desperately trying to reclaim it—or obliterate it. Give and take. The world demanded that he give; the demons demanded that he take back. In his art, he concealed his images within layers of paint, systematically weaving them into an impenetrable web of lines and dribbles, spills and drips. Show and conceal; give and take. He veiled his art just as he veiled his life, to protect himself from the world without and the terrors within.

Against the incitement of the storm, Smith tried to calm his friend. He knew better than to refer directly to Jackson's drinking. Nothing was more likely to set him off again than an effort to take away the bottle or suggest that he had had enough. Besides, he would just get in the car and race down the slick, dark highway looking for more. Desperately, Tony filled the air with art talk, probably about Pollock's recent falling-out with Betty Parsons, at whose gallery the two men had become friends and over whose eccentricities they had shared more than a few laughs. Gradually, the rage began to subside. At some point, Jackson put down the knife and took up a cigarette and a bottle of bourbon.

The studio was cold and dark, a palpable reflection of Pollock's creative state. The yellow light of the candelabrum spread across the rows of paintings that lined the walls: small black-and-white ones recently returned from Sidney Janis in front; huge "classic" ones like *Autumn Rhythm* and *Number 32* looming in back, their monumental calligraphy stark in the dim light. Pollock held the candelabrum aloft and walked to the kerosene stove in the corner. The grim poetry of Jackson moving unsteadily through the dark, holding the light in front of him, surrounded by the huge apparitions of his paintings could not have escaped the poet in Tony Smith. When Jackson lit the stove and flames began to shoot from the flue and lick the ceiling beams, the vision turned demonic. "For Chrissakes, Jackson, put it out," Smith blurted. Obediently, Jackson picked up the iron lid with a pair of pliers and dropped it over the fire. A few minutes later, he relit it.

On the floor lay a painting that Jackson had been working on recently, a network of delicate circles painted with a light, tentative brush—unlike anything he had done before. Seeing it, Smith thought of something George Grosz had told him once: "When a painter works in circles . . . he is near madness." Look at van Gogh, he had said.

To get Pollock "out of himself," Smith suggested that they do a painting together. Between swigs of bourbon, the two men unwrapped a fresh roll of Belgian linen and unfurled it across the studio's cement floor. Jackson searched through a box of paint for the right color to begin. The first tube he pulled out was cadmium red; so was the second; and the third. After four or five more tries, he cried out in exasperation, "I can't start a painting with cadmium red!" and threw the tubes down. Gently, Smith volunteered to begin. He reached into the box and pulled out a tube of cadmium orange. "Well, I come from Orange, New Jersey," he joked. He squeezed a long line of orange at the edge of the canvas, then laid a piece of waxed paper over the line and walked on it. Where he stepped, the paint oozed out, forming a trail of uneven blotches.

"So that's the way you do it," Jackson sneered. "Here's how I do it." In a sudden, sweeping motion, he grabbed a big bucket of black Duco in his paw-like hands and began to pour it on the canvas. For just an instant, he could have been the "old" Jackson Pollock, the Jackson Pollock who, four years before, had stunned the world with his inexplicable skeins of paint; the Jackson Pollock whose image would be indelibly etched in the public consciousness for decades after his death: a brooding, slope-shouldered figure in a black T-shirt, bent over a huge canvas, flinging lariats of paint from a stick or dribbling them from a stiff brush, stepping lightly into the middle of the canvas, his arm describing circles in the air, moving laterally, rhythmically, throwing tight loops of glistening paint in lace-like lines across the expanse of white, then stepping back to look, wholly focused, as the lines continued to unwind out of his unconscious, into his eyes, and finally, in another burst, onto the canvas. "Forget the hand," Barnett Newman said of Pollock at work. "It's the mind—not brain, but *mind*—soul, concentration, gut. I've seen him come out of his studio like a wet rag." For just a moment, through the alcoholic haze, Smith must have glimpsed the apparition of that Jackson Pollock moving among his candlelit creations.

The demons demanded recognition. For Pollock, success was more than a goal, it was a visceral necessity. Born the youngest in a family of five boys, all vying ferociously for scraps of attention from a distant father and a granite-faced mother, Jackson learned early the hard art of breaking through. Neighbors remember him as a "cry-baby" and a "mama's boy," always running to his mother to bewail some imagined abuse. Behind a facade of robustness, as a child and even as an adult, he was sickly and accident-prone. As an adolescent, he learned to test his mother's tolerance with alcohol and his father's with failure. During the long years of anonymity in Depression-era New York when he was cleaning floors or silk-screening neckties, he would wander the streets at night in a drunken stupor, shouting at passersby, "I'll show them someday." Even the untouchable Picasso was the object of his vaulting envy. "That fucking Picasso," he would fume. "He's done everything."

In his harrowing exploits of drunkenness—assaulting policemen, driving insanely, destroying property, terrorizing parties, peeing in public (the list is endless)—Pollock was only testing. One friend likened him to "Peck's bad boy, who later apologizes and says 'I didn't mean to do it.' Jackson wanted you to suffer forgiveness." His frequent drinking binges almost always ended the same way: someone—first his brothers, then Lee—would come to the bar where he had passed out or pick him up out of the gutter and carry him home. Even the fights he provoked were exercises in forgiveness. "He didn't want to really hurt anybody," remembers Herman Cherry.* "He'd start a fight and then try to get out of it. It's like insulting somebody, then going up and kissing them and saying, 'Oh, I didn't mean it.' "

No one in Jackson's life was tested more searchingly or suffered more forgiveness than Lee Krasner. From the beginning of their relationship in 1941, the boundaries of tolerance were redrawn almost daily. Drinking, of course, was the fundamental, continuing provocation: what he said when he was drunk, what he did, what he threatened to do. At times—when he turned his phonograph up full blast in the middle of the night or upended the table at a dinner party—tolerance was relatively easy. At other times, when he drove ninety miles an hour down rural Fireplace Road or flaunted his mistress in front of her, it wasn't easy at all.

As it mixed with Smith's blotches of orange, Pollock's black Duco turned a "bilious green." Tony muttered, "It looks like vomit," but to keep Jackson's mind off his problems he pressed ahead, grabbing a brush and another color and "laying it on" with calculated abandon. Jackson joined in and they "splashed and drooled" paint until the luminous expanse of Belgian linen was covered with a half-inch of the bilious green. As he often did, Jackson applied the paint with basting syringes made of thin glass with a rubber bulb at one end. When a syringe clogged, he would fling it at the canvas in disgust and fill another with paint. When that one clogged, another. Each time he threw a syringe down, it shattered against the concrete floor. He went through a dozen syringes until the paint surface around him glinted with shivers of glass. Defiantly, he took off his shoes and waded through the dark, sparkling slime in

---

* Quotes framed in the present tense (e.g., he says, she recalls) are taken from the authors' interviews. All other quotations, with a few exceptions, are from printed sources cited in the notes.

his bare feet, daring Smith to follow. Numbed by the cold and the bourbon, Smith waded in behind him.

Only in his art could Pollock find the concealment, the recognition, and the forgiveness he craved. Before the canvas, his demons were transformed into muses, and the result was an art that, like its creator, tested the bounds of tolerance. The final target of Jackson's hunger for attention was the world, and his art was the provocation. "Abstract painting is abstract," he said. "It confronts you." His paintings "caused a kind of havoc," wrote the *New York Times* of the drip paintings in the 1950 Venice Biennale. Like a well-placed insult in a crowded bar, they touched off "violent arguments." "Compared to Pollock," marveled one critic, "Picasso . . . becomes a quiet conformist, a painter of the past."

Jackson Pollock found himself on the leading edge of the Abstract Expressionist movement for reasons that had little or nothing to do with abstraction or expressionism or art itself. He was drawn to that position by the same forces that had been directing his art from the beginning. As a child, he had shown no inclination toward drawing or painting and, more pointedly, no proficiency. His decision to become an artist was born less out of artistic inspiration than out of the compulsion to compete with his brothers and to test his parents' love. For the rest of his artistic career, he piled outrage on outrage, searching for new, ever more unpalatable risks. The great successes of 1949 and 1950, which another artist might have taken as definitive approval, Jackson saw as only an invitation to the next step. "He was always in transition," said Betty Parsons. "His vibrations, to me, were always those of a driven creature. There was futility at the end of all his rainbows."

Like the drunken binges that grew wilder and more destructive, the car rides that grew faster and more reckless, the rages that grew sharper and more abusive, Jackson's art reached always for new outrages, new tests, all of them built on the original outrage of which Jackson was always preciously aware: that he was *an artist who could not draw*—at least not the way artists were supposed to draw. He would eventually force the world, just as he had forced his mother, his brothers, and finally Lee, to give him the attention he craved; to suffer forgiveness for his outrages; not just to tolerate him, but to love him, or at least his art; to accept him, and finally to concede that he was a great artist.

By morning, Tony Smith had returned to the house to clean off and sober up. Lee was waiting to help. "We spent a long time getting glass out of my feet," Smith recalled. Together they carried Jackson, who had passed out in the studio, back to the house. In the kitchen, while Jackson slept fitfully in a chair, Lee bathed his feet. The painting that the two men had begun lay on the studio floor, stiff with wet paint and broken glass. Over the next six months,

Jackson would return to it again and again, scraping away the bilious green, applying new layers of yellow, red, light blue, aluminum, and finally—using a long piece of two-by-four—eight deep blue vertical "poles."

Ultimately, painting was the only way Jackson Pollock could appease the demons that tormented him. In the veil of paint, he could conceal himself, and in the celebrity that followed, satisfy his hunger for attention; he could best his brothers and command his parents' love. In the end, painting was a way to test the world, to probe its heart, and to make it suffer forgiveness.

Twenty years after Tony Smith's visit, sixteen years after Pollock's death, the same painting—Jackson titled it *Blue Poles*—was sold to the government of Australia for two million dollars. No American painting had ever sold for more, and in the entire history of Western art, only works by Rembrandt, Velázquez, and Leonardo da Vinci had commanded more "respect" in the marketplace. Even Picasso, who had "done everything," had never done better than one million.

The world had forgiven Jackson Pollock—even if it didn't yet know what for.

Part One

THE WEST

I

STRONG-MINDED WOMEN

One image dominated Jackson Pollock's imagination. Like all five Pollock brothers, he could close his eyes and see a figure emerging from the shadow of a porch into the bright Phoenix sun: her thick, pale ankles; her black dress; her stout frame, round as a tree trunk; her abundant bosom; her white gloves and intricate lace collar; her huge, fair-skinned face obscured by a black veil from the brim of her hat to the right angle of her jaw; her light brown hair coiled and pinned at the nape of her neck. "My earliest impression of my mother," says Charles Pollock, reaching back almost eighty years, "is of a woman dressed in the most elegant fashion, climbing into a four-wheel buggy, grabbing the reins, and going off to town behind two very proud horses. It took some strength to keep those horses from running away or tipping the buggy over, but Mother always had control."

For all her power over him, Jackson Pollock knew surprisingly little about his mother, Stella. In a 1944 interview, he described her ancestors as "Scotch and Irish," ignoring or forgetting the strong current of German blood that ran in her veins. He claimed she came from pioneer stock, savoring, undoubtedly, the image of his forebears playing their small roles in the great drama of westward expansion, of pioneering men and devoted women suffering the hardships of an untamed continent.

In fact, for three generations in Stella's family, it was the women who pioneered and the devoted men who suffered.

Godfrey Augustus Speck set this improbable pattern when he stepped off a boat in Baltimore harbor in 1774—by mistake. Hardly the energetic, fortune-seeking immigrant of family legends, Speck had never entertained the notion of traveling to America. He was a simple twenty-year-old journeyman in Dresden, Saxony, when a gang of thugs, "recruiting" for the Hessian king, shang-haied him to America to help George III put down the rebellion in the United Colonies.

By 1779 Speck had met and married a sixteen-year-old Virginia girl named

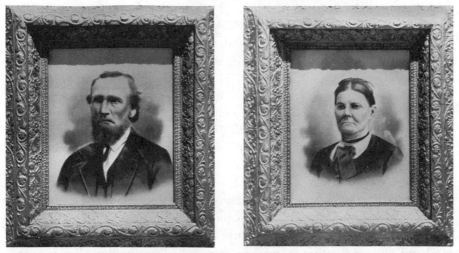

Archibald and Eliza Jane Speck, Jackson Pollock's great-grandparents

Sarah Townsend. Hers is the first appearance of a woman in the recorded history of the Speck family, and an auspicious debut it was. After bearing four children in eight years, she loaded the family possessions into a handcart and dragged her unwilling husband over a hundred miles of rough roads to more promising land in the south of Maryland. By 1800, she had borne four more children and moved her family twice more—first to Virginia, then across the Appalachians into the Ohio Territory. There, in what might have been an effort to curb his wife's wanderlust, Godfrey Augustus built her a stone farmhouse near Freeport.

Following in the family tradition, Sarah Speck's second child, Samuel, attached himself to Jane Leach, another raw-willed woman with little tolerance for domesticity or motherhood, although a talented "weaver of woolens and carpets." Ignoring her husband's wishes and, presumably, his advances, and defying the hard odds of frontier mortality, she quit childbearing after her fourth child, at the age of twenty-nine, and devoted herself exclusively to sabotaging her only daughter, Sarah. Forbidden by her mother to marry, Sarah Speck—"a beautiful and promising young lady"—died a spinster at the age of eighty-six.

In 1837, Jane Leach Speck's oldest son, Archibald, married Eliza Jane Boyd, a young Irish girl whose father, William Boyd, had mastered the linen loom as an apprentice in southern Ireland before coming to America. Another of his daughters, Belle, earned a local reputation for her fine linen and embroidery work, and a granddaughter, Lettie, became an accomplished watercolorist. If one searches Jackson Pollock's ancestry for the first signs of creativity, they are here among the Boyds of Ireland. Eliza Jane bore four children before concluding, on the basis of too little land and too many children, that she could never fulfill her ambitions in Ohio; that, once again, it was time to move on.

She wasn't alone. In the 1840s and 1850s, thousands of settlers in the Ohio

Valley came to the same conclusion and began to move farther west, first in a trickle, then in a deluge. Most, like the Specks, were second- and third-generation pioneers whose parents or grandparents had struck out from the East Coast, filled the land with a surfeit of sons, and now were pushing the next generation deeper into the continent. They joined the continuing flow of foreign-born immigrants escaping famine in Ireland and military conscription or political persecution in Germany, as well as those fleeing debts of one sort or another by "declaring bankruptcy with their feet."

Archibald and Eliza Jane, Jackson Pollock's great-grandparents, set out for the new promised land in 1844. Like most of the settlers on the road to Cincinnati, they were bound for the Black Hawk Purchase, otherwise known as the Iowa Territory. (No one could agree on the meaning of the name. Some said it was Sioux for "he who paints pictures," but most preferred the more inspiring translation, "the beautiful land.") Enticing accounts of the rich farmland and clement weather in the new territory had appeared in Ohio papers as early as 1835, soon after the capture of the last Indian leaders at the Black Axe River in southern Wisconsin. "It may be represented as one grand rolling prairie," read one such account, widely reprinted by railroads, banks, and seed companies. "For richness of soil; for beauty of appearance; and for pleasantness of climate, it surpasses any portion of the United States." Between 1833 and 1850, some 200,000 settlers responded to the glowing reports and the promise of land for themselves and their children.

By Mississippi steamer, the trip from Cincinnati to Fort Madison at the southeastern tip of the territory could take as little as two weeks with good connections, compared to four or five months for the overland route. From Fort Madison, it was a relatively short ten-mile wagon ride to the new town of West Point, where, in all likelihood, either Archibald or Eliza Jane had relatives waiting to help them get started. There they bought some land for $200 a quarter-section, or about $1.25 an acre, and set about carving a farm out of the wilderness.

Despite the richness of the land, it wasn't an easy task. For millions of years, nature had been generous to Iowa, depositing on its lumpy morainal substructure more than a quarter of all the top-grade soil on the continent. But separating the settler from it was a vast sea of "blue stem," a thick covering of prairie grass, "higher than a horse's back," knotted into a thousand-year-old mat of roots reaching a foot or more into the black soil. When farmers like Archibald Speck tried to turn a furrow with the small European hand plows they had used back in Ohio, they discovered that it was rich soil, all right—some of the richest, blackest loam in the world—but the richness was buried under lifetimes of hardship and hard work, of terrible sacrifice for the benefit of the next generation. Those who were ambitious only for themselves quickly moved on from Iowa, usually farther west. For those who remained, family and land became as tightly intertwined as prairie grass and prairie soil.

Archibald Speck was lucky to get even one corner of his land planted in his

first Iowa spring. Even if there had been time, he could scarcely afford the
$3.00 or more per acre charged by the local prairie breaker to bring in his team
of eight oxen and his huge plow wagon with its iron-covered moldboard and
hard steel share to cut a two-foot-wide furrow in the prairie mat. And clearing
the land was only the beginning. Hardly a day passed without a threat of some
kind. Except for occasional wild snowstorms that could "freeze chickens to
their roosts," the weather was generous to farmers during the middle decades
of the nineteenth century, but recurring waves of rust, scab, and orchard blight,
as well as plagues of grasshoppers, wildly fluctuating grain prices, and even
occasional Indian raids, kept farmers like Archibald Speck perpetually on the
edge of financial and emotional ruin.

It would have been a struggle even for a hard, adventurous man, but Archibald Speck was neither. His dreams, like those of many frontier men, were
incongruously modest for such a lavishly fertile land: "to get land, to better his
own and his children's condition, and to be left alone in the process." The
womenfolk had a scornful term—"do-less"—for men like Archibald Speck,
men with dreams but without the blind determination and resourcefulness in
adversity that the frontier demanded.

Among the Specks, as among many Iowa families, it was the women who
made the dreams come true. It was the women, strong-willed and resourceful,
shepherding their men through the hardships of frontier life, who were celebrated in local lore and family legends. Typical was the oft-told tale of a young
couple whose wagon came unhitched as they were fording a river. The horses
bolted and the wagon began to roll back into the deep, swift water. While the
husband sat on the sinking wagon seat lamely yelling "Whoa," the wife
grabbed the reins from his hands, jumped down into the mud, and wrestled
the frightened horses to shore. Another popular story told of a grandmother
who saved the family's precious milk cow from choking to death by reaching
deep into its throat and pulling out a wad of hay—while the men of the family
stood by "wringing their hands." Men whose wives died on the trek west were
notoriously disconsolate and "lost" for years; some never recovered. Women
whose husbands died, on the other hand, would routinely repair to the nearest
town or relative, remarry, and press on.

In August 1861, Barclay Cappoc of Springdale, Iowa, accompanied John
Brown on his raid at Harpers Ferry and became Iowa's first casualty of the
Civil War. (By the time the darkness passed, five years later, some 70,000 Iowa
men had died, most of them from disease. Unlike troops drawn from the East
Coast who fought through the fields and woods of Georgia and Virginia, prairie
soldiers fought and died in the malarial swamps of the lower Mississippi valley.)
News of the war soon reached Fairfield, Iowa, where the Specks had moved
after the birth of their fifth child, Cordelia Jane—known to everyone as Jennie
—in 1848. Samuel Speck, their oldest son, was among the first of the town's
young men to join the ragtag corps of volunteers who drilled on the road at

night while the small boys played fife and drums. On July 4, the men planted a "Liberty Pole" in the center of town while the women sewed a giant flag and made picnic lunches.

In the Speck household, the festive mood that greeted "the War of Rebellion" was short-lived. Jennie's older sister, Mary, died three days after the holiday celebration; brother Samuel soon marched off, never to return; another sister, Elizabeth, died in November at the age of seven. The quick succession of tragedies had a profound effect on Jennie Speck. For the rest of her life, relatives and friends would describe her as if she were two people: the warm, risible, slightly irreverent, and unpredictable girl from before the war and the measured, humorless, severe woman from afterward.

It was the severe side of Jennie Speck that found its natural expression in a lifelong "union" with the Presbyterian church. Even among their God-fearing Iowa neighbors, the Presbyterians were considered "stricter than the Methodists or even the Christians," and Jennie was strict even by Presbyterian standards, chastising young girls for playing cards on the "almost Sabbath" (Saturday night), and forbidding boys who had worked hard all week to play baseball on Sunday. Children were allowed to sing, but only "p'sams"; even hymns were too worldly. She would tolerate no drinking or swearing in her presence, and dancing she considered "the last straw."

Work was the only sufficiently godly recreation, and Jennie was proud of her handiwork; often boasting to her daughters about the "40 yards of blankets [and] 107 yards of carpet" she had woven by the time she was sixteen, as if the sheer quantity of effort were the best measure of a soul's worth. One chronicle from the period describes a group of Iowa women sitting around quilting and "talking about what they considered happiness to be." The answer, they all agreed, was "Something to do . . . even if [it was] only winding and unwinding a ball of yarn." Jennie Speck learned early that a woman should never be idle, that a trip to town was an hour of crocheting, an evening was a shirt, a Sunday was a tablecloth, a snowstorm was a quilt. "Busy hands," she would say, are the Lord's workshop.

The Civil War opened up vast new fields of opportunity to Iowa's busy, strong-minded women. Bereft of college-age men, the University of Iowa began to admit women, becoming the first coeducational state university in the country. For the first time, women were hired as elementary school teachers, store clerks, government workers, and even farmhands to replace men gone to war. Newspapers urged women to come out of the home to aid the war effort. "Any woman who neglects all other duties, and devotes herself to the avocations of warlike times is a heroine forthwith," declared one editorial. Jennie Speck even heard stories in school about older girls who disguised themselves as boys and enlisted in the infantry.

Theodore Tilton, a popular reform speaker from New York who lectured after the war in towns throughout Iowa, including Fairfield, was struck by the "spirit of equality" that animated Iowa men and women. In 1866, he predicted that "Iowa would be the first state in the Union to achieve the political equality of the sexes." With that objective in mind, suffragist speakers fanned out across the state, taking the message to every town, no matter how small. "Women were classed with paupers, criminals, and idiots in being denied the right of property and suffrage," they told their large, predominantly female audiences, and they deserved a better fate. As a woman who had carried the burden of her family since the death of her sistiers, Jennie Speck must have shared their outrage. She might even have joined in the wave of vocal protests that led, in 1873, to passage by the Iowa legislature of the first comprehensive women's rights bill in the country. (The bill was conspicuously silent on the issue of women's suffrage, however. That fight would take another fifty years.)

In October of 1873, only a few months after passage of the reform bill that greatly expanded the rights of married women, Jennie Speck married John Robinson McClure.

The Specks and the McClures had lived in neighboring counties in south-western Ohio for at least a generation before coming to Iowa. The two families had made the trip within five years of each other, following exactly the same river route. At that point, however, although they continued to live less than fifty miles apart, their lives took very different courses.

On the boat trip from Ohio in 1850, John Robinson's father, McKee Mc-Clure, contracted cholera (he was "exposed to cholery on the rivery," Jennie later wrote). By the time the boat arrived at Burlington, he was gravely ill and the rough twenty-five-mile wagon ride to the farm of his uncle, James Mc-Clure, finished him. With her two-year-old son, John, the young widow, Ann Reid McClure, lived for a while with relatives until her plight attracted the attention of a brother-in-law, James R. Willson. In 1854, Willson dispatched his eldest unmarried brother, Adam, age thirty-seven, to rescue the young mother from widowhood.

John McClure never took his new father's name and, as far as can be told, never really felt a part of the large family of twelve that Ann McClure bore for him. By the time he was eighteen, John had moved to Sharon, where he was probably working on his uncle James's farm when he met Jennie Speck.

A childhood of abandonment had left John McClure withdrawn and dis-trustful. In later life, neighbors who knew him would refer to the "McClure Trait"—the pained reticence, the slowness of speech, the stony reserve—that he passed on to most of his children. In a photograph taken when he was an old man, his face is a mask, but his eyes betray the lifelong burdens of sweet-ness and sensitivity. In the same picture, Jennie sits in her high white collar, teeth clenched, her eyes blank walls of rectitude and determination.

Soon after his wedding in October of 1873, John McClure took his new wife farther west, across the Des Moines River at Ottumwa and into the more fertile hills of south central Iowa. On a grassy knoll just a few miles north of the little town of Mount Ayr in Ringgold County, he built a log house and began a

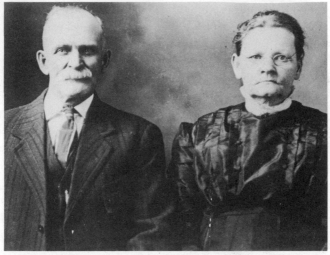

John and Jennie McClure, Jackson's maternal grandparents

family. On May 20, 1875, Jennie McClure bore her first child, a girl, and named her Stella.

As a first child on a small frontier farm, a son would have been more welcome, certainly, but there was plenty of work to keep a girl's hands busy. At the age of three, Stella was initiated in the restless, numbing routine of a frontier woman's life: build a fire, thaw the pump, fix breakfast, refill the lamps, empty the bedside "thundermugs" in winter; purge the flies in summer. There was always mending to be done and knitting. Jennie took in sewing to earn extra money for sugar or cloth, but it was always the last thing done, usually late at night. Monday was for washing; Tuesday, ironing; Wednesday, mending; Thursday, shopping; Friday, baking; Saturday, cleaning; Sunday, church-going and Bible-reading. Jennie McClure strictly enforced the rule of rest on Sunday; even Sunday supper was prepared the day before. "They wouldn't even hardly go out the door on Sundays," a neighbor recalls.

For a farm woman, cooking was the highest art, and from an early age, Stella proved extraordinarily talented. At six, she could make peach, plum, and grape butter; watermelon molasses; pumpkin leather (cooked, dried pumpkin meat); and hominy. When her father butchered a hog or steer in preparation for the long winter, she would fry the meat down, pack it in big stone jars, and cover it with lard. (The odor lingered for days.) She dried corn and packed it in salt; canned fruits; stored pumpkins, squash, apples, potatoes, cabbage, beets, and turnips in the root cellar, covered with dirt and straw. The first pie in spring was always dried apple and peach.

When two more daughters, Anna Myrtle and Mary Elizabeth, were born, five-year-old Stella tended them while Jennie helped with the farm work. "She had to be quite a strong individual," says a granddaughter who lived with Stella for fourteen years. "She took a lot of responsibility very early in terms of raising

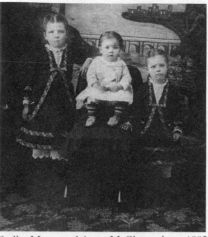

Stella, Mary, and Anna McClure, about 1885

the kids." By 1885, Stella was a short, sturdy ten-year-old strong enough to work shoulder to shoulder with her father in the fields and barnyard. Perhaps it was the added responsibility of playing son to her quiet, melancholy father that gave her the premature self-confidence and steely determination friends later marveled at. As Anna grew into the quiet, thoughtful one, and Mary into the girlish effervescent one, Stella was already developing the stone face, the emotional reserve, and the implacable will that would steady her, and confound those around her, through the crises ahead.

Partly, of course, it was just the Presbyterian way. Jennie McClure had joined the Mount Ayr United Presbyterian Church immediately upon arriving in 1874 and raised her children in the straight and narrow. The Presbyterians believed there was only one road to salvation and they were on it. "They didn't think you could get to heaven by short cut," says an old resident of Ringgold County. "If you weren't immersed you were hell-bound."

The Presbyterians were known for being "hardshelled"—secure in the rightness of their routing, impervious to the vagaries of fate. Whether windfall or catastrophe, good harvest or blight, they accepted it without unseemly rejoicing or lamenting, because it didn't alter the fundamental reality of salvation. To respond to events in daily life, to laugh or cry, was to legitimize their claim on happiness, when good Presbyterians knew that salvation was the only genuine source of happiness, and that salvation could be secured only through the church: reciting catechisms, singing psalms, reading the Bible, resting on Sundays, and avoiding the dark constellation of prohibitions—dancing, drinking, card-playing—many of which were, in themselves, temptations to false happiness or false grief.

Stella's hard shell was put to the test early.

Although two sons, Samuel Cameron and David Leslie, were finally born in 1883 and 1885, they came too late to prevent their father's farm from failing. Not that a boy, or even several, would have made the difference between

success and failure on John McClure's eighty acres. Not only had he started
with too little land, he had probably started too late. Most of the best land in
Ringgold County had been bought up by 1870, four years before his arrival.
What was left were odd lots, rocky patches, and timbered and hilly parcels that
no one had bothered to break. Locals called them "heartbreak deals." For
John McClure, the farm was a toehold at best, and it never developed into
anything better.

In his first full season of farming, 1875, a grasshopper plague devoured his
fields of corn and oats. The next year, his hogs died in a wave of hog cholera
that swept through the county. He bought more hogs with the slim profits from
the year's harvest, but the cholera returned the following summer and the hogs
died again. There was plenty of corn the next two years, 1878 and 1879, but
too much corn meant low prices. At tens cents a bushel, he could barely make
the mortgage payments. Because the land was gratuitously bountiful, there was
always food on the table. But in 1880, months of storms and perpetual rain
flooded the fields and washed the crops into the swollen streams. Inflated by
demand from the railroad crews who were laying track in the county, the price
of corn shot up to fifty cents a bushel, but John McClure had no corn to sell.
In the spring of 1881, after the planting, the rain returned and he watched his
crops rot in the fields. After the flood of May 1881, he planted another crop,
but this time there was no rain. For six months, there was no rain and his corn
turned brown. Another year went by and John McClure had nothing to take to
market except a few melons and vegetables. In the spring of 1882, corn was
eighty cents a bushel.

That fall, to make ends meet, he took a job as a mason, bricklayer, and
plasterer in the tiny town of Tingley, eight miles north, where the coming of
the Humeston and Shenandoah Railroad had sparked a construction boom.
For the next five years, he laid sidewalks and foundations in Tingley while
clinging to his eighty acres near Mount Ayr, trying, against continuing waves
of blight, drought, rot, and grasshoppers, to keep the farm alive. Jennie made
it known that she would prefer life in town, but it was the hour-long wagon
rides into work, longer and more treacherous in winter, that finally brought the
McClure family, now grown to eight, to a farm one mile west of Tingley. For
Stella, age twelve, the move would offer a first taste of something new and
better.

Due to Thomas Jefferson's obsession with classical symmetry and order,
Tingley township is easy to locate. In 1783, Jefferson had proposed dividing
the trans-Appalachian lands into "hundreds," parcels consisting of ten units,
each ten miles square. The Land Ordinance of 1785 opted instead for town-
ships six miles on a side, sixteen to a county. By 1855 the land had been
surveyed and the section corners fastidiously marked with stones, posts, pits, or
mounds. Each township was further divided into nine school districts, each
district two miles on a side, and finally into mile-square "sections," each of

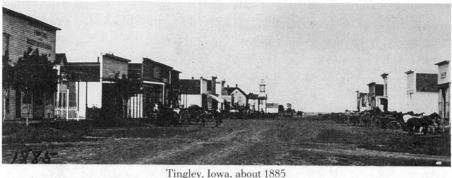

Tingley, Iowa, about 1885

them numbered and outlined by dirt roads. The result was a grid of numbing regularity superimposed on the prairie's casual roll. On a map of Iowa, Ringgold County is the fourth county from the left on the bottom row; in Ringgold County, Tingley township is second from the right on the top row; and the town of Tingley is in school district number 5—middle row center—in sections 16 and 21.

When John McClure and his family moved nearby—to section 18—in 1887, Tingley was two neat rows of low frame buildings on either side of a wide dirt road. The town's short roster of buildings and businesses spoke economically of its concerns: three churches, three general stores, two lumberyards, and one each of grocery store, hardware store, drugstore, meat market, law office, hotel, farm implement store, blacksmith shop, furniture store, paint shop, and livery stable. There were only four hundred people and even fewer trees. But, like most Iowa towns, Tingley was ambitious; no one ever considered calling it a village. Someone planted elms along both sides of Main Street, someone else started a town band, and plans were in the air for an opera house.

Stella McClure probably had little contact with Tingley during the three years she spent on the farm west of town. Her time was consumed by the work left undone when her father went off on masonry jobs, her share of the chores, and the duty of caring for five brothers and sisters, none of whom was old enough for heavy work.

In 1890, when Jennie McClure became pregnant again in what was probably a last try at another boy, it was simply assumed that fifteen-year-old Stella would take charge of the family—including the youngest, two-year-old Euphonia Isabell—called Phony—who had contracted a high fever. On May 7, for reasons unknown, Phony went into convulsions. With no time to run for help, Stella tried to stop the seizures by holding her tightly, but the spasms continued until the child died in her arms.

Stella left no record of her reaction to Euphonia's death. She never spoke of it again, either within the family or to her own children. Perhaps she consoled herself in the birth of another sister, Martha Ellen, exactly one week later. The McClures apparently accepted Phony's death with resignation, as yet another temptation to false grief. The death of an innocent, after all, was a chance to reaffirm the optimism of the true believer: "A little flower of love," reads the 1879 gravestone of a two-year-old Tingley girl, "that blossomed but to die, transplanted now above, to bloom with God on high."

Soon after Euphonia's death, John McClure surrendered to economic reality and moved his family into a small house on the west end of Main Street in Tingley.

For his eldest daughter, it was a liberation.

Life in town meant fewer chores and a chance to pursue her adolescent craving for a more genteel life. Except during the canning season, the Ladies' Missionary Society and the Ladies' Social Club met weekly in their stiff white skirts to discuss an astonishingly ambitious range of assigned topics, from Raphael to Lord Byron. "Art and art consciousness," wrote a traveling art lecturer in his memoirs, "[are] present mainly in the five largest cities of the land, plus an attenuated dribble that [runs] through the women's clubs of the country." Given the obstacles they faced, these small groups of Tingley women had to have a burning commitment to learning and to bettering themselves. The nearest library was fifty miles away, the nearest college, a hundred miles. To hear traveling lecturers like Ralph Waldo Emerson (speaking as a "Man of the World"), or Bronson Alcott (holding forth on "The New England Mind") they had to journey to Davenport, Cedar Falls, or Webster City and pay fifty cents.

The men of Tingley, of course, took no part in such pastimes. The world of art and literature, or self-improvement and learning—except as it related to "book" farming—was almost exclusively a female domain. A man's community activities, other than church and holiday celebrations, began and ended on Saturday night when the stores stayed open until midnight and all the men gathered at Heyer Brothers General Store (on the porch in the summer, by the stove in the winter) to swap stories.

Although Stella never learned to sing or play an instrument, she could have taken lessons from one of the traveling piano teachers like Daisy Smith, who hitched up her buggy in the morning and saw twenty or thirty students in a week. Both boys and girls were welcome, anybody with fifty cents, but the boys usually had work to do on the farm. There were traveling art teachers, too. Unlike the local music teachers, they were usually out-of-towners and more often men than women—a young single woman traveling alone would have scandalized a Presbyterian community like Tingley. Every student painted the same assigned scene, following the teacher step by step as he demonstrated and explained the technique. These strange and often single men who pulled into town with their colorful books and exotic skills made the hearts of young girls like Stella McClure race with anticipation. At least one old Tingley resident remembers Stella attending the watercoloring class of an itinerant art teacher and painting the Castle at Chillon, a scene that also served as the backdrop in a Mount Ayr photographer's studio. For a girl who had seldom traveled more than a day's ride from home, it was a faint but treasured glimpse of a broader, richer, more colorful world. Years later Stella told one of her daughters-in-law, "When I was young I wanted to study art but I never was able to."

About the time Stella left school and began to cast about in the small pond of Tingley for the makings of an adult identity, her aunt, Flora Estella, moved into the area. Although separated by seventeen years, the two women had enjoyed a unique affinity since Stella's childhood, when Aunt Stella often journeyed from Fairfield to visit her older sister, Stella's mother, Jennie. Their common name became, in young Stella's eyes, a secret bond, one that was reinforced as she grew older and began to look more and more like her aunt: the same stout, big-boned body, the same broad face and strong features. In fact, as family members were quick to note, she looked more like her heavy-framed aunt than her diminutive mother. By the time young Stella was in her teens, the gap between their ages had become irrelevant. At Eliza Jane Speck's funeral in 1889, fourteen-year-old Stella wrote in her aunt's autograph book:

When you are in a distant land
And view the writing of my hand
Although my face you cannot see
Then think Dear Stella think of me
       Your niece Stella

By now, time and fondness permitted young Stella the liberty of addressing her aunt by her first name.

Whatever distant land Aunt Stella visited following her mother's death, she returned to Iowa and moved to Tingley soon afterward. There she set for her young niece a daily example of what it meant to be a lady: promenading in fine dresses of silk and taffeta, using linen napkins, and inviting lunch guests by sending sealed invitations. She decorated her house in ornate Victorian style with flowerpots lining the staircase. Every afternoon, she would stroll into town for shopping or church or a social gathering, wearing a dark blue dress with a lace collar, a veiled hat, and white gloves. She sewed most of what she wore and was particularly fond of intricate lace and crochet work. Such exquisite finery, seen for the first time, made a deep impression on Stella and the other young girls of Tingley. Recalling a white collar of crocheted grapes that Aunt Stella wore to church, one of them later said: "I sat in the pew behind her and stared at those grapes all through the sermon. They fascinated me." Although makeup was considered an irreligious sign of worldliness, Aunt Stella risked a dusting of fine European powder with a slight rose tint that accentuated the mask-like quality of her face. Unfailingly clean and immaculately manicured, she was "correct as much as she could be, living in such a small community," recalls a woman who knew her. "She was among the few who served their meals well, on beautiful tablecloths, and kept their houses nice, and dressed up in the afternoon and walked uptown in their good clothes the way they did in those days."

Aunt Stella's exaggeratedly ladylike demeanor may have been, in part, compensation for the bulk and indelicacy of her own body. Beneath her lace collars and veiled hats were broad shoulders; thick, straight arms and legs; a wide, curving back; a strong, protruding jaw; and heavy, masculine features. Aunt Stella may also have felt that she deserved better from life than Tingley, Iowa. She had seen something of the world beyond and knew there was more to it than Tingley could offer. The townspeople sensed her aloofness. "She was a big woman and very stern, and she walked real straight," recalls one who knew her. "She was not a friendly type of person." According to another acquaintance, "It was kind of hard for her to smile."

Young Stella watched her aunt with keen, admiring eyes. She saw the way Aunt Stella despised "shoddy" goods and shoddy workmanship, the way she insisted on the finest quality material when she sewed or the best ingredients when she cooked. She studied the severity of her aunt's expectations, the rarity of her smile, the way she held back her words, weighing every sentence, giving away as little as possible. Stella came to see her aunt not just as a namesake and a look-alike, but as the inevitable fulfillment of her own inchoate personality, more so than her own mother. Jennie McClure made rag carpets and heavy cloth; Aunt Stella created fine lace and intricate crochet. Her mother cooked for a large family; Aunt Stella served fine meals for a few invited guests. Her mother was a pioneer woman; Aunt Stella was a lady. There was never any doubt which one Stella wanted to be.

But years of playing eldest son to her father, and older brother to her siblings had left in Stella a deep stain of masculinity that resisted both her aunt's lessons in refinement and her own ambitions. She had developed a masculine walk and a way of speaking that was "kind of short and loud, like a man's." She could be direct and forceful to the point of abruptness. "She knew what she wanted, and what she thought was worthwhile, and she knew how to get it," recalls her son Charles.

By 1893, when she was eighteen—an age when most Tingley girls were already married—Stella had shown little interest in the ritual of courtship. She wasn't at all suited to the role of shy, self-denying virgin that the ritual seemed to require, much preferring the company of her younger brothers, Cameron and Leslie, whom she called Cam and Les. Jennie McClure had turned over to her the responsibility for disciplining the two boys, age seven and five, but Stella enjoyed the camaraderie too much to play the stern parent, even when their "devilment" landed them before the justice of the peace. (During the ten years Stella was responsible for him, Les fell behind four grades in school.) As the oldest and the biggest, she was entitled to pitch in their sandlot baseball games and even played the prankster herself from time to time. "Once, she

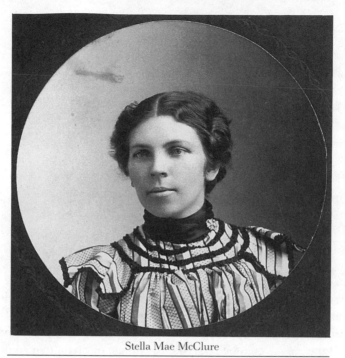

Stella Mae McClure

dressed up like an old hobo or tramp to scare them," recalls Cameron's son, Dean McClure. "The get-up was so convincing that they chased her with a pitchfork."

As she approached her twentieth birthday in 1895, however, Stella McClure was growing restless. Her aspirations to ladyhood were continuously frustrated by household chores and small-town routine. Her maternal instincts and sexual urges, increasingly intertwined and indistinguishable, could no longer be satisfied by roughhousing with her younger brothers. And always there were vague, persistent images, like the Castle at Chillon, of something better out there.

In the summer of 1895, two events brought Stella's growing frustration into sharp focus. In May, her sister Anna graduated from high school. Despite an accelerating, undiagnosed illness, she planned to attend Parsons College in the fall. Then, in August, Aunt Stella, now thirty-seven, married a local farmer and handyman, Benjamin Lorimor. The marriage of her mentor and model to a relatively poor and charmless man might have had more of a disillusioning effect on Stella if she herself hadn't already become involved in a relationship. Sometime earlier that year, probably at a school party or church outing, she had been introduced to one of her sister's classmates, a slight young man with a boyish face named LeRoy Pollock.

2

SENSITIVE MEN

I

f Jackson Pollock knew little about his mother, he knew even less about his father. When Jackson was nine, Roy Pollock abandoned his family and, except for occasional visits, did not return until after Jackson himself left home at the age of eighteen. Unlike the image of Stella that so dominated Jackson's imagination throughout his life, his father's image was never more than a vague silhouette moving in the distance of his earliest memories. "His father was a mystery to me," says his wife, Lee Krasner. "Once, I said to him, 'What was your father like?'—it was always mother, mother, mother—but he didn't say anything that registered."

Even Roy Pollock knew very little about Roy Pollock. He knew that he had been born LeRoy McCoy and that, at the age of two, he had been given to a family named Pollock. If he knew anything more about his real family, he kept it to himself. Years later, his sons believed that their father had been adopted by the Pollocks because both his parents died at the time of his birth. The McCoy family Bible, dutifully kept for a hundred years, doesn't even mention LeRoy's name.

Roy Pollock didn't know that he was descended from a long line of idealistic, independent-minded men, the first of whom, Alexander McCoy, came to America from County Donegal in Ireland in 1774—the same year that Godfrey Augustus Speck was shanghaied in Saxony—and settled in Pennsylvania. The first Alexander McCoy (there would be one in every generation) was an intelligent and conscientious man. Although a devout Presbyterian himself, he was impressed by the religious tolerance in the Quaker colony. In the Revolutionary War, he supported independence, but refused on moral grounds to join the fight, volunteering instead to serve as a chaplain in the Revolutionary Army despite his lack of formal religious training. After the war, he read with Charles Nisbet, the first president of Dickinson College in Carlisle, Pennsylvania. In 1795, he was licensed as "reverend" by the Presbyterian church and installed in the tiny frontier outpost of West Alexander near the modern Pennsylvania–West Virginia state line.

Of Alexander McCoy's multitudinous descendants, many followed his lead into the Presbyterian ministry (including Roy Pollock's brother, John McCoy), and all, including Roy, shared his legacy of social concern, progressive politics, and democratic morality. Among these was his grandson Alexander, who, instead of a life in the ministry, chose life with a minister's daughter. In 1832, at the age of twenty-three, he married Martha Pattison and, over the next twenty years, a period of remarkable stability and calm for a frontier family, raised twelve children in Ohio County, Virginia (now West Virginia), just across the state line from West Alexander. In 1852, the McCoy family joined the wave of settlers who hopscotched their way west in the 1850s. They stopped for a few years in Knox, Ohio, before moving on in 1858 to Monmouth, Illinois, where they waited for the country to spend itself in the Civil War. The outcome of the war opened up new possibilities for settlers like Alexander McCoy. As long as Missouri was a slave state, his conscience wouldn't allow him to settle there. But in 1867 he took his family to Jackson County, Missouri, on what he hoped would be the final leg of a fifteen-year journey.

By this time, his seventh child, also named Alexander, was twenty-three and in need of a wife. Unfortunately, the younger Alexander had inherited his great-grandfather's thoughtful, introspective conscience but not his strength of purpose. Throughout his life, Alexander's moodiness and indecision would leave him vulnerable to more strong-willed souls around him, especially his first wife, Rebecca McClelland—Becky—a tall, robust, forthright woman of Irish ancestry, a year older than Alexander and filled with maternal fervor. After the birth of two sons, John and Joseph, the family moved to a more promising spot near Rebecca's brother's farm in south central Iowa. The year was 1874—the same year that John and Jennie McClure packed their wagons and headed for the same promising spot.

Being a conscientious McCoy, the elder Alexander provisioned his son and his young family as best he could before they set out: a milk cow for the children, a horse, a few pigs and chickens, whatever furniture and clothes could be spared, and even a few pieces of family china to make the prairie life seem just a bit less desolate, all loaded in or tethered to a single wagon. It was not a hoard by any means, but it was at least a head start.

Somewhere on the trip from Missouri to Iowa, in one brief, terrible moment, the McCoys lost everything. They were crossing a river, swollen with spring rains, when the raft carrying their wagon and stock broke loose and capsized. The children swam safely to shore and Alexander helped his wife to shallow water, but everything they had brought, except the little money he had with him, was swept away by the river.

It was only a taste of the hardships to come. Although he did manage to secure a small farm, Alexander McCoy was caught at the bottom of the economic and social ladder in Ringgold County. In 1875, Becky had a third child, a girl she named Nina, and, two years later, on February 25, 1877, a boy, LeRoy. Soon after his birth, she complained of fatigue and began to lose weight. A nagging cough grew more persistent until, by the time LeRoy was two, he had become accustomed to the sight of his emaciated mother coughing up blood.

At some point in her struggle with tuberculosis, Becky McCoy sent word to Missouri for her mother, Elizabeth McClelland, now seventy-six, to come and look after her four grandchildren. The task wasn't an easy one. Sometime in 1878, three-year-old Nina began to show the same symptoms that had reduced her mother to a pale, withdrawn ghost. Sitting in the closed cabin, unable to escape, LeRoy watched his mother and sister being slowly consumed.

On February 28, 1879, three days after LeRoy's second birthday, Nina died. She was buried in the little cemetery behind the Presbyterian church in Eugene, Iowa. Two months later, Rebecca McCoy was placed beside her.

Within a year of his mother's death, LeRoy McCoy was no longer living with his own family. In the official Iowa census of 1880, he was listed as belonging to the household of James M. Pollock, age forty-five, and Lizzie J. Pollock, age forty-four. Exactly how LeRoy McCoy came to be in the Pollock house has been a source of speculation among family members and local historians ever since. Some stories claim that *both* of LeRoy's parents died; some that he was formally adopted (not true); some that the McCoys and the Pollocks were in fact related (also not true). Several focus on the deathbed declarations of Becky McCoy. In the tenderest terms, they tell of Becky summoning Lizzie Pollock to her bedside and begging her to take care of little LeRoy after her death. One story tells of the tragic death of Lizzie Pollock's own son and how Alexander surrendered LeRoy to her as an act of compassion. The number of explanations is an indication of how fundamentally inexplicable the event was: with his mother-in-law and two older sons still in his household, Alexander McCoy gave his three-year-old child to a couple who were not related, not wealthy, and considered "a bit on the scruffy side" by other townspeople. Although he soon moved back to Missouri, married a landed woman, and continued raising a family in relative prosperity, as far as is known, he never sent for, communicated with, or acknowledged the existence of his son LeRoy.

At age three, LeRoy McCoy suddenly found himself in a new world, a world even colder and more alienating than the old one. His new father, James Madison Pollock, called Matt, had come to Iowa from Ohio in 1871 with only a wheelbarrow full of belongings, his wife, Lizzie, and an adopted son, Frank. After a decade of hardship and sacrifice, he had managed to double his acreage and fill his barn with livestock. Despite his apparent success, however, Matt Pollock was not a popular or even respected man in Ringgold County. He attended church every Sunday, but avoided the ancillary church activities that earned a man his neighbors' respect. He was considered single-minded to the point of ruthlessness in his effort to improve his lot in life.

Lizzie Pollock easily made up for her husband's slack attention to "God's work." Her fellow believers revered her as "strong and courageous"; the uninitiated considered her "a religious fanatic," determined not only to do God's will but to enforce it on others. As president of the Women's Christian Temperance Union, Lizzie—with her tall, angular figure, her deep, harsh voice, and reputation for severity—became a well-known figure throughout the county. "She was very strong in her ideas," recalls her nephew. "She made everybody toe the mark." A family member who knew her says with some understatement, "She didn't approve of everybody." Most of all, she didn't approve of weakness, physical or moral, in the face of adversity. She once scolded a woman for jumping at the sight of a mouse. To her sons Frank and LeRoy, Lizzie Pollock was a loving mother in the same way she was a loving Christian: righteous without compassion, demanding without compromise. "She had a very loyal heart," says a woman who knew her, "but she was too severe to show it."

Growing up with a distracted, obsessed father and a stern, undemonstrative mother, LeRoy withdrew further and further from the world. Although very little is known about the early years after his "adoption" by the Pollocks, the image that emerges is of a small boy alone in a house he never considered home while the father he feared but never loved worked in the fields and the mother he feared and loved but never understood, threw herself into God's work. At an age when a year is a lifetime, LeRoy Pollock spent lifetimes alone, laying the foundations of his adult personality: solitary, introspective, fearful, uneasy with people, and sensitive "to an unnatural degree."

In 1884, probably unknown to seven-year-old LeRoy, his real father died in a diphtheria epidemic in Butler County, Missouri. The reports Alexander McCoy had received in Iowa of a rich widow had proved true. His estate consisted of 360 acres of prime Missouri land, including hundreds of head of livestock and a large, white frame house. Under the terms of his will, LeRoy McCoy, perhaps forgotten by now, received nothing.

By the time LeRoy was ten, Matt Pollock was hiring him out to Walter Edie and other farmers in Ringgold County to raise extra capital. He was not growing up as big as his father would have liked—it would be a few more years before he could handle a plow as well as his brother Frank—but he was strong for his size, and durable. Matt Pollock made his best money when he could offer a package deal: a horse, a plow, and a boy to work them.

There was nothing unusual about young boys being farmed out as extra hands in rural Iowa. It was often the logical compromise between those with too much land and those with too many children. The arrangement proved so lucrative that entrepreneurs brought in trainloads of orphans from the East Coast who were adopted by local families for a fee and then hired out. Of course, profit wasn't the only motive at work. "Sometimes a kid wouldn't get along with the parents so he was farmed out to whoever would take him," says one local historian. But for Matt Pollock, nothing was more important than the ascent from poverty. He sent young LeRoy as far away as Missouri and Arkansas to join the huge gangs that worked the big farms along the Mississippi. For years, Roy Pollock kept a picture of one of those gangs, a panoramic photograph of a dozen teams of horses, wagons stacked twenty feet deep with hay, an enormous barn, and a hundred men scattered through the field—black spots in a sea of grass. One of those spots was Roy Pollock.

In fact, the work suited young LeRoy. In the fields, he could be alone with his thoughts and away from the people he feared. For him, work was easy; it was coming home that was hard. There are stories that LeRoy ran away from home during these years, but there was no need to run away. The work was escape enough. Far from resenting the furrow and the plow to which he was virtually chained, he learned to love the land and to love working on it: the feel of "the horses straining against the walking plow" turning up the fresh, black soil; the sweet smell of "new-mown hay, as the mower makes a swath into the tall strands of hay, scaring baby rabbits out of their nests." Over the years, he became extraordinarily skilled in raising crops and breeding animals. His sons called him "a craftsman of the soil."

It was probably during his long trips to Missouri or Arkansas that LeRoy discovered an even more potent form of escape—alcohol. Liquor wasn't easy to come by in Tingley. After drunken railroad workers started a disastrous fire in 1882, the town cracked down on saloons and bars. In 1894, decades before the Nineteenth Amendment, Iowa passed its own version of Prohibition. For the determined, liquor could always be found or made, but consuming it was a furtive, antisocial activity. LeRoy must have often heard his mother intoning the pledge of the WCTU, Tingley chapter: "We promise to abstain from all ferment, malt, and distilled liquors, including wine, beer, and cider . . . anything whereby thy brother stumbleth or is offended or is made weak." Fearing her wrath, he undoubtedly refrained from drinking at home. But much of his youth was spent in other people's fields, away from his mother's reproving eyes. On a work gang, on the farm of a more tolerant neighbor, or with his brother Frank, LeRoy began his lifelong struggle with alcohol—a struggle that he hid from his mother, just as he would try, years later, to hide it from his wife and children; a struggle that his youngest son, Jackson, by some unknown mechanism, would eventually inherit.

The same year that LeRoy began high school, 1892, James B. Weaver, the Populist candidate for President of the United States, polled more than one million popular votes, many of them in Iowa. Among those cheering Weaver on was LeRoy Pollock. Iowa had been a fertile field for populist sentiments since the early 1870s when it boasted the largest Grange membership of any state in the Union. Since then, the lot of the small farmer had gone from hard to intolerable. In addition to the familiar blights of crop disease, locust, flood, and drought which wreaked havoc on farm economies from 1880 to 1900, farmers felt themselves increasingly at the mercy of bankers, railroad profiteers, big-city commodities dealers, and other "nonproducers." In many states in the West and South, the Populists organized local Farmers' Alliances, which won regional and sometimes statewide political victories. In Iowa, however, land-owning farmers like Matt Pollock, deeply suspicious of the Populist platform's socialist subtext, its plan to nationalize the railroads, and its support for the emerging labor movement, resisted the new party. As a result, Iowa men voted safely Republican, as they had in every presidential election since 1856.

LeRoy Pollock, on the other hand, enthusiastically embraced the socialist implications of Populist reforms. From his first encounter with socialist ideas —probably among the work gangs in Missouri and Arkansas, both of which voted Populist in the 1892 election—LeRoy responded to their call for fairness and equality. For years he had worked hard to enhance other men's profits and, unlike most Iowa sons, had no assurance that his foster father's farm would one day be his. The big farms were worked by men who spent their lives performing "alienated labor"—a relatively rare phenomenon in family-farmed Iowa. He had seen how fluctuating grain prices and interest rates could destroy a man who gave his life to the soil. After the election of 1892, he followed the Populist cause through the depression of 1893 and the Pullman strike of 1894 —the strike in which the world first heard of Eugene V. Debs. Over the next three decades, as his sons grew up, he would continue to support the causes of his youth: the labor movement—including even the radical Wobblies—and the populists in the name of their successors, the socialists. In 1917, he celebrated at the news that the workers of Russia had taken control of their government. Of his five sons, two would become active in the labor movement and one would join the Communist party. The other two would become artists.

When he entered high school in 1892, LeRoy Pollock was a shy, withdrawn, and rather small fifteen-year-old boy with dark brown hair, hazel eyes, a pre-maturely developed body, and a perpetually serious expression. Three years later, when he graduated (a rare achievement matched by only 25 percent of the farmboys in Ringgold County), he was a darkly handsome young man who compensated for his diminutive size with masculine posturing and who yearned for adventure. He had several close friends among his classmates, an older girlfriend named Stella McClure, and a yen to see the world. He was also no longer LeRoy Pollock; sometime during high school he had decided to call himself simply Roy.

After graduation in 1895, Roy and a classmate, Ralph Tidrick, laid secret plans for a raft trip down the Mississippi River in pursuit of their high school heroes Huck Finn and Tom Sawyer. If Matt and Lizzie Pollock caught wind of the plans, they surely objected, but the two friends set out nevertheless in the summer of 1895. In Burlington, they caught a flatboat and rode it as far as Missouri where they stopped to work the September harvest and earn some money. They may have stopped again in Arkansas before reaching their real

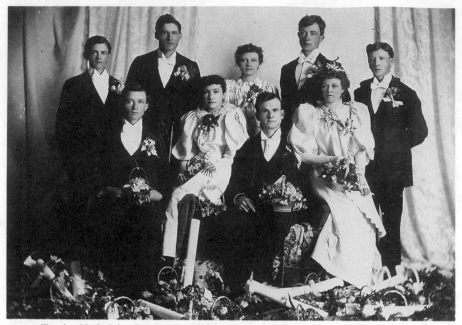

Tingley High School senior class, 1895: Ralph Tidrick, back row, second from left; Anna McClure, back row, center; and Roy Pollock, far right.

destination, New Orleans. It was a trip that lived in Roy Pollock's imagination for the rest of his life, and one of the few stories from his youth that he shared with his sons—with each one individually, ritually—as they came of age.

When Roy and Ralph arrived in New Orleans, they found work at a hotel in exchange for room and board. They had been there just long enough to learn a little French when Ralph took sick with malaria. For a few days, Roy nursed him, unsure what to do, no doubt fighting the images of sickness, death, and guilt that must have welled up from his own past. Finally, Ralph sent a letter to one of his brothers explaining their dilemma and asking for ten dollars. The letter fell into the hands of Ralph's father and within a few days, two train tickets for New Orleans to Tingley arrived at the hotel. Upon their return, the doctor told Roy, "It's a good thing you got him home when you did or you would have brought him home in a box."

Around Christmas 1896, Ralph and Roy again laid plans to leave Tingley. This time they sought adventure and escape in the 51st Volunteers of Iowa, Company M, a unit based in Red Oak, Iowa, just two counties west of Ringgold. The exact sequence of events isn't clear, but Matt Pollock must have uncovered the plan because, on February 16, 1897, just nine days shy of Roy's twentieth birthday, he and Lizzie formally adopted LeRoy McCoy. The brief handwritten "indenture" specified that "said Roy McCoy shall hereafter be called Roy Pollock [and] That said child is given to the said James M. Pollock and Lizzie J. Pollock for the purpose of adoption as their own child." People in Tingley preferred to believe that Matt just wanted Roy to inherit part of his estate. More likely, it was Matt Pollock's last attempt to control his dreamy ward: as an underage, legal son, Roy would need his adoptive parents' consent to enlist.

In April 1897, Ralph Tidrick boarded the train in Tarkio, Missouri, where he had been attending Tarkio College, and headed for Red Oak. Keeping it a secret to the last, he had written his family that on the way through Tingley, he would "throw his suitcase out the window of the train to let them know he had gone to the service." Roy Pollock watched as the train passed and the suitcase landed next to the tracks.

Roy Pollock and Stella McClure were formally introduced sometime prior to May 1895. For Stella, the slight, young-looking Roy was only a small step away from the boys she had been raising. In their company, she had always felt both comfortable and in control. The shy, introspective Roy allowed her to dominate, which she was used to doing; and to mother, which she liked to do. For Roy, the plump, big-bosomed, older-looking Stella must have seemed a feast of maternal love after years of hard crust from the bony, thin-lipped Lizzie. But Stella also must have recognized in Roy the same urge for something better that Aunt Stella had instilled in her. They were both dreamers; both were dissatisfied with their lives so far; both yearned, in their own way, for escape.

The first time Stella brought Roy home to her parents, John and Jennie McClure were deeply disappointed. The McClures had spent years inching their way up Tingley's strict social pecking order and now their eldest daughter was being courted by the foster son of a "ne'er-do-well" farmer. A socially prominent Tingley woman said some years later, "People considered that the Pollocks were a little on the trashy side. They were not one of the establishment. The McClures, on the other hand, *were* the establishment." Even in a town of three hundred people, there were strict class lines, and Roy Pollock, knowingly or unknowingly, was trying to cross them.

Gradually, however, the McClures warmed to the shy, boyish Roy. "He was a very quiet man who listened intently," recalls one of his daughters-in-law. He "always seemed interested in what other people were saying." Instead of treating him as the product of a bad family, they began to see him as the victim. The fact that he was in high school with their own bookish, fragile Anna may have been the key to their slow favor. "People were able to climb up by their own merits," recalls a Tingley resident, "and I would say, by the time LeRoy was graduated from school, he was just as acceptable as anybody." By 1895, John McClure had embraced his daughter's suitor, teaching him the skills of masonry, plasterwork, bricklaying, and wallpapering and occasionally using him as an apprentice. Even Roy's socialist ideas didn't seem to trouble the McClures—an indication of just how winning and unthreatening he could be. For some time before and after the election of 1896, John and Jennie teased their daughter about being courted by the "lone Socialist in Ringgold County."

In 1896, like so many of their ancestors, Stella and Roy began a long journey west, although at the time neither was aware it had begun. That winter Stella's sister Anna returned from Parsons College in Fairfield before the end of her first year. She had always been a sickly child, but when she was helped off the train in Tingley, the family could see she was dying. The diagnosis was tuberculosis. For a while Stella and her sister Mary, a practical nurse, cared for Anna at home, but she drifted closer and closer to death. Desperation in the McClure house ran so deep that when the Denver and Rio Grande Western Railroad distributed fliers boasting of the curative powers of the Manitou mineral springs in Colorado, the family determined that Anna should try the cure, and that, because she was too weak to travel alone, Mary should go with her.

In 1898, after long but unsuccessful treatment, Anna returned to Tingley to die. While seeing to her sister's final needs, Mary enthralled her family with stories of Colorado's beauty and promise. She undoubtedly also told them about John Keicher, a young railroad conductor whom she had met during her vigil in Colorado Springs. Soon after Anna's death on January 31, 1898, Mary returned to Denver, and two years later, in 1900, a letter came announcing her intention to marry Keicher.

Whether Stella traveled to Colorado to attend Mary's wedding or simply to visit is not known. But once there, she found work and decided to stay. Roy must have been stung by her willingness to leave him in Tingley, but they apparently continued to communicate. Some time during late March or early April of 1902, as soon as the spring thaw made travel feasible, they were undoubtedly together because not long afterward Stella discovered she was pregnant. She wrote Roy, leaving him no real alternative but to marry her and legitimize the expected child. It was the first of many decisions that Stella would make for her family. Both Stella and Roy kept the awkward news from their families in Tingley. To everyone except Mary, who must have known the truth, Stella explained her condition by claiming, as she did for the rest of her life, that she and Roy had been married secretly in Denver early in 1902 but that he had been forced to return to Iowa on family business. In Tingley, Roy worked to set aside some money and made plans to join his premature family someplace where there were more economic opportunities—preferably someplace far away from Iowa.

The plans must have taken longer than he expected because on Christmas Day 1902, Stella delivered a baby boy, whom she named Charles Cecil, while Roy was still in Tingley. It was another three weeks before he headed west to join his wife and new son. At about the same time, Stella boarded a train in Denver, probably carrying her new baby, and headed northeast. They met on January 13, 1903, in the little town of Alliance, Nebraska, near the junction of the Union Pacific and the Kansas Pacific mainlines.

One can only imagine what County Judge D. K. Spracht thought when two strangers—a small, boyish-looking man and a large, buxom woman in her late twenties carrying a three-week-old infant—stepped out of the cold and into his law office. He must have wondered why "Estella May McClure" who listed her residence as Denver, and "Lea Roy Pollock," of Tingley, Iowa, were applying for a marriage license in a little prairie town like Alliance, far from either place. Nevertheless, he issued the license, and the next day, Wednesday, January 14, 1903, Stella and Roy were married by Pastor Sanders at the Alliance Methodist Episcopal Church.

Alliance was not only out of the way (no small matter, under the circumstances) it was also on the way to the new home that Roy and Stella had chosen. A few days' train ride up the Chicago, Burlington & Quincy line was the brand-new town of Cody, Wyoming—the perfect place, they thought, to start a brand-new life.

3

STELLA'S BOYS

Fifty years before Jackson Pollock wore cowboy boots on Fifth Avenue or threw what one critic called "lariats of paint" across the canvas, Buffalo Bill Cody stood in the saddle to acknowledge the cheering of the crowd in Covent Garden and tipped his Stetson to a smiling Queen Victoria. At every stop on his tour—Paris, Vienna, Rome, and Berlin—the response was tumultuous. His legend had preceded him. In dime novels and newspaper headlines, Buffalo Bill had become a symbol of the American West, a place where everything—the men, the danger, the emotion—seemed more vivid and more authentic than in real life, a place where legend and reality met.

Like the man, the town that bore his name was caught between the real West and the legendary West. The Pollocks could have sensed the contradiction in the town's character from the moment they stepped off the train. Unlike older western towns, Cody did not evolve from a crossroads, a train stop, or a bend in a river. It was invented by a group of wealthy landowners in the Big Horn Basin looking to cash in on the wave of young families in search of a fresh start, families like Roy Pollock's. Unwilling to share the wealth with the Burlington Railroad, which already stopped at the DeMarais Hot Springs (called "Stinking Waters" by the Indians) on the north side of the Shoshone River and which owned much of the surrounding land, the developers picked a site on the south side of the river, leaving the station marooned in the middle of a treeless bench of sagebrush and sandy soil. When newcomers like the Pollocks asked the station master, "Where's the town?" he would point south, past a trestle bridge over the Shoshone to a scattering of houses sprinkled on a grid of streets off in the distance so far that on summer days the heat waves coming off the ground obscured it altogether.

Cody's developers took pains to offer the familiar amenities of life in the East—a new schoolhouse with four classrooms, a hospital with two doctors on staff—but they also recognized that the new settlers had a yen to be a part of

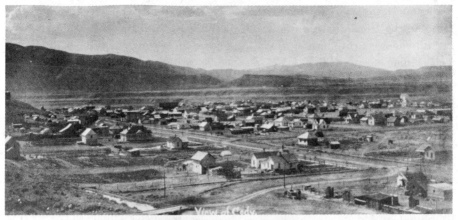

Cody, Wyoming, about 1908

the Wild West they had read about in novels and travel journals. So they recruited Buffalo Bill Cody, also a local landowner, to join their company and lend his Wild West credentials and name to the new town. To heighten the romantic illusion, they warned newcomers to "look out for wild Indians" and advised women to carry smelling salts in case they accidentally came upon a raiding party.

When the Pollocks arrived in 1903, the old West had not entirely disappeared from the area. Small parties of Crow, Arapahoe, Shoshone, and Sioux Indians, keeping well out of the settlers' paths, still came to the Stinking Waters as their tribes had done since 7000 B.C., to take advantage of their magical, curative powers. Old cowboys still hung around the schoolhouse to watch the pretty young schoolteacher. An occasional mountain lion strayed into town and startled an unwary shopper. Among Cody's most popular "occupations," according to the local paper, was "short range pistol practice with dudes and tenderfeet for targets, a dude being one who wears a white shirt, talks like a spelling book and refuses to go to bed with his boots on." But no matter how hard they talked, how much they drank, or how often they emptied their six-shooters into the air, the cowboys, like the Indians, knew they were an endangered species. The spirit of pioneering and independence that had fueled the West for a century was being replaced by the spirit in which Cody was founded, the spirit of enterprise. Boasted one local paper, "There is more enterprise, energy, and public spirit in this community of half a thousand souls than there is in an eastern city of half a million." Work had already begun on a canal and a dam on the Shoshone River to control flooding in the valley and bring water to neighboring areas. In the center of town, Buffalo Bill had just finished building the Irma Hotel, an $80,000 sandstone showcase, with stone sills, hardwood flooring, and a carved cherrywood bar sent by Queen Victoria as a gift to her favorite cowboy.

Film companies had already come to Cody to make "documentaries" about the Wild West; "eastern gentlemen" enrolled in the Wild West Cavalry School to become "genuine western riders in a short time"; tourists admired the paintings by Frederic Remington on the walls of the Irma Hotel. There were even "school marm" tourist trips through the most rugged stretches of nearby Yellowstone canyon. The Cody post office received a letter from a girl in Indianapolis: "Dear Sir: Will you please send me a nice young cowboy." The postmaster tacked up a notice that if he couldn't find one, "he may go himself."

On November 1, 1903, the year the Pollocks arrived, a gunman robbed the First National Bank of Cody and killed the teller. Not far away, in Cody's first movie house, *The Great Train Robbery*—the first western—was playing to a full house every night.

In Cody's boom-town economy, Roy Pollock was able to find a job almost immediately. He began by washing dishes at the Irma Hotel, but soon impressed the manager with his skill at plastering and carpentry and was promoted to building handyman. To good, solid citizens like Roy Pollock, with families, jobs, and the intention to stay for a while, the Lincoln Development Company made houses available in town for no money down, no interest, and no fixed mortgage payments. The house the Pollocks chose, which stood by itself on Salsbury Avenue at the north edge of the 1901 town plat with an unobstructed view of the river, was comfortable by frontier standards: a parlor, dining room, bedroom, and kitchen. Comparing it to the crowded farmhouses in which they had grown up, Roy and especially Stella must have felt themselves already on the road to a better life.

When winter came to the Big Horn Basin, the stream of tourists taking the cure at the old Indian sulfur springs dried up, the influx of settlers slowed as the railroad changed to a lighter winter schedule, and the transient dam workers moved south to the big projects in Arizona and California. With business at the hotel slack and a second son, Marvin Jay, recently arrived, Roy was forced to look for small indoor construction and repair jobs: plastering, carpentry, wallpapering. By late winter, he was working on a surveying job for the Sunlight Copper Mining Company—hard, hazardous work even in good weather. On a late winter trek in the rugged Rattlesnake and Cedar mountains west of Cody, his surveying crew was caught in an unexpected snowstorm and Roy was one of three men ordered to carry a rare 500-pound sample of copper ore back to town as a mineral exhibit. On the return trip, the group ran into fifteen feet of snow and was "forced to dump the 'exhibit' there," according to a newspaper account of the adventure. "Meantime, the public would just have to take their word for the size of the marvelous thing."

It was the first of many times that Roy Pollock strayed from home.

Some time in the next year or two, Roy and a friend from Tingley, Tom Archbold, found regular work at a rock-crushing plant on the banks of the Shoshone River just above the depot bridge. It was dirty, exhausting work, but it provided a steady income and a daily escape. (The Pollock children grew up believing, inaccurately, that their father was a part owner of the plant—a notion

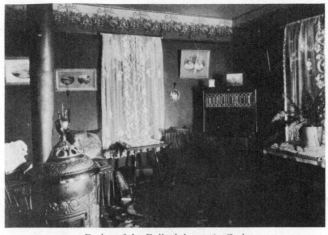

Parlor of the Pollock house in Cody

advanced by Stella, perhaps, who urged her husband to find a more dignified job.) To supplement his income, Roy continued to do plastering work in the winter and masonry and cement work in the summer and earned a reputation as a quiet, solid worker. "People respected him," says Francis Hayden, a Cody resident who remembers Roy Pollock. "I never heard anything bad against him, and at the time Cody was too small a town to keep any secrets."

Whatever Roy Pollock could earn—as a dishwasher, handyman, plasterer, surveyor, or mason—Stella Pollock could spend.

No matter how many extra jobs he worked, there was never enough left over to satisfy her extravagant aspirations. Most of the money went to decorating their little house in the ornate late-Victorian style that she had admired so much at her aunt's house in Tingley: an Aubusson-style carpet ornamented with garlands and multicolored flowers for the parlor; photographs of Charles and Marvin Jay and small prints of country landscapes, each in its own heavy baroque frame; a wide wallpaper border echoing the intricate garland motif of the carpet; in the dining room, a floral wallpaper and two long collages of pansies; next to the kitchen, a sturdy dresser for displaying her collection of serving bowls and Sunday china. The windows were hung with sheer lace curtains scrolled at the edges. On every horizontal surface, she placed either a crocheted doily or an embroidered tablecloth, creating an intricately patterned, graciously cluttered environment—all of it her own handiwork. "She ran the house," recalls Frank Pollock, "no doubt about that. Whatever was in that house was mother's influence." The results so pleased Stella that she arranged for a neighbor to take photographs of the interior and kept them until her death.

Relieved of the rigors of farm life, she devoted more and more of her time to the decorative sewing and refined cooking she had learned from Aunt Stella. She subscribed to the *Ladies' Home Journal* and studied each issue for new patterns and recipes. The Cody Trading Company ("The Big Store that Sells

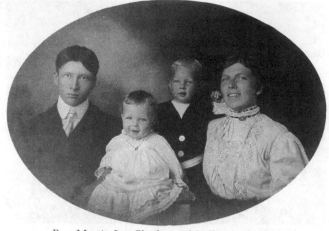

Roy, Marvin Jay, Charles, and Stella, about 1904

Everything") never seemed to run out of meat, vegetables, canned fruit, milk, butter, all the things that had consumed her life back in Tingley. She would stroll for hours through the store's four long aisles: one for groceries; one for dishes, furniture, and paintings; one for pots and pans; and one for clothing and dry goods, including yards of material in every conceivable color and pattern. When she wanted something still finer, she would walk across Sheridan Avenue to the Ladies' Emporium where the aging and eccentric Nelli Bruce had "all the latest in summer fashions." The former wife of a saloon owner who wore a small diamond embedded in her front tooth, "Poker Nell" could have found no more eager and knowledgeable a customer than the young Stella Pollock. Through her magazine subscriptions, Stella followed the developments in fashion with a keen eye, showing a particular fondness for the latest effusively lacy styles. In a formal picture of the Pollock family taken about this time, she sits closest to the camera, her head cocked proudly, smiling broadly, wearing a white lace blouse with pleated front, puff sleeves, high collar, and a profusion of crochet and lace. On the other side of the picture, his hair impatiently combed, staring resignedly into the camera, sits Roy Pollock.

In the same photograph, poised between their parents, are Charles and Marvin Jay—"Chas" and "Mart" in the family shorthand. Stella's arm holds Charles close at her side while one-year-old Marvin Jay wears a frilly lace dress that marks him unmistakably as his mother's. Roy's arm rests limply on the table beside him. The photograph both announces a battle and records its outcome.

From the start, it was an uneven contest. Roy, who had never had a real father himself, knew little of fatherhood and treated his sons more or less as Matt Pollock had treated him: supervising their work, administering occasional discipline, and setting down a strict hierarchy of privileges. Stella, on the other hand, "would get up and do the cooking and the laundry and part of the milling and do all the baking," boasts Frank Pollock. "She also made all of

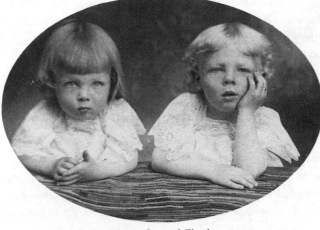

Marvin Jay and Charles

our shirts. We never wore store-bought shirts until we were fifteen or sixteen years old. She had the busiest hands of any person I've ever known." In many ways, Stella was a child's idea of a perfect mother—in part, no doubt, because her notions of motherhood had been formed when she herself was a child. She indulged her sons just as she had indulged her rambunctious brothers, never laying down rules and never punishing. On the rare occasions when Roy dared to spank them, she refused to speak to him for days. When four-year-old Marvin Jay threw a tantrum because Charles was attending school without him, Stella demanded that school authorities admit Jay to the class as well.

Only a few months after the family portrait was taken, Stella took Charles and Marvin back to the photographer's studio, this time without Roy. This was to be a picture of her sons as she wanted to remember them. She had been grooming them in the interim, letting their hair grow long—Roy did the family barbering—and making the special long lace blouses with little lace wings that they would wear. In the spirit of Victorian sentimentality that shaped her aesthetic world, she posed them as the *putti* in a Raphael painting she had seen illustrated in one of her magazines.

Roy Pollock didn't surrender his children without a fight. When Charles was five, Roy took him on a buggy ride (a rare treat) up the newly opened canyon road to the site of the Shoshone dam. About the same time, he introduced Charles to the Orange Athletic Club in Cody where there was almost always a wrestling or boxing match to watch. None of this attention was lost on Charles, who for the rest of his life would mimic his father's cocky walk, his macho mannerisms, his way of standing with his arms roguishly akimbo.

In August 1907, a third son, Frank, was born.

A year later, Roy Pollock moved his family to the north section of the Sant Watkins sheep ranch, at the base of the twin-peaked Hart Mountain three miles northeast of town. Stella couldn't have been happy about the move. Life in Cody had been relatively easy, even gracious by Iowa farm standards, and the little house on Salsbury Avenue had finally begun to resemble Aunt Stella's house in Tingley. The prospect of living on the Watkins ranch, even as the foreman's wife, in a two-room frame house that was comfortable but hardly fine, must have left her cold. In a rare display of determination, however, Roy pressed ahead. A sheep ranch foreman was paid about $400 a year in 1908, more than a dam worker could earn in a construction season, and room and board were provided. Roy was also eager to return to the kind of work he knew best. The Roy Pollock who knew by heart the nesting behavior of sage grouse and loved the smell of just-turned soil had never felt at home in the din and dust of the rock crusher—or among the lace and garlands of his own house. Moving to the Watkins ranch, with its fields of alfalfa, barnyard stock, and long silences interrupted occasionally by the boisterous camaraderie of the sheep-herders, was both an escape and a return to the only kind of home he had ever known.

It was also a last chance to regain control of his family.

Ever since the Johnson County War a decade before, sheep ranchers like Sant Watkins throughout Wyoming and as far away as Colorado had been jumpy. In that bitter sixteen-year feud over grazing rights between homestead-ers and the "hired killers" of the Wyoming Stock Growers' Association, five people had been killed, all of them sheepherders. The killing had never reached Cody, but tensions still simmered beneath the placid sagebrush land-scape. In 1907, cattlemen raided Linn's Sheep Ranch on Trapper Creek in the Big Horn Mountains, tied up the herder, put dynamite under his chair, and "blasted him to bits." Then they dynamited the 400 sheep he was tending. The next year, a similar raid in the same area killed 600 to 700 sheep, burned two wagons, and "ran the herder off into the brush."

Around the time of the last raid, Roy Pollock decided to accept Sanford Watkins's offer of the foreman job. He must have been influenced in his decision by Watkins himself, a tall, distinguished-looking old-timer who had homesteaded near Cody before the turn of the century and who viewed the rising tensions with concern but not alarm. Roy was among those who admired Watkins, so much so that when his fourth son was born in May 1909, he named him Sanford, which Stella immediately shortened to Sande.

Once settled on the ranch, Roy put Charles and Jay to work bottle-feeding the lambs who had lost their mothers. In summer, the two boys roamed the dry, treeless hills far from the ranch house, where Stella tended her two newest babies, Frank and Sande. "At every opportunity," says Charles, "we would tear off down to the Shoshone river and listen to the coyotes off in the distance." Herding sheep was lonely work. After shearing in the spring, a herder went out on the range for as long as six months, living alone in a four-by-eight-foot camp wagon with a bunk, a stove, and a water barrel, interrupted only once a week by a camptender who traveled from herder to herder with supplies of food, water, and the latest gossip. Winter brought herders, camptenders, and

10,000 sheep onto the ranch, transforming it into a community of colorful characters with stories to enchant and terrify small boys. "They were fascinating people," recalls Jay, "with fascinating names like Rattlesnake Pete and Mosey Bill. They had beards, and told stories about life on the range." The stories these hard, lonely men told, relayed and embellished by his older brothers, eventually became the basis of Jackson Pollock's knowledge of a frontier he never experienced firsthand. Years later, when he enthralled friends with tales of cattle rustlers and prairie wolves, or painted images of frontier life— covered wagons, cowboys, and lost steers—he was only echoing the stories his brothers told and conjuring images from cowboy yarns spun late on a winter night long before he was born.

In the late fall of 1909, Roy traveled to Tingley to stand vigil at his father's deathbed and comfort his mother. The trip must have awakened old anxieties, because soon after his return to Cody in early 1910, he began to drink. He had probably been drinking steadily, if moderately and secretly, since coming west. While living in Cody, where there was one bar for every twenty people, he never lacked for opportunity. The local papers were filled with complaints about "16 year old boys buying whiskey at the back doors of saloons" and drunken cowboys "shooting up the town and making unusual and indecent noises on the street." Community indignation peaked when a dam worker died "after an overdose of whiskey" outside the Thomas Saloon. The Woman's Public Service League was formed—"ladies of the town on the trail of vice and corruption"—and the town paper published an editorial plea: "Let's Trample Evil," but the rate of consumption was unaffected. In 1908, according to the local census, alcoholism was the primary cause of death among Cody men.

Roy did most of his drinking during the Cody years not in town, where he had to face Stella, but on his frequent hunting trips into Yellowstone with friends like Tom Archbold. "He was an outdoorsman," remembers Frank Pollock. "He hunted for deer and bear and elk. He went with other fellas, ones that he worked with, and they didn't leave town without a supply of booze with them." Later, on the Watkins ranch, he was always ready to share a bottle with one of his workers, especially in winter when the hard-drinking herders congregated. Besides, "there was plenty of reason to drink," says Frank, himself a recovered alcoholic. "It was so goddamned *cold*." Stella apparently knew about Roy's drinking, but as long as it was confined to hunting expeditions, didn't object. When he drank at home, however, she "put her foot down," Jay Pollock remembers. "She said, 'No more.' " It was the first sign of a much deeper struggle that would erupt ten years later and tear the Pollock family apart.

Sometime in the winter of 1910–11, Roy began to feel short of breath. He tired more easily and earlier in the day. At first he probably attributed it to the harsh winter—when the temperature was ten below zero, a sixty mile per hour wind could take anyone's breath away—an explanation that seemed more credible when Tom Archbold developed the same symptoms. At the Cody

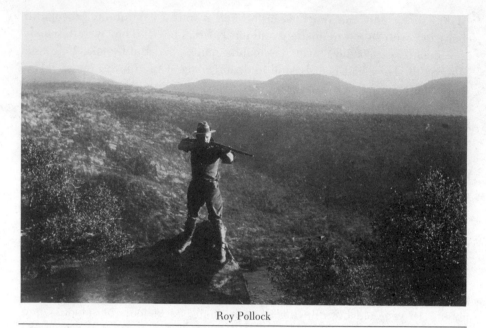

Roy Pollock

hospital, Dr. Frank Waples couldn't diagnose the problem with certainty, but he urged the Archbolds to leave Cody and make their home in a more forgiving climate. By the time they left in the spring of 1911, Tom's health had deteriorated even further. Roy's symptoms faded the next summer, and Stella was briefly optimistic, but they returned again with the cold weather and a visit to Dr. Waples brought the same advice: leave Cody.

The following winter (1911–12), Stella decided it was time to go. Roy's health was the designated reason, but hardly the only one. Work on the Watkins ranch, although good, wasn't the work Roy knew and loved from his youth; it wasn't even a farm; and, most important, it wasn't his. For Stella, ranch life was rough and lonely; winters made her trips to town—her lifeline —almost impossible; the Lower Sage School near the ranch was too small and poorly taught; and, as always, she yearned for something better. "My mother was the restless one," recalls Charles. "She was always looking for greener pastures."

With the news of Tom Archbold's death in early 1912, Stella made up her mind. As soon as possible, Roy would travel to California in search of a new home while she returned to Tingley with her sons for a last visit before moving farther west.

But nothing could happen, none of these momentous changes could begin, until after the birth of their fifth child, which was due, according to Dr. Waples, in January 1912. Stella was hoping for a girl, finally, to take home and show off. Roy, too, wanted a girl. "My dad always said, 'I've got a house full of boys,'" Frank remembers. " 'How long am I going to have to carry on until I get a *girl* out of this woman?' "

■ ■ ■

When Dr. Frank Waples looked out his window on Sunday morning, January 28, 1912, he was relieved to see blue sky. It had been snowing when he went to bed, but the morning wind had already blown the night's accumulation off the roads, leaving only long, white scars where wagon tracks had frozen and filled with snow. Blue sky and clear roads meant that he could cover the eight miles out to the Sant Watkins ranch in a couple of hours or less. Stella Pollock had reported "irregularities" during her pregnancy, alerting Dr. Waples to the possibility of a difficult delivery. When Roy arrived by horse that morning to tell him that Stella was in labor, Dr. Waples decided it would be best if both he and the local midwife, Annie Howath, who had assisted at the delivery of the last two Pollock boys, were present.

Dr. Waples's familiar, affable bedside manner must have been a source of some comfort to Stella as she suffered through labor for the fifth time. Roy wasn't in the room; as usual he was off with the sheepherders who were camped out at the ranch for the winter. Nor did Stella's sons show much interest in the activities around their mother's bed. When Charles was told another baby was due, he replied nonchalantly, "Oh, that's nothing new. There'll be another one by Christmas."

Soon after the final contractions began, Dr. Waples realized that something was wrong. Some unseen problem in the womb prevented the baby from moving even as Stella followed his instructions to bear down harder. When the head finally appeared through the birth canal—an alarmingly dark bulge straining to emerge—Dr. Waples saw the shiny, blue-black cord wrapped around its neck. He quickly cut the cord, disentangled the baby, and held it aloft to spank some life into it. When Stella saw her child for the first time, its head was deep blue, the color of a bad bruise (she later exaggerated the story and said it was "black as a stove"), and its 12¼-pound body was limp. Even after the first few slaps, there was no sign of breathing. Stella later admitted that, at the time, she feared it was stillborn.

The baby, another boy, lived, but Stella paid a price for him. According to Dr. Waples, she could never bear another child. He was named Paul Jackson Pollock: Paul for a reason that only Stella knew; Jackson for the beautiful lake at the base of the Tetons where Roy used to go hunting with his friend Tom Archbold, who had just died. In accordance with an old McClure tradition of using the middle name, or perhaps at Roy's insistence, the boy was called Jack from his first, traumatic day. "I guess mother knew he was the last one," says Frank Pollock. "So she always referred to him as the baby of the family, even into his teens. She'd got this whole clan, and she'd say, 'Here's my *baby.*' "

Within weeks of Jackson's birth, just as he was becoming accustomed to the world, it began to change around him. Carried in Stella's arms, he began a journey that would cover five thousand miles through eight states with only two brief stops along the way—almost nine months of continuous travel.

For the other brothers—Charles, nine; Jay, seven; Frank, four; and Sande, two—the trip was a kaleidoscope of new sights and experiences. They had never ridden a train before or been outside the Big Horn Basin. "We discovered things that we'd never seen before," Charles recalls, "Indians selling trinkets at the stations, prairie dogs popping out of their holes." In Iowa, there was snow on the ground, and when the train stopped in Tingley, Stella's father was there in his sleigh to meet them. When they returned to Cody, Stella spent a few months packing, selling the household goods, and waiting for word from Roy, who had left for San Diego in October. In November, she placed a short classified advertisement in the Park County *Enterprise*: "For Sale: All my household goods, baby buggy, canned fruit, and everything. Call at the house."

When the letter from Roy finally arrived, it instructed Stella to bring the family and meet him in National City, a new California fruit-growing town wedged between San Diego and the Mexican border. Leaving Cody on November 28, 1912, when Jackson was exactly ten months old, the train took a long, right-angle course through Montana and Idaho to Seattle, across Puget Sound, then down the coast through Oregon and California. In all, the trip took more than a week, requiring more than half a dozen changes of train.

For four of the Pollock boys, the journey was yet another adventure. But for little Jackson, squirming and blinking toward his first birthday, traveling was a more anxious experience. The usually doting Stella was suddenly preoccupied with four rambunctious sons, including two-year-old Sande, who required vigilant supervision. Throughout the trip, except in rare moments of privacy, Jackson was denied the usual breast-feeding and, for much of his first year, experienced his mother from the perspective of a piece of cherished baggage, bundled in layers of lace, staring up into her impassive public face hidden behind the veil she always wore while traveling.

The reunion in National City was not a happy one. In the months since they had last seen him, Roy had been unable to find either a farm to work or a place to live. He was drifting from one temporary job to the next, working here as a plasterer on a construction job and there as a hired worker on one of the big farms in the Imperial Valley. Stella had arranged for the family to stay at the house of a friend from Tingley, a Mrs. Edelmann, who lived on Sixth Street in Coronado, a small resort town on the narrow isthmus across San Diego Bay from National City.

It was already clear to everyone, especially Stella, that Jackson was the most beautiful of her babies. He had his mother's broad face and sensuous mouth, but his father's refined features and vulnerable eyes. He had three deep dimples—one on each cheek and one on his chin—which he would keep the rest of his life, and thick blond hair, which he would lose. Stella might have doted even more on her beautiful new baby if it hadn't been for an epidemic of mumps and measles that swept through the family soon after they arrived in Coronado, leaving Roy sterile. "That was the end of the Pollock family," Charles recalls.

Sterility wasn't the only setback Roy encountered in Southern California. Like thousands of other Iowa farmers who flooded the area between 1900 and 1920, Roy Pollock came dreaming of a farm that combined Iowa soil and California sun. But only a few scraps of land were still available and only wealthy landowners could afford them. Then, in January 1913, a devastating freeze—not only the fruit on the trees but the trees themselves froze and split open—shook the region's economy and its image as an agricultural paradise. Farmers like Roy Pollock began to look elsewhere for cheaper land and more predictable weather.

Among the places he looked was Phoenix, Arizona.

Roy had been in contact with Leonard Porter, a distant relative in Louisiana who planned to move to Phoenix in August, and on his recommendation, visited the area in the late spring of 1913. Impressed by what he saw, he returned to Coronado and, without waiting to make specific arrangements, prepared his family to move. Frank was sent ahead with Mrs. Edelmann, who was joining her husband in Phoenix, and on August 11, 1913, the rest of the family followed with a few household furnishings that had been stored since the move from Cody.

After a year and a half, the period of transition and uncertainty that had begun soon after Jackson's birth was almost over. It was prolonged for a few more weeks in Phoenix while Roy made the final arrangements to buy from Hart and Sydney Baker a twenty-acre plot of land six miles east of town on the road to Tempe. The family stayed in a rooming house in Phoenix until the day in September when Roy took them to the Five Point Livery Stable at the corner of Van Buren Street and Grand Avenue, rented a horse and buggy, and drove them out through the dust of Sherman Street to see their new home.

4

SENSITIVE TO AN UNNATURAL DEGREE

In February 1913, a huge show of paintings and sculptures by Claude Monet, Henri Matisse, Pablo Picasso, and dozens of other artists opened at the 69th Regiment Armory on Lexington Avenue and Twenty-sixth Street in New York City. Public reaction ranged from skepticism to outrage. Marcel Duchamp's *Nude Descending a Staircase* drew "shrieks of laughter" from a crowd that was unable "to discover the lady or the stairway." A room filled with paintings in the new Cubist style, eight by Picasso, was dubbed the "Chamber of Horrors." In March, Picasso left for a vacation in Ceret, France, with his mistress Eva. Securely prosperous and widely acclaimed, he was untroubled by the ridicule in New York and already beginning to play with a newer, more whimsical Cubist style than the one on display in the Chamber of Horrors. In April, Henri Matisse accompanied a critic through a Paris exhibition of paintings from his just completed trip to Morocco. In an effort to explain why he had simplified his images almost to the point of abstraction, Matisse told the critic, "I tend toward what I feel; toward a kind of ecstasy. And then I find tranquility." That summer, Claude Monet, still in mourning after the death of his wife and suffering from cataracts, found personal solace and great art in the flowering arches of his garden at Giverny.

In September, Jackson Pollock, age one and a half, saw his new home for the first time.

Eventually, all of the events of 1913 would have an impact on Pollock's art. At the time, however, and for the next five years, his entire world—visual, emotional, psychological—was bounded in a nutshell of land a quarter of a mile by an eighth of a mile. To a child, it was a universe—including his house, his father's farm, and all the neighbors he knew—a universe at least as rich and fertile to a sensitive eye as the history of Western art.

And no one's eye was more sensitive than Jackson's. "He looked at things psychedelically," says Nick Carone, a close friend at the end of Pollock's life.

"He didn't see them with the retina, he saw them with his mind. He would look at an ashtray like he was trying to get at its molecular structure. And then he would touch it, move a butt or a matchstick with his fingertips. He was organizing that phenomena, putting it right. He was going to make it his." Even as a child, according to his brother Sande, Jackson was, like his father, sensitive "to an unnatural degree." Barefoot, dressed in bib overalls, his blond hair shining in the Arizona sun, Jackson explored his little universe: both the outer landscape of adobe houses and dusty yards, and the inner landscape of sibling rivalries and unreturned love. Then, detail by detail, he took that universe and "put it right." Through fantasy, he created his own landscape, a private world of images that, for the rest of his life, would haunt his dreams and preoccupy his art.

In the front room of the little adobe house on Sherman Street, his father's bookcase was the most sacred object. Two of the shelves were low enough for Jackson to peer through the diamonds of leaded glass at the rows of grainy black and brown leather spines etched in gold. Above the glass, beyond a little boy's reach, was an expanse of dark, glossy wood with a keyhole at the top and, above that, another row of books so far up that he had to step back to see it. The floor in front of the bookcase was covered with a grass rug where he and his brothers often fell asleep after lunch when Mother warned them out of the midday sun, and at night when Dad read to them from one of his books. Next to the bookcase stood the chair where Dad smoked his pipe and read, or Mother sewed. Mother read too, but she read with scissors in her hand, cutting out recipes and pictures from her magazines. In the basket at the foot of the chair were several spools of white thread and a metal crochet hook. If his father's magic came from the bookcase, his mother's came from the basket. Proof of it filled the room: dark tabletops were broken into fragments by it, pillows were turned into snowflakes, chairs floated on clouds of it, and the bright Phoenix sunlight shimmered through curtains of it. "I can remember her sitting and crocheting these things," says her grandson, Jonathan Pollock, who many years later shared Jackson's boy's-eye view of Stella's handiwork. "I used to watch her working. It was so intricate. I couldn't figure out how she could make something so complicated. The designs were intricate but the compositions were always well-balanced."

It was just a few sleepy steps from the grass rug in the front room to the bedroom where all five Pollock boys slept from November through March when it was too cool to sleep outside. Three iron bedsteads filled the small room: one for Charles and Jay, one for Sande and Jack, and one for Frank, the third son, marooned in the middle of the family. Even in the winter, they slept in the nude: five small bodies crowded together on sheets their mother had sewn. A teddy bear marked Jackson's bed. "For some time he had felt that he was too big to have it around," recalled brother Sande, but he was "unable to banish it to a trunk.'"

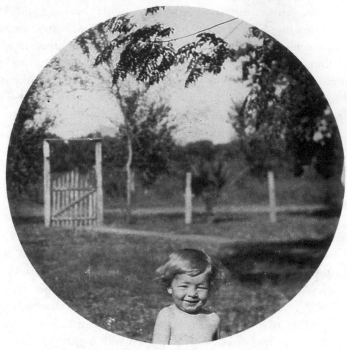

In the front yard of the Phoenix farm

In the wood dresser against the wall Mother kept their clothes. The top drawer, also beyond Jackson's reach, held the pastry-like stacks of handmade lace blouses and gowns that had belonged in turn to each of her sons. Knowing that Jackson was her last, she dressed him in petticoats and lace until well past his third birthday. In the middle drawer were his brothers' clothes: well-worn denim overalls for work and corduroy knee pants for school, stacks of soft chambray and blue gingham shirts, long black socks, and belted jeans that Jackson longed to wear—"They'll never stay on you," his father would say when he pleaded for a pair. For Stella, the dresser was a display case: like her children, a sample of her handiwork. "We were always groomed," recalls Frank Pollock, "however poor we were." Charles remembers "the pride that my mother had in the cleanliness and good looks of her five children." Near the dresser, five pairs of shoes were lined up from small to tiny, hardly worn. Every fall, Stella went into Phoenix and bought each of her boys a new pair "because she didn't want us to go to school and have the teacher think we couldn't afford shoes," says Frank. But sitting on the floor by the dresser in May, they still looked brand new. "It was more comfortable to go barefooted," Frank explains, "so every day we stuck them on a pomegranate tree on the way to school and picked them up on the way home."

From the bedroom window, Jackson could see the front yard in the white light of noonday. The big umbrella trees were the focus of activity on the quiet side of the house. They offered a cool home to the red-winged blackbirds, shielded the sparse grass from the sun, and cleared a shady spot for dinner on a hot night. Most of the year, the front yard was also a bedroom. The Pollocks would drag the heavy bedsteads out and array them under the trees with only sheets to protect them from the mosquitoes. "It'd be so hot we couldn't breathe," remembers a Pollock neighbor. "So we'd jump in the irrigation ditch and wet our clothes. Then we'd sleep in wet clothes to keep ourselves cool." The path from the front door passed through the shade of the umbrella trees out to a gate between tall cottonwood posts. Cottonwood trees had been planted all along the roadside *acequias,* or ditches, to provide shade, but they made unreliable fence posts. "You'd plant a cottonwood post," Charles Pollock recalls, "and first thing you know you'd have a damned tree. So you'd cut it down again for firewood, stick in a new post, and that one would sprout branches. We did a lot of fencing on the place." The shady *acequias,* lined with a cushion of grass, made a convenient place to wait for the mailman who brought Mother's and Dad's magazines mostly.

No room beckoned Jackson more irresistibly than the kitchen at the back of the house, where he could almost always find his mother. Dominating the room and the house, like the tryworks of a whaling ship, was a huge, black iron stove. The flames in the firebox danced furiously from morning to night, so hot that Jackson could feel the heat on his face from across the room. He wasn't allowed near. In the mornings, Mother moved around the stove with impunity, adjusting the black pot handles that jutted out over the edge of the stovetop. Looming over the stove, a huge kettle of water, poised just below boiling, added curls of steam to the heavy kitchen air. On wash days, Stella emptied the kettle into a galvanized washtub on the porch and sat with the washboard between her knees torturing the dirt from overalls and shirts. On Saturdays, it was Jackson's turn in the tub.

When Mother opened the oven door, Jackson could just glimpse the pans of bread before being hit by the wall of heat and smell. The oven door was always opening up to surprises that made a boy want to stay in the kitchen forever. "Stella loved to bake," remembers her grandson, Jonathan. "I remember apple pie very vividly, and cookies. When I came home from school I was always drawn to the aroma coming from the kitchen." At Christmas there was special candy in the oven and roasted walnuts on the stove. The acrid sweetness of burnt sugar and the cannonade of popping corn filled the house for hours as Stella labored around the blazing stove through the night preparing Christmas candy and long strings of dyed popcorn to decorate the house "from corner to corner."

The warm smells and sweet feasts attracted flies as well as wanton boys to the kitchen. Especially during the summer when the nearby barnyard was ripe and the windows wide open, great sheets of flypaper hung around the room like banners, stirred slightly by an occasional breeze. When the smooth black paper became heavy and encrusted, Stella took it down, rolled it gingerly, and tossed it into the firebox where it crackled brightly for a few seconds, then flaked into nothing.

On the counter beside the stove Mother kept a simple nine-by-twelve-inch book bound in imitation red leather like an old ledger. "It had all her recipes in it," recalls Stella's granddaughter Jeremy Capillé. "It was all handwritten and she had a very spidery, beautiful handwriting. On the side of each recipe were little notes, like 'this is especially good,' or 'after you've taken it out of the oven, don't forget to let it cool,' or 'try letting it sit overnight.' She wrote personal notes, too, like 'Made this cake for Jack's fifth birthday.' And it was so full of her handwriting, with cards clipped on at almost every page, that there was no order to it. You would find a recipe for dumplings right next to one for carrot cake."

The kitchen's secret was the cellarway: a small, shallow hole in the ground beneath the house where, even in the inescapable summer heat, there was always a stale remnant of coolness in the air. Jackson seldom ventured down alone; but he had descended with his mother and seen her take the cover from one of the crocks and ladle buttermilk into a pitcher. He had himself groped in the butter jar, sniffing the sweet damp smell, and pulled out a pat of butter wrapped in moist cheesecloth; fetched apples from the barrel for pie; and brought up sweet milk for oatmeal—although he preferred to use the cream he skimmed off the top of a fresh pan of milk from the barn the way his brothers showed him.

Outside the back door, a path led to the barnyard. Jackson often stood for hours at a time behind the safety of the screen door, staring at the busy, dusty world of the barnyard, so different from the world of doilies and lace gowns his mother had created inside. Unlike the soft, curtained interior light, the light in the barnyard was pure and clear as glass, so bright that it threw a glare up from the hard-packed earth. At noon the sky was ice white; in the evenings, limpid blue.

Jackson was at his post by the back door every morning when Stella stepped outside to prime the pump that stood hard by the kitchen door, then disappeared around the side of the house to tend her rose garden. A long flume ran from the pump along the top of a rickety trestle on the right side of the path to the water tubs for the livestock on the other side of the barnyard fence. After Mother had watered her roses and filled her two buckets for cooking and cleaning, Dad would come out and work the squeaky handle for a long time until the distant tubs were magically full. As he grew bolder, Jackson explored the whole length of the trestle aqueduct, although he was never tall enough to see the water in its course.

To the left of the path, opposite the flume, stood the outhouse with its five holes. "The Sears, Roebuck catalogue was the toilet tissue," Frank Pollock remembers. "It was tissue-thin paper, my god, a thousand pages it seemed like. You could sit there and read and look at these pictures and wish you could have this and that, then rip off a page." In the corner stood a can of lye to keep away the relentless flies. Like most farmhands, the Pollock boys shunned the outhouse whenever possible, preferring to make evanescent designs on the

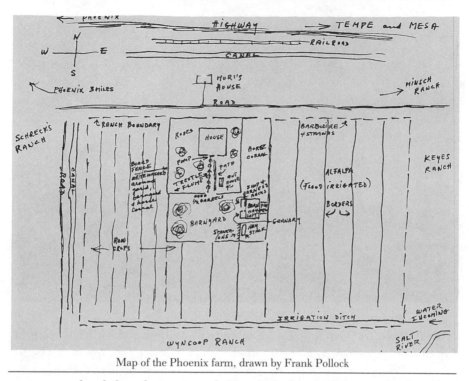

Map of the Phoenix farm, drawn by Frank Pollock

nearest patch of dry, dusty ground. Young Jackson often saw his brothers urinating in the fields or in the far corners of the barnyard, sometimes competing to see who could reach farthest. Too young to compete, he would retreat to the outhouse, sitting in sullen, fly-plagued privacy even to urinate—a habit that persisted for the rest of his life, even after he was old enough to make the same long yellow arcs his brothers made.

Beyond the outhouse, on the other side of a whitewashed board fence, lay the vast, undifferentiated expanse of the barnyard. From the gate to the back fence fifty or sixty feet away, the ground was a table of brown dust strewn with yellow straw and sticks and a few traces of grass. Three large cottonwood trees cast skittish, doily-like shadows in the dirt. The barnyard was home to Patchwork, a female cat who would stand by during milking until one of the boys pointed a nipple her way and shot a stream of milk into her mouth, and Gyp, a white, short-legged dog with a brown patch around one eye.

Gyp had inherited the fighter's temperament of his bull-terrier father and the survival instincts of his collie mother. The Pollocks would give him up for dead many times in his seventeen years. Once a neighbor borrowed him for a hunting trip and abandoned him in a canyon a hundred miles from Phoenix. "We were all sick about it," recalls Frank, "but a few days later, Gyp showed up. Made it home by himself." Gyp might have been a "great companion" and a "member of the family," but he was also a fighter. "He would never let another dog on the place," Frank remembers. "No one had the nerve to pull Gyp off of a fight for fear he'd turn on them. Dad had to use a pitchfork

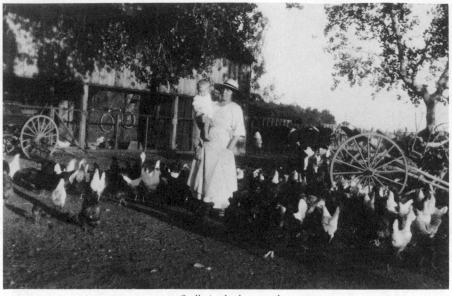

Stella in the barnyard

to break them up. Gyp killed a lot of animals and other dogs." The sight of
Gyp in a killing frenzy could be traumatic. Evelyn Porter Trowbridge, a neighbor and playmate of Jackson's, remembers seeing one particularly vicious dogfight. "Gyp got into it with a stray, and it was the most horrible thing I ever
witnessed."

Gyp was only one of the dangers waiting for two-year-old Jackson beyond
the barnyard gate. (For some time after arriving in Phoenix, he refused to
venture past the kitchen door without his mother.) The real denizens of the
barnyard were the dozens of chickens, fully half his size, that roamed aimlessly
in the dirt and straw. Clutches of them swept nervously back and forth from
house to barn, exploding in squawks at the slightest disturbance. When he tried
to feed them, they pressed in on him, bullying him, surrounding him in a
waist-high frenzy of pecking beaks, beating wings, and beebee eyes. After only
one traumatic encounter, Jackson was given the easier job of collecting eggs
which, because the chickens were free to wander, was more like a treasure
hunt than a chore.

Past the barnyard, Jackson's knowledge of his world grew fainter with every
step. The gray-board barn and horse corral on the east side of the yard were
home to even bigger and more awesome creatures. Jackson never ventured
over the corral fence where his father kept the family's four or five horses when
they were not hitched to a plow or a wagon. (Sande couldn't walk for three
weeks after one of the horses kicked him for "getting too familiar.") Jackson
seldom neared the pen behind the barn where six big hogs and their offspring
kept the family supplied with bacon, chops, and lard. The only farm animals
he saw often were the milk cows, between eight and twelve of them, lined up
at the water trough or in their stalls during milking time. Although he never

milked a cow himself, he watched his older brothers every morning before breakfast as they spread the hay in the manger, waited for the cows to thrust their heads through the V-shaped stanchions, then slipped the loose board over their necks, trapping them. The white stream of milk made a metallic buzz as it hit the empty bucket, then, as the bucket filled, "softened to a steady purr."

Jackson could reach the hayloft at the top of the barn only with his father's help. When Patchwork chose to have her kittens in the loft's seclusion, Dad hoisted him up to see the tiny, mewing litter. The hayloft was replenished through an opening at one end equipped with a Jackson fork; its crescent-shaped metal talons could grasp a bale or a huge bundle of hay and unload a wagon in half the time it took a man with a pitchfork. Dad also used the fork when he wanted to butcher one of the big hogs. "He killed the hog with a gunshot between the eyes," remembers Frank, "then hung it up by the hind legs, cut its throat and let the blood drain out, dropped it into a barrel of scalding hot water and scraped off the hair."

Beyond the barn and corral was his father's domain. Although only twenty acres, it seemed endless. Only on rare occasions was Jackson allowed to tag along behind his older brothers as they left the familiar barnyard through a gate in the whitewashed fence and climbed the low embankment that surrounded the fields. From the top of the rise, he could see his whole world: the small adobe house surrounded by trees on one side, the green-striped fields on the other, everything encircled by the brown, crenellated horizon of North, South, Squaw, and Camelback mountains and, here and there, distant stands of trees marking other farms and other worlds. Laid out before him, the fields were a study in symmetry and order. Along the south side of the farm, its razor-straight course marked by a line of unkempt greenery, an irrigation ditch brought water from some unseen source whenever Dad paid the water man, the zanjero. "How many feet do you want?" the zanjero would ask, noting the answer in his little book along with the time the water should be turned on and for how long. By some magic, exactly at the appointed hour, the water would flow through the ditch and into the gate leading to the fields. To Jackson, the periodic coming of the water meant a swim and, for a few hours afterward, a chance to play in the changing landscape of receding puddles it left behind.

Running perpendicular to the irrigation ditch, along its full length at intervals of eighteen feet, like the tines of a comb, were low banks of sandy soil that divided the fields into long green strips or "borders." The banks allowed each border to be flooded separately depending on the crop and the weather. Within the strict grid of thirty-six borders, the patterns were constantly changing. A staggered irrigation schedule meant that some borders were silvered with new water, others—recently flooded—were dark brown, and others had dried to the light sandy color of the barnyard. One border would be filled with big-leafed melon vines and hundreds of watermelons, another with a soft green cover of strawberries. Tomato plants grew in ostentatious disorder next to more modest cucumber vines, rangy cantaloupes just across from regiments of corn.

Here and there stood patches of sweet potatoes, yams, okra, and anything else that could be loaded in the wagon and taken to the farmers' market in Phoenix. Most of the borders, however, were given over to alfalfa. Its sweet fragrance hung over the fields even on the hottest days, its bright green young shoots or purplish mature blossoms waving in the rare breeze and spilling across the grid.

From his vantage on the embankment, looking across the field of constantly changing stripes, Jackson could see his father: a tiny, distant figure, bent over the ground, plowing a field, seeding a furrow, tending a shoot, harvesting a crop, alone in a vast arena. He seemed to Jackson a tireless figure, like his mother, but more distant and working on a far larger scale. Where his mother crocheted her intricate designs on pillowcases and tablecloths, his father worked on a canvas that stretched from horizon to horizon.

In the geography of Jackson Pollock's childhood, there was also a hell—a forbidden place that both fascinated and terrified.

Half a mile west along Sherman Street, Jackson's universe came to an abrupt end. The green alfalfa gave way to sand and sagebrush, the road descended, and high gravel banks rose up on either side. Farther still, the land suddenly fell away and the road plunged into a deep gully several hundred feet wide. A dry wash of white sand curved through the bottoms. The road narrowed, then snaked its way down the steep walls of "bare, rain-washed earth" and across a little wooden bridge spanning the creekbed. "Here and there rocks cropped out and a cactus thrust up its spears," Sande Pollock recalled. This was the arroyo, a forbidden territory of lizards and rattlesnakes and man-eating coyotes, of magical cacti filled with water, and supernatural stillness—the ideal place for a sensitive child's exaggerated fears and private demons to take up residence. Whenever Sande suggested going to the arroyo, Jackson reminded him that "Mother wouldn't like it." When the family rode through in the wagon, he would beg the driver to "stay on the road." On the rare occasions when Sande shamed him into exploring it, he was paralyzed with fear. According to Sande's account of one such trip: "If the brush rustled, [we] jumped."

On the other side of the arroyo lay the Mesquite Camp, a tuberculosis sanitarium on the outskirts of Phoenix. To Jackson's brothers who rode the milk cart every morning (Roy Pollock had a contract to supply the sanitarium with milk), there was nothing mysterious about the rows of tent-like shelters with their screened porches, wandering patients, and unnatural quiet. To Jackson, however, who had heard of it but never seen it, who knew only "that there were sick people in it and that it used up a lot of milk," the sanitarium remained for the rest of his life, like the arroyo that guarded it, a landscape for nightmares.

Beyond the irrigation ditch and barbed-wire fences of his father's farm, Jackson saw little of the outside world. The Porters, who lived a few farms over, a mile down the road, were sharecroppers, poorer than the Pollocks, and considered "lower class" by others in the area—Jay called them "backwoods people"—but they were friendly and they were family, albeit distant, so the two clans often spent summer Sundays together over watermelons or ice cream. The Schrecks lived just across the lane to the west in a small frame house distinguished by the automobile displayed proudly out front. Like Roy Pollock, Adolphus Schreck had moved to Arizona partly for health reasons, bringing his young family with him. (The eldest daughter, Ellen, was just old enough to play with Jackson.) Half a mile east, Jacob Minsch ran a big, relatively prosperous farm with a machine shop that Roy used occasionally. To the south lived the reclusive Mr. Wyncoop, the neighbor who had abandoned Gyp in the canyon. According to the stories whispered by local children, Mr. Wyncoop was a "retired prospector" with a hoard of gold buried somewhere on his ranch. He owned the land the Porters worked but lived alone, tinkering with his inventions, and supplying grist for the local rumor mill.

Of all the inhabitants of the outside world, none played a more important role in Jackson's private world than the Moris, a Japanese family that lived just north across Sherman Street. Yoshiro Mori had been a houseboy in Santa Cruz, California, before marrying Ayame Hamasaki, a recent arrival from his hometown of Kumamoto, Japan, and moving his family to the Salt River valley in 1913, about the same time that the Pollocks arrived from Coronado. With the help of a local missionary—who signed the deed because Japanese were barred from owning land in Phoenix—the Moris moved into a tiny but handsome brick house with green trim, set back from the road at the end of a lane of chinaberry trees. Jackson often walked down the lane to play with Shizuko Mori, a shy little girl his own age, and Akinabu, her round-faced younger brother. He rode in the Moris' truck and watched as the father made bread and danced around the stove while it baked. He watched the mother, who spoke no English, dressed in a long white dress, quietly preparing dinners of Japanese vegetables. He studied the strange-looking newspaper that arrived every week from Los Angeles, so unlike his parents' papers and magazines, and stood enchanted at Ayame's elbow as she wrote letters to relatives in Japan, creating pages of intricate calligraphy with hand movements even finer and more delicate than those of his mother crocheting.

Because the Pollocks never went to church, family trips outside the neighborhood were rare. Once a year, the circus came to Phoenix and the whole family took a day off—"probably the only day off in the whole damn year," according to Frank. They watched the noontime parade through the center of town and spent the afternoon in the big tent. In five years, the only other family outing was a "hayride picnic" with the Porters to Camelback Mountain. It may have been on this trip that Jackson first heard the story of the Hohokam—the civilization that had flourished in the same valley more than a thousand years before. The road to Camelback paralleled the course of the old Hohokam canals that had connected a vast network of communities ("the most complex urban civilization outside of Mexico in prehistoric times," according to one

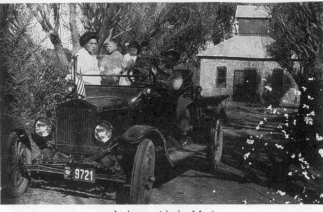

Jackson with the Moris

historian). Jackson could see from the road the remains of Hohokam adobe houses, some of them several stories high, as well as the faded routes of their long, narrow canals, a few of which had been excavated by recent settlers to carry water again after ten centuries of disuse.

From the top of Camelback, Jackson could survey the whole Salt River valley, forty miles long, ten miles wide, bounded by the Superstition Mountains on the east, the White Tank Mountains on the west, and the black lava flows of Squaw Peak on the north. However much the panoramic view piqued his curiosity about the world outside the envelope of farm and family, he had few opportunities to explore it. He was always "too young": too young to accompany his father to the farmers' market in Phoenix every week, too young to sit next to him in the wagon, too young to eat breakfast with him in a *real* restaurant in town, too young to have "anything to do with the farming operations," according to brother Frank. He was also too young to tag along with Charles and Jay when they struck out for Phoenix along the railroad tracks that ran just north of the farm. Returning from one such adventure, they questioned their father about the letters "I W W" scrawled on walls and fences along the way. His sympathetic explanations of the International Workers of the World and its struggles against capitalist exploitation were among the first disturbing hints they had that the world beyond Camelback was not only vast but also troubled.

For the most part, Jackson knew of that world only when it came to him. Visitors to the Pollock farm were rare; even a passing car was a special event. (In 1913, there were only 646 cars in all of Phoenix.) Although the mailman stopped at the Pollocks' box on the road only once or twice a week to deliver magazines and an occasional letter from relatives, Jackson waited eagerly in the roadside ditch every day for the calamitous noise of his car. Sande remembered that Jackson told his mother, "I think I'll be a mailman when I get big. Then I'll have an automobile and drive all over the country."

On Saturdays, small bands of Apache Indians would sometimes stop their wagons at the Pollock farm to buy melons. During the week, Roy would stack the flawed melons by the side of the barn—the good ones went to market— and then sell them to the Indians for a nickel apiece. The Pollock boys had heard the terrifying stories of the Apache wars, which had ended only twenty-five years earlier. The older boys had even seen Indians on their trips into Phoenix, although only the peaceful Pima and Maricopa Indians, not the legendary Apaches. Jackson and Sande, who had heard their older brothers talk of having seen Indians in Cody, were especially captivated by these strange-looking people with their long black hair and bright ornaments. "The women were decked out in colorful dresses with bold patterns," Frank Pollock recalls. "The bucks wore jeans and belts with silver buckles. Sometimes they were made out of snakeskin. And they always had rings and bracelets. They were a sparkling people."

On rare special occasions, Jackson rode into Phoenix with his mother. From the moment he climbed into the old buggy, took off his shoes, curled his toes around the dashboard, and pushed his straw hat back the way his brothers did, he was rigid with curiosity. The horse, Brown Jim, balked and whinnied nervously when cars rattled by. Over the flat, treeless approach, Jackson saw the big new buildings of Phoenix, the just completed state capitol building and YMCA, the cupola of the fire station, and the twin spires of the opera house. Mother's destination was inevitably Goldwater's Store at the corner of First and Adams. Amid the hardships of farm life, Goldwater's was an oasis of self-indulgence, an extravaganza of style and finery unlike anything in Cody, where Stella and her sons could browse through four floors of furniture imported from Vienna, finger the finest clothes from Chicago and New York, and ride the first elevator most Phoenicians had ever seen.

In town, Jackson also saw the blacksmith who repaired his father's wagon— the first black man he had ever seen; he heard Mexicans talking excitedly about Pancho Villa's return after the assassination of Francisco Madero (he recognized Villa's name from the stories his brother Charles told about Villa's raids across the border); he saw the Chinese peddlers' "village," a street lined with wagons from which Chinese families sold vegetables, and Indians surrounded by their handiwork—baskets, pots, silverware, beads, blankets, turquoise jewelry. Especially on Saturdays when the whole countryside came to shop and sell and trade, and the stores stayed open late, the streets of Phoenix formed canals of color and energy, of strange faces and curious details, all of them rendered impossibly vivid in the blazing Arizona sun.

5

AN ORDINARY FAMILY

When Roy Pollock agreed to buy Hart Baker's twenty acres of irrigated land, he thought he finally had what he wanted. At last, no one was looking over his shoulder or telling him what to do; at last, the ghost of James Matt Pollock had been exorcised. "Here he'd finally got ahold of something," says son Frank, "something that was *his.*"

Liberated, Roy threw himself into farm work with an intensity that often bordered on anger. Using the skills he had learned so well as a for-hire farmhand back in Ringgold County, Roy coddled and coaxed his stock with such a loving hand that, in time, his pigs were fatter and his cows more productive than any of his neighbors'. "He loved animals and the animals seemed to love him," says Frank. "He could get them to do anything." He worked the same magic with the soil, winning blue ribbons for his produce at local fairs; growing fatter melons, taller alfalfa, and more of it per acre. He introduced new crops to the sandy Phoenix soil, like the yams his cousin Leonard Porter had brought from Louisiana. Roy was so proud of his farm and its productivity that he invited his widowed mother to come to Phoenix and see it. When a traveling photographer came to the door, Roy posed his family with slices of his biggest watermelon and proudly sent copies of the picture to all his relatives. "Dad was just showing off," says Frank.

But the isolated life of a hired hand, concerned only with the productivity of soil and stock, had not taught Roy *all* the skills that an Arizona farmer needed. In Iowa, he didn't have to think about market prices or shipping costs; his father was paid regardless of market conditions. In Arizona, however, working hard wasn't enough. At the glutted, fiercely competitive farmers' market in Phoenix, it wasn't enough to produce the biggest, sweetest melons or the most milk per cow. Unsold, even blue-ribbon produce was worthless. "My father knew how to make things grow and he knew how to care for animals," Charles Pollock remembers, "but he didn't know how to make money doing it."

But Roy Pollock was "a very quiet type of fellow" whose sons saw little of his borning frustration. What they saw was a man buried in work from before dawn until long after dark. Charles and Jay, eleven and nine, helped as they could, but neither showed any real enthusiasm for farm work. Charles delivered papers in the afternoons to earn spending money—none of which was contributed to the family kitty; Jay escaped to school after the morning milking; and Sande and Jackson were too young for real work. Frank, at six, was eager and willing but not much help. To some extent, all the Pollock boys followed the example of their mother who, despite Roy's pleading, steadfastly refused to take any part in running the farm. "Mother's day was spent largely in the kitchen cooking and sewing," Frank remembers. "She spent very little time in the yard. While we were working, she was always writing letters or reading magazines."

Stella's quiet war of attrition soon began to take its toll. Isolated and disdained by his own family, Roy withdrew further into his work. As in Tingley, the fields became his refuge; work, his escape. Daughter-in-law Elizabeth Pollock remembers, "Stella used to talk about the rare occasions when they'd dress up to go somewhere. By the time she got the children all dressed to go, LeRoy would forget he had his good clothes on and would go outside and muck around and get dirty." In apparent retaliation, Roy redoubled his efforts to make men of his overmothered sons. "Jackson didn't talk about his Dad much," recalls Peter Busa, a close friend twenty years later. "Except there was this emphasis on manliness—if you have boys, you have men. That was his father's philosophy." When the time came for the bloody business of castrating the young pigs and calves, Roy made sure that all five boys participated—the oldest helping, the youngest watching. Almost inevitably, such strategies backfired. "I helped with that awful business," Charles recalls ruefully. "You had to tie the animal down on its back first. It was a gory mess and they squealed like crazy. I couldn't understand how Dad brought himself to do it."

Outside of the daily routine of meals and chores, there was little time for contact between father and sons. Occasionally, just before bedtime, Roy would take a book from the glass case and read to Charles and Jay by the light of the kerosene lamp. Sometimes, he would give the book to them, sit back, close his eyes, and listen as they read to him; sometimes drift off into stories about his trip down the Mississippi with Ralph Tidrick, about his adoption by the Pollocks, or about his belief in "the higher power of nature." On those increasingly rare evenings, the older brothers caught a glimpse of the sensitive, romantic man-child that Roy Pollock always struggled to conceal—the father who scolded them for shooting at birds with slingshots or destroying eggs in the nest; the farmer who, at the sight of a beautiful sunset, never failed to "look up from his plow and stare until it was gone."

Jackson Pollock never saw this side of his father. By the time he was old enough to stay up and listen, the readings had become rare events. "With the younger sons he didn't have that much contact," says Frank, who also grew up

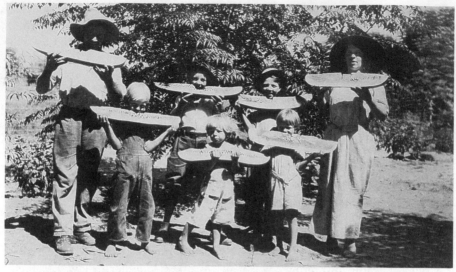

Roy, Frank, Charles, Jackson, Jay, Sande, and Stella in Phoenix, about 1915

too late. "After the first two, I think he kind of gave up." Whether working distantly in the fields or sitting unapproachably in the light of the kerosene lamp, Roy Pollock would remain a dark figure at the far edge of Jackson's world, a figure that he longed to be near but despaired of reaching. According to Sande, whenever his father left the farm, Jackson would stand at the gate and cry.

In place of fatherly affection, Roy Pollock gave his sons a strict system of duties and privileges modeled after the one his father had imposed on him. A boy couldn't wear Levi jeans, "the kind without the bib," until he was five, shoot a gun until he was nine, or drive a team until he was ten. As the oldest, Charles was given the choicest jobs and the most enviable privileges. On his trips every morning to deliver milk to the sanitarium, he drove his own cart drawn by his own pony. When the boys walked to the fields, they walked in order of age, their rank reflected in the implements they carried: Dad in front with the horse, Charles next with the plow, Frank with a hoe, Sande with a shovel, and Jackson "tagging along behind without the dignity of even a shovel over his shoulder," according to Sande.

Stella further fanned the flames of rivalry by dividing her boys into two groups; the "Low Steps," Sande and Jackson, and the "High Steps," Charles and Jay, because "when they stood in a row they made regular stairsteps." (Frank, as usual, occupied a filial limbo.) Between the two groups, the dividing line ran deep. The Low Steps were usually assigned to Mother's work in the kitchen, the High Steps to Dad's work in the barnyard. In the mornings, "the High Steps were awakened first . . . but they could never resist the temptation of pulling the covers off [the Low Steps], or sprinkling water in their faces," according to Sande. In the evenings, only the High Steps were allowed to churn

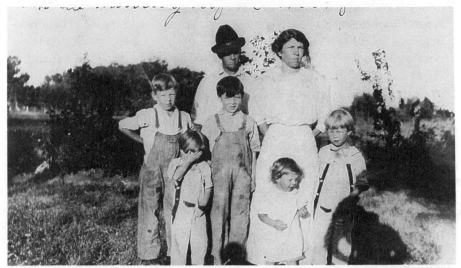

Roy and Stella with (from left) Charles, Sande, Jay, Jackson, and Frank

Mother's butter. Roy let footraces, which the High Steps invariably won, determine who could ride next to him in the wagon, and when Stella went into town, the High Steps were always first in line for the two extra seats. During most of the Phoenix years, the High Steps went to school while the Low Steps stayed home.

Despite the gulf that separated them, the High Steps seemed to take a special pride in their youngest brother. "Jackson was the baby," says Jay, "and for that reason, it seems to me we went overboard feeling responsible for him, taking care of him so that he didn't get in trouble." In their enthusiasm to indulge him, however, they quickly spoiled him. Unlike his brothers, Jackson was never required to work. "We didn't ask him to help out around the house," Jay remembers. But to Jackson, such enforced idleness may have felt more like ostracism than privilege. He would linger at the kitchen door or at the edge of the fields, begging to be given some trivial task, like pulling carrots or radishes for his mother, or inspecting the borders for gopher holes for his father. When work was allocated, he insisted "I will too" so often that the phrase became a favorite taunt within the family. On the rare occasions when he was given a responsible task, his overeagerness often resulted in embarrassment and failure. Sande later recorded one such incident.

As I ran along the top of the embankment I saw that Jackson and Gyp were in mad pursuit of an excited gopher. . . . I was just behind them, when Jackson made a flying tackle and caught the tip of the gopher's tail. Jackson, flat on his stomach, panted,"I got him!" Then he let out a yell and jumped up as the gopher turned and fastened its teeth in his finger. "Ouch! Oh, ouch!" screamed Jackson. "Take him off! Oh, take him off!" I was frightened too, but the sight of blood and Jackson's pain forced me to act. I grabbed the gopher and started to pull. "Wait! Don't do that!" yelled Charles, as he came running to us. "You'll hurt him worse—here, hold Jack's arm—" As I did as I was told, Charles hit the gopher on the head with a rock. The little animal dropped to the ground without a sound. . . . Jackson was shaking from head to foot and his face was so white the freckles stood out browner than ever across his nose. . . . "It is pretty bleedy," sniffed Jackson, trying to keep back the tears.

Jackson's brothers may have deferred to him as the baby of the family, and protected him from work, but underneath they resented his privileges and envied his idleness. "Jackson was a dandelion," says Frank. "We didn't pay much attention to him. We did the work and, if there was any playing to be done, Jack did it. Maybe he fed a chicken or two. That's easy to do. Maybe gathered an egg. He never milked a cow—but I sure did." Like all emotions in the Pollock family, such resentments rarely, if ever, surfaced. But Jackson undoubtedly sensed them in the teasing and impatience that greeted his every effort. According to Sande, when the family planned a trip to Camelback Mountain, Jackson was "busy running from one person to another, begging to be told what mountains *really* would be like." But no one would tell him. As Jackson grew up, his brothers would continue to extract payment for the child-hood privileges they had conferred on him. "They used to refer to him as 'baby' up into his teenage years," remembers Marie Pollock, Frank's wife, "and he *hated* it." All of Jackson's brothers would later insist, with Frank, that "there was never any rivalry between us. We were never in competition with each other. Never. Just wasn't so." But Jackson knew otherwise. Thirty years after leaving Phoenix, he told his friend Clement Greenberg about a recurrent night-mare in which his brothers tried to push him off the edge of a cliff.

Only in his imagination could Jackson close the gap that separated him from his brothers. Almost as soon as he could talk, he began appropriating events from their lives and recasting them to include himself. He talked about "his trips to the mountains" long before he had seen a mountain; about the birth of Brown Jim, the family horse, although he had been only a baby at the time; about a flood in the arroyo that he had only heard about from Sande. Years later, Sande recalled the exchange.

"Remember the time there was water in the creek bed?" Sande said at the dinner table one night.

"I remember," said Jackson.

"No, you don't, you were too small," said Sande.

"But I *do* remember," Jackson insisted. "The water came down—it was muddy and yellow and there were branches and sticks in it—and it poured over the bridge and over the banks and over the rocks—and it roared—and the rain came down. . . ."

"You don't remember that at all," said Sande. "You were too little."

But Jackson went on, "and the next day the water was gone again—it was gone to the ocean."

Nothing made Jackson feel more like an outsider than sex. "Mother and Dad felt we didn't need to be told the facts of life," says Frank. "We learned that from the animals. We grew up with roosters and hens, dogs and bitches, boars and sows, bulls and cows, studs and mares. Sexual activity was everywhere." Jackson's older brothers occasionally let slip tantalizing insinuations, but they never dared to ask (or entertain) any questions among themselves about sex. "You wouldn't confide to anyone, least of all your brothers, that you didn't know anything," Frank remembers. "You would just imply that you were experienced." But when the neighbor, Mr. Mori, accused Frank of "making mischief" with his daughter Shizuko, Frank denied the charge. "I told him we weren't into anything," he recalls. "I didn't even *know* about such mischief." Later, Jackson bragged to Sande that he, not Frank, had been caught and reprimanded for "playing doctor" with Shizuko.

For the rest of his life, Jackson would play with reality in the same way, both in his life and in his art, taking the real world—his age, his sexual inexperience, an unseen flood—and elaborating on it, gradually transforming it into the world as he wanted it to be, or the image that he wanted to see.

If Jackson could have changed places with any of his brothers, it would have been Charles. Charles enjoyed a catalogue of privileges that piqued the envy of all his brothers. He could read like his father (and increasingly took Roy's place under the kerosene lamp); he could play marbles, shoot a gun, chew gum, and blow bubbles. He could even whistle—a skill that Sande and Jackson spent endless hours trying to match. Because he had his own horse, a pinto pony named Prince, Charles could also travel. For him, trips to Phoenix were not special occasions at all; he went every day to pick up the papers he delivered for the Arizona *Republican*, often stopping on the way at the only movie house in town to watch the latest serial adventure of Pearl White. Jackson and Sande listened raptly to Charles's tales of the movies and of his trips to the traveling circus, the motorcycle velodrome, and the fairgrounds where he watched "Model T Polo," a wild game in which players rode stripped-down cars with foot-operated gears.

Of all Charles's privileges, none was more envied than his special relationship with Stella. "I was the first born and the first to strike out," says Charles. "Inevitably, I suppose, that showed in Mother's feelings." At Stella's insistence, Charles quit his barnyard chores and began pursuing his own interests at an early age. "We had eight or ten cows in Phoenix," Charles recalls, "but I never learned how to milk. I managed to escape that." According to one family member, "Just like Grandma Pollock, Charles's dream was to escape being a farmer. That was their dream." When Stella drove the skittish Brown Jim into town, it was always Charles who accompanied her—"in case she got tired."

On a trip to Goldwater's Department Store, she bought denim for the other brothers' shirts, but silk pongee for Charles's. "I had the idea that I wanted something special," Charles recalls. With money from his paper route, he also bought a pair of Florsheim kangaroo-skin shoes—"the most expensive shoes you could buy. My mother gave me a taste for quality materials."

But the most important reason to admire and envy Charles was that he could draw.

As early as Cody, Charles had begun to take an unusual interest in the visual world. Even before he could read, he would linger over cartoons in the Cody papers, like Mutt and Jeff, Buster Brown, Happy Hooligan, and Little Nemo. Later, when the family moved to the Watkins ranch, he experienced an artistic epiphany while exploring the dry sagebrush hills nearby. Inside an abandoned log schoolhouse, its interior illuminated only by streaks of light angling between the window boards, he found hundreds of sheets of lined foolscap scattered across the floor, each sheet covered with handwriting in the Palmer method. "The elaborate pattern made a tremendous impression on me," he recalls. By the time the family settled in Phoenix a few years later, Charles considered himself an artist.

Soon after their arrival, he began painting lessons with "Mrs. Warner," a Swiss immigrant who lived with her husband in the desert between the Pollock farm and Tempe. "She painted in oils, so that's what I did," Charles recalls, "and she introduced me to Payne's Gray and other colors I had never heard of." Charles's search for something better, his mother's search, found its fulfillment in the feel of sable brushes and the smell of linseed oil. "At twelve or thirteen," says Frank, "Charles was always drawing. My Dad thought he ought to be on the farm more, but Mother would say, 'He's entitled to it.' "

Charles turned all of his attention and energy to the new pursuit. At home, he cut illustrations out of Stella's *Ladies' Home Journal* and Roy's *Country Gentleman* to create a "library of art." He cherished these illustrations, he told later interviewers, "and learned to make judgments about their relative merit." At the Wilson School, he befriended a talented Japanese classmate, Ginsu Matsudo, who "could draw the most elegant vase or bowl."

None of this was lost on Jackson, who watched his older brother's exciting life with wide-eyed envy. He saw the way Charles cut illustrations from magazines with his mother's scissors, the way he rode off on Prince every Saturday to his lessons with Mrs. Warner, the way he took out his pad and began to sketch when Mr. Wyncoop asked him to make a drawing of a submarine he had invented. "I think we were all influenced by Charles," says Frank. "I know I was." Sande put the point more bluntly. "Charles started this whole damn thing," he told a *Time/Life* reporter forty-five years later. In 1957, in the brief interlude between Jackson's death and her own, Stella told an interviewer from the Des Moines *Register:* "When Jackson was a little boy and was asked what he wanted to be when he grew up, he'd always say, 'I want to be an artist like brother Charles.' "

In return for adoration, Charles gave Jackson the minimum attention nec-essary to transact family business—which, among the quiet and insular Pol-locks, was little indeed.

Of all the brothers, only Sande gave Jackson the attention he craved. Lumped together as the "Low Steps," they became a single unit within the family, almost indistinguishable as individuals. "It was always 'Jack and Sande,' " Frank remembers, " 'Jack and Sande this, Jack and Sande that.' They were like two burrs on a dog's tail." As a role model, Sande was a world apart from Charles. Where Charles was refined and sensible, Sande was rough and hot-headed. Where Charles was detached and icily self-contained like his mother, Sande was adventurous and high-spirited. Where Charles cut pictures out of magazines, Sande shot birds off of power lines with his slingshot and, if he had been old enough, would have eagerly joined his father on hunting trips.

Jackson's joyous hours with Sande might have been enough to offset his deepening sense of alienation from the rest of the family if Stella hadn't made the mistake of putting him in Sande's charge—a task that Sande soon grew to resent. Around the house, Jackson needed constant supervision; in the fields, he prevented Sande from undertaking more responsible jobs for his father. In 1915, when Sande should have joined his older brothers at the Wilson School, Stella kept him home so he could continue to care for Jackson during the day.

Sometime in 1916, the drama of "Jack and Sande" was played out in one brief, traumatic episode. It began in the barnyard of the Pollock farm amid the fluttering chickens and flying dust. For Jackson, it was an unusually quiet and lonely day: Dad Pollock was out in front of the house with the zanjero arrang-ing for the next irrigation day; Stella was with her mother-in-law, Lizzie Pol-lock, who had come to Phoenix for a visit. The three oldest brothers were all at school. Sande and an older neighborhood boy, Charles Porter, were playing in the barnyard around the chopping block—a half-stump where Dad and the High Steps split cottonwood for the kitchen stove—pointedly ignoring Jackson. Eager to be included, Jackson fetched a small log from the woodpile, carried it to the chopping block, and picked up the ax that lay nearby. According to Sande, "Porter saw Jack and said, 'You're too young to handle an ax. Tell me where you want it cut.' " Jackson placed his right index finger on the spot where he wanted the blow to fall, and Porter awkwardly raised the long-handled ax. "It was a regular man-sized ax that I was usin'," Porter recalls. "I didn't have too much control over it." When the blade struck, it caught Jack-son's finger just above the last knuckle.

The little fingertip hit the ground and almost immediately an old bull rooster —fourteen pounds and "almost a pet"—waddled over and began pecking at it. (No one actually saw the rooster swallow the fingertip, but when Charles Pollock returned from school and searched around the chopping block, it was gone.) It was a few long seconds before any of the boys realized what had happened. Porter threw the ax down and ran home. Jackson—who was "too

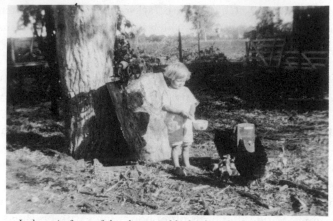

Jackson in front of the chopping block where he lost his fingertip

shocked to cry," according to Porter—stuck the "bleedy" stump in his mouth and followed Sande in search of their mother. Stella reacted with chilling Presbyterian calm. "It was just another one of those things that happened to the Pollock boys," Frank remembers. "Mother was a realist, and whatever happened, she just took it in her stride." After covering the wound with sugar and wrapping it in a bandage, she led a bewildered but still tearless Jackson out the front gate, commandeered the zanjero's horse and buggy, and drove into Phoenix to see Dr. Monacle.

While Stella was calm and Jackson remained paralyzed, Sande was "the one who got sick," he later admitted. Although he must have felt, at some level, that Jackson had gotten what he deserved, Sande had also faltered in his duty to take care of Jackson and, in so doing, had failed his mother. For years afterward he would harbor feelings of inadequacy and guilt as well as anger over the incident. For Jackson, too, the episode at the chopping block had a double edge, one that emerged only years later as he recounted the story in different ways to different friends. In 1923, when the Pollocks returned briefly to Arizona, he told Evelyn Minsch that he had "laid his finger on the block and dared Porter to 'Cut it off.' " "The boy thought Jack would pull his finger away at the last second," Minsch recalls, "but he didn't." In the 1940s, Jackson told Axel Horn that he and some friends "were bored and hanging around the chopping block when one kid picked up the ax and said, 'Somebody put your finger down.' " "The way Jack told it," says Horn, "it wasn't an accident. It was a dare, and he took it." Late in his life, Jackson told an East Hampton neighbor that it was Sande who had wielded the ax.

And, in a way, it was. In a test of manhood, Jackson had offered his finger, and in his eyes Sande, not Porter, had cut it off. But the loss of a fingertip was a small price to pay for the bond that was created between them in that instant, a bond of love and guilt, sacrifice and resentment, that would hold them in the same unresolved embrace for the next forty years.

■　■　■

From the moment she laid eyes on the tiny adobe house in the middle of the desert, Stella hated it—hated it in the same silent, tenacious way she had hated the farm where she grew up. She had left the Watkins ranch longing for another house like the one in Cody: simple but dignified, a house she could decorate to her ladylike taste. Instead, Roy had brought her to this shabby little mud hut with its rough walls, uneven floors, and a barnyard just outside the back door. Every summer her resentment was rekindled when the poorly built house began to molt like a desert insect. "The heat would strip the plaster off the outside," Frank Pollock remembers, "and every damn year Dad would have to re-plaster sections of the house. Mother always insisted that he at least do that."

The Pollocks' neighbors soon noticed that the new woman in their midst was not happy to be there. She seldom paid visits to nearby houses, never invited neighbors or their children into her house, and, except when she traveled into Phoenix, was seldom seen about. "She thought she was a little bit more society than the rest of the farm folks around there," recalls Charles Porter. "She had a little bit of an air to her. I don't think she appreciated farming too much." Indeed, in later years she would refer to it as "low-down drudgery."

At night, Stella pored over her magazines, newspapers, and catalogues, following with furtive pleasure the genteel life of Henry Field's family as related in the latest edition of the Henry Field catalogue, and wrote letters to relatives, especially her mother and Aunt Stella. During the day, she rarely ventured into the barnyard, preferring instead to tend her private flower garden where she grew rare flowers and rosebushes with seeds ordered from Iowa. The rest of her time was spent cooking, baking, and sewing—activities appropriate for a farm, but performed in a way that underscored her disdain for real farm life. When she cooked, she preferred new recipes taken from magazines, recipes that required extra time and special ingredients. For every meal she prepared a variety of foods, and always in extravagant quantities. She used only the best ingredients, whether store-bought or appropriated from Roy's market wagon. "She boasted that she would take the best for herself and sell what was left," recalls Stella's daughter-in-law, Marie Pollock, "where farmers usually do it in the reverse." When she sewed, she neglected the everyday mending chores, preferring to labor over the latest patterns from the Ladies' Home Journal or to crochet another tablecloth for her collection. "She was an exquisite seamstress," says another daughter-in-law, "and she wouldn't work on any material unless it was the finest procurable—if it wasn't, she did without."

As in Cody, Stella refused to discipline her brood. "If you did something that was kind of foolish she might say, 'Where is your head?' meaning you ought to know better," says Frank, "but she never reprimanded or spanked us—ever." In fact, she had other, more effective ways of maintaining her iron grip. Food, for example. In Stella's hands, meals became a daily ritual of control. She prepared elaborate, enticing offerings which ensured that her boys would come home every evening. "If you had done something she didn't like," Frank remembers, "she might cut you out of a piece of pie or something. That would be pretty harsh." Despite the modern facilities available in Phoenix, she refused to take her sons to doctors or hospitals even in the direst emergencies. (Jackson's trip to Dr. Monacle was a rare exception.) No one, in fact, was allowed to come between her and her children. If they insisted on attending school events or going on Sunday trips, she would refuse to go along, perhaps fearing that the presence of other adults, including Roy, might dilute her authority. "Whenever Dad would read to us," Jay remembers, "Mother wouldn't participate. She would always find something else to do." She urged them to stay away from neighborhood kids and, despite her own religious upbringing, kept them out of church. Whatever her sons' needs—social, medical, even spiritual— Stella and Stella alone would take care of them.

Far from encouraging the "independent and adventurous" boys Sande later bragged about, Stella's protectiveness produced a family of timid, fearful sons, of such delicate sensibilities that any contact with the outside world produced near panic. On trips into Phoenix, they recoiled from strangers and kept close by her side. When a neighborhood Catholic family, the Schrecks, took Charles to church, he was terrified. "They were kneeling and crossing themselves," he remembers, "and it just paralyzed me with fear." When a rare argument broke out between Roy and Stella at the dinner table, Charles burst into tears. "At that time, the slightest raising of voices might have set me off," he recalls. When Frank was finally confronted by a doctor—to have adenoids removed— he "ran for his life." "They had to subdue me with chloroform," he remembers. "I suppose I made Mother nervous."

To avoid making Mother nervous, the Pollock boys learned to read her moods with exquisite care and avert her displeasure at all costs. They all remembered one especially vivid and disturbing image of their mother from Phoenix. "She would tie chickens to the clothesline by their feet," Charles recalls, "then she would grab them and cut off their heads one by one. That was pretty shocking." Jackson especially could never forget the sight of his mother gripping a huge knife in her hand—the same hand that spun such delicate webs of lace—slicing off one head after another and throwing them into a pile, the blood draining from the suspended bodies, covering her hands and the knife blade, dripping onto her white apron, making shiny, dark spots in the dirt at her feet.

No one needed Stella's love or read her moods more acutely than her baby, Jackson. When he returned to her even after an afternoon's absence, he would invariably ask, "Did you miss me, Mother?" Once, when Stella and Jackson were driving into town—one of their rare moments alone together—a huge bull, apparently escaped from its pen, charged their spring buggy. The horse reared in panic, overturning the buggy and throwing Jackson and Stella to the ground. Although they were quickly rescued by a passing farmer—who slapped Jackson to stop his crying—the incident so traumatized five-year-old Jackson that he had vivid nightmares of terrifying bulls and terror-stricken horses for the rest of his life.

Far longer and more desperately than any of his brothers, Jackson clung to the needful childlike behavior that bound him to his mother. "He would always run to his mama crying," recalls Akinabu Mori, who was two years younger and considerably smaller than Jackson. "He was a mama's boy, always a crybaby, always running to the mama telling on me—'Oh! He said something *bad*, Mama!' " But Stella paid little heed to Jackson's special needs, treating him with the same hovering detachment as she did all her sons. Her reticence only confirmed Jackson's vague but already powerful feeling that he had some-how disappointed her. Sande remembered his sadly telling a visitor one day: "[Mother] wanted me to be a girl, only I wasn't."

A quarter-mile down the road, Jackson found a playmate to help him act out his reparative fantasies. Evelyn Porter, Charles Porter's sister, was a year younger and, like Jackson, "a very timid child." Evelyn, who was called Evie then, recalls that "we were the only agewise playmates in that area, so we became very close friends." During Jackson's daily visits to the Porter house, the two would "play house out under the trees," Porter remembers. "I wore rompers and Jack wore the same thing. No shoes, of course. We were definitely barefoot kids. I had a little tiny puppy at that time, Trixie, and we had a little tea table. The doll would sit in one chair, Trixie in another, and Jack and I would sit down with them for a tea party. He was just a real sweet farmboy." The tea parties at the Porters' became such a regular event that when a pho-tographer passed through, Evie and Jack dressed up in their Sunday best and recreated the scene for the camera.

Jackson had seen Sande playing his own version of "house" out under the umbrella tree in the front yard. He had built a miniature farm with its own alfalfa field, a canal filled with water from a leaky bucket, a barn made from a crate, wagons made of matchboxes and spools, and cows and horses made out of sticks. Sande, of course, played the daddy. In the fantasy world he shared with little Evie, however, Jackson was free to recast his family and himself as he wanted them to be. "When we were playing house," Porter recalls, "he always insisted on playing the mother. He was the momma, and I was the papa. One time I remember we argued about a little pair of blunt-nosed scis-sors. They were mine, and I wanted to play with them, but he insisted that the momma should have the scissors of the house and *he* was the momma."

As late as 1916, Jackson didn't know that his family was heading for a crisis. Of all the brothers, only Charles, who rode to the farmers' market every morn-ing with his father, saw it coming. "We'd get up at four in the morning, hitch up the horses and go into the market with a load of produce. When it didn't sell, Dad would have to start peddling it to restaurants door to door. That was a painful and humiliating experience for him. But Mother never knew. He would throw away what was left before we got home so she wouldn't see it."

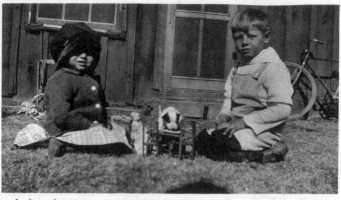

Jackson having a "tea party" with Evelyn Porter and her dog Trixie

Even at age fourteen, Charles could see that the problem was "a glutted market." What he couldn't see were the complex forces—some within his father's control, some not—that were driving the Pollocks toward bankruptcy. By 1917, due to the development of a long staple hybrid by big landowners and the explosion in demand following America's entry into the First World War, cotton had replaced alfalfa as king of the Salt River valley. As more and more farmers went "cotton-crazy" or just diversified beyond alfalfa, the dairy industry declined. Between the big new consolidated dairies and the cheap dairy products being shipped in on an improved rail system, small farmers like Roy Pollock were being squeezed out of the dairy business. Besides, the unusually sandy soil on his farm could never have sustained the kind of intense cultivation necessary to compete in the new marketplace. "All the land around there was sandy," remembers Akinabu Mori, who stayed on an adjoining farm for another thirty years after the Pollocks abandoned theirs, "but [the Pollocks'] place was even sandier than other farms in the same area. When the ground is like that, the water goes down fast and it doesn't hold the fertilizer. The ground was so poor to start with it was a wonder he could grow anything."

Roy Pollock might have been able to hang on to his farm, as the Moris hung on to theirs, if his family had been willing to endure greater hardship. "There were times we went hungry for a week with no food at all," Mori says, recalling his family's plight during the Depression. "We would spend all our money for seed and have to wait for the crops to come up to eat." In fact, the cotton boom in Phoenix fizzled three years after it started and those farmers who had stayed with dairy and truck farming during the craze became suddenly prosperous.

But Roy Pollock had to contend with forces that other small farmers didn't. Stella's "big city" tastes were driving the family toward financial ruin. "Mother was a spendthrift," Frank recalls. "When she went shopping, she would buy yards of cloth and hundred-pound bags of sugar and flour. She *loved* to spend money." According to Charles, Stella was "hopelessly extravagant. Any reasonable farmer would have considered it an outrage, but Mother didn't see anything outrageous about it." (Years later, daughter-in-law Marie discovered just how extravagant Stella could be. "She was staying with us, and even though Frank was earning $60 a week, she used to go out and buy a pound of butter every day for $1.05. She spent 10 percent of our entire income on butter. I said, 'Stella, how about using some margarine for frying?' And she said, 'Absolutely not.' It had to be real butter, and she used it like mad.")

Stella not only blithely spent the family money, she also steadfastly refused to help earn more of it. Although she spent hours crocheting and baking, "she never sold or tried to sell anything she made," Frank recalls. "She wasn't interested in selling." Just as she distanced herself from barnyard chores, she refused to take part in marketing the farm produce. "She only went into town to go shopping," says Frank. "My god that woman loved to shop!"

As the financial noose closed tighter around Roy, it was inevitable, even in a family so atomized and uncommunicative, that tensions would surface. In November 1916, the Pollock boys were surprised and puzzled when their parents argued openly for several days, ostensibly over politics. "Dad was for Wilson and Mother was for Hughes," recalls Frank. "Hughes was announced as the winner and Mother was gloating. The next day the decision was reversed because the votes from California put Wilson on top and it was Dad's turn to gloat." The real focus of the rising tensions wasn't politics, however; it was, as always, control of the family. Having lost the struggle over Charles and Jay in Cody, Roy Pollock was determined to make a farmer and a father's son out of Frank. He talked about sending him to agricultural school in Iowa and pushed him early into a farmer's routine of hard work and responsibility. But the effort backfired. "When you're a kid and you're down there pulling sweet potatoes out of the sand, you get tired of it in time," says Frank. "You'd never want to admit it. You'd never give up because you wouldn't want your dad to think that you couldn't do it. But after a while you resent clawing in the dirt."

When the son he hoped would work beside him began to think of farming as "clawing in the dirt," Roy Pollock must have known he was beaten. "He had dreams," says Frank, "and I think that was the end of them."

But Stella had dreams too, for herself and for her sons, and by 1917 she was pursuing them openly. She sent away for brochures distributed by the chambers of commerce in dozens of California cities, looking once again for "something different, something better." "She had it in her mind that the schools in California were better than those in Arizona," Frank remembers, "and she thought her boys ought to have as good an education as she could get for them. She also wanted a better material life for us." Whether or not Stella confronted Roy in a moment of uncharacteristic openness, the ultimatum was clear: either he would leave the farm or she would leave him—return to Tingley, perhaps —and take the boys with her. "She refused to stay in that environment any longer," says Frank. "If he stayed, he would stay alone." There was no question where his sons' sympathies lay. "Mother was the dominant one," Frank concedes. "She had the love of five boys behind her. If she wanted something better, if she wanted to leave, we were ready to go with her. It wouldn't have been too much of a job to uproot us from that farm where we were just milking cows and feeding chickens." Probably without a word of protest, Roy agreed to go and numbly set about the task of finding a buyer for the farm.

On May 22, 1917, a public auction was held at the farm of L. R. Pollock on Sherman Street between the hours of nine and twelve in the morning. A large crowd turned out, kicking up dust in the barnyard as they milled around the implements that Roy had laid out neatly on the ground. Afraid of strangers and unused to crowds, Jackson sought refuge in the kitchen and watched the strange events from behind the familiar safety of the screen door. When the auction finally began, the bidding was fast as the cows, horses, pigs, and calves were brought one by one up to the auctioneer. The crowd was enthusiastic and the prices good—up to $2.25 for a laying hen—but the day went painfully slowly for a few of the spectators. "It was a sorrowful thing," Frank remembers. "Your friends are the calves and the cows. But everything went." Throughout the morning, Stella graciously passed out the last of the watermelon.

Soon after the auction, the Pollocks boarded a train for the destination that Mother had chosen: Chico, California. To Frank, who watched the unfolding of the last days in Phoenix with sharp, guilty eyes, the significance of the departure was clear in his father's face: "It was the end of my dad."

6

ABANDONED

Over the next six years, the Pollock family would fall apart—not slowly and inadvertently, but precipitously and deliberately—while Jackson watched in helpless silence. Driven by her restless yearning for "something better," Stella would move her family, or what remained of it, in and out of seven houses in six years, as if the demons that plagued her could be left behind like bad soil or inclement weather. No matter where she went, however, faces continued to fall away from her dinner table.

In the summer of 1917, the Pollock family stepped off a Southern Pacific train in Chico, California. At first sight, Chico must have seemed full of promise. Despite the discovery of gold (and then diamonds) half a century earlier in the mountains nearby and the successive waves of fortune hunters that followed, the town's population had risen steadily to a respectable seven or eight thousand by 1917. Farming and churchgoing were still the primary local activities, although the Diamond Match Company maintained a mill nearby where huge timbers from the mountains were splintered into kitchen matches. The heat and dust of Main Street in midsummer must have reminded the Pollocks of Phoenix, but Roy, who had a farmer's eye for nature's subtle distinctions, could see clouds clinging to the low Sierra foothills off to the east and, beyond that, mountains green with pine and aspen and streaked with the August red of Indian paintbrush. Here, at least, rain seemed possible. Within the city limits, low, green rows of young almond, walnut, peach, and pear trees, stands of myrtle and pomegranate, and blue *Brodiaea* in the scattered grain fields attested to the fact that there had been a spring and a fall was on the way. If Roy Pollock could see beyond the emotional defeat that Chico represented, he saw a land that, even in the drought of summer, looked promisingly fertile compared to the dustbowl of Phoenix.

Just across the Big Chico River stood the stately Bidwell mansion, home of

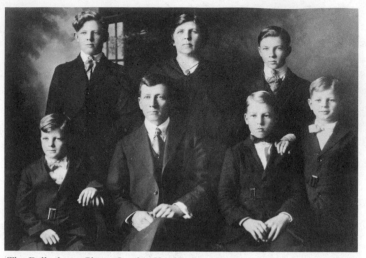

The Pollocks in Chico: Sande, Charles, Roy, Stella, Frank, Jay, and Jackson

John Bidwell, whose 20,000-acre estate, granted when California was still a Spanish possession, included all of Chico and most of surrounding Butte County. Bidwell had accomplished what Roy Pollock had once dreamed of: carving an empire out of the wilderness. Now his widow roamed the huge house and ruled Chico like a frontier dowager empress, dictating the town's growth and character and treating the remaining Indians with Presbyterian noblesse oblige. Reviewing her stacks of promotional pamphlets, Stella must have figured, rightly, that over the years, Mrs. Bidwell had brought a measure of eastern culture and refinement to the town her husband founded.

In February, more than half a year after arriving, Roy and Stella finally sold their farm in Phoenix and found a small place on Sacramento Avenue west of town for a price they could afford. Like Chico itself, the eighteen-acre plot of peach, prune, and apricot trees was Stella's choice more than Roy's. "It was the most unlikely place in the world for a dirt farmer to buy," recalls Charles, then fifteen. "He really knew nothing about fruit trees." But Stella knew something about houses. Built at the turn of the century when the craftsman movement was beginning and the new railroads offered cheap lumber to encourage building, it was a handsome frame house with a proper front porch, a parlor, pine floors, and—for the first time in Jackson's memory—indoor plumbing. The builders had obviously taken some uncompensated care in finishing the window frames and the door surrounds; they even boxed the eaves, giving the house the refined, "dressed up" look of Aunt Stella's house in Tingley. For Stella, the decision to buy was an easy one; she didn't even bother to venture out back amid the long rows of peach trees to see the barn, the windmill, and the tank house. Roy, resigned to his wife's will, made only a cursory inspection —if he made one at all.

■   ■   ■

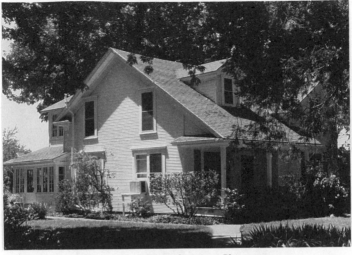

The Pollocks' house in Chico

The physical geography of Jackson's life may have been dramatically altered by the move to Chico, but the emotional terrain remained ominously unchanged.

As a teenager, Charles Pollock was an attractive, if incongruous, blend of his father's small-scale machismo and his mother's small-town sophistication. Like Roy, he was drawn to the easy camaraderie of other men (at five feet five, he was the runt of a high school gang known as "the dirty seven"). Yet he was also an artist and wanted the world to know it. "Charles *looked* like an artist," recalls a neighbor and schoolmate. "He had long hair like an artist. Never saw a barbershop. We knew he was an artist from the first day." Some days he played the rogue, posing in rumpled jeans and a chamois shirt with the sleeves turned up the way Roy wore them, hands akimbo, the brim of his cap carefully peaked so the shadow fell just so across his face—or, without the cap, letting his hair fall rakishly over one eye. Other days he played the dandy, strutting all day in a high starched collar and a broad silk cravat tied in a perfect cylindrical knot, with a tie pin and polished shoes, his pompadour carefully coaxed into place with a little grease and a meticulous combing. In a secondhand store in Chico, he found a fancy gray men's dress vest with pearl buttons and wore it until it fell apart. "Charles always had a taste for elegant things," says one member of the family. "That was his mother in him." Like all the Pollock boys, he was obsessed with women's breasts; yet, when the occasion called for it, he could spoon like a gentleman, writing love letters and decorating them with "lovely ornamental borders."

For Charles, this balance of masculine and feminine, precarious as it was, came naturally. Even at fifteen, he carried it off with such confidence and flair that it must have looked easy to an adoring and impressionable six-year-old Jackson, who for years afterward would mimic his oldest brother's habits and mannerisms, his clothes, his life-style, even his choice of career, in a vain

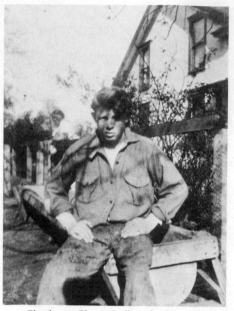

Charles in Chico; Stella in background.

effort to replicate his success at life and love. Several years after leaving Chico, Jackson had his picture taken wearing the same cap that Charles wore, at the same rakish angle, the same worn jeans and the same chamois shirt with the sleeves turned up just so. But somehow the effect was never quite the same.

Charles had long demonstrated an enthusiasm for any activity—from paper routes to art lessons—that took him away from home. In Chico, no longer saddled with farm chores, he became a virtual stranger. He still came to the dinner table from time to time and Stella still lovingly displayed his drawings and paintings around the house for her other sons to see, but the center of his life had moved elsewhere: to school, to new friends, and to his growing interest in art. His withdrawal was devastating to Jackson. In a poignant effort to prevent it, he tagged along wherever Charles went—even on dates. "Jack used to follow us around," remembers Hester Grimm, one of Charles's several girlfriends in Chico. "It didn't occur to him that he couldn't be with Charles any time he wanted to." On such occasions, Charles could be cruelly dismissive. "He'd be tagging along with his nose always running," Grimm recalls, "and Charles would snap at him, 'Go home, Jack.' "

Even as Jackson clung to Charles, another member of the family was slipping out of his life largely unnoticed. In the last year of World War I, Jay Pollock went into Chico with a friend and tried to enlist. The recruitment officer rejected him as too young, but Jay had other ways of courting danger. After school, he and his friends would walk west to the Sacramento River and see who could jump from the tallest tree. "They would dive out of those trees nude from forty or fifty feet," remembers Frank, who sometimes tagged along. "It scared the devil out of me."

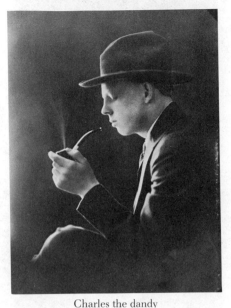

Charles the dandy

Although short even for a Pollock, Jay was the athlete of the family. In his premiere football game as a 132-pound halfback, he "got so goddamned excited that I was in on every play. I was making a hell of a motion out there." The next day, the school paper headlined: "Pollock Tore Up Campus Like a Wild Steer." Teammates called him "Punk" and "Squirt." "He was a fighter," remembers a still-admiring Frank, "and quick and tough and hard as nails." In his freshman year, he won Chico High's annual boxing tournament, clobbering a series of older and beefier opponents. By the time he was a junior, nobody would fight him, so someone suggested having a "battle royal—eight men in the ring at once, last man standing takes the prize." When the fight began, Jackson and his brothers watched from the stands as eight boys, weighing as much as 180 pounds, flailed away at one another indiscriminately in the crowded ring. When blood began to flow too freely, however, the officials stopped the fight. "What the hell's the matter with these guys?" Jay demanded indignantly as the other fighters began to leave the ring. "Let's finish this thing."

In Chico, Roy went about tending the orchard in an absent, melancholy way. Among the neighborhood children, he earned a reputation for moodiness. "I recall us boys avoided him when we were around," remembers Wayne Somes, a regular playmate of the younger Pollock boys. "He was kind of distant—remote." Family dinners, never conversational showpieces, became contests of silence. "After a brief time in Chico, Dad's spirit was pretty well licked," Frank remembers. "He couldn't forgive Mother for pressuring him to give up their toehold in Arizona." Even Charles, watching from a distance, understood his

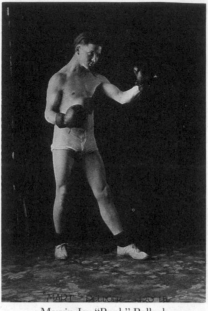

Marvin Jay "Punk" Pollock

father's frustration: "Chico was a fruit ranch and he didn't know anything about almonds and peaches and apricots. He knew how to make crops grow—nothing at all about fruit." Without conviction, Roy tried to learn. He attended pruning demonstrations offered by the county agricultural commissioner. He joined the growers' cooperative on Sacramento Avenue where the neighborhood peaches, apricots, almonds, and plums were brought to be cleaned and dried—a laborious process even for the stalwart. For a season's crop, Roy took home a few dollars a ton. Compared to the back-breaking job of cutting alfalfa or irrigating row crops, it wasn't hard work, but "his heart wasn't in it," recalls Frank. "And no wonder. He didn't know how to fit into that kind of economy. Mother would tell us, 'Don't bother Dad. He's got the blues.' "

In early 1918, Roy discovered an alkaline strip 200 feet wide and a half mile long running lengthwise through the farm. From the back door of the house at one end almost to the property line at the other, nothing except Sudan grass or maybe alfalfa would grow, certainly not the additional fruit trees that were needed to make the land profitable. Suddenly, the farm's usable acreage—already the bare minimum—was cut in half. Frank remembers that his father had planned to plant more peach trees like those in front, or apricots or almonds, with pumpkins underneath, perhaps, for extra income. In obvious desperation, he took a job working the rice fields of nearby Willows, where he contracted a case of malaria that weakened his already frail health. At the Pollock dinner table, of course, nothing was said, but everyone knew that buying the Chico farm, like moving to Chico in the first place, had been Stella's doing.

Disregarding the mounting financial problems and the strained silence that had descended on her marriage, Stella clung tenaciously to her routine. She continued to spend money on the house, wallpapering for the second time in a year in the spring of 1919. Her meals were as lavish as ever and the baked goods as abundant. If she felt the accusing looks of her husband and sons, she never let on. "She wouldn't show any of this to the family," Frank remembers. "Her pride was impenetrable." She blamed the family's economic misfortunes on outside forces—the war, the armistice, the Wilson administration, the Jews. "I heard her say one time that the Jews have all the money," one of her sons recalls, "and all we needed to do was get in on some of it." The facade finally cracked in the summer of 1919 when she began to complain about severe headaches. She blamed them on the "Northerners," the hot dry winds that blew through Chico during July and August, but the family knew that the winds that caused Stella's headaches came from a quadrant not marked on any compass. "Mother didn't really like the town of Chico for personal reasons," Frank recalls. "She had sized it up and decided there was something better out there."

Despite the warning signs, Jackson's world remained deceptively calm. In September 1918, to his great delight, he joined Sande at the Sacramento Avenue School, a neat clapboard structure a few hundred yards down the road from the Pollock farm, with two big rooms (four grades to a room), a shingled belfry, and a long front porch where the girls huddled together whispering and giggling, while the boys roared through recess. The teacher was a ferocious woman misnamed Grace Belle, known among the students as "the Tartar." After school, Jack and Sande escaped into the flat, spacious country around Chico. If they were lucky, Frank could be persuaded to take them down to Grape Way and across the Big Chico Creek to the cookhouse on the huge Phelan Ranch. There, a Chinese cook, imported all the way from San Francisco, would give them each a slice of banana cream cake. In the summer, they could cool off in the creek out back or, if it was dry, hike down the road to the Sacramento River where the big boys jumped naked from the tall trees. There were ball games and slingshots (Roy forbade them to shoot at the mosquito-eating dragonflies) and "once in a great while" a movie in town at one of the theaters on Broadway.

Meanwhile, events and forces far beyond Jackson's control were propelling his family toward yet another financial disaster. The end of the war in Europe, marked by the Armistice on November 11, 1918, meant that millions of American soldiers no longer needed supplies and millions of European farmers could go back to their fields. The resulting drop in demand and surge in supply sent the price of farm goods around the world plummeting into a depression that would persist, with only occasional relief, for twenty years—until the next war. Roy Pollock was only one of thousands of farmers who had been seduced by high wartime prices and government calls (delivered by President Wilson's food administrator, Herbert Hoover) for increased production, and had borrowed commensurately. The $4,000 that Roy owed on his little plot of flawed land represented only a tiny piece of the $6.7 billion worth of farm mortgages in 1920–a figure that had doubled during the war years. In 1920, American farm families' income accounted for 15 percent of the national total. Eight years later, the farmers' share had dropped to 9 percent. Caught in this vast ebbing tide, Roy Pollock struggled to survive. "Dad had to put a third mortgage on the farm," recalls Frank, the only brother who worked on the Chico farm. "It was the first time I ever heard of a third mortgage."

Seizing the excuse of financial necessity, Stella again determined that the family should move, that the answer to their problems was to start over, yet again, someplace else. "Mother was always willing to give up what she had for something beyond that might be more favorable," says Frank. Of course, Roy had his reasons, too. His time in Chico had convinced him of the dismal long-term prospects for small farmers. For both Roy and Stella, moving was a way to avoid the terrible truth that their marriage and their family were on the verge of collapse.

From the long list of available properties, the Pollocks chose a small hotel and some property in the town of Janesville, about 120 miles northeast of Chico. On December 31, 1919, they sold their Chico farm for $3,500—a loss of $500—and one month later bought a "property known as Dakin or Janesville Hotel" for $10 down and a mortgage of $6,000, due on or before January 1, 1925. Only desperation could explain such a wildly misconceived purchase. Although the deed included 140 acres, only a small part of the land was clear and level, and that, according to a collateral agreement, would continue to be farmed by the seller, J. B. Rice. The Pollocks' only clear title was to the hotel, a few cherry trees, and a small field for grazing a handful of sheep. Once again, Roy was stumbling into a business that he knew nothing about. "They were just grasping at straws," says Frank.

As in Chico, the combination of Roy's inexperience and Stella's blind determination invited disaster. Just as they had failed to discover the alkaline strip, they neglected to inquire about the hotel's occupancy rate or the level of traffic through Janesville, a crucial factor for a hotel in a town with a population of only two hundred. Belatedly, Roy tried to visit the property for a second look in early February 1920—after title had passed—but turned back when the Ford roadster he had bought for the trip died in a winter storm on the mountainous passage. Far from breaking the cycle of debt and borrowing, the Janesville mortgage added $2,000 in debt at a time when the area's agricultural economy was depressed and hotel rooms rented for $1.50 a night. Nor would the move to Janesville cure Stella's headaches. The weather on the eastern edge of the Sierra Nevada was far more severe than in Chico, with long winters, brief summers, and frequent ferocious windstorms created when hot air rising from the desert to the east sucked steamy air off the Pacific. By far the gravest miscalculation, however, was Stella's belief that the move to Janesville would keep her family together. If anything, it hastened the collapse. On the eve of the move, Charles and Jay announced their intention to stay with friends in

Chico to attend high school and, afterward, visited Janesville only two or three times in two years.

After a train trip from Chico to Susanville, where the snow was hip deep, Roy rented a wagon to take his family and possessions the last twelve miles to Janesville. Just a few miles out of town, the dirt road turned the corner of Thompson Peak and plunged down the mountainside, dropping thousands of feet in three heart-stopping miles. Looking down from the road, the Pollocks could see Honey Lake stretched out like a mirage over seventy thousand acres in a semi-arid valley of sagebrush, sand dunes, and salt flats. Along the mountains on the western rim of the valley, a straight line where sagebrush met pine marked the shores of an ancient inland sea, now dried to a shallow puddle of saline water that disappeared entirely in the dry season. Just above the line, hidden among the pines on the slopes of Diamond Mountain, lay Janesville.

For eight-year-old Jackson, it was a hostile, lonely town. Where Chico had been open and sun-filled even in winter, Janesville was dark and claustrophobic—a dungeon with tall pine trees for walls. The "town" consisted only of Orlo Wemple's combination general store and post office, the Odd Fellows Hall, the bank, and the hotel. In summer, the big burl tree in the middle of the highway that passed through town hid the buildings from each other. In winter, howling winds and frigid temperatures turned every house into an island, cut off sometimes for days from its neighbors. When it rained, the dirt roads clogged with "gumbo mud" (mud studded with axle-breaking rocks). Where Chico, like Phoenix, had beckoned a shy little boy to explore the world around him, Janesville was grim and punitive. Isolated by harsh weather and bad roads, people lived private, insular lives. "We had very little communication," recalls a woman who was fourteen the year the Pollocks arrived. "It was a lonely life—especially for a child."

Because Janesville sat at the foot of the Sierra Nevada, the last barrier on the emigrant trail to the golden valleys of California, most of the townspeople were descendants of settlers or prospectors who had come in search of easy riches but lacked the fortitude to carry them over the top. In the sixty years since the town's founding, a process of reverse selection—a weeding out of the most ambitious and most capable—had produced a populace that was by turns dissolute, spiteful, ignorant, and suspicious: the dross of westward expansion. The day the Pollocks arrived in late February 1920, a neighbor brought his family over to greet the new owners. "That was a rough family," remembers one old resident. "They had a cattle thief and a criminal and the girls weren't too good either." Frank Pollock recalls, "Their attitude was you have to fight your way through this life." One of the boys told Frank that if he refused to fight the town bully, "we'll stick you in a hollow oak tree and pelt you with acorns."

Surrounded on all four sides by a high fence, the Janesville school was a one-room microcosm of the town itself. "They were a bunch of rowdy buggers," recalls Gordon McMurphy, one of Jackson's classmates, "big kids who

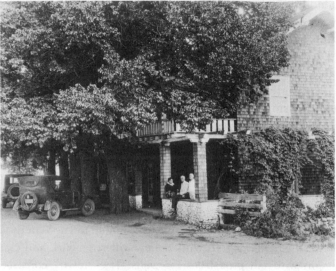

The Diamond Mountain Inn

made it pretty miserable for the teachers and everybody." The classroom taught by Mrs. Drake, who lived quietly at the Diamond Mountain Inn, and Miss Smith, her attractive young assistant and the object of Frank's schoolboy crush, was more often a battleground than a place of learning. "One time Erwin Tuckey flew a paper airplane," McMurphy remembers, "and [Mrs. Drake] went back there to stop him and he started to give her some lip—he was a low child and thought he could talk his way out of anything. So she grabbed him out of that seat and threw him down on the floor and fell astraddle of him and took a history book—one of those advanced history books—and she pounded his head with it."

Unable to make new friends among his hostile, clannish schoolmates, and trapped inside by the weather, Jackson retreated into the private world of the Diamond Mountain Inn.

Built in 1872 as a stagecoach stop between Reno and Susanville, the inn had seen settlers, gold prospectors, diamond miners, and the usual entourage of gamblers and confidence men. Its clientele had changed little since the days of Black Bart, California's most famous highwayman, who robbed a stage just across the county line near Quincy—although the traffic had thinned considerably. A salesman would straggle through occasionally, in need of a night's rest and a meal, but most of the Pollocks' handful of guests were, like the schoolteacher Mrs. Drake, permanent residents. The most regular of these was a group of surveyors working on the Baxter Creek Irrigation Project near Susanville. "They drove down every night after work," Frank recalls, "and they had dinner with us and slept there. Next morning, they had breakfast and Mother made lunches for them. They liked Mother's cooking." It was a rowdy group that enjoyed a drink, a laugh, and a ribald story. Roy reveled in their fellowship, Stella tolerated them, while Jackson stood at a safe distance and watched as these strangers replaced his brothers at the dinner table.

The hotel itself was a brooding building, covered with weathered dark brown shingles and guarded by six tall elms with rails in between where riders could tie their horses. In summer, elm leaves exploded over the front porch, blotting out the sun in the upstairs guest rooms, and ragged sashes of wild ivy hung from the porch beams. Inside, the shadows cast by deep porches and the broken light filtering through the latticework of branches left the big rooms cool and melancholy even on the hottest, brightest days. The small bar in the front corner of the building facing the street had been closed, officially at least, for two months when the Pollocks arrived. Prohibition had just become the law. "The bar only offered soda pop," says Frank, "and served a few cowboys who danced to an accordian. My mother put her foot down about hard liquor being served although bootleggers were everywhere." Behind the bar was the dining room where Stella served family and guests at a big boardinghouse table. Beyond was the kitchen, more spacious and better equipped than anything Stella had seen before, and beyond that a bedroom for "the help." Upstairs, a single long corridor served the hotel's twenty guest rooms. Over the years, previous owners had opened up rooms one by one, as money for furniture, linens, wallpaper, and fixtures became available. The result was a mélange of furnishings, all styles and shapes, mostly idiosyncratic family heirlooms that settlers had lugged west then discarded at the last minute because the wagon was too heavy, the river too high, or the money too low. Jackson and his brothers were now the beneficiaries of this accumulation of misfortune. Eerily empty and suffused with broken light, the upstairs guest rooms were a small boy's wonderland. "I remember fantastic hardwood chests," says Frank. "Some had marble tops and some had mirrors. We never got tired of exploring up there." Against Janesville's climate and people, against the mounting tensions in his own family, Jackson found a temporary refuge.

Soon he discovered another refuge, one both more insulating and more enduring.

One morning in April of 1920, as soon as the winter snow had melted and the spring mud began to harden, small groups of Indians appeared on the road in front of the Diamond Mountain Inn. They were members of the Wadatkut ("seed eaters"), a small offshoot of the Northern Paiutes, on their way to the annual Bear Dance. When the first white man settled in Honey Lake valley in 1853, the Wadatkut "headsman," Babakukua ("big feet"), had ridiculed an old shaman for predicting that "white-skinned people" would eventually overrun the Wadatkut valley. By 1920, all that remained of the Wadatkut was the Bear Dance, a few old legends, and a disappearing language.

Compared to the "sparkling" Indians Frank had seen in Phoenix, the Wadatkut must have been a disappointment. Coming from their jobs as domestic servants and farmhands, dressed in print dresses and denim work shirts, they

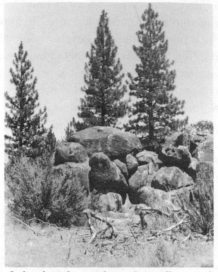

Indian burial ground near Janesville, site of
the annual Bear Dance

hardly fit a schoolboy's romantic visions of buffalo hunts and raiding parties. Yet they were still Indians, and the remoteness of their flat, broad faces still exerted a powerful attraction. "Jack, Sande, and I followed them out to the burial grounds in the mountains," Frank remembers, "and listened to the chanting in the pine trees."

About three miles out of town they came to a clearing where more than a hundred Indians were gathering for the ceremony. The spot, chosen for its proximity to the ancient Wadatkut village of Kasawinaid, long since vanished, was appropriately funereal—a desolate shelf of sagebrush and gnarled trees strewn with granite boulders sculpted by nature into pyre-like formations. As the Pollock boys watched from the surrounding pines, the crowd gradually formed a circle in a clearing between two piles of boulders. To one side, a tall curved pole, stuck in the ground and festooned with long streamers of sagebrush bark dyed red with yam and black with coal, announced the ceremony. There was a moment of quiet and expectation. Then suddenly a tall figure wearing a long bearskin jumped from behind the boulders and, with a loud shriek to clear his path, pushed into the ring. Little boys jumped, girls squealed. The current headsman, Hele Joaquin, Babakukua's grandson, and the other old people around the ring closed their eyes and began to chant together loosely in a low, nasal hum as ancient melodies floated up from childhood memories. In the middle of the circle, the bear danced and chanted loudly. The old men shifted their weight back and forth to the unbeaten rhythm. The circle undulated. Occasionally the bear would dance close to the ring, shake his wormwood tassles threateningly, and pull someone into the circle with him. Young boys would rush to the breach and poke at him with sticks. The bear would play with them and coax them to join him in the dance. Gradually, the circle began to fill and the ring began to thin. After an hour, the clearing was filled with lines of chanting dancers and clouds of yellow dust.

When Stella cut herself on a tin can and had to be hospitalized for blood poisoning, Roy hired an Indian woman named Nora Jack to assume her hotel duties and act as nurse. "She was a fine, statuesque, beautiful woman," Frank remembers, "extremely kind and generous. She stayed a couple of weeks and became a friend of the family forever." While living at the hotel, Nora Jack beguiled the youngest Pollock boys with local Indian legends. For the Wadat-kut, every object and every activity in the real world had a significance in the spirit world. "Feasting, dancing, and painting . . . were modes of religious ap-peasement," writes a student of local Indian culture. "Natural forces, disaster, the noises of the night, the rustling of the forest's limbs and leaves, vivid dreams, all had supernatural portent connected with the unknown world of demonology."

From his concealed position near the Janesville burial grounds, and later at Nora Jack's knee, Jackson learned for the first time the power of mysticism. Having grown up in a family that was never religious, a family that never even attended a church service, he might have been puzzled, but surely he was intrigued. Like the Wadatkut who had been terrorized since prehistory by the bears that descended from their mountain lairs to forage for food, Jackson had felt threatened since infancy by forces that he neither understood nor con-trolled. In the Bear Dance, the Wadatkut could, through fantasy, release their anxieties and defeat their fears; the imaginary could overcome the real. For a boy who had spent much of his childhood in a fantasy world, the Bear Dance and Nora Jack's tales were both revelation and confirmation. Physical senses were an artificial limitation. Demons could be appeased. There were other landscapes, no less real than the Janesville burial grounds, where bears were harmless and mothers were loving and fathers doted on their sons. For the rest of his life, Jackson's "other reality" would assume different shapes and names —Krishnamurti, Jungian psychology, Hindu mysticism—but in the end, only the other reality of art, which he hadn't yet begun to explore, would placate the bears that terrorized him.

The coming of summer brought some relief from the claustrophobia of Janesville life. But if Jackson hoped it would also bring his family back together, he was soon disappointed. After graduating from Chico Grammar in early spring, Jay immediately took a job on a friend's cattle ranch in Altebertus, about twenty-five miles north of Susanville. He stopped briefly in Janesville on his way there, but disappeared after a few days with a vague promise to stop again before school in the fall. Jackson's beloved Charles didn't even make a token visit. With "Cat" Grimm, his girlfriend Hester's brother, he drove di-rectly from Chico to the bustling lumber camps around Westwood where he soon found a summer job hauling logs. Frank accepted a job with Dr. May, a physician who "dropped in from somewhere," stayed one night at the hotel, and decided to put out a shingle in Janesville. During the summer, Dr. May took his practice on the road and he needed a companion on overnight trips along the edge of Honey Lake to the Nevada border.

Since moving his family to Janesville, Roy Pollock had grown progressively more isolated and irritable. During the spring, he tended his few sheep, his cherry orchard, and vegetable garden with exaggerated devotion, leaving the hotel early in the morning and not returning until supper, lavishing on two or three acres the restless care that had nourished twenty in Phoenix, while Stella maintained a busy routine of cooking and cleaning for both family and guests. "In Janesville," says Frank, "my mother worked much harder than my dad." In late June or July, an old neighbor named Guthrie approached Roy with a business proposition: Guthrie would sell Roy's vegetables door-to-door from the bed of his Model T truck in exchange for a share of the profits. Roy accepted listlessly but quit soon afterwards, haunted undoubtedly by memories of Phoenix. More and more, his only joy was the time he spent with the team of surveyors who gathered each night at the dinner table to swap stories and defy Prohibition.

In Janesville, once again, Roy Pollock was carried toward a crises not just by demons from his past, but by the vast, contrary tide of history. Despite Stella's prodigious labors, which earned her dining room a local following, the hotel continued to lose money. By the end of the first year, they had paid off less than one percent of a five-year mortgage. The Pollocks were feeling the first effects of the automotive revolution in America. "The automobile did the same thing to all the rural areas here," says Tim Purdy, a local historian. "You could travel so much further that there was no longer a need for so many places close together. A whole way of life—and a lot of livelihoods—were lost." What the car did to the hotel business, the Eighteenth Amendment did to the saloon business. If it hadn't been for permanent guests like Mrs. Drake and the crew of surveyors, the Diamond Mountain Inn would have closed much sooner.

Finally, in midsummer, Jackson's wish for a family reunion came true, although not in a way he would have hoped. It began with the arrival of Roy's brother, Frank, Frank's wife Rose, and their adopted daughter Betty Nelson, from Casper, Wyoming, where Frank owned a prosperous secondhand furniture business. Roy had always admired his brother's shrewdness and success in business, his bravado, and his taste for ostentation. "He collected gold and diamonds," his nephew and namesake, Frank, remembers. "He was bald, bow-legged, bow-armed and he walked with a strut." His taste for show extended even to his wife, the former Rose Fivecoats of Nebraska, a tall, raven-haired woman, considerably younger than her husband, with a "doeskin complexion" and "two or three diamond rings on each hand." They were a warm, effusive pair whose presence must have buoyed the dispirited Pollock household, even as their ostentatious display of financial and marital success underscored Roy and Stella's failures.

In August, Charles visited Janesville for the first time. It was the search for a job, not family devotion, that finally brought him home. In two months of work around the Westwood logging camps he had been fired from one job for romancing a co-worker's daughter and quit another after a day and a half for fear of bodily injury. Stella, Jackson, and Sande gave him a hero's welcome regardless. She made his favorite meals for a week while the two boys listened raptly to tales of his logging camp adventures, and Charles made passes at Betty Nelson, a pretty, blond, blue-eyed sixteen-year-old with "a conspicuous nose kind of prominent in her face," according to Frank, and—most eye-catching to Stella's sons—big, firm breasts. Soon after Charles's arrival, Jay returned from his summer in the mountains, completing the impromptu re-union and joining the pursuit of Nelson. "God almighty," Charles recalls, "Jay and I were chasing her all over the place. You could make a Tennesse Williams story out of it—two boys and one pretty girl in this little hotel."

For Roy, the appearance of Stella's old ally, Charles, with his colorful stories, his spending money, and his carefree sexuality, turned out to be the final indignity. Charles made no attempt to hide his disdain for the failed venture of the hotel—"I had no idea what they thought they were doing with that place," he recalls—and with the self-absorption of youth ignored his parents' financial plight. Stella had laid down the rules in Phoenix: Charles's money, whether paper-route change or lumber-boom wages, was Charles's money, to be spent on silk pongee shirts, pearl-buttoned vests, or whatever else Charles's cultivated tastes dictated.

Soon after he arrived, Charles caught his father drinking in the darkened little bar downstairs.

Stella must have suspected for some time: his long, unaccounted-for hours in the barn and the garden, his loud, late night carousing with the surveying crew, his deepening alienation and depression were all familiar warning signs. Even with Prohibition, home brew was as close as the next-door neighbor's still. But to have the truth confirmed, and presumably relayed to Stella, by Charles, had to be more than Roy Pollock's threadbare pride could take.

His resentment spilled out at the dinner table. The occasion was a political discussion between Roy and a hotel guest about the upcoming presidential contest between Democrat James Cox, standing in for the ailing Woodrow Wilson, Republican Warren G. Harding, and Socialist Eugene V. Debs, a man whom Ray had held in awe since high school. Suddenly, Charles jumped into the debate. "I got up on my high horse," he recalls, "and gave Dad a piece of my mind," attacking Wilson and the League of Nations and parroting the anti-union views popular among his friends' parents, whose farms depended on cheap transient labor. At that, Roy exploded. He lashed out in frustration at the repeated failure of the socialist cause. He lashed out at the country's rejec-tion of Debs. He lashed out at the critics of Woodrow Wilson, whom he had come to embrace in Debs's absence, a man who, not unlike himself, was emotionally besieged and clinging desperately to a dream that was beyond salvaging. He lashed out at a son who had never really been a son in the way he wanted one.

The final blow came from Roy's youngest sons. Later that year when the sheep escaped from their barn, Roy confronted Frank, Sande, and Jackson and demanded to know who was responsible. All three claimed innocence. Even after Roy threatened to beat the truth out of them, they remained defiant, invoking, in their attitude if not in their words, their mother's protection. Challenged by his own children, Roy erupted in a red-faced rage. Smashing an old barrel, he grabbed one of the long, curved staves and began beating all three of his defiant sons at once. "It scared the devil out of us when he jumped on that barrel," Frank recalls, "and it hurt like hell." When she heard of the thrashing, Stella warned her husband, "Don't you ever lay a hand on those boys again!"

In the end, of course, it was Stella who was the object of Roy's rage. She had brought him to this abandoned hotel in this abandoned town and made him suddenly superfluous. She had uprooted him from the soil in Phoenix, sandy as it was, and tried to transplant him among the strange orchards in the alkaline soil of Chico. She had squandered the money in Cody on wallpaper and baby clothes. She had stolen his sons. In one form or another—in a word, a look, a political argument, a blind rage, at the dinner table or by the barnyard gate— everything spilled out, and all that was left was to leave. Says Frank Pollock, "My dad decided he wasn't going to take any more of it."

It's not clear exactly when Roy Pollock abandoned his family. He may have accompanied the surveying team that was staying at the hotel on short trips as early as the summer of 1920. He was certainly gone in October of the same year because the Lassen County voter registration records list him as a Republican, indicating that Stella registered in his behalf. He may have returned to Janesville several times to transact business, including the exchange of the hotel for a small farm near Orland, California, about twenty miles west of Chico. In any event, by the spring of 1921, he was gone.

7

LOST IN THE DESERT

lmost from the moment Roy Pollock walked away from the Diamond
Mountain Inn, Stella Pollock waged a determined campaign to deny,
or at least conceal, the fact that her husband of nineteen years had left
her. She planted articles in the *Orland Unit* announcing the family's arrival
and in the *Lassen Advocate* lamenting their departure. "L. R. Pollock traded
off his place for a property in Chico [Orland]," the *Advocate* noted on July 15,
1921. "We understand that Mr. Pollock will make his home there soon. We
should be very sorry to lose these neighbors." For the move to Orland, she
recruited Roy's brother, Frank, now settled in Chico, to load the household
goods onto a railroad car and accompany them on the circuitous, two-day milk
run through Reno and Sacramento to Orland. When the car pulled into the
Orland station filled like an ark with two each of horses, cows, pigs, and a pen
full of chickens, the *Orland Unit*—"The Only Absolutely Honest Newspaper
in California"—mistakenly announced the arrival of "F. Pollock . . . with a
carload of household goods and other personal property, to make his home at
this place."

The farm Stella had chosen, three miles east of Orland on the road to Chico,
consisted of a handsome house, a dilapidated barn, a windmill, and a small
orchard surrounded by eighteen acres of tired alfalfa that no farmer would
have chosen. "It was an old stand," Frank recalls, "and it should have been
plowed under." As always it was the house that attracted her. Neighbors described it as "one of the better houses around the countryside." Although it
had once been the hub of an active dairy farm, she made no effort to coerce
Frank, dispirited by his father's absence and disillusioned with farming, into
assuming full-time farming duties. She had no intention of returning, even
temporarily, to the life of a farmer's wife. Between school, odd jobs, and visits
to Charles and Jay in Chico, Frank desultorily tended the fields and milked
the two cows: on rare occasions, Jack and Sande helped with the raking or

picked listlessly at the orchard; and every few days Stella hand-churned the butter. Once or twice, she even put a sign by the road announcing "Hay for sale." "We'd pick up maybe a few dollars," Frank recalls. But the money that kept her family fed and clothed came from the check that arrived every month in the mail from the distant, unacknowledged Roy. The activity on the farm was merely a charade.

In a sense, the land itself was a charade.

Like so much of the Sacramento Valley, the land around Orland was flat, treeless, arid, and inhospitable—hardly the bountiful land promised by the railroads, land developers, and chambers of commerce. Water, rerouted from the mountains and stored behind the East Park Dam, lent to those farms that could afford to buy it the transitory appearance of fertility. But when the water dried up, as it had during the winters of 1919 and 1920, the desert quickly reasserted its claim. "They had to line the irrigation ditches with cement or the water would just disappear between here and there," recalls one old Orland resident, "fifty yards from the creek to the farm and it would be gone." In town, the workmen paving the main streets with blocks of Warrenite had to use mining bits to drill through the kiln-dried earth and the movie theater advertised "blocks of ice in the blowers." The wealthy built a swimming pool while the poor, mostly farmers, talked of drilling wells or building another dam. Some, like LeRoy and Frank Birch, lost their farms and lived with their livestock in an abandoned barn—cows on one side, family on the other. Others, like the dairyman, Mr. Peterson, came in from a day in the sweltering sun, sank into a bathtub of cold water, and died.

Then, in the spring of 1921, just before the Pollocks arrived, the rains finally came, "storm after storm," enough to fill the East Park reservoir four times over. The talk of wells and new dams ebbed, exposing once again the myopic boosterism so characteristic of small western towns waiting for a boom that never came.

Unable to support their families on the standard forty-acre plot, local farmers were often forced to take second jobs. But because cheap Russian pickers harvested most of the prunes and almonds, many residents were forced to look outside the Orland area for additional work. Thus, no one thought much of it that Stella Pollock's husband was never seen working his little plot of land along the well-traveled road between Orland and Chico, or that Stella always had money when she came to shop at Pearce & Frank's or the People's Store on Orland's gap-toothed main street.

At home, Stella maintained the pretense of a normal family life. "I knew their father wasn't around," recalls Stuart Cleek, a schoolmate of Jackson's and one of the few friends who visited occasionally, "but they never spoke of him." "Mother seemed to get along fine without Dad," Frank remembers. "I never heard her complain. After all, she still had her boys. She had gotten what she always wanted." Stella kept up the charade until the late fall of 1921 when she complained of pain and took to her bed. Frank rode the spring wagon into

Orland and summoned a doctor, but never discovered the nature of her affliction. He wrote to Charles and Jay in Chico of their mother's sudden illness, but neither one traveled the few miles to her bedside. Only when Roy made a brief appearance at Christmas did Stella's health begin to improve, and then only for a few days.

Just at the moment when Stella had finally "gotten what she always wanted," her sons began to desert her. One by one, following their father's lead, they forced themselves into various exiles as if to validate his departure with their own and, perhaps, in the process, reestablish a lost bond.

On a frigid New Year's weekend in December 1921, Charles appeared in Orland for the first and last time to announce that, with only three months remaining in his senior year, he had quit high school and was leaving for Los Angeles to "get involved in the art field."

The news couldn't have been welcome. Even if her restlessness often interfered, Stella had always encouraged her sons' education—"Get all of it you can," she used to say, "because they can't take it away from you"—and had always hoped that at least some of her sons would enter what she loftily called "the educated professions." Just a few months later, Jay appeared in Orland. Mumbling vague protests about feeling "isolated" and searching for "something that seemed more important," he announced that he too was quitting school. Roy arranged a surveying job for him in the mountains, and he returned to Chico at the end of summer to begin his junior year, but soon after the football season ended, he left school again, permanently this time.

Frank was next in line. Although outwardly submissive, he, too, harbored grievances against his mother. "I hated the moves," he remembers. "You make a bunch of friends, and then you have to leave them. It wasn't good for me, and I'm sure it wasn't good for Sande or Jack." Too young to make a final break like Charles and Jay, he gradually removed himself from Stella's orbit, hiring himself out to other farmers in the area: winnowing and raking hay for a few dollars a day and the excuse to stay away from home until dark. In the fall of 1922, when a neighbor offered him a daily ride into Chico, he leapt at the chance to attend high school, where he was particularly enchanted by Homer's *Odyssey* and the adventures of its wandering king. Although still bound to a bare minimum of farm chores, he often spent nights in Chico with Uncle Frank and Aunt Rose and their distracting daughter Betty Nelson, putting Orland and Stella as far from his thoughts as Homer's poetry and Betty Nelson's breasts could take him.

Despite his long absences, Roy remained blameless in his sons' eyes. "The checks came without fail," Frank remembers. "He was very responsible. You get used to not having your Dad around." His rare visits were anticipated breathlessly and when he arrived, looking strong and weathered, the long absences were instantly forgotten. In November 1921, barely able to wait for his father's Christmas visit, Sande wrote him a letter.

My Dear Father:

Sunday afternoon and it is kind of hot & not much to do so I thought I would write a line to keep me busy. Our gun had a rag caught in it and we got it out this morning and we went hunting Jack killed a owl and we shot at some rabbits but didn't get any. The rabbits here are all jack Rabbits & they don't sit up so we just have to shoot at them on the run I killed one on the run a few days ago . . . You asked me what school I liked be[s]t Lassen or here all of us boys like it here far the best our teacher is sick don't know if she will be all right or not. . . . She Christian science and they don't get better very fast some times. Well I guess I'll have to close with lots of love.

        Santy.

        P.S. Christmas is coming slow isn't it?

Marooned on her little eighteen-acre island of parched, treeless land with no car, less and less money for shopping, and no electricity for late night sewing, Stella clung to the fiction of a family for as long as possible. The neighbors saw her only fleetingly, collecting eggs from the chicken shed in the morning, hanging laundry, pulling vegetables from the little garden out back. Through the scorching summer of 1922 and into the fall when Frank began school in Chico, she held out. But mortgage payments on the Orland farm were increasingly hard to meet. Sometime around the end of the year, just as Sande and Jackson began the long anxious vigil for their father's Christmas visit, Stella once again set her mind to move. She would sell the Orland farm and take the remnant of her family back to Arizona, where Roy had found another surveying job.

It was not an inevitable decision. Despite their financial dilemma, Stella didn't *have* to follow Roy. She could have rented a house in Chico for far less than the Orland mortgage payments and maintained her charade on Roy's monthly checks. By any measure, Arizona had been a humiliating ordeal for her; it was the last place she would have chosen for a home, no matter how temporary. The only explanation is that she had finally acknowledged that her family was falling apart and her sons needed a father after all.

The trip to Phoenix in May 1923 was a reunion only out of desperation. The family lashed what possessions they could to the bumpers of a 1920 Studebaker Special 6 (partial payment for the farm) and consigned the rest, including Roy's glass-front bookcase, to a Chico warehouse. "We were down to the end of the line," Frank remembers. "None of us knew what Mother and Dad hoped to accomplish by going to Arizona." Jay, who had fled to a cattle ranch after quitting school for the second time, returned home to help with the driving as far as Los Angeles, where Charles had found him a job. Gyp, the bull terrier, rode between two duffel bags tied to the front fender. "It was a rough trip for him," says Frank recalling the time Gyp rolled off onto the side of the road when the car was going full speed on a straightaway. "But he was a tough dog —no pup, you know."

The week-long trip was hard on the younger Pollock boys in a different way. A week was more time than they had spent with their father in years, and they were eager to make the most of it. But, sitting on either side of the stone-faced Stella in the backseat, they didn't dare try. "He wasn't exactly a stranger," says Frank of those frustrating days on the road, "but we couldn't be very intimate with him." More than five hundred miles went by in silence.

The Pollocks arrived at the Porter farm on the east side of Phoenix just after sundown in early June. The two families were together for only a few days— enough time for some celebratory group photographs—before Roy disappeared again, headed for the Tonto National Forest northeast of Phoenix, leaving Stella and her sons in a tiny rented house in one of the city's grimmer neighborhoods. "We went there without knowing what the hell we were going to do," Frank remembers.

It may have been as long as several months before Stella paid a call on Jacob Minsch, a modestly successful local farmer and dairyman whom the Pollocks had known distantly during their earlier stay. Stella had learned from Charles (who stopped in Phoenix on his way to Los Angeles) that Mrs. Minsch had died the year before in a freak car accident and that Jacob was hard pressed to tend a 140-acre farm, a busy dairy, and a family of four without the help of a wife. Minsch, a rangy, "raw-boned" Kansan with a raucous laugh, appreciated Stella's Teutonic reserve (his wife had been German, his parents Swiss), and within days, the Pollock boys moved into the white frame bunkhouse out back with Wilbur, Orville, and young Jay Minsch. "It was an obvious arrangement," recalls Dolly Minsch, Jacob's only daughter, who was ten at the time. "They needed a home and my father needed a housekeeper."

Between the winter of 1920–21 when Roy Pollock walked away from his family and the summer of 1924 when the Pollock family, still without Roy, left Arizona for the second time, Jackson Pollock grew up.

Just how remarkable a transformation took place in the interim can be seen in two pictures, taken only two years apart. The first shows Jackson with his fellow students at the Walnut Grove School in Orland in early 1922. He stands at the end of the second row, stiff and formal even compared to his self-conscious schoolmates: hands awkwardly at his sides, shirt hastily tucked in, pants pulled high, belt tightened, hair combed, cuffs buttoned. He has prepared elaborately for this confrontation. His expression is darkly inquisitive, almost pained, as he concentrates on the photographer as if looking from a great distance, squinting to rivet the details. He is still the "mama's boy" from Phoenix, the sensitive child haunted by fantasies and insecurities, unsure and suspicious of the world, sifting every experience for threatening signs. While Sande looks over his shoulder with an impish, impatient smile and Frank stands in back with a wide open aw-shucks grin, Jackson looks out from his rigid body like a sentinel surveying hostile countryside.

Two years later, in a picture taken on an outing with the Minsches near

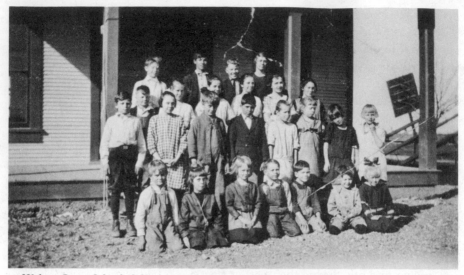

Walnut Grove School, Orland, 1922: Jackson, second row, far left; Sande, third row, far left; Frank, back row, second from right.

Phoenix, Jackson sits impromptu on the edge of a rock, leaning forward, as if squatting in midstride, ready to spring up and out of the picture. His body is loose and angular, all joints and limbs, one elbow resting on his knee, the other braced to keep his relaxed frame from falling over. His clothes are loose and comfortable, sleeves rolled up, shirt billowing out over his belt in empty folds, hat cocked at a rakish angle. He tosses a roguish smile at the camera, almost a smirk, which betrays not even a trace of self-doubt.

With only slight revisions, this is the Jackson Pollock who will eventually intrigue, frustrate, and win the art world, the Jackson Pollock whom Thomas Hart Benton will take in and love as a son; the Jackson Pollock whom Lee Krasner will call "the sexiest thing on two legs." Even at this age, there were other, less flattering sides not caught by the camera: a dark streak of self-abuse that will turn ugly as he grows older and discovers alcohol. But here, even at age twelve, crystallized in adolescence, is the legendary Pollock charm. In the last picture of Jackson, taken on the day he died, he sits precariously on a boulder with his mistress on his lap, his legs apart, clothes loose, leaning forward, tossing the remnants of a roguish smile.

The first signs of transformation appeared soon after the family moved to Orland. The frightened little boy who had always cautioned his adventurous brother, "Mother wouldn't like it," was replaced by an enthusiastic accomplice. "They had a mischief streak in them," recalls Stuart Cleek, who accompanied the "fun-lovin' " Pollock brothers on many of their adventures. "They was always getting something wrong with somebody," Cleek says enigmatically. "Never mean or anything. They just had a lot of high life." It was the kind of high life, apparently, that caught the attention of Bessie Trowbridge and Helen Sabelman, their teachers at the nearby one-room Walnut Grove School. Cleek

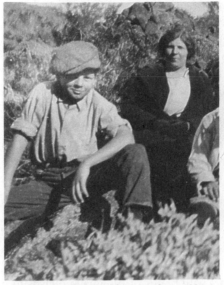

Jackson and Stella, Phoenix, about 1924

recalls that he and the Pollock boys were kept after class on numerous occasions. "We'd just sit there and look at the clock and laugh and wink at each other." On the playground, both Sande and Jackson were known for their prowess at "hand-e-over," a fast-moving game of elimination much like blind man's bluff, which often ended with the two of them in play and the rest of their schoolmates in "jail." After school, they often lit out for the vast stretches of sagebrush and wild grass that surrounded Orland to hunt brush rabbits, gophers, ground squirrels, and any bird they could hit. Hunting was one of the few memories they had of their father.

Jackson's brief exposure to Roy's ingratiating machismo on the return to Phoenix only accelerated the transformation. Egged on by the Minsch boys, he began to range farther over the same landscape that six years earlier had held all kinds of unnamed terrors. With Sande, he hunted and hiked along the Salt River and its crazy grid of tributary canals, swimming in the pooled water and digging caves in the steep embankments. To the astonishment of the Minsch children, whose father frequently "whacked" them with a green peach branch, Jackson operated free of constraints. Roy, Charles, and Jay had all left, Frank was seldom home for long, and Stella seemed wholly indifferent. "Have all the fun you can," Frank remembers her saying, "because one day it will all be a memory." Among the neighborhood boys, Jackson earned a reputation as a daredevil and provocateur. On January 28, 1924, he and Orville Minsch took a frigid midnight swim in the canal to celebrate his twelfth birthday in Huck Finn style.

But the transformation from Mama's boy to Peck's bad boy was never complete. When he accidentally killed the eccentric Mrs. MacDonald's cat while showing off his deadeye aim with a .22, he pleaded with his friends not to tell on him. "He was afraid of what she might do to him," says Dolly Minsch. When Sande invited him to skip classes at the Monroe School, he refused, afraid that his absence might be discovered. The new image might allay and even beguile the outside world, but it could never touch Jackson's troubled, irresolute inner world.

Fortunately, during this same three-year period, he discovered something that could.

For the first seven or eight years of Jackson Pollock's life, art existed solely as an activity—something that people, notably his brother Charles, *did*; a skill no different from blowing bubbles, shooting marbles, or whistling—all of which Charles also did; no different from his mother's crocheting or his father's reading. Until Chico, when Stella began to display some of Charles's watercolors, he had little if any sense of the permanence of art. Charles's brothers marveled at the act of making a drawing; but once the act was finished, the drawing had no more independent significance than a bag of marbles. Despite occasional encounters with bands of Indians and visits to Indian ruins, Jackson never experienced Indian art firsthand and therefore never had an opportunity to see the seemingly isolated act of creation as part of a larger and, in some cases, coherent culture.

In Janesville, he had marveled at the artistic skills of his schoolmates Orlo Shinn and Cecil Williams. "They were darn good drawers," Gordon Mc-Murphy remembers. "Whatever would come into their minds, that's what they could draw. They were freehand drawers, either with chalk on a blackboard or on paper. I don't think they learned it; it was just a natural gift. And they could spin a rope, you know, and do rope tricks, and they could draw a horse bucking in any position." In Jackson's childhood world, spinning a rope and drawing a horse were commensurate skills.

From these same experiences, Jackson had begun to learn something else: not about art, but about artists. Orlo Shinn and Cecil Williams were both Indian boys, the only two who dared to cross the strict racial line that divided whites from "diggers" in towns throughout the West. Their unique position made them outcasts on both sides of the line. (Both also died young under unusual circumstances: Shinn was kicked to death by loggers in a whorehouse in Westwood; Williams died in an unexplained fight in army boot camp.) Although he never knew of their fates, Jackson must have sensed their alienation and sympathized with it, even as he envied their remarkable skill and the attention it attracted.

If Shinn and Williams were only a fleeting, subliminal glimpse into the link between art and psyche, Monteze LeMaster was a long unblinking look. She was the oldest of Jackson's schoolmates at the Walnut Grove School: a tall, dark-haired girl with large features and a wounded look. At fifteen, she was two years behind in her schooling, perhaps because of family duties, perhaps because Orland High was too far away for a poor family without a car. Her story was the story of many farm girls in the area—except that Monteze Le-Master could draw. "That girl was sure handy with a pencil," one of her classmates recalls. Handy but not happy. "Monteze was older and bigger and knew everything already," says Helen Finch, another classmate. "She was miserable 'cause she was different." On Friday afternoons at 1:50, when the school had its weekly art lesson, Mrs. Trowbridge would usher her to the front of the class, where, pencil in hand, she would glumly draw a picture for her admiring classmates. "She always did it reluctantly," recalls Finch, "like she wanted to be someplace, anyplace else."

Other people may have helped shape Jackson's early attitude toward art, but no one had the impact Charles did. After the family moved away from Chico in February 1920, the two saw each other only on the rare occasions when Jackson accompanied Frank into Chico to see Jay play football or box, or to visit Uncle Frank and Aunt Rose. Even then, Charles gave Jackson only passing attention. It was primarily through Stella and Frank that news of Charles's exploits filtered back to Jackson. He saw, for example, that in 1920 and 1921, Charles was drawing cartoons and illustrations for the Chico High School paper and yearbook: drawings in the rakish Art Nouveau style of Aubrey Beardsley, which Charles later dismissed as "awful" and "filthy." On one of his trips, Jackson undoubtedly saw the collection of color reproductions that Charles began to clip on the sly from copies of the *Studio* in Orland's Carnegie Library. "I couldn't resist stealing them," Charles explains. "I had never seen a museum or gallery." It was a tame assortment of landscapes, still lifes, and mythological scenes, primarily English, in cool, restrained contrast to the wildfire burning in the salons of Paris.

The most important influence on Charles's art during these years was an attractive, aristocratic spinster art teacher named Angeline Hardcastle Stansbury. "She would always encourage him to keep up and do whatever he could with his talent," recalls a girlfriend of Charles's who often accompanied him to the big Victorian house in Chico where Miss Stansbury would greet them in high lace collar and black crepe skirt and offer them wine and fruitcake. Teacher and student continued to correspond after Charles arrived in Los Angeles in the summer of 1922 and enrolled—at her urging, with her recommendation, and with a $175 loan she had arranged—at the Otis Art Institute.

Among Charles's many discoveries at Otis was a magazine called the *Dial*, a monthly collection of serious fiction, poetry, commentary, and book reviews sprinkled with black-and-white reproductions. Charles called it "a revelation," and in his enthusiasm, began to mail copies home to Orland. If his intention was to encourage his younger brothers' interest in intellectual pursuits, rather than just to display his budding erudition, the *Dial* was wildly off-target. The issues he sent included short fiction by D. H. Lawrence and Thomas Mann; commentary by Bertrand Russell and Ezra Pound; and poetry by William Carlos Williams, Wallace Stevens, and T. S. Eliot, including the first appearance in America of "The Waste Land"—hardly the kind of introduction to

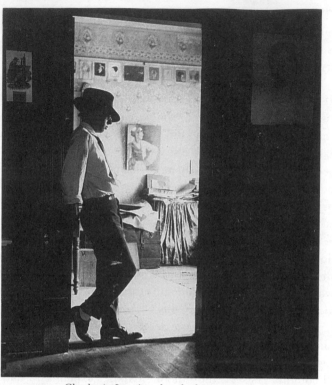

Charles in Los Angeles: the big-city artist

literature likely to lure two farmboys, eleven and thirteen, back from a hunting expedition or in from a game of "hand-e-over."

But if Charles's aim was off, his timing was impeccable. Estranged from their father and ignored by Stella, Sande and Jackson were thrilled by their oldest brother's attentions, however distant and misdirected. They may have taken only an occasional bite from the *Dial*'s cornucopia of articles, but they devoured the pictures. Though small, the illustrations amounted to a comprehensive catalogue of avant-garde art. The line drawings of nude women by Pablo Picasso and photographs of nude sculptures by Ernesto de Fiori must have riveted Jackson and Sande's adolescent attention. Some pictures, like the one of Constantin Brancusi's bronze *Bird*, undoubtedly puzzled them, while others, like the German Expressionist Franz Marc's painting of a horse or Gino Severini's neo-Romantic fresco of three harlequins may have struck a sympathetic chord, however brief and inarticulate its vibrations. Of the art criticism —Roger Fry on Jean Marchand and Hans Purrmann on Matisse—Jackson couldn't have made any sense. But his sensitive eye would have lingered on the illustration of Matisse's *Les Capucines*, with its everyday objects and dancing figures.

The loose collection of thoughts and images that had been accumulating in Jackson's mind since Phoenix—from memories of Charles's painting lessons to his admiration of Monteze LeMaster—coalesced around these issues of the

Dial. Over the next few years, he and Sande would begin to sketch and talk with increasing conviction of becoming artists when they grew up. Forty years later, lying in the hospital on the night before he died, Sande would talk of the spell the *Dial* articles had cast, recalling to a surprised Charles the wonder and excitement that he and Jackson had shared as they pored over them together.

While Jackson struggled with limited success to cope with the split between his parents, his brother Frank was undergoing a similar struggle, and discovering how wrenching it could be. Since leaving Phoenix in 1917, he had lost a year at Phoenix Union High School, and the indignity of lagging behind his former classmates proved too much for the insecure and sensitive Frank. Soon, he began to cut classes, then whole days. Sande, who often joined his older brother's truant adventures, missed more than half the school days that year, cruising the streets of Phoenix with Frank in the family Studebaker.

At night, with other friends, Frank discovered a more potent form of rebellion. "We'd drive out of town on a sandy road in the middle of vacant desert. Just when you thought you were past civilization, somebody would have a tent out there, and they'd be making this home-brew called white mule—because it kicked like one. We'd pay maybe a quarter for a drink, and in thirty or forty minutes we'd be crazy and fighting each other. I fought a cactus once, wrestled with it until it tore me up. Then I'd start vomiting. I vomited all over that goddamned desert." Even Sande, for all his enthusiasm, couldn't keep up. "We'd buy in the morning and drink all afternoon. We'd go to movies or Vaudeville shows and I'd think they were hilarious because I was half-crocked." Where was Stella? "Mother was permissive," says Frank. "And anyway, she didn't know what the hell was going on. If Dad had known, I would have gotten a beating. Such monkey business would have been tended to."

Eventually, as Frank clearly intended, both Stella and Roy found out. "One day Sande came in from an alley while I was in a pool hall assaying a shot," Frank recalls. "He tapped me on the shoulder and said the truant officer was coming to get me. So I dropped the cue, ran out into the alley, and jumped in the car. I said, 'I'm quitting school,' and Sande said, 'Me too.' We drove out to the ranch and I told Mother, 'I quit school,' and Sande said, 'Me, too.' " If Frank was hoping, finally, for some words of reproof, some concerned anger from his mother, Stella didn't oblige. "She simply accepted it," Frank recalls, "and made a fast decision: instead of waiting for the school year to be over, she decided we'd take off right away."

Stella's decision to leave Phoenix was not as sudden and unconsidered as it may have seemed to her outlaw sons. Earlier in the year when Jacob Minsch announced his intention to remarry, Roy had arranged for Stella to work the summer as a cook at the Carr Ranch, a rustic retreat in the mountains east of Phoenix where city folk escaped the summer heat. In some ways, the trip was a homecoming for the Pollock family. The Studebaker roared past the farm on

Sherman Street and followed the Salt River east toward Mesa. Just past Apache Junction, the road started to climb out of the desert, pine and juniper began to spring from the rocky hillsides, and the river cut deeper and deeper into the valley. In ways that the Pollock boys, especially Frank, may have sensed as the road wound up the Salt River Canyon toward the Roosevelt Dam, they were confronting the past. In the vast reservoir that stretched behind the dam, they saw for the first time the source of the water that had irrigated their father's Phoenix farm, the water that the zanjero sent, the water that puddled in the *acequias* and silvered the tines of alfalfa, the water that poured through hidden gopher holes and turned the hot dust black, the water on which Roy would have built his "empire." The water represented the family life they had not known since leaving Phoenix seven years before and the father they hadn't lived with in almost as long. Only days before leaving the Minsches, Stella had learned that the warehouse in Chico where all their worldly possessions were stored had burned to the ground. Everything, even Roy's glass-front bookcase with the diamond-shaped panes and all his books, had been destroyed.

The Pollock family had come full circle since abandoning Roy, and now, with nothing to show for their wandering, the survivors were coming home to him.

Of course, as usual in the Pollock family, nothing was said about this unusual reunion. Stella had already arranged to move her family, without Roy, back to California in the fall. After three and a half years of strained absence, the summer in the mountains would be their last chance at reconciliation.

The Carr Ranch lay at the end of sixty miles of gravel road, north of the copper mining towns of Globe and Miami on the slopes of Aztec Peak in southeast Arizona's Sierra Ancha. To the summer visitors from the desert around Phoenix, the dry crumbly slopes with their balding cover of pines may have looked like a forest, but to the Pollock boys, who had lived within the solid green walls of Janesville, the countryside seemed invitingly open. The ranch itself was a cluster of about a dozen one-room sleeping cabins around a generous old farmhouse, a "dance hall"—simply a floor with a roof over it where fiddlers played on Saturday nights in the summer and "all the cowboys came out and the cowgirls cut up"—a general store and post office, and, out behind the big house, a half-dozen "housekeeping cabins" for the staff. Stella ran the big kitchen while young Apache girls from the nearby White Mountain reservation in exaggerated "native" costumes slipped back and forth into the dining room, quietly serving the food and clearing the big boardinghouse tables. "It was a family-style operation," Frank recalls, "just the kind of operation Mother was used to." Without electricity, the nights were long but cool and starry; the days, impeccably blue.

A few miles north of the ranch toward the Mogollon Rim where, two years before, Zane Grey had built a cabin and begun to immortalize this corner of Arizona, Roy's team of government surveyors made their summer camp.

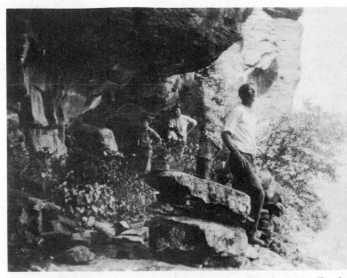

Exploring Indian cliff dwellings, Tonto National Forest, 1924: Frank leading, followed by
Sande (left), Roy, and Jackson

During the week, they hiked the rocky forests rerouting the old road to keep the grade below 6 percent. On the weekends, Roy came down to the Carr Ranch to be with Stella. The visits, it seems, were part of their unspoken bargain.

On Labor Day, September 1, 1924, the last day of summer, Roy invited Sande and Jackson on a day-long hike to the Indian ruins on Cherry Creek. The ruins lay about ten miles due east of the ranch, on the other side of Aztec Peak's 7,000-foot flank. The hike promised to be long and arduous and Roy hesitated to take twelve-year-old Jackson along, but Sande's pleading finally persuaded him. In the pale gray predawn, the car carrying the two boys, their father, and a local guide climbed slowly up Cherry Creek Canyon between Aztec and Sombrero peaks until the road ended at the edge of a wide wash. The rest of the journey was on foot over trackless, rocky forest floor. The sun quickly sucked up the morning mist and by the time the group reached the canyon floor, where they ate lunch, it was forehead high and blistering hot. The rocks on the side of the creek burned Sande's back as he stretched out for a brief rest with his feet dangling in the stream. Jackson sat beside him and watched as his father climbed a nearby boulder and urinated onto a flat rock below, creating a distinctive pattern on the sun-baked surface.

Farther down the canyon, they could see the cliff dwellings high above the treetops, sealed into a dark niche in the canyon's sheer yellow sandstone walls about a hundred feet above the creek and sixty feet below the rim of the overhanging bluff. The climb up the face of the cliff was difficult and at times harrowing. Once on the ledge, Sande discovered a small doorway on the back wall leading to an enclosed room. He crawled into the darkness, followed by the beam of his father's flashlight. Inside, he saw on the wall opposite the doorway the unmistakable imprints of human hands. Jackson scrambled in behind him and together they marveled at this unexpected sign of life in such a dead place, handprints left by cliff builders six hundred years before when the mud plaster was still soft. Sande placed his small hands in the imprints and was startled to find that they fit perfectly. Jackson thought that must mean that the dwellings had been built by a "race of pygmies," but Roy explained that in tribes like this one, women did the masonry work.

While Roy and the guide lit pipes and sat on the edge of the cliff planning the route down, Jack and Sande continued to explore. It was Sande who discovered the strange hole about eighteen inches in diameter in the ceiling of one of the back rooms and called his father. Roy found a precarious toehold on the back wall and climbed high enough to grab the lip of the hole and haul himself up to where he could see into the blackness above. According to Sande, Jackson became suddenly terrified and begged his father, "Don't try to go in," but Roy ignored the pleas and poked his head up into the hole, wedging his shoulder against the rim for support. After probing the darkness with a flashlight and discovering that the cave was big enough, he announced, "I'm going up." At that, Jackson became "hysterical." But before Roy could respond, he heard a rumbling from nearby in the darkness. Sande remembered him yelling "Look out below" in the instant before the stone hit him.

He had thrown his arm up to protect his head, but both were now pinned against the rim of the opening. The impact knocked his feet from their precarious toeholds on the wall. For five long, anxious minutes, as Jackson and Sande watched helplessly, their father dangled from the opening, his legs beating the air above them, searching desperately for some support. Sande remembered vividly Jackson's panicked screams: "Do something! Do something!" Finally, somehow, Roy found a foothold and the leverage he needed. With a great heave, he managed to move the stone just far enough to free his arm and drop to the floor. According to Sande, his father's only comment as he stood up and brushed himself off was a laconic, "That was a close one."

On the long hike home, Roy said little, and within days the Studebaker with Jack and Sande in the back seat pulled out of the Carr Ranch without him.

8

JACK AND SANDE

The only thing surprising about the Pollocks' move to Southern California was that it had taken so long.

In the twenty-five years since Stella McClure had left Tingley to visit her sister in Denver, thousands of her fellow Iowans had taken a more direct route to the golden valleys south of the Tehachapi Mountains. In the 1920s alone, some 160,000 Iowans (almost 7 percent of the state's population), driven by skyrocketing land prices at home and seduced by the boosterism of Harry Chandler's All-Year Club in Los Angeles, climbed into their Dodges and Oldsmobiles and headed west, joining like-minded refugees from other midwestern states in what became "the first great migration of the automobile age." By the middle of the decade, the official button of the Iowa State Society, showing an ear of corn, a pig, and the motto: "Hog and hominy," was a common sight throughout Southern California. Strangers greeted one another on the streets of Los Angeles with the question, "What part of Iowa are you from?" and an anonymous wag rewrote Rudyard Kipling's famous quatrain:

On the road to old L.A.,
Where the tin-can tourists play
And a sign says "L.A. City Limits"
At Clinton, Ioway.

For two blistering hot days in early September 1924—one of the years of peak migration—the Pollocks' Studebaker took its place in the sorry parade of cars with Iowa, Missouri, Ohio, and Kansas license plates that inched and stalled their way toward the Pacific Ocean.

About sixty miles east of Los Angeles, near the town of Riverside, the Pollocks fell out of line and found a campground.

Riverside had to be Stella's choice. Founded as a colony settlement in 1870 for "people of intelligence and refinement," Riverside had grown into an island of considerable culture on the high, dry plains of south central California. The ideals of the founders had been reinforced around the turn of the century by an influx of English families following the establishment of two major English citrus farms in the area. While their numbers were never great, the Britishers' influence, in a land starved for cultivation of both soil and spirit, was deeply felt. Homegrown patricians founded the Casa Blanca Tennis Club in 1883 and the Riverside Polo Club in 1892. Dressed in the latest London fashions, they took Sunday drives up Victoria Avenue to the Victoria Club on Victoria Hill to watch the real Englishmen take their Sunday strolls.

In 1873, when the Department of Agriculture shipped two budded navel orange trees from Bahia, Brazil, to Mrs. Luther C. Tibbets of Riverside, the final, American ingredient of success was added to Riverside's mix: money. As California's population exploded, so did the local market for navel oranges, and as refrigeration methods improved, so did the national market. Riverside became a haven for culture *and* capital. Oranges became a source of both revenue and status. "To own a well-stocked corn-and-hog farm in the Middle West undeniably confers a sense of solid well-being and plenty," wrote a local historian, "but to own an orange grove in Southern California is to live on the real gold coast of American agriculture." Money and prominence brought civic pride and its manifestations in stone: an ornate city hall, a massive Beaux Arts courthouse, and, as Stella undoubtedly was aware, an excellent school system.

With its perennial sun, Riverside attracted leisure-class vacationers as well as leisure-class farmers. By the time the Pollocks arrived, it was the premier winter resort on the West Coast, and the town's premier hotel, the Mission Inn, was the finest tourist hotel west of the Mississippi. Its fairy-tale silhouette of dormers, arches, buttresses, and bell towers in the famous "mission style" gave Riverside a uniquely Old World flavor with a flamboyant, entrepreneurial twist —a mixture of old and new that would itself become a Southern California tradition.

This was the small, prosperous, cultivated, highly literate, and deeply conservative community to which Stella Pollock brought her three sons in the fall of 1924. A week or two after their arrival, she found a suitable house to rent at the corner of Chestnut Street and Twelfth Avenue, only a few blocks from the tourist resorts, tree-lined boulevards, and Victorian facades of downtown. The house itself was another of Stella's proud attempts to give her family at least the appearance of stability and prosperity. "I never thought of them as being poor," says a friend who visited the Pollocks often at the Chestnut Street house, "because Mrs. Pollock was always so generous." Built about 1910, the six-room, one-and-a-half story bungalow may have caught Stella's eye with its chalet-style bargeboards, spandrels, exposed rafters, and carved corbels. A deep porch with elephantine columns resting on fake-stone piers overhung the front door on the Chestnut Street side. The house was set high on its lot to allow for a street-level garage underneath the porch. Although built from the same basic plan as other houses in the neighborhood, number 1196 offered enough refinements—diamond-shaped mullions in the transoms, sidelights at the door, upper sashes in the windows—to satisfy Stella's appetite for distinction.

In Riverside, after five years of increasingly distant and halfhearted supervision in Roy's absence, Stella finally gave up parenting altogether. According to Robert Cooter, a classmate of Sande's who often accompanied the youngest Pollock boys on hunting trips, "If we wanted to ditch school and go rabbit huntin', they'd go to Mrs. Pollock and say, 'Mom, we're goin' rabbit huntin'.' And she'd just say, 'Here's fifty cents, get yourselves a box of shells.' *My* mother wouldn't do that." Unlike Cooter, who delivered newspapers and telegrams and bagged groceries on Saturdays, neither Sande nor Jackson ever held a part-time job. According to Cooter, they didn't need to: "[Stella] was always good to them and gave them spending money." She didn't even require them to perform chores around the house, despite the presence of several boarders, who always created extra work. The kids in the neighborhood were understandably envious: "I thought they were an ideal family," Cooter recalls.

In fact, the Pollock family was in the final stages of its slow death—and Stella wasn't the only one trying to lower her emotional stake in its survival. For Frank, the self-destructive rages of previous years had been replaced by an eagerness to finish high school and get out with some dignity. By senior year, he had been elected president of his class—a long way from cactus-wrestling in the Arizona desert. As far as Jackson was concerned, however, he might as well have been gone. Between writing for the school newspaper and the yearbook, acting in school plays, and delivering groceries from the back of a Model T truck after school, Frank was seldom home. From his downstairs bedroom adjacent to the front door, he could slip in and out largely unnoticed. Saturdays he worked at Sevaly's Market and summers on a maintenance crew emptying trash cans and cleaning latrines at camps in the San Gabriel mountains. "I didn't pay any attention to Jack in Riverside," Frank admits. "I didn't even know he was around."

With all the other members of the family deserting him, in body or in spirit, Jackson clung ever more tenaciously to Sande.

In later years, Jackson Pollock would win fame as "the cowboy painter," an artist who twirled "lariats" of paint on a "cattle range" of canvas. At one point, after his death, a rumor would buzz through European art circles that he had actually *been* a cowboy, throwing his admirers "into rapture."

In fact, Sande, not Jackson, was the first "cowboy" in the Pollock family, just as Charles was the first painter. It was Sande who had been fascinated since childhood by stories of cowboys and Indians, gunfights and stagecoaches. It was Sande who, over the years, had mixed colorful scraps of family history, popular imagery from dime store novels, and bits of schoolboy gossip to create an idealized portrait of a Wild West he wished he had known. "Saddles and horses and boots and guns, all this was a very big part of our childhood expe-

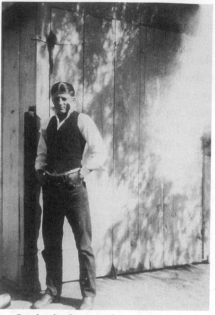

Sande, the first "cowboy" in the family

rience," he boasted to an interviewer in 1949. But it was only fantasy. In fact, neither Sande nor Jack ever owned a horse or a saddle (Jack was afraid of horses and never learned to ride); the guns they used were single-shot .22s, not six-shooters; and they rarely killed anything bigger than a rabbit on purpose. The closest either had come to the *real* Old West was Janesville, where, according to Sande, "the cowboys would get bored, and if there was a pretty teacher, they would go to school with us and sit next to the 8th grade . . . with their chewing tobacco, and boots, and six-shooters." The surveyors who stayed at the Diamond Mountain Inn, although not exactly gun-toting cowboys, were mostly old-timers who had seen the West in wilder days and, like the sheepherders in Cody, enjoyed the adulation of a wide-eyed boy. "All the old codgers would sit around our stove and talk about gunfights and rustlers," Sande told the same interviewer. "When we got there, it was all over, but it was just over." At some level, Sande's obsession with the past undoubtedly reflected the estrangement he felt from his own family, especially now that Roy had actually joined the surveyors and gone to live in what was left of the Old West. Like Jackson, Sande had come too late, falling just outside the favored inner circle of brothers who, for a while at least, in Cody and Phoenix, had been part of a real family. By the time he and Jackson arrived, "it was all over, but it was just over."

The pool halls of Phoenix had given Sande a brief taste of the cowboy freedom he longed for—freedom from school, freedom from Stella and her needful baby, freedom to play with the big boys. But all that ended with the move to Riverside: Frank abandoned him, school corralled him, and Jackson, as always, clung to his shirttails. Jackson was bigger now—a full inch taller than Sande and bigger boned—so their wrestling contests were more evenly matched, but being "the runt of the family" didn't sit well with Sande either, so he set out to find new ways of proving his manhood. A punching bag appeared in the backyard on Chestnut Street.

Jack and Sande couldn't have found a better proving ground than the countryside around Riverside. The town, with its close-cropped polo field and vast armies of citrus trees, may have been an island of cultivation, but all around it, just on the other side of the irrigation ditches was an ocean of dry, rocky wilderness. North of the Santa Ana River, the Jurupa Mountains heaved up from the Riverside plateau. Farther back, the San Gabriel and San Bernardino mountains heaved even higher. Beyond them, walled off from Southern California, was the great oven of the Mojave Desert. Without the mountains to keep out the heat and dust of the desert and to snatch moisture from the ocean winds coming off the Pacific, the area around Riverside would have long since baked to a barren crust. Even with the mountains, water was hardly abundant. The Santa Ana River, one of the three driest rivers in America, could have been the inspiration for Mark Twain's comment that he had fallen into a California river and "come out all dusty." But Pacific breezes refreshed the air even when the ground was parched, and the mountains spun clouds from their moisture. It was this combination of ocean air, arid terrain, and bald, brown, undulating mountains that made Southern California unique, a place where "the land does not hug the sky," in the words of a local historian. "It is the sky that is solid and real and the land that seems to float."

The same air and light and openness that had lured farmers from the other side of the continent and made the fantasy business feel at home in Southern California now drew Sande Pollock, with Jackson in pursuit, into the wilderness to live out their fantasies. They bought wide-brimmed cowboy hats, buckskin jackets, and cowboy boots, borrowed a six-shooter and holster, and took each other's picture. Except for weekend trips into the mountains, however, most of their hunting was done on school days in clean shirts and corduroy pants. Even within the city limits of Riverside there were more than 16,000 acres of unwatched orange groves where they could roam and hunt, as they had in Orland and Phoenix, for birds, ducks, quail, and the ubiquitous rabbits. A short five miles out Fourteenth Street, between Box Spring Canyon and the Atchison Topeka and Santa Fe roadbed, the rabbit hunting was always good. "We used to get on our bicycles after school and ride out there and get rabbits for dinner," Robert Cooter remembers. Jackson was a "pretty good shot," better than Cooter, but "Sande was better than him," Cooter recalls. At the end of the hunt, it was Sande who skinned and dressed the day's kill.

But Sande was Charles Pollock's brother, and therefore an artist as well as a cowboy. Ever since Orland, when Charles's copies of the *Dial* began arriving in the mail, Sande had been sketching off and on in spare moments. In Phoenix, he was often seen with a sketch pad in hand. "I thought Sande would turn out to be the artist in the family," says Dolly Minsch. "He was always doing drawings. Jack wasn't." By the time he reached Riverside High, Sande had already become, like Charles at the same age, a young artist in training. "Sande was very, very talented," recalls Claire Peterson, who attended Alice Richardson's art classes at Riverside High with Sande. "Most of us were just doing watercolors, but Sande and one other girl were doing oils. They were just that advanced."

Striking a balance between hunting and troublemaking on the one hand, and being Mrs. Richardson's favorite student in an art class filled with girls on the other, would have been far easier for the surefooted Charles than it was for Sande. To resolve these contradictory callings, Sande began packing a sketch pad on trips into the fields and hunting expeditions. "He would sketch a squirrel on a fencepost, or a coyote sittin' in a field," says Robert Cooter. Without the fussing and "fancifying" of art class, drawing could be a manly, outdoorsy pursuit that even Roy Pollock might approve. "We'd be out huntin'," says Cooter, "and he'd just pick up a piece of brown paper and start drawin' something." Wherever Sande went, of course, Jackson followed. He, too, bought a sketch pad and pencils to go with his hat and boots. "Jack got inspired into drawing through Sande," recalls a schoolmate and friend of Sande's. "Sande was always drawing, and he was good at it. Jack just followed in his footsteps."

On Saturdays, Jack and Sande would walk the eight blocks from their house on Chestnut Street to the Mission Inn. "The Pollock boys and I used to go there and explore all the time," Robert Cooter remembers. "All of us kids have been *all* over that place." After sneaking past the doorman, they would pause to listen to Joseph and Napoleon, the macaws, in the lobby, then wander through the Cloister Court into the baronial music room with its elaborate Spanish Renaissance furniture, flags, full-length portraits, and antique statuary. Not far away they saw the Spanish Art Gallery where Rosa Bonheur's splendidly romantic *Old Darby* and solemn *Roman Warriors* were displayed beside tiers of obscure portraits and landscapes. At one end of the long room hung William Keith's wall-size painting, *The California Alps*, a huge, luminous canvas that must have caught a curious Pollock eye with its familiar terrain; the other end of the room was filled by a towering baroque altar from a Mexican church, its gilded profusion set ablaze by the sunlight angling in from clerestory windows. Other Saturdays, they saw the fantastically ornate furniture that the king of Bavaria had given his mistress Lola Montez, all ebony, brass, and mother-of-pearl; a great gilded Buddha from Japan; an eight-foot bronze dragon with gilded flames shooting from its mouth; Chinese porcelains and Italian ceramics; Tiffany lamps and Persian rugs; medieval armor, Spanish cannons, and ancient Chinese bells. Downstairs, in a maze of hallways known as "the catacombs," there were Indian and Mexican artifacts as well as hundreds more paintings on display. "When a boy has been through there," says Cooter, "he never forgets it."

∎ ∎ ∎

Robert Cooter was a short, curly-haired country boy with big ears, a mischievous smile, and a talent for trouble. From their first encounter in the ninth
grade at Manual Training School in 1924, Sande and Cooter were, in Cooter's
phrase, "practically cleft together." They spent most of their time on the hillsides overlooking Riverside, skating and sledding high in the mountains in
winter; hunting rabbits lower down all year around. When they felt especially
fearless, they sharpened their aim on the rattlesnakes that came out to sun on
the hot rocks. At first, they were accompanied almost everywhere—even to
church on Sunday mornings—by Jackson and Cooter's younger brother Leon,
a short, sweet, chubby boy. As a matter of necessity and symmetry, the two
younger brothers, only a few months apart in age, developed a friendship
although, unlike Sande and Cooter, they seldom ventured off on their own—
"nothing more than bicyclin' or maybe going skating," Cooter recalls.

Of these regular foursomes, Cooter remembers only that Jackson seemed in
constant competition with Sande. From sharpshooting contests to "peeing
competitions," "he didn't care about anything except Sande's attention" and
approval. "Jack was a different nature entirely," says the easygoing Cooter, still
puzzled after sixty years. "I just didn't know what to think of it."

Sometime after his sixteenth birthday in May 1925, Sande bought a stripped-
down Model T Ford. It cost only twelve dollars, and "there wasn't much to it,"
Cooter recalls: a flatbed frame with an engine, a steering wheel, a windshield,
two leather seats, and a handsome set of all-white cornhusker tires. Making
these remnants function, even with both Sande and Jackson working on it, was
a never-ending challenge. According to Frank, the car spent more time in the
backyard than on the streets. But it worked often enough to be an attractive.
alternative to the Market Street livery stable, which rented Model T's at fifty
cents an hour (Buicks at one dollar) for special occasions. Through several
years of backyard tinkering, climbing mountain roads, and cruising through
the fields of filaree around Riverside, the car became a pretext for togetherness.
"Jack and Sande spent a lot of time in that stripped-down Ford," Frank remembers. "Their life together revolved around it."

With the Model T also came a new kind of freedom. Weekend trips could
now extend far up into the mountains, or even across them to the desert
beyond. Most of their adventures, however, were centered around the small
community of Wrightwood about forty miles north of Riverside in the San
Gabriel Mountains where a few of Sande and Cooter's classmates' parents
owned cabins. As soon as the Model T rattled out of sight of home, they would
pull out a plug of Piper Heidsieck chewing tobacco and tear off a chaw. "It
really felt free to be away from Mother," recalls Frank, who had a summer job
at nearby Big Pines.

In spring, the slopes of the Pine Mountain Ridge were jumping with mountain quail (at other times of year the boys had to roll a rock down the mountainside to startle the quail and rabbits from their shady redoubts). In summer,

the visits often stretched to a week or two—the piney mountain air was a welcome respite from the heat and dust of the mesa. To cool off, they would drive the Model T to the edge of Wrightwood, throw it out of gear and "just coast that thing down the six percent grade all the way from Wrightwood to Cajon Pass about twelve miles away," Cooter remembers. "That was an experience." Usually it was Sande who led the group in its most perilous adventures —like the time he found a shortcut down the mountainside. "He went over to the side of the mountain that was covered with sulfur shale," Cooter recalls, "and he sat down on his butt and held his gun up in the air and he just slid all the way down to the bottom."

On overnight expeditions, the boys often stayed at a road camp in Lone Pine Canyon between Cajon and Wrightwood. Beside a gravel pit carved into the side of a hill, federal road builders had left a rock-crushing plant, a shed for graders and trucks, and a tiny community of "tent-shacks" (wooden floors, wooden sides, and screen windows with an army-style pyramid canvas top) around a crude, pine mess hall. From the camp, road crews could fill potholes, improve grades, and repair culverts after the spring runoff. The boys pitched their tent in a nearby clearing and ate with the road workers at the long table surrounded by stools. In the late dawns and early dusks of winter, the hall was lit by lanterns and warmed by an old-fashioned wood-burning stove.

In this unlikely setting, Jackson and Sande were reunited with their father.

Little is known of Roy Pollock's move from Arizona to California in 1924 or 1925. By the summer of 1925, however, he was foreman of the Lone Pine Canyon road camp and had begun to put down shallow roots in the area, about a forty-five-minute drive from his family in Riverside. Within a year, he had held back from Stella enough of his paycheck to buy a small piece of hillside land near Wrightwood where, with the help of a friend, Lyndon Bement, he built a small cabin on stilts. During one of his summers at Big Pines, Frank came over to help dig out space underneath for a car. Roy spent many weekends and holidays alone in his cabin, reading mostly, venturing "home" to Riverside only for short visits at Thanksgiving and Christmas. Even when Jack and Sande and their friends were visiting the road camp, he remained aloof. "They didn't do things together," Robert Cooter remembers. "He didn't go on camping trips with us. He liked his job and he encouraged us to come up, but he couldn't spend much time with us except to eat now and then." After years of awkward reunions, apparently, a reticence had come between Roy Pollock and his sons. "It was hard for Dad to regain his past position," says Frank. "When he just came in for holidays or between jobs, and when he'd been gone for so long, we wouldn't likely confide in him." Nor he in them. For the rest of his life, Roy would communicate his feelings to his sons only in letters, sometimes sent from camps as close as twenty or thirty miles away.

During their stays at the road camp, the boys came to know the four or five year-round workers who served on their father's crew. Louis Jay was, after

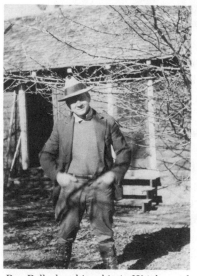

Roy Pollock at his cabin in Wrightwood

Roy, the unofficial leader of the group, a tall Texan with a hard drawl who wasted few words at work but made up for it after a few shots of whiskey. Jay (everyone called him by his last name) had worked with Roy Pollock at other road-building sites and had even spent a few days at the house in Riverside, so he was no stranger to the Pollock boys. He claimed to be a cowboy—a real cowboy—a claim that Jack and Sande never doubted. With his broad, cured face, dark eyes, and vaguely malevolent lower lip, "he was certainly different than anything we had ever known firsthand," Frank remembers. "He was rough, and he had a mouthful of white teeth." Robert Cooter remembers him as "a strong, husky-looking guy who wore cowboy boots and big buckles on his belt." Whether or not he was the genuine article, Jay certainly had the cowboy aura, sitting around the fire after supper, spinning vivid and often coarse tales from his cowboy past between long, dramatic draws on his pipe. Jay's sidekick, Fred Wiese, also a Texan, was shorter, grayer, more reserved, and in general "not nearly as interesting" as Jay, according to Frank Pollock.

Emboldened by Louis Jay's example and liberated by the Model T, Sande, Jackson, and the Cooter brothers began to venture farther and farther from Riverside, over the mountains and into the great Mojave. When Jay and Wiese transferred to a road maintenance gang near the Grand Canyon sometime in 1926, the boys jumped at the chance to join them. That summer, after fourteen years of wandering back and forth between barren, undistinguished pockets of cultivation, Jackson Pollock finally began to explore some of the great natural spectacles of the American West. In southern Utah, they drove the Model T to the sagebrush rim of Bryce National Monument and hiked into its mammoth white and orange amphitheaters cut through layers of limestone and sandstone by water erosion. They explored Zion Canyon, fifteen miles of carved rock given its name by Mormon settlers who were convinced that only God coul[

have sculpted such a place. Farther north, near the small Utah town of Cedar City, they hiked and hunted on the high Markagunt Plateau, a game-rich cedar forest surrounding a 2,000-foot escarpment of rosy limestone cliffs streaked with iron and manganese oxide that glinted silver and metallic white in the fierce summer sunlight.

In Fredonia, Arizona, just across the Utah state line, the Model T hit the gravel road that led to the North Rim of the Grand Canyon. They crossed the high plateau the Indians called Kaibab, or "reclining mountain:" a hunter's extravaganza of wild turkey, coyote, fox, and deer. Thirty miles into the forest, eighteen miles shy of the canyon, they came to the road camp where Louis Jay and Fred Wiese worked maintenance on the North Rim road. After pitching their tents, they sat on the front porch of the V.T. Ranch lodge and enjoyed the hot, dry evening breeze as air from the unseen canyon, heated during the day, emptied into the surrounding night. With a pair of binoculars, Sande counted more than 200 deer grazing in the vast pasture that stretched toward the canyon rim.

At the road camp, Louis Jay introduced his young band of followers to another cowboy-turned-road worker named simply "Red." Red hailed from Provo, Utah, but he knew the North Rim country "better than an Indian." "How'd you guys like to go mustang huntin' before you go home?" Red asked. Cooter had heard of the big herds of wild horses, or cayuses, descended from the horses brought by the Spaniards in the sixteenth century, that roamed freely in the high mountain meadows and inaccessible sagebrush plateaus of Arizona, Utah, Wyoming, and the Pacific Northwest. They belonged to western legend, remnants and reminders of what the whole West had been once: "wild as a cayuse," untamed, and by most accounts untamable. Like most legends of the West, the mustang herds were increasingly victims of progress. In the water hole "hideaway" where they were headed, a Los Angeles meatpacking company had built a corral so herds could be trapped and loaded into trucks for "processing."

With Red as a guide, the boys drove back across the Kaibab Plateau, out of the forest and into the hot sagebrush flats around Fredonia. Around noon, at Cain Springs, they turned off the road and headed west across the dry, rough ground. "Every once in a while we'd come to a wash and we'd have to dig the bank down with shovels and picks to cross it," Cooter remembers. By sundown, they arrived at a ridge around the watering hole where, Red assured them, the herd would come to drink early the next morning. "We camped there," Cooter recalls, "built an open fire on the ridge beside the hole, cooked and slept on the ground." At first light, before the horses arrived, they descended to the narrow draw that served as a gateway to the hole. From there, Red figured, the shooting would be best. Before they could reach their positions, however, they heard the rustle of horses' hooves echoing from deep within the canyon. "We was just a little late getting there," Cooter recalls, "so Red says to get down and be real quiet or the horses might see us and get scared away." On their

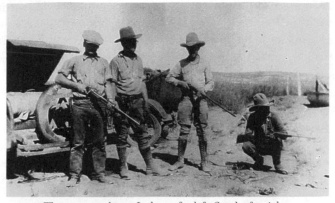

The mustang hunt: Jackson, far left; Sande, far right.

knees, they crawled the final few feet into position as the tight knot of horses appeared in the draw and moved nervously toward the watering hole only a few dozen yards away. "They had long manes hanging way down," Cooter remembers, "and tails that hit the ground. They were beautiful animals and they shook their long manes."

Then the shooting began. At the first thunderlike volley, the herd exploded. A few horses fell almost immediately, the rest were at full gallop within seconds, stampeding through the draw, heads lowered, manes unfurled, a twister of muscle and legs and clouds of yellow dust passing just feet from where Jackson and Sande stood frozen in fear and startled wonder. They could hear the rumble of hooves for a long time after the last horse disappeared, leaving a thick haze of dust and three or four dark shapes on the canyon floor. "We killed a few," Cooter recalls mournfully. "We just walked off and left them. They were beautiful horses, and I can't believe we could just shoot them and walk off. But we did. And I'm ashamed of it to this day."

After a summer of exploration, the return to school in September 1926 wasn't easy. Sande went off to high school while Jackson, who had just graduated from Grant Elementary School, moved on to the Manual Training School on Chestnut Street. The sense of alienation and dislocation was heightened by two quick family moves sometime in the first half of 1926—perhaps while Jack and Sande were away in Arizona. By September the Pollocks were living in a cramped bungalow on North Street—smaller, cheaper, and less desirably located than the Chestnut Street chalet, but just a quarter-mile southeast of Riverside High. Soon after school began, Sande and Robert Cooter went out for "soccer ball," and the after-school rabbit-hunting expeditions of previous years came to an end.

The most devastating blow, however, came in the fall of 1926, when Sande Pollock discovered girls.

With his blue eyes, sandy hair, compact, muscular body, and masculine reticence, Sande had never been at a loss for girlfriends. "Sande was a ladies' man," says Cooter. "He could get any gal he wanted, pretty near." In some ways, Riverside in the 1920s may have been a sophisticated enclave, but in others it was still a small town, a town dominated by the punitive sexual morality of conservative Calvinist Republicans. If a seventeen-year-old boy in Riverside hankered for something more than "kissing and petting," he had to go to Los Angeles, or, if he didn't want to drive so far and wasn't particular, to D Street in San Bernardino on a Saturday night where the Mexican girls sat on their porches and called to passersby. In Riverside, the closest Sande came to sex was the attenuated symbolism of "weenie bakes," chaperoned dances, and "button, button, who's got the button," a parlor kissing game at which he excelled. For the first few months of the school year, Cooter remembers, Sande "was never without a girl."

But he was often without Jackson. "Jack wasn't in our little clique," says Cooter.

After years of hunting, drawing, driving, and playing cowboy, here, finally was something Jack couldn't do with Sande. Not that he didn't try. "We'd go on these dates to weenie bakes or to the movies," Cooter remembers, "and Jack would come with us. Sande would have a girl and I would have a girl— but Jack, he would be alone." After a while, no doubt feeling awkward and ignored, Jackson gave up trying and stayed home, "puttering" absently around the Model T, drawing occasionally, and waiting for Sande to return. Leon Cooter, who also liked to tinker with cars, joined him at first. "Now, Leon was slow on starting to date," says his brother Robert, "but eventually he started bringing girls along with Sande and me and our dates. But Jack never did. I can't remember Jack *ever* dating. I remember wondering, 'Why isn't Jack interested in girls?' Just like that."

The final blow came in January of 1927 when Sande met Arloie Conaway, a pretty, slight girl with soft, bobbed hair, big eyes, and a way of looking up through her eyelashes that "made you want to put your arm around her." He had been watching her appreciatively for some time, trying to devise a scheme to meet her when Robert Cooter invited him on a weekend outing in the San Bernardino Mountains, an outing that included Conaway. "I liked him when I first met him," remembers Arloie, who was especially struck by his "beautiful blue eyes." The feeling was mutual—Cooter called them "a matched pair"— and they began a relationship that would last the next thirty-five years.

Jack and Sande had often passed the Conaways' big white house on Pennsylvania Avenue, with the two giant palms in front, on their way out to Box Springs Canyon. Now Sande stopped there almost every day, always alone. "We saw a lot of each other," Arloie remembers. "We used to go target shooting out in the hills around Riverside." On weekends, they often relived their first blind date with trips into the San Bernardino Mountains, often accompanied by Cooter and his girlfriend, Margaret Lucius, but never by Jackson.

If Sande had seen little of his brother before, he saw almost nothing of him

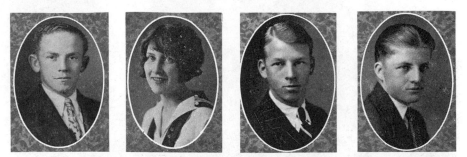

Riverside High School, class of 1928, left to right: Robert Cooter, Arloie Conaway, Frank Pollock, Sande Pollock

now. Although he talked often about Jackson—"I sensed that he felt responsible for taking care of Jack," says Arloie—he made no attempt to bring Arloie into the family. "I didn't meet Jackson until after they left Riverside," she recalls. Through the winter and early spring of 1927, Jackson stayed home while the Model T rusted in the yard, the guns and boots sat in the closet, and his sheaf of drawings grew thicker. "I suppose Jack felt neglected," Frank recalls with characteristic Pollock understatement. "He may even have felt a little hurt. He certainly wasn't getting the same cooperation from Sande he always had."

In the spring, Jackson lost a "great companion" when Frank had to take Gyp out behind the house and put him to sleep with chloroform. A few weeks later, he almost lost Sande, too. At track practice one day, Sande started a cross-country run with Robert Cooter but collapsed halfway through. He was rushed to the hospital just across Magnolia from the school, where the doctors determined that his appendix had ruptured. "They got him to the hospital just in time to save him," Cooter remembers. "He damned near lost his life." Stella was summoned from the house not far away and, presumably, Jackson as well. (It was a week before anyone bothered to call Arloie.)

Sande spent three weeks in the hospital, a Pollock record that would stand until Jackson broke it ten years later at a sanitarium in New York. The only lasting damage was to Roy, who was forced to sell the little cabin near Wrightwood to pay the hospital expenses. Without that anchor, he drifted back to his old friends Louis Jay and Fred Wiese, who were still working near the Grand Canyon. From Arizona, he arranged jobs for his two youngest sons on the expanded summer road crew in the area.

It was the answer to Jackson's prayers. In late June of 1927, after weeks of trying to put the Model T in working order, he and Sande left Riverside, crossed the mountains near Wrightwood, and headed down into Barstow and the white summer heat of the Mojave. On one particularly barren stretch of road, Sande looked out and saw a wheel rolling alongside, passing in the next lane. It took him a few seconds to realize that the wheel was from *his* car. The Model T was cruising comfortably on three wheels.

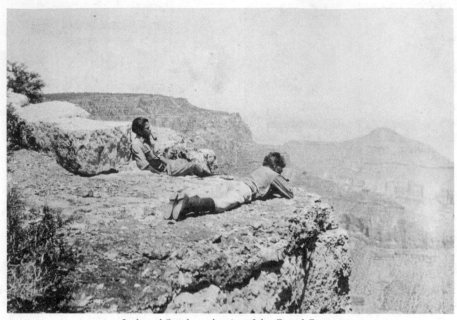

Jack and Sande at the rim of the Grand Canyon

For two months, Sande and Jackson lived and worked near the Grand Canyon, visiting it—often just for a look—almost daily. From the North Rim, where they camped, it was eighteen miles to the opposite rim, a mile to the canyon floor, and fifty-six miles from east to west. Within those walls stood black volcanic peaks, vermilion buttes, and "contorted" rock formations that had once been lofty mountains before the river whittled them down to precarious columns. Of the geology of the canyon, the Pollock boys probably knew very little, but hours of sitting and watching, as the sunlight moved through the cliffs and cloud shadows drifted over and rain turned the gray to black and the red to umber, created impressions that lasted a lifetime. "That experience was etched in Sande's memory," Arloie remembers. "He always talked about sitting on the rim and watching thunderstorms down in the canyon."

The real drama of the summer, however, was played out in the unsettled strata of Jack and Sande's relationship. During the day, they saw each other only occasionally. With an experienced surveyor guiding him, Sande drove a "reconnaissance truck" out ahead of the main survey party, identifying landmarks, roughing in the road's centerline on a strip map, and marking the spots where the surveyors should set their instruments. Jackson stayed behind with the main party of four or five men, marking with stakes the line of levels along the centerline and, while the transit man and chain man moved to the next station, roughing out the course of the roadway with more stakes.

With the long summer light, workday evenings at the camp were short—barely enough time for one or two stories from Louis Jay before the lights began to go out in the hip-roofed tents. Roy Pollock, perhaps intentionally, had

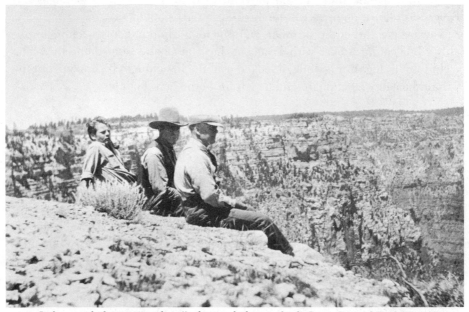

Jackson with the two "cowboys" who taught him to drink, Louis Jay and Fred Wiese

arranged to work on a different crew from his sons, so Jack and Sande saw little of him that summer. When there was enough daylight left after work, they usually spent it at the canyon rim, smoking calabash pipes like the ones that Roy and Jay and the other men smoked. Only on the weekends was there time for play. As the youngest members of the crew, Jack and Sande were inevitably the butt of some cowboy humor, especially from Louis Jay, who had taken a mischievous liking to the Pollock boys. "Jay was rough and ready and playful and teasing," says Frank, who knew him from Wrightwood. "He would try to get a laugh out of you with some kind of monkey business."

It was in that spirit of Saturday night shenanigans that Jay, himself a drinker, began to push the bottle at Sande and Jackson. " 'What the hell?' " Frank remembers his attitude. " 'You work all week, what are you going to do for fun on the weekend?' " Alone among these older men, anxious to prove their manhood—both to the crew and to each other—Jack and Sande eagerly joined in the fun. From the start, Jackson had a lower tolerance for alcohol than Sande. Later in life, various doctors would describe his "chemical vulnerability" and friends would marvel at how little liquor it took for him to lose control. The road workers noticed the difference right away, and the sight of fifteen-year-old Jackson reeling around the campfire pie-eyed on a Saturday night became a favorite source of amusement. For Jackson, such indignities seemed a small price to pay. "He was becoming one of the boys," says Frank, who had undergone a similar initiation in Phoenix, "which is especially important when you're the youngest." Drunkenness was humiliation, but it was *manly* humiliation. Besides, when he stumbled too close to the fire or stayed down too long,

Sande would pick him up and put him to bed. After months of neglect in Riverside, almost no price was too high for Sande's attention.

Toward the end of the summer, with the long trip home approaching, probably while cutting stakes with a hatchet, Jackson's hand slipped and the blade went into his leg. For a while, it looked as if the bone might be broken, but the wound healed well enough, and he left for home on schedule.

In September, Jackson joined Sande at Riverside High. For the first time in years, the two brothers walked to school together and even took some of the same classes—in particular, a woodworking class where they made simple pieces of furniture. But it wasn't enough to reverse their growing estrangement. Reunited again, Sande and Robert Cooter resumed their campaign of troublemaking and roughnecking. Classmates dubbed them "the Gold Dust Twins" after the twins pictured on packages of Gold Dust cleanser—not, as Sande preferred to tell it, after a pair of Wild West bandits. The two boys also resumed their weekend expeditions into the San Bernardino and San Gabriel mountains—without Jackson again.

Without Sande, Jackson was adrift. His grades, which had already begun to falter at the Manual Training School, slipped even further. The facade of cowboy machismo that had been his pass into Sande's world began to crumble, exposing the timid, frightened little boy who used to hide behind the screen door in Phoenix. Old feelings of isolation and abandonment returned, resurrected in part by the intimidating immensity of Riverside High School and exacerbated by his failure, through years of obsession with Sande, to make other friends. When forced to choose between football, physical education class (both relatively brutal activities in an agricultural community in the 1920s), and ROTC (a harmless routine of marching and meetings), Jackson chose the latter. His decision surprised and disappointed not only his classmates, who had assumed that any boy Jackson's size would play football, but especially his brothers. Too small to play themselves, Frank and Sande had been counting on their big baby brother to relive the gridiron heroics of Jay "Punk" Pollock in Chico. "I wondered," says Frank, "why a big guy like that wouldn't want to go out for football and prove his manhood."

The answer became clear to Sande on one of the by now rare reunions of the Pollock and Cooter brothers for a camping trip into the mountains. As Jackson recounted the story to a friend years later, the four boys had gathered at the high school to set out when they were confronted by three or four classmates looking to settle an old score—hardly a surprise, given the Gold Dust Twins' reputation. Sande and Robert Cooter were ready to "mix it up," but Jackson refused to fight. After failing repeatedly to rouse his little brother to action, Sande, frustrated and angry, accused him of being "yellow." Thirty years later, Jackson had forgotten the outcome of the confrontation, but not the accusation.

Stripped of his macho pretenses, Jackson reverted to the needful, self-jeopardizing behavior that had always guaranteed his brother's attention in the past. Sometime during the first semester, with memories of the Grand Canyon undoubtedly fresh in his mind, he began to drink. In Riverside, as in most small, conservative towns during Prohibition, liquor was hard to come by, but not impossible. And to find an example of secretive drinking, he didn't have to look far.

Unknown to his friends, Frank Pollock continued to drink throughout his years as a leader and model student at Riverside High. "The truth of the matter is I used to get terribly drunk," Frank remembers. "But I was senior class president and I didn't want anybody to know. I'd get home and I'd be so damn sick, I would head for the toilet and vomit and vomit and vomit." Jackson, who spent a great deal of time alone at home, may have heard Frank staggering to the bathroom late at night and felt in some way vindicated in his own furtive drinking. As the episodes became more frequent, however, and the need for alcohol more urgent, Jackson's secret inevitably escaped. Robert Cooter remembers discovering that Jackson was making his own crude liquor by putting raisins in apple cider to speed fermentation. If Cooter knew, Sande knew, which was undoubtedly what Jackson intended.

Also in the fall, probably in response to Sande's accusation and clearly under the influence of alcohol, Jackson slugged one of the student officers in the middle of ROTC parade drill. According to Sande, the officer dressed Jackson down in front of the other students because his "leggings were falling apart" (the cadets wore the wind-around leggings common in World War I). Instead of shrinking, as he had before, Jackson grabbed the officer's coat and sputtered, "You're a god damned son of a bitch," in front of the whole platoon. For that infraction, according to Sande, he was court-martialed and "kicked out" of ROTC. In hindsight Sande may have exaggerated the confrontation, especially Jackson's bravado, but the fact that he remembered it at all indicates how successfully Jackson accomplished his real goal.

Soon after the ROTC incident, Jackson began to think about quitting school. (Leon Cooter, his only friend, had dropped out earlier in the year to work for Western Union.) By late November, the notion had developed to the point where either Jackson or Stella felt obliged to write and tell Roy. From his road camp in Hemet, California, only twenty-five miles southeast of Riverside, Roy responded in a letter that arrived at the beginning of Jackson's Christmas break on December 18. In the seven years the two had been separated, it may have been the first letter Jackson received from his father.

Dear Son Jack—

Well I have just gotten in and I have been thinking of you a great deal your case is sure a problem to me. I would so much like to see you go on through high school as I know if you could you would be in a better position to start into something. Education should really be a mind train- ing—a training to make you think logically. The problems you solve today give you strength to solve a little harder ones tomorrow and so it goes. It takes a lot of application and concentration and interest in your work in fact a hunger for knowledge and power of mind.

Then, in a remarkable confession that only hints at the agonies of self-deprecation and depression he had suffered in seven years of homelessness, Roy opened his heart to his youngest son:

I am sorry that I am not in a position to do more for all you boys and I sometimes feel that my life has been a failure—but in this life we can't undo the things that are past we can only endeavor to do the best possible now and in the future with the hope that you will do what is best for your own good.
                    I am your affectionate
                    Dad

In the short term, the letter served its purpose. Jackson returned to school on January 3, 1928, and hung on for another two months. Ultimately, however, it proved counterproductive. In a brief letter, Roy Pollock had expressed more concern and affection for Jackson than in all the previous sixteen years. From the heights of inaccessibility he had revealed himself in intimate detail to a son who grew up reveling in a casual glance—all in response to a threat to quit school.

On March 8, Jackson made good on his threat, telling Fred McEuen, the vice principal, that he was headed for Arizona, although with Sande still in Riverside and his father in the Jacinto Mountains not far away, it's unlikely that he went anywhere.

For the next six months, Jackson Pollock virtually disappeared. During that time, Sande, who graduated on June 18, left for Los Angeles where brother Jay had arranged a job with the *Los Angeles Times;* and Frank, who also graduated, worked for few months at his old job in Big Pines before buying a $135 ticket on the S.S. *Manchurian* and sailing to New York City to rendezvous with Charles.

Jackson, by contrast, from the day he quit school until the day he reenrolled in Los Angeles the next fall, left only one trace—a summer job at a road camp in Crestline, just north of Riverside—and only one clue to why the intervening six months were "lost." On a night when school was still in session, about one o'clock in the morning, Frank was awakened by a knock at the door. "It was a schoolmate from another class," he recalls, "and he said, 'Jack's down at the restaurant drunk and raising hell.' " The student led him to a small café in downtown Riverside where Jack was "all over the counter." "I guess he went in there to get a cup of coffee," says Frank. "He was cutting up with the waitress and having a helluva time. That's the first time I remember Jack being smashed."

9

LIGHT ON THE PATH

B y the time he arrived in Los Angeles in the summer of 1928, Jackson
Pollock was, for the first time in his life, virtually alone. A process that
had begun inconspicuously in Chico, when Charles and Jay stayed
behind to finish high school while the rest of the family lurched ahead to
Janesville, ended in a nondescript bungalow on West Fiftieth Street near Exposition Park, in the concrete wasteland of south Los Angeles.

Stella had accompanied him on the short drive from Riverside, with her few
possessions piled unceremoniously in the back seat of the Studebaker. Upon
arrival, in what was by now a ritual of threadbare dignity, she spread her
crocheted doilies, hung her lace curtains, and nailed to the living room wall
the prized pictures by Charles—"they were the first things she would show
when anyone came in," recalls a visitor. Largely deserted by her husband and
sons, she had seen her life whittled down to little more than window-shopping
by day, sewing and letter-writing by night. She gave the impression, even to
strangers, that she felt her maternal duties had been discharged.

For a while, Sande, too, shared the West Fiftieth Street house. Instead of
joining his brother on the summer work crew at Crestline, he had come to Los
Angeles, eager to begin his lucrative job at the *Times* and to be closer to Arloie
who, while recovering from a bout of anemia, was staying with her cousin in
Long Beach. Over the next two years, Sande would spend most weeknights at
the Fiftieth Street house, sleeping on the living room sofa to save rent, but his
days were devoted to the job, his evenings to a new set of friends, and his
weekends to Arloie. As Jackson surely saw, the days of "Jack and Sande" were
over. "In Los Angeles, they lived in the same house," says Arloie, who visited
occasionally, "but they had nothing to do with each other."

As usual, school offered Jackson little comfort. Like Riverside High, Manual
Arts was a sprawling education factory punching out diplomas on a double-
time schedule. Its 3,200 students, drawn largely from the thousands of new

homes that stretched to the horizon down dozens of new streets, were insistently middle class and upwardly mobile, reflecting—and often embodying—the dreams of their parents, most of whom had migrated within the previous decade to what L. Frank Baum first called "the land of enchantment." All but a handful were white, well-manicured, and as indistinguishable as their parents' bungalows, dressed in the unofficial uniform of corduroy pants and V-neck sweaters for the boys, belted dresses and "dress-low heels" for the girls. "School is a business," the rule book advised, "and clothes appropriate for business should be worn." Editorials in the school paper exhorted boys to clean their "cords" regularly, and girls to "desist" from wearing makeup. A boy could be given demerits for combing his hair in the hall while a girl with long hair was expected to keep it pinned up and out of sight.

From his first day, September 11, Jackson's career at Manual Arts was an unfolding disaster. Having grown up competing for his family's special attention, he had learned to stand out, not blend in. Antagonistic to athletics, ill prepared and unmotivated for academic work, uninterested in girls, and socially inept, he was a misfit in a school and a community that prized fitting in above all else.

It was this sense of alienation as much as his interest in art that brought Jackson into the erratic orbit of Manual Art's most eccentric faculty member: Frederick John de St. Vrain Schwankovsky, the head of the art department.

Schwankovsky—or Schwany, as the students called him—was a handsome man with a distinguished profile and dark brown hair swept back from his high forehead. Most students, as well as faculty, considered him a benign "kook," a charlatan, or an "extremist," depending on whether they were discussing his personal habits, his art, or his politics. "He was on one side of the wall and the entire school on the other side," recalls one of Jackson's classmates. "Very few sympathetic confreres. They would have gotten rid of him if they could have." They nearly succeeded when Schwankovsky brought nude male models into his drawing classes, igniting a furor that subsided only when he agreed to cover the models from the waist down.

For Schwankovsky, eccentricity was a family legacy. His father's father had been an Anglican minister of Polish-Russian ancestry who lived in Catholic Ireland for years before coming to Quaker Pennsylvania in the nineteenth century. His father, Frederick, Sr., a seller of pianos and sheet music in Detroit, had tried to train his son for the family business but succeeded only in turning him into "an unhappy young man." Somewhere along the line, Frederick, Jr., had inadvertently acquired a consuming passion for art. So in 1908, he fled to the East Coast in search of training, first at the Pennsylvania Academy of Fine Arts, then, in 1910, at New York's Art Students League.

Schwankovsky's wife, Nellie Mae Goucher, introduced him to mysticism. Her parents often held séances and spoke to spirits. (The ghost of Charles Dickens was a frequent visitor on such occasions and Schwankovsky came to think of him as "their guiding spirit." Later in life, Nellie Mae—whom her children considered "the practical one in the family"—would read tea leaves, consult a Ouija board, and list "out-of-body experiments" as her favorite hobby.) Soon after marrying, Schwankovsky brought his wife to the home of fantasy, Hollywood, where he found a job as a set designer at the old Metro Studios working on silent movies. When Metro was absorbed into the new movie giant Metro-Goldwyn-Mayer, Schwankovsky was laid off and forced to take a job—temporary, he told himself—at Manual Arts High School.

No better than a competent artist whose Cézanne-like landscapes, still lifes, and movie star portraits never rose above the level of family curiosities, Schwankovsky remained at Manual Arts for thirty-two years—designing stage sets for school plays, organizing a fencing team, instituting a "color week," and singing an occasional solo at school assemblies. In class, he would sweep through the room in his shirtsleeves, pausing only long enough to deliver a few instructions in his theatrical baritone, then sweep out as if still trailing the long velvet cape that he wore at Nellie Mae's frequent musical soirees. Dark rumors circulated among the students about his involvement in cults, Eastern religions, and radical politics—nothing seemed impossible. To taunt his critics, he formed a cabalistic society known as the Phrenocosmian Club, described with a mixture of admiration and perplexity by the 1930 yearbook as "that deeply philosophical organization which exists without parties and without dues."

Although a conservative painter who later criticized "artists with no firm base in drawing who just splash the paint on the canvas," Schwankovsky encouraged his students to "expand their consciousnesses" as artists through experiments with color and materials. According to his daughter Elizabeth, who often posed as a model for his classes, he advised them to "let your mind go and paint whatever's in your thoughts." He read poetry and played music while they sketched, encouraged them to paint their dreams, just as he often painted his own, and taught them innovative techniques. In one of his favorite experiments, students poured oil paints onto glass plates covered with water, or watercolors into alcohol and turpentine. The droplets of color would swirl and burst and re-form, making "crazed looking" patterns in the liquid. When the plate was put on a pottery wheel and spun, the paint drops whirled into vortices of color. If a student was quick and dexterous, he could capture the image by laying a piece of heavy paper over the plate, sucking the fine bubbles of watercolor and alcohol up into abstract clouds of quick-setting color. Schwankovsky also borrowed techniques for covering a canvas from his days as a scenic designer. "He did a lot of mixing media," his daughter remembers. "He tried everything he could think of—combining materials, mixing matte surfaces with shiny ones. Anything to break out of the mold."

Jackson welcomed Schwankovsky's experiments. They held out the promise that one didn't have to be a draftsman—in the conventional sense, at least—to be an artist. Although his classmates found a certain "energy" and "rhythm" in Jackson's work—"especially in the sculptures he was doing, almost like high reliefs," one of them recalls—no one, least of all Jackson himself, had any

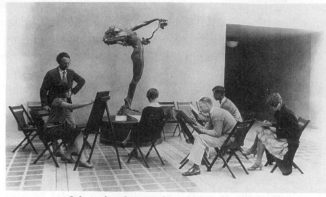

Schwankovsky, standing, with drawing class

illusions about his technical skills. After years of watching Charles's effortless sketching, then Sande's, he was still, at this early date, acutely aware of how inept a draftsman he was. "[Jack] couldn't make images out of other images," Sande said once. "If you had seen his early work, you'd have said he should go into tennis, or plumbing."

Nevertheless, Jackson was soon drawn into Schwankovsky's inner circle of students, a small but diverse group of misfits with artistic and intellectual aspirations. Dominant among them, both for his statuesque height and precocious facility with a pen, was a darkly handsome, sharp-featured boy named Philip Goldstein (later Philip Goldy, then Philip Guston). At fifteen, Goldstein was an accomplished cartoonist who had been "drawing seriously" for three years. Like almost all his classmates, he was born elsewhere—in Montreal—but, by the standards of the day, could claim native status, having lived in Los Angeles for ten years by the time Jackson arrived. This in combination with his talent, his success with women, and his close relationship with Schwankovsky made him almost immediately an object of Jackson's competitive envy—another Charles.

A less conspicuous presence at the little gatherings in the art department office was Harold Hodges, a slight, shy boy who had been banished to the West Coast by a disapproving stepfather back in New York. At school, his effeminate manner and his talent as a sculptor had driven him into Schwankovsky's circle, where he alternately brooded and anguished over his estrangement. At the edge of the group, drawn to Schwankovsky more by intellectual curiosity than by artistic ability, was Donald Brown, an eager, gangly boy whose adolescent manner and pleasant face hid a "dreamy" intellectualism and precocious melancholy. Brown was as much a prodigy of literature as Goldstein was of art. At sixteen he was reading the novels of James Joyce and John Dos Passos and the poetry of e. e. cummings and the French Surrealists André Breton and Paul Éluard. He had ferreted out the latest avant-garde publications like *transition* and established himself in Los Angeles's embryonic literary community.

For Jackson, the supercilious Goldstein, the effeminate Hodges, and the cerebral Brown were, each in his own way, as unreachable and unsupportive as his three oldest brothers had been. What he needed most among Schwankovsky's disciples was an unthreatening ally: a Sande. He found one in Manual Tolegian.

It's difficult to give an accurate account of Manuel Tolegian prior to his meeting Jackson Pollock in the fall of 1928. Tolegian was an inveterate embellisher of history, especially his own. Like Jackson, he told his life not as it was but as he wished it had been. Born Jeriar Tolegian on October 18, 1911—although even his birthdate varied in the telling—and raised in and around Fresno, California, Tolegian, like Jackson, had been shaped by a childhood of transience and emotional dislocation. Never free of financial problems, Jeriar's father, Manuel, shuttled his family from city to country looking for construction jobs or farmland to work. In the early twenties, after losing his modest savings in one of the brief but devastating downturns that foreshadowed the Depression, he moved to Los Angeles and opened a small grocery store. A year later, he died of cancer. At age fifteen, Jeriar Tolegian, like Jackson, faced the loss of his father. Soon afterwards, he began calling himself by his father's name and spinning fantastic tales about his father the architect and builder, who made a fortune in the construction business, designed stained-glass windows, illuminated manuscripts, wrote poetry, and, most implausibly of all, encouraged his son to pursue a career in art.

The five boys roamed everywhere together, both at school and afterwards at Tolegian's house where Manuel had converted a backyard chicken coop into a makeshift "studio." Squeezed into the tiny, windowless coop, they spent endless hours thumbing through art books and copying their favorite images. The fruits of their labors—pencil sketches after Piero della Francesca, Uccello, and other Renaissance masters—lined the coop's rough-plank walls. Jackson did his best during these sessions, but next to the accomplished drawings of Goldstein, Hodges, and even Tolegian, his best wasn't nearly good enough. "He worked hard trying to make conventional drawings," Tolegian recalled, "but he just didn't have what it takes." Occasionally, his envy and frustration erupted into violence. One afternoon at school, he tried to throw Goldstein, the most talented of the group, down a flight of stairs.

In a ceremony of considerable significance to him, Jackson taught the other boys how to smoke a pipe, despite Mrs. Tolegian's injunction against tobacco chewing and smoking. Manuel's family recalls the strange sight of the tiny chicken coop shrouded in a suspicious, aromatic haze as pipe smoke curled out through the cracks. At Don Brown's house, the group attracted the attention of Don's younger sister, Alma. "The guys would all pile into my brother's bedroom and plan whatever they were planning," she recalls. "There were never any girls, just these boys—and they would sit around for hours then suddenly light out as if they had to put out a fire." Alma remembers Jackson as "an explosive young man. You never knew exactly what he would do next. Mother wasn't sure she liked Don going out with him at night. She worried that Jack might lose control." (In late 1933, Alma Brown visited Jackson's house and met Jay Pollock. The next summer they were married.) In Don Brown's bedroom, Jackson encountered an extensive collection of books on recent French art and artists: Cézanne, Gauguin, Redon, Picasso, Matisse, Derain.

Occasionally, but not often, considering its proximity to the school, the group descended on the Pollock house on West Fiftieth Street where, according to Tolegian, "Jack's mother never said no to anything Jack did." Stella would welcome the five boys with food and turn her head when they lit up pipes. On school nights, Philip Goldstein would sometimes sleep over to avoid the long ride home on the Venice Short Line.

In addition to a new family, Schwankovsky offered Jackson a new way of coping with the problems of alienation and identity that he had inherited from his old family: religion.

In the summer of 1928, alone at the work camp in Crestline, Jackson had written his father explaining his "philosophy of religion." It was an unusual step for a boy raised in a family that never went to church by a mother who was openly areligious and a father who had flirted with atheism. The Pollocks had kept a painting of Jesus on the wall of the Phoenix house when Jackson was growing up, but their Presbyterian devotion had faded considerably over the years. Jackson's inspiration may have been his cordial relationship with Leon Cooter, who, like all the Cooters, was a devout churchgoer, or even his fellow camp workers at Crestline, many of whom came from San Bernardino, a Mormon settlement that still retained its founding fervor. Clearly, whatever their source, Jackson's first religious thoughts were little more than the freefloating speculations of a pensive, depressed teenager on the "meaning of it all." "I think your philosophy on religion is O.K.," Roy wrote in response from his road camp in the Kaibab Forest on September 19, 1928.

> I think every person should think, act & believe according to the dictates of his own conscience without to much pressure from the outside. I too think there is a higher power a supreme force, a Govenor,* a something that controls the universe. What it is & in what form I do not know. It may be that our intellect or spirit exists in space in some other form after it parts from this body. Nothing is impossible and we know that nothing is destroyed, it only changes chemically. We burn up a house and its contents, we change the form but the same elements exist, gas, vapor, ashes, they all are there just the same.

In 1928, with thoughts like these taking root in the rich soil of his anxieties, Jackson arrived in "the most celebrated of all incubators of new creeds, codes

---

* In excerpts from Pollock family correspondence, errors of spelling, syntax, and punctuation have been preserved except where indicated by brackets.

of ethics, [and] philosophies"—Los Angeles. Called by some the "shrine of fakers," Los Angeles had become a haven for "every religion, freakish or orthodox, that the world ever knew." Attracted, like everyone else, by sunshine and mild winters, and by the limitless supply of older, infirm, and simply naive newcomers, cults that offered mysterious new curative powers—allopathy, homeopathy, osteopathy, chiropractic, faith healing, Christian Science— proved especially popular. So did the doctrines of rebirth or reincarnation: "I am told," remarked one skeptical resident, "that the millennium has already begun in Pasadena, and that even now there are more sanctified cranks to the acre than in any other town in America." Even mainline Christianity—which "ranked as a leading industry (just behind real estate and motion pictures)"— was touched by the cult fervor. Despite the questions surrounding her brief disappearance two years before, Sister Aimee Semple McPherson was still packing the Angelus Temple for her evangelical extravaganza.

Through this fractious carnival of cults, Schwankovsky served as Jackson's guide. Although raised an Episcopalian, Schwankovsky responded enthusiastically to the opportunities for religious "experimentation" that Los Angeles offered, and at various times described himself as a Buddhist, a Hindu, and a Rosicrucian. It was his love of experimentation, combined with his attraction to Eastern religions and his tendency to pick and choose desirable elements from a variety of sources, that finally led him to the Theosophical Society.

Schwankovsky may have been involved with the society as early as his student days in New York City. According to one report, he was a personal friend of Helena Petrovna Blavatsky, the Ukrainian aristocrat's daughter who founded the movement in 1875 for the purpose of "diffus[ing] information concerning those secret laws of Nature which were so familiar to the Chaldeans and Egyptians but are totally unknown by our modern science." Although an unlikely prophetess—obese, slovenly, foul-mouthed, and penniless at the time of her "elevation"—Madame Blavatsky possessed a powerful and prolific imagination. In two decades, she managed to build the society into one of the largest of the mystical enthusiasms that swept through the middle and upper classes of Europe and America in the second half of the nineteenth century.

Like many of these spiritual movements, Theosophy (meaning "divine wisdom") was an attempt to rescue old religious beliefs—free will, immortality, spirituality—from the emerging threat of science, particularly Social Darwinism with its seemingly inexorable natural forces, vast time scales, and self-sustaining mechanisms. Blavatsky's innovation was to *use* science, rather than reject it, in the search for higher truths. She urged "the unity between science and religion" in the quest for the "single, primitive source" of truth from which all the world's religions flowed. The new theory of evolution, she argued, didn't contradict old beliefs in reincarnation and life after death; it helped explain them. Just as man evolved from animals, man could evolve through various levels of spirituality toward a higher reality. The great religious figures of the past, from Buddha to Christ, had all reached the final stage of spiritual evolution, the "Universal Over-Soul."

In the spirit of eclecticism that appealed to Schwankovsky, Blavatsky borrowed liberally from Eastern religions and the occult to flesh out her theory of spiritual evolution. The seven levels of evolutionary development, called the "cycle of incarnation," were borrowed from Hinduism, while those who had reached the final stage of spiritual evolution were called "Masters" or "Adepts," a term common in Western occultism. Adepts existed on the "astral" plane—a dimension that could not be fully perceived with the physical senses—although Adepts could take physical form in order to communicate their wisdom to mortals (Blavatsky in particular) and select followers could take "Astral" form to visit the Adepts.

Despite Madame Blavatsky's involvement in an embarrassing séance hoax and several schisms within the movement, the Theosophical Society grew into a worldwide organization with headquarters in Benares, India, and Ommen, Holland. Under the guidance of her successors—an attractive British feminist and member of the Fabian Society named Annie Besant, and an unsavory English colonel, William Leadbeater, whose irrepressible pederastic enthusiasms caused more than one scandal for the society—it reached its peak membership, 45,000, the year Jackson Pollock moved to Los Angeles.

The real explosion in the movement came in the 1920s when a magazine article predicted that the next step in mankind's spiritual evolution would take place in Southern California. Based on Madame Blavatsky's theory that races, as well as individuals, pass through stages of spiritual development on the path to perfection, the article cited psychological tests administered to California schoolchildren that revealed a surprising number of prodigies and predicted that "a new sixth sub-race" would arise in the Ojai area. The news was a lighted match on the dry California landscape. According to the biographer of Annie Besant, "theosophists all over the world turned their eyes toward California as the Atlantis of the Western Sea." Besant herself came and, acting on the orders of a "Master" speaking to her from the Astral world, purchased 465 acres of farmland as a home for the new race in the Ojai valley, a scenic spot about 70 miles north of Los Angeles already well-known as an occult refuge, thanks largely to Edgar Holloway, a famous eccentric who claimed to have come to Ojai in the form of "a great flying fish."

In time, Besant would also bring to Ojai a young man she called "the new Messiah"—"the incarnation of God," "the Divine Spirit," "the Literally Perfect"—Krishnamurti.

As early as 1889, Madame Blavatsky had predicted that the world was ready to receive a new "World Teacher" in the line of Christ and Buddha. Twenty years later, in 1909, Annie Besant revived the prediction before an audience in Chicago. "We look for Him to come in the Western world this time," she said, "not in the East as did Christ two thousand years ago." When Colonel Leadbeater discovered him bathing near the society's headquarters in Adyar, India, however, the "new Messiah" was indeed an Easterner, a slight, dark, fourteen-year-old Indian boy with delicate features and mesmerizing eyes named Jiddu Krishna. The eighth child of an impoverished Brahmin who was himself a Theosophist, Krishna had, according to Leadbeater's report, "the most wonderful aura [I] had ever seen, without a particle of selfishness in it." After the boy's extensive training in India and England, Besant was ready to announce to the world "the definite consecration of the chosen vehicle." In May 1929, Jiddu Krishna, now called Krishnamurti, "beloved Krishna," arrived in Southern California and before a capacity crowd of enraptured followers in the Hollywood Bowl gave his first American lecture on the subject of "Happiness through Liberation."

Frederick Schwankovsky was among the sixteen thousand who heard Krishnamurti's message of liberation, individualism, and happiness that day. He may also have joined the thousand followers who attended the Ojai camp in May 1928, at which Krishnamurti spoke daily. Eventually, Schwankovsky would become a personal friend of the Messiah, hosting dinners for him at his Laguna Beach studio. But even as early as the fall of 1928 when Jackson Pollock joined his small circle of disciples, Schwankovsky burned with missionary zeal, proclaiming Krishnamurti "the mouthpiece of the new age and the new art." He introduced his students to a key Theosophical tract, *The Light on the Path* by Mabel Collins, as well as Krishnamurti's own *Life in Freedom*, a small volume of addresses from the 1928 Star Camps at Benares, Ommen, and Ojai. They were difficult books, and Jackson, never a good reader, probably relied heavily on conversations he heard between Schwankovsky and students with more agile intellects like Goldstein or Brown for his knowledge of Theosophical ideas.

Within the year, Jackson himself would be sitting at the foot of the Master.

Fifteen years later, in therapy, Jackson reportedly told his doctor that he "was looking as a youngster for a way of life and came under the influence of Krishnamurti and Theosophy." More than thirty years later, his widow, Lee Krasner, would recall Jackson "often speaking of Schwankovsky and Krishnamurti." Despite the difficulties of often impenetrable jargon and fantastical doctrines, sixteen-year-old Jackson Pollock was clearly entranced. He wrote his brother Charles several times, explaining the theories as best he could and urging him to read *The Light on the Path*. "Every thing it has to say seems to be contrary to the essence of modern life," he wrote, "but after it is under stood and lived up to i think it is a very helpful guide. i wish you would get one and tell me what you think of it." Jackson even offered to send Charles a copy if he couldn't find one in New York.

Charles viewed his baby brother's new enthusiasm with characteristic sangfroid: "He tended to get hooked on fads," Charles recalls thinking, "starting from early on." There was, however, far more to Jackson's strong and unchar-

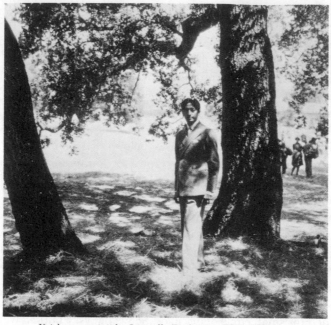

Krishnamurti, "the Literally Perfect" at Ojai, California

acteristically lasting devotion than simple peer-group pressure, adolescent impressionability, or competition for a teacher's favor. In the ideas themselves, Jackson found something that struck home.

To a boy who had been struggling his entire life to fit in—to his family, to his school, to the role of artist—Krishnamurti preached that the effort to fit in was not only futile but misguided as well. "If you make yourself into a type," he warned, ". . . you have not the capacity to choose, and hence you will become an automaton, a person that is dead." To a boy who felt alienated from the world, *The Light on the Path* glorified alienation: "Through all time the wise men have lived apart from the mass." Like most cults, Theosophy allowed the sufferer to see his affliction—whether illness or loneliness or age—as a necessary stage on the road to happiness, a transitional state filled with unperceived promise. "The moment you are really struggling in sorrow," Krishnamurti said, "and feel that sorrow in its uttermost depths . . . sorrow then becomes a soil through which you must grow, a soil for nourishment, not a thing to be avoided." The outcasts became the chosen few, the alienated became the enlightened, the afflicted became the favored—like the lotus "which plows through mud and slime, pushing its way upward to the Sun, finally becoming a thing of joy and beauty." Krishnamurti offered solace for Jackson's inadequacy at drawing ("The appreciation of beauty is within yourself") and for his lack of verbal facility ("I have often wondered whether it is worth while talking at all . . . through experience alone can you grow"). Even his chronically poor academic performance was transformed by Theosophy's alchemy into a blessing ("It is indeed those who suffer and struggle and not necessarily those who are learned in books that understand"). Krishnamurti spoke to Jackson's oldest and deepest anxieties. To Jack "the baby," who longed to be talented like his brother Charles, or manly like Sande, Krishnamurti said, "Each one has to make his own path." One can never arrive at "self-perfection," he cautioned, by "dwelling in the shadow of another."

Finally, Theosophy armed Jackson against the fear that he could never live up to his brothers' examples, that he could never prove "to myself nor anybody else that i have it in me," as he wrote to Charles. If his desire was strong, said Krishnamurti, if his "spirit" was right, "hard work"—at least in the sense of arduous training—wasn't necessary. The facility that Charles and Phil Goldstein had acquired through years of painstaking practice, Jackson could achieve through "the swift knowledge, which is called intuition with certainty." Inspiration was to be cherished more than schooling, impulse more than intellect, because "intellect, left to itself, will only waste its energies in systematization and in this way will become divorced from life." Thus the true task of the artist was to bypass the intellect and "make a living link between inner feelings and external actions." For Krishnamurti, the test of all truth—and later, for Jackson, the test of all great art—was "Does it flow spontaneously from an inner impulse?"

The only way to forge the link between impulse and action, said Krishnamurti, was to rebel.

10

A ROTTEN REBEL

Jackson was no stranger to radical politics. As early as Phoenix, when he heard his father's sympathetic explanation of the IWW, or saw him celebrate at news of the Bolshevik Revolution, he had been exposed to socialist sympathies. At Manual Arts, Schwankovsky urged students to pursue "an heroic idealism . . . which will make a new and better world," and introduced his privileged inner circle to the magazines and writers of the intellectual left. Even Theosophy occasionally spoke in an explicitly political voice on such issues as capital punishment, prison reform, and aid to the handicapped. But it was the city of Los Angeles itself—as it reflected and magnified the nation's right-wing paranoia—that finally pushed Jackson into the turbulent world of radical politics.

Against a background of hysterical avarice in the last few years before the Depression, Los Angeles had embarked on a witch-hunt for "subversive" political elements, especially Communists and union organizers and the intellectuals who supported them. While preacher "Fighting" Bob Shuler broadcast his nightly KGEF crusade against books "not fit for heathen China or anarchistic Russia," the police arrested writer Upton Sinclair for trying to read the Constitution to a rally of strikers, and the superintendent of schools removed the *Nation* (Roy Pollock's favorite journal) from library shelves throughout Los Angeles. Teachers who advocated public ownership of utilities were branded Bolsheviks, and both the Better America Foundation and the *Times* kept an extensive network of paid spies on the boards of liberal and progressive groups. "Reds" and "pinks," broadly defined, were prosecuted under the Criminal Syndicalism Act, and their meetings—in homes, halls, and public parks—broken up with the generous use of teargas and billy clubs. The *Times* routinely announced police "shove days": "This will be 'shove Tuesday' for the Los Angeles police," read a typical article. "The communists plan to stage another demonstration today, according to Capt. Wm. ["Red"] Hynes, which means

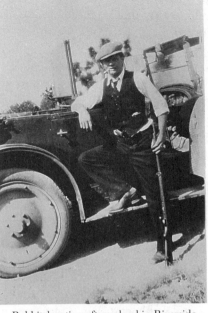

Rabbit-hunting after school in Riverside

that 500 police will be in readiness. If the communists demonstrate, the police men will shove and keep on shoving until the parade is disrupted." In this charged atmosphere, even the simply unemployed were suspect. City-sponsored national advertising campaigns attracted workers to Los Angeles from around the country, but if they couldn't find jobs when they arrived— which they often couldn't—they were arrested for vagrancy. ("Unemployment is a crime in Sunny California," quipped one observer.) During Jackson Pollock's first year at Manual Arts, Los Angeles police made more than 12,000 arrests for vagrancy.

It isn't clear how soon Jackson or any of his fellow students became aware of this larger political context. Throughout the 1928–29 school year, Phil Goldstein was doing illustrations for the Manual Arts student paper, the *Weekly*, on subjects as distant from radical politics as proper school spirit ("Respect Upper-Classmen," "Go Out for Athletics," and "Join in School Activities") while Don Brown worked on the literary magazine and contributed occasional poems to the *Weekly*. Like most high school students, their first concern was with high school. For some, although not for Jackson, concern for social injustice and oppression in the larger world would follow, but the teething injustices were the ones closest to home, the oppressions that weighed the heaviest, the ones that limited their own freedom.

Of these, the weightiest by far was the pervasive obsession with sports.

The entire country had been in the throes of a sports mania since the end of the First World War. In 1926, Knute Rockne brought his legendary fighting Irish of Notre Dame to the Coliseum to face USC for the first time. (The home team lost in an electrifyingly close game, 13–12.) The next year, just a year before Jackson arrived, seventy thousand fans crowded into the Coliseum to see the Chicago Bears led by Red Grange prove to the skeptics that "professional" football was a viable concept. From their vantage just across the street from the Coliseum, only blocks from USC, Manual Arts students were swept up in the sports craze. Their football team, the Toilers, was always a contender for the fiercely contested city championship. During the fall, nothing else mattered. The entire week preceding a big game was dedicated to whipping up student support. At pre-game rallies, the ROTC band played, "yell leaders" led the student body in school fight songs, and coaches introduced their players to whistles and whoops and clamorous applause. Wins were reported in six-inch banner headlines on the front page of the *Weekly;* while losses were blamed on the failure of school spirit: "Student Body Overconfidence Kayos Manual's Dream," the paper headlined after an upset loss to Los Angeles High that cost the Toilers the championship in 1928.

Jackson's antagonism toward sports and the mania it generated had been set as early as Riverside. At Manual Arts, he was joined in his rebellion by Manuel Tolegian and Phil Goldstein who, like Jackson, avoided the school's phys. ed. requirement by hiding under the gymnasium bleachers. On October 10, 1928, a program in the auditorium that was billed as a "musical assembly" featuring a recital by Schwankovsky and a local soprano was disrupted by the yell leaders who jumped onto the stage and, to thunderous cheering, led the audience through the standard round of fight songs. A month later, following a disastrous loss to Los Angeles High, the entire assembly was given over to a rally highlighted by a skit lampooning "high school slackers"—students who refused to support the team—and their leader, "a high school fairy," whose appearance on stage triggered gales of derisive laughter from the audience.

Sometime in February or March, Jackson and the others struck back. They wrote and printed a small brochure and, early one morning, with Manuel Tolegian's help, slipped copies into student lockers and faculty mailboxes. Beneath a drawing of a dog wagging its tail contributed by Goldstein and titled "Shall the Tail Wag the Dog?" it read:

STUDENTS OF MANUAL ARTS:

We present for your consideration the serious problem of good judgment in relative values in this high school. We deplore most heartily the unreasonable elevation of athletic ability and the consequent degradation of scholarship. Instead of yelling, "hit that line," we should cry, "make that grade." Give those letters to our scholars, our artists, and our musicians instead of animated examples of physical prowess. Give our offices to executives instead of varsity men. Our last president was a living example of the system we advocate. There have been such men elected but they have been few and far between. It will mean a great change in our present policies. If the change is not made, Manual, the school we know and love is doomed. It is all very good to win victories but what good are they if we have nothing behind them? School success depends first upon administrative reputation. Interscholastic victories are matters of secondary importance. We must have victory at home before we are worthy of victory abroad. Too much emphasis have [sic] been placed on the physical end of school life; too little on the mental. We have before us a difficult task. Let us face it bravely. STUDENTS, MANUAL NEEDS REFORM. ARE YOU MEN ENOUGH TO GIVE IT?

The exact nature of Jackson's role in this experiment with rebellion isn't known. Though he may have helped print the brochure, most accounts agree that he had little to do with the actual writing—variously attributing the contents to Goldstein, Don Brown, or even Schwankovsky.

Wherever the responsibility fell, the consequences fell on Jackson alone. The next day, the vice principal appeared in Schwankovsky's class accompanied by a janitor who had seen a boy distributing the leaflets the previous morning. When asked to identify the culprit, the janitor surveyed the anxious classroom and pointed at Jackson, who was led away to the principal's office.

Not long afterward, another broadside appeared, this time a vague lashing-out against the faculty and the penalties imposed on dissent—presumably Jackson's.

STUDENTS OF MANUAL ARTS

There is in this high school a certain group, that has, for a long time looked with extreme disfavor on the oppressive and tyrannical methods in vouge [sic] with the present faculty. We feel that we can no longer remain silent. We make no rash statements, but we hold and defend tenaciously those principles of personal liberty for which our forefathers gave their lives. We wish to ask the following questions.

1. Why is it that inefficient or unjust teachers and heads of departments are placed over us?

2. Why is it that the honerable [sic] ward of students, inrespect to injustice, is mocked at, and disbelieved?

3. Why can not a student express his or her opinion of teachers or office officials without being in danger of direct or indirect punishment?

Any student with a brain above the mental age of twelve, and with the experience of a term in this highschool knows the anwsers [sic] to these questions. We ask you first to think, then organize, and finally to act. We do not wish a revolution, but rather a peaceful change, we want fair treatment. WHICH WE ARE NOT GETTING.

The power and might of a school lies in its student body. You are as a gaint [sic] sleeping. AWAKE AND USE YOUR STRENGTH.

Jackson seems to have had more of a hand in this second broadside. In addition to the characteristic spelling errors and Krishnamurti-like closing, there is a new, more desperate tone, reflecting perhaps Jackson's panic as he stood on the verge of yet another incomplete semester, his third in just two years of high school.

If the second brochure was intended to soften the resolve of his prosecutors (hence the apologetic "We do not wish a revolution" and the patriotic allusion to "forefathers"), it had just the opposite effect. While both students and faculty had openly debated the impact of the sports craze on the school's academic standing, accusations that teachers were "tyrannical" "inefficient" and "unjust" were more serious, although not, by themselves, cause for dismissal. (About the same time, a *Weekly* editorial accused the faculty of being "biased and unjust" and the school's "worst enemies.") When Jackson was expelled sometime in March, it was probably for accumulating too many total demerits under the school's complicated disciplinary code rather than for his involvement with the "inflammatory" brochures alone.

Apparently, despite some accounts to the contrary, Jackson was the only one punished so severely. Goldstein may have been suspended briefly, but he continued to contribute to the *Weekly* illustrations of football heroes, Uncle Sam, and "Senior Hat Day," which belied his involvement in any anti-establishment plot. Don Brown retained his position as editor of the *Spectator* until his family's departure for Alhambra in June, and Manuel Tolegian submitted a series of woodcuts of famous personalities—Charles Lindbergh, von Hindenburg, Herbert Hoover—that appeared in the *Weekly*. "I wanted to graduate!" he later said in defense of his failure to admit his role in the protest.

Whether Jackson intended it or not, his expulsion had at least one desirable and entirely foreseeable effect: it attracted his father's attention. In fact, Roy or Stella, or both, felt the crisis was so urgent that, sometime in late March or early April, Roy made an unprecedented, midseason trip from his road camp at Santa Ynez about ninety miles northwest of Los Angeles. No record exists of their confrontation in the little bungalow on West Fiftieth Street—if indeed it was a confrontation—but Roy's attitude toward school was well known: "Either you go to school or you go to work. He'd give you the choice," Frank Pollock recalls, "but he'd say you've got a better chance if you go to school." Only a few months before, Roy had written Jackson: "The secret of success is concentrated interest, interest in life, interest in sports, and good times, interest in your studies, interest in your fellow students. . . . Write and tell me about your schoolwork." Jackson's antics had forced him to leave work and deliver the same message in person. His mere presence under such circumstances was tantamount to a fit of rage in the emotional lexicon of Roy Pollock, even if harsh words were never spoken.

On one point, at least, Roy seems to have been explicit: he would not tolerate idleness. A year before, when Jackson was contemplating leaving school in Riverside, Roy had written him: "If you are well satisfied that [staying in school] is impossible at present I suppose the thing to do is to go to work at something

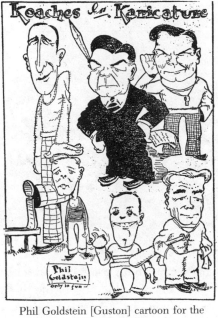

Phil Goldstein [Guston] cartoon for the
Manual Arts *Weekly*; Sid Foster, center.

where you can gain knowledge and training by practical experience." Although
Jackson would have preferred to stay in Los Angeles with his friends, Roy
insisted that he spend the summer working at the road camp instead.

As soon as Roy returned to Santa Ynez, however, Jackson plunged back into
the world of radical politics. The spirit of rebellion, freed from the constraints
of high school, carried him into the broader underworld of union organizers
and genuine Communists, the world that was being genuinely oppressed by
Captain Hynes's Red Squad, police "shove days," and syndicalism indictments.
He attended Communist meetings at the Brooklyn Avenue Jewish Community
Center in East Los Angeles where Communists and union organizers often
met. How frequently he attended these meetings, who else attended, and how
actively he participated is not known—although strangers always frightened
him and, even among friends at Manual Arts, he tended to avoid group discus-
sions. It was during these nighttime forays that Jackson must have learned
something about the nexus between radical avant-garde art and radical politics.
He certainly learned of the Mexican muralists, José Clemente Orozco, Diego
Rivera, and David Alfaro Siqueiros, who were agitating for a revolution in
Mexican politics as well as a renaissance in Mexican art.

While he was absent from school, Jackson also plunged back into religion,
even more deeply than before.

On Monday, May 27, 1929, he set out with Schwankovsky, Tolegian, and
Goldstein on the seventy-mile trip to Ojai where, for an entire week, they would
hear Krishnamurti speak. As the car descended into the scenic valley, they
could see the campground at the far end of the table-flat fields, row after row

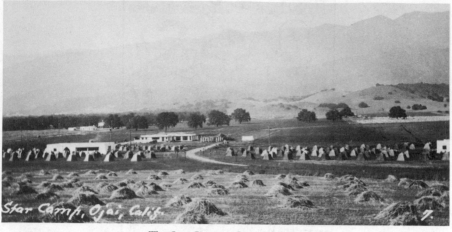

The Star Camp at Ojai, California

of carefully pitched tents—enough for two thousand followers—a grove of oak trees, a few low buildings, and the blue hills of the Sierra Madre beyond. At fifteen hundred feet above sea level, the air was drier than on the coast, warmer during the day, and cooler at night. "Imagine Italy, the Riviera, and the best parts of India rolled into one," wrote Lady Emily Lutyens, wife of the famous British architect, Edwin Lutyens, and a Krishnamurti intimate, "and you have this place."

The camps were organized more like military engagements than religious revivals. For the $45 entry fee, members received accommodations in a two-person tent and three meals a day. They were expected to bring their own "sheets, blankets, soap, towels, etc." or buy them at the camp shop. Banking services were provided, as was mail delivery. The members performed all of the camp work, from preparing food to standing night guard, on a volunteer basis.

The next morning, on the light-flecked ground beneath the oaks, Jackson gathered with the others for the first of Krishnamurti's talks. When the "Divine Spirit" finally appeared, the crowd fell into such a profound silence that the rustling of leaves could be heard even in the faintest breeze. Some members fell at Krishnamurti's feet, "overwhelmed by this marvelous rush of force." "It reminded one irresistibly of the rushing, mighty wind, and the outpouring of the Holy Ghost at Pentecost," wrote a witness at a similar meeting. "The tension was enormous. . . . It was exactly the kind of thing that we read about in the old scriptures, and think exaggerated; but here it was before us in the twentieth century." At the center of this vortex of attention was a thin, fragile man who looked only half of his thirty-four years. "An odd figure," according to Lady Lutyens, "with long black hair falling almost to his shoulders and enormous dark eyes which had a vacant look in them." Although he had undoubtedly seen photographs and heard Schwankovsky's descriptions, Jackson could not have been prepared for such an elegant, asexual presence. Krish-

namurti wore a custom-made white shirt, sometimes open at the collar, with
an impeccably tailored suit that Charles Pollock would have envied. When he
spoke, the words came effortlessly, without notes or pauses or false starts. "Like
many others who have tasted mystical reality," explained an admirer, "the
experience gave him a sense of inner authority and self-confidence." When he
finished, he took questions from the audience:

> QUESTION: Isn't the theory of individual freedom really anarchy?
> KRISHNAMURTI: If the individual is not happy, as he is not at the present
> time, he is creating chaos and anarchy around him, by his selfishness, by
> his cruelty. . . .

For six days, Jackson attended these daily talks, wandered with his friends
through the surrounding countryside, listened to concerts of Bach and Oriental
music, watched plays by James Barrie and George Bernard Shaw and a dance
interpretation of Krishnamurti's poems, and ate at the long tables beneath the
timbered pergola. In the evenings, he sat with the others around a campfire
and listened to followers of the Master bear witness to his message. On Thursday evening, Krishnamurti appeared again, lit a fire, chanted two Sanskrit
hymns, and, while a trio of concealed musicians played classical music, recited
some of his own poetry:

> Ah, come sit beside me
> Open and free.
> As the even flow of clear sunlight,
> So shall thine understanding come to thee.
> The burdensome fear of anxious waiting
> Shall go from thee as the waters recede before the rushing winds.
> Ah, come sit beside me.

In the midst of so much emotional turbulence, both at school and at home,
Jackson quickly succumbed to the sunlight, serenity, and soft voices of Ojai.
He may have met Krishnamurti personally on this trip, but even from a distance
he must have been reassured by the sight of the "vague and dreamy" teacher
who looked the same age as Jackson yet spoke with confidence and fluency;
who was, in his way, as much a misfit as Jackson, and yet held thousands in
thrall; who dressed like Charles, yet spoke a language of revolt. It was as if
Krishnamurti had taken the jagged fragments of Jackson's world and magically
assembled them into a life of serenity and self-fulfillment.

Krishnamurti didn't recruit disciples—"Be rather the disciple of understanding," he told his audiences—but such humility was lost on Jackson. By the
time the Ojai camp concluded, he had found a new ambition: to "follow the
Occult Mysticism." He grew his hair long and combed it back behind his ears
as the Master did. He began to wear his shirt open at the neck, the long collar
wings folded out over the peaked lapels of his well-tailored jacket—the way
Krishnamurti wore his. He refused to eat meat.

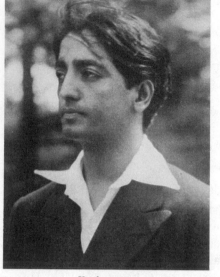

Krishnamurti

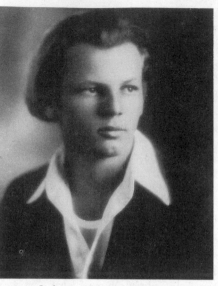

Jackson at Manual Arts, 1929

It was in this "spiritual" state that Jackson went to meet his father and begin work on the road crew at Santa Ynez.

On the first of July, Jackson and Stella drove up the coast, past Ojai and into the Santa Ynez Mountains. Stella spent two weeks at the road camp, "cooking and washing dishes," before returning to Los Angeles. On July 22, she left to visit her mother in Iowa.

The month that Jackson spent living and working with his father—what Roy called "batching together"—wasn't anything like the long-sought reconciliation it might have been a few years earlier. Jackson later told a friend that he had gone to the camp only to earn money and, from the moment he arrived, "wanted to come back." Nevertheless, the first few weeks with Stella in camp went smoothly enough. On July 20, Roy wrote to Charles and Frank in New York, "[Jack] is getting along fine he reads quite a lot of good magazines & doesn't seem to get lonesome for the city." Even after Stella's departure, Roy's grim optimism and their common Pollock reticence combined to create the appearance of tranquillity, even when the temperature reached an incendiary 106 degrees in the shade. "[Jack] is a very good & pleasant companion," Roy wrote a week after Stella's departure, "always in a good mood."

The mood didn't last. At some point during the summer, a fistfight erupted between father and son, ostensibly over Jackson's desire to return to Los Angeles. Perhaps Roy disapproved of his son's exaggerated self-involvement. "I do not think a young fellow should be too serious," he had written Jackson the previous fall. "It is no use to worry about what you can't help, or what you can help, moral 'Don't worry.' " (It was the credo of a man who, unlike Jackson, had come to terms with himself, however unfavorable those terms might have been.) Perhaps Jackson's indecisiveness seemed to Roy too much like indifference. "The secret of success is concentrated interest," he had also written. Perhaps Jackson's dismal school record and vague ambitions smacked too much of laziness, or, at least, a laxness of spirit that must have seemed a grave sin to a man whose pride had survived so many indignities. Whatever the spark, clearly Roy felt profoundly disappointed by his son. The truth, bitter as it must have been for Jackson, was that Roy Pollock thought, and perhaps had always thought, that his fifth son would never amount to much. "Dad would have been *astonished*," says Charles, "that anything ever became of Jackson."

All that's known for sure about the fight or about what followed is that Jackson came home from Santa Ynez, by himself, a month early, and never worked with his father again.

Back in Los Angeles, Jackson was more alone and lost than ever: Stella lingered in Iowa, the Manual Arts gang dispersed over the city, and Schwankovsky spent the summer at his studio in faraway Laguna Beach. Sande, the only brother within reach, inhabited a distant world of salary checks, expensive suits, and friends he never brought home. He still spent his weekends at the big Victorian house on Pennsylvania Avenue in Riverside where Arloie nursed her sick father and dropped hints about marriage. In response, Sande pled penury—then returned to Los Angeles, spent $600 on a new Model A roadster coupe with a rumble seat and lent Robert Cooter several hundred dollars to buy a gas station in Phoenix.

With no one to buoy him up, Jackson drifted deeper and deeper into depression and, in all probability, drink. Behind him was the painful memory of his father's rejection; ahead, the dismal prospect of another school year. In his desperation, he reached out in the most unlikely direction: to Charles. In a long, disjointed letter, he poured out his problems to his brother, detailing the turmoil at Manual Arts, his involvement with Krishnamurti, his experiment with radical politics, and even his now waning interest in art. That Jackson would turn to Charles, whom he had not seen in fours years and who, before that, had barely acknowledged his little brother's existence, betrays the depth of his desperation. The two had not exchanged a single letter in the eight years since Charles left home.

During all those years, though, Jackson had never lost faith in his big brother, the artist, who had gone to the big city—first Los Angeles, then New York—to become famous. "[Jack] held Charles in reverence," says a friend from this period. "He had picked his bags up and gone to New York, and he had done things that were so professional, and so accomplished. All the way up and down the line, whatever Charles had done, *that* was the thing to do."

Jackson's letter was not only an offering, it was a dark, pessimistic chronicle that alarmed the usually sanguine Charles. Within days, he drafted a long and thoughtful reply and, as was his practice, copied it in careful calligraphy onto fine paper.

From the moment it arrived, Charles's letter was a turning point in Jackson's life. His rekindled interest in art and his decision to become an artist both began to take conscious shape in the hours he spent reading and rereading—"with clearer understanding each time"—this rare, lengthy, and fatefully well-timed token of Charles's concern.

> Your letter has confounded me and I am inescapably lead to write you a long letter to attempt if possible to persuade you of the folly of your present attitude towards the problems of life. I do this without wishing to meddle in your own personal problems, but only because I am interested in you and because I have myself gone through periods of depression and melancholy and uncertainty which threatened to warp all future efforts.
>
> I am sorry I have seen so little of you these past years when you have matured so rapidly. Now I have the vaguest idea of your temperament and interests. It is apparent tho that you are gifted with a sensitive and perceptive intelligence and it is important that this quality should develop normally and thoroughly to its ultimate justification in some worthy endeavor and not be wasted.

In his letter, Jackson had apparently described at some length his frustration and alienation at school, as well as his intellectual insecurity. It's clear from Charles's response that Jackson was contemplating not returning to Manual Arts in September.

> I know well this is no easy matter and that the problems of adjusting oneself to the standards of the contemporary school system, if one is equipped with intelligence and a sensitive spirit, are at times almost insuperable. Still wisdom and understanding we must achieve one way or another. . . .
>
> It would be well to finish school if you can if at all possible or tolerable not because it means anything in itself but because ground work is necessary however ineptly it is provided. . . .

Charles had little patience for Krishnamurti or for his views, and even less for Jackson's proposal that he follow Krishnamurti to his camps in India and Holland and, monk-like, dedicate his life to the search for his "individual truth."

> The philosophy of escape to which you have momentarily succumbed is a negation which should have no place in twentieth century America. If one thing is more certain than another it is that we are born into potentially one of the most magnificent countrys in all of history—into a material prosperity before unheard of . . . [that can be] the possible means to an ideal and humane civilization. I am unwilling to believe that with your gifts you are willing to forego the challenge, for a contemplative life that can have no value because it ignores realities—for a religion that is an

anachronism in this age—for adherence to an occult mysticism whose exponents in this country are commercial savants. . . .

In an effort to counter the despairing tone of his brother's letter and offer some constructive advice, Charles seized on Jackson's statement that he was still interested in art—a statement that must have come as a revelation to Charles who, when he left home, knew only of *Sande's* budding artistic ambitions.

> I am delighted that you have an interest in art. Is it a general interest or do you consider you may wish to become a painter? Have the possibilities of architecture ever interested you. This is a field of unlimited rewards for a genuine artist, once intelligence and the unaccountable wealth of the country begin to command real talent. One of the finest architects in the country Lloyd Wright is living and working in Los Angeles. I do not think he is finding an outlet for his capacities but the time may not be far away when such men will be recognized. If architecture appealed to you there might be a splendid opportunity to serve an apprenticeship.
>
> My interest in mural painting definitely related to architecture has lead me lately to think of returning to Los Angeles if I could get work with Wright. Are you familiar with the work of Rivera and Orozco in Mexico City? This is the finest painting that has been done, I think, since the sixteenth century. "Creative Art" for January 1929 has an article on Rivera and "The Arts" October 1927 has an article on Orozco. I wish you could see these and also an article by Benton in Creative Art December 1928. Here are men with imagination and intelligence recognizing the implements of the modern world and ready to employ them.

Charles's letter may have been a plea for accommodation with the world, but it was the tone of self-assurance, even defiance, that stuck with Jackson and gave him renewed strength as he began the school year. Without realizing it, Charles had added his persuasive voice to Krishnamurti's call for revolt.

> Do not believe so early that you are ill placed in this world and that there is nothing you are fitted to do. There are many pursuits supremely worthy of your best efforts and for which the qualities you possess, are a first necessity. Finding your way may be difficult but in the end the torment of uncertainty will be only a part of experience. Do not believe in an easy way to freedom. The way to freedom physical or spiritual, to be enduring, must be won honestly. . . .
>
> I would be very glad if you would write me in greater detail of your interests.

Armed with his brother's reassurance, Jackson returned to Manual Arts on September 10, 1929, cocky and defiant. Left uncut since Ojai, his hair had grown provokingly long. He wore his loose, open-collared shirts in the style of

Krishnamurti while the other boys wore cardigans; and high, lace-up surveyor's boots instead of saddle shoes or wingtips. The effect was that of a "ham actor," one classmate recalls: everything seemed calculated to attract attention—most of it unfavorable. "I really think he did it just to rebel, just for the heck, the kick of it," said Manuel Tolegian. "Restrictions were all right for some people but not for him." Friends like Tolegian must have sensed the self-destructiveness in Jackson's desperate clamor for attention. Why else would a quiet, painfully reticent and "seclusive" youngster, comfortable only "in the background," invite such public ridicule?

Jackson flouted the school's course requirements as blithely as he ignored its dress code. Under rules that applied to all Los Angeles high schools, students were required to take courses in English, history, laboratory science, math, and the arts. In the fall of 1929, Jackson ignored the requirements, enrolling instead in two English classes, both taught by a favorite teacher, and two art classes: Schwankovsky's life drawing and Hazel Martin's clay modeling. Even in this, Jackson seemed to be courting humiliation. His sketches were still embarrassingly crude—"rotten," "cold and lifeless," he called them—and the two English classes, American Literature and Contemporary Literature, both required oral presentations: "[When I had] to talk in a group," he admitted in a letter to Charles and Frank, "I was so fightened that I could not think logically." For Jackson, however, enrolling in a course didn't necesssarily mean attending. Tolegian remembered that, no matter how much Jackson juggled his schedule, "he just wouldn't attend any classes."

If Jackson was looking for a confrontation, whether to prove himself or to punish himself, he soon found it.

On the first day of school, fifty Manual boys responded to the notices posted by Coaches Sid Foster and Jim Blewett recruiting "prospective gridiron heroes." With only five of fourteen starters returning from 1928, the turnout was disappointing, and word soon began to circulate that the coaches and varsity players were scouting the student body for additional "beefers"—big kids who hadn't played the game but who had the necessary bulk to block the line. This year there was an added urgency to the call because Manual's "purple and grey hoghiders" were favored by local sportswriters to win the city championship if they could win their season opener against the Parrots of Poly High, a game already being billed on campus as "the battle of the ages." In the frantic, informal draft that preceded the game, Jackson was an obvious candidate. With his broad, vaguely bullish face, big-boned limbs, and square-set body, he looked like a football player despite the long hair and eccentric clothes. Even if he wasn't directly approached by coaches or players, he was a walking reminder of the plague of "slackers" that beset the school: a beefer who wouldn't play ball. In an editorial that appeared shortly before the decisive game, the *Weekly* publicly castigated—perhaps with Jackson specifically in mind—such traitors to school spirit.

It's a ghastly or something-or-other shame when . . . the number of candidates is shockingly low. Are we a school of "little boys" and non-patriots? . . . We want a winning team and we are positive that every loyal student of Manual does too.

Around the same time, Jackson was ambushed in the hall at school by a group of football players. Probably incensed by his appearance as much as his slack school spirit, they pinned him down and cut off his long hair. Then they dragged him into a nearby bathroom and forced his head into the toilet. If it was humiliation Jackson wanted, he had finally found it.

Soon afterward, he was hauled before Coach Sid Foster, a "mean, short-tempered" man who also happened to be the head of the physical education department. Whether Jackson was there to explain his refusal to play for the team or because he had once again run afoul of the school's phys. ed. requirement isn't recorded. What is recorded, by Jackson himself, is that the confrontation eventually "came to blows." (It was the third time in as many years Jackson had lashed out at an authority figure: the ROTC officer at Riverside, his father at Santa Ynez, now Coach Foster). Within minutes, he found himself in the office of the principal, Dr. Albert E. Wilson, known to faculty and students as "the Czar." To Dr. Wilson, a humorless, stiff-necked man of Scandinavian rectitude, no crime was worse than tardiness and, according to a school chronicler, "no alibi had validity." (He was also known for his interest in and sympathy toward the arts—a sympathy that would later work to Jackson's benefit.) If Jackson had not come to Wilson's attention before, his record of absences, tardiness, and incomplete semesters spoke too eloquently now. Wilson expelled him. "He was too thick to see my side," Jackson complained to Charles and Frank. "He told me to get out and find another school."

Despite Jackson's boast to Charles and Frank that "I have a number of teachers backing me so there is some possibility of my getting back," only Schwankovsky and Jackson's English teacher came to his defense. Stella, only recently returned from Iowa, also met with Wilson and asked him to reconsider. Frank Pollock recalls that he was shocked when he learned that his mother had pled on Jackson's behalf: "That's the first time that mother ever took part in any school activity." Yet even if such efforts had been successful, Jackson must have realized, after four of the last five semesters had ended prematurely, that high school was no longer a viable option; he had used up his last chance. His speculations about returning alternated between resignation and unreality:

If I get back in school I will have to be very careful about my actions. The whole outfit think I am a rotten rebel from Russia. I will have to go about very quietly for a long period until I win a good reputation. I find it useless to try and fight an army with a spit ball.

Speculation aside, Jackson seemed bent on self-destruction. Only days after being expelled, he was in trouble again. He and "another fellow loaned two girls some money to run away," he dutifully reported to Charles and Frank:

> We were ignorant of the law at the time. We did it merely through friend ship. But now they have us, I am not sure what the outcomes will be. The penalty is from six to twelve months in jail. We are both minors so it would probably be some kind of a reform school. They found the girls today in Phoenix and are bringing them back.

In all likelihood, the other "fellow" was Phil Goldstein, a notorious "ladies' man." Goldstein began the year as art editor of the *Weekly*, but was abruptly and inexplicably demoted to "assistant" after the October 1 issue—almost precisely the time that the episode with the two girls was discovered by school authorities.

The dire consequences Jackson feared never materialized. Instead, from the end of October through the first part of 1930, he withdrew into another period of seclusion and depression. A year of rebellion had left him humiliated at school, alienated from his family—especially his father—and still unable to make a pen move gracefully across a piece of paper. Instead of "growing like the Lotus" he was stumbling from one crisis to another, troubled by his own moroseness and plagued by nightmares. Old feelings of inadequacy and guilt, never far beneath the mask of political posturing and Theosophical resignation, welled to the surface. He toyed fatalistically with the idea of running away to Mexico City, "if there is any means of making a livelihood there."

Only the letter from Charles held out hope. As the Manual Arts football team ground through a disappointing season, and Sande lit out in his brand-new Ford for the big white house in Riverside, and the country skidded toward financial collapse, Jackson languished in the bungalow court off Vermont Avenue, reading and rereading the small pages of his brother's elegant, High German calligraphy. With the letter as inspiration, old fantasies were revived. He dutifully subscribed to *Creative Art* magazine, as Charles had recommended—"it gives me a new outlook on life," he enthused—and sought out the articles on Rivera, Orozco, and Benton (although he found only the first). Inevitably, more recent fantasies were discarded. "I have dropped religion for the present," he wrote Charles in submission. "Should I follow the Occult Mysticism it wouldn't be for commercial purposes."

Between brief spells of optimism, Jackson's depression lingered through Christmas and into the New Year. As if on cue, the nation plunged past him. Longer and longer lines of the unemployed, homeless, and hungry formed outside private missions in the city's slum sections to receive their ration of rancid scraps from restaurant garbage (city officials refused to set up soup kitchens, convinced they were breeding grounds of unionism and socialism). The crash itself disregarded such fine distinctions, crushing bourgeoisie and

proletariat indiscriminately. In tony Pasadena, the first of seventy-nine people
—most of them bankers, stockbrokers, and real-estate speculators—jumped to
his death from the scenic bridge across the Arroyo Seco, soon nicknamed
"Suicide Bridge." In the spirit of indefatigable boosterism that characterized
Los Angeles, a fiesta was planned, with floats, evangelists, and movie stars, in
the hope that it would "lift the city out of the commercial doldrums by lifting
its spirits." After all, the *Times* reported, "much of the Depression is psychological." For Jackson, even being readmitted to school on a part-time basis in
January—due to some combination of Schwankovsky's influence with Dr. Wilson and Stella's insistent pleas—did little to lift his spirits. "This so called happy
part of one's life youth to me is a bit of damnable hell," he wrote to Charles at
the end of January:

> if i could come to some conclusion about my self and life perhaps there i
> could see something to work for. my mind blazes up with some ill[u]sion
> for a couple of weeks the[n] it smoalters down to a bit of nothing[. T]he
> more i read and the more i think i am thinking the darker things become.

As he approached his eighteenth birthday, Jackson was feeling increasingly
embarrassed by his lack of a girlfriend. Charles, after all, had never been
without female companionship, and school friends like Phil Goldstein were
already in a position to be "choosy about girls." "Jackson just didn't have
girlfriends like the rest of them," recalls Don Brown's sister Alma. In late 1929,
as the peer pressure mounted, Jackson received word through Stella, the family
news broker, that Charles had met the woman he would eventually marry,
Elizabeth Feinberg, in New York. Within a year, Arloie Conaway would press
Sande into serious discussions about marriage, and Frank would begin courting Marie Levitt, his future wife. Jackson, meanwhile, remained conspicuously
celibate.

Sometime in the fall of 1929, Harold Hodges invited him to a party in the
big house on the corner of Gramercy and Forty-third Street where Hodges
boarded. The party turned out to be a "musical jam," a small gathering of
high-minded young musicians who performed for an audience made up of
other "artsy kids" from Manual Arts. At some point during the evening, Jackson watched as a short, serious-looking girl in a severe dress adjusted herself
at the piano and began to play. Her black hair, extravagantly long, fell over the
back of the bench. She played with an intense, authoritative touch and, when
she finished, walked stiff and unsmiling back to her chair. Jackson was attracted by her talent and the confidence it gave her; she found him handsome,
"clean," and charmingly awkward. Besides, her long, plain face and direct
manner had won her few looks from the other handsome boys at school. At a
deeper level, each undoubtedly recognized a fellow rebel.

The girl was Berthe Pacifico, a junior at Manual Arts. She had been born
Bertha, but despised the name and readily agreed to her concert agent's suggestion that she change it to Berthe, which she pronounced in a single syllable,

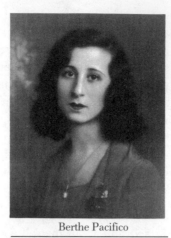

Berthe Pacifico

"Burt," without the fussy schwa. Her conversation was similarly brusque and unadorned. She tended to pounce on questions as if they were small fires— "Holy Cow, no!" Forthright and full of opinions, she hardly fit the coquettish image of the other girls at Manual. "In fact, she was *overly* serious," recalls a classmate, "without much of a sense of humor."

Although attracted to Jackson—she had recognized him from campus immediately—Berthe wasn't about to let him interfere with her rigorous five-hour-a-day practice schedule. "Right after school Jack would come over and listen to me play till dinner," she recalls. "He was like a mouse, so quiet you wouldn't even know he was there." And so persistent that Berthe occasionally felt "like I had to kick him out." Sometimes he tagged along to lessons and recitals. Everywhere he went he took a small sketch pad in his shirt pocket. "He'd sketch my head, my hands, my face," Berthe remembers, "but he especially liked to draw my hair. I had long, heavy hair." With what little money he could earn or borrow, Jackson bought her gifts: a small gold locket in the shape of a cross with enamel inlay and matching earrings that she never wore; a pair of silk lounging pajamas piped in black satin. In her rough way, Berthe was touched by the gifts. "It must have taken all the dough he had," she remembers thinking.

Soon Jackson began staying for dinner at the big Victorian house on Dalton Street only six blocks from school. The Pacifico family generally approved of him—"He was always a good polite boy; clean as a whistle and never showed dirt," recalls Berthe's sister, Ora Horton—and eventually let him drive the family Hudson up to the Baldwin Hills, a site for the upcoming Olympics that was still just rolling fields and swampland. There, he would stop the car, pull a package of tobacco from his pocket, and roll his own cigarettes in brown paper. At times like these, says Berthe, or when they were alone on the piano bench of the mahogany Kranich & Bach in the parlor, "all he was interested in was smooching if he could." Only once, when they were sitting on the bench, did she allow him a kiss.

Berthe may not have satisfied all of Jackson's romantic needs, but for a while, at least, she satisfied the most pressing one. Returning from his afternoons of Beethoven, Chopin, and Gershwin, he regaled his mother and Sande with stories that were gradually disseminated through Stella's letters to the rest of the family. He brought her proudly to the bungalow court to introduce her to Stella—"she was always pleased to see me," Berthe recalls—and to share the dinner table, two-by-two at last, with Sande and Arloie. Eventually, he would show her off to all the brothers. Yet the sketches he drew of her, hundreds of them presumably, remained hidden—even from Berthe. "All the time I was playing, that darn old pencil never stopped," she recalls. "But he would never let me see what he did." At times, he would go off by himself with his pencil and pad and work furiously while Berthe watched from a distance.

The harder he tried, however, the more frustrated he felt. "I am doubtful of any talent," he wrote Charles in October, "so what ever I choose to be will be accomplished only by long study and work. I fear it will be forced and mechanical." In the Pacificos' parlor, in Manual Tolegian's chicken coop, and in Schwankovsky's drawing classes, he continued to sketch, but his thoughts turned more and more to other media in a desperate effort to reconcile his ambitions with his inadequacies. "Architecture interests me," he wrote Charles, "but not in the sense painting and sculptoring does." The reference to painting was largely wishful—no one at Manual Arts taught oil painting, and Jackson never enrolled in Schwankovsky's watercolor class. In "sculptoring," however, Jackson found a thread of hope. "I have started doing some thing with clay," he reported to Charles in January, "and have found a bit of encouragement from my teacher." The teacher, Hazel Martin, although not a particularly accomplished sculptor herself, apparently saw that the undisciplined Jackson needed encouragement more than honesty. According to another student, Martin was never sure when Jackson had completed his sculptures: "There was a group of figures Jack had done but they were very, very vague, almost abstract, and she said, 'Why don't you get hold of Jack and tell him to finish these so I can fire them.'" Jackson informed her that they were already "finished."

Most of his fellow students were similarly baffled, although a few had begun to see, especially in his sculptures, signs of an oblique, unconventional talent. "Some of his work had a lot of energy and we admired that," recalls a classmate who later became an artist.

But the pen still frustrated him. On the last day of the winter term, he wrote Charles:

> . . . my drawing i will tell you frankly is rotten it seems to lack freedom and rhythem it is cold and lifeless. it isn't worth the postage to send it . . . the truth of it is i have never really gotten down to real work and finish a piece i usually get disgusted with it and lose interest . . . altho i feel i will

make an artist of some kind i have nver proven to myself nor any body else that i have it in me.

When the second semester began on February 3, 1930, Jackson was permitted to enroll only in Schwankovsky's life drawing class and Mrs. Martin's clay modeling class, and only on an ungraded basis. Despite the opportunity to concentrate his efforts, his inadequacies were only further underscored by the arrival that term of a new classmate, Harold Lehman.

Lehman was everything Jackson Pollock wasn't: brash, self-confident, erudite, articulate, and extraordinarily talented. He could also be, like Goldstein, self-impressed and supercilious. Having just moved from New York to Hollywood, he concluded that California in general, and Manual Arts in particular, was a cultural wasteland. His talent, however, was undeniable. Trained in a world-renowned casting studio at age fifteen, Lehman was an accomplished sculptor and a master caster by the time he arrived in Martin's clay modeling class. "She had never seen anything like it," he recalls. "It was just unbelievable that a young kid like myself could do all this technology. Nobody in the school knew anything about it." Technology aside, the sculptures themselves were in the best academic tradition: lifelike in detail, flawless in execution. His sketches displayed an astonishing precision of line and sensitivity to shape, proportion, and shading. Of all the artists Jackson had encountered, and perhaps ever would encounter, Lehman came closest to that ideal of effortless accomplishment expressed in the term "gifted." There was no doubt: Harold Lehman was extravagantly gifted. At his first show in Los Angeles a few years later, he would be hailed by newspapers as "a great genius" and "unbelievable talent." During his two years at Manual Arts, art teachers from other districts would approach him with inducements to change schools—"as though I was a football player." For months, his bust of Abraham Lincoln was prominently displayed in a glass case outside the school auditorium.

For most of his classmates, Lehman felt only contempt; but for Jackson, with his guileless admiration and athletic body, he felt the impatient, possessive affection of an older brother. The unlikely pair went browsing through the bookstores along Broadway and Spring Street in lower Los Angeles, hunting for bargains on art books and secondhand magazines. In Lehman's neighborhood, Hollywood, they visited Stanley Rose's bookshop and gallery, where the very latest in controversial avant-garde literature (James Joyce, Luigi Pirandello, Gertrude Stein) was always available, along with books on the modern European masters. Lehman took Jackson to the Los Angeles County Museum and the tiny handful of galleries—Daltzell-Hatfield and Stendhal—that exhibited modern French paintings. Jackson took Lehman to Manuel Tolegian's backyard to see the chicken coop, which Lehman called "picturesque" but declined to enter because he "didn't like to draw in groups."

Like Charles, Lehman was an unapproachable figure, at home in a world from which Jackson felt excluded. If, on a trip to a bookstore or museum,

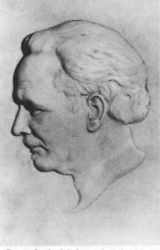

Bas relief of Schwankovsky by
Harold Lehman

Jackson tended to forget the distance that separated them, he had only to put
pencil to paper to remind him. The scraps of knowledge he had gathered from
Charles's articles and Schwankovsky's class were lost in Lehman's lavish monologues on the Renaissance, Matisse, Picasso, and Cubism, which he "didn't
really get." In the spring of 1930, Schwankovsky arranged for Lehman and
Phil Goldstein—not Jackson—to take an evening class in life drawing at Los
Angeles High where the models posed nude. In June, the *Weekly* announced
that Goldstein had been awarded a scholarship to the Otis Art Institute for the
coming fall. It would be another year before the two prodigies began holding
meetings to play Stravinsky recordings, discuss the filmmaking theories of
Eisenstein and Dovchenko, or give reports on philosophical tracts. But Jackson's comfortable little family of fellow students was, largely due to Lehman's
dervish intellect, already drifting in that direction and, with each drift, leaving
Jackson further behind.

In mid-June, Charles and Frank returned from New York in a 1924 Buick.
Their arrival at the bungalow court off Vermont Avenue marked the beginning
of one of the Pollock family reunions that invariably foreshadowed an upheaval
in Jackson's life.

Charles had changed considerably since his departure in 1926. Four years
in New York had taught him the rudiments of humility and accommodation.
He was no longer the high-handed, thin-skinned dandy who would shoo his
youngest brother away or burst into self-righteous indignation at the dinner
table. In his long, careful letters to Jackson, as well as his commitment to
Elizabeth Feinberg, he seemed prepared at last to care about somebody other
than himself. In that new spirit, he sat down and told Jackson his story.

After walking away from the Orland farm, he had stopped briefly in Phoenix before arriving at his final destination, Los Angeles. By a stroke of luck, one of his first acquaintances there was a prominent local art critic, Arthur Millier, who promptly arranged a job for him as a copyboy at the *Times*. Eventually, he worked his way into the art department where his job included "layout, fancy lettering for the Sunday supplement, and scaling photographs."

As soon as he had saved enough money, he enrolled at the Otis Art Institute and moved to nearby Echo Park, within sight of the revolving gold cross of Aimee Semple McPherson's Angelus Temple. The routine at Otis was deadly dull, consisting mostly of drawing from casts and live models. For news of more exciting developments, like the works of Matisse and the French School, he had to rely on magazines, word of mouth, and traveling exhibitions. One show in particular, an exhibition of Mexican painters at Exposition Park, had captured his imagination. The brooding, polemical, often violent paintings of Orozco, Siqueiros, and Rivera proved to Charles that art could be more than plaster casts and sketching classes. Soon, rotogravures and layouts lost their appeal. "I got bored with my job," he recalls, "so I gave it up, thinking that I would go to Mexico." Then one day, while browsing in the little Japanese fruit stand where he had bought the *Dial*s for Jack and Sande, he picked up a copy of *Shadowland*, a movie magazine that featured articles on painting and music. In it, he found an article by Thomas Hart Benton.

On the recommendation of Arthur Millier, he dropped plans for Mexico and headed instead to New York City to enroll at the Art Students League where Benton had just joined the faculty. At Benton's apartment near Abingdon Square, Charles was "received with open arms." Within a few months, he was a fixture both in Benton's class at the League and in the Bentons' household. By 1927, they had found him a roomier flat in the same building and by 1928, they were inviting him to their summer house on Martha's Vineyard. In exchange for baby-sitting her infant son, T. P., Rita Benton offered him genuine Italian spaghetti and helped him find work designing motion picture display cards for a Long Island printing firm.

Charles repaid his teacher's generosity with total devotion. "Whatever talent I had when I came to New York was nonexistent," he says. "I had only enthusiasm, excitement, and a burning desire to study with him." Under the influence of the pragmatic, earthbound Benton, Charles's conception of art, and the artist, had also changed. Instead of a "pretty pasttime" appreciated, if not created, largely by women, art to Benton was an athletic event, a manly exercise involving structure and movement and muscle. The new view of the artist extended even to Benton's wardrobe, which the clothes-conscious Charles quickly adopted, trading in the white spats and silk vests of Los Angeles for the rumpled shirts and suspenders that Benton considered the uniform of manhood.

For the first few weeks, after Frank left for Big Pines, Jackson had the new, more approachable Charles all to himself. Together they drove to the little town of Claremont, thirty miles east of Los Angeles, to see the mural that

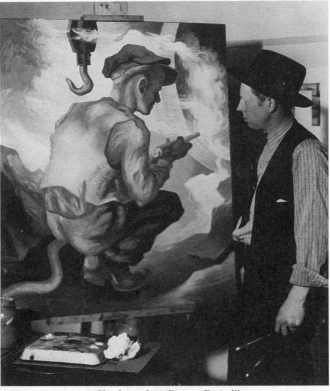

Charles in his "Benton Period"

Orozco had recently finished at Pomona College. In a vast Gothic arch at one end of the student refectory, they saw the giant figure of Prometheus filling the space above the fireplace. Painted in harsh, bleak browns and grays, he stood twenty feet tall, yet still seemed somehow crowded into the triangular space, pressed down on one great trunk-like knee, surrounded by a rabble of smaller figures, arms outstretched, in a chorus of fear and despair.

It wasn't a "fine" painting in the classroom sense: the legs were too big for the body, the hands ill-formed, the head too small—all "mistakes" that Jackson himself had made countless times. It looked nothing like the perfect drawings of Harold Lehman or Phil Goldstein. But it possessed an undeniable power. It seemed to prove everything Charles had been saying about muscular art and a new kind of artist. And if Jackson missed the emotional intensity of the image, the directness of the style, the political implications of the subject matter, or the potential of mural-size painting, Charles was there to point them out and offer explanations, however incompletely understood. More than any book or article, Charles's admiration conferred on this unfamiliar art a new and indelible fascination for Jackson.

Sometime around the Fourth of July, Charles and Stella left for Wrightwood to visit Frank and Roy. Sande and Arloie joined them for a while, sleeping together in a tent beside the cabin, with Stella's blithe acquiescence, before

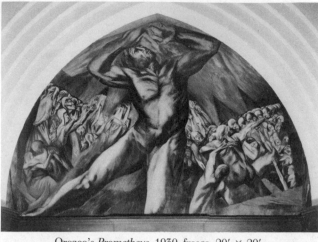

Orozco's *Prometheus*, 1930, fresco, 20′ × 20′

Sande returned to his job in Los Angeles. In the midst of so much movement, and despite his hunger to be with Charles, Jackson remained in Los Angeles, memories of the fight with his father in Santa Ynez the previous summer still fresh in his mind.

Without Charles, Jackson sank back into a restless depression. The unexpected arrival of his cousin Paul McClure provided some distraction but little comfort. Through a sweltering July and August, Jackson remained cloistered in the tiny bungalow, sketching furiously and turning over in his mind what Charles had told him. "He only seemed to be interested in seeing things he could reproduce," McClure remembers. When McClure could engage him in conversation, it was invariably about Charles. "It was clear that Jack idolized Charles. He wanted to do what Charles did. He said, 'Charles can do this so I guess I'll try it.'"

In early September, as Charles and Frank were preparing to return to New York, they urged Jackson to join them. "If you want to be an artist," Frank remembers Charles saying, "there's only one place to be, and that's where it's all happening. That's New York." The summer had shown Jackson that there was nothing, and no one, in Los Angeles to hold him. Before leaving, however, he went to Berthe Pacifico's house and asked her to marry him and come to New York. "We could live in Greenwich Village," he argued, "and you could go to music school." Over her mother's vehement objections—"She thought we were too young"—Berthe said yes to marriage but no to New York, dismissing Jackson's dreamy plans with a wave of her hand. "You're so naive," she sighed.

On September 10, 1930, the Buick left Los Angeles carrying one more Pollock brother than when it arrived. For a change of scenery, Charles, who did most of the driving, decided to take the northern route through Utah, Wyoming, Nebraska, and Missouri, then coasted Route 40 into New York. In one of the brief pockets of conversation about New York, school, art, Benton, and "the big question," which Charles recalls was "what is it all going to add up to," the subject of names arose. Jackson had assumed that as an artist he would use his full name: Paul Jackson Pollock. Charles thought that was "too long," and Paul Pollock "didn't sound very interesting." He suggested that Jackson stick with Jackson. "It sounded more forceful, it seemed to me, or euphonious, if you like," Charles remembers. "Jackson Pollock had a certain ring to it."

Jackson's family never called him Jackson, however. To them, he would always be Jack.

Part Two

NEW YORK

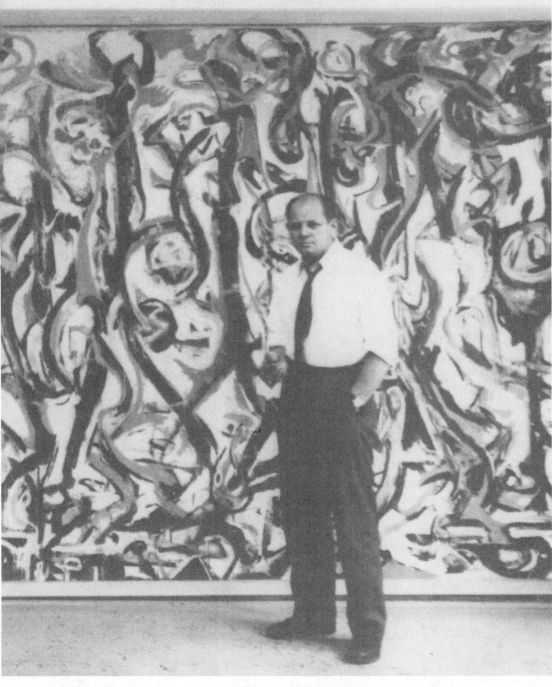

II

THE BEST PAINTER IN THE FAMILY

To Jackson's eye, New York in the fall of 1930, almost a full year after the great crash, was still a city of lofty ambition. He could see it in the skyline, where the unfinished Empire State Building's 102-story silhouette stretched even native necks in astonishment. Beside it, the Chrysler Building, with its steel crown, and other, lesser towers—Woolworth, Chanin, Waldorf—stood in random array, many still showing their skeletons and topped by construction cranes. During the late twenties these buildings had become the city's arrogant symbols, simultaneously solid and ephemeral, real and delusional, part hard Manhattan schist, part weightless aeries, thrusts of form and energy that deserved their name, stolen from sailors' efforts to describe the topmost sail on a high-masted schooner: moon-sail, cloud-raker, sky-scraper. Like a stone armada in the full furl of ambition, they sailed in what Malcom Cowley called "dynamic immobility" through the island's deep, unyielding granite.

Jackson could see the ambition in the "amplitude and onrush" of street life; in the long lines of men waiting outside burlesque houses on Forty-second Street, bathed in Mercurochrome light; in the crowded, smoky balconies of movie houses that specialized in triple features, where the homeless often spent the night; in the cheap carny fair of vivid, vulgar amusements that went on perpetually just off the elegant avenues; in the start-stop steeplechase of 25,000 cabs through canyons already clogged with newsstands, vendors, carts, beggars, shoeblacks, kiosks, flower girls, and trams, all of them washed by the "eddy and mill and bustle of the common, garish crowds." On Broadway, he could see it in the dazzling hues of neon that ringed Times Square. He could see it below the streets, where seven million people every day funneled through the dark passages of New York's subway system and into the clattery cars, pressed together "like dried figs done up in cellophane." He could see it as he traveled the "licorice ribbon" avenues north toward Harlem on the Third, Sixth, or

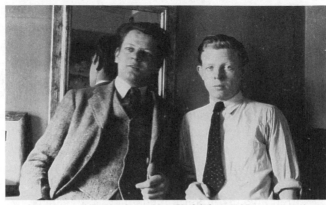

With Charles in New York, about 1931

Ninth Avenue Els. Down each passing street, glimpsed blinkingly, he could see the contrasts that fueled the ambition: out one side, the limestone town houses and towers of celebrity; out the other side, tenement shells in endless rows of anonymity.

New York was the city of ambition because it was where ambitious people were drawn, like Melville's wise man to water. They put up with the noise, the filth, the conflict and confusion, even grew addicted to the mindless intoxication of it all. They proclaimed themselves—like Whitman, Melville, Thomas Wolfe, and thousands of others in the ceaseless flow of talent—natives of Manhattan and accepted the permanent status of stranger. It was a city, wrote John Dos Passos, "full of people wanting inconceivable things."

No one wanted inconceivable things more than Jackson Pollock.

But New York was Charles's world: the last in a long line of special places, beginning with the sanitarium in Phoenix, in which Charles was at home, and Jackson merely an uneasy guest. He slept on Charles's couch, ate meals prepared by Charles's girlfriend, Elizabeth, and followed Charles as he settled back into his orderly, exotic New York existence. "In a sense, Charles was sort of a surrogate father," Frank recalls of Jackson's first days in New York. "He was an adviser and a counselor and he guided Jack." Everywhere they went together, Jackson felt the admiration that his oldest brother enjoyed. "He was very suave and very subtle," remembers a classmate at the Art Students League, "but his head was screwed on straight." The Bentons welcomed him as an artist—he could "out-Benton Benton," according to Rita—and as a friend, favoring him with an apartment on Union Square, a suitcase full of Benton's early abstract works, and invitations to the Benton summer home on Martha's Vineyard.

Charles, and perhaps Benton, too, helped introduce Jackson to the contentious world of American art in the early 1930s. He had already gleaned bits and pieces of art news from Schwankovsky and more knowledgeable students like Goldstein and Lehman, but nothing could have prepared him for the civil war brewing in New York. In the two decades since the 1913 Armory Show, the reign of American realist painters like Robert Henri and George Bellows had been challenged by the Cubist and Fauvist revolutions of Picasso and Matisse. American artists like John Marin and Marsden Hartley—and even former realists like John Sloan—espoused the new ideology: subject matter was subordinate to form; the future of art lay in abstraction, not, as Sloan now said, in "the disease of imitating appearances." Even Thomas Hart Benton had clambered aboard the modernist bandwagon in the twenties, painting brightly colored Synchromist works under the influence of his friend Stanton Macdonald-Wright, exhibiting with Macdonald-Wright and Morgan Russell at the Anderson Galleries in the important Forum Exhibition of 1916, and fraternizing at Alfred Stieglitz's radical modernist "291" gallery.

But the decade of rootless prosperity, uninhibited experimentation, and international disillusionment that followed the war had generated a counter-revolution, a movement "back" toward traditional values, both in the art world and in the nation: a "country-wide revival of Americanism," Benton called it. Even as Warren G. Harding called for "not heroics but healing, not nostrums but normalcy, not revolution but restoration," Edward Hopper set out to make a pictorial record of alienated America, and William Gropper painted the plight of the poor and the dispossessed. By 1930, caught up in the tide of isolation and introspection that swept the nation, these and other artists had begun to reverse the fortunes of international modernism in America.

The "American Wave" had not yet crested, as Jackson could see by the Impressionists and Post-Impressionists enshrined in the Museum of Modern Art and the Fifty-seventh Street galleries. In fact, the term wasn't coined until 1931. But its momentum was clearly building. "There can be little doubt that the ascendancy of abstraction in the artistic universe is on the wane," wrote Walter Abell in the *American Magazine of Art* in 1930; abstraction was nothing more than an adventure—"an adventure which is all but over." Alfred Barr noted that, from 1925 to 1930, only five articles on modern art appeared in the two most important journals devoted to art. Already the American Wave had begun to draw additional strength from political artists like the Mexican muralist José Clemente Orozco who believed that abstraction was for the elite while art should be for the people—an argument that the Depression had rendered grimly persuasive. "The way of George Bellows, the early John Sloan, and Thomas Eakins was being revived after the novelties of the famous Armory Show of 1913 had worn off," wrote one of the new realist painters. "An Americanist movement, though it was not clearly defined, was in the air." Within a year, the author of that statement would emerge as the new movement's most articulate spokesman: Thomas Hart Benton.

While waiting for Benton to arrange his admission to the Art Students League, Jackson signed up for the free sculpture classes at nearby Greenwich House, a neighborhood association on Barrow Street that offered a variety of art-related activities. The class was given by Ahron Ben-Shmuel, a skilled stonecarver, at the Greenwich House annex two blocks away on Jones Street.

Without a salable skill, Jackson was forced to rely on Charles—and occasional small contributions from Stella—for food and supplies. (Despite the high unemployment rate, Charles held down two jobs: as a free-lance illustrator of movie cards and as a part-time teacher at the City and Country School on West Thirteenth Street.) Such assistance, however kindly proffered, only reminded Jackson that after eighteen years, Charles still had everything Jackson wanted: the admiration of his colleagues, Benton's favor, a girlfriend, a job, steady money, independence, and emotional resolution—something that must have seemed to Jackson particularly far from his reach. Elizabeth, who had been charmed at first by Jackson's "youth, dimples, and the flash of those beautiful teeth," began to sense the darker feelings that moved beneath the surface. "Jackson seemed jealous of everybody that he came in contact with in New York," she remembers, "especially Charles. Although he could always be charming when he needed to, he began to develop a sulking, resentful attitude." "When Jackson first got to New York," says another family member, "he spent much of his time overcoming his sense of competition with [Charles]. He needed to say, 'Here I am. Now look at *me*.' " As so often in the past, Jackson determined that the only way to be recognized was to best his oldest brother. "Before he could be the best painter in the world," recalls Gerome Kamrowski, a friend and fellow artist, "Jackson had to be the best painter in the family."

In late September, he left Charles's apartment and rented a room of his own a few blocks away.

Jackson began classes at the Art Students League on September 29, 1930. Located in a sand-colored French Renaissance building on West Fifty-seventh Street, the League was unlike any school he had attended before: the building, with its carved pilasters, arched windows, and marble hall, grander; the students, especially compared to those at Manual Arts, more diverse. In the halls, there were no monitors, dress codes, or demerits to haunt him; in the bathrooms, no gangs of football players waiting to enforce conformity. It was, in the words of a student who attended in the thirties, "wonderfully loose."

Lemuel Wilmarth had wanted it that way when, in 1875, he and a handful of students bolted from the National Academy of Design and founded the League in a spare room over Weber's Piano Rooms on lower Fifth Avenue. Rejecting the deadening drudgery of the old "alcove" system in which students labored for years drawing from plaster casts before being allowed to work from a live model, they set out to recreate the unstructured, collaborative environment of the "Parisian ateliers." Despite its modest beginnings, the League prospered mightily and by 1892 took its place in the grand French Renaissance palazzo designed by Henry J. Hardenbergh, the architect of the nearby Plaza Hotel and the distant Dakota. But the League's goals remained humble and its attitude toward the Prussian curricula of most art schools, hostile. In 1930, fifty-five years after its founding, there were still no required courses, no efforts to regularize instruction, no set terms, no grades, and no attendance records. Enrollment was month-to-month, with no limit on the number of months a student could linger in the same class, as long as the relatively stiff fee of twelve dollars per class per month was paid or, in cases of financial need, excused. Policy decisions were made and rare disciplinary cases handled by the Board of Control, a group of twelve students and teachers elected by League members. The board was also responsible for inviting artists to teach at the League.

The combination of laissez-faire administration, excellent facilities, and earnest students had, in the League's short half-century, attracted a varied and distinguished roster of artists to the faculty: William Merritt Chase, Thomas Eakins, Augustus Saint-Gaudens, George Bellows, Robert Henri. Like the students and the faculty, the resulting curriculum was a potpourri. "One reason why the League is first among the art schools of this country," said John Sloan, the former "militant illustrator" and 1913 Armory Show veteran who, in 1931, became the League's president, "is that it furnishes such a varied menu of nourishment for the hungry art student, ranging from the conservative to the ultra-modern. A student at the League can choose his studies much as he can choose his food at an Automat."

In such an unstructured, stimulating environment, Jackson should have flourished. Without the rules, the coaches, the teachers, and the requirements that had always stymied him, the energy of his pent-up rivalry with Charles should have been released. Instead, he found at the Art Students League only what he had found elsewhere: frustration. For regardless of the auspicious freedom and opportunities, sooner or later he had to confront the common denominator of the art school experience, the moment when pencil touched paper.

For Jackson the dreaded moment came in Tom Benton's Studio 9. Alone on the fifth floor at the top of the stairs, Studio 9 had the cozy air of a converted attic, a cul-de-sac where classes were never disturbed by other students passing noisily in the hall. During the day, sunlight sifted through the frosted north-facing windows, filling the room with soft, even light. In the evening, when Jackson had his first class, the windows formed a faint blue backdrop to the glow of funnel lamps.

His first impression was probably similar to that of another student, Axel Horr (later Horn), who walked into Benton's class two years later:

> They were all huddled in a tight group around the model stand in one corner of the room. Seated on stools and holding drawing boards on their laps, each student was busily scratching out a drawing with a grocer's pencil on brown wrapping paper. Several squatted on the stand itself, forming a solid group whose core was the model. She was a young girl with the pleasing fruity contours and surface textures of a warm peach.

She also sat on a stool and was distinguishable from the rest because she was nude and without a drawing board. Otherwise she seemed as occupied and involved as everyone else.

Benton didn't believe in elaborate introductions or gradual immersion. With criticisms scheduled only twice a week, Jackson could easily have begun Benton's class, as Horn did, without Benton. The class "monitor"—a student who collected monthly fees in exchange for the waiver of his own fee—probably made a few housekeeping remarks, but the business of the class went on, undistracted by the appearance of a new student.

Benton's first scheduled visit was the next day, Tuesday, September 30. Class veterans recognized his impatient footsteps on the stairs and knew to have their questions ready by the time he reached the fifth floor hall. He would call out, "Anybody want criticism?" from the studio doorway, and if there were no immediate responses, quickly disappear. "He wouldn't go near you unless you asked him to look at something," says Horn who, like most of the students, seldom did. At first, Jackson may have been among the many students who went weeks without exchanging a word with their teacher. When summoned to a question, Benton might offer anything from general comments about "the rhythm," "the nature of the structure," or "the nature of the relationship between solids and voids"; to a demonstration, taking a pencil or charcoal to sketch a "correction" on a student's drawing; to a lecture. Often his comments were unrelated to the picture in front of him. "He seemed to talk more about life than about art," Herman Cherry remembers. "He'd been through the art-for-art's-sake stuff and wanted to get back down to earth."

Benton's classroom manner may have been relaxed, but, as Jackson soon discovered, his teaching method was anything but. Fifteen hours of studio time each week were devoted almost exclusively to drawing from nude models. Through his occasional critiques and choice of monitors, Benton conveyed what he thought to be the artist's true objective—"to be able to articulate and express the softness, the tensions, the recessions and the projections of the forms that together make up the human figure." Benton's folksy term was "the hollow and the bump"—a term that became synonymous with the distinctive undulating lines of his own work. For Benton, these recessions and projections were a pictorial equivalent of the "Baroque rhythms characteristic of Michelangelo's" muscular sculptures; his models were chosen for their hollow-and-bump muscular definition and posed to emphasize their contours. He encouraged his students to explore the landscape of the human form by touching the models' naked bodies—male and female—"to identify the direction and shape of a particular muscle or bone." (Ticklish models soon learned to avoid Benton's classes.)

The real work of the class was done outside the classroom. Peter Busa, a League student in the early thirties, recalls that Benton "was less interested in looking at what we were doing than in principles and ideas." The path from

Studio 9 to the League's small library on the second floor was well-worn by
Benton students sent to analyze the works of his favorite old masters: Michelangelo and Tintoretto for their spatial rhythms; Rubens and Rembrandt for
their complex compositions and tonality; Dürer, Schongauer, and Cambiaso
for their cubistic exercises; and Signorelli, Massacio, Mantegna, Brueghel,
and even Assyrian bas-reliefs for good measure. El Greco's attenuated figures
and exaggerated contours were particularly hospitable to Benton's hollow-
and-bump analysis, and Jackson's earliest sketchbooks are filled with El Greco
studies. In his life class, Benton directed students to examine drawings as well
as finished paintings. "When you look at a finished work," Busa remembers
him saying, "you're just seeing the skin of the building. Look at the *drawings*."
But for Benton, analysis involved far more than looking. Another League student, Mervin Jules, recalls the painstaking way Benton had them analyze the
old masters:

> Every part of the picture had to be broken down into block forms and then
> reconstructed—everything from a horse's pelvis to the turn of an out-
> stretched hand. After that, you would break down the tonality—in other
> words, where did the light come from? When you had done that, you
> would take a piece of transparent paper, put it over the drawing, and,
> using a variety of whites and blacks, fill in the block figures to indicate the
> structure of the tonal relationships.

"Benton demanded a lot of work," a classmate of Jackson's remembers. "His
students didn't spend much time in the lunchroom."

After Schwankovsky's relaxed experimentation, Benton's rigors were like a
cold bath. Jackson's lack of facility, an embarrassment at Manual Arts, became
a grotesque handicap in a school where, among the serious students, some
degree of facility was assumed. Recalling these early classes, Benton told an
interviewer in 1959: "[Jackson] was out of his field. . . . His mind was absolutely incapable of drafting logical sequences. He couldn't be taught anything."
Even tracing—the grade school exercise of covering an old master reproduction with a piece of translucent paper and tracing the outlines of major figures
in order to understand their spatial relationships—was a "horror" to Jackson.
Such exercises revealed a lack of control over a pencil that at times verged on
a physical disability. Whether from impatience or from lack of coordination,
he simply couldn't discipline his hand to follow the lines beneath the tracing
paper. "Every damn time, instead of tracing, he would set the paper next to
the drawing and copy it freehand," recalls Peter Busa. Even then, he would
avoid the more difficult parts of the body, leaving blank circles for faces and
lopping off hands altogether.

Despite the frustrations, Jackson worked furiously, bent over his sketch pad,
making the small "hairy scribble-scrabble" pencil strokes characteristic of Benton's students. "He would labor over the most infinitesimal detail," recalls

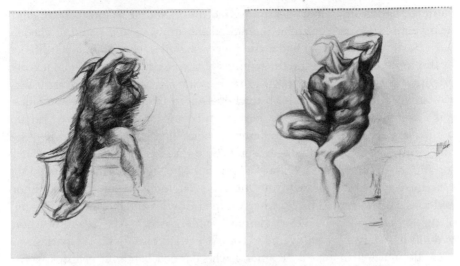

Two studies of figures from Michelangelo's Sistine Ceiling, early 1930s,
pencil and colored pencil on paper, 13⅞" × 16⅞"

classmate Joe Delaney, "that's how sensitive he was. He wasn't happy until he
had the thing like he thought it ought to be, but it never was." He would work
and rework a hip, or a thigh, or a fold of drapery, until it was black with pencil
marks. "Jackson's drawings were easily the 'hairiest,'" wrote Axel Horn in his
memoir of Benton's class. "They were painfully indicative of the continuous
running battle between [Jackson] and his tools." Delaney remembers one class
in which Jackson, in the middle of a sketching frenzy, suddenly threw his pencil
down and jumped up from his stool in frustration. "I've had enough," he cried
out, shattering the usual classroom quiet, "I gotta get the hell outta here," and
ran from the studio. "Everything Jack did in his student days was a struggle,"
brother Charles remembers, "a struggle to get things to come together the way
he wanted them to. I don't know if it was a question of drawing per se, but it
was a question of getting things down on the paper in some kind of organized
way that suited him."

In that first class, only a few seats away from Jackson, sat a well-dressed,
As always, Jackson's frustration and bitterness were exacerbated by the obvious talents of those around him. The League was a touchstone in the fragmented artistic world of New York in the early thirties, and many of the city's
most ambitious artists, drawn by the faculty, came there to test their gifts.
Buoyed by the constant flow of faceless students "just going along for the ride,"
these ambitious and accomplished young people floated in and out of League
classes, staying as long as they could afford the fees or cadge financial aid. "We
were all young," recalls one of Jackson's classmates, "and we all thought we
were geniuses and we were going to be the greatest artists that ever lived."

In that first class, only a few seats away from Jackson, sat a well-dressed,
articulate student named Fairfield Porter, a twenty-three-year-old Harvard
graduate who, according to rumor, had made a life sketch of Trotsky while on
a grand tour of Europe. But it was his self-assurance with a pencil, not his

patrician background, that Jackson envied most. Not far from Studio 9, eighteen-year-old Harry Holtzman monitored the drawing and painting class of A. S. Baylinson. Holtzman had arrived a year before Jackson, already inflamed by the works of Cézanne and the writings of Roger Fry. While Jackson labored mightily at cubic forms and Renaissance exercises in "spiralic countering," Holtzman experimented with abstraction—more than a decade before Jackson's first abstract work. While Jackson tried to master the hollow and the bump, another League student, James Brooks, had already rejected it—"too much rolly polly," he scoffed—and embraced Picasso. Through Charles, Jackson met Herman Cherry, a fellow Californian who, after less than a year at the League, had worked his way into the inner circle of Benton protégés. Short and tough like Benton himself, Cherry joined Charles and the "Missouri gang" of Benton intimates: Joe Meert, Bernard Steffen, Archie Musick, all of whom had left the Midwest to study under Tom. Meert, a close friend of Charles, was a gentle, reticent man, "a dreamer," who painted beautiful pictures with a "poetic" brush. He and Charles were generally acknowledged to be Benton's best and favorite students. The presence of fourteen-year-old prodigy Nathan Katz (who later changed his name to Nathaniel Kaz) made it impossible for Jackson to claim any special consideration as the "baby" of the League. After winning an art prize in Michigan at the age of ten, Katz had come to New York and earned his high standing among the older students with his exquisite anatomical drawings and a seemingly unlimited capacity for bathtub gin.

Through Benton, Jackson found a job in the cafeteria working as a busboy in exchange for meals. There, he often saw Arshile Gorky in the company of attractive women and Russian wolfhounds, holding court in dark personal splendor. "Towering well over six feet," according to one biographer, "with a romantic shock of dark hair falling across his forehead, a full moustache, and large brooding eyes," Gorky cut an impressive figure. He hadn't attended classes at the League since 1926, but still visited the cafeteria often, partly to impress new students like Jackson with his tall, caped presence and arrogant erudition, but mostly to woo young female students like Josephine Fox or Stephanie de George. In a "very sad Russian voice," Nathaniel Kaz remembers, he would plead with them: "Come to my studio, be my *vooman*, I give you *everything*." But de George only laughed, rebuffing his advances, sometimes in the middle of the crowded cafeteria, because, according to Kaz, "she wanted a man with money, not genius, and who the hell was Arshile Gorky anyway?"

Even Manuel Tolegian, with whom Jackson lived briefly during this period, began to seem a threat. One classmate remembers that "Jack wasn't terribly competent as a draftsman while Tolegian was pretty accomplished." Although often together, their constant "joking and kidding around" took on a new edge. "They would insult each other continuously," recalls the same classmate. "Jack would call Manuel a Turk, which annoyed him no end. It seemed friendly enough, but they were getting in their jabs." Tolegian's budding pretensions to literary and artistic erudition only exacerbated the rift. Classmates remember him as "very dapper" and socially "aloof," except at prestigious League functions. In the cafeteria, where he shared cleanup duties with Jackson for a while, he tried to mimic the Continental hauteur and "outlandish jargon" of fellow Armenian Gorky. "Tolegian was very verbal, and he was always explaining what he was doing," recalls Axel Horn. "Always rationalizing it, always defining it." Soon after arriving in New York, he began to write poetry.

Overwhelmed by the ambitions of others, Jackson withdrew behind a wall of reticence and resentment. Most of his fellow students saw only a shy, moody boy "with his high heel boots and his fresh young face." On meeting Jackson for the first time, Axel Horn noticed his expression—"the smile barely tightening the corners of the mouth, the squint as if looking through early morning mountain haze, the knitting of the brows in what seemed to be (and was indeed) a continual attempt to comprehend a bewildering and complex world." To others, the same expression seemed "stupefied" or "just plain dense." "Jackson always seemed to be in a daze," one classmate recalls. At a time when most League students were inflamed by the battle over the appointment of George Grosz, a German expressionist, to teach at the League, and arguments raged in the cafeteria (and the press) about the struggle between Sloan and Jonas Lie for control of the board and the democratic soul of the League, Jackson rarely offered an opinion. Even in classroom discussions, he remained resolutely silent. When pressed for a "specific" response, he would offer lamely, "I do everything in general." "I don't think he could have carried on an intelligent conversation about art in the *least*," says Nathaniel Kaz. In his autobiography, Benton describes Jackson's losing battle with words:

> He developed some kind of language block and became almost completely inarticulate. I have sometimes seen him struggle, to red-faced embarrassment, while trying to formulate ideas boiling up in his disturbed consciousness, ideas he could never get beyond a "God damn, Tom, you know what I mean!" I rarely did know.

Less than a year after arriving in New York, Jackson began to repeat the cycle of withdrawal and depression that he had left Los Angeles to break. After the flurry of letters to Charles the previous year, the flow of correspondence to family members dried up. The rare letters he did start often languished on his desk, sometimes for months, unfinished. Completed letters went unmailed. He began to destroy his drawings so ruthlessly and indiscriminately that Charles had to intervene to save what he could. "Jack was on the outside looking in," Elizabeth Pollock remembers, "and full of envy toward those who were able to enjoy open, natural, commonplace pleasures."

Inevitably, Jackson turned to alcohol for the feeling of belonging that eluded him when sober. In New York, bootleg whiskey was as close as the speakeasy behind the League on West Fifty-eighth Street ("Just knock on the door and tell them Benny sent you"). If Jackson didn't want to leave the building, he could put a dime or a quarter into one of the collections that regularly made the rounds in the cafeteria and buy a share in a bottle of bathtub gin with a fancy English label. Once drunk, Jackson had plenty of friends: fellow drinkers like Joe Delaney, the son of a black Methodist preacher from Knoxville, Tennessee, and Bruce Mitchell, a handsome, troubled boy from upstate New York. Nathan Katz and, at first, Manuel Tolegian, were often along on Jackson's binges, and sometimes older students like Joe Meert and Bernie Steffen. For different reasons and to different effects, almost everybody at the League drank. More and more often, Jackson would disappear to some bar, and, for an evening at least, he was the best painter in the Pollock family. "We would gear up and have a *hell* of a good time," Joe Delaney remembers. "Not where we got sogged, not where we didn't know what we was doing, but just to the peak of truthful expression to each other." On one such occasion, at the peak of truthful expression, Jackson confided in Delaney, "Joe, you know I *am* great."

Despite his growing frustrations, the threats he saw everywhere, and the strange, grisaille landscape of his first New York winter, Jackson clung to his ambition—"It always seemed to me that he wanted to be number one," remembers Kaz—working quietly but furiously at school during the day, drinking and railing every night to prop himself up for the next day. It was a flirtation with despair, and only one man kept him from crossing the line.

12

BENTON

On a summer day in the early 1950s, after the great drip paintings, after the triumphant shows, Jackson Pollock was relaxing on the Coast Guard Beach near East Hampton with Franz Kline and Syd Solomon. All three artists were disillusioned and depressed. "We were bemoaning the lack of interest in art among most Americans," recalls Solomon. Someone suggested half in jest that, if all else failed, they could "just chuck it all and go teach old ladies to do watercolors." The three men laughed, and a running joke was born. Thereafter they would always kid one another about a "fall-back" career among the ladies' clubs of America.

Like the other artists of their generation, Pollock, Kline, and Solomon were acutely aware that, for the great majority of Americans, art was old ladies' business. They had inherited an aesthetic world shaped by Victorian sentimentality and administered, almost exclusively, by women. Men who strayed into that world were considered, at best, unproductive, at worst, homosexual, by those outside it. While fathers, like Herman Cherry's, demanded of their sons, "What the hell are you going to do for a living?", mothers, like Jackson's, cultivated their sons' artistic ambitions like hothouse flowers.

The forces that shaped these antagonistic views were gathering energy as early as the middle of the nineteenth century when industrialization began to transform women from producers into consumers and, at the same time, art into leisure. Where Jennie McClure wove rugs that she sold to neighbors, daughter Stella made lace for her curtains and frilly clothes for her babies. Stella may have worked hard, as hard in some ways as her mother; but her aspirations were far higher. Where Jennie aspired only to keep the family fed, Stella aspired to a life of finery and leisure—the life promoted in her stacks of women's magazines. She joined the millions of women who, according to Ann Douglas, a feminist and cultural historian, swept aside the old, cliquish, largely male market for more challenging fare and replaced it with an immense new market for sentimental literature and art. "American culture," writes Douglas, "seemed bent on establishing a perpetual Mother's Day"; on satisfying the "enormous need of its authors and readers for uncritical confirmation of themselves and instantaneous satisfaction of their appetites." In the 1850s, *Uncle Tom's Cabin* was a thunderous success while *Moby-Dick* languished in obscurity. The era of American "mass culture," feminized and sentimentalized, had begun.

This was the burden of history, concentrated in childhood training, that Jackson and his fellow artists inherited. It was a distinctly American legacy. Nowhere else were there so many fathers who, like Roy Pollock, considered it a crime against nature to be unmanly or "unproductive," and so many mothers who, like Stella, confirmed their aspirations by instilling in their sons delicate sensibilities and a respect for "culture." Given their upbringing, it was inevitable that male artists in the art world of the thirties, forties, and fifties would be condemned to a constant struggle to appease their insecurities, to reconcile their fathers' injunctions with their mothers' aspirations; that they would all but exclude female artists from their company; that they would pass women around like bottles of whiskey; that they would feel compelled to walk the barroom gauntlet, snarling insults, hurling profanities, and picking fights in a running parody of masculinity. "In all that aggression and machismo," recalls Leslie Fiedler, who occasionally visited New York's most famous artists' bar, the Cedar, "there was always a trace of hysterical desperation."

No artist was more desperate than Thomas Hart Benton.

Twenty years before Jackson Pollock drank, raged, and bullied his way into popular iconography, Benton had already begun to cast a Paul Bunyonesque shadow on the landscape of American art. No one cussed more fluently. "Benton's language made *me* blush," says Mervin Jules, a Benton student in the early thirties, "and my language was the language of a labor organizer for the National Maritime Union." No one could hurl such flaming insults or ignite such outrage. Museums were run, Benton told a group of reporters in 1935, by "a pack of precious ninnies who walked with a hip swing in their gaits and affected a certain kind of curve in their wrists." No one painted on a grander, more ambitious scale. At the age of thirty, he began an epic mural cycle of seventy-five large panels in which he hoped to capture the whole sweep of American history. No one's rages were more titanic. In a fight with Burl Ives, a hulking, six-foot-four folk singer, Benton grabbed a poker from his fireplace and, according to a witness, "just about bashed Ives's skull in." No one made more enemies or kept them longer. "Leftists attacked him as a chauvinist," notes the introduction to his autobiography, "rightists accused him of radicalism, even Communism . . . [those in the] museum world have dismissed him as an Ozark hillbilly . . . and even some liberals have been fearful [of] his provincialism." No one was more of a *man*. "He was short but powerfully built," Herman Cherry recalls. "His voice was deep, he was strong, and he was

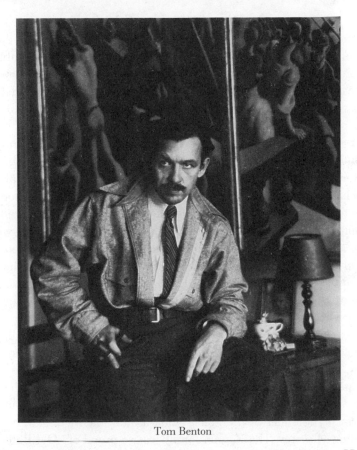

Tom Benton

purposeful. He told marvelous stories about going to whorehouses. He was as masculine as a man could possibly be, masculine in every sense of the word."

It was in this last and greatest of his roles, the role of the "man's man," that Benton made his most lasting contribution to American art. Such was its power that, despite rejecting his art and denouncing his political views, an entire generation of artists was shaped by Benton's archetypical machismo. What Hemingway was to a generation of writers, Benton was to a generation of American painters, the ideal against which, consciously or unconsciously, they measured themselves—as drinkers, as fighters, as rebels, as provocateurs, as womanizers, as debunkers, as outsiders, as Americans, and as artists.

No one felt the force of Benton's oversized personality more fully or was more transfixed by it than Jackson Pollock. No one outside the Pollock family would have a more enduring influence on Jackson's development until, more than ten years later, he passed into the hands of Lee Krasner. Even then—long after Benton's theories of art, his style, and his classroom techniques had sifted into Jackson's subconscious or out of his art altogether—the irresistible imprinting force of Benton's personality remained. In his mannerisms, his profanity, his pugnacity, his drunkenness, his vulgarity, and his misogyny, Jackson proved a willing, often predisposed, student. But at a deeper level, the two men, separated in age by more than twenty years, were not so much teacher and student, or even surrogate father and surrogate son, as they were partners in a struggle—a struggle rooted in their profound ambivalence toward art and toward the role of artist. Ultimately, Benton's power over Jackson was based on the deep, unspoken sympathy that passed between them, on the tendency of like material to take like forms, of like pasts to produce like men.

At first glance, Thomas Hart Benton and Paul Jackson Pollock would seem to have little more in common than birthplaces on the same side of the Mississippi River. Unlike Cody in 1912, the little town of Neosho in southwestern Missouri had been settled for half a century by 1889, the year of Benton's birth. In Cody, there were no houses like the one that Benton's father built on the high ground overlooking the town, a proud house of wood and stone, with such "marvels" as a tin-lined bathtub, central heating, and a glass-walled conservatory. On April 15, 1889, Thomas Hart Benton was born within its handsome walls in rustic splendor while, 250 miles to the north, fourteen-year-old Stella McClure went sourly about her farm chores and twelve-year-old LeRoy Pollock plowed his neighbors' fields.

Although Tom Benton claimed his ancestors were "southern hill people" and therefore "frontiersmen" rather than "tidewater aristocrats," the Bentons were—by Tingley standards at least—nobility. The "great hero of the tribe" was Senator Thomas Hart Benton who for thirty years had been the Democratic voice of the United States Senate, adviser to Presidents, champion of small farmers, defender of the gold standard, and enemy of slavery, even in slaveholding Missouri. The Benton family was so proud of "Old Bullion Benton" that they made sure there was at least one Thomas Hart in every generation. So no one was surprised when Maecenus Eson ("M.E.") Benton, whose father had also been Thomas Hart, gave his firstborn son the family's best name.

Like Old Bullion, Tom was both cursed and blessed by the Welsh blood of the Benton clan. He had the Benton physique—short and stocky, tending toward portly in age—and the Benton disposition: moody and choleric in private, proselytic and combative in public. "From obscurity in pre-Revolutionary North Carolina, through its adventures in frontier Tennessee," Tom Benton wrote at the end of his life in an account undoubtedly tainted by hindsight, the Benton clan "was always engaged in conflicts, either of its own making or of the making of its enemies. It was a family fated, it would seem, for turmoil."

In fact, most of the turmoil in Tom Benton's family centered around his father, M.E., and his mother, Lizzie Wise. They were, at best, an improbable pair. He, according to his unsympathetic son, "was not, in any sense, a romantic figure—short, thick-necked, with reddish skin, a red beard and a protruding belly." She, on the other hand, by Tom's enamored telling, was "a tall, willowy, black-haired and brown-eyed Texas beauty" who "sang and tinkled at the piano." She was the spoiled baby in a family of thirteen Waxahachie Wises, a "Celtic"-looking clan of Scotch-Irish origin that had, at some point in its history, shared the Carolina hill country with the Welsh Bentons before moving on to Texas. Just as the Bentons had bequeathed contentiousness to their descendants, the Wises had passed along an innate dignity arising from an unshakable belief in their own moral superiority. Being simple and largely uneducated people, the Wises had interpreted their pride and touchiness as signs of religious "electness." This was especially true among the strong-minded women of the clan who, according to Tom, "found themselves apppointed brides of Christ or, if not quite that, numbered among his closest intimates."

In her youth, Lizzie Wise had shared her sisters' self-righteous devotion, but gradually her aspirations fixed on more temporal rewards. Like Stella McClure, she longed for the life of refinement, the life of luncheons and fringed parasols, formal parties and "pictures on the wall"—in short, the life of a lady. Maecenus Eson Benton, with his successful practice, his political aspirations, his big house and tin-lined tub, was her key to that life.

In public, these ominously contrary personalities proved surprisingly complementary in advancing M.E.'s political career. The new Mrs. Benton, in her St. Louis gowns, played the gracious hostess at her husband's frequent political dinners. In an era when only men could vote, her "brunette handsomeness" won the support of more than one state party leader, and her strange refusal to invite other women to her parties had few political repercussions. The combination of her charm and his bonhomie—along with his populist views on eastern bankers and railroad tycoons—soon made M. E. Benton a likely candidate for the United States Congress.

Whatever its public advantages, the marriage was, from the outset, a private disaster. "Lizzie Wise may have been, probably was, a docile bride-to-be, complaisant and sweet of tongue," Tom Benton wrote years later, "but once she got her papers, she spit the bit of the marriage vow out of her mouth and asserted herself." The Benton line of "plain men of the people" collided with the superior Wises, and the result was an unceasing campaign of domestic warfare.

Using a potent combination of threats, wiles, tears, and frequent fainting spells, Lizzie quickly trained her new husband to submission. Immediately after becoming pregnant, she evicted him from the marriage bed and, except for those occasions on which she conceived three more children, never welcomed him back. The Benton children were often awakened in the middle of the night by their mother's indignant screams when their father tried to enter her room. Tom Benton, who lay awake frightened on many such nights, later recalled: "I was aware of the anger and sense of outrage she felt for days following." To Lizzie, "sex was a plain manifestation of the Devil, and though it had to be put up with in marriage, was a nasty thing."

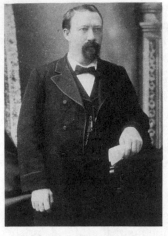

Maecenus Eson Benton

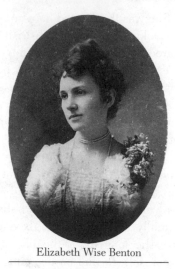

Elizabeth Wise Benton

The ultimate battleground for M.E. and Lizzie Benton was the nursery, and no one saw more combat than their firstborn, Thomas Hart. "I was conditioned very early in my life to accept strife and argument as basic factors of existence," he later wrote, "as inescapable concomitants of human association." M.E. may have given the boy his family's best name, but Tom Benton, with his dark Celtic complexion and Wise family features, always belonged to Lizzie. From an early age, he accompanied her into her dressing room, where his father was forbidden, to admire her clothes and, later, advise on her choice of dresses. Like young Jackson, he watched his mother's "busy hands" as she did her fine embroidery and crewelwork. She designed the clothes he wore, and he, in turn, later designed patterns for her needlework. Like Stella Pollock, Lizzie tended a flower garden, doting especially on roses. Her gardening "was done more in the spirit of the artist," Tom wrote admiringly, ". . . the one expression of her ego which reached beyond self concern into an area of objective accomplishment." Young Tom took an "unusual interest" in the artistry with which his mother arranged flowers from her garden for her dinner table and worked closely with her on the elaborate preparations for her frequent luncheons, dinners, and parties. "Her taste in general was that of the American ladies' magazines of the nineties," Benton wrote. "She possessed an aesthetic responsiveness, a disposition to take pleasure in the qualities of things." Benton's most vivid memory of his mother, like Charles Pollock's memory of Stella, was of "rid[ing] in a high, fringe-topped buggy with my mother around the town square behind a big white horse she calls Rex [while] men bow to her and tip their hats."

Whenever Tom wandered away from home, Lizzie packed him a lunch, and he invariably returned with a gift of wildflowers or persimmons. In the evening, he joined her on her promenades around Neosho's town square in his white pants and blue jacket with the brass buttons. When he reached "the mooncalf age," she convinced him that boys who masturbated at night died in their sleep

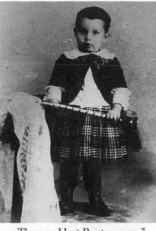

Thomas Hart Benton, age 3

and went to hell. Until he left home, she planned all his parties—systematically excluding all females except herself.

Tom Benton may have felt at home in his mother's world of place cards, Paris fashions, and persimmons, but he never stopped longing to be a part of another, very different world.

Like Roy Pollock, M. E. Benton was a man who felt truly comfortable only in the company of other men. A jovial, expansive man with an ear for the earthy idioms and rhythms of the Ozarks, he spent as much of every day as possible in his law office entertaining political cronies with jokes and stories and political wisdom packaged in colorful anecdotes. The men who filled his office were not unlike him. Tom Benton described them as "expository men who drank heavily, ate heartily, and talked long over fat cigars, the ends of which they chewed." Theirs was emphatically, if not pathologically, a man's world, "always reeking with cigar smoke," and from the very start, Tom Benton felt excluded from it.

M.E. missed much of his son's childhood traveling the state on prolonged trips, "erecting and mending political fences." But as Tom must have sensed, there was more to his father's absence than the demands of a political life. Like Roy Pollock, M. E. Benton began early to withdraw from his family. His son remembers him as "a perpetually serious, dour and sometimes irritable and suspicious man who could barely keep his temper under control." Intensely private, he developed "an addiction to odd and inexplicable ways of self-communion." He was often overheard talking vigorously to himself, and spent hours adding, subtracting, and dividing enormous figures with no apparent significance on any handy piece of paper. Out of political necessity, he continued to entertain, but as soon as the last guest had departed, he would retire "in moody silence to the library and lose himself in [his] curious arithmetical game."

Tom's early efforts to earn a place in his father's distant, male world invariably went awry. Knowing M.E.'s passion for hunting, Tom practiced hard to perfect his aim. But when M.E. challenged him to kill the woodpeckers that were making holes in the eaves of the Neosho house, he balked. He did manage to wing one of them, but the sight of the wounded bird flapping pathetically at his feet so unnerved him that he refused to ever pick up a gun again. Among M.E.'s hunting buddies he became known as "the worst game-shy hunter there ever was."

In 1896, M. E. Benton won a seat in Congress and the domestic battles moved to the far grander stage of Washington, D.C. With "visions of a fabulous Washington life," Lizzie threw herself into the round of political and diplomatic receptions and, with her tall Texas beauty and natural graciousness, quickly became a welcome ornament on the Washington party circuit. Observers sometimes commented that "the homeliest man in Congress" was married to the prettiest wife in Washington.

Soon Lizzie set her sights on a bigger house in a better neighborhood. Mindful of his Missouri constituency and the need to "keep his Washington life as unpretentious as possible," M.E. resisted, sparking a series of fierce confrontations, one of which Tom recounted in his memoirs:

> After hearing some unusually angry exchanges between my parents I ran into our little A Street parlor to find my mother lying on the floor at my father's feet with only the whites of her eyes showing. . . . [My] father was red-faced and grim and when he shoved me hurriedly out of the room I sensed something serious was happening.

By fall of the following year, the Bentons had moved to a more "socially proper address." Like Stella Pollock, Lizzie Benton was bent on realizing her magazine fantasies regardless of the consequences.

Convinced by his embroidery patterns and flower arrangements that Tom was an artistic genius, Lizzie fanned every faint ember of inclination with gifts of "drawing pencils, inks, crayons, tablets, and sheets of drawing paper." She kept his pictures close at hand to show visitors and fished for compliments at every opportunity. By the time Tom entered the Force School in Washington, his mother's guests "were saying that I should have some training," Tom recalled, "even saying that I was a born artist." Lizzie needed no prodding. She arranged for a series of art tutors, beginning with an elderly woman who taught Tom to paint watercolor wreaths on place cards, followed by more formal lessons at the Corcoran Gallery and then at the Western High School in Georgetown.

In a futile effort to make the enterprise more palatable to M.E.—who, according to his son, considered art a pastime for old ladies and effeminate men —Tom confined his drawings to subjects of indisputable masculinity: trains in the beginning; then, when the battleship *Maine* was blown up in Havana Harbor in 1898, exploding battleships. At the onset of the Spanish-American War, he began drawing soldiers "parading behind waving flags or shooting off guns in imaginary battles." When M.E. gave him a set of books on Indians, Indians began appearing in Tom's sketchbook. When Lizzie tried to redirect his talents to more suitable, genteel subjects, Tom resisted. One early art lesson ended in "bitter disappointment" when he discovered that the teacher painted only flowers. "As a depictor of battleships, marching soldiers, wild Indians and heroes of mythology," Tom wrote, "the 'sissy' subject matter of my teacher revolted me."

Benton would later argue that his father had "something like a Puritan aversion to images, an uneasiness before them." In fact, M. E. Benton's aversion was to his wife and her ruinous cultural ambitions, and, by association, to his son's artistic aspirations. The more he felt threatened by the first—over which he had no control—the more he detested and discouraged the second. Although he never outright forbade drawing lessons or art classes, M.E. did dismiss the effort as a waste of time, vainly protesting, "The boy has got to *learn* something." But the drawings and the classes—like the dresses and the parties—continued, while M.E. commiserated with his cigar-smoking pals at the office who, Tom later wrote, "were sorry he had such a queer duck for a son."

In 1902, Lizzie was introduced to President Theodore Roosevelt. As the author of a biography of Old Bullion, Roosevelt took a special interest in the Missouri Bentons and Lizzie was, of course, "overwhelmed by the President's chivalrous attentions to her." Her year as a regular guest at the White House was "seventh heaven" for her, according to Tom, "probably the happiest time of her life."

Swollen with pride in her new presidential liaison, Lizzie returned to Neosho in the summer of 1903 "to teach the home folks how Washington society behaved." Under her careful supervision, the Neosho house was refurbished, indoor plumbing added—the old tin-lined tub discarded—and new debts incurred. At the frequent gatherings of M.E.'s political supporters, she served Washington-style dinners on new settings of china and silver with multiple courses and multiple wines. Neosho—where, according to Tom, people "set all the food out at once"—had never seen anything like it.

Such ostentation proved political poison for M.E. Before long, Tom recalled, the talk of the town was that the Bentons had become "mighty uppity."

[My father] constantly admonished my mother, urging her to hold back and keep things simpler, not to dress too splendidly, and above all not to talk too much about "how we do it in Washington." "It's these folks that send us there, Mizzuz, don't shame them," he said. They bickered about this a lot, often at supper after my mother had put on too fancy a luncheon.

But she had a good defense then that always worked. "Don't criticize me before the children, Mister," she'd say and lean back in her chair and wipe her eyes.

All summer long, unrepentant, Lizzie promenaded around Courthouse Square in full Washington array. "Mother outshone them all," Tom crowed. Not until after their return to Washington in the fall did M.E. finally broach the possibility that he might lose the 1904 election, whereupon Lizzie "went into hysterics and faints, crying out against his lack of courage and his 'abandonment' of the future of his children." "You can't take them back to that little country, Mister," Tom remembered her crying. "You have to give them a chance in the world."

Nevertheless, on November 8, 1904, M. E. Benton was defeated in his bid for a fifth term in Congress.

Lizzie Benton was at a party when the news came. A friend's diary entry records her reaction: "[She] leaned against the wall dead white, as if she would faint, her pallor not relieved by the glow of the deep red velvet hat and dress in which, like Mary Queen of Scots, she had arrayed herself for her execution." The Bentons returned to Neosho in the summer of 1905. Soon afterward, when the crates and boxes from Washington arrived, Lizzie suffered a nervous breakdown. She took refuge in her bed and two of her sisters were summoned from Texas to tend her. M.E., too, withdrew from the world. What the sale of the Phoenix farm had been for Roy Pollock, the election defeat of 1904 was for M. E. Benton. Never again did he participate actively in politics. Instead, he began to suffer "moody spells" and spent more and more time behind the doors of his study adding long columns of numbers.

Unlike his mother, Tom Benton felt shamed and chastened by his father's defeat and, back in Neosho, immediately set about mending his errant, sissified ways.

He began by abandoning art. Instead of drawing and painting, he prowled the alleyways around Courthouse Square, picking fights, then running home proudly to show his father the bloodstains on his clothes. In his paranoia, M.E. blamed the "scoundrelly Republicans" who had taken over Neosho for setting the local boys on his son, but was pleased by Tom's triumphs. The fights continued for several weeks until the church ladies began to complain about the "quarrelsome" Benton boy.

He threw himself into farm chores and part-time work, and began meeting clandestinely with other boys at the swimming hole "where we added to our linguistic powers and learned the arts of chewing and smoking tobacco." Despite being only 5 feet 2¾ inches (his full adult height), he joined the Neosho high school football team. When he was cut from the squad after only a few games because bigger opponents were beating up on him, he turned to wrestling, a sport in which tenacity—which he had in abundance—counted more than size. About the same time, as a kind of consolation, he became obsessed with the accomplishments of Napoleon, for whom he developed "a hero worship so infatuated that I could think of nothing else." He also began to drink —a badge of manhood available even to a boy only 5 feet 2¾.

By the summer of 1906, however, he was back under Lizzie's spell and drawing again. Between spasms of exaggerated masculinity, he would repair to her dressing room or rose garden for prolonged indulgences in the very "sissy" behavior he decried. On Saturdays, he would practice boxing in the morning, follow the older boys to burlesque show matinees in the afternoon, then escort Lizzie to the opera at night. There, sitting in his starched shirt beside his bejeweled mother and watching Wagner's *Tannhäuser* or *Parsifal*, he was often moved to tears and would run home in the throes of enchantment to make pastel drawings of his favorite scenes.

About the same time, in another futile bid for his father's approval, he began referring to drawing and painting as "picture-making," a term borrowed from his grandfather, Pappy Wise, whom Tom much admired as a "saddle-maker" and "violin-maker." If M.E. objected to his son becoming an artist, he would become instead a "picture-maker" and work with his hands like a carpenter or cobbler.

Mortified by such talk—no son of hers was going to be a carpenter—Lizzie introduced Tom to her piano teacher, Mr. Calhoun, "a big city man of the world" with cultivated manners and expensively tailored suits. Unlike the gaunt, laconic Pappy Wise, Mr. Calhoun was "a little puffy about the mouth and chin" and "a great talker" who enthralled Tom and Lizzie with tales of his journeys in Europe, his frequent visits to the Bayreuth Festival, and his love of Wagner. "We could hardly believe he was a resident of Jasper County," Tom wrote. "He was all so big city." Enchanted, Tom showed Mr. Calhoun his drawings and pastels.

> He was most enthusiastic about my pictures and told me that I was the most remarkable boy he had ever met, that I was already close to being a real artist and that I must let nothing stop me from becoming a professional one. "You must go to art school," he said, "and then Paris."

For a while at least, listening to stories about Paris and *"La vie de Bohème,"* Tom forgot about "picture-making" and Pappy Wise. "[His] stories and flatteries had their effects," Benton wrote. "He made me feel I was something special and belonged, like himself, to a special world."

In the summer of 1906, however, instead of enrolling in art school, Benton signed on as a rodman with a surveying crew marking out boundaries at the mining properties around Joplin. It was hard, hands-on work that undoubtedly made M.E. happy. Joplin was "a wild boomtown . . . the sinful enticements of which were notorious all over southwest Missouri," and in later years, Benton would portray the summer as a restless boy's liberation, the product of "that

irrepressible itch, so common among western boys, to be up somewhere, to
have done with home, family, and familiar things."

On Saturday nights I went into town and looked things over. There were
friends of the family in Joplin, respectable people, but I steered clear of
them. I'd left home mainly to get away from contact with respectability.
. . . I went in the saloons, drank beer, and put nickels in the slot machines.
I was really a man, seventeen years old now, and foot-loose.

In fact, Lizzie Benton had carefully supervised and approved all the summer
plans, insisting that Tom live with relatives in Joplin—the "respectable people"
that he claimed to avoid—and that he visit Mr. Calhoun's studio regularly in
order to meet "the right kind of young people." Instead of frequenting saloons,
drinking beer, and putting nickels in slot machines, Benton spent most Saturday nights sitting in a hotel dining room, sipping Benedictine aperitifs, and
listening raptly to Mr. Calhoun talk about his upcoming trip to Paris. On one
such occasion, the older man suggested that Tom accompany him "and see
what a city of art is like." Benton "became excited" at the talk of Paris and
promised to take it up with his parents.

But Mr. Calhoun had something else on his mind.

I caught the strange way he was looking at me. His eyes were like girls'
eyes, when they want to tease you. . . . But I knew exactly what they were
saying because I'd been approached by queers in Washington and had
learned from the older boys there what such people were after.

"Embarrassed and revolted," Benton bolted from the table. By his telling, he
never made contact with Mr. Calhoun again, although he "remembered for
years the sad look on the face of this usually so self-possessed man when [he]
departed."

Nevertheless, the following year, Benton took Mr. Calhoun's advice and
enrolled at the Chicago Art Institute. Two years later, he made the trip to Paris.

In his autobiography, Benton recorded a very different version of how he
came to choose art as a career. In the manner of a western movie, it began in
the House of Lords bar and whorehouse in Joplin, Missouri, during the hot
summer of 1906. He was standing at the bar, drinking a beer and staring at a
painting of a nude woman that hung on the wall behind rows of bottles.
Suddenly a group of "grinning fellows," seeing him absorbed in the painting,
began to harass him. "They laid into me with all the obscenities bearing on the
picture they could think of," Benton wrote. "They made me hot with embarrassment." Rising to the challenge, young Tom insisted that he was studying
the picture not because the girl was naked but because he was an artist and he
wanted to see "how it was done."

"So, you're an artist, Shorty?" one of the men asked with a snicker.

"Yes, by God!" he answered. "And I'm a good one."

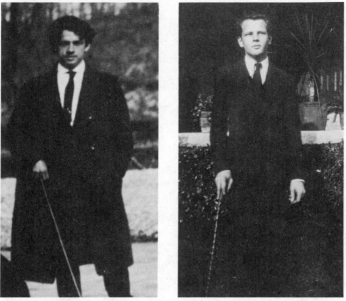

Thomas Hart Benton and Jackson Pollock in their respective dandy periods

"I don't think that it had ever seriously occurred to me before," he wrote, "that I wanted to be an artist. Certainly, until the kidding in the House of Lords, I had never declared myself one."

This was the story Tom Benton wanted the world to believe—and, undoubtedly, wanted to believe himself; a story filled with the local color and characters of the real American West; a story in which women were little more than one-dimensional objects of lust; a story that could make Pappy Wise—even M. E. Benton, perhaps—understand how a man could want to be an artist.

In fact, all of Tom Benton's works, from his first drawings of trains to his great murals, were indelibly stamped with his mother's mark. Everything else —drinking, fighting, cussing, carousing—was apology, offered sometimes desperately, sometimes bitterly to the unyielding father he carried with him. When he first returned to Neosho from Washington bearing the guilt for his father's defeat and began his campaign of brawls and drunken binges, Benton himself called it a period of "rehabilitation." By that definition, most of the Benton legend that grew up over the next fifty years, most of the Tom Benton that Jackson Pollock knew, was rehabilitation. Even the paintings themselves—the "huge masculine figures with bulging muscles," the enormous murals, the preoccupation with western themes of men and mastery and camaraderie— were a form of "rehabilitation." So were the constant battles—artistic, political, and personal—that he fought as desperately as brawls on Courthouse Square.

At the Chicago Art Institute, he grew his hair long under a derby hat, wore what he called a "genius outfit," and exulted in the taunts and scuffles his appearance incited among the neighborhood toughs on the city's South Side. In Paris, "he bought himself a Balzac stick . . . wore tight, tailor-made suits, a black flowing cape, and a French beret . . . eager to look the part of a successful Left Bank artist." Friends called him "le petit Balzac." But there was, as always, a price to be paid, an apology to be made, an urgent need for "rehabil-itation": in Chicago, he worked out furiously at a local gymnasium; in Paris he was "notoriously drunk most of the time, fighting in cafés and quarreling with girls."

But he never let go of Lizzie. In the years to come, she would abandon M.E. to live with Tom in New York. Later, Tom would follow her to Great Neck, Long Island, where they lived together until he joined the navy. She would offer and he would accept her help in avoiding combat duty in World War I. He never spoke of girlfriends to her and, when he finally married, spent his honeymoon at her house. Over his wife's objections, he invited Lizzie to spend the summers with him on Martha's Vineyard, then helped her build a perma-nent house nearby. Into her last years, he continued to make designs for her embroidery and crewelwork.

Tom Benton was caught forever in a scene that he had witnessed as a boy while visiting Pappy Wise. At the train station in Waxahachie, Texas, a line of volunteers was being loaded onto a train that would take them to fight in the "Spanish War":

> As the last of the line reached the coach steps there was a terrified scream
> and one of the boys jumped out of the line and ran away from the train.
> The regulars caught him and brought him back. When he was pushed up
> the steps of the coach he cried out "Maw, Maw, Maw," like a little boy.
> All of the women about us wept and some of the men. I cried too.

Benton rushed home to draw the incident, but it wasn't the drawing that fixed it forever in his memory. At the end of his life, Tom Benton could recall the scene in photographic detail because he had replayed it almost daily for seventy years.

This was the Tom Benton that Jackson Pollock met for the first time in September 1930. Benton was forty-one years old at the time and, outwardly at least, a model of everything Jackson longed to be; the ideal combination of his father's exaggerated masculinity and his mother's artistic aspirations. Under-neath, however, beyond Jackson's seeing, was a still-desperate search for emo-tional resolution—a contest of identity and aspiration almost identical to Jackson's own.

13

JACK SASS

For Tom Benton's favor, Jackson could compete with Charles on level ground, even perhaps—for reasons he couldn't have imagined—favorable ground. "[Jackson] had no money and, it first appeared, no talent," Benton wrote in his autobiography, "but his personality was such that it elicited immediate sympathy."

Exactly why Jackson elicited Benton's sympathy or why Benton elicited Jackson's in return, neither man was likely to explore. From the beginning, however, they must have felt a mutual, unspoken recognition that they were on the same errant trajectory, both victims of what Thomas Craven called "some strange irregularity of development." Even Jackson's classmates recognized their special kinship. "There was a rhythm between Jackson and Benton from the time they met until the time Jackson died," says George McNeil, a classmate at the Art Students League. "The rhythm was physical, gestural. The two men were *bonded*, you could almost say." Joe Delaney had a simpler view: "Benton was a stange shot, and he was inclined to be a more personal guy with people who were strange shots like he was. And Jackson was the strangest shot of all."

Strangely, it was Jackson's very lack of ability that cemented the bond between student and teacher. "Jack's talents seemed of a most minimal order," Benton later wrote. "He had great difficulties in getting started with his studies, and, watching other more facile students, must have suffered from a sense of ineptitude." If Benton had sympathy for Jackson's plight, it was because he had heard many of the same criticisms during in his own student days. Even his friends considered his early works "halting," "badly imitative," and "crude." "[Tom] made his bow to the current isms," wrote his close friend, critic Thomas Craven, "but without grace or that ease of mind which lends the illusion of conviction to imitation." According to a Benton biographer, "lack of technical facility, and frustration," had driven Benton into a depression that

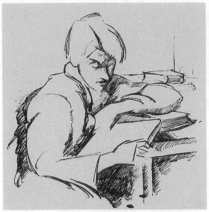

Jackson Pollock, Thomas Hart Benton,
c. 1935, ink on paper, 8½″ × 11″

lasted for most of his first year in art school, during which he was "notoriously drunk most of the time." Just as Jackson withdrew from cafeteria discussions at the League, Benton had shied away from the Paris cafés frequented by artists like George Grosz and Diego Rivera because, he said, "they were all more talented and capable than I."

Benton also shared with Jackson the reassuring conviction, born of his own self-doubts, that "great talents"—like those of Harold Lehman or Phil Goldstein, or even Charles—"were not the most essential requirements for artistic success." He pointed Jackson toward artists like Albert Pinkham Ryder, the reclusive painter of late romantic landscapes and seascapes, who couldn't draw a boat as finely as contemporaries like Winslow Homer, but could capture in his turbulent brush strokes its pitch and roll on a roiling sea. "Intense interest," said Benton, the *ambition* to be a great artist, was what mattered most; "and that [Jackson] had." In fact, it was the uneasy combination of artistic shortcomings and overreaching ambition that most reminded Benton of himself as a student. Like Jackson, he had suffered classroom indignities and the whispered ridicule of fellow students without surrendering his dreams of greatness. "I [liked] the idea of being a genius," he wrote of his early student days at the Art Institute in Chicago, "and grew resentful of those who questioned it." Later, in Paris, when he met Stanton Macdonald-Wright, the California painter, he wrote: "We agreed on only one thing . . . that all in Paris, but ourselves, were fools." At the League, Benton served Jackson in the same conspiratorial way, throwing, in his suspended skepticism, a lifeline to Jackson's ambition. "I had seen too many gifted people drop away from the pursuit of art because they lacked the necessary inner drive," he wrote in his autobiography, expressing a thought that he had often shared with Jackson. "Jack's apparent talent deficiencies did not thus seem important."

As a student, Benton, too, had been impressionable and eager to please, jumping from one influence to another, from Impressionism, to Neo-Impressionism, to Cézannism, to Cubism, to Synchromism, to Constructivism, always "casting around for solutions." In politics, his views had changed "with every whiff" of fashion. After meeting a Marxist named John Weichsel in New York in 1916, he declared himself a Marxist. Later he met the philosopher John Dewey and adopted Dewey's more pragmatic view of history—just as easily as Jackson modeled himself after the mystical Krishnamurti, only to be remolded a few years later by the hard-headed Benton. In a phrase that could apply as well to Jackson, Benton complained of the "lurking uneasiness underlying all my contacts with the world."

Beneath the similarities, however, Benton felt another kind of appreciation for the boy he saw in Studio 9 every Tuesday and Friday, hunched over his sketch pad, scribbling furiously. Ever since Neosho, he had been especially attracted to young men less sophisticated than himself. Most of his boyhood friends were rough, "uncultivated" country boys. During his service as a navy draftsman in Norfolk, Virginia, he fondly recalled being "thrown among boys who had never been subjected to any aesthetic virus . . . boys from the hinterlands of the Carolinas, from the Tennessee country, from all over the South, in whom I discovered, despite all the differences in our experiences, bonds of sympathy." For years after his vivid experiences among the sailors of Norfolk, he made long summer trips to the South, abandoning his wife and "disappearing into the hinterlands," often taking along favored students like Bill Hayden, "a very young, very good-looking" man, according to his account, with whom Benton shared the back of a station wagon—"fixed up as a sort of combined kitchen, bedroom, and workshop"—for months at a time during several such sojourns. In picking favorites among his League classes, he was guided by the same standard, almost invariably choosing westerners and other "uncultivated" types.

Benton's preoccupation with his own sex was balanced by an indifference to the opposite sex that verged on misogyny. According to his biographer, "He was inclined to ignore his female students completely." One of those students recalled that "Benton didn't think women should be painters." Rita Benton, with considerably less reticence, used to tell friends that "Tom hated women because of his mother."

Later, in the 1950s and 1960s, Benton grew less circumspect in his displays of interest in rustic young men, once commenting on the "beauty" of Italian peasant boys: "Who wouldn't be attracted to them?" While he continued to vent his rage against the reign of "pansies" in the art world and recoiled at even the most casual physical contact with other men, he found it increasingly difficult to disguise his exaggerated preference for the company of younger men, and his virulent attacks on homosexuality began to sound shrill and defensive. "Tom," his sister Mildred warned him late in life, "you're protesting too much." Eventually, not only his sister but his son, several of his close friends, and his biographer began to believe that, all along, Tom Benton had been fighting a losing battle with his own homosexual urges.

Whatever the sources of his teacher's affection, Jackson reveled in it. Deprived of his own father's attention for so long, he found in Benton's sympathies the male approval that had always eluded him. Benton even looked like Roy Pollock: the same short stature, the same self-conscious pugnacity, the same creased face and big, leathery hands. For the first time in his long struggle to prove himself, Jackson had finally found an ally.

He quickly seized the advantage. In class, he tried to replicate Benton's technique and subject matter "down to the last brush stroke," according to one classmate. Imitating Benton's Regionalist style was common among his students, but Jackson embraced Regionalism not just as a technique but as a philosophy and a life-style. He "tailed after Benton like a puppy dog," recalled Harry Holtzman. "Whatever Benton did, he wanted to do too." If Benton saw himself as "a western artist," then Jackson would be a westerner, too—the most western of them all. He began by spreading stories about his "frontier family," about the cows he milked while growing up on a ranch in Wyoming, about the wild stallions, wolves, and buffalo that had been a part of his boyhood. When he began appearing in the League cafeteria dressed in cowboy regalia—"high-heel boots, cowboy hat and so forth"—he was so convincing that fellow students like Reginald Wilson who had heard Jackson's Wild West stories assumed "it was no costume." "Jackson always walked around wearing his cowboy hat," remembered another classmate, Philip Pavia, "and he had complete contempt for all of us 'foreigners,' as he called us. He loved the West and the Midwest." When Benton asked him who his teachers had been in Los Angeles, he replied, with down-home derision, "Only California nuts!"

Charles's girlfriend, Elizabeth, thought she saw Jackson's campaign for what it was: a contest with Charles for Benton's favor. "In the beginning he presented himself to Benton as kind of a laddy boy and wheedled around to get what he wanted," she recalls. "He wasn't at all the sweet dear boy some people thought he was." Even Jackson's friends, many of whom had labored in Benton's classes for a year or more and had seen Jackson's clumsy drawings, sensed that ambition was at work behind the appearance of the idolizing student at the feet of the master. "He was highly committed," recalls one of them, "a very intense person with a good sense of reality and a good sense of how he could take advantage of certain relationships."

Whether out of ambition, or empathy, or emotional need, over the next few years Jackson's campaign to win a place in Benton's innermost circle—and, in the process, to displace Charles—succeeded. But success had its price. Benton may have claimed a kinship with his fellow Norfolk sailors, men whose "egos were not of the frigid, touchy sort developed by brooding," but no one was more preoccupied with self, no one more given to brooding than Tom Benton. Beneath the posturing, he was no more the heartland man's-man than Jackson was the uncultivated country boy. To Jackson, however, who knew little if anything of Benton's past, the ideal of the macho artist seemed to answer many

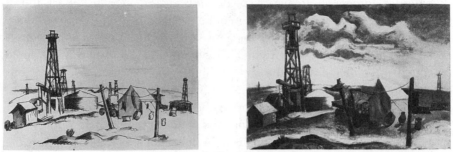

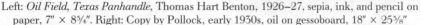

Left: *Oil Field, Texas Panhandle*, Thomas Hart Benton, 1926–27, sepia, ink, and pencil on paper, 7″ × 8¾″. Right: Copy by Pollock, early 1930s, oil on gessoboard, 18″ × 25⅜″

dark, nagging questions. Was art a "sissy" activity? Benton's answer was to expunge the feminine by exaggerating the masculine—by drawing masculine figures with a muscular line; by discussing art in hard-boiled, hillbilly terms; by sketching in a man's world of whorehouses and gymnasiums; by talking, dressing, cursing, drinking, and fighting like a man.

But Benton's preoccupation with the male persona, as well as the male physique, came from a different source altogether. For Jackson, there was no synthesis, no resolution in Benton's ideal artist, only, somewhere down the road, a confrontation with his own inchoate feelings. In the interim, Benton's ideal, with its implied license on "masculine" behavior, only exaggerated the symptoms of Jackson's problems—the self-abusive drinking, the violent outbursts—without beginning to address the problems themselves. It succeeded only in giving Jackson's rage a voice and a character, not in giving it rest.

In the fall of 1930, Benton began work in earnest on a set of murals for the New School for Social Research, his first major mural commission. The school, founded only a decade earlier by a group of progressive scholars and educators, was just completing its handsome new home at 55 West Twelfth Street. It had already commissioned a mural from José Clemente Orozco when, after protests from Benton supporters, the school's director agreed to offer an additional commission to "an authentic American" artist. Benton's mural would fill the third floor boardroom, a generous space, about thirty feet square, at the back of the building looking south over a garden toward Eleventh Street. Orozco, as at Pomona, was given the dining room.

As Benton's favorite new student, Jackson was undoubtedly privy to much of the planning process. If he was frustrated by the close work and extended concentration required in class he must have despaired as he watched his mentor's laborious preparations for the New School murals. As a teacher, Benton could be a taskmaster and disciplinarian; as an artist, he was meticulous to the point of preciosity. After choosing his theme—technology and the transformation of American society—he began by sorting through his vast store of sketches for appropriate images. "He had a bureau drawer just chock full of sketches that he'd made all over the country," a student recalls. From these reams of sketches, gathered over the previous five years on "walking tours" into the hinterland, sifted and resifted, a "general image of America" began to emerge. Benton then divided the sketches into broad themes: industry, regions of the country, people and popular culture. Gradually, through a long series of preliminary oil sketches, he subdivided the three themes into nine smaller panels to be arranged around the doors and windows of the boardroom.

Within the panels he subdivided his material again into scenes. A *Changing West* panel would include scenes of oil drilling, pipe welding, surveying, cow-poking, and sheepherding. Some scenes he could borrow directly from his sketchbooks—the oil rigs from his record of a 1927 trip to the Texas panhandle, for example. Others required new sketches. For a panel on the steel industry, he traveled to a Bethlehem Steel plant in Maryland to sketch scenes of workers on the forging line. He posed family members, friends, and students for featured figures. His wife and son posed with Caroline Pratt, founder of the City and Country School, for the scene representing education; Charles's girlfriend, Elizabeth, posed for a scene in a movie house; Max Eastman, the editor of *The Masses* and a Benton friend, posed for a subway scene with Peggy Reynolds, a well-known burlesque performer; Alvin Johnson, Benton's patron, sat for a "signature" scene in which he shares a glass of bootleg hootch with Benton himself. At this stage in the laborious process, Benton invited Jackson to the studio for what he called "action posing." Although he later denied including Jackson's likeness anywhere in the murals, Benton made numerous sketches of his body, posing him pantomiming various activities depicted in the background: harvesting crops, sawing logs, surveying, mining coal, forging steel.

Next, to help refine the compositions and, in particular, to establish the right balance of light and dark areas, Benton fashioned a clay bas-relief, or diorama, of each section of the mural and, using a naked light bulb to exaggerate the shadows, lighted the scene from various angles. Occasionally, he would paint the little figures to see how color affected the intensity of the light. From these clay models (adapted from a technique used by the Renaissance painter Tintoretto), Benton produced yet another set of studies, in watercolor, distemper, and egg tempera, in an exhaustive effort to anticipate and resolve any problems that might arise when the actual painting began: the interaction of colors, the effects of washes, the placement of highlights.

As interminable as these preliminaries must have seemed to Jackson, Benton could justify them. Like the Renaissance masters he admired, he had chosen to work in egg tempera—dry pigment mixed with egg yolks and water—a medium so difficult and out of favor that he was forced to turn to a 400-year-old text for instruction. Considered a draftsman's technique because of its potential for precise lines and sculptural modeling, tempera offered Benton more control than oil. It could be applied in layers to produce deeper, more translucent colors and, when dry, was more durable and longer-lived than oil.

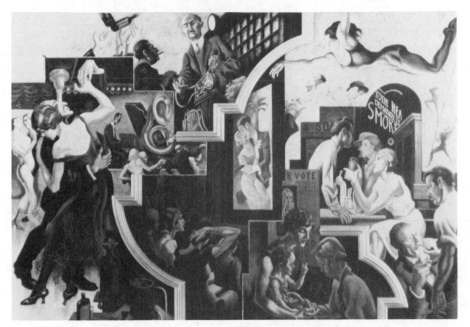

City Activities with Dance Hall, Thomas Hart Benton, panel from the New School murals,
1930–31, distemper and tempera on linen with oil glaze, 92″ × 134½″. Elizabeth Pollock
posed for movie patron, center; Rita and T. P. Benton for mother and child, center right;
Benton himself for the drinker at far right.

Finally, its historical association with the Italian Renaissance appealed to artists
who, like Benton, advocated a renaissance in American art. But tempera was
an unforgiving medium. Oil paint could be retouched—a slip, an errant drop,
the wrong brush, or even a change of heart about a color could be easily
corrected. Mistakes in egg tempera were forever. It was, in short, the perfect
medium for a meticulous planner like Tom Benton.

When the preparations were finally complete, months later, the work moved
into a large loft space arranged by Alvin Johnson on Twelfth Street not far
from the New School. Before Benton could start painting, however, he had to
construct the mural's nine panels. Egg tempera made special demands on the
painting surface as well as the artist, and Jackson, working beside Benton and
his chief assistant Herman Cherry, found himself involved in another elaborate
preliminary step. On wallboard reinforced with one-by-three-inch cradling,
they glued heavy linen, then spread seven coats of gesso—a paste-like mixture
of glue, water, and whiting—and two coats of Permalba, a commercial com-
posite oil paint that brought the panels to a frosty white. All nine hundred
square feet of surface were then sanded down to a smooth finish. Without
assistance, Benton drew a proportional grid on each panel and then painstak-
ingly transferred and enlarged, square by square, the images on his sketches to
the pearly linen panels. When the blueprint was complete, he began by roughing in the images with an underpainting of distemper, a quick-drying mixture
of glue, pigment, and water also borrowed from Renaissance muralists.

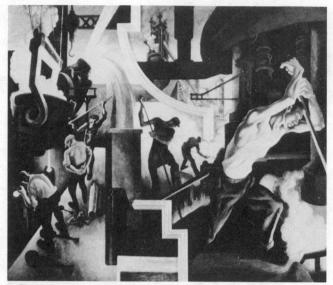

Steel, Thomas Hart Benton, 1930–31, distemper and tempera on linen with oil glaze, 92″ × 117″; Jackson posed for worker at right.

Finally, the panels were ready to be "painted." Benton worked alone—no one else touched the canvas. When Jackson was present, he merely watched. It was the first time he had seen an accomplished artist at work on a project of this magnitude. During this last stage of painting, Benton was "an artist of incalculable energy," according to Thomas Craven, "driving himself constantly, and . . . working from twelve to fifteen hours a day." But the energy Craven speaks of showed itself in Benton's commitment to his art and his attention to detail, not in his brush. He worked systematically, meticulously, seldom departing from his detailed plan. "There was a formula and he followed it," says Mervin Jules, who assisted Benton on a later mural. "It was all very mechanistic, passionless. Everything was seen in terms of rendering light and dark, modeling, and use of color. That's why it was so easy for his students to 'do' a Benton painting."

For Benton, the passion had already been expended at the point of contact, at the place on a Tennessee road where he stopped to sketch a farmer, or at the bar in Borger, Texas, where he caught the face of a "big-boned" oilman in a few quick lines. The challenges had been confronted and overcome in endless sketches and studies, in the effort to make the image of the oilman harmonize with the other figures in the scene and that scene with other scenes in the panel. By the time the Texas oilman reached the smoothed surface of *Changing West*, he was nothing more than an element in a larger design, an area of color and shading and form in an unforgiving medium. "He drained people of their humanity," says Jules. "They became mannequins." Craven called him a "master designer . . . an artist who can resolve and harmonize diverse and

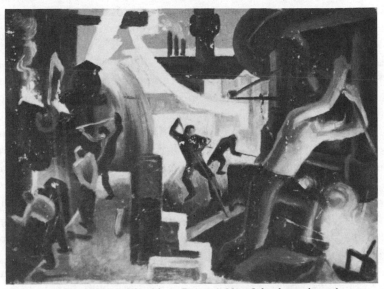

Jackson's copy of *Steel* from Benton's New School murals, early
1930s, detail from oil on gessoboard, 18″ × 25″

seemingly impossible contradictions of subject-matter," but acknowledged that
his art lacked "greater depth of feeling."

As he watched his teacher—painting finally—deeply concentrated, but always in control, Jackson must have tried, and failed, to see himself. So far, at
least, "depth of feeling" was about the *only* thing he had.

The mural project drew Jackson even more deeply into his teacher's professional and personal life. More and more often, after class or a day at the studio,
Benton would invite him back to the apartment on Hudson Street. From the
League, they would ride the subway to Fourteenth Street where crowds of
unemployed men shuffled into the giant Art Deco mouth of the recently
opened Salvation Army Temple. From the studio, it was only five cold blocks
past Abingdon Square between rows of dark and idle warehouses. Jackson had
visited the Benton apartment earlier in the fall, but always as Charles's little
brother. By early 1931, with Frank holed up at Columbia growing daily more
disenchanted with New York, and Charles trying to juggle his teaching job
with his commitment to Elizabeth, Jackson usually came alone. In the unde-
clared contest with Charles, he could claim his first victory.

In his autobiography, Benton would argue that there was nothing unique
about Jackson's visits. "I was given to treating my students like friends," he
wrote, "inviting them home to dinner and parties and otherwise putting them
on a basis of equality." That may have been true later, but when Jackson began
his regular visits, he was the *only* League student who enjoyed the privilege of
casual access. Not even fellow Missourian Joe Meert or chief assistant Herman

Cherry accompanied Benton home in the evenings. Later in 1931, when Benton organized a musical group, Monday night rehearsals would bring a crowd of students into the Hudson Street apartment, but few were fed and fewer still came back between rehearsals.

At the Bentons', Jackson created a new, more affectionate family than the one he had left behind. Like Charles and Frank before him, he often sat with four-year-old T.P. when his parents were away, showering the pensive dark-haired boy with the kind of attention that had been so lacking in the Pollock house. Although taciturn around Tom and Rita, Jackson would blossom into long hours of animated conversation when alone with T.P., telling endless stories about "the spooky mythology of the West" that always made their way back to the Bentons the next day through T.P.'s excited retelling. Such lavish attention wasn't lost on T.P., whose own father seldom made time for him. "Jack became the boy's idol," Benton wrote in his autobiography, "and through that our chief baby-sitter."

Jackson also quickly became the Benton's chief floor scrubber, window washer, and general fix-it man. "[Rita] was always finding little tasks for him to do," remembers her niece. Whatever the job, Jackson was paid in cash (fifty cents for a night of baby-sitting, five dollars for a day of scrubbing) when cash was available, in food when it wasn't. If Manuel Tolegian accompanied Jackson for chore duty, Rita invariably put him to work washing rugs—an assignment that Tolegian considered an ethnic slur. Elizabeth Pollock, ever-vigilant against exploitation, thought Rita "took advantage of the boys who formed a coterie around Tom. She *used* them." If so, Jackson didn't seem to mind. On Hudson Street, he not only competed with Charles, he became Charles—the oldest, the favored son—gradually taking the place in Rita's eyes that he had always wanted in Stella's.

No woman could have satisfied Jackson's fantasies of a mother more amply than Rita Benton. Like Stella in her youth, she was a robust, broad-hipped, big-breasted woman who loved to cook. But there the similarities ended. Where Stella was Scotch-Irish and German, Rita Piacenza was unmistakably Italian, the daughter of a coppersmith from a little town outside Milan, who had come to America as a girl but never lost her accent. (She considered English a barbaric language.) "She was a professional Italian," says her niece, Maria Piacenza. "She always kept her accent. She knocked those WASP guys dead with it." Where Stella's features were broad, Rita's were fine, if slightly boyish ("like something out of Michelangelo," according to her niece). Where Stella withheld, Rita was profligate. Her clothes were always loose, her short chestnut-colored hair bounced, and her big hips swung from side to side when she walked. When she was amused, which was often, she let out a "beam-shaking" laugh. Where Stella glowered and congealed in reproval, Rita mocked and scorned and railed. Where Stella nodded and cut an extra piece of pie when pleased, Rita swooned and stroked and flattered, and made enough spaghetti for fifty. "She was the mother of the world," recalls a neighbor on

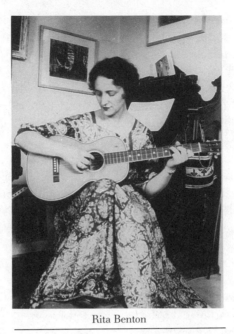

Rita Benton

Martha's Vineyard who often saw Rita walking barefoot through the dune grass, her breasts bouncing and her big skirt filled with sea breeze. "She was the eternal mother," says Piacenza. "Mother with a capital M. She just adored and worshiped children, her children, *all* children."

For Rita, as for Stella, all men were essentially children—and none more so than Tom Benton. In 1917, he had been her teacher in a free art class sponsored by the Chelsea Neighborhood Association. She found his posturing very childish, very American, and very appealing. In his autobiography, Benton described Rita as a "slim, dark-eyed, and beautiful" girl who "wore a red hat." Beauty or no, he gave her the same abbreviated treatment he gave all the women in his class. But Rita persisted. For five years, through Tom's navy duty in Norfolk, through long summer absences and frequent trips to his mother's house in nearby Great Neck, she pushed the relationship inexorably toward the altar. Lizzie Benton tried everything to prevent the marriage—railing, pouting, fainting. She called Rita's Italian background unworthy of a Benton. But Rita was determined to wrest Tom from Lizzie's lace grip. Finally, despite skepticism from every side—Tom's friends "were certain, knowing about [his] experiments, that it would be impossible for [him] to live permanently with any woman"—Tom and Rita were married on February 19, 1922, at Saint Francis Xavier Church in New York. After a short reception at the Piacenza apartment, however, the newlyweds took a taxi directly to Lizzie Benton's house in Great Neck where they spent the next three months under Lizzie's reproachful glare. Eventually, Benton would come to call Rita "Mommie," but he always referred to Lizzie as "Mama."

The evenings Jackson spent at the Benton apartment on Hudson Street provided him with a view of a marriage completely unlike the one he had grown up with. Instead of long silences and lingering tensions, there were frequent verbal skirmishes, mock rages, tirades of profanity, and fierce, sudden rebukes. Neighborhood children stopped routinely at the Benton door to expand their vocabularies. "They were always hollerin' at each other," recalls one of those children, Margo Henderson, "and he used words that made a child's hair curl." Another guest remembers Tom yelling to Rita from the kitchen when he wanted dinner, "Goddammit, woman, get in here," and Rita calling back in a sharp, accented retort: "Don't be *vulgar*, Tom." "Whatever abuse she got from Tom," says Maria Piacenza, "he got his back. She had her way of knocking him down—little things she would do in front of people to embarrass him." Her favorite retaliation was to impugn his carefully cultivated macho image. "She would say things like 'Poor Tom, he's always so *tired*,'" Piacenza recalls, "with all the implications that carried. She got her own back." When Tom drank too much, she would reprimand him firmly: "*Italian* men don't get drunk!"

The transparency and fireworks of the Bentons' relationship must have shocked Jackson, but beneath the exaggerated repartee, he undoubtedly saw their unwavering mutual commitment. "Tom was Rita's man, totally dependent, but acted as if he were not," said friend and neighbor Roger Baldwin. "Rita had the European woman's approach to marriage, was very possessive, but knew when to leave him alone."

Tom Benton presented himself in public as a model of masculine prerogative, but in private he "put *everything* in Rita's hands," according to a family friend. Even before their marriage, Rita surrendered her own artistic aspirations and turned her considerable skills as a bargainer and promoter to fulfilling her husband's ambitions. In their early years together, she earned rent and food money by designing hats and posing for fashion periodicals. To keep him focused on painting, she would buy his clothing, cut his hair, and read his mail. Later, she placed paintings with collectors, solicited mural commissions, arranged exhibitions, negotiated fees, cultivated dealers, and always, in the midst of everything, tirelessly promoted Tom Benton. "In a business sense," says a friend, "she *made* him."

Theirs was the exact opposite of the bargain struck by Roy and Stella Pollock. Where Stella had condemned Roy's weaknesses and subverted his ambitions, Rita accepted Tom's inadequacies and supported his aspirations. For Jackson, it became the model of what a professional marriage should be.

Among the stories with which Jackson captured young T.P.'s imagination were the adventures of a boy-hero named "Jack Sass," adventures that took place in a world of "wild stallions, shadowy white wolves, lost gold mines, and mysterious unattended campfires." "We received early reports of [such things] from our admiring son," Tom Benton recorded in his autobiography, "and about the imaginary hero Jack Sass, who had explored, solved, or conquered all these mysteries." No other record of these tales exists. Years later, Jackson would occasionally tell a story from his childhood to an intimate friend, but the tales of Jack Sass represent his first effort to take stock of his troubled past and put it in some order. In all likelihood, there were tales of unknown menaces lurking in deserted arroyos, runaway horses, Indian burial grounds, mountain bears, canyon thunderstorms and dangerous Indian ruins, herds of wild cayuse, axes in the barnyard, and wolves in Cody that only his brothers had seen—the whole range of unknowns and uncontrollables that had haunted his childhood, dredged up to be "explored, solved, or conquered" in fantasy. "Jack Sass," Benton wrote, "was, of course, Jack Pollock without the frustrations."

14

THE OLD LOVE

In early June 1931, Jackson left New York for a hitchhiking trip to Los Angeles with Manuel Tolegian. Ostensibly, it was a sketching trip, fashioned after those that Benton took with chosen students to see the real "American Scene." But in fact, like Benton's annual expeditions, it had far deeper significance. In Tom Benton's iconography, the road was the place to which all true men inevitably returned. "Inherent restlessness" was a prerequisite to masculinity; a longing for the road as natural as a longing for sex, and often related. "The bonds of marriage did not lay very heavily on my back," he confessed in his autobiography, "but I began to feel rather too well tamed and to itch for freedom." By exhortation as well as example, Benton had urged his male students to experience America as America and themselves as men, and Jackson was determined to answer the call. Finally, at age nineteen, he would stike off on his own—or very nearly—without Sande's support or Charles's supervision.

At the farmers' market in Union Square, Tolegian found a Pennsylvania truck unloading strawberries. "I just went up to [the driver] and said, 'If we unload these strawberries from the truck would you give us a ride to where you're going?' And he said, 'Sure, go ahead,' . . . and we slept in the truck all night long." Using the same strategy at subsequent stops, the pair hopscotched as far as Cleveland. Without pausing to record the hot, grim stillness of the factories along the Cuyahoga, they took a streetcar to the west side of town where the roads went due west to Toledo and Chicago and southwest to Dayton and Indianapolis—and they waited.

Suddenly, they found themselves among the vast wandering population—almost two million people, most of them young—who had spilled out onto America's roads in the first years of the Depression. For hours they waited, thumbs out, among the throngs of unemployed men and displaced families who dragged themselves from town to town "in search of a solvent relative or a generous friend," according to a contemporary magazine account. In another two or three days of travel, much of it on foot, they reached Indianapolis, where the crowds of drifters who had collected for the recent Memorial Day car race were still lingering in the rail yards and the cheap coffee shops with no place to go.

Tired and apparently frustrated by the slow progress, Jackson argued for jumping a freight train to St. Louis. To Tolegian, who was "terrified" of being robbed, the idea of entering the world of bums and hoboes—where, it was well known, people were murdered for less than a fiver—was sheer madness. "Manuel was afraid he'd get killed," says his wife Araks. "It meant grabbing onto a moving train, and Manuel knew he couldn't do it." After only a week on the road, the two friends parted company. Tolegian arrived in Los Angeles only four or five days later with the help of several long rides. Jackson, truly alone now, missed the train: "I got thrown out of sight, the damn thing was going to fast," he reported afterward. He had to settle for a slow ride to Terre Haute along Route 40 where the hitchhikers were so thick that the road looked like a parade route. Somewhere along the Indiana leg of the trip, he reported on a postcard to Charles: ". . . experienced the most marvelous lightning storm . . . I was ready to die any moment."

One night in Terre Haute, he had a run-in with the local police—undoubtedly while trying to live up to Tom Benton's example. Exactly what happened isn't known, but Jackson's cryptic reference to "miners and prostitutes" in a letter to Charles and Frank indicates that it involved all the elements that, over the next ten years, would become a kind of formula for his most self-destructive binges: sexually available women; tough, abusive men (in this case, the dark-faced miners who worked the bituminous coal fields around Terre Haute); and the ubiquitous bootleg liquor. As in so many of the later episodes, the night ended with Jackson in jail.

In St. Louis, he followed the other transients to the vast "Hooverville" that stretched along the city's riverfront. In the confusion of corrugated tin shacks and driftwood lean-tos, thousands of homeless and unemployed, black and white, suffered through the heat, the stench, and the flies of summer. Heading out of the city on Route 40, he found the hitching even slower than before. The only cars on the road, it seemed, were "spavined Fords" crammed with destitute families and their bundled possessions. The poor who drove had no room, the still-employed couldn't afford long trips, and the still-rich weren't disposed to pick up nineteen-year-old boys traveling alone. Jackson was lucky to catch an occasional day-tripper commuting between neighboring towns: from St. Louis to Fulton (where he mailed a postcard to Charles); across the Missouri River to Boonville; to Sweet Springs where the traffic picked up into Kansas City. Beyond Topeka, the last ripples of the Ozarks flattened into the great endless plains—"where the curvature of the planet was apparent to the human eye." Through Manhattan and Salina, past foreclosed farms, idle machinery, dry, overcultivated fields, and stretches of road where cars were as rare as trees,

Jackson mostly walked. The great exodus was still to come, but the combined droughts of water and money had stopped all inessential movement across vast stretches of shadowless land.

As the wait between rides grew longer and the summer sun hotter (record high temperatures and low rainfall were already loosening the soil that, in a few years, would be swept away in the "black blizzards" of the dust bowl), Jackson grew increasingly impatient. In southern Kansas, probably near Wichita, he tried again to jump a freight train. This time he succeeded.

From the moment he climbed aboard, Jackson entered another world: "a new social dimension," Eric Sevareid called it in his memoirs of a similar trip, a "great underground world" whose inhabitants "eat from blackened tin cans, find warmth at night in the box cars, take the sun by day on the flat cars, steal one day, beg with cap in hand the next, fight with fists and often razors, hold sexual intercourse under a blanket in a dark corner of the crowded car." If Jackson had hoped to avoid the congestion of the highway shoulders by climbing into an empty boxcar, he soon discovered his mistake. Almost a million Americans, most of them young and male, inhabited "the jungle," as it was called. "There were more people ridin' the freight trains than they was ridin' the passenger trains," remembers Joe Delaney, Jackson's classmate who rode the rails on and off throughout the thirties. It was a variegated crowd, as Jackson later wrote to Charles and Frank, including "cutthroats [as well as] the average American looking for work." There were career hoboes like the famous Tex, King of the Tramps, whose insigne—"Tex-KT"—was carved on privy seats and penciled on flophouse walls from Maine to California. But there were also criminals and derelicts in the jungle, as well as truant teenagers, city hustlers on the move, evicted families, foreclosed farmers, and hundreds of thousands of young men who had no job and didn't want to be a burden on their families.

The trains carried Jackson south across the west-pointing finger of Oklahoma, then out onto the white griddle of the Texas panhandle. Four years before, as Jackson knew, Tom Benton had come the same route, sketching the boom towns and oil derricks that had found their way into the *Changing West* mural. Now Jackson watched as the train passed black oases of oil rigs shimmying in the heat and false-front shops on one-street towns in the middle of country as barren as a speculator's promise. Inside the metal cars, the temperature climbed well past a hundred, forcing the whole population onto the roofs and the flat cars to feel the hot wind. Cause for celebration was the discovery of a refrigerated car, or "reefer," carrying some perishable delicacy to an oil baron in Amarillo or Lubbock. A big chunk of pilfered ice, placed just upwind, could add a chill to even the hottest breeze. Across Texas and into the high desert of New Mexico, stopovers were rare. Hundreds of miles rolled by between Tucumcari, Santa Rosa, Albuquerque, and Gallup.

For a boy like Jackson who had always been pampered and provided for in one way or another, the freights had to be a hard initiation. Unless he was

willing to beg or steal, even the youngest and most charming traveler went
without food. A loaf of bread cost only a dime and a full meal only a quarter
most places, but dimes and quarters represented hours of work, and work was
the scarcest commodity of all. Some "boes" raced the sunrise and one another
to be at the local A&P by 4:00 A.M. when the bread trucks left their morning
delivery by the back door. Latecomers had to look for handouts at coffee shops
or queue for hours in city soup lines. Most restaurants would give a bum a cup
of coffee ("You didn't have to say anything, they could see you were on the
road just by lookin' "); a few might even fix a sandwich with leftovers that
weren't worth saving.

Like any demimonde, the jungle was controlled by unseen forces that preyed
on newcomers. Communities were rated and itineraries planned according to
the citizenry's generosity with handouts and the temperaments of local railway
"deeks" who patrolled the freight yards. Old boes knew which train operators
deliberately left a few boxcars open and vacant to avoid the chaos of hoboes
clambering over a moving train, jumping from car to car in search of an
"empty," or clinging to the tender, faces blackened by flying coal dust. Such
generosity was rare, however. As Jackson undoubtedly discovered, most of the
time nothing came easily on the rails. At most freight yards, the deeks were
ready with clubs and revolvers to clear the trains of unticketed riders. Texas
sheriffs in particular were notorious for rounding up bums and locking them
away for months at a stretch.

It was not a life for the timid or the vulnerable—and Jackson was both. "You
almost hit bottom," says Delaney. "As a matter of fact, you *do* hit bottom.
When you're out there with no money and no destination, you're just another
animal—and a dangerous one, too." The most common danger for young boys
like Jackson was the older men who prowled the populated railroad embankments and the crowded express runs—called "hot shots." Sevareid describes
his first encounter with homosexuality in the jungle: "[I] rather imagined it
was something confined to certain boys' schools in England and the Bohemian
quarters of Paris. Suddenly it was all around me. I noticed men with glazed,
slightly bulging eyes and uncertain voices who traveled in company with boys
in their teens. The men were referred to as 'wolves.' " There were, of course,
young wolves as well as old—boys who rode the rails from town to town,
seeking out the cafés where homosexuals congregated, separating a prosperous-
looking one from the pack, and earning enough in a few nights to last for
months in the jungle. Sevareid describes a "well-built, remarkably attractive"
boy of sixteen who in a single night could coax his victims into giving him
everything they carried—including their clothes. Almost every young newcomer was tested—by the old wolves if he was penniless, by the young ones if
he had something of value. "If you were a lamb, they'd walk on you," recalls
Delaney, describing the inevitable confrontation. "If you were not a lamb,
they'd find out quick. They'd look in your eyes and see from your pulsations
that they're gonna have trouble with you if they keep movin' your way."

What happened to Jackson during the week or more he spent riding the rails between Kansas and California, if anything, isn't known. Years later, in drunken candor, he told Manuel Tolegian that his time on the trains had been "terrible" and "scary." Another League classmate remembers Jackson listening with unusual interest and sympathy to his stories about being assaulted in the jungle and admitting that "he had also had some homosexual experiences when he was younger." Whatever happened, the trip clearly took its toll. Jackson arrived in Los Angeles on June 29 a physical wreck. A friend who saw him soon afterward remembers, "He looked so different I hardly recognized him. All that beautiful blond hair had been chopped off and it was just hanging out in tufts. His face was all pimply. Even his ways and disposition had changed." Jackson was so exhausted and disheveled that even a week later when Stella, who had been away, saw him for the first time, she wrote to Frank and Charles in distress: "[Jack] looks very tired from his trip needs a rest & get fed up as he went with out eats more than once on his trip. I would have been worried sick if I had known he was bumming the freight train, he sure took lots of chances of getting killed or crippled for life."

Still, when the time came to report his trip to his brothers and the Bentons back in New York, Jackson was determined to put a manly face on it. In terms that could have come directly from his mentor's mouth, he transformed his ordeal into a postcard-perfect tour, as upbeat as Benton's New School murals. "My trip was a peach," he wrote. "I got a number of kicks in the but and put in jail twice with days of hunger—but what a worthwhile experience. I would be on the road yet if my money had lasted." Instead of a hard-hit, drought-ridden area, Kansas became the place where "wheat was just beginning to turn and farmers were making preparations for harvest." Instead of the "grim misery" of a shantytown on the St. Louis riverfront, Jackson reported seeing "negroes playing poker, shooting craps, and dancing along the Mississippi." The miners and prostitutes in Terre Haute, he wrote, "gave swell color" then added, in a flourish of Bentonesque anti-capitalism, "their both starving—working for a quarter—digging their graves." Of his days riding the rails, he speaks only of the "interesting bums" he met, and concludes with vacant rhetoric: "the freights are full, men going west men going east and as many going north and south a million of them."

For a few days after his arrival, Jackson recuperated in the hot California sun at a "swell place" that his old friend Don Brown and Sande had rented on Montecito Drive. Situated on the grassy hills just a few miles northeast of downtown Los Angeles, the house enjoyed a panoramic view of the growing city that, on days when the desert wind cleared the air, stretched all the way to the curved blue line of the Pacific. Eager to resume their relationship after a year of intermittent letters, Jackson contacted Berthe Pacifico within days of his arrival and invited her to the Montecito Drive house. Despite her own waning interest—she had begun dating another Manual Arts student—Berthe

arrived the next day with her sisters Ora and Pauline just as Jackson and Sande
were finishing a crude mural on the garage door. The young women were
shocked by what they saw. Jackson had been drinking and the trials of the
recent trip showed on his face and in his manner. "I couldn't stand to look at
him," Berthe remembers, "he was such a mess. He just wasn't the person I
knew." Ora couldn't conceal her disgust. "He looked awful and I told him so,"
she recalls. Stung by the rejection and emboldened by alcohol, Jackson quickly
turned abusive. He grabbed Pauline and tried to kiss her. When she resisted
("I didn't want him to even *touch* me, he looked so dirty," Pauline said afterward), there was a brief, awkward struggle, then perfunctory good-byes, and
Berthe Pacifico left Jackson's life forever. "After that we never saw him again,"
says Ora. With the summer barely begun, Jackson had lost his only claim,
however tenuous, to sexual prowess.

After the heat of the day on Saturday, July 4, Jackson, Sande, and Arloie
drove to the relative coolness of Wrightwood. Roy Pollock had been laid off
from the park service at Big Pines the previous spring, but had found work on
the federal roads project near his old camp and had even managed to arrange
a job for Jay. The reunion at Wrightwood was even more subdued than usual,
shadowed as it was by the realization that the Depression had finally caught up
with the Pollock family. The "raw food" rage of two years before was now an
economic necessity; there was simply no money for meat. While Roy and Jay
had found jobs and Sande still earned a solid wage at the *Times,* a certain
anxiety clung to conversations about the future. "[Jay] and I are still working,"
Roy wrote Charles, "but do not know how long it will last. Sande still has his
job . . . [but] a lot of fellows have been laid off while he stays on." After a week
of looking for a place on the work crews with Jay and his father, Jackson
returned dejectedly to the house on Montecito Drive with Sande. After they
left, Roy confided in a letter to Frank, who was also without a job, "Hope [Jack]
finds something to do [in Los Angeles] but it will be almost a miracle if he
does."

Idle and restless, Jackson drifted back to his old circle of friends from Manual Arts. In the year since his departure, former Schwankovsky favorites like
Harold Lehman and Phil Goldstein had achieved considerable notoriety in the
small, emerging Los Angeles art world. While Jackson was struggling to control the bump and the hollow, they had begun to form their own independent
artistic circle with Lorser Feitelson and Benton's old friend, Stanton Macdonald-Wright, as mentors. They had their own avant-garde gallery, Stanley
Rose's bookshop in Hollywood—described as "a combination cultural center,
speakeasy, and bookie joint"—and their own prominent collectors, Walter and
Louise Arensberg, at whose Hollywood house, designed by Frank Lloyd
Wright, they could view works by Picasso and Brancusi, as well as Duchamp's
Nude Descending a Staircase, which the Arensbergs had purchased from the
Armory Show. Like Benton, both Feitelson and Macdonald-Wright looked to
the Italian Renaissance for inspiration, but had served their terms in Paris and

exposed their students to Cubism and Surrealism. Under their influence, Goldstein had abandoned Otis and advanced to an idiosyncratic style of his own, combining the empty architecture, reclining statues, and blank-faced mannequins of Giorgio de Chirico with the Mannerist distortions of the late Renaissance in paintings of startlingly professional quality. Meanwhile, Harold Lehman was organizing trips to the Philharmonic, private playings of new classical recordings, and weekly reports on philosophical tomes.

In the midst of so much accomplishment, Jackson's insecurities quickly resurfaced, and his relationship to the old gang during the summer, although cordial, was never comfortable. He must have felt the widening gap that separated him from the others, although his comments reveal some uncertainty as to who was drifting away from whom. "The old bunch out here are quite haywire," he wrote to Charles in August, "they think the worse of me tho."

At a reunion of the "old bunch" early that summer, Jackson saw a new face: a short, slender, solemn young man in wire-rim glasses, fine Worumba coat, and domed Borsalino hat. Jackson was attracted by his directness and intensity —so unlike the glibness of Lehman or Tolegian—as well as his well-articulated radical ideas about art and politics. It wasn't until they were well into the conversation that Jackson realized he had spoken to this young man once before. The previous summer, he had seen an article in the paper about students at a Los Angeles area high school organizing a demonstration to protest the presence of American marines in Nicaragua and had called one of the protest leaders, a student named Reuben Kadish. This was the same Reuben Kadish. "That cemented our relationship," says Kadish. "He was a bad boy, I was a bad boy. We felt the same way about each other right from the beginning." The more the two men talked, the more surprising it seemed that they hadn't met sooner. Kadish had known Marie Levitt, Frank Pollock's girlfriend and future wife, since their childhood together in Ontario, California. Like Jackson, Kadish had gone to New York the previous fall, looking for some direction after being expelled from high school, only to return at midyear and enroll at the Otis Art Institute. There, he had met Phil Goldstein, and the two soon established their own studio. Ultimately, however, Otis proved as frustrating for Kadish as high school. "It was a very regimented kind of place," he remembers. "You couldn't take life drawing until you did cast drawing and you couldn't do this until you did that." By spring, Kadish and Goldstein's independent "studio" had become an embarrassment to Otis and they were asked to leave. "You don't need Otis," the dean told them. Soon afterward, only a few weeks before Jackson's arrival, Kadish had met Sande Pollock.

Although fate seemed determined to bring them together, Jack Pollock and "Rube" Kadish were an improbable pair: the bookish Russian Jew with his intense visage, quick walk, and close-cropped hair, and the broad-faced American boy with his hank of blond hair, cowboy boots, and dimples. Where Jackson's ancestors had arrived in America before the Revolutionary War, Kadish's had only just preceded the Great War, having fled czarist persecution

in the Lithuanian town of Vilna. His father, Samuel Shuster, had come through
Germany to the Russian-Jewish community in Chicago where he took a new
name and started a house-painting business specializing in *faux bois* and mar-
bling (techniques that Georges Braque would soon introduce into the Cubist
vocabulary). In 1920, when their first child, Reuben, was seven, the Kadishes
moved to Los Angeles in search of a better climate for Samuel's chronic bron-
chitis. Not until Reuben took a trip across country in 1925 to visit his uncle in
New York City did his artistic ambitions begin to coalesce. Leib Kadison had
formed a theatrical company, the Vilna Troupe, in the flourishing Jewish
community around lower Second Avenue, premiering plays like *The Dybbuk*.
Kadish remembers his uncle as a "culture vulture" who introduced him to
painter friends like David Burliuk and took him to galleries and museums. On
one such visit to the Metropolitan Museum, fourteen-year-old Reuben had an
epiphany. "I was looking at a Courbet nude," Kadish remembers, "and I totally
succumbed to the erotic aspects of it. I made a choice right there that I wanted
to be an artist."

More than his facility or his learning, both of which were formidable, Jackson admired Kadish's feeling for art, for art's power to arouse, to persuade, to
grip. In contrast to Goldstein's facile manipulations and Lehman's cold, intellectual precision, which had always made Jackson feel inadequate, Kadish's
approach to art was, like his radical politics, direct, earnest, and utterly committed. Kadish, whose own work lacked the uncerebrated urgency he espoused,
envied Jackson's enormous reserves of raw artistic energy. From the beginning,
he saw what it would take the world another two decades to see: this crude,
intense, untrained nineteen-year-old possessed an "imaging power" that, for
all his lack of technical facility, could bring inanimate objects to life. "Jack had
a way of making magic out of things," Kadish remembers. "When he looked
at something, it was as if it had been created for him alone, for him as an
artist."

Through the rest of July and into the record-setting heat wave of early
August—every day for two weeks, temperatures soared past 100 degrees—the
two boys visited museums and galleries together, searching out works of art
that captured the directness, the immediacy, the emotional energy about which
Kadish waxed eloquent in the evenings over beer. In the Southwest Museum,
not far from the house on Montecito Drive, they saw Southwestern and Plains
Indian artifacts—some displayed in recreated environments—and Pacific
Coast Indian baskets: from the thick coiled willow-splint baskets of eastern
California to the delicate sea-grass baskets of the Aleutian Islands. At the Los
Angeles County Museum near Exposition Park, not far from the Pollocks' old
bungalow court on West Fiftieth Street, they bypassed paintings by the old
masters and exhibitions of local art and headed for the deserted cellar to
wander the "ethnographic" exhibits of South Pacific cultures—glass cases
filled with boldly sculptural ceramic bowls from the Pava cultures of the South
Pacific, carved knife hilts and sword handles brought back from the Philippines

by sailors, tapa cloths in vivid geometric designs. "We had to lie down on our bellies sometimes to see what was in the bottom of the cases," Kadish remembers. "Marvelous things were just stuck back in there. At the time, those things were thought of as mere ethnological data, but we didn't care. We would eyeball them for hours rather than waste our time with the show that the Los Angeles County Art Association was putting on upstairs. We knew where the vigor was, where the real energy was."

In mid-August, Roy sent word from Wrightwood that two jobs had opened up at the camp. With work scarce and the Los Angeles sun sizzling, Jackson reluctantly accepted, inviting Manuel Tolegian to join him on what turned out to be an ill-fated expedition. The work was sawing felled trees into standard lengths that could be chopped into stove wood for winter. The sawing was done with long two-man saws like those depicted by Benton in his *Midwest* mural. One man pushed, the other pulled, for ten to twelve hours a day. Even for men who had spent their whole lives in the camps it was exhausting work. For Jackson and Manuel, dissipated by a year of subsistence living in New York, it was slow, backbreaking agony. Every morning, a supervisor came by, recorded the size of their pile, and paid them accordingly—usually in small change. Even the normally unmovable Stella felt something like pity. "Jack and Tolegian are cutting wood," she wrote to Frank, "[and it's] sure hard work. They can't cut very fast until they get used to hard work again."

In the mountain air, the boys had hoped for some respite from the record heat in the valley, but none came. Between the sun, the exhaustion, and the frustration that had been simmering all summer, tempers flared. Arguments broke out about who was doing most of the work on the two-man saw. On a ride into camp to get the saw blade sharpened, Manuel accused the supervisor —a friend of Roy's—of taking wood from the pile during the night. Infuriated, Jackson grabbed the blade that was braced between them and shoved the cutting edge against Manuel's neck. In the struggle to protect himself, Manuel let go of the wheel and the car swerved perilously toward the precipice at the edge of the road. "He said he was going to cut my throat," Tolegian later told his wife. "For a minute there I really feared for my life."

Soon afterward, Tolegian left Wrightwood, and soon after that, the work ran out. In several weeks of bone-tiring effort, Jackson had earned almost nothing. "I have finished up my job today," he wrote to Charles in late August, "and after figuring things out there is damned little left—barely enough to pay for my salt." For several weeks, however, he lingered at the camp instead of returning to Los Angeles. Except for his time with Kadish, the summer had left him socially alienated and creatively paralyzed. "I haven't done any drawing to speak of," he confessed to Charles.

For Roy Pollock, the summer—especially Jackson's last idle weeks at camp —only confirmed his worst fears about his youngest son. Now fifty-four, Roy had spent most of the previous year depressed and ill, alternately worried about keeping his job and about staying healthy enough to work. More and more, as his savings dwindled, he was haunted by thoughts of his own failure. Earlier that summer he had written Frank in New York, "I wish we were all back in the country on a big ranch with pigs cows horses chickens—don't you? The happiest time was when you boys were all home on the ranch." To Roy, Jackson seemed to be dangerously adrift at a time when even skilled workers, desperate to work, were standing in breadlines. His artistic career, unlike Charles's, held little promise of employment. Even the self-centered Tolegian had sensed the tension between them, later describing Roy's relationship with Jackson as "the most unfatherly thing I ever saw." In the provocative August heat, Roy couldn't contain his exasperation for long. At some point he lashed out as he had the previous summer, making clear to Jackson just what a dismal future lay in store for him.

Again, Jackson turned to Charles for consolation and guidance:

I don't know what to try and do—more and more I realize I'm sadly in need of some method of making a living—and its beginning to look as tho I'll have to take time off if I'm ever to get started. To make matters worse, I haven't any particular interest in that kind of stuff. There is little difficulty in getting back there—and I suppose I can find something to do—what is your opinion?"

Charles apparently answered quickly, encouraging his little brother to return to New York, because on Tuesday, September 22, Jackson left for Oklahoma City, the destination of a woman who paid him to drive her car. The summer had only sharpened the conflict inside him, only widened the gap between his frustrations and his ambitions. "Dad thinks I'm just a bum," he wrote Charles, "while mother still holds the old love."

In New York, too, the reception was mixed.

Embittered by Jackson's bid for Benton's favor and furious at Charles for acquiescing in it, Elizabeth greeted his return with a late-autumnal chill. "Most women were like Rita," Elizabeth recalls. "They babied him and stroked him. *I* gave him a cold glassy eye when I realized what he was doing to Charles." Nevertheless, as a money-saving measure, Charles arranged for Jackson to sleep in his Tenth Street studio and to share meals, many of them prepared grudgingly by Elizabeth, in his new apartment at 47 Horatio Street. By contrast, the Bentons, especially four-year-old T.P., greeted Jackson's return with warm celebration.

His artistic ambition rekindled by the summer with Kadish, Jackson attacked his work and for a while at least, the obstacles seemed to yield. At the League, he registered again for Benton's class, now called Mural Painting, but so unchanged from the previous year that decades later Benton insisted he had never taught a course in mural painting. Even more than the previous year, Benton's favor worked to Jackson's advantage. Between classes, unknown to the other students, the two met for private tutorials at the apartment on Hudson Street, where Benton corrected Jackson's drawings and demonstrated technique by sketching directly on his student's pad. Due in part to these special sessions, Jackson began to distinguish himself in class. While Mervin Jules's academic versions of anatomy (the product of four years of training at the Maryland Institute) earned a "great heavy X" from the teacher, Jackson's cruder but more energetic efforts were, by Benton's laconic standards, lavishly rewarded. "I used one of his rough analytical diagrams as an example for my class," Benton later wrote, "to show that it was not a copy that we were looking for, even a cubistic copy, but a plastic idea."

Outside of class, however, Jackson continued to find nothing but failure and frustration. He joined the regular lunchroom crowd that craned to hear the lively dialogue between Arshile Gorky and Stuart Davis, who had just joined the faculty. "Gorky had an influence on all of us without teaching us," recalls Philip Pavia. "He really impressed Jackson." When Jackson tried to mimic Gorky's studio jargon and historical analysis, however, the effect was less than convincing. "Jackson tried very hard to become cultivated—to acquaint himself not only with the visual arts but with literature," says Whitney Darrow, who came to the League in the summer of 1930, "but he had no academic skills whatsoever. For him, everything was a matter, not of the intellect, but of emotion." Still, Jackson struggled with ideas, trying to make them his own by writing sequences of key phrases, like trails of crumbs, to help him retrace an argument. On the back of a page in a volume of the *Publications of the Bureau of Ethnology* that he and Charles had bought at a secondhand bookstore, he wrestled with the editor's argument that any philosophy develops in three stages: discernment, discrimination, and classification. "Man starts with impression of general situations," he scribbled in his barbed-wire handwriting.

Gradually handling things (getting familiar with
the content of such general situations) he makes distinctions
The distinctions he classifies. (names)
From these come inferences.

Such efforts left most of his circle unimpressed. Elizabeth Pollock, by now Jackson's nemesis, recalls: "I never heard him carry on a logical conversation in which one and one added up to two." Even his indulgent mentor acknowledged Jackson's shortcomings. "His mind was absolutely incapable of logical sequences," Benton said. "He couldn't be taught anything." But when Jackson grew despondent over his lack of verbal facility, Benton was quick to supply a defense: "The deep wellsprings of the visual arts are in fact nearly always beyond verbal expression."

Jackson tested not just his verbal limits but his artistic limits as well. Having seen Goldstein's deft paintings during the summer, he ventured into oil paints for the first time (Charles undoubtedly bore the additional expense) and found himself once again engaged in a "continuous running battle" with his tools.

"Jack fought paint and brushes all the way," classmate Axel Horn later wrote. "They fought back, and the canvas was testimony to the struggle. His early paintings were tortuous with painfully disturbed surfaces. In his efforts to win these contests, he would often shift media in mid-painting." Horn recalls a particular portrait on which Jackson had tried, in succession, lacquers, oils, chalks, pencil, and ink in his struggle to make peace with the image. But even Benton's generous eye saw little of value in the result. He called Jackson a "damn fine colorist"—a dubious accolade, given that most of Benton's contemporaries considered Benton himself a dreadful colorist—but thought his paintings lacked "the human element." Whether or not Benton expressed his bleak assessment, Jackson was acutely aware of it. He had only to look around his apartment, where Charles's paintings lined the walls, to see how far his work fell short of genuine accomplishment—on Benton's terms, at least. On one of his rare visits to the Horatio Street studio, Frank remembers being surprised to find only Charles's paintings on display; Jackson had turned all of his to face the wall.

Not until the following spring, at the second annual Washington Square Outdoor Show, did Jackson summon up the courage to exhibit his work. In late April 1932, along a stretch of sidewalk on MacDougal Alley, Jackson Pollock had his first public showing. He waited all day, sitting on the curb, posing in his red bandanna for a charcoal portrait by Joe Delaney, and hoping for a buyer—only five to ten dollars for a signed original. But no one bought.

The single bright spot in Jackson's life continued to be the Benton apartment on Hudson Street where T.P. listened in thrall to the further adventures of Jack Sass and Rita laughed her big laugh while stirring a kettle of her famous spaghetti sauce. In the fall of 1931, however, the coziness and exclusivity of life with the Bentons was threatened by the arrival of the Harmonica Rascals.

Tom had first conceived the group the previous spring. Depressed and listless following the completion of the New School murals, he had begun toying with his son's harmonica and discovered that he had a natural talent for the instrument. That spark—Benton called it "a revelation from heaven"—touched off a conflagration of enthusiasm that eventually consumed all of his students as well as Rita and T.P. He began with pieces by Bach, Purcell, Couperin, and Josquin des Près, but soon turned to more suitably rustic fare: folk songs, hillbilly ballads, and country blues. "We commenced charging a nickel when anybody missed a note," Benton wrote in his autobiography, "[but] that became rather expensive as we increased the complexity of our music and we had to abandon it." Benton had an almost comic enthusiasm for making music: he stomped, hooted, and "danced" through every number. Loosened up by bootleg liquor, others joined in until the floor shook and the lights shuddered.

Despite the circus-like atmosphere, Benton's students ignored these Monday-night "musicales" at their peril. Sooner or later almost all of them joined in: Charles on the mouth harp ("I was no damn good"), Tolegian on

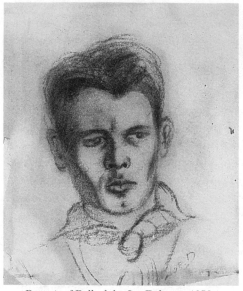

Portrait of Pollock by Joe Delaney, 1932,
chalk on paper, 10″ × 7¼″

the harmonica, Rita and Axel Horn on the guitar, Bernie Steffen on the dulcimer, and eventually little T.P. on flute, playing songs like "In the Good Old Summertime" and "The Jealous Lover of Lone Green Valley." For those with no training or facility, there was always a kazoo or a comb with tissue paper. Eager to outdo the others, Jackson (who had already tried and failed on the harmonica years before in Wrightwood) bought a used violin and tried teaching himself to play fiddle. After only a few frustrating hours of practice, he smashed the instrument to pieces and settled for the mouth harp, Charles's instrument. With a little instruction from Tolegian, he learned to play it well enough to join the band, although real mastery eluded him. "[I] can't play a damned thing— much," he confessed in a letter to his father, "but it kinda puts me to sleep at nite and I kinda get a kick out of it." In a phrase that could have applied to all of Jackson's life at the time, Benton said he played "enthusiastically, if not terribly well."

Sometime after the first snowfall, the Harmonica Rascals were forced to suspend their rehearsals when Tom Benton took to his bed with a high fever. The illness—Jackson thought it was typhoid or "the grip"—couldn't have come at a more inopportune time. Persuaded by the success of the New School murals and Rita's backstage promotion, Juliana Force of the new Whitney Museum of American Art had asked Benton to paint another series of murals for the museum library. "Hard luck to get sick just as he gets a job," Jackson wrote home. Hard luck for Benton, but not for Jackson, who, with Benton sick in bed, was able to spend more time alone with Rita—watching T.P., assuming Tom's share of the chores, even accompanying her occasionally on social outings. She flattered him endlessly—"from the beginning she called him a ge-

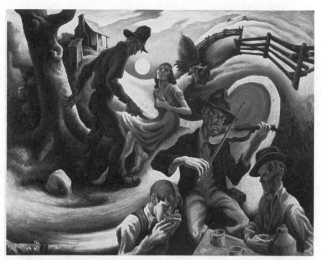

The Ballad of the Jealous Lover of Lone Green Valley, Thomas Hart
Benton, 1934, oil and tempera on canvas, 41¼″ × 52½″.
Jackson posed for the figure playing the harmonica.

nius," recalls her niece—cooed over his looks in her sultry voice, smoothed his
frustrations, and tested his diffidence. "She was a very flirtatious woman,"
recalls one of Jackson's fellow students, "very vivacious, very Mediterranean.
She had a way of making you feel, as you sat at a table with twenty other
people, that she had cooked this meal especially for you."

For the first time in his life, Jackson felt the weightlessness of seduction.

It was not the first time Rita Benton had crossed the line between flirtation
and seduction—not even the first time with a Pollock. In 1928, her fancy had
been struck by Frank Pollock, who arrived in New York blond and suntanned
from an eighteen-day cruise through the Panama Canal. Then as now, the
attraction ran both ways. "She had winning ways that were pretty damned hard
to resist," Frank recalls. "Her lips were different than Mother's. She had an
angular face and polished skin, black hair and sparkling eyes—a voluptuous
Italian, very voluptuous. I wasn't used to being in such company." Despite
Charles's warnings, Frank soon found himself alone with Rita in the Bentons'
kitchen. "She said she'd been reading a book, *The Well of Loneliness*, about
lesbianism, and I said, 'That's terrible!' But it was her way of bringing up the
issue of sex, and I got very uncomfortable with just the two of us there." Late
one night, he accompanied Rita and some friends to a Harlem club. Halfway
through the floor show and a dozen drinks, while a male stripper named Snake
Hips bumped and ground through a twenty-minute "serpent dance," Frank
felt Rita's hand on his knee. "I was unused to that sort of thing, and all I can
remember is my embarrassment," says Frank. "I couldn't believe it was true."

No doubt, Jackson wanted desperately to believe it *was* true. Six awkward
months with Berthe Pacifico, culminating in a few family dinners, were all that
stood between him and his worst fears of sexual failure. More than his pam-

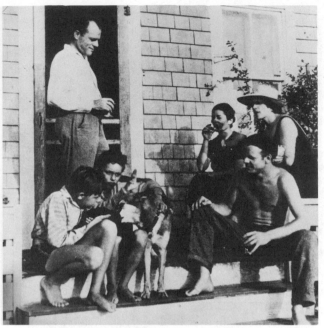

At Martha's Vineyard: Jackson in beret, Rita Benton in hat,
T. P. Benton with dog

pered childhood, more than his exemption from chores, more even than his incompetence as an artist, it was his unconquered virginity that marked him as an outcast among the Pollock brothers.

Tom Benton, too, set a demanding standard of sexual prowess. When asked about the "social life" on his sketching sojourns, he would respond with a lascivious chuckle: "You know how dogs are—well—I was like that. When the urge came on me, it came on me, that's all. Nothin' to it." Jackson had no way of knowing that Benton's whorehouse tales were as tall as Louis Jay's cowboy legends told around a Kaibab campfire. All around him, he saw fellow students living out Benton's Rabelaisian fantasy. "We were geniuses," says Herman Cherry, "and we all had girls—we were either living with one or trying to live with one." From the suave interloper, Arshile Gorky, who "liked sexy women and never had a shortage of them," to Manuel Tolegian, who corresponded faithfully with Araks Vartabedian, his future wife, on the West Coast even as he scoured New York for more immediate gratification. Of the many attractive models who hung around the League, Mervin Jules recalls that "you rarely were turned down if you propositioned them." Even fifteen-year-old Nathan Katz was a regular at the League's twenty-five-cent Saturday night parties where girls sometimes ran naked and half drunk into Fifty-seventh Street and where the Midtown Precinct paddy wagons ("Black Marias") made regular stops. "It wasn't uncommon for girls to come to these binges without any clothes on," Katz remembers. "I danced with one and all she had on was charcoal dust. When I walked away, I realized that half her costume had come off on me."

Despite the sexual opportunities surrounding him, Jackson remained inexplicably aloof. "He was so handsome, as good-looking as any movie actor," says Elizabeth, "but I never saw him with a girlfriend. I never *could* understand why he seemed so terrified of women." Benton later attributed Jackson's reticence to " 'blocs,' psychic obstructions [that] constantly afflicted him. . . . He would get 'stalled' in drawing, in painting, in all kinds of activities he attempted, including those of sex." In the end, sex was even more frustrating for Jackson than art. "The drawing at least he had an opportunity to struggle with," says Axel Horn. "There weren't too many women who were willing to let him struggle with them. There'd need to be some sort of follow-up. He'd have to offer something more if there was to be a continuing encounter. And there never was."

Until Rita Benton. Whether Rita intended to seduce him or not, Jackson perceived in her attentions, for the first time in his life, the mixture of maternity and sexuality to which all the Pollock brothers were inevitably drawn. For the first time, sex seemed like a possibility.

As early as the forties, rumors of Jackson's "affair" with his teacher's wife were circulating in the art world—most of them started by Jackson himself. Frank recalls a conversation with Jackson in 1954: "He told me right outside the door to his studio that he had had an affair with Rita. I was kind of shocked, but then Sande came over and confirmed it. We just gossiped among brothers." "I was very shocked," recalls B. H. Friedman, Jackson's friend and first biographer. "He said it just this way: 'I used to fuck her.' Period." Rumors spawned plausible scenarios. "I could see her initiating him into sex as a favor," suggests one of Jackson's League classmates, "doing it to help him resolve some awkward problems—doing it in a motherly way. Spaghetti and sympathy, you might say." Even Tom Benton later heard the rumors and deferred to their plausibility. "Of course, feeling the way [Jack] did about Rita," Tom told an interviewer in 1964, "he came to resent me."

In fact, it was an affair, like others to come, that existed only in Jackson's imagination. That Rita flirted and teased, perhaps even tormented Jackson, is undeniable. (It would be years before she fully understood her role in his groping search for sexual fulfillment.) Her attentions may have been intended to flatter his masculinity and reinforce his sexual confidence, but they had exactly the opposite effect. Almost two decades later, in a moment of utter honesty, Jackson admitted to his wife, Lee Krasner, that "Rita Benton played with me and titillated me and got me all excited, but when it came to the moment of truth, she wouldn't go through with it."

Rita's rejection, combined with the continuing creative frustration and a bitter cold winter, plunged Jackson into a deep depression. In the studio, he would sit with his head in his hands, unable to work, for days at a time. He had never stopped drinking, but now the gray, snow-laden clouds brought with them the old despair, the old emptiness that he hadn't felt since Los Angeles. Occasional nightly binges became weekend binges, then week-long binges. Sometimes he would disappear for days, waking up on a friend's couch or in the sawdust on a speakeasy floor. Typically, the binges began with friends like Joe Delaney and Bruce Mitchell, somewhere in Chelsea. From there he would stumble uptown to Nathan Katz's skylight studio in the Lincoln Square Arcade, with its Atwater-Kent and its upright piano for dancing. Katz was usually too drunk to care if Jackson wandered in for a few drinks, then wandered out again without making a contribution. "I was drunk for three solid years," Katz recalls, "from the age of fourteen to seventeen. It wasn't so uncommon."

On Saturday nights, Jackson could pay his way into the League dance where flasks and bottles passed back and forth as briskly as girls. Lionel Hampton's silver band filled the room with brassy jazz, and scuffles broke out like little whirlpools on the crowded dance floor. Jackson never danced: when sober, he was too shy; when drunk, it made him dizzy and sick. Mostly he watched the crowd, reeking of corn liquor, then turned and left for the next party. Afterward, he would push through the snow to a penthouse party on Central Park West or the Upper East Side where many of the League's rich-boy dilettantes lived—"Those were suave affairs," says Joe Delaney who, as a black, wasn't always welcome. Of course, by the standards of the day, anybody with a job was considered wealthy. On weekdays, the speakeasy on Fifty-eighth Street was always open if Jackson was sober enough to remember the password. With whatever dimes and quarters he could earn from Rita and occasional dollar bills from Stella, he bought bathtub gin from a bootlegger named Jack Frost. "It was all right," remembers Katz, who drank his share of it. "At least we didn't go blind." Cheaper but more dangerous was corn whiskey, trucked in from North Carolina or Pennsylvania in barrels. And even that was nectar to the bums Jackson passed shivering in the street, who were reduced to squeezing Sterno through a sock.

On Christmas Eve, 1931, Jackson and Tolegian were reeling between parties, enjoying the holiday lights on Washington Square, when they passed a group of worshipers carrying candles down the dark corridor of Bleecker Street. They followed the group east, past the Bowery, and into the elegant Greek Revival Church of the Nativity on Second Avenue. "Jackson walked right up to the altar," Tolegian recalled, "and knocked everything over—the candles, the cross, the chalice, everything." When the police came, Tolegian accompanied Jackson to the police station where, in all likelihood, Charles bailed him out.

Jackson's winter was filled with scuffles and brawls and Saturday night bouts, some as far as 125th Street in Harlem. More than once the binges ended when the police wrestled him to jail—or, if he was too drunk to walk, dragged him there. Tolegian was present one night on a Hudson River dock when Jackson, "angry at civilization," flung himself into the icy water. "I had to jump in and save him," Tolegian recalled. "Otherwise, he would have drowned." As early as 1932, Katz remembers, "it was common knowledge that Jackson was suicidal."

The rages that drinking brought on were neither accidental nor arbitrary. Elizabeth remembers that Jackson "coldly and deliberately worked himself up into these rages *in order to* say the insulting things he said." Deliberate or not, they managed to hit with uncanny accuracy at the sources of Jackson's greatest frustrations: at those who stood in the way of his ambitions. To his more accomplished classmates he could still be reticent and deferential when sober; but when drunk, he became a provocateur, critical of their work and skeptical of their manhood. Sometimes, one classmate recalls, "he'd look you over real quick, almost as if he was deciding whether to punch you in the nose or not." The more clearly he recognized another's talents, the more likely he would.

In the case of brother Charles, the ultimate source of frustration, Pollock family protocol required that Jackson find more indirect ways of expressing his resentment. "Outside, he could be very charming and lovely in his manners," Elizabeth remembers, "but once he was in our house, he was sulky and lazy. He didn't want to be cooperative. Jackson gave about as much back in the way of gratitude as if Charles had been some kind of strange landlord that he rented from."

Women were Jackson's other, special victims. Handsome, shy, and boyishly charming when sober, he turned "pugnacious and ornery" toward women with the least excuse of alcohol. His natural inarticulateness was transformed into cold, subversive silence; his macho pretensions into wildly offensive language; and, occasionally, his emotional rage into physical abuse. "He'd walk up to a woman at a party and stick his big face in hers and say something in a rough, threatening way," one classmate remembers. As his reputation spread through the League—"He made the women afraid," Philip Pavia recalls—Jackson was forced to rely increasingly on fantasy instead of drunkenness to appease his sexual ambitions, spinning out in lunchroom tales the sexual mastery that eluded him in reality. "He bragged about a lot of conquests," one classmate remembers. "But it was pretty evident that they didn't culminate to the extent that he claimed they did."

Only rarely did other members of the Pollock family glimpse Jackson's darkest side. On a visit to the Tenth Street studio-apartment early in 1932 with Frank, Marie brought along a girlfriend, Rose Miller, a quiet, modestly attractive girl—"bubbling, not dramatic," according to Marie—with dark curly hair, olive skin, and "no particular interest in the arts," but eager to meet new men. On the way to Jackson's apartment, the two women "made the mistake of buying a bottle of whiskey," Marie remembers, "not knowing what the effect was on Jack, not knowing about the Pollocks and alcohol. This was kind of early in the game. It was just the smart thing to do—this was in the days of Prohibition. We bought it to have a little party and to be friendly with Jack."

The "party" began well enough. Rose took an instant liking to the brooding, awkward boy with the hazel eyes and quizzical squint. At first she thought the handsome paintings around the walls were Jackson's, forcing him to explain that *his* paintings were the ones turned to the wall. With an ax, Jackson cut small pieces of hard-to-come-by wood and fed them to the potbellied stove. In the warmth and glow, Marie quickly forgot her lingering annoyance at Jackson (on her last visit, he had put her new hat at the bottom of the closet, then piled a party's worth of coats on top of it). As the whiskey was passed around, Frank shared the latest family news (Sande's job at the *Times* was in jeopardy), complained about New York (the Depression might defy optimistic predictions and drag on for another year), and lamented the prospects for a career in journalism.

Before anybody realized what was happening, Jackson was drunk.

He began to paw at Rose menacingly. She tried to brush it off, but the more she ignored him, the bolder he became. "He got very rough," Marie remembers, "not saying sexual things, just being abusive to her, manhandling her, pushing her. I'd never seen him that way before—he was usually this sweet young guy." Marie grabbed Jackson and tried to pull him away. This wasn't the tantrum of a petulant little boy deprived of his way, Marie recalls thinking, "it was just mean. I was afraid he would hurt her." His face already red with anger, Jackson turned on Marie and exploded. A winter of discontents spewed out in one volcanic rage. For all his self-inflicted suffering, nothing and nobody would bend to his will, not even pencils and brushes. For all the spinning ambition that he had brought back from the summer, he was more isolated and embattled than ever. For all the work, and the years of wanting, he was still the last and least, the little brother yearning for the attention of an increasingly cold and distracted family in an increasingly cold and distracted world.

In an instant, he grabbed the ax from beside the stove and held it over Marie's head. "You're a nice girl, Marie, and I like you," he spat at her. "I would hate to have to chop your head off." After a few seconds of frozen silence, he turned and brought the ax down into one of Charles's paintings hanging on the wall. The force of the blow split the canvas and buried the ax in the wall behind it.

Jackson had chosen, half consciously perhaps, not only one of Charles's best paintings, but also one of the few that he had managed to sell. It was in the studio only because Charles had borrowed it back from the buyer to show at an exhibition. Even Charles—unemotional, unmovable Charles—was visibly angry when he returned. With Elizabeth's approval, perhaps at her insistence, he told Jackson to find another place to live.

But the family could never desert Jackson entirely. When one brother grew tired of caring for him, or resentful of the imposition or of Jackson's ingratitude, another one took his place. It was a pattern that would be repeated often in the next few years, as each brother, in turn, served his term as Jackson's keeper. "Jackson's four brothers behaved toward him as if he had been a disabled child," Elizabeth remembers, "as if one leg was shorter than the other, or one arm withered, or he had a speech impediment. All four brothers recognized that he was flawed in some way, and that they had to protect him."

Now it was Frank's turn. Although comfortably settled in an apartment on West 114th Street only blocks from both his day job peeling potatoes and his night job at the Columbia law library, Frank moved to Midtown and took a room with Jackson. In a cramped, windowless space hidden in a dilapidated warehouse building not far from Macy's, the two brothers spent the rest of the winter and spring. "It was on a corner and there was a small speakeasy on the ground floor," Frank recalls. "In the middle of the night, maybe two or three o'clock, they'd bring barrels of beer and drop them through the sidewalk to the basement. You'd hear the thump. It was illegal, of course." The room was only large enough for a double bed and a chest of drawers, but between Frank's two jobs—beginning at five in the morning and ending at midnight—and the long commute, the two brothers hardly noticed each other. "We were there together only the few hours of the night that I slept," Frank remembers.

One night, stumbling through the dark toward the edge of the bed, Frank found someone else in his place. Rose Miller had returned to Jackson's life.

After the night at Charles's studio, no one could have been more surprised than Jackson at Rose's persistence. While not a beautiful girl, she was, to Frank's eye, "attractive and wholesome." And also, apparently, very lonely. Before being introduced to Jackson, she had frequently accompanied Marie and Frank to the movies. "Frank would hold my hand during the first act," Marie recalls, "and Rose's hand during the second act. She didn't have a boyfriend." Although "reserved" and "feminine," Rose was, like Marie, a headstrong Jewish girl who had crossed the country on her own—the two had met at a residence for working women in Los Angeles—and was never without a job or money in her purse. She approached Jackson with the same calm determination and pioneer sense of purpose. "There's no question in my mind," says Frank, "that *she* seduced *him.*" In preparation for one late-night rendezvous in Jackson's room, Marie bought a dozen red roses and put them in a milk bottle on the chest next to Jackson's bed. "I left them there for Rose and Jack," Marie recalls, "because they were going to have their big encounter that evening."

What happened that evening is not recorded, but the relationship soon sputtered out. Although Rose had money, the two never went out or joined Frank and Marie for dates, nor did Jackson ever venture to her parents' house. Their liaison was bounded by the low-ceilinged·space above the speakeasy. "She was only with us two or three evenings," Frank remembers. On the last occasion, Frank returned from work, rapped softly on the door, and was surprised when Rose appeared, alone and dressed and obviously eager to leave. "*I* wouldn't have turned her out of bed to go home alone from that address in the middle of the night," Frank remembers thinking. "It was midnight. I would at least have taken her to the subway. At *least*. But Jack didn't even get out of bed. He didn't stir. I just climbed in in her place."

By summer, the relationship was dead. "Rose wrote me and said she didn't know what happened," Marie recalls. "The interest just wasn't there—on his part, that is, not hers."

15

INTO THE PAST

The rescue effort continued through the spring of 1932. Alerted by Charles and exhorted by Stella, the Pollock family responded with an outpouring of letters to shore up Jackson's sagging spirits. From Wrightwood, Roy made the usual apologies and recommended several articles in the *Nation* to his son's attention. Sande complained that he had been cut to part-time status at the *Times*. Even the long-silent Jay, who had thrown himself into union activities that would eventually lose him his printing job, wrote a homiletic letter about "finding himself." Stella sent several letters, inquiring in characteristically circumspect terms about the adequacy of his diet, his sleep, and his wardrobe. The subject of Jackson's coat became a momentary *cause célèbre*, Stella apparently believing that his problems could be traced, at least in part, to an ancient, tattered blue coat he had worn since high school. Eventually, Frank dutifully stepped forward and, despite being deeply in debt, took Jackson to Macy's and bought him a new corduroy coat for twelve dollars. Stella also sent money, scarce as it was, and Sande enclosed a reproduction of a painting. Perhaps at Stella's instigation, Charlie Brockway, a family friend from Riverside, came down from Boston and visited Jackson in his small room over the speakeasy.

Out of Jackson's hearing, a consensus emerged in the family that he was having "growing up" problems, exaggerated by the easy availability of bootleg liquor and a decadent New York life-style, but nothing beyond the normal pangs of adolescence—"the usual stress and strain of a sensitive person's transition from adolescence to manhood, a thing he would outgrow," according to Charles. The best antidotes, the family agreed, were wholesome activity and close supervision, provided by Charles and Frank respectively. Even with more than a million jobless in New York City, Charles managed to find Jackson part-time work as a janitor at Greenwich House. But it was only a temporary solution. With Charles applying for a fellowship in Los Angeles, and Frank planning a trip to the West Coast with Marie in June, what would become of Jackson alone and jobless in the emotional hothouse of a New York summer?

Everyone breathed easier when, in April, Charles's fellowship fell through. Rather than spend a summer baby-sitting Jackson under Elizabeth's wrathful glare, however, Charles arranged for him to join Frank and Marie on their trip west. To cover his expenses, Jackson persuaded Whitney Darrow, Jr., the Princeton graduate, budding cartoonist, and distant cousin of the famous lawyer Clarence Darrow, to come along, citing the salubrious effects of "getting away from the suffocating, closed-in city and out into the green countryside again." His share of expenses would be "$25 to $30," Jackson told him, less than he earned for a single cartoon. "I had never been west of Geneva, New York, and I saw it as a wonderful, unique opportunity," Darrow remembers. J. Palmer Schoppe, another League student, wanted a ride only as far as his home in Salt Lake City.

On May 29, 1932, the five set out in a bright yellow 1926 Packard 6 touring car that Marie had bought for $165 and the Pollock boys had done their best to put in working order. With Frank and Jackson taking turns at the wheel, they followed the northern route through New York, Ontario, Michigan, Illinois, across the Mississippi and out onto the warped tabletop of Iowa farmland. They passed within fifty miles of Tingley without stopping. The high point of the trip came in the unlikely town of York, Nebraska, about a hundred miles southwest of Omaha, where Marie's uncle was shocked to find his young niece traveling with four unshaven, unmarried young men "looking very wild and woolly." "He was president of the Rotary Club and owned half the town," says Marie. "I think we embarrassed him."

In Cheyenne, Wyoming, a sudden gust of wind tore the canvas top off the Packard. As if on cue, the skies over the Medicine Bow Mountains, usually cloudless in June, turned dark, and heavy rain followed them all the way to Salt Lake City where Schoppe disembarked. Turning south, they stopped at Bryce Canyon National Park where, five years earlier, Jackson had come with Sande, Robert Cooter, and the cowboy Louis Jay. Unfortunately, Jackson spent most of the visit in a pool of mud, struggling in the rain with one of an endless succession of flat tires. The rest of the trip retraced a familiar route: from the Arizona border near the Kaibab Plateau, down into the Mojave, then up again into the San Gabriel Mountains and the familiar pine smells of Wrightwood. They spent the last night at Roy's old road camp. "There were no beds," Darrow recalls, "so we slept on the floor. We didn't bring any warm clothing, and the cabin was on top of a mountain. I've never been so cold in my life." The next morning, they descended into the valley of orange groves around Riverside.

Like the trip, the summer that followed was a step back into the past. Without the remotest possibility of a job, Jackson spent most of the summer at Stella's house on Montecito Drive overlooking Los Angeles. It could have been the Chestnut Street house in Riverside: Sande, whose increasingly precarious job paid the rent, shared a bed with Jackson; Frank slept on the couch in the living room; and Roy came down from the mountains occasionally to share a meal with his family. One night, Darrow, who had rented a place in Santa Monica, came for dinner. "They were very simple people," he remembers, "and I felt out of place as the stranger from back east. Jackson's mother was a solid woman and obviously the power in the family. His father was a hard worker and a drinker, from what I could tell. The dinner conversation was on the simplest level."

One of Jackson's few joys that summer was the reunion with Reuben Kadish. The two would sit for hours in the kitchen on Montecito Drive earnestly talking art and politics while Stella preserved fruit and vegetables in mason jars. Kadish's conversation was filled with the revolutionary rhetoric of the exiled Mexican muralist, David Alfaro Siqueiros, who had come to Los Angeles in 1931 and formed a small "workshop" of young painters. Stirred by Siqueiros's Communist politics (he had been jailed for anti-government trade union activities in Mexico) and by the visceral power of his paintings, Kadish had become his ardent disciple, assistant, and occasional chauffeur. "He was a vigorous, charismatic man," Kadish recalls, "and I was happy to do anything for him." In the year since Jackson's last visit, Kadish had assisted Siqueiros on several outdoor murals that tested both traditional painting techniques and public tolerance in a city where unions were still anathema. One, *Crucifixion*, depicted the Latin American peoples bound to a cross and, above them, perched like a vulture, the eagle of American capitalism.

Through his "workshops," Siqueiros hoped eventually to build an international "syndicate of painters" that would serve the workers' revolution with inflammatory public works like *Crucifixion.* (Kadish signed his next mural, for a Communist club in Los Angeles, "Syndicate of Painters," raising a howl of protest from local papers.) Kadish had already introduced Siqueiros to a number of his friends, including Phil Goldstein and Sande Pollock, so when Jackson arrived for the summer, he eagerly arranged a meeting. In preparation, the two trekked across town to the Chouinard School of Art to see Siqueiros's murals depicting a labor organizer rousing a crowd. But Jackson reacted coolly both to the art and, when they finally met, to the artist. "Jackson dismissed Siqueiros," Kadish remembers. " 'Orozco is the *real* artist,' he said," referring to Siqueiros's more prominent countryman, José Clemente Orozco, " 'and his *Prometheus* is really the thing to look at.' "

Although deeply impressed by the strength and immediacy of Orozco's work, Jackson continued to struggle with Tom Benton's notions of form and control. Buttressed by Sande and Kadish, he passed the summer in relative calm, producing yet another round of tortured drawings. Even after two years at the League, sketching was still not an easy process. Every new piece of paper was another battle with spontaneity, every line laden with risks. Nothing "right" happened automatically. Even his most successful attempts were little more than crude, jagged imitations of Benton's sure, undulating lines. At a time

when Kadish was proselytizing for Siqueiros and Benton was painting alongside Orozco, Jackson must have sensed the affinity between his errant imitations and the work of the Mexican muralists—in their energy, their directness,
and their emotional freedom. Where Benton insisted on cerebral control, the
Mexicans offered a broader range of possibilities, an acceptance of risk. Where
Benton denied the spontaneous, they embraced it. Jackson had admired Orozco's *Prometheus* from the moment Charles showed it to him, but at some point
he must have begun to feel a kinship with it that Charles, in all his Bentonesque
refinement and exquisite sensibility, could never know.

At the same time, away from the rigors of League classes, New York, and
the rivalry with Charles, another kind of drawing began to appear among the
run of "hairy," undistinguished imitations Jackson produced over the summer.
Occasionally, his battle with spontaneity turned into a rout—the proportions of
a figure, begun impatiently, would go wildly astray; a doodle would grow
uncontrollably to fill a page. When, in frustration, he chose not to correct a
mistake but to pursue it, the result was an image that looked nothing like the
others. What began as the folds of a saint's drapery in an El Greco study would
be transformed into an Orozco-like interplay of lights and darks. An outline of
a torso would become a skein of swirling lines. Among Jackson's efforts, these
were still the discards, born more out of frustration than inspiration and invariably first to be thrown away. But in his conversations with Reuben Kadish
among the mason jars, Jackson may already have begun to glimpse their
significance. "I told him what Gauguin said," Kadish remembers, "that one
day somebody is going to come along and work with color and tone—and
without any image that has any reference point in nature. And the result is
going to be like music."

Except for a short trip with Whitney Darrow to Ensenada, Mexico, and,
undoubtedly, some commotion surrounding the Tenth Olympiad being held at
the Coliseum in Jackson's old neighborhood, the summer passed languidly,
and, in September, Jackson and Darrow laid plans to return to New York by
the southern route. (Frank and Marie returned separately.) In a clattering old
Ford that Darrow bought for $100 on Jackson's recommendation, the two set
out across the high deserts of Arizona, New Mexico, and the Texas panhandle.

For the first time in years, Jackson felt in control, and the confidence made
him buoyantly charming and high-spirited. On the familiar stretches of bright,
barren road, he could play older brother to Darrow's timid city boy—Sande to
Darrow's Jack. "I never had been to the desert before," Darrow recalls, "but
you could tell Jackson was in his element." At Jackson's insistence, they
avoided towns and rooming houses and slept out on the open desert, freezing
all night amid snakes and cacti, then baking all day in the black coupé. When
Darrow took the wheel, Jackson leaned back on the passenger side, propped
his dusty cowboy boots on the dashboard and played his mouth harp "until the
coyotes complained," or rolled a cigarette of Bull Durham tobacco and lit it

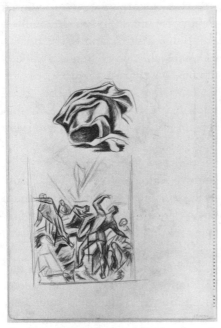

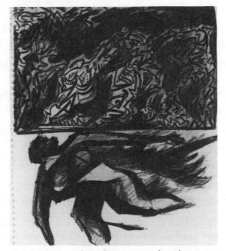

Mid-1930s, ink and crayon on lined paper,
8½″ × 7″

Detail, mid-1930s, pencil and colored pencil
on paper, 18″ × 12″

with a flick of his thumbnail across a big Diamond kitchen match. "Jackson was always doing the Benton thing," says Darrow. "We were out west and he wanted me to know how good he was out there. We tried chewing tobacco, even, but when we spit it out the car window, it blew back in our faces." At night, Jackson built a campfire. "Once he shot a rabbit and we ate it. I guess his family were hunters." In the morning, Jackson was up in time to watch the sun rise—"he loved that kind of thing"—and to cook up eggs and bacon or a can of beans. "We almost never ate at a restaurant," says Darrow, "and we almost never stopped."

When they did stop, never for long, it was usually to sketch. Using a brand-new set of Chinese ink sticks—rectangular crayons of water-soluble color that, in the waterless desert, he had to moisten with spit—Jackson felt an unfamiliar rush of confidence. "He would spit on them and slash away at the desert scenes with earth colors," remembers Darrow, who, because he saw himself more as a cartoonist than as a draftsman, mostly watched. Facing the landscape of his childhood and feeling the freedom that the Pollocks always connected with the open road, Jackson soon abandoned any effort at "spiralic countering" or "bumps and hollows" and yielded to spontaneity. "He did a desert scene with the cactus and the sun coming from behind," Darrow recalled, "putting it down on the paper with great physical energy," applying the colors "liberally . . . in a frenzied, un-Benton manner."

Benton's subject matter, however, was inescapable. Through Amarillo and the Texas panhandle, Jackson saw the oil derricks and decaying one-street towns that Benton had painted in *Changing West*. In Arkansas, they detoured to see plantation workers harvesting the September cotton just as Roy Pollock had seen them thirty-seven years before with Ralph Tidrick, and just as Benton had painted them. Heading south to New Orleans, they watched black workers unload bananas and load cotton bales onto boats tied along the Mississippi—"the negro—swell stuff," Jackson wrote his mother. In the hill country of Tennessee, they toured the heart of Benton's America, traveling roads that Benton had walked only a few years before, glimpsing a Benton sketch in every town and every turned head.

Ten days after setting out and with ten dollars left in their pockets—just enough to have the Ford towed away—they arrived in New York. For Jackson, after the frustrations of the previous winter, the trip had been a modest triumph capping a recuperative summer: no scenes, no tantrums, no binges. "He was a very likeable, warm person," Darrow recalled. "I don't remember ever having any contretemps with him, or any unpleasantness." Even on the same thirsty stretches of desert where Jackson had first experienced drunkenness, there had been no drinking—the surest sign that his confidence had recovered, at least partially, from two disastrous years of competition with Charles. "I remember we bought a cold bottle of milk at a country store in the desert," says Darrow, who wasn't a drinker. "Our drinking problem was finding something to quench our thirst. We never drank alcohol the whole trip."

By the time he reached New York, Jackson was filled with an optimism for the coming year that even Elizabeth's cold reception couldn't deflate. Charles had not so much forgiven the ax incident as purged it from his memory, and was again ready to assume his caretaking duties. Over Elizabeth's acid objections, Jackson immediately moved into Charles's new studio at 46 Carmine Street, a relatively spacious two-room apartment in an old house on what Jackson called "a happy Italian Street" in the West Village. Elizabeth, who now worked part-time at a real-estate agency in nearby Washington Square, had located both the studio and an apartment across the street where she and Charles set up permanent housekeeping for the first time, sharing a single ground floor toilet ("a stinking relic of another time") with a Scottish couple. During the summer, between trips to their tent on the sand dunes, they had already moved Charles's studio into the front room and Jackson's bed and few paintings into the smaller back room. Jackson and Elizabeth crossed paths only at dinnertime, when they shared a bowl of spaghetti and a glass of California wine by candlelight—for a while Charles was too poor to have the electricity turned on—and glowered at each other across the table. "He never looked me in the eye," Elizabeth recalls. "He feared me greatly, as well he should have, because I had the sharp tongue of a snake."

At the Art Students League, the reception was considerably warmer. The new term began on Monday, October 3, with a triumph: Benton, returning late from Martha's Vineyard, appointed Jackson class monitor. To most students, the position was little more than a bureaucratic necessity, but to Jackson it meant both financial relief—as monitor he would be exempt from the twelve dollar monthly fee—and acceptance. After two years of struggle, Benton had finally acknowledged him as an artist. Coming on top of the summer in Los Angeles, the drive back, and Charles's forgiving reception, the appointment was just one more sign that pieces of the stubborn puzzle were finally beginning to fall into place. For the first few weeks of class, Jackson greeted students with a "pleased smile on his face" instead of the moody cowboy reserve his class-mates had come to expect. For the first time, he obviously felt like he belonged among them.

Consistent with the League's laissez-faire philosophy and long-standing practice, Jackson approached most of his bureaucratic duties with a noncha-lance that bordered on neglect. "I don't think he took the attendance, because nobody cared about attendance," says classmate Axel Horn. "He would know who was registered and who wasn't so he could identify a crasher. But he didn't care, and neither did anybody else, really. It was that low-key. If there was too much of a draft, he would close the window." Only one aspect of the job received Jackson's special attention: the selection of models. Despite its billing as "mural painting," Benton's class was still a "life class" in which drawing from a nude model was the central ritual. Models served week-long stints, then moved on to other classes and other schools. Male and female models usually alternated weeks, but Jackson's attention, like Benton's, focused almost exclu-sively on the males. "He was pretty careful about choosing them," Joe Delaney remembers. "He wanted them to have as perfect a body as he could get." Benton had long ago realized that masculine bulges illustrated the theory of hollows and bumps far better than feminine curves. As a result, his favorite models came not from the standard group that made the round of League classes but from the male world of bars and gyms. They were men like "Tiger" Ed Bates, a black man with "a beautifully developed figure," whom Mervin Jules had found through Bates's brother, a bouncer at the Apollo Theater; and Hank Clausen, a burly, blond Swede who posed during the day and wrestled "professionally" at night. Both Bates and Clausen were among Jackson's, and Benton's, favorites. Clausen posed and wrestled on the West Coast as well, and often returned with news from Macdonald-Wright's class at Otis. Every Mon-day, Jackson would "pose" the model on a chair or stool to emphasize his rippling anatomy. At every class for the rest of the week, the model would hold the same pose. "Benton was a muscle and bone man," says Whitney Darrow, "and I remember Pollock poking and pinching the models to show the other students where the muscles were and how they felt. The models were a little squeamish sometimes. I don't think models would allow that today."

Benton still appeared every Tuesday and Friday at the top of the stairs and solicited questions, but the students who knew him sensed the distraction in his voice. Over the summer, he had completed the murals for the library of the Whitney Museum entitled *The Arts of Life in America*. The attendant publicity, on top of the critical attention still being given the New School murals, had begun to pull him away from the League and into a vortex of celebrity and controversy. Not that he fought the current. The New School murals had enhanced his reputation, but had done nothing to relieve his persistent financial problems. (Benton summarized their economic impact on his life by saying, "I improved my brand of whiskey.") The Whitney commission, on the other hand, had allowed him to pay off debts and helped create a bull market for his paintings that Rita deftly exploited.

Benton's murals had caught the public eye at a time when America was becoming fashionable again. After a decade in which legions of American artists, writers, and critics had virtually abandoned their country—some literally—to the "Babbitts, Rotarians, and boosters," the hardships of the Depression brought quiet celebration. Ernest Hemingway, F. Scott Fitzgerald, John Dos Passos, and others of the "lost generation" returned home from Europe. In 1932, the year that Benton completed the Whitney murals, William Faulkner wrote of his Mississippi home in *Light in August,* John Steinbeck turned for the first time to his native California for *Pastures of Heaven,* James Farrell revisited the streets and pool halls of his impoverished Chicago youth in *Young Lonigan,* and John Dos Passos published the second book in his U.S.A. trilogy. In the same year, the best-selling nonfiction book was *The Epic of America,* by James Truslow Adams, a self-critical journey into America's past.

Even at the time, Benton recognized that he had been caught fortuitously on the crest of a wave "much wider and deeper than art." "We were psychologically in tune with our time," he wrote. "We could hardly have avoided some kind of success." His murals gave form to the pride and idealism that swept the country in the midst, paradoxically, of its worsening plight. Within the art world, the murals also crystallized the decade-long conflict between "European" abstraction and home-grown realism. In the twenties, painters had gone on a stylistic exodus. Many, like Benton, had studied abroad and brought the abstraction of Picasso and Matisse back to a baffled public. In the thirties, these artists felt the same homeward tug that writers felt. Abstraction was foreign; realism was American. And of the realists—the *truly* American painters—Tom Benton was the most visible, the most vocal, and, according to *Time* magazine, "the most virile." The other leaders, Grant Wood and John Steuart Curry, worked quietly in the media vacuum outside New York City: Wood in Stone City, Iowa, painting the same rolling fields that Roy Pollock had worked as a boy (as of 1932, Wood and Benton had not even met); Curry in Westport, Connecticut, painting the natural and psychological landscapes of his native Kansas. Thus, without a contest, the mantle fell to Benton. Almost overnight, he became the champion of a nationalistic movement in art that its critics inaptly dubbed "Regionalism." "Neither Wood, Curry, nor I," Benton protested, "ever held ourselves, either in space or time, to any American region."

In many ways, the newest "ism" in American art had found the perfect spokesman in Tom Benton. Almost a decade before the term "American Wave" was coined, at a time when, according to Frederick Lewis Allen, the cocktail parties of New York and the cafés of Paris still bristled with criticism of America as "a standardized, machine-ridden, and convention-ridden place," to which "people with brains and taste naturally perferred the free atmosphere of Europe," Tom Benton had already undergone a personal repatriation.

For a man as obsessed with his own past as Benton, it was perhaps inevitable that his art would eventually serve to illuminate—or obfuscate—the backward path. His early years as an artist had been marked by a series of attempts to break away from his own roots, all of them unsuccessful. In 1911, he returned to Missouri after three years in Paris and showed his abstract Synchromist paintings to M.E. "His father took one look at the splashes of color," writes Benton's biographer, " . . . and thought his son had gone mad." Benton, who had so far avoided the rigorous abstraction of his Synchromist mentors, Morgan Russell and Stanton Macdonald-Wright, moved to New York unable to purge the last vestiges of representation from his work. After another thirteen years in the city, years in which he struggled through "semi-abstract" and "highly-generalized" styles, he returned to Neosho in 1924 to be at his father's deathbed. Once again, ancient family dynamics—unpaid debts and the hope for a final reconciliation—had a profound impact on his artistic development. He wrote movingly of the experience in his autobiography:

> I cannot honestly say what happened to me while I watched my father die and listened to the voices of his friends, but I know that when, after his death, I went back East I was moved by a great desire to know more the America which I had glimpsed in the suggestive words of his old cronies. . . . I was moved by a desire to pick up again the threads of my childhood.

Thus began Benton's ten-year-long search for his own past—and, almost coincidentally, America's; a search that began predictably in the hill country of Tennessee near his father's boyhood home and led eventually to the New School and Whitney murals at a time when the country itself, shaken by economic tragedy, was also "moved by a desire to pick up again the threads" of its past.

Benton was quick to take advantage of being in the right place at the right time, filling his frequent speeches and interviews with the flag-waving populist rhetoric he had heard as a boy on his father's campaign tours. "It is high time," he wrote in *Arts* magazine, "that native painters quit emulating our collectors by playing weathercock to European breezes." The press was as taken by his raw, colorful language as the public was by his easy, colorful paintings. According to his biographer, he was "poised and quick to top his last picture, blast at his adversaries, or have a hilarious good time with the press, where he said he usually drank enough to work up a good story." He attracted near-fanatic sponsorship among newspaper critics like America Firster Edward Alden Jewell of the *New York Times,* who called *America Today* "the most genuinely American murals yet produced." Benton himself offered a weighty intellectual defense of Regionalism, citing everything from nineteenth-century French

Positivism to post–Civil War social history, but it was his populist rhetoric, filled with down-home imagery and charged with emotions from his own past, that captured the public mood. "The arts of our pioneers were simple arts perhaps," he wrote, "but they were genuine and they were assiduously cultivated. In the backways of our country many of them have survived up to this day, and in little churches hidden away in the depths of our mountains, it is possible sometimes to hear music that is, though simple, just as genuinely music as any that may be heard in the churches of the great cities." Even in these early salvos, ringing with God and country, old friends could hear Benton the pugilist warming up for a genuine fight.

What had begun as a justification of realism quickly became, in Benton's contentious hands, a blitzkrieg against abstraction. "We can afford to ask whether a tablecloth and an apple, in terms of human value, are worth all the effort expended in trying to make them pictorially interesting," he wrote as early as 1924, the year of his father's death, referring to the still-lifes of Cézanne, to which much of modern abstraction traced its roots. "Still-lifes and their geometrical counterparts, which are equally poor in meaning are dignified by cryptic and highsounding titles and explanations—an endeavor is made to project meaning into a totally empty vehicle." By 1932, Benton had revived these arguments and distilled them, through careless and sometimes inebriated public comments, to their demagogic essence. Only a few years later he would declaim to a reporter in New York, "If it were left to me, I wouldn't have any museums. I'd have people buy the paintings and hang 'em in privies or anywhere anybody had time to look at 'em. . . . Nobody goes to museums. I'd like to sell mine to saloons, bawdyhouses, Kiwanis and Rotary clubs, and Chambers of Commerce—even women's clubs." Benton had turned from extolling the virtues of "our pioneer and simple arts" to another, darker populist tradition: intellectual-bashing—charging that the eastern establishment was, in effect, perpetrating a fraud on the honest people of the aesthetic heartland. "There is hope that art may again become a living thing," he wrote, "of interest to plain living people, rather than a collection of objects strung up on the cold walls of institutions run for aesthetic dilettantes, amateur philosophers, and generally in memory of dead vanities."

Abstractionists responded to Benton's argument with cries of outrage. "We *hated* it," remembers George McNeil, who later helped found the American Abstract Artists. "We felt about it the way people think about Creationism now —backward and *dumb*, just plain dumb." The leftist press accused the Regionalists of "incipient Fascism." Arshile Gorky dismissed Regionalism as "poor art for poor people"; others scoffed at its nationalistic claims, noting pointedly that Benton's mural technique was borrowed from Italian masters. "By a curious paradox," wrote a prominent dealer, "Mr. Benton stridently went native in an Italian sarong and Mr. [Grant] Wood preached love of his country in parched Flemish."

But Benton's blend of grass-roots rhetoric and artistic revanchism threw others into a panic of self-doubt. Most abstract artists were strongly political—Communists or Communist sympathizers—and many were already uneasy with the essential elitism of abstract art. As Orozco and the other Mexican muralists had pointed out, if art should be for the people, then how could one defend an art the people couldn't comprehend? "While most rejected the Regionalist adulation of the virtues of rural America," artist Jerome Kainen later said, "they respected its call for social responsibility in art."

Soon, however, politics triumphed over art. Instead of seeking an alliance with Social Realist artists like Hugo Gellert or Louis Lozowick, Benton tried to smite them with his nationalist sword. He told a meeting of artists at the John Reed Club that they "couldn't paint anything *real* about America because their European-derived Communist preconceptions wouldn't permit real experiences of American institutions." For a while, the Social Realists continued to embrace Benton—in January 1933, his works, as well as those of Curry and George Biddle, were represented in a show at the John Reed Club called "The Social Viewpoint in Art." In the end, his opposition proved hugely beneficial to the Social Realists, whose Marxism became an attractive alternative to the Regionalists' chauvinistic nationalism. In an ironic turn, Benton's crusade gave added legitimacy to the notion that art could be used as an instrument of social enlightenment or as propaganda, a notion that over the next decade would propel American art in directions Benton never imagined.

Through the fall of 1932, the controversy escalated. With Thomas Craven as his "hatchet man" and the press largely in his camp—his sharp, off-color remarks made good copy—Benton traded blows with his adversaries, alternating hyperbole, demagoguery, and personal vilification. When Benton claimed that "there are no artists in Paris—none at all" at a time when Picasso, Matisse, and Braque were working there, even his admirers cringed. His detractors responded with apoplectic derision. "Benton was a dirty name," McNeil remembers. "We respected the motives of the Social Realists, but Benton we had absolute contempt for. He was beyond the pale. In a Fifth Avenue café, you couldn't even talk about him. You wouldn't acknowledge that he existed. He was like refuse." When critics *did* talk about Benton, it was with the same scorn later heaped on Father Coughlin, Martin Dies, and other "narrow-minded, mean-spirited, rabble-rousing" public figures of the thirties. Benton responded to his accusers with broadsides against the entire art world, leveling what to him was the most devastating charge of all—effeminacy. In increasingly crude and caustic terms, he blamed effeminate men, especially homosexuals, for abstraction's stranglehold on contemporary art.

Far be it from me to raise my hands in any moral horror over the ways and tastes of individuals. If young gentlemen, or old ones either, wish to wear women's underwear and cultivate extraordinary manners it is all right with me. But it is not all right with the art which they affect and cultivate. It is not all right when, by ingratiation or subtle connivance, precious fairies get into positions of power and judge, buy, and exhibit American pictures on a base of nervous whim and under the sway of those overdelicate refinements of taste characteristic of their kind.

At the League, Jackson and his fellow Monday night musicians leapt to Benton's defense, forming what Axel Horn called a "hard core of devotees . . . who carried [Regionalism] to the level of a cult." In the lunchroom, where Benton was increasingly referred to simply as "that son-of-a-bitch," Jackson joined his teacher's attacks on Picasso and echoed his homophobic diatribes. "He liked that kind of talk," Philip Pavia remembers. Without the leavening of Benton's agile intellect, however, Jackson's argument seldom rose above "a very primitive level." When Mervin Jules tried to explain his view that the Impressionists' use of color was more "realistic" than the modeled forms of "realists" like Benton, Jackson responded with a terse "Oh, yeah? That's *your* folly." Pavia recalls trying unsuccessfully to explain to Jackson the hypocrisy of Benton rejecting European influence while embracing the "wop culture" of the Italian Renaissance. "Jackson wasn't a talker," says Milton Resnick. "He would challenge you, but it was all more like 'You want to *fight?*' " Jackson's visceral tactics proved more useful at a public forum at the John Reed Club where Benton's "outlandish statements" so agitated the audience that the meeting erupted into a "yelling shambles." When an "enraged Commie" threw a chair at the podium, Jackson and his fellow students jumped onto the stage and formed a cordon around their leader.

Soon the number of students in Benton's class began to fall precipitously, from twenty-nine when Jackson first enrolled in 1930, to only seven in the fall of 1932. Benton's raw language and the harshness of his criticism had always frightened away the "menopause crowd" of elderly women who made up much of the League's total enrollment. "If they signed up, they soon gave up," recalls Mervin Jules, another of Benton's student bodyguards. But now, with the temperature of the public debate rising, attendance had fallen perilously close to the League's unofficial minimum. Shaken by the prospect that the course might be canceled, Benton sent Jackson and the remaining "faithful Bentonites" in the class to the League cafeteria during the next monthly sign-up period to recruit "new, naive, and uninformed" students to fill the class. "Conscripts like that didn't last very long," says Jules, "but at least they met the quota."

Despite Jackson's fierce loyalty, Benton was increasingly preoccupied by the larger controversy, and their time together dwindled. Now when Jackson came to Hudson Street for dinner, other guests—critics, writers, journalists, anyone who might help advance the cause—held center stage. "We had many ardent discussions at our table with dinner guests," Benton recalled years later, "[but] Jack never entered these. . . . He had no verbal facility. He had read too little anyhow to be at ease with the subjects discussed." In particular, Jackson

seemed incapable of understanding the theories behind Regionalism: "He followed a Benton *example* but this was in matter of form rather than of content,"
Benton observed. "He did not have . . . my interests in history." Jackson still
posed for occasional sketches and helped prepare Benton's gesso panels; he
still played in the Monday night musicales; but more and more he felt cheated
and abandoned by his mentor.

In the late fall of 1932, when rumors spread that Benton was being considered for another major mural commission, Jackson saw an opportunity to
recover his lost place. Despite Benton's refusal to hire him for the Whitney
murals the previous summer ("Jack would not have been qualified for such
work," Benton wrote), Jackson began working on a series of clay and plasticine
models, painted black and white, like those his teacher had done in preparation
for the New School murals. Whitney Darrow remembers Jackson's crude maquettes as "swirling objects, objects with interesting curves and strong forces"
which he anxiously brought to the League for Benton's critique. According to
Mervin Jules, who also submitted maquettes for Benton's approval, there was
never any doubt about their purpose: "We were all hopeful that we might get
to work on a mural."

In December 1932, Benton accepted a commission from the state of Indiana
to paint a mural depicting Indiana's "social history" for an exhibit at the 1933
Chicago World's Fair, a task that would take eight months. In the end, he
avoided deciding which students to take with him by taking none. Before
leaving, however, he did help arrange for Jackson to become a full member of
the League, entitling him to use the graphics workshop on Saturdays. It was
an honor that offered little consolation.

Only days after Benton left, Jackson received word that his real father was
seriously ill.

In fact, Roy Pollock had been ill for some time. He was only fifty-five years
old and still stronger than any of his sons, but the years of road work and camp
living had taken their toll, both visible and invisible. In a photograph that he
gave to Frank during the summer of 1930, he stares at the camera, tight-lipped
as always, holding his huge saddle-leather hands like a schoolboy, his bright
blue eyes struggling behind folds of tired flesh. For all the physical rigors of his
life, his real suffering had not been at nature's hands.

Not that the elements hadn't inflicted their share of injuries. Ever since
Cody, winters had been especially hard on Roy—"too many cold drafts and
too little hard work," he would say. During the previous few winters at the
county road camp near Wrightwood, colds and bouts of flu had become as
inevitable as snow. So no one thought anything of it when he came home for
the New Year's holiday on the last day of 1932 feeling unusually tired and
running a fever. Assuming it was again flu, Stella nursed him over the weekend, and he returned to camp in time for work on Monday, January 2. With
Sande's job threatened and Jay in and out of work, Roy's paycheck was more

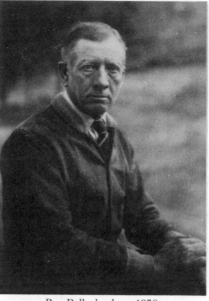

Roy Pollock, about 1930

vital than ever to the family's survival. As soon as he was gone, Stella left to spend a few days with a friend in Riverside.

After only two days at camp, Roy collapsed and came home. Unable to reach Stella by phone, Marie Levitt, who was visiting at the time, and whom the family already treated like a daughter-in-law, did what she could to make him comfortable. She didn't need a doctor to tell her his condition was more serious than flu. Sande and Jay agreed: their father would never miss work for something as simple as a common cold. When Stella finally returned, she reacted with a calmness that startled Marie: "It seemed like she was prepared to withstand anything." Nevertheless, she agreed, without her usual resistance, to take Roy to the French Hospital on College Street in central Los Angeles, where, after a series of inconclusive tests, doctors suggested it was perhaps flu after all. "They said, 'Go home and rest, and sit in the sun, and you'll get better,' " Marie remembers.

But Roy didn't get better. Instead, for three weeks, he fought increasingly prolonged spells of weakness, fever, nausea, and sweats. His temperature hovered around 100 degrees. Stella searched her red-leather-bound cookbook for the scribbled notes indicating that, on some day over the previous thirty years, Roy had liked a particular recipe. But even his appetite faded in and out, putting him for long periods beyond the reach of her most potent medicine. Despite his deteriorating condition, Stella kept the news of his illness from Charles, Frank, and Jackson for as long as possible. In a letter she wrote to Jackson shortly before his birthday, however, between reports on old friends like Reuben Kadish and cheerful inquiries about summer plans, her fears show through:

Los Angeles has sure been hard hit this year earthquakes then Griffeth park fire over one hundred men burned to death the million $ hill fire that destroyed the water shed back of Montrose & Glendale that is why the floods was so terrible through that section lots worse than ever was told in the papers over three hundred killed lots of bodys they never will find.

In fact, Jackson may already have heard about Roy's condition through Marie, who, increasingly distraught over the lack of improvement and the inadequacy of the prescribed treatment, had already broken the family silence in a letter to Frank.

Finally, on Monday, January 30, with Roy's temperature at 102 degrees and the spells growing more severe, Stella and Marie took him to Los Angeles County General Hospital on North State Street in East Los Angeles where Marie had arranged for her uncle, Dr. S. S. Rynin, to examine him. The same day, Jay informed his brothers in New York of Dr. Rynin's preliminary diagnosis: "Malignant Anaconditis . . . a bad case of heart leakage." His description of the affliction was crude—"the heart muscle develops on the inside as well as on the outside leaving no room to take care of the blood rushing in"—but it clearly conveyed the gravity of the situation. "It will be awfully hard to impress on [Dad's] mind to be reasonable in activity, if not some strain might end it any time." In the same letter, Jay reported that Sande had finally lost the last part-time remnants of his job at the *Times*. For a while, at least, Roy would continue to receive a percentage of his wages, but that would not last long.

News of Roy's illness took Jackson by surprise. The same day Jay's letter arrived, he sat down to write his father. In typical Pollock fashion, there are no overt pleas for or professions of love, just a strained effort to prove to his father that he is worthy of it. He talks of school and classes that are "damned hard work." "If I'm able to learn anything," he writes of a new class, appealing to Roy's respect for perseverance, "I'll take it full day and stick with it for three or four years—then the rest of my life." In response to his father's persistent doubts about his ability to support himself as an artist, Jackson writes, "artists are having it better now than before . . . the pot bellied financiers are turning to art as an escape from the some what blunt and forceful reality of today."

In a kind of desperate refrain, Jackson returns again and again to Roy's socialist rhetoric. New York life is "hard on the bums," he writes, "[but] after all, they are the well-to-do of this day. They don't have as far to fall." He defends Benton as a worthy model because "he has lifted art from the stuffy studio into the world and happenings about him, which has a common meaning to the masses." He urges his father not to worry about money, because "no one has it. The system is on the rocks so no need try to pay rent and all the rest of the hokum that goes with the price system." Finally, in closing, he invokes his father's tireless optimism: "We have had extremely fine wheather as a matter of fact it has, fore the most part, been like spring—a bit chilly at times, but just enough to put some pep in a fellow."

By mid-February, tests had confirmed Dr. Rynin's diagnosis. Roy Pollock was suffering from "malignant endocarditis," a bacterial infection of the valves of the heart. Since the bright days on the Phoenix ranch, Roy had known he had a "leaking heart valve," caused perhaps by a childhood bout with rheumatic fever, or an even earlier malformation in the womb. Perhaps he did not know—perhaps he chose to ignore—that a leaking heart was a vulnerable heart, that the harder he worked, the faster it leaked and the more vulnerable he became. "It is a case of too much hard work," Jay wrote the brothers in New York, "his strong muscular body being overtaxed, until it became a weakness."

Once the diagnosis was confirmed, the outcome was inescapable. "It is fatal," Jay wrote. "Doctors admit they are helpless, it may linger on for a year or end in a week."

Even at the time, some members of the family sensed an eerie appropriateness in Roy's illness, a black poetry that Frank—next to Roy, the most poetic soul in the family—captured half jokingly in the epitaph, "My father died of a broken heart." Roy's affliction was due not to a chance bacterium snagging on a healthy heart, but to an inherent defect as incurable as a childhood of loss and alienation, as indelible as the image of a dying mother in an Iowa farmhouse. As far as Roy had traveled away from Tingley—down the Mississippi, to Wyoming, Arizona, and California—as hard as he had worked to heal the defect of a loveless, exploitative family, he could never stop the leak. "I sometimes feel that my life has been a failure," he had written Jackson five years before, "but in this life we can't undo the things that are past we can only endeavor to do the best possible now."

Stella received the news stoically and insisted that no one tell Roy. In his letter, Jay warned his brothers: "We have not told Dad of the seriousness of his trouble, so in your letters don't mention that part." When Roy returned from the hospital soon afterward, Stella chatted about arrangements for the summer and laid plans for a trip to New York so Roy could meet his first daughter-in-law. To make his days more comfortable, she opened the convertible couch, put on a second mattress, and piled it with pillows so he could sit up and see out the east windows in the dining room "the beautiful golden hills" that led like timeworn steps to the San Gabriel Mountains beyond. On a clear day, he could see the white shroud of Old Baldy suspended in the sky above Wrightwood. Stella gave him what she could—"sunshine fresh air and flowers"—but the "drenching nightsweats" and high temperature only grew worse. The constant pain he bore "without a murmur." Marie and Arloie came often while Sande and Jay joined the millions looking for work. On February 28, Roy's fifty-sixth birthday, a telegram arrived from Charles, Frank, Jackson, and Elizabeth. "He enjoyed hearing from you boy's," Stella wrote back, "did him so much good for he was proud of each one."

On Saturday morning, March 4, Roy Pollock turned on his radio and waited to hear the new President, Franklin D. Roosevelt, begin his inaugural address, wondering, along with tens of millions of other anxious Americans huddled around their radios, "what Roosevelt's answer to disaster [would] be." According to Frederick Lewis Allen, it was a chilly, gray day in Washington, D.C., but the announcer was filled with "the synthetic good cheer of his kind, bearing down hard on the note of optimism, in fact, for he [knew] that worried and frightened people [were] listening to him." After the oath was administered, another voice came though the crackling ether: a strong, Yankee voice. "President Hoover, Mr. Chief Justice, my friends," it began:

> This is preeminently the time to speak the truth, frankly and boldly. Nor need we shrink from honestly facing conditions in our country today. This great nation will endure as it has endured, will revive and will prosper. So, first of all, let me assert my firm belief that the only thing we have to fear is fear itself.

No one could have savored the moment more than Roy Pollock. For forty years he had seen the folly and injustice of the economic system, a system that had brought a full measure of hardship to his own life, from his childhood of alienated labor, through his high school days as Tingley's lone, embattled socialist, and into a life buffeted and finally defeated by market forces—crop prices, war quotas, land speculation—that even his powerful hands could not control. When the voice on the radio blamed "the rules of the exchange of mankind's goods" for the disaster that had befallen the country, it was almost as if his old hero Eugene V. Debs had returned to claim his victory. "The money changers have fled from their high seats in the temple of our civilization."

The speech was over in less than ten minutes, but Roy's elation lasted the rest of the day as he searched the airwaves eagerly for newscasts to hear the reactions. At times, Jay found it hard to believe his father was as sick as the doctors said he was. "He took it all in a fine spirit and fighting," he remembers. The next morning, Sunday, the radio was on again early, in time for the first bulletins that Roosevelt had declared the following week a national "bank holiday," officially extending the "holidays" that most states had already imposed to stem the tide of bank closings. The radio stayed on through the live broadcast of the Mormon Tabernacle Choir from Salt Lake City, which opened and closed with the beckoning lines of a Mormon hymn:

> Come, come, Ye Saints,
> No toil or labor fear;
> But with joy wend your way.

Soon afterward, around noon, Roy began to complain about shortness of breath. The pain followed—"great pain," Jay remembers. "[We] thought the critical time was near." But Stella resisted calling a doctor; shortness of breath, she explained later, "[was] the only thing that seemed to be the trouble." For almost six hours, after a lifetime of silence, Roy cried out while Stella tried to calm and comfort him.

Finally, at about six o'clock, Jay left to bring the doctor. For the next two and a half hours, Roy and Stella were alone together. She held him tightly as he struggled for breath, thinking, she said later, about how "her parents had made fun of her because she was being courted by a socialist, the only one in the county at that time." She reassured herself that Roy would never want to live with an incurable disease—they had talked about it once, in the abstract —especially one that kept him inside, stockaded in pillows, separated from the land whose moods he knew so well. She herself had tried that in the first years of their marriage, to bring him inside, into the Victorian parlor of her girlhood dream, into the city house in Cody with its lace curtains, into the chalet bungalow in Chico, even into the frontier finery of the Janesville hotel. But, as in Phoenix, he was always running outside again, even in his Sunday suit, to get his big hands dirty, looking in the Arizona sand for the fragrant black soil and endless furrows of *his* boyhood dream. For Roy, inside was a place where nightmares happened, where his mother and sister had died, where his father had abandoned him, where Matt Pollock had trapped him, Lizzie had broken him, and Stella and her boys had betrayed him. But he was inside now, cradled in Stella's arms, breathing harder and harder, drawn by the old emptiness that Becky McCoy had left when she died.

At about eight-thirty, just as Jay was opening the door, Roy looked at Stella and tried to speak. "Mother," he began in a gasping whisper, "I don't think I can last till morning . . . " He wanted to say more, Stella thought, but before he could, his flawed heart finally gave out. She held him for a long time. The lone socialist of Ringgold County had finally come in from the field.

After calling Sande in Riverside and arranging for the body to be removed, Jay drove to the Western Union office and, at 1:27 on the morning of March 6, sent a telegram to his brothers in New York: "Dad passed on 8:30 tonight we can take care of everything."

16

OUT OF THE VOID

In New York, the long-awaited telegram stirred little apparent grief. Charles left a message at the Columbia law library: "Tell Frank that his father has died." Even after the message was relayed, Frank had to be coaxed into taking the rest of the day off. "I already knew Dad was dying," he explains. By late morning, the three brothers had gathered in Charles's studio for a reading of the telegram and a "moment of silence." They quickly dismissed as too expensive the possibilities of telephoning or traveling to Los Angeles for the funeral. Besides, they couldn't get at what little money they had—Roosevelt had closed the banks. "The fact that we couldn't go to the funeral didn't really affect us much," Frank recalls. "A funeral was something we had no experience with." At Charles's direction, they agreed to write letters.

Throughout the gathering, Jackson remained stone silent. "I simply have no memory of any effect [Dad's death] had on Jack," says Charles. Frank, too, noticed Jackson's odd calm but dismissed it: "Dad was a father to Jack for a much shorter period of time. And Jack seemed to be able to withstand these shockers without tears. I can't remember his ever crying in his adult life." A few days later, Jackson mailed a short letter to Stella, Sande, and Jay.

> I really can't believe Dad is gone. With all your letters we were unable to fully realize the seriousness of his illness. I wish we could go there—it is hard for you three to have to shoulder everything—and being there makes it much harder. Please, mother, don't let yourself get too upset—it is one thing unavoidable in life, but of course not as young as dad. I am glad, tho, that he was not bed fast for a long periods, and didn't have to suffer great pain . . . This is poorly put—but will let it go—and will write soon.

On Friday, March 10, Roy's body was immured in a crypt in the mausoleum at Forest Lawn Cemetery in Glendale. For a man who had worked and loved the earth, it was the final indignity, but burial was too expensive. Stella, Jay,

Sande, Marie, and Arloie drove the short distance to the cemetery at the foot of the Santa Monica Mountains, where they were joined by Robert and Margaret Louise Archbold, their cousins from Santa Ana, and a few of Roy's leather-skinned co-workers from the road crew at Wrightwood. It was, like Roy's life, a brief, modest ceremony that deserved tears but received none. Stella retained her stony poise throughout and never visited the crypt again.

Only hours after the mourners had dispersed, the earth began to shake. In just a few minutes, from Long Beach to Pasadena, hundreds of buildings, including Manual Arts High School, collapsed into piles of bricks and clouds of dust. According to local newspaper accounts, the vibrations of the quake shook extra eggs from chickens and caused the lame to walk. Even the hill under Montecito Drive felt the jolt. Mourners in another era might have taken the quake as some kind of omen, but the Pollock family went on about their lives as if nothing had changed.

In fact, everything had changed. For the first time, Charles and Frank rebuffed Stella's plea for them to return to Los Angeles that summer, even though they had made similar trips every summer for three years. In letters home, they claimed there was no money for travel, but even at the time, Marie doubted their excuses: "If it had been Stella who died and Roy who needed them," she remembers thinking, "you can be sure they would have made the effort." Poverty didn't prevent Frank from crossing the country to visit Marie that June, or Charles from traveling to the world's fair in Chicago. In late March, Jackson wrote his mother, "I can only wish that we were there with you. . . . We will all try and come home this summer," but when offered a free ride in May, he refused it. What all of Roy's sons were thinking, only Frank, Roy's favorite, was willing to admit: "Dad deserved a better break than he got. If he'd stayed in Arizona he would have been a tremendous success and become a wealthy man." Roy's death had begun sixteen years before when Stella insisted on leaving Phoenix; it wasn't the hard work that had killed him, it was the betrayal. "Mother still had her boys," Frank thought but dared not say. "She'd gotten what she wanted after all. She wanted this family and she'd got it. She didn't miss Dad too much."

For Jackson, Roy's death was every bit as devastating as his sudden departure from Janesville twelve years earlier. From the Carr Ranch to Santa Ynez, through a succession of arguments and fistfights, Jackson had never stopped angling hopefully for his father's approval. Increasingly, however, one obstacle had come between them: Jackson's desire to become an artist. While never overtly hostile to any of his son's ambitions, Roy Pollock had been convinced since Jackson's high school days, perhaps before, that his fifth son was feckless and irresolute, that an indulgent family had protected him for too long from hard work and self-reliance. In Roy's view, Jackson's interest in art represented just another refuge from the character-building vicissitudes of the real world;

and his life in New York, under Charles's aegis, just a perpetuation of the state of dependence that had always been at the root of his troubles.

Jackson had tried every means of appeasement. In a letter written only a few months after his summer at Wrightwood in 1931, he had tried mightily to persuade his father that his commitment to art was genuine and that an artist's "work" was little different from a road builder's:

> I'm going to school every morning and have learned what is worth learning in the realm of art. It is just a matter of time and work now for me to have that knowledge a part of me. A good seventy years more and I think I'll make a good artist—being a artist is life itself—living it I mean. And when I say artist I don't mean it in the narrow sense of the word—but the man who is building things—creating molding the earth—whether it be plains of the west—or the iron ore of Penn. Its all a big game of construction— some with a brush—some with a shovel.

On other occasions, he wrote admiringly of Benton, of his painting "jobs," of the sheer physical effort involved in large murals, and of his "struggle with the elements of every day experience." Benton was the kind of man Roy Pollock might have worked with or drunk with, Jackson told his father, a stranger to Stella's pretensions to culture and Charles's precious calligraphy; in short, an artist *and* a man. But the reality never lived up to the illusion Jackson labored to create. In December 1932, Benton refused to hire him as an assistant on the Indiana murals, and the League rejected his application for a teaching position (citing "bad habits"). To Roy Pollock, of course, any man who couldn't get a job, no matter what he called himself, was "just a bum."

In January, Jackson's situation took another turn for the worse when he enrolled in John Sloan's drawing class. He may have hoped that Sloan, whose career had begun with cartoons and whose paintings demonstrated a similar journalistic empathy for American anecdote, would be as indulgent a teacher as Benton. Like many other artists, Sloan had been inspired to switch from realism to modernism by the 1913 Armory Show and used his drawing class to introduce students to the "European" Cubism that Benton noisily denounced. Yet his conversion to modernism had somehow misfired. Instead of working toward a more radical painting style, he had developed a watchmaker's preoccupation with methodology and craft, focusing on a particular way of modeling a figure by shading with hatches and crosshatches to achieve sculptural volume.

Whatever it was, it was a world apart from Benton's "hollow and bump," his emphasis on rhythm even at the expense of proportion. After two years in the League, Jackson was suddenly adrift again; suddenly a beginner. "Benton tolerated Jack's attempts to draw," recalled Manuel Tolegian who, like Jackson, moved to Sloan's class after Benton's departure. "In fact, all of his teachers at the League were tolerant of him, all except John Sloan. But no matter how hard Jack tried, he just couldn't draw realistically. It was an impossibility."

In February, Jackson quit the class. A month later, Roy died and, with him, all hope of persuasion. No longer restrained by Bentonesque illusions, the old demons returned.

In March 1933, Jackson abandoned painting altogether. Long frustrated by his lack of facility, he forsook the tainted art of Charles and Stella and set out to create an artistic identity of his own, one that would appease the ghost of Roy Pollock.

He turned to sculpture.

As a young man, Roy had learned the rural mason's craft, laying foundations and sidewalks alongside his future father-in-law, John Robinson McClure. On his marriage certificate, he proudly listed his occupation as "mason." Jackson had undoubtedly heard his older brothers' stories of Roy's days in Cody, working at the rock-crushing plant, lugging ore samples, doing odd masonry jobs. Later, he had seen his father at work in Arizona and California, routing roads around rock formations, clearing boulders from roadbeds, and spreading gravel. Jackson's most vivid images of his father—working against the rock-strewn horizon in Phoenix, catching a gila monster behind a stone on Camelback Mountain, urinating on a flat rock near the Carr Ranch, trapped by a boulder at the Cherry Creek Indian Ruins, camping on the rim of the Grand Canyon—formed a web of unconscious associations that surfaced decades later in boulder-like sculptures and a fascination with earth-moving.

From the time Jackson was old enough to work, Roy had been openly urging him to study masonry and "do what is best for your own good." Even after Jackson left for New York, returning for summers at Wrightwood with enthusiastic accounts of Tom Benton and his new commitment to art, Roy reminded him that he needed "a method of making a living" and that masonry was a sellable skill. In strained populist rhetoric, Jackson responded that the work of the artist and the work of the mason were in fact the same thing. "That's the new artists job to construct with the carpenter—the mason," he wrote, referring to the construction of Rockefeller Center, which was rising only blocks from the Art Students League. "The art of life is *composition*—the planning—the fitting in of masses—activities." But his growing frustration with Benton's meticulous technique and Charles's head start made him increasingly receptive to Roy's injuction. "Sculptoring I think tho is my medium," he wrote in February 1932, in a transparent effort at reconciliation after the confrontation in Wrightwood. "I'll never be satisfied until I'm able to mould a mountain of stone, with the aid of a jack hammer, to fit my will. . . . I would like to get work in a rock quarry—or tomb stone factory—where I could make a little money and at the same time learn something about stone and the cutting of it." In January 1933, only days after hearing that his father had been taken to the hospital, Jackson enrolled in his first sculpture class.

Even as early as Chico, when he collected birds' eggs and brought them to his father for identification, Jackson had looked at objects with a sculptor's eye.

In Agnes Martin's clay modeling class at Manual Arts, his abstract figures had "found a bit of encouragement"—enough for him to join with a group of students who arranged to have their sculptures professionally fired and glazed. He had hauled dozens of blocks of limestone and sandstone to Manuel Tolegian's backyard where he would chip away at them tirelessly with a hammer and chisel. Jackson later told Tony Smith that "he originally came to New York to learn 'to sculpt like Michelangelo.' " Even after a year of total immersion in Benton's drawing class, he returned to Los Angeles in the summer of 1931 and, with the help of Reuben Kadish, fished a boulder from the Los Angeles River and spent long days pounding at it. "From the start, Jackson had an intense interest in sculpture," recalls Kadish, who twenty years later became a sculptor himself. "The whole time he was studying with Benton, he never lost that interest." By the summer of 1932, when Leonard Stark gave him a book on Michelangelo's sculpture, Jackson was already familiar with the works of John B. Flannagan, the brooding, alcoholic Irishman from North Dakota whose powerful, primitivistic little figures of rabbits, birds, and fish defied all the rules of neoclassical sculpture.

Despite this long-standing if erratic interest, Jackson was still a novice when he joined a stone-carving class at the Greenwich House annex on Jones Street in January 1933. What he lacked in training, however, he made up in conviction. "I have joined a class in stone carving in the mornings," he wrote his father proudly. "I think I like it. So far I have done nothing but try and flatten a round rock and my hand too, but it's great fun and damned hard work."

Jackson's teacher at Greenwich House was Ahron Ben-Shmuel, a thirty-year-old darkly handsome sculptor of Egyptian Jewish descent who, even in an art world filled with eccentrics, seemed as strange and exotic as Fedallah on the *Pequod*. Born Archie Levitt in New York, Ben-Shmuel had begun his career carving wooden forms for his taxidermist father, and after an apprenticeship as a "monumental carver," had assisted sculptor William Zorach. An insular, forbidding man, often described by friends as "angry," Ben-Shmuel considered students a necessary but unwelcome burden. "He wasn't a teacher at all," according to Isidore Grossman, Ben-Shmuel's apprentice in the late thirties. "He never talked to you about your work. He'd just give you a piece of stone and you'd carve away at it—and that was the last you'd see of him. "After Sloan's demands, Ben-Shmuel's indifference must have been a welcome relief to Jackson, even at the price of a flattened hand.

Despite their obvious differences, Ben-Shmuel, the Egyptian Jew, and Benton, the Missouri Welshman, had their similarities. Choleric, opinionated, vulgar, and exhibitionistic, Ben-Shmuel presented an even more exaggerated caricature of masculinity than Benton. "He was a very tough, off-the-streets-of-New-York guy," recalls Reuben Kadish. "Tough and foul-mouthed. Everything was 'fuck' and 'shit' and all the rest of it, which indicated that he wasn't going to be one of those faggy art types." Although never a drinker, he could out-Benton Benton in his outbursts of profanity and violence. "He had the

filthiest mouth in creation," recalls Nathan Katz, who had also heard Benton
in a rage, "and he didn't care who was around. He called his neighbors 'moron
motherfuckers' to their faces." Friends thought of him as a "gentle eccentric"
with "lots of personality" whose "outlandish" behavior was calibrated for shock
value. Enemies labeled him "weird," "nuts," and "crazy as a bedbug." Even
more so than Benton, he treated women with brutish, humiliating hostility.
"To him, they were always 'wenches' and 'bitches,' " recalls a student. "You
know, 'Bring my coffee, you bitch.' He was constantly talking about what a big
cocksman he was and how he liked to *fuck*." Yet, like Benton's, his tales of
conquest were purest fiction; he rarely socialized with women, and he married
late in life, leaving a trail of speculation about impotence and latent homosexuality.

Soon, Jackson was working as a studio boy at Ben-Shmuel's private studio
at 35 Jane Street, not far from Eighth Avenue. It was an old frame building
with an unpretentious door leading to an open courtyard where Ben-Shmuel
kept his blocks and often worked alfresco even in the winter. Upstairs, the
Cubist painter Byron Browne kept an apartment and studio. Nathan Katz, who
was only fourteen when he served as Ben-Shmuel's apprentice, recalls the job
as "helping him with what he was working on and cleaning up the studio."
Katz also kept his own sculpture there and recalls his teacher as "very tough to
work with. *Very* tough." Like Jackson, Ben-Shmuel was an undisciplined
worker and the work, haphazard. Depending on his mood, months could
elapse between the first hammer blow on the pitcher, a crude chisel, to break
the corners off a big block of Barre granite and the last ring of a flatter, more
precise chisel on the lips of a young woman. During periods of activity, the
incessant pounding of the iron hammer was accompanied by a running monologue of angry, articulate invective. "He thought everybody was pretty terrible," Katz recalls. "If he liked you, he liked you. If he didn't, he hated you
vehemently." But the turbulence of Ben-Shmuel's conversation never reached
his chisel. Years of carving—from tombstones to doorsills, in everything from
velvety Tennessee marble to odd chunks of domestic sandstone picked out of
demolition rubbish—had given him a feeling for the stone, the craftsman's
"sixth sense" he called it, which told him more about the form in the stone
than his eyes ever could. Although he occasionally worked in fired clay or cast
in bronze, and his style ranged from the near-abstraction of Flannagan to the
rounded monumentalism of his mentor Zorach, the underlying aesthetic was
always that of the carver. "He knew how to cut granite," says Milton Resnick,
a friend in later years. "He knew his tools and he knew how to keep them
working. He knew all the tricks—he thought of them as secrets of a kind."

If Ben-Shmuel was proud and pugnacious like Tom Benton, it was partly
because he, too, was fighting a war with the past. A few decades earlier, he
wouldn't have been considered a sculptor at all, or even an artist. In the eighteenth and nineteenth centuries, a "sculptor's" work began not with a pitcher
and a block of stone but with elaborate drawings and small maquettes. From

these a wood-and-metal armature was built on which the sculptor worked bits of clay, slowly building up the forms: shaping, kneading, and smoothing the pliable material into mythical figures, allegorical scenes, portraits of the famous or wealthy, or one of the period's other favorite subjects, most of them only a few feet tall. The *Balzac* of Auguste Rodin, the *Seated Lincoln* of Daniel Chester French, even Bartholdi's Statue of Liberty all took shape as lamp-size objects on an atelier tabletop. When finished, the small clay original could be transformed, via a plaster cast, into bronze—or it could first be enlarged to life-size or larger in plaster or clay, using a pointing machine, before being cast. Or it could be carved. Only at that point was a stone carver brought in and a suitable block of stone secured. The carver would take a series of precise measurements of the original with a pointing machine and transfer them to the uncut block, indicating where stone needed to be chipped away. Early carvers used a plain hammer and chisel to transfer the design to marble; their successors worked with compressed-air chisels. Either way, the result was an exact or an enlarged copy, roughed in and often finished by the carver, not the sculptor. Even Rodin typically left every hammer stroke to other hands. For the most part, hammers, gouges, and chisels were the carver's tools, not the sculptor's. Carving was a craft; sculpting was an art. Sculpture not done from a clay model —building decorations, monument inscriptions, and the like—was tradesmen's work.

The technique had deep roots and a distinguished lineage. The sculptors of the Belle Epoque who preceded Ben-Shmuel inherited it from Michelangelo, who borrowed it, in turn, from the Romans, who stole it from the late Greek sculptors, who were the first to free stone of its own weight, modeling nymphs in mid-flight and windblown tunics that defied gravity. During the first decades of the twentieth century, however, in the same revolt against academicism that produced Picasso's *Guitar* and Brancusi's *Kiss*, American artists like Flannagan and Zorach denounced the traditional division between sculptor and carver. The only authentic sculptor, they argued, was the sculptor who worked directly with his material. In 1921, Horace Brodsky, an American critic who championed the cause of "direct carving," dismissed traditional sculpture as "a sea of marble *patisserie*."

Jackson responded enthusiastically to the theories of Flannagan and Zorach as related by Ben-Shmuel with characteristic vehemence and vulgarity. Only a month after joining the Greenwich House workshop, he quit Sloan's drawing class at the League and enrolled instead in a second sculpture class, Robert Laurent's evening "modeling" class. Laurent was an Americanized Frenchman—"a native of Brittany and Brooklyn"—whose direct carvings combined the naiveté of Flannagan's works with the Continental finesse of French modernism. "Quite delicious," wrote critic Henry McBride of Laurent's sculptures. "They betray all sorts of primitive touches inextricably interwoven with the present day feeling." Although he shared the new preference for working directly in stone and wood, Laurent felt equally comfortable modeling in clay or in plaster and frequently cast his larger works from plaster originals. Such flexibility, a benign disposition, and inherited wealth exempted him somewhat from the ideological wars being waged by the other leaders in the movement toward direct carving.

In Laurent's class, held nightly in the basement studio, as in Benton's, students worked from a nude model, beginning the week with a lump of clay scooped from the clay bin. "If what you did was good, you could cast it," recalls Philip Pavia, a classmate of Jackson's who had been sent to Italy to study sculpture by his caster-carver father. "If it wasn't, it would go back into the bin." The challenges were also the same as in Benton's class—proportion and control—and Jackson encountered the same "blocs" that frustrated him in every medium. Intimidated and insecure, he clung to the few techniques of which he could claim some mastery. "He just wanted to make small figures like the ones he did for Benton's murals," recalls Pavia who was, like most of the other students, a full-time sculptor and accomplished modeler. "He was just imitating Benton. There *we* were, serious sculptors, and here he was doing these little Bentonesque figures with big arms, workmen types." When Laurent saw these oddities on one of his twice-weekly visits, he was, as always, mildly encouraging. "He was really a fatherly type of teacher," Pavia recalls. "Whatever you did was all right with him. He just encouraged you. He didn't direct you too much." (A typical comment: "Well, you might take off a little bit dere and a little bit dere.") Behind the cultivated pleasantries, Laurent may have recognized what Pavia and the other students had seen, what Mrs. Martin had recognized four years before: "Pollock had the rhythm down," Pavia remembers. "He really had a feeling for it."

But a feeling for it wasn't enough to satisfy Jackson. Nor were the regular parties at Laurent's nearby apartment, or the after-class "field trips" to the speakeasy on Fifty-eighth Street where, in the twilight of Prohibition, the doors were always open and beer was suddenly legal. Laurent's class was, ultimately, another art class, rooted firmly in the same aesthetic and academic tradition as Sloan's or even Benton's.

With Roy Pollock's death in March, Jackson turned his back on that world and embraced his father's old demands: self-sufficiency and gainful employment. Immediately after hearing of Roy's death, he wrote Stella: "I had many things I wanted to do for you and Dad—now I'll do them for you, mother. Quit my dreaming and get them into material action. . . . I'm still lazying around with no definite indication of my earning anything thru my work." Three weeks later, he was still obsessed and unreconciled with his dead father. "I always feel I would like to have known Dad better," he wrote Stella, "that I would like to have done something for he and you—many words unspoken—and now he has gone in silence." Later the same week, Jackson finally did something for his father: he dropped out of Laurent's modeling class, and the League, and devoted himself exclusively to "sculpture"—or as he described it in his letters home, "cutting in stone." "It holds my interest deeply," he wrote. "I like it better than painting."

For the rest of the spring, Jackson worked with Ben-Shmuel at his studio on Jane Street and at the Greenwich House Annex where he was given access to space and materials in exchange for part-time janitorial work. Starting with an iron hammer and a pitcher, then switching to a chisel, he would chip at a small block for days before even a corner of a figure would begin to emerge from the void of stone. If the angle of the chisel was too deep or the hammer blow too hard, the block could crack through; too shallow or too soft, the chisel would ricochet harmlessly off the stone in a little explosion of dust. Like Ben-Shmuel, he worked without plans or drawings, just a vision of the image in the stone. After Benton's elaborate mural preparations, cubistic studies, and volumetric models, after Sloan's precise cross-hatching and Laurent's "little bit dere," Jackson must have thrilled at the manly directness of the carver's art, at the bravery of setting a cold chisel against a blank face of stone and just *beginning*.

True sculptors, Ben-Shmuel argued, were engaged in a process of discovery, "persistently searching in their own minds, [bringing] forth in three dimensions their personal and peculiar mental entrails." But while Ben-Shmuel could pick the image from his "mental entrails," project it into the stone, and hold it there for the weeks, or sometimes months, required to free it, Jackson's mind was in constant turmoil. The images rising out of his unconscious changed too quickly, the stone responded too slowly, each chip proved too conclusive. In drawing and painting, he had been able to work and rework his images, trying to fix them by recording their changes, often in different media, forcing the variations into a single furious image. The chisel, however, was both too slow and too final. The image would change from hammer stroke to hammer stroke, shifting in the void and sometimes fleeing altogether, forcing Jackson to abandon stones in various stages of incompletion. Axel Horn, who visited the Jones Street Annex, remembers Jackson's frustration. "Jack showed me some of the stones he was working on. They were incomplete and showed the evidence of a tremendous struggle. The material was resisting him horribly." Although he continued "cutting" for some time, Jackson must have realized early that sculpture—or at least Ben-Shmuel's kind of sculpture—wasn't suited to his imagination or his disposition. His "mental entrails" were too chaotic, too unsettled, too layered, too protean, for such a resistant, brittle, unforgiving medium.

Of the pieces Jackson did produce, only one reached completion; only one image remained fixed in his mind long enough for him to hammer it out of the void. Strangely for Jackson, who avoided painting or drawing faces whenever possible, it was a small stone head, a mere four inches tall. Only the face has fully emerged from the stone. It is the face of a dead man—sad but resigned. It is a death mask for Roy Pollock.

■   ■   ■

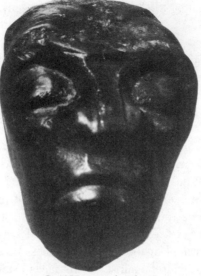

C. 1933, stone, height 4"

Late in the spring, Jackson accompanied Ben-Shmuel to his summer place near Upper Black Eddy, Pennsylvania, an old house at the end of miles of double-rut country roads in rural Bucks County northeast of Philadelphia. The house was surrounded by a huge stone yard, an unkempt garden of Ben-Shmuel's favorite materials: limestone, sandstone, Tennessee marble, and a geography of granites: Westerly, Barre, Scotch, and Coopersburg. The yard served also as a stockade to protect Ben-Shmuel from hostile neighbors. "The natives hated him because of his vile mouth," recalls Isidore Grossman, a Ben-Shmuel apprentice who later assisted Jacques Lipchitz. "He was always cursing and getting into fistfights with the locals and I would have to defend him." While in Bucks County that spring, Jackson met a lesser-known sculptor named Richard Davis, a slight, delicate man in his late twenties who considered himself another of Ben-Shmuel's "students." The scion of a wealthy New York family, Davis was also an avid collector of his teacher's work and frequently made the hundred-mile pilgrimage to Upper Black Eddy from his own summer house near Cresco in the Poconos. Jackson undoubtedly looked forward to such visits as a release from the tyranny of Ben-Shmuel's moodiness and as a chance to break the unaccustomed dry spells with his teetotaling teacher by sampling the local beer with the cosmopolitan Davis.

Despite Ben-Shmuel's volatile temper and dark moods, however, despite the prospects of three months without alcohol, Jackson decided to spend the summer in Upper Black Eddy as a studio boy rather than cross the country with Frank or Manuel Tolegian in order to visit his mother—as he had promised he would. "[The apprenticeship] will afford [Jack] an opportunity to acquire some practical experience," Frank wrote Marie, struggling to explain Jackson's change of heart, "and the summer in the open will do him good. He regrets

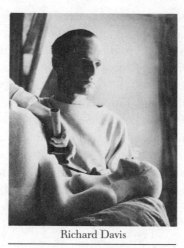

Richard Davis

not coming home, but money there is scarce, and he doesn't want to tax the family."

In fact, Jackson's failure to visit his mother in the months following Roy's death was part of a pattern. During the same months, he avoided Charles and Frank as well, spending great stretches of time with Ben-Shmuel on Jane Street or in Bucks County. In early April, he moved with Charles and Elizabeth from Carmine Street to a larger apartment at 46 East Eighth Street—an entire floor for $35 a month—but stayed only a short time. Within weeks, he left for Ben-Shmuel's Pennsylvania house to spend the summer.

There is no record of what happened when Jackson arrived in Upper Black Eddy in May of 1933 or why he suddenly departed soon afterward. It may have been loneliness—he was, for the first time, completely on his own, without a family member within hundreds of miles. It may have been the discovery of some previously unknown aspect of Ben-Shmuel's eccentric character. He was capable, for example, of flashes of extreme violence as well as bizarre personal habits. "He had a pathological hatred of butter," Grossman remembers. "If he saw it on the table, he would throw it off, like he saw the devil, and say, 'You get syphilis from butter.'" Or it may have been that the lack of alcohol over-taxed Jackson's limited powers of abstinence and self-control. Whatever the reasons, he waited only until Richard Davis's first visit of the season to desert. It was not, apparently, an amicable parting. He never returned to the studio on Jane Street or to the Greenwich workshop, and seldom mentioned Ben-Shmuel's name again.

The remaining months of the summer Jackson spent at Davis's even more isolated cabin on the slopes of Seven Pine Mountain in the Poconos. Hidden in a dark, thickly wooded hollow known locally as the Devil's Hole, the house was spare and rustic, with big fireplaces in the living room and bedroom and a potbellied stove in the kitchen. Even on the brightest summer days, leaves obscured the sunlight almost completely and the silence was broken only by the rustle of squirrels and deer, the murmur of pheasant, and, occasionally, the glottal call of a wild turkey. "Going into that hollow was like going into Count Dracula's castle," recalls a local resident who often hunted in the area. "It got real foggy in there and you had to be careful not to shoot somebody by accident or get lost."

How Jackson spent the long summer days in Devil's Hole is not known. Davis told his part-time maid, Ettabelle Storm, that Jackson was his "house-boy," although she continued to perform her usual housekeeping chores. The two men apparently sketched together in the outlying studio, which was connected to a second small room by a covered breezeway. Occasionally, Davis would arrage for models to come from New York and pose for a weekend of sketching and sometimes modeling in clay. When he felt a clay sculpture was particularly successful, he would take it to the city and have it cast. The two men quickly established a domestic routine. They would come to Storm's house in the morning for milk from her cow and vegetables from her garden; later, they would cook the evening meal together—often Davis's favorite, lamb stew, which Jackson learned to prepare. When there was a square dance at the fire hall in nearby Cresco, Davis and Jackson would accompany Storm and her new husband. "We'd have them to our house first," Storm remembers. "We'd play cards and drink beer. We made our own beer. Then we'd go dancing. I was only seventeen or eighteen and Jack was just a kid like me." More than a few attractive young girls at the fire hall dances admired the "good-looking" older man and his "tall, husky" younger companion, Storm recalls, but "there were never any girlfriends. No, no, no. No girls at all." Several times during the summer, Jackson and Davis made the two-hour journey into New York and stayed at Davis's penthouse on Central Park West.

Beyond these bare outlines, nothing is known of the three months that Jackson and Davis lived together. Although Jackson continued to visit the Pocono cabin frequently throughout the fall and winter, he never spoke of the summer or of Davis to his family or friends. Instead, he used Davis's support to distance himself even further from his mother and brothers. With summer earnings—or perhaps with Davis's direct subsidy—he rented a room in a brownstone on East Fifty-eighth Street and tried for the first time to live on his own. Despite Benton's return from Indiana and the proximity of his rooming house, he failed to register for classes at the League. He still visited now and then—fellow students recall seeing him occasionally in George Bridgman's drawing class and once in the lunchroom arguing with Arshile Gorky—but many of the old friendships languished. He stopped writing letters home and, in conversation, no longer mentioned his family or bragged of Charles's accomplishments.

Asserting his independence was only the first step in what appeared to be a desperate new drive to prove his manhood. Although no longer in Benton's class, he faithfully attended the revived Monday night meetings of the Harmonica Rascals, reveling more than ever in Benton's cartoonish bravado and bonhomie. When visiting for supper, he would linger after Tom left for his evening class to savor Rita's flirtatious attention, then return to the rooming house and hint heavily to friends of their illicit affair. The rumor spread quickly, fed by Jackson's calculated silence and drunken braggadocio. At League parties, alcohol—available legally as of December 5, 1933, for the first time in thirteen years—became the magic touchstone. Around women, it transformed him into "a dog in spring," alternately insatiable and abusive. Axel Horn recalled seeing Jackson at one party "roaring like a Satyr in hot pursuit of a frightened nymph through the corridors. . . . Out of the mildest and most recessive person I knew had emerged a fire-breathing dragon!" Around men, it transformed him into a "wild Indian," "a maniac," a "Mr. Hyde." "He was a mean drunk," Mervin Jules remembers. "We often had to pull him away from an argument in order to prevent a fight." At a Puerto Rican dance hall in Harlem, his pugnacity triggered a knife fight with "strangers" that could easily have proved fatal, although he apparently emerged from it unscathed. "If Americans get in a fight," he reportedly told a friend afterward, "they punch each other. But they don't have to die. Up there, in Harlem, somebody has to die."

Not even a brush with death could sober him up for long, however. Around Christmas time, the Harmonica Rascals were invited to perform at the town house of Joel Elias Spingarn, a professor at Columbia and social activist who often invited groups of like-minded friends to his elegant house on the Upper West Side to share views on human rights, economic reform, and the threat of fascism in Europe. For this holiday get-together, a formal affair, Spingarn's young wife, Amy, a former student at the Art Students League, had hired additional staff, laid in extra supplies of liquor and a banquet of hors d'oeuvres, and made special arrangements for her former teacher Tom Benton and his little harmonica group to entertain her guests.

When Benton arrived, he was accompanied by Jackson, Manuel Tolegian, and the other players, as well as Maria Piacenza, Rita Benton's attractive niece who had only recently left high school in Brooklyn and entered the "sophisticated Bohemian" world of her uncle Tom. At the Spingarn house, "the maids greeted you and butlers circled around handing out gold-tipped cigarettes," Piacenza recalls. "I'd never seen anything like it." The group played through its repertoire with Benton stomping the floor, Tolegian playing the harmonica, and Jackson struggling with the mouth harp. "I didn't know what to think about Jackson," Piacenza remembers. "He was a beautiful young man, a very handsome boy, and very silent. It was very difficult to communicate with him except when he was drunk, which was often."

When the music stopped, Jackson headed straight for the bar.

After a few drinks, Maria could see that Jackson "was just looking for a fight. There was a certain strangeness about him; he was suddenly offended by the bourgeois atmosphere." At one point, he staggered up to a couple of men in tuxedos and muttered something about "stuffed shirts." Fists flew, and the bar

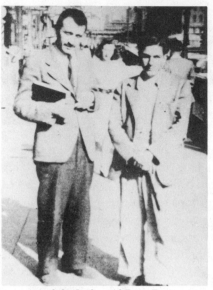

Arshile Gorky and Peter Busa

was demolished. After that, "it was a free-for-all," Piacenza recalls. "All I remember is that Jackson grabbed my hand and we ran, because the cops were coming. I felt badly because these people hadn't been anything but kind and hospitable. But Jackson was exultant, so thrilled with his bruised knuckles."

If Jackson hoped to win Maria's girlish heart with such derring-do, it must have come as a blow when she began dating Manuel Tolegian. Ever since the summer at Wrightwood, the two old friends had been drifting apart, but the combination of Tolegian's one-man show at the Ferargil Galleries in 1934 and his success with Maria proved to be more than Jackson could tolerate. Joe Delaney recalls a drinking bout one night about this time when Jackson blurted out, "I don't give a damn about Tolegian!" Although he later denied it, Manuel told several people that sometime during the fall, he awoke in the middle of the night and saw Jackson standing over his bed, drunk and brandishing a knife. Piacenza tried to mend the rift by inviting both men to a spaghetti dinner on the roof of her apartment building, but they immediately fell to drinking and quarreling. "Then they had this crazy fight," Piacenza recalls. "They rolled around on the roof and at one point they rolled out to the edge. I was just in terror. I *knew* they were going to fall off and I'd find them both dead at the bottom."

About this time, Jackson found a new friend, one untainted by the past, a short, soulful young man named Peter Busa, who had just taken a room at the boardinghouse on Fifty-eighth Street and enrolled at the League. A refugee from college—after two years at Carnegie Tech he could no longer afford the tuition—and from an Italian-American family in Pittsburgh whose savings had been wiped out by the crash, Busa provided the perfect ear for Jackson's

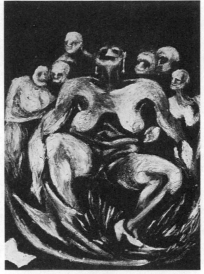

Woman, c. 1933, oil on Masonite,
14⅛″ × 10½″

mounting anxieties. The two spent long hours together in the little rooms on Fifty-eighth Street ridiculing their suspicious and parsimonious Irish landlady who served baked beans every night, discussing Benton's methods, sketching, and drinking. Like Jackson, Busa had only recently lost his father, a painter of church murals from Sicily. He, too, had left his family to perform a vague but urgent penance. In a soft, confessional voice, he told Jackson of being assaulted by the "wolves" while riding the rails and, in turn, assaulting the next fresh young prey that entered the jungle. "That common experience of riding the rails gave us something to talk about from the first day," Busa remembers. "It sealed our friendship."

The conversations with Busa were Jackson's first opportunity to explore territory that had always been forbidden in his own family. "He told me that he had a problem and that he was trying to go through with it," says Busa. "And I said, 'Is it alcoholism?' and he said, 'No, that's only part of it. It's what causes alcoholism.' But when he started to get to his problem, I would say, 'What is it?' and he would break down and cry and say he didn't know himself." At that point, Busa would just listen patiently. "I was sure he had had encounters with men," Busa remembers, "and I think he was troubled by some of those experiences. He didn't need anybody to tell him he had homosexual drives. All I used to say was 'Any port in a storm.'"

Throughout the fall and winter, Jackson caromed between weekend visits to the cabin in Devil's Hole and free-fall binges of alcohol and machismo; between soul-searching conversations with Peter Busa and random explosions of anxious rage. "He was unrecognizable from one minute to the next," recalls Maria Piacenza. Busa, who heard the tales of each new outrage through the League grapevine, was puzzled by "the two Jackson Pollocks." "I was aware

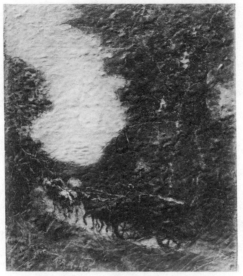

Sentimental Journey, Albert Pinkham Ryder,
oil on canvas, 12″ × 10″

of the contradictions in his behavior. So I said to him, 'Hell, all this crap about you going around and raising hell—I find you very gentle.' " To which Jackson replied, "Never mistake gentleness for weakness." The spiral of self-abuse—the spiral from which his family had rescued him two years before—was again spinning out of control. Friends found it harder and harder to coax him home "upright." He would careen into the street, daring cars to "run me over," punch out store windows, then lapse into "comatose" silence. Binges that two years before would have ended on a friend's couch now ended abruptly in the gutter. At a League party on a night boat up the Hudson, with the sound of jazz echoing across the dark river, Jackson unscrewed all the light bulbs, throwing the crowd into darkness, then climbed unsteadily to the top of the railing and flailed about wildly. "He was waving his arms," recalls Philip Pavia. "He called out, 'I'm gonna jump. I'm gonna jump,' and we all laughed our heads off." Suddenly Jackson turned his back to the crowd and looked into the darkness as if he really *was* going to jump. Nathan Katz, Bernie Steffen, and several others grabbed him and wrestled him to the deck where he turned strangely docile and vacant. "Jackson always left you with a feeling of emptiness," says George McNeil, "as if he was living in an abyss."

Sometime during the tumultuous fall of 1933, Jackson returned to painting. Presumably he continued to sculpt on weekend visits to the Devil's Hole cabin, but it would be another ten years before he returned openly to the medium. Yet the emotional needs that had compelled him toward sculpture remained unmet. When he began to paint again, the images that emerged were not the postcard western scenes of Tom Benton; they were dark, brooding images of death. Working from a skull he had "borrowed" from Bridgman's anatomy studio, he painted the scenes that still haunted him: a huge woman with

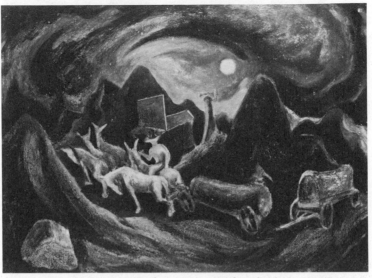

Going West, 1934–36, oil on composition board, 15⅛″ × 20⅞″

pendulous breasts surrounded by five emaciated figures and a disembodied skull; a woman hovering—perhaps mourning—over the skeleton of a large animal as a crowd of skull-faces closes around her. The style is no longer Benton's. There are still echoes of the hollow and the bump in the droop of a breast or the bend of a knee, but the complex interplay of short, undulating lines has been replaced by threatening swells and unexpected jabs and every-where the marks of the turbulent brush that Jackson had struggled for so long to control. Instead of Benton's mannered cheerfulness, there is the obsessive moodiness of Albert Pinkham Ryder, whose works he would have seen at the Ferargil Galleries where Benton exhibited. Studying Ryder's small, heavily impastoed canvases (and, undoubtedly, the monograph on Ryder prepared by the Ferargil's director, Frederick Newlin Price, in 1932), Jackson's eye was drawn to the images that reflected his own ordeal: tenebrous images like *Sentimental Journey*, in which a hearse-like wagon, driven by a man in a top hat, wearily rounds a bend into the moonlit distance. In *Going West*, Jackson painted the same wagon, transposed to the land of his childhood, rounding the same ominous bend surrounded by apocalyptic swirls of angry sky and churning landscape. In another of the paintings illustrated by Price, *Death Rides the Wind* (which later was determined to be a forgery), a mounted Grim Reaper charges across a barren landscape in the eerie ecliptic half-light of a hidden moon, his victim, apparently, an unsuspecting steer grazing beneath a skeletal tree. In Jackson's two versions of the same scene, the Grim Reaper is transformed into a cowboy and the steer into a skeleton, but death remains a constant.

In the same paintings, memory intrudes for the first time in Jackson's art—not the convenient, picturesque memory of Benton's murals or Jackson's earlier Bentonesque works, but specific memories from his own childhood: the threat-

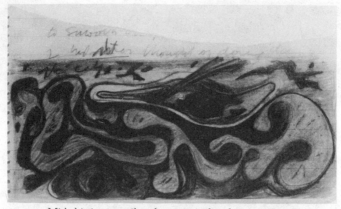

Mid-thirties, pencil and crayon on lined paper, 4″ × 7″

ening bull outside Phoenix, Stella's overturned wagon, the cayuse stampede near the Grand Canyon. In paintings like *Going West* and *The Wagon*, the past insinuates itself in the Roy-like figure of a wagon driver urging his horses ahead of him, in a windmill tower from Chico, a long-line skinner from Cody, or a water caisson from Orland. In one untitled work, unusually large for this period, Jackson paints a farm family gathered in their barnyard among the chickens for what could be a formal portrait. The featureless totemic figures of a mother and father loom huge on each side of the canvas (a composition he will return to again and again in coming years). The mother, who towers over the father, cradles one faceless child in her arm while another peers out warily from behind her. A tiny, doll-like child sits precariously on the skull-faced father's knee. In the foreground, two older children, knowledgeable in the mysteries of sex, urge together a cow and a bull. The roiling barnyard threatens to rise up and engulf them; the dark sky is streaked with ominous flashes of orange and red. Everywhere, like smoke from two fires, Jackson's bleak, uncertain past intertwines with Ryder's dark, turbulent style. Skies lower menacingly, the ground convulses, the sun and moon, often obscured, offer little light, figures move in faceless chiaroscuro. They are not nightmare images, but anxious dreams caught at the first moment of unaccountable darkness, when the potential for terror is first perceived.

Peter Busa recalls that Jackson's obsession with his father's death had led him to questions about "fate" and "chance" and "what he had done to deserve it all." Someone—Richard Davis, perhaps—had given him a copy of *Moby-Dick*, and Jackson had laid siege to it repeatedly—"he must have tried to read it not once but ten times," Busa recalls—perhaps identifying with Captain Ahab's obsessive search for meaning in the seeming arbitrariness of life:

All visible objects, man, are but as pasteboard masks. But in each event—
in the living act, the undoubted deed—there, some unknown but still

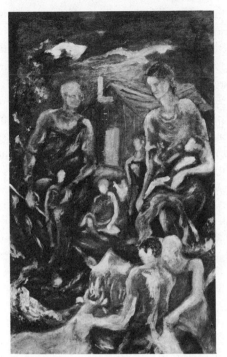

Untitled (Family Scene), 1930–1934,
tempera on Masonite, 26¼″ × 42¼″

reasoning thing puts forth the mouldings of its features from behind the unreasoning mask. If man will strike, strike through the mask!

Jackson's obsession with finding a pattern in the arbitrary—the face behind the mask—led him first to sidewalk poker games and three-card monte. "He liked to gamble," Busa recalls, "and in New York, in those days, if you wanted to gamble, all you had to do was walk around the corner. It appealed to his notion that there is some logic in chance, that there has to be a certain rhythm to the way things happen, that there is no such thing as arbitrary or random." In Greenwich Village, in the early hours of the morning, he would follow with fascination trails of urine left by police horses on patrol. "One time, a policeman caught him at it and nearly hauled him in," Busa recalls. "But I said, 'No, you've got the wrong person here. He'll give you a thesis about it.' I said, 'He's going to college and this is part of his work.' The cop was really baffled, and he let us go. But Jackson had a fascination with that kind of thing."

In his drawings, Jackson turned to "doodling" to explore the arbitrary. For the first time, patches of doodling appear in the margins of letters and notes and larger sketches, spreading indulgently across other images—sometimes geometric, sometimes swirling, sometimes reworked with colored pencil or wash. Occasionally, an entire sheet is filled with a pattern gone out of control —or just allowed to happen—perhaps hiding an earlier image.

In the same year, Jackson painted his first self-portrait. It was the appropriate culmination to a period of self-absorption, self-deception, and self-abuse. In it, the twenty-two-year-old Jackson paints himself as a child. He is nine or ten years old—his age when Roy Pollock left home—harrowed, emaciated, hollow-eyed. He stares out of the Ryderesque gloom, half in darkness, struggling to conceal his fears. The painting was not based on an old photograph; it is the face that Jackson Pollock saw in the mirror. It *is* the void. Maria Piacenza saw the painting after it was completed. "I felt it was so revealing," she remembers. "It was the painting of a madman. It was the very painful, very exposed painting of a very turbulent man. . . . There was all this hatred boiling up behind this little boy's face." With the other paintings, the self-portrait marks the beginning of a new period in Jackson's art. He has found a new and inexhaustible subject matter: the frightened child in the mirror. Instead of America's past or Benton's past, he has discovered the backward path, the path back into his own past and his own subconscious. He will pull the image out of the void.

17

THE DARING YOUNG MAN ON THE FLYING TRAPEZE

Reports of Jackson's latest outrages eventually reached their intended audience. Late one midwinter night in 1933, Bruce Mitchell and Whitney Darrow appeared at Charles Pollock's door on Eighth Street to announce that Jackson had been arrested and taken to the Jefferson Market jail not far away. He had gone on a rampage in a local nightclub and assaulted a cop. Although he later dismissed the incident as "something minor," at the time Charles was anxious enough about the prospect of a criminal prosecution to enlist the help of Ernest Howe, an Englishman and friend of Elizabeth's, to testify in Jackson's behalf. At the arraignment the next day, Howe, a grave, elderly man who barely knew the accused, persuaded the judge to let Jackson off with a "severe admonishment."

Whether or not Jackson had learned a lesson, the family certainly had. After only two or three months on his own, Jackson was invited back to live in the Eighth Street apartment with Charles and Elizabeth. Another rescue effort had begun.

For the most part, the family accepted it with practiced resignation. "I had hoped Jack would spring out for himself this year," Frank wrote Charles as 1933 came to an end, "but I suppose conditions make the present set-up the wiser." Elizabeth was far less sanguine. "He came with this peculiar dissatisfied, selfish temperament to two young people who were greatly in love and deeply involved in their own lives," she recalls. "He and I conducted ourselves as if we were armies under truce." Over Elizabeth's objections, Charles devoted increasing amounts of time and energy to keeping his little brother preoccupied and sober. Through the wall that separated Jackson's small studio from the rest of the apartment, Charles maintained an uncharacteristically conscientious vigil. "I had my studio in front so I could be aware of Jack, of his physical movements," he remembers. "I knew he was having a hell of a struggle." As often as possible, he would stop at Jackson's door and "ask to see what he was working on." Probably at Charles suggestion, both brothers prepared sketches for a proposed mural at Greenwich House. Charles, technically accomplished and intellectually *au courant* as always, depicted a pushcart vendor being run down by a large truck (the workingman's fate in an oppressive capitalist system); while Jackson, working summarily in oil on brown wrapping paper, evoked Benton's Monday night "musicales" with a murky blue Ryderesque drawing of five men playing instruments. Despite the bonds that always connected their artistic lives, it was the first and only project on which the two brothers cooperated.

Buoyed by Charles's solicitude, Jackson survived the winter—increasingly his most troubled season. In late spring, the therapy continued with a long visit with the Bentons on Martha's Vineyard. Rita, who had heard reports of Jackson's drinking through her niece, Maria Piacenza, was especially eager to help.

For part of May and June, Jackson uncoiled and dried out in the Vineyard's briny sunlight. "Without alcohol he was very quiet," Benton recalled, "not morose, just quiet. He had charm for us. I guess we had that for him. From the stories I've heard I am inclined to believe that he was happier during his Martha's Vineyard visits than at any other time in his life." With Rita, Jackson picked blueberries and dug clams from the shallow inlets nearby. Eight-year-old T.P. taught him how to sail. Tom recruited him for gardening, house painting, and chopping firewood. Every day around noon, the family would "strike out across the moors" to join other summer residents at the beach for a picnic lunch and sunbathing in the nude on the hot sand—an activity that Tom had introduced to shocked islanders years before. If he wanted to be alone, Jackson wandered the hills around Menemsha, occasionally sketching or painting pastoral scenes and ocean vistas. When the sun finally began to lower behind the Gay Head lighthouse, Rita would lay out a feast of spaghetti with squid, vermicelli with clams, lobster, or the freshest fish from the Menemsha fishermen; then Jackson would retire early to the converted chicken coop out back—dubbed "Jack's Shack." With no radio, no cardplaying, no phonograph and a regular 4:00 A.M. rousting, the days ended early.

But there were limits to what could be expected, either from a surrogate family or from the Vineyard's sea air. Rita, after all, was a source of anxiety as well as comfort. And the intimacy and isolation of the little shingled house only aggravated the unspoken rivalry with Benton. Although still largely oblivious to the cause, Tom sensed the contradictions that underlay Jackson's impenetrable moodiness. "He was mostly a silent, inwardly turned boy," Benton recalled later, "and even in gay company carried something of an aura of unhappiness about him."

In midsummer, Charles and Jackson set out in a 1926 Model T Ford on what would become an 8,000-mile cross-country trip. It was Jackson's fourth such journey in five years.

■ ■ ■

When Stella Pollock was unhappy, she spurred her family to some new place, where, she vaguely hoped, fate would treat them more kindly. Unable to confront problems, she saw movement—the simple accumulation of miles—as the ultimate solution at times of crisis. Her sons had learned the lesson too well. For more than a decade, in an era when travel was arduous, time-consuming, and often dangerous, they ricocheted around the country, logging thousands of miles in ancient cars in a vast, transcontinental catharsis of motion. Long before Tom Benton urged his students to experience back-road America, Jackson Pollock had sought solace at the wheel of a stripped down Model T on the roads outside Riverside; and long afterward, his first instinct in a crisis was to pile up miles against it—the faster he drove, the more quickly they accumulated—searching for the destination or the escape velocity that Stella had never found.

The pretext for the 1934 trip was to make good their year-old promise to visit their widowed mother in Los Angeles. But there had to be more to it: the route was too roundabout, the pace too languorous, and the stay in Los Angeles too brief. By Pollock standards, preparations were unusually elaborate. They packed bedrolls and folding cots in order to avoid hotels, and cooking utensils to save money on food. "We prepared our meals on wood that we found along the highway," Charles remembers, "and at night we just found a place in a churchyard or schoolyard and set ourselves up." The route took them first through the coal-mining regions of southwestern Pennsylvania, through Uniontown and across the Monongahela River into West Virginia, where the mines were mostly idle and the towns desperately bleak. Near Charleston, winds blowing through the empty open pits covered everything within miles, including passing cars, in a shroud of black dust. Since 1929, both the price and the production of coal had plummeted. In a company town, after the company deducted rent, the cost of explosives, and insurance, even a miner who brought out as much as forty-five tons of coal in a month was deeper in debt at the end of the month that he had been at the beginning. Miners were forced to assign their children "eating days"—seldom more than three a week.

First stop was Harlan County, Kentucky, just across Tug Fork in the Cumberland Mountains. In 1931, striking Harlan County miners had fought a pitched battle with machine-gun toting deputies at the Battle of Evarts, leaving four dead and sparking a confrontation between mine owners, the United Mine Workers, and the National Guard. The Communist party had been quick to exploit the violence and the kangaroo trial that followed (in which miners were tried for murdering a deputy), calling them the opening salvos in the class war predicted by Marx. In the three years since, Harlan had become a mecca for the radical New York intelligentsia. A distinguished train of writers and intellectuals, including Theodore Dreiser, John Dos Passos, Sherwood Anderson, Edmund Wilson, and Malcolm Cowley, had made the pilgrimage from New York, but the war had been lost. By the time Charles and Jackson passed through, the union movement had disappeared from Kentucky and its last sympathizers had been hounded out of the mines.

From Harlan, the brothers followed Daniel Boone's Wilderness Trail through the Cumberland Gap and out onto the rolling blue-pine plateau of the Great Smokies. To avoid retracing the route through Alabama that Jackson and Whitney Darrow had taken on their return from California in 1932, they turned due west at Knoxville and wound through Tennessee's long, lateral spine. Past Nashville, the road finally plunged into the 200-mile-wide Mississippi trough; from the Tennessee River to Memphis, there was hardly a hillock. In Memphis, where Benton had stopped to see Beale Street, "home of the blues," and paint a few drowsy street scenes, they saw the mile-wide Mississippi on the last leg of its extravagant journey, looping and curling in its path like "a long, pliant apple-paring," in Mark Twain's phrase. Impatient for New Orleans, they turned south at Memphis and sliced straight down through a still, sultry Mississippi summer, over the Tallahatchie, Yalobusha, and Yazoo rivers —names were all that remained of the region's original inhabitants—and out onto the broad steamy delta—10,000 square miles of Mississippi silt, floated grain-by-grain from as far away as the banks of the Shoshone River in Cody, Wyoming.

For Charles, the visit to New Orleans was more than a sight-seeing tour. For the first few decades of the century, New Orleans had been the home of Storyville, the country's only legalized red-light district. Tales of its tinseled demimonde of antebellum "palaces" and rows of street-side "cribs," where pleasures of every kind were available for twenty-five cents and up, had inflamed his adolescent imagination. Although Storyville had been officially closed for more than fifteen years, the legend lingered, as did the considerable economy that had grown up around it. Scattered but not discouraged, the celebrated procuresses of New Orleans—like Countess Willie Piazza, Josie Arlington, and Lulu White, along with hundreds of smaller "independents"— filtered back into the surrounding areas, including the French Quarter, to carry on the New Orleans tradition. "Everything goes as it will," boasted a local underground guide suggestively, "and those who cannot be satisfied [here] must surely be of a queer nature."

In all likelihood, this was Charles's real destination. More than a diversion to keep Jackson out of New York (and out of trouble) for the summer, more than just general therapy for his troubled soul, the visit to Storyville may have been planned to solve what the family believed was Jackson's *real* problem: his lagging, and perhaps errant, sexual development. Whether or not rumors had reached his ear, Charles had plenty of reason to be concerned. Frank had undoubtedly reported the cold reception given Rose Miller. Elizabeth was quick to point up Jackson's utter lack of interest in a serious, consistent relationship. And, even at twenty-two, Jackson had yet to show any real enthusiasm for the kind of sexual anecdote that preoccupied Charles. Among his brothers, Jackson's inactivity had become uncomfortably conspicuous. Here, in what remained of the fabled Storyville, Charles might be able to help his youngest brother regain his sexual bearings.

That night, he took Jackson to the red-light district. "The women were sitting in the doorways inviting us in," Charles remembers. " 'Any way you like it for a quarter.' " Which way Jackson liked it isn't recorded. In fact, Charles remembers nothing else about the evening except that neither he nor Jackson ever spoke of it again—an inauspicious sign, given the Pollock brothers' tireless enthusiasm for tales of sexual conquest.

Beyond the Mississippi, the Great Plains had become "the new Sahara." Across the half of Texas that wasn't already desert, from Beaumont to San Antonio, Charles and Jackson witnessed the desolation at the southern rim of the dust bowl. Jackson had seen it coming on his trip in 1931, but since then, the summer of 1933 had turned millions of acres of topsoil across the Midwest into fine powder. On Armistice Day that year, a great dust storm had risen up on the Dakota prairies and obscured the midday sun as far away as Albany, New York. Roads, houses, animals, and people disappeared under the moonscape left by the "black blizzard" of 1933. Little had changed when the Pollock brothers came through seven months later. Temperatures seemed stuck above 100 degrees, every second farmhouse stood deserted, farm machinery and shed roofs poked out from under drifts "deeper than a man is tall." At El Paso the road became clogged with farm families in jalopies even more ancient and decrepit than the Pollocks'—"square-shouldered" 1925 Dodges, 1927 La Salles, battered 1923 Model T Fords, and trucks piled high with mattresses, cooking utensils, and children—all of them headed, like Charles and Jackson, for California, the land of promise. "It was the year of the great Okie migration," Charles recalls, "and the drought. We saw it all."

Finally, after stopping for a few days outside Phoenix to visit with old friends, the Minsches and the Moris, Charles and Jackson arrived in Los Angeles sometime in late July.

They couldn't have been prepared for what they found.

The Depression had finally overtaken the Pollock family. Sande had lost his lucrative job at the *Times* shortly before Roy's death, and no one had been able to find steady work since. For a while, Jay worked on the road in his father's place and Sande joined up with Reuben Kadish to paint *faux bois* on office safes. "We'd get twenty-five bucks for a job," Kadish remembers, "which was a *lot* of money." But soon those jobs, like most jobs in Southern California, dried up or were siphoned off by cheaper labor—the homeless thousands that Charles and Jackson had seen crowding the roads. When Frank returned in the summer of 1933, there was another mouth to feed and still only intermittent work—ten days in a power plant, seldom more than few hours a day, always at bone-lean wages. Over the winter, Frank and Sande tried to sign up with the newly created Civil Works Administration (by January, four million people nationwide were making fifteen dollars a week with the CWA), but corruption in the local program shut them out. Stella had stopped paying rent on the Montecito Drive house when Roy died, and with even store-bought food now an extravagance, expanded her backyard garden. Jay spent everything he had saved on a milk goat, then started saving again for a few rabbits and chickens. In the spring of 1934, he felt compelled to reassure Charles, "We are eating regularly and shall continue to manage by some means. . . . With milk, eggs and meat from our back yard ranch we can manage until something can be done about this rotten situation." The Pollock family had been relatively poor for years, but now, for the first time in anyone's memory, they were sliding unchecked toward impoverishment.

No one felt the reverse of fortunes more acutely than Sande. For four years, even after the crash, his job at the *Times*'s rotogravure plant had shielded him from the rising tide of anxiety both in his own family and in the society beyond. He developed expensive tastes—in cars, in clothes, and in friends. "Sande was making a lot of money," Reuben Kadish recalls, "and he spent it all. A thirty dollar pair of shoes, a hundred and eighty dollar suit." Money also made it easy to commute to Riverside for weekends with Arloie. When not in Riverside or at the house on Montecito Drive, he would disappear into the city with a group of feckless, self-indulgent friends who were always getting into costly "jams" from which Sande felt obliged to rescue them. "Most of [them] aren't worth the powder to blow them up," Jay complained to Frank.

When the layoff finally came and the money stopped, Sande was devastated. Like millions of other men who were thrown out of work in the early thirties, men who relied on their jobs for a sense of identity, he clung for as long as possible to the habits of affluence. "Even when he was unemployed and he came to my place of work," Kadish recalls, "everything was natty. Never blue jeans. We were graining safes, and we were using paints and solvents. But Sande always came dressed in a suit. That was the way he'd worked at the *Times*." When denial failed, Sande, like Jackson, resorted to alcohol, self-abuse, and fast driving. Returning drunk from a party in Los Angeles, he ran his car into a telephone pole. "He just made for the pole," recalls Marie Pollock, who was sitting in the rumble seat. "That was his target." At another party, he climbed to the roof of a house and tried to jump to a nearby tree. "He missed the tree," Marie remembers, "but he was so drunk he didn't hurt himself." His frustrations often found release on the Ascot Speedway outside Los Angeles, where he raced cars around the track at the unheard of speed of 90 miles per hour; or on trips to San Francisco when he covered 450 miles in as little as six hours.

During the flush years, Sande had abandoned the sketch pads and paints of his childhood, preferring to enjoy the artistic exploits of Charles and Jackson vicariously. But with new friends like Reuben Kadish and Phil Goldstein replacing the old circle of hangers-on, his interest in art returned. In late 1932, at Kadish's urging, he joined a "fresco class" taught by Siqueiros. Soon he was

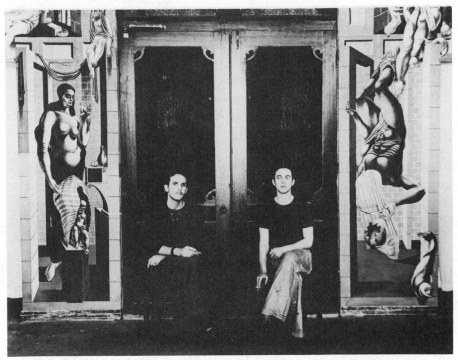

Phil Goldstein and Reuben Kadish in front of mural on which Sande Pollock assisted

assisting Kadish and Goldstein, learning both painting techniques and radical politics.

But Sande's devotion to art was always more a product of circumstance than a consuming passion. "He wasn't as developed in his desire to be a painter as Phil or I or Jack, or anybody else in that group," Kadish remembers. "He just wanted our company." Jackson, too, sensed how sublimated and mutable his brother's artistic aspirations were. "While your out of work," he wrote soon after Sande joined Siqueiros's workshop, "keep close to your art." Closeness— whether to a job, to art, or to a brother—was all that mattered to Sande— having something or someone to care for. For a while, after Jackson went to New York, his errant friends had met that need. With his sculpted features, compact, muscular body, and winning country-boy ways, he made friends easily. "There was a warmth about the man that was very, very appealing," says Kadish. But behind the warmth and the masculine reserve, there was a profound emptiness that neither Kadish, who left with Goldstein for Mexico in the spring of 1934, nor Arloie, in her uncomplaining self-sufficiency, could fill. Sande had to have a special charge, someone equally incomplete, to placate his own demons.

When Jackson left Los Angeles with Charles only a few weeks after arriving, Sande was, for the first time in all the comings and goings of the previous years, genuinely heartbroken. "We sure missed you was lonesome after you left," Stella wrote Charles and Jackson. "I felt so sorry for Sanford he broke down and cried he hated to see you leave would like to of gone with you."

The inevitable took only another month and a half. During that time, Jackson, barred by Elizabeth from returning to the Eighth Street apartment, found a cold-water flat on Houston Street; while Sande, in Los Angeles, continued to make lame arguments to Arloie: "Without money we can't get married, so if we can't get married, maybe we should stop dating for a while and see other people."

Sometime in October 1934, Sande arrived in New York—"with 34 cents in my pocket and California clothes." He had come to resume the job he seemed born to: taking care of Jackson. No one was ever more suited to the task or performed it better—which was fortunate, because over the next few years, Jackson would need it more than ever before.

The New York to which Sande came to rescue his brother was itself in need of rescue. Five years of depression had wrung the last drops of energy and optimism from the fabled city of the twenties. "The proud unsinkable 'Titanic' of New Capitalism," Lewis Mumford observed, "had hit an iceberg and capsized." Even Roosevelt seemed powerless to reverse the gray tide of "stringency and strain." In the twenty months since the New Deal had been dealt, prices had risen, incomes fallen, and a vast migration begun. Honeymoon recovery efforts like the NRA had failed, sixteen million people were still jobless, and another million on strike (1,800 strikes were called in 1934 alone). Full-scale class warfare had broken out in some cities and seemed in the air almost everywhere. For those who, unlike Jackson, cared to look beyond the dizzying blur of personal and national traumas, there were even more ominous signal fires overseas: the death of Germany's von Hindenburg and the ascension of Adolf Hitler, the civil war in Spain, border clashes between Ethiopian and Italian troops. "Among New York intellectuals," says a historian of the period, "there was a tremendous sense of foreboding and darkness. Spengler was popular. *The Decline of the West* hung over the city like a dark cloud."

On the streets, sights that once elicited shock or rage or compassion had become commonplace: the "wobblies" in the parks, huddled glumly on benches carrying their belongings in paper bags; legions of men in gray clothes with gray faces leaning against the walls, blocking the sidewalks, waiting for Mr. Hearst's coffee wagon, harvesting butts from the sidewalk and newspapers from the rubbish, lining up in every open space to sell single gardenias for fifteen cents, or apples or oranges or newspapers, or to shine shoes, or just to beg. On sunny Indian-summer days, thousands of them filtered into midtown. From under bridges and cardboard lean-tos, from subway stations and railroad terminals, from the Hooverville in Central Park's drained reservoir, from the vast emergency shelter on the East River docks where the stench of human bodies was "less sweet than cows, less fragrant than horses," they crawled together—first to form the "serried rows" of breadlines, then to fill the gray parks and street corners. They were not "bums" in the traditional American sense. A guard at a city shelter told Matthew Josephson, "Nowadays, we're getting a very good class of people. Half of them aren't bums at all." They were mostly the unemployed, a vast and ubiquitous new class—as many as one million in New York alone during the worst years. Not all were homeless. Beyond Lexington Avenue on the east and Sixth Avenue on the west lay endless rows of "Depression shanties," corrugated tin villages where the pavement was broken and the despair palpable, where babies died of malnutrition and men dropped dead in the streets and strangers were found frozen to death in abandoned warehouses in the winter. In more permanent neighborhoods like the Village, little girls clutched their dolls and detailed their families' plights to other girls playing relief workers in a game called "Going on Relief." Boys played a rougher game called "Picketing," in which they yelled "scab" at each other and staged fierce mock street fights. In the fancier neighborhoods, conversation often turned to suicide. A popular joke concerned the hotel clerk who inquired of guests: "Do you want a room for sleeping or for jumping?"

By the standards of a city in which one out of four workers was jobless and one out of ten jobless was also homeless, Jackson and Sande Pollock fared relatively well. The "apartment" Jackson had found south of the Village was nothing more than the top floor of an abandoned commercial building that stood by itself amid the piles of rubble and Depression shanties—sometimes indistinguishable from each other—that lined Houston Street. Probably rent-free, it was a bare, barn-like space without heat or hot water. "To get their attention, we'd have to throw rocks at the windows," remembers Maria Piacenza, who often stopped by with her girlfriend, Madeline, on their way home from work at Klein's department store. "We'd see their heads way up there in the sky, and they'd come down and we'd have to climb all these stairs up to the studio, which was really just a big bare place." To discourage Arloie from joining him in New York—which she was eager to do—Sande wrote of the dismal conditions: "It's a *terrible* place, a pigsty in the city!" "Sande didn't want me to come," Arloie remembers. "He said it wasn't fit for a woman, and it got so cold at times they had to burn their furniture." Pigsty or not, Piacenza and others visited often—although when they came for dinner they had to bring their own pots and pans. And if the place "wasn't fit for a woman," it was primarily because Sande and Jackson had painted crude "pornographic murals" on the flaking plaster walls. "They were kind of naughty," Piacenza recalls. "There were guys peeing all over, that sort of thing. Madeline and I tried very hard not to notice them."

With the help of the Bentons, the brothers found a job at the City and Country School on West Thirteenth Street, a progressive school for children ages three through twelve founded on John Dewey's principles of "learning through doing." Tom and Rita had known the school's founder, Caroline Pratt, and her partner, Helen Marot, for some years, having often summered with them on Martha's Vineyard, and in all likelihood had already introduced Jackson to the two elderly women. Within a few years, Marot would be drawn into the drama of Jackson's decline and the Pollock family's desperate efforts to arrest it, but even as early as the winter of 1934, she and Pratt were generous, if somewhat distant benefactors. For cleaning the five-story school every night and "swabbing it down" once a week, they paid the two brothers five dollars apiece—half what a salesgirl at Klein's like Maria Piacenza made, but enough to buy food and fuel. Jackson, whose only experience with a regular job had been on his father's work crews, resented the demeaning routine of emptying trash cans and cleaning latrines. "He just wasn't capable of functioning in the way you needed to for regular work," recalls Reuben Kadish.

Rita Benton, another of Jackson's guardian angels during the bleakest days of the Depression, searched for ways to supplement the lean wages at the City and Country School, but found that "Jack was a very proud and sensitive young man [and] there was no way of giving him money." Over the years she had tried various subterfuges to pass along a few extra dollars—arranging make-work odd jobs, inflating T.P.'s baby-sitting hours, ordering milk delivered to Jackson's door anonymously—but by the winter of 1934, even the Bentons had few dollars to spare. Despite Tom's increasing visibility—he appeared on the cover of *Time* in December 1934—the market for his large paintings had all but evaporated. In a depressed art market filled with nervous, cash-strapped collectors, only his small and relatively inexpensive ceramic bowls and plates moved well.

At Rita's prompting, Jackson attended the free ceramics workshop taught by Job Goodman at the Henry Street Settlement House as part of the so-called "teachers' project" of the 1932 New York State work relief program. With additional tutoring from Benton, Jackson was "quickly successful," according to Tom, "producing some handsome and very salable works" that Rita displayed in her ad hoc gallery for young and unknown artists in the basement of Tom's dealer, the Ferargil Galleries. "We opened December 1st and ran through to the Christmas holidays," Rita recalled. "Jack Pollock, Manuel Tolegian and I cleaned up the place. Mr. Benton and I bought the paint for the walls. . . . By December 24th, we had sold thousands of dollars worth of paintings." Over the next six months, she sold every bowl and plate that Jackson produced—except for six, which he presented to her as gifts. Touched but ever pragmatic, Rita insisted on paying for them.

Sometime during the winter of 1934–35, the second winter of the New Deal, Jackson and Sande joined the four million families and seven million single people receiving direct government aid. For the million and a half of those who lived in New York City, the help came just in time. The winter was mercilessly long and brutal. After a blistering summer, the temperature plummeted to the teens and single digits and seemed to die there. Week after week, papers carried reports of "a general increase in malnutrition" and of clinics and relief agencies "so overcrowded they can offer adequate relief to no one." Jackson and Sande could easily have encountered one of the dozens who died of starvation that winter, floating through the snow in a final, painless delirium. It was the year of William Saroyan's story, "The Daring Young Man on the Flying Trapeze," about a young man starving to death, wandering the city streets feeling the giddiness of imminent death, hanging in midair, "the form without the weight," floating back and forth between "the trivial truth of reality" and "the tiny, tangible atom of eternity," between life and death, on a trapeze of delirium. "Starvation," wrote Alfred Kazin in praise of Saroyan's story, "expressed perfectly the sense of the outer world in 1934 as implacable, ungiving."

For Jackson and Sande, the winter was cold and grim, but not, in fact, threatening. Between the job at the City and Country School, occasional money from the sale of Jackson's bowls, and a few dollars in relief payments, the two brothers seldom went hungry. At times, they were, by Depression standards, almost flush. Reginald Wilson came by often and accompanied them to the Restaurant dei Lavoratori, a neighborhood eatery at 92 West Houston. "It was one of our favorites," Wilson recalls, "a splendid restaurant, very modest, where you could get a pretty decent dinner for under a dollar." If, at other times, they couldn't afford a dollar—when Jackson spent the money from the sale of a bowl on a bottle of whiskey—there were other, less splendid restaurants where a penny bought coffee or day-old bread and twenty-five cents bought a meal. If all else failed, they could have joined the 81,000 who daily endured the rudeness and degradation of the breadline for a tin bowl of vaguely vegetable stew, three slices of stale bread, and a tin cup of watery coffee—although Charles, who remained employed throughout the period, would never have permitted the Pollock family to suffer such an indignity.

"They were sort of living hand to mouth in the city," recalls Axel Horn. "There were just no holds barred. At least that's the impression one got." It was an impression the Pollock brothers relished. Jackson liked to tell the story of his encounter with a well-dressed man walking his dog on lower Fifth Avenue. "I started petting it, saying 'nice dog,' " he told T. P. Benton and others. "Then I jumped up and said to the man, 'You son of a bitch, you feed that dog when I'm starving,' and I slugged him. And then the cops came. They gave me a terrible beating, and I wound up in the hospital." (In fact, it was the dog owner, not the cops, who gave Jackson the beating, according to Rita Benton, who was called by the police after they took Jackson to St. Vincent's Hospital for head injuries and charged him with assault and battery. The charges, like so many others against Jackson, were later dropped.)

Sande also bragged and railed about the hardships of the Depression, about how he and Jackson were reduced, like millions of their fellow workers, to stealing food to stay alive. "Trying to wring a bare existence out of this goddamned city," he wrote Reuben Kadish in the depths of their poverty, "takes most of ones time. The rest of the time is spent holding ones nuts in one hand to keep them from freezing and stealing potatoes with the other. The suffering of thousands of people in this city alone is appaling."

If Jackson and Sande did steal food from the streets that winter, they were moved, not by the delirium of starvation, but by the bad-boy spirit of the Gold Dust Twins, thinly veiled in political rhetoric. "Sometimes people stole as a badge of honor," recalls another artist who lived through the Depression in New York and saw fellow students at the League eating out of garbage cans. "They wanted to show people that they weren't taking things lying down." In fact, Jackson and Sande always had enough money for liquor, occasionally enough for restaurant dining, and even a little extra to send home to Frank on his wedding day. When they had money to spend, they spent it as they always had—as their mother had—on the best. "Even during the Depression, with very little money," recalls Elizabeth Pollock, "there was a kind of strange dandiness about them, that to a New Yorker like me seemed queer at times. . . . Compared to my instincts, which were always bargain-basement, they went to the top floors for the best, even if it meant going without other things."

Together again for the first time since Riverside, away from Stella and Arloie, "Jack and Sande" quickly reverted to the old games of cowboy machismo they had played in the orange groves and sagebrush gullies of Southern California. On the gray streets of Manhattan, however, the effect was altogether different. Short and stocky even in his tall cowboy hat and boots, drawling out country phrases like "tighter than a gnat's ass," Sande cut an unintentionally comic figure that only Jackson found convincing. "Sande was like a folly," recalls Gerome Kamrowski, a fellow artist. "The only time you saw a cowboy in Manhattan was when the rodeo was in town—except for Sande. And Jackson was right there beside him wearing jeans and boots. They were the Wyoming kids." Instead of roaming the San Gabriel Mountains in a stripped-down Model T, they explored the bars and nightclubs of the Village. There, among the remnants of Prohibition-era seediness and Depression-era despair, they continued the old search for manhood and belonging that had begun around a campfire on the rim of the Grand Canyon.

"They were both drinking," recalls Axel Horn, who witnessed their drunken antics often, "but it only had a marked effect on Jack. Sande would drink a lot, but he would never go wild the way Jack did." Now, as then, Jackson stumbled and reeled and took the falls. "He would erupt in every direction at once. He would start chasing women, he would throw things around, yelling, and challenging everybody." Now, as then, Sande picked him up and put him to bed. He "was always there to see that, when Jack was going out of bounds, he was controlled," says Horn, "even if that meant he had to come in and knock Jackson out cold—I saw that happen several times." "Sande took care of him," recalls Reginald Wilson, "got him out of jams, got him home safely from bars. Jack would never have survived without him."

But there was also something deeply provocative in Sande's solicitude, a license to "screw up" that Jackson understood only too well. "The real problem started when Sande arrived and began making all of Jack's decisions for him," Manuel Tolegian said later. "He should have let him alone." But "Sande's job was Jack," as Reginald Wilson recalls, and without Jackson's excesses, without the drinking and the self-abuse, Sande would have been without a job. At a benefit for the Art Students League held at the Palm Garden in 1935, an argument between Jackson and Harold Anton, a fellow artist, boiled over into the first pushing stages of a fight. Instead of pulling Jackson away, Sande leapt onto his shoulders and began flailing at the taller Anton. "They were like the James brothers," recalls Peter Busa, who watched in astonishment. "It was like fighting a giant with four hands." When Anton backed away, Jackson started reeling through the startled crowd, hugging Sande's legs while Sande "looked for the tallest people he could find and hit them in the mouth." According to Busa, "They nearly caused a riot."

Nothing had changed since the day in the Phoenix barnyard when Jackson offered up his fingertip. The two brothers were still locked in their mutual, self-destructive embrace. Despite months of drunken binges, late night searches, barroom fights, and long walks home, Sande never tried to prevent Jackson from drinking, and Jackson never tried to quit. Instead, surrounded by deprivation and starvation, he escaped on the familiar trapeze of drunkenness to an atom of the past where he had been briefly happy. It was his private delirium, less final than starvation and, behind the histrionics, deeply satisfying. With Sande close by again, he had no fear of falling.

18

A GREAT HOPE FOR AMERICAN PAINTING

O n the morning of August 1, 1935, Jackson and Sande Pollock awoke
to startling news: "They're hiring artists." People dashed through the
streets of the Village, clutching paintings under their arms, spreading
the news from door to door. May Tabak Rosenberg, whose husband Harold
would become a leading art critic in the 1950s, was one of those who heard the
alarm. "They were shouting with the excitement of children at a zoo," she later
wrote, " 'Hurry. Grab some paintings. Hurry! Grab anything you've got framed
and come along. Hurry.' "

In the "exhilarating madness" that followed, details were hard to come by.
Fragments of explanation flew back and forth on street corners and in cafeterias: the government had set up an "Art Project," they would pay painters to
paint, "one had to sign up that very day," the pay was more than twenty dollars
a week. After years of destitution, of languishing in cold-water flats and empty
galleries, most of the Village's two hundred artists and art students could hardly
believe their ears. "It was like winning a lottery for ten million dollars," recalls
one of them. "We couldn't believe that you got paid *steady*, twenty-three dollars
a week, just to paint. It was the craziest thing we ever heard of."

The rescue had come just in time.

In the six years since the crash, the American art world had virtually ceased
to exist. Prices had dropped to one-third of their 1929 levels, imports had
plummeted over 80 percent, and the production of artists' materials was off by
almost half. Artists who moonlighted in commercial illustration suffered a
higher ratio of unemployment than either the Kentucky coal miners or the
Okie farmers whom Jackson had seen on his last trip west. The success of radio
had devastated the market for magazine and newspaper illustrators, leaving
only a residue of movie- and travel-poster artists like Charles Pollock. Sculptors
were prohibited from working on billions of dollars' worth of public construction—virtually the only construction being done—under the government's

cost-cutting prohibition on decorative stone work. Even scarce private dollars —lured by special cooperative galleries like Rita Benton's—had largely evaporated. A group of New York artists approached European buyers offering to trade their works for "anything reasonable." Those artists who continued to paint did so only "out of habit," according to one account, "[standing] before their easels painting pictures they knew no one would buy." They didn't need a presidential commission to tell them in 1933 that "for the overwhelming majority of the American people the fine arts of painting and sculpture, in their non-commercial, non-industrial forms, do not exist."

So it wasn't surprising that the initial jubilation that greeted the government announcement was followed by suspicion and disbelief. Even after the artists who had signed up on August 1 returned the following week and received their first check for $23.86, doubts lingered. Some wondered out loud if banks would cash the checks; few had bank accounts. "Then a scout appeared with good news," May Rosenberg recounted. "The liquor department at Hearns Department Store on 14th Street would cash the checks of all customers. The artists trouped down in a body. Drink and be merry; for tomorrow, you're fired, was the mood. Nobody believed it would last a month, if that." During those first weeks, artists spent every new penny as quickly as possible, on the theory that "the government couldn't get money out of a rolling stone." They had dental work done—many for the first time since 1929; bought concert and theater tickets, fancy meals, and lots of liquor—anything that a vacillating government couldn't repossess.

Gradually, as the weekly checks from the U.S. Treasury continued to arrive, the money "began to seem real," and its implications began to sink in. "Before that I had no idea that you could make a living as an artist," remembers Peter Busa. Mercedes Matter, the daughter of abstract artist Arthur B. Carles, and herself a painter, recalls: "It was marvelous. You can't imagine how wonderful it was to get that money just to *paint*. It was the most important thing that ever happened to me or to this country as far as art was concerned." Even those artists who had hesitated at first soon flocked to the new program. Willem de Kooning quit his $250-a-month job designing window displays for A. S. Beck shoe stores. "I decided that if I worked at a job I was poor," a friend remembers him saying. "If I painted, I just didn't have any money." For most artists, who, like Jackson and Sande, had been living on a trickle of relief payments and an occasional odd job, however, twenty-three dollars a week was a fortune. They "really had a field day," recalled May Rosenberg.

They began to look for *space*, and instead of cheap apartments rented places with decent light, paying as much as twenty or thirty dollars a month for an abandoned small business loft with cracked john, broken walls, tin ceilings, and a skylight. They became skilled carpenters and plumbers, shrewd electricians who knew more than just how to wire a lamp. Teaching and helping each other, they installed sinks and lights and kerosene heaters and gas stoves . . . all at practically no cost. They painted thousands of acres of floors and walls and tin ceilings among them, investing God knows how much time and energy, so that dingy, depressing fire-traps became enviable, spacious islands of serenity.

But new studios, new life-styles, and in more than a few cases, new partners were only the first and most superficial of the changes that emerged from the exhilaration of August 1935.

In an astonishingly short time, the modern art world in America was born.

As Jackson and Sande knew from personal experience, the "art project" announced that summer was not the government's first attempt to aid unemployed and destitute artists. As early as 1932, then-governor Franklin Roosevelt had authorized a special work-relief program for New York's artists. Devised by state relief director Harry Hopkins, the program directly affected only about a hundred artists, but it made classes—like Ben-Shmuel's sculpture workshop at Greenwich House—available to a large number of young artists, like Jackson, who couldn't have afforded them otherwise. When, three months after the inauguration, artist George Biddle wrote his former Groton schoolmate, now President Roosevelt, urging direct federal support for artists, his plea fell on sympathetic ears. By November 1933, Hopkins, now director of the Civil Works Administration (CWA), was providing federal funds to continue the "teachers' project" in settlement houses and boys' clubs around New York.

But Biddle and others around Roosevelt, including Hopkins, felt that more direct, systematic aid was needed. In December, they succeeded in setting aside a small portion of the CWA's vast work-relief allocation to fund the Public Works of Art Project (PWAP). Under the authority of the Treasury Department, PWAP would hire artists to create art "of the best quality available" for the embellishment of public buildings. Although modest by comparison to later efforts, PWAP was a landmark. For the first time, the United States government was directly subsidizing the arts.

Inevitably, the program ignited a fire-storm of controversy. In the field, agents were besieged by marginal and self-styled "artists." "The first applicant in Los Angeles," writes a historian of the New Deal's art projects, "was a plumber who 'did a little painting.' He was followed by a flood of little old ladies who painted little scenes from nature, art students, and down-at-the-heel commercial artists. Fully three-fourths of Southern California's applicants were not bona fide artists." Because state, not federal, officials examined each applicant's bona fides, standards varied wildly. As Sande and Frank discovered when they applied unsuccessfully for CWA jobs in the winter of 1933–34, local politics could frustrate the best of federal intentions. In areas like Southern California where officials were hostile to relief efforts and to avant-garde art, too few artists qualified. In New York City, where the climate was more hospitable, too many qualified. Artists were put to work cleaning and repairing the city's statues and monuments.

Not that the New York program was free of rancor. There, federal largesse only fueled an artistic debate that had been smoldering for years between modernists—typically young, left-leaning, and unemployed artists who shared Biddle's belief that artists should follow the example of the Mexican muralists and document the "historic social revolution" of the time—and traditionalists who were generally older and better paid. When Juliana Force, director of the Whitney Museum of American Art and a modernist, was appointed PWAP regional chairman, the presidents of all the major art societies charged that she "identified with a definite art movement" and would favor "a very small percentage of those artists professionally engaged." Jackson and Sande, still under Benton's sway, sided with Force's conservative critics. "There is a woman in charge of all art projects," Sande wrote Reuben Kadish, "a political designing woman who will stop at nothing to see that her clique of fa[i]ries are given work. She is a bitch and actually amounts to an Art Dictator and is rapidly becoming a very serious menace to Art in general here in N.Y." John Sloan took a more sanguine view, characterizing the fierce infighting that accompanied each new federal initiative in the arts as "the natural result of throwing corn in the chicken coop. There are bound to be feathers flying."

Feathers flew at the White House, too, where the ideological battle lines had been drawn over a replacement for PWAP. Treasury's Edward Bruce proposed a plan that eliminated "need" altogether as a basis for supporting artists. Quality would be the sole criterion. Knowing that Congress would resist funding a work-relief program not based on need at a time of so much need, Bruce proposed that the program be supported by setting aside one percent of construction costs on federally funded building projects for "embellishments." Hopkins, on the other hand, was formulating a far grander scheme that called for "ending the dole, expanding the rural rehabilitation projects, and giving other relievers jobs on useful projects." In the democratic spirit of Hopkins's proposal, an artist would be treated more or less like any other worker and given a job appropriate to his or her skill at a wage that was "adequate for the maintenance of health and decency." The tug-of-war for Roosevelt's support was still going on when, on April 28, after only four and a half months, PWAP funding ran out and more than 3,700 artists were thrown back on the dole. Fed up with a fickle bureaucracy, artists grew increasing militant. Between 1934 and 1935, membership in the Artists Union more than doubled.

While many of the PWAP's projects in New York were simply abandoned, some were transferred to the local work-relief agency, the Emergency Relief Bureau (ERB), among them Job Goodman's ceramics class at the Henry Street Settlement House, which Jackson had attended the previous winter. Sometime in early 1935, Jackson signed up for another Goodman class, this one in life drawing, also sponsored by the city's relief agencies. Although little more than a rehash of the procedure Benton taught at the League (the thirty-eight-year-old Goodman was, in fact, a former Benton student), the class did at least provide live models and free materials. In February, Jackson was pulled from the relief rolls and, based on his carving experience with Ben-Shmuel, assigned to the monument restoration project, another of the programs rescued from PWAP. The pay of $1.75 per hour was relatively princely, but the work—cleaning the pink marble Firemen's Memorial at 100th Street and Riverside Drive with solvents—was dirty, tedious, and, in the middle of winter, with winds spinning off the icy Hudson, frigid. The daily commute north—one hundred blocks on the grimy Ninth Avenue El—undoubtedly tested his limited capacity for adversity and abstinence.

Both the weather and the working conditions improved in spring when Jackson was assigned to clean the equestrian statue of George Washington in Union Square, only a twenty-minute walk from the loft on Houston Street. By that time, Sande had joined him and the job became just another excuse for drinking and bad-boy bravado. Maria Piacenza remembers taking a break from her job on Union Square one afternoon that spring. "A big crowd had gathered around the statue and there were Jackson and Sande, hamming it up, scrubbing the horse, making a big point of scrubbing the rear end and the underparts. Everybody was howling."

It wasn't long before Jackson somehow managed to attract the opprobrium of his supervisors in a program that was supervised very loosely, if at all. In June, he was demoted from "Stonecarver" to "Stone Carver Helper," and his pay was cut in half, to eighty-five cents per hour. He continued on the restoration project another month, glumly cleaning the Augustus Saint-Gaudens statue of Peter Cooper in the traffic-congested oven of Cooper Square.

Meanwhile, in Washington, the hiatus in art subsidies over the winter of 1934–35 had given Roosevelt's opponents time to mount an attack. The art projects, they argued, were "New Deal boondoggling" at its most wasteful and wrongheaded. "That the government should provide artists and white-collar people with 'useless' projects was stigmatized as both immoral and ruinous of the economy," according to Matthew Josephson. Still, Hopkins pushed ahead with his plan for a mammoth work-relief program that would include large-scale subsidies to artists. A straight-talking Iowan whose Presbyterian heritage revealed itself in a tenacious commitment to social morality, Hopkins responded to his critics with indignation: "Hell, [artists] have got to eat just like other people." To those in Congress who insisted that artists should be "put to work with pick and shovel," Hopkins fired back defiantly, "That is all they think about, money to repair the streets. . . . We are not backing down on any of these projects. I think these things are good in life. They are important. . . . The plain fact is we haven't done enough."

The artists agreed. By the summer of 1935, two years of on-again-off-again subsidies, restrictive "quality" controls, short-lived programs, and biased selection processes had left many angry and suspicious. Sande Pollock wrote to

Reuben Kadish in July, describing the economic "piss pot" in which most artists found themselves: "Conditions here in general and particularly for the artist are certainly not improving in spite of the large gestures and bullshiting from official Washington. There has been and is much talk of more Projects but it is the usual circle of procrastination."

In the same month, Roosevelt finally resolved the battle between Bruce and Hopkins by approving both their proposals. Almost simultaneously, the Treasury Relief Art Project (TRAP), under Bruce, and the Federal Arts Project (FAP), under the vast umbrella of Hopkin's CWA, opened for business. With a relatively high percentage of non-relief artists and lofty aspirations, TRAP was soon dubbed "the Ritz" of the relief projects. Status-conscious artists, especially those already comfortable with the "approved" style and subject matter, were attracted to TRAP's better wages and elitist reputation. Manuel Tolegian was the lone TRAP artist among Jackson's friends. It was Hopkins's FAP, however, with fourteen times more money and, eventually, ten times more artists on its payroll, that greeted Jackson and his friends on the morning of August 1, 1935, with the unprecedented promise of "$23.86 a week to do nothing but paint."

The FAP was, in fact, only one small cog in the mammoth engine of work-relief that started up in the summer of 1935 with the creation of the Works Progress Administration (WPA). The WPA was the realization of Hopkins's dream of taking America off the dole and putting it back to work. "Those who are forced to accept charity," he said, "no matter how unwillingly, are first pitied, then disdained." Within the next six years, the WPA would employ an average of 2,100,000 workers, spend $2 billion, and begin work on almost a quarter of a million projects, from raking leaves to building airfields. Against this epic panorama, the art projects played a relatively minor role. Only 5 percent of WPA funds (about $46 million) and 2 percent of its employees (about 38,000) were allotted to all the creative and performing arts including the Federal Music Project, Theater Project, and Writers' Project.

In the vast oceans of funding with which Roosevelt and Hopkins tried to "prime the pump" of the economy, it was only a few drops, but its impact on the artistic community was diluvial. Within four months, two thousand artists had joined the WPA payroll. In New York City, where, according to Matthew Josephson, there were only two hundred serious artists at the time, more than a thousand signed up. By the following year, almost six thousand were employed nationwide. Although screening procedures varied from stated to state, in New York City, virtually anyone on relief who could produce a framed painting was suddenly a self-supporting artist. Among all the industries and businesses affected, directly and indirectly, by work-relief efforts, only the art "business" achieved essentially full employment.

In a community as small, insular, and arcane as the art world, such massive intervention inevitably produced massive dislocation. Harry Hopkins had tried to minimize the side effects of federal subsidies by consulting experts like

Audrey McMahon, administrator of New York's aid programs for artists, and appointing Holger Cahill, a museum curator and art lover with catholic tastes, as FAP's director. Nevertheless, the marriage of government bureaucracy and artistic license was troubled from the start. "We were the backward natives and they were the British colonists," says Peter Busa, who, like most of Jackson's friends, joined the WPA early. "The government was going to civilize us, only we didn't want to be civilized in that way. It was a real clash of cultures."

When he applied for FAP work, Sande discovered that "two people with the same last name living in the same house" could not both draw WPA checks— a regulation apparently designed to spread federal money among as many households as possible. To be eligible for his $23.86, he either had to move out of the Houston Street loft or change his last name. As always, Jackson's needs came first. Within weeks, Sande Pollock became Sande McCoy. "I have changed my name," he wrote Reuben Kadish in July 1935, "so as not to be known as Jack's brother—political reasons."

WPA regulations also forced many artists to confront for the first time, albeit in a specious form, the question of what kind of artist they wanted to be. According to project guidelines, painters produced either murals or easel paintings—never both—and were divided accordingly. Predictably, Sande, whose only artistic experience was the mural work he had done in Los Angeles with Siqueiros, Goldstein, and Kadish, was assigned to the mural division. Jackson, with scores of paintings to his credit and only passing experience with mural painting, should have joined the easel division, but, unwilling to be separated from Sande, joined the mural division instead. The choice was made easier, no doubt, when Job Goodman was assigned an FAP mural and asked Jackson to assist him.

By choosing murals, Jackson also avoided the dreaded "force account," which required easel painters to show up at a supervised location, check in, and paint for a specified number of hours each week. "There was one place on Fifty-seventh Street where you could work," recalls painter George McNeil, "and that was the only place. Of course, I didn't like that, and neither did anybody else. It meant breaking up your day, like going to an office to work." In the mural division, Jackson was spared the public indignity of these "easel factories," although he didn't escape discipline altogether. Mural supervisors were free to establish their own disciplinary standards, and Job Goodman was well known as "kind of a martinet," a Benton ideologue who demanded regular attendance and an honest day's work at his studio on Sixteenth Street or at the site. Otherwise, mural division artists were subject only to occasional "inspections" by traveling supervisors—usually fellow artists and often sympathetic friends—who expected only "some evidence of getting someplace."

Government intervention gave new pitch and moment to long-simmering political disputes within the artistic community. With a firm grip on state FAP screening committees, traditionalists could gerrymander skill classifications to favor their own. Whether an artist was classified "unskilled, intermediate, skilled, or professional" determined the amount of his or her paycheck. At TRAP, artists were explicitly encouraged to do objective works for the project and abstractions on their own time. In the rare instances where modernists wrested control of the perquisites from traditionalists, the flow of favoritism was reversed. In New York City, a small but zealous group of abstractionists led by Burgoyne Diller and Harry Holtzman managed to create a small protectorate for abstract artists in the mural division, assigning murals to prominent abstractionists like Arshile Gorky, Stuart Davis, Byron Browne, Jan Matulka, and Ilya Bolotowsky.

Even such small-scale rebellions, however, were often thwarted by regulations requiring every mural to have a sponsor—a school, public library, or similar institution willing to receive it. Sponsors tended to favor the traditionalists: a fashion school requested a mural depicting "the story of Costume"; an airport, the history of aviation. Goodman's mural, *The Spirit of Modern Civilization*, on which Jackson worked, was installed at Grover Cleveland High School in Queens, while Lee Krasner's abstract design for WNYC went homeless. Of the more than one thousand murals begun in the program's first year, only a tiny fraction were abstract. "There were lots of us working on abstract murals," recalls George McNeil, "but the whole thing was sort of mythical. We'd do murals and nothing ever came of them. They were never put in place." In a letter to Reuben Kadish, Sande Pollock (now McCoy) lamented the plight of the artist trapped in a politically accountable bureaucracy: "If and when an artist is given a chance at a wall he is bound hard by a stinking Art Commission headed by the superpatriot, Jonas Lie. So as a result what few murals are being done are merely flat wall decorations of the lowest order."

Frustrated and resentful of government regulations, artists waged a guerrilla war against the bureaucracy. Sande Pollock's name change was just one of thousands of skirmishes—some fought in the name of artistic freedom, some in a Robin Hood–like redistributional game—between artists and project officials who were often just other artists. Many held part-time jobs and concealed the extra income, using it to rent better apartments—which also went unreported—or to spend summers in the country. No act of "subversion" was more widespread than pilfering from WPA supplies. "We figured on a 25 percent loss over our allotment from stealing," recalls Charles Mattox, who in the first years of the project assisted the supervisor of technical projects, sculptor David Smith, and manned the supply window at the WPA distribution center on Thirty-ninth Street. "A lot of the artists were very resentful that they couldn't just take what they wanted." In bureaucratic retaliation, Mattox and Smith carefully calculated how much sizing and how much paint were required to cover a canvas—"we took into account if somebody used more impasto"— how much thinner the cleanup would consume, and how much "mileage" a painter could get from a brush, and doled out supplies strictly according to the formula.

Eventually, Holger Cahill, FAP's director, managed to blunt the most insensitive regulatory intrusions. He abolished the hated "force account" rule, allowing artists to paint in their own studios by their own clocks. Not long afterward —probably not coincidentally—Jackson transferred from the mural division to the easel division. Under the new rules, artists were required only to report periodically to the WPA office (usually once a month) and to produce a minimum quota of paintings (usually one every month to six weeks), and even these loose requirements could be readjusted to suit an individual's working habits.

Meanwhile, the glacier of government largesse was fundamentally reshaping the artistic landscape. Largely relieved of the need for part-time work, artists had more time to spend with one another. At the WPA offices, at the Artists Union, in lofts and bars and cafeterias, they met and talked and, for the first time, felt a genuine sense of community. "What a break it was," recalls Peter Busa. "We were all young, and there was no such animal at the time as a master of fine arts degree, so the WPA really amounted to a graduate program in art. It was an experience we shared. It was really the first art community I was ever aware of." Stories circulated of artists helping other artists, usually by shielding them from inane regulations. "There was a wonderful feeling of people being *for* each other," says one of the few women artists on the project. "We were all together and we all cared—about serious things, about each other." The project was "like one big happy family," says another artist.

Already, in the bars and coffee houses of the Village, a group identity was beginning to take shape that would endure for more than two decades, a male identity based largely on machismo and beer—what Charles Pollock called "the fraternity of painters." "The project changed many things," says Ibram Lassaw, a sculptor, "but most of all it changed the image of the artist. It put an end to the idea that being an artist was somehow unmasculine." Rooted in the furtive pleasures of Prohibition, drinking would become the new community's central ritual. Already, WPA paychecks triggered check-cashing sprees "not unlike payday binges in the army or navy."

In time, the barroom machismo spilled over into artistic competitiveness and bitter feuds. "All artists made enemies," recalls Charles Mattox. "The better they were, the more enemies they made. There was a lot of rivalry on the project." Personal enmities, aggravated in turn by political manipulations of project money and favors, deepened old rifts—political, philosophical, and artistic—further fragmenting the community beneath the surface of homogeneity and self-help. Within a decade, critics would drive the wedges of their favor into these rifts and split Jackson's world apart.

Finally, the projects changed the relationship between the community of artists and the society at large. Such a change had always been part of Roosevelt and Hopkins's master plan. The projects, they hoped, would become a "symbol [of] people's interest in [the artist's] achievement." Even TRAP's Edward Bruce hoped that government support would "[bring] to the artist for the first time in America the realization that he was not a solitary worker." By 1936, however, the projects had already begun, not to bring the artists and their public closer together, but to drive them further apart.

At a time when a saleswoman at Woolworth's earned $10.80 for a fifty-hour week and many others made as little as $7.00 a week, when Ph.D.'s were camping in Morningside Park and professional men were still sleeping in the subways, Jackson and his fellow artists, only a few of whom had children to support, were earning $23.86 a week for unsupervised work, at home, often in rent-free apartments. In return they were required only to produce one painting every four to six weeks, a painting that, in most cases, disappeared into permanent storage. Even compared to others on work-relief, artists were a pampered lot. The average WPA worker (most of whom were classified as construction workers) cost the government only $60 a month, compared with $100 a month for each artist. "The people who worked on the WPA were really part of an aristocracy," recalls Reuben Kadish. "Almost every artist I knew was more flush than they had ever been before."

The world-owes-me-a-living attitude that first showed itself in widespread cheating and pilfering was given political legitimacy by radical union groups beginning with the Unemployed Artists Group in 1933 and later the Artists Union. Founded the same year as PWAP, the Artists Union formalized the emerging sense of community, reflecting both the common experience of the project and the common perception of the bureaucratic enemy against which only a united voice could be effective. Pointing to the close relationship between artists and the state in Communist countries, these groups argued that the government had an affirmative *duty* to support artists. To the extent that the projects "deprived workers of the right to work in their chosen occupations," they were inadequate. Not all artists shared this view, but most, like Jackson, came to view the weekly Treasury check as more than a temporary windfall. By the time World War II brought an end to governmental subsidies, seven years later, the artistic community had become addicted to a life-style and a level of prosperity largely unheard of in the Bohemian days before the projects. Stripped of their privileges, artists would welcome with open arms the new breed of entrepreneurial dealers who appeared after the war, hoping both to recapture the old prosperity and to replace the old "symbol of people's interest" with the new. "There's no doubt that government sponsorship led artists to think they couldn't live without sponsorship of some kind," says Reuben Kadish. "That's one thing Pollock learned, too: somebody else has got to put up the dough."

In the spring of 1935, Tom and Rita Benton left New York. On a lecture tour to the Midwest earlier that year, Benton had been invited to serve as director of painting at the Kansas City Art Institute. To sweeten the offer, a group of prominent Missourians, impressed by Benton's Indiana mural at the Chicago fair, dangled the prospect of a similar commission. (Eventually, the Missouri legislature, persuaded by Benton's unassailable political and artistic credentials, authorized $16,000 for a mural in the statehouse.) Citing a boom in art-related activities in the country's heartland, Benton tried to put a regionalist face on his departure: "I began to feel that I, a western artist, the better part of whose work was motived by western subject matter, should find a way of being part of the change that was coming in my homeland."

In fact, Benton had long since overstayed his welcome in New York. Years of rhetorical jousting in *Art Digest* and *Art Front* magazine, punctuated by drunken outbursts, had left him few allies and legions of enemies. Even close friends like Lewis Mumford, who enjoyed Benton's company but whose political affinities were with the modernist camp, had come to think of Benton's art as just another of his embarrassing personal eccentricities. At the same time that his self-portrait appeared on the cover of *Time* and the country enjoyed a wave of government-subsidized "Regionalist" art, Benton sulked and brooded through his last, unproductive winter in New York. In April, after twenty-three years, he emptied his studio on East Eighth Street, packed his paintings and furniture in a truck—probably with Jackson and Sande's help—and left for Missouri, telling a newspaper reporter in a parting shot that New York "had lost all masculinity."

Four months later, Charles Pollock left for Washington, D.C., to take a position with the Resettlement Administration, a government agency that relocated poor farmers, offering them better land, newer equipment, and free training. The two departures were not unrelated. Benton had intended to take Charles with him to assist on the mural in Jefferson City, but mysteriously withdrew the invitation at the last minute. "I think it had to do with Rita and Elizabeth," says Charles in retrospect. "It was a simple matter of the wives not getting along." The aborted trip forced Charles to reassess his foundering career. Although his paintings had been exhibited at the Ferargil Galleries, reproduced several times in magazines, and even given a favorable mention in the *New York Times*, he was no closer to supporting himself as an artist than he had ever been. Movie posters, art classes, and Elizabeth's salary were still his mainstays. He could have signed on to the Project, but his pride precluded anything that smacked of the dole. "To get on the WPA, you had to be at poverty level," he recalls, "and I didn't want to go out that way." For years, Tom and Rita had been his only regular patrons—seldom buying but often making introductions, lobbying for gallery showings, and arranging jobs. Without them, the prospects were dim indeed. Elizabeth's vigorous, Rita-like campaign to woo prospective buyers had met with little success, and her bitterness was beginning to show in ways other than hostility toward Jackson. In California, Stella was talking of selling quilts to stave off poverty. The family's dignity was at risk. The Resettlement Administration appeared to offer a way out. Because relocation was often especially traumatic for rural, uneducated farmers, the agency had established a Special Services Division to help them preserve their cultural heritage. As part of that effort, musicologist Charles Seeger had begun recording and documenting American folk music. Charles's job would be to illustrate the volumes of sheet music that Seeger's project generated. Sometime in August, he gave Sande and Jackson the key to the Eighth Street apartment and, with Elizabeth, gave up on New York after nine years of trying.

A year earlier, the loss of *either* Benton or Charles would have thrown Jackson into another round of self-abuse culminating in emotional collapse. By 1935, however, his fragile world had more or less stabilized around Sande. Just as the projects had relieved Charles of the financial burden of supporting Jackson, Sande had relieved him of the emotional burden. "If any kind of situation presented itself that would be difficult for Jack to cope with," recalls Reuben Kadish, "Sande took care of it." Jackson continued to drink, often to the point of incapacity, but without the self-destructive determination of previous years. The two moved out of the Houston Street loft and into the spacious and, by comparison, luxurious apartment on Eighth Street. It was accepted without discussion that Jackson would take the large front room with its ideal north light—the room that had been Charles's studio. For his bedroom, Jackson took the small adjacent room he had used before, and Sande moved into the big bedroom in back. A tiny room off the living room was designated as Sande's studio, although he seldom used it.

In this hothouse of financial security and Sande's care, Jackson thrived. The move to Eighth Street, in fact, marked the midpoint of a two-year period of relative emotional tranquillity and extraordinary creative activity.

As early as the spring of 1934, even before Sande's arrival, Jackson had shown signs of recovering from the year of confusion and depression that followed his father's death. Intrigued by a set of lithographic prints that had been pulled for Charles by Theodore Wahl, a Kansas native well known among Benton students, Jackson eagerly sought out Wahl's print shop on MacDougal Street in the Village. "He came blasting in and said, 'I want to do a lithograph,' " Wahl remembers. Despite Jackson's ignorance of the lithographic process, Wahl gave him a prepared stone "just to get rid of him." As if refreshing his memory—it had been almost a year since he had created a completed image—Jackson rapidly sketched on the stones images that still showed the marks of Benton and Ryder: horses and farmhands, threatening skies and turbulent landscapes. Later that spring, at Martha's Vineyard, he sketched the sea, the rocky coast, and the sailboats in Menemsha Harbor with an unusually lucid hand. With Benton's help, he experimented with watercolor, duplicating on paper the style of his Bentonesque oils on canvas. First on the Vineyard, then on the trip across country with Charles, he recorded images—some on paper, more in his memory—that would reappear over the next years in other moods and other forms. A field of Mississippi cotton pickers would be transformed into a tranquil Bentonesque anecdote in oil, a simple watercolor of Vineyard Sound into the heavy impasto of a Ryderesque sea, a bather emerging from the ocean into a mythic figure on a ceramic bowl.

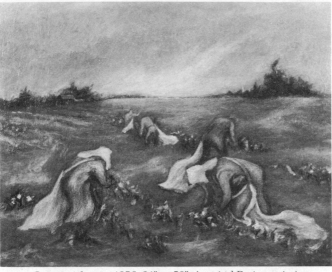

Cotton-pickers, c. 1936, 24″ × 30″. A typical Project painting.

Jackson was already developing a habit that would later confuse and frustrate art historians in their efforts to date his often undated paintings or to trace the "line" of his stylistic development. Although still firmly rooted in Benton's classroom, he had begun to experiment freely with other styles, other moods, other media. "By that time he was beginning to reach out for different solutions," recalls Reginald Wilson. "You could sense his ambition." A Bentonesque study would be followed by a Ryderesque seascape, and that by a semiabstraction, all in a single creative breath. By early 1935, Sande's arrival had rekindled his interest in the Mexican muralists and another style was added to the shifting mix. In February, even as the Brooklyn Museum was exhibiting one of his works for the first time (a small, presumably Bentonesque watercolor or gouache quaintly titled *Threshers*), Jackson was painting the vast, lewd mural in the style of Orozco on the walls of the Houston Street loft. By the time he saw his first full-scale exhibition of Ryder's paintings at the Kleeman Galleries in late 1935, he had already visited the Museum of the American Indian at Broadway and 155th Street, awakening deep childhood memories of burial grounds and cliffside dwellings.

Nowhere did Jackson experiment more exuberantly than in the ceramic plates and bowls he produced at Rita Benton's urging during the winter of 1934–35. On the cramped, unlikely surfaces of these multicolored pieces, he displayed for the first time the full range of his influences and invention. In the bottom of an eight-inch bowl, an obscure brown figure stands at the seashore as the sun sets behind a thunderhead of clouds in a confusion of dark red, blue, and white. Stormy sea mirrors stormy sky. On a nine-inch oval platter, a sailboat crosses a bright Vineyard sea while ominous, Ryderesque clouds threaten to choke the sun. At the bottom of an ashtray, a Social Realist tableau in shades of rust, yellow, blue, and black disintegrates into near abstraction as two workmen wrestle a pneumatic drill in a burst of terse, vibrating lines. On the open range of an eighteen-inch plate, a Bentonesque cowboy is caught in the grim, un-Bentonesque business of shooting his lame horse while, in an incongruously playful touch, the ground sparkles with dabs of white, and, in the sky beyond, a purple Ryderesque storm gathers vengefully. In a shallow seventeen-inch bowl, an attenuated Promethean figure rises from the Vineyard waves like a Michelangelo nude and turns his Bentonesque back to watch a sailboat flounder in a churning Ryderesque sea.

A visit from Harold Lehman, who moved to New York in September, reintroduced Jackson to the old masters. With Lehman tirelessly leading the way, the two toured New York's museums and galleries, especially the newly opened Frick on Fifth Avenue. "They had El Grecos and Goyas and Rembrandts," Lehman remembers, "and Jackson made a copy of a little El Greco, *Expulsion from the Temple.*" Not long afterward, at Sande's invitation, Reuben Kadish and Phil Goldstein arrived from half a year in Mexico and camped out briefly on the Pollock brothers' floor. They brought with them a youthful disdain for the stylistic crudities of the Mexican muralists, especially Rivera, but a renewed enthusiasm for Siqueiros's "kinetics" and Orozco's emotional plasticity. In early 1936, Jackson submitted a mural proposal in the style of Orozco.

With Kadish, Jackson visited the Museum of Natural History on Central Park West, reliving summer trips to the basement displays of Oceanic art at the Los Angeles County Museum. "We would go straight to the large carvings in the Northwest Coast Indian room," Kadish recalls. "Those pieces were very communicative." Meanwhile, at the WPA office on King Street and at cafés and cafeterias around the Village, Jackson listened to Arshile Gorky wax eloquent on Rouault and Picasso, and a group of European artists who called themselves Surrealists.

With new and old images shifting and recombining in his imagination, Jackson reached out in every direction to capture them. At Job Goodman's studio on Sixteenth Street, he experimented with modeling for the first time since his abortive efforts in Robert Laurent's class three years earlier. The opportunity arose serendipitously when Goodman, in preparation for the mural, insisted on making wax maquettes as Benton had done. "Making these Renaissance maquettes was driving [his assistants] crazy," recalled Charles Mattox, the Project supervisor who oversaw Goodman's mural. "So nearly everybody working there was using wax to make things of their own." Like schoolboys, the assistants would wait for the lunch break when they could create "things which were quite free," according to Mattox. It isn't known how long these furtive sculpting sessions continued, or how many pieces Jackson completed, but at least one work satisfied him enough to justify the effort of casting it in bronze at a small foundry on Court Street in Brooklyn. It was a small, complex piece of interpenetrating limbs, of a bird-like creature and a man-like figure embracing, or fighting, across a barrier of driftwood-like convolutions. In the midst of work on a Bentonesque mural, while submitting

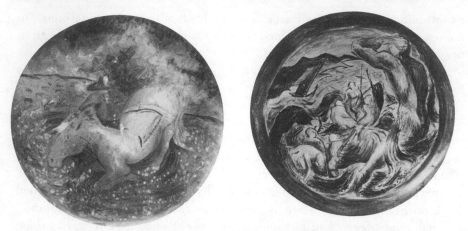

Left: C. 1934, enamel on porcelain plate, 18″ diameter, signed on back, "For Rita / Jackson."
Right: C. 1934, enamel on chinaware bowl, 17″ diameter

mural designs in the Mexican style, listening to Harold Lehman's endless monologues on Raphael and Rembrandt, and visiting the totemic images of the Northwest Coast Indians, Jackson created a sculpture that crossed the threshold of abstraction. Yet, within a year, he would submit to the easel division a series of placid Bentonesque landscapes hardly distinguishable from his earliest classroom work; and twenty years later, at the end of his life, he would still be "experimenting" in the style of Orozco.

Such an outpouring of creativity and experimentation did not go unnoticed. For the first time in his life, Jackson began to hear a murmur of accolades. After his visit to Martha's Vineyard in the spring of 1934, Benton wrote, "I think the little sketches you left around here are magnificent. Your color is rich and beautiful. You've the stuff old kid—all you have to do is keep it up." Mingled with the praise were reservations—the same reservations Jackson would hear often over the next twenty years. "You ought to give some time to drawing," Benton couldn't resist adding, "but I do not somehow or other feel the lack of drawing in the stuff left here. It seems to go without it." Sensitive to his student's depression, Benton may have exaggerated his praise, but even talking in private with their niece, Maria Piacenza, Tom and Rita insisted that Jackson was "a genius." (Years later, looking at Jackson's work in retrospect, Benton was more circumspect. "By 1934," he wrote, "Jack was showing compositional ability of an unusual sort.")

The broader public judgment, to the extent Jackson perceived it, was more reserved. Of the three paintings that he exhibited during this period—*Threshers* at the Brooklyn Museum, *Cotton Pickers* at the Temporary Galleries of the Municipal Art Committee, and *Cody, Wyoming* at the Ferargil Galleries—only the last one "sold"—in exchange for a suit of clothes. Yet a consensus was forming among his friends that Jackson, in Charles's phrase, "had something cooking." Charles Mattox remembers seeing Jackson's sketches for proposed murals and thinking "he was one of the better people in that group." When

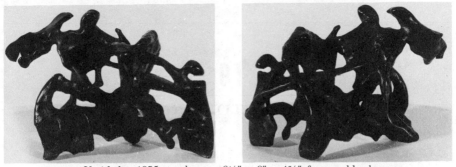

Untitled, c. 1935, cast bronze, 6½″ × 9″ × 4¾″, front and back

Reuben Kadish arrived in New York in the winter of 1935–36, he could see that Jackson's "self-confidence had begun to coalesce because various people thought that he had a helluva lot on the ball." One of the people who thought so was Burgoyne Diller, the supervisor of the mural division. Another project artist, Jack Tworkov, recalled a conversation with Diller. "[He] told me about a painter he considered one of the most talented on the Project. He looked upon him as a great hope for American painting. He named Pollock and it was almost the first time I heard the name."

19

AN ANTIDOTE TO REGIONALISM

It was at this creative peak that Jackson once again encountered David Alfaro Siqueiros, the revolutionary Mexican painter whose dynamism and fecundity were legend among militant young artists. Only four years earlier, both men had come away from their first brief meeting in Los Angeles strangely untouched. This time they struck sparks.

After leaving Los Angeles—at the request of local officials—Siqueiros had gone to Buenos Aires, where he continued to pursue his ambitious vision of a worldwide "syndicate of artists." In February 1936, he arrived in New York to represent Mexico at the American Artists Congress. Under the sponsorship of George Gershwin, he remained in New York and, within weeks, began organizing another "workshop" of artists like the one Kadish, Goldstein, and Lehman had joined in Los Angeles. It was to be "a laboratory of traditional and modern techniques in art," according to Siqueiros's introductory statement, read to the Artists Union by Jackson's old classmate, Harold Lehman: "We shall experiment with all the modern tools which can be employed by the artist. . . . We invite all of you to come and work with us and help us in the building and developing of what we have started."

At thirty-eight, Siqueiros was still "the naughty boy of Mexican art," a man of adolescent temper tantrums ready to "throw down his painting machines at any moment [and] rush out into the street to make a demonstration, or throw stones at capitalistic windows." Born in Chihuahua, Mexico, in 1898 to a libertine father, Siqueiros, like Jackson, had been scarred by a childhood of inattentive parents and insensitive schooling. At thirteen, he was jailed for the first of many times; at fourteen, he left home to join the revolutionary *Batallón Mamá,* an army of children who fought to overthrow Porfirio Díaz; by fifteen, he was a battle-tempered lieutenant. The rest of his life had followed more or less the same pattern, as the war moved off the battlefield and into the streets, into words, and into his painting. "The ideal goal of art," he wrote in 1923,

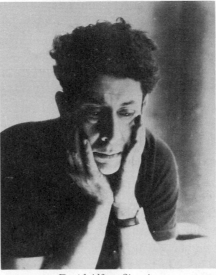

David Alfaro Siqueiros

". . . should be one of beauty for all, of education and of battle." Although not a heavy drinker, he shared Jackson's predilection for violence and "uncontrollable excesses." When he spoke, especially in English, he fired words like a rivet gun. "It didn't matter whether he was talking about peanuts or politics," recalls Reuben Kadish. "Everything was explosive." He was, according to one observer, "a man on fire."

Also like Jackson, Siqueiros was capable of disarming warmth and charm. His revolutionary zeal for "the class war" often showed itself as a childlike idealism, and his fiery intensity generated a potent charisma. "Things happened around him," recalls Axel Horn, who joined the workshop soon after Sande and Jackson, "and that made you want to be near him." When Sande, who had worked at the fringe of the Los Angeles workshop, brought Jackson to the studio on Union Square and introduced him to Siqueiros, there was, according to witnesses, a deep, instant bond between them. "They had a great rapport," recalls Reuben Kadish. "They seemed to reflect each other in a strange way. Each felt the other's intensity. When you put them in the same room, they really bounced off each other." Another friend remembers them as "extremely *simpático*." Almost immediately, they established a barroom physical rapport, beginning most workdays at the studio with five minutes of arm wrestling and horseplay. More than once, assistants found them on the floor "twisting and wrestling," rolling over each other in adolescent play.

In April, when Jackson and Sande arrived, Siqueiros's huge loft on the top floor of 5 East Fourteenth Street was bustling with preparations for the upcoming May Day celebration. While outside an unusually warm spring brought Union Square to an early boil, inside more than a dozen artists—including Lehman, Horn, Clara Mahl, Louis Ferstadt, and George Cox, a group of young sculptors, and a "core" of Hispanic artists who traveled with Siqueiros

—worked feverishly on banners, posters, and a giant float. Many also worked on the Project (Cox was working with Jackson on the Job Goodman mural); all worked without pay. "People contributed time and energy because this was a way of being current," Axel Horn remembers, "a way of being in the avant-garde of the art enterprise, of contributing to the development of new ideas." Although Siqueiros addressed all his co-workers as "comrade," and all the participants thought of themselves as "practicing artists" rather than students, a de facto hierarchy was observed, with the master's inner circle of Hispanic artists on the uppermost rung. Harold Lehman, who had worked with Siqueiros in Los Angeles, assumed an informal supervisory role over the American artists. Although irritated by Lehman's arrogance—"He spent much of his time indicating how good he was," recalls Horn—most of the others, including Jackson, generally deferred to his considerable skill. At the other end of the ladder, Jackson and Sande "followed directions" and "acted basically as assistants," according to Lehman, laying in color over large areas after forms had been blocked in by others. "Jackson never took a central role," Horn remembers. "He never generated the ideas. He never masterminded any of these things. Not because he was junior, but because that wasn't what he felt secure doing. Lehman and Siqueiros did most of the painting."

As May 1 approached, the workshop grew more chaotic: paints, panels, tools, pieces of float, and bits of scenery piled up in the big open space. Throughout the day, spray guns hissed, the compressor chugged, drill presses and jigsaws whined, hammers pounded, and the rumble of Union Square rolled in through the open windows. Artists shouted to one another across the din. Even Charles Pollock, who visited his brothers in the workshop in mid-April, was roused from his usual sangfroid, later describing the scene as "outlandish." Indeed, compared to Studio 9 at the Art Students League, where both Charles and Jackson had practiced spiralic countering, Siqueiros's workshop was a brave and dazzling new world, a calamitous introduction to a new way of thinking about art. "You can't imagine how appealing this experience was to young people," says Reuben Kadish, "how different it was from what we'd run across in art school, in life drawing. [Siqueiros] was overturning the whole idea that the only thing worthwhile in art was what was being represented, the whole neoclassical ideal, the whole Greco-Roman tradition."

In his studio, Siqueiros generated a "torrential flow of ideas and new projects" with a child's eye for investigation and surprise. Paint itself was a source of endless discovery, especially the new industrial paints like Duco—a synthetic nitrocellulose-based paint developed for automobiles. (Siqueiros's passion for the new paint earned him the sobriquet "Il Duco.") Synthetic resins like Duco were not only stronger, more durable, and more malleable than organically based oils, they were *new*: products of the technological era. What medium could be more fitting for an art that "belonged" to the workers of that era? "Lacquer had so many possibilities," recalled Axel Horn, "that we tried everything. We threw it around, we dripped it, we sprayed it, we chopped it with axes, we burnt it, just to see what would happen." They applied it in gossamer-light veils of spray and in thick, viscous globs. For a hard edge, they sprayed it through stencils or friskets. For texture, they added sand and paper, pieces of wood and bits of metal. "It was like high school chemistry class," said Horn. "When the teacher leaves the room and there's a mad dash for the chemical cabinet. You grab things and throw them in the sink and throw a match in to see what will happen." Mistakes ("failed experiments") could be scraped off easily—the new paints dried to hardness "almost instantly." Instead of canvas duck or Belgian linen, they used concrete walls, Masonite panels, and plywood boards nailed together like siding on a house—industrial surfaces for industrial paints. "As early as 1936," claims Harold Lehman, "we had already announced the death of easel painting."

New materials demanded new methods, new ways of creating images. A painter should work the way a *worker* works, Siqueiros believed. In applying paint, he should use a spray gun; for plaster, a plaster gun. In one corner of the Union Square workshop stood a silk-screen frame, long considered merely an industrial tool for sign-making. Siqueiros used it to reproduce original works of art as well as posters and placards for the May Day celebration. To create a likeness, Siqueiros relied on the new, more accurate technology of imaging: photography. For portraits, he would photographically enlarge smaller portraits onto giant Masonite panels, then paint the enlarged images with an airbrush. "A lot of people were using these materials, these techniques," Horn recalls, "but he came along and said, 'This is all usable in art.'"

No matter how large the image, Siqueiros never worked from a drawing or a cartoon, preferring to work directly—in "partnership" with his materials. He studied the dynamics of paint—its density, its viscosity, its flow rate—in an effort to incorporate those dynamics into the image, letting the paint itself help create the painting. In an experiment similar to one Jackson had seen in Schwankovsky's classroom, Siqueiros fastened a plywood board to a lazy Susan ("liberated" from a local cafeteria) and poured different color paints directly from the can onto the board as it spun, producing "striking halations of color," according to Horn. "Accidental" images were also created by pouring paints of different colors onto a board, then pouring thinner on top. As the thinner began to flow it would form rivulets through the layers of color, creating "the most fantastic, weird patterns," Harold Lehman recalls. Patterns, in turn, suggested images. By directing the flow of paint—guiding it with a brush, tipping the surface—Siqueiros could "seize" the image and develop it. "Many of his images started the same way," says Lehman, "with automatic dissolvings of paint from which he would pick out images and develop them. That wasn't just one of Siqueiros's techniques, it was *the* technique." Sometime that year, on a visit to Axel Horn's apartment, Jackson laid a canvas on the floor and tried to duplicate Siqueiros's technique by dripping paint across it.

For Jackson, Siqueiros's workshop fulfilled the promises Benton had made but never kept. Where Benton, despite attacks on European modernism, "aes-

thetic orthodoxies," and "conformist principles," always remained unshakably
rooted in the traditions of Western art, Siqueiros offered a genuinely new vision
of what art could be. Where Benton searched through four-hundred-year-old
tomes to reconstruct the formulas and techniques of Renaissance mural painting, Siqueiros reached into the hardware store of technology for spray guns
and silicones and asbestos panels, and talked proudly of "putting out to pasture
'the stick with hairs on its end.' " Where Benton wrought murals and easel
paintings and sketches just as Michelangelo or Tintoretto had done centuries
before, Siqueiros painted floats as well as murals, banners, placards, and rally
decorations. After having observed Benton through the long weeks of preparation on the New School murals—assembling the sketches, gessoing the
panels, mixing the tempera, lighting the plasticine models, transferring the
cartoons—Jackson must have felt liberated as he watched the spry, wiry Siqueiros standing over a twenty-five-foot-square painting laid out on the floor
in front of him, spray gun in hand, shooting a jet of Duco at an image the size
of a boulder. According to Axel Horn, "the possibilities inherent in the experimentation at the Siqueiros workshop offered [Jackson] a way out of his lack of
technical facility." Even Charles, who visited the workshop only once, was
struck immediately by the subversive power of what he saw—the "violation of
accepted craft procedures," "accidental effect," and "scale." "The whole ambience," he later wrote, "was an antidote to regionalism."

And to other ailments as well.

For all his brusqueness and bluster, for all his denunciations of "fairies,"
Tom Benton's art always belonged to the world of Lizzie Wise and Stella
Pollock, the world of sable brushes, well-turned lines, pretty colors, and Renaissance *contrapposto*. It was an art of refinement, control, repression, and
indirection that Jackson was never able to reconcile with his search for a
masculine self-image. Siqueiros, on the other hand, was an artist that Roy
Pollock would have liked: for his politics, his workmanlike approach to the
artist's trade, his deep respect for materials, his ardent involvement with his
work, his pragmatic concern for the usefulness of his labor, even the scale of
his works. Before his father's death, Jackson had tried to persuade him that an
artist was just a worker whose business was "composition," like the carpenter's
or the mason's. Benton, he bragged, had "lifted art from the stuffy studio into
the world and happenings about him, which has a common meaning to the
masses." Now, three years later, it was Siqueiros, not Benton, who delivered
on that boast.

Throughout April, as preparations for the May Day celebrations accelerated
and the workshop staff swelled with volunteers, Jackson spent most of his time
on the wood-frame armature for the chicken-wire and papier-mâché float. The
design, conceived by Siqueiros and his entourage, called for a large central
figure representing a Wall Street capitalist holding in his outstretched hands a
donkey and an elephant—indicating that "as far as the working class was
concerned, both political parties were controlled by enemies of the people"—

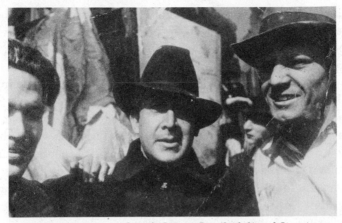

At the May Day parade with George Cox (far left) and Siqueiros

and a large ticker-tape machine which, when struck by a giant, movable hammer emblazoned with the Communist hammer and sickle, would break apart
and spew tape over the capitalist figure. Siqueiros called it "an essay of poly-
chromed monumental sculpture in motion" and intended it to represent both
the enormous political power of Wall Street and the unity of the North American peoples in their determination to overthrow the capitalist system.

With access to a car (Charles had recently signed over his Model A Ford to
his younger brothers), Jackson instantly became "the person to go get something if it was needed," according to Horn. On the morning of May 1, he and
Sande helped carry the float's giant pieces down the fire escape, reassembled
them in the street below, then towed them to the parade staging area. The
celebrations were bigger and more peaceful than ever as labor groups and
political activists from around the country put aside factional differences and,
under the surprisingly benign eyes of 1,500 New York police, celebrated the
fiftieth anniversary of the Haymarket riots. Kicked off by a fat Hitler look-alike
with bloodied hands, the "shuffling line" of marchers included "all grades and
classifications of organized workers," according to the next day's *Times*, "from
garment makers, striking ship-builders, teachers, lawyers, writers, dancers and
actors to boondoggling WPA workers." "The public ate it up," recalls Harold
Lehman, who followed the float nervously, fearing it might fall apart. "They
gave us support all along the route, except for a few reactionaries shouting
epithets." Later, standing as spectators among the throng that filled Union
Square to hear the speeches at parade's end, Jackson and WPA friend George
Cox posed proudly for a photograph with an uneasy-looking Siqueiros.

With the end of the celebration and approach of summer, the workshop
emptied. Newly flush, WPA artists made plans to leave New York for the
summer; Siqueiros began work on a series of private commissions to earn
money for the next round of political activity. "He was always working," Lehman recalled. "At such [quiet] times people would drift off and only the central
core would remain—the Mexicans, other Latins, and a few, very few, Ameri-

cans." Neither Jackson nor Sande was among those few who remained. By the end of May, less than two months after arriving at the Union Square studio, they stopped coming altogether. Others who did return remember seeing the Pollock brothers working on and off at the workshop until early the next year when Siqueiros left to join the Republican Army in Spain, but the immersion was over. It had been an experiment, not an education.

It did, however, give Jackson a vivid glimpse of what was possible: in scale, in materials, in methods, even in fundamental assumptions about the nature of art. It now remained only to realize those possibilities—a task that frustrated even Siqueiros. "I am at more unrest with the problems of form in art than ever," he wrote in December 1936, in a letter to all those who had participated in the New York workshop. "I have not yet crossed the bridge of experimentation that will put me on the road to production."

The summer that lay ahead was as bright with promise as any that Jackson could remember. He not only had freedom, thanks to the easel division's lax work rules, he had a car with which to exploit it and, thanks to the WPA, the money with which to enjoy it. Best of all, he had Sande, whose companionship had made the worst year of the Depression tolerable and now promised to make the best year even better. Not since the halcyon summer days in Riverside when they would slip the stripped-down Model T out of gear and let it glide down the mountain from Wrightwood had Jackson felt such a prolonged limbo of happiness.

As in Riverside, the Pollock boys celebrated by taking to the road. A trip north to see Orozco's new murals at Dartmouth College was only one of several long drives into the surrounding countryside that filled the short weeks of spring. They also went west to coal country, and southwest into the rolling farmland and low wooded hills along the Delaware River. "God damn beautiful son-of-a-bitch country," Jackson called it, shouting into the wind from the rumble seat of the Model A. When, in early summer, the opportunity arose to join the legions of Project artists who could finally afford to desert the city, Jackson leapt at it. With memories of Wrightwood and visions of long country days with Sande undoubtedly in his head, he made arrangements with Bernie Schardt, a neighbor, and Reginald Wilson, a League classmate, to rent an old "Dutch" farmhouse on sixty acres of land. For all four, the cost would be only fifteen dollars a month.

Just how long Sande waited before telling Jackson the news isn't known. He may have accompanied the others to the house near Erwinna, Pennsylvania, during the first weeks of summer, giving Jackson at least a few days of the old pleasures. By the end of June, however, he was compelled to give up his secret: he had proposed marriage to Arloie and she had accepted. She would arrive from California in a few weeks.

20

THIS UNNATURAL MASS OF HUMAN EMOTIONS

For a while, Jackson found consolation in the lolling green hills and off-road solitude of Bucks County. The house, like most of those that dotted the hillsides, was little more than an old stone shell, overgrown with rhododendron and blackened with age, its deep front porch yawning out of the underbrush. All around, stands of soybean, corn, and winter wheat rose and fell in shaggy disarray. Like many farms in Bucks County, this one had died years before in the first plague of bank foreclosures that followed the crash. During the summer, limpid sunlight and a reprieve of wildflowers in the hip-high grass lent the old house a tentatively festive air.

The misfortunes of Bucks County farmers had proved a windfall to New York's burgeoning population of artists and writers. Flush with WPA money and time, they rushed to the kind of country life that, during the twenties, had been reserved for the genuinely well-to-do. As in Greenwich Village, the accommodations were often Spartan—few Bucks County farmhouses had heat or water or bathrooms—but they were enough to create the illusion of comfort and leisure. Just down Geigle Hill Road from Jackson's farmhouse, S. J. Perelman was already making notes for his series of pieces in the *New Yorker* on life in Bucks County. Not far away, novelist Josephine Herbst set neighborhood gossips buzzing with rumors of her Communist sympathies. The year Jackson arrived, Dorothy Parker and her husband, Alan Campbell, bought a farm in the same township, Tinicum. While the house was being modernized, they held court at Dyer's Mill restaurant in nearby Doylestown, often accompanied by Herbst and out-of-town guests like Lillian Hellman. Only two miles away, in Frenchtown, on the New Jersey side of the river, both Arthur Koestler and Nathanael West settled in for the summer. Between these pockets of reputation were hundreds of stone farmhouses sheltering hundreds of unknown writers and artists who, like Jackson, didn't think five or ten dollars was too much to pay for a month of escape from the city heat.

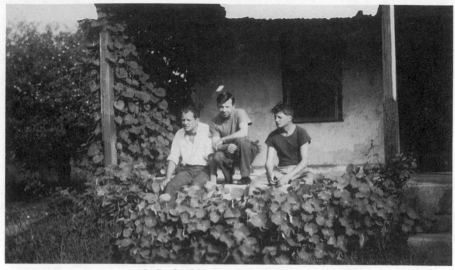

In Bucks County with Jay and Sande

Despite the opportunities for socializing, Jackson spent most of his days painting on the big front porch with Schardt and Wilson or one of their frequent guests. According to Reuben Kadish, who visited regularly, "There was a lot of running off into the woods to draw trees or roots coming out of the swamp. That kind of thing." Most evenings were spent around the old-fashioned country range where the three bachelors "took turns trying to cook something that our mothers used to make," Wilson recalls. For a break from the isolation and one another, they would drive down Geigle Hill Road toward the river, past Stover's Mill, through a covered bridge and into the town of Erwinna where they bought supplies and traded jokes with the locals at Williams's store. A cluster of sturdy stone houses hard by the Delaware Canal, Erwinna had never boomed in the western sense; but, like the farmhouses in the surrounding hills, it had known better times. Before 1930, when mules still pulled barges along the canal, cozy Erwinna had seen its share of drinking, card-playing, and shooting by canalers, the men who ran the barges filled with Lackawanna coal and Bucks County grain down to markets in Bristol and Philadelphia. Now, for anything like the boisterous nightlife of Erwinna in its glory days, visitors had to drive to Revere, about seven miles northwest, where they found no town at all, just two buildings on either side of Rock Ridge Road, one a store, the other a hotel, the Paul Revere. "It was a tiny little place where we used to go to play pool and have a beer," Wilson remembers.

But nothing matched the solitude and escape Jackson found behind the wheel of a car. Even more than painting, driving was the activity that filled the long summer days and helped him forget what was waiting for him on his return to New York. It was as if he had traveled so many miles with Sande that now *any* traveling, even without Sande, was a way of holding on to him. Jackson could often be seen flying down the rough, gravel roads between

Erwinna, Revere, and Doylestown in the Model A Ford, trailing a plume of dust across the rolling quilt of the Piedmont Lowlands. From the pine slopes of Flint Hill in the north to the Atlantic Coastal Plain in the south, on quick trips into the city for WPA submissions, Jackson piled up hundreds of miles against the inevitable. "Jack was a thrilling driver," recalls Wilson, who accompanied Jackson on many of his trips. "He drove very fast and accepted any space that opened up to him, and he was incensed if he felt anyone was infringing on his rights." This may have been the summer that Jackson and Kadish—a frequent stand-in for Sande—took off for Bethlehem, Pennsylvania, twenty-two miles northwest of Erwinna, to sketch at the mile-long Bethlehem Steel mill. Sitting outside the factory fence, sketch pads in hand, the two were "captured" by Bethlehem Steel guards and hauled into the office. "They wanted to know what we were doing," Kadish remembers. "They kept us there, made all sorts of threats, and took all our drawings. Finally they let us go." On the way out of town, the two stopped at a bar where, after telling their story, they were toasted as heroes by local steelworkers, all "big Poles," Kadish remembers, "huge, huge men."

Jackson crammed as many miles as he could into the weeks prior to Arloie's arrival, but nothing, not even alcohol, could forestall the impending panic. On the eve of his return to New York in mid-July, Schardt and Wilson were startled from their rooms by a loud noise on the roof. Outside, Wilson recalls, they "saw Jackson running back and forth along the peak of the roof, waving his fists at the moon and shouting, 'You goddamn moon, you goddamn moon!' "

On July 25, 1936, a wiltingly hot and humid Saturday in New York City, Sande Pollock married Arloie Conaway. It had been almost nine years since their blind date to the San Gabriel Mountains. Along the way, Sande had contrived delay after delay and Arloie had outlasted each one without complaining. When she arrived in New York, he tried one last feint; ostensibly for political reasons, he insisted that the wedding be conducted by a black minister. In the final masochistic act of their long masochistic courtship, Arloie spent a week searching the alien city in vain before Sande finally relented. The wedding took place at City Hall with a drunken Jackson and a total stranger standing witness.

As was her way, Arloie slipped into the apartment on Eighth Street with barely a ripple of disruption. Only in Sande's bedroom, now their bedroom, did she allow herself the self-expressive luxury of an old-fashioned wrought-iron bed painted white and covered with a patchwork quilt. Sande cleared one of the three sections in the hall closet. "I was very aware of coming into a situation that I didn't want to upset," Arloie remembers. "And I leaned over backwards not to change things too much. I didn't want to intrude on their relationship." She wore her extravagantly long, light brown hair in a ring of tight braids like a crown and seldom ventured into the front room, which, although open to the back hall, was considered Jackson's space. She passed the days in the bedroom sewing, or in the kitchen, where her skill as a cook soon began to attract visitors like Harold Lehman, who arrived regularly around dinnertime three or four days a week.

But Jackson wasn't appeased. Within a week of the wedding, he accepted an invitation from the Bentons to come to Martha's Vineyard and urged Sande to join him. Only days after vetoing a honeymoon as "too expensive," Sande packed his suitcase and joined Jackson on a sketching trip from New York City, through Connecticut and Rhode Island to Woods Hole, Massachusetts. There they caught the ferry to the Vineyard where the Bentons, who now lived in Kansas City, continued to spend their summers. For two weeks, Arloie paced the Eighth Street apartment in the sweltering August heat. "It was a strange city and I didn't know anyone," she remembers. "I never felt so alone in my life."

Sande's marriage was only the last and most dramatic in a series of events that lent Jackson's sexual dilemma new urgency. In April of 1935, Frank had married Marie, leaving Jackson alone in the family without even a prospect of marriage. "His brothers betrayed him by getting wives," said one old friend. Everywhere Jackson turned, he saw the same threat. With WPA money in their pockets, more and more of his friends who had postponed commitments during the general abstinence of the Depression began to make plans; marriage became thinkable again. In 1936, Phil Goldstein bunked in the Pollock's Eighth Street apartment for several weeks and bragged about his beautiful bride-to-be, Musa McKim; Herman Cherry passed through town morose and dispirited by a broken love affair; Bruce Mitchell, Jackson's old drinking buddy from the Art Students League, married Olivia Dehn; Bernie Schardt, his Bucks County housemate, met his soon-to-be-bride Nene Vibber; and even Manuel Tolegian, while still on the prowl in New York, began to make marital noises with the faithful Araks in Los Angeles.

At twenty-four, Jackson was still struggling to find his sexual footing. For a long time after the debacle with Rose Miller, most of his experiences with women had been brief, crude, drunken exchanges at parties and in bars. From Ahron Ben-Shmuel, he had learned frightening new ways to express his hostility, ways that made Tom Benton's caustic misogyny look pale and chivalrous by comparison. "Ben-Shmuel put every contact with women, no matter how casual, on a sexual basis," recalls his student Nathan Katz. "He would run up to women on the street and grab them by their box." According to another student, "he liked to humiliate women by talking about their period, or their sagging breasts. He humiliated them by vocalizing what seemed to be most forbidden." It was a repertoire of abuse to which Jackson would resort again and again in an effort to protect himself from the forbidding demands of intimacy.

At one party, Elizabeth Pollock made the mistake of introducing him to the hostess, a bright, single woman in her late thirties, described by Elizabeth as "a lovely person." After "vacuuming up the wine," Jackson spent most of the evening sitting in a corner, glowering at the festivities. Suddenly, without warning, he stalked across the room to the woman and roared, "You are the ugliest goddamned old bitch I ever saw!" Family members began to comment to one another about how it was "unnatural for [Jackson] not to bring women home." At one point, aware of the gossip and undoubtedly stung by it, Jackson tried clumsily to put a stop to it. Arriving home in the middle of the day, Charles and Elizabeth heard "scuffling" and "a girl's frightened protest" on the fifth floor landing. "Jackson was trying to shove a young woman back into his room and she was fighting back," Elizabeth remembers. "He pushed her, really shoved this girl ahead of him through the door. She looked scared to death as he slammed the door behind them." Through the wall, Charles and Elizabeth heard arguing, then, only minutes later, the sound of Jackson "brutally shoving her along the hall and following her down the stairs."

Sande's arrival in the fall of 1934 saved Jackson from more serious abuses. As in Riverside, his companionship satisfied Jackson's need for intimacy and, at the same time, reaffirmed his manhood. "Sexually, Jackson was always a solitary guy," says a fellow artist who met Jackson around this time. "Rather than having any kind of a sustained relationship with some other person, he had that family relationship with Sande." Abetted by hard times, which made "dating" unaffordable, Jackson spent two unthreatened years with Sande, his sexuality safely confined to dance-floor outbursts and barroom antics. He no longer even bothered to fabricate affairs as he had for years at the Art Students League. After moving into the privacy of the Eighth Street apartment, he avoided any repetition of the scene on the landing. "I never saw a girl up there," recalls Harold Lehman, who visited often.

Sometime prior to Arloie's arrival, Jackson was seen several times with a woman named Sylvia, "a very plain girl," Axel Horn recalls, "rather tall and very diffident—just like Jackson"—who was "obviously having trouble finding a man. They must have gravitated together by virtue of both being unhandy in love—kindred souls." Remembered mostly for her height and fuzzy blond hair, Sylvia appeared so infrequently in Jackson's life that most of his friends, including Lehman, never met her and those who did never learned her last name.

Immediately after returning from Martha's Vineyard in August, Jackson jumped in the Model A and roared off to Bucks County to rejoin Bernie Schardt and Reginald Wilson. Two months later—long after the trees had begun to turn, long after the other temporary residents (including Schardt and Wilson) had fled to the city—Jackson was still there, as if in hiding, driving through the hills as the color drained out of them. He found a small farmhouse near Frenchtown on the New Jersey side of the river that the owner gratefully let for five dollars a month. It must have seemed the perfect place for his self-imposed exile: a one-room cell with eighteen-inch-thick stone walls, a lean-to kitchen, and a sleeping loft. Outside there were no trees nearby to protect it from the cold winds that blew down the Delaware Valley from Canada, only a rusty pump and a field of old clumped soybean.

Nevertheless, on his brief trips into the city, Jackson talked of staying the winter in Frenchtown, bragging to Sande that he had persuaded Sylvia to join him in the country. "He had this romantic notion that they would spend the winter together in this little house," Arloie remembers. Whether Sylvia actually went or how long she stayed is not recorded, but, according to Reuben Kadish, Jackson was incapable of spending more than "a couple of hours" alone with a woman. "He had no idea how to strike up a conversation with the opposite sex," says Axel Horn, "or how to maintain a conversation once it began." If Sylvia did go, she may have stayed long enough for Jackson to paint a portrait of her. ("He must have been thrilled that somebody was finally willing to pose for him," says Horn, into whose hands the portrait later passed. "It was not very deft. Jackson was struggling to evoke a particular person but having a hard time with the paint." Horn later threw the painting away.) If, as seems more likely, Sylvia never visited the little stone house outside Frenchtown at all, or visited only briefly, then Jackson spent the month of October sitting alone in the desolate farmhouse, drinking to stay warm, and driving around the barren hills, concealing his lie with an elaborate charade.

Late that month, undoubtedly while drunk, he demolished the Model A. In reporting the accident to Charles, Sande made the usual excuses. "Jack had the misfortune of collideing with some bastard," he wrote, "and as a result the old Ford has been permanently lain to rest. The other man's car was damaged to the extent of eighty bucks which it appears Jack will have to pay." Saddled with a bill for eighty dollars, confined by the winter to his tiny, drafty cell, confronted for the first time with real loneliness, Jackson quickly capitulated. In early November, he returned to the Eighth Street apartment, explaining tersely that the little farmhouse was simply "too cold." Soon thereafter, Arloie noticed that Sylvia had dropped out of his life.

Almost immediately, the trouble started. Jackson resumed the nightly forays to the bars along Thirteenth Street, Fourteenth Street, and Sixth Avenue, just as if Sande were still along. By midnight he was drunk, and by two or three he was reeling, violent, sick, and disoriented—or unconscious. Bartenders turned him away or threw him out, sometimes as soon as he appeared in the doorway. He would buy drinks without money, then move on to another bar and order drinks all around. Every evening, Sande would struggle not to notice Jackson's absence for a few hours, then, around midnight, like clockwork, begin the search. "[Jackson] would disappear and we would go around walking, trying to find him," remembers Reuben Kadish, who often joined the search. "We would go to the familiar haunts like the clam bar on Eighth Street." Sometimes they would return after hours of fruitless searching only to find Jackson passed out on the couch. More often, they found him on the street, bellowing at the moon, or slumped over a bar owing money. It was a scene they had played out hundreds of times. If Jackson was violent, Sande might have to ride him down, or pacify him with a hard right to the jaw, but it always ended with Jackson falling onto Sande's shoulders in childlike submission for the long, slow walk home. "I remember Sande really *dragging* Jackson up those stairs," says a neighbor who often heard the "clump and slide" of the brothers' late night return. Once inside the apartment, they would stagger to the kitchen where Sande would set Jackson carefully in a chair and pour him coffee. Even then, Jackson could suddenly erupt in violence or burst into tears, but whatever happened, Sande sat beside him, held him, and talked soothingly until he fell asleep.

There was an air of ritual about these episodes. Jackson seldom ventured beyond the "familiar haunts" and Sande, according to Arloie, "always seemed to know where to go find him and bring him home." More clear-eyed witnesses, like Reginald Wilson, saw the petulance beneath the pyrotechnics. "The most important thing for Jackson was that Sande be willing to put his relationship with Arloie on hold whenever Jackson needed him," says Wilson. But to hold on to Sande, Jackson had to keep raising the stakes. So the binges grew more frequent, more self-destructive, and more prolonged. By Christmas time, he was disappearing for three and four days at a time and returning in an "indescribable state."

Arloie was both terrified by Jackson's rages and angered by the almost nightly intrusions into her married life, by the early morning shuffling and murmuring of the affectionate ritual being played out in the next room. Unlike Elizabeth, she continued to profess the tenderest feelings for Jackson, but she recognized the challenge implicit in his nocturnal antics and responded firmly. "I told Sande I didn't want to see [Jackson] in that state," she remembers. Thereafter, when she heard them staggering up the stairs, she locked herself in the bedroom and refused to come out until Jackson had gone to bed. Faint, unrecognized, and later denied, the battle lines were drawn.

Instead of retaliating directly against Arloie, Jackson turned his rage on other women. At the Saturday night dances sponsored by the Artists Union, he would accost them in reeling fits of belligerence, randomly grabbing and kissing them. "He would come on very strong," Peter Busa remembers. "He approached women almost like a dog, bending down and smelling them. He could tell by the smell if a gal had her period, and if she did, he would tell her so." Lurching across the dance floor, he would break into couples, belch obscenities, and, invariably, provoke fights. From these, too, Sande often rescued him. "He used to get thrown out of the Union dances almost every Saturday for starting fights," Charles Mattox remembers. Too drunk to be daunted, he would stumble from the Union's loft at Sixteenth Street and Sixth Avenue to the nearest subway and take the A train to Harlem, where he would "try to pick up whores," recalls Busa, who didn't dare accompany him.

It was almost as if Jackson had embarked on a campaign to cut himself off from any possibility of a relationship. "He always did the wrong thing and said the wrong thing," Reuben Kadish recalls. "He always got drunk at the wrong time. Women were a constant source of disappointment." Only once during the drunken winter of 1936–37 did his offensive defenses break down. At an Artists Union party around Christmas time, he stumbled up to a dancing couple and, stepping between them, took the woman clumsily in his arms. She was slightly older with an intriguingly unattractive face—prominent nose, heavily lidded eyes, and a protruding mouth that she kept closed to hide her bad teeth —but a taut, proud body. She was, apparently, far more pliant than Jackson had expected. He pulled her closer and began rubbing his body against hers. "Do you like to fuck?" he whispered in a beer-soaked grumble. When she felt his erection, she pushed him away. "It was like when a dog gets on your leg," recalls an eyewitness. "He was trying to have an orgasm." Indignant, the woman slapped him hard across the face. The blow must have startled Jackson into something like instant sobriety because, according to one witness, he quickly apologized. What happened next was even more out of character. "He started to charm me," the woman told a friend years later. "I was intrigued and liked him and we went home together." If anything happened there, its memory quickly disappeared in the alcoholic fog that obscured much of the thirties. Four years later when the woman reappeared in his life, Jackson had forgotten both the incident and her name—Lee Krasner.

Inevitably, Jackson's roiling emotional life spilled into his art.

The 300-mile trip to Dartmouth College in New Hampshire, with Sande, Bernie Steffen, Phil Goldstein, and Reginald Wilson to view Orozco's mural cycle, *Epic of American Civilization,* had rekindled Jackson's long-standing obsession with the painter of *Prometheus.* According to Peter Busa, Jackson kept a large reproduction of the Pomona mural prominently displayed in his studio, and, when asked, readily offered the opinion that it was "the greatest painting done in modern times." His hyperbole was, at least in part, an echo of the enthusiasm Kadish and Goldstein had brought back from Mexico the previous winter. Although generally disdainful of the "much heralded Mexican Renaissance"—Rivera's stylistic "crudities" and Siqueiros's "shitty" painting —they had come away with a new, more complex appreciation of Orozco. Goldstein, whose own paintings at the time were, if anything, too deftly calcu- lated, faulted Orozco for being "dominated by emotion," but praised the plas- ticity of his forms. For Jackson, however, expressionism and emotion were the keys to Orozco's power. The vast mural cycle in the basement reading room of Dartmouth's Baker Library was more than a tour de force of composition and plastic form, it was a landscape of images that struck Jackson with galvanizing force.

On seventeen panels of overlapping scenes, shifting moods, and assaultive imagery, Orozco had exposed the errant path of Mexican "civilization," from Aztec human sacrifices to the coming of Cortez to twentieth-century militarism. Out of this kaleidoscopic procession, Jackson's eyes were drawn to two images

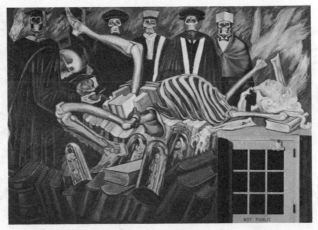

Gods of the Modern World, José Clemente Orozco, 1932–34, fresco, 120″ × 119″

in particular. One was a nightmarish vision of modern education in a panel called *Gods of the Modern World*. In what appears to be a satanic ritual, five skull-faced "academics" preside as a grotesque skeletal figure—half human, half animal—gives birth on a bed of books and specimen bell jars. Another skull-faced figure in mortarboard acts as midwife, holding the tiny skeletal fetus while the mother kicks her bony leg high in the air in a reflex of pain. The other image—at the far end of the cycle, near a doorway—was a huge Prometheus-like figure, striding out from the shadows into sun-like yellows, oranges, and reds, a titanic Christ straining at the edges of the panel, looming at the threshold of the picture plane as if the next step forward would be onto the reading room floor. On the ground between his legs lies the massive cross from which he has descended; in his hand, the ax he used to chop it down. He is surrounded by the ruins of the corrupt "civilization" he came to destroy— discarded armaments, religious icons, cultural fragments. Like Prometheus, he has suffered: his hands and feet are stigmatized with gaping holes, his legs are flayed, exposing the bloodless muscle tissue beneath, his face is scarred with pain. If the Pomona *Prometheus* showed suffering, Orozco's avenging Christ described volcanic agony.

Jackson made sketches of the mural while in Hanover, then returned to New York and put them aside. On the trip to the Vineyard with Sande after the wedding, he sketched a few placid landscapes and watercolor seascapes, just as he always had. It wasn't until he returned to New York in November and was forced to confront his own demons that Orozco's demonic imagery began to reverberate in his imagination.

Throughout the winter, when not drunk or recovering from a binge, Jackson explored the dark landscape that Orozco had shown him. His sketchbooks are filled with skeletal, half-human beasts, pregnant women—some of them carry- ing skeletal animals in their wombs—crosses and chains, skulls, and flayed bodies. In several drawings, figures spring from the womb already nailed or

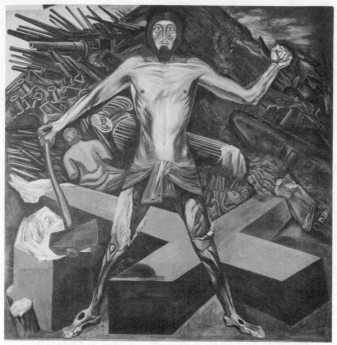

Modern Migration of the Spirit, José Clemente Orozco, 1932–34,
fresco, 120″ × 126″

chained to crosses, some already reduced to skeletal carcasses. In one painting done that winter, Jackson depicted Orozco's skull-faced academicians towering over a prostrate figure. In another, he borrowed the entire nightmare tableau of *Gods of the Modern World* to explore his own vision of hell: a skeletal "mother beast" lies prone, surrounded by a crowd of leering skull faces as she gives birth to an unseen infant. Bending over her in an almost fetal position is a faceless female figure that could be mother, infant, midwife, or all three.

Not since the dark, Ryderesque "family portraits" that he painted after his father's death—the brutal images of a naked mother with huge, pendulous breasts, surrounded by her brood of skeletons—had Jackson entered so unblinkingly the underworld of his unconscious. For almost two years after Arloie's arrival, the problems that tormented him in the outer world were played out, with wrenching candor, in his art. And once again, the central figure was Stella Pollock. In the real world, Stella may have been unassailable, but on canvas or Masonite or paper, she became his nemesis: a grotesque figure, naked, faceless, bloated, and brutalized. In the real world, Jackson could express his rage only indirectly, in endless barroom binges and dance-hall scenes, in self-abusive brawling and public humiliation. In his art, however, using Orozco's grim vocabulary, he learned to express the inexpressible. Through the brutality he inflicted on perpetually faceless female figures, he found a way to enact his ancient fantasies of retribution. Through his obsessive mixing of images of birth and suffering—fetuses nailed to crosses, crucifixes springing

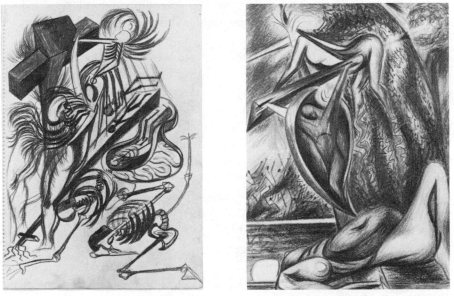

Both 1936–37, pencil and crayon on paper, 14″ × 10″

from the womb—he could portray his misery and at the same time vent his rage at Stella for delivering him into that misery. She became the skull-faced midwife and executioner of Orozco's mural as well as the pregnant skeleton bearing her skeletal baby into a world of suffering.

To Orozco's ghoulish images, Jackson added one from the deep recesses of his own past. Since watching Stella control the horses hitched to her buggy—just as she controlled her husband and sons—Jackson had seen horses not just as symbols of masculinity but as reminders of sexual ambiguity. The pregnant carcass in Orozco's mural, with its huge skeleton and beastlike skull, may have triggered this old association. As a succession of women—Rita, Arloie, Sylvia, and soon Becky—raised tormenting doubts about Jackson's own sexuality, horses began appearing in his art, sometimes as skeletons, sometimes attached to human bodies, often in mid-transformation, becoming birds or bulls—other animals connected with masculinity that had obsessed him since childhood.

Even in the midst of this winter-long Walpurgisnacht, Jackson somehow managed to resurface in the real world often enough to paint a series of placid landscapes and anecdotal Bentonesque scenes. Like all Project artists, he was aware that the FAP paid for supplies by selling submitted works and that agreeable representational images were more likely to be accepted because they were more likely to be sold. After 1936, however, such paintings had become mere exercises, thinly and quickly painted as if he were impatient with the ruse. His real artistic energy was directed elsewhere. From the imminent wreck of his emotional life, his imagination had salvaged new subject matter and a new style perfectly suited to record his descent. Just as Siqueiros had begun the process of liberating Jackson from traditional materials—"the stick with hairs on the end"—Orozco had cracked open the Pandora's box of Jackson's unconscious and, in so doing, begun the liberation of his imagination.

The Christmas celebrations, including a turkey from Rita Benton, only pushed Jackson deeper into despair. Drinking binges and recovery days had begun to consume so much work time that even the "exercises" he did to meet the FAP's lax requirements had become a burden. "Not having much luck with painting," he wrote Charles in a tone of hopelessness reminiscent of the worst days at Manual Arts. "Got my last painting turned back for more time—they didn't like the form in the water—if it had been a good picture I wouldn't have consented."

Just at this time, several parties to honor Siqueiros were held on the eve of his departure for the Spanish Civil War. When asked to suggest names for the guest lists, the Mexican artist singled Jackson out from among all the assistants in his former workshop: " 'You've got to get Jackson. You've got to get Jackson!' " Reuben Kadish remembers him insisting. The first noisy celebration took place at a Basque restaurant on the West Side; the second at an artist's loft. Siqueiros sported a huge ivory-handled revolver given to him by Mexican well-wishers. At one point, just as the drunken guests were set to toast the departing warrior, they discovered he had disappeared. Pollock, "whose scatalogical bellowing was usually much in evidence on such occasions," according to Axel Horn, was also missing. Both men were soon found under a table—wrestling. Still recovering from too much drink at the first Siqueiros send-off, Jackson had gotten roaring drunk at the second, and lunged at the guest of honor. The two men had often "horsed around" together, but this time Jackson wasn't playing. "He was killing him," recalled Horn, who watched in horrified silence as the two men rolled around clutching each other's throats, each "silently attempting to choke the other into unconsciousness. Jack in a wild exhilarated effort and Siqueiros in a desperate attempt to save himself." The deadlock was broken only when Sande rushed to the scene and knocked Jackson unconscious "with a deft right to the jaw." Four of the guests carried Jackson to the Model A and Sande took him home.

By now, Sande had run out of excuses. When, in the late fall, Charles wrote to broach the possibility of Stella moving to New York and living with Sande and Arloie, Sande rejected the idea out of hand. For family consumption, he cited financial constraints and the uncertain future of Project funding, but privately he confessed to Charles that such a move "would be fatal for Jack." It had finally sunk in that Stella was part of the problem, not the solution, and that Jackson's "episodes" were not the transient adolescent phenomena the family had always hoped.

In January 1937, Sande took the final step. Based on "a succession of periods of emotional instability . . . usually expressed by a complete loss of responsibility both to himself and to us," Sande concluded that Jackson was "mentally sick" and should see a psychiatrist. It was an unprecedented and undoubtedly agonizing admission in a family that routinely protected itself with repression and denial: Jackson needed help not just for his drinking but for his past. "As you know," Sande wrote Charles, "troubles such as his are very deep-rooted, in childhood usually, and it takes a long while to get them ironed out." In his search for a psychiatrist who would "help [Jackson] find himself," Sande turned to Caroline Pratt and Helen Marot at the City and Country School. Marot, with her connections in the city's small community of Jungian analysts, was especially interested in Jackson's troubles. The psychiatrist whom she recommended to Sande was undoubtedly drawn from among fellow Jungians like Cary Baynes, a woman who had known Jung and translated several of his books. Although Sande was clearly impressed by the analysts's credentials and even optimistic about the results, most of the family shared Jay's wife, Alma's, early skepticism. "Jackson didn't really want to be helped," she said, "he wanted to be taken care of."

About the same time he began therapy, Jackson set out with fresh determination to follow his brothers' lead and find himself a woman. An opportunity presented itself in early February when Tom and Rita Benton came to town and Rita organized a party at the Pollocks' Eighth Street apartment. The occasion was an exhibition at the Municipal Art Galleries that included works by many of Benton's former students who had since graduated to the Project. Inevitably, the old Harmonica Rascals played: Bernard Steffen on dulcimer; Sande, Manuel Tolegian, and Benton himself on harmonica. But Jackson's attention was elsewhere. Throughout the evening he stared at a "slim and pretty" young woman with shoulder-length brown hair who sat on a high stool at one side of the big front room, her back against a window, playing a banjo and singing Tennessee ballads in a high, sweet voice. She was "a lovely girl with a perfect voice and a sweet face," and Jackson, according to Reuben Kadish, "went absolutely gaga."

Her name was Becky Tarwater. Her voice was clear and poignant, her accent was marked by the pleasant, rolling cadences of the hill country, and the name was her own, not a manager's invention. Yet at twenty-nine Becky was not quite the backwater ingenue she appeared to Jackson. Born "Rebecca" to a well-to-do family in the eastern Tennessee town of Rockwood, she had been destined for Wellesley College via a prestigious Philadelphia girls' school when "the theater bug bit." Along with her equally talented sister Penelope, she had enrolled in the Kingsmith Studio School in Washington, D.C., where she studied and taught music and dance for more than eight years.

Despite her extensive training, including a year in Paris, Becky had never ventured far from her roots. "We were hillbillies," she says, "and in our family, everybody sang. . . . My grandmother taught me the most beautiful songs, like 'Bonnie Annie Laurie' and 'Barbara Allen.' " In fact, when she arrived at Jackson's doorstep, she had just come from recording "Barbara Allen" as part of Charles Seeger's folk music project at the Library of Congress. While in

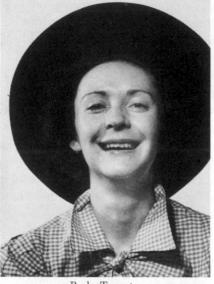

Becky Tarwater

Washington, she had met Charles Pollock who introduced her to Bernard Steffen, an old Art Students League classmate. It was Steffen who had brought her to the Pollock's crowded apartment that night.

Jackson's instant infatuation did not escape notice. "It was very touching," Reuben Kadish recalls. "Jack was like a dodo. He just stared and stared as if she'd hypnotized him." Becky remembers only that he was a persistent listener. "I think he enjoyed the playing," she says. When she stopped playing, however, Jackson continued to stare; and when she left, he followed her out the door. Although drunk as usual, something apparently prevented him from staging the usual drunken scene in the hallway. "He just followed me," Becky remembers. "I would go down a few steps and he would follow, some steps back. When I stopped, he stopped." On the street, "he stayed at a distance behind and when I would turn around to look, he would duck in a doorway. I think it was all teasing." Finally, at the Astor Place subway station, she turned on him and said, softly but firmly, "Jack, I don't want you coming home with me. I am perfectly all right." A friend had arranged for her to stay at the Allerton, a hotel for young women on Fifty-seventh Street, and she feared his appearance there might cause a scandal.

Jackson immediately began planning their next encounter, an event almost guaranteed because she had left her banjo behind in the Eighth Street apartment. He sat up at night picking at the five double strings and asked friends to recommend "a good instruction book" for the banjo. "All I'm able to do so far," he wrote Charles in frustration, "is to get it out of tune." But making music together was only the beginning of Jackson's fantasy. Over the next several months, he began to construct in his imagination an intense, elaborate affair. To Arloie and Sande especially, and to friends like Kadish and Tolegian, he declaimed his infatuation. "He was very much in love with her," Kadish remembers. "He was just crazy about her."

The reality, however, wasn't nearly so intense. Although she returned to the apartment a number of times for dinner, Becky never thought of Jackson as anything more than a friend—"a tortured, sensitive person who was very touching." In the four or five months of their acquaintanceship, Jackson never showed her his paintings or took her to galleries or museums or introduced her to his friends. Their only encounters, in fact, were several more dinners at the Eighth Street apartment where he could show her off to Sande. "We never went out on a date, or to dinner, or anything of that sort," Becky says. On the rare occasions when they talked on the telephone, Jackson never spoke about his family, his past, his ambitions, or his paintings—"painting and anything of that sort just wasn't on his mind," she remembers. He never told her of his therapy or visited the converted church on Lexington Avenue where she sang the nightly entr'acte in a cabaret production of *Naughty Naught.* Nor could he have probed too deeply into Becky's life or thoughts. If he had, he would have discovered that her childhood boyfriend and the man she intended to marry, Mason Hicks, was finishing his internship and residency at Bellevue Hospital and lived only a few blocks from the club where she sang.

Despite such yawning gaps, Jackson and Becky shared enough moments both to sustain his fantasy and to give her some sympathy for his plight. He could be charming—especially when he showed up at the starched-shirt Allerton wearing "a great big cowboy hat"—but seldom laughed. "He was really almost like two people," Becky remembers. "I found him a tortured and unhappy person, but also very sensitive and very sweet. He seemed so complicated. . . . I thought he had too much awareness for his own good." Although she never saw him drunk, she occasionally felt the aftershocks. One day, while walking together, they saw a woman leading a tiny dog on a leash. "This infuriated him," Becky recalls. "He walked over to the woman and started to kick the dog. He was infuriated that somebody could be so infatuated with a dog. I was terrified the police would come." After that incident, fear crept into her fondness. "He was always gentle and sweet with me, but I was afraid to be with him in public, afraid he might create an awkward situation or embarrass me."

Kept alive by dinners and an occasional kiss, the fantasy carried Jackson through the winter. By spring, it had displaced reality altogether. The drinking continued, however, unseen by Becky and unchecked by continuing visits to the psychiatrist. Straining to be optimistic, Sande wrote Charles that he noticed "slight improvement in [Jack's] point of view" after six months of therapy. But the situation was still critical—so critical that he couldn't leave Jackson alone.

Earlier in the year, Charles had moved to Detroit to take a job as a layout editor and political cartoonist for *United Automobile Work,* the weekly newspaper of the United Automobile Workers Union. Soon after arriving, he wrote and invited Sande to join him—hoping that with two solid incomes, they could afford to offer Stella a home. Despite the precariousness of his future on the Project and the hardships of New York, Sande rejected the offer. Jackson was his first responsibility. "Without giving the impression that I am trying to be a wet nurse to Jack," he replied, "honestly I would be fearful of the results if he were left alone with no one to keep him in check." Then, in a step back from the dire implications of his own words, he added, "There is no cause for alarm, he simply must be watched and guided intelligently."

In the wilderness of drinking binges, subterranean rivalries, ineffectual therapy, and arrested creativity, Becky Tarwater remained Jackson's only oasis. "I always felt that I was with him at a time when he was so mixed up in his own life," Becky remembers, "that he couldn't find his way. He didn't seem to know where he was. I think that's why he was attracted to me."

When the time came for her to leave New York and return to Tennessee, she waited as long as possible to tell him. When she did, he asked for one last meeting to say good-bye. They met before lunch in the unlikely fluorescent glare of a White Castle restaurant not far from the Eighth Street apartment. He walked in carrying a single white gardenia and gave it to her. "It was so sweet," she remembers. "That was the side of him that was so really wonderful." Then, surrounded by white tile and the smell of hamburgers and onions, Jackson asked her to marry him. She paused for a minute before replying, thinking about the question without giving it serious consideration. It had no relevance to the relationship that had preceded it. "Our backgrounds, everything about us was so different," she says. "I would have been the worst person in the world for him, and he for me, and I had the sense to know it. . . . I knew he was very troubled and I wasn't that strong. I was too much of a coward. I couldn't handle it." She thought about Sande and Arloie. "They had a wonderful marriage and I thought he wanted to marry someone like [Arloie] who could provide something like that for him. . . . It would have been lovely if he could have had a life like Sande's, with an adoring person like Arloie. That's what he seemed to want, and I knew I wasn't that person." But instead of revealing her thoughts, she explained to him in the gentlest terms her plans for a career and how incompatible they were with marriage. If she did marry, she said, it would be to her childhood sweetheart from Rockwood, Mason Hicks. When she finished, she took the gardenia and walked away. Jackson never saw her again. "It was really poignant," she recalls. "He seemed to understand how I felt about him and didn't hate me for it."

Sitting with Becky in the White Castle, Jackson may have seemed understanding, but as soon as she was gone, he collapsed in despair. According to Manuel Tolegian, he "went berserk," setting off on a drunken binge that lasted almost a week. Reuben Kadish remembers how Jackson would "sit in a corner and brood" over "the girl of his dreams who disappeared," the pain made worse, no doubt, by the loneliness of an empty apartment—Sande and Arloie had moved to the country for the spring and summer. Never one to suffer in solitude, Jackson left to join them.

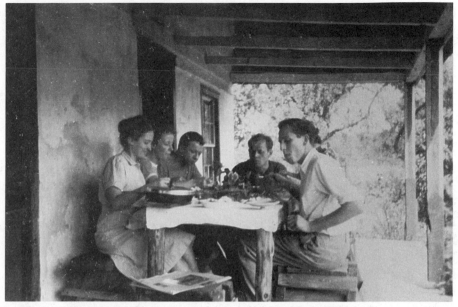

Arloie, Musa Goldstein, Jay, Jackson, and Phil Goldstein in Bucks County

This time, however, the green hills of Bucks County offered little solace. Except for Reuben Kadish, who visited occasionally, almost all of Jackson's circle had broken up and reformed in twos. Sande had brought Arloie, Bernie Schardt had brought Nene, and Phil Goldstein, who rented a house nearby, came by often to show off his beautiful young bride, Musa. To Jackson, their relentless coupling must have been a painful reminder of his own solitude. By mid-July, after a brief, uneasy stay, he left Bucks County to pursue the only fantasy that still held hope.

The boat trip to Martha's Vineyard was excruciatingly slow. If Jackson hadn't been so despondent, or hadn't come alone, the overnight steamer down the wide, dark corridor of Long Island Sound might have offered a brief moment of calm in a life skidding perilously close to chaos. The New Bedford Line's night boat from New York was famous for its exuberant decor, luxurious accommodations, and sophisticated ambience, even in the more crowded steerage compartment, where passengers were segregated by sex. But Jackson was haunted by thoughts of Becky Tarwater, to whom he had just sent a furtive letter and, undoubtedly, by memories of the previous summer when he and Sande had escaped to the Vineyard together.

Early the next morning, July 21, the boat arrived in New Bedford where Jackson transferred to a ferry bound for the Vineyard. Two and a half hours later, with the summer sun full up over the Atlantic, he stepped out on the long pier at Oak Bluffs. The town of gingerbread houses was already bustling with the activity of a holiday resort: children roller-skating on the boardwalk and riding the merry-go-round; couples strolling past the dance hall and sunbathing on the beach. In his desperation, Jackson had come for the first time unannounced and uninvited, so there was no one at the end of the pier to welcome him. Knowing that the Bentons had no phone, he called the general store in Chilmark and asked the clerk to carry a message to the Benton house, about a mile down the road. He addressed the message specifically to Rita, not Tom, asking her to pick him up at the Oak Bluffs boat landing.

It was several hours before the clerk, who was alone in the store, found someone to relay the message up the hill. In the meantime, Jackson grew restless. While exploring the little Carpenter Gothic shops along Lake and Circuit avenues, he found a liquor store and bought a bottle of gin. He would later claim that it was intended as a present for Tom, but social niceties quickly yielded to private anxieties. "After a while," Benton later reported, "he opened the bottle and took a swig—and he was off." In Chilmark, Rita finally heard the news of Jackson's arrival and rushed off in the family's Stutz to fetch him. By the time she arrived at the boat landing, however, Jackson's patience had long since run out. After calling the general store a second time, he had decided to get to Chilmark on his own. With the last of his money, he rented a bicycle and set out across the eighteen-mile-long island with drunken resolve. Before long, however, the gin started to "take hold." When he saw a group of girls crossing the street ahead of him, "He promptly took out after them, yelling like a wild Indian," according to Benton's colorful retelling of the day's events, "and chased them onto the sidewalk. After that, disregarding all remonstrances, he chased every girl he saw in the street."

This image of Jackson Pollock drunk on Martha's Vineyard, his bag tied to the back of his bike and a bottle of gin in one hand, weaving down the quiet streets of Oak Bluffs, bellowing and scattering girls in front of him, became a regular source of amusement to Benton and later chroniclers. "When [Tom] heard what had happened," writes Benton's biographer, "[he] thought it was so funny, [he] almost wished he'd done it himself." In fact, behind the picture of comic ineptitude and playful harassment that Benton painted was the reality of Jackson in a moment of genuine rage. The menace felt by the women who scrambled out of his path was real. It was the same menace that Pauline Pacifico had felt when Jackson grabbed her in the driveway on Montecito Drive, that Rose Miller had felt when he pawed her drunkenly, that Marie Pollock had felt when he threatened her with an ax, that the woman in the hallway had felt when he wrestled her into his room while Charles and Elizabeth looked on in disbelief.

Eventually, Jackson lost his balance, fell from the bike, and gashed his face. The police, who had been summoned by one of his victims, arrested him for drunkenness and disturbing the peace. At the courthouse in Edgartown, he pled guilty to both charges. Unable to pay the ten dollar fine, he was led off to the empty county jail. That evening, the Edgartown sheriff called the Chilmark general store and told the clerk to inform the Bentons that Mr. Pollock had been arrested and would be spending the night in jail. The next morning, the entire Benton family, including eleven-year-old T.P., drove to Edgartown and brought Jackson home. After paying the fine, Benton dismissed the whole incident as "only a matter of fun."

Jackson spent the next three weeks suspended between Rita's ambiguous affection, which had brought him to the island, and the despair that had followed him there. Alternately relaxed and moody, he spent most of the days with Rita: clamming in Nashaquitsa Pond, shopping in Menemsha, picking wild berries in the moors overlooking the sound. When not with her, he retreated into solitude, often walking the back route of cattle paths, past the scrub oaks and patches of wild strawberries, to view the Atlantic from the top of the Wesquobsque Cliffs. He painted a few small works, including a little oval picture of T.P.'s sailboat that he gave to Tom's visiting nephew, also named Thomas Hart.

One day a letter arrived for Jackson at the little post office on Beetlebung Corner. Becky had written from Tennessee and, in even gentler terms, repeated all the things she had said that day at the White Castle, hoping, apparently, that further explanations might ease the pain. They had just the opposite effect. Soon after the letter arrived, he wandered onto a windy hillside and, with exquisite care, painted a tiny study of a wild tuberose—one of the thousands that grew in bouquets along the stone walls and in luxurious vines on the gray-shingled houses and barns.

When, in mid-August, he returned to New York and an empty apartment— Sande and Arloie had left again for Bucks County—he carefully wrapped the little painting and sent it to Becky, along with a note:

Darling Becky—

You will excuse the stupid pencil. I received your letter at the Chilmark, with understanding I overstayed my vacation up there, I returned this week & I loved the island too well (life, flowers, and real love of the earth). It has been very depressing coming to this unnatural mass of human emotions, but am making all effort to settle myself to some good creative work.

. . . About your plans, Becky, I am very glad you are doing what you want to do, and I feel you have showed much common sense by doing it. at this time I am going thru a tremendous emotional unrest. With the possibility that I will do better in the future. I realize very well now that I couldn't have made a happy life for you. With the help of the broad Atlantic Ocean I have come to realize this too. [B]efore I forget—the passions of a tuberose—have you ever seen one—if not I send you [this] one. Becky I offer all my love, and happiness to your grand future. I hope you will drop me a line now and then, and when you are in town you will come to say hello . . .

My fondest respect,
Jackson

In a postscript, he added: "I will do as you wish with the banjo—keep it love it send it etc. Jackson".

(Becky Tarwater never did claim her banjo. Only two months after receiving Jackson's letter, she married Mason Hicks and returned to New York, where he started a practice. For the next twenty years, she followed Jackson's career from a distance. She saw his picture in magazines and newspapers and thought, "Good for you, Jackson! Good for you!" But she never dropped him a line or came to say hello. Once, she saw an announcement for a Pollock exhibition. "I would love to go to that," she remembers thinking. "I would have liked to see Jackson again, to walk up and say 'Remember me?' " But she never did. "I had another life and it would have been foolish to go outside it. Once a relationship is over, it's over." According to Reuben Kadish, it was never over for Jackson. "If Becky had come up to him," says Kadish, "he would have gone on a three-week drunk.")

By the time Sande and Arloie returned to the city in mid-September, Jackson's binges had resumed with unprecedented ferocity. According to Reuben Kadish, Jackson suddenly seemed intent on only one goal: "complete self-obliteration." Neither Sande nor Kadish had thought it possible for Jackson's mental state to sink any lower than it had the previous winter, but suddenly it seemed that he had finally slipped the last few notches into genuine madness. Six months of therapy had been undone in one frustrating summer. "He was going berserk every time he drank," recalls Kadish, who often assumed Sande's duties as "wet nurse." "He was going berserk and doing *awful* things, getting himself in intolerable situations." More and more often, his binges exploded in violence. Hardly a night went by that he wasn't the cause of a fistfight, or the victim, or both. When he reappeared after a binge, his clothes would be "filthy and foul smelling," as if he had slept in the gutter—which he often had. Many bars in the neighborhood refused to serve him, but he could never remember which ones because he could never remember what he had done, where he had done it, or when. As he ventured farther from the familiar hangouts, he became harder to retrieve at two or three in the morning. More and more often, strangers would find him passed out in the street. Most just walked by, taking him for a stray from the Bowery; some called the police. A few tried to help him home by searching for a phone number or address or by coaxing a name out of him. Some knew him already. "I was walking down Sixth Avenue with friends," Nathan Katz recalls, "when I saw Jackson being thrown out of a bar—actually rolling out onto the street. I turned him over and said, 'Jackson, what the *hell* are you doing? Get up! I'll walk you around.' And he said, 'No. Leave me *alone!*' With two big bouncers still standing in the doorway, he said, 'The bastards just threw me out! I'm going back.' I said, 'Are you *crazy?*' But no matter how much I pulled on him, he kept crawling back, *dragging* himself along the sidewalk back into this place they'd just thrown him out of."

In a rare moment of candor, Sande confessed to Charles that he was "worried as hell" about Jackson's condition.

At the Eighth Street apartment, Arloie struggled to maintain her benign neutrality in the face of escalating indignities. One morning she walked into the kitchen and found the tablecloth cut to shreds. Jackson had attacked it with a butcher knife. The almost nightly scenes when he returned to the apartment had lost their ritualistic, post-coital calm. Jackson was often still violent and abusive when he came up the stairs, and the job of pacifying him took longer and longer. "He would come back wild," Kadish remembers, "wild as can be. You can't *imagine* how wild."

Even before the latest round of binges, Arloie had felt threatened and imprisoned by Jackson's rages. She had vowed never to have children while living under the same roof with him. But the new threats required more direct action. Soon after returning from Bucks County—perhaps at Arloie's insistence, certainly with her approval—Sande built a partition that closed off the front room from the rest of the apartment. He tried to soften the blow by explaining to Jackson that he would get "a private studio."

Even with a private studio, however, Jackson's work slowed to erratic spurts. Every binge was followed by at least a day, sometimes several, in which he would lie in bed or sit motionless in a chair, petrified by "horrendous feelings of guilt." "The *remorse!* Oh God, he was so remorseful!" Nene Schardt recalls. "He couldn't remember what he'd done, but he knew by people's silence that whatever it was, it must have been awful." Arloie remembers walking by the door of the little bedroom at the end of the hall and seeing him sitting motionless on the edge of the bed, his head in his hands. For hours, sometimes days, he remained in a state of suspended depression, never talking either about the binges or about his guilt and never apologizing—"just silent about the whole thing," says Kadish. Nor did he paint. Except on rare occasions, he never painted while drunk or while suffering through the low, slow, silent decompression that followed. Eventually, he would come into the kitchen and begin to eat. It was the first sign of recovery. "Finally, he'd wiped himself clean," Kadish remembers, "and then he could get back to work."

Before, the cycle of drinking and depression had usually permitted Jackson a few days of "calm sea" between binges, enough to do four or five paintings and dozens of drawings. But now the cycles were closing up, even overlapping sometimes; he would recover in the afternoon and disappear the same night. As a result, during the winter of 1937–38, the small explosions of activity that had sustained him in the past were fewer and briefer. He did manage, as usual, to transform some of the sketches and watercolors from the Vineyard trip into oil. (It was probably one of these summer watercolors that he exhibited at the opening of the new WPA Federal Art Gallery on Fifty-seventh Street—his only public showing of the winter.) To fulfill the increasingly onerous WPA requirements, he reached for the tranquil banality that eluded him in real life, painting feathery landscapes and lifeless Americana. In the midst of his private agony, these works must have seemed incongruously placid, almost as if they had been done by another hand. More cathartic were the harsh, angular, Orozco-like drawings and occasional paintings that continued to bubble up from his subconscious.

In early December, the momentum of Jackson's fall was broken by a visit from Tom Benton, who came to New York to receive an award from the Limited Editions Club. At a reunion of the Harmonica Rascals, he invited Jackson, Sande, and Manuel Tolegian to Kansas City for the Christmas holidays. To the Pollocks, the prospect of travel was always therapeutic, but for Jackson there was the additional lure of seeing Rita again. Only days before the scheduled departure, however, Tolegian, whose car was to provide the transportation, contracted mumps and Sande pulled out. Not to be denied, Jackson purchased a bus ticket and, with only change in his pocket, left from the Port Authority bus terminal on a thirty-eight-hour Greyhound bus ride through a bleak midwest winter to Kansas City.

The reception at the Bentons' two-story limestone house on Valentine Road was mixed. Rita was, as usual, warm and maternal, grown wider and more bosomy in the years since Jackson first met her. Benton, however, was harder and cooler than he had been on the Vineyard, due perhaps to a brewing political upheaval at the art institute where he was director. The self-conscious simplicity of earlier years had already begun its slow transformation into the grotesque caricature of Benton's old age. He seemed to drink perpetually now; his short fuse had grown shorter, his language, impossibly coarser. His relationship with Rita had changed, too, as Jackson must have noticed. The reality of mother and son showed more clearly through the charade of husband and wife. "He would be yelling and drinking and carrying on," recalls a Kansas City friend, "then Rita would yell downstairs, '*Tom!* Come to *bed!*' And he would just stop and go upstairs."

For most of Jackson's two-week stay, Benton was away at the art institute during the day, leaving Jackson virtually alone with Rita. T.P. received so little of his former baby-sitter's attention that later he wouldn't be able to recall the visit at all. Just as firmly and deftly as she managed Tom's career, Rita took Jackson's financial plight under her care, encouraging him to paint in the studio while Tom was away and, when he obediently produced four small winter landscapes, arranging to sell two of them to friends. The sales produced enough money to pay for Jackson's return ticket.

At night, when Tom returned, Jackson usually left the house and lost himself in a round of holiday parties with Benton's students from the institute. One of those students, Lawrence Adams, remembered two parties, "stag affairs," where "there was considerable drinking" and "feats of strength," including Indian wrestling. Always more comfortable with horseplay than with conversation, Jackson happily joined in "the usual student brawls" and was "accepted as one of Benton's boys from New York," said Adams. Far from Sande and feeling daily closer to Rita, Jackson caught a brief glimpse of open sky, his drunken antics blending, for a change, into the background of seasonal high spirits and roughhousing.

It was only a matter of time, however, before the desperate fantasy that had brought him to Kansas City broke through the polite pretenses. On the eve of his departure, made bold by liquor, he finally poured out to Rita the feelings that had been secreted in his imagination for so long. Seven years of forbidden longings and private looks, of envying her husband and caring for her child; seven years of watching her sunbathe nude on King's Beach or probe the bottom of the pond with her foot in search of clams and, finding one, throw her head back and shake with laughter; seven years of maternal affection and sensual enticement were crowded suddenly into a few brief moments of breathtaking openness. He told her that he loved her and that he always had, that "she was his ideal woman and the only one he had ever loved." Then, in a final spasm of fantasy, he asked her to marry him.

How Rita responded to Jackson's outburst is not recorded, except that "she turned him down." Whether she did so gently, as Becky Tarwater had tried to do, or with a wise laugh and a dismissive toss of her head, the effect was devastating: seven years of fantasies erased with a nod.

His first reaction was rage, directed not at Rita but at Tom, whose fame and facility, in Jackson's tortured calculus, stood between him and the only woman who could bring him peace. According to an account that Benton later gave a friend: "After [Rita] turned him down, [Jackson] ran to Benton and said, 'Goddamn you, I'm going to become more famous than you.' " The second reaction came that night when Jackson left the house on Valentine Street and plunged into the circuit of parties and bars and self-obliteration. He returned early the following morning, "so sick with overdoses of whiskey" that Rita immediately dressed and drove him to see a doctor. Even Benton finally recognized Jackson's "disease." "The doctor told me later that his habits were 'confirmed,' " he wrote.

The binge in Kansas City was only a prelude. After a perfunctory visit to Charles in Detroit, Jackson returned to New York and threw himself back into the maelstrom. Within a month, Sande wrote Charles, and behind the grim optimism and the continuing reluctance to blame Jackson, his desperation shows:

> Our plans for the summer are very indefinite except for one important thing which is to get Jack out of New York. It has only been with a commendable and courageous effort on his part that he has held himself in check . . . [he] needs relief badly from New York.

Shortly thereafter, probably at Charles's urging, Benton invited Jackson on a six-week sketching trip beginning on May 28. During March and April, however, the binges continued and Jackson's output slowed to a standstill. The new, more stringent WPA check-in and production requirements became an almost impossible burden. By 1938, the Project was under constant pressure to trim its rolls, and rules that had once been enforced loosely, if at all, were suddenly threatening. On a day when Jackson was supposed to submit a painting at the WPA office, friends remember seeing him running through the streets in his pajamas with a painting under his arm, racing to beat the deadline. Other days, sitting in his room "horrendously sick and absolutely immobile," he missed the deadline altogether. Desperate to keep him on the Project, Sande let friends search the studio and pick paintings to submit on his behalf. When they couldn't find an appropriate canvas, or missed the deadline, Burgoyne Diller, now supervisor of the easel division, would "cover" for him.

Despite the continuing binges, Sande still hoped as late as May that the trip with Benton would reverse Jackson's decline. When Jackson finally applied for a leave of absence later that month, however, his request was denied—he had been absent too many times already. It was, apparently, one setback too many. Sometime soon afterward, he disappeared.

He was gone for four days on the longest and most determined effort at self-obliteration of his life. He may have hoped, or even intended, that it would be his last. For four days, he wandered the streets of the Bowery on the Lower East Side, drinking "sherry wine and rotgut" around the clock, passing out in the gutter, in other men's urine, being nudged awake by police only to begin drinking again. On the fourth day—filthy, violent, incoherent, and sick—he was taken to Bellevue Hospital. The doctors told Sande that he had suffered "a breakdown." With grim resignation, over Jackson's objections, Sande sought Helen Marot's help in arranging to have his brother committed to a mental hospital.

It wasn't until June 9, however, when he was formally dismissed from the Project for "continued absence," that Jackson finally accepted the inevitable. "He had been on the Bowery and he knew that wasn't for him," recalls Reuben Kadish, who visited him at Bellevue. "He wasn't just an ordinary slobbering drunk. He was going in a different direction entirely."

On Monday, June 12, Sande drove Jackson thirty-five miles north to the New York Hospital at White Plains and left him there.

21

RETREAT

An extravagance of stone and plum-colored brick, surrounded by a wrought-iron fence, the New York Hospital—or Bloomingdale's, as it was called—loomed over the sleepy countryside around White Plains like a dark Victorian fantasy. "It was a huge old asylum," a patient later wrote, "a private asylum, less grisly in some respects than public asylums like Bellevue or Wingdale, but grisly enough."

Fearful of hospitals, deprived of alcohol, and cut off from his family, Jackson must have spent the first few days alternately terrified and despondent. Strangers in white coats gave him the first complete physical examination of his life, the first neurological exam, the first X rays. Bearing his folder marked "chronic alcoholic," he was shuttled from clinic to clinic, specialist to specialist—internist, opthalmologist, otologist, laryngologist, dentist, urologist. In the men's ward, nurses in white caps hovered like gulls, alert to signs of "tenseness, depression, anxiety, sexual preoccupation, hypochondriasis and compulsions [or] fear of insanity." The hospital staff considered these the "outstanding mental symptoms" of alcoholism. Everyone, even the other patients, had been taught to watch for "suicidal preoccupation."

Jackson was classified a "voluntary patient," although the doctors at Bloomingdale's put little real stock in voluntarism; the temptation to leave was too great. So Jackson, like all voluntary patients, was required to sign an application for "inebriate certification." After an examination by two outside doctors to verify that he was indeed "an inebriate and a proper subject for treatment," the application was approved by a Westchester County judge, and Jackson was remanded to the hospital's care "for a period not exceeding 12 months." Although still officially a voluntary patient, he could no longer leave without his doctor's permission.

The first few weeks of therapy were "centered around the principles of rest, increased nutrition and fluid intake, and proper elimination." Alcohol was

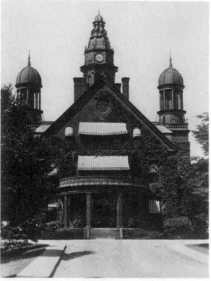

New York Hospital in White Plains, New
York; known as "Bloomingdale's."

strictly banned and patients were put to bed. Those who couldn't sleep were
given prolonged baths, steam-cabinet sessions, warm wet packs, ultraviolet
light treatment, and massage, all of which were considered preferable to seda-
tive drugs. Jackson was also placed on a diet "rich in calories" and "abundant
fluid intake." Proper elimination was ensured by the regular indignity of "colonic irrigations." Although designated a "free" patient—meaning he could
walk the halls and grounds at will—Jackson was never free enough to refuse
treatment. Mail and packages were routed through the office where they were
checked for contraband. Patients who refused a proper diet were force-fed or,
if necessary, tube-fed. And for those who resisted the beneficial effects of warm
baths and proper nourishment, who persisted in their "impulsive, stuporous, or
negativistic behavior," shock treatment was the ultimate form of enlightenment.

   The second stage of treatment was "occupational." Patients were offered a
wide range of physical activities to keep their hands and minds occupied during
the ordeal of withdrawal. From its founding in 1821, at a time when other
asylums still relied on shackles, bars, and bloodletting, Bloomingdale's had
distinguished itself as a pioneer of "moral management"—a new, more humanitarian way of treating the mentally ill. Its well-to-do patients were given
privacy, clean accommodations, spacious grounds, supervised outings, and otherwise treated "as rational beings insofar as possible." Over the years, this
benign handling of embarrassing family problems had earned the gratitude of
many of New York's richest families—Macys, Whitneys, Goulds—and their
generous support had transformed the old asylum into a veritable resort. Luxurious facilities for bowling, shuffleboard, billiards, sunning, and card-playing

had been added, as well as two fully equipped gymnasiums, six tennis courts, and a golf course. Women usually joined supervised exercise and dance classes while male patients, many of them under thirty, participated in "competitive games and strenuous physical exercise," often out of a belief that their recovery would be accelerated by "sweating out the poison." Inside, in the spacious parlors filled with fine Oriental carpets and Victorian furniture, men and women in mufti read and relaxed. Around the pianos, knots of patients prepared for the frequent evening entertainments. In the barrel-vaulted assembly hall, patients rehearsed on stage for an upcoming play or operetta. During the day, free patients like Jackson could wander the grounds to enjoy the lush, exotic flora—reputedly planned by Frederick Law Olmsted—and inspect the lavish outlying "guest villas" that were reserved "for the insane of wealthy families." In the evenings, staff members organized parlor games, dances, informal social gatherings—any activity that provided "a substitute for the relaxing effect of alcohol."

Except for a few charity cases like Jackson, most of the patients at Bloomingdale's—the troubled but well-socialized black sheep of wealthy families—thrived in the familiar, spa-like atmosphere. One doctor described them as a "breezy, affable, argumentative, demanding and disarming" lot. Like voyagers on a long cruise, they made the best of their "voluntary" confinement together.

But for Jackson it was a different story. Always intimidated and socially inept in groups, he suddenly found himself marooned in a sea of strangers, deprived of liquor to help assuage the awkwardness, afraid to participate in competitive games, and undoubtedly haunted by visions of Sande and Arloie spending the summer in Bucks County without him. Soon after arriving, he wrote Sande a brief note, concluding wistfully: "Imagine you are getting a lot of food off the farm by now."

The faint echo of childhood was no coincidence. In the real world, Jackson had retreated to the sylvan tranquillity of White Plains, but in his mind, he had returned to the forbidding sanitarium near the Phoenix ranch—the distant and terrifying place beyond the arroyo where people were sick and never got well. Recalling Jackson's first few weeks at the hospital, one of his doctors later said, "[He] was rather anxious, as sensitive people often are, and suffering from depression. There was a lot of calming down to be done and building up of his self-esteem."

Although assigned to Dr. Edward Allen, a highly respected, New England–born and Harvard-educated staff doctor, Jackson's case caught the eye of James Hardin Wall, the hospital's assistant medical director and resident expert on alcoholism and its treatment. A courteous, genteel South Carolinian, Wall had come to Bloomingdale's as a resident in 1928 and taken an early interest in the treatment of "alcoholic psychosis" at a time when alcoholics were still considered interlopers by the other mental patients. Since then, he had conducted several studies of alcoholic patients and was compiling careful records in preparation for a long-term study of alcoholism in men. Jackson suited perfectly the study's protocol and soon became Dr. Wall's special project.

A confirmed Freudian, Wall began by encouraging every patient to "unburden himself and to tell his life story in his own words." Despite Wall's gentle, circumspect approach—"The patient must be convinced of real interest on the part of the therapist," Wall later remarked—Jackson barricaded himself in a stony silence. When Wall turned in frustruation to Sande, he encountered the same defensiveness as well as a memory that was alternately inaccurate and self-serving. Gradually, however, Wall's persistence and reassuring southern charm wore down Jackson's defenses and, one by one, the demons of his inner landscape began to emerge into the open for the first time.

Although the records of Jackson's psychotherapeutic sessions remain confidential, it's clear from Wall's later writings that much of what he discovered about Jackson's past confirmed his own emerging theories about the origins of alcoholic psychoses. Like more than half of Wall's patients, Jackson was not the only member of his family with a drinking problem, although to Wall, it would have been Roy's (or Frank's or Sande's) *example*, not his genes, that led Jackson astray. "The example of a relative who uses alcohol to help him manage his problems is of dynamic significance in personality formation," Wall wrote only six years after treating Jackson. According to his research, mothers of alcoholics were typically "aggressive [women who] dominated not only the fathers of the families but the patients, whose lives they sought to direct." "In the case of male patients," Wall wrote, "the spoiling, pampering and protective type of mother was common." Fathers of alcoholic men, on the other hand, typically "took no part in disciplining their offspring, and in several instances deserted their families when the children were young." In almost every way, Roy Pollock fit Wall's model: "a weak individual who set a poor pattern for his son to follow," an alcoholic who "lacked forcefulness, and [was] too calm and placid, giving in to the mother and the children."

According to Wall, the combination of dominating mother and weak father subverted the normal identification process. Unable to identify with the submissive, or absent, father, male alcoholics tended to develop a "pathological but ambivalent fixation on the mother." As a result, Wall found his male patients "were likely to be too close to their mothers . . . and seemed to develop a feminine approach to life and its problems." For most alcoholic men, like Jackson, this skewed identification began to take its toll during adolescence, when exaggerated sexual demands enforced by peer pressure turned the close maternal relationship into "a source of growing resentment and conflict." Not surprisingly, adolescence was also when most male alcoholics began to drink. "When drinking begins with puberty," Wall reported, "and unfortunately becomes associated with sexual prowess in the mind of the patient, we see the beginning of a pattern in which a fundamental human relationship is placed on a false basis." Thus, Wall wouldn't have been surprised to learn that Jackson was "fundamentally afraid of women" or that his relationships had all ended in disappointment or disaster. Although few of his patients during these years demonstrated "overt homosexuality," Wall saw such behavior as nothing more than an exaggerated display of the mother identification and "effeminate approach to life" that underlay most alcoholic psychoses. Among the reasons cited by male patients for seeking therapy—including disappointment in love and the marriage or death of a relative—the second most common was "conflict over homosexuality."

In a move apparently intended to reinforce Jackson's ill-formed identification with his father, Wall shrewdly assigned him to the hospital gardening detail. From the wide assortment of occupational diversions (basketry, bookbinding, block printing, broom-making, cooking, chair-caning, knitting, leather tooling, printing, rug-making, weaving) Wall guided Jackson into metalworking—despite the availability of painting, drawing, and sculpting—in an apparent effort to bolster his masculine self-image. "Metal work and wood work appeal quite often," Wall wrote, "as the [male] patients consider them employment of a masculine nature."

The few copper plaques and bowls that Jackson hammered out in the metalworking shop during the summer confirmed Wall's analysis. Around the outside of one small copper bowl, he depicted a line of nude men cavorting in sexual revelry. On a plaque, a huge, muscular male nude sits astride an emaciated, stumbling steer. The sexual subject matter and the fact that Jackson worked from drawings suggest that these were calculated efforts, probably done at Wall's urging to help Jackson explore his sexual identity. Sande later recalled that Wall "attached great importance to [Jackson's] interest in drawing the male nude." These works represent Jackson's first *conscious* attempt to probe his own unconscious with his art. The process had begun years before, but it wasn't until the summer at Bloomingdale's and the prodding of Wall's Freudian preoccupations, that Jackson took the final step. By the end of his stay, the process had become explicit. After fashioning a large copper plaque showing two male nudes in a combative embrace surrounded by allegorical figures, Jackson gave it to Wall along with, for the first time, an explicit interpretation of the images. "He spoke of it as the cycle of man," Wall later wrote. "Moving away from infancy and parents, mating, the chaos of life [at the] top, man helping another to the left and death at the base. I can hear him talking now as he pondered this out."

But Jackson had other, more surreptitious reasons to impress Wall with his newfound powers of insight.

As early as August, just two months after being admitted, Jackson was restless to go home. But Wall had determined that a minimum of six months was necessary for effective rehabilitation. Most patients stayed nine months, and some lingered for a full twelve, the maximum allowable under the inebriate certification guidelines. The only way Jackson could win an early release was to convince the doctors that he was fully recovered. With the same combination of eager ingenuousness and creative angst that had attracted Benton and Siqueiros, he set out to charm Wall. "He was an intelligent and cooperative patient," Wall recalled, "and made real progress fairly soon." By late August, a tentative release date had already been set and extended. By early September, Jackson received permission to return to New York for a brief visit, a privilege that clearly signaled the final stages of treatment. "My time here has been extended to the end of Sept.," he wrote Sande early in the month. "Can you come up here one day this week and get me? Any day that is convenient for you—I will come back by train."

In his campaign for early discharge, Jackson's art played a persuasive role. Through it, he could demonstrate the "interest and curiosity . . . in working out his inner problems" that Wall considered essential to a successful recovery. Thus the copper bowls and plaques, with their exaggerated masculine imagery and thoughtful accompanying narratives, became tangible proof of Jackson's near-miraculous rehabilitation. "It was obvious that here was a talented artist," said Wall. "I [saw] a sweetness and strength in his work just as I did in him." The present of the copper plaque was for Wall, apparently, the clinching evidence. (Perhaps he saw himself in Jackson's flattering depiction of "[one] man helping another.") "It really [was] a lovely object," Wall concluded, "and he really was a lovely person." On September 30, after only three and a half months and with a promise "never [to] drink again," Jackson was released.

It was a disastrous precedent. By charming his therapists, Jackson not only squandered a unique opportunity for genuine rehabilitation, he also established a pattern that would control his therapy for years to come. Wall and Allen were only the first of many doctors who, despite Jackson's continued drinking and repeated relapses, were persuaded to cut short or forgo his treatment; the first of many who were distracted by his art or beguiled by the voyeuristic pleasures of treating an artist. Not surprisingly, Wall came away from the summer convinced of Jackson's recovery and the effectiveness of his brief therapeutic experience. "My recollection," said Wall, "is that . . . we felt good about our work with him as a patient." More than a decade later, on the occasion of a Pollock exhibition at the Betty Parsons Gallery, Wall wrote Jackson, "I remember you very pleasantly and always enjoyed working with you," and invited his former patient back to White Plains for a friendly reunion.

Jackson, on the other hand, came away from Bloomingdale's brimming with resentment, angry at Wall for prying into his private world and angry at himself for letting him in. He told friends that his confinement had been "a waste" and, later in life, seldom mentioned the lost summer. On the rare occasions it came up in conversation, he "would get really furious," according to one friend. "He wanted to *completely* wash his hands of it." Several years later, when Attilio Salemme, a fellow artist who had also spent time in a mental institution, reminded him of their common experience, Jackson stormed out of the room. Even a decade later, he was still fulminating. "He told me he didn't think [the therapy] was very effective," recalls Roger Wilcox, a close friend in the late forties and fifties, "and he didn't think it was good for him either. He said it was Sande's idea and he just went along with it and he was sorry he did."

Back on Eighth Street, Jackson's efforts to stay dry, however halfhearted and ineffectual, were quickly undermined by well-meaning friends and family. Only days after returning home, he received a letter from Tom Benton, who apparently had heard the full story. "I am very strongly for you as an artist," he wrote, "[but] you're a damn fool if you don't cut out the monkey business and get to work." Although the accolade was undoubtedly welcome, the advice was both belittling and ambiguous. Given his distrust of psychoanalysis and his fondness for whiskey, it wasn't clear whether Benton meant "monkey business" to refer to the drinking or to the therapy. Rita's letter, in the same envelope, was clearer and more reassuring but fingered old wounds:

> I was worried about you for 4 months, and can't tell you how relieved I was to hear from you. We all hope & pray that you settle down & work— & we mean *work hard paint hard*—so few have the ability to say something thru their work—You have—Tom & I and many others believe in you.

Unfortunately, most of the "many others," like Peter Busa and Axel Horn, knew only that Jackson "had gone away for a while to dry out." No mention was ever made of psychological problems or therapy. "Willy and Walter," the owners of the nearby Cedar Bar, had received only a cryptic note from Jackson early in the summer: "I can't get into town for a few days," he wrote. "Will you let Sande McCoy cash my checks and have a couple on me—thanks." Undermined by uninformed friends and inadequate follow-up, Jackson's resolve didn't last long. "He really tried to stay on the wagon," Arloie remembers, "but the first time a friend offered him a drink, of course, he took it, and— boom!"

Once Jackson began drinking, the last months of 1938 offered ample excuse to continue. In late September, Adolf Hitler and Neville Chamberlain met in Munich while the world waited anxiously to be delivered from a war that seemed increasingly unavoidable. In October, closer to home, Charles and Elizabeth provided Stella Pollock with her first grandchild. (Finally, at age twenty-seven, Jackson was no longer the "baby" of the family.)

Of most immediate concern, however, was the perilous state of the Federal Arts Project. As early as mid-September, while still at the hospital, Jackson had appealed to be rehired at his old job in the easel division. Every week, through October and November, he visited the WPA office on King Street to check on his application. Every time, he was turned away by a bureaucracy paralyzed with apprehension. In Washington, the summer hearings of Texas Congressman Martin Dies's Committee to Investigate Un-American Activities had struck a mortal blow at Federal One, successfully branding it "a hotbed for

Communists" and "one more link in the vast and unparalleled New Deal propaganda machine." Even before Roosevelt's humiliating loss of congressional support in the midterm elections, most WPA bureaucrats and artists sensed that the end was near. On November 23, Jackson was finally readmitted —with a cut in pay. Amid the growing anxiety, it must have seemed a Pyrrhic victory. Only weeks later, when Harry Hopkins, the old New Deal warrior, resigned from the WPA, anxiety turned to despair. "From all appearances," Sande wrote Charles in early 1939, "this may be our fatal year."

During the weeks of uncertainty following his return from Bloomingdale's, Jackson tentatively resumed work. On the advice of Dr. Wall, who scheduled several follow-up visits to White Plains during October and November, he continued the "identity therapy" begun that summer with metalworking. For several months, he shied away from painting and concentrated instead on "masculine" activities like sculpture and lithography. Partly in an effort to raise money while he waited for a Project job, he also painted a number of ceramic bowls. It was a medium that appealed to him both for its easy marketability and for its relative freedom. Canvas and easel were circumscribed by formalities; they bore the burden of training, of classes, of composition, of Charles and Benton and all the other competitors. A bowl or a plate, on the other hand, was an invitation to play—a cheap and disposable license to spontaneity in which he could safely explore his own artistic future.

On one bowl, executed during the last months of 1938, he painted a scene that he referred to as "the story of my life." On the right, a Bentonesque male nude shoots an arrow at two distant horses galloping across a sky streaked with red clouds. On the left, a mother figure from Orozco—even to her Mexican face—crouches to give birth. In the center, an infant curls fetus-like in a blossom of flames. At the bottom, a sailboat tosses on a surging Ryderesque sea. Whatever specific meaning Jackson attached to this impenetrable allegory, if any, the imagery is clearly a summing-up of everything that has gone before, a roll call of his unconscious and the idioms he has learned to express it. After the stay at Bloomingdale's, he is marshaling his forces, rehearsing the summer's lessons, testing the new, conscious connection between art and the unconscious.

Later, on a bowl that he presented to Dr. Wall on one of his return visits, Jackson painted a swirl of red, yellow, and blue nude forms floating around a single figure, glowing like Orozco's *Man on Fire*, in the center. On the sides, nudes dance in a near-abstraction of curved lines. When he gave it to Wall, he described the image—probably for Wall's benefit—as "the flight of man." Wall responded in kind by commenting approvingly on the beauty of the female forms. The same forms appear again on a bowl Jackson sent the Bentons after Christmas, only by now their abstracted dance has moved just out of legibility. The lines are still there—dense motions of black, blue, and green against a yellow ground—but the confining reality of figures is gone. Jackson has invented his own imagery, as psychologically charged as Orozco's, but as

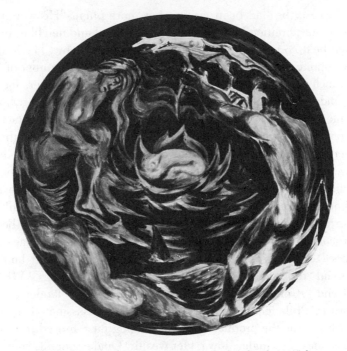

"The story of my life," c. 1938, enamel on porcelain bowl, 11⅛" diameter

personal and disembodied as his own unconscious. Reuben Kadish remembers that "after [Jackson] left Bloomingdale's, he began using the accident for the first time. The images became much more abstract, as if they had gone underground."

Jackson's neighbor, Ed Strautin, was probably the first to see the next breakdown coming. As late as January, Sande and Arloie still pointed with hopeful pride to the "improvement" Jackson was showing. Artist friends were distracted by the quality and confidence of his recent work. But Strautin, an amiable Lithuanian housepainter, saw the troubled man, not the aspiring artist. Sometime after the New Year, he noticed that Jackson was even quieter than usual. "It got so you couldn't get him to say a word in a half-hour," Strautin's wife, Wally, recalls, "and when you did, he'd say one word at a time and that was all. We could see he was getting more depressed every day." The breakdown that followed—probably another prolonged binge—caught everyone else, especially Sande, by surprise.

Exasperated to the verge of despair, Sande turned again to Helen Marot.

Jackson had been visiting Marot's brownstone on Twelfth Street on and off since the winter of 1934 when he and Sande worked at the City and County School. During the hellish months preceding his hospitalization, she had offered both a sympathetic ear and practical (if unheeded) advice on treatment and recovery. Seeing a crisis coming, she had worked with Sande and arranged Jackson's eleventh-hour admission to Bloomingdale's as a charity patient.

Since his release, he had been visiting her more often. "He would come at midnight or later," remembers Rachel Scott, a friend and neighbor of Marot's, "and when he'd come up he'd be half overseas, you know. He couldn't talk until he was pretty well lit." One can imagine that, after a summer of Freudian analysis, much of it focused on his relationship with his mother, Jackson had begun to understand the role that Marot played in his life. Wall, who knew of Marot's interest in the case, may even have prescribed more contact between the two, both to monitor his progress and to help Jackson work through his "ambivalent fixation" on Stella. Whatever the cause, by the time of the second breakdown, Marot had finally been drawn into the center of Jackson's turbulent emotional world. One night very late, Scott woke up to the sound of Jackson pounding on Marot's door screaming, "Let me in, let me in!"

As a surrogate mother, Marot was everything Stella had never been: combative, articulate, irreverent, empathetic. Where Stella favored lace and veils and shopped compulsively, Marot wore mannish clothes and bookkeeper's spectacles and "didn't pay much attention to clothes and things." Where Stella was stout and "strong-bottomed," Marot was spare and slender as a Shaker chair. Born in Philadelphia two months after the assassination of Abraham Lincoln, Marot was the product of an upbringing far removed from the Presbyterian grimness of Tingley, Iowa. Her wealthy Quaker parents supplemented her solid education with tutoring and exhortations to intellectual and moral betterment. "I want you to think for yourself," her father, Charles Henry Marot, a bookseller and publisher, used to tell her, "not the way I do." For the next fifty years, Marot pursued her father's advice with a vengeance. An early crusader for child labor laws, she rose quickly in the leadership ranks of both the trade union movement and the women's rights movement of the early 1900s. With an unusual combination of pragmatism and ideological zeal, she organized strikes, wrote tracts, and investigated labor abuses. She even served briefly on the editorial board of the radical pamphlet *The Masses* until a controversial Supreme Court decision by Oliver Wendell Holmes, Jr., suppressed it. "Whatever she undertook," recalls her friend Lewis Mumford, "she was always an insurgent."

In fifty years on the barricades of social reform, Marot became a divining rod for ideas, people, and movements. Along the way, she won the friendship and respect—sometimes grudging—of fellow reformers like Samuel Gompers, Louis Brandeis, Thorstein Veblen, John Dewey, and Mumford. Then, in 1919, she gave it all up. "[She] dropped the preoccupations of a whole lifetime," Mumford wrote, "as if they were so many soiled garments." Moving with her old friend Caroline Pratt to the house on Twelfth Street, she retreated into a private study of psychology and anthropology. "She had seen all the movements she had worked in and for, with an almost religious dedication, go wrong," Mumford wrote, "and she was determined to get to the bottom of this miscarriage by working back to the earliest [childhood] patterns of human behavior."

Fifteen years later, at the age of seventy, she met Jackson Pollock.

Far from embittering her, the years of frustrated idealism had left Marot with a relaxed appreciation of human frailties—a "vein of unabashed romanticism," Mumford called it—that invited openness and intimacy even from someone as reticent as Jackson. Although never trained as a psychologist or psychoanalyst, she fell into the role naturally. Her conversations were filled with "swift insights into the human situation [and] warm response to the sufferings of others." "Jackson always seemed to be more relaxed if there wasn't a sexual element in a relationship," says Peter Busa, "and I think it helped him explain his problems to older women like Marot." Jackson may also have been relieved that Marot was more interested in him as a person than as an artist. Although as a child she had played with Maxfield Parrish, and later served on the editorial board of the *Dial*—the magazine that Charles Pollock sent home to his brothers in Orland—Marot always cared more about the human "creative impulse" that produced art than about the art itself.

Basing her theories on the work of behavioral scientists like Sir Charles Scott Sherrington and James Bryan Herrick rather than the more popular Freud and Jung, Marot argued that impulses were the physiological building blocks of all human behavior and that the true purpose of education was to isolate and restructure those blocks in a way that ensured continued "growth and development." Because impulses could be directed, no action was truly spontaneous. Actions that appeared spontaneous were, in fact, "reflexes" of the unconscious. If the summer at Bloomingdale's had shown Jackson *what* to paint, Marot's ideas may have given him a first hint of *how* to paint. Instead of adopting conscious symbols—crosses, pregnant women, horses, or bulls (as Orozco had done)—Jackson could paint by impulse, bypassing the conscious mind altogether. The more spontaneous a painting, or a brush stroke, the more accurately it reflected the unconscious.

Despite their frequent conversations and Jackson's apparent candor with her, Marot never considered herself anything more than a friend and confidante. When he suffered a second breakdown in January, she didn't hesitate to recommend that he resume professional therapy. But not at Bloomingdale's. For some unknown reason, neither Marot nor Sande pressed Jackson to return to the hospital. Apparently, no one even bothered to inform Dr. Wall of the relapse. Perhaps Jackson was discomfited by Wall's incisive analysis. Perhaps Sande, obsessed with family pride and privacy, wasn't prepared to concede failure. Whatever the cause, the decision set another dangerous precedent. For the rest of his life, Jackson would move from doctor to doctor as restlessly as Stella moved from house to house, staying with each just long enough to relieve the immediate anguish, exercise his charm, and absorb the vocabulary, but never long enough to be helped. What seemed to many a frustrated search for emotional resolution was, in fact, a flight from exposure. Years later, when his agony, like his art, became a public concern, Jackson's wife and friends would complain bitterly about the incompetent therapy he had received in early adulthood. In fact, with rare exceptions, Jackson got exactly the therapy he wanted —seldom less, never more. "[Therapy] never grew him up in any way," observed Fritz Bultman, an artist who met Jackson in 1940. "He used it as a crutch."

Frequent changes in therapists also meant frequent changes in therapeutic strategies. The first and most critical of these came in early 1939 when Helen Marot, searching for a therapist to replace the Freudian Wall, turned to her friend Cary Baynes, a leader of the small Jungian community in New York. Baynes, in turn, recommended the newest member of that community, a young analyst named Joseph Henderson.

Once a week, more or less, for the next year and a half, Jackson visited Henderson's small office-apartment on East Seventy-third Street. Like so many of Jackson's ambivalent attempts at therapy, however, the sessions with Henderson would prove of far greater benefit to his art than to his psyche.

22

ARCHETYPES AND ALCHEMY

Joseph Henderson had just returned from nine years of study in Europe, including an apprenticeship with Jung, when Cary Baynes recommended him to Helen Marot. At the relatively advanced age of thirty-five, he was still an inexperienced analyst struggling to make a name for himself in a city overrun with German analysts, mostly Freudian, fleeing the incipient war in Europe. Grateful for Baynes's patronage, and intrigued by the opportunity to work with an artist, he agreed to see Jackson gratis.

Henderson was a short, slight man with an aquiline nose and pointed jaw that gave his face the sleek aerodynamism of an Art Deco sculpture. Behind the meticulously cultivated facade of Continental elegance, however, lurked a boy, like Jackson, bred in the American backwoods. Born in 1903 in Elko, Nevada, Joseph Lewis Henderson was the ambitious scion of an ambitious frontier family. His great grandfather had been the second governor of Nevada, his father a prominent cattleman, his uncle a United States senator. Although serenely uninterested in his family's empire, Henderson brought the family ambitions with him to a gilt-edged eastern education. At Lawrenceville Academy, he attached himself to a promising young teacher named Thornton Wilder who introduced him to both psychology and art. When Wilder went on to graduate work at Princeton, Henderson followed as an undergraduate. Afterward, "at sea over his future," he drifted through the "salons" of Berkeley, California, until he met the Bayneses. They gave him a reproduction of Jung's painting *Mandala of a Modern Man* and a copy of Jung's book *The Seven Sermons to the Dead*, and instantly he knew what direction his life would take. "I decided right there and then," he said, "that, if I possibly could, I would have to go and meet the man who had written this."

From the start, Henderson was determined to distinguish himself among the army of adoring analysts-in-training who gathered at the Hotel Sonne in Küsnacht, near Jung's beautiful lakeside Zurich home. In a bid for the master's

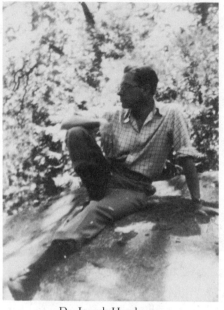

Dr. Joseph Henderson

attention, he announced that his destiny as an analyst had been revealed to him in a dream. (For the rest of his life, he would make career decisions by "asking his dreams for guidance.") But Jung was unimpressed. He told Henderson curtly, "If you're really interested in analysis, go to medical school first." Henderson did just that, enrolling in premedical studies at the University of London. The night before his final graduation exam, however, he dreamed about a "white horse running over a dark sea" and being killed by an eagle, and took that as a sign that medical school was *not* his destiny—an insight that was confirmed the next day when he failed the exam. Eventually (after yet another dream about a "ray-like, black fish") he did pass and, in 1934, consummated his assimilation into the European intelligentsia by marrying Helena Darwin Cornford, great-granddaughter of Charles Darwin. While in medical school, he returned often to Zurich where he "swallowed Jung whole," according to one colleague, and joined the inner circle of apostles whose training consisted of being analyzed by the fifty-five-year-old master.

In the fall of 1938, Henderson brought his wife and daughter to America. From the start, he had difficulty adjusting to the relative isolation and anonymity of New York. Despite his social connections through Cary Baynes and old Princeton friends like Wilder, professional recognition eluded him. The earlier arrival of Freudian emissaries like Otto Rank and Sandor Ferenczi, as well as Freud's lecture tour in 1909, had staked a prior claim on public attention. Even Jung's belated lectures at Yale in 1937 did little to loosen Freud's grip on New York. Only outside the city, especially farther west, where there was "a puritanical reluctance to grant the libido total creative monopoly," were Jungian ideas finding a truly favorable climate. Late in 1938, not yet licensed and still unknown, Henderson watched as his old schoolmate, Wilder, was awarded the Pulitzer Prize for his acclaimed Broadway play *Our Town.* Soon afterward, a "large, self-contained man" named Jackson Pollock walked into his office.

Still fresh from his sessions with Jung, armed with theories and eager to build a reputation, Henderson decided to make Jackson a model case. An artist himself, Jung had developed elaborate theories on symbology and the "imaginal mind." If he could prove these theories using Jackson, Henderson might attract the master's attention and jump-start his stalled career. "For him, Pollock was just an example for a Jungian study of an artist," says a friend to whom Henderson recounted his early experience with Pollock. "What interested him was how artists 'fit the Jungian package.'" Because Jungian theory dictated that analysis focus not on the past but on the future—the search for the "innermost self"—Henderson disdained questions about Jackson's history: his mother, father, family situation, childhood, or sexual experiences. To avoid polluting his analysis with the errors of others, he refused to look at Jackson's hospitalization or previous treatment records. He also refused to speak with the previous therapist, Dr. Wall, Marot, or Sande. "[Jackson] was taken simply as he presented himself," Henderson said later. As a result, he knew only what Jackson chose to tell him. "[Jackson] explained that he did not feel the way he looked," Henderson recalled, "that he was in a diminished state of being as a result of his problems with alcohol, [and that] he thought of himself as less of a person than [his] brother." All Henderson knew of Sande was that he "saw to it that Pollock got to his appointments and home again without losing his way or going into a bar." Although aware of Jackson's drinking, he chose to ignore it. Jung had taught that as long as such behavior was "managed" in a way that allowed "the emergence of the true self," the analyst didn't need to be concerned with it. The "managing" job, of course, was Sande's. Later, Henderson would joke, "it may be that his drinking was necessary to keep him afloat, if you'll pardon the expression."

Without family, past, friends, or previous therapy to talk about, Jackson had little to say. Watching him sit edgily in an office chair, Henderson thought "he seemed preoccupied with his inner thoughts and feelings." Occasionally he would make a halfhearted effort to "talk about himself," Henderson later wrote, but "would do so in an impersonal manner, and then only refer to the most superficial aspects of his life." For weeks, Henderson endured these long, unproductive sessions—"This was not even counseling," he admitted—and with each frustrating hour, no doubt, felt his career breakthrough slipping away.

Until Jackson brought in a drawing.

It is impossible to understand the impact of Jackson's art on Henderson and on the course of his therapy without understanding the world of ideas in which Henderson lived—the world of Carl Gustav Jung.

Every person, Jung believed, has the potential to become a healthy, well-adjusted human being: one in whom the four personality coordinates or "functions" (intuition, feeling, sensation, and thinking) are "integrated" into a balanced whole. Under normal conditions, a person's inner potential or "embryonic germ-plasm" emerges into consciousness only after a long and arduous journey of self-discovery that Jung called "individuation"—the process of becoming an individual. According to another key Jungian theory, every individual is also born with a "collective unconscious," a set of instinctive patterns, both images and behaviors, that represent the accumulated psychic experience of the race. Jung called these instinctive patterns "archetypes" and theorized that they play an important role in the individuation process. The journey from germ-plasm to "integration" is an interior one, Jung said, but it is marked by the emergence of archetypes along the way, indicating that a person has "discovered" a certain pattern in the collective unconscious and raised it into the light of conscious recognition. Thus, by following the archetypes that emerge in a person's consciousness—through dreams, for instance —a therapist can track a patient's progress on the path to integration.

But archetypes are more than just the by-products of the individuation process. According to Jung, they are preexisting psychic phenomena stored in the unconscious whether or not they're ever discovered. Therefore, a person who has lost his way (whose personality is out of balance) can be "reintegrated" if only he can recognize the appropriate archetypes. Jung saw this as the therapist's job: not to review the past to determine where and why a patient went off the path, but instead to help the patient see the way back to the path by directing him to the archetypes that mark the way. For Jung, unlike Freud, the value of a symbol was primarily therapeutic, not diagnostic. Each time a patient, with an analyst's help, "recognizes" an archetype in his own unconscious, he makes another step toward integration, toward health.

In this world of curative symbols, Jung considered artists "the symbol-makers." "The creative process, insofar as we are able to follow it at all," he wrote, "consists in an *unconscious animation of the archetype.*" Artists are favored with a special sight—the "visionary mode"—that gives them extraordinary access to the unconscious world of symbols and archetypes. "The artist reaches out to that primordial image in the unconscious," Jung wrote, "and in the work of raising it from the deepest unconsciousness he brings it into relation with conscious values, thereby transforming its shape, until it can be accepted by his contemporaries according to their powers." When confronted with true art, Jung claimed, "we are astonished, taken aback, confused, put on our guard or even disgusted. . . . We are reminded of nothing in everyday, human life, but rather of dreams, night-time fears and the dark recesses of the mind that we sometimes sense with misgiving." Just as Aristotle's tragedian traps his audience into "recognizing" half-known truths, Jung's visionary artist relates "genuine primordial experiences" to his audience, leading to a "synthesis of the individual and the collective psyche" that brings each member of the audience one step closer to integration. As a group, artists constitute a priesthood that can provide therapy for the entire society, bringing it into "balance" just as symbols bring the individual psyche into balance.

Jung formulated his theories about art and artists partly in reaction to what he saw as Freud's denigration of art as "substitute gratification" for neurotics seeking escape from reality—what Jung called the "genetic fallacy." Where Freud explored the personal conditions in which a work of art was created, Jung focused on the work's psychic significance. "It is art that explains the artist," Jung wrote, "and not the insufficiencies and conflicts of his personal life." Freud argued that the unconscious symbols in a work of art reveal repressed events from the artist's life and the analyst's job is to work with the patient to bring those events into consciousness and "work through them." Jung believed instead that symbols represent current events that can lead to health. By identifying those symbols and encouraging the patient to provide analogies, an analyst can help a patient "dream the myth onwards" toward the ultimate goal of individuation. Where Freud seemed to reduce art to little more than a diagnostic tool or biographical study, Jung celebrated art's healing powers and the role of the artist as visionary. "What is essential in a work of art," Jung wrote, "is that it should rise far above the realm of personal life and speak from the spirit and heart of the poet as man to the spirit and heart of mankind. The personal aspect is a limitation—and even a sin—in the realm of art."

As soon as he saw Jackson's drawing, Henderson grasped its value as a therapeutic tool—and as a career opportunity. Why he didn't inquire about Jackson's work earlier, given Jung's emphasis on symbol-making, isn't clear. Dream interpretation was Henderson's preferred method of therapy, and he may have tried others only after Jackson refused to talk about his dreams.

Thereafter, each session focused on one or two works. The early offerings, done before the therapy began, were Orozcoesque in style, filled with "human figures and animals in an anguished, dismembered or lamed condition," Henderson recalled—a vein of vivid, disturbing images that Henderson mined enthusiastically, identifying the symbols and trying to engage Jackson in a dialogue about their significance. To one of these early sessions, Jackson brought a turbulent gouache done in primary colors and heavy black outline, depicting a crucifixion reminiscent of Orozco's *Migration of the Spirit* at Dartmouth. With Jackson apparently taking notes, Henderson explained the four personality functions and assigned a color in the gouache to each: intuition, yellow; thinking, blue; feeling, red; and sensation, green. (With only three primary colors to work with, he was forced to assign "sensation" to a small patch of smeared black with a slightly greenish hue.) According to Henderson, the violent movement and distortion of the four figures in the work confirmed that Jackson's four personality functions were dangerously out of balance. The "intuitive" yellow of the crucified figure indicated that "[Pollock's] own highly developed function of intuition needed no help from anyone, but did need to be rescued from time to time from a crucifying sense of isolation." Among the

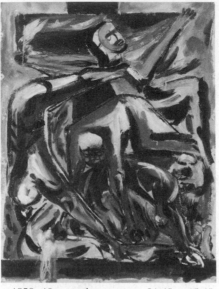

1939–40, gouache on paper, 21½″ × 15½″

few encouraging signs, said Henderson, were the cross (as distinguished from the crucifixion), which represented the axial archetype, and a red circular dot in the upper right corner representing the sun. Both of these appeared to be new "ordering symbols"—or signposts on the road back to integration.

Henderson later described this interpretive/therapeutic process as one in which "the analyst (out of knowledge of comparative mythology) and the patient (from his innate subjective sense of the significance of archetypal imagery) collaborate in producing a background or context from which the individual meaning of the archetypes may emerge." Unfortunately, Jackson refused to collaborate. "He did not have free associations," Henderson lamented, "nor did he wish to discuss his own reactions to my comments. . . . I had to be content with saying only what he could assimilate at any given time, and that was not much. There were long silences. Most of my comments centered around the nature of the archetypal symbolism in his drawings."

Such "comments" would have ranged from basic definitions and simple notions (e.g., two forms in the same drawing represented "the battle of opposites" in Jackson's psyche), to deeper, more complicated analyses. In response to a drawing of a tree with a snake coiled at its foot which Jackson brought in, Henderson would have explained that the snake "would normally seek to encompass the principle of psychic growth as suggested by the trunk of the tree, from which it could then reach into the discriminating and productive levels of unconsciousness suggested by the branches." In Jackson's case, however, the coiled snake indicated "a movement of regression back to the state of unconsciousness [called] *uroboric*, expressing the inactivity and isolation of the infantile state."

Each new interpretation required additional explanation. To explain Uroborus, Henderson showed Jackson Jung's illustration of a tail-biting snake in *The Secret of the Golden Flower*, and explained its significance: "a simple form of mandala which represents integration"—an explanation that in turn required him to explain mandalas and the Jungian belief in "a psychic birth-death-rebirth cycle." Henderson also revealed one of the basic tools of Jungian pictorial analysis: curved lines and rounded forms indicate a feminine impulse; straight and jagged lines indicate a male impulse.

The more deeply he delved into the symbology of Jackson's drawings, however, the more uneasy Henderson must have felt. In Jungian theory, only if an artist works spontaneously out of his unconscious (in what Jung called "the visionary mode") is his art "a genuine, primordial experience." Otherwise, the artist lapses into the self-conscious or "psychological mode" and his art becomes "something derived or secondary . . . a symptom of something else." So the success of Henderson's "experiment," both for Jackson's therapy and for his own career, depended entirely on the drawings' continued spontaneity. Previous psychological profiles of artists—Jung himself had analyzed the symbolism of Goethe's *Faust*, Dante's *Divine Comedy*, Wagner's Ring Cycle, and Melville's *Moby-Dick*—had never confronted this problem. In those studies, Jung and his disciples had confronted only the finished works, not the artists themselves in an ongoing therapeutic setting.

As their weekly sessions continued and Jackson became increasingly familiar with Jungian theory and terminology, Henderson faced the growing likelihood that the drawings he was interpreting were, in fact, no longer "true symbolic expressions," but mere processed images, calculated to *illustrate* Jungian symbols rather than discover them.

Even if Jackson came to their initial sessions untutored in Jungian psychology (as seems likely), even if the drawings were initially spontaneous (as seems likely), even if he continued to bring the drawings without Henderson's prompting (as seems unlikely), such a state of innocence could not have lasted for long. Jackson was too impressionable a student, too needful of attention, and too adept at ingratiating himself into the favor of father figures like Henderson to resist the bait of his analyst's predilections, however much Henderson struggled to conceal them (as seems unlikely). Nene Schardt, who, with her husband Bernie, lived in the Eighth Street apartment for several months while Jackson was seeing Henderson, recalls him coming home from the sessions and talking about what he had "learned." According to Schardt, Henderson told Jackson "what happened in the drawings from an unconscious point of view." "They [Jackson and Henderson] discovered all this material from the unconscious in Jackson's 'doodles,' " she remembers, "and symbols that dated way back in culture." Although he never read any of Jung's numerous works —two of which were available in English translation by 1939—Jackson gleaned enough from his sessions with Henderson to attempt an explanation of the distinction between "anima" and "animus" in a letter to Charles. "He was thinking of incorporating that in a painting," Peter Busa recalls.

Inevitably, Jackson's enthusiasm for these new ideas and images was recycled into the drawings he brought to Henderson. Symbols "discovered" and explained by Henderson quickly became leitmotifs in Jackson's weekly offerings: the circular Chinese Tao, representing the union of opposites; the vertical "axis mundi" representing "ego-strength"; the crescent moon, representing the female; the snake, representing the unconscious; crossed lines (or arrows, or arms) representing the conflict of opposites, especially male and female; the pelvic basin, representing birth or sex or mother or all three; the mandala, representing integration. Occasionally, Jackson would sketch an image one week, test Henderson's reaction, then repeat it the following week in a more finished form. To assert his masculinity, he drew exaggeratedly angular figures and, in two doodles, riotous jumbles of jagged lines. Despite the blatant self-consciousness of such efforts, Henderson continued to treat each new drawing as a "spontaneous" vision.

By mid-1939, Jackson was producing images tailor-made to his analyst's needs. Yet Henderson's interpretations grew increasingly elaborate and abstruse. One pencil and crayon drawing from this period, in particular, provided him with a synopsis of Jackson's case so apt and illustrative of Jungian theory that he used it for decades thereafter as a teaching tool. In it, Jackson drew two headless humanoid figures leaning against each other to form a triangle, their outstretched arms crossing at the apex like tentpoles. Between them stands a short pillar surmounted by an oval-shaped area containing a branch with four leaves. A snake coils around the pillar's base. Above and behind the central grouping is a "schematic female torso," sketched lightly in yellow crayon. On either side, a bull and a horse peer out from behind the torso. According to Henderson, the pole was not a simple phallus; it represented both the axis mundi and Jackson's newfound ability to organize his psychic life so as to avoid falling back into the "jaws of the world monster" as he had in the past. The two figures, really more like giant legs, symbolized the recovery of Jackson's "reality function" following his crippling breakdown. The crescent shapes, general pelvic-basin configuration, and confusion of anatomical features represented opposites brought into harmony, while the central oval shape containing the small plant suggested "the principle of psychic growth or development." In short, Henderson concluded that this seminal drawing, freshly dredged from Jackson's unconscious, announced the progress of his inner self toward integration during the months of therapy. What he failed to mention was that Jackson had already sketched the same image at least seven times in the months since Henderson had first explained it.

The charade dragged on into the winter of 1939.

As a true believer in the curative power of archetypes, Henderson may have thought that Jackson's weekly drawings, however calculated and self-conscious, continued to have some genuine therapeutic value. Jackson's reasons for persisting in the fiction were more complex. Although reluctant to discuss Jung's ideas in any depth, and at times incapable of doing so, Jackson

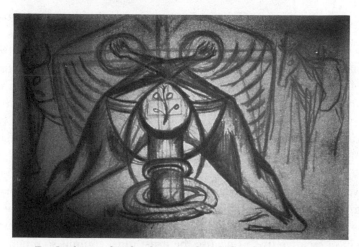

To Henderson, this sketch summed up Jackson's inner journey,
c. 1939–40, crayon and colored pencil on paper, 12¼" × 18¾".

was nevertheless intrigued by them. Certainly he appreciated both the high
standing Jung conferred on artists and his emphasis on the role of the unconscious in art. But he also responded to the mystical undertones of Jungian
concepts like the collective unconscious, the visionary mode, and the archetype.
A childhood of fantasy had left him susceptible to promises of spiritual escape,
especially at times of crisis. In that respect, Jung was merely the successor to
the Bear Dance in Janesville and Krishnamurti at Ojai.

But the conspiracy with Henderson also fulfilled a more basic, more selfish
need. Around Henderson, Jackson was safe. In their weekly sessions, there
were no probing questions about Stella or Roy or Sande, no efforts to dredge
up painful memories from Phoenix or Janesville or to coax out awkward sexual
confessions. Henderson never even asked Jackson about his most recent self-
destructive binge. After the first few sessions, the hour settled into a reassuring
routine of long, abstract monologues as Henderson moved methodically
through each drawing, pointing and explaining: no talk of romantic failures or
sexual identification or manic-depression. Jackson and his past remained safely
off limits. Only the drawings mattered. Only the drawings were needed "to
help [Jackson] structure his thinking function toward achieving a more rational
and objective view of his life and his art," according to Henderson. What
happened in the real world meant nothing compared to what happened in the
unconscious one.

In the real world, of course, Jackson continued to drink.

After one particularly self-destructive binge, Helen Marot telephoned Henderson to question whether the artist was being "adequately cared for," Henderson recalled. Marot, who had little patience for intellectual rigor at the
expense of human suffering, undoubtedly demanded to know what kind of
psychiatric therapy would ignore the most pressing problem in a patient's life
to concentrate on interpreting sketches. Henderson politely responded that

carrying Jackson's "reality function"—that is, keeping him out of bars—was Sande's job, not his. And besides, Jackson always appeared sober at their sessions. Years later, Henderson claimed to be "astonished" in retrospect at "how little I troubled to find out, study, or analyze [Jackson's] personal problems in the first year of his work with me, and especially do I wonder why I did not seem to try to cure his alcoholism." The justification for such "unorthodox analysis," he offered, was that it benefited Jackson's art. "My duty was therefore to promote the welfare of this individual quality in him," Henderson wrote, "rather than to rescue or reform his suffering ego."

In his ungenerous fatalism, Henderson may have been echoing Jung himself. "The lives of artists," Jung wrote in 1933, "are as a rule unsatisfactory—not to say tragic—because of their inferiority on the human and personal side. . . . There is hardly any exception to the rule that a person must pay dearly for the divine gift of creative fire." Because the artist must commit so much energy in one direction, Jung reasoned, it is almost inevitable that the natural balance of functions would be upset. (Jung had studied Picasso's paintings and determined that the artist belonged to "the schizophrenic group.") Who was Joseph Henderson to jeopardize a "divine gift of creative fire" by curing the creator?

If the sessions with Henderson were a therapeutic failure, they were also an artistic triumph. In addition to exploiting a rich new iconography, Jackson succeeded, as he had at Bloomingdale's, in transforming psychological insights into artistic breakthroughs. Jung's theory that art was therapeutic nudged Jackson away from the dark, self-absorbed images of Orozco and Ryder. He began to experiment with lighter strokes, more playful images, and more open compositions. In Jackson's long escape from the tyranny of facility, Jung's view that genuine art originates in the unconscious ("Everything in the unconscious seeks outward manifestation") played a key role. Coming immediately after the experiments at Bloomingdale's, such ideas reinforced Jackson's growing reliance on spontaneous image-making rather than the careful, scientific methods he had tried to learn from Benton. Already in his last drawings for Henderson, Jackson had begun to drop the old search for the "correct" line, the representative line, the line that Charles could draw and he never could, and turned his struggle inward to discover the "right" line, the line unrelated to the outer world but perfectly expressive of the inner one. "He could pull a painting out of nothing," recalls Peter Busa. "He worked by looking in rather than looking out. He once said that if you could paint what's inside you'd need more than one lifetime to do it."

Henderson made one other lasting, if inadvertent, contribution to Jackson's art. Having been raised by a Navajo nanny, Henderson was, by his own account, "obsessed" with Indian culture. While still in medical school, he had visited the Zuni and Sia tribes to see the corn dances, and the Hopis to see the famous snake dance. Only months before returning to America, he had given a lecture on these rituals to the Analytical Psychology Club in London. Because he believed, with Jung, that a colonizing people "inherit" the racial memory of the natives they displace, Henderson assumed that Jackson's unconscious already contained Indian imagery and encouraged him to "dredge it up." Despite his frequent visits to the Southwest Museum in Los Angeles and the Museum of the American Indian in New York, Jackson's initial efforts were surprisingly uninspired: two penciled doodles on a sheet of gouaches that he made about this time, one of intertwined snakes (a motif that Henderson had shown him) and the other an Indian in feathered headdress, as much a caricature as any cigar-store mannequin.

But his imagination had been engaged. Guided by Henderson, he began to explore the wealth of imagery in the brilliantly colored sand paintings of Henderson's Navajo; the bold geometry of the painted skin shirts of the northwest coast Tlingit and Tsimshian tribes; and the complex and subtle sculptural massing of the Haida totem poles he saw on trips to the Museum of Natural History with Reuben Kadish. Using an "Indian palette" of bright yellow, red, blue, green, and black, he painted gouaches of geometric Indian motifs: feathered arrows, shields, snakes, birds, and lightning bolts. He was especially intrigued by the brilliant carving and inventive distortions of shamanistic masks, from the tortured forms of the Haida to the "alarming aspect" of the horned Kwakiutl to the unexpected delicacy of the Tsimshian.

On a visit to the Museum of Natural History about this time, Jackson encountered Paul Wingert, a noted scholar of American Indian art. Wingert, astonished to find a young painter staring intently at objects that most people still considered curios, asked, "Why are you interested in these things?" "This is art," Jackson declared; to which Wingert replied, "Nobody else seems to think so."

It was the animal imagery of these objects that particularly intrigued Jackson, Peter Busa remembers. "He was fascinated by the way two animals, sometimes more, would be combined in the same image." To celebrate a mythological past in which humans existed in absolute harmony with nature, artists of the Kwakiutl, Bella Coola, Haida, Tsimshian, and Tlingit tribes often depicted humans learning skills from animals, or mating with animals and giving birth to "supernatural" offspring. The animal past and the human present were brought together in carvings that often combined human eyes, ears, or nostrils with the paws, tails, or fins of an animal.

Jackson recognized these images as if they had sprung directly, in midtransformation, from his own protean imagination. Since early childhood he had responded with both fascination and fear to animals, whether they were the inhabitants of his familiar barnyard world—chickens, bulls, horses—or the bears, coyotes, and mustangs that roamed his fantasy world. Like all objects, these animals were constantly undergoing a process of transmutation in his imagination, changing from form to form, from animal to human and back to animal again, as readily as objects moved through space in the real world. Now, fixed in masks and carvings, they began to appear in Jackson's art, both

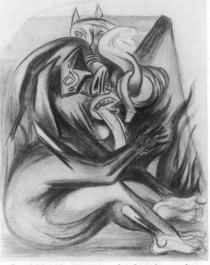

C. 1939–42, crayon and colored pencil on
paper, 14″ × 11″

in the drawings he brought to Henderson and in his paintings. The style was
new, but the subjects were still deeply evocative of his own past: a bull attacking
a woman in a blur of erotic desire; a bull transforming into a man, or vice
versa; a horse transforming into a snake; a snake coiling abstractly inside a
woman's womb. These were the changing images he had tried unsuccessfully
to capture in the "hairy drawings" he did for Benton and in the unfinished
carvings for Ben-Shmuel. In Indian imagery, he had finally found a vocabulary
for putting down in two dimensions these shifting and elusive images from his
unconscious.

In his therapy with Wall and Henderson, as in his artistic encounters with
Benton and Orozco, Jackson had shown his ability to absorb ideas, recycle
them through his unconscious and into his art, and, in the process, make them
his own. By the middle of 1939, his pictorial language had already transcended
the esoteric world of Jungian iconography. "What is interesting about Pollock,"
says fellow artist George McNeil, "is that he came from very bad influences
like Benton and the Mexican muralists and other anti-painterly influences, and
yet, somehow, in a kind of alchemy, he took all the negatives and made them
into a positive. It's a mystery. The rest of us were following the right path and
therefore the magic didn't issue."

After almost a decade of "bad influences," it only remained to be seen how
Jackson's alchemy would work on more refined substances. If he could transform even the lead of Henderson's Jungian archetypes into hints of genius,
what "magic" would issue when he confronted the pure gold of Pablo Picasso?

23

INTIMATIONS OF IMMORTALITY

For America as well as for Jackson Pollock, 1939 was a year of anticipation, suspended at the end of the endless thirties like a question mark. The Depression had passed (or so the government claimed) but nothing had taken its place exactly. Certainly not prosperity. Nine and a half million people were still out of work, hundreds of thousands still clung demoralized to the WPA lifeline, and the news from Europe grew more ominous every day. The result was a vacuum, a stillness into which people read the future according to their moods.

Nothing captured the air of urgent ambivalence like the world's fair that opened in the meadows of Flushing, New York, on April 30, 1939. Jackson Pollock was among the millions who paid seventy-five cents to gawk down the flag-draped, tree-shaded Constitution Mall, file through the ultramodern color-coded exhibits, and pose before the fair's centerpiece, the Trylon and Perisphere—the only fair buildings painted stark white. The surrounding pavilions, in pastel colors and garden settings, covered almost 1,200 acres, every acre permeated by a relentless optimism too self-conscious to be entirely convincing. The theme of the fair was "The World of Tomorrow" (reassurance was the subtext), and everywhere the future was on display. At the Westinghouse pavilion, visitors were introduced to the medium of the future, television, and signed their names to a time capsule destined for the year 6939. On the Farm of the Future at the Borden's exhibit, machines, not farmer's or farmer's sons, did the milking. At the General Motors building, the Futurama ride took fairgoers through the car-filled, care-free world of 1960. When it was over, each visitor was given a blue and white button proclaiming, "I Have Seen the Future."

For Jackson, the summer of 1939 marked the first anniversary of his hospitalization. Although still in therapy with Henderson and still "having problems with living and painting," as Sande wrote Charles in March, at least he was back *in* the world, not watching it from behind the fence at Bloomingdale's. In June, he accompanied Sande and Arloie and a group of friends to a big farmhouse near the town of Ferndale in Bucks County, only a few miles up the road from the house in Frenchtown where he had spent a miserable few weeks two years before. Jackson always found comfort in the Pennsylvania countryside, but this summer he seemed especially susceptible to its tranquilizing beauty. "He was so moved by the hills, by the fields, by the beauty of it," recalls Nene Schardt who used to ride with Jackson in an open car down the back roads. "I would say how beautiful it was, and he would say, 'You don't talk about it, you *inhale* it. It becomes part of you. It goes through a creative process in your psyche and then it comes out.' " For the moment, however, Jackson seemed more concerned with his psyche than with the creative process. Although he spent hours on the road and on the trails that crisscrossed the hills behind the farm, he seldom sketched. "He didn't even take sketch pads with him the way he used to," Schardt recalls. "He didn't do things on the spot anymore." For relief from the relaxation, he would trek to a nearby abandoned quarry for a wade in the knee-deep water or ride into town to buy supplies or just to watch the Amish amble in and out. At night, activity focused around the big cast-iron stove in the kitchen. Most of the food came from the backyard garden and the neglected fruit trees around it. Except for baking an occasional pie, he seldom helped with what was known as "the farming."

Without electricity, there were no appliances, no lights, and no late nights. Butter and beer were kept cold in the well. Guests materialized almost every evening. Some, like Jackson's brother Jay and wife Alma, and Joe and Margaret Meert, just moved in. Others, like Ed and Wally Strautin and Phil and Musa Goldstein, rented farmhouses nearby, but "everybody shopped together and made food together," Wally Strautin remembers. "It was a crazy summer." After dinner, in the long hours of waning light, the conversation turned to art or to gossip, brought back from frequent trips into the city to submit work, report to WPA supervisors, or pick up checks.

The summer had an immediate, if temporary, therapeutic effect. For the first time in years, Jackson tried to control his drinking. A friend's wife remembers seeing him at a loft party that summer. "Everyone was drinking except Jack Pollock," she says, "and I thought, 'Well, he's pretty straitlaced.' Then somebody said to me, 'He can't drink. He has a problem.' "

When Jackson looked beyond the idyllic summer, however, the future must have seemed far less benign. Storm clouds had been gathering over the WPA since the previous fall when the Dies Committee loosed its anti-Roosevelt wrath on Federal One. In January 1939, a new Congress, smelling blood, cut fifteen hundred artists from the project rolls. In March, Sande wrote Charles: "We have been investigated on the project. Don't know yet what the result of it all will be." With a fraudulent name-change on his conscience, Sande feared the worst. "Should they ever catch up with my pack of lies, they'll probably put me in jail and throw the key away."

In July, the ax fell, not just on Sande but on the entire Federal Arts Project. All artists who had been on the federal payroll for more than eighteen months were automatically terminated. Overall, more than 775,000 workers lost their WPA jobs that summer. In addition, all WPA employees were required to swear a loyalty oath. Renamed the WPA Art Program and demoted from a federal project to a bundle of state projects with reduced federal funding, the Project survived the summer purge but only as a shadow of its former self. Those lucky few who survived the cuts became subject to the vagaries of state and local control. (Within months, many local officials would demand a return to the dreaded force account requiring artists to report to central workshops.) The unlucky, including Sande, went on relief. Jackson was spared only because the stay in Bloomingdale's had interrupted his seniority. In May of the following year, his eighteen months would be up.

On September 1, 1939, with crowds still elbowing their way into the General Motors exhibit to goggle at the World of Tomorrow, German troops invaded Poland.

Sometime during the future-obsessed year of 1939, Jackson Pollock undoubtedly contemplated his own future. While many artists responded to layoffs and cutbacks on the Project by demonstrating in the streets, occupying WPA offices, confronting police with linked arms, and being dragged off to jail, most knew that the grand old ship was sinking. The prospect of life without the Project brought artists like Jackson face-to-face with a fact that had been largely forgotten in the decade since the crash: for a vanguard artist in America, there was no such thing as success. Of the generation of American artists who had returned from Paris in the twenties filled with modernist fervor, none had reached even the nethermost niches in the pantheon with Picasso and Matisse. A very few, like Jan Matulka and Vaclav Vytlacil, had won teaching positions at generally conservative bastions like the Art Students League. Many, like Benton and Max Weber, had abandoned some or all of their modernist ideals. The vast majority had labored through the first half of the decade in the same impoverished obscurity that befell artists of every stripe.

The Project had brought relief, but not redemption. The modern movement remained firmly rooted in Paris. "In the late thirties there was a feeling that American art could never achieve the status, could never become the aesthetic equal of French art," recalls Lee Krasner. "Absolutely no one thought American painting could rival French painting, then or ever. I don't remember anybody who even *thought* in those terms at the time." Even Arshile Gorky, an artist as talented, knowledgeable, urbane, and accomplished as any in Jackson's generation, held out little hope. One evening in the late thirties, he and a group of artists met in Willem de Kooning's studio to discuss the dilemma of American painting. Gorky opened the meeting with the bleak pronouncement: "We are defeated," then proposed an unorthodox solution. "Gorky suggested we work on a group painting," recalled Lee Krasner who was also in the room.

"[He said,] 'one person could draw better, another person has better ideas, another is better at color. What we have to do is sit and talk this over and come up with a thought. Then we'll all go home and do our separate things and bring them back and decide who should draw it, who should paint it, who should color it.' " The plan never went any further. According to Krasner, the artists repaired to their studios, took one look at their easels, and threw up their hands in despair.

Gallery shows became the American artists' lifeline to the "force and vitality" of French painting. Like colonials ogling fine, finished goods from the motherland, they flocked to Pierre Matisse, Valentine Dudensing, Julien Levy, and the other predominantly European galleries to see works by the Cubist, Expressionist, and Surrealist masters. "One knew exactly which galleries to go to to see what you wanted to see," said Krasner. "We'd look forward to those shows with enormous anticipation. It wasn't a case of you *might* see this or that; we went with a great sense of hunger."

At the summit of the distant and inaccessible peak of European artistic achievement stood Pablo Picasso. "He has painted everything and better," claimed one observer, "he has exhausted all pictorial sources. . . . Picasso is devastating." Gorky said wistfully that he would be content to achieve even a "little bit" of Picasso's quality. Some critics were beginning to question whether there *could* be art after Picasso. "At that time," says Lionel Abel, "people were saying, how can you be a revolutionary after Picasso? How can you do *anything* different after Picasso?" One critic declared unequivocally: "Picasso is the greatest painter of the past, present, and future."

This was the prospect that Jackson faced in 1939 when he looked into his own future: the piled centuries of Western art reaching back to Lascaux, rooted immovably in European soil, and surmounted by the towering figure of Picasso.

Jackson had no way of knowing, of course, that the world was on the verge of upheaval; that within three years, America would come to rescue the "European tradition;" that within five years, New York would replace Paris as the center of the art world and American art would topple the piled centuries of European preeminence; or that within ten years, Jackson himself would confront Picasso on level ground.

The person who gave Jackson his first glimpse of this heroic future—and helped make it possible—was John Graham.

An aristocratic Polish refugee from the revolutionary excesses of his adopted homeland, Russia, Graham had little in common with his predecessor in Jackson's life, Tom Benton. Although clearly fond of Jackson, Graham played a role that was always primarily artistic, not emotional—a healthy change from the ambiguities of the relationship with Benton. Graham also represented a final rejection of Benton's facile "America First" notions—a rejection that Jackson had been rehearsing for years in his experiments with Siqueiros and

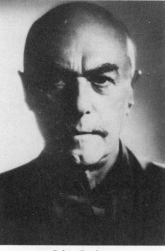

John Graham

Orozco. In befriending the cosmopolitan Graham, who traveled to Europe often and claimed to know Picasso, Jackson announced his readiness to confront the Europeans.

Like Benton, Graham was an extraordinarily physical man. He was known to receive friends in the nude and perform acrobatic tricks while conversing. (Even in his sixties, he could do a headstand without using his hands.) Strong and sinewy like Roy Pollock, with powerful hands and arms and ice-blue eyes, he dominated people with energy rather than size. "You always knew the moment you entered a room where Graham was," said painter Ludwig Sander, "[and] that he was the superior being in that room." Decked out in striped silk shirt, flannel pants, double-breasted waistcoat, watch and chain, cuff links, flowing cravat, and sometimes even a monocle (all bought at secondhand stores on Third Avenue), he walked with the ramrod back and slightly bowed legs of the cavalry officer he had once been. Every morning, he shaved his entire head, leaving only his imperiously arched eyebrows and a mustache that rounded the corners of his thin lips at a demonic angle. "He was a showman," says Ron Gorchov. "Anything to amuse people."

Dazzlingly well read and widely acquainted, Graham was a fountainhead of eccentric, unequivocal, and often inconsistent opinions. Willem de Kooning recalled seeing him marching in a May Day parade in the thirties, enthusiastically chanting "We want bread!" while waving a hand clad in an elegant beige chamois glove. When Jackson met him in 1939, Graham had only just begun to show an interest in Theosophy, alchemy, numerology, astrology, and the occult—interests that would later lead him to declare himself "a universal genius in communication with occult higher powers." Already he believed that "any repetitive act—even one as ordinary as ironing clothes—was a form of prayer and put one in touch with Divine Powers." More than anything, he hated smoking (because it was "primitive," not because it was unhealthy) and concrete ("the proliferation or use of concrete is the most destructive force in modern society," he warned). "He never hated anything or liked anything for the same reason everybody else did," recalls Graham's friend Roger Wilcox.

Aside from a pragmatic preference for rich women, Graham was an avowed fetishist. More than once, a female sunbather on Coast Guard Beach near East Hampton opened her eyes to find Graham staring at her feet. "With women, he had fetishes," says Wilcox—a foot fetish, a fetish for crossed eyes, even a blood fetish. At parties, Wilcox remembers overhearing an exchange between Graham and a woman to whom he had just been introduced:

GRAHAM: "Do you bleed much?"
WOMAN: "I don't understand. What do you mean?"
GRAHAM: "I mean do you bleed much? Women bleed, you know, and I would love to see you bleed."

When asked why many of the women in his paintings showed wounds on their necks and cheeks, Graham responded, "Because all women should be wounded." Yet women remember him as "utterly charming," "extremely elegant," and "very sophisticated." "It would be nice," says Hedda Sterne wistfully, "if all artists were such fascinating personalities."

The origin of Graham's personality—more like a Byzantine mosaic of eccentricities—is one of the minor mysteries in the history of modern art. Unlike Benton, who wrote extensively of his youth (and with increasing honesty as he approached death), Graham was a ruthless editor of the past. "No one knew *anything* exactly about him," Sterne remembers. "He could have had any kind of past." Legends filled the vacuum, including claims that he was an intimate of the imperial family (he kept a portrait of Czar Nicholas on his desk). Graham exulted in the enigma and replenished it regularly with revisions of his story, new versions of himself that grew increasingly bizarre and contradictory as he grew older. Eventually, he claimed that an eagle had left him stranded on a rock in the middle of the ocean where his mother, a sorceress, found him. "When I grew up," he wrote, "[mother] explained that I was the son of Jupiter and a mortal woman and that is why He had to send me to live with the human beings though I was not altogether human." His age, like his origin, changed according to his mood. At various times, he claimed to be 100, 460, and 2000. Finally, presumably to put the matter to rest, he claimed to be immortal.

The records indicate that John Graham was actually Ivan Gratianovitch Dombrowski and was born in Warsaw in 1887. Several versions of his ancestry survive: that he was descended from a Scottish mercenary employed by the czar's army; that he was the son of a Russian count and an Englishwoman; that he was the scion of an aristocratic White Russian family. There *was* nobility in his blood—German on his mother's side, Polish on his father's—although considerably diluted. His family was, apparently, among the many dispossessed Polish gentry who fled to Kiev (where Graham was baptized) after the uprising of 1863 when Poland was still partitioned. The Dombrowskis must have brought with them some wealth, for, despite the systematic repression of émigré Poles, he attended the Imperial Lyceum and the University in Kiev, obtained a law degree, married, and fathered two children. When Russia entered World War I, he joined a unit of the imperial cavalry with the colorful name "the Circassian Regiment of the Wild Division," under the command of the czar's younger brother, Grand Duke Michael (later, briefly, Czar Michael II). He held the relatively low rank of cornet. Years later, Graham shamelessly embellished his cavalry experience, claiming that he belonged to the czar's household guard. In fact, he served most of his tour on the Romanian front, one of thousands of cavalrymen in the grand duke's beleaguered division and far from Czar Nicholas's battlefield headquarters at Baranovichi. Nevertheless, Graham proved an excellent horseman and, apparently, a brave soldier, receiving the St. George Cross for valor at least once (and perhaps as many as three times, by his telling).

In 1918, the war ended and the revolution began. Although Graham later claimed that he joined the counterrevolutionary movement in the Crimea, was imprisoned by the Bolsheviks (in the same cell with the czar), and miraculously escaped a death sentence, the record indicates that he either fled or was smuggled across the reconstituted Polish border to Warsaw and simply headed west, pausing only long enough for his second wife, Vera, to have a child in Germany before boarding a steamer in Southampton bound for New York.

Although he had apparently shown little interest in art while in Russia, Graham enrolled in John Sloan's class at the Art Students League and quickly distinguished himself. Among the eager Americans starving for legitimacy, he found a receptive audience for his exuberant self-inventions. To them, he presented himself as a Continental artist, an exponent of Cubism, who had made the mandatory pilgrimage to Gertrude Stein, Paul Éluard, and André Breton, and hobnobbed with the avatars of the avant-garde—Picasso in particular. (Throughout the twenties and thirties he continued to boast of frequent trips to Europe to catch up on the latest developments and see former associates —although all such claims were later thrown into doubt.)

While his art would remain generally unappreciated until long after his death, Graham's genuine intellect, ostensible Parisian connections, and eccentric personality won him an almost immediate following among his younger fellow artists. A biographer lists his credentials: "a connoisseur of art and women, a witty and acerbic teller of tall tales and adventure stories, a proselytizer for Cubism, and a discoverer of gifted young artists." Eventually, his circle of "discoveries" included Arshile Gorky, Stuart Davis, Jean Xceron, Adolph Gottlieb, Dorothy Dehner, and Willem de Kooning, whom Graham introduced in the mid-thirties as "the best young painter in the United States." Another of Graham's protégés was a young sculptor named David Smith who summered near him at Bolton Landing, New York. "His annual trips to Paris kept us all apprised of abstract events," Smith later wrote. Clement Greenberg called Graham "a missionary in the wild."

In 1933, separated from his third wife, Elinor, and frustrated—perhaps by his own work, which had become little more than a spirited imitation of Picasso's cloisonnist style, perhaps by the rising anti-modernist tide in New York art circles (the tide that would sweep Thomas Hart Benton to notoriety)—he stopped painting altogether and joined a small, quasi-religious group of Russian émigrés who lived together in a crumbling brownstone that Graham called "the monastery." Vowing to live "a suffering and spartan life," he begged food in neighborhood markets and in winter kept a large bowl of snow on the table "to freshen the air." A friend who saw him about this time remembers a John Graham very different from the tightly strung, charismatic man whom Jackson met five years later. "He reminded me of a Jewish tailor," says Gerome Kamrowski, "a bit stooped, with an uncommanding voice and a mild personality."

But Graham was a changeling. In 1935, he turned up in Paris, charming his way through the galleries, ateliers, and cafés of the avant-garde art world. David Smith, who was also in Paris that year, wrote: "[Graham's] introduction and entry to private collections made my world there." At home, too, Graham burst out of obscurity with a ground-breaking article, "Primitive Art and Picasso" (which caught Jackson's attention) and an erudite, opinionated, and slightly wacky book, *System and Dialectics of Art*, in which he named Jan Matulka, Milton Avery, Stuart Davis, Max Weber, David Smith, Willem de Kooning, Edgar Levy, Boardman Robinson, and S. Shane among the "young outstanding American painters" and added daringly that "some are just as good and some are better than the leading artists of the same generation in Europe."

The book may have brought Graham to the attention of the Baroness Hilla Rebay, the autocratic German director of the Guggenheim collection. In 1938, unfazed by his low opinion of Kandinsky, the star of her collection, Rebay hired Graham as a secretary to arrange grand private showings at the Plaza Hotel and to help plan the transfer of the collection to a more permanent home. In 1939, after returning from a trip to Mexico, he and his fourth wife, Constance, rented an apartment at 54 Greenwich Avenue and began looking for new employment. The same fall, Jackson's friends Nene and Bernie Schardt, who had been bunking temporarily in the Eighth Street apartment, moved to 56 Greenwich Avenue where their apartment shared a fire escape with Graham's. Nene Schardt recalls that Jackson and Graham met soon afterward—at the Schardts' apartment, or perhaps at the Waldorf Cafeteria on Sixth Avenue where Graham became a regular, or at one of the Saturday afternoon teas that Graham hosted in his studio.

In the many hours they subsequently spent together in Graham's apartment, Jackson, then twenty-seven, and Graham, who had just turned fifty, forged a close, improbable bond. "Jackson had a unique place in John's life," one friend remembers, "over and above that occupied by Gorky or any of the other painters." Not surprisingly, the savvy Graham was drawn to Jackson's passion and naiveté. "He thought Jackson was a primitive, a proletarian," recalls artist Ron Gorchov, a later Graham protégé. "He was a little bit snobbish about Jackson, but he also thought he was very deep. To him, Jackson was a kind of bumpkin —but with a profound nature." Constance Graham remembers how her husband raved about Jackson's work when he returned from his first visit to the Eighth Street studio: "He said that Pollock was really crazy but that he was a great painter."

It is almost impossible to overstate the effect such accolades had on Jackson. For the first time in his ten years as an artist, he was being taken seriously, not just by a teacher or a colleague, but by a man who he believed had been to the mountaintop and met Picasso, Matisse, Mondrian, and the others, a man who spoke with the full authority of Western art. "Graham was the *link*," says Lillian Olaney, another young artist at the time. "He was the bee spreading the honey." Reuben Kadish remembers the surge of confidence he felt just being in Graham's presence. "He was an individual who came from Europe, who was so far above an ordinary aesthetician. You went in there and he was the guru. You just sat at his feet and listened. And if he said something to you, like your work was exciting, it really *meant* something."

Graham was the first to see what was happening in Jackson's art, the first to express, even distantly and conditionally, the possibility that it might contain the seeds of genius. "Who the hell picked him out?" Willem de Kooning later asked rhetorically. "It was hard for other artists to see what Pollock was doing —their work was so different from his. . . . But Graham could see it."

Graham's neighbor Nene Schardt remembers hearing "many great discus-sions about art" lasting late into the night when Jackson came to visit. Although usually subdued, Graham became animated when talking about art. One account pictures him pacing his dark, art-filled apartment, his bald head shining in the yellow light from the antique Franklin stove, pausing to explain a Gabonese nail fetish, "theorizing, speculating, speaking in rapid-fire declarations, [filling] friends' ears with artists' talk and intimate anecdotes about the giants of the twentieth century. Thus, that Mondrian ate only one egg a day became intermingled in the minds of his listeners with the idea that it was the 'edge of the paint' that mattered. [To Graham] art was a way of life as well as a way of seeing."

For the next two years, Jackson would see the world through Graham's eyes.

He would see African art. As early as the 1920s, Graham had spoken of African art as "the greatest of all arts." By the late 1930s, his Greenwich Street apartment bristled with exotic artifacts, including a Yoruba mask-helmet, a Gouro war mask, and a Gabonese sorcerer's mask, many of which he had acquired while assembling an even more distinguished collection for Frank Crowninshield, the publisher of *Vanity Fair*. Proudly, lovingly, Graham displayed his collection to Jackson and other visitors. In the middle of a conversation, he would pick up a favorite piece and stroke it appreciatively as he talked, describing it as "lyric," "majestic," or "awesome," explaining how it was based on "wholly different principles" from the art of the West—on what Graham called "spiritual emotions."

He would see the link between art and the unconscious. Graham's admiration of primitive art, like Henderson's, reflected his belief that "Primitive races . . . have readier access to their unconscious mind than so-called civilized people." But Graham's belief in the power and importance of the unconscious went far beyond Henderson's timid symbology. "It should be understood," Graham proclaimed in his landmark 1937 article, "that the unconscious mind is the creative factor and the source and storehouse of power and all knowledge, past and future." The challenge to the artist, he believed, was to plunge "into the canyons of the past back to the first cell formation" and "bring to our consciousness the clarities of the unconscious mind." No one, of course, had done more plunging into the canyons of the past than Jackson Pollock. For more than a decade, under the guidance of thinkers as diverse as Krishnamurti and Helen Marot, Jackson had been playing with the unconscious at the margins of his art, tantalizing his anxious analysts with drawings and plaques that were neither fish nor fowl, neither pure art nor valid psychological insight. He seemed to be waiting for a signal, a sign of approval—from the world of art, not the world of psychoanalysis—that an imagery pulled from "inside" was worthy of being called art. John Graham gave him that signal.

He would see line. Unlike some other European modernists who believed that color was the essence of painting or composition, Graham argued the preeminence of *line*. "Gesture, like voice, reflects different emotions," he wrote in *System and Dialectics*. "The gesture of the artist is his line, it falls and rises and vibrates differently whenever it speaks of different matter." Among Western masters, Graham especially admired the great draftsmen: Paolo Uccello, Ingres, Cézanne, and Picasso. He also introduced Jackson to a whole new way of thinking about the link between art and the unconscious: *écriture automatique* or "automatic writing." In the effort to tap the unconscious, Graham believed, line was the most sensitive seismograph: especially when freed from the dictates of conscious manipulation and allowed to be "automatic." The handwriting must be "authentic and not faked . . . [not] conscientious but honest and free." No lines, of course, were more honest and free than Jackson's. The more he tried to discipline his hand, in fact, the more it seemed to exercise a will of its own, responding to signals coming from someplace beneath consciousness, someplace where images bore only a passing resemblance to objects in the real world. Even before meeting Graham, he had forsaken the old struggle for the "correct" line, as Benton defined it, and embarked on a search for the line that reflected his inner vision. But it was Graham who gave that line a name.

He would see new possibilities. "Imitation of nature, technique or trained skill have nothing to do with art," Graham declared in *System and Dialectics*. "No technical perfection or elegance can produce a work of art." No one, of course, felt the lack of technical perfection and elegance more acutely than Jackson. Surrounded by draftsmen like Goldstein, Tolegian, Lehman, Meert, and Schardt, he continued to be plagued by doubts about his "natural abilities" as late as 1940. That summer, he wrote Charles that he was still waiting for his work to "clear up." Graham's words calmed those doubts.

Emboldened by Graham's support and liberated by his ideas, Jackson finally began to pursue the truly personal imagery that was, for Graham, the ultimate test of genius. "A work of art is neither the faithful nor distorted representation," Graham wrote in *System and Dialectics*, "it is the immediate, unadorned record of an authentic intellecto-emotional REACTION of the artist set in space." No artist's "intellecto-emotional" experiences were more immediate, more unadorned, or more authentic than Jackson's. "It wasn't something he was conscious of," says Wally Strautin. "It was never 'I want to do this because I want to get there.' That was not him at all. Jackson painted from an inner compulsion."

And he would see Picasso.

Jackson had first encountered Picasso in 1922 when he saw reproductions of his sketches in the copies of the *Dial* that Charles sent to Orland. By the time Jackson reached the Art Students League, Picasso had become the focus of intense controversy among American artists. Upstairs in Studio 9, Benton reviled him and his followers, while downstairs in the cafeteria, Arshile Gorky (who was already in contact with Graham) extolled him as the world's greatest living painter. At least once during his summers in Los Angeles, Jackson had gone with Kadish, Goldstein, and Lehman to the home of Walter Arensberg where several of Picasso's Cubist paintings were on display. In 1934, he and Sande had gazed at Picasso's *Three Musicians* through the windows of the New York University library. During his Benton years, he had seen reproductions of Picasso works in *Cahiers d'art* and an occasional Picasso show at one of the commercial galleries in Midtown, but their impact was still muted by Benton's old antipathy.

Then, in January 1939, he saw *Guernica*.

Unfortunately, Jackson never recorded his impressions of the momentous event, but he did return again and again to the Valentine Dudensing Gallery on Fifty-seventh Street, where, to raise funds for refugees of the Spanish Civil War, the Artists' Congress exhibited Picasso's huge masterpiece painted to protest the saturation bombing by Axis planes of a small, undefended Spanish town. Sometimes Jackson came alone, sometimes with others, to make sketches, to exchange hushed comments, or just to stand and be overwhelmed by the great, gray monolith of it. Eleven feet high and twenty-five feet long, it loomed in the modest gallery space like a ship run aground, its images enlarged to supernatural proportions: a hand with fingers the size of limbs, a severed head as big as a boulder, a horse rearing up to the ceiling, a woman screaming with a tongue like a sword, another clutching her dead baby, another standing at her window gasping in recognition, another running to the scene of devastation in frantic bewilderment. Everywhere, the world has turned to spikes and shadows and shattered limbs. Not since his pilgrimage with Charles to Orozco's *Prometheus* had Jackson responded so viscerally to a painting. When, on one of his many visits, he overheard a fellow artist make a disparaging remark, Jackson challenged him to "step outside and fight it out."

Guernica was Jackson's real introduction to Picasso. Almost immediately, its stark imagery began to appear in the drawings he took to his sessions with Joseph Henderson: drawings of misshapen, screaming figures with their heads thrown back, their teeth bared, mouths open revealing sword-like tongues. In November, Alfred Barr's mammoth Picasso retrospective opened at the Museum of Modern Art with the fanfare and reverence of a coronation. In *Art News* Alfred Frankfurter crowned Picasso "the master of the modern age," "the painter who . . . has influenced the art of his time more than any other man," "the most fertile and most advanced artist of the twentieth century," "an accepted classic almost unto the academies." Meanwhile, in Graham's dark, sculpture-filled apartment on Greenwich Avenue, away from the public hoopla, Jackson's private confrontation with the artist whom Graham referred to as "Le Maître" had already begun.

Transfixed, Jackson listened to Graham's glistening—perhaps fictionalized, undoubtedly embellished—accounts of meeting Picasso, sharing a bottle of wine with him, discussing Western art, watching him paint. Every personal anecdote came festooned with accolades: "Picasso drops a casual remark," Graham said, "and a score of artists make a life's work out of it." For the rest of the winter and all the following year, Jackson came often to Graham's apartment and "communed" with Le Maître.

The Picasso Graham most admired was the Picasso of *Girl before a Mirror*, the "cloisonnist" Picasso who assembled fragments of pure color, like enameled shards, and set them in heavy black outlines. Graham admired such works both for their power and for their honesty. Stripped of modeling and perspective, they made no attempt to create the illusion of depth. The Renaissance, Graham claimed, with its naive insistence on the third dimension, was "the period of the greatest decadence in art." It was Picasso's genius to "refute modeling or three-dimensional painting as a make-believe art." (Only a few years later, Clement Greenberg would take up Graham's argument under the banner of "flatness.") One day he would assail the puritanical Anglo-Saxon obsession with hygiene—on which he blamed the American disdain for accident and personal touch—the next day expound on the inherent limitations of different mediums.

Like Graham's theories, Picasso's art enthralled Jackson not because it was new but because it was so unexpectedly familiar. In it, all the threads, all the vague notions that had been lurking in his own paintings, struggling toward expression for more than a decade, came together. He saw the influence of primitive art, as in Picasso's seminal work of 1907, *Les Demoiselles d'Avignon*

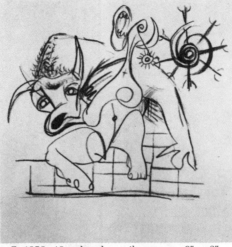

C. 1939–40, colored pencil on paper, 9″ × 8″

(a work that Jackson later told Lee Krasner had been "terribly important to him"), in which the artist borrowed the image of an elongated mask from the Dan tribe of West Africa. He saw an affirmation of the relationship between art and the unconscious. "Picasso's painting has the same ease of access to the unconscious as have primitive artists," Graham wrote, "plus a conscious intelligence." He saw a rejection of facility. Here was an artist of dazzling technical skill who, in order to achieve an authentic image, had rejected facility.

Using Picasso's preparatory sketches for *Guernica* as models, Jackson began to make drawings that, for the first time, create their own reality rather than wrestle with the more familiar one. Gone are the errant Benton lines and the tentative doodles. These are sure, lyrical, expressive works in which the lines loop and curl, widen and narrow with near flawless confidence. A woman throws back her head, opens her wide-oval mouth and screams. Horses rear in terror, a bull paws the ground: each one defined precisely, sparely, by a few fluid lines.

Jackson also recognized in Picasso's art the mutating images of his own unconscious. In *Les Demoiselles d'Avignon*, Picasso transformed prostitutes into half-human creatures with the faces of African masks. In *Girl before a Mirror*, he caught the body of a young woman with breasts like ripe fruit in the middle of a transformation into some luxuriant vegetal form. These and other of Picasso's images, like *Sleeping Nude*, fascinated Jackson throughout this period, and he began to experiment with transformations of his own. In one series of paintings, human heads transform into the Eskimo masks he saw illustrated in Graham's article, "Primitive Art and Picasso." In *Reclining Woman*, a female figure stretches out languorously on a long horizontal canvas. Despite her voluptuous breasts, there is something dissipated and barren about her, betrayed by the bony hand, the savage mouth, and the stunted, dog-like legs. She is the ghoulish female figure from Jackson's Orozcoesque drawings, only now

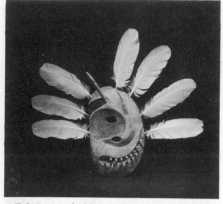

Eskimo mask, Hooper Bay region, Alaska

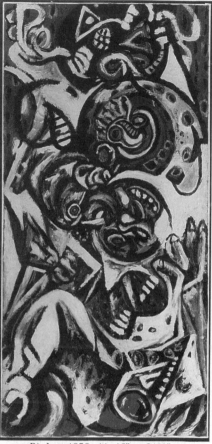

Birth, c. 1938–41, 46″ × 21¾″

he captures her in mid-transformation, between skeleton and odalisque, between life-threatening and life-affirming, beckoning from a bed that is at once menacingly barbed and lushly inviting.

In other works, Picasso drew unknowingly on Jackson's most personal imagery, his childhood bestiary. In ink drawings and gouaches from the *Guernica* period, the same archetypal menagerie of chickens, horses, and bulls appears in ever more bizarre combinations and transformations: a bird-headed man carries a dying bull; a chicken transforms into a feathered horse; a man with the head of a bull lugs a dead mare; a single figure combines man, woman, and horse in an explosion of limbs and hooves and faces and flaring nostrils. Like *Guernica*, these drawings spoke to Jackson in a language of the unconscious that few other artists could have understood as well.

But of all Picasso's images, none captivated Jackson's imagination like the bull. During most of the late 1920s and thirties, bulls appeared in dozens of Picasso's works in every medium and every incarnation, from the real bulls of the *corrida de toros*, disemboweling horses and goring matadors, to the fantastic bulls of classical mythology. To Jackson, Picasso's obsession, which he followed

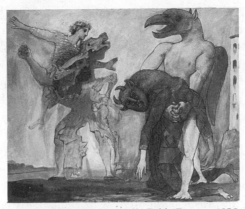

Composition with Minotaur, Pablo Picasso, 1936,
ink and gouache on paper, 17¼″ × 21½″

in the pages of *Cathiers d'art,* was yet another confirmation: the distant and vastly enviable Picasso had fixated on the very same animal that had prowled and terrorized Jackson's unconscious since childhood. Following Picasso's example as well as his own inner vision, Jackson began to fill his paintings and drawings with bulls, both real and fantastical. John Graham may have told him that the Surrealists looked upon the Minotaur's horns "as symbols of Eros (libido) and Thanatos (the death wish), the poles of the Freudian psychodynamic for the functioning of the unconscious," and that the Minotaur's home, the labyrinth, was actually a metaphor for the unconscious. But to Jackson the Minotaur was only a bull caught in the inexorable process of transformation that governed all the images in his unconscious. It was the bull that overturned his mother's buggy, transforming into the farmer who scolded him, transforming into the father who didn't love him, transforming into all the men who threatened his vulnerable world.

Even as he listened to Graham and devoured Picasso, however, Jackson was already transcending both of them. Never technically capable of duplicating Picasso's imagery, he had no choice but to process it through his own vision and retell it in his own line. In that way, Jackson's lack of technical facility had become a blessing. Even as he was studying with Graham, other more technically proficient artists like Gorky and de Kooning were retooling their imaginations to see the world through Le Maître's eyes. Even as they occupied themselves with works that were obviously derived from Picasso's Surrealist masterpieces, Jackson—forever locked inside his own head, behind his own eyes—began to integrate the lessons of Picasso with the lessons of the American Indian and finally the lessons of the past into paintings of astonishing originality. The terrified animals of *Guernica* become the terrifying animals of his childhood—shrill birds, fierce horses, and menacing bulls. The benign, expiatory transformations of primitive masks become grotesque man-beasts, and Picasso's voluptuous women are turned back into terrorizing harpies.

In *Bird*, which Pollock painted about this time, a huge bird-like creature stretches its wings almost to the edges of the canvas. Beneath it lie two severed heads—one female, perhaps, one male—in Picassoid profile. At the top, a single eye peers out threateningly from the canvas. The bird is at once terrified and terrifying. The elements are arranged formally, as in an Indian painting, the style is Picasso's, the drawing is crude, the subject could be borrowed from Jung or from American Indian art, or both. But the image is unequivocally Jackson's because the terror is Jackson's. The bird is, in fact, a barnyard chicken, dredged up from memories of the Phoenix farm, terrifying to a two-year-old boy confronting it eye-to-vulnerable-eye, but also terrified of its own fate in Stella's bloody hands.

Even after years of artistic "training" with Benton, Ryder, Siqueiros, and Orozco, even after Henderson and Jung and Graham and finally Picasso, Jackson's tumultuous unconscious was still the engine that powered his art.

24

THE WAGES OF GENIUS

S ince the days of sketching rabbits and fence posts in the hills around
Riverside, Jackson's sole ambition had been to be the best painter in the
Pollock family. The fire of that ambition had propelled him through
almost a decade of hardship and frustration. By 1939, however, Charles had
taken a position teaching calligraphy at Michigan State University, Sande was
looking for a "real" job to support his family, and Jackson had come about as
far as desire and intensity could bring him. In his late twenties, his hairline
already receding, facing a future without the indulgence of the Project, he
could no longer play the charming naïf or the enfant terrible. Potential, even
recognized potential, was no longer enough.

By confronting him with Picasso, Graham gave Jackson a new Charles to
pursue and harnessed his childhood fire to a larger ambition: to be a serious
artist, perhaps even a great one.

Jackson began by redrawing his circle of friends. "He knew that one single
artist was not going to be able to operate on his own," Reuben Kadish recalls.
"He had gotten this idea from Benton that you've *got to get a group together.*"
Up to now, Jackson's group had been shaped primarily by his emotional needs
—especially the need for fraternal camaraderie. Beginning in 1939, he finally
began to venture into the small community of avant-garde painters with whom,
through Graham, he felt a growing artistic affinity. Surprisingly, despite his
encyclopedic connections and his reputation for making introductions, Graham
seldom acted as intermediary. No matter how eager he may have been to bring
together such future luminaries as Stuart Davis, David Smith, and Willem de
Kooning, one Graham scholar suggests, "[He] preferred to keep Pollock to
himself."

Nevertheless, over the next few years, Jackson managed to meet many of his
fellow protégés: David Smith, whom Graham had identified as "the best sculp-

tor in America"; Smith's wife, Dorothy Dehner, also a sculptor; Edgar Levy, yet another of Graham's "young outstanding American painters"; Hedda Sterne, a Romanian artist who emigrated to the United States in 1941; and Gorky's studio-mate, the Dutchman, de Kooning. It was a diverse group, held together loosely ("one knew who was painting and what their work was about") by shared ideals and a common sense of estrangement from the conservative mainstream in American art. Gathering ad hoc at places like the Waldorf and Stewart's cafeterias, Ratner's, Romany Marie's, and the Jumble Shop, they would talk animatedly of the recent shows from Paris, the current issue of *Cahiers d'art*, or "Graham's latest account of what Picasso was up to," and share the usual complaints about rejection and injustice. Harold Rosenberg called these "the years of hanging around."

Gradually, half consciously, Jackson drifted away from old friends. Some left the city as Benton had: Reginald Wilson to Woodstock, New York; Stuart Edie to Iowa; Archie Musick to Colorado. Others, including Joe Meert, Bernard Steffen, Bruce Mitchell, Nathan Katz, and Joe Delaney, faded into a limbo of fondness and neglect. Remnants of the old gang continued to meet from time to time at a German bar on Thirteenth Street to horse around, play cards, and, of course, drink, but the fire had gone out of their fellowship as surely as it had gone out of the Regionalist movement.

For Jackson, the transition from the physical, barroom world of the Harmonica Rascals to the rigors of cafeteria debate was never easy and never complete. Socially reticent and intellectually insecure, he seldom joined the impromptu discussions that were the lifeblood of Graham's inner circle, preferring to remain at the periphery, meeting people one at a time as circumstances permitted. For everyday companionship, he turned to less threatening friends, most of whom he had met on the WPA: men like Louis Bunce, with whom he canvassed the commercial galleries "trying to get a foot in the door"; Bernie Schardt, who often accompanied him on vacations to New Jersey; Louis Ribak, a former student of John Sloan's; and Fred Hauck, who "went ape" over Jackson's work and won his grateful affection.

New friends were not the only sign of new ambitions. Graham had convinced Jackson that a *serious* artist was also a *knowledgeable* artist. Compared to Graham's breathtaking erudition and near-photographic memory, Jackson's understanding of art history and theory was fragmentary and haphazard at best: Ryder and the Renaissance from Benton, modern sculpture from Ben-Shmuel and Robert Laurent, the Mexicans from Kadish, Sande, Goldstein, and Siqueiros, and finally an introduction to American Indian art from Henderson. Between these low hills of familiarity were broad plains of ignorance. His visits to museums and galleries prior to 1939, although a more common feature of his life than books, had done little to level out the uneven landscape. When friends came to town, he would spend days, sometimes weeks, touring the galleries to view the latest shows, but between binges, months would pass without a single sortie to Fifty-seventh Street. Museum visits, too, were more a function of camaraderie than connoiseurship, and often concluded with "a couple of ales at McSorley's." Accompanied by Sande, Reuben Kadish, Harold Lehman, and sometimes others, Jackson continued to visit the Museum of Natural History, and occasionally the Hispanic Society of America, as well as the uptown Fifth Avenue museums, the Frick and the Metropolitan. Everywhere he went, he found something that caught his eye: at the Hispanic Society, the "flamelike vibrancy" of the El Greco paintings; at the Frick, a reproduction of an Italian Renaissance fresco showing "a horse sniffing a corpse with dilated nostrils"; at the Metropolitan, the Etruscan figures ("Jackson thought they had such conviction and strength," Lehman remembers). Sensitized by Henderson and Graham, both of whom he was now seeing regularly, he also began to look more closely at the collections of primitive art on view at the Museum of Natural History and the American Indian museum. In January 1941, he and Graham attended the exhibition "Indian Art of the United States" at the Museum of Modern Art and watched as Navajo artists executed sand paintings on the gallery floor.

Also under Graham's tutelage, Jackson began to cast his visual net more widely among avant-garde styles. He followed closely the shows of Max Ernst, Yves Tanguy, and the other Surrealists at Julien Levy's gallery. At Paul Rosenberg's, he studied the works of Expressionist masters like Paul Klee, Wassily Kandinsky, and Max Beckmann. (In July 1941, Sande wrote Charles: "[Jack's] thinking is, I think related to that of men like Beckman [sic].") At both Valentine Dudensing and Pierre Matisse, where important exhibitions of work by the School of Paris were on continual exhibition, he saw the paintings of Joan Miró, the Spanish Surrealist whose biomorphic images and whimsical touch would have a lasting, if delayed, effect on his own work. More and more often, in a clear break from the past, he attended these exhibitions alone. "When you're a serious artist," Nene Schardt remembers him explaining, "you don't go to shows in gangs."

After a decade of drifting through the backwaters of Regionalism and Mexican muralism, what brought Jackson finally, belatedly, to the swift currents of Picasso and the School of Paris? Critics, and even friends of Jackson's, detected behind his timely shifts in allegiance a lively art-political savvy. "There's no doubt," says Gerome Kamrowski, "that Jackson had a sense of where his career should go. He joined Benton when Benton's star was on the rise, then jumped to Picasso when Benton began to fade."

How calculated were Jackson's career moves? How sophisticated was his reading—intellectual or political—of art historical trends? How much did he actually understand, for example, of the labyrinthine abstractions of Graham's *System and Dialectics*, the metaphysics of Analytical and Synthetic Cubism, or the arcana of Jungian philosophy? At the time, Jackson's acquaintances often read into his long silences and rare, cryptic statements a failure to grasp the intellectual issues—an inference made more plausible by his self-evident lack of reading. In fact, it's fair to say that he knew only those specifics that he could assimilate in conversation, and although extraordinarily absorbent, he never achieved mastery of the analytic subtleties of any of the theories that informed his art. What understanding he had was intuitive, not intellectual. "He had an aesthetic intelligence," said Joseph Henderson, "but not a philosophic intelligence. . . . Basically uneducated, he took in a lot and his intuition was highly developed . . . his imagination was turning over ninety miles a minute." A later therapist concludes that Jackson was "highly intelligent, much more so than he appeared, but it was all intuitive. His inability to express ideas went both ways—he couldn't absorb words and he couldn't use them, but he picked up the subtlest nonverbal signals. . . . His intelligence functioned in the unconscious without transposing itself into the conscious."

For Jackson, the process of analysis never left the canvas; it never made the leap into words. "All his great feeling and intelligence is there in his painting," says Reuben Kadish. "His sharpness and discrimination were all focused toward painting. When you went to a museum with him, he didn't say much, but he had a very professional eye." Ideas independent of images were not so much incomprehensible as irrelevant. A fellow artist remembers that Jackson had "no interest in the nature of Cubism as such. He didn't want to talk about it, but he'd go look at the paintings any time." According to Kadish, "he understood the *intensity* of the paintings, and that was it. When Mondrian said something good about his stuff, he was excited. When Matta was responsive to his work, he got just as excited. And there can be nobody further apart then Matta and Mondrian. The image was the only thing that mattered."

The same can be said of Jackson's political savvy. He related to other people with the same startling, intuitive acuity that he brought to art. While incapable of manipulations that unfolded over time or involved groups of people, he was exceedingly effective at working his will in private. Nor was he above using his considerable powers to charm, cajole, or hurt the major players in his life, both personal and professional. "Jackson knew how to pick just the right thing to say in order to destroy you emotionally," recalls Roger Wilcox. "He did that to one friend after another." Yet nothing he did appears to have been carefully plotted. Thus, if Jackson was drawn from one type of image to another, from Benton to Orozco to Picasso, it was not in pursuit of either theoretical resolution or long-view political advantage. It was, instead, a natural, half-conscious movement dictated both by an acute aesthetic intuition and by a need for approval with deep roots in his past. If the moves appeared to be the product of uncanny political foresight, it was only because Jackson's childhood plumb lines were extraordinarily long and sensitive.

By the middle of 1940, Jackson began to see the fruits of his new efforts. "Jack is doing very good work," Sande wrote Charles in May. "After years of trying to work along lines completely unsympathetic to his nature . . . [he] is coming out with an honest creative art." More and more, friends who had dismissed him, however fondly, as a troubled youth were responding to him as a serious artist. Rachel Scott recalls an unannounced visit about 1940: "One night, Jackson was having dinner with neighbors whose windows looked directly into ours. When he got bored, he walked out and came over to our apartment. He was half overseas at the time, but he was *very* intelligent. He had a wonderful long talk with my husband [Bill Scott], who was also an artist. Afterward Bill said, 'That man's *brilliant.*' " Even old friends like Reuben Kadish began to notice a new "aura" about Jackson—a combination of the old intensity and the new confidence. "He had a way of firing the situation," Kadish remembers. At a poker game in which matches served as chips, Jackson pounded the table to punctuate a point about Picasso and a box of matches burst into flames. Says Kadish, "It was clear that Jackson had the spark to make things happen."

In late May 1940, after a visit to Jackson's studio, Helen Marot called Dr. Henderson to give him the good news. "I saw Jackson Pollock last night," she reported, "and he talked for hours in a stormy but fascinating way about himself and his painting. I don't know but it seems to me we have a genius on our hands."

Soon after Marot visited his studio, Jackson was laid off the Project—his eighteen months were up. A week later, on June 3, 1940, Helen Marot died.

The combination of blows shattered his fragile new confidence. The night of Marot's death he plunged into the most ferocious binge of booze and violence since Bloomingdale's. This may have been the night that he destroyed dozens of his own paintings, slashing them repeatedly with a kitchen knife and throwing the shreds out the window, where they floated to the street like multicolored streamers. According to Kadish, Jackson saved his special wrath for the old Bentonesque paintings that still lined the studio walls. "He didn't want the world to see that he had had any contact with Benton."

At first, Henderson tried to dismiss the binge as merely "a truly glorious wake [for] a special friend." As the "regressive" behavior continued in Marot's absence, however, even Henderson finally had to admit that their sessions were having little, if any, real therapeutic effect. No doubt fearing that the relapse might undermine the validity of his Jungian therapeutic methods altogether, Henderson belatedly—and probably at Sande's insistence—abandoned the analysis of Jackson's drawings. "Thence forward [I] dwelt upon his personal conscious problems," he recalled, "rather than upon the imagery of the unconscious." (He may also have deigned to recommend *The Common Sense of Drinking*, a practical and very non-Jungian self-help book for alcoholics that Jackson read about this time.)

For the first time, Henderson began to ask questions about his patient's past and family experiences. He soon "discovered" the truth about Jackson's childhood of "human deprivation on the personal level" and his "need for the 'all-giving mother.' " He even reported a diagnosis: Jackson was suffering from a schizophrenia-like disorder characterized by alternating periods of "violent agitation" and "paralysis or withdrawal." Henderson unhelpfully compared this form of introversion to the mental state of a "novice in a tribal initiation rite during which he is ritually dismembered at the onset of an ordeal whose goal is to change him from a boy into a man." Jackson's seemingly endless drunken binges were, according to Henderson, like the "wild paroxysms" of a Kwakiutl Indian induced by drinking salt water. Both were a hopeful prelude to an emotionally healthy adult future. Jackson was undergoing a "ritual death" from which he would emerge "by a ritual rebirth."

In a later description of Jackson's case, Henderson laid the blame for the relapse squarely on Marot's death. "He had in fact suffered from considerable isolation due to emotional deprivation in early childhood, and this had not yet been adequately compensated," Henderson wrote. "He had begun to compensate in a close relationship with a sympathetic older woman friend, whose interest in him he had learned to trust, but unfortunately, she died before he had attained the security of a really new position."

Whether Marot's death in fact touched off the long depression that followed, or merely coincided with one of the periodic downturns that marked Jackson's emotional life, the effect was the same. Without a job and without Marot's maternal support, Jackson quickly reverted to old habits. "He had made up his mind to drink," recalls Nene Schardt, "and nobody could stop him. The motivation was suddenly too strong. It was just a compulsion. He had had a period when he was all right, then suddenly it was broken." As always, Jackson's art suffered first. His productivity plummeted—he told a friend that he "wanted to paint very badly," but "that was just no longer possible"—a paralysis made more frustrating by the successes of the recent past. As his expectations had risen, so had his capacity for disappointment (a dynamic that would be repeated, with devastating effect, a decade later).

As in the past, Jackson expressed his frustration by lashing out at his competitors. Drunk and raving, he descended on Arshile Gorky's apartment at 36 Union Square. Gorky, who was six feet four and "*immensely* strong," received him civilly until Jackson called his paintings "nothing but shit," whereupon Gorky threatened to throw him down the stairs. At an exhibition of Manuel Tolegian's works, he tore paintings off the wall and routed patrons from the gallery. Tolegian's successes on the Project (one of his paintings had been bought by the White House) and at the Ferargil Galleries still rankled. Later, Jackson laid siege to the apartment building that Tolegian managed at 25 Vandam Street, hurling stones at the windows, breaking them one by one with methodical madness.

No successes, however, rankled more sharply than Philip Goldstein's. Even before he arrived in New York in 1936, Goldstein had been the subject of an article in *Time* magazine. Although his mural designs for the WPA met with no more success than Jackson's, he frequently entered small, well-publicized public competitions and routinely won. In 1938, his mural design for the WPA pavilion at the New York World's Fair was accepted, along with one by Anton

Refregier. Jackson spent the next year listening to the raves it earned from critics and public alike. At the end of the summer, Goldstein's mural, *Maintaining America's Skills*, was awarded, by public vote, first prize for the best outdoor mural of the fair. Not long afterward, Jackson wrote Charles, barely disguising his dejection and bitterness: "I haven't been up to all these competitions. . . . Phil [Goldstein] and his wife have been winning some of the smaller jobs. I'm still trying to get back on the project."

When he wasn't staggering drunk in the street or waging war on rivals, Jackson spent the days recovering in his studio as he always had, head in hands, sitting motionless for hours at a time. More and more, the schizophrenia-like state that Henderson had described was playing itself out in a binary drama of "depression and elation." Disconsolate, he wrote Charles later that summer: "I haven't much to say about my work and things—only that I have been going thru violent changes. . . . God knows what will come out of it all—it's pretty negative stuff so far." For the first time since the early thirties, he contemplated suicide. One friend remembers seeing a drawing he had done of a male figure "hanging by a cord." "I took it to be a hint of suicide," she remembers, "but I thought it was too delicate a subject to talk about."

During the months after Marot's death, Jackson spent more time than ever in John Graham's apartment on Greenwich Avenue. He undoubtedly found some solace in Graham's belief that a profound nature and genuine talent often invite emotional disaster. "Regrets, sorrow, loneliness and eventual collapse"—these, said Graham, "are the wages of genius." Acutely aware of Jackson's unsuccessful therapy with Henderson and his drinking problem, Graham allowed their discussions of art to assume a psychotherapeutic dimension. (Despite his interest in Jung's theories of the unconscious, Graham felt that, therapeutically, "Freud was on the right track.") Later, in retrospect, friends would say that Graham acted as Jackson's "lay analyst," a label that Graham himself rejected. According to another artist whom Graham helped through similar difficulties, his therapeutic method consisted of "nothing but listening."

In September, after having several dreams about cross-country train trips, Joseph Henderson packed his bags and left for San Francisco. The New York psychoanalytic community, dominated by Freudians, had proven "too stifling" for his capacious ambition. (Henderson would later found the C. G. Jung Institute of San Francisco, one of the leading centers for Jungian studies in the United States.) His departure, only four months after Marot's death, apparently caused not the faintest trauma in Jackson's life, not even a modest binge. Jackson gave him a gouache as a going-away present.

Arguably, Henderson's most important contribution to Jackson's emotional well-being was his choice of a successor: Dr. Violet Staub de Laszlo. A Swiss-born analyst and student of Jung, de Laszlo had just arrived in New York from London where she and Henderson had studied together. Henderson did not choose a female successor by chance. "It is frequently efficacious," he later

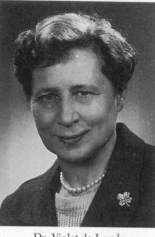

Dr. Violet de Laszlo

wrote, "for a man with this type of mother-complex to be treated by a woman analyst capable of playing the mother role temporarily." A stout, amiable-looking woman in her early forties with a diffident manner, matronly air, bright blue crescent eyes, and a round Alpine face, de Laszlo quickly filled the void in Jackson's life left by Helen Marot's death—despite her own efforts to "avoid involvement that might get in the way of his therapy." Twice a week for the next year, Jackson eagerly made the long trek up to the apartment building at 27 West Eighty-sixth Street where de Laszlo lived with her two sons.

In some ways, the sessions merely recapitulated his experience with Henderson; the first few consisted of near-total silence. "I learned almost nothing about his childhood," recalls de Laszlo, who had not discussed Jackson's case with Henderson in advance. "It's hard to convey how little he said in words. He was enormously inhibited." Once again, the deadlock was broken only when Jackson began to bring drawings to their sessions. Unlike Henderson, however, de Laszlo proffered a minimum of Jungian interpretation. "We just sat together and looked at the drawings," de Laszlo remembers, "and I picked out various elements that told me something. It was a search in common, really —totally unsystematic and based on mutual sympathy. I didn't condemn, I didn't criticize. I tried to be understanding." Mutual sympathy and understanding from a maternal figure were, of course, precisely what Helen Marot had provided, and precisely what Jackson needed most. Only a few months after the sessions began, he tried to arrange to see de Laszlo outside the confines of analysis. "I would have liked to have seen him outside my office," she remembers, "but he lived so far away and spent the greater part of his time in a drunken or semi-drunken state. So although he would have welcomed it, and I would have welcomed it, it didn't fit together." Jackson did, however, bring John Graham, who was contributing toward de Laszlo's fee, to one of their regular sessions.

In May, Jackson persuaded de Laszlo to write his draft board and request a deferment on psychological grounds. She balked at first, believing that "the army would be good for Jackson, that it would make a man of him," but finally acquiesced and, on May 3, 1941, wrote the examining medical officer of local draft board 17:

Dear Sir,
Mr. Jackson Pollock has been referred to me by Dr. J. L. Henderson. Pollock has been coming to me for a number of psychoanalytical interviews during the past six months in connection with his difficulties of adaptation to social environment. I have found him to be a shut in and inarticulate personality of good intelligence, but with a great deal of emotional instability, who finds it difficult to form or maintain any kind of relationship. I would say that the problem is fairly deep-seated and not due to any superficial tendencies towards evasion, or to immaturity of outlook.

Although he has not during these months shown any manifest symptoms of schizophrenia, yet in the course of the interviews, it has become evident that there is a certain schizoid disposition underlying the instability. It is for this reason that I venture to suggest that Pollock be referred for a psychiatric examination.

Three weeks later, Jackson underwent the suggested examination at Beth Israel Hospital. After obtaining another statement from de Laszlo verifying that he had been admitted to Bloomingdale's, he was classified 4-F, unqualified. (He later told a friend that the army "rejected" him because he was "neurotic.") It must have seemed an easy solution at the time, but in the long run, Jackson always made himself pay for what he perceived as moments of unmanly weakness.

Bolstered by de Laszlo's support and reinstated on the WPA in October, Jackson began to paint again. By the summer of 1941, he was enjoying the sunshine and seclusion of Bucks County for the third year in a row. "He seemed to have his drinking under control," recalls Eda Bunce, who joined the Pollocks and the Schardts that summer. "I never saw him drink." The most momentous event of the summer was the discovery of an old, abandoned Packard, over which Jackson, Bernie Schardt, and Louis Bunce labored like boys for weeks.

Beyond the hedgerows of Bucks County, however, the future hurtled ahead in directions that the World's Fair, now a distant memory, had never foreseen. By the summer of 1941, almost all of Europe had fallen to the Nazis. Paris, the artistic center of Jackson's world, disappeared behind the wall of German occupation. Picasso was one of the few artists who remained in the city. (When a German officer visited Le Maître's studio and saw reproductions of *Guernica*, he asked admiringly, "Did you do this?" To which Picasso replied, "No. You did.") Matisse had retreated to Vichy Nice and most of the others, including the Surrealists, had fled in a decorous rout to the high ground of New York. On June 22, while Jackson tinkered with the old Packard, three million German soldiers swept across the Russian border toward Moscow.

Closer to home, the WPA staggered toward extinction. After 2,500 murals, 17,000 pieces of sculpture, 108,000 easel paintings, and 240,000 prints, public tolerance and government money had finally run out. The furor over "communist infiltration" and "Bohemian chiselers" had dealt the final blow. Artists who complained shrilly that Communists deserved federal jobs or that reporting to workshops "consumed the precious morning light" sounded increasingly like the "ingrates and subversives" the Hearst papers accused them of being. "A winter of ups and downs," Sande called it, "with the latter in the majority." Thousands, like Sande and Jackson, had been on and off the Project, some more than once, living in perpetual fear of the next round of legislative harassment. Purge begat purge, beginning with loyalty oaths in 1939 and consummating in a congressional mandate to rid the WPA of Communist sympathizers, past and present. "They're dropping people like flies on the pretense that they are Red," Sande wrote Charles in October, "for having signed a petition . . . to have the C[ommunist] P[arty] put on the ballot. We remember signing it so we are nervously awaiting the axe. They got 20 in my department one day last week. There is no redress. . . . I could kick myself in the ass for being a damn fool—but who would of thought they could ever pull one as raw as that."

Artist George McNeil sums up the raw deal that most artists felt the war had handed them: "It was the best of times followed by the worst of times. During the thirties, we were young and optimistic, but then the war in Europe started and everything turned to dirt and grit. All the fantasy in life came to an end."

Jackson's private world, too, was turning to dirt and grit. Stella, who had moved to Tingley in 1939 to care for her mother, was already testing the chilly family waters for a new place to live as Jennie McClure's condition worsened. When Charles again suggested New York, Sande responded with barely concealed panic. All the ugly secrets he had been withholding from the family came pouring out in a letter to Charles—Jackson's hospitalization, the subsequent treatment, the discovery of a "definite neurosis," "depressive mania," and "self-destruction"—all leading to the inescapable conclusion: "Since part of [Jackson's] trouble (perhaps a large part) lies in his childhood relationship with his Mother in particular and family in general, it would be extremely trying and might be disastrous for him to see her at this time."

But Sande had other, unstated reasons for saying no. After seven years in New York, he had reached "a kind of limbo," Reuben Kadish remembers, "where nothing really counted." Despite the talent he had shown in adolescence, Sande's efforts to become an artist had always been halfhearted, crippled by his time-consuming commitment to Jackson's welfare and by their common past. "He felt that he was nothing," says Kadish, "that he was only good enough for the most demeaning, the least rewarding jobs. He was always just a helper." For the last seven years, Sande had helped Jackson. Now, with the end of the Project only months, even days away, with a wife to support and, he hoped, a child someday, he began to see that others needed his help more.

In the early spring of 1941, Arloie announced she was pregnant.

Jackson's old support system was crumbling. Just as the childhood rivalry with Charles could no longer propel him artistically, the bond with Sande, after twenty-nine years, could no longer sustain him emotionally. More than the beginning of the war or the end of the WPA, that realization was undoubtedly the real terror in *his* World of Tomorrow.

In the closing months of 1941, three events combined to save him from that future. In November, John Graham invited him to participate in a show of French and American painters at the McMillen Gallery the following January. Jackson's paintings would hang for the first time beside those of Picasso and Matisse. In December, the Japanese attacked Pearl Harbor, bringing the United States into the war and accelerating the movement of the international art world to Jackson's doorstep.

And sometime in between, Lee Krasner appeared at his studio door.

25

LENA KRASSNER

According to a family legend, Lena Krassner was conceived on January 14, 1908, the day her mother, Anna, joined her father in America.

They had parted three years before and half a world away in the tiny Ukrainian village of Shpikov just north of Odessa. There, at the station, surrounded by sobbing relatives and skeptical neighbors, Joseph had vowed to work hard in America and send the money for his wife and four children to join him. It was a promise heard often at the station near the *shtetl*—one that wasn't always kept. "A person gone to America," recalled a fellow emigrant, "was exactly like a person dead." But Joseph Krassner was a reliable man and the money did come, more than $200—a fortune several times over in a community where economic activity among Jews was severely restricted and malnutrition commonplace. It was just enough for five steerage tickets from Odessa to Bremen to New York.

Like hundreds of thousands of other Russian Jews, the Krassners came to America to escape a biblical litany of afflictions. Beginning in 1881, anti-Semitic pogroms, incited by the procurator of the Russian Holy Synod, had repeatedly swept across Russia, routing millions of Jews from their communities. On April 20, 1903, in Kishinev, the capital of Bessarabia, a group of workmen armed with picks and shovels stormed the city's Jewish section, killing 120, injuring more than 500, and burning almost 100,000 people out of their homes. Even more than the pogroms of the 1880s, the massacre of 1903 unleashed a tidal wave of new Jewish emigration. Those who stubbornly remained faced conscription in the Russian army following the outbreak of the Russo-Japanese War in early 1904. Even a man as devout and oblivious as Joseph Krassner could no longer ignore the peril, could no longer peddle his tobacco and perform his duties as *shuka* to the town's rabbi secure in the conviction that the historical forces descending on him were nothing more than the "troublesome trifling of the gentile era."

In 1905, the same year mutineers from the battleship *Potemkin* faced the bayonets of the czar's Imperial Guard on the steps of Odessa's port, Joseph Krassner left his family in nearby Shpikov and sailed from the same port to the land where, according to one immigrant, all the men "were tall and slender and . . . wore yellow trousers and high hats"—America. Three years later he greeted his family at Ellis Island.

The reunited Krassner family settled into a small house on Jerome Street in the East New York section of Brooklyn, not far from the Blake Street Market where Joseph rented a stall and sold fish. Jacob Riis had already declared the area a "nasty, little slum," but compared to the mud-and-dung world of Shpikov, it was indeed the promised land.

Yet the Krassners remained strangely untouched by the new world around them. Like many of the one and a half million Jews who immigrated from Eastern Europe at the turn of the century, they didn't really leave the *shtetl* behind; they brought it with them. On Jerome Street, the old family unit quickly sprang back into shape with Joseph assuming the role, common in Russian Jewish households, of the distant and revered authority figure "whom one did not speak to or about lightly." Moody and introspective, he was always the first to "assert the moral right" but the last to exercise physical discipline. "If we needed to be spanked," recalls one of his daughters, "all he had to do was raise his strap and that was enough. You'd run like hell in the other direction. But he never came after you." Like most of the elder men in the *shtetl*, Joseph spent more time at the synogogue than at home or at work, leaving the affairs of this world, business and family, to his wife and children so he could devote himself to affairs of a higher order.

Anna Krassner was a contentious, pragmatic, grim-faced woman a decade younger than her husband, but careworn far beyond her years. "She was all business," recalls one of her daughters. If she was hard on her children, it was because she herself had missed childhood. Married at eleven, she had borne five children before turning twenty. One had died, leaving three daughters—Edith, Esther, and Rose—and a son, Anna's pride, Izzy (later called Irving). The older sisters helped at the market, lifting heavy loads of pike, carp, and whitefish, and "doing all the things that should have been done by the man in the family." Irving stayed home with Anna and helped plan the family finances. Unlike her taciturn husband, Anna was short-tempered and confrontational. She never punished by "hitting," but instead "would lose her temper with her mouth," according to daughter Ruth, often reducing her children to tears with barrages of verbal abuse. On those rare occasions when she sought escape from the burdens of the temporal world, she turned not only to religion but, like many *shtetl* women, to mysticism: the world of spirits and curses and supernatural powers. Her mother-in-law in Russia, Pesa Krassner, had been a psychic and fortune-teller, and she passed the same fears and superstitions on to her children. At the sound of thunder—considered an especially potent ill omen—

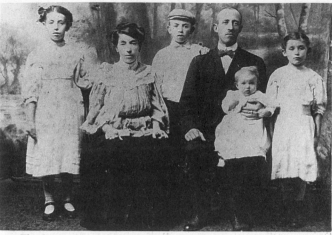

The Krassners, about 1908; Lena (Lenore) on her father's knee,
Izzy (Irving) standing center.

she and her daughters would run to the kitchen stove and clutch each other in
sheer terror until the storm passed.

This was the family into which Lena Krassner was born on October 27,
1908. It was, from the beginning, a family already in decline and disarray: a
distant and often absent father; a moody, shrewish mother who pined loudly
and often for her home in Russia; older sisters approaching marriageable age;
and a usurpative son deeply involved in an Oedipal triangle. It was also a
closed, complete unit, hostile to newcomers, even by blood, with its roots thousands of miles away. "Any member of the family," Lee later complained,
"could always break out in a language I couldn't understand"—a cacophony
of Hebrew, Russian, and Yiddish with only "a smattering of English." Outsiders called her Lenore, but the family always used her Yiddish name, Lena.
It was, she said, "like living in some litttle ghetto back in Stalingrad or somewhere." Or like living with a family of strangers. Years later, she described her
childhood self as "an oddball" and "an outcast," and admitted that her earliest
memory was of a burning desire to leave home.

When Lenore was three, another child was born. Her Yiddish name was
Udel (which, when mangled by her first grade teacher, became "Adele"), but
outside the family she would be known as Ruth. Although constant companions, the two youngest sisters were never intimate. In a picture taken while
both were in elementary school, they pose on the front steps of the Jerome
Street house wearing identical Sabbath coats, their hair cut in identical page-
boys. Ruth's hand rests lightly on Lee's knee; Lee's arm reaches behind her
sister's shoulders in a feint of possessiveness. Lee knows enough to smile; Ruth
stares uncomfortably into the camera, obviously unused to her older sister's
solicitude. "I didn't look up to her," Ruth recalls. "She had no influence on
me and I had none on her. We had *nothing* in common."

In fact, Ruth left more of a mark than she knew. She was not only Anna's

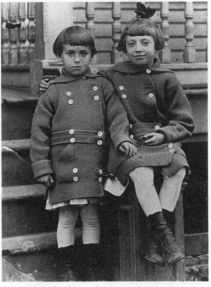

Udel (Ruth) and Lena, about 1916

favorite, and therefore exempt from the "work-until-you-drop" rules imposed on her older sisters, she was also the prettiest in the family. Not that any of Joseph and Anna Krassner's other children were attractive. Most had inherited either their father's jutting chin and protruding eyes or their mother's long nose and shallow brow. Lee, unfortunately, had inherited both. Ruth, on the other hand, looked hardly like a Krassner at all, and relatives came from far away to admire her and vie for the privilege of showing her off or taking her on weekend trips—trips on which Lee was never invited.

Jealous of her baby sister, alienated from the rest of the family, and desperate for attention, Lee turned inward. "From an early age," comments John Bernard Myers, a friend in later years, "Lee had to invent a life for herself." Like Jackson, she created a fantasy world to compensate for the inadequacies of the real one. Dressed up in her Sabbath clothes, to which she always added a special touch like a bow or a sash, she would promenade down the dilapidated street, stopping at each house to pay "a social call." Because East New York, along with neighboring Brownsville and New Lots, was a way station for Jews from all over Europe, Jerome Street offered a world's fair of exotic cultures to stimulate a little girl's imagination. A German family, the Lehmans, lived on one side; a French family, the Granvilles, on the other. "There were always wonderful odors of strange food in the air," Lee recalled years later, "different foods, different languages, different cultures. It was a very European atmosphere. It made me feel very grown up."

As both the only son and, in his father's absence, the only male, Irving dominated the Krassner family. Indeed, he terrorized it. In close alliance with Anna, the source of all domestic authority—"She almost treated him like he was her husband," Ruth recalls—Irving meted out physical punishment with

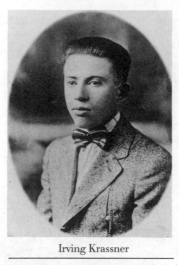

Irving Krassner

as much relish as his dour sense of responsibility would permit. "You had to be afraid of my brother," Ruth recalls. "If he said he was going to smack you, he *smacked* you. He didn't threaten, he just did it. We *died* when he was around."

Even so, Lee adored him. Long before she could read, she would follow him to the library and sit at a safe distance holding a book, her eyes darting back and forth between the indecipherable pages of *Grimm's Fairy-Tales* and the sight of Irving slowly and intently turning the pages of Gogol, Tolstoy, or Turgenev. In the evenings, she would plead with him to read to her—"from whatever book he happened to have, it didn't matter," says Ruth. Even when he raised his hand threateningly against her pestering, she persisted. At school, she learned to read on her own only reluctantly and, later in life, would coax, cajole, and trick friends into reading to her aloud. At home, it was a rare privilege when Irving allowed her to listen to his recordings of Enrico Caruso.

Everything that Charles Pollock was to Jackson, Irving was to Lee. In the rush to make herself over in his image, she adopted his mannerisms, his temper, even his bilious disposition. "Irving was a tough nut," Ruth recalls. "He didn't take any crap from anybody, and he could put you down pretty good. So Lee became even *tougher* than he was. Irving had a temper, but you'd have to step hard on his toes before he would lose it. Lee would go off without warning." Later in life, family members referred to Irving and Lee as "the immovable object and the unstoppable force."

When Irving renounced Judaism, Lee, at age twelve or thirteen, quickly followed suit. "I crashed into the living room just as my parents were having tea with a doctor who was a distant relative," Lee recounted later, "and [I] announced that I was through with religion." (Lee's jealousy of Anna, whose intimacy with Irving she coveted wildly, turned mother and daughter into lifelong enemies. "She was always getting back at my mother," says Ruth.

"Everything that went wrong in her life was Mama's fault. . . . Mother haunted her to the *grave*.")

But nothing pleased Irving. Where Jackson had received at least moral and logistical support from his oldest brother, Lee met with open hostility. "She wanted Irving to be close to her," Ruth recalls, "but he never was. *Never*." Essentially mean-spirited, manipulative, and misanthropic (he never married), Irving had only a sadist's interest in Lee's adulation. The harder she tried to please him, the more abusive he became. Later in life, "if Lee didn't do what he wanted," says Ruth, "he just walked away from her. Every once in a while, she would be difficult and he'd smack her down *fast*. He would say, 'If you don't shut your mouth, I'm walking out and you'll never see me again.' And she knew that's just what he would do, so she shut up."

At the age of five, Lee Krasner was already locked in a contest that would shape all her future relationships with men. With unwavering masochistic determination, she would always seek out men as remote, abusive, and implacable as Irving, and lose herself in them with the same guileless abandon. A half dozen times over the next three decades she would repeat the cycle, each time with another man and a fresh determination to make the old formula yield a new result.

Because confrontation and abuse were the only forms of attention she could elicit from Irving, she learned to cultivate them. At school, she refused to sing Christmas carols that proclaimed "Jesus Christ [was] the Lord" because, she protested, "he just wasn't mine." At home, she denounced the Jewish faith to her *shuka* father and bridled at the role her faith assigned to women. As a teenager, she came to see the cosmopolitan neighborhood of her girllhood as an unbearable "condition of slavery" and her neighbors, however colorful their origins, as hopelessly mundane Americans. Convinced that the world operated by the same harsh rules as her family, she entered that world hardened by her years with Irving and prepared to do battle. "You couldn't just have a conversation with Lee," says Ruth. "Oh, no! She'd bite your head off even before you had a chance to say hello!"

Later in life, Lee frequently spoke of "colliding" with people, even when referring to chance encounters on the street. It was a revealing word choice. For her, all interactions between people *were* collisions: the more traumatic, the more explosive, the more satisfying. Addicted from infancy to the highs of aggravation and abuse, she sought them out, always living, as Fritz Bultman observed, "on the edge of antagonism," waging a secret war on self-control and civility, searching for the hidden enmity she sensed in every encounter, always testing for the rejection that would be her vindication.

For Lena Krassner, art was the ultimate collision.

Nothing in the record explains where her first artistic impulse came from. Although, as a child, she loved to copy the pictures of beautiful ladies from newspaper advertisements, Lee later claimed that the desire to pursue art as a career was "haphazard," that it simply "sounded more alive than secretarial work." The only artwork in the house on Jerome Street was Irving's reproduction of a painting of Queen Isabella giving her jewels to Columbus. But Irving's passion was reserved for the giants of Russian literature and for Enrico Caruso, not for art. His frequent trips to the library and evenings in front of the Victrola did, however, introduce Lee to the possibility of aesthetic fulfillment, to the existence of a world where beauty was not physical and rewards were not necessarily tangible.

In 1922, fourteen-year-old Lena graduated from P.S. 72 in Brooklyn and applied to Manhattan's Washington Irving High School, the only high school in the city that permitted girls to major in art. Her application was rejected. It was only the first of many rejections to come: in her family, at school, in her religion, in the art world, in society itself. It was a path that promised endless collisions.

Like all their neighbors on Jerome Street, the Krassners had come to America to find financial security. But centuries of Talmudic scholarship had also instilled in Jewish families like the Krassners an almost reverential appreciation of culture, which they called by its Russian name: *iskusstvo*. Ibram Lassaw, an abstract sculptor whose family had traveled from the Ukraine to Egypt to America, remembers conversations he overheard as a child, when friends from the old country would sit around the samovar and talk in Russian about *iskusstvo*. "I didn't know what the word meant, but I could tell from the tone of their voices that they had great respect for it." The area of the Ukraine where the Krassners had lived was, in fact, the capital of Jewish culture in Russia during the czarist days, and Odessa, "the Paris of the East."

Even in Odessa, however, art never commanded the reverence that literature or theater or even music did. "The graphic arts had absolutely no place in our lives," said Maurice Sterne, a painter who grew up in the Baltic region of Russia. The same Talmudic culture that sanctified words had been denuded by the biblical injunction against graven images. Except for decorated candlesticks, prayer shawls, and other objects used in worship, it was a culture virtually without a visual tradition. To become an artist was to live "outside the boundaries of respect," stripped of both the financial rewards conferred by business and the dignity conferred by *iskusstvo*. In time, Lee and the other Jewish artists of her generation would help reshape the art world into a form more consistent with the values of their parents—a form more responsive both to financial imperatives and to the written word. At the time, however, no such synthesis seemed possible. To become an artist was to leap from a high cliff "into the gentile unknown"—without benefit of culture, religion, or family to cushion the fall.

But Lee's rebellion went even further. Unlike her male counterparts, Lee was also rebelling against her sex—or at least against the role her sex traditionally played in Jewish culture, described by Irving Howe as "a combination of social inferiority and business activity." Jewish girls were supposed to be "quiet and modest" and, if at all possible, to have a job—at least as a shopgirl, preferably as a teacher. (Teaching was considered a dignified way of earning a good salary without trespassing on male prerogatives.) Once married, Jewish women were expected to do as Anna Krassner had done: manage their families —even to the extent of supervising children at work in a family business—but not to have opinions and certainly not to voice them.

Like other Jewish girls locked by tradition into "the progression from shop-girl to housewife," Lee found herself inspired, or at least made restless, by ideas never heard in the *shtetl* in Shpikov—American ideas. Jewish girls "came to value pleasure in the immediate moment," according to Howe; "some were even drawn to the revolutionary thought that they had a right to an autonomous selfhood." Like Stella Pollock and her magazine-reading *consoeurs* in the Midwest, Jewish women quickly carved out "a niche of privacy within the cluttered family apartment, [where] they responded to the allure of style, the delicacies of manners, the promise of culture." For the rest of her life, Lee lived in both these worlds, alternately struggling to establish her autonomy and yielding to the belief that "a woman alone, not a wife and not a mother, has no existence"; avoiding marriage, but seldom living without a man; insisting on her independence, but refusing to learn to drive until she was in her forties; flaunting her artistic ambition, but often putting aside her work for long periods to concentrate on pleasing a man. In every relationship, she played out the dilemma of her generation, while underneath, the older, private battle with Irving continued to rage.

Yet, for all Lee's noisy rebellion, her family hardly noticed. If her parents were less disappointed with her than they would have been with a son, it was because they didn't have the same high expectations. "A girl who sacrificed a career for the arts," says Ernestine Lassaw, who once shared Lee's creative ambitions, "didn't have much of a career to sacrifice." It was the final, parting insult; one that deprived her of the climactic collision she so desperately sought. Eventually, she exacted her revenge, first by dropping an *s* from the family name, then by changing her first name altogether, from Lenore to the sexually ambiguous "Lee." Years later, when a friend asked her what her parents had contributed to her career as an artist, she replied dryly: "A mauve sweater."

After a dismal year in a pre-law program at Girls' High School in Brooklyn during which she supported herself by decorating lampshades, china, and felt hats, Lee reapplied to Washington Irving and this time was accepted. Unfortunately, the thrill of commuting to Manhattan and studying art did nothing to improve her grades. In fact, art was her worst subject. In later years, she derived a sly pleasure from repeating her art teacher's caustic remark: "I am going to pass you in art with sixty-five, not because you deserve it, but because you have done so well in all your other subjects." But poor grades and teachers' ridicule only emboldened her. After graduating in 1925, she applied to the Women's

Art School of the Cooper Union for the Advancement of Science and Art, located in Cooper Square on the edge of Greenwich Village, and was accepted. To celebrate, she made a score of small paintings of flowers and gave them to all her old friends in Brooklyn.

Like Alfred Kazin and a generation of artists and intellectuals who grew up in Brooklyn, Lee Krasner was in a "terrible rush to get away from everything [she] had grown up with." And the place to get away to was Manhattan. For years, she had lived in its shadow, never more than an hour away by trolley (even less by the newly built El), catching occasional glimpses of its hurly-burly glamour. "[It] revealed a style of life that was as alluring as it at first seemed frightening," wrote Matthew Josephson, another refugee from Brooklyn. "Its intensely metropolitan character and electrifying tempo seemed to drain the neighboring borough of all attraction, making it by comparison utterly provincial." In 1926, in the last golden years before the Great Depression, Lee crossed the Brooklyn Bridge and began her new life as an artist. Decades later, she reminisced: "Coming over the bridge was like arriving in another world . . . like suddenly being in Paris in 1900. It was my salvation."

No sooner had she shaken herself free of the past, however, than she began to recreate it in her new surroundings. Like Jackson, she didn't really escape her family by coming to Manhattan, she merely recast it. For the rigidity and oppressiveness of *shtetl* home life, she substituted the strict discipline of traditional academic training. (At Cooper Union, classes were organized according to "alcoves." In the first alcove, students drew from plaster casts of hands and feet; in the second, from casts of torsos; in the third, from casts of the full figure. Not until the fourth alcove did live human models appear.) To play Irving's immovable object to her unstoppable force, Lee found Charles Louis Hinton, a sculptor and instructor in the second alcove. Hinton made no secret of his distaste for Lee's work (he called it "messy") although he did eventually promote her to the third alcove, according to Lee, "in utter disappointment and desperation." "I'm going to promote you," Hinton told her, "not because you deserve it, but because I can't do anything with you." In her odd way, Lee relished Hinton's grudging promotion more than the ones she earned.

To play out the other side of her relationship with Irving, the side of self-denial, subordination, and emulation, Lee turned to another of her instructors, Victor Semon Perard. A graduate of the École des Beaux-Arts in Paris and the author of numerous books on drawing and anatomy, Perard cared less about originality than about technique, especially his own technique. Lee proved an unusually adept, admiring student, and developed a drawing style so indistinguishable from her teacher's that when Perard began work on an instruction manual, he hired Lee to provide some of the illustrations. Lee was elated. "Victor Perard was the first one who bought my art," she says. "I got paid something like ten dollars for it and I thought, This is *easy*." In the summer of 1928, she enrolled in George Bridgman's drawing class at the Art Students League with expectations of a similar success but with very different results.

Even after she adjusted her academic figural technique to please Bridgman's more casual taste, he continued to be "disdainful of her work." According to a friend, Lee was "infuriated" by Bridgman's rejection but also, oddly, "drew strength" from it.

During the same summer, while sharing a studio with a group of friends on Fifth Avenue at Fifteenth Street, Lee modeled for Moses Wainer Dykaar, a well-known portrait sculptor who worked in the same building. It was Dykaar who suggested that Cooper Union "was no place for a young artist of real ambitions," Lee recalls, and encouraged her to apply to the National Academy of Design, one of the most prestigious art schools in America at the time. Although her record was hardly exemplary, the academy accepted her, on the chilling condition that she start the whole arduous process over again back in the first alcove, drawing from casts.

Lee arrived at the National Academy of Design at 109th Street and Amsterdam Avenue in September 1928, the same year Jackson Pollock entered Manual Arts High School. At the first class, her high hopes, inflated by the elegant Victorian surroundings and the cosmopolitan student body, were abruptly dashed when the instructor walked in. It was Charles Hinton, her nemesis from Cooper Union. "We looked at each other and realized it was futile," Lee recalled, "because at the Academy he couldn't promote me. It took a full committee to do that. So we were stuck with each other again, and so it went."

Once again, the rigid academic discipline proved too much like the repressive home life she was trying to escape. "At the Academy, I was very busy trying to do my best like everybody else," she said later, "only I never could make it. For the life of me, it wouldn't come through looking like Academy." Just how long and hard she exerted herself is open to question. Only four months after arriving she was placed on probation. By the end of her first year, in a rigid, conservative school where even the most accommodating students "rarely got along with their teachers," she had earned a reputation among students and faculty alike as "a nuisance," "impossible," "smart-alecky," and "too sure of herself." One teacher noted in her file, "This student is always a bother."

The inevitable collision came in the fall of 1929. After a full year bottled up in Hinton's cast drawing class, Lee was determined to break out. There was only one way: she would have to submit an oil painting that met the "approval" of a full committee of the faculty. In the summer after her first year, she set out to do just that, working at her parents' new house in Huntington, Long Island, to escape the city heat.

Fittingly, it was a self-portrait. Her figure fills the largish canvas. She catches herself at her most important activity, painting. The corner of a canvas juts in from the right; she wears a painter's smock over her light, short-sleeved blouse. One hand tightly clutches a quiver of brushes and a dirty rag, the other is hidden behind the canvas, laying on the very paint that depicts the act. Despite the studio accoutrements, she stands against an Impressionistic background of shaded tree trunks and sun-speckled underbrush. Warm sunlight strikes her

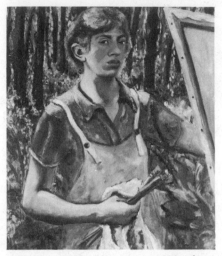

Krasner's *plein air* self-portrait, 1929, oil on
linen, 30⅛″ × 25⅛″

back and bare neck. The face is skeptical, vulnerable, and defiant, all in one
slight, side-long glance. She hasn't misrepresented the facial features, only
softened them with shadows and a complexion like marble. This was the way
Lee Krasner wanted to be seen—and judged.

In the fall, she took the painting to the faculty review committee. Raymond
P. R. Nielsen, a portrait painter and the jury chairman, looked at it once and
waved it away. "That's a dirty trick you played," he said, wagging a finger at
her. "Don't ever pretend you painted outdoors when you painted indoors." Lee
explained how she had hung a mirror on a tree and suffered through heat and
bugs and the mirror's glare, but her words fell on deaf ears. Nielsen and the
other judges refused to believe that a beginning student could produce even a
modestly successful *plein air* portrait. Surprised and probably cowed by Lee's
uninhibited protests ("His reaction was very shocking to me," she recalled),
Nielsen passed her anyway—on probation.

But Lee refused to heed the warnings. In December, she was caught trying
to paint a fish still life that had been set up for another class in the basement,
an area that was off-limits to women. The penalty was a brief suspension for
"painting figures without permission."

Later that winter, on a Saturday after class, Lee and a group of fellow
students took a subway from the academy to 730 Fifth Avenue to see "Painting
in Paris from American Collections," a show of modern French painting including works by Picasso, Matisse, and Braque at the newly opened Museum
of Modern Art in the Heckscher Building. For Lee, the exhibition "really hit
like an explosion." On the following Monday, the same group reassembled at
the academy and staged a minor coup. In the studio before class, they pulled
down the heavy red velvet drape against which the models posed—its Victorian
solemnity was suddenly a symbol of everything repressive about academy tra-

dition—and kicked the model's stand away from the wall into the middle of the room. When the model, a black man, appeared, and began taking off his "brightly-checkered lumberjacket," Lee recalled, the group shouted, "No! Keep your jacket on!" Just then the instructor walked in and saw the anarchy to which his class had been reduced. "I can't do anything with anybody!" he cried and stalked out of the room.

One of Lee's co-conspirators that day was a tall, dark, extravagantly handsome man with whom she had fallen madly in love.

Igor Pantuhoff had what Irving Krassner had: an aura. In 1928, the year of Lee's arrival, he won four of the academy's principal prizes for artistic excellence and was unanimously acclaimed the school's most promising student. Two years later, he won a traveling scholarship stipend, the equivalent of the prestigious Prix de Rome. Even in hard-luck, Depression-era New York, Igor appeared to lead a charmed life. So charmed that when he told stories about his childhood ordeal of escaping Russia, he found more puzzlement than sympathy among the women who inevitably flocked to him at parties. To them the stories seemed somehow unreal—like the romantic inventions of a Hollywood screenwriter.

In fact, Igor's entire life was suffused with the gauzy, glamorous unreality of a thirties movie. At six feet two, he was a striking presence in any crowd, moving with a lithe theatricality, embellishing his comings and goings with flamboyant gestures. When he spoke, his deep, golden baritone, with a hint of an accent, carried over the babble of ordinary conversation. With his high forehead, dark eyes, and exquisitely dimpled chin, he was as handsome as any of the era's leading men: Ronald Colman, Robert Taylor, William Powell. "That's the first thing anyone would remark about him," recalls Ronald Stein, a friend for thirty years. "How handsome he was. He looked like Errol Flynn." Thus it seemed only fitting that at a gala charity auction some years later, Igor made the winning bid for the evening's choicest lot: a dance with the actress Veronica Lake. When the couple took the floor—he in elegant black tie, she in a shimmering gown—they seemed the perfect pair. It was also typical of Igor that he made the winning bid "without a cent in his pocket."

The next day, their picture appeared in the New York papers and everyone wondered who that other movie star was swirling across the dance floor with Veronica Lake.

It's not entirely clear who he was. Like many fugitives from the 1918 Revolution, he *claimed* to be a White Russian of noble blood—a cousin to the czar. He was only seven years old when the revolution forced his family to flee, first to Turkey, then briefly to Paris where he later studied painting in an academic atelier, then finally to America where he joined his aunt Olga, a devotee of religious cults and vegetarian regimes, who had married a wealthy Florida businessman. If eccentricity and flamboyance ran in the Pantuhoff family, they ran through Olga's line. "She was a worldly, charming, sophisticated woman,"

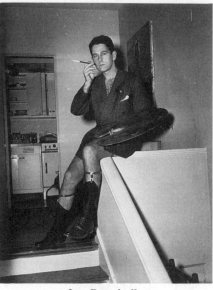

Igor Pantuhoff

recalls Muriel Francis, a longtime friend of Igor's, "but a little bit of a crackpot. She would pin her dress up around her waist and get down and scrub the floors with her hat on."

Igor represented everything that had been missing from Lee's life, everything she had left home, family, religion, and Brooklyn to find. Where the Krassners were poor and working class, Igor was rich and aristocratic—or at least appeared to be, in his impeccably tailored suits and his twelve-cylinder, yellow-and-chrome Lincoln convertible. Where Joseph and Irving were remote and laconic, Igor was garrulous, extroverted, and thrillingly attentive. Where Lee was a drab child of East New York, Igor was the darling of Paris. Where Lee was a Jew, Igor was a White Russian—as far from a Jew as one could get at the time. (According to May Rosenberg, "The only thing his family knew about Jews back in Russia was how to kill them.") Where Lee was short and *zaftig*, Igor was tall and sleek and strikingly handsome. Where Lee was struggling to become an artist, Igor seemed born to it.

Igor's attraction to Lee is harder to fathom. Most of his friends dismissed it as just another of Igor's eccentricities—of which there turned out to be an alarming number. "There was something off about Igor," recalls Muriel Francis, "something that wasn't quite straight. He was always charming, but you could see there was a darker side."

The darker side was alcoholism. Igor was "a notorious drinker," according to Ronald Stein, Lee's nephew. "I've never seen anybody drink so much and live." Lee may not have known about his drinking when they met in 1929, but she no doubt sensed the needfulness and vulnerability that underlay it. When she did discover it, sometime during the thirties, "she only loved him more," recalls May Rosenberg. "[She] said only a man desperately in need of something he can't get turns to alcohol."

With her usual abandon, Lee threw herself into the relationship. In 1932, when Igor returned from his fellowship year in Rome, they moved into an apartment together.

Soon afterward, Lee quit her career as an artist. After years of struggle and confrontation, almost at the moment of her most exciting artistic discoveries, she decided to "withdraw from the field." In fact, it was more like a rout than a withdrawal. She not only left art, she retreated all the way back to the most traditional and secure aspiration a young Jewish woman could have: teaching. She enrolled in a teacher training program at City College of New York.

Lee later tried to explain the sudden reversal as a financial necessity. It was the depths of the Depression, after all, and *somebody* had to make a living. But no excuse could conceal the truth. Even Lee must have realized that at a critical moment in her career, her will had failed; that for all her style and rhetoric, her fire didn't burn hot enough. There were too many others, like Jackson Pollock, who survived the worst of the Depression without surrendering their ambitions; who built fires out of floorboards in abandoned buildings and stole food so they could buy canvas.

Abandoning her Bohemian independence, she accompanied Igor to society parties, nightclubs, dance halls, and fashionable uptown cafés, riding proudly next to him in the yellow Lincoln. She danced the steps he taught her. She wore the clothes he chose: a severe black outfit for casual wear; brightly colored stockings to show off her legs; an exotic evening dress he assembled from bits and pieces; a nun's habit to a costume party. "Part of the understanding between them was that [Igor] would choose all of her clothing," recalls May Rosenberg, "even though Lee continued to pay for it. After that, she was always magnificently dressed." Igor also designed her makeup, sometimes using several shades of mascara or painting wide circles around her eyes, then adding a final touch of a few vividly colored feathers in her hair or, occasionally, a bright red wig.

Lee fell willingly into the hands of her Pygmalion. Within a few years, the homely and rebellious little Jewish girl from Jerome Street, Brooklyn, was transformed into a chic, smart, acerbic young woman. Fritz Bultman remembers her "sparkle and gaiety." "[She had] a kind of arrogance that blinds people and makes waves happen," recalls Lillian Olaney, who met Lee soon after her transformation. "She had the kind of animal energy and voluptuousness we later came to call sex appeal."

To support their gay life-style, Igor forsook modernism and took up portraiture. Even in the Depression, a portrait artist could earn a decent living if he was facile and discreet. "He did mostly pretty women and their children," recalls Muriel Francis, "or just pretty women, and all with beautiful swan-like necks." Always intending to return to modernism when he could afford to, Igor

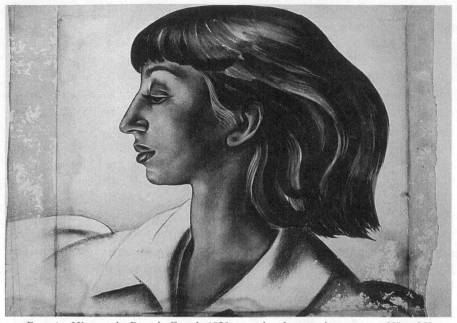

Portrait of Krasner by Pantuhoff, early 1930s, pastel and watercolor on paper, 22″ × 25″

religiously attended gallery openings and museum exhibitions with Lee in tow, sharing his sharp aesthetic judgments and educating her eye to the new art. "He came in with books on Picasso and copies of the *Cahiers d'art* long before anybody else did," Fritz Bultman remembers. He introduced her to his friends Gorky and de Kooning, and when the modernist teacher Hans Hofmann opened a school in New York, he was among the first to sign up. But the money and glamour of society work proved more addictive than the aesthetic adrenaline of modernism. According to a friend, "Igor sort of struggled between wanting to be a serious painter and wanting to live in the world of the beautiful people."

It wasn't just a matter of money, however. When John Little asked Pantuhoff how much he was paid for a portrait of a society lady, he replied: "How much you get paid depends on how well you sleep with her." Igor often boasted of his amorous adventures with sitters and, in the tiny art community, gossip inevitably reached Lee. "Friends tried to tell her," says Little, "but she refused to listen." When other artists complained about his snobbery, his facile painting style, his drunken insults, or his moral lassitude, Lee either closed her eyes or made excuses. If he spent his talent on society portraits, it was because he wanted to be generous with his friends, she would say. If he cursed sweet-tempered James Brooks in a drunken frenzy, it was because Brooks taunted him. "If Igor left to go get drunk, and there was a catastrophe," recalls May Rosenberg, "Lee would hold everyone to blame except him."

Even when Igor turned his abuse on her, in public, Lee never protested. "She was so madly in love with him that she forgave him anything," according to Little. When Igor said to a friend in her presence, "I like being with an ugly woman because it makes me feel more handsome," she didn't wince. "He tormented her," says Fritz Bultman, "but she never complained. The masochistic part of Lee loved every minute of it."

In fact, despite the rising chorus of complaints, Lee clearly was determined to live the rest of her life with Igor. In the mid-thirties, they moved into a large apartment among the dilapidated warehouses on the lower West Side, sharing the cavernous space with May and Harold Rosenberg and another tenant. Lee took Igor to visit her parents in Greenlawn, Long Island, where Joseph and Anna Krassner had bought a small farm, and to Ocean Avenue in Brooklyn, where her sister Ruth had settled with her husband, William Stein. The sight of Igor's sleek yellow convertible brought the entire neighborhood to their windows, "with their mouths hanging open," Ruth remembers. "[Igor] was so stunning coming out of that car." Afterward, he would take Lee and Ruth to dinner at an expensive restaurant. "When the waiter brought the check, Igor would whip out a hundred dollar bill, and nobody could break it," Ruth Stein recalls. "'In *those* days, a hundred dollars was a great deal of money. So he would sign for it. Of course he never paid a *penny*. He probably did all of New York on that hundred dollar bill."

If the Krassner family treated Igor like an in-law, it was because they thought he was one. Throughout the thirties, Lee led her parents and sisters to believe that she and Igor were married. "They never volunteered any information," says Ruth, "but one time he said, 'Don't you ever *wonder* about our relationship?' And I said, 'Well, you're married, aren't you?' He didn't deny it."

The problems began in 1934 when Lee, after two years of studying at City College and working as a waitress in Greenwich Village, decided she wanted "no part of teaching" and began to paint again. When PWAP, the government's first assistance program, opened its doors in early December, Lee was at the front of the line waiting to sign up.

The renewed sense of competition went almost unnoticed at first. Although both still harbored modernist dreams, they were working in different worlds: Igor in the recherché world of society portraits, Lee in the workmanlike world of the early projects. But a collision was inevitable.

One night, Igor came home and regaled Lee and the Rosenbergs with stories about the exciting new ideas being explored at the school. That same night, Lee decided that she would go there, too.

Hofmann's "school" occupied a single large room, designed by the European architect Frederick Kiesler, in a building at 38 West Ninth Street. When Lee walked in, wearing her most Continental outfit—a tight skirt and black blouse, net stockings, and high heels—she saw a familiar tableau: about twenty students working intently at their easels. But this clearly wasn't the National Academy of Design. On a table facing the easels someone had carefully placed a red ball, a length of brightly colored cloth, a playing card, and a piece of broken pottery with a Kleenex tissue draped over its edge. Behind this assemblage hung a crumpled sheet of cellophane. A lamp had been placed so that its light raked the cellophane into fragments of light and shadow.

The school's volunteer registrar, Lillian Olaney (later Mrs. Frederick Kiesler), was impressed by Lee's "animal magnetism" and "voluptuousness." She barely paused long enough to look at Lee's portfolio of academy drawings before rushing downstairs to Hofmann's tiny cubicle on the main floor to tell him that "a unique student, a girl by the name of Lee Krasner," wanted to enroll. "You must give her a scholarship," Olaney insisted. Hofmann agreed immediately and Olaney explained to Krassner what she would need: Strathmore paper, charcoal, a charcoal eraser, and a board. A few days later, Lee returned for her first class, ready to make a fresh start.

Before long, however, Jerome Street reasserted itself. "She really raised hell," recalls John Little, another student. "She was very pushy in class, especially with the women. If a woman set up an easel between her and the model, she'd just push her way through." A few of the female students, like Olaney and Ray "Buda" Kaiser (later Mrs. Charles Eames), did respond enthusiastically to Lee's urbanity and style, but most shared the assessment of Maria Piacenza, Rita Benton's niece who was also a Hofmann student at the time, that Lee was "mad at the world." "She always acted as if life had been unfair to her," Piacenza remembers. "She was a woman, and people didn't take women seriously." She was an artist, and it wasn't easy to make your way as an artist in the thirties. Then she was Jewish, which she didn't seem to want to be . . . and she certainly didn't like being ugly. She always acted as if she had these four big chips on her shoulder and she dared you to knock one of them off."

To older-brother figures like John Little, George McNeil, and Fritz Bultman, however, Lee was the life of the party. In an era when "hanging around" was the primary activity and conversation was the dominant form of entertainment day and night, Lee Krasner was a dazzling talker. "She was very lively and forthright," recalls George McNeil, "outspoken and gay. She would make known her opinions of people and things, very clearly." "She was always vociferous and she always had a great liveliness about her," Fritz Bultman remembers. Although by no means an intellectual—she resisted reading throughout her life—Lee had an acute sense of people, a quick caustic wit, and an extraordinary ear for words and phrases. When familiar words failed her, she invented her own ("this was a *prestate* to the state we're talking about"). When they bored her, she left them out entirely ("And then the minister said, 'Do you take this cloppety clop clop—I do"). John Little recalls walking down Madison Avenue with Lee when she spotted a late landscape by the French artist Maurice Vlaminck in a gallery window. "It looks like it was painted with cold cream," Little remarked. "Too bad it wasn't painted with vanishing cream," Lee shot back.

In the Hofmann school, reactions to Lee's painting were mixed. Some fellow

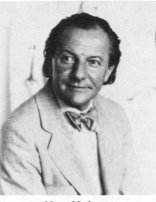

Hans Hofmann

students, like George McNeil, considered her "a painter's painter, a professional artist." "Lee was taken *very* seriously by the other students in the school," says Lillian Olaney. Others, like Beatrice Ribak, thought "nobody took Lee Krasner seriously as an artist. She was no more a good artist than she was a good looker." To Lee, however, the only approval that mattered was Hofmann's, and from her first day, mustering all the emotional resources of her past, she set out to win it.

Like John Graham, Hans Hofmann was among the small, adventurous band of European "missionaries" who, beginning in the 1920s, brought the new gospel of modernism to young American artists. In 1930, at the relatively late age of fifty, Hofmann had traveled to the University of California at Berkeley, then to the Chouinard Institute of Art in Los Angeles, and finally, in 1932, to New York. Unlike Graham, who acquired—or invented—his expertise after arriving in America, Hofmann brought with him an encyclopedic knowledge of European modernism and a genuine familiarity with the giants of the new movement. Drawn to Paris, the mecca of modern art, from his native Bavaria in 1904, he remained there for ten years, rubbing elbows with Picasso, Braque, Derain, and others during the very years when they were creating their revolutions of Cubism and Fauvism. Hofmann also brought with him a rigorous pedagogical training—something almost unheard of in an artistic movement that was still in the process of discovering and defining itself. As a student alongside Matisse at the Grande Chaumière, an atelier in Paris, he had acquired both a passion for teaching and an admiration for Matisse's work that suffused his pedagogical theories. When war broke out in 1914, he returned to Munich and established his own school modeled on one Matisse had opened in Paris.

In New York, Hofmann taught briefly at the Art Students League but found the atmosphere—permeated by traditional thinking and Benton's rhetoric—inhospitable. In 1933, he left the League and established the first of his "schools." Students were drawn not only by his European experience but also

by his charismatic personal style. Unlike Benton, who took little pleasure in
teaching, Hofmann flourished in the collegial environment of the atelier and
in his role as its *"cher maître."* He was an imposing man—"as strong as a
mountain," according to one student, "and as big"—with a "good German
ego" to match. Suave and detached one minute, buoyant and enthusiastic the
next, his classroom presence was catalytic, combining equal parts of tempera-
mental artist, supportive teacher, and irrepressible showman. It was a combination that, in the quarter century between 1933 and 1958, left a permanent
mark on an entire generation of American artists. "He brought Paris to New
York," says one former student. "We were all ignorant. He really brought the
word."

"The word" was that traditional art wasn't really art at all, just reproduction
—a clever but wrongheaded effort to imitate nature. Unlike the traditional
painter who "pretended," by the use of tricks like perspective drawing, that
the image was three-dimensional, the modern artist recognized and embraced
the limitations of his medium: in particular, the *flatness* of the canvas and the
inertness of the colored pigment.

Hofmann's critique of traditional art was nothing new. Even his sermon on
the flatness of the canvas, although seldom heard before in American classrooms, had been preached by Maurice Denis as early as 1890 in Europe. His
analogy of color to music had been made by Gauguin at least as early as 1888.
What *was* new, and truly inspirational to struggling young painters like Lee
Krasner, was the way he applied these grand abstractions to the artist's core
dilemma: what to do with a blank canvas.

European modernism may have liberated painting from "the tyranny of
reality," but in the process it created a whole new set of problems. If the
common goal was no longer to reproduce reality in some compelling way, by
what rules did an artist apply paint? What connection was there between one
brush stroke and the next? How could an artist judge whether the last stroke,
or the next, was right or wrong? When was a painting "completed"? And when
it was completed, how could an artist—or a critic—make judgments about it,
or compare it to other paintings? By what articulable standards was a painting
by Matisse "great," or one Matisse painting "better" than another, or Matisse
a better artist than Dufy? These were the pressing questions to which Hofmann
offered answers.

In any painting, he argued, various tensions are created from the moment
the first dab of paint is applied: tension between the dab and the empty canvas,
between the color of the dab and the color of the canvas, between the space
covered by the dab and the space outside it. A second dab affects all those
tensions and creates new ones. If the next dab is a different color, a whole new
set of tensions is created—between warm color and cool color, between receding color and advancing color, between luminous color and tonal color. Add a
line and the complications multiply geometrically—tensions between inside
and outside, solid and void, direction and stability. And so on, dab by dab,

color by color, line by line. ("Put a spot on the surface and let the surface answer back!" he would say.) Hofmann described each tension as a "push-pull" of competing forces or elements and urged his students to "activate the surface" with the energy of these tensions. The ultimate goal, of course, was to *control* the tensions so they achieved the state that Hofmann considered the goal of all great art: "equilibrium." A painting that sustained an equilibrium between push and pull, between force and counterforce, created an alternate reality, one far more profound than any mere academic depiction of the natural world.

Hofmann's version of the artistic process may have been abstruse but at least it was a version that could be debated, practiced, replicated, and, not least important, taught. During his twice-weekly rounds of student work, he hammered at the same themes, exhorting students to "keep the picture plane flat," "make the colors sing," and "give the most with the least." He frequently commented that a student drawing "lacked sufficient push and pull," or "had a hole in it"—that is, the equilibrium was disrupted. Sometimes, a bad painting would spark a long exegesis on "how to handle color" or "why colors worked or didn't work with each other." At other times, the comments were arrogantly terse: "this is wrong, and that's wrong, and the color is tonal, and you're losing the picture plane." He often referred to "the mythical perfect picture [that was] just waiting to be painted." More than anything, Hofmann provided a common language for talking about modern painting and thinking about quality, a language that avoided simpleminded verisimilitude without slipping into the deep ooze of subjectivity.

Hofmann had his detractors. Some students found him "pompous, blustering, [and] egocentric," and dismissed his favorite aphorisms—"Do not make it flat! But it must stay flat!"—as more gibberish than genius. But most, like Lee Krasner, hung on his every word. "It was just wonderful," recalls George Mercer. "We'd come out of class gasping, all refocused in new possible directions." Even when he got carried away with his own ideas, and his fractured English dissolved into German, they would sit reverentially to the end. According to Larry Rivers, who attended the school years later, Hofmann "beefed up the timid hearts" and "puffed up" the delusions of grandeur "until you saw clearly your name in the long line from Michelangelo to Matisse . . . to Hofmann himself."

Hans Hofmann proved the perfect object for Lee Krasner's ambivalent affections. With a telling mix of fondness and resentment, she later recalled how Hofmann "would come up to me, look at my work, and do a critique half in English and half in German, but certainly nothing I could understand." When he left the room, she would ask a fellow student, "What did this man say to me?" With her instinct for antagonism, Lee quickly detected Hofmann's chauvinism. ("Hans thought women were better artists than men *until* they fell in love," says May Rosenberg. "After that the man gets stronger and the woman gets weaker.") One time he commented on a drawing of Lee's, "This is so good that you wouldn't know it was done by a woman."

To Lee, they were fighting words. Soon, a guerrilla war developed between the autocratic teacher and his most assertive female student. "A number of times," she recalls bitterly, "he would walk up to me and take the charcoal out of my hand and start working on my drawing." In class one day for a biweekly critique, he stopped in front of a drawing that Lee considered particularly good. (It had attracted several compliments from other students.) After looking at it only briefly, Hofmann untacked it from the easel and ripped it into four pieces. He rearranged the pieces on the easel and announced, "*This* is tension," then walked away.

Like a chastened child, Lee said nothing at the time, but later complained furiously to friends. "I had a total fit," she recalls. Nevertheless, she went on to become Hofmann's most ardent admirer and imitator at the school, mouthing his clichés—"This has got a hole in it," and "Keep the picture plane flat"—and, according to fellow students, trying desperately to make the "perfect picture" Hofmann always talked about. "She wasn't a great mind," says May Rosenberg, "but she was an acute mind, and she could pick things up with great ease when she wanted to."

Lee undoubtedly would have picked up Hofmann's painting style as well as his vocabulary if it hadn't been for the master's legendary reticence. Although sometimes arrogant, Hofmann harbored grave doubts about his ability as an artist, and literally hid his paintings from all but his closest friends. He even barred students from his studio, offering the excuse that "he did not want them copying him." Unable to imitate the work of the artist she worshiped, Lee turned to the work of the artist that Hofmann worshiped: Matisse. She had used Matisse as a model before arriving at the school, but in the effort to please Hofmann, she resorted to outright imitation, borrowing, in some of her paintings, the pointillistic "broken touch" of such early Matisse paintings as *Study for Joy of Life* (which was shown at the Museum of Modern Art in 1936); in others, Matisse's color, his mature painterly technique, even his subject matter.

But Hofmann was also "one of the leading exponents" of Cubism in America and, along with John Graham, an ardent admirer of Picasso. Lee remembered how, in class, her teacher's favor seemed to "swing like a pendulum" between the two giants of modernism. Inevitably, Lee swung along with it, executing reams of charcoal drawings based on Picasso's Cubist sketches, and paintings, like *Abstract Human Figure*, based on Picasso's cloisonnist works. In 1939, she saw *Guernica* and, for a while at least, stopped swinging. "It knocked me right out of the room," she said. She meant it literally. At her first sight of the painting, she left the gallery and circled the block "four or five times" before returning for a second look. For a while, all of her paintings paid homage to Picasso's flat areas of color and thick black outlining.

Then, in 1940, at an exhibition that included three of her Picassoid abstractions, she met Piet Mondrian, the Dutch master of the *de Stijl* movement who

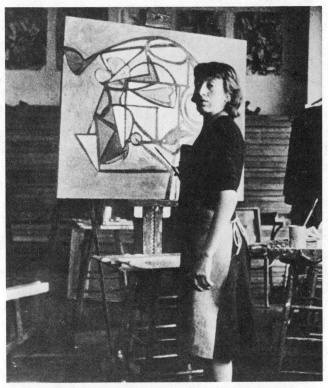

Lee in Hans Hofmann's studio, early 1940s

had recently arrived in New York. In his late sixties, Mondrian was an imposing, charismatic man: ascetically lean, elegant, and quintessentially European. Lee was overwhelmed. By the time Mondrian got around to looking at her paintings, she was "queasy" with anticipation. "Very strong inner rhythm," he commented gently. "Stay with it."

Hardly resounding praise, but Lee treasured it anyway. "Oh, it was beautiful, just beautiful," she said. "I have remembered that for a long time, for a long, long time, and still remember it." She had experimented with Mondrian's spare style before, but the encounter transformed her overnight into a passionate devotee. Together with Perle Fine, a fellow student at the Hofmann school, she began turning out paintings of black grids inlaid with red, yellow, and blue rectangles that were virtually indistinguishable from Mondrian's own. For a while, "nothing existed except Mondrian," she later admitted. "Mondrian at that point took over my life."

Even as Lee's career coalesced, her personal life disintegrated. After several years on West Fourteenth Street where May Rosenberg "never heard voices raised," Lee and Igor moved to a new apartment on East Ninth Street. Their new roommate, Michael Loew, saw a very different couple. Instead of the gay, glib sophisticate she had been, Lee was now "an intense, serious person who didn't go for small talk or nonsense," according to Loew. Igor's fecklessness and infidelity were now out in the open—"He was a real man of the world but wild, running around with women"—and after years of tranquillity with the Rosenbergs, Lee's antagonism had found a voice. "I could hear them scrapping a lot," Loew recalled. Other friends remember how Lee began to bridle under Igor's abuse. He would say, "I'm not anti-Semitic, I'm anti-Jewish," and she would lash back, "You son of a bitch," and the fights would last for days. (Igor's family's refusal to even meet his Jewish girlfriend was a continuing source of friction between them and may have been behind Lee's apparent resistance to real marriage.) When Igor pressed her to begin a family, even without a marriage, she refused. "She told him she wouldn't *think* of spoiling her figure," recalls Lee's sister Ruth. Among Lee's friends, a rumor circulated that she had aborted Igor's child. It was sometime during this period of growing friction that Lee stepped onto the dance floor at an Artists Union party with a big, clumsy drunk from "someplace out west" named Jackson Pollock and, according to some accounts, tried her own hand at infidelity.

By 1937, the years of sparkle and gaiety were over, although it was another two years before the relationship ended. Lee, who had begun as Igor's eager work of art, was intently pursuing her own art at the Hofmann school. At the end, "she hardly had time for Igor," says Fritz Bultman. "She was much too busy developing her *own* career." In the meantime, Igor, who had begun the decade amid such acclaim, slid even deeper into frivolousness, dissolution, and drunkenness, reduced to peddling his portraits among the first-class passengers on ocean cruises. The two fates seemed strangely connected: the higher Lee rose, the lower Igor fell. "The problem," says May Rosenberg, who knew them best, "was that Lee was getting more and more attention." To most of Lee's modernist friends, it was an act of charity to overlook Igor altogether. On a visit to Lee and Igor's apartment, Harold Rosenberg complimented her paintings but not his. "That kind of thing was happening more and more," May recalls. "People began to forget to ask about Igor's work." According to Lillian Olaney, "No one considered him even so much as a threat to Lee's professionalism as an artist. He wasn't to be taken seriously." Not even by Lee. At first warily, then more and more stridently, she began to chastise him for his frivolous ways. "She felt defrauded," May Rosenberg recalled, "seeing that this drudge was not the man who had presented himself to her as a romantic genius who had won prizes, scholarships, and great expectations."

Finally, sometime in 1939, Igor disappeared. "Lee was so frightened," says May, "she called the police and checked the listings. It never occurred to her that it was over." But it was. A week later, she received a letter from Florida, where Igor had joined his family, asking her to return the portrait he had made of her. "Until the letter arrived," May recalls, "she refused to believe that he had really left her." It would be at least a year before she saw him again.

Despite the long denouement of rivalry and alienation, Lee was devastated. A confrontation, no matter how rancorous, she could have survived; abandonment was worse than death. "When she lost Igor, when he walked out without a word," May remembers, "that was nearly a fatal blow."

For the next two years, Lee immersed herself in art and politics. She organized demonstrations for the Artists Union to protest dwindling government subsidies. Splitting with the mainstream of Hofmann students, she joined the American Abstract Artists (AAA), a group that followed Mondrian's lead in rejecting *all* subject matter, although she continued to mix with friends from the Hofmann school. As always, she preferred the company of men, and while many of the males from the old circle were homosexual, they at least provided social diversion. George Mercer, a slender, handsome, Boston-born and Harvard-educated painter, became a regular companion. Like Igor, the patrician Mercer inhabited a different world entirely from that of Lena Krassner (among his friends at Harvard were David Rockefeller and Joseph Pulitzer)—although Lee had little patience for his workmanlike paintings or his WASP social reticence, and the liaison generated little heat.

But trips to galleries, all-day movie binges, political debates, and endless Jumble Shop chatter couldn't begin to fill the void left by Igor's departure. Lee was looking for something more, something special.

She glimpsed it briefly one night at the Café Society Uptown on East Fifty-eighth Street, where Harry Holtzman had arranged a party for Piet Mondrian, who had recently recovered from an illness. While Hazel Scott sang, Lee and the stately Mondrian, whom she adored, walked to the edge of the dancers and waited for just the right number. When the music changed to a boogie-woogie, Mondrian whispered, "Now!" in her ear and together they swung onto the floor. Even at sixty-eight, Mondrian "had a wonderful sense of rhythm [and] liked very complicated dance steps." Lee was a stylish, flattering partner—another legacy of the gay years with Igor. Heads everywhere turned and seemed to follow them. "I thought, 'Of course, they're looking at us,' " Lee remembered. " 'Of course, they're looking at us because I'm dancing with Mondrian.' " But when she swung around, she saw that they weren't looking at her after all, but at "some movie actor and a divine-looking woman" behind them.

To Lee, these years of emptiness and incompletion must have seemed a kind of punishment. Like Igor's departure, they carried a warning. She had confronted him too directly, pushed too hard, attracted too much attention, demanded too much, collided too often. The early years, the years of submission and self-denial, had been relatively happy; the years of competition had been unmitigated hell. She would know better next time.

Just to remind herself, she scrawled on the wall of her studio some lines from her favorite poem: Rimbaud's "A Season in Hell":

To whom shall I hire myself out?
What beast must I adore?
What holy image is attacked: What hearts shall I break?
What lie must I maintain? In what blood tread?

George Mercer was among the hundreds of thousands of men drafted in the last weeks of 1941. Within days of hearing the news, Lee Krasner climbed the long stairs to Jackson Pollock's studio.

26

LEGENDS

Lee Krasner loved to tell the story. At seventy-five, she would sit in her stiff-backed chair in the front room of the house on Long Island and repeat it to curators, dealers, scholars, students, friends, any one of the endless train of visitors who came to pay homage to "the widow Pollock." Normally, she had little patience for any of them. Normally, their questions about Jackson annoyed her. In the twenty-five years since his death, she had answered every question about him a hundred times, often in print, and that was enough, she thought. But she was never too tired or bored or annoyed to tell the story about the day they met.

In a deep, rutted voice, she would begin with John Graham's visit to her studio on a cold morning in early November 1941. The artist Aristodemos Kaldis had brought him by to see Lee's work. The two men caught her at the front stoop on Ninth Street. "[Graham] looked at me and said, 'You're a painter,' " Lee recalled. "I thought, 'My God, that man has magical insight,' and I said, 'How do you know?' He pointed to my leg and I had splatters of paint on it." Next came the part about the penny postcard. Graham sent it to her soon after his visit. She had kept it for forty years, and if it was in the house, she would pull it out. "I am arranging at an uptown gallery a show of French and American paintings with excellent publicity, etc.," Graham had written. "I have Braque, Picasso, Derain, Segonzac, S. Davis, and others! I want to have your last large painting."

Lee was overwhelmed. Even at the hundredth telling, her voice filled with excitement and surprise. "This is big-time stuff," she would say, slipping into the present tense. "Graham is arranging a show of European greats and just a few Americans, maybe three or four, and he wants to include *me*." Immediately, she wanted to know what other American artists would be included in the show. When Graham gave her the list, only one name was unfamiliar: Jackson Pollock. "I was astonished because I thought I knew all the abstract

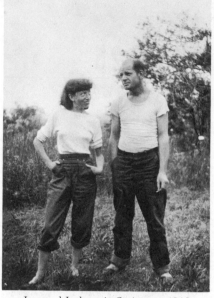

Lee and Jackson in Springs, c. 1946

artists in New York." Reluctant to ask Graham who he was—"that might have broken the spell"—she canvassed her friends at the Artists Union and the AAA, demanding "Who the hell is Jackson Pollock?" But no one seemed to know. She asked Willem de Kooning, who was also on Graham's list, but he shrugged his shoulders. Finally, at an opening at Edith Gregor Halpert's Downtown Gallery, she collided with Louis Bunce, a friend from the WPA. "By the way, do you know this painter, Pollock?" she asked offhandedly. "Sure," said Bunce, "he lives just around the corner from you."

"I was in a rage at myself," she later said, "simply furious because here was a name that I hadn't heard of [and] all the more furious because he was living on Eighth Street and I was on Ninth." She wasted no time in correcting the oversight. "Something got into me and I just hoofed it over to Pollock's studio and introduced myself."

She "bounded" up the five flights of stairs and knocked at Jackson's door. "I found out later that this wasn't everyday traffic," she would add parenthetically, "Jackson didn't usually answer the door." But this time he did. "I knocked, he opened," she would continue in her tersest Dashiell Hammett style. "I introduced myself and said we were both showing in the same show. He said 'Come in.' " At this point in the story, she sometimes felt obliged to mention their previous encounter at the Artists Union dance in 1936. "Actually, we had met once years before," she would add quickly, "but I had forgotten about that first meeting and so had he."

Over the years, Lee used a variety of words and phrases to describe her reaction when she stepped inside Jackson's studio and saw his paintings for the first time. The sight "impressed" her, "moved" her, "overwhelmed" her, "blasted" her, "stunned" her, and "bowled [her] over." She "felt the presence of a living force that [she] hadn't witnessed before." She "felt as if the floor was sinking." She "fully understood the enormity of what Pollock had done." She "almost died." In one interview, she quoted herself saying simply: "My God, there it is!"

In all her tellings, Lee rarely offered further details. She rarely spoke about Jackson—what he looked like, how he acted, what he said—or about her reaction to him. It was almost as if he hadn't been there. She rarely talked about what happened *after* those first few minutes when the floor sank. She did tell one interviewer that when she commented favorably on a painting, Jackson said, "Oh, I'm not sure I'm finished with that one." To which Lee replied, "Don't touch it!" In another interview, she indicated that before she left, they made arrangements for him to visit her studio. But tidbits like these were offered grudgingly. To Lee, the story of their first encounter had only one message: Lee Krasner had fallen in love, instantly and irrevocably, not with Jackson Pollock, but with Jackson Pollock's art.

It was a dramatic and satisfying story and Lee repeated it often. But neither conviction nor repetition could make it true.

When Lee climbed the steps to Jackson's studio in November 1941, she already knew the man she was going to see. According to several acquaintances, she not only remembered her embarrassing encounter with Jackson at the Artists Union party ("He was the one who stepped all over my feet"), she had been following his career from a distance ever since. In fact, she had probably marked Jackson as a possible lover long before she came to his door. Certainly the prospect was on her mind. Colleagues at the Artists Union remember that she had been trying unsuccessfully for some time to fill the void left by Igor Pantuhoff's departure. "She was having plenty of problems finding a man," says Axel Horn, "and that's how she gravitated to Jack. She was not a handsome woman, but she had a great deal of aggressiveness and she came on strong with men. My impression was that most men, like me, were rather repelled by her." Lee, who had turned thirty-three just weeks before the visit to Jackson's apartment, was beginning to worry that "no guy was ever going to marry me." According to one friend, she described herself on the eve of their meeting as "an old maid. A fucking old maid." She had picked Jackson out of the crowd once and had kept an eye on him ever since. The McMillen show provided the perfect opportunity for a second try.

When she arrived, Jackson wasn't in his studio, he was sitting in his small bedroom at the front of the building, head in hands, recovering from a binge the night before. When he opened the door, she saw no paintings, only a tiny, cluttered, malodorous cubbyhole. Eventually, he took her next door to his studio where, among hundreds of Martinson coffee cans, the paintings were stacked haphazardly against the walls, hidden behind dilapidated wicker chairs. Some were based on Picasso, some on Orozco; a few dated back to

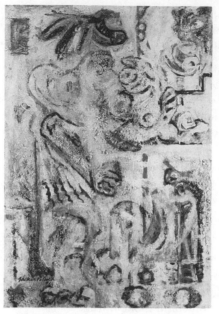

The Magic Mirror, 1941, oil and mixed
media on canvas, 46″ × 32″

Benton days—those that had survived the rampage after Helen Marot's death. *Masqued Image, The Magic Mirror,* and *Bird* were there, obscure and unprepossessing, scattered among the dross, none much larger than three by four feet. All in all, it was not an impressive showing. Promising, undoubtedly, or Graham would never have added Jackson's name to his list, but hardly the stuff of serendipity. "It's impossible that [Lee] or anybody else was 'bowled over' by his work at that point," says Axel Horn, who still visited the apartment occasionally. "That was 1941, which was too early to be that spellbound by the quality of his art. He was still very unformed as a painter."

Whatever her later accounts, at the time Lee apparently agreed. Close friends remember her coming away from that first encounter madly in love with Jackson ("She found him the most beautiful thing that ever walked on two feet") but unconvinced of his artistic ability. While she confided to friends like Mercedes Matter and May Rosenberg that she had "met someone she liked very much," she didn't at first even mention that he was an artist, much less a great artist. In letters to George Mercer, she never referred to Jackson's paintings, but was "just full of *him,*" Mercer recalls: " 'He was indescribable, he was magnificent, he was tremendous.' " Later, Lee admitted that one of her strongest impressions from that first day was not of the paintings, but of his "fantastic, powerful hands." A month passed before she worked up the courage to ask Mercedes Matter to come to Jackson's studio and honestly assess his work.

Mercedes didn't share Lee's reservations. "Mercedes spotted his work right off as being terrific," recalls Betsy Zogbaum. "She was the first one. Lee followed Mercedes's lead." But not until Mercedes's husband Herbert also visited the studio and added his approval. Then, finally, Lee joined the small but growing chorus of praise that Graham had started. By that time, she was already "terribly in love." "When they first came together, it was not because she recognized any innate ability in him," says a friend who knew both Lee and Jackson before they met, "it was because he was there and available."

Not without some effort, however. If Lee's aesthetic response to their first meeting was hesitant, Jackson's emotional response was nearly comatose. In her subsequent revisions of the story, Lee liked to skip directly from her first sight of the paintings to "living together"—so inevitable was their union. In reality, the process was far slower and considerably less romantic. Even after Lee wrung from him a commitment to visit her studio, weeks passed before Jackson showed up. When he did, he quickly discovered that Lee wasn't exactly cut from the mold of Stella Pollock. "I asked him if he wanted coffee," she remembers, "and he said yes, so I turned around and headed back to the hall to get my coat and said, 'Let's go.' He looked confused and I said, 'Well, if you want coffee, we'll have to go down to the drugstore to get it. You don't think I make it here?' I've never seen anyone so shocked." In fact, she had never turned on the gas in the kitchen; she had no idea if the stove even worked; and her cupboards were completely bare.

During this second encounter, Jackson remembered, or Lee gingerly reminded him of, the Artists Union loft party where they first met. Lee may have thought this represented progress—especially if their previous encounter consisted of more than just a clumsy dance—but it was far from the whirlwind courtship she later described. Another month went by before Jackson took her on their first official "date"—to the opening of the McMillen show. In between, she visited his studio several more times and they went out occasionally for beer or coffee, but nothing more. One friend remembers seeing them together before the McMillen show, "but he wasn't really *serious* about her." It was an embarrassingly slow start for a woman who, at the National Academy of Design, "never went anywhere without a diaphram." "If a guy interested me, really interested me," Lee once said of her student days, "I slept with him because I wanted to know him better and wanted him to know me better. That was my morality."

Eventually, Jackson came around. He began to see in Lee's persistent attentions the potential for the exclusive maternal relationship that Stella had never provided. "He had found a 'mommy,'" says Elizabeth Pollock. Like Rita Benton, Lee exuded confidence and control. "She barely touched the floor," according to Ethel Baziotes, "and that effortlessness in her attracted Jackson. He did not have that fluidity in his temperament with people." What Lee lacked in traditional attractiveness (one of Jackson's friends said she looked "like a goat") she more than made up for with a lithe, sensual body and eager sexuality. "Jackson was by far the more dramatic-looking of the two," recalls Gerome Kamrowski. "He was almost like Brando. But Lee was very dramatic when she talked and argued." Besides, she had big, firm, pneumatic breasts that would create a sensation among his brothers. Like Berthe Pacifico, she was also talented, a quality that had always attracted Jackson. Arloie recalls that on the rare occasions when he talked about Lee around the apartment, he usually referred to her painting: "He thought she was a very good painter for a woman."

Lee was drawn both to Jackson (presumably as early as 1936), and to the alien world from which he came. "I thought of Jackson as 100 percent American," she later admitted. "He was American—at least five generations back. Other artists I knew were born elsewhere or were born here just after their parents arrived." To a Jewish girl born nine months after her mother stepped off a boat from the Ukraine, Jackson was, in fact, more exotic than the mysterious White Russian, Igor Pantuhoff: a native of that most foreign of all lands, the one west of the Hudson.

Finally, Graham's imprimatur gave Jackson the requisite aura: the special something like Mondrian's reputation or Igor's flamboyance or Hofmann's charisma, that was, for Lee, the most powerful of aphrodesiacs. (She had already tried unsuccessfully to seduce at least one of the other artists on Graham's McMillen show roster, Willem de Kooning.) One night that January, she was walking back from Graham's apartment with Graham and Jackson when a short, "funny man with an overcoat down to his ankles and wearing a homburg" approached them and embraced Graham "very warmly." Graham introduced him—"This is Frederick Kiesler"—then turned to introduce Jackson. "And *this*," he said, searching for the right words, "is Jackson Pollock"— his deep voice expanded to fill the empty square—*"the greatest painter in America."* The sound of the phrase combined with the frigid air to take Lee's breath away. After a long pause, Kiesler, another of the early modernist missionaries, slowly lifted his homburg and bowed "almost to the sidewalk," Lee remembers. When he straightened up, he turned to Graham and asked in a stage whisper, "North or South America?"

That was all the confirmation Lee needed. By the time the McMillen show opened, two months after her visit to the studio, both she and Jackson had found what they were looking for. As Lee expressed it, they had "meshed." "We knew that we had something to give each other, some answer to each of our particular kinds of loneliness." Clement Greenberg, who knew Lee already and would soon meet Jackson, had a somewhat less sympathetic view. "They took to each other because no one else would have them," he said. In the end, the story that Lee loved to tell was accurate in at least one regard: there was a certain inevitability to their union. They were, Ethel Baziotes remarked, "psychologically embedded in each other."

"American and French Paintings" opened at McMillen, Inc., on January 20, 1942. Although largely ignored by war-preoccupied New Yorkers, the show was a milestone for Jackson. His painting, *Birth*, a turbulent canvas of Picassoid heads transforming into Indian masks, hung in the company of works by Picasso, Rouault, Modigliani, Matisse, Braque, Bonnard, Derain, and de Chirico. The roster of American artists wasn't as exclusive as Lee had hoped (she later misled people to believe that she and de Kooning were the only other Americans in the show). It included Stuart Davis, Virginia Diaz, Pat Collins, Walt Kuhn, and H. Leavitt Purdy, as well as two of Graham's Russian friends, Alexander Vasilieff and David Burliuk. In such a crowd, it was unlikely that anyone, especially among the Americans, would be singled out by reviewers, but Jackson was. In a review titled "Mélange," James Lane wrote that Jackson's painting "resembles [Stanley William] Hayter in general whirling figures." Hardly a rave (Lane thought Diaz "walked off with the show"), but it was at least something to show for a decade of work, and it came at a good time. A week after the exhibition opened, Jackson celebrated his thirtieth birthday.

For Lee, the McMillen show was a milestone of a different sort; her painting, an abstraction derived from Picasso, hung between works by Matisse and Braque. "Just being in that show and being with Pollock," she recalled, "the whole newness of it all overwhelmed me."

In her newfound enthusiasm, Lee rushed to show Jackson off. She took him first to meet her "uptown" friends, the Matters. A ravishingly beautiful woman, Mercedes Matter had modeled with Lee in the thirties and attended Hofmann's school. Her husband, Herbert, a Swiss-born graphic designer and photographer, had known the Giacometti brothers in Europe, as well as Josef Albers and Fernand Léger. Inevitably, the Matter town house on East Forty-second Street became a "meeting place" for painters, sculptors, critics, curators, and designers. Léger had lived on the third floor when he first came to America in the late thirties. ("He was an incredible cook," Herbert remembers.) Alexander Calder had kept his *Circus* in the basement. When the Matters entertained, their guests included Peggy Guggenheim, James Johnson Sweeney, and James Thrall Soby, the chairman of the department of painting and sculpture at the Museum of Modern Art.

But on this night, their only guests were Lee Krasner and Jackson Pollock. For Lee, it was the first of many frustrating social events. "We sat in the living room and tried to talk," she remembers, "but Jackson didn't say a word." Neither did the equally laconic Herbert. The two women "talked a blue streak," until Mercedes excused herself to bathe the baby, and Lee, hoping the two men might "find their voices" if left alone, joined her. "After a while we stopped and listened for some sign of life from downstairs," Mercedes remembers. "But there wasn't any. Not a sound. We panicked. I said to Lee, 'Oh, my God, you've got to go down.' " In fact, in the silence, the two men were laying the foundations of a close friendship. "After the women disappeared," Herbert Matter remembers, "Jackson said, 'It's really a wonderful time to be living.' That gave us plenty to think about the rest of the evening."

Lee's friends from the Hofmann school were not so easily impressed. The women especially—an articulate, aggressive group—rejected the newcomer out of hand. "I can't say that he came into my life with flags flying," admitted Lillian Olaney. "[We] were a small group of prejudiced snobs and we had a high regard for Lee. He seemed beneath her." Jackson suffered from being compared to the glamorous extrovert who preceded him in Lee's life. "We were all very fond of Igor," Olaney recalled, "and of that kind of flamboyance. So when Jackson came along, we thought that Lee was in a sense compromising herself." Herbert Matter may have been won over by Jackson's quiet strength, but most of Lee's friends took it as a sign of mental deficiency. "He seemed like a drag on Lee," said Olaney, "like she was the teacher and he was her slow pupil." They also had grave reservations about his art. "We took our painting very seriously and we weren't sure where all this higgledy-piggledy painting of his fit in the line of modern art." Their suspicions were confirmed when they discovered that Jackson had studied with Benton, modernism's archenemy.

In general, the men in Lee's circle were less hostile, although still far from enthusiastic. Before the McMillen show, Lee took Jackson to Willem de Kooning's studio on West Twenty-first Street and introduced him to the widely respected young Dutchman. "I don't think either one was very impressed with the other," Lee recalls. On the day she had arranged for him to meet John Little, who was about to leave for the navy, Jackson disappeared. "He's probably at a bar," Lee said, indicating that even this early in their relationship, she was aware of the hazards ahead. When Jackson showed up later that night, Little "rather liked him. He was very quiet and shy. He didn't try to make an impression. He wasn't a bully like some of my artist friends." Clement Greenberg had much the same reaction when he ran into Lee and Jackson on the sidewalk outside the liquor warehouse where he worked as a customs appraiser. "There was Lee with this guy in a gray felt hat with a top coat," Greenberg remembers. "He looked so bourgeois in it." Taking her cue from John Graham, Lee said, "in her uncouth way, 'This guy is going to be a great artist,' " according to Greenberg. "Jackson looked embarrassed. He had a nice open face. He didn't say much and smiled reluctantly."

Undaunted by the reactions of Hofmann's circle, Lee finally summoned the courage to introduce Jackson to Hofmann himself. After puffing up five flights of stairs, the fastidious Hofmann was "absolutely aghast" at the sight of Jackson's unkempt studio. "The Hofmann school was immaculate," Lee recalls. "We didn't scrub the floors with lye but we might as well have. You could eat off them." Jackson's studio, in contrast, was "an incredible mess," with hundreds of coffee cans scattered about, filled with dried and drying paint. In the middle of the devastation, Hofmann found Jackson's palette with a brush lying on it. When he picked up the brush, the entire palette came with it. "With this you could kill a man," Hofmann muttered. "That's the point," Jackson replied. From that high point, the encounter swiftly deteriorated. "Hofmann, being a teacher, spent all the time talking about art," Lee remembered. "Finally, Pollock couldn't stand it any longer and said, 'Your theories don't interest me. Put up or shut up! Let's see your work.' " As Jackson undoubtedly knew, Hofmann rarely showed his work even to close friends, so the two men just glared at each other in silent stalemate.

From such social debacles, both Lee and Jackson learned their lessons: Lee stopped staging elaborate introductions to her friends while Jackson practiced ignoring them. The compromise worked well, although it produced some awkward moments. When May Rosenberg visited on one of her weekend trips from Washington, D.C., where Harold had taken a job in the Office of War Information, she was surprised to find "a silent-looking man in dungarees" in Lee's studio. "He just sat there," Rosenberg remembers, "and Lee didn't introduce him. She didn't say anything about him then, or at lunch afterwards. On the way out I said good-bye to him. I thought he was a janitor, or somebody who was deaf or half-witted, and she was giving him little jobs to do. When I came back the next time, I was shocked to find him there again. *Then* Lee told me that this was Jackson Pollock."

Lee and Jackson's relationship may not have stirred much enthusiasm in Lee's circle, but at 46 East Eighth Street, it was greeted with barely restrained joy and sighs of relief. Arloie found Lee "a very straightforward, take-charge kind of woman" when they met for the first time in mid-December. "She inspired confidence: in us, and in Jackson." Arloie had good reason to be hopeful; no one was more anxious to be rid of Jackson. For years she had maneuvered to keep from becoming pregnant, waiting for the day when she and Sande could afford a place of their own. Finally, as a kind of ultimatum, she had borne a child, Karen, on November 9, 1941. "She got pregnant in order to break up the household," says her son Jason McCoy. "She had been living with Jackson for six years and that was enough." Arloie wasted no time in taking advantage of Lee's arrival. In early 1942, at her insistence, Jackson began spending most nights at Lee's studio. When he returned to the Eighth Street apartment during the day, the common door was kept locked.

In February, Jackson's landlord summarily raised the rent for the second time in a year, citing the exigencies of war. "The gouge is on," Sande wrote Charles, "and we're the victims." Jackson, who had planned to stay in the apartment even if the unthinkable happened and Sande moved out, now faced the even more unnerving prospect of looking for a new place to live—on his own for the first time in a decade. At the last minute, Sande appealed to the landlord, pleading poverty and his small baby. "I had a talk with the landlord and it seems we may have come to terms," he wrote Charles in March. "I rather hope so as moving [would] be difficult at this time."

Extremely difficult, given Sande's job prospects. Despite repeated eulogies, the Project still clung to life, but between the draft and the boom in war-related industrial production, the end was imminent. In a national emergency, no one could justify make-work for the able-bodied. Sande had been laid off a second time in 1941 when the mural he had been working on since 1938 at the Marine Air Terminal was finally completed. Already, Project workers were being reassigned to the war effort and Project rolls were considered "shopping lists" for local draft boards. Particularly terrifying to Sande was a rumor that the army would begin drafting married men with children who were not "employed in war production." In May, with help from Bill Hayden, Jackson's drinking buddy from the Art Students League, Sande found a job as a carpenter for the Sperry Gyroscope Company in an old piano factory in Deep River, Connecticut, which had been hastily retooled to produce gliders for the army.

In the midst of this upheaval and uncertainty, Stella Pollock wrote that she was coming to New York. At the age of ninety-four, Jennie McClure had finally died. As a twelve-year-old girl, she had watched her brother march off to be killed in the Civil War. Her husband had died on the eve of the First World War. Friends remarked that three wars were enough to kill even a strong-minded Iowa woman like Jennie McClure. After a brief stop in East Lansing to see Charles and Elizabeth, Stella headed east to visit the Low Steps. Although nothing was said, it was understood that she was coming to stay.

Even with Lee's support, the news of Stella's impending visit proved too much for Jackson. The night before she was scheduled to arrive, he vanished. The next morning, Lee was awakened by an anxious knock at the door. It was Sande, wanting to know if Jackson had slept overnight at Lee's. "No, why?" she asked, puzzled and distraught. "He's at Bellevue," said Sande gravely. He asked her to go with him to the hospital. "What the hell happened?" she demanded as she threw on clothes and rushed out the door. It was the first time for her. "I was a little shell-shocked," she later admitted.

When they arrived at the hospital, Jackson "looked awful," Lee remembers. "They told us they had found him on some street someplace. He had blacked out totally." At Jackson's bedside, Sande ticked off instructions: "Put him to bed, feed him milk and eggs, and pull him together in time for dinner tonight with Mother." Clearly, this wasn't Sande's first time. Lee listened dutifully and Sande left to be with Stella. When Jackson opened his eyes, he saw only Lee. He was her responsibility now. "Is this the best hotel you can find?" she drawled.

Lee did as Sande instructed and the dinner came off, as dinners always did in the Pollock family, without a hint of friction. "It was my first meeting with Mother," Lee recalls. "I was overpowered by her cooking. I had never seen such a spread as she put on. She had cooked all the dinner, baked the bread— the abundance was fabulous." During dinner, she whispered to Jackson in disbelief, "Did you people eat this way every day?"

Lee never understood Jackson's battle with his mother. Having cut the ties to her own family so early, she couldn't comprehend the power that Stella continued to exercise over her sons. "Lee was terribly suspicious of family as a reason for anything," says Jason McCoy. "It was a blindness she had." Jackson's hostility only perplexed her. "It was easy for me to get along with [Stella]," she says, "[so] I thought, what the hell is wrong with Jackson? Why is he always going on about this mother of his? She's a very nice lady." At the time, Lee didn't even connect the Bowery binge with Stella's arrival.

Not everyone who met Stella during her stay in New York was so purblind. Ethel Baziotes came to dinner at the Eighth Street apartment and vividly recalls the tension between mother and son. "Coming up the stairs, we could hear music so loud that everything was vibrating. That was a danger signal right there." Once inside the apartment, Baziotes felt "danger in the air":

> [Jackson] was very strange that night. You felt that anything you said might lead to something. Stella was wearing something dark. She was a handsome woman, but you couldn't read her at all. She was like an American Indian woman. She sat like statuary the entire evening and didn't move once, but she followed everything. The relationship between her and Jackson was very taut. Everything was understood between them without talking. She followed him perfectly and he followed her. It was like two cats sitting near each other. They had nothing to do with one another, but there was an energy going back and forth all the same. . . . All during dinner, I kept thinking of what Willa Cather said about the family being the enemy of art.

The three months of Stella's visit were a test for Jackson. Mother and son never spent a night under the same roof. Every night, one or the other stayed at Lee's. "My grandmother had to be protected from the terrors of my uncle," says Arloie's daughter Karen. During the day, Stella shopped and "held audience," usually at Lee's apartment. She pressed both Jackson and Lee to bring their artist friends around for her to meet. Not once during her stay did she offer a comment about Jackson's art, although she did, according to Lee, "seem proud of Jackson's artistic friends." It was only the first hint of how Stella would revel in Jackson's later success. His was the world she had driven her family across the American West in pursuit of.

In August, Arloie, Karen, and Stella joined Sande in Deep River. The "eccentric cowboy," who had come to New York eight years before to be an artist, moved into a small apartment with his new family—and Stella. In so doing, he merely traded burdens. He left the Eighth Street apartment and his artistic aspirations to Jackson, and Jackson to Lee. "[Sande] had devoted a hell of a lot of time and energy to taking care of Jack," says a family member. "In some ways his life was blighted as a result. I don't think that's too strong a word to use." Now it was Lee's turn.

The minute Sande moved out of the Eighth Street apartment, Lee moved in and, like Sande, was almost immediately "swallowed up" in Jackson's needs. "She totally negated herself," Fritz Bultman recalls. "It was such a shock that a woman so strong could subordinate herself to that extent." Everything other than Jackson seemed suddenly "irrelevant," Lee recalled. "He was the important thing. I couldn't do enough for him. He was not easy. But at the very beginning, he was accepting of my encouragement, attention, and love." Just as Arloie and Sande had done for six years, she ran the household: buying groceries, washing clothes, "keeping house," even doing Jackson's personal errands like shopping for family presents. She had "a wonderful sense of the mechanics of living," says Ethel Baziotes, that "meshed well with Jackson's inadequacies." "He couldn't do anything for himself," Clement Greenberg recalls. "If he went to the train station to buy himself a ticket, he'd get drunk along the way." According to Wally Strautin, "[Lee] had to remind him to eat."

But for Jackson to eat, Lee had to cook—something she had never done. Almost overnight, she went from bare cabinets to collecting recipes, planning menus, and baking bread. She labored for hours in her tiny kitchen, preparing elaborate meals for two. "I wanted that role," she said later. "I couldn't suddenly not be a woman, not be in love." Peter Busa ran into her at the Waldorf Cafeteria one morning. "She was in a terrible rush," Busa recalls. "She said, 'If I don't get upstairs, Jackson will be furious that his breakfast isn't ready.' " She dressed to suit Jackson, just as she had dressed to suit Igor, swapping Continental chic for domestic propriety. In just a few months, she transformed herself from a "Bohemian vamp" to a "Peck & Peck girl." She also became Jackson's voice, corresponding with his relatives, making his phone calls, even speaking his thoughts. "She was always saying, 'Pollock thinks this, Pollock thinks that,' " May Rosenberg remembers.

Finally, Lee performed what was for her the ultimate act of self-negation. For the second time in her life, she virtually stopped painting. "She was so busy with Jack that she didn't have any time for herself at all," recalls Wally Strautin. Although she kept her studio on Ninth Street, she returned there rarely. The same paintings remained on the easels for more than a year. "I guess it was never a complete stop," says Fritz Bultman, "but what *is* a complete stop? Death? The lapses were so long that there couldn't have been any artistic relationship between one spurt and the next." For the next three years, Lee would not complete a single painting. Later, she would refer to this as her "blackout" period, as though she had lost all consciousness of herself and seen only Jackson and Jackson's art. "She never missed an occasion to talk about Jack's work," Strautin recalls, "but she never mentioned her own." For a long time, only Jackson's paintings hung in the Eighth Street apartment. "In that household," says Reuben Kadish, "there was one painter and that was Jackson." Some of Lee's friends thought Jackson was to blame for the work stoppage—"He made her give up painting," says Milton Resnick, "like a lot of artists who made their wives give up." Mercedes Matter remembers Lee complaining that her painting "was a problem for Jackson." But Lee had reasons of her own to quit. "Her painting had driven Igor away," says May Rosenberg. "She was careful that the same thing didn't happen to her again with Jackson."

Beginning in the spring of 1942, Lee's supporting role in Jackson's life extended even to the Project. Caught up in the patriotic fervor following the bombing of Pearl Harbor, WPA administrators eagerly offered the beleaguered remnants of their work force to the secretaries of war and navy. In March, the art, museum, and craft projects were reorganized under the WPA War Services Subdivision. Purely "creative" projects were scrapped and those few artists who didn't leave the Project to enlist or take jobs in defense industries were put to work painting camouflage for tanks and ships, or designing propaganda posters. Among the projects abandoned was the mural commission at radio station WNYC that Lee had been promised for years. Furious at the last-minute betrayal, she signed a petition to President Roosevelt demanding that the project be taken out of local hands and that artists be allowed to contribute to "the culture of this country." But when offered a position as supervisor of a War Services project, she took it without protest. The job was to design nineteen department store window displays announcing war-related training courses at local schools and colleges. As director, she not only could design the displays, she could also choose her assistants. Her first choice, of course, was Jackson. From April through September, she accompanied him to the WPA studio and watched him work—or loaf—with an indulgent eye. "It was like he was appointed by the queen to be on that project," recalls one of Jackson's co-workers. "Lee certainly looked out for him."

Jackson's drift away from old friends, which had begun under Graham's influence, accelerated under Lee's. Even relatively recent friends like the Schardts and the Strautins no longer played the quotidian role that they had when Sande and Arloie shared the apartment. "She protected him," recalls Nene Schardt. "After Lee came into the picture, we were in the shadows, all the old friends. She didn't keep us away; he just didn't come over as often." When Reuben Kadish stopped by on leave from the army or Peter Busa paid a visit, Lee was courteous and correct, but even they felt the heavy curtain of her concern being drawn around Jackson. The most prominent victim of what Lee later called a "shedding" process was Jackson's analyst, Violet de Laszlo. From her first encounter with Lee, de Laszlo sensed that her role in Jackson's life was being preempted. "Jackson was usually drawn to women as emotional refuges," de Laszlo recalls, "so I wasn't surprised that he found a refuge in Lee. And I thought she was good for him. She knew what she was doing, what he needed at the time." When de Laszlo's sessions with Jackson ended sometime before the summer of 1942, the parting was amicable on all sides. "It was a natural development," de Laszlo says. In gratitude, Jackson offered her any painting in his studio, but she refused, saying she didn't want to confuse the professional relationship.

The departure of de Laszlo and Jackson's increasing isolation from other friends gave rise to rumors: Lee was manipulating Jackson, "systematically disengaging him from his earlier friends," "getting rid of anybody who couldn't help him," grooming him for artistic success (no one yet dreamed of financial success). The rumors, chary at first, eventually grew into a full-scale legend: "She was much brighter than he was and she ran his career," says Lionel Abel, stating it in bold outline. "She carried the ball for the enterprise. She thought the whole thing out from the beginning: how to put him over and make him a big success. How to attack rival painters and rival movements."

As in any good legend, almost everybody found some serviceable truth. Jackson's friends, who found it hard to believe that he would abandon them so summarily, could blame Lee for coming between them. Lee's friends—many of whom, like Lillian Olaney, felt that Lee had "diminished" herself by pairing with Jackson—could console themselves that she hadn't surrendered her artistic ambitions altogether, just rechanneled them. According to some, "there would never have been a Jackson Pollock without a Lee [Krasner]." "All of Pollock's intelligence came from Krasner," said Ilya Bolotowsky, who had enjoyed a brief sexual encounter with Lee in the 1930s. "Jackson was guided by a definite apparition, meaning Lee," said Isamu Noguchi. "She was the agent, be it angel or witch."

In reality, Lee didn't plot or contrive grand schemes; she didn't even give directions. In the beginning, she had only her passion, her fantasy, and a keen sense of how to realize both. "I couldn't walk in and tell Jackson to do this or do that," she said later, "even if I had wanted to." The telling point, of course, is that she *didn't* want to. Being dominated was the fantasy, not dominating. The challenge was not to work her will, but to anticipate and fulfill Jackson's. "Jackson and Irving were just alike in that way," says Lee's sister, Ruth Stein. "If Jackson wanted things a certain way, that's the way they were." The ruthless, manipulative Lee Krasner of later years began as an anxious housewife hurrying home to fix her husband dinner. Hans Hofmann later recalled that "she gave in all the time [to Jackson]. She was very feminine." On matters of business, especially, she deferred to Jackson's judgment—as she did throughout their years together. "Lee had no real business sense," says Clement Greenberg. "In a showdown, she would go to pieces. It was Jackson who had the courage of his convictions. Lee manned the phones and did the detail work."

Whatever Lee did, she did out of passion, not personal ambition. If she kept Jackson from others, it was because she wanted him to need her more. If she shielded him from competition or attacked rival painters, it was because she understood his insecurity and was quick—often too quick—to see a slight. If she introduced him to "people who could be influential in getting him to the top," it was because she genuinely believed in his talent—as seen through the magnifying glass of her infatuation. If she stopped painting, it was because she wanted to spare him the competition—not, as some claimed, because "Jackson insisted on it." She would never have let it come to that. "Lee was completely devoted to Jackson and his work," says Wally Strautin. "Completely. That's why she gave up everything she had and everything she was."

(After Jackson's death, Lee would cling to his paintings tenaciously, resisting pressures to sell them en masse, instead doling them out cautiously to the right museums and collectors for the right prices over a period of almost thirty years. At her death, hundreds of his works remained in her personal collection. According to some, she was simply manipulating the market, keeping the supply of Pollocks low and the price high. Friends praised her sagacity. Some went even further. "Mrs. Jackson Pollock," wrote Harold Rosenberg in 1965, "is often credited with having almost single-handedly forced up prices for contemporary American abstract art after the death of her husband." But Lee's motivations were in a different sphere entirely. Prices and markets never mattered to her as much as Jackson did. Even forty years after their first meeting, her actions were based less on market savvy than on an older, more enduring calculus. "It wasn't that she was trying to raise the prices," says Donald McKinney, who worked with Lee in setting the prices for Jackson's paintings during the 1960s; "it was partly that she couldn't make up her mind, and selling a work required making up her mind. But even more it was a matter of love. It was simply that she loved him so much, she didn't want to let go of anything, not the smallest drawing, unless she absolutely had to. She didn't want to let go of anything that represented *him.*")

The legend also gave Jackson no role in his own "discovery." Lee alone made it happen. More "articulate and cool-headed, as well as more aggressive and 'political' " than Jackson, she had the connections and she made the introductions that launched his career. As for Jackson, he was at best a pawn in Lee's grand scheme; at worst, a hindrance. To illustrate the latter, Lee delighted in telling the story of Alexander Calder's disastrous visit to Jackson's studio early in 1942. "After looking at the paintings, [Calder] said, 'They're all so *dense.*' He meant that there was no space in them. Jackson answered, 'Oh, you want to see one less dense, one with open space?' And he went back for a painting and came out with the densest of all. That's the way he could be." The message was clear: Lee didn't just make Jackson's career for him, she made it *in spite of* him.

In reality, of course, she had considerable help: from her own friends, especially the Matters, who had arranged Calder's visit, from Jackson's friends, and even from Jackson himself. John Graham, whose McMillen show had launched Jackson's career, barely knew Lee at the time of the show, whereas Jackson had been a regular companion for two years. It was Jackson who took Lee to tea at Graham's Greenwich Avenue apartment where, Krasner recalls, "you didn't talk, you listened." Another of Jackson's friends, Reuben Kadish, helped with the most precious asset of all—buyers. On leave from the army in 1942, he brought Jeanne Reynal, the artist, and Emily Davis, the collector, to the Eighth Street studio. When he returned to San Francisco, he persuaded Dr. Grace McCann Morley, the director of the San Francisco Museum of Art, to visit Jackson on her next trip east. Eventually, all three women would buy major Pollock paintings.

■ ■ ■

Nowhere was Lee's hand more evident, according to the legend, than in Jackson's art. Wrote one commentator: "Lee's influence on Jackson, which everyone who witnessed it describes as profound, was to turn him away from the crude and barbaric expressionist modes that reflected primitive and archaic styles and to direct his attention to the sophisticated cosmopolitan art of the School of Paris." In this and similar versions of the legend, Jackson invariably appears as the "bumpkin" to whom Lee revealed the wonders of modernism. "Krasner put [Jackson] in touch with the aesthetics of modernism," writes Barbara Rose, "and a more international, sophisticated view of art than Benton's narrow provincialism." "She helped Pollock a great deal through her intelligence and background," said Ilya Bolotowsky, "because he originally was a Benton student." It was as if Jackson had walked out of Benton's studio and into Lee Krasner's arms. The legend ignored not only Jackson's two years with Graham but even the art itself, which, according to one visitor to the McMillen show, "was immediately recognized by other painters as wise in the ways of School of Paris art."

But to Lee's friends at the time and to purveyors of the legend ever since, an artist's pedigree was almost as important as his art. In order for Jackson, the bumpkin student of the discredited Benton, to sire great art, his thin, Regionalist blood had to be mixed with the true blue blood of modernism. Unaware of Jackson's extensive contacts with Graham, many modernists saw Lee Krasner as the only link between Jackson and the modernist mainstream. *Her* pedigree, through Hofmann, was impeccable. (Hofmann later said, "[Pollock] was never a student of mine, but he was a student of my student.") As Jackson's star rose, the legend-builders claimed more and more credit for Lee until, after Jackson's death, some even argued that "any ultimate assessment of their relative roles" in Jackson's art was "impossible."

Lee apparently began their relationship determined to enlighten Jackson. For two or three months, beginning with a misguided effort to recruit him for Hofmann's school, she urged him to "convert" to modernism and repent his numerous sins. "When I first met Pollock, we disagreed on many things," she said later. In fact, they disagreed on almost everything: She criticized his paintings for "not [being] abstract enough"; he ridiculed her for painting from life. He didn't understand Cubism or care much for it; she pooh-poohed Jung. She was constantly revising her works; he "preferred a one-shot deal." He didn't appreciate Matisse or Mondrian; she reviled Siqueiros (who was rumored to have had a hand in Trotsky's assassination). He even maintained a residue of respect for Benton; Lee wondered how anyone "could take [Benton] seriously as a painter." Jackson didn't think enough about painting; Lee wouldn't "just shut up and paint." One of the few things they had in common was an admiration for Picasso and *Guernica*. But even that touched off arguments: Lee distinguished the formal properties (which she admired) from the psychological properties (which she dismissed), while Jackson refused to separate the two. They were long, loud, captious months. In an unguarded moment, Lee admitted it was "a violent transition and upheaval." Even love, apparently, couldn't bridge the artistic gap. On Eighth Street, Jackson continued to work through Picasso and Jung while, on Ninth Street, Lee, still painting at this point, continued to labor over Hofmannesque abstractions. Once, when Jackson was visiting her studio, Steve Wheeler remembers seeing her "try to show Jackson how to make the 'perfect picture' that Hofmann always talked about."

The antagonisms finally came to a head in Jackson's studio. "[Lee] was trying to tell Jackson what he was doing, what Cubism was," recalls Peter Busa, who was there, "but Jackson was tuning her out as usual." In a fit of pique, Lee grabbed a brush from Jackson's palette and, to emphasize a point, thrust it toward the unfinished painting on Jackson's easel. Busa couldn't tell if she meant for the brush to make contact or not, but it did, leaving a conspicuous dark red blotch. Jackson exploded, "Go ahead, you work on the fucking thing!" and stormed out of the room.

According to Lee, it was several months before their relationship recovered. In the interim, apparently, she had learned her lesson. "It was the last time we talked about aesthetics," she admits laconically, "for a long time." In fact, she never again broached the modernist agenda with Jackson. Abandoning ideological warfare, she retreated to the relative safety of what she called "shop talk"—terse, concrete comments about individual works. "[Jackson] would— speak specifically of the painting in front of him," she said. On trips to museums and galleries, they communicated in a "shorthand" of grunts and nods and appreciative noises. Occasionally, one or the other would mutter, "Great painting!"

In time, Lee would vehemently deny that she and Jackson had ever had any artistic discussions—or, by implication, any disagreements. "I practically had to hit him to make him say anything at all," she told one interviewer. "We never discussed our work." "We didn't talk art," she said on another occasion. "We didn't have that kind of relationship at all." It was as if the first few rancorous months had never happened.

Gradually, Lee's artistic ideals, like everything else, were caught in the undertow of infatuation. She abandoned Hofmann's method of working from "nature"—still lifes, models, landscapes—and tried to work "from inside"— "the way Jackson did." She consciously tried to "lose Cubism," "to jettison all objectivity, and reach inside herself for imagery." She had set out to convert Jackson and ended up being converted by him. "Pollock was too demanding," says a friend. "He was too powerful for Lee. He just obliterated her artistically. She didn't know where he drew his power from, and she never came close to that source herself."

To her credit, Lee never claimed that she did. That part of the lore was largely the product of other mouths and other agendas. "I daresay that the only possible influence that I might have had," she once said, "was to bring Pollock an awareness of Matisse"—a claim corroborated by Jackson's shift in 1942 from the turgid browns and reds of Orozco to the incandescent pinks and purples and turquoises of Matisse. She also could have claimed, but didn't, the substantial cumulative impact of her "shop talk": that slight but persistent current of offhand comments, appreciative nods, and puzzled looks that, over time, undoubtedly affected Jackson's artistic course. "Lee was crucial to Jackson, no doubt about it," says Clement Greenberg, "but not in introducing him to new art, which he already knew, or even in training his eye, which was his own. Her real contribution was in telling him what was good and what was bad in his own work, in being his editor."

Ultimately, Lee's *real* contribution wasn't artistic at all, at least not directly; it was emotional. She gave Jackson what Stella had always refused to give: total devotion, exclusion of all others, complete primacy—even over her own career—and sexual fulfillment. It was the resolution Jackson had sought unsuccessfully for thirty years. "Jackson was a person waiting to be born," recalls a friend, "and Lee saw right away what to do to make him happy. He was her artwork." She created, for the first time since 1934, when Sande came to New York, an emotional open space where, for a while at least, Jackson could wrestle the demons inside without being overwhelmed by them. "Her impact was beyond words," says Ethel Baziotes. "She kept a deep sense of his needs and the needs of his art. Both would have been quite different without her."

With her, and with the order she brought to his emotional life, Jackson could finally focus his tumultuous psychic energy on painting. At almost the same moment, the tides of war were changing the face of the art world, bringing new people and new ideas into his orbit. It would prove a fateful coincidence. Contrary to legend, Lee didn't drag Jackson into the mainstream of Western art. She didn't have to. It came to him.

27

A WELLSPRING OF INSPIRATION

Shoppers who looked in the windows of Bonwit Teller at the corner of Fifth Avenue and Fifty-sixth Street on the morning of Thursday, March 16, 1939, were shocked by what they saw. Many stopped and stared. Some exchanged bemused smiles. A few rushed straight to the manager's office to complain: they had seen many "screwy" window displays before, but nothing like this—nothing so "risqué" or "extreme." The manager tried to explain that the store had hired "the World's No. 1 Surrealist" to design a window, but it didn't help. "It's not art," said one customer, "it's perversity."

No one would have enjoyed the brouhaha more than the artist responsible for it, Salvador Dali. Only two weeks after arriving from Paris, he had been asked to create a Surrealist "folly" for two of Bonwit's windows. He had labored all through the previous night with the store's bewildered window crew bringing his vision to life. In one window, entitled "Day/Narcissus," a mannequin, clad only in long red hair and a few green feathers, stepped into a bathtub lined in black Persian lamb and filled with water. Three disembodied hands floated eerily on the water, each holding a mirror. The walls were tufted in purple leather and studded with mirrors. In the other window, "Night/Sleep," a mannequin lay naked on a bed of what appeared to be red-hot coals. Above her was the head of an animal, described by one reporter as "a stuffed trophy" and by another as "a water buffalo headboard." Dali helpfully identified it as "the decapitated head and the savage hoofs of a great somnambulist buffalo extenuated by a thousand years of sleep."

While Dali might have been pleased with the reaction of Bonwit's customers, Bonwit's management was not. By noon, the feather-clad figure in "Day" and the sleeping figure in "Night" had been removed and replaced by two standing mannequins in smartly tailored suits. But by then word of Dali's windows had spread through the nearby Fifty-seventh Street galleries and from there to Greenwich Village. When Jackson Pollock and Peter Busa heard the story, they headed off to Midtown to see "what work of art had caused such a ruckus." Meanwhile, Dali, who had been catching up on his sleep at the St. Moritz hotel, decided to inspect his handiwork. On seeing the altered windows, he screamed and "stormed" into the crowded store, "sizzling in Spanish and French," according to one account. He had been "hired to do a work of art," he declared *appassionata*, his famous mustache quivering with rage, not to have his name "associated with typical window dressing." Utterly unappeased by the store's manager or, in turn, the store's lawyer (who spoke both Spanish and French), Dali rampaged through cosmetics and hats until he reached the offending windows. Once inside, in full view of the crowd that had gathered on the street, he began dismantling his creation. When he yanked at the tub, it came loose from its moorings, slid forward and crashed through the window. Startled and off-balance, Dali followed it onto the sidewalk.

"We had just walked up," Busa remembers, "when we heard the crash of this big plate window and we looked and there was Dali sitting next to this bathtub in the middle of the sidewalk. . . . Jackson laughed about that for days." Jackson may also have noticed in the paper the next day that a night court judge suspended Dali's sentence for disorderly conduct. "These are some of the privileges," said the judge, "that an artist with temperament seems to enjoy."

Dali's antics announced to an unprepared America that the Surrealists had arrived. Within the next three years, he would be joined by virtually the entire Surrealist movement: Nicolas Calas, Marcel Duchamp, Max Ernst, André Masson, Roberto Matta, Gordon Onslow-Ford, Wolfgang Paalen, Man Ray, Kay Sage, Kurt Seligmann, and Yves Tanguy, as well as the group's imperious leader, André Breton—all of them swept in on the vast tide of European artists and intellectuals fleeing the war in Europe. The same tide brought the leaders of other movements, from Cubism (Léger) to de Stijl (Mondrian), but none came with as many followers or arrived amid such fanfare; none could boast such articulate spokesmen, such disciplined ranks, such newsworthy high jinks, or such galvanic rhetoric. "To many young American artists like me," says Peter Busa, "it seemed like, finally, here was an art movement that had everything."

In fact, Dali's antics only betrayed the disarray at the heart of the Surrealist movement. In twenty years of trying, no artist, not even one as inventive and visionary as Picasso, had been able to capture, in a coherent imagery, Surrealism's abstruse, literary essence. There had been many attempts, many partial or temporary successes, and even some great art, but the promise was still unfulfilled.

It wasn't a surprising predicament for an art movement that began by denying that art existed at all.

Like many nihilistic theories, Surrealism sprang from the despair and disillusionment that followed World War I. That war, so inexplicable, so avoidable, and so costly, had convinced many European artists and intellectuals, especially the young who had seen their generation decimated, that traditional bourgeois society was bankrupt. Frustrated, angry, and guilt-ridden, they denounced traditional painting and sculpture for their cozy alliance with the discredited order. They dismissed traditional works of art as "jewels for the bourgeoisie" and gleefully flouted artistic conventions. In 1919, Marcel Duchamp exhibited a photograph of the *Mona Lisa*, the great icon of Western art, on which he had painted a mustache and goatee. The following year, Francis Picabia affixed a stuffed monkey to a canvas and labeled it "Portrait of Rembrandt, Portrait of Cézanne, Portrait of Renoir." Even the movement's name reflected a taste for the arbitrary and the absurd. A group of artists inserted a knife in a dictionary and landed by chance on the French word for a child's hobbyhorse: *dada*. The leading Dadaist poet, Jacques Vaché, put the movement's philosophy in a nutshell: "ART does not exist."

But if art did not exist, then neither did artists. Some Dadaists, owning up to their new philosophy, abandoned art altogether. In 1920, Duchamp gave up "anti-art" in favor of engineering and chess. Others, like Vaché, abandoned everything by committing suicide. The majority, however, realizing that nothing would come of nothing, underwent a timely "dialectical transformation." After three years of bickering and recrimination, presided over by the autocratic Breton, the old movement regrouped around the less nihilistic proposition that art, when properly construed, was not the tool *of* irrational forces, it was a tool for *exploring* irrational forces. Dada became Surrealism.

In Europe, it was the era of Freud and psychoanalysis—an era dedicated to the notion that rational life is governed by irrational forces. In the great soul-searching that followed the Great War, every new intellectual movement took its turn on the Viennese doctor's couch. Breton visited Freud in Vienna in 1921 and later wrote him a letter that Freud described as "the most touching I ever received." But Breton had little interest in the therapeutic essence of Freud's theories. He didn't want to *cure* disturbances in the psyche, he wanted to *exploit* them: to open a window on the disorderly inner world, not close it. According to one historian of the Surrealist movement, "Without too much respect for the detail of Freud's model of the mental processes, [Breton] seized on the idea that there is a vast untapped reservoir of experience, thought and desire, hidden away from conscious, everyday living." The way to tap that reservoir, said Breton, was through dreams, free association, word games, and hypnotic trances—any kind of mental activity that was "dictated in the absence of all control exerted by reason," or "outside all aesthetic or moral preoccupations." The Surrealists called such mental activity "psychic automatism" and hailed it as "the true function of thought." An artist who could thus liberate his imagination from reason, aesthetics, and morality would produce artworks that reflected a "superior reality." Breton summarized his theory in the famous credo: "I believe in the future resolution of the two states, apparently so contradictory, of dream and reality, in a sort of absolute reality, of *surreality.*"

Breton's elegant theories proved far easier to express in words than in images. Artists, understandably, had trouble ridding themselves of "all aesthetic preoccupations." Did Breton's injunction against conscious control apply to content or style? To the choice of images or to the manner in which those images were rendered? In capturing the "omnipotent" dreamworld, should an artist recreate, as accurately as possible, the images that he has seen in dreams? Or should he try to paint while in a dreamlike state—a state in which conscious control is minimized? Around this core dilemma, Surrealist art quickly degenerated into polite civil war.

In one camp, artists like Salvador Dali and René Magritte "illustrated" their dreams, rendering bizarre but recognizable images in trompe l'oeil detail. Borrowing liberally from Freud, Dali created a vocabulary of feverish sexual imagery (disembowelment, masturbation, castration, hermaphrodism) and called his images "hand-painted dream photographs." Magritte also used psychoanalytic theory, basing his images of room-sized apples and levitating rocks on Freud's contention that dream dislocations reveal important unconscious associations. But to convey these modern psychological insights, both Dali and Magritte relied on literal images painted with the academic precision of nineteenth-century neoclassicism.

In the other camp, a group of artists led by Jean Arp and Joan Miró experimented with images that were not merely records of a previous unconscious experience, but direct *products* of the unconscious. They called their method of creating images "automatism," because the artist's actions were, theoretically, automatic—"dictated in the absence of all control by reason." To achieve truly automatic images, they deprived themselves of all the artist's traditional crutches: time, planning, content, facility, and conventional materials. Oscar Dominguez pressed black gouache between sheets of glazed paper, then peeled them apart to see what patterns the squeezed pigment had formed. Max Ernst, in a process called *frottage*, placed sheets of paper over rough objects, such as floorboards, then rubbed with a soft pencil, creating ghost-like images. Wolfgang Paalen waved a lighted candle in front of a canvas, leaving a trail of burns and smoke stains in a technique known as *fumage.*

No artist was more determined to liberate himself from the "finessed mechanics of the *peinture-peinture* tradition" than André Masson, a graduate of the École des Beaux-Arts who had been severely wounded in the trenches of the Western Front. He began conventionally enough with pen and ink, just "let[ting] his hand travel rapidly over the paper, forming a web of lines from which images began to emerge." When the intrusions of technique (the drag of the pen, for example) continued to plague him, he switched to an unfamiliar medium, spreading glue on the surface of a canvas, sprinkling it with sand, then dusting away the residue to reveal patches where sand had stuck to the glue. Still unsatisfied, in 1927 he began to apply paint directly from the tube, laying the canvas flat and squeezing the paint from above in long thick lines.

They were prescient experiments. Yet, after only a few years, Masson abandoned them and returned to a more comfortable, illusionistic style. Perhaps his "over-literary imagination" was ill suited to the demands of creating art in the absence of all aesthetic preoccupations. He had come closer than any of his confreres to achieving the Surrealist goal of tapping the unconscious, but it would take another artist—one with a richer, more accessible, more impacted unconscious—to turn Masson's taphole into a wellspring of great art. "The subconscious is our wellspring of inspiration," said composer Virgil Thomson. "Some need to use a pump. Others have only to cap a gusher."

In their search for a genuine Surrealist imagery, European artists were virtually ignored by Breton, whose first and only love was literature. A poet and essayist by training, he preferred to explore the unconscious through elaborate word games, at which he excelled. Art he considered merely a "lamentable expedient," a form of expression that served primarily as a springboard to literary discussion (a view he would bequeath to a generation of American art critics). He was especially hostile to abstract art. According to Breton, only works with "pictorial themes" that were "transposable into language" qualified as Surrealist. By the time of the Second Manifesto in 1929, he had virtually deleted abstraction from the Surrealist canon. Automatism, he said, was a way of life, not a style of painting. Fallen from favor, Masson abandoned the movement while Dali was elevated to the unofficial post of court painter.

It was the approved, illusionistic form of Surrealism that first reached America. As early as 1932, the dealer Julien Levy treated the New York art world to the latest innovation from Paris: "Newer Super-Realism," a show that brought together works by de Chirico, Dali, Max Ernst, Masson, Miró, Picasso, Pierre Roy, Marcel Duchamp, and one American, Joseph Cornell. Although Levy included several artists who were not technically Surrealists, he otherwise hewed closely to the party line laid down by Breton (as he would continue to do for the next ten years), showing only works that delivered on the promise implicit in the title of the exhibition. The critics compounded Levy's error, lauding the new movement as "the return of trompe l'oeil painting." One reviewer defined Surrealism as a style in which "the artist sees his subject clearly [and] paints it sharply."

It was a definition that was bound to alienate most young American artists. In fact, except for Levy and a few critics, illusionistic Surrealism was virtually without allies in the American art community. Militant young abstractionists like Lee Krasner deplored its reliance on nineteenth-century trompe l'oeil techniques. Regionalists like Tom Benton dismissed its psychological subject matter as hopelessly un-American. Even the few critics who praised the new movement suggested that it take up American subject matter—a proposal that would have left Breton aghast. The arrival of Salvador Dali in 1934 on the first of his many trips to America won no new friends for Surrealism. While his flamboyant personality, public antics, and exuberant speech-making brought him widespread public attention, they only reinforced the impression that Surrealism was a one-room mansion in which most American artists would never feel at home. Only those few who read French and followed developments in the magazine *Minotaure* knew of Surrealism's other side still hidden from American view.

Not until February 1936, when Alfred Barr presented "Cubism and Abstract Art" at the Museum of Modern Art, was the other side revealed. Many American artists learned about automatism and "abstract Surrealism" for the first time from the show's catalogue, written by Barr. Both show and catalogue concentrated on works by Masson, Miró, Klee, and Arp that illustrated automatic techniques. Barr described these works as "done in a state of semi-hypnosis in which conscious control is presumably abandoned." By including such notions in a Cubist exhibition, Barr not only enlightened American artists, perhaps including Jackson, he also conferred on abstract Surrealism instant legitimacy.

The following December, Surrealist art finally burst on the American scene with the largest exhibition ever presented at an American museum. "Fantastic Art, Dada and Surrealism," also mounted by Barr, was a kaleidoscope of nearly seven hundred entries that attracted more critical attention than any exhibition since the Armory Show of 1913. It included Man Ray's *The Lovers*, Max Ernst's *The Hat Makes the Man*, and Meret Oppenheim's *Fur-Covered Cup, Saucer and Spoon* as well as works by "every artist associated with the movement in even the most remote sense." After being lulled by Dali's harmless antics for half a decade, American art finally woke up to the grand ambitions and dark power of the Surrealist vision. With the notable exception of Lewis Mumford, however, most critics did not appreciate the shock. They called it a "sham," a "maelstrom," "a farce," "a huge absurdity," "the supreme hoax." Martha Davidson, writing in *Art News*, argued that the public was "bound to be amused or outraged," and that if some of the paintings "repulse the visitor they have achieved precisely what they set out to do." Davidson was not the only critic who was put in mind of Kurt Schwitters's terse summary of Dadaist aesthetics: "All an artist spits is art."

Arshile Gorky was among the handful of American artists who dismissed the criticism and embraced the art. In many ways, Gorky was the first American Surrealist: the first to recite Surrealist manifestos, the first to read *Minotaure*, the first to incorporate Surrealist theory into his paintings. He was soon joined by William Baziotes, an artist from Reading, Pennsylvania, and Gerome Kamrowski, a student at the New Bauhaus in Chicago who arrived in New York in the fall of 1938 and met Baziotes the following summer at a party in honor of Wolfgang Paalen. Fresh from the ideological battles with Regionalism and Social Realism, these artists rejected Dali's figurative, illusionistic imagery out of hand. "We considered Dali an illustrator," recalls Peter Busa, another early

American Surrealist, "and that was the dirtiest word you could call an artist."
But *abstract* Surrealism was a revelation. The profusion of automatist techniques appealed to a community of artists obsessed with plastic concerns. Over
the new few years, American artists would seize this tantalizing, inchoate new
concept and make it their own. "Automatism," said Robert Motherwell, "was
the first modern theory of creating that was introduced into America early
enough to allow American artists to be equally adventurous or even more
adventurous than their European counterparts."

More so than any painter since Masson, Baziotes took Surrealist theory at its
word. Like Gorky, he carefully studied the organic shapes of Miró and Jean
Arp, and experimented with automatist techniques such as *coulage* (poured
paint). He rode the subway to Columbia to study Rorschach ink blots. He also
tirelessly disseminated Surrealist theory to his wide circle of friends, one of
whom was Jackson Pollock.

There's no way of knowing how Jackson responded to the theories of Surrealism as Baziotes explained them. How quickly did he see the many parallels
between Surrealist theory and his own art as it emerged from Orozco, Bloomingdale's, and Jungian analysis? How surprised was he to hear (months, presumably, before his first encounter with John Graham) echoes of his own
highly personalized method of working from the unconscious in Baziotes's
explanation of automatism? How soon did he realize that he was better
equipped—artistically and psychologically—than any other American artist to
realize the promise of Surrealist theory?

Clearly, his discussions with Baziotes had an edge of déjà vu. Sometime in
the fall of 1939 or the following winter, the two men arrived at Gerome Kamrowski's studio on Sullivan Street arguing heatedly about whether Jackson's
experiments at Siqueiros's workshop in 1936 constituted "automatism" as defined by the Surrealists. Baziotes, who refused to believe that Surrealism had
been upstaged by a discredited Mexican muralist, "was bringing [Jackson] over
trying to win an argument," Kamrowski recalled. "He was enthusiastically
talking about the new freedoms and techniques of painting and noticing the
quart cans of lacquer asked if he could use some to show Pollock [the tech-
niques]." On a canvas of Kamrowski's that "wasn't going well," Baziotes began
dribbling white paint in a spiral motion using a palette knife. After a minute or
two, he stood back and "interpreted" the spirals as a "bird's nest." He then
handed the palette knife to Jackson who made some "quick whipping movements of the wrist, flinging the paint onto the canvas," according to Kamrowski,
but when he was done, "declined to comment on any meaning." Before long,
Kamrowski joined in with a palette knife of his own and the "demonstration"
quickly degenerated into a "very free kind of activity." When they stopped,
Kamrowski felt Baziotes had "made his point," but Jackson was still "puzzling
the thing out."

Jackson had good reason to puzzle. Baziotes's demonstration *was* a reprise of Siqueiros's workshop. Now, as then, an errant rivulet of paint might suggest the outline of an animal; a burst of spray paint, kinky hair; a swirl of lines, a bird's nest. There was nothing new in that. What may have puzzled Jackson was that the Surrealist theory of automatism, as explained by Baziotes, *promised* much more than that, more than da Vinci's game of reading the cracks in the wall. The theory, at least, was much closer to Jung than to Rorschach. Images were supposed to *originate* in the unconscious, not merely find labels there. "Everything wells up and is given as it appears," wrote Max Ernst. "The great thing is for the show not to be lost, and it is here that the artist's hand intervenes, not to add but to record." What truth of the unconscious was "recorded" by a swirl of lines that could be read as a bird's nest *or* a bale of wire *or* a tornado funnel? For all his trying, Baziotes hadn't yet gone beyond "doodle-reading" to solve the fundamental Surrealist problem: how to establish a minimum of conscious, artistic control over the creation of an unconscious image.

Still, Jackson learned an enormous amount from the gentle Baziotes. The son of Greek immigrants, Baziotes was another of the surrogate father/brother figures to whom Jackson was inevitably drawn. He had all the qualifications: short and wiry and powerfully built like Roy; an ex-boxer like Jay (he considered boxing the most "psychologically useful" preparation for painting); charming, sociable, and well read like Charles. His family, like Jackson's, had suffered financial ruin in the Depression. His "education" had consisted of selling newspapers, shining shoes, standing guard for bootleggers, working in a hat factory, and making stained glass, before he finally enrolled briefly in Leon Kroll's class at the National Academy. Wherever he went, he took an umbrella (whatever the weather) and his wife Ethel, a woman of piercing intelligence, epic devotion, and Byzantine serenity. One friend recalled seeing them "dressed like a proud working couple on a gray Sunday stroll . . . they were 'one bone and one flesh,' bonded for life and perhaps beyond."

From 1939 on, Baziotes was Jackson's liaison to the small but active American Surrealist community that existed before the arrival of the Europeans. In the spring of 1940, they saw a show of works by Wolfgang Paalen, the Austrian Surrealist who had studied with Hofmann in Munich. Paalen's eerie dreamscapes with their abstract backgrounds created by the use of *fumage* and foregrounds filled with jagged forms (knives, skeletons, and the beaks of terrifying birds) only underscored the connection between automatic writing, as John Graham was explaining it at the time, and the Surrealist games of Baziotes. That same month, Gerome Kamrowski saw Jackson and Baziotes emerging from a Miró exhibition at the Pierre Matisse Gallery. Jackson, of course, had been familiar with Miró's organic forms and elegant compositions since at least 1938 when Sande began work on the Marine Terminal mural under James Brooks, an ardent Miró admirer, but he had much to learn from Baziotes about Miró's biomorphic inventiveness, which was increasingly evident in Baziotes's own work.

Still, Baziotes's experimental heart remained with Masson whose more recent illusionistic paintings were shown jointly at the Willard and Buchholz galleries early in 1942. There Jackson may have seen for the first time the dribbled color and mazy, wandering line of the reclusive Frenchman. The technique, of course, was nothing new. Jackson had been squeezing paint directly from the tube on and off since the Siqueiros workshop. In 1940, he had ransacked the workshop of Theodore Wahl emptying all his tubes of paint directly onto a single canvas. "When I returned, the place was a mess," recalls Wahl, "and I didn't have to ask who did it." But Masson's images were much more than a mess. What had been, in Siqueiros's hands, a craftsman's technique, and, in Jackson's, a form of doodling, was, in Masson's, a new way to create subtle, psychologically expressive abstract images.

By the winter of 1942, Jackson was conducting his own "Surrealist experiments" at every available opportunity. Peter Busa remembers him sitting at a table in a WPA studio "squeezing paint out of a tube and just seeing where it went." "He talked about the 'free agent,' " Busa recalls, "the element in Surrealism where you don't touch the canvas, where you just let the paint fall." Years later when a friend asked Jackson, "How much did the Surrealist movement affect you?" he responded, "The only person who really did get through to me was Masson."

Clearly, in a different but no less profound way, Bill Baziotes "got through" to him as well. The two men had what Ethel Baziotes calls "an unconscious collaboration." More than anyone before or after, Baziotes shared Jackson's uneasy relationship with his art. "When I am away from my canvas," he wrote, "I look at the world as realistically as I can. And when I return before my canvas, it is there that the world becomes mysterious. It is there when a few brushstrokes start me off on a labyrinthine journey." Like Jackson, Baziotes approached the act of painting like a fighter entering the ring to do battle with demons. "What happens on the canvas is unpredictable and surprising to me," he said. "Once I sense the suggestion, I begin to paint intuitively. The suggestion then becomes a phantom that must be caught and made real. As I work, or when the painting is finished, the subject reveals itself."

Baziotes also taught Jackson that "to talk about art is to be tainted," that "too many veils should not be lifted." According to his wife, he agreed with Matisse that "artists should have their tongues cut out." He also rejected "the affectations of scholarship," in the belief that "there were some places where words shouldn't trespass," says Ethel Baziotes. He spurned critics and dealers and even museum directors in order to avoid being "caught in their web" of words and wrangling and inevitable compromise. The worst fate that could befall an artist, in Baziotes's estimation, was to become a "phony"—an artist who abandoned "his own kingdom" in a misguided search for acceptance and approval. It was a lesson that Jackson learned well—perhaps too well.

In the winter of 1941, Jackson may have accompanied Baziotes to Gordon Onslow-Ford's lectures on Surrealism at the New School for Social Research. If he did, what he heard was reassuring, but hardly new; Onslow-Ford argued that the artist should "look within himself" for subject matter. The lectures did, however, mark the beginning of the end for the short-lived independent Surrealist movement in America. Onslow-Ford, an English artist who had been in Europe since 1937, had come to preach the *true* gospel of Surrealism, Breton's gospel. Everything that existed before was apostasy. (Years later he still claimed to be "the person who introduced Surrealist painting to New York.")

The Europeans had arrived.

The visit of the European Surrealists to America has often been trumpeted as a great catalytic episode in American art. "It was the challenge of ideas that created a tremendous movement," said Pierre Matisse, whose New York gallery benefited lavishly from the sudden presence of the European artists he exhibited. "It was the *possibilité* of American artists meeting [the Surrealist artists]." "Their being here was overpowering," says Ethel Baziotes. "Its importance can't be overstated. These were fascinating men with highly perfected artistic ways. They had form, and the Americans were searching for form. The ideas the Europeans brought with them were utterly fascinating. They were catalytic. It was like one flame meeting another and making a larger flame."

The metaphor is unintentionally apt. In fact, the Surrealists' visit generated considerable friction, heated controversy, and smoldering resentment, but little creative fire. Surrealist *ideas*—ideas that had crossed the ocean years before—proved catalytic, but the visit itself proved divisive and counterproductive for both hosts and guests. Far from galvanizing the Surrealist movement in America, it drove American artists out of the Surrealist fold in search of new solutions under new labels, blackened the name of Surrealism, and obscured its contribution to American art for the next quarter-century.

To begin with, very few American artists actually *met* their new guests. Unlike other European visitors such as Mondrian and Léger who "really enjoyed the New York scene," the Surrealists tended to remain clannish and aloof. They frequented the same cafés, Larré and the Free French Canteen, where they sat, ate, and conversed only with one another, complaining about the weather, the food, the hectic pace, and "longing for the bistros of Paris." They gathered for parties at the homes of those few Americans, like Bernard and Becky Reis, who had both the money to subsidize their high style and the cultural insecurity to suffer their condescensions. In the summers, they vacationed together, clustering in enclaves like the Hamptons where they were fed and indulged by American Francophiles Sara and Gerald Murphy. Some, like Masson, "kept away from everything" by moving to Connecticut. "They were terrible snobs," says Clement Greenberg. "The Americans were too grubby." Few of the Surrealists could speak English well and some of those who could, refused to.

Only occasionally did the Surrealists reach across the cultural barrier to embrace the natives. Marcel Duchamp and Kurt Seligmann, in particular, made an effort to be accessible. Gorky was a favorite of Breton and Tanguy,

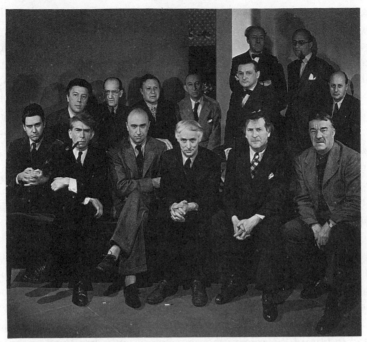

Artists in exile. Left to right, front row: Roberto Matta Echaurren, Ossip Zadkine, Yves Tanguy, Max Ernst, Marc Chagall, Fernand Léger; second row: André Breton, Piet Mondrian, André Masson, Amédée Ozenfant, Jacques Lipchitz, Pavel Tchelitchew; in back: Kurt Seligmann and Eugene Berman.

and the Matters, of course, were always *bienvenu*. But most of the newcomers restricted their communications to the few Americans who, like Mercedes Matter and Fritz Bultman, could speak French. "The Surrealists arrived like visiting royalty," writes May Rosenberg, "bearers of sacred visions to the heathens; trippers among the lollipops."

The pitch of arrogance and contempt was set by Breton, who, according to Max Ernst, "insisted in thinking everything not French *imbécile*." From the moment he arrived, bowing and kissing ladies' hands, dispensing *les mots justes*, Breton embodied European Surrealism at its haughtiest. Some were beguiled. "Breton may have spoken fifteen minutes with you," recalls Ethel Baziotes, "but that fifteen minutes would last the rest of your life." Others smarted under his "autocratic and priestlike condescensions." Admirers called him *le pape* ("the pope") and treated him with a reverence that struck their American hosts as unnatural, if not perverse. "It was amazing the respect all these grown men gave [him]," said Becky Reis. "It was ingrained in them that he was superior." Breton exercised his authority with a whim of iron. "He was full of prejudices," said David Hare, the editor of Breton's short-lived magazine *VVV*. He refused to learn English—fearing it might pollute his classical written French— wouldn't eat eggs, and abhorred homosexuality. He ordered one of his followers, Nicolas Calas to marry or face excommunication. He particularly relished parlor games in which he used his immense power to inflict small indignities. His favorite was *La Vérité*, a game of his own devising, in which players were required to reveal their deepest emotional secrets. Peggy Guggenheim, who despised the game, called it "a form of psychoanalysis done in public. The worse the things that we exposed, the happier everyone was." Especially Breton, who enforced the rules of the game with the humorless intensity of a schoolmaster, screaming out *"Gage!"* ("Foul!") at even the most minor infraction. "He got mortally offended if anybody spoke out of turn," Guggenheim recalled, "part of the game was to inflict punishment on those who did so." Punishment consisted of "being brought blindfolded into a room on all fours and forced to guess who kissed you."

The Surrealists' oblivious, self-indulgent life-style struck many as gallingly frivolous and irresponsible against a backdrop of battlefield dispatches and wartime shortages. "In this country the visitors displayed a life-style that was staged and elegant," wrote May Rosenberg. "Languid or passionate, they seemed to be having a good time, an intellectually suave time." What were Americans to think of a community that found it *amusant* when Leonor Fini decorated her apartment with piles of autumn leaves and perfumed excrement? The whimsy, lyricism, and hedonism of their art and poetry seemed almost calculated to offend the more pragmatic, masculine, and Puritan sensibilities of their hosts. Their absolute, unquestioning obedience to Breton smacked of totalitarian mind-control. Their obvious disdain for America seemed at best ungrateful and at worst—with Americans fighting to free Europe—treasonous. (Dali triggered a furor when he exhibited a painting depicting an American plane being shot down.) Their precious preoccupation with matters literary, their disdain for "the brush," seemed maddeningly obtuse and *retardataire*.

To make matters worse, the European interlopers were co-opting more and more of the attention of American dealers, collectors, and museums—of which there was already an acute shortage. Not just uptown dealers like Julien Levy, who had always shunned young American artists and taken aesthetic marching orders from Breton; not just "the Museum of Modern Art people" like Barr, who had always favored Continental artists. What really stung was the way in which even beginning collectors, notably Bernard Reis, "swallowed all Gallic innovations whole." "[Reis's] only money was spent on Europeans," recalled Robert Motherwell. "To the degree that he had any American paintings I am sure we gave them to him."

Proximity to the Europeans bred not only contempt and resentment but also a more realistic assessment of their art. Willem de Kooning, for example, found himself in the same studio with Léger and the French abstractionist Jean Hélion, who had recently escaped from a prisoner-of-war camp. "One day I looked at what I was doing," de Kooning later told Lionel Abel, "and I said it's just as interesting as what they're doing. And it was, too." Abel remembers that "it meant a lot to [Bill] to be able to compare himself to a first-rate painter like Léger." Similar epiphanies were occurring throughout the community of

American artists. David Smith said of Mondrian and Lipchitz, "We have met them and we have found that they were humans like we were and they were not gods." Jackson Pollock, too, began to ask the inevitable question. "I don't see," he told an interviewer in 1943, "why the problems of modern painting can't be solved as well here [in America] as elsewhere."

By the end of 1942, despite Breton's last-ditch effort to salvage his hegemony with the publication of *VVV*, Surrealism was a movement in disarray, its earlier convictions undermined by factional infighting and the trauma of dislocation. American artists, filled with newfound confidence and emboldened by the pervasive "can-do" attitude of wartime America, crowded into the breach.

In the ensuing scramble, Jackson Pollock was little more than a bystander. By 1942, he was known widely, if not well, and generally perceived, mostly on the strength of Graham's recommendation, as "a diamond in the rough." Among the American Surrealists, the front-runners should have been Gorky and Baziotes. But neither man was suited to the political battlefield. Although Gorky was extremely knowledgeable and widely respected, his aesthetic sensibilities were too changeable for him to play the role of ideologue. ("Gorky is like a cow," Jackson told a friend. "You know, they forage and eat, and then they get back in the stable and they're still chewing. . . . Gorky will look at Picasso for hours, then go back to his studio and make a Picasso in the Gorky style.") In 1943, Gorky spent nine months at a farm in Virginia—the first of many long stays outside New York—and was already showing signs of moodiness and emotional isolation. Baziotes was the more likely candidate. Among all those who later claimed the title of "founder of the American Surrealist movement," Baziotes was the one who deserved it most. Yet he was determined to avoid the contest for power and credit. "He cared only about the integrity of the search," says Ethel Baziotes. "He was completely aloof from the audience. . . . We both knew critics and dealers and museum directors quite well, but he never moved in their orbit." That, of course, was precisely the orbit in which the contest would be fought.

One artist who didn't share such qualms was Roberto Sebastián Matta Echaurren, known simply as Matta. Basque by origin, Chilean by birth, Matta had lived in Paris where he studied architecture with Le Corbusier before joining the Surrealist circle in 1937. Despite his reputation as a libertine, Matta was received by the prudish Breton as "a loved son, the heir apparent." In 1939, however, almost two years ahead of the main wave of European artists, he forsook Paris and came to New York. Unlike the Europeans who were to follow, Matta was young, spoke excellent English, mixed often with American artists, and made friends easily. Robert Motherwell's reaction was typical: "He was the most energetic, poetic, charming, brilliant young artist that I've ever met." "Matta was like a firebrand," says Becky Reis. "He could ignite the imagination and the enthusiasm of anybody about the arts, a very explosive personality." In the year before Breton's arrival, Matta "touched base with everyone," nestling his way deep into the ranks of those Americans who considered themselves Surrealists.

As the lone "European" Surrealist in New York (other than Dali who was by now completely discredited) Matta could play the Promethean role that suited his ambition. In Paris, he had been a promising protégé. Alone in New York, he was a "genius." At the age of thirty, with only a handful of paintings to his credit, he was given a show at the Pierre Matisse Gallery, an honor that none of his American friends could claim. But Breton's arrival changed all that. "No one paid any attention to him after [the Europeans] arrived," recalls Steve Wheeler, a young artist at the time. "He was pushed back into the shadow. The older Surrealists who were around the triple V magazine would have nothing to do with him. They considered him an upstart."

Spurned by Breton and the others, Matta plotted his revenge. According to Wheeler, "He said, 'Fuck you, guys, I'm going to have my own movement.'" The only place to start a new movement was, of course, among the Americans. "By allying himself with the younger American painters," says Wheeler, "he could arrogate power to himself." Largely through his contact with Baziotes, Matta concluded that automatism was the only Surrealist idea that retained any viability for American artists, and he moved quickly to promote himself as its champion. Soon after John Graham's McMillen show, he began to lay secret plans for an event that would upstage Breton and, in one audacious stroke, end European artistic hegemony. "He wanted to show the Surrealists up as middle-aged grey-haired men who weren't zeroed into contemporary reality," according to Robert Motherwell. The show would feature only American artists—and Matta. "He realized that if he made a manifestation by himself, or even if he had a beautiful show by himself," said Motherwell, "the Surrealists could say, well, he's a Surrealist and he's very talented; but if there were a group who made a manifestation that was more daring and qualitatively more beautiful than the Surrealists themselves, then he could succeed in his objective of showing them up."

Matta outlined the plan to Baziotes, hoping he would help recruit his friends to the new movement, but Baziotes once again refused to get involved. He did, however, provide a list of the artists he thought might respond to Matta's pitch, a list that included Gorky, Kamrowski, Busa, de Kooning, and Pollock. But with anti-European resentments already percolating among the Americans, Matta was determined to find a local co-sponsor to give his new movement an American imprimatur. He selected Robert Motherwell, a young, unknown artist from California whom he had met on a trip to Mexico in the summer of 1941. To the aristocratic and class-conscious Matta, Motherwell seemed like the perfect choice: educated at Stanford and Harvard, polished, cosmopolitan, articulate, ambitious—in many ways, an American version of Matta himself.

It was, in fact, a disastrous choice.

●   ●   ●

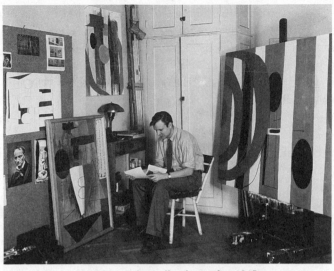

Robert Motherwell in his studio, 1943

Robert Motherwell's name appears for the first time relatively late in the chronicle of American Surrealism. In 1937, in the wake of the Museum of Modern Art's Surrealism shows, when Gorky and Baziotes were already reading *Minotaure* and experimenting with Surrealist imagery, Motherwell was a twenty-two-year-old graduate student at Harvard, drifting toward a Ph.D. in philosophy. In 1939, when Baziotes took Jackson to Kamrowski's studio to settle a dispute over automatism, Motherwell was teaching philosophy at the University of Oregon. By 1940, he had come to New York but, by his own admission, didn't know any American painters and didn't care to meet any. Preferring "the French milieu," he studied engraving with Kurt Seligmann and took to hanging around the edges of the growing refugee community. It wasn't until the summer of 1941, on the trip to Mexico with Matta, Matta's wife, and Barbara Reis (Bernard and Becky's daughter), that Motherwell was finally introduced to Surrealism. "In the three months of that summer," he said later, "Matta gave me a ten-year education in Surrealism." In Mexico City, he visited Wolfgang Paalen, whose show Baziotes and Jackson had seen at the Julien Levy Gallery the year before. On the same trip, he also found a wife—a dark, stunningly attractive Mexican actress named Maria Ferrera, described by a friend as "a little, capricious ariel floating around."

On his return from Mexico, Motherwell began to paint seriously for the first time and, with Matta as a sponsor, redoubled his efforts to ingratiate himself into the community of European artists. At first, they were intrigued by his brashness. While most Americans remained standoffish, if not hostile, Motherwell—describing himself as "imbued with French culture"—strode fearlessly into the Surrealists' gatherings and engaged them in intellectual conversation. "I would talk to Max Ernst," he recalled. "[He] probably was the first painter before me to have a degree in philosophy and . . . was perfectly

willing to talk about intellectual things." In public, Ernst and the others tolerated the nervy young American, often teasing him with arch, ambiguous comments—"You have a tremendous capacity to grow"—that he invariably took
as compliments. He later told an interviewer that in the course of "ransacking
the cultural world for talent," the Europeans were particularly impressed by
his intelligence, style, and good looks. "He was pleasant to look at," says Roger
Wilcox, whose wife, Lucia, was a frequent host to the Surrealists in the Hamptons, "he looked so cherubic with his round face, and he was very polite and
very eager." Breton even picked Motherwell to be the first editor of *VVV* (part
of his halfhearted effort to build bridges to the American artistic community),
although he was fired before the inaugural issue appeared.

In private, however, the Europeans ridiculed him. According to Lucia Wilcox, "He used to come and insinuate himself into this crowd but they simply
didn't pay any attention to him." Ernst dismissed him as "a joke." Breton, who
considered all Americans naive, deplored his intellectual pretensions and referred to him demeaningly as *"le petit philosophe."* Even Matta, in an unguarded moment, agreed that he was "a windbag and a pompous ass."

In 1942, however, Matta had a use for his new protégé. To prepare for the
decisive "manifestation" that would establish their new movement, Matta and
Motherwell launched an intensive campaign of recruitment and indoctrination.
Using Baziotes's list, they visited the artists' studios with their message. Motherwell would arrange the meetings and make introductions—"he had a tremendous facility for gathering ends together," recalled Peter Busa—then
Matta would explain the movement: the need for a "revolution of the young
'inside' Surrealism"; the need for Americans "to develop some sort of unified
direction in their art"; the need to "show up the Surrealists as a group of
dogmatic painters no longer attuned to the contemporary world"; and the need
for "reliance on truer versions of the technique of psychic automatism." Motherwell would follow with an eager, lengthy explanation of Surrealist theory.
One artist recalled being "annoyed because he talked more than Matta did."
During the spring and fall of 1942, Matta and Motherwell took their act to the
studios of Gorky, Pollock, de Kooning, Kamrowski, and Busa, meeting with
mixed reviews. Gorky was bemused, de Kooning indifferent. Kamrowski and
Busa were interested, however, and Pollock was "exhilarated." "He was
thrilled that Matta liked his work," recalls Reuben Kadish. Including Baziotes,
Matta now had six artists—himself, Motherwell, Baziotes, Busa, Kamrowski,
and Pollock—enough to make a movement.

Years later, Motherwell would claim that he used these sessions to "initiate"
Pollock and the others into "the Surrealist mysteries"—a version of history that
elicited howls of laughter and derision from the artists' friends.

On October 14, 1942, the European Surrealists staged their first New York
spectacle, the "First Papers of Surrealism" show at the Whitelaw Reid mansion
on Madison Avenue. The American art world had never seen anything like it.

Duchamp, the master of ceremonies, strung two miles of string around the columns of the old mansion's interior to create an airy skein as a backdrop against which the paintings would be auctioned. The sound of children playing echoed through the marble halls as a troop of youngsters, hired by Duchamp, played football, hopscotch, jacks, and jump-rope in the ballroom. Guests were encouraged to join them. In assembling the show, Breton cast the net of Surrealism wide. In addition to Miró, Masson, Ernst, Seligmann, and Magritte, he included Picasso and Klee, two artists who had resisted the Surrealist label. He even deigned to hang works by Americans Baziotes, Motherwell, and David Hare, although their presence was somewhat compromised by their proximity to pictures of Superman and Father Divine. Despite the growing rift between them, Breton also included Matta. Dali, however, was beyond forgiveness. All in all, it was a convincing display of vitality. If the Surrealists were dispirited, if their domination of the art world was threatened, there was no sign of it among the marble pillars and amused patrons on opening night.

In the shadow of Breton's extravaganza, Matta began work on his manifestation. Peggy Guggenheim, whose new gallery, Art of This Century, opened only a week after the "First Papers" show, had already expressed interest in Matta's plans for a show of the "new American automatists" and seemed to share his ambitious vision of topping Breton. Now Matta had the idea, the artists, the strategy, and the sponsor. All he needed was the art.

To recreate the sense of "community" that Breton exploited so masterfully among the Europeans, Matta arranged for the artists and their wives to meet for dinner and "games" at his Twelfth Street apartment, a dramatic, open space with curved canvas walls designed by Frederick Kiesler. The game was "the Exquisite Corpse," the most famous of the Surrealist parlor games developed in the twenties by Tanguy and Duchamp using children's games as models. It began with one player writing a word or a line on a piece of paper, then folding it and passing it to the next player, who added another word or line without looking at what came before. When everybody had contributed, the paper was unfolded and the resulting "poem" read aloud. (The game's unusual name came from the first sentence derived by this method: "The exquisite corpse shall drink the young wine.") According to Ethel Baziotes, the purpose of the game was "to locate a common meeting of the psyches." The result, however, was usually something between Haiku and nonsense. A "poem" that Jackson wrote in the margin of a drawing about this time is typical:

>   the effort of the dance
>   the city with horns
>   the thickness of white.

Disappointed with their first efforts, Matta's guests tried rearranging the lines. (The job fell to Motherwell, the intellectual among them.) When that didn't work, they decided to "cheat," by requiring that all contributions relate to a common topic, like "What is a Fox?" Motherwell recalled that "one rainy night one of the subjects was rain, and an extremely beautiful poem resulted from that."

The guests seated around on Matta's canvas chairs (also designed by Kiesler) and passing pieces of paper included Robert and Maria Motherwell; Bill and Ethel Baziotes; Peter Busa and his wife-to-be, Jeanne Juell; Matta's wife, Ann; Lee Krasner; and, sitting by himself in a corner, Jackson Pollock. "Jackson didn't participate too much," recalls Ethel Baziotes. "He didn't want to have anything to do with something so revelatory. . . . It was a constant source of anguish." The gregarious Matta was confounded by Jackson's antisocial reticence. He called Jackson "*fermé*. A closed man." Only when the group made automatic drawings of males and females and psychoanalyzed them did Jackson come to life. "Jackson was the best at that," recalls Peter Busa.

Although Matta clearly intended such evenings to be regular events, attendance began to fall off after the first few sessions. Jackson came only two or three times—at least once without Lee. Motherwell tried for a while to continue the work at his apartment on Eighth Street and Jackson attended at least one session there, but interest quickly waned. After no more than six evenings, and perhaps as few as two, the effort was dropped.

Far more important to Matta's plans was another group that began meeting at his studio on Ninth Street every Saturday afternoon beginning in October 1942. These were the sessions at which he would shape his new movement. No hors d'oeuvres were served, no games played, and, consistent with Surrealist misogyny, no wives invited. (The Surrealists "treated their wives like French poodles," Lee Krasner complained.) Otherwise, the participants were the same: Baziotes, Kamrowski, Busa, Motherwell, and Pollock. Matta recalled that Jackson "resented most this idea of a group," but came anyway, persuaded by Matta's reputation and his enthusiasm for Jackson's work. The purpose of the sessions, as set forth by Matta, was "to find new images of man." The program was simple, direct, and inflexible: they would make automatic drawings based on specific themes. One week, they concentrated on "natural elements"—fire, water, earth, air—and tried to capture their unconscious reactions on paper. The next week, they thought about "what it would be like to go swimming if you were blind." Much of Matta's explanation of automatist methods and theory was familiar to the Americans, but according to Kamrowski, "he brought such energy to the subject that in a way it didn't make any difference what he said."

One theme in particular obsessed Matta: "the hours of the day." Time had been a preoccupation of the Surrealists since de Chirico's timelessly vacant piazzas. From Dali's melting watches to Giacometti's *The Palace at 4 A.M.*, the very concept of "surreality" implied a dreamlike exemption from traditional rules of time and continuity. Matta hoped that by applying the true principles of automatism, he could make a new and powerful statement about the relationship between time and space and the unconscious. "Surrealism was largely a night world (of dreams)," said Kamrowski. "Matta wanted to create a similar world for day hours." If he succeeded, he would have outdone the Surrealists on their own terms.

But Jackson and his colleagues weren't interested in Surrealist terms. They wanted to make paintings, not statements. To them, Matta's plan sounded suspiciously like one of Breton's efforts to use art as mere sugar-coating for metaphysics. Still, out of deference to their host, they agreed to try it. At his direction, they kept logs of their daily activities and thoughts for the purpose of discovering "what common images might cross their minds at identical hours." Lee Krasner remembered Jackson returning from one session bewildered by his instruction to "draw the hours of the day." Although impressed by Matta's drawings, the Americans grew increasingly unhappy with his "dogmatism." "We worked pretty well together, except Matta was getting more and more polemical about it," recalls Peter Busa. "We were more interested in the formal possibilities and the mechanics of it, [but] Matta felt that was kind of not very cultured." According to Kamrowski, "Matta got to the point that he wasn't pushing automatism so much as he was pushing this mediumistic shit—the fortune-telling and divination aspect of Surrealism that none of us cared about." Least of all Jackson, who complained that it was "too much like a game and not serious," and balked at keeping a log—"It reminded him of homework," says Busa. The meetings, friendly at first, turned "intense." Once, when Matta was demonstrating the Surrealist technique of *fumage*, Jackson turned to Busa and said in a stage whisper: "I can do that without the smoke."

The end came at a meeting in late winter when Matta proposed that each person take home a pair of dice, which he would roll every hour on the hour and record the numbers that came up. "That was more than Jackson could take," recalls Busa. "He just got up and walked out."

Soon after Jackson left, Peggy Guggenheim withdrew her support from Matta's plans for a manifestation. Her interest had never been more than exploratory, and although she, too, bridled under Breton's regime, she wasn't yet ready to join a palace coup. Instead, she offered Matta's young Americans, including Jackson, an opportunity to contribute to a collage show planned for the spring of 1943 at Art of This Century. Matta, too, was having second thoughts about a break with his Surrealist mentors, brought on in part by the unexpected recalcitrance of his American protégés. "Matta's allegiances were always torn," says Ethel Baziotes. Before accepting him back into the fold, however, Breton exacted a bizarre revenge. "There was a meeting," recalls Hedda Sterne, "and Matta had to atone by branding himself—I don't know where on his body."

Matta's capitulation left Robert Motherwell as the heir apparent to the "American automatist movement"—a movement that had yet to exist anywhere outside of Matta's ambitions. Motherwell, after all, had been Matta's handpicked American liaison; had accompanied him on recruitment visits; had proven himself socially, politically, and artistically astute; was an excellent organizer; and best of all, knew Peggy Guggenheim, whose new gallery and flamboyant life-style had already catapulted her into a position of prominence that rivaled Breton's. Without Motherwell's influence, Jackson believed, Guggenheim would never have extended the collage show invitation.

Certainly no one wanted a position of power and influence more than Motherwell. As a newcomer and bystander at Surrealist events, he had seen, more clearly than most, Breton's immense power. The sight left him both awestruck and envious. Harry Holtzman, a close friend at the time, recalls that soon after Matta's surrender, Motherwell burst into his studio exclaiming, "Breton terrifies me. . . . He can make or break an artist." Holtzman tried to calm him. "What the hell do you care about him for? We don't need these guys to tell us what we should think." "That's all right for you," Motherwell responded, "but I want power. When I get power I can take that point of view."

As much as Motherwell wanted power, no one wanted to give it to him. The Europeans mocked his ambitions and the Americans resented them, responding to his pretentiousness with a mix of indignation and derision. To them, he was a baby-faced newcomer—articulate and persuasive, perhaps, but without a single legitimate claim to leadership. Where had *he* been when they were struggling through the Depression, Benton's broadsides, and the ideological warfare of the Project? Where were *his* paintings? As of 1942, very few artists had even seen Motherwell's early painterly abstractions, and some of those who had seen them questioned their integrity. When a friend arrived unexpectedly at Motherwell's studio in the early forties, he found the artist on his knees, assembling tracings of forms from a Miró painting. "These were not authentic paintings," says Roger Wilcox, "and Jackson and just about everyone else knew it."

Such shortcuts were to be expected of a man who had spent the previous five years earning a Ph.D. in philosophy from Harvard. "He was a literary, intellectual sort of person," says one former member of the club, "and at that time that was extraordinary. He wasn't rooted in painting. All the rest of us were." And yet he wanted to lecture them, in a tone laced with condescension, on theories of art that had been common currency for years. Not surprisingly, most American artists were deeply insulted.

The real insult, however, had nothing to do with art. It had to do with money: Robert Motherwell was the son of a banker.

For artists like Pollock, who had scraped through the Depression, who had resigned themselves to the indignities of the public dole, who had joined the Communist party or at least marched in its parades, whose families had been devastated by foreclosures and bankruptcies, it was the ultimate, unforgivable sin. "Motherwell was born with gold spoons sticking out of his ears, nose, mouth, and asshole," says Harry Holtzman, expressing a view that most artists shared. "He never suffered for a moment. He never knew want." Although he later denied it, Motherwell apparently made no effort to hide his legacy at the time. With no visible means of support, he lived in a spacious apartment on

Eighth Street and summered in Mexico and other exotic locales. In his defense, he argued that his father, the president of San Francisco's Wells Fargo Bank, had also been ruined in the crash, but to a generation convinced that bankers *caused* the crash, that only seemed like poetic justice. He maintained that he received only fifty dollars a week from his father, but that was twice the wage on the WPA, and friends suspected that his mother provided additional subsidies.

Most artists, however, kept their resentments to themselves and treated Motherwell with the same diffidence, even deference, they reserved for the Europeans with whom he was increasingly identified. Many, like Jackson, were intimidated—if not by the reality of Motherwell's intellect, then by the illusion of his power, money, and connections. "Jack had a way of making sure that he didn't neglect someone who might be or might become an individual of importance," recalls Reuben Kadish. "He had respect for Motherwell's status, if not for Motherwell himself." If, as Motherwell claimed, he introduced Jackson to Peggy Guggenheim in October 1942, it was all the more reason for Jackson to maintain cordial relations. "Alliances were beginning to be formed," says Steve Wheeler. "Jackson knew that Motherwell was no good as an artist, but he also knew that Motherwell had power, so he wasn't going to come out and tell Motherwell he was full of shit." Soon after Motherwell's first visit and probably with Lee's help, Jackson arranged for Motherwell to meet Hofmann and de Kooning. The results were hardly encouraging. Not only was Hofmann hostile to the psychoanalytic aspects of automatism, as explained by Motherwell, but Jackson managed to drink too much jug wine during their short visit and had to be carried back to his apartment by Motherwell and the elderly Hofmann. "It was a helluva job," Motherwell recalled. The meeting with de Kooning also misfired. Jackson had apparently forgotten to inform him of the meeting time and he was asleep when Motherwell arrived.

In another uncharacteristically politic gesture, Jackson suggested that he and Motherwell work together in preparing their collages for Peggy Guggenheim's show. "He had been painting much longer than I had," Motherwell said later, "and had a much more professional set-up than mine in terms of space, light, and materials." Given Jackson's resistance to working in groups and his distaste for Motherwell, it seems unlikely that he would share his studio for any reason other than political expediency, combined, perhaps, with pressure from Lee. The two spent a long afternoon in the spring of 1943, during which Motherwell was shocked by Jackson's "attack on the material." He tore the paper, spit on it, and burned the edges with a kitchen match. "Generally, he worked with a violence I had never seen before," said Motherwell. "I can still remember watching him with a mounting tension, fearing I don't know what." Such incidents only underscored the differences between Jackson and the cerebral Motherwell who had noted with disdain the T-shirt Jackson was wearing the day the two first met. (In a classic left-handed compliment, Motherwell professed admiration for Jackson's "left-handed intelligence" and compared him to "Marlon Brando in scenes from *A Streetcar Named Desire*," except that "Brando was much more controlled than Pollock.")

Motherwell might have succeeded where Matta had failed, even without the love of his countrymen. He was by far the most eloquent and persuasive spokesman for the two galvanic ideas of the decade: automatism and an end to European domination. American artists of every stripe could agree, in the abstract at least, that painting was more important than theory and that the time had come for them to take their rightful place beside the European masters. His theory of "plastic automatism" fused Surrealist philosophy with the modernists' plastic concerns, but it remained only a theory—text without illustrations. Like Breton and Matta before him, Motherwell still lacked the most important ingredient for a new movement: compelling art.

Matta had been right: to steal the limelight from the Europeans and inspire American artists to their best efforts, a "manifestation" more beautiful and more compelling than anything seen before was needed. If the images were right, the movement would coalesce on its own. Despite his enthusiasm, his soirées, and his workshops, Matta had been unable to elicit the necessary creative spark. Interest in his new movement, both among artists and among dealers like Peggy Guggenheim, dissolved in frustration. Motherwell, for all his political machinations, had also failed. But their efforts left behind an unexpired impetus for change and an expectation, urgent and pervasive, that a triumphant manifestation was just around the corner; that after wandering through the decades in search of expression, Surrealist ideas, rooted in Freud and the disillusionment following World War I, would finally find appropriate images; and that those images would, like the ambient war, affirm America's new position of leadership in the world.

In short, the American art community was primed for a breakthrough.

28

EXCITING AS ALL HELL

In the dying days of the Project, still on the government payroll, and safe in the emotional haven created by Lee, Jackson painted his first master-pieces. They appeared almost by surprise. The spring and summer of 1942 had been a total loss. Between Stella's arrival, Lee's attentions, the Project's uncertainties, and Sande's departure, Jackson had been too busy coping, or failing to cope, to manage more than a few perfunctory drawings. In September, however, Lee's move into the Eighth Street apartment gave him the courage to confront, for the first time openly and confidently, the demons that had tormented and congested his imagination for more than a decade, while the lessons of the past few years—Graham and Picasso, Henderson and Jung, Matta and automatism, Miró, Matisse and even Siqueiros—gave him a rich new vocabulary of images. The result, in three paintings all done in the last three months of 1942, was an imagery far more original, compelling, complex, and accomplished than anything he had yet produced.

In *Stenographic Figure*, a grotesque female sits across a table from a timid, emaciated male figure. She offers him something (food, perhaps), her great gray paw reaching across the canvas in a gesture that is both generous and menacing. It is a subject—the possessive, all-providing, castrating female— that has haunted Jackson's art since the early thirties, but the imagery is star-tlingly new. Stella, who visited Jackson and Lee in New York several times during the months when the work was painted, has been transformed from the implacable monster of Jackson's Orozcoesque drawings into a familiar, if still frightening, domestic harridan. Her breasts are no longer huge, limp, and empty, but round, firm, and full, like Lee's. In fact, Stella has become Lee, recognizable by her sharp tongue, bug eye, and withering gaze, as well as her ambiguous gesture of possessiveness. The male figure, although still intro-verted and self-negating, is no longer a skull-headed victim, and no longer a child. Gone is the oppressive bleakness and vicious caricature of the drawings of skeletal females. Gone, too, are the burned-out palette and furious brush strokes of Orozco. In their place are the luminous, self-confident colors of Picasso and Matisse. The vision is no longer nightmarish and claustrophobic, but suddenly spacious and brightly lit. To underscore the newfound sense of playfulness—an echo of the Miró retrospective he had seen earlier the same year—Jackson covered the canvas with a scrim of numbers, letters, lines, and doodles. Clearly an afterthought (some or all were added after the signature), these graffiti were probably a sly allusion to the automatist experiments going on in Matta's studio at the same time. Peter Busa, who saw the paintings at several stages, recalls that Jackson had originally included whole words, but later decided they were too distracting and used instead "arbitrary scribbles" and "numbers that he considered lucky" (especially 4 and 6, both of which had appeared recurrently in his street addresses).

An even more direct tribute to Lee is *Moon Woman*, a painting in which Jackson depicts the vulnerable, intimate face of female sexuality that Lee had shown him for the first time. The woman's head is gently rounded, her features inscribed in careful, Piccasoid profile. There are no bared teeth or wild eyes. One of her hands is drawn up toward her mouth in a gesture of apprehension or maidenly reticence. The other holds a flower. Instead of claws, she has plump, round fingers. Her body is a series of sensuous black lines draped in pinks and delicate shades of blue—baby, teal, sky, and aquamarine—surrounded by a sumptuously flattering field of raspberry shading to plum. On the left side of the canvas is a line of blue ovals, each inscribed with a simple design, laid out like a jeweler's assortment of cameos. After the bestiary of the Henderson drawings and the obscene earth mothers of earlier years, *Moon Woman* is an astonishingly tender and lyrical work, no doubt reflecting the sense of release and fulfillment that Jackson found in the first few months of life with Lee.

Sexual fulfillment also allowed Jackson to confront on canvas for the first time the most sensitive topic of all: his own sexual identity, the inner struggle between masculine and feminine imperatives that had been pulling him apart since Evelyn Porter's tea parties in Phoenix. In *Male and Female*, the confrontation is once again across a table. On either side, tall black figures face each other in a cubistic showdown. On the right, partially hidden behind a blackboard-like slab on which Jackson has painted more numbers, is a figure with the curvaceous breasts and pink skin of the Moon Woman as well as the grotesque Picassoid head with dangling jaw of the harpy in *Stenographic Figure*. But there is also a suggestion of genitals and an ejaculation. The figure on the left is equally ambiguous, with shapely breasts and luxurious lashes on its displaced Picassoid eyes, as well as testicles and an exuberantly long, flaccid penis. Only one thing is not at all ambiguous: Jackson's elation at having finally discovered his own potency. As the figure on the right ejaculates, a white column to the left shoots a celebratory jet of yellow, red, and black into the air where it spreads out like fireworks in a multicolored burst of automatist drips and splatters that hints—for the first time—at the great drip paintings to come.

The elation was short-lived. In December 1942, events in the outside world cut short Jackson's productive euphoria. After more than seven years, Franklin Roosevelt gave the WPA "an honorable discharge." The art projects had finally reached the end of the road. Within a few years, government warehouses would quietly begin auctioning off thousands of unallocated canvases *by the pound*, along with old copper and scrap iron. Murals were covered over with institutional green paint, lost, or in some cases indignantly destroyed, while easel paintings, according to one account, "went home with bureaucrats, to dank storerooms, or to incinerators." When a cache of hundreds of Project paintings, including several by Jackson, turned up at a secondhand store in Manhattan two years later, the news created a sensation. A plumber had bought the whole lot at government auction for four cents a pound, intending to use the canvas as pipe insulation. He sold it only when he discovered that "pipe heat and oil paint produced an unattractive smell." When they heard the news, artists, including Jackson, rushed to reclaim their works at three to five dollars apiece (twenty-five dollars for murals).

Both Lee and Jackson stuck with the Project to the bitter end. After finishing the department store window displays in October, Lee was given another project in the War Services Division designing posters for navy recruiting stations. She promptly retrieved Jackson from a Project sheet-metal training job in Brooklyn where he had spent a brief but humiliating eight days (at a forty dollar cut in salary), then recruited the rest of Matta's "workshop"—Peter Busa, Gerome Kamrowski, and Bill Baziotes—for her team. The result was "the most unregimented group of artists that you can imagine as far as carrying out a project," Busa recalls. "We spent most of our time making automatic drawings instead of war propaganda." Two months later, the pink slips came.

Despite all the warning signs and years of anticipation, few artists were really prepared for the end when it arrived. Many had forgotten what it was like to find and keep a regular job. The young ones had little or no memory of an art world without government largesse. In seven years, the art community and the Project had become almost synonymous. "The question on everybody's mind," recalls one artist, "was 'Is there life after the WPA?' "

Like many artists, Lee, Busa, and Baziotes opted for one of the government-sponsored vocational training programs designed to ease the transition from government payroll to the real working world. At a "salary" of seventeen dollars a week (about half what the projects paid), they enrolled in a mechanical drafting course at the New York Trade School on East Sixty-seventh Street in Manhattan. According to Lee, they were given "hunks of machinery" to draw and pages of lettering to copy. After years of creative freedom, it may have been witless drudgery, but at least it paid the rent.

That wasn't enough, however, to assuage Jackson's pride. Although assigned to a similar course in Brooklyn, he either never went, was fired, or quit after just a few days. When Stella came to visit in February, she found him unemployed and only planning "to take a course of some sort" at some future date. Still, Lee's seventeen dollars a week wasn't nearly enough to pay for rent, clothes, food, and materials. Although Jackson, like many artists, had liberated as much canvas and paint as he could from the WPA store before it closed (wrapping his legs with canvas and striding out with stiff-legged nonchalance), artists' supplies were becoming increasingly expensive as the war interrupted and diverted lines of supply. When he was reduced to shoplifting tubes of paint, even Jackson had to acknowledge that they were "dead broke" and that the only solution, however unpleasant, was to find a paying job.

Through his old Art Students League friend, Joe Meert, he landed a night job as a "squeegee man" silk-screening designs on lipstick tubes, neckties, scarves, and plates at Creative Printmakers, a breezeless back-room sweatshop on Eighteenth Street. Between financial need and affection for Meert, Jackson managed to struggle through two months of ink and noise while his consumption of alcohol soared and his productivity sank.

It was becoming increasingly clear that if Jackson was ever to be productive again, he had to find a reliable means of support. For a while, Lee hoped that she could provide it, but she lost her first drafting job after only five days and, according to her, "that was the end of that career." Besides, Jackson didn't want her to work. "Other artists were being supported by their wives," said Lee, "but Jackson didn't want me out working. He wanted me home." With Jackson unable to hold a job and paint at the same time, and Lee unemployed, there was only one solution: "Jackson was totally determined to live from the sale of his paintings," Lee recalled.

It was a preposterous notion. Apart from the Project, no American avant-garde artist had ever lived entirely on proceeds from the sale of his art. None had even tried. Most had other jobs—as dentists (Herbert Ferber, Seymour Lipton) or designers (Willem de Kooning, John Little)—or had wives with jobs (Adolph Gottlieb, Barnett Newman). A few, like Motherwell and Bultman, had family money. But no one had dared throw himself on the mercy of a "market" for contemporary American art that, in reality, didn't yet exist. The Project's stated aim of integrating the work of creative artists into America's daily life had failed miserably. In 1940, after five years of "education," the American public still spent less than $500,000 on contemporary art. The entire market—including the vast traditionalist establishment—supported only 150 American artists at a level of $2,000 a year or better. To make matters worse, by 1942, the influx of European masters had siphoned off what little interest there was in modern art. New York dealers, mostly Europeans themselves, fought for the privilege of representing the visitors. American museums like the Guggenheim and the Museum of Modern Art courted them. American collectors like the Reises and the Murphys threw parties for them, put them up, and bought their paintings. When Gypsy Rose Lee, the stripper-turned–national icon, began to collect modern art in the early forties, a friend recalls, "she wouldn't look at anything except Max Ernst."

In fact, for a young, avant-garde American artist looking to make a living from painting, there was only one place to turn. Only one person was a prominent collector and gallery owner with both the money and the bravery (or eccentricity) to buy paintings from relatively unknown artists—even American artists. That person was Peggy Guggenheim.

The role of savior of American avant-garde art was a new one for Peggy Guggenheim. Like many of the American elite at the time, she had spent most of her life in the thrall of European art—and European artists. The sole joy in a childhood otherwise "filled with torments" had been the trips that she and her father, Benjamin Guggenheim, had taken to Europe every summer. When Benjamin died on the *Titanic* in 1912, Peggy began a lifelong search, on the Continent they had shared, for a man to replace him. As soon as she could, she fled her family—"those stupid, staid, bourgeois people"—and her country to join the wave of expatriates who filled the cafés and nightclubs of Paris in the twenties. She frequented chic Montparnasse watering holes like the Dôme and the Rotonde, conspicuous in her long lamé dresses, with her shaved eyebrows, bobbed hair, and twenty-inch cigarette holder. Enchanted by her visits to the great salons of the day, she began holding her own salons at a Montparnasse studio. Julien Levy, who arrived one evening with Marcel Duchamp, found "the place was crowded. Hemingway, Pound, Cocteau, Gide . . . I don't know who all was there."

While in Paris, Peggy met and married Laurence Vail, a handsome, charming, volatile idler who carried an American passport but, having been born and educated on the Continent, "was more French than expatriate." Peggy called him "the King of Bohemia." Six years and two children later, she walked out of the marriage, fed up with Vail's spectacular public rages—he once attacked a chandelier in a restaurant—and his incestuous relationship with his sister, Clotilde. Within a year she had found a new lover, a Byronic, alcoholic Englishman named John Holms, whose accent "thrilled her." A talented writer and an even more talented conversationalist—"He talked like Socrates," Peggy bragged—Holms spent the next five years, the happiest of Peggy's life, alternately educating her and infuriating her with his drinking. When Holms died during a routine operation as a result of the interaction of anesthesia and alcohol, Peggy blamed herself: she had neglected to inform the doctors that he had been drinking the night before. "Everyone I love dies," she wailed.

After several more failed relationships, Peggy gave up on men—temporarily at least—and turned to art. Although she personally preferred the old masters, collecting them would have been unthinkably conventional. Avant-garde art, on the other hand, "carried with it the power to scandalize." With the help of Marcel Duchamp, she assembled a collection of abstract and Surrealist works

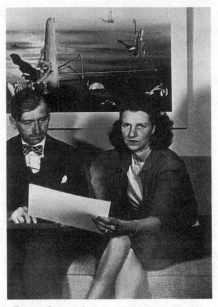

Peggy Guggenheim with Herbert Read in
front of a painting by Yves Tanguy, 1939

and, on January 24, 1938, opened her first gallery in London, Guggenheim Jeune.

A lover of eccentricity, Peggy was inexorably drawn to the high style and hedonistic excesses of the Surrealists, especially to a young, married painter named Yves Tanguy, who soon became her passion, both in art and in bed. (Peggy had notorious difficulty distinguishing between artists and their art.) "Tanguy really loved me," she insisted in her memoirs, "and if he had been less of a baby I would have married him . . . but I needed a father, not another son." She also reported affairs with Roland Penrose, the wealthy English writer and artist (who, according to Peggy, would only sleep with a woman if he could bind her wrists—"It was extremely uncomfortable to spend the night this way, but if you spent it with Penrose it was the only way") and Samuel Beckett, a green-eyed Irishman whose poetry Peggy considered "childish."

After several years of financial losses, Peggy decided to close Guggenheim Jeune and open a museum instead. "I felt that if I was losing that money I might as well lose a lot more and do something worthwhile," she said. Incapable of halfway enthusiasms and never shy about seeking advice, she enlisted the help of the leading British art critic, Herbert Read, as well as Nellie van Doesberg, widow of the de Stijl painter Theo, and Howard Putzel, a young American dealer, and began acquiring paintings for the planned museum at a rate approaching one a day. Never as wealthy as her family name promised, she set a limit of $10,000 for any single painting, and often bought works directly from her artist friends for less than $1,000. Like her father, she could be both generous and inexplicably parsimonious in her personal life. Other than sex, art was her only indulgence. "She allowed herself one dress a year and she paid no more than $125," recalls her friend and, briefly, paramour David Porter. "She wore the same pair of dirty tan boots and one dress at openings for a whole year. She spent her money by giving it to artists and buying pictures, and I admired her enormously for that."

The approaching war put an end to Peggy's plans for a museum (she worried that the Germans would bomb her paintings) and eventually drove her from Paris, along with her Surrealist friends. Before leaving, she tried to place her paintings in the safekeeping of officials at the Louvre, but "they decided that my collection wasn't worth the trouble of saving," she recalled. For Peggy, as for Europe, the threat of war had made it impossible to ignore the United States any longer. She had not been home since the death of her favorite sister, Benita, in 1927, and had vowed she would never return. But the necessities of war overrode old wounds. In early 1941, she packed up her collection and shipped it to New York marked as "household goods."

But she still wasn't ready to return. *Anyplace* in Europe, she seemed to feel, was better than America. With her entourage, she repaired to Marseilles in Vichy France, where much of the Surrealist community (Breton, Masson, Brauner, Dominguez, Lam) had gathered in a dilapidated villa for a last stand against exile. There, on the eve of America's entry into the war, she fell in love with yet another European artist, the German Surrealist Max Ernst—a suave, "exquisitely-made" man ten years her senior. "He had white hair and big blue eyes," she later wrote of Ernst, who often painted threatening birds, "and a handsome beak-like nose resembling a bird's."

Finally, on July 13, 1941, Peggy flew from Lisbon to New York aboard the Pan-American Clipper. She brought with her the flesh-and-blood souvenirs of her European happiness: her ex-husband, Vail; their two children, Sindbad and Pegeen; her mentor Breton (separately by ship, via Martinique); and her lover, Ernst. (As a German national in America on the eve of war, Ernst proved to be an embarrassment—although Peggy didn't embarrass easily. After Pearl Harbor and the declaration of war on Germany, she married him. "I did not like the idea of living in sin with an enemy alien," she quipped.)

From the moment she arrived, Peggy treated New York more like a hotel than a home. Surrounded by Surrealists, she set out to recreate on the new continent the life-style she had been forced to abandon on the old.

In a city awash with refugees, it was a relatively easy task. On an East Side cul-de-sac, she found a huge town house overlooking the East River. Distorted through the old panes of a big bay window in the baronial two-story living room, Fifty-first Street could have been London's Cork Street or the Boulevard Montparnasse. There, amid round-the-clock revelers, surrounded once again by her beloved art collection, she picked up where she had left off. In shoe-black hair, blood-red lipstick, lizard-green eye shadow, and huge unmatched earrings (her clothes artfully torn to show she had nothing on underneath), she moved among her guests offering cheap whiskey, potato chips, and outrageous commentary. Around her, knots of guests complained in overheated French about American food and longed for the day when they could return to France; Breton choreographed his vicious games; and Ernst sat in his ornately carved ten-foot Victorian throne in front of the bay window, looking, according to one guest, "Mephistophelean." The local press, thoroughly beguiled, referred to the house as "Surrealism's headquarters" in America and dubbed Peggy its "financial angel." "She practically supports the group by collecting its pictures," wrote a reporter for *Time* magazine, "[and] plans next fall to open a Manhattan museum where they can be shown."

The projected gallery was, in fact, a revival of the earlier plans for a London museum, which had been so rudely interrupted by the war. And Peggy saw no reason to change anything just because she was in America. It was, from beginning to end, a European project. Ernst and Breton would serve as advisers; Ernst's son, Jimmy, would be her secretary; and Frederick Kiesler, the Romanian-born "impresario without portfolio," who had been in the United States since 1926, would design the gallery. Within this inner circle, Howard Putzel was the sole American.

For the double loft that Peggy found over a grocery store on West Fifty-seventh Street, Kiesler designed a space as insular and self-contained as Peggy's apartment. All views of New York were banished. Skylights and windows were blacked out. Materials were chosen without regard to wartime shortages (or, to Peggy's chagrin, expense): linen, gumwood, fluorescent lights. Kiesler's goal was to "break down the physical and mental barriers which separate people from the art they live with." Paintings were stripped of their frames, suspended away from the walls, thrust toward the viewer on sawed-off baseball bats, and propped up on movable stands. The walls themselves, made of movable canvas panels, curved and bulged indeterminately in the background to avoid defining the space or providing a static reference point. All this would allow the paintings to "interact" with their environment while the gallery itself remained oblivious both to place and time, to America and to the war.

Peggy's goal was to open the gallery with "as thorough a sample of modern masters as possible." Using the list prepared by Read and van Doesburg in Paris, and accompanied by Ernst, Breton, and Putzel, she descended on the New York galleries. In weeks of shopping, she added to her already impressive collection of works by Duchamp, de Chirico, Miró, Malevich, Archipenko, Giacometti, Klee, Lipchitz, Ozenfant, and Tanguy. For breadth, she threw in an early Cubist Picasso and a Mondrian gouache. As for American artists, she bought only one piece by her longtime friend and jeweler, Alexander Calder (whom she had met in Paris and didn't consider American at all), and one work by the abstract painter John Ferren, whose wife, Inez, was publishing the catalogue for the opening.

Like the show it documented, the catalogue was a tour de force of European chauvinism. Breton wrote a lengthy introductory essay on the "great physico-mental stream of *Surrealism*"—in French, of course—which Vail translated into faithfully overheated English. Breton also contributed the idea of including pictures of the eyes of each of the artists represented in the show (to underscore his theory that reality is not as important as how the artist *views* reality) and wrote a brief biographical sketch to accompany each grainy photograph of bushy eyebrows. The catalogue also included a short preface by Jean Arp, articles by Ernst and the English sculptor Ben Nicholson, and, again for balance, a short piece by Mondrian, a Futurist manifesto, and a Realistic manifesto. Ernst designed the cover and Vail contributed the title: "Art of This Century." Peggy liked it so much that she adopted it for the gallery itself. As a last, poignant touch, Peggy dedicated the catalogue to her English lover John Holms, who had been dead for almost nine years.

The opening of the Art of This Century gallery on October 20, 1942, was an unalloyed triumph. Except for the pulsating lights that made it hard to see the paintings and "drove people crazy," Kiesler had accomplished the seemingly impossible: he had outdone the Surrealists' First Papers exhibit at the Whitelaw Reid mansion the week before. The wall-to-wall opening-night crowd milled through his creation, dodging paintings, toasting Peggy, and exclaiming their admiration, usually in French. They stared at Kiesler's "seven-way" chairs, upholstered in bright shades of linoleum, which could be used as seats or tables or lecterns or easels; at the turquoise floors and sail-like walls; and at the "kinetic gallery," a kind of penny arcade of contraptions, including a conveyor belt of paintings by Paul Klee—push a button, see a Klee—a giant pinwheel of Duchamp's works, and a shadow box containing a portrait of Breton. Someone dubbed it "Coney Island."

The press, invited to a special preview, responded with ambivalent delirium. "Surrealist Circus!" cried the *Mercury*. "Isms Rampant," headlined *Newsweek*. One writer described it as "a sort of blend between an alchemist's dream, a nightmare, and a first-class hangover." Even when the reviewers were skeptical, they were never, never bored. "My eyes have never bulged further from their sockets than at this show," wrote the New York *Sun* reviewer. It was exactly the kind of breakthrough Peggy had hoped for. In a wartime world starved for extravagance, she and her European entourage had startled the art community to attention. "She made a big impression," Julien Levy conceded enviously. "[She] got here at a time when everything was ready to burst."

The gallery may have been a triumph for Peggy, but for most American artists, it was yet another defeat. They, too, were electrified by Kiesler's audacious design. (After surviving for a decade on the hardtack proletarian galleries of the Depression, they welcomed the indulgence.) "When you walked into Art of This Century," recalls Reuben Kadish, "you knew there wasn't any other place in New York that supplied as much energy and as much vigor." But their exhilaration was edged with despair: not a single member of their ranks was represented in Peggy's "thorough sampling of modern art." (John Ferren, the lone American on view, had spent most of the 1930s in Paris.) Even the First

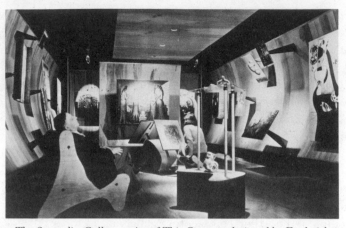

The Surrealist Gallery at Art of This Century, designed by Frederick
Kiesler, who is seated at left in one of his seven-way chairs.

Papers show had included a few token American artists. Peggy had promised that her gallery would be a "research laboratory for new ideas," that it would "serve the future instead of recording the past." Did that mean that American art had no place in the future? Breton and Ernst apparently thought so, and Peggy, with all the authority of her new position, seemed to agree. As thrilled as American artists were with the triumph of Art of This Century, they had to wonder if they would ever get to share in the glory.

In fact, even as she moved among the delighted patrons on opening night in her white dress and unmatched earrings (one by Calder, one by Tanguy), Peggy was already growing disenchanted with her European mentors. Her restless eye was already scanning for something new—an art, an artist, a lover. Perhaps all three. She never bothered with fine distinctions.

It's difficult to know when the estrangement began. Having been raised by a philandering father, a "dizzy" mother, and a series of sadistic nannies, Peggy had always been susceptible to resentment, distrust, infidelity, and fear of infidelity. Sooner or later, they poisoned all her relationships—with movements as well as with men. She was always either deliriously happy or deeply disenchanted with the present. The first overt sign of souring in her decade-long infatuation with the European Surrealists was a dispute over an advertisement for her gallery in Breton's journal, *VVV*. In anticipation of the opening, Ernst had promised her free space in exchange for her generous patronage, but Breton, whom she was supporting at the time, reneged, explaining that *he* "had sacrificed to truth, beauty and art" so why shouldn't she? Peggy was livid at the ingratitude. Her daughter Pegeen, equally incensed, called the Surrealists *"mesquin"* (cheap), an accusation that Breton considered a serious breach of decorum coming from a seventeen-year-old girl. The skirmish resulted in the cancellation of a show of *VVV* covers scheduled at Art of This Century in March

1943. In the show that she hastily assembled to fill the gap, Peggy pointedly included three works by Breton's nemesis, Salvador Dali.

But the rift ran far deeper than money. The tiff with Breton may have disappointed and embittered her, but Max Ernst's infidelity broke her heart. She had steadfastly refused to see it coming, although their marriage had never been the mad flight of passion that Peggy longed for. "She was in love with him," recalls Ethel Baziotes, "whereas he respected her and found her interesting. Their temperaments were too violently opposed." In the summer of 1942, unknown to Peggy, Ernst had rented a house in Amagansett, Long Island, where he met secretly with a beautiful young American Surrealist painter named Dorothea Tanning. By the time the gallery opened in October, Peggy could read her fate in Ernst's lethargy—he seldom arose before she left in the morning. In retaliation, she set about seducing Marcel Duchamp, whose priestly detachment alternately aroused and infuriated her. By all accounts, except Peggy's, the attempt failed, giving her yet another reason to divorce the Surrealists. In December, Ernst took personal charge of selecting the paintings to be included in a show entitled "31 Women" scheduled for January. Peggy was later able to joke that the exhibition should have been limited to thirty. One of the thirty-one was Dorothea Tanning.

By March of 1943, Ernst had moved out. Between Ernst's departure and Breton's enmity, most of the Surrealist circle deserted Peggy's big town house on the river. Only five months after their triumphant show, she and her favored coterie of European artists had separated in recrimination and disillusionment. Her situation was much like that of American artists who had embraced the Europeans on arrival, only to reject them on closer inspection. Thus, when the critic Klaus Mann (son of Thomas Mann) launched a blistering assault on the Surrealists in the February 1943 issue of *American Mercury,* calling them "parlor anarchists" and claiming that the entire movement was a sham, it was no surprise that Peggy failed to leap to their defense. "I am not the supporter of surrealism," she wrote in a letter to *Art Digest,* "neither am I its defender."

With the departure of Ernst and Breton, Peggy was forced to turn elsewhere for guidance. James Johnson Sweeney, who would soon become chairman of the painting and sculpture department at the Museum of Modern Art, was promoted to the unofficial position of chief spiritual adviser, but remained aloof from gallery affairs. Howard Putzel, an extraordinarily knowledgeable and peripatetic impresario of young American artists, replaced Jimmy Ernst as Peggy's secretary, factotum, and "whipping boy." Matta, whose close association with American artists saved him from being tarred with Breton's brush, became the sole "European" Surrealist in Peggy's inner circle. (It was during this period that Peggy expressed interest in Matta's plan for a show of "American automatists.") Together, Sweeney, Putzel, and Matta pushed Peggy and Art of This Century in a radically new direction. For the first time, she sought out young American artists whose works she considered Surrealist in spirit.

She also began to reevaluate, in light of her changing tastes, the works of American painters whom she had dismissed only a few months before. Among these was Jackson Pollock.

Dismissing Jackson in the early forties was easy to do. Unlike the paintings of Matta and Masson, Jackson's works didn't enjoy the flattering light of Breton's theories. Nor were they finely crafted objects like the hand-painted dream photographs of Dali or the near academic canvases of Magritte. They weren't exquisitely modulated like Tanguy's dream landscapes or elegantly composed like Miró's abstract "magnetic fields." Although Jackson was far from a theorist, his paintings took the theory of "automatism," with its emphasis on spontaneity, psychic energy, and unconscious imagery, very seriously, and they demanded the same of the viewer. "You had to work to like them," recalls Peter Busa, "they were not easy paintings." Jimmy Ernst called them "shocking." "But the closer you looked and the more you thought about them," says Busa, "the more you saw and the better they looked." To those who still clung, furtively or unconsciously, to old notions of elegance, accomplishment, and style, however, Jackson's dense, turbulent, rough-hewn canvases remained an acquired taste.

Sweeney had first brought Jackson's work to Peggy's attention in early 1942. That spring, Herbert Matter, an old friend, had approached him brimming with enthusiasm (a comparatively agitated state for the restrained Matter) after a visit to Jackson's studio. Sweeney's response was polite but noncommittal. "He was a little like Calder," Matter remembers. "If it didn't come from Europe, he wasn't interested. . . . He wouldn't promise anything, just that he would go look." (Sweeney remembers agreeing only because "Matter and I looked at pictures the same way.") After visiting Jackson's studio, Sweeney reported back to Peggy: "I told her I thought this man was doing interesting work." He may even have introduced her to Jackson at the time, but once that was done he considered his duty to Matter discharged. "It was between Peggy and [Jackson] after that," he says. In the spring of 1942, of course, Peggy had other art and other artists on her mind, especially Max Ernst. She didn't forget the encounter—David Porter remembers that when Jackson's name came up in conversation, she commented, "Sweeney tells me he's a very important artist"—but neither did she pursue it.

The next voice that whispered "Pollock" in Peggy's ear was Howard Putzel's. No one would have a more critical or more unsung role in Jackson's career than Putzel, an overweight, alcoholic, epileptic homosexual with a passion for art and an unerring eye for quality. Behind the cigarette holder and owlish glasses, beyond the weakness for martinis and gourmet meals, lurked a Promethean enthusiasm for modern art. "He paid twenty dollars a month, but he simply had to have the picture," recalled Julien Levy, from whom Putzel bought a very early Gorky painting. In conversation, he often choked on his own ardor, stuttering uncontrollably as his fat cheeks turned crimson. Despite ill health, poverty, and a troubled personal life—including a wealthy mother who considered him "an insane and embarrassing nuisance" and refused to support him—Putzel managed Peggy's affairs and the gallery with frantic efficiency. Peggy showed her gratitude by abusing him relentlessly ("she treated him like a slave," recalled her son, Sindbad), but that was part of the odd bond that held them together.

Jackson met Putzel in the summer of 1942 during a brief visit to New York by Reuben Kadish. Putzel and Kadish had known each other in Los Angeles where Putzel, a New Jersey native raised in San Francisco, ran a gallery on Hollywood Boulevard—the successor to Lorser Feitelson's Hollywood Gallery of Modern Art. As early as 1934, Putzel had alerted the small and close-knit Los Angeles art community to Surrealism and by 1937 was selling works by Tanguy, Ernst, and Miró to his gallery's small clientele of "movie people." Unfortunately, even Hollywood wasn't yet ready for Putzel's modernist vision, so in 1938 he closed his gallery and traveled to Paris, where he met Peggy.

Of all the people who later claimed to have recognized Jackson's genius on first sight, Howard Putzel was one of the few who did. According to Reuben Kadish, Putzel used the word "genius" the minute he saw Jackson's paintings. He used it again soon afterward in a letter to Gordon Onslow-Ford. "He wrote to me that he had discovered an American genius," recalled Onslow-Ford. "It was Jackson Pollock." Inevitably, the word soon found its way to Peggy—Putzel was incapable of suppressing his enthusiasm—but once again she turned a deaf ear. Putzel persisted, showing her some of Jackson's work and perhaps pointing out his contribution to the "Artists for Victory" show that ran at the Metropolitan Museum throughout 1942—all to no effect. Even a favorable recommendation from Matta, whose "workshop" Jackson was attending during this period, apparently drew a blank. Jackson's conspicuous absence from the First Papers of Surrealism at the Whitelaw Reid mansion didn't help Putzel's case. In fact, of all the young Americans, Peggy's personal favorite was Baziotes, whose work had been "approved" by Breton and included in the First Papers show.

After the departure of Breton and Ernst in March 1943, Putzel gingerly proposed Jackson's name for inclusion in the upcoming international collage show scheduled at Art of This Century in April. This time, Peggy agreed. Besides, she had already solicited a collage from Gypsy Rose Lee. How could she say yes to a striptease artist and no to Putzel's genius?

Jackson's contribution to the collage show, prepared alongside Motherwell and since lost, earned a favorable word from Peggy's friendly critic at the *Nation*, Jean Connolly. But Putzel had grander plans for Jackson. As soon as the collage show closed, he persuaded Peggy to revive Herbert Read's proposal, formulated for the London museum, for a "Spring Salon for Young Artists." In its revived form, the show would be made up almost exclusively of American artists, a sign of how far Peggy, with Putzel's nudging, had come in the seven months since the gallery's opening. Except for Marcel Duchamp and Piet

Mondrian, even the judges would be American: Sweeney, Soby, Putzel, and Guggenheim. The rules were simple: any artist under thirty-five could submit works to the panel (although rumors persisted that Peggy "edited" the submissions before the jury saw them). From the works submitted, the judges would choose the best forty or fifty, using a voting system designed to eliminate biases. As soon as the competition was announced in *Art Digest*, the floodgates of Greenwich Village opened. Artists who had been locked out of the gallery world for years lined up outside 30 West Fifty-seventh Street with canvases under their arms. Howard Putzel spared Jackson that indignity by coming to the Eighth Street apartment and selecting the paintings he thought Jackson should submit, one of which was *Stenographic Figure*.

But Putzel's scheming was in vain. No matter how carefully or how often he led Peggy to the well, she steadfastly refused to drink. When presented with *Stenographic Figure*, she dismissed it as "dreadful." On the day the jury met to make their selections, her only thought of Jackson was how Putzel and Matta would react when none of his paintings made the final cut, as she was sure they wouldn't.

Mondrian was the first of the jurors to arrive—he wanted to have plenty of time to give every work fair consideration—and while Peggy and Putzel rushed about with last-minute arrangements, he began to examine the entries that Peggy had arrayed against the walls of the gallery. Tall and professorial in a double-breasted suit and horn-rimmed glasses, he walked slowly from painting to painting. When he came upon *Stenographic Figure*, he stopped and stroked his chin. Looking over, Peggy saw him "rooted" in front of the Pollock and rushed to apologize. "Pretty awful, isn't it?" she said, more as a statement than a question. "That's not painting, is it?" Mondrian didn't reply. A few minutes later, he was still staring at the Pollock. Peggy, increasingly uneasy, felt called on to elaborate her opinion. "There is absolutely no discipline at all. This young man has serious problems . . . and painting is one of them. I don't think he's going to be included." Mondrian stroked his chin a few more times. "I'm not so sure," he finally said. "I'm trying to understand what's happening here. I think this is the most interesting work I've seen so far in America. . . . You must watch this man."

Peggy was stunned. "You can't be serious," she said. "You can't compare this and the way you paint." Mondrian responded patiently, as if instructing a student, "The way I paint and the way I think are two different things."

Peggy protested no further. What was gibberish from Putzel was gospel from Mondrian. After almost two years of resisting Jackson's art, she was converted in a matter of minutes. As each juror entered the room, she pulled him over to the Pollock and said, "Look what an exciting new thing we have here!" (Years later, Peggy would boast, "Pollock was easily accepted by me. His art was so overwhelming and wonderful I loved it right away." It would be easy to see cynicism or mercantile savvy, or both, in Peggy's reversal, but Jimmy Ernst, who witnessed the scene, had a more sympathetic view. "She was willing to listen, she was willing to be told, she was willing to see. . . . There was nothing phony about it.")

The oft-repeated story of what Lee Krasner later called "Mondrian's nod," soon worked its way into Pollock legend: the septuagenarian dean of abstract art had reached across a vast ideological gulf and embraced the young American expressionist. It was the ultimate endorsement. Of all the European masters, only the titan himself, Picasso, could have pronounced a more compelling judgment. For American artists, the story came to signify the passing of the true flame of abstraction from the old world to the new. It also seemed to foreshadow the coming alliance between abstractionists and disenchanted Surrealists. Peggy Guggenheim, the wife of Max Ernst and patroness of Breton, had agreed with Mondrian, the founder of de Stijl, about a painting by Jackson Pollock. From such an unlikely conjunction, a new movement was bound to spring.

As grandly satisfying as it was, the tale of Mondrian's nod was, in fact, only half the story.

Mondrian had not come to Peggy's gallery that day purely in the spirit of accommodation. He had accepted the invitation to serve on the jury only because he feared that his protégé and sponsor, Harry Holtzman, who was on the West Coast when the salon was announced, would not be treated fairly by the other jurors, especially Peggy. It was the least he could do for Holtzman, a Hofmann student who had rescued him from a desperate, impoverished existence in a Paris garret in 1940. ("I would be dead now, if it were not for Harry," Mondrian would gently insist.) "He wrote me," recalls Holtzman, "and said the only reason he was on the jury was that he wanted to be sure I would be in [the show], because Peggy didn't like the kind of thing I did." With the help of Fritz Glarner, a Swiss émigré artist who also considered the elderly Dutchman his "master," Mondrian retrieved one of Holtzman's sculptures from storage and submitted it to the jury.

On the morning of the selection, he was apparently determined to teach the iconoclastic Mrs. Ernst a lesson in impartial judging. By selecting a painting that was outside the well-known parameters of his own taste and by defending it, he could demonstrate the kind of open-mindedness he expected Peggy to accord Holtzman. Nothing, of course, violated his tenets more egregiously, or better demonstrated his open-mindedness, than Pollock's frenetic, graffiti-covered canvas. Jimmy Ernst recalls Mondrian elaborating his defense of Pollock's work with a pointed plea for tolerance. "Everybody assumes that I am interested only in what I do in my work," he reportedly said to Peggy, "[but] there are so many things in life and in art that can and should be respected." The subtle stratagem worked. The jury "respected" both Holtzman's sculpture and *Stenographic Figure*.

To Peggy's delight, so did the critics. "For once the future reveals a gleam of hope," wrote her friend Jean Connolly in the *Nation*. Of the thirty-three artists represented in the show, she said, "They are all promising," although she did single out works by Matta, Motherwell, and several others as "paintings it would be a pleasure to own"—a friendly bow to Peggy's commercial imperatives. "There is a large Jackson Pollack [sic]," Connolly added, "which, I am told, made the jury starry-eyed." It was a comment that sounded better than it was. Either she had no opinion of her own, or she chose to withhold it and preserve the appearance of enthusiasm by substituting a bit of pre-show publicity, undoubtedly supplied by Peggy. Writing in the New Yorker, Robert Coates was both more enthusiastic and less circumspect. Recognizing that the show was split between "those twin branches of advanced modern painting, abstractionism and surrealism," he saw Jackson's work, "with its curious reminiscences of Matisse and Miró," as the most promising hybrid on view. "We have a real discovery," he concluded.

Jackson was elated. "Things really broke with the showing of that painting," he wrote Charles proudly in July. Even more thrilling than Coates's review was the story of Mondrian's nod, which he heard from Putzel. "I was there when Jackson heard it, for Christ's sake," says Reuben Kadish, "and I remember how excited he was that it was Mondrian who had made the decisive move, that Mondrian had picked him. He was so excited, he was like a kid."

But excitement didn't pay the rent.

For a lucky few, Art of This Century's first season brought some financial as well as critical success. Motherwell sold his collage for $85. Baziotes's two paintings in the Spring Salon were bought for $150 each. But Jackson wasn't so lucky. Mondrian may have nodded at Stenographic Figure, but he didn't buy it, and neither did anybody else. The financial slide that had begun in January continued into the spring. In April, Jackson was still working nights at the silk-screening shop, growing more depressed with each passing week; Lee was still in training to be a draftsman; and Peggy Guggenheim had yet to buy her first Pollock painting. Despite Putzel's optimism, the day when Jackson could support himself on his painting seemed further away than ever.

Jackson found temporary relief when a job opened up at the Museum of Non-Objective Painting, the new home of the Guggenheim collection, where his friends Sam Fabean and Robert De Niro worked. Museum policy was to hire young artists to fill all staff positions, from manager to janitor, provided they strictly adhered to nonobjective principles. To help Jackson over that hurdle, De Niro had developed a method for "forging" nonobjective drawings that would satisfy the museum's requirements. "He would make pastiches out of reproductions of works in the museum collection," recalls a friend, "and then copy them in drawings."

With or without De Niro's help, Jackson quickly produced a sheaf of nonobjective drawings and, on April 14, took them to an interview with the museum's director, the eccentric Baroness Hilla Rebay, who, in a heavy German accent, pronounced them either "cosmic" or "nicht cosmic." When he returned home, Lee helped draft an ingratiating note ("I have been very interested in the work you have been doing, and the Museum of Non-objective Art, for some time . . ."), which closed with a heavy-handed hint ("I would like to continue working in this [nonobjective] direction, but find it impossible at this time as I am working at night with little energy left for painting and drawing during the day light"). For good measure, Jackson included a hastily composed "biography," the sole purpose of which was to repeat the code words that De Niro had coached him to use: "subjective spacial," "spacial intensity," and, as often as possible, "non-objective." Transparent as it was, the strategy worked. Rebay immediately sent a check to help pay for art supplies, and, after receiving another obsequious letter, offered Jackson a position as "custodian and preparator of paintings." He began work on Saturday, May 8.

As his father had discovered more than a decade earlier, Jackson Pollock was ill suited to the rigors of regular employment in every way. But working for the Baroness Rebay wasn't regular employment; it was a trip through the looking glass.

Founded only four years before, the museum was a trysting gift from the aging copper tycoon Solomon Guggenheim to his improbable mistress, the Baroness Rebay. Instead of minks and jewels, he bought her works by Kandinsky, Klee, Vlaminck, Chagall, Arp, Moholy-Nagy, Delaunay, Campendonck and, her own personal favorite, Rudolf Bauer—known to the staff as "Bubbles Bauer" for the candy-colored circles that were his trademark. She displayed most of her baubles (the objective paintings remained in the Guggenheim suite at the Plaza) in a converted two-story automobile showroom at 24 East Fifty-fourth Street. The walls, windows, and couches were all covered in gray flannel; the air filled with Bach. A guard stood at the tunnel-like entrance and a receptionist sat at the front desk to answer questions. All this, according to one staffer, to service "about two visitors a day."

Every morning the baroness, a short, stout woman, would arrive with the latest copy of *Modern Screen Romance* under her arm, "very well dressed but always a little unkempt," carrying her lapdog and spitting orders in Katzenjammer English. She was usually followed by Bauer, a comic-book "Junker general" in dove gray spats, white linen shirt, gold cuff links, and ascot tie. The baroness had rewarded his "execrable" art with such misguided largesse that he now lived in "baronial splendor on the Jersey shore" and often came in to see the museum's growing collection of his work. As the baroness and her entourage passed, the guard at the door would alert the rest of the staff. She had been known to discharge people for recommending visits to other galleries, for marrying without her permission, even for painting an objective picture. With employees and artists alike, "she was a Nazi," recalls Lucia Salemme, the gallery's receptionist when Jackson began work there. She hired spies to monitor conversations between employees and "write down what visitors and staffers were saying about the collection." An artist herself, she felt free to "improve" canvases submitted to her by young artists by adding a triangle here or a spot there. The staff responded to her Prussian rule with relentless guerrilla warfare. "Everyone made faces and jumped around and clowned behind her back," recalls Salemme, "and they made fun of some of the art she had, especially the Bauers and Rebays." When a wall sculpture by Moholy-Nagy fell and broke, one staff member, mistaking the pile of fragments for trash, simply "swept it up and threw it away," recalls Leland Bell, who worked as a guard at the front door. Bell, whose real job was to keep the baroness supplied with movie magazines, once greeted a visitor by gleefully calling out to the staff, "We have another inmate!" Another time, he slipped a Bing Crosby record into the sound system, interrupting the Bach and igniting the baroness.

For the first few months on the job, Jackson worked the noon-to-six shift, confined to the basement, building and repairing the massive wooden frames (called "baguettes") in which the baroness encased her Kandinskys and Bauers. Except when he cleaned, hung pictures, or ran the service elevator, he seldom had a chance to participate in the antics upstairs. Every day at lunchtime, Bell would retreat to the basement and the two would argue good-naturedly for exactly half an hour. "He would ridicule Arp," Bell recalls. He'd say, 'I could do an Arp easy!' He made faces about Mondrian and he hated Klee, especially, because Klee only did little works, nothing big." Bell's visits were Jackson's only release. He rarely saw De Niro, who had the night shift as janitor and watchman, or Jean Xceron, who worked alone in the storehouse. The work was easy, if boring, but Jackson resented the imposition nonetheless. Because he seldom rose before ten or eleven in the morning, it effectively robbed him of the prime daylight painting hours while leaving his evenings perilously free. The night silk-screening job had at least kept him occupied during the hours when he always found it easiest to drink—not that he found it hard at any hour.

Meanwhile, he waited for some word from Peggy Guggenheim. In early June, the Spring Salon began its third week and there were still no sales. He took some solace in the fact that the Baroness had decided to boycott the show. According to Bell, Jackson lived in terror of being found out as a "figurative" painter. "He worried a lot about losing his job over that," says Bell.

The combination of uncertainty about the future and long stretches of tedious, lonely work took its toll. One night, De Niro came in late for his shift and discovered that a slop-sink faucet had been left on, the elevator pit and parts of the basement were already flooded, and Jackson was nowhere to be found. On another occasion, the baroness tongue-lashed the staff "for leaving the basement cluttered" and demanded that it be cleaned up before they left that night. When several staff members returned to the museum after supper to do the job, they found Jackson "drunk and wrecking the whole basement, throwing furniture around like a maniac."

Finally, in mid-June, Putzel stopped by Jackson's studio to deliver some good news: Peggy was coming to visit.

Putzel had worked too hard for too long to leave anything about the meeting to chance. He started coming by the Eighth Street apartment every night, often staying for dinner, to brief Jackson on a subject that Putzel knew better than anybody: Peggy Guggenheim. "He told Jackson what to do, and how to be-have," Lee remembered. "Jackson was thoroughly prepared."

Or so Putzel thought. Unfortunately, the day Peggy had chosen to visit, Wednesday, June 23, also happened to be the day of Peter Busa's wedding. Jackson would have to rush back from the ceremony to keep the appointment. Even from a distance, Lee saw trouble coming: a crowd of people, free liquor, professional anxiety—it all added up to disaster, and she begged Jackson to skip the wedding. When he refused, she resolved to shepherd him there and back rather than wait for Peggy by herself. Not until they arrived at the house on Fifteenth Street where the ceremony was to take place did Lee discover that Jackson was to be best man. Otherwise, the afternoon unfolded exactly accord-ing to her worst nightmares. Surrounded by drinkers and semi-strangers—the guests, all in suits, included Gerome Kamrowski, Fritz Bultman, Tony Smith, and Tennessee Williams—Jackson camped beside the bar. By the time the ceremony began, he was reeling. During the vows, he was heard to mumble, "What a dumb thing, to get married," and just before the Unitarian minister called for the ring, he passed out. With infinite composure, Lee stepped for-ward, pried the ring from his fingers, and handed it to Busa.

But the problems had just begun. After getting Jackson on his feet, she guided him unsteadily back to Eighth Street, hoping the walk would clear his head. When they arrived, however, he was still woozy and incoherent and Peggy was due any minute. With mounting desperation, she dragged him to the nearby Waldorf Cafeteria and force-fed him coffee. (In Lee's hilariously sanitized retelling of the story, "[Jackson] suggested that Krasner accompany him to the corner drugstore for a cup of coffee.") The moment he was coherent and self-supporting, she hustled him back to the apartment.

Just as they reached the stoop, Peggy burst from the front door of the build-ing "almost incoherent" with rage. Striking a pose of epic suffering against the stair rail and looking like an avant-garde Medea in unmatched earrings, tat-tered dress, and ankle socks—giving a full view of her unshaven legs—she cursed the five flights of steps she had just climbed in vain, bewailed her weak ankles, and bitterly denounced those, particularly Putzel and Lee, who had made her suffer such an indignity. Only after fifteen or twenty minutes of coaxing by both Lee and Jackson (who had sobered up quickly at the sight of Peggy) did she agree to climb back up to the studio and look at the paintings. Inside the apartment, the first thing she saw was a group of paintings signed "L.K." (To save money, Lee had recently relinquished her Ninth Street studio and was storing her paintings in Jackson's apartment.) "L.K. L.K. Who the hell is L.K.?" Peggy snapped impatiently. "I didn't come to look at L.K.'s paintings."

Peggy showed somewhat more enthusiasm for Jackson's work—she was particularly taken by a gouache drawing, *Burning Landscape*, which she later bought—but she still had reservations. Putzel had been urging her to give Jackson a "solo" show at the Art of This Century. Such a bold gesture would

have signaled not only her support for Jackson's art but also her break from
the European Surrealists and her newfound interest in American art in general.
She had already taken the first tentative steps in that direction with a late 1942
show featuring the works of the American Surrealist Joseph Cornell and, in
February, with a solo exhibition for the French abstractionist Jean Hélion. But
to feature Jackson, who was neither a Surrealist *nor* a European, would be to
step beyond the point of no return. Although still partial to Baziotes's work, she
had managed by now to internalize Mondrian's assessment of *Stenographic
Figure*. According to Lee, she called it "the most beautiful painting done in
America." As of June 23, however, she still wasn't ready to take that last step.
Instead, she told Lee and Jackson before leaving that she would send Marcel
Duchamp to look at the paintings. His reaction would settle the matter once
and for all.

It was not an encouraging prospect. As Putzel had no doubt already told
Jackson, Duchamp's reaction to *Stenographic Figure* had been anything but
enthusiastic. Since then, Jackson had encountered the fifty-six-year-old Duchamp only once, at Art of This Century, soon after the show closed. In a rage,
he had ripped a copy of Duchamp's salon poster from the wall, torn it up, rolled
it into a ball, handed it to the stunned Duchamp, and said with a snarl, "You
know where this goes."

The next day Jackson returned to the museum and shared his anxieties with
Leland Bell. "He wasn't very optimistic about his chances with Duchamp,"
Bell remembers, "and even if Duchamp said yes and Peggy Guggenheim gave
him the show, worried that it might flop, and then the baroness would find out
he wasn't really a nonobjective artist and he would be fired." Only a few weeks
later, *Bell* was fired after one of the baroness's spies overheard him recommending to a visitor a Mondrian show at another gallery. Jackson was brought
up from the basement and given Bell's old job as guard and doorman, a move
that put him back into contact with sunlight and people. By now, however, he
was too anxiety-ridden to care. "He didn't fraternize with anybody," recalls
Lucia Salemme. "He gave the impression of being a loner. He seemed very
secretive—like he had other fish to fry."

In early July, Duchamp finally made his anxiously awaited appearance.

Fortunately, Jackson had underestimated the Frenchman's notorious indifference. As Lillian Olaney said, "[Duchamp] didn't give a goddam." No one
who knew him was surprised that Duchamp was the last of the European
artists to arrive in America. Although capable of pomposity, he "didn't mind
wearing old clothes and having a bowl of soup for dinner," recalls Ethel Baziotes. He also "didn't mind" Jackson's art, although that was as far as his
enthusiasm went. His report to Peggy following his visit amounted to little
more than *"pas mal."* From the laconic Duchamp, however, even "not bad"
was considered a rave. Suddenly the forces pushing Peggy in Jackson's direction were irresistible: Sweeney, Matta, Putzel, and now even Duchamp. She
had no reason left to say no: Jackson Pollock would be her new protégé.

Putzel worked out the details. Jackson would be given a one-man show the following November at Art of This Century. To ensure that he could "work in peace" on preparing the show, Peggy would pay him a fixed sum of $150 each month for one year. At the end of the year, the total amount advanced ($1,800) would be deducted from the proceeds of all sales during the year, minus a one-third commission. Thus, for Jackson to make any additional money on the contract, the gallery would have to sell more than $2,700 worth of his paintings. If the gallery sold less than that, he would have to make up the shortfall with paintings. In addition, at Putzel's urging, Peggy would commission him to paint a mural for the entrance hall of her new apartment (the ghost of Max Ernst still haunted the old one). Putzel was eager to see "whether a larger scale would release the force contained in Pollock's smaller paintings."

For an American artist, it was an unprecedented deal. Even among the Europeans, it was rare for an artist to receive anything more than informal and irregular support from dealers or collectors. "Matta's arrangement with Pierre Matisse was perhaps the only one," says Lionel Abel. In one grand gesture, Peggy had shown her aesthetic faith in Jackson's future and her financial faith in the future of the art market. It was, in its own way, a bolder statement than the gallery itself.

Jackson was understandably ecstatic. When Putzel brought the offer to Eighth Street, Lee was away visiting her parents on Long Island, but Jackson couldn't wait. "Have signed the contract," he wrote her during the week of July 15, ". . . it's all very exciting." Soon afterward, he walked away from his job at the Museum of Non-Objective Art. It's unclear whether he quit or was dismissed. A friend recalls Jackson saying that he "left and didn't go back" when the baroness "took a heavy ruler and tore a piece off" one of his drawings and said, "It looks much better that way." A co-worker remembers that he was "canned for talking back to the old Kraut." Jackson probably came closest to the truth when he said, "Between the canned music and the craziness of the director I got myself fired."

Jackson was ready to paint. Finally, he could earn money as an artist. He was no longer his father's ne'er-do-well son. He had fulfilled his boyhood promise to "quit my dreaming and get them into material action." Peggy Guggenheim had lifted the last emotional obstacle to creative fulfillment. Now, beneath a conjunction of emotional tranquillity, artistic inspiration, and financial security, he began to work furiously. He tore out the wall between his studio and Sande's old studio (now nominally Lee's) and put up a stretcher for the mural he was to paint for Peggy's apartment. It was a vast expanse of blank canvas, nine by twenty feet, but Jackson was undaunted. Suddenly, everything seemed possible. "It looks pretty big," he wrote Charles triumphantly, "but exciting as all hell."

29

BEHIND THE VEIL

By August 1943, the cap was off the gusher again and paintings poured out at a rate of almost two a week. The studio, always in disarray, was suddenly bursting with big, vibrant, shiny-wet canvases drying too slowly in the sultry summer heat, the thick air made impossibly thicker by the smells of turpentine and linseed oil and scores of paint cans perpetually open. Paintings leaned against chairs and tables and one another until the room looked, according to one visitor, "like somebody had knocked over a giant house of cards." Somewhere in the chaos, a bulky, hunched figure in a sweaty T-shirt and speckled pants, a cigarette clinging to his lip, worked feverishly on a canvas that, to casual visitors, had looked finished weeks ago. Jackson kept three or four paintings "open" at all times. He would work on one or two while the others dried. But no painting was safe. On one day, a canvas that had languished in the corner for months might catch his eye. The next day, he would repaint it entirely. Glancing up from a newspaper, he might spy some "imperfection" and, reaching awkwardly around the back of a chair, correct it with whatever brush was closest at hand, then return to the paper. Almost every inch of a canvas was worked and reworked a dozen times. He applied paint quickly, not carefully, in short, decisive bursts, testing colors and forms and even composition as he went. It was a risky way to work—Peter Busa likened it to "playing at craps"—but it was the way Jackson worked best.

Almost immediately, he recaptured the palette, energy, and ease of expression that had distinguished the paintings of the previous winter, completed just before the Project ended. If anything, the seven months of uncertainty and relative inactivity had given him even more perspective on the lessons of the previous four years. In *The Moon-Woman Cuts the Circle*, he gave pictorial life to a Jungian image by combining it with elements from his personal iconography (Stella's knife) and biomorphic shapes from Miró. Decades later, Jungian scholars would seize on the painting's title, a reference to an ancient Indian

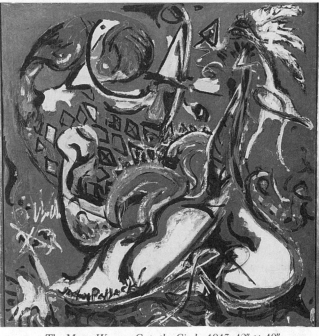

The Moon-Woman Cuts the Circle, 1943, 42″ × 40″

myth (in which a young man sees a girl swinging from a grapevine on the moon and, in a jealous fit, cuts the vine, sending the girl plummeting to the earth), and tease from its obscure imagery an elaborate Jungian analysis. In the process, they would attribute to Jackson a careful reading of recondite Jungian texts and a sophisticated knowledge of Indian lore. In fact, even while under Henderson's care, Jackson's interest in Jungian esoterica amounted to little more than schoolboy enthusiasm. By the summer of 1943, Henderson and de Laszlo were distant, if fond, memories, and Jungian iconography had been subsumed into Jackson's vast, personal storehouse of imagery—stripped of its ideological finery and reduced to those essential elements that served *his* vision, not Jung's. *Moon-Woman*'s fanciful title might have been supplied by one of several friends; or, more likely, lingered in Jackson's imagination until it suggested an image. Once a painting was begun, however, no myth—not even one Jackson knew well—could control the movement of the brush. He could no more follow a program for a painting than he could follow the lines of a model. Jungian arcana yielded to Indian imagery, which yielded to Miró, and then to immediate compositional needs. There is no indication that Jackson ever approached a blank canvas with more than just a "general notion" of where it would take him. (When asked if he had a "preconceived image" in his mind when he began a painting, Jackson replied with a touch of incredulity, "No, because it hasn't been created [yet], you see.")

Jackson had always worked that way. His earliest Benton sketchbooks document the struggle between subject matter and technique, between reality and improvisation. Unable to subordinate his errant line to the "fact" of the model, he had been forced early to cope with the compositional challenge of images that grew and transformed in unpredictable ways. By 1943, only the terminology had changed: what Benton called "ineptitude," John Graham called "automatic écriture" and the Surrealists called "automatism." By any name, it was the only way Jackson knew how to paint.

On one canvas, completed in August, he began with the rough outline of a bull, an image rich with personal meaning, standing against a distant horizon —as simple and straightforward as a Bentonesque sketch. Then he began to surround and obscure the outline with a delicately stippled "sky" of drips and dribbles and specks of color—a Surrealist dreamscape of blue-green, yellow, and umber. When the background threatened to envelope the bull, he took a wide brush and reworked the outline in black. At the same time, he complicated the image by adding heavy black calligraphy in the margins. On one pass, he turned the bull's shaded, indistinct underbelly into an irregular serrated line suggesting teats—perhaps to explore the issue of sexual ambiguity, perhaps because some previous reworking had accidentally suggested them. Then he left it to dry, still unresolved: a heavily worked image on an abstract ground surrounded by automatist doodles. When he returned to it days, perhaps weeks, later, he again tried to sharpen the central figure, using white highlights to reduce the "multiple exposure" effect of repeated outlining. When he was finally satisfied with the central image, he covered over much of the old stippled sky and distracting calligraphy with broad strokes of battleship gray, then signed his name.

The picture became known as *She-Wolf.* The discrepancy between the title and the image did not go unnoticed. "When I saw it for the first time," Axel Horn recalls, "I could have sworn that this was an attempt by Pollock to paint a calf. I looked at it, and I said, 'He's been trying to paint a calf.' Then I read the title, *She-Wolf,* and I figured somebody had superimposed the title on it." Like many others, Horn suspected that Lee or Sweeney or Putzel had chosen the name, either because he misread the image (the teats were confusing) or, more likely, because he preferred the mythic "She-Wolf" to the more prosaic "Cow" or "Bull." (Struck by the title, Peggy Guggenheim asked Lee if *she* had posed for it, to which Lee replied tartly, "Of course I did.") Whatever its origins, the name meant little to Jackson. He almost never began a painting with a title in mind and, afterward, often took suggestions for titles from friends and visitors. He detested titles that attempted to "explain" the imagery in a painting and, later in his career, would resort to numbering his paintings to prevent people from searching for the title in the image. The painting called *She-Wolf* was never intended as a comment on the reality of bulls or wolves. It was a statement about a different reality altogether. In the 1943 paintings, more so than ever before, "[Jackson's] unconscious came through," said his friend, James Brooks. "In a sense, he walked right into another world."

■   ■   ■

In the burst of paintings that preceded the Guggenheim show, Jackson grappled with an old dilemma: how to reconcile the real world with the world of his imagination. For years, the dilemma had focused on facility: could he draw a man that looked like a man, or a bull that looked like a bull? Or would he create a drawing that more closely corresponded to the image in his own unconscious—a man becoming a bull? Or perhaps an image that wasn't recognizable at all but conveyed, in an iconography even Jackson couldn't explicate, revelations from his unconscious? In the decade since Benton's class, he had tried a number of ways to reconcile these different realities—Orozco's psychologically charged imagery, Picasso's transformations, Jungian symbology, and finally automatism—but none had proved adequate. None had captured both the complexity and the energy of the unconscious image. Pure abstraction had also failed him. In his few experiments, especially on ceramic bowls, the abstract passages lacked the psychological intensity that identifiable images from his past could call forth. The image of a bull—or a woman or a knife or a table—with all its childhood resonance, had the power to propel Jackson through an entire painting. Abstraction, especially the formal kind preached by Hofmann and practiced by avowed automatists like Motherwell, lacked that crucial, cathartic energy.

But representation held its own hazards. Images resonant and powerful enough to energize a painting proved also deeply threatening. They were the very images—of devouring females, charging bulls, and ambiguous sexuality —that Jackson needed most to suppress. Throughout his life, the periods of the greatest emotional upheaval were also the periods of the most explicit imagery. For two years after Bloomingdale's, nightmare images of grotesque women and unwanted, skeletal babies had haunted his imagination. All the darkest and most monstrous truths had roamed virtually unchecked through his conscious world—disguised as anxieties only liquor could quell—and through his art, in works like *Bald Woman with Skeleton* and *Naked Man with Knife*. With Lee's support, he had brought these demons under control, and even begun to confront them, in paintings like *Stenographic Figure* and *Male and Female*. But the fear persisted, as did the need for abstraction and the concealment it offered.

Unfulfilled in both worlds, Jackson played on the borderline between them, wavering back and forth between the recognizable and the obscure, between representation and abstraction. No paintings reveal his dilemma more clearly than three he painted over a period of twelve months beginning in late 1942. In all three, the basic image is one of people gathered around a table, an image drawn directly from his childhood. Sidney Janis referred to *Search for a Symbol*, the first of the three, as "personage[s] over and about the conference table." The figure on the left is the female, recognizable by her flowered dress and long eyelashes; the one on the right is the male. Between them, superimposed on the table, are fragments of another figure, a figure that Jackson has chosen to obliterate. Only a pair of eyes, a few biomorphic shapes, and two arms

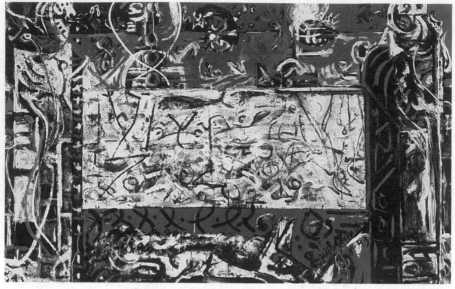

Guardians of the Secret, 1943, 48¾" × 75"

remain. At some earlier stage, apparently, the central figure was attached to the female by an umbilical cord, and one of its arms was flung around her. The other arm, now lying disembodied on the table, appears to be connected to the penis of the male figure on the left. It is an unsettling bond, made threatening by the nearby presence of a chicken—always, for Jackson, a symbol of castration and dismemberment.

Only seven or eight months later, Jackson conjured the same demons in another painting, *Guardians of the Secret.* Again, the scene is of figures gathered around a table. In the finished painting, only two figures are apparent, one at either end of the table, as in *Stenographic Figure, Search for a Symbol,* and *Male and Female.* Other figures are faintly suggested, obscured beneath a profusion of shapes and colors. But a photograph taken in Jackson's studio while *Guardians* was in progress, reveals not two but five people seated around the table—three on the far side and one at either end. At some point in its creation *Guardians* was a group portrait of the Pollock family at the dinner table. It even included Gyp, lying at the foot of the table at the bottom of the picture, with his distinctive long snout, white eye patch, and brown paw. Only the loving portrait of Gyp survived the reworkings that followed, however. The figures in back, brothers presumably, were reduced to abstract motifs unrecognizable even as human forms. The figures on either side, Stella and Roy, remained, but not as the readily identifiable figures in the photograph. By the time Jackson was finished, they had been transformed into featureless "totemic figures," stark amalgams of lines and shapes and colors that merely suggest a human precedent.

But where was Jackson in this family portrait? Did his failure to include

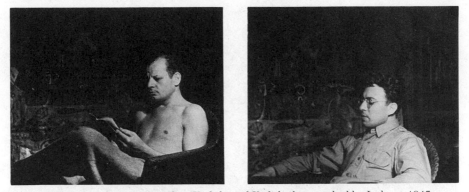

Jackson photographed by Reuben Kadish, and Kadish photographed by Jackson, 1943;
Guardians of the Secret, in progress, in the background.

himself reflect his continuing sense of alienation, ten years after Roy's death? The answer probably lies somewhere in the maze of black-and-white calligraphy that covers the tabletop around which the Pollock family has gathered. The photograph of *Guardians* in progress reveals nothing about what lies under the numbers and automatist doodles added at the last minute (like those in *Stenographic Figure*), except that it was very different from what appears in the finished painting. As in *Search for a Symbol*, the central figure in *Guardians* is missing, blotted out at the last minute by Jackson's compulsive need to hide and hide from the truth.

By the end of the year, he had returned to the same subject a third time. On the largest canvas of his career so far, an arena almost five by eight feet, he wrestled again with his conflicting needs for revelation and for concealment. The result is a painting of furious, exploded imagery, filled with figures caught between two worlds, figures that jerk in and out of reality—a limb here, an eye, a face, a hand, a penis, a pair of haunches—but relate to each other only as line, shape, and color. Unlike *Guardians*, nothing is left unjumbled by abstraction. The table is still there, a faint blue oval this time, and figures hover around it—one on the left, three on the right, perhaps more in the background. Unlike *She-Wolf*, here Jackson hasn't made a last-minute effort to sharpen the primary figures by filling in the background or highlighting their outlines. Background and figures and calligraphy vie fiercely for attention. In the confusion, Jackson dares to lift the veil on the central figure that remained hidden in *Guardians*, but only enough to reveal tantalizing fragments. In the center of the table, an animal of some sort lies on its back, its hind legs pumping the air. Its mouth appears to be open as if crying out. It may be disemboweled. The figures gathered around could be preparing to feast on it. Beyond that, meanings are swallowed up in abstraction—as Jackson no doubt intended. The painting's title, *Pasiphaë*, is, like so many of Jackson's titles, a late graft. Even Jackson's original title, *Moby-Dick*, has no discernible relation to the painting. But the implications of *Pasiphaë* for Jackson's art are clear. He has wrestled his

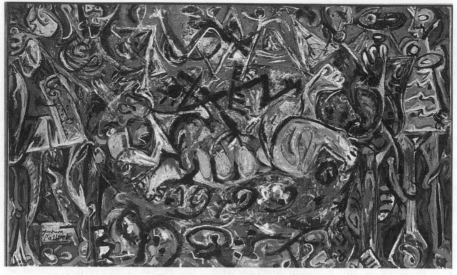

Pasiphaë, 1943–44, 56⅛″ × 96″

imagery up to the borderline of abstraction, with all its psychic power and personal resonance intact.

Before the year is out, he will cross that line.

While Jackson probed the imaginary world, events rushed by in the real one. Putzel came by the Eighth Street apartment often to offer encouragement, enjoy Lee's cooking, nudge Jackson to work faster, and generally avoid the loneliness of his one-room apartment on East Fifty-seventh Street. The visits were meant to be reassuring, but as the November 9 opening approached, it was usually Putzel, a notorious worrier, who needed reassuring. Every time he appeared at the door, panting from the long climb, Lee thought he looked more tense and harried than ever. His reputation with Peggy, as well as the gallery's reputation, depended on how Jackson's show was received, both critically and commercially. Nervous that no collector would gamble on one of the large-scale canvases that Jackson increasingly favored, Putzel pleaded with him to drop work on the giant *Pasiphaë*, just begun, and concentrate on producing "small pictures" for more timid buyers. During September, Jackson obliged with *Wounded Animal*, a mere thirty by thirty-eight inches, and several abstract exercises that he left untitled. By the time Art of This Century opened in early October with an exhibition of works by de Chirico, all the major paintings for the show were finished and delivered. Jackson spent the last anxious month preparing a few more small-scale works, including a number of gouaches and drawings. Meanwhile, the huge stretched canvas for the mural, covering the entire east wall of his studio, remained untouched.

While Jackson and Putzel shared dinners, openings, and a Segovia concert in the months preceding the show, Peggy Guggenheim rarely saw her new protégé. It wasn't the split with Ernst that distracted her—normally, emotional trauma sent her straight to the gallery to bury herself in business. This time, it was lovesickness. Soon after learning of Ernst's infidelity the previous winter, she had met a handsome redheaded young Englishman named Kenneth Macpherson and fallen rapturously in love. "She really flipped for him," said Lee Krasner. Despite being married and resolutely homosexual, Macpherson proved the perfect mate. "[He] came into my life when I most needed him," Peggy later wrote. "He immediately gave me a sense of peace, and when I sat with his arm around me I was perfectly happy, happier than I had been for years." In September, she and Macpherson moved into a duplex apartment in a double brownstone on Sixty-first Street (for which she had commissioned the mural from Jackson). Although they lived on separate floors and Peggy treated him "less as a lover than as a girl friend," Macpherson was a source of great comfort. "You can have an affair, you know, without sex," Peggy insisted. With his support, she even managed to survive the agonizing divorce from Ernst without the usual histrionics.

With so much happening in her personal life, Peggy gladly left the gallery to Putzel, incuding the job of shepherding Jackson toward the November show. The few times she did meet with him, she found him intriguing "in a man/ child sort of way," although his taciturnity made her self-conscious and uncomfortable (she said he reminded her of "a trapped animal who should have stayed in his burrow"). More and more often, when Peggy had something to say to Jackson, she spoke to Lee Krasner.

No one worked harder preparing for Jackson's show than Lee. Using the pay phone in the nearby Waldorf Cafeteria, she scheduled Jackson's increasingly crowded days—the comings and goings of visitors (she kept them to a minimum until he finished the paintings), inquiries about the exhibition, arrangements for transporting works—and maintained a running dialogue with Putzel. "In spite of the fact that I'm not working," she wrote Stella, ". . . I seem to be kept busy every minute." When brothers Frank and Sande came to town, Lee baby-sat their children. She kept Stella informed of "the wonderful things happening" and picked out shoes for her sixty-eighth birthday (which Jackson promptly lost). Such remarkable devotion didn't seem odd to Stella. According to Arloie McCoy, the family had led her to believe that Lee and Jackson were already married.

Lee seemed to thrive in her new role. Some friends thought it suited her particularly well. "As I remember her in the Artists Union," says Axel Horn, "she had a flair for promotion, for publicity." Ethel Baziotes thought Lee "had developed an executive temperament on the WPA. She could say very difficult things without any strain." But May Rosenberg and other old friends saw Lee's new role in a less flattering light. "Lee turned out to be a terrific saleswoman," says Rosenberg. "She was very clever. She had the quality of a peasant. She operated as if everybody was looking out only for himself." Jackson's friends were divided on the question of whether Jackson would have fared so well without Lee's promotional instincts. Some, like Peter Busa, thought Jackson "couldn't sell a heater to an Eskimo" and, even if he could, "didn't want to have anything to do with promotion." Others, like Gerome Kamrowski, recall that Jackson understood well the importance of public relations. "For somebody so unverbal," says Kamrowski, "he always managed to say hello to a critic or a collector."

Everyone agreed, however, that Lee did one job better than Jackson ever could have: managing Peggy Guggenheim.

"In general," writes Peggy's biographer, "those people who found Peggy most generous or got along best with her were those who needed her the least." Unfortunately, no one needed Peggy more than Lee Krasner did—a fact that Peggy never for a moment let her forget. After commandeering her to stuff and address twelve hundred announcements for Jackson's show, Peggy dressed her down in front of the staff for making mistakes on three of them. "She bawled the hell out of me for the nine cents I was wasting," Lee remembers. On a cab trip together, Peggy told the driver to stop and, while Lee watched aghast, "stood over a manhole, picked up her skirt, and peed." Peggy had a way, said Buffie Johnson, "of making it clear to others that they really didn't count for much." On another occasion, Peggy invited Lee and Jackson to her house for dinner with "a few people" but asked Lee to come early and see if the meat loaf was done "the right way." When Lee arrived, she found "two maids peeling potatoes" and "a huge amount of meat." The party, it turned out, was for fifty people, and Peggy was waiting anxiously for Lee to prepare the meat loaf. "It was not exactly what you'd call a catered situation," Lee recalled acidly.

Behind the abuse, there was, undoubtedly, some kind of skewed affection between the two women. Peggy treated her sister Hazel with the same fond cruelty, and Lee had accepted Irving's abuse with the same masochistic resignation. "They would quarrel, be friends again, then quarrel some more," recalled David Hare, who often saw Lee keeping vigil in the gallery while Peggy took her usual three-hour lunch. "They were quite alike." In fact, although separated in age by twelve years, they were more alike than either would admit. Both were the wayward children of large and fractious families. Both were distinctly unattractive women who relied on wit, style, and insouciance in lieu of looks. Both were proud of their bodies (Peggy so much so that, even at forty-five, she intentionally wore dresses that allowed her breasts to "pop out from under the fabric," according to one friend). Both had a taste for homosexual men as lovers. Both were "made of alloyed steel," according to Clement Greenberg, and "used to getting ascendancy over people."

Given their similarities, their antagonism was inevitable. To Lee, Peggy was a "kookie," nymphomaniacal, manipulative "bitch" with "too much money and not enough taste." To Peggy, Lee was a shrill, overreaching *klafte*, a perfect example of the grasping, lower-class Russian Jew that her German-Jewish relatives had tried to keep out of America, a woman who "should have been out holding a job" to support Jackson rather than sponging off Peggy.

More than one mutual friend, however, suspected that the real bone of contention between the two women was Jackson. "He was grateful for the chance to do the mural," Lee later said, "he was appreciative, but she wanted him in her bed every night to prove it."

Lee suffered the many indignities of her new role in uncharacteristic silence. In a thank-you note to Jackson after one of his many dinners at the Eighth Street apartment, Putzel referred to Lee as "your cordon bleu chef." After twenty years on her own in New York, after countless classes, the Hofmann school, WPA battles, and one delirious evening with Mondrian, Lee had given up her studio, moved in with an emotionally troubled alcoholic, gone back to modeling for money, relegated most of her paintings to storage or the trash heap, taught herself to cook, indentured herself to Peggy Guggenheim, and for what? If, at this point in her relationship with Jackson, she allowed herself to ask that question, she undoubtedly looked to the coming show, now only weeks away, to answer it.

As the day approached, Jackson allowed himself a cautious confidence. Putzel had done his job well, informing Jackson of every faint breeze of enthusiasm that passed through the gallery prior to the show. "Mrs. Goodspeed wants your show for Chicago [Arts Club]," he wrote in early October, "and Caresse Crosby wants it for her gallery in Washington, D.C. Hope there won't be enough [paintings] left." "[James Thrall] Soby dropped in this afternoon," went another Putzel confidence-builder, "and is mad about your work. . . . [He] predicts you will be THE new sensation this season and, moreover, that unlike past seasons' sensations that you will last." Putzel was by no means the only source of encouragement. In three months of preparing for the show, Jackson had entertained a number of guests in his studio and enjoyed an embarrassment of praise. Reuben Kadish had come through New York in the summer of 1943, on his way to India and China as an artist-correspondent, and reported being "overwhelmed." "I knew I was seeing something important," he said later, "a new volcano had erupted on the American scene." During the same visit, Kadish's friend Jeanne Raynal had been captivated by *The Magic Mirror*. When she returned to San Francisco in August, she wrote and bought it for $500. It was Jackson's first major sale. Soon afterward, Dr. Grace McCann Morley of the San Francisco Museum offered Jackson an exhibition of drawings and eyed *Guardians of the Secret* longingly (she would eventually purchase it). Reginald Wilson, who had witnessed Jackson's earlier struggles, came by the studio while on leave and was dumbstruck by the changes in his art and in his life. "My God, the place was filled with paintings, and Jackson was on top of the world," recalls Wilson, who found *She-Wolf* particularly "overwhelming." "And I had been worrying what would become of him." Sidney Janis, a collector and writer who had visited Jackson the year before at Lee's urging and selected a painting for his coming exhibition "Abstract and Surrealist Art in the United States," visited again in September and was also startled by the metamorphosis in Jackson's art in only a year. "I enjoyed very much the visit to your studio," he wrote soon afterward. "I think [*Search for a Symbol*] the most provocative painting by an American I've seen yet." (Janis eventually reproduced *Guardians of the Secret* in his exhibition catalogue and *She-Wolf* in his book.) Lee's friend, Clement Greenberg, his aspirations now turned from creating art to criticizing it, also climbed the steps to the studio, as did James Johnson Sweeney, who came several times, once to buy a drawing and once to offer Jackson a job teaching art in Buffalo, New York. "I don't think he'll take it," Lee wrote Stella, "but it certainly gave him a lift to get the offer." In fact, of all the visitors to the studio that summer and fall, only Jackson's family withheld judgment on the new works—a failure of generosity that Lee would never forgive. Frank took one look at the new works and clearly thought his baby brother had gone off the deep end. "I think my painting had him worried," Jackson wrote Charles.

The sweetest victory, perhaps, was a visit from Harold Lehman the week before the opening. Jackson took his former high school classmate to Art of This Century to show off the already installed paintings and introduce him to Peggy and Putzel, whom Lehman had known at his Los Angeles gallery. "Jackson was constantly telling me, 'See how I'm progressing in the art world,'" Lehman remembers. "'The Museum of Modern Art is buying a painting and this is my show, and isn't it great.'" Great for Jackson. Less so for Lehman, who had moved to Woodstock, New York, and who, despite his dazzling facility, was still virtually unknown.

A week before the show, Jackson was in a mood to savor such ironies. He had just delivered the last of Putzel's "small works," including *Conflict*, an oil painting he gave to Sweeney; *Burning Landscape*, which he would sell to Peggy; and several gouaches and drawings. Putzel was pleased. "These small pictures are (on the whole) better than the other small pictures," he wrote, ever supportive. On November 1, a public announcement of the show appeared in *Art Digest*, where Putzel's friendship with editor Maude Riley ensured prominent and favorable treatment. The article included a biographical sketch of the artist —"born in Wyoming, later lived in California and in Arizona"—and a ringing endorsement from Peggy, probably penned by Putzel. "I consider this exhibition to be something of an event in the contemporary history of American Art," she was quoted as saying. "I consider [Pollock] to be one of the strongest and most interesting American painters."

Perhaps if Peggy's praise had been slightly less fulsome, slightly more detached, Jackson might have been better prepared for what followed. At Peggy's request, James Johnson Sweeney had written a brief introduction for the exhibition catalogue. Jackson read it for the first time when the printed catalogues arrived at the gallery only a few days before the show.

"Talent, will, genius," as George Sand wrote of Flaubert, "are natural phenomena like the lake, the volcano, the mountain, the wind, the star, the cloud." Pollock's talent is volcanic. It has fire. It is unpredictable. It is undisciplined. It spills itself out in a mineral prodigality not yet crystallized. It is lavish, explosive, untidy.

But young painters, particularly Americans, tend to be too careful of opinion. Too often the dish is allowed to chill in the serving. What we need is more young men who paint from inner impulsion without an ear to what the critic or spectator may feel—painters who will risk spoiling a canvas to say something in their own way. Pollock is one.

It is true that Pollock needs self-discipline. But to profit from pruning, a plant must have vitality. In art we are only too familiar with the application of self-discipline where deliberation would have been more profitable. Pollock can stand it. In his early work as a student of Thomas Benton he showed a conventional academic competence. Today his creed is evidently that of Hugo, "Ballast yourself with reality and throw yourself into the sea. The sea is inspiration."

Among young painters, Jackson Pollock offers unusual promise in his exuberance, independence, and native sensibility. If he continues to exploit these qualities with the courage and conscience he has shown so far, he will fulfill that promise.

The further Jackson read, the more incensed he became. At the last word, he threw the catalogue down and repeated, through clenched teeth, the word that really stung: "undisciplined." Sweeney, however well meaning, had touched a nerve. "Unpredictable," "not yet crystallized," "untidy," "will risk spoiling a canvas"—for Jackson, they all meant one thing: "undisciplined"—a charge that resonated back to high school and the humiliations of Benton's class. "He was furious," Lee remembers, "really mad. I'd never seen him so angry." Terrified that he would confront Sweeney, Lee—who thought it was a "fine introduction"—somehow convinced Jackson that a thank-you note would be both more appropriate and more politic. Sweeney, after all, served actively on the Junior Advisory Committee at the Museum of Modern Art, which had already expressed an interest in acquiring *She-Wolf.* "Dear Sweeney," the note began, using Lee's customary form of address, "I have read your forward to the catalogue, and I am excited. I am happy—The self-discipline you speak of will come, I think, as a natural growth of a deeper, more integrated, experience." In closing, Jackson consciously or unconsciously betrayed Lee's hand. "Many thanks," he wrote, "*We* will fulfill that promise—"

After writing the letter, Jackson continued to smolder. Only days before the opening, he took *Search for a Symbol* to the gallery for a meeting with Sweeney. It was a small, restrained picture from the same period as *Stenographic Figure.* According to some versions of the story, he had repainted it after reading Sweeney's introduction to make it even more "disciplined." As he showed it to Sweeney, he reportedly said, "I want you to see a *really* disciplined painting."

■　■　■

The show that opened on November 8, 1943, did not rivet the eyes of the artistic world or rocket Jackson Pollock to instant notoriety. Only later, in retrospect, would it achieve mythic status. Most of those who came shared Clement Greenberg's reaction: "I wasn't bowled over at first. I didn't realize what I'd seen until later." If the show was revolutionary, it wasn't because of Jackson's paintings, it was because, for the first time, an American avant-garde artist was being given serious commercial and critical attention.

It wasn't a large crowd at Art of This Century on that unseasonably warm November night. There was plenty of room in the white-walled "Daylight Gallery" to stand back and examine the show's sixteen paintings, ranging in size from the tiny *Conflict*, little more than a foot square, to the imposing *Guardians of the Secret*, and in price from $25 for a drawing to $750 for *Guardians*. The crowd was dotted with uniforms—the war had finally reached Fifty-seventh Street. Ibram Lassaw, the pioneer abstract sculptor, had come on leave from Fort Dix. Lee's friends George McNeil and John Little came in their immaculate navy whites. Greenberg and Kamrowski also attended, along with Herbert and Mercedes Matter who had lent their untitled painting, a gift from Jackson, to the exhibition. Jackson himself stood unsteadily in the middle of the room where Peggy had placed him between herself and Sweeney. "Sweeney did so much to help me make Pollock known," Peggy later wrote, "that I felt as though Pollock were our spiritual offspring." Some thought he even looked a little like their child, standing stiff-legged and clean-shaven, in a suit and tie, with his hands clasped tightly in front of him and his eyes searching the turquoise floor, nervously saying hello as Peggy made her flamboyant introductions. He reminded one guest of "a little boy dressed up for Sunday school."

Lee wasn't deceived by appearances. She stood at the desk near the door, answering questions, handing out catalogues, and glancing at Jackson "sixty times a minute." *She* knew he was drunk. Not drunk enough to make a scene, perhaps, but drunk enough to attract unkind attention. Becky Reis, who hadn't met Jackson until Peggy introduced them that night, was sure he had consumed "at least a quart of liquor." Of Jackson's friends who attended, more were disoriented by his suit and tie than by the weaving line he made on his way to and from the bathroom. Afterward, over Lee's protest, Peggy threw a party for Jackson that ended up in Kenneth Macpherson's apartment.

The first reviews of the show appeared not in the papers or the magazines but in the bars and coffee shops around Greenwich Village. There, opinion was split. The European Surrealists, Peggy's *former* darlings, publicly claimed Jackson as one of their own—Max Ernst called him "a wild man like Soutine"; Matta commented, "very Masson"—while privately they ridiculed him. Roger Wilcox recalls that, despite their vaunted admiration for the primitive in art, the Surrealists scorned Jackson's "lack of cultivation"; it was one thing to travel to the American Northwest in search of primitive artists, another thing entirely to accept one as their social and artistic equal. According to Lee Krasner, the

Surrealist community felt that Peggy had forsaken not only them but her standards as well: "The entire outgoing group were furious at her for taking on someone like Pollock."

Jackson's friends tended to agree with Reuben Kadish that "he had cracked the whole thing open," but many artists were less than enthusiastic. Morris Kantor, a painter who had known Jackson on the WPA, "burst a blood vessel," according to a friend. "He said, 'That isn't painting!' He just blew his top." More than one visitor to the show scribbled obscenities in Peggy's guest book. Others just walked out. "Pollock unnerved me," said one. "I had to leave. Either the guy is too sick . . . I just couldn't take it." Balcomb Greene, the first chairman of American Abstract Artists, was reminded of Stuart Davis's definition of abstraction: "a belch from the unconscious."

When the printed reviews finally began to appear in mid-November, it was clear that the show had been every bit as provocative as Putzel had predicted. Not since the gallery's opening had there been such an outpouring of publicity. The *Times*, the *Sun*, the *New Yorker*, the *Nation, Partisan Review, Art News, Art Digest*, and *View* all featured reviews.

But if Jackson was clinging to the childhood hope for unalloyed praise, he must have been deeply disappointed. None of the critics was kinder than Sweeney and some were considerably more cruel. Henry McBride, writing in the New York *Sun*, likened the works to "a kaleidoscope that has been insufficiently shaken. Another shake or two might bring order into the flying particles of color—but the spectator is not too sure of this." There were, to be sure, some nuggets of extravagant praise. In his review for the *New Yorker*, Robert Coates called him "an authentic discovery." "His color is always rich and daring," wrote Coates, "his approach mature, and his design remarkably fluent." "We like all this," said *Art Digest.* The show's smaller works drew a disproportionate share of the accolades, especially *Wounded Animal* and *Conflict*, which one reviewer pronounced "among the strongest abstract paintings ever produced by an American."

Most critics, however, followed Sweeney down the middle of the road— admiring Jackson's audacity, indulging his unruliness, and expressing conditional optimism about his future. "Most of the abstractions are large and nearly all of them are extravagantly, not to say savagely romantic," wrote Edward Alden Jewell in the *Times*. "Here is obscurantism indeed, though it may become resolved and clarified as the artist proceeds." "Mr. Pollock's forcefulness, coupled with a persistent tendency to overwork his ideas, leads him into turgidity," said Coates. "Pollock is out a-questing," wrote *Art Digest*'s reviewer, "and he goes hell-bent at each canvas . . . plenty of whirl and swirl."

No one, however, captured Sweeney's tone of benign ambivalence more articulately than Clement Greenberg in one of his first art reviews for the *Nation.* "[Pollock] is the first painter I know of to have got something positive from the muddiness of color that so profoundly characterizes a great deal of American painting," Greenberg began, insistently balancing every positive with a negative. "The mud abounds in Pollock's larger works, and these, though the least consummated, are his most original and ambitious. Being young and full of energy, he takes orders he can't fill . . . he spends himself in too many directions at once." In *Guardians of the Secret*, "space tautens but does not burst into a picture," whereas *Male and Female* "zigzags between the intensity of the easel picture and the blandness of the mural." Even Greenberg's conclusion was inconclusive. "Pollock has gone through the influences of Miró, Picasso, Mexican painting, and what not, and has come out on the other side at the age of thirty-one, painting mostly with his own brush"; *but*, added Greenberg ominously, "in his search for style he is liable to relapse into an influence."

There was only one aspect of Jackson's show about which the critics were unambiguously enthusiastic: he was *American.*

Two years after Pearl Harbor, the country was at war body and soul. Daily battle reports from Italy, Africa, Russia, and the Pacific filled the front pages. Only two weeks before the show opened, American marines had invaded the fiercely defended Tarawa atoll in the Pacific and suffered horrendous casualties. The grim details headlined the newspapers for weeks and touched off yet another tidal wave of war bond appeals, rallies, and speech-making in a city already saturated with newsreels, ration tickets, propaganda posters, and soldiers in transit. Inevitably, critics brought to Peggy's long-awaited showing of an American avant-garde artist some of the same patriotic fervor that filled the airwaves and editorial pages. "[Jackson's] abstractions are free of Paris," exulted the reviewer for *Art News*, "and contain a disciplined American fury." Critics especially reveled in Jackson's all-American past and projected it into his work wherever possible. "His work is personal," said one, "though occasionally one feels an Indian influence." The *New Yorker* review referred to Jackson as "a young Western artist" in the first sentence and, while acknowledging that Picasso was an influence, noted that his influence had not detracted from "the basic force and vigor" of Jackson's art. Greenberg's entire essay was suffused with what Hilton Kramer later called "a sense of history on the march" never before seen in American art criticism, a sense of embracing, ineluctable optimism—an artistic Manifest Destiny.

Jackson was stunned and demoralized by the probationary tone of the reviews. Outrage would have been easier to accept. During the first week, he went to the gallery often "in case a collector came in," Lee Krasner recalls, but after the reviews began to appear, lost interest. Lee, of course, continued to arrive every morning at ten when the gallery opened (beating Peggy by an hour or more), and often stayed until after it closed at six. When she returned to the apartment, Jackson would ask if anything had sold, and every day she would have to say no. At the end of the show's three-week run, only one drawing had been bought—by Kenneth Macpherson, who, according to Peggy, was never really enthusiastic about Jackson's work.

Meanwhile, the canvas for Peggy's mural remained untouched, stretched out along the east wall of the studio, exactly where it had been since July, when Jackson had eagerly torn out the wall to Sande's old studio to make room for it. More and more often, when Lee returned from the gallery, she found Jackson sitting in the front room, his arms folded over the back of a chair, staring at the white void, "getting more and more depressed." He tried drawing sketches and "cartoons"—something he rarely did—but none of these small images "made the leap" to the huge canvas. In desperation, perhaps at Lee's suggestion, he considered other possibilities. Peter Busa remembers him struggling with "studies" for a giant collage. "I told him, 'Look, Jack, this isn't the Project. You don't have to get the plan approved by a committee. Treat it like an easel picture, just bigger.'" But size wasn't the problem. The imaging process that over the previous months had produced more than a dozen canvases—all prodigal of imagery, layers and layers of imagery, fighting and obscuring each other in dense little squares—that process had suddenly and inexplicably broken down. When Bill and Ethel Baziotes came to dinner on December 23, the canvas was still untouched.

Friends like Reuben Kadish knew that the block wasn't on the canvas; it was in Jackson's head. "I thought it was a gestation period," says Kadish. "Whatever it was that was taking place was taking place *inside*. Other artists drew sketches, Jackson's preparations were all internal. I felt, when it was ready to come out, it would come out." But Peggy Guggenheim wasn't willing to wait indefinitely. Sometime in December, she informed Lee that she expected the mural to be delivered in time for a party that Jean Connolly was giving in her apartment in January. When Lee balked, Peggy reminded her that the canvas should have been finished in time for the November show. She also apparently hinted that the monthly stipend of $150 might be withheld if Jackson didn't come through.

Despite the deadline, Jackson and Lee spent Christmas and the New Year in Deep River, Connecticut, with Stella, Sande, Arloie, and their daughter Karen, now two. The visit didn't turn out to be the reunion of "Jack and Sande" that Jackson undoubtedly anticipated. The two brothers had seen each other only once or twice in the previous year and a half. During that time, a huge gulf had opened between them. Sande was "enduring" life in a town he described as a "dump," working seventy-eight hours a week to support his new family. He had little time to recapture the old days with his petulant baby brother. Everything that Jackson had known of Sande—the stocky, swaggering little troublemaker in Riverside; the pipe-smoking companion on the rim of the Grand Canyon; the daring young man in the cowboy hat on the streets of New York—had vanished without a trace. "Sande was proud of Jack," says James Brooks, "but he gave up on him when he moved away. He decided he wanted to be a real father on his own. Jackson just didn't fit into that."

Back in New York, with only a week before Connolly's party, Jackson locked himself into the studio and Lee out. Every now and then when he emerged, she could see the canvas through the doorway, still blank. Eventually, he ordered her out of the apartment altogether. She retreated to her parents' house on Long Island, hoping that while she was away, Jackson might find whatever it was he had lost. But when she returned the day before the deadline, he was still sitting and staring at the empty canvas. John Little found her later that day in a state of panic. "I don't know what I'm going to do," she said. "The canvas has to be ready tomorrow morning and Jackson hasn't even *started* yet." When Little offered to go into the studio, Lee wouldn't let him for fear of disturbing Jackson. Little remembers, "She could only wring her hands and say, 'I don't know what's going to happen tomorrow.' "

Just after nightfall, Jackson began to paint. "I had a vision," he told a friend years later. "It was a stampede." Apparently the week with Sande had summoned up memories of an earlier time, of the Grand Canyon and wild horses on the run. On the right side of the canvas, in gigantic strokes of black, he caught the figures that moved like shadows between unconscious and imagination: "Red" from Provo, Lewis Jay, Cooter, Sande. Suddenly the mustang herd appeared, behind and around them, exploding through the narrow draw, a chaos of haunches and legs and unfurled manes, charging across the huge canvas in graphic black panic. No sooner were the bold outlines down, however, than the images began to change, overlap, combine, and obliterate one another. New figures appeared and old ones were transformed. Humans became horses; horses became bulls. Eventually the stampede was joined by "every animal in the American West," according to Jackson's own account. "Cows and horses and antelopes and buffaloes. *Everything* is charging across that goddamn surface." Across this panorama, Jackson laid a frenzy of swirling lines: lines that multiplied on themselves, lines that curved around the black poles like the muscles of a Bentonesque nude, lines in teal and raspberry and yellow, lines that highlighted the obscure and obscured the obvious. Then, with white, he filled the spaces between the lines, risking mud with every broad stroke on the wet canvas. Finally, under splatters of yellow and red, the last fragments of recognizable images disappeared. Nothing remained of the original stampede except furious energy, panoramic chaos, and primal alarm. For the first time since his experiments on ceramic bowls in 1938, Jackson had pushed the image beyond representation, beyond scrutiny, behind the veil.

By nine the next morning, fifteen tumultuous hours after he began, Jackson was finished. Lee stepped into the studio and blinked in disbelief. "When I saw her that day," John Little remembers, "she ran up to me and said, 'You won't believe what happened. After you left, he went to work, and this morning the painting was finished.' She couldn't believe it."

As soon as the paint was dry to the touch, Jackson broke down the stretcher, rolled the canvas, and transported both to Peggy's apartment building on East Sixty-first Street. When he reassembled it in the low, ground-floor elevator lobby, however, he discovered it was too long—by almost a foot. Sleepless, distraught, and close to panic, he telephoned Peggy at the gallery. "He became quite hysterical," Peggy recalled. That was before he began to drink. Knowing that Jackson would be in her apartment that day, and "knowing his great weakness," Peggy had hidden her liquor before leaving for the gallery. But Jackson soon found it. His calls became more and more frantic. He pleaded with her to "come home at once and help place the painting." Finally, she called Marcel Duchamp and David Hare and persuaded them to rescue Jackson. "Peggy wanted us to tack it up," Hare recalled, "but it missed by eight inches so we cut eight inches off from one end. Duchamp said that in this type of painting it wasn't needed. We told Jackson, who didn't care." By then, Jackson was too drunk to care. Weaving and incoherent, he walked into the apartment where Connolly's party was already under way, crossed the room, unzipped his pants, and peed in the marble fireplace.

The demons were loose again.

30

FRUITS AND NUTS

For Jackson Pollock, success was its own punishment. Every artistic peak of his career was followed, usually within months, by an emotional freefall. Some friends saw such plunges as merely cyclical, like phases of the moon, that came and went without regard to the events in his life. Others, like Lee, related his depressions to his drinking, and his drinking, in turn, to his exhibitions. "Jackson usually drank before and after the shows," she said later. Still others, like Peter Busa, were forever being surprised. "Each time he stopped drinking, I just thought he was cured," Busa recalls, "and I'd always congratulate him. He'd say, 'Yeah, I don't need that stuff anymore.' And then he'd be just as bad as he ever was."

In different ways, all of them were right. There was certainly a pattern to Jackson's depressions, or at least to the periods when he seemed most vulnerable to depression. Plotted on a graph, his emotional life would have been a wavy line with two-year intervals between crests. From his despair following Sande's discovery of girls in 1926 to his breakdown in 1938 to the binge in 1942 preceding Stella's arrival in New York, even-numbered years had been especially brutal. But Lee was also right. The pattern of depression and drinking was to some extent responsive to events in Jackson's life; it could be altered —for the worse, as when Roy's death precipitated a collapse in 1933; or for the better, as when Lee's presence ameliorated the effects of Sande's departure in 1942. In the same way, the pressure of preparing a show, the anxiety of an opening, even the tone of reviews could speed up or slow down the next wave.

And Busa was right, too: no one was more surprised than Jackson each time a wave overtook him.

Even the equivocal acclaim that greeted his first show was enough to speed the decline of 1944. Routine money allowed him to buy liquor routinely. After a decade of Prohibition and Depression, alcohol had become a status symbol;

success was measured by what one drank. "When you were broke you drank coffee," recalls Herman Cherry. "The minute you had enough money to buy alcohol, that meant you were prosperous. If you could buy whiskey instead of beer, you had made it." Success also brought new people into Jackson's life: collectors, dealers, curators, and other artists. They wanted to visit his studio, to have lunch with him, to interview him. Eager to promote her new protégé, Peggy tried to accommodate them. She arranged meetings with potential buyers and lunches with museum officials, not realizing how toxic the combination of strangers and alcohol could be for Jackson. "He behaved like a pig," recalls Peggy's sister, Hazel, who sometimes accompanied Peggy on business lunches.

Of course, the more notorious Jackson became, the more tolerant people were of his embarrassing lapses and the further he had to reach to elicit the same level of outrage. At one lunch in the dining room of the Chelsea Hotel, he vomited on the carpet, sending guests and waiters scattering in every direction. Even Peggy had her limits. Eventually, she stopped trying to "show Jackson off" to his public and discouraged him from coming around the gallery. Jackson was still capable of self-control—the Philadelphia collector Mrs. H. Gates Lloyd described him as "perfectly nice" after their meeting—but such politesse was quickly becoming the exception. The rule was what Charles experienced on a visit to New York in early 1944. "I took some friends out to dinner at Ticino's on Thompson Street, and Jack was absolutely awful," Charles recalls. "In the middle of the meal, after making a mess of it, he just got up and left." Steve Wheeler remembers seeing Jackson sitting alone on a park bench in the middle of Washington Square early one morning. "It was a very painful sight," Wheeler recalls. "He had very little to say, just feints and grunts. So we went over to a bar and got tanked up."

As Jackson stumbled closer to the edge, the successes mounted. *Guardians of the Secret* went to Cincinnati for the February opening of Sidney Janis's "Abstract and Surrealist Art in the United States," then began a five-city tour of the country; that same month, *The Moon-Woman Cuts the Circle* and *She-Wolf* went to Providence, Rhode Island, where they joined a second traveling exhibition, the Museum of Modern Art's "Twelve Contemporary Painters," with an eleven-city itinerary; soon thereafter, a nameless "smaller work" found its way to David Porter's G Place Gallery in Washington, D.C.; in May, *Male and Female* was shown at the Pinocatheca gallery; and in November, *The Mad Moon-Woman* appeared at the Mortimer Brandt Gallery on Fifty-seventh Street. Amid the traffic, there were a few sales: Thomas Hess bought *Wounded Animal*; Kadish's friend, Jeanne Reynal bought *The Magic Mirror*; and Mrs. Lloyd, who had thought Jackson "perfectly nice," bought *Male and Female* out from under the indecisive nose of Grace McCann Morley of the San Francisco Museum of Art.

Like the collectors, the press appeared to be warming to Jackson. Robert Motherwell contributed a commentary to the winter 1944 issue of *Partisan Review* in which he masterfully lauded Jackson while promoting himself:

"[Pollock] represents one of the younger generation's chances. There are not three other painters of whom this could be said." Clement Greenberg saw the big mural in Peggy's apartment building and instantly abandoned the ambivalent tone of his earlier review. "I took one look at it," he recalls, "and I thought, 'Now *that's* great art,' and I knew Jackson was the greatest painter this country had produced."

In the meantime, Jackson continued to reap the benefits of wartime jingoism. By 1944, American art, like American armed might, seemed to be headed toward worldwide victory, and Jackson Pollock was portrayed as leading the charge. He was not only quintessentially American (de Kooning and Gorky were too foreign; Baziotes, too recently arrived; Motherwell, too patrician; and Rothko, too Jewish), he was the breakthrough artist, the one who had established a beachhead in the European stronghold at Art of This Century. For their Februrary 1944 issue, the editors of *Art & Architecture* asked Jackson to submit a short essay on his view of the destiny of American art. When he balked at such a literary assignment, they suggested an interview instead. Still nervous, apparently, Jackson accepted the help of the interviewer, Robert Motherwell, in formulating his answers.

Where were you born?
Cody, Wyoming, in January 1912. My ancestors were Scotch and Irish.
Have you traveled any?
I've knocked around some in California, some in Arizona. Never been to Europe.
Would you like to go abroad?
No. I don't see why the problems of modern painting can't be solved as well here as elsewhere.
Has being a Westerner affected your work?
I have always been impressed with the plastic qualities of American Indian art. The Indians have the true painter's approach in their capacity to get hold of appropriate images, and in their understanding of what constitutes painterly subject-matter. Their color is essentially Western, their vision has the basic universality of all real art . . .
Why do you prefer living here in New York to your native West?
Living is keener, more demanding, more intense and expansive in New York than in the West; the stimulating influences are more numerous and rewarding. At the same time, I have a definite feeling for the West: the vast horizontality of the land, for instance; here only the Atlantic Ocean gives you that.

The rising strain of nationalism in art did present one problem for the avant-garde community, however: how to distinguish itself from the discredited Regionalist movement of the 1930s. Jackson (and Motherwell) addressed the issue directly.

How did your study with Thomas Benton affect your work, which differs so radically from his?
My work with Benton was important as something against which to react very strongly, later on; in this, it was better to have worked with him than with a less resistant personality who would have provided a much less strong opposition.
Do you think there can be a purely American art?
The idea of an isolated American painting, so popular in this country during the 'thirties, seems absurd to me, just as the idea of creating a purely American mathematics or physics would seem absurd . . .

But Jackson wasn't prepared to deflate completely the balloon of patriotism that was lofting his career. "An American is an American," he added, conceding what would have been unthinkable among avant-garde artists in the thirties, "and his painting would naturally be qualified by that fact, whether he wills it or not." He did not, however, join the Regionalist denunciation of European art. True to modernist gospel, he admitted that "the important painting of the last hundred years was done in France." But the encomiums were strictly *retrospective.* "American painters," he said, "*have* generally missed the point of modern painting from beginning to end." The message was very clear and very popular: the days of abject submission—past, present, and future—of second billing and second-class citizenship for American art, were over. In a period of isolationism, the Regionalists had argued for a separate American art. In the midst of war, the avant-garde was laying the groundwork for a triumphant American art.

For many of the same reasons the American press rallied to Jackson, Alfred Barr detested him. Barr, the tweedy, cultivated product of Princeton and Harvard's Fogg Art Museum had first come to the attention of the founders of the Museum of Modern Art as a twenty-seven-year-old art teacher at a women's college outside Boston. In the fifteen years since being appointed director, he had dedicated himself to bringing European culture to the benighted classroom of America. His heart, as well as the collection of Post-Impressionists, Cubists, and Fauvists he had assiduously gathered, was firmly rooted in European modernism. The museum's American works, by artists such as Charles Burchfield and Marsden Hartley, had been chosen largely to document the influence of European giants like Braque and Picasso. The notion that American abstract artists, especially mavericks like Jackson Pollock, deserved a place in Barr's temple of modernism was almost enough to unnerve the usually poised, patrician director. According to Lincoln Kirstein, a close friend and Harvard classmate, Barr's prejudice was "more anti-abstract than anti-American," but by the mid-1940s the two were virtually interchangeable. "I think it's fair to say that the main support for the Abstract Expressionists came not from Barr but from Sweeney," says Kirstein, who admits that he, too, was "very unsympathetic to Pollock."

In May 1944, Barr was asked to approve the museum's purchase of *She-Wolf*.

It had been eight months since James Thrall Soby first recommended the purchase and six months since the museum put the painting on reserve. In the interim, Sidney Janis, the head of the advisory acquisitions committee, and James Johnson Sweeney had been waging an intense, covert campaign to persuade Barr that *She-Wolf* was worth its $650 price tag. Janis had decided to substitute the work for *Guardians of the Secret* in his forthcoming book, *Abstract and Surrealist Art in America*, while Sweeney had arranged to have it included in the museum's traveling show from February through May. By May, when Barr made his decision, the painting had already been seen by a national audience and had acquired a respectable exhibition history. Janis also tried to persuade Peggy Guggenheim to lower the price. "He said they couldn't afford more than six hundred dollars," Lee Krasner recalled. "Would she drop the price to four hundred and fifty?" Peggy shot back, "Go tell them to tell my Aunt [Mrs. Simon Guggenheim, a prominent supporter of the museum] to make up the difference."

At a lunch meeting with the earnest, proper Barr, Jackson was on his best behavior. "He didn't say a word," recalled Dorothy Miller, wife of the WPA's Federal One director Holger Cahill, who was assistant curator of painting and sculpture at the time. "[He] just sat there listening to Alfred talk all through the meal. When finally Alfred asked some questions, [Pollock's] answers were to the point. And it wasn't a strain either—in fact, a very pleasant lunch, and I thought him very touching." If Barr needed further convincing, he found it when he opened the April issue of *Harper's Bazaar* and saw an article by Sweeney entitled "Five American Painters." One of the "five" was Jackson Pollock and one of the few paintings reproduced, in color, was *She-Wolf*. According to Lee Krasner, it was the *Harper's* article that "clinched the deal."

At their meeting on May 2, the acquisitions committee voted to purchase *She-Wolf* and Robert Motherwell's collage, *Pancho Villa Dead and Alive*. (The pairing of Jackson's painting with a work by Motherwell, who was more closely identified with the Europeans, may have been yet another effort to placate Barr.) Although still "not particularly enthusiastic" about Jackson's work, according to Sweeney, Barr reluctantly accepted the committee's recommendation, and two days later the purchase order was issued. Only six months after Jackson's show at Art of This Century, another bastion of European hegemony had fallen. When she heard the news, Peggy wired Jackson and Lee:

VERY HAPPY TO ANNOUNCE THE MUSEUM BOUGHT SHE WOLF FOR $600 TODAY.
LOVE PEGGY GUGGENHEIM.

Peggy had good reason to be elated. Only three weeks before the MOMA sale, at Putzel's urging, she had renewed Jackson's contract for another year on almost identical terms. The sale of *She-Wolf* brought the total proceeds from sales of his paintings to almost $1,500, or $150 *more* than she had paid

Jackson in the nine months since the original contract was signed. In addition, she now owned a twenty-foot mural that had drawn critical raves. Suddenly alert to the possibility that she might actually make money by sponsoring him, Peggy, for the first time, "dedicated" herself to the task of promoting Pollock with all her manic energies. "I worked hard to interest people in his work," she wrote proudly, "and never tired of doing so. . . . One day Mrs. Harry Winston, the famous Detroit collector, came to the gallery to buy a Masson. I persuaded her to buy a Pollock instead." Intrigued by the notion of creating a reputation, Peggy made a point of selling Jackson's works to the *right* buyers—she called it "getting him into the right hands"—and often gave drawings as presents to collectors and rich friends, hoping to lure them into making larger purchases.

The sale of *She-Wolf* was a turning point for Jackson as well, but in the opposite direction. For the same reason the contract looked better and better to Peggy, it looked worse and worse to Jackson. It forced him to confront the near impossibility of selling more than $2,800 worth of paintings in any one year and thereby "earning out" his yearly advance. After all, the November show had represented the best of two years' work and the next show at Art of This Century was not scheduled until April of 1945. At that rate, he would be living on $150 a month—less than the combined income he and Lee had made on the Project—for the foreseeable future. Only a month after proudly informing Charles of the contract renewal, he wrote with more than a touch of bitterness, "I am getting $150 a month from the gallery, which just about doesn't meet the bills. I will have to sell alot of work thru the year to get it above $150." While Charles may have been sympathetic, the rest of the family was dumbfounded. How could an artist who had received so much attention, including a picture in *Harper's Bazaar,* earn so little money? Privately, they huffed about "slight recognition" and disparaged "the same low figure" of $150 a month. Soon after *She-Wolf* was sold, Stella complained to Charles that "of course [Jackson] didn't get any cash out of it," then added, in obvious bewilderment, "I guess he thinks he is lucky to have his contract renewed for another year."

With sentiments running in such contrary directions, friction was inevitable. Jackson began to question both Peggy's ability as a dealer and her commitment to him. He complained to Putzel that she wasn't putting enough money into promotion and advertising to earn her hefty one-third commission. Months went by without a sale while Peggy made arrangements for upcoming solo shows for "competitors" like Baziotes, Motherwell, David Hare, and Mark Rothko. The 1944 Spring Salon for young artists in May included only one small colored drawing by Jackson alongside major paintings by Baziotes, Hedda Sterne, Jimmy Ernst, and Attilio Salemme. The salon also sparked a blistering attack on Peggy's integrity in *Art Digest* as well as a wave of criticism from those who "detected a decline in the level of talent that Guggenheim was exhibiting." Rumors persisted that Peggy would close the gallery and return to Europe as soon as the war was over—a prospect that seemed suddenly less remote when the Allies invaded France in early June. Even more unsettling were hints that Howard Putzel might quit the gallery, leaving artists on their own to deal with the mercurial Miss Guggenheim. The uncertainty was enough to prompt Motherwell to write Baziotes suggesting they "look out for themselves as soon as possible since [Peggy] could guarantee nothing for the future." Artists like Motherwell and Baziotes, of course, could go to other dealers— both, in fact, were already being wooed by Sam Kootz—but Jackson was bound by contract to Peggy, with or without Putzel.

By May, Jackson's anxiety had reached the critical stage. Putzel tried to reassure him: "Probably—possibly, I mean—you may be really launched by the beginning of 45," he wrote with a hesitation that was not at all reassuring, "and much more solidly or enduringly than sales pressure and advertising could have effected, with no need for social playing up."

To Peggy, Jackson's dissatisfaction seemed like outrageous ingratitude. She had put up with his "rather wild and frightening" style of painting, his huge, unwieldy canvases, his shrewish girlfriend, his surly disposition, and his drunken antics without too much complaining (for her). Compared to Motherwell, whose works she considered "much weaker" but sold "much more readily," Jackson was a dealer's nightmare whose turgid canvases and "devilish" behavior made a difficult job impossible. Given the obstacles he threw up, she thought, her efforts had been remarkably successful. "I did sell [Jackson's works] all the time," she insisted, "not very much, but a little bit. . . . He didn't help me sell his pictures at all 'cause he was so drunk all the time." To her, the $150-per-month payment so denigrated by the Pollock family was not just a generous, unprecedented favor, it was a major sacrifice. Because of it, she complained, "I concentrated all my efforts on selling [Pollock's] pictures and neglected all the other painters in the gallery, many of whom soon left me."

In fact, Jackson and his family, accustomed as they were to Stella's misplaced notions of "only the best," had wildly underestimated Peggy's parsimony. In restaurants, she would ostentaciously add up the bill while suggesting under her breath that her guests should "go out and get a job and stop living off of her." At her own dinner table, the fare was "generally spartan," and she closely monitored her guests' consumption. If someone failed to clean his plate, Peggy would pointedly scrape the leftovers back into the serving bowl, muttering to herself, "It's too good to waste." "She did not create around her an atmosphere of easy giving," understates her biographer, ". . . especially if one were on the receiving end of her generosity." (That Jackson expected "easy giving" from Peggy was only the first, ominous indication of how ill prepared he was for the financial challenges ahead. Throughout his career, he was never able to appreciate the economic constraints on others—especially his dealers—to educate his family's expectations, or to control his own spending.)

Success was not only less profitable than Jackson had expected, it had hidden costs. By far the most unexpected and devastating of these was the transformation of his circle of friends. Some, like Balcomb Greene, simply disliked the art. Hard-line abstractionists like Fritz Bultman felt that Jackson's imagery had been sucked into the tar pit of Surrealism that surrounded Peggy Guggenheim. "There was," said Peter Busa, "a kind of isolation between all of us after we started to show." John Graham was the first to break off contact altogether. According to a mutual friend, Graham felt Jackson had betrayed Picasso and the modernist tradition. Yet by 1943, Graham himself was drifting away from modernist dogma toward the alchemical and mystical imagery that would dominate his later works. Lee Krasner suspected that "Graham abandoned Jackson because he used to say that an artist lost his soul when he became famous," but there's no indication that Graham thought less of Picasso on account of his extensive celebrity. Bill Baziotes was another artist who distrusted success—Jackson's or anyone else's. As far as Baziotes was concerned, Jackson had been caught in "the web"—his term for the network of dealers and directors who were "always ready to snare an artist and devour him." Arloie McCoy remembers that "Nene Schardt was resentful, too, because Jackson got what her husband Bernie didn't. They wouldn't say it, but the resentment was there." Even Reuben Kadish, who had recently returned from India, began to cool noticeably.

For someone who so desperately needed approval, the effect of so much withdrawal was devastating. To fill the gaps, Jackson once again turned to alcohol, the perennial comfort and penance. Since the last wave of drinking binges, however, he had found a new theme with which to torture himself and those around him. "You'd go to a party with a pretty girl," Harry Holtzman recalls, "and he'd come up and take her hand and not let go of it and say, 'You know, I'm a great artist.' It was pathetic." Beatrice Ribak remembers Jackson drunk, "going around bragging about this new thing that he had found and what he was going to do with it. Nobody took him seriously, but Jackson would just brag at the top of his lungs." In May, drunk and belligerent, he burst into Louis Ribak's studio on Twenty-first Street. "Jackson tried to tell him that he shouldn't be doing that kind of representational work," Beatrice Ribak recalls. "He should be doing what Jackson was doing. There was a lot of yelling, but when my husband wouldn't listen, Jackson picked up a hammer and said, 'I'm gonna kill you.' It was really kid stuff."

Success also thrust Jackson into unfamiliar company. Soon after the November show, egged on by Peggy and Lee, he began appearing at the frequent parties and dinners given by prominent collectors like Bernard Reis and Jeanne Reynal as well as Peggy herself. They were giddy, garrulous events, where Matta entertained with his hilarious stories and Motherwell held forth on Mallarmé. In the midst of so many strangers and such intimidating social fluency, Jackson seemed "a lost soul," even more painfully conspicuous for his silence. When he spoke, it was usually through Lee, although, according to a friend, "one sometimes wondered if Pollock himself would have replied in the same words." Most of the time, he simply "smiled and sat quietly," recalls May Rosenberg, and drank. "If someone came in and said, do you want a drink, he'd say yes—like a good little boy, or even more like a good little girl. He felt that they bought his art, so he had to be nice to them."

It was only a matter of time before Peggy tried to have sex with Jackson. Given her reputation, both Lee and Jackson must have been surprised that she waited as long as she did. Both had heard the stories about her bizarre sexual appetites, about her affairs with Tanguy and Penrose, about the long lists of lovers she kept, about her claims to have slept "with practically every man she had ever met," about her ability to make love anywhere, any time, even "with the window-cleaner watching." A sexual omnivore, Peggy pursued men, women, and even, according to one particularly lurid account, dogs, with a frankness that never lost its power to shock. Her preferred prey, of course, was "anything in pants," but otherwise she made no distinctions, pursuing hetero-sexual and homosexual men with equal fervor. "She tried awfully hard to go to bed with Alfred Barr," recalled Dorothy Miller. Some people suspected that she actually preferred homosexual lovers because they "were more likely to put up with a middle-aged woman" and "like[d] the idea of a woman being inter-ested in them." One friend thought that Peggy's whole approach to sex was "homosexual": "She was around them so much," said John Richardson, "she picked up the one-night stands."

One of those "one-night stands" was Jackson Pollock. Sometime in early 1944, on a night when Lee was out of town and Jackson was too drunk to make excuses, Peggy managed to lure him into her bedroom. According to Lee, she had been trying for some time, insinuating that if Jackson was *truly* grateful for her patronage, there was only one way to prove it.

But it wasn't fidelity or sobriety that had kept him out of Peggy's bedroom for so long. Even after two years with Lee, Jackson continued to be plagued by sexual anxieties. The resolution that Lee had brought was fragile, and nothing threatened to shatter it like Peggy's nymphomaniacal demands. The evening climaxed in fiasco—although the exact details varied in the telling. At different times, Peggy claimed that Jackson fell asleep, that he vomited in her bed, that he urinated in her bed, and that "he threw his drawers out the window," all of which could have happened. As for the sexual event, Peggy said only that it was "very unsuccessful," which, given Peggy's indiscriminate appetite and willingness to fabricate sexual triumphs, must have meant it was truly humili-ating. When asked about the incident years later, Jackson responded as he always did to questions about his rumored sexual exploits: a knowing smile, a crude joke, and an enigmatic grunt to leave the impression that "he probably did, but if he didn't, it was because she wasn't worth it." Several friends recall him saying, "To fuck Peggy you'd have to put a towel over her head first."

But Peggy's unrestrained sexuality wasn't nearly as threatening as the forbid-den sexuality of those around her.

With the departure of the puritanical Breton, who disapproved of any sex outside marriage, and the arrival of Macpherson and his entourage of "Athenians" (Macpherson's preferred term), Peggy's apartment quickly filled with a "pandemonium" of homosexuals from both inside and outside the New York art community. Most had been exempted from war duty as "undesirables." They "were around because no one else was around," recalled Peggy's son, Sindbad, who served in the army; "most everyone else was drafted."

Not quite everyone. Caught like a clam in this teeming, exotic, evanescent tidal pool of gay New York was Jackson Pollock.

The war had already wreaked havoc on Jackson's shaky sexual self-confidence. The deferment that was supposed to spare him the trauma of military service had inflicted a different kind of trauma as he watched friends like Kadish, James Brooks, George McNeil, John Little, Burgoyne Diller, Ilya Bolotowsky, Wilfrid Zogbaum, George Mercer, Ibram Lassaw, and even brother Frank go off in uniform. Although few of them crossed the ocean and fewer still saw combat, they at least were "in it," taking part in the great endeavor. They were not among the dross of manhood that remained behind in mufti, described by Sindbad as "those that were too old, or queens, or 4F." Between these categories, neither Sindbad nor the American public drew fine distinctions. A young, able, unmarried, apparently healthy male like Jackson who was not on his way to war was presumed to be defective in some dark, unspeakable way. The fact that Jackson was an artist suggested the darkest explanation of all. When Robert Motherwell appeared before his draft board, the first question was, "Are you a homosexual?" When Motherwell answered no, the board didn't believe him, insisting that anyone who lived in Greenwich Village and was an artist *had* to be a homosexual. Motherwell called their attention to his marriage, but the board granted him an "undesirable" exemption regardless. In Selective Service announcements, artists were routinely lumped with "hairdressers, dress and millinery makers, designers, and interior decorators," in a group whose bravery, patriotism, and manhood were all suspect.

The gay courtesans who reveled every night in Peggy's apartment fit the unflattering stereotype perfectly. Like their hostess, they were utterly oblivious to the war. According to Sindbad, who visited his mother on leave, "If they hadn't seen me in uniform, they wouldn't have known I was in the army. All those people behaved as if there were no war." They drank, played games, staged skits, and drank some more. No one talked of the battle for Monte Cassino, the relief of Leningrad, or the race riots in Detroit. The only clues to the conflict engulfing the rest of the world were the occasional bewildered young sailors dragged in by Parker Tyler or sometimes by Peggy herself. When tempers flared, the bone was usually artistic or amorous, seldom political.

Peggy's "rich fruits" (May Rosenberg's term) included a small contingent from the Museum of Modern Art. If the party began to sag, the friskiest of them would remove his clothes, dart through the crowd naked, and ascend the sweeping stairs to the delighted laughter of the regulars. In such flights of Dionysian excess, nothing was forbidden and no one in the room was off limits.

Among the blushing bystanders who attracted his share of amorous attentions was Jackson Pollock.

It's impossible to know just how far Jackson was drawn into the circle of homosexuality that surrounded Peggy Guggenheim. According to one account, Jackson and the MOMA streaker "used to frolic together," and sometimes, when Jackson was drunk enough, would disappear into Peggy's guest room or Macpherson's apartment upstairs where sexual "free-for-alls" were common. Given Jackson's paralyzing anxieties, however, it's unlikely that he could engage in any sexual activity, especially homosexual activity, so blithely—even with the help of alcohol. Yet homosexuality was clearly on his mind in the year following the first Guggenheim show. Despite the threat it posed to his own sexual identity, he immersed himself in the gay subculture of the New York art community, frequently visiting George's Tavern on Seventh Avenue, a block south of Sheridan Square, where a group of homosexuals and others from the New Bauhaus in Chicago often congregated. "It wasn't really a homosexual hangout," recalls one regular patron, "because it wasn't very open then. They didn't make you proclaim what you were at the door, but that's what it amounted to." Fritz Bultman's old family friend, Tennessee Williams, often joined the group at George's, offering tart, black commentary on what he called "the big lie." "I was sitting at a bar with Fritz and Tennessee Williams," Peter Busa remembers, "and Tennessee said, 'You know, Peter, the world is divided into fruits and nuts.' "

Jackson was also a frequent guest at the Gramercy Park apartment of John Little, who returned from navy duty in 1944, where he often saw Little's friend, Ward Bennett. Jackson may have been confused about his sexual identity, but Bennett—a "sandy-haired," athletic-looking, twenty-five-year-old former Hofmann student—picked up very clear signals. "I didn't go to bed with him," Bennett says, "but he was definitely interested in me. I mean I would have gone to bed with him, but I was not interested in Jackson. I liked him very much—he was so sweet and such a dear when he was sober and so crazy when he was drunk. I'm sure it would have been possible if I was interested but I really wasn't."

Others were. One of the young artists who frequented George's "was very attracted to people like policemen and truck drivers and big rugged characters like that," according to Peter Busa. "So he doted on Jackson, who could have picked this guy up and thrown him across the room." Busa recalls hearing the same person brag about how he waited until Jackson was "loaded" and "defenseless," then led him to the house that he shared with Tennessee Williams on Eleventh Street. "What could Jackson do if [this guy] wanted to screw him in the ass? I know it happened," Busa insists. "Friends of mine talked about it and laughed about it at times." Contacted years later, the man Busa named would only admit coyly that he had "kissed" Jackson once or twice. But, says Busa, "he has these elegant terms he uses now."

If Jackson's anxieties ever permitted a homosexual act, it probably followed the scenario described by Busa: a drinking binge to the brink of oblivion, a passive role (to avoid the demands and implications of taking the initiative), and a smaller man who, in some deep recess of Jackson's subconscious, may have recalled Sande and a childhood of shared beds. (A decade later, when the issue of homosexuality would surface again in Jackson's life, the reported encounters were almost identical to the one described by Busa.) As early as 1944, at least one person took accounts like Busa's seriously: Lee Krasner. "Lee knew that he was interested in me," recalls Ward Bennett, "and it drove her up the wall." Years later, she confided to several close friends that "[Jackson] liked men. He always had this tremendous thing about homosexuality. He was rather anxious about it, you know, wondering whether . . ." Later, Reuben Kadish would tell an interviewer, "I know Jackson had sex with men as well as women," and confirmed that Sande "worried terribly" that his younger brother was gay.

Next to the testimony of those closest to him, the most persuasive proof of Jackson's homosexual involvement is the explosion of self-hatred that accompanied it. During the late winter and early spring of 1944, he reached an apogee of drinking and self-abuse unseen since the months preceding Bloomingdale's. John Little remembers him picking a fight with a prizefighter in the Cedar Bay—"the guy turned around and grabbed Jackson, and said, 'Would you like me to flatten your nose?' "—then heading off down the street stopping at every bar. By two or three in the morning, he would be weaving and bellowing in the empty streets: "I'm gonna fuck you all, I'm gonna fuck the world." "Fucking" became an obsession. "One thing he loved to do," recalls Steve Wheeler, "was to take me around and knock on doors at night. These were women he knew. And he'd say, 'I'm gonna get fucked tonight, Steve.' And I'd say, 'Go ahead, help yourself.' So we would go through the Village and as soon as they'd hear Jack's voice, and hear how drunk he was, they'd turn the lights out. . . . I think he was trying to prove to me that he could go out and get laid. But he never did. He'd wind up stewing in his beer at a bar somewhere."

Usually at George's Tavern. More and more often, Jackson's nocturnal rampages ended in the gay company where they began. One night, Rita Benton's niece, Maria Piacenza, found him at George's and, at Jackson's request, invited him back to her apartment to see her paintings. Once there, Jackson immediately found a bottle of whiskey and "practically swallowed that thing down within minutes," Piacenza remembers, "and began reeling and rocking around the apartment." Eventually, she managed to steer him out to a restaurant "to get some coffee or food into him." But that, too, was a mistake. "As soon as we got inside, he began to literally break up the joint. He really tore that place apart before they grabbed him and me and threw us the hell out. It was so embarrassing." On the sidewalk, several men came out of the shadows and gathered around Jackson. "I didn't know what they were up to, but they acted like they knew him," says Piacenza. Angry, humiliated, and certain that if she called the police, they would take Jackson to Bellevue, Piacenza walked away.

"I just left the son of a bitch there," she says. "That's all. He had nothing to steal. And they didn't look like they intended to rob him. They hung around him waiting for me to leave. What they did afterward I don't know."

Jackson's forays into the gay demimonde, like the sexual fiasco with Peggy, betrayed his deteriorating relationship with Lee. The previous fall, on the recommendation of her friend Sarah Johns, Lee had begun regular visits to a homeopathic doctor named Elizabeth Wright Hubbard for treatment of persistent stomach pain. Part dietician and part psychoanalyst, Hubbard believed in the interrelatedness of emotional and physical health and often prescribed behavioral cures for physical ailments. It may have been at Hubbard's urging that, soon after Jackson's November show, Lee began to assert her independence. Almost single-handedly, she persuaded Peggy to mount a show in March for Hans Hofmann. Even with Putzel's support, it was a hard fight. "Peggy was reluctant about Hans," Lillian Olaney remembers. "As far as the Surrealists were concerned, Hofmann could drop dead. But Lee really took up arms for him." Afterward, Peggy regretted her decision—"she was convinced [Hofmann] gave the gallery a bad image," Lee said—but for Lee the show was an encouraging success.

Jackson apparently accepted this temporary diversion of Lee's attentions. According to one account, he even helped persuade Peggy to mount the Hofmann show and subsequently accepted a share of the "blame." But, as always, he found a way to make his objections known. When Putzel and Betsy Zogbaum came by the Eighth Street apartment to take him to the opening of Hofmann's show, Jackson insisted on first going across the street to buy some supplies. He returned a few minutes later, stumbling drunk and covered with paint. "In that short time, he had gotten drunk," recalls Zogbaum, "and the tubes of paint he bought had squeezed out all over his one good suit. It was a ghastly sight."

Sometime in early 1944, Lee brought her easel back from Reuben Kadish's studio on Twelfth Street, where she had taken it temporarily when Jackson tore out the wall of her studio to make room for the giant mural, and set it up in Jackson's old bedroom. There, for the first time in two years, she started a fresh canvas. Much had changed in those years. Jackson had shown her a new way to paint and, as when Igor Pantuhoff came home from the Hofmann school, she was determined to try it herself. "I gave up the model and still life," she recounted. "I began with a blank canvas and nothing in front of me." Rejecting Hofmann and "the Cubist grid," she tried, like Pollock, to paint "from the inside out." "It was only after Pollock made some impression that [Lee] began to reorient herself," recalls Steve Wheeler, another Hofmann student. "Instead of trying to make the perfect picture that Hofmann always talked about, she started doing what Pollock was doing—a little freehand drawing, a little smearing around." When Lee reached inside, however, she came up empty-handed. Paint accumulated on the canvas—sometimes an inch thick—but the images refused to coalesce. "I was putting masses of paint on canvas and nothing would happen," she recalls, "just tons of paint going nowhere." She called it "sitting on the easel," and later admitted, "It was all very frustrating."

If Jackson never told Lee, "I don't want you to paint" (as Lee later claimed), it was because he never had to. Two years before, they seemed to have reached an unspoken agreement: he would profess respect for her as an artist—"a good woman painter," he often called her—and she, in return, would abandon her artistic ambitions. Despite Lee's protest that "I didn't hide my paintings in a closet; they hung on the wall next to his," no one remembers seeing them there and a few visitors recall specifically that her work was "nowhere in evidence." "Whoever came into that house came to see Jack's work," Reuben Kadish recalls, "not Lee's." Her return to the easel, frustrating and unproductive though it was, disrupted the delicate balance of egos. "It upset Jackson," Betsy Zogbaum remembers. "He was always basically insecure, and when Lee started painting again you could see that it ate at him."

In early June, Tom Benton came through New York on his way to Martha's Vineyard. "The bell rang one day and I stuck my head out, looked down, and saw this foreshortened face of Benton looking up at me," Lee recounted. Jackson ran down the five flights and greeted his former teacher, whom he hadn't seen in two or three years, "effusively." Almost immediately, at Jackson's prompting, Benton asked to see Lee's paintings, a prospect that horrified Lee. "I knew what was in my studio," she recalled ruefully. "Jackson also knew . . . this is during the point at which my canvases were building up into gray masses and no image came through. It [was] not a good state of affairs." Nevertheless, she led Benton to her studio and gamely showed him one of her "gray slabs." "I stood in front of the canvas and from Benton there was no word," Lee recalled. "The silence was brazen." He stood there looking "a little awkward, a little embarrassed," until finally, Jackson, having made his point, suggested that they get a beer.

Lee did her best to explain away the incident—"I was having a rough time and I didn't care who knew it"—but Jackson's hostility was impossible to ignore. Soon afterward, while Lee was out of her studio, Jackson took a brush and reworked one of her unfinished canvases. Years before, she had tested him in the same way, touching a brush to his canvas to probe the boundary between love and integrity. Now it was her turn to be tested. When she returned and saw the painting, she exploded in "total rage," slashed the offending canvas and refused to speak to Jackson for days. Referring to the long chill in their relationship that followed, she later said, "at that time I didn't really love people or things."

The incident only brought to the surface resentments that had been brewing for two years. At that stage, "they were so competitive that they couldn't even work in the same house together," recalls Reuben Kadish, who shortly thereafter welcomed Lee back to the vacant room next to his studio. "He couldn't stand having her around while he was working. She couldn't stand being around him. It was suddenly like a male-eat-female thing, that kind of antagonism. She was being digested into oblivion by his presence."

Just when a showdown seemed inevitable, Jackson and Lee decided to take a vacation. In mid-June, they sublet the Eighth Street studio to Bernard Steffen and left for Provincetown, Massachusetts. It wasn't the first time—or the last —that they tried to solve a problem with a change of scenery.

But scenery was the only thing that changed. The isolation and exposure of a Cape Cod summer acted like a magnifying lens, focusing the anxiety and resentment of the previous winter to an incendiary point. Even the long drive up the coast turned out to be an ordeal. Lee had pointedly arranged for them to ride with her old boyfriend Igor Pantuhoff in his eye-catching, yellow-and-chrome Lincoln. Never comfortable around the glib White Russian, by the end of the all-night trip Jackson was bristling with jealousy. For a few days, the threesome enjoyed the panoramic view of Provincetown Bay from Hans Hofmann's house on Miller Hill where John Little and Ward Bennett had rented a room. To Jackson, Hofmann was yet another reminder of Lee's former life —and of her painting—whose mere presence could set him to sulking. On the day of their arrival, Jackson was forced to accompany Little and Lee into Hofmann's studio where Sam Kootz, who had just signed up Hofmann for his new gallery, was choosing the paintings for Hofmann's first show. Because of Lee's role in arranging the show at Art of This Century, both Little and Kootz deferred to her eye in making selections. According to Little, Jackson watched the proceedings in "seething" silence.

Jackson retaliated by taking an inordinate interest in the charcoal drawings being done by Ward Bennett. "I was just a student," Bennett recalls, "but he used to come over and see what I was doing all the time." The two men often walked the beach together. At one point, to Lee's chagrin, they even collaborated on a painting. "It was a piece of canvas that we found on the beach," says Bennett. "We just put some paint on it. It was just a lark." Lark or not, Lee was livid. She had not traveled three hundred miles to see Jackson spirited away by someone else, male or female. She made that point clear to Maria Piacenza, who was also visiting the Cape that summer. When Jackson saw her on the street, he rushed toward her "with great enthusiasm," Piacenza remembers. "Why don't you come over to the studio and have a drink with us?" he started to say before Lee interrupted. "Jackson, we have an appointment this afternoon." "Well, how about coming over tomorrow?" he pressed. "Tomorrow, we are going to the gallery," Lee countered. "She just fixed it," Piacenza recalls. "It was clear by the third invitation that she wasn't about to let this happen, so I said, 'Well, Jackson, I'll see you around,' and I walked away and didn't see him the rest of the summer." A few days later, Jackson introduced Lee to Nene and Bernie Schardt. The meeting was cordial enough—the two couples even took pictures of each other—but it was clear to Nene Schardt, too, that "Lee didn't think we were good enough for her," and the foursome never got together again.

The guest arrangements at Hofmann's house soon became unworkable, and, less than a week after arriving, Lee and Jackson agreed to move. It would be about the only thing they agreed on that summer. The new place was closer to the center of town—a small apartment on the second floor of an old boat house on Bradford Street, known as the "back road" of Provincetown because its houses were cut off from the town's magnificent harbor view. From their narrow, one-room aerie, Jackson and Lee could see "only a sliver of blue between some of the houses if they craned their necks," according to a neighbor. Otherwise, the house was a charming picturesque Cape Cod original, clad in mist-gray, rain-streaked shingles, and only a few minutes' walk from the beach.

For a few days, Lee was hopeful. They went every day to swim and sunbathe at New Beach where Lee tanned while Jackson burned. "I've taken a crew cut and look a little like a peeled turnip—or beet," he wrote Sande. In the late afternoons, they could watch the brightly painted boats of the Portuguese fishermen coming in from the "back side"—the local waters just offshore— and the "trippers" returning low in the water from their week-long venture to the teeming deep waters of Stilwagen and Georges banks, their mid-decks heaped with a silver booty of haddock and cod. Or they could idle down Commercial Street, the town's main street, where, to Jackson's mortification, he was almost the only civilian male of military age. The lights no longer blinked out at sundown as they had at the height of the U-boat scare when Max Ernst was expelled from the town because jumpy officials feared he would signal submarines from his seaside windows. But gasoline allowances were still tight and cars were a rare sight. There was, as always, plenty of salt air, sunshine, and fresh fish, which the fishermen supplied free to local artists "to bring good luck." "Provincetown looks much better to me now," Jackson wrote Stella and Sande.

The summer idyll was soon shattered, however, by the arrival of two unexpected guests. The first was Howard Putzel, looking fluorescent pale, urban, and out of place among the leather-skinned locals. He had come to announce that he was quitting Art of This Century and establishing a gallery of his own. He was fed up with being Peggy's "sandwich boy." He also reported that Peggy was planning to close her gallery after the next season and give her collection to the San Francisco Museum. Still bound to Peggy by contract, Jackson was dazed by the news. Putzel had been his chief champion and protector in the face of his boss's fickle pleasure. Now it appeared that Putzel would abandon him to Peggy, and, soon afterward, Peggy would abandon him to the unknown. Rumors about Peggy's return to Europe, encouraged by Robert Motherwell, who was anxious to take other artists with him to a rival dealer, had been circulating almost since her arrival, but as of 1944, no date had been set and no disposition of the collection had been decided on. In this regard, Putzel's report seems to have been the product of anxiety and wishful thinking rather than inside information. Nevertheless, Jackson received it as gospel. "Howard has quit the gallery," he wrote Sande the day after Putzel's arrival, "which I'm sorry to hear about. Peggy plans to close the gallery after next winter."

But the news about Peggy couldn't have been as painful as what followed: Putzel invited Lee to join his new gallery. In the midst of his renewed anxieties about the future, it was a devastating blow to Jackson and he struck back in the only way he knew how.

One obvious target was Hans Hofmann. Not only had Lee arranged his show at Art of This Century, she had shepherded him into the contract with Sam Kootz—a favor that seemed all the more galling to Jackson in light of Peggy's imminent departure. Even worse, Lee had set up her summer studio in Hofmann's house—another sign of independence that must have rankled. Socially, Jackson and Hofmann had always been "like sandpaper against one another," according to George Mercer, and their first social contact of the summer had done nothing to improve relations. In one famous exchange, Jackson tried to draw Hofmann into an argument about art. "Jackson was trying to get across to [him] his concept of the image," recalls Fritz Bultman, who was also in Provincetown that summer. "He said that if you painted out of yourself, you created an image larger than a landscape." According to Lee, Hofmann responded by suggesting that Jackson "work from nature," as Hofmann usually did, especially in Provincetown where he found the beach and sea great sources of inspiration. "I *am* nature," Jackson responded defiantly, throwing a rare morsel of profundity to generations of writers and critics. Most versions of the exchange end with Pollock's Cartesian pronouncement, but, in fact, Hofmann had the last word: "Ah, but if you work from inside you will repeat yourself." Jackson, realizing perhaps how salient and prophetic a riposte it was, fell glumly silent.

Bested in verbal sparring, Jackson resorted to more familiar weapons. At a gathering at Hofmann's studio early in July, drunk and determined, he clambered up to the balcony where Hofmann painted and often slept. When Hofmann and one of his students, Fred Hauck, reluctantly pursued him up the stairs, Jackson grabbed the easel and hurled it down at them. Fortunately, his aim was off and the easel flew past. Hofmann was too startled to say anything but Miz Hofmann was furious. She instantly banished Jackson from the house, and neither Jackson nor Lee saw the Hofmanns again that summer.

The other unexpected guest that summer was Tennessee Williams. According to one story, he "dropped in" on Jackson and Lee and stayed, "living out of a suitcase," for several weeks before renting a room over the garage of Karl Knaths, the American Cubist painter. "He was always a freeloader," says John Myers, relating the story told him by Lee, "and he freeloaded on them until they couldn't stand it anymore." What Lee couldn't stand, however, wasn't the dozens of meals that Williams cadged, or the daily visits when he biked over on breaks from writing *The Glass Menagerie*, or even his cavorting with Jackson

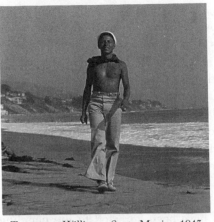

Tennessee Williams, Santa Monica, 1943

on the beach—"he used to carry me out into the water on his shoulders," Williams wrote in his memoirs, "and to sport about innocently." What really made Lee frantic with worry were the times, increasingly frequent, when Jackson and Williams would disappear together into the Cape's cool, foggy nights.

As Lee feared, Jackson was being drawn back into the gay demimonde they had left New York to escape. The temptation came not directly from Williams —he called Jackson "just a little bit heavier from beer-drinking than was attractive to me"—but from the group of six or eight men who met every night at Julian Beck's studio on Captain Jack's Wharf just off Commercial Street near the center of town. A nineteen-year-old student at Yale University, Beck had been an aspiring painter until a year before when he met Judith Malina, his future wife. Malina had turned Beck's head to the theater and converted one corner of his dilapidated studio into a makeshift stage. (Three years later, the two would found the influential Living Theater.) "They were always putting on little theatricals," Ward Bennett remembers. "They were open to anybody who wanted to come in. It was very Parisian." But there were other activities going on in Beck's studio designed for a more select audience. The balcony was the designated place for sex, mostly male-to-male, although a female occasionally wandered in, and voyeurs were always welcome. "The whole place was quite homosexual," Bennett recalls. The regulars on Captain Jack's Wharf that season were Beck, Williams, a young Harvard Law School student named Bill Cannastra, and, by midsummer, Jackson Pollock. Around them floated an ad hoc "lunatic fringe," which Williams described as "a collection [that] could not be found outside of Bellevue or the old English Bedlam."

By far the craziest of the lot was Cannastra. Williams called him "one of the aboriginal 'beats,' " a "beat before there were 'beats.' " Setting out from Beck's studio around midnight, Cannastra would lead a group of six or eight, including Jackson, out into the deserted streets of Provincetown in search of open windows or parted curtains through which they might catch a glimpse of sexual activity. "We would go up and down fire escapes, looking at people screwing,"

Bennett remembers. "This guy knew exactly where everybody was, where sex was going on in Provincetown. Not just man and man, but regular sex." According to Williams, Cannastra was similarly familiar with the environs of Harvard. "He had a map of the town of Cambridge with X's marked to indicate the location of window shades that were likely to expose an exciting peep show." Each nocturnal tour was "carefully mapped-out," and Cannastra would return, "rocks off, about 2 A.M.—sometimes with rapturous reports on intimacies he had witnessed through those lucky windows." In Provincetown, another of Cannastra's favorite haunts was the Catholic cemetery behind the Pilgrim Monument where, one night that summer, a local girl broke her leg while cavorting with "that gay bunch" from out of town, and Jackson and Cannastra were arrested.

Jackson may well have been attracted to the gangling, dark-haired, light-eyed Cannastra, whom friends described as "beautiful" and "poetic looking." Certainly, the two men shared the same demons. Sober, Cannastra was "extremely quiet and terribly sweet," according to his friend Nell Blaine, and spoke with a disarming stammer. Like Jackson, he was fond of "spinning fantasies," Blaine recalls, only his medium was words not paint. Drunk, he was "completely altered, a wild man with a death wish." "When Bill was drunk," says Blaine, "his poetic imagination came out in absolutely bizarre ways. He crashed a costume party I gave and he came as a ghoul, with his face and his feet painted silver. He brought his valuable collection of opera records and scattered them on the floor, then turned a beer keg on and started dancing on the records with his bare silver feet. He was jumping around on the broken records covered with beer and his feet were bleeding. Then he went into the kitchen and turned on the oven and stuck his head in to see how long he could last. Then he went outside, jumped up on the hood of a car and started leaping from one car to another."

Cannastra's friends called him a "frustrated artist" and blamed his self-destructive antics on "sexual problems."

For Jackson, too, the summer quickly turned to self-obliteration. The nights out with Williams and Cannastra, the bizarre scene at Julian Beck's studio, the desires that he may have felt, even the sporting with Williams in the surf, all demanded punishment or denial of some kind. Sex always had a price, but forbidden sex proved particularly costly. Even as he continued his nocturnal visits to Captain Jack's Wharf, he began frequenting the local bars—the Old Colony Tap, Cookie's Tap near the boatyard on Commercial Street where the fishermen drank, or Mac's Bar on the east side—anyplace where he could drink his way into oblivion, or, better yet, into a fight. Chaim Gross crossed his path at the Lobster Pot. "I was with a friend, and [Jackson] was drunk and belligerent," Gross recalls. "He insulted me without any reason, trying to pick a fight. He was an angry person." In the same angry mood, Jackson ran into Leland Bell, his friend from the Museum of Non-Objective Art. "It was a horrible scene," Bell remembers. "He was drunk and he started talking about

Klee and Arp and sneering, egging me on. He said, 'If you like that shit you'll never be a painter,' and I just said, 'Fuck you, to hell with you, Jackson.' " When people started avoiding him, Jackson moved to the front of the bar, sitting near the windows, "so he could see everybody," says Gross. At the slightest provocation, he would leap up, fists clenched, knocking over glasses, swearing at the top of his voice, and "begging for a punch." Ward Bennett recalls the sight of Jackson, dead drunk, pissing defiantly in the middle of a crowded barroom floor, daring anyone to stop him.

By August, Lee was frantic. Between the escapades with Williams and Cannastra and the drinking binges, she seldom saw Jackson anymore. They still swam together occasionally, but most of her nights were spent in a hollow-eyed search from bar to bar. Maria Piacenza remembers the poignant sight of Lee "wandering around town trying to look unconcerned saying, 'Have you seen Jackson?' She spent the summer, every minute of it, vaguely looking for Jackson. It couldn't have been easy." When he finally did appear, usually in the early morning hours, his condition confirmed all Lee's worst fears. "Jackson was in such shape in Provincetown," recalls Ward Bennett, "that Lee just brought him home and cleaned him up and put him to bed, and then got him going again the next day." The rolls of canvas that she had arranged to have sent up from New York sat in the studio unopened.

In desperation, Lee turned to Jackson's family. On the way back from a visit to her ailing father in mid-August, she stopped at Sande's house in Deep River. Within two weeks, the entire family, including Stella, descended on Provincetown. As Lee hoped, Jackson's nightly forays stopped. By Labor Day, Tennessee Williams was gone (he accompanied Bill Cannastra back to Harvard where he finished *The Glass Menagerie* in Cannastra's law school dorm room surrounded by headstones stolen from local cemeteries), and Jackson rounded off the summer with two weeks of sunbathing, reminiscing, and "damn swell swimming" with Sande in the waning cape sunlight under Stella's oblivious gaze.

Jackson had won. He had not only alienated Lee from her mentor Hofmann but also effectively prevented her from doing "a god-damned bit of work" all summer. Even more remarkably, his antics had brought Stella and Sande from Connecticut to rescue him. In more ways than either Jackson or Lee could have known, the summer had been a glimpse into the future. Like Sande before her, Lee was firmly locked in Jackson's ambivalent embrace. She had spent the summer in an agony of uncertainty, searching and waiting, worrying and listening and, after the ordeal, still cared.

Jackson's future was written more obscurely in the fate of Bill Cannastra, whom he never saw again. After graduating from law school, Cannastra found "a very strong woman" and, for a time, stopped drinking. But it was a short-lived victory. On the eve of their marriage, the woman "had second thoughts," according to a friend, "and went away to Chicago." Cannastra returned to drinking. Soon afterward, on a subway train in New York, he leaned out a window as the train rushed forward and was decapitated by a column.

31

ESCAPE

O nly a few weeks after Jackson and Lee returned from Provincetown, the 1944–45 season began. Peggy reopened her gallery, the parties recommenced, and Jackson, brittle and rootless as ever, was quickly swept up in the resumed flow of alcohol and anxiety. By October, he was "getting just as drunk as he ever had been getting," according to Reuben Kadish, who had seen Jackson hit bottom before. At a dinner with the Hofmanns arranged by Lee to patch up the summer rifts, Jackson drank, sulked, drank, fulminated, drank some more, and finally passed out. It was a familiar routine: listless days and long nights out—Lee never knew where—ending in a ritual of forgiveness when Jackson appeared at the doorway "filthy dirty and falling all over himself."

As winter came on and the trees around the corner in Washington Square turned charcoal gray, Jackson virtually stopped painting. A large canvas—*There Were Seven in Eight*—begun the previous spring in the afterglow of the Guggenheim mural, leaned unfinished against the living room wall. It was all he could do to accompany Reuben Kadish to Stanley William Hayter's Atelier 17 diagonally across from the Eighth Street apartment. There, in a nondescript loft, the two old friends etched copper plates, pulled proofs, and shared reassuring silences. During the day, the workshop was a mecca for European artists like André Masson, Joan Miró, and Marc Chagall, who had worked with Hayter at his workshop in Paris before the Germans put a bounty on his head for printing leaflets that described "how to make a Molotov cocktail to throw at German tanks." But Jackson "couldn't work with people around," according to Kadish, so they came only at night and on weekends when the studio was deserted. (Kadish had worked for Hayter as a printer and kept a key.) Hayter himself, a warm but peripatetic man "filled with brio," would occasionally join them for a beer at one of the local bars favored by Atelier artists or at Hayter's house on Waverly Place.

In the smoky darkness of the White Horse Tavern, the Hotel Albert bar, or the Cedar, in the momentary transition between sobriety and forgetfulness, Jackson talked "about the source of inspiration and about the limits of working from the unconscious," Hayter recalled. Obsessed with the months of impotence, artistic and otherwise, since the Guggenheim mural, "he pointed out that there is a problem when you have plumbed the depths in how to go beyond that level and produce further content." But such flashes of introspection were rare and fleeting. After just a few beers, Jackson was "lost" again—where he apparently wanted to be.

By November, even the local bartenders refused to collaborate in his head-long run at self-obliteration, and he was forced to recruit friends as intermediaries. John Little recalls coming home to find Jackson sitting, shivering on the stoop, waiting for him. "The first words out of his mouth were, 'Let's go and have a beer.'" They went to the bar at the Hotel Albert, but as soon as they sat down, the bartender came charging out, yelling at Jackson, "You get out of here or I'm calling the police!" Outside, Little asked, "What did you do to him, Jackson?" "Well, I was in there yesterday," Jackson explained with a sheepish grin. When they tried a "crummy nightclub" just across the street, the same thing happened. "They took one look at Jackson and said, 'Oh, no, you're not coming in here!'" Little recalls. "This would happen five or six times a night, so he was pretty well known." Despite the obstacles, Jackson always found a way to drink. By the first snowfall, he was wandering the streets again, as he had done in the thirties, stumbling over dirty snowbanks, stopping cars, and yelling at passersby. One friend remembers seeing him urinating in the snow, "spraying the stream from side to side, and bellowing, 'I can piss on the whole world!'"

As the days grew shorter, the binges grew longer. "He spent a lot of time disappearing," recalls Kadish. "Not just for hours but for days." There was one difference from the thirties. Now when he fell down on a bar counter or a snowbank, it was Lee's name, not Sande's, that he called out as he drifted into unconsciousness. And it was Lee, not Sande, who waited at home, alternately sullen and hysterical, angry and terrified, listening for his voice in the street or his footfall on the stairs. "Every time Jack disappeared," Kadish remembers, "Lee would get frantic and start making excuses, looking for someone to blame. She would pace around the apartment saying, 'Jackson will be here any minute.'"

In fact, Jackson was slipping away, and nothing Lee or anyone else did, apparently, could stop him.

When Lee turned to the Pollock family for help, she received only tempered sympathy. Sande and Arloie had already begun barricading themselves against the unpleasant memories of their six-year ordeal with Jackson, and Stella, at Sande's insistence, remained largely oblivious to the problems. Occasionally, she would come to the city and "baby-sit" Jackson during Lee's trips to see her family on Long Island—trips that became increasingly frequent after her father fell ill in 1943—but Jackson never misbehaved while Stella was there. Lee never ceased to be amazed at the strange tranquilizing power, first demonstrated in Provincetown, that Stella held over Jackson, and would have installed her permanently in the apartment if Sande had permitted it. No one else seemed capable of slowing Jackson's fall.

Instead, she did the next best thing: she found another Stella.

Even before the summer, Lee had tried unsuccessfully to persuade Jackson to resume therapy. The debacle in Provincetown only redoubled her determination, and the experience with Stella suggested a solution. Sometime in the fall of 1944, she persuaded him to visit her doctor, Elizabeth Wright Hubbard. Although officially an M.D., Dr. Hubbard was far more than a family doctor. Her unconventional "holistic" approach to treatment took her well beyond the realm of physical ailments. "She believed that her job was half psychology," recalls her daughter, Elizabeth Wright Hubbard II, "and she alienated many patients when she said things like 'the reason your son has asthma is because of you, madam.' " Hubbard preferred to treat whole families (sometimes including family pets) instead of individuals and was eager to receive Jackson as a patient. His first interview began with a series of "psychological" questions such as "Do you like thunderstorms?" and "How do you feel about your mother and father?"

Normally, Jackson would have fended off such efforts to probe his psyche, with a combination of charm, evasion, and belligerence. Instead, as Lee must have anticipated, he was transfixed by Hubbard. With her "enormous bosoms," somber clothing, steel-gray hair, tight corset, square jaw, erect posture, and deep, masculine volice (on the phone, people invariably said, "Yes, sir"), Elizabeth Hubbard *was* Stella Pollock. "She reminded me of Stella from the first time I saw her," says Reuben Kadish. "She had the same stature, the same stance, the same feeling that a lot of western women have—not saying much, but when they say it they mean it." Although a product of Manhattan, not the West, Hubbard was indeed a formidable woman who had made a place for herself in the overwhelmingly male world of medicine. A member of the first graduating class at the Columbia College of Physicians and Surgeons to include women, she had won a coveted residency at Bellevue—also the first ever awarded to a woman. Defying the contumely of her colleagues, she had left the mainstream of medicine to study homeopathy in Geneva, then returned to teach its immunological principles at Hahnemann Medical College in Philadelphia. "She was in the vanguard of women who *did* something," says her daughter. "She had the power. She was like a good witch, a white witch." From her office at 20 East Eighty-fourth Street, Hubbard provided free treatment to the poor and tended to the holistic needs of a patient list that included, at various times, Darius Milhaud, Georges Auric, Alexander Calder, Lily Pons, Marlene Dietrich, and, by early 1945, Jackson Pollock.

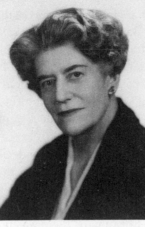

Elizabeth Wright Hubbard

Hubbard's help came just in time. With only a few months remaining before the scheduled March exhibition at Art of This Century, Jackson had virtually nothing to show. In the months immediately after finishing the Guggenheim mural, he had produced only a handful of exhibition-quality paintings, all of them in the same dense, rhythmic, abstract style. He had tried variations: sharp, jagged lines instead of great, flowing curves in *The Night Dancer*; smoky, turbulent browns instead of bright teal and turquoise in *Night Ceremony*. In *Night Mist*, he even stepped back across the line of abstraction toward the fragmented imagery of *Pasiphaë*. But by summer, the creative momentum of the previous year had dissipated completely. His perfunctory efforts at Hayter's workshop in the fall had produced more frustration than art. "He discovered that [etching] wasn't his medium," Reuben Kadish remembers. The resistance of the material, the reversal of the image, the intervention of the acid, and the general intractability of the process were all unsuited to Jackson's abrupt, impatient muse. "He was separated from the final product and he found it very frustrating." In early 1945, Jackson learned that Peggy had scheduled his one-man show at the Arts Club of Chicago for March, the same month as the New York show. He now had two shows to paint.

With no new art to exhibit, Jackson had forfeited a prime pre-Christmas slot at Art of This Century. The first show of the season went to William Baziotes, who had emerged from a long creative slump in time to take the place of a postponed Giacometti exhibition. Three days after the Baziotes show closed, Robert Motherwell's multimedia extravaganza opened (featuring forty-eight works compared to Jackson's fifteen). If the fecundity of his fellow artists didn't rankle Jackson, then surely their reviews did. Baziotes's work was "spontaneously designed and painted in a fever of inspired intent," wrote Maude Riley in *Art Digest*, and his gouaches revealed a "boundless wealth" of color. Even Clement Greenberg raved, calling Baziotes "unadulterated talent," a "natural painter and all painter," and Motherwell "almost too much of a good thing." But no success galled like financial success, and in the booming wartime economy, both shows, especially Baziotes's, were solid sellers.

With his shows and contract renewal approaching, his studio empty, and Peggy's receipts languishing far below the $2,800 break-even point, Jackson watched his colleagues' successes from a sinkhole of envy and depression, consoled only by Greenberg's dictum that "the future of American painting depends on what [Motherwell], Baziotes, Pollock, and only a comparatively few others do from now on."

Hubbard's support couldn't reverse Jackson's decline, but it did provide the eleventh-hour fix of emotional energy he needed to rescue the March shows. Reuben Kadish recalls being stunned when he walked into the studio a few weeks before the opening. "It had been empty only days before. He did everything at the last minute. . . . For months there was nothing, and then suddenly there were a dozen paintings. There had been this tremendous, explosive kind of work period." There was no time to break new ground. Subject matter, size, color, and complexity were decided by the exigencies of speed. For the Chicago show, he painted a series of horses—a familiar subject in an equally familiar Picassoid style, more draftsmanlike than painterly. For Art of This Century, he did a number of simple Miró-like works in which vivid monochromatic backgrounds describe images in bare canvas with accents in pastels and sgraffito (by scratching the wet paint to reveal the white ground, he could avoid waiting for the paint to dry). Not all was lost in haste, however. In the sgraffito paintings especially, speed and economy produced some stunning effects. In one, a gangly horse, lying on its back, legs in the air, appears suspended like a sculptural void in a block of brilliant purple. The few larger paintings that Jackson scrambled to finish by March were also more recapitulation than exploration: *Totem Lesson 1* harked back to the fragmented imagery of *Pasiphaë*, only this time in confectionery shades of purple and salmon; while *Totem Lesson 2* and *Two* echoed the totemic forms and confused personal mythology of *Guardians of the Secret* and *Male and Female*. In the long-unfinished *There Were Seven in Eight*, Jackson's review of the past reached a frantic climax. Almost every style from the previous five years, from *Magic Mirror* to *Gothic*, appears in this sprawling, desperate, cacophonous canvas. Only a year after the perfection of the Guggenheim mural, Jackson had lost his way.

When it came time to name the paintings, Jackson's despondency manifested itself in a black-mass litany of titles—*Horizontal on Black, Square on Black, The Night Dancer, Night Ceremony, Night Mist, Night Magic*—as well as a veiled reference to Helen Marot in the title of one painting, *Portrait of H.M.* (Marot's spirit may have been conjured by the appearance of the equally maternal Hubbard.) The work continued at a feverish pace until just days before the opening. In March, Kadish brought David Slivka, a young California sculptor, to the studio to watch Jackson in the final throes. "He was working fu-

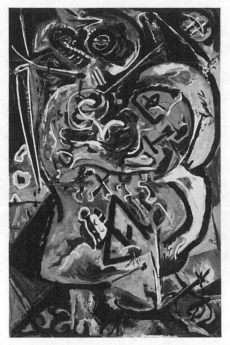

Totem Lesson 1, 1944, 70″ × 44″

riously with the brush," Slivka remembers. "I was still a bit green, and I had never seen anything like it. It was thrilling to watch."

When the show opened on an extraordinarily hot Monday, March 19, 1945, the crowd was larger and more enthusiastic than it had been fifteen months before. A few hardy visitors, including Stella Pollock, trooped eight blocks in 80-degree heat to see the giant mural in Peggy's apartment building. But the reviewers still had reservations. While most admired the energy and expressiveness of his brushwork, they divided over the question of what it all meant —if anything. In the *Times,* Howard Devree questioned whether Jackson's "big, sprawling coloramas" were "clarified enough in the expression to establish true communication with the observer." He also likened some of the paintings, "with their pother of paint and flying forms," to an "explosion in a shingle mill"—resurrecting, without irony, the snide description first applied to Marcel Duchamp's *Nude Descending a Staircase* at the 1913 Armory Show. Parker Tyler, a mouthpiece for the European Surrealists who were still stewing over Peggy's defection, sniped in *View* that Pollock's "nervous, if rough, calligraphy has an air of baked-macaroni" and concluded that, despite his "strong feeling for *matière,*" Pollock "does not seem to be especially talented." In *Art News,* Maude Riley complimented Jackson's relationship with his paint, but complained about his "belligerence . . . toward all other things" including "the subject, and you and me." She concluded with a by now familiar lament: "I really don't get what it's all about."

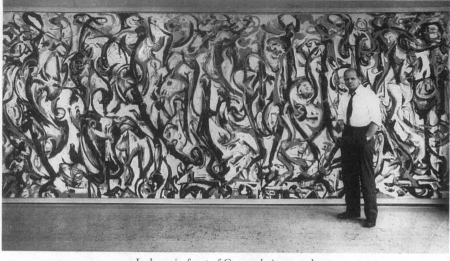

Jackson in front of Guggenheim mural

Of all the critics, only Clement Greenberg dared to issue a blast of unequivocal praise. "Jackson Pollock's one-man show," he wrote in the *Nation*, "establishes him, in my opinion, as the strongest painter of his generation and
perhaps the greatest one to appear since Miró." Except for a Hofmannish
quibble about abrupt color juxtapositions that created "gaping holes," Greenberg abandoned the ambivalent dialectic of his previous review. "I cannot find
strong enough words of praise," he confessed. Pollock was not only the best
painter since Miró, he was the answer to Cubism—the answer to the question
that had been haunting American art for almost a decade: "Is there art after
Picasso?"

To his fellow critics, craven doubters, Greenberg offered a stunning rebuke
designed, consciously or unconsciously, to consolidate his position as the
preeminent critic of avant-garde art. "There has been a certain amount of self-
deception in School of Paris art since the exit of cubism," he wrote. "In Pollock
there is absolutely none, and he is not afraid to look ugly—all profoundly
original art looks ugly at first." If other critics responded unfavorably, they were
not looking closely enough, Greenberg implied; they were the dupes of their
own parochial tastes. What mattered was not whether a painting pleased the
eye—the average eye is naive and indolent—but whether it was "original," a
determination that required not just a trained eye, but a clairvoyant eye—
Greenberg's eye. For a generation of American artists, like Lee Krasner,
trained to imitate the already digested and accepted, Greenberg had turned
the world upside down, and Jackson, the complete original, was now on top.

But even Greenberg's paean couldn't lift Jackson's spirits. Unlike the critics,
Jackson knew how much time and how little artistic distance separated the
Guggenheim mural from *Night Ceremony*. He knew how quickly most of the
paintings had been produced, how relatively shallow and stingy of imagery they

were—how much better they could have been. He must have known, too, that, Greenberg's accolade notwithstanding, the second show wasn't the prodigal, cathartic event that the first had been. (Years later Greenberg himself admitted that his review of the 1945 show was, in part at least, a delayed reaction to the first show.) Such realizations—combined with the lack of sales—drained the juice from Greenberg's praise and left Jackson disconsolate. Even money lost its reparative power. When his contract came up for renewal in April, Peggy reluctantly agreed to double his monthly allotment in exchange for all the paintings he produced in the coming year minus one. But here, too, Jackson could believe that the largesse was partly a lie. Baziotes and Motherwell had defected to Sam Kootz's new gallery in February, and Peggy was desperate to keep Jackson from joining them.

By May, the pent-up frustrations, disappointments, and self-doubts of the previous year had reached the flash point.

When Phil Goldstein returned to New York in 1945, he was no longer Philip Goldstein, he was Philip Guston. Four years of teaching in Iowa City, Iowa, where Jews were still a rarity, had persuaded him to finalize a change he had been contemplating since high school when he signed his cartoons "Phil Goldy." The years in Iowa had reshaped his art as well. Influenced both by a Regionalist hegemony in the Midwest and his wife Musa's taste for sentimental subject matter, he had painted a series of allegorical works culminating in a large canvas filled with harlequins and wide-eyed children called *If This Be Not I*—a title taken from Musa's favorite Mother Goose story about an old woman who lost her identity.

Guston's transformation shocked his old friends in New York. On the WPA, his accessible subject matter and accomplished brush had made him a frequent prizewinner. But in the four years since, the New York art world had changed and Guston's new works looked to many like provincial curiosities, best described by a term Clement Greenberg had recently added to the critical vocabulary: "kitsch." When his exhibition (with titles like *Halloween Party* and *Sentimental Moment*) opened at the Midtown Galleries in January 1945, it still won the enthusiastic plaudits of the traditionalists who had once dominated the Project. Juliana Force gave his paintings "a place of honor" at the Whitney Museum on Eighth Street, and a group of critics and writers, when asked to name "living masters, American or foreign," who were "headed for immortality," put Philip Guston at the head of their list. But in the increasingly powerful avant-garde community, his quaint canvases had become an embarrassment to those who knew him and a laughingstock to those who didn't.

To Jackson, Guston had always been a lightning rod for frustration and envy as well as admiration. Ever since Manual Arts—when Guston could draw and Jackson couldn't, when Guston had girls and Jackson didn't—he had been the Charles figure against whom Jackson could act out his deep store of childhood resentments. For more than a decade, Jackson had suffered his successes—his

artistic encomiums, beautiful wife, and paying jobs—as personal affronts, galling reminders of Jackson's own shortcomings made almost intolerable by Guston's overweening ego. "Phil was in competition with everybody," says Herman
Cherry. "Whether it was personally or artistically, he was going to top everybody. He had fantastic ambition." Now, with the success of *If This Be Not I*,
Guston was once again enjoying the fruits of success that Jackson felt should
have been his.

Soon after V-E Day, May 7, 1945, Sande gave a party at the Eighth Street
apartment for the "old gang": friends from the Art Students League, the WPA,
and California, many of whom had recently returned from the war. Caught in
New York between the Midtown show in January and the Carnegie Institute's
annual competition in October (in which he would take first prize), Guston
joined his old friends. It wasn't long before the fireworks began. "The drinking
got heavier and heavier," recalls Harold Lehman, who also attended, "and the
noise got louder and suddenly there was Jackson, muttering and trying to
express himself—you know how the tongue thickens with liquor. He suddenly
got up and yelled at Phil: 'Goddamn it, I won't stand for the way you're
painting! I won't stand for it!'" Lehman, who was standing with Guston at the
time, remembers that he was "thunderstruck." Jackson's words—which had
been on everyone's mind—sucked all other sound from the room. "[Phil] was
really stricken," Lehman recalls. "You could see it in his face. . . . He had
already begun to see himself as being passed by, being behind and out of date.
Jackson's explosion merely brought it to the surface in front of all the people
who meant something to him." There are various accounts of what happened
next. Guston later told friends that Jackson threatened to throw him out a
window, triggering a long-drawn-out fistfight in which the two artists almost
killed each other. Lehman remembers Guston standing in shocked silence
until the sounds of the party slowly rose and closed around him. Other witnesses maintain that Guston "broke down and cried." No one else remembers
a fight. (Some would later claim that as a result of the confrontation in Jackson's apartment, Guston abandoned the sentimentalism of *If This Be Not I* and
began experimenting with abstraction.)

By the middle of 1945, Lee was desperate. The winter binges and incidents
like the one with Guston had convinced her that Jackson needed to be rescued
both from his friends and from himself.

She began by insisting that he marry her. After three years in which, by her
own admission, she had been "absolutely against it," she suddenly issued "an
ultimatum—either we get married or we split." Lee later attributed her startling reversal to the death of her father—"At that point it just snapped and
suddenly I wanted to be married." But she had never felt constrained by her
father's orthodoxy and, in the thirties, had lived openly with Igor Pantuhoff,
allowing her family to believe they were husband and wife. Lee also described
her betrothal to Jackson as a whirlwind affair (like their first meeting): "I said

[to Jackson] 'You will have to make the decision.' He said to me, 'I have made the decision. We get married.' I asked, 'When shall we go to City Hall to get our license?' " In fact, from the day in November 1944 when Joseph Krassner died to the day the license was finally secured in October 1945, the process took more than eleven months.

In the meantime, Lee laid plans to take Jackson away for the summer. She had rediscovered the terrible truth that Charles and Sande had learned a decade ago—that Jackson fared even worse than usual in the city heat. Yet, after the disaster of the previous summer, another trip to Provincetown was out of the question.

In early July, Reuben and Barbara Kadish packed their two children, three bikes, and one dog onto "the Cannonball" at Pennsylvania Station for a summer on the eastern tip of Long Island where they had sublet a beachside "shack" from Bill Hayter. They left believing that Jackson and Lee would be spending the summer on the Cape. Soon after they arrived, however, a letter came. "They wrote saying that they were going to find it impossible to go to the Cape this year," Kadish recalls. After talking it over with his wife, Kadish issued an invitation. With more than a month of the summer already gone, Jackson accepted eagerly, "cleaned up his brushes," sublet the Eighth Street studio to Sande's old friend James Brooks, just back from the war, and hopped the first train east. Lee, although wary of Kadish, was relieved to leave the city and finally to have Jackson more or less to herself.

For Jackson, it was an idyllic summer. The little house sat at the edge of Gardiners Bay, so close to the water that high tide lapped at the foundations and fish were sometimes left stranded at the kitchen door. From within a few steps of the front porch, they could see Accabonac Harbor to the west, ripe and untended like a virgin continent, and, to the east, the bay, the sound, and the ocean beyond, differentiated only by the quality of light they reflected. A soft, briny breeze swept through the old board walls and boled curtains, carrying the distant sounds of fishing boats and the bells at Barnes Landing. The house itself was "very tiny and very shabby," according to Barbara Kadish, with a leaky roof, hand-pumped water, and no electricity, but Jackson spent too little time indoors to care. In the mornings, he and Kadish would wade out into the chilly water, trailing aqueous clouds of mud as they searched the bottom for clams—just as Rita Benton had taught him. Later, after a few beers on the porch when the sun was at its highest, they would climb crazily into the rowboat and zigzag out to where the waves started and catch some fish for dinner. "One time he caught a blowfish," Kadish remembers. "That blowfish started puffing up and popping around in the boat, and Jack got so excited he was jumping up and down like a kid. I thought he was going to jump right out of the boat."

There were pleasures on the leeward side as well. Back up the Amagansett-Springs Road, only a few minutes by bike, the dunes and scrub oak of Louse Point gave way to potato fields and, a few miles farther on, the little town of

Amagansett. With the Kadish's dog running alongside, Jackson and Reuben would race down the narrow road, only recently paved, and into town for supplies, mail, telephone calls, and as much beer as they could balance on the back of a bike. The bicycle circuit usually included a stop at Harold and May Rosenberg's place on Neck Path, where Jackson doted on their three-year-old daughter, Patia. On weekends, Bill Hayter and his wife Helen would come down from town for clamming, barbecuing, and Lee's incomparable clam chowder. David Slivka took the train out from New York and stayed one night, sleeping on the porch. Robert Motherwell was building a house in the neighborhood, but Jackson saw him only once all summer, "bicycling somewhere." "There was a respectful exchange between them," Kadish remembers. But from the porch at Louse Point, Motherwell's maneuverings and Guggenheim's parties—even Howard Putzel's fatal heart attack on August 7—seemed as far away as the war in the Pacific. A few days later, when the strange, garbled news came that a new bomb had been dropped on Japan and the war would soon be over, Jackson was lying on the beach and didn't even open his eyes.

Lee didn't share his serenity. The summer had rescued Jackson from New York, but it hadn't rescued their relationship. "She thought the summer was going to be a very therapeutic thing for Jack," recalls Kadish. "That it was going to be a cure-all, that they were going to have this romantic thing, walking along the beach, that he'd never want to be doing any drinking, that he'd never want to carouse or separate himself from her ever again." Instead, unable to drive a car and unsteady on a bike, she spent most of the summer in and around the little fishing shack, cooking, talking with Barbara Kadish, and tending the Kadish children—all activities which, according to Reuben, "she couldn't stand." What walks along the beach Jackson did take were usually with Kadish and, as Lee feared, hardly a day went by when the two men didn't drink. Jackson wasn't sleeping in doorways, as he would have been in New York, but he wasn't working either. "She was furious that whole summer," recalls May Rosenberg, "because Kadish and Jackson were doing some drinking. They were playing games, laughing, and telling jokes, instead of painting."

When they agreed to reshingle her leaky roof, Rosenberg remembers, "the first thing they asked for was a beer. Then they got up on the roof and started tearing everything up until they were sitting on the exposed beams with their legs hanging down, joking and laughing and banging away at it. Before you know it, they had to have more beer." The party lasted only until Lee arrived. "She caught me passing some beers up to them," May remembers. "They were perfectly grown up men—they could have gone and gotten beers for themselves. But she was absolutely livid." Lee spent much of the summer livid, playing Aunt Polly to Jackson's Tom Sawyer and Kadish's Huck Finn. When the two "boys" fell while trying to race their bikes through a patch of fresh tar and came home covered with it, Barbara Kadish laughed. Lee stewed. When Barbara finally coaxed Lee into the boat to do some fishing, a sudden storm caught them and began blowing them out toward the ocean. "She didn't know how to row, and it looked bad for a while," Barbara recalls. "I got us back safely, but when we hit the beach, Lee was ready to faint. . . . She wasn't very physical."

A storm was one of the few things that Lee couldn't blame on Reuben. If Jackson drank too much, it was because Kadish drank with him; if he became "impossible" when drunk, it was because Kadish "always found a way of excusing him"; if he was playing jacks in the street or doing handiwork for the Rosenbergs instead of painting, it was because Kadish encouraged him. "She blamed Stella, she blamed Sande, she blamed me, she blamed everybody around the countryside," Kadish remembers. (Later, Lee would take revenge on the Kadishes by using her most powerful weapon, her ability to reshape history by telescoping or omitting events and people she found disagreeable. In subsequent interviews, she reduced the six weeks with the Kadishes at Louse Point to "a weekend." In 1956, she banished Kadish from Jackson's funeral and backed down only when the Pollock family threatened to boycott the services if Kadish was not permitted to attend. In hate as well as love, she knew no moderation.)

Lee dreaded returning to New York. Despite Kadish's bad influence, the summer had at least succeeded in reversing Jackson's long decline. He had been drunk on the porch at Louse Point, at times very drunk, but without a car and with no bars around the corner, he was at least controllable. There was none of the awful uncertainty, the hours of waiting that had consumed so many nights the previous year. Without Kadish and the distractions of summer, she apparently concluded, Jackson might be able to work again. Sometime in late August, while accompanying the Kadishes on a preliminary tour of some of the local houses for sale, she made inquiries about winter rentals in the area. Soon after their return to New York, she popped the question. "I said to Jackson, 'What do you think of the idea of our going out there and trying it for the winter? We could rent the Eighth Street apartment, bring some canvas and see how we like it.' " Jackson was stunned. "He said, 'Leave New York? Are you crazy?' "

A few weeks later Jackson announced, "We're leaving New York." It was Lee's turn to be stunned. "In just that short time, he had completely flipped," she recalls. "I had no idea what happened."

Jackson later said that he changed his mind suddenly after spending several sleepless nights on the sofa at Eighth Street waiting for James Brooks to find another apartment. It was a typical Pollock explanation: terse, pragmatic, unsubtle, and utterly adrift from the truth. In fact, the reasons for his reversal were many and complex, with roots reaching back to childhood. Like marriage, the country offered Jackson a chance to emulate his brothers, Charles and Sande, who had left New York to start their families. The country was where Roy Pollock had lived. (In the fall of 1945, Frank, too, moved to a farm to take up where Roy had left off.) The country was the place to have children, and after a summer of playing with the Kadishes' children and Patia Rosenberg, Jackson was eager to be a father. The country was also escape, a place where Jackson could deny the dark corners of his life in the city. "Pollock didn't basically move *to* [the country]," said Dan Miller, "he was moving *away* from something. . . . He told me that himself. . . . There were conditions in New York that had developed that he wanted to get away from, associations." But finally, the country was just someplace new, someplace different, someplace *else*, a blank canvas where Jackson could try again to make his world right. Like Stella, he had to believe that anything was possible further down the road.

Once Jackson agreed, Lee moved with startling swiftness. Axel Horn saw Jackson in a bar that fall, staring into a mug of beer and looking "slightly stunned." "I said, 'What's the problem, Jackson?' and he said, 'You know we just got a house, but I don't know how we did it,' " Horn recalls. "He couldn't figure it out." Within days, perhaps hours, of Jackson's *volte-face*, Lee telephoned the real-estate agent who had shown the Kadishes several houses during the summer. "Jackson liked one house in particular," Lee remembers, "and he said, 'That's the house we're going to live in.' " When she learned that house had been sold, she contacted Robert Motherwell, who had been recruiting other artists to join him in the East Hampton area. Motherwell quickly arranged a meeting with Ed Cook, a part-time real-estate broker.

Among the places Cook showed them was a two-story, turn-of-the-century farmhouse on Fireplace Road in Springs, a small community near Amagansett. It was a handsome, solid-looking house set on five open acres, with old trees in the front yard, a barn and several outbuildings in back, and a breathtaking sweep of grass down to Accabonac Creek and the harbor beyond. With its asymmetrical, shingled facade, wide eaves, shutters at the windows, broad front porch, and bay window on the side, it was a house Stella Pollock could have loved. The inside, however, was only a modest improvement over the "shack" at Louse Point. There was electricity, at least, and running water in the kitchen, but no bathroom and no heat. The rent was $40 a month or, if they chose to buy, $5,000—all in cash, non-negotiable. Cook considered it "a steal." Lee was ready to rent, but, to her astonishment, Jackson wanted to buy. "Well, of course we didn't even have the forty dollars to pay rent," Lee said later, "not to speak of *buying* a house, so I said, 'Jackson, have you gone out of your mind?' His answer was: 'Lee, you're always the one who's saying I shouldn't let myself worry about the money; we'll just go ahead and do it." They settled on a compromise instead: they would rent the house for six months with an option to buy within that period. Perhaps by the following April, Jackson seemed to think, a miracle might happen—or Lee might make one happen. Stella had bought houses on slimmer hopes. When they signed the contract, they had to borrow the forty dollar security deposit from Cook.

Lee's next hurdle, marriage, proved more daunting. Like Sande, who had demanded a black minister at his wedding, Jackson insisted on a last minute test of devotion. "He wanted a church wedding," Lee recalls. When Lee suggested simply going down to City Hall and getting a license instead, Jackson shook his head. "Uh-uh. I'm not a dog. No license. A church wedding or nothing." Grimly, Lee began a citywide search for a church that would marry a "non-practicing Jew and an unbaptized Presbyterian." She enlisted May Rosenberg to help in the search. "We called every church in the phone book," says Rosenberg, who couldn't remember the name of Jackson's religion and referred to it as "some small western denomination." Even the rabbis said no. Finally, May called a Dutch Reformed church "where I heard the minister was liberal, and I said to the man, 'I have a real problem and I expect you can solve it because you're Dutch. Unless these two people are married in a church there will be no wedding, and it's a sin that they should continue living together without being married, so it's up to you.' " To her amazement, the minister, Charles J. Haulenbeek, agreed—"God will understand," he said. (He was less sure about his congregation. According to Lee, he asked that the couple "be very quiet about it, not [make] an issue out of it.")

Jackson had one last hoop. He wanted May Rosenberg as one of the two required witnesses. Lee wanted Harold Rosenberg and Peggy Guggenheim, but Jackson wouldn't have Harold, only May. (Neither wanted any family member present.) When asked, Peggy responded frostily: "Why are you getting married? Aren't you married enough already?" She wanted to know who else would be there. When Lee told her May Rosenberg, Peggy refused to attend. (She confused May with another woman with whom she had had editorial disputes over the manuscript of her memoirs.) Lee went back to Jackson. "If May isn't there, I won't be either," he bluffed. So on Thursday afternoon, October 25, 1945, only Jackson, Lee, and May Rosenberg met under the Gothic arches of the Marble Collegiate church at Fifth Avenue and Twenty-ninth Street. The church's custodian, August Schulz, who lived in the building, provided a second, somewhat dispassionate witness. Lee was exhausted—she and May had spent the morning in a frantic, last-minute search for a hat to wear, as required by the pastor. Jackson was sober—Lee was not about to have the debacle of Peter Busa's wedding repeated. Of the three, May was by far the most elated. "It was a beautiful ceremony," she recalled. "The minister made a beautiful speech. He spoke about religion, and their religions, and God. It was beautiful. I was transformed."

After May treated them to a celebratory lunch, Lee and Jackson returned to the apartment, which was in the final, chaotic stages of moving. Within minutes, Ray Eames, Lee's friend from the Hofmann school and now the wife of designer Charles Eames, arrived unannounced from California. "I told her we had just gotten married," Lee remembers, "and she turned around and went back down and came back with champagne, and we celebrated." Jackson called Jay and his wife, Alma, who were living temporarily in Flushing, to share the good news. "It was a total surprise," Jay remembers. Later that afternoon, they arrived at the apartment to congratulate the newlyweds. "Jack looked the same to me," Jay recalls, "except maybe a little more sheepish." Amid the crates and boxes and rolls of canvas, the talk of a new house and a new life in the country confirmed a theory Alma Pollock had had for some time. "The marriage did what it was supposed to do," she remembers thinking, "it gave Lee more control."

A week later, the final preparations were complete. The apartment had been rented (James Brooks took the front room, Jay and Alma the back). The paintings had been packed off to Art of This Century, either for safekeeping or because, under the terms of Jackson's contract, they belonged to Peggy. Only sketchbooks, unfinished canvases, a few gouaches, and a mountain of supplies would make the trip to Springs. Separately, Lee had packed a few of her paintings for the trip. With Putzel dead and his gallery closed, there was no place else to put them. The ones that weren't worth moving she had long since destroyed. At the last minute, forewarned of the frigid winter winds off Block Island Sound and the rigors of a heatless house, Jackson bought Jay's collection of a dozen Indian blankets and rugs. Jay accepted a painting in return, but because all the paintings were packed away, he would have to pick it out later. (He never did. After Jackson's death, Lee refused to honor the arrangement.)

Finally, on the weekend of November 3, as a "northeaster" blew in and swept the streets black with rain and sleet, Jackson and Lee climbed into the cab of a butcher's truck they had borrowed from May Rosenberg's brother and set out into the midday darkness.

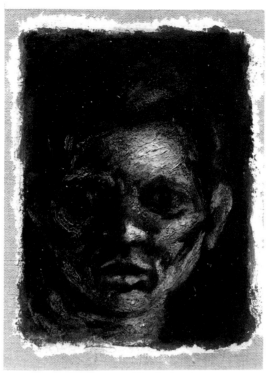

Self-portrait, 1933, 7¼″ × 5¼″

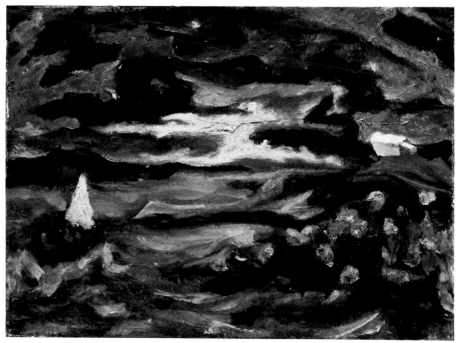

Seascape, 1934, 12″ × 16″

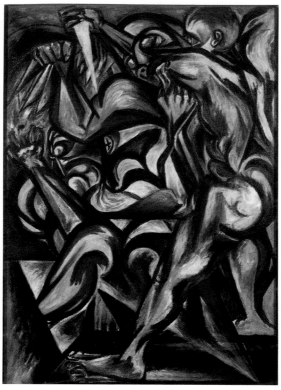

Naked Man with a Knife, 1938–41, 50″ × 36″

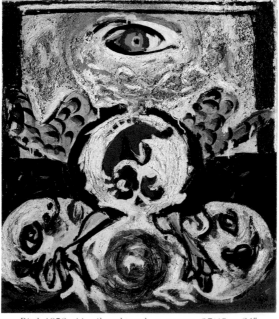

Bird, 1938–41, oil and sand on canvas, 27½″ × 24″

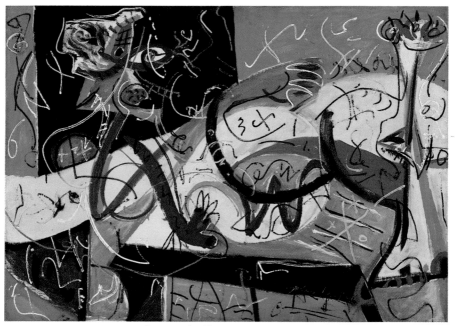

Stenographic Figure, 1942, 40″ × 56″

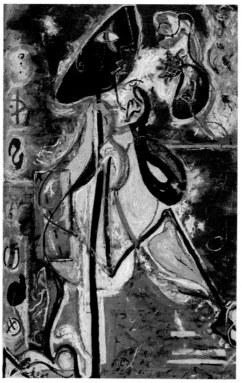

The Moon Woman, 1942, 69″ × 43″

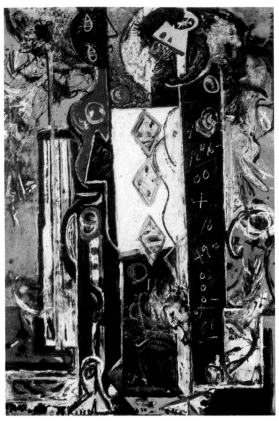

Male and Female, 1942, 73″ × 49″

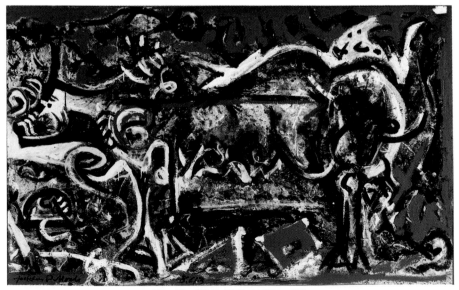

The She-Wolf, 1943, 41⅞″ × 67″

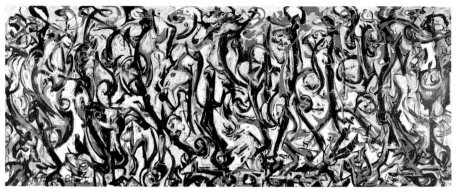

The Guggenheim mural, 1944, 7′11″ × 19′9½″

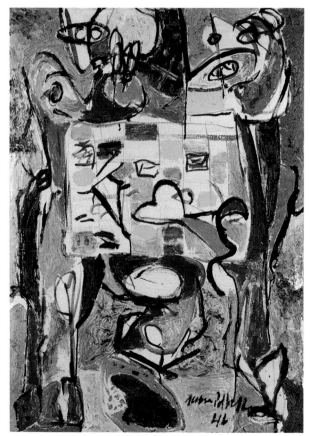

The Tea Cup, 1946, 40″ × 28″

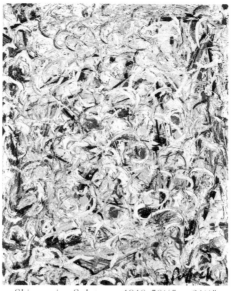

Shimmering Substance, 1946, 30⅛″ × 24¼″

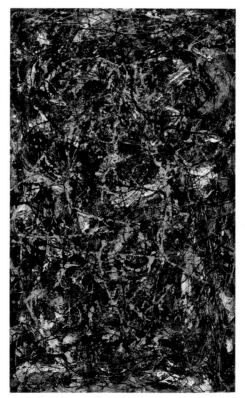

Full Fathom Five, 1947, oil on canvas,
with nails, tacks, buttons, key, coins, cigarettes,
matches, etc., 50⅞″ × 30⅛″.

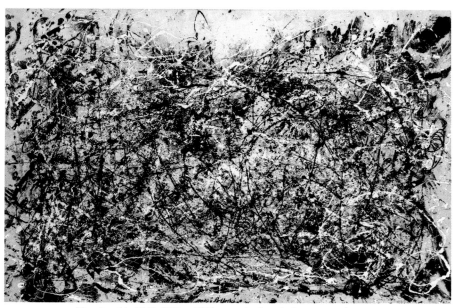

Number 1A, 1948, 5'8" × 8'8"; note the handprints across the top.

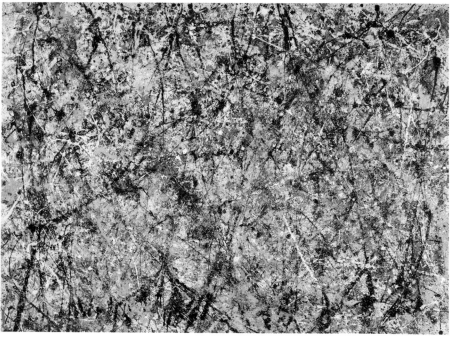

Lavender Mist (Number 1, 1950), oil, enamel, and aluminum paint on canvas, 7'3" × 9'10"

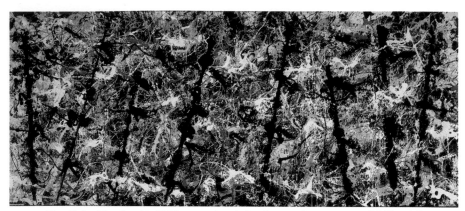

Blue Poles (Number 11, 1952), enamel and aluminum paint on canvas, 6'11" × 16'

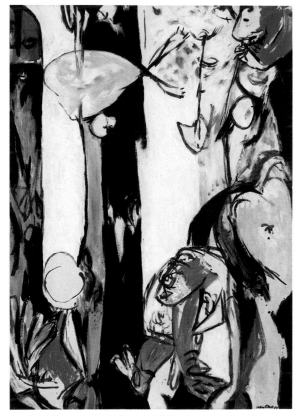

Easter and the Totem, 1953, oil, enamel, and
aluminum paint on paper, 82¼" × 58"

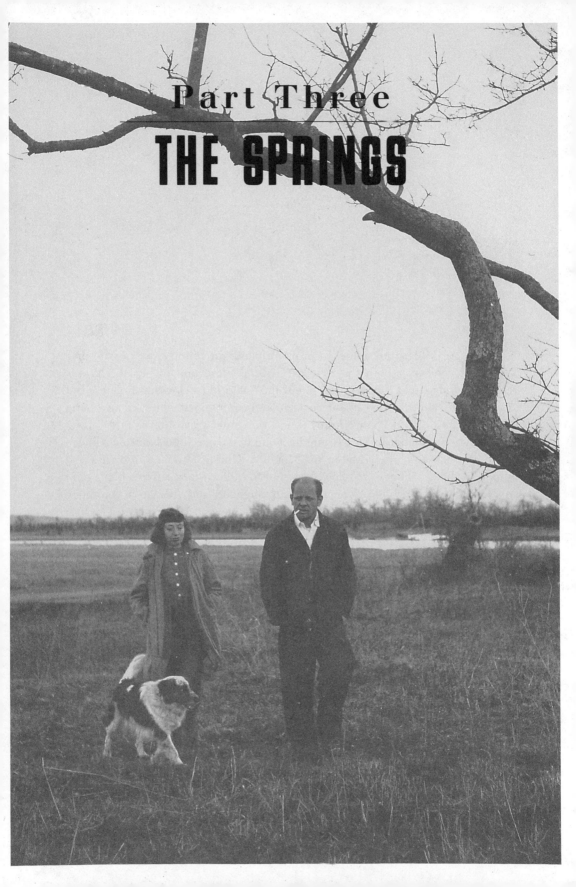

Part Three

THE SPRINGS

32

STARTING OVER

Dan Miller, the one-eyed airplane pilot and country savant who presided over both the Springs General Store and the local Masonic lodge, told many stories about the "wild-hide" Jackson Pollock. But his favorite was the one about Jackson's encounter with an old farmhand named Charlie who "didn't know much but could drive horses and mow." One day, just as Charlie was reining his team to the porch post outside Miller's window, Jackson clattered by in his Model A. Charlie watched him pass and shook his head. "That old Pollock," he said to Miller, "lazy son of a bitch, ain't he, Dan?" Miller, who liked his new artist neighbor, said, "What do you mean he's lazy?" Charlie shook his head again for emphasis. "Why I never seen him do a day's work," he said, "did you?"

If Jackson came to Springs, a loose cluster of houses just across Accabonac Creek from Louse Point, looking for an escape from the prying eyes, public rebukes, and private alienations of New York City, he came to the wrong place. He would have fared much better just a few miles south of Springs in the tiny summer community of East Hampton where the residents—patrician relics, mostly—understood artists. For a hundred years, a parade of painters and sculptors, including Thomas Moran, Childe Hassam, Augustus Saint-Gaudens, and Winslow Homer, had been tutoring them in the idiosyncratic ways of creativity. From the Tile Club of the 1870s, which met weekly to paint on eight-by-eight-inch Spanish tiles, to the Quonset hut of Robert Motherwell, artists and their eccentricities were woven into the loose summer fabric of East Hampton life. (Thomas Moran helped found the Maidstone Club, an exclusive retreat for tennis, swimming, and golf where Hassam and, later, Motherwell were active members.) In 1931, the town even erected a handsome white brick building, Guild Hall, to showcase their contributions: Impressionist oil paintings of bathers at the seashore, watercolors of the "almost English" countryside, sketches of clambakes and fishermen and local scenery. Even the

Surrealists, with their European hauteur and bizarre games, had been accepted there. Max Ernst, Jean Hélion, Fernand Léger, even Breton, had strolled the beaches and streets of East Hampton and nearby Amagansett, admiring the "Parisian" sky, without attracting attention—except from the occasional gauche tourists who would stop at a local gas station to ask, "Where can we find the Surrealists?"

But Springs was another world entirely. Where East Hampton was diverse and cosmopolitan, Springs was inbred and backward: a proud, petty, introverted community of fishermen and farmers held together by a dense thicket of intermarriage, a place where the toilets were still outdoors, artists were still slackers, and men's fortunes were still more closely tied to nature than to the stock market. East Hampton had Guild Hall; Springs had the Masonic Lodge. East Hampton had golfers' brunches at the Maidstone Club; Springs had potluck suppers at Jungle Pete's Bar and Grill. To East Hamptoners, anyone or anything from Springs was "below the bridge"—said with an inflection that made it sound like the dark side of the moon.

It had always been that way. Despite its proximity to East Hampton, Springs had always been closer in spirit to its northern neighbor, Gardiners Island, a mysterious crescent of land lodged between the fork tines of eastern Long Island. In 1639, an English engineer named Lionel Gardiner who already owned most of the South Fork, including the early settlements of Southhampton and Springs, bought the island from the Indian "sachem," Wyandank. For most of the three hundred years since, Gardiner and his descendants had ruled their private fiefdom from the huge manor house on the southern tip of the island. The English sailors who accompanied Gardiner settled not on the island, Lionel's private reserve, but in Springs, the nearest "mainland" town, where they proved to be just as proud and insular as their laird. When Jackson Pollock arrived in 1945, Springs was still dominated by the same handful of families—Bennett, Miller, King, Parsons, Lester, Talmage—who still made their living from the sea and still spoke with the cockney accent of Lionel Gardiner's crew. Everyone was "bub"—as in, "Yessir, bub." Women were always "dolly," and children were "yowns." Words were often doubled for emphasis: "Yes, yes." About the only thing Springs residents had borrowed from the new world in three hundred years was their name. They called themselves Bonackers after the tribe of Accabonac Indians that had once inhabited the land around the harbor and creek that also bore their name.

Even the Great Depression and World War II had left Springs relatively untouched. Neither had much affected the yearly harvest of clams and scallops from the sea and potatoes from the fields. Roosevelt's unemployment compensation had somewhat eased the seasonal cycle of abundance and scarcity, but at the general store, Dan Miller still spent half the year taking cash and the other half giving credit. Lee Krasner assumed that the hardship and dilapidation she saw around her were just remnants of the Depression. "She felt cast down by the fact that these people were living in such conditions," recalls a friend. "Even though the rest of the country had recovered, here these people were stuck in dire poverty." Soon after her arrival, Lee offered to paint the postman's cart—"just to spruce it up and give it a gay appearance"—but to her astonishment, the offer was refused. A coat of paint wouldn't have made it better, only different. "Bonackers are Bonackers," went one favorite East Hampton saying, "and that's enough for *them.*"

In such a small, placid, constant community, Jackson's arrival attracted considerable attention. Charlie the farmhand wasn't the only one of Dan Miller's customers who followed the exploits of "the newcomer with two last names." In the first few weeks, rumors flew. It was said that he worked only after midnight; that he slept till noon; that he was backed by big money from New York; and, hardest to believe, that he planned to make Springs his year-round home. At Jungle Pete's, Merton Edward told how Jackson had arrived in the middle of a nor'easter only to discover that his house was locked and he had lost the key. So he came to Edward's door, dripping wet, figuring that Merton might have a key that worked "since Merton's house was the same age as Jackson's." That story was always good for a laugh or two and another round of drinks. For weeks thereafter, people often talked about "the strange city couple that had moved into the old Quinn place" and were struggling through the winter without a car or coal. They would point Jackson out to their neighbors and say, "There goes that crazy artist" when he rode by on his bicycle to Miller's store. Young boys would sneak up to the windows and peer warily through the icy glass hoping for a glimpse of him. "Did you see the way he wears a rope instead of a belt to hold up his pants?" one neighbor asked another, or "Did you notice that he never shaves, dresses up, combs his hair, or goes to church?" They noted how often he bought booze at Dan Miller's store, how often he appeared at Jungle Pete's—only a mile down the road from his place. They listened sharply to the first reports from his neighbors: that he didn't act "uppity" like artists were supposed to; that he seemed like an "ordinary guy." One of them even ventured a Bonacker compliment, calling Jackson "common as dirt." By the time Bonackers like Ed Hults finally said "helloo" to their new neighbor, he was already a local celebrity.

But celebrity had its dark side. Jackson may have rented for the winter, but he was still one of the summer people at heart. The Bonackers called them "drifts," with a curl of the lip. Jackson may have been an artist, but, like the other drifts, "he didn't go out and work with a hammer and saw," said Ed Cook, a Springs resident at the time of Jackson's arrival, "or go fishing or anything like that, so he was still a drift." Drifts were a fickle, self-indulgent and useless lot who hogged the beaches in summer and fled before the first frost. Worst of all, they had money. "They could buy anything they wanted to," Cook recalls. "And their kids, if they got in a little bit of trouble, they could buy their way out of it." The proud Bonackers also sensed the reciprocal disdain of drifts like Balcomb Greene who found the locals "so dumb I didn't want to spend much time with them." Even well-intentioned drifts like May Rosenberg couldn't find anything better to say about the Bonackers than that they were "unspoiled."

But the drifts, like the fish and the clams, were one of the area's indispensable natural resources on which the Bonackers depended for part of their meager livelihood. Ultimately, it was that dependence that separated them from Jackson. He wasn't disdainful (although Lee was) or rich (although rumors of rich backers persisted), but he certainly wasn't a Bonacker. When, in a moment of unguarded enthusiasm, he said to George Sid Miller, "I'm going to be a Bonacker same as you someday," Miller replied dryly, "You only got to wait four hundred years." In Springs, as everywhere, celebrity had its price.

When Jackson and Lee broke into their new home on a stormy November night in 1945, Lee finally had what she had always wanted: Jackson alone—no meddlesome family, no bars, no drinking buddies, no parties, no Peggy, no gays on the make. This time, she would make it work; this time, she would retake control of their lives and make it possible for Jackson to paint again.

She soon discovered that nature was her most powerful ally. The winter of 1945–46 was one of the worst of the decade. When the winds blew from the northeast, they carried rain and snow from Canada; from the south, hurricanes. Even hundreds of miles out, a storm could hurl eighty-mile-per-hour gusts of wet wind across the open sea, into the mouth of Gardiners Bay, past Louse Point, across Accabonac Harbor, and against the first obstacle in their path—their house, rattling windows and whistling through the loose boards. All through November and December, the howling ocean winds turned trips to the outhouse into perilous adventures. "I opened the door this morning," Jackson wrote friends in New York, "and never touched ground until I hit the side of the barn five-hundred yards away—such winds." Not even a craving for liquor could drive him outside in such weather. It was everything he could do to keep the kitchen stove stoked with firewood, huddling in Jay's Indian blankets, endlessly smoking cigarettes and drinking coffee to stay warm. "It was hell," Lee recalled later, "[no] fuel, no hot water, no bathroom. It was a rough scene."

On the rare days when the weather let up and the sky brightened—it almost never turned blue—Lee had to rely on her wits to keep Jackson at home. For the first few weeks, there were always jobs that needed to be done around the house. The owners had left the place in a shambles, "stuffed with belongings," and desperately in need of cleaning. To set up his studio, Jackson spent days clearing one of the upstairs bedrooms. Then the living room had to be readied so Lee could paint there (when a storm blew in, it was too cold to paint anywhere). No sooner was one job done than something else broke: after a heavy rain, the water pump in the basement gave out; the porch floor began to sag; the living room flue wouldn't open. Jackson didn't even have time to think about the outbuildings: a barn stacked to the rafters with cold, rusty farm implements and road equipment and a tool shed so full the door wouldn't open. Besides, if they decided not to stay, or couldn't raise the money to buy the house, all their work would be for nothing. In frustration, Jackson wrote Louis Bunce: "The work is endless—and a little depressing at times."

Even when the frustration and privation became too much to bear, Jackson had no place to go. Without a car, he was limited by the range of a bike: some days no more than a mile—the exact distance to Jungle Pete's. He had been there several times in the first weeks, not for liquor but for the huge country breakfasts served by Nina Federico, the bar's crusty owner. It was Federico who had lent Jackson two dollars he needed to buy the bicycle. Jungle Pete's, like the Bonackers themselves, wasn't given to public displays. There was none of the usual drinkers' camaraderie that Jackson relished; only single men and occasional pairs, standing apart from one another in a swirl of cigarette smoke and be-bop music, as sentinel and unsmiling as coastal rocks. For months, no one even bothered to say hello and Jackson would sulk home after only a beer or two. "He wasn't very friendly with the locals at first," recalls Roger Wilcox, "and they were pretty unfriendly with him."

The only other convenient source of liquor was Dan Miller's store a few hundred yards down the road—close enough to be accessible during all but the worst storms. Jackson bought paint and supplies there when he couldn't hitch a ride into East Hampton with Julien Levy. It was easy enough to pick up a case or two of beer and "put it on the books" like everything else at Miller's store, although in winter there was no place to drink it except at home under Lee's disapproving glare.

Jackson soon discovered that the most effective tranquilizer available at Dan Miller's store wasn't booze, it was Miller himself. Stern and "strictly business" with most of his customers, Miller took an instant liking to his new neighbor from the city. The two often spent hours together in the office next to the store. Miller, who loved the sound of his own voice, did the talking and Jackson listened: the more mystical and "highflown" the topic, the more enthusiastically Jackson grunted and nodded in agreement. A drinker himself, with a prodigious beer belly to prove it, Miller was a born psychologist who saw through Jackson's gruff reticence. Before long, their talks had assumed the role of therapy—the kind of informal, nonthreatening therapy that Jackson responded to best.

Lee didn't try to prevent the meetings with Miller, but she didn't like them. From the beginning, she eyed the Bonackers with a mix of suspicion and contempt: suspicion of their designs on Jackson and contempt for their bumpkin ways. Like Stella in Phoenix, she kept aloof. "Lee would just say hello and that was it," recalls Ed Hults, a local plumber. "She holed up in there and never got very involved in the community." Many of the local workmen who came to the house over the next ten years saw Lee Krasner for the first time at Jackson's funeral. She did go to the store once or twice with Mary Louise Dodge, a neighbor who owned a car, and Allene Talmage saw her occasionally at parties, "but she stuck pretty much to her own group," Talmage remembers, "and if you stopped by to chat, she sure never invited you in."

Bonackers weren't the only ones that Lee turned away. Soon after arriving, Jackson wrote Reuben Kadish a letter filled with enthusiasm for the house and the rigors of country living. Fondly recalling the summer on Louse Point, he urged the Kadishes to come to Springs and look for a place of their own. When they arrived on a fittingly frigid day in January, however, it was Lee who met them at the door. "We were going to stay with them," Kadish recalls, "but when we arrived, Lee said, 'I guess you're here to get Jack drunk again,' and that was it." Infuriated, Barbara Kadish said to her husband, "Let's get away from this witch," and the two stalked back out into the cold. They didn't return to the house until Jackson's funeral ten years later. In the spring, they bought a farmhouse in rural New Jersey instead. Jackson, apparently unaware of the encounter with Lee, wrote Kadish in February: "When can we expect you out?"

Roughly the same scene was repeated when Jim Brooks and Charlotte Park came out, "despite Lee," and camped in Montauk, where they later bought a house. William and Ethel Baziotes, also invited by Jackson, made it through the front door but had to leave soon afterward "because Lee wasn't feeling well." Even Lee's own family was banished temporarily. "We were close in New York, then she moved out [to Springs] and all of a sudden we were unclose," says her sister Ruth. Jackson's family fared slightly better. At Jackson's insistence—he wanted to show off his new house—they came for Thanksgiving dinner. But otherwise only one guest regularly penetrated the emotional *cordon sanitaire* that Lee had thrown around Jackson: Stella Pollock.

Lee was just beginning to understand Stella's power over him. No matter how overmastering his rage seemed, no matter how inconsolable his depression, Stella could subdue him. Her mere presence had a hypnotic effect. At the sight of her tightly corseted body, bright shoes, and immaculate handmade clothes, Jackson became a child again. Self-obsessions flowed backward into their childhood tributaries and he was suddenly all adolescent apprehension and alertness, sensitive to her every look—charming or sullen, defiant or deferential, "bad boy" or mama's boy, changing from minute to minute according to the imperceptible choreography of her approval. "Pollock had a strong face," said Tony Smith, ". . . [but] next to his mother, he looked like a little boy." Her arrival might be preceded by a wild one-night binge, her departure followed by an explosive rage—"as if he had been holding himself in check," one friend observed—but as long as she was nearby, he was utterly, eerily quiescent.

Lee both resented Stella's power, and envied it. She considered Stella "an ignorant bore," according to May Rosenberg, and bristled in her company. But Jackson's needs came first, and in early 1946, Jackson needed to prepare for an April show at Art of This Century. Lee had managed to fill his first two months in Springs with household chores and endless repairs, but no painting.

Now the storm season was past, the muddy footprints on the path to the outhouse were preserved in ice, snow had transformed the landscape, and Jackson was spending more and more nights at Jungle Pete's. Even more troubling to Lee, he had begun looking for a cheap secondhand car. Meanwhile, the rolls of canvas they had brought from New York sat, still wrapped, in an upstairs bedroom. Thinking no doubt that Stella's presence would ensure a week of untroubled workdays, Lee made the arrangements for her to visit in January. Jackson spent the entire day before her arrival baking pies and cakes "to prove to his mother he could do it," according to Roger Wilcox. That night, he disappeared into the snowy darkness and stumbled in, drunk and delirious, near dawn. But when Stella's train pulled in, he was there to greet her with a boyish grin.

One afternoon, Jackson walked into the kitchen were Stella, Lee, and May Rosenberg were waiting to go to lunch. In the bright winter sunlight, he looked at Lee and his mood turned instantly black. "What is that on your face?" he demanded.

"Just a little rouge," Lee replied in the little-girl voice she often used to defuse such moments.

This time it didn't work. "Jackson hit the ceiling," May Rosenberg recalls. "He shouted, 'No wife of mine is going to wear makeup!' " Lee jumped up and shouted back, "But your *mother* uses rouge!" "That was it," says May. "Then there was a *real* brawl. He became really violent. I had never seen him hit anybody, but he was getting very close. . . . His mother sat there watching as if in a theater. I was petrified."

Finally, Stella stepped in. "Sit down, Jackson," she ordered, and he did. "It's true," she confessed, "I do use rouge." "But you never used to," he protested in what sounded to May like the hurt voice of a ten-year-old boy. "I did it for you, Jackson," she explained. "When your father died, my eyes were swollen and I looked terrible. I didn't want you boys to see me like that. I knew you would be frightened. I only did it for my boys." At this point, according to May, "her eyes welled with tears." "It was," Stella said, "a sacrifice for *you*."

While Lee and May watched in astonishment, Jackson was transformed. "He reacted like someone soothed," recalls May. "He sat next to her, put his head on her shoulder, and swayed back and forth with her, like a mother and her baby." Lee and May were "speechless."

Stella's visit was soothing in other ways. To Lee's delight, Jackson began painting again for the first time since the move. During the week she stayed, he started four or five canvases, including the largest one since 1944. In *The Child Proceeds*, he painted a woman giving birth to a child—part fetus, part man—who stands facing his mother with an arrow through his heart. In *Sun-Scape*, he evoked the Arizona horizon in the background and, against it, the memory of chickens hanging on the line. A severed head lies on the ground, hidden in a tangle of denial. Finally, on the big canvas that Jackson himself named *Circumcision*, he explored his most private anxieties in his most private

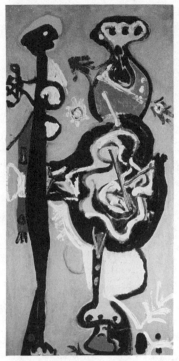

The Child Proceeds, 1946, 43" × 22"

imagery, combining the *horror vacui* of *Pasiphaë* and *There Were Seven in Eight* with the even deeper horror that Jackson, who had escaped childhood uncircumsized, still felt in his mother's presence.

Lee had another reason to be delighted with Jackson's productivity, no matter how troubling its source: she had decided to make the situation in Springs permanent.

For Jackson, the country was still an excursion. "Lee and I are trying the country life for a while," he wrote Louis Bunce early in 1946. "[It's] a good feeling to be out of New York for a spell." But Lee was sure she had found what she was looking for—and what Jackson needed. Since their arrival, he had remained more or less sober. If there were occasional lapses at Jungle Pete's, at least the long decline of the last two years had been reversed. She still longed for Manhattan—"I'm a city person," she confessed—but had grown used to having Jackson all to herself. For that, the hardships and deprivations of country living seemed a small price to pay.

But with only three months left in the purchase option on the house, she still needed $5,000. The local banks weren't much help. One of them had refused Jackson a $100 loan to buy a car. They would offer a $3,000 mortgage, but Lee would have to produce the $2,000 downpayment. There was only one place where she could find that kind of money: "Mrs. Moneybags," Peggy Guggenheim.

Perhaps anticipating such an emergency, Lee had been trying to repair her shaky alliance with Peggy ever since their last round over Jackson's contract. As a conciliatory gesture, she agreed to edit parts of the manuscript for *Out of This Century*, the scandalous memoir that Peggy had written the previous winter. In a paroxysm of insecurity and exhibitionism, Peggy was distributing copies of the manuscript to members of her circle, hoping for a validation that never came. Lee was one of many who thought Peggy "could have done better to have gotten on the analyst's couch rather than write the book," but for diplomacy's sake, she kept her opinion to herself and even arranged for Jackson's work to appear on the front and back of the book jacket.

When Lee finally came forward with her request for the $2,000 loan, however, Peggy relished the opportunity to say no, adding caustically, "Why don't you go ask Sam Kootz?" Incensed, Lee did just that. "I went to see Kootz," she recalled, "and he agreed to lend us the money but only with the understanding that Jackson would come over to his gallery." That, of course, was precisely the answer Lee had hoped for, and she gleefully relayed it to Peggy, who reacted predictably. "How could you do such a thing," she exploded, "and with Kootz of all people! Over my dead body you'll go to Kootz." Torn between her fury at Lee and her genuine concern that Jackson might desert the gallery, Peggy consulted Bill Davis, a collector and friend, and David Porter, both of whom advised her to make the loan. She even visited Springs in early February to assess for herself the truth of Lee's claim that Jackson was "more happy and productive" in his new surroundings.

By the following Friday, she had capitulated. "Things couldn't have turned out better!" Jackson wrote Reuben Kadish triumphantly. "Peggy and Bill [Davis] were here over the weekend & she liked the place and got the spirit of the idea." Once Peggy came through, the rest was easy. The East Hampton Bank agreed to provide a $3,000 mortgage and the sellers, the Quinns, agreed to throw in all the contents of the house and barn for an additional $150. Dealing with Peggy on the terms of the loan proved more arduous. She agreed to deduct $50 from Jackson's $300 monthly allowance until the interest-free loan was repaid. In exchange, however, she insisted that Jackson put up three big paintings, including *Pasiphaë*, as collateral. By the end of February, the loan documents were signed and the sale was closed. For the first time in his life, Jackson owned a house. "All there is to it now is a hell of a lot of work," he wrote Kadish, "and it doesn't frighten me."

After the excitement of buying the house, the April show was anticlimactic. Almost half of the eleven paintings on exhibit had been painted the previous year, before the move to the country. Of those done in Springs, only *Circumcision* and *The Little King* spoke with full conviction. Jackson admitted as much soon after the show closed. "Moving out [to Springs] I found difficult," he wrote to Louis Bunce, "change of light and space and so damned much to be done around the place. [B]ut [I] feel I'll be down to work soon." For Jackson, the show was primarily an excuse to see New York again and briefly reimmerse himself in the fast-flowing currents of the art world. In a quick survey of his fellow artists prepared for Bunce, who was in Oregon, he betrays a certain nostalgia for the more concentrated, center-stage life he had left behind.

> Joe Meert is in NY and getting some painting done between jobs—some exciting stuff, abstraction with a personal touch. Jim Brooks . . . is back from the army and painting abstractions. . . . Baziotes I think is the most interesting of the painters you mentioned—Gorky has taken a new turn for the better—from Picasso thru Miro—Kandinske and Matta. Gottleib and Rothko are doing some interesting stuff—also Pousette-Dart. The Pacific Islands show at the Museum of Modern Art—tops everything that has come thru this way in the past four years. Spivak is working toward abstraction. Byron Brown continues along the same slick pace. . . . Guston has fallen to repeating a formula—and of course his stuff gets weaker instead of growing.

Given how limited an effort Jackson put into it and how little new ground it broke, the April show was received with surprising kindness by the critics. "Jackson Pollock is one of the most influential young American abstractionists," *Art News* concluded, "and he has reinforced his position in a recent exhibition." One critic lodged a flattering complaint against Jackson's "surface virtuosity," saying it "frequently forbids him to the promised land of plastic realization." Clement Greenberg, writing in the *Nation*, excused the show as "transitional." "Pollock's third show in as many years," wrote Greenberg, "contains nothing to equal the large canvases, 'Totem I' and 'Totem II' that [Pollock] exhibited last year. But it is still sufficient—for all its divagations and weaknesses, especially in the gouaches—to show him as the most original contemporary easel-painter under forty."

The show probably would have received far closer scrutiny, for good or ill, if the entire art world had not been preoccupied with the publication of Peggy's *Out of This Century* in March. One reviewer suggested that "Out of My Head" would have been a more appropriate title, "considering the nymphomaniacal revelations and other mad doings related in the book." Despite almost universal condemnation—the press labeled Peggy "an urge on wheels" and her world, a "Boudoir Bohemia"—the book was seen under every arm on Fifty-seventh Street.

By the time the *succès de scandale* reached its peak, however, Jackson was back in Springs where he was surprised by a far more momentous event: the coming of spring.

It came early that year. Prodded by the Gulf Stream and its warm escorting winds, the tiny pink blossoms of the dune-hugging bearberries had already begun to appear. They were only a hint of the transformation to follow. Caught unaware, local farmers quickly plowed up the green blanket of ryegrass in preparation for potato planting. Fishermen dipped their vast seines into the currents of striped bass and bluefish that passed near shore in shimmering migration. In the sky, gannets, shearwaters, and ocean gulls flew by on their way north, only to be joined in the swift invisible currents by local plovers and sandpipers on their short round-trip to arctic nesting grounds and by Canada geese bound for the great northern tundra.

Jackson hadn't seen a true country spring for twenty years, not since the spring harvest in the yellow fields below Janesville. According to Lee, it affected him profoundly. "He spent hours, sometimes whole days walking around the first spring we were there," she recalls. "He was like a kid, exploring every-thing"—the saltwater marsh that fringed the tidal waters of Accabonac Harbor, the tall spartina grass that parted like fur in the sea breeze to reveal colonies of black ducks and terns, the grass-choked "crick" that flowed from the fresh-water springs that gave the town its name. In high boots, or sometimes barefoot, Jackson tracked the intimate topography of the marshlands—the hills, or hum-mocks, decorated with hudsonia; the valleys, or pannes, where glasswort, pale green in the spring, thrived in the spongy, salt-saturated ground. Occasionally he would stumble on a huge boulder half buried in the teeming water and blanketed with vegetation. Geologists called them "glacial erratics"—huge rocks scooped up on the mainland and dropped here by retreating glaciers. On the landward side of the harbor were small stands of oak, red cedar, and marsh elder—most of the big trees had gone down in the 1938 hurricane; on the seaward side, the sandy marshes of Louse and Gerard points.

Jackson never missed a chance to walk the crescent-shaped ridges that hemmed the shore near the points. "He loved to go out and look at the dunes," Lee recalled later. He would sit on a grassy crest for hours, gazing at the mild spring sea as it slowly rebuilt the beaches that had been torn away by winter storms. In the distance, he could see the boats of the Bonac fishermen trap-fishing in Gardiners Bay while, overhead, gulls and terns floated from breeze to breeze like paper kites and now and then an osprey plunged for fish. In the lee of the dunes, beach plums grew and pitch pines hunkered on the windy slopes. Around the freshwater slacks at their base, cranberries reddened in the sun, red-winged blackbirds built their nests, and muskrat and quail rustled in the blueberry-dotted brush.

Buoyed by Lee's attentions and the unexpected joys of the onrushing spring, Jackson began what was, probably, the happiest year of his life. Yet for all his psychological sophistication, he almost certainly failed to understand his new-found happiness. Even as he laid out and plowed an ambitious garden of vegetables and melons, even when he adopted a mongrel collie and named it Gyp after his boyhood companion, even as he proudly surveyed the land and talked about "his farm" and "what he was going to do with it," Jackson apparently never realized that he was replaying the past.

Lee neither understood the reasons for Jackson's contentment nor cared to. It was enough that he had finally found a level spot in a life that only a year before had seemed to be nothing but peaks and valleys. "There were times

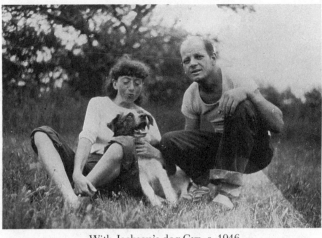

With Jackson's dog Gyp, c. 1946

when [Jackson] was happy," Lee once reminisced about the early years in Springs. "He loved his house, he loved to fool around in his garden." He also loved Lee. She was, after all, a crucial part of his re-creation. For the first time since 1942, the delicate balance of their relationship held steady. "When I'd rant and rave about someone being a son of a bitch," Lee recalled, "he'd calm me down considerably." She later described it as a "cozy, domestic, and very fulfilling" time. They slept long and late, spent middays rooting in the garden —Jackson did the digging and planting, Lee the watering and weeding—and afternoons working inside—Jackson painting in the upstairs bedroom, Lee cleaning the house, shopping, and preparing dinner. (For most of the first year, her easel stood folded and unused in a corner of the living room.) Sometimes, in the late afternoon, they would bicycle together into town through the sweet, heavy smell of new-sown potato fields and roadside cherry saplings in bloom. Other times, he would gesture for her to join him on a walk to the marshes and dunes, "or we would sit on the stoop for hours gazing into the landscape without exchanging a word," Lee remembered. For a while, at least, New York and Provincetown and the inexorable cycle of Jackson's troubles were forgotten.

On the weekend of May 17, just when the pink and white dogwoods were at their height, Stella, Sande, and Arloie came to Springs to celebrate Stella's seventy-first birthday. For a few days, as Jackson proudly showed off his house and his garden, past and present came together.

In a burst of painting that coincided with Stella's visit, Jackson recorded their fleeting union. In *The Water Bull*, he summoned up the bull that frightened his mother's horse, the overturned wagon that spilled them onto the road, the gloved hand of the farmer who slapped him—all in the sun-bleached colors of the Arizona desert. In *The Tea Cup*, he relived an afternoon of "playing house" in the cool shady colors of Evelyn Porter's porch with her little dog Trixie looking on. In *Bird Effort*, he captured the sharpness and confusion of bird

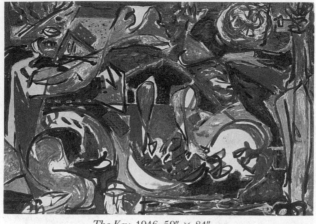

The Key, 1946, 59″ × 84″

beaks and wings and the threat of a knife blade. In *Yellow Triangle* and *The Key*, he returned to his favorite image, the family table, spread with food and flanked by still, diffident figures obscured by an obsession of brush strokes. Stylistically as well as psychologically, these paintings from the spring of 1946 are suffused with an unapologetic nostalgia. After two years of turgid, humorless colors and heavy impasto, Jackson returned to the looser limbed, more thinly painted style of 1943 paintings like *Stenographic Figure* and *Search for a Symbol.* In the afternoon light that flooded his second story studio, surrounded by spring, he rediscovered a Matisse-like palette of clear reds, lime greens, violets, peaches, pinks, and teal blues, as well as a spectrum of watercolor-like pastels unused since *The Magic Mirror.* In his art as well as in his life, Jackson was making an inventory of the past: rehearsing earlier styles, colors, and images even as he resurrected Roy Pollock; taking stock, both creatively and emotionally, of what he had achieved; and savoring, if only briefly, the long sought sense of resolution.

But Jackson, like Stella Pollock, was restless. No sooner had he settled into the house, the life-style, and the art than he began to hanker for changes in all three. He began, as Stella often did, by fixing up the house. During the summer and fall, he painted the upstairs bedrooms, cleaned out the barn and tool shed (salvaging a few objects to hang on the walls), put in a crude bathroom, enclosed part of the back porch, and hired Whitey Hustek to paint the entire exterior—white over the old brown shingles, blue on the shutters. Jackson thought it looked "grand."

But the big project of the summer was moving the barn. Ever since the closing, Jackson had been eyeing the old structure restlessly. Standing halfway between house and harbor, it was too far away for a studio—especially in the winter—and too close to the harbor for a garage. Lee also complained that it blocked her view of the water. The solution was to move it up, toward the house, and over, out of the line of sight. Roger Wilcox, a recently arrived

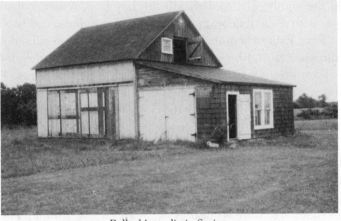

Pollock's studio in Springs

neighbor with an acute mechanical sense, offered to help. His plan was simple enough: they would tie the four walls together with beams to keep them from spreading, jack the building up off its rock foundations (there was no floor), set logs underneath and simply roll it into place. It would be a slow process—the new site was five feet higher than the old and fifty feet to the north—but, even after Jackson pulled a ligament in his right arm while laying the cement foundation, they figured they could do it themselves.

When moving day, June 10, arrived, progress was excruciatingly slow. "Every time we leveraged it up and pushed it along," recalls Wilcox, "it only moved about five inches." Wilcox suggested that Jackson find a local fisherman with a seine-hauling winch on the back of his truck, but Jackson "didn't want to bother those guys." By the end of the day, however, when the barn had budged only about "four or five feet," Jackson had run out of patience. "Shit," he said, "we're never going to get it up there." The next day, he recruited a local fisherman who deftly fitted the building with wooden skids, hooked it to his truck, and hauled it up onto the concrete base. Within a few days, Jackson had removed the temporary supporting beams and knocked a huge hole for a window high up on the north wall. When Lee suggested that he put in another window lower down, Jackson replied, "No, no, I don't want to be disturbed by the outside view when I'm working." For all his love of the harbor view and the country spring, Lee remembered, "he wanted his studio completely closed off."

It was an impossible request, as Jackson must have known. The turn-of-the-century structure had never been more than a partial shelter from the elements —abused in summer, abandoned in winter. Scores of freezes and thaws had shrunk and curled the old boards till broad slits of daylight showed between them. Knotholes sent lasers of sunlight through the perpetually dusty interior. In the main "room," an eighteen-by-twenty-four-foot space porportioned for tractors and wagons, the walls rose twelve feet and the gable another six. On the west wall, two big sliding doors hung on rusty tracks and rattled at every breeze. On the south side, underneath the hay trap, someone had added a storage room with a small door up off the ground, windows, and two big access doors of its own. Everywhere inside, the gray-brown water-stained walls were studded with shelves and hooks and makeshift storage. Overhead, chunks of mortar fell from the roof lathing, and old rags plugged the joints. The height of the ceiling made the space look bigger than it was, so that even after Jackson filled the shelves and the floor near the walls with a confusion of paint cans, brushes, thinners, easels, canvases, stretchers, tools, and a few pieces of old furniture, the place still looked empty and echoed like an abandoned mine.

Inside this lofty, dilapidated space, Jackson's art proved even more intractable than the barn. The paintings he had done in the spring, like *The Tea Cup* and *The Key*, were certainly accomplished—an achievement that must have brought him some pleasure—but they explored no new ground. He had used the same Matisse-like colors and compositions with more energy and insight three years earlier in *Moon Woman*. Stylistically, he seemed to be moving backwards. Restless, but unsure of a direction, he continued to retrace his path. In *The Blue Unconscious*, a big canvas begun before the move to the barn but finished afterward, familiar images—a table flanked by totemic figures with the family dog underneath—began to break up into more obscure fragments, just as in *Guardians of the Secret* three years before. In *Something of the Past*, the images almost disappear completely (except for the faint trace of the family dog, hunkering down, as in *Guardians*, asleep or afraid, at the very bottom of the picture). Just as in late 1943, Jackson was playing at the boundary between abstraction and representation. In *Something of the Past*, as in *Pasiphaë*, he struggles to sustain the emotional urgency of the unconscious imagery even as it flirts from behind a veil of abstraction. Two and a half years after the Guggenheim mural, riding another crest of emotional resolution and professional success, Jackson was again poised for a breakthrough. Psychologically and artistically, he had spent two years retreating from, then recovering, the pitch of creative intensity that produced the Guggenheim mural and *Gothic*, his first true nonfigurative masterpieces. Like the manic-depressive cycles of his drinking, the cycle of his art was giving Jackson a second chance. This time, he grasped it.

It's impossible to know exactly what events, in what combination, led Jackson from his halfhearted restatement of earlier styles in 1945 and 1946 to the astonishingly original "dripped" images that began to appear only six months later. Surely, Lee's lavish support brought a degree of psychological stability and sexual fulfillment that made it possible for him to concentrate on work. (The next four years would be the longest uninterrupted period of productivity in his life.) The steadying influence of home ownership and a rural life-style no doubt contributed to the feeling of domestic security—a feeling that must have been incalculably gratifying to a boy whose childhood home had begun to disintegrate almost as soon as he entered it.

In the shorter term, however, there were at least two events, both of which seemed relatively insignificant at the time, that nudged the angle of Jackson's trajectory just enough to alter his ultimate destination.

The first was the decision, made sometime in the spring when he was still working in the house, to lay a canvas flat on the floor. At the time, it was merely a practical solution to a practical problem: the five-by-seven-foot canvas for *The Key*, attached to a curtain stretcher, was too big to stand upright in the small, low-ceilinged upstairs bedroom. Even on the floor "[it] took up the whole space," Lee recalled. "He could barely walk around it." For years Jackson had been turning paintings around on the easel, propping them on their sides or upside down in order to solve a problem or just to see them from a different perspective. Occasionally, he had even worked on a canvas while it was askew. But the new arrangement allowed unlimited access to any side at any time. Perhaps because of the cramped conditions in the bedroom, the change had little effect on *The Key*. But as soon as Jackson moved to the converted barn, where any picture, no matter how big, could be propped on an easel, he began to experiment with the new technique, working mostly on his knees, moving from one side to another, creating and revising the image from every angle.

The effects of the change began to show immediately. In *The Blue Unconscious*, probably the first painting produced in the new studio, he was able to achieve the same kind of fragmentation of the image as he had in *Pasiphaë* without resorting to heavy overpainting. Painting parts of the image from all four sides, he discovered, *automatically* fragmented the overall image as seen from any one side. It also reflected more accurately his own way of seeing, in which objects had to be rotated and absorbed from a variety of angles before they were truly *seen*. Finally, he discovered a strange new satisfaction in working on a canvas placed on the floor, in walking around it, standing over it, and bending down beside it. Something about this new way of working satisfied a deep, inarticulate need, a need that, once aroused, would begin to seek fuller, more direct gratification.

The second decisive event was the arrival of Clement Greenberg for a weekend visit in July.

Despite Greenberg's unfaltering support of Jackson's art, the two men had had little personal contact in the four years since they were introduced. For most of that time, Greenberg had pointedly avoided the company of artists, whom he considered, as a rule, "dumb and boring." "The art world was not the center of gravity for me," he recalls. "I was more like a tourist in it." Actually, more like an exile. He had tried and failed to make a place for himself in the literary circle at the *Partisan Review*, where he briefly served as an editor from 1938 to 1940. Considered both pompous and intellectually mediocre by some of his colleagues, including Philip Rahv and Delmore Schwartz, he soon began casting his critical eye in other directions. "As for [Greenberg] becoming

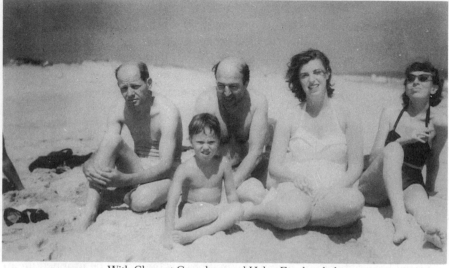

With Clement Greenberg and Helen Frankenthaler

an art critic in the first place," wrote William Barrett, recounting a theory of Rahv's, "the reason for that was quite simple: the fact was there were too many literary critics around, and Clem thought it would be easier to avoid the competition by going into the field of art." He was right. After nothing more than a summer session at the Art Students League, several lectures at the Hofmann school, and some gallery-going with Lee Krasner and Igor Pantuhoff, he handily won a post as art critic for the *Nation*, where one of his first reviews covered the opening of a show by a young, unknown artist named Jackson Pollock.

From their joint debut, artist and critic seemed ideally matched: Jackson's energetic, uncouth, ambitious paintings and Greenberg's masculine, earnest, ambitious prose. Still, it wasn't until almost three years later, at Lee's prodding, that the two men began a friendship. Although contemptuous of art critics in general and skeptical of Greenberg's intelligence in particular, Lee was resigned to his importance. "He's helping us get on our feet," she told John Bernard Myers. "It's important to get in print, to be written about." "She thought of him as a necessary evil," says her nephew Ronald Stein, "a person to be used and manipulated to get exposure for Jackson." Thinking, perhaps, that Jackson needed a champion more than ever now that he had moved out of New York, she put Greenberg high on the short list of people who were invited to enjoy a weekend in Springs that first summer.

From the moment his train pulled into the East Hampton station, Lee played the charming, savvy hostess. "Lee and I would sit at the kitchen table and talk for hours," Greenberg remembered. "We'd drink coffee and go to bed at three or four in the morning." An alert but sad-faced man with a prematurely bald, egg-shaped head that made him look both older and more pedantic than he was, Greenberg relished these sessions with Lee and later acknowledged that "she was damn significant for me. I was learning from her all the time." Most of what he learned was "warmed-over Hofmann," according to a friend of Lee's, which he then repeated back to her with the proprietary certitude that marked all his conversation.

That certitude would soon become the watermark of his criticism, the product of both deep-rooted intellectual insecurity and a long, cold immersion in Marxism. It was, after all, the revolutionary spirit of American abstraction— fighting to overthrow both the art establishment and European hegemony— that had attracted him to the avant-garde in general and Jackson Pollock in particular. By 1946, he had retired the prewar Marxist vocabulary, but his view of art, and of art critics, was still shaped by a tenacious belief in "historical inevitability." Like soldiers in the class struggle, artists either did or did not advance the cause; they marched either with history or against it. The art critic's job was to define the cause and, within the limits of persuasion, rally the soldiers to it.

Greenberg's "cause" was the flatness of the canvas. Because a painting was nothing more than a two-dimensional surface spread with visual data (i.e., paint), he argued, its "beauty" could be judged only by reference to the formal properties of the paint on the surface, not by reference to an extraneous reality or a transcendent metaphysic. Imagery of any kind, because it suggested a third dimension and therefore violated the flatness of the picture plane, was forbidden. "Content is a morass," he once said. Painting is painting is painting— shiny smears on a flat surface, strokes and colors interacting with one another. "Picasso, Braque, Mondrian, Miró, Kandinsky, Brancusi, even Klee, Matisse and Cézanne, derive their chief inspiration from the medium they work in," he wrote in 1939. "The excitement of their art seems to lie most of all in its pure preoccupation with the invention and arrangement of spaces, surfaces, shapes, colors, etc." Of course, as Greenberg well knew, Hofmann had said essentially the same thing years before, and Maurice Denis, Roger Fry, and several others, years before that; but, as a true intellectual, disdainful of painters, Greenberg needed a higher authority. He found it in positivism, the notion that knowledge is based only on the "positive" data of experience and therefore phenomena can be studied only in terms of their formal relationships to other phenomena. "Ours was an age of science," wrote William Barrett in *Truants*. "Positivism was the scientific philosophy of our time, and [Greenberg] had, above all, to be in tune with the deeper *Zeitgeist* of history." Later, Greenberg would add to the unlikely combination of Marxism and positivism an even more unlikely reliance on the German moral philosopher, Immanuel Kant. ("It was not that Greenberg 'got Kant all wrong,' " wrote Barrett, "but that he seemed to have read only the first thirty or forty pages of Kant's work.") In 1946, Greenberg's theories, like his influence, were still in their infancy, but his sense of certitude had already reached maturity. "My generation were all geniuses," he once admitted. "We didn't think it was right to take suggestions."

But it *was* right to give them. And when he entered Jackson's studio in late July, that's exactly what he did.

Inside, *Blue Unconscious* stood on one wall drying, nearly finished. On the floor, Jackson had begun work on *Something of the Past*. Greenberg looked long, "squinting, with brow furrowed, lips pursed, and fingers pressed beneath his eyes to help them focus," according to one account of a similar visit. "Sometimes his look was quick, sometimes long. Either way it was frequently followed by a judgment. The painting was first-rate, or second-rate, or missed altogether." This time, Greenberg's eye was drawn to the painting on the floor with its dense tangle of yellows. It reminded him, he would later recall, of Jackson's mural for Peggy Guggenheim, which he had already called "Jackson's best," and of *Gothic*, another painting he admired. To him, both of those earlier works, with their deeply buried imagery, all-over compositions, and exuberant surfaces, perfectly exemplified his theories: in them, paint was paint; surface was surface; and neither, apparently, aspired to more. Since 1944, Greenberg had watched with increasing disappointment as Jackson retreated from "his own manifest destiny" by reintroducing imagery. To him, *Blue Unconscious* was just another example of that retreat, although he did admire the fragmentation of the figures and the variously textured paint surface. But the new painting, as yet unnamed, seemed to hold real promise, not merely saving graces. Finally, according to one version of the tense enounter, he pointed to the painting on the floor and said slowly, his Brooklyn accent thinly disguised by an acquired southern drawl, "That's interesting. Why don't you do eight or ten of those?"

When Greenberg spoke, Jackson listened. Like Lee, he knew how much Greenberg's support had done to buoy his career over the previous three years. Paul Brach remembers him years later being "flattered and grateful that Clem spoke for him." The same gratitude extended to any critic who ventured a flattering comment. A friend remembers seeing Jackson in the fifties, clutching a copy of a favorable review. "Even though it was full of the critical clichés of the day, Jackson was very respectful of it. He was in awe of critics or anyone who could affect your fate that much." Of course, Jackson also had acute political instincts. "Be nice to Clem," he once told Fritz Bultman. "If he likes your work he'll help you."

Jackson couldn't have been surprised by Greenberg's enthusiasm for *Something of the Past*. He knew of the critic's praise for the Guggenheim mural and *Gothic*, of his belief that pure abstraction was the only legitimate form of painting, and of his admiration for all-over composition. Only a few months before, both men had attended Janet Sobel's 1946 show at Art of This Century and come away "struck" by her small canvases of all-over linear abstractions. Sobel, a self-taught, fifty-two-year-old grandmother from Brooklyn, whom Greenberg considered slightly balmy, had followed a career path much like Jackson's, although considerably shorter. Beginning in 1939 with primitive representational images, she had developed a highly personal, quasi-Surrealist style in which "facial features and other forms evolved out of a web of seem-

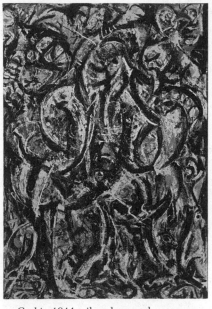

Gothic, 1944, oil and enamel on canvas,
84⅝" × 56"

ingly totally abstract linear rhythms." Later, Greenberg would claim that Sobel's show, and one painting in particular—*Music*, with its "overall design of
pine-needle strokes, with hidden faces and figures"—had a significant "influence on Pollock's work."

In fact, Sobel was only the last in a long line of influences that had brought
Jackson to *Something of the Past*. From the earliest doodles in his Benton
sketchbooks to the abstract motifs that first appeared on his ceramic pieces,
Jackson had been experimenting with "all-over" composition—evenly distributing picture elements over the available space. One untitled painting from the
period, obviously a prescient experiment, bears a startling resemblance to later,
fully realized all-over works. Among his drawings for Joseph Henderson,
tucked between Surrealistic monsters and Picassoid profiles are sheets of abstract and semi-abstract "doodling," sometimes confined to the center of the
page, sometimes edge-to-edge. The "automatic" drawings of Matta, which
Jackson so much admired, although not edge-to-edge, suggested a tangle of
lines that could be expanded to cover the picture plane in an elegant, all-over
web. In paintings like *Stenographic Figure*, Jackson used the graffiti of automatism, spread evenly over the picture, both to obscure the figures and to soften
the hard compositional regime of figures and background. Jackson may well
have seen Sobel's 1944 show or the illustration of *Music* in Sidney Janis's book,
Abstract and Surrealist Art in America, but he certainly saw a showing that same
year of Mark Tobey's "white-writing" pictures at the Willard Gallery. The
dense web of white strokes, as elegant as Oriental calligraphy, impressed Jack-

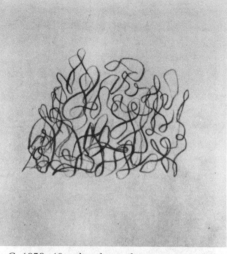

C. 1939–40, colored pencil on paper, 8″ × 8″

son so much that in a letter to Louis Bunce he described Tobey, a West Coast artist, as an "exception" to the rule that New York was "the only place in America where painting (in the real sense) can come thru."

In Provincetown, the same year as Sobel's and Tobey's shows, Jackson and Ward Bennett worked together on an old piece of canvas they found on the beach to produce an image that, while it didn't yet fill the picture frame, showed that Jackson was still haunted by the possibilities inherent in the Guggenheim mural. Back in New York, he began a new, more conscious set of experiments toward all-over composition in his sketchbook. On several sheets, he filled the middle ground with teeming jumbles of lines and forms like whirlwinds flinging about bits of detritus. These represent the dark side of Matta's cerebral webs, the angry side of Tobey's congested cityscapes. They haven't yet grown to fill the page like Sobel's sinewy clusters of color, nor have they lost the personal imagery that served as a contact point for Jackson's unconscious. But they do form a clear path through the stylistic missteps and retreats of the 1945 and early 1946 paintings, a lifeline connecting the great mural of 1944 with the fragmented images of the paintings Clement Greenberg saw when he walked into Jackson's studio in 1946.

For the rest of the summer and fall, Jackson pursued the path marked out by *Something of the Past*. In paintings like *Eyes in the Heat, Croaking Movement, Earth Worms,* and *Shimmering Substance,* he covered the canvas from edge to edge in thick, "suffocatingly packed" swirls of paint. Imagery that had been poised on the edge of abstraction in *The Blue Unconscious* disappears completely beneath a turbulent sea of small brush strokes and heavy impasto that all but ignores the edges of the canvas. Would Jackson have pursued these all-over images without Greenberg's encouragement? Did Greenberg redirect him down a path from which he had retreated once before, after the Guggenheim mural, or merely legitimize a path on which he was already embarked?

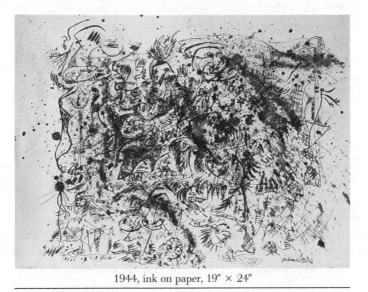

1944, ink on paper, 19″ × 24″

Paintings like *Earth Worms* and *Shimmering Substance* can easily be seen as Jackson's reponse to Greenberg's request to "do eight or ten of those." And despite the elbow room in the new studio, all the paintings from this period are, by Jackson's standards, small and tentative: the largest, *Croaking Movement*, only 4½ by 3½ feet; the smallest, *Shimmering Substance*, a mere 2½ by 2 feet. Clearly, even as he painted them, Jackson felt the critic peering over his shoulder. When he finished *Eyes in the Heat*, he told Lee, "That's for Clem."

Such responsiveness paid off. In his review of the same paintings (and a Dubuffet show) the following February, Greenberg proved predictably enthusiastic. After beginning with a statement of principles—"It is the tension inherent in the constructed, re-created flatness of the surface that produces the strength of [Pollock's] art"—he compared Jackson and Dubuffet:

> Pollock, again like Dubuffet, tends to handle his canvas with an over-all evenness; but at this moment he seems capable of more variety than the French artist; and able to work with riskier elements—silhouettes and invented ornamental motifs—which he integrates in the plane surface with astounding force.

Finally, Greenberg pointedly applauded the disappearance of explicit imagery from Jackson's work. "Pollock has gone beyond the stage where he needs to make his poetry explicit in ideographs," he wrote. "What he invents instead has perhaps, in its very abstractness and absence of assignable definition, a more reverberating meaning."

If it bothered Jackson or Greenberg that the latter was reviewing paintings he had had a hand in shaping, neither complained. Both had gotten what they wanted: Jackson, a favorable review; Greenberg, substantiation of his theories.

It was a fortuitous beginning for a symbiosis that, in the coming decade, would prove first highly beneficial, then disastrous for Jackson and his art.

Through the rest of the summer and fall, Jackson coasted on an unprecedented tide of support. Every weekend in July and August a new set of house-guests caught George Schaefer's taxi at the East Hampton station and asked for "the Pollocks' place." Bill Davis—next to Peggy, Jackson's most ardent collector—and his wife Emily; Herbert and Mercedes Matter, who had just returned from California; Fred and Janet Hauck. Lee even let Jackson invite Ed and Wally Strautin, his blue-collar neighbors from Eighth Street, for Labor Day weekend. Springs was particularly beautiful in the late summer when mallow roses and sea lavender crept into the marsh grass, and goldenrod filled the margins of the fields.

The scene was so breathtaking that Jackson hated to miss even a day of it. During the entire summer, he took only two brief trips into New York—one in June, another in September when Peggy finally announced what had been rumored for years: she was closing the gallery. Howard Putzel's death the year before had proved to be the fatal blow, although Peggy, still furious at his ingratitude, would never admit it. Since then, deprived of his unerring eye, the shows had steadily declined in quality and many of her earlier discoveries had defected to other galleries. "Everything got to be too much," she complained. The 1946–47 season, she had decided, would be her last.

Desperate to exceed his minimum for the year and generate some extra money for the new house, Jackson begged for one more show before the final closing. Peggy joylessly obliged, thinking no doubt that, despite the short time since his last show, Jackson's works were more likely to sell than those of some of the other painters she had been showing. The best she could do at this late date, however, was to squeeze him in from January 14 to February 1—a graveyard slot, too soon after Christmas and too long before spring.

On their trips into the city, Jackson and Lee stayed with Jay, Alma, James Brooks, and Charlotte Park in the apartment on Eighth Street, in the little room beside the studio where Jackson had lived briefly in the mid-thirties. The familiar surroundings conjured old ghosts. "He was up and down," Charlotte Park recalls, "fine for a while, and then, with a drink or two, as bad, as wild as he ever was. We worried because Sande wasn't there to protect him from himself."

Once back in Springs, however, Jackson appeared to be in control for the first time in years. When he drank—which was often—it was in search of companionship, not oblivion. By fall, he had even begun to earn acceptance among his fellow drinkers at Jungle Pete's. Gradually, they introduced him to the other Bonacker hangouts: the bar at the Nursery View Cabins; Frank Eck's Elm Tree Inn near the firehouse in Amagansett, and, farther still, Cavagnaro's —"the only bar in East Hampton where the Bonackers would go," according to one customer, "because nobody put on any airs." Before long, the Springs police had added Jackson's name to the list of local drinkers who were likely to need a ride home. "In the first years Jackson was here," recalls a Pollock neighbor, "the police could afford to be protective. His drinking was still just a joke."

Along with new places to drink, Jackson discovered a new drinking companion that summer. Tall and gaunt with an amiable hound-dog face, Roger Wilcox was "the kind of man you want to tell your life's story to," according to one friend. The two men had actually met twice before, once in the late thirties through John Graham and again at a Guggenheim opening. But it wasn't until they were introduced again at Ralph Manheim's house in April of 1946 that the friendship took hold. Wilcox, like Jackson, had just bought an old house in Amagansett and needed some escape from a powerful, possessive wife (one friend described Lucia Wilcox as "a powerhouse like Lee"). But it was drinking that sealed their bond.

Wilcox was a man of some mystery. He didn't have a job and never seemed to work, yet was obviously better off than the Pollocks. He claimed to live well on the royalty payments from obscure inventions: a machine that sculpted wall-to-wall carpet, another that counted threads in textile manufacturing. "I just go to the mailbox every month and get a check," he would say offhandedly when people inquired. Then there were the questions about his mysterious military service. (Later, he would admit that he worked in "intelligence operations.") He was even evasive about his age, although he was clearly older than Jackson, perhaps by a decade.

Not that Wilcox refused all talk of the past. Over beer in the booths at Jungle Pete's, he would entertain Jackson for hours with stories from his astonishingly dense and variegated life: his troubled childhood in south Florida when Miami was still "a wilderness around a bay"; killing his first rattlesnake with a hoe at the age of three; jumping from job to job and state to state—sign painter in Florida, electrical engineer in New York, architect in Texas, designer in Ohio, artist in New York (after only a few months, he decided he didn't have the "compulsion" to be an artist). At each stop along the way, Wilcox would "use his brain instead of his back," inventing some new device to make the work easier and himself richer. By the time he turned twenty, he had made and lost a fortune in the booming neon light business. Ten years later, on the verge of a second fortune, he decided to quit the world altogether and turn "primitive" on a deserted island off the coast of Florida. That lasted about four months, he recalls, "long enough to build a cabin." He was just too restless and sociable to lead a hermit's life.

The next stop was Key West, a curious cross between a navy town and an artists' enclave. With his dry humor and amiable manner, Wilcox soon planted a foot on both sides of the line: consulting for the navy during the day and mixing with writers like Tennessee Williams and Elizabeth Bishop by night. He became a regular crew member on Lester Hemingway's boat, where he often encountered Lester's infamous older brother, Ernest. "He was a preten-

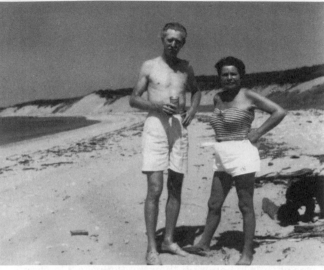

Roger and Lucia Wilcox

tious ass," Wilcox remembers, "a big, macho pretender. When it came to a showdown he had someone else do his fighting for him. He was always trying to write what he wished he was for real. Physically, he was a big guy, but he wasn't worth a damn."

Jackson was especially impressed by Wilcox's vast circle of acquaintances. In only six months as an artist, he had befriended almost as many artists as Jackson had in all of the thirties. In childhood, he had known Ernest Lawson and Maurice Prendergast, members of The Eight. At the gallery school in Columbus, Ohio, he met the Regionalist triumvirate: Benton, Wood, and Curry. In New York in the late thirties, he was equally welcome in the realist circle of Ben Benn and the modernist circle of Gorky and de Kooning that met every night at Stewart's Cafeteria. His calm intelligence and straight speaking were highly regarded, especially in the anxious and polemical world of young American artists. It was this "solidity," so rare in the volatile thirties, that had attracted the attention of Lucia Christofanetti, a Syrian-born Surrealist painter, on a trip to Key West. In 1945, Lucia was living in East Hampton with Max Ernst, Dorothea Tanning, and the remnants of the Surrealist community that she had known in Paris and had supported during their American exile, when Wilcox returned from war duty and married her. Only a few months later, the newlyweds were introduced to Jackson Pollock.

Lucia welcomed her husband's new friend with effusive Damascene hospitality. Not since Rita Benton had Jackson encountered a more reassuring maternal figure. Lee, on the other hand, fearing that Wilcox would turn out to be another Reuben Kadish—a perpetual temptation to drink—remained standoffish. She made no effort to hide her resentment of their nights out together and cast a jealous, sidelong look at every mention of Lucia.

■   ■   ■

Even as Jackson's career was finally regaining its momentum, the complications of the past were entwining themselves in the present. The reversal
began when he suggested starting a family and Lee unexpectedly refused. "She
said she wouldn't have a child by him," recalls May Rosenberg, "*ever.* He had
been drinking in the past, and she didn't want to have a child because she
didn't know when he might start drinking again." (Years later, she would be
more direct, telling a friend, "I wasn't about to have a child with a crazy
person.") Whatever the rationale, the announcement shattered Jackson's
dreams of joining his father and brothers in creating a family. "He went berserk," recalls May Rosenberg. "The whole thing was to be married and have
children." According to Rosenberg, Jackson suddenly felt Lee had "tricked"
him into the marriage.

In the joys and successes of the summer, however, the crisis soon passed,
indicating that, at some level, despite his protests, Jackson was probably just as
happy not to share *this* mother's love with a family of siblings. As one friend
commented, expressing the opinion of many, "He was enough child for one
family."

It was Lee, not Jackson, who emerged from the episode scarred. Convinced
that Jackson might leave her to start a family elsewhere, she began to see
betrayal in every unreturned glance. Upon arriving back from a short trip to
the city and discovering that Jackson had taken Maria Motherwell for a spin in
Motherwell's prized MG convertible, she erupted in a jealous rage. Maria was
a beautiful woman who "would flirt with anybody," according to Roger Wilcox.
Over Jackson's protestations of innocence (probably valid), Lee banished the
Motherwells from Jackson's life. Motherwell recalled that the next time he
stopped by the house, Jackson came out to the car and told him apologetically,
"Lee forbid me to see you anymore." Although hardly affected by the estrangement—Jackson never liked Motherwell's work and later called him a "son of
a bitch" and a "phony"—Jackson was duly chastised. For the rest of the
summer and fall, whenever women came to the house when Lee was away, he
received them coolly—on the porch.

The momentum of the spring and summer carried Jackson through the
storms of fall. Working regularly in the lowering sky and waning light, he
completed all the paintings for the January show by the end of November. To
maximize the number of works in the show, he sent both the earlier, representational paintings from the spring and the all-over canvases he had painted
since Greenberg's visit in July. To justify what looked like a gross stylistic
discontinuity, he gave each group its own name: "Accabonac Creek" for the
paintings done in the upstairs bedroom; "Sounds in the Grass" for those finished in the barn (including *The Blue Unconscious*).

After riding in to New York from Springs with the Rosenbergs, Jackson and
Lee spent Thanksgiving with Jay, Alma, Sande, Arloie, Karen, and Stella in
Deep River. "[Jack and Lee] both look so well since they have been out of the

city," Stella boasted to Frank, "he has done some swell painting this year." On Saturday, however, after proudly inviting the family to come to Springs for Christmas, Jackson cut the holiday short. He was anxious to return to Springs and the barn.

To Lee's astonishment, even with the show packed off to New York and the winter settling in, Jackson continued to paint. On the coldest mornings, he would fix himself a mug of "hobo coffee," wrap himself in every piece of clothing he owned, and fight his way to the barn. Inside, condensation would coat the old boards with frost and little drifts of snow would build up in the open spaces between. But the light! According to Lee, on days when it snowed, "there was this incredible white light and Jackson would indulge in the experience of light then because of the luminescence of the snow." But the light was fleeting. Between the late start, the bitter cold, the relentless drafts, and the numbness in his hands, he was lucky to last an hour or two. "But what he managed to do in those few hours," said Lee, "was incredible."

The Christmas reunion was snowed out, but on December 30, Stella arrived for a two-week stay. The next day, New Year's Eve, huge gray clouds swept down from Canada and burst with snow. For days, the white of the sky and the white of the ground were indistinguishable; the white creek disappeared into the white harbor and the white ocean beyond. On one of these brief days of pure light, bundled against the cold, with only a cigarette for warmth, his hands so numb he could barely hold a brush, Jackson Pollock altered the course of Western art.

33

MEMORIES ARRESTED IN SPACE

I t was a simple gesture. In one hand he held a can of oil paint, thinned to the consistency of honey. In the other, a stick—probably the one he used to mix the paint with turpentine. On his knees beside a small canvas, he dipped the long stick in the can of paint then waved it over the canvas. From the end of the stick, held at a downward angle, a fine line of paint dribbled onto the canvas below. It formed a tiny stream. As the paint on the stick ran out, the line thinned, then choked to drops. He repeated the gesture. Each time, he learned something new: if he slowed his movement, the stream would puddle; speed up and it narrowed; move closer to the canvas and it smoothed; farther away and it rippled. Pass followed pass. The strands began to overlap and interweave. A sweep of his arm produced a rough circle while a flick of the wrist launched an extravagant ellipse. By adding more thinner to the paint, he could fling the line even farther. He learned about tools: a stiff brush held more paint than a stick, a full circuit or two, but it always threatened to flood the line. When he shook it, the stream turned to rain. That, too, he could control by thinning the paint, loading less paint on the brush, or holding the brush higher above the canvas. A stick required more reloadings but produced a finer, more consistent line and, when the paint was especially thin, a dew-like wash. Each discovery was woven into the densening web.

Why did Jackson Pollock begin to drip paint? What was the source of his inspiration? The question has preoccupied artists, critics, and art historians since the drip paintings first appeared in 1947. Stories of his "discovery" are legion. According to one, he was working on paper when a recalcitrant pen began to "dribble and blob." Most of the stories involve an accident of some sort: thinning the paint too much, spilling paint, throwing a brush in anger. One specifically suggests that he kicked a pot of paint over one of Lee's pictures. Whitey Hustek, the local housepainter, believed that Jackson had been inspired by looking at the board on which Whitey cleaned his brushes. But

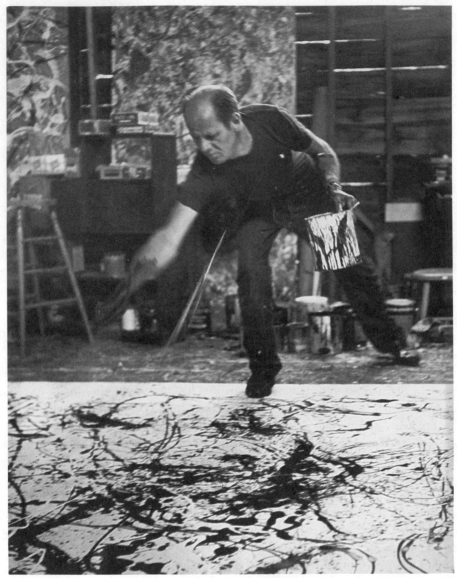

Pollock at work, 1950

most Bonackers tended to credit the far simpler explanation that Jackson discovered the drip when he was drunk.

Fellow artists were less kind. Many denied there had been a "discovery" at all. With the rigor of hindsight, they found precedents for Jackson's drip technique everywhere: the Surrealists had thrown paint over their shoulders; Max Ernst had dripped paint from a bucket; Masson had dribbled glue. "It was Wolfgang Paalen who started it all," argues Fritz Bultman. Others credited Onslow-Ford or Picabia; still others Miró. Jackson's success had many American fathers as well: Baziotes had dripped long before Pollock; so had de Kooning and Resnick and Kamrowski and Gorky. "All that dripping came from Gorky," insists Philip Pavia. An obscure artist, Misha Reznikoff, claimed he was throwing paint at the canvas as early as the mid-thirties. "Everybody was doing drips," says Bultman. Even the sculptor David Smith returned from the first showing of Jackson's drips muttering, "I did drip paintings too." Hans Hofmann claimed to have done drip paintings as early as the 1920s while still in Munich. Miz Hofmann, infuriated at Jackson's success, spread the rumor that Jackson had seen Hofmann's drip technique in the early forties and had deliberately stolen it.

Where the artists left off bickering, the critics and art historians began, spilling gallons of ink in disputations over the true "origin" of dripping. Some found it in the shamanistic rituals of primitive tribes, some in the techniques of Navajo sand painters, some in the "fundamental rhythms" and "improvisatory" riffs of jazz. Clement Greenberg, predictably, found it in the cool imperatives of form and paint. "[Pollock] wanted to get a different edge," Greenberg hypothesized. "A brush stroke can have a cutting edge that goes into deep space when you don't want it to." Decades later, admirers of Lee Krasner found it in the "divisionist preoccupation with splintering, fracturing, and dispersing" in Lee's paintings at the time. Commentators turned somersaults to link Jackson's drip technique to the grand tradition of European modernism. "I do not think it exaggerated to say," Greenberg wrote, "that Pollock's 1946–50 [drip] manner really took up Analytical Cubism from the point at which Picasso and Braque had left it." It remained to subsequent scholars to fill the gaps in Greenberg's grand vision or, as Hilton Kramer said, "to turn the history of recent art into Wagner's Ring."

In fact, Jackson was *not* the first artist to drip, pour, spill, splatter, or throw paint at a canvas. As early as 1877, the art critic John Ruskin accused James McNeill Whistler of "flinging a pot of paint in the public's face" for splattering specks of red and gold to suggest fireworks in *The Falling Rocket.* As Jackson's fellow artists were quick to point out, many of them had, at one time or another, applied paint to the canvas without touching it. *All* of them were surrounded every day by multicolored splatters, drips, and flecks on the floor, on the easel, on their clothes. Some, like Hofmann, had used splatters for "marginal or 'coloristic' effect." Some, like Ernst and Masson, had devised new ways of applying paint in search of the "accidental" image (Ernst poked holes in the bottom of a paint-filled bucket, then swung the bucket back and forth over a canvas). Some, like Baziotes and Kamrowski, squeezed paint from a tube and let it fall in "automatic" patterns. (Paint from a tube was too thick to drip or pour.) Jackson both knew of Ernst's experiment and had taken part in Baziotes's. In fact, the "revolutionary" drip paintings that appeared in 1947 were not even *Jackson's* first drip paintings. Eleven years earlier, he had poured paint in Siqueiros's workshop and seven years before that, dripped paint onto a plate of glass covered with water in Schwankovsky's classroom. As early as 1934, he had spattered paint on the bottom of a ceramic bowl for Rita Benton. In 1943, for iconographic reasons, he dripped and looped paint onto parts of *Male and Female*. The following year, for the first time, he poured paint onto a canvas for essentially formal reasons. As recently as 1946, he had experimented with dripping only to retreat to more conventional techniques.

What happened in Jackson's barn in the first few days of 1947 was not the discovery of a new technique. There was no need for him to thin his paint too much, throw a brush in anger, accidentally dribble ink, or kick over a pot of paint. The technique was already at hand. What it lacked was a vision—a way of seeing that would bring its delicate, evocative lines to life, an imagination fecund and vivid enough to keep those lines suspended through a thousand loops, making each new loop as tensile and expressive as the last. In early 1947, Jackson found that vision in himself. Like all his discoveries, it was the result of going backwards, not forward: an epiphany of the past. "Painting is self-discovery," Jackson once said. "Every good artist paints what he is."

In some ways, the drip paintings were a logical next step. As soon as Jackson began to paint on the floor in the summer of 1946, it was virtually inevitable that he would return, if only briefly, to his experiments with dripping. From Schwankovsky to Siqueiros to Baziotes, those experiments had always taken place on the floor. To lay a canvas on the floor was to invite dripping, intended or not. But this time around, the technique had new resonance. For years he had been using a variety of techniques to conceal, or at least obscure, his imagery—more out of personal reticence than artistic conviction. That summer, however, Clement Greenberg conferred on this old imperative a new legitimacy. The purpose of art, he argued, is to "continue the flattening-out, abstracting, 'purifying' process of cubism." Because "purity in art consists in the acceptance, willing acceptance, of the limitations of the medium of the specific art," imagery of any kind defiles that purity. In his review of the 1946 show, he had praised Pollock for "submit[ting] to a habit of discipline derived from cubism." It was clear from Greenberg's reaction to *The Blue Unconscious* that, in his opinion, merely fragmenting the image wasn't enough. It had to be obliterated. ("If there is anything Pollock was set against in his poured pictures," Greenberg later said, "it was iconography.") Yet Jackson relied on the emotional power of unconscious imagery to energize his paintings. Only in the Guggenheim mural and *Gothic* had he been able to maintain that same level of energy and unconscious "truth" over a large canvas without evoking overt imagery. To reconcile his own need for urgent images with Greenberg's call for an end to iconography, Jackson returned to the solution of the mural, only on a far smaller scale. In the series of all-over works that immediately preceded the first drip paintings, he laid down literal images—described by Lee as "heads, parts of the body, fantastic creatures"—then covered them with layers of overpainting.

This curious, back-and-fill process puzzled Lee. "I asked Jackson why he

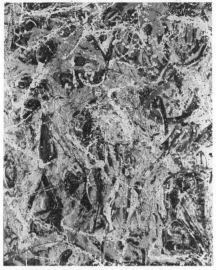

Galaxy, 1947, oil, aluminum, and gravel on
canvas, 43½" × 34"

didn't stop painting when a given image was exposed," she later recounted. "He said, 'I choose to veil the imagery.' "

At first, Jackson's experiments with pouring had little effect on this procedure (an indication that they were, indeed, experiments). In *Galaxy*, one of his first drip paintings, brushed-in images are still discernible beneath the layers of poured paint. Only the "veil" has changed. Instead of a heavy brocade of tight curvilinear strokes, it is now a lacy, translucent curtain flecked with aluminum. Jackson was clearly pleased with this new use for an old technique (it also saved him from the backbreaking, knee-numbing job of covering every inch of a big canvas with heavy impasto). In the paintings that followed, like *Watery Paths* and *Magic Lantern*, he reveled in the new possibilities of density and complexity. In *The Nest* and *Vortex*, he evoked his early experiments with Baziotes and Kamrowski. Almost immediately, the brushed images began to disappear completely behind ever more complicated, exuberant latticework. The lines and flecks of paint took on a new importance; dripping became no longer just another way of obscuring images, but a new way of creating them.

From the beginning, Jackson's overactive imagination had seen the world in a special way. Sande recalled the flights of fantasy in which he rearranged actual events to suit his emotional needs. He would sit for hours staring at objects, fingering them "as if he would crawl inside them." "When Jackson looked at something," recalls Nick Carone, a close friend in later life, "it was as if he were getting into the pores of it, the most minute molecular structure of it, the level at which even the most insignificant thing, like an ashtray, has life and is constantly moving." What was static to most people was, to Jackson's hyperactive imagination, a blur of perspectives and potentials. That had always

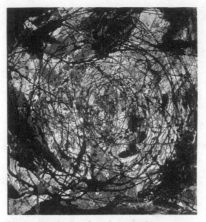

Vortex, c. 1947, oil and enamel on canvas,
20⅝″ × 18¼″

been Jackson's problem with reality, both in life and on canvas: it changed too much, too often; it vibrated with too many possibilities to be put down with clarity or precision. In his sketches for Benton, he had tried furiously to freeze the images. But even as he put them down they shifted in his mind's eye, rotated to another position, or transformed into something else entirely, leaving behind a trace of hairy lines and frustrated cross-hatchings. His brief experiment with sculpture had been even more of a failure. As he slowly chipped away on the outside of a block, figures and faces spun like dervishes on the inside. Primitive art and Picasso had shown him a way to begin to capture the transformations he saw, and Jung had provided an appealing conceptual framework, but even as late as 1947, he was still searching for a way to make the world see the world his way.

There was more to Jackson's vision than a vivid imagination, however. If he saw movement where no one else did, if objects seemed to rotate and transmute in space, it was partly because, in his eyes, they sometimes did. For as long as he could remember, Jackson had been afflicted with hallucinatory spells. They came without warning and could be as short as an instant or as long as several minutes. In the late 1940s, after years of silence, even with Lee, he described the affliction to Roger Wilcox. "With his eyes wide open, in a normal situation, he would suddenly begin to see all these swirling images," Wilcox remembers Jackson telling him, "a swirling of lines and images, swirling tangles of lines. It was like *real*. . . . He wanted to know if there was something wrong with his eyes or with his sanity." Having done some research on visual phenomena in connection with an invention, Wilcox reassured him, "It's just a temporary malfunction in the optic nerve. It's inside your head, not in your eyes." Jackson was relieved. "At least there's nothing wrong with my eyes," he said. (Later, Wilcox researched the problem in medical and optical journals and concluded on the basis of Jackson's description that "it was just a temporary malfunction in the optic chiasm, triggered by a malfunction of the perceptual circuits in the occipital lobe of the cerebral cortex and projected onto the retina." The generally accepted medical term for this painless visual disturbance is an ocular migraine.) At first, according to Wilcox, Jackson didn't recognize the connection between his dripped images and the swirling visions. "He said when he did the first drip painting, he knew it was something familiar, but he didn't know what." Not until after he had painted several more did the full recognition come. "Then he realized he had seen those images before he painted them," says Wilcox. "He told me that."

Jackson had finally found what was, for him, the perfect image: an image that freed him from the lifelong consternation of pencil and paper, brush and canvas, chisel and stone, all the tools that had proved too slow, too fixed, and too explicit; an image that allowed him to attenuate the heavy, obscurantist energy of the brush into the lyrical, long-winded energy of the line; an image that could capture every spin, every transformation in his imagination's eye, no matter how fleeting. The line of paint that he cast from the end of a stick or stiff brush could begin as the profile of a head, change into a bull, a horse, a bird, and a knife, all in the time it took the first drips of paint to reach the canvas. He would pull the art out of himself "like a magician," in George McNeil's phrase. The rapid unspooling of his imagination and the inherent unpredictability of the paint also produced a flow of "accidents" that he could leave or exploit in a running dialogue between automatism and control. "He painted like a machine," said Nick Carone, "but the machine was clicking away on another level. It was a conscious, unconscious dialogue. . . . It was a thing in perpetual motion." When he was "*in* a painting," the images were indeed perpetual. "I don't know where my pictures come from," he once told Clement Greenberg. "They just come." When the spool ran out temporarily, he would set the canvas aside and wait, sometimes for a few hours, sometimes for days, for the next outpouring.

The final breakthrough came when the long line of imagery leapt off the surface entirely and Jackson began to work in the air above the canvas, tracing the unwinding images in three-dimensional space. "Jackson told me that he wasn't just throwing the paint," recalls Nick Carone, "he was delineating some object, some real thing, from a distance above the canvas." Lee called it "working in the air," creating "aerial form[s] which then landed." Another eyewitness described how Jackson would "take his stick or brush out of the paint can and then, in a cursive sweep, pass it over the canvas high above it, so that the viscous paint would form trailing patterns which hover over the canvas before they settle upon it, and then fall into it and then leave a trace of their own passage. He is not drawing on the canvas so much as in the air above it."

It was the final liberation from the frustrations that Jackson had always found on the surface—in reality. He could now work openly with the images that energized his art without risking exposure or Greenberg's censure. No matter how explicit the "aerial forms," when they landed they became unreadable skeins of paint—what one writer called an "alien code." Occasionally—inevitably—an image would float down to the canvas still in recognizable form, later giving rise to speculation that other images lay buried beneath the welter of lines and that even in the densest abstraction, Jackson was a figurative painter in hiding. In fact, he never stopped being a figurative painter, according to Lee, but his figures were ephemeral creations, "airy nothings" that existed only momentarily in midair loops of paint, then disappeared, leaving behind their vacated "skins" on the canvas. Jackson hadn't abandoned the figure; he had, like the Cubists, transformed it. Instead of fragmenting it, he wrapped it in line, then saved the wrapping, thereby "tricking the censor," in Paul Brach's phrase, "painting in the air and letting gravity make the picture." The personal iconography that had obsessed his inner vision for years—the world of Stella and the dinner table, barnyard chickens and menacing bulls—was never more than a dimension away. It hovered *above* the surface, not beneath, its "organic intensity, energy and motion made visible" in the skein of paint below—according to Jackson's own description. He called his new images "memories arrested in space."

Jackson's new way of painting offered another, even deeper gratification. Since childhood, he had connected the act of painting with Stella and Charles: the emphasis on texture and touch, the sensuousness of color, the concern for quality, the pride in craftsmanship, the hours of solitude. Jackson always showed an appreciation for the "gorgeousness of paint," says Budd Hopkins, "a concern with physical loveliness." He also shared Stella's culinary obsession with ingredients. Even in the lean years, he seldom settled for less than the best. At the slightest trickle of money, he would run off to Joseph Meyer's to shop for a new set of brushes and the finest quality paint. "Who else ran around and found all that silver and gold and metallic paint?" asks Hopkins. "Who else worried so much about the way paint falls when it drips and runs or splatters when it's thrown?" Even the most skeptical reviewers at the time couldn't fail to notice Jackson's "strong feeling for *matière*." Like Stella, he took great pains in preparation, carefully unrolling a length of canvas, cutting it precisely, smoothing it flat with his big hands, straightening and patting the corners as if he were laying out the sleeves and back of a chambray shirt.

But the new technique changed all that. It took him away from the canvas—where Stella did her close work—and back to the upright position from which Roy Pollock did his manly work, from his mother's tight wrist movements to his father's broad arm gestures. More than one visitor to the studio noticed that Jackson's relationship to the canvas was like that of a farmer to his field. "The way he stood, the way he looked at the canvas, the way he worked it, always made me think of him like a farmer," says Herbert Matter. "The paintings were his rocks, his trees, his earth. Art was his landscape." Tony Smith also sensed that "his feeling for the land had something to do with his painting canvases on the floor . . . it seemed that [the canvas] was the earth, that he was distributing flowers over it."

The canvas may have been Jackson's field, but it wasn't flowers he was distributing. He told several friends that when he stood back and looked at one of the first drip paintings, a memory suddenly "popped into his head." "He saw himself standing beside his father on a flat rock," recalls Patsy Southgate, a neighbor in Springs, "watching his father pissing, making patterns on the surface of the stone . . . and he wanted to do the same thing when he grew up." To Jackson, who even as an adult urinated from a sitting position, the sight of his father urinating on a rock or in the field had become an archetype of masculine potency, an archetype worked even deeper into his unconscious by years of "peeing competitions" with his brothers. By the time he was an adult, pissing—especially in public—had become the ultimate assertion of masculinity—sometimes the closest he could come to sexual potency. "We'd be in a bar drinking," Roger Wilcox recalls, "and instead of going to the men's room, he'd go outside and take a leak just outside the door. We'd be out driving and he'd stop by the side of the road in broad daylight and take a leak. He'd just get out and not take any precautions, keep the door open, not watch out to see if anybody was coming. He'd just do it." Peter Busa remembers Jackson's obsession with urination. "He was always unbuttoning his fly and taking a piss," says Busa. "One of his brothers told him that in Europe, if you were on a date and you couldn't find a public *pissoir*, you could just go up against a building, with your date right there. He was fascinated by that." At home, he seldom used the bathroom, telling visitors, "I'm from the West and you always go to piss in the backyard." Not only did he urinate in Peggy Guggenheim's fireplace—and perhaps her bed—he did the same thing in the guestroom beds of friends like May Rosenberg, Lucia Wilcox, and Margaret Meert—and often in the bed he shared with Lee.

Standing over the canvas, flinging a stream of paint from the end of a stick, Jackson found the potency that had eluded him in real life. When a woman asked him, "How do you know when you're finished [with a painting]?" Jackson replied, "How do you know when you're finished making love?" For all his problems with impotence and bedwetting, Jackson could "control the flow" in the studio. Creative potency, like sexual potency, came down to a peeing contest. "Tchelitchew had it," he would say, "but he pissed it away." Inevitably, a rumor began to circulate that Jackson *did* urinate on his canvases. John Graham, who had by now rejected abstract art—calling it "slapdash art"— said, "When a child pees on the street, it's charming, but when an adult does, it is not charming." But Jackson was still a child, flinging his belated assertion of manhood across the canvas the way he had seen his father do it. By pouring paint, whether dribbling it in slow curves or flinging it in thin, taut loops, Jackson could play Roy Pollock—even though in the intricacies of the built-up image and the gorgeousness of the paint, he would always be Stella.

Years later, Max Kozloff wrote: "When, finally, [Jackson] lifted the instrument off the canvas, and skeins of liquid, shaken and jolted by their flight through space, came raining and splattering upon the surface, the turgid, ham-fisted Pollock kicked up his heels in the most gracile pirouettes American art had ever known. Dripping, that aerial sphincter of his consciousness, literally enabled him to change identity in midstream."

34

A PERFECT MATCH

By early 1947, Lee was nervous. She had inherited both her mother's superstitiousness and her father's grim fatalism: the better things were, the more uneasy she became—and things had never been better. Despite the cold, Jackson was working more diligently than ever. "He was a hundred percent work at that time," recalls Roger Wilcox, who visited the studio almost daily. Lee didn't know quite what to think of the new paintings, but she trusted Jackson's instincts. "Everything I saw in his studio interested me," she said. Due largely to Stella's frequent visits, he was drinking less and sleeping more—as much as twelve hours a night. Lee spent the first few hours of every day tiptoeing around the house to avoid waking him.

The success of his show in January 1947 only added to her anxiety. No one seemed to notice the strange disjointedness of the paintings: eight big, colorful figurative works and seven small, busy abstractions. The reviews, although few, were generally positive. Greenberg came through, as expected, with praise for the all-over paintings, calling them "a major step in [Pollock's] development." More surprising was his kind treatment of the earlier "ideographs" like *The Tea Cup* and *The Key*, which he had snubbed in the studio. He especially liked their Matisse-like colors, which, he maintained, were responsible for "the consistency and power of surface of [Pollock's] pictures." Greenberg used the opportunity to strike another of his favorite themes: "As is the case with almost all post-Cubist painting of any real originality, it is the tension inherent in the constructed, re-created flatness of the surface that produces the strength of [Pollock's] art." Jackson's new palette also caught the eye of Ben Wolf at *Art Digest*. Citing the "thoughtfully related pastel colors" of *Shimmering Substance* and the "controlled yellows" of *Something from the Past*, he promised that the show was "bound to intrigue the color-conscious gallery gazer." At *Art News*, there was an almost audible sigh of relief that Jackson's "latest pictures such

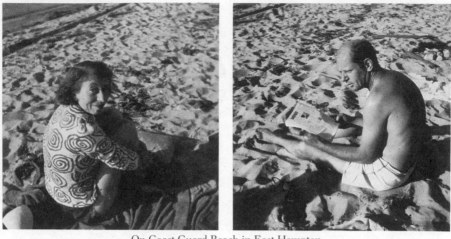

On Coast Guard Beach in East Hampton

as *The Key*, being broader and more colorful, make it easier to assimilate the basic energy which flows through all his canvases."

The only commotion during the show's short, two-week run, was caused by Peggy Guggenheim herself. With only four months left before the gallery was scheduled to close, she was desperate to sell anything she could. In addition to the sixteen paintings in the current show—all of which, under the terms of Jackson's contract, she owned—she had dozens of unsold paintings from previous shows. In a last-ditch effort to sell the giant mural, she opened the lobby of her apartment building yet again to gallery visitors. "Peggy was desperate toward the end," says Sidney Janis. "She was begging people to buy a Pollock."

Peggy's pitch, shameless as it was, worked. The show sold well, beginning with Bill Davis's purchase of *The Tea Cup* and *Shimmering Substance* even before the opening. Although Jackson saw none of the money, the favorable response buoyed him through the winter. It did just the opposite to Lee. By spring, she had "become subject to an unreasonable dread," according to May Rosenberg. Whenever she was alone in the house while Jackson was asleep, "she would suddenly become convinced that it was much too quiet, that [Jackson] had stopped breathing. Each time this happened she told herself that it was all nonsense, but soon she would become uncontrollably frightened again and no logic could reassure her."

Briefly, in early spring, Lee's anxiety appeared justified. Only weeks before Peggy's scheduled departure, Jackson was still without a new gallery. For months, Peggy had been peddling him up and down Fifty-seventh Street, looking for someone, anyone, on whom she could unload her $300-a-month burden. Not only did she have another year to pay on Jackson's contract—an obligation she now considered outrageously onerous—she also had dozens of unsold Pollock paintings, the future value of which would depend largely on the shrewdness and diligence of her successor. For the same reasons that she wanted to sell, however, no one wanted to buy. The high-rent dealers in European modernism, Pierre Matisse and Curt Valentin, "wouldn't touch" Peggy's stable of young American painters. "I must be going blind," Valentin scoffed. "I can't see them at all." Matisse dismissed their work with a mangled cliché: "It isn't my fish." Julien Levy was closing his gallery. Sam Kootz, who two years before had offered to take Jackson on, had since acquired Robert Motherwell and Bill Baziotes from Peggy and was no longer desperate enough to put up with a drunk. Betty Parsons, a former socialite who had opened a new gallery the previous October in part of Mortimer Brandt's old space, admired Jackson's work—"I'm crazy about him," she said—but couldn't afford his contract. She took three of Peggy's other artists—Mark Rothko, Barnett Newman, and Clyfford Still—but passed on Pollock when Peggy insisted that Jackson and the contract were a package deal. With time running out, Peggy tried even more unlikely possibilities such as Marian Willard, galleries that handled realists like Edward Hopper and Jackson's mentor, Tom Benton. But still no takers.

Finally, at her wit's end, she returned to Parsons and offered a compromise. If Parsons would promise to give Jackson a show the following season (1947–48) and act as Peggy's agent in regard to the Pollock paintings she already owned, then Peggy would continue to pay Jackson's $300 monthly allowance until the contract expired on February 15, 1948. Of course, as long as Peggy was providing the subsidy, she insisted on sticking to the original arrangement whereby all of Jackson's new work would belong to her, with one exception of Jackson's choosing. To sweeten the offer and to encourage Parsons to work hard in Jackson's behalf, Peggy offered to let her sell the new works as she saw fit and retain a full commission. On sales of earlier paintings, however, Peggy would set the prices and receive *all* the proceeds. It was, by Peggy's standards at least, an extraordinarily generous offer. Parsons could show Jackson for an entire year, risk-free, for the cost of a single show.

But Parsons balked. Like Kootz, she was concerned about Jackson's reputation as a violent drunk. Twenty years before, she had divorced her first and only husband on account of his drinking and had fled golden-era Hollywood because "there was such heavy drinking all the time." Twice burned, she apparently thought it prudent to visit Springs and see for herself if, as Lee claimed, Jackson had "settled down."

It was the meeting of two worlds: Parsons, the high-strung graduate of Miss Randall McKeever's Finishing School, former Newport and Palm Beach debutante; Pollock, the son of an Arizona dirt farmer. Born in the family house at 17 West Forty-ninth Street—later demolished to make way for Rockefeller Center—Parsons was an unstable mix of New England aristocratic asceticism and southern dissipation. Her father, a Wall Street broker ruined by the crash of 1929, was the descendant of Yale's first rector; her mother, a New Orleans belle with effervescent French blood in her veins—"Thank God for the French!" Parsons would exclaim—who read voraciously and drank juleps with

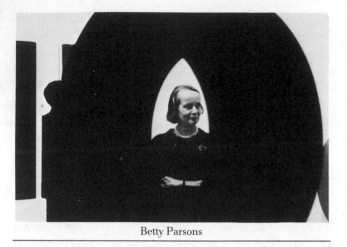

Betty Parsons

breakfast. Elizabeth Pierson Parsons inherited both her father's reserve and her mother's longings. After an adolescence of society balls and finishing school, she wangled her way into a class with Gutzon Borglum, the sculptor of Mount Rushmore. Her early marriage to Schuyler Livingston Parsons ended three years later in a divorce, the first in family history. (Infuriated by the scandal, her grandfather cut her out of his will.) To Parsons, the breakup was a godsend. It not only rid her of the alcoholic, homosexual Parsons but also allowed her to pursue freely the two great passions of her life: art and other women.

Like so many others, Betty Parsons had experienced her epiphany at the Armory Show in 1913 when she was thirteen years old. Eight years later, after her divorce, she moved to Paris where she studied sculpture in the same class as Alberto Giacometti and joined an expatriate circle that included Gertrude Stein, Alice B. Toklas, Sara Murphy, Alexander Calder, Man Ray, Isamu Noguchi, Hart Crane, Max Jacob, Tristan Tzara, and Harry Crosby. With her high cheekbones, straight, short hair, slim hips, and "da Vinci forehead" she looked like a finely fashioned piece of Art Deco sculpture. Men in the streets often mistook her for another archetypal woman of the era: Greta Garbo. "If you look at Betty, you see the Sphinx, the Garbo-like quality, the remoteness," said Saul Steinberg. When she returned to the States in 1933 and moved to California, she met and befriended the real Garbo as well as Marlene Dietrich and other movie stars. Back home in New York, she added Martha Graham and Eleanor Roosevelt to her distinguished, all-female inner circle.

In Springs, Parsons and Pollock circled each other warily. She was intimidated by Jackson's reputation as a ticking time bomb. "His whole rhythm was either sensitive or very wild," she said. "You never quite knew whether he was going to kiss your hand or throw something at you." She "loved his looks"—his vitality, his "enormous physical presence"—and thought he looked taller than he had the previous year when Barnett Newman introduced him to her at a party. The combination of Jackson's brooding volatility and exaggerated male physicality unnerved her. "Betty would get nervous about any goddamned thing," recalls Gerome Kamrowski. "She was a society dame."

It was the "society dame" in Parsons that, in turn, unnerved Jackson. Her "rapid-fire bursts of nervous laughter" and "small truthful girlish voice," grated almost as much as her Social Register background. Jackson also knew of her lesbianism and, according to his friend Harry Jackson, felt threatened by it. In the end, however, he seemed placated by her admiration for his art which, in her romantic, literal view, reflected the great open spaces of the American West. Even when he took her to the studio to view the new "drip paintings" (he didn't yet call them that) she flattered him with a nervous little laugh that at least appeared to indicate appreciation. "Betty worked on the principle, if you didn't understand it, it was probably good," recalls Hedda Sterne, a friend and investor in Parsons's gallery, "because you very seldom *like* something really new." Aware that Parsons was Peggy's only buyer, Jackson put on his most charming face for the rest of the weekend. "He held her hand and wheeled and dealed and played for position," recalls Harry Jackson. "He wasn't just cultivating her, he was courting her."

The effort paid off. When Parsons returned to New York, she accepted Peggy's offer. In May, Peggy had the papers drawn up—a formality that surprised Parsons, who considered verbal contracts binding—and the two women signed. No one, however, rested easier. In Springs, Jackson grumbled about Parsons being "not as tolerant" and "not as forceful a dealer" as Peggy and complained about being shut out of the process. "I'm not a slave," he protested to Roger Wilcox. "They can't sell me." Parsons, too, was leery of the new arrangement and further aggravated Jackson by refusing to sign a separate contract with him. Despite her enthusiasm for his art, she couldn't help feeling that Peggy had "dumped" him in her lap "because nobody else would risk showing him." Peggy, in turn, was leery of *both* Jackson and Parsons. In a parting gesture of distrust, she asked James Johnson Sweeney to keep an eye on them for her.

At the end of the day, Saturday, May 31, 1947, Art of This Century closed its doors for the last time. Kiesler's revolutionary multi-use chairs were auctioned off, the curved gumwood walls of the Surrealist gallery went to the Franklin Simon department store, the collection itself was put in storage, and, with only her two Lhasa Apsos, Peggy left for Venice. She would never see Jackson or speak to him again.

By her second summer in Springs, Lee had perfected the routine. Everything was geared to Jackson's needs. In the morning, before he woke, she cleaned the house and tended the garden—being careful to take the phone off the hook so its ringing wouldn't wake him. Guests, especially those who had known Lee in her Bohemian days, were astonished by the obsessively tidy house she kept. (Charlotte Park quipped, "that's probably why Jackson drinks so much.") After breakfast, around one o'clock, Jackson would retreat to the barn and Lee would start to work on the phone. She maintained a list of people—collectors, dealers, artists, friends—with whom she kept in constant touch. If Jackson had a question for Parsons, she added that to her list of calls. "Jackson was afraid to call his gallery," according to a friend, "whether it was to ask for a hundred dollars or to see if there had been any sales. It was difficult for him to assert himself." Not for Lee. She enjoyed the daily manipulations and collisions of commerce. "Trade was in [her] blood," said May Rosenberg. On a slow day, she had enough time after telephoning to work again in the garden, shop, prepare dinner, or, later in the summer, can and preserve foods for the winter. Whatever happened, she was always ready by five or six when Jackson emerged from the barn ready for a beer and a walk to the beach. From there, the day usually drifted off into dinner and conversation with the Wilcoxes, the Matters, or the Rosenbergs, all of whom Lee considered "safe company."

Lee also took the precaution of loading the summer weekends as far in advance as possible with safe houseguests. The safest, of course, was Stella, who came several times during the spring and summer. She thought Jackson's new drip paintings were "swell"—the same word she used to describe his garden. Elizabeth Wright Hubbard was another of Lee's approved visitors. With her "heavy hocks, crusty hair, and stained black dress," she would descend on Springs for a weekend, shepherding her restive family. Jackson, as always, enjoyed the company of children. "He took me in the barn and showed me his pictures stacked up against the wall," recalls Merle Hubbard, who was ten at the time. When Merle asked, "Why are you spilling paint, silly?" Jackson laughed. "One of the things he loved about us," says Hubbard's daughter, Elizabeth, Jr., "is that we were such philistines about painting." Another safe visitor was Ruth Stein, Lee's sister, who came with her husband, William, and their twelve-year-old son Ronnie. The two sisters had been estranged for several years, but Jackson's fondness for Ruth overrode family squabbles. "He was the most wonderful host at that time," Ruth recalls. "We never wanted to go home."

Whenever guests came, Lee spent most of her time in the kitchen. She had taught herself to cook Stella's way. "It was American-type cooking," recalls Ronald Stein, "pot roast and gravy and stuffing and potatoes and salad." To Ruth, who had been raised on a Jewish-Ukrainian diet of pahrkas, knedler, and tsimis, the midwestern fare seemed exotic. Occasionally, Jackson would invade the kitchen to bake a pie—"but only when he was in the mood," according to Stein. "Another time, he might dry the dishes, but generally he left everything to Lee."

The same rule governed every aspect of their life together: Lee directed and Jackson went along, except now and then when Jackson chose to assert himself. "Lee would do everything," recalls Stein, "and then something would come up and Jackson would say, 'Yes, we're going to get the plumbing fixed,' and Lee wouldn't argue, and the plumbing would get fixed—and then Lee would go back to running the show." Running the show meant reshaping the world

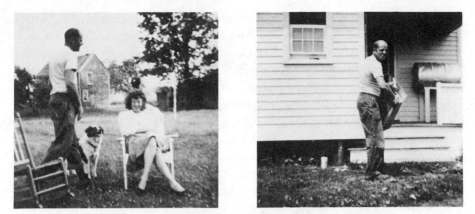

A summer afternoon in Springs, c. 1948, with Gyp and Jackson's
pet crow, Caw-Caw (on Lee's head).

to serve Jackson's needs, to minimize his worry and maximize his time at work. She schooled visitors in his moods, telling them when and how to approach him. "She would say, 'Ask him this way, say this, say that,' " recalls Stein, "and she was usually right." It was the perfect match: Jackson created and Lee made it possible for him to create. "That was what we thought we had to do in those days—be nurturing," says Patsy Southgate. "It was masochism, all right, but for turning out a Hemingway or a Pollock, it was well worth the candle."

Clement Greenberg was another frequent houseguest. Often with a young girlfriend in tow, he would accompany the Pollocks to the beach or ride bikes with Jackson into East Hampton. During his visit that spring, he took Jackson and Lee to see a private collection of paintings by Miró in one of the huge "cottages" near the water in an area that locals called "the city development." On every visit, sooner or later, Greenberg and Jackson would retreat to the barn to look at paintings and talk about "the direction of Jackson's art." Greenberg was deferential but definitive. "I'd say a picture was good or bad, or a piece of a picture was good or bad," Greenberg recalls. "That's the only way I talk." Jackson listened intently and later would lead friends through the studio proudly pointing out, "Clem likes this, Clem likes that."

What had begun as a political imperative was becoming, in addition, a genuine friendship. For Greenberg, Jackson's companionship provided an antidote to the insecurity he always felt among the *Partisan Review* crowd. Often slow and ponderous of speech, especially in the company of articulate talkers, he found in Jackson the ideal, undemanding listener. He was attracted to Jackson's taciturn machismo, so different from his own querulous, defensive posturing: so direct, so uncalculated—so American. Like Lee Krasner, Greenberg had spent much of his adulthood trying to escape the past. "Who in his right mind would want to be Jewish?" he would ask rhetorically. Born in Brooklyn to Lithuanian Jewish parents, he had learned Yiddish and English at the same time. His family lived briefly in Virginia and, for the rest of his life, he clung—not entirely convincingly—to the cultivated southern accent he learned there. After college, he spurned the family wholesale dry goods business and sat at home for two and a half years "in what looked like idleness," teaching himself Latin, French, Italian, and German. When he finally capitulated and worked briefly for his austere, implacable father, he discovered that "my appetite for business did not amount to the same thing as an inclination."

Since then, Greenberg's war with the past had expressed itself in macho posturing, ardent Marxism, and, after his divorce in 1936, an even more ardent misogyny. At a party at Peggy Guggenheim's apartment shortly before her departure for Europe, Greenberg's "sounding off" so provoked Max Ernst that he dumped a large ashtray full of ashes and cigarette butts on Greenberg's bald pate. In her unpublished memoirs, May Rosenberg recorded the incident:

Clem leaped up to throttle Ernst (almost half Clem's size and much older). He might have succeeded, since Ernst was overcome with laughter at his own joke. But Niko Calas (young, long, lean, handsome, and fragile) took a roundhouse swing at Clem and—to everyone's surprise—connected! Probably Clem lost his footing, for it is hard to believe that Niko's punch could have knocked a baby down. Anyway, there's Niko staring down at Clem sitting on the floor, practically under the piano. Ernst and the guests are convulsed with laughter, and Clem's girl, overcome with horror, is pressing a couple of aspirin and a glass of water on the dazed Clem. Who swallows as he is bid, and seconds later begins yelling that he's allergic to aspirin, that he has been poisoned!

"Clem's girls" were typically bright, naive, extremely young, and willing to pay a high price for admission to the New York art world. "I was awed by the man and thrilled by the company he kept," recalls one of them. But Greenberg charged dearly for such thrills. "He was always terrorizing me," says Phyllis Fleiss, who dated Greenberg during these years. Finding a half-dead mouse in a gutter on Park Avenue, "he picked it up by the tail and dangled it in front of my face," Fleiss recalls. "I screamed, of course, and ran, but he chased after me with this mouse. He had a sadistic streak a mile wide."

The common theme, in Greenberg's life as in his criticism, was provocation. "To be attacked universally is a favorable sign," he said. "If you're not against most opinion, something is off." It was this same instinct for provocation that had attracted Greenberg to Jackson's provocative art in the first place. "He had the whole Trotskyite syndrome," says Fleiss. "Anything that was popular he wasn't going to like. He had to find an art that was totally shocking, that people were totally against, and *that's* what he was going to like." In Greenberg's eyes, he and Jackson were fellow provocateurs.

Jackson, in turn, was flattered by Greenberg's attentions. Clem had been to college, spoke several languages, had a seemingly encyclopedic knowledge of literature, and always talked, in front of Jackson at least, with ringing conviction. As a high school dropout, Jackson's respect for book learning, traceable perhaps to Roy Pollock's glass-front bookcase, ran deep. Too deep, many of his friends thought. "He was a country boy in awe of the big-city, East Coast Jewish radical intellectual," says Paul Brach. When Greenberg expressed an opinion, Jackson never challenged it in his presence and even in his absence was wary of contradicting him. Fritz Bultman recalls a conversation with Jackson about mysticism—a subject anathema to Greenberg—after which Jackson felt obliged to say, "Don't tell Clem any of this."

Although he "listened intently to everything Clem had to say," as one friend recalls, Jackson never really understood Greenberg's theories—the theories that would eventually secure his place in the hierarchy of twentieth-century art. Milton Resnick was only one of many friends who saw that Greenberg's ideas "were always a mystery to Jackson." "He couldn't get a hold of them," says Resnick. "Surfaceness, Cubist space, and all of the things that Greenberg was saying, it just didn't take. And if he felt honest with you, if he felt he could open up, he made it clear how little he really understood." Ultimately, of course, neither Greenberg nor Jackson cared if Jackson understood. Enlightenment wasn't really the point. Their mutual needs were met regardless of words. "Jackson was never a bore," Greenberg once said. "He didn't have to talk in order to be interesting."

Jackson wasted no time in taking advantage of his new friendship.

Infuriated by the news in 1947 that Phil Guston had been awarded a Guggenheim Fellowship, he wrote John Myers for information on how he could apply for one. During September and October, he labored over a statement for the application. Even if Greenberg didn't actually write the two short paragraphs, his ideas and critical technique permeate them. In his review of the January show, Greenberg had announced the "historical death of 'easel painting.' " ("Pollock points a way beyond the easel, beyond the mobile, framed picture, to the mural, perhaps—or perhaps not.") In the very first line of his statement, Jackson picks up where Greenberg left off: "I intend to paint large movable pictures which will function between the easel and mural." Echoing Greenberg's praise of the Guggenheim mural, Jackson boasts, "I have set a precedent in this genre in a large painting for Miss Peggy Guggenheim which was installed in her house." Like Greenberg's reviews, Jackson's statement is imbued with a sense of art history on the march. "I believe the easel picture to be a dying form and the tendency of modern feeling is towards the wall picture or mural." In order not to appear too radical, however, the statement closes on a modest note. "I believe the time is not yet ripe for a *full* transition from easel to mural. The pictures I contemplate painting would constitute a halfway state, and an attempt to point out the direction of the future, without arriving there completely."

At about the same time, Harold Rosenberg helped Jackson with another statement, this one for the premier issue of *Possibilities*, a magazine of commentary edited by Rosenberg and Robert Motherwell. The article sounds more like Jackson than the Guggenheim application does, but Greenberg's influence is still detectable.

My painting does not come from the easel. I hardly ever stretch my canvas before painting. I prefer to tack the unstretched canvas to the hard wall or the floor. I need the resistance of a hard surface. On the floor I am more at ease. I feel nearer, more a part of the painting, since this way I can walk around it, work from the four sides and literally be *in* the painting. This is akin to the method of the Indian sand painters of the West.

The Guggenheim application was rejected, and *Possibilities* folded after the first issue. But in the process, Jackson had acquired, through his contact with Greenberg, a basic vocabulary of ideas which, half understood and highly simplified, would fill his public statements over the next ten years.

In the October issue of the prestigious British publication *Horizon*, Greenberg finally spoke out in his own voice. It was a clarion call, outrageously arrogant and dismissive even by Greenberg's standards: Matisse wasn't as "hard-headed" as Cézanne—despite the latter's "paranoia"; American art had been obsessed with "the aberrated and deranged"; only Picasso's Cubist works were great; Kandinsky lost it when he "discovered the Spiritual." All the great themes are unfurled. "Pollock's strength lies in the emphatic surfaces of his pictures . . . that thick, fuliginous flatness which began—but only began—to be the strong point of late Cubism." "It is its materialism, or positivism . . . that made painting the most advanced and *hopeful* art in the West." But in art as in people, Greenberg's ultimate obsession was America and Americanness. After dismissing Morris Graves and Mark Tobey as "so narrow as to cease even being interesting," he pronounced the ultimate judgment: "The most powerful painter in contemporary America and the only one who promises to be a major one . . . [is] Jackson Pollock." Why? Because "the feeling [his art] contains [is] radically American. Faulkner and Melville can be called in as witnesses to the nativeness of such violence, exasperation and stridency." Finally, after naming David Smith the American sculptor whose art, "like Pollock's, might justify the term major," Greenberg concludes that Pollock "relieves us somewhat of the necessity of being apologetic about American art."

Two months later, *Time* magazine scornfully reported Greenberg's pronouncements in a one-column article entitled "The Best?" The message was delivered subtly by juxtaposing snippets of Greenberg's fuliginous praise with small pictures of works by each of the three artists he singled out: Pollock, Smith, and Hans Hofmann. "Is any good art being painted in the U.S.?" the article began. "Britain's highbrow magazine *Horizon* scanned the U.S., and found three little sunbeams peeping through. 'The most powerful painter in America,' wrote Manhattan Critic Clement Greenberg, is Jackson Pollock, who painted this." The reproduction of *The Key* that followed, contrary to later reports, was not printed upside down, but, reduced to a 1½-by-2½-inch, black-and-white blur, it might as well have been.

A month before his first show at the Parsons gallery, Jackson felt stronger than ever before—physically, emotionally, and creatively. After a Thanksgiving visit to Springs, Stella wrote Frank: "Jack was busy getting his painting stretched for his show which is the 5th of January [1948] he has done a lot of swell painting this year. They both look wonderful done both of them a lot of good to be out of the City and they are very happy with their home." Happiness at home translated into confidence in the studio. Through the summer and fall, the paintings grew steadily larger, more complex, and more daring. Soon Jackson was laying out canvases that were too big to cover from a kneeling position. Standing over and maneuvering around a canvas while pouring paint with one hand and holding a can of paint with the other involved a new set of logistics and a new repertoire of movements. He also began experimenting with the density and texture of the web, from the open skein of *Reflection of the Big Dipper* to the impenetrable thicket of *Sea Change*. He found he could loop the lines, as in *Vortex*, or lay them straight, like a bed of pine needles, as in *Phosphorescence*. He could inscribe them sharply on the matrix of paint, as in *Shooting Star*, or let them bleed into one another and into the canvas, as in *Cathedral*. He experimented with materials, adding gravel, nails, tacks, buttons, keys, combs, cigarettes, or matches to give the surface texture and using metallic aluminum paint to enliven and enrich the painting surface. (Later Greenbergian critics would make much ado over such playful experiments, seeing in them efforts to provide realistic content without violating the ban on figuration, or to give the illusion of depth without violating the integrity of the picture plane.) He also began experimenting with enamel—regular house paint—which he could buy in the large quantities he required far more cheaply than oil paint at Dan Miller's store down the road.

By December, Jackson had completed all the paintings for the show and invited his neighbors, Ralph and Mary Manheim, into the studio to help name them. (At least one, *Cathedral*, had already been named, if not at Greenberg's direction, then certainly with his full approval. In the *Horizon* article, he had equated the spirit of Jackson's paintings to that of the great Gothic cathedrals.) Manheim, a translator of French and German literature, tended, predictably, to the romantic and the literary with names like *Enchanted Forest, Lucifer, Phosphorescence, Magic Lantern, Sea Change, Full Fathom Five,* and *Watery Paths*. According to Lee, Jackson relished their earnestness and admiration as he stood back, arms folded, quietly "vetoing or approving [suggested] titles."

The week before the show opened, Jackson and Lee went into the city and stayed with Lee's sister Ruth Stein on lower Fifth Avenue. On the eve of the opening, unable to sleep, Jackson stayed up talking with Ruth. "He had a gift for making you feel like you were the chosen person," Ruth recalls. Ruth Stein had a gift of her own; she had inherited her grandmother's psychic powers.

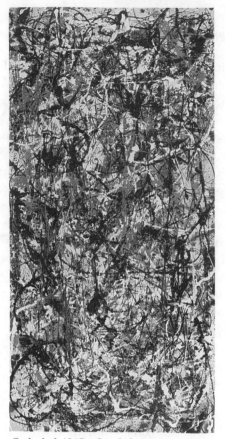

Cathedral, 1947, oil and aluminum paint on
canvas, 71½″ × 35¹⁄₁₆″

More than once before, she had astonished Jackson with her clairvoyant insights. This night, "he wanted to know about his future as an artist," she remembers. "What I saw for him and whether or not he would be successful." Ruth put Jackson's big hand in her lap and intently traced the deep creases. "You are going to be a very famous painter one day," she told him. Jackson laughed and said, "I should set up a booth at the show where you can read everybody's fortune, so if my paintings don't sell, at least I can make money from you." "We both laughed," Ruth remembers, "but he really believed it. God, did he believe."

Measured by Jackson's expectations, the show was a disaster. No one knew what to make of these great tangled webs of paint, many of them laced with aluminum, glowing in the windowless void of Parsons's gallery. Robert Coates, the critic for the *New Yorker*, lamented: "There are times when communications break down entirely." The handful of opening night guests shuffled back and forth on the scrubbed wood floors, some brimming with hostility, (Hedda Sterne found it "all too Dionysiac"); others searching for something to say (Joe

Glasco, another painter, could only repeat "radical, radical, radical"). The evening, and the show, might have been saved by Peggy's irrepressible personality, proselytic fervor, and unabashed huckstering, but Betty Parsons was no Peggy Guggenheim. Where Peggy worked the crowd like a politician, Parsons hovered at its edge "like a protecting priestess," aloof and slightly mortified. Where Peggy dug deep for buyers, Parsons seemed to avoid them. "Collectors were afraid to ask her the price of paintings," recalls Herbert Ferber, one of her artists, "because it seemed that she didn't really want to sell them." Jackson had undoubtedly heard stories about Parsons's *laissez-faire* attitude—"I give them walls," she would say, "they do the rest"—but seeing it deflate the debut of his new paintings was, apparently, too much to bear. Although he remained sober, if tense, through the opening, as soon as the last puzzled guest left, he rushed off with family and a few friends to the bar at the Hotel Albert. After three double bourbons, he snatched Alma Pollock's hat and tore it to pieces.

The critics treated his show less kindly. Overnight, it seemed, the tolerance that Jackson had wrung from them in the four years since his first show vanished. "Lightweight," said the *Art News* reviewer, "a perverse echo of Tobey's fine white writing," nothing but "crashing energy" and "monotonous intensity." Coates's review in the *New Yorker* also paid left-handed respect to Jackson's "tremendous energy" and even complimented some of the smaller paintings, but Coates's verdict on most of the major works, including *Lucifer*, *Reflection of the Big Dipper*, and *Cathedral*, was unsparing: "mere unorganized explosions of random energy, and therefore meaningless." In *Art Digest*, Alonzo Lansford even revived the snide tone that hadn't been heard since Parker Tyler's reference to "baked macaroni":

> Pollock's current method seems to be a sort of automatism; apparently, while staring steadily up into the sky, he lets go a loaded brush on the canvas. . . . This, with much use of aluminum paint, results in a colorful and exciting panel. Probably it also results in the severest pain in the neck since Michelangelo painted the Sistine Ceiling.

Only Clement Greenberg stood firm, not only reaffirming his controversial support of Pollock—"[this show] signals another step forward on his part"—but even questioning the judgment and good faith of those fainthearted critics who disagreed: "[Pollock's] new work offers a puzzle [only] to all those not sincerely in touch with contemporary painting." It was a classic display of Greenbergian fireworks, filled with culinary metaphors (the aluminum paint produces "an oily over-ripeness"; this new phase in Pollock's development needs further "digestion"), niggling criticisms ("the artist's weakness as a colorist"), and unsupported razor-fine distinctions (*Gothic* is "inferior to the best of his recent work in style, harmony, and the inevitability of its logic"; *Enchanted Forest* "resembles *Cathedral*, though inferior in strength"). After sounding some familiar themes ("In this day and age the art of painting increasingly rejects the easel and yearns for the wall"), Greenberg concluded with a provocative bang: "Pollock will in time be able to compete [with John Marin] as the greatest American painter of the twentieth century—no other American artist has presented such a case."

But his dominant theme was art history on the move. More so than in any previous review, he strained to fit Pollock into the logically unfolding *Zeitgeist* of modern art. "Since Mondrian no one has driven the easel picture quite so far away from itself [as Pollock has]." Of *Cathedral*, which he considered the strongest picture in the show, Greenberg wrote, "[It] reminds one of Picasso's and Braque's masterpieces of the 1912–1915 phase of cubism." By tying Jackson firmly to such pillars of modernism, Greenberg was shrewdly responding to those who criticized his championing of Pollock. No one doubted the genius of Mondrian, Picasso, or Braque; no one questioned the revolutionary importance of Analytical Cubism. Flatness was the undisputed grail of modernism, according to Greenberg, and now it had fallen into Jackson Pollock's hands. He was, in short, Picasso's legitimate heir.

To make such a claim credible, however, Greenberg had to argue that Jackson's breakthroughs were the result of his immersion in the theory and practice of Analytical Cubism, that Jackson had engaged in an artistic and ideological dialogue with Picasso, that he had been steeped in what Greenberg liked to call the "culture" of painting. "It is Pollock's culture as a painter that has made him so sensitive and receptive to [this] tendency [toward an emphasis on surface]," Greenberg asserted.

Even as he made it, Greenberg must have known from his frequent visits to Springs that such an assertion was false. Jackson's primary interest in Picasso was not in the artist's Analytical Cubist paintings, but in the cloisonnist works of the 1920s and 1930s. Those aspects of Jackson's paintings that Greenberg attributed to the legacy of Picasso, Braque, and Mondrian—restricted palette, shallow space, and all-over composition—either had come to Jackson indirectly from less "distinguished" sources (such as Tobey) or had never come at all. His "dialogue" with the giants consisted largely of a monologue delivered by Greenberg. To several friends, Jackson admitted that he neither understood nor cared for Analytical Cubism. His paintings came from a different source altogether. The only person other than Greenberg who might have sensitized Jackson to the possible Cubist implications of the drip paintings, Lee Krasner, considered them irrelevant. (According to Greenberg, Jackson later told him that Lee "didn't agree" with his theories about Jackson's art—especially his designation of Jackson as "a late Cubist.")

But Greenberg wasn't interested in what was, only in what should be. In the service of his grand vision of the progress of modern art, facts became irrelevant. Never a stickler for historical accuracy and grateful for Greenberg's support, Jackson gladly went along. He, too, had a vision that superseded facts.

The reviews were bad, but the worst was yet to come. In February, the last of Peggy's $250 checks arrived in the mail. Jackson had already signed a one-year contract with Parsons for the following year, but it included no provision for a monthly allowance. Nor was there any chance of "overage" from the January show. Sales had been dismal. Jackson's startling new paintings had left most collectors as well as reviewers "feeling that their dog or cat could have done better." (In galling contrast, a simultaneous showing at the Artists' Gallery of gouaches of clowns by a former vaudevillian named Walter Phillips sold out the first day.) By the time Jackson's show closed, only two paintings had been sold, not including the one that Bill Davis, who was traveling in Europe, had arranged for Lee to choose and set aside for him. But the exact count was academic. Under the terms of the old contract, all the proceeds went to Peggy.

Within a month of Peggy's last payment, the Pollocks were destitute. To save on coal, they heated only one floor of the house at a time, closing off the upstairs during the day in order to keep the downstairs tolerably warm. At $21 a cord, wood for the kitchen stove was an unaffordable luxury. When the weather turned frigid, they would abandon the house altogether and retreat to the city. On one such visit, Jackson called on Barnett Newman and his wife Annalee on East Nineteenth Street. "He and Barney went around the corner to the New Star Market so Jackson could cash a ten dollar check," Annalee Newman remembers. "It bounced."

In Springs, Jackson tried other ways to make ends meet. To pay off a $56 grocery bill at the Springs General Store, he offered Dan Miller a painting. Miller, who felt everyone was entitled to some credit, accepted the offer—to the amazement of most locals, especially his wife, Audrey. When she refused to allow the painting in her house, Jackson lent three more for her to choose from. Eventually, Miller took the first one, but hung it on his office wall at the store. (After Jackson's death, he sold the painting for $7,300.) But Dan Miller was the exception. Most of Jackson's creditors "wouldn't take his paintings on a bet," according to a neighbor. Like most of the townspeople, they considered his plight pathetic but predictable—a cruelly appropriate fate for a crazy artist.

By March, the situation was so desperate that for the first time since the end of the Project, Jackson was forced to look for a job. Lee offered to go to work instead, but Jackson's pride wouldn't allow it. He "made a real issue of it," according to Lee. He went to Julien Levy, who had taught for years at the Art Students League, and asked about a teaching position at his alma mater. Levy explained sympathetically that "because of his behavior it couldn't be considered." When Jackson approached his old friend Peter Busa, who was teaching at Cooper Union, another traditionalist bastion, the reaction was the same. "He came to see me in class," Busa remembers, "and he said he wanted to teach. I looked around at these students—what they were doing was nothing like Jackson's stuff—and I said, 'What the hell would you teach here, Jack?' He didn't even say anything. He knew I was right. So he just turned around and walked out." Despairing, Jackson turned to John Little, who had made so much money designing fabrics before the war that he kept his work secret from Trotskyite friends like Lee Krasner. "Jackson came to me and said, 'Maybe I could do some textiles,' " Little recalls. But nothing came of it. When a fabric factory opened in nearby Montauk, Jackson and Roger Wilcox walked the twelve miles to Montauk to sign up. (Wilcox's old Ford was out of commission.) They found jobs all right, at a dollar an hour, but the employers wouldn't advance them the money to fix Wilcox's car. Without transportation, the job was unthinkable, so they walked back, still unemployed.

Betty Parsons sympathized with Jackson's plight and did what she could to generate some income from her huge store of Pollock paintings. "I tried to sell a few things by offering a discount," she recalled, "very unprofessional—and Peggy would have been furious. I even appealed to a couple of clients on a charity basis, an even worse mistake." But nothing seemed to work.

In the end, it was Lee's determined salesmanship that saved them. As part of her constant campaign to promote Jackson among her friends, she had pressured Fritz Bultman, who in turn pressured his sister, Muriel Francis, into visiting Parsons's gallery. When Francis, a New Orleans–born impresario and agent, expressed an interest in buying *Shooting Star* from the January show, Parsons immediately wrote Peggy in Venice, bewailing "the terrible financial condition of the Pollocks" and asking her to forgo the proceeds from the sale so the money could go directly to them, thereby "saving them from immediate financial embarrassment." In return, Peggy would receive some future work in place of the one sold. On April 12, a week after Parsons's plea, Peggy wired a terse approval of the arrangement. Both Parsons and Lee were shocked that she offered no additional assistance. "[Peggy] just disappeared," said Parsons. "Either she was childish or inhuman." Lee didn't see a choice. "The idea of [Peggy's] dedication to Pollock was fanciful," she said later. "When she was off, she left him high and dry—that was her great dedication. . . . [S]he said bye-bye, hope you can swim." Two days after Peggy's approval, Francis bought *Shooting Star* for several hundred dollars on an installment basis, and Parsons rushed a check to the Pollocks. She didn't bother to deduct her commission. Jackson later told an interviewer, exaggerating only slightly, "We lived a year on that picture, and a few clams I dug out of the bay with my toes."

The same month that *Shooting Star* sold, Willem de Kooning's first show at the new Egan Gallery opened to nearly unanimous raves. What Greenberg, and only Greenberg, had said about Jackson, others were suddenly saying about de Kooning: "A singular concentration of passion and technique . . . fierce energy . . . virtuosity . . . voluptuousness." Within days, the Museum of Modern Art bought a painting from the show and the art world began to buzz with recognition. (Among artists themselves, de Kooning had been admired for years.) Inevitably, the to-do raised Jackson's competitive hackles. Especially at a time when his own career was faltering, it must have seemed that the spotlight was already moving on. During a party at Jack the Oysterman's fish restaurant on Eighth Street after the de Kooning show, Jackson "came in like a cannon," Ethel Baziotes remembers. "He lashed out at everyone, and no one could say anything to please him. He was insulting to his good friends in a way I'd never seen before. Everyone was white with fear. I mean there was the threat of physical violence. You didn't know if he would pick something up and throw it at you." Breathing fire, he approached Arshile Gorky, who stood against a wall quietly whittling a long pencil to a fine point with a pocket knife he always carried. As Jackson weaved toward him, Gorky "looked at him in the eye in a way that said, 'Be careful,'" Baziotes recalls. Jackson planted himself directly beneath Gorky's shadowed brow and launched into a train of obscene invective, most of it directed at Gorky's paintings. Without taking his eyes off Jackson, Gorky lifted the pencil toward him, leaned forward, and continued to whittle. At each stroke, the knife came closer to Jackson's throat. "Pardon me, Mr. Pollock," Gorky finally interrupted, "you and I are different kinds of artists." For a tense moment, the two men stared at each other, eyes locked. "It was like a stage play," says Baziotes. "They were taking each other's measure." The tension was broken when Bill Baziotes called out from the crowd, "Jackson, why the hell don't you shut up?" And he did.

A month later, the same artists set aside their incipient rivalries to fight an old common enemy: the continuing resistance of the art establishment to American abstract art. As late as October 1947, Greenberg had noted in *Horizon* that avant-garde artists in America still had "no reputations that extend beyond a small circle of fanatics, art-fixated misfits who are isolated in the United States as if they were living in Paleolithic Europe." The latest indignity was a statement by James S. Plaut, director of the Institute of Modern Art in Boston, justifying the institute's decision to change its name from "Modern" to "Contemporary." Plaut's manifesto was, in fact, a broadside attack on the integrity and sincerity of "modern" art, which he accused of "obscurity and negation" as well as intentional deception. After an earlier protest in Boston, a group of New York artists led by Bradley Walker Tomlin, who also exhibited at the Parsons gallery, began to agitate for a show of support from New York artists. Out of a planning session at Stuart Davis's studio came a demonstration at the Museum of Modern Art in May. Jackson was among the artists who marched and carried placards denouncing reactionary art critics as well as the museum itself for continuing to favor European art and artists. As far as Jackson had come in the last decade, the art world still lagged frustratingly behind.

Since the move to Springs, summer had become the season of renewal for Jackson. In a reversal of the pattern that had ruled his life in New York—when winters were productive and summers perilous—winter was now a fallow season, filled with gallery business, trips to New York, and cold, early nights. Summer was increasingly a time to roam the countryside, see friends, and *paint*. The studio was partly to blame. Although he could and sometimes did use the barn in winter, the sunlight was brief and the discomfort daunting. While in summer, except on the hottest days, the barn was a shady redoubt, cooled by a high ceiling and a perpetual breeze from Accabonac Harbor. No matter what crises threatened, no matter where Jackson was in his cycle of depression, the coming of summer never failed to boost his spirits.

The summer of 1948 began with another, more tangible boost. In mid-June, he received a letter from the Council for the Eben Demarest Trust Fund announcing he had been selected as the beneficiary of the trust income for the following year. The Demarest Trust, established in 1938 by Elizabeth B. Demarest of Pittsburgh, provided a single annual grant to an artist "who wishes to escape dependence upon the public sale of his work." The estimated total of the award was only $1,500, not enough to replace Peggy's stipend, but enough to forestall financial collapse for at least another year. The amount would be paid out in quarterly installments, the first due in October. Among the names listed on the council's letterhead, only one was even vaguely familiar: John H. Sweeney, a relative, apparently, of James Johnson Sweeney, one of Jackson's earliest champions. Exactly what role, if any, Sweeney played in arranging the council's unlikely selection of Jackson is not certain. (According to Betty Parsons, he "pried" it out of them.) Parsons had been trying for some time without success to secure a subsidy for Jackson, but the news came as a surprise to her. Peggy Guggenheim, who was in regular contact with Sweeney from Venice, may have planted a seed, but the most likely moving force behind the award was Lee, whose indefatigable behind-the-scenes campaign on Jackson's behalf brought her into regular contact with Sweeney.

For Lee, summer was the campaign season, the season of strategic invitations, weekend houseguests, social arrangements, and quiet promotion. During the summer of 1948, the guest list included John Little, Betty Parsons, Fred and Janet Hauck, Barnett Newman, Wilfrid and Betsy Zogbaum, Sam and Edys Hunter, James Brooks and Charlotte Park, George Mercer, and, of course, Clement Greenberg. This may have been the summer that Lee took Bill Davis's advice and invited Lincoln Kirstein, an intimate of Alfred Barr, for a weekend. Lee also mined the rich and growing vein of summer residents, people like Gerald Sykes, a novelist and philosopher who wrote for the *New York Times*, and his wife, Buffie Johnson. "It seemed to me," says Johnson, "that Lee had her eye on my husband as a writer who would be useful to work on, to help promote Jackson." The same was undoubtedly true of Joe Liss, a successful television writer, and his wife, Millie, who seemed to the impoverished artists both rich and famous.

Despite the lack of funds, Lee always found the few dollars necessary for weekend entertaining (just as Jackson always found money for beer). For truly special occasions—when Greenberg came—she would take a few precious dollars and buy steaks at Dreesen's Market, the "society" butcher in East Hampton. While Jackson barbecued in the backyard, Lee remained inside, doing the real business of the evening—showing her folders full of photographs, reviews, and announcements. During the week, she was careful not to invite overnight guests for fear of disrupting Jackson's work, but there were always visitors. Herbert and Mercedes Matter and Gustaf and Vita Peterson had rented a spacious house on Fireplace Road for June and July, and almost every day, the women would stop to pick up Lee on their way into town. Later in the afternoon, when he was finished in the studio, Jackson would seek out Herbert, who was filming a movie on Alexander Calder in the area, or walk to the Matters' house and join the women and children for a few hours on the beach nearby before the sun set. On weekends, when Gustaf (Peter) Peterson came out from the city, the three couples would drive to one of the ocean beaches in East Hampton, where the men would play poker or twenty-one while the women watched the children and swam. Peterson, who had fled Germany in the late thirties to avoid Hitler's draft, found Jackson "immensely American."

These were idyllic times for Jackson. "He played with our kids like he was one of them," says Vita Peterson.

One day, the same kids came racing into Jackson's studio in bare feet and ran onto a half-finished canvas, tracking little footprints of paint. "Mercedes and I cringed," recalls Peterson, "but Jackson only laughed. He said, 'Oh, no, no, never mind. Let them come in,' and the footprints just became part of the painting." On the beach, Jackson and the children would play in the sand or collect pebbles together. "He had that gentleness himself," Peterson recalls, "a childlike quality that children were attracted to." On weekday afternoons, when the other men were away, he would sit in the dune grass and tell stories about his own youth, about milking cows, hunting in the desert, jumping trains, riding the rails, and seeing the country. Both the children and their mothers were particularly fascinated by the adventures of a wondrous dog named Gyp.

Each day in the studio, the same images from the past unspooled from his imagination and took shape in the air.

The same needs that drove Jackson to turn women into mothers and children into siblings also shaped his friendships with men. Gradually, just as in the thirties, he began to gather around him a family of surrogate brothers. There was John Little, the courteous, handsome southerner with whom Jackson often fished but seldom talked. After Little bought a dilapidated old saltbox house nearby, Jackson took a day-to-day interest in the arduous, year-long renovation efforts. There was Roger Wilcox, a more approachable companion who shared Jackson's habit of spending long hours in a bar, sipping beer in absolute silence. Wilcox was also a source of whiskey, which, by 1948, Lee had banned from the house in the belief that it would take Jackson longer to get drunk if he drank only beer. There was Herbert Matter, whose quiet, reassuring company Jackson sought out eagerly in the lazy summer afternoons. Matter was only thirty-nine at the time, but his European sangfroid and Swiss taciturnity, so much like Charles's, made him seem older, almost paternal. On trips to beaches in Montauk and East Hampton where Matter shot the ocean sequences for his documentary on Calder, Jackson sometimes acted as guide and bearer, carrying the heavy boxes and tripods, asking occasional questions, but mostly just following Matter through the dunes in silence.

Around Harold Rosenberg, on the other hand, there was rarely silence. "Never have I known anyone who could talk with such unflagging, manic brilliance," said Irving Howe. "I used to think, when visiting his studio, suppose I were suddenly to drop dead, would he stop talking?" The huge, affable Rosenberg mesmerized Jackson with his jokes and dazzlingly erudite commentary. That Jackson understood little of what was being said came as no surprise to Rosenberg who, according to Roger Wilcox, believed that most Americans, "especially Gentiles," were "intellectually sloppy almost to the point of illiteracy." But his relationship with Jackson never approached an intellectual level. According to May Rosenberg, the two men enjoyed "doing boy things" together, like playing poker, fishing, and throwing stones. Despite his game leg, Harold would indulge Jackson's childhood fondness for wrestling. "They were like puppies or kittens at play," recalls May. It was an odd and never entirely convincing friendship, the cerebral Rosenberg and the impulsive, physical Pollock, but it served reparative fantasies on both sides. "Harold had a younger brother about Jackson's age who died," says May, "and he would tell Jackson what to do. If Jackson was being difficult, Harold would say, 'That's *enough*, Jackson. Sit down and behave yourself.' And Jackson would do it. He just beamed when Harold treated him like a little brother."

Also in the summer of 1948, Jackson added two new "brothers" to his surrogate family. One was Tony Smith, the charming Irish storyteller and drinking companion whom Jackson had known distantly in the early forties. (At that time, Smith considered Pollock a boor and his art "pure chaos." He later described their first meeting as a "disaster," saying Pollock was "so sullen and intense, so miserable" that he said to himself, "I've got to get out of here. I can't stand this guy.") Smith was just one of a number of people—Mark Rothko, Barnett Newman, Gerome Kamrowski—who reentered Jackson's life through the Betty Parsons Gallery. Jackson had been impressed by the "floating" panels Smith designed for an exhibition of Kamrowski's works at the gallery in February and soon afterward invited Smith and Parsons to Springs to explore the possibility of doing something similar for his next show. Ultimately, Smith rejected the panel idea—he felt Jackson's paintings were too big —but this time the chemistry between the two men was more favorable and the encounter produced an almost instantaneous intimacy. Smith even reversed his opinion of Jackson's art, calling it "great" and "thrilling." Although the two men saw each other only once or twice that first summer, they laid the foundations for a friendship that would profoundly affect Jackson's creative and emotional life.

The other new brother that summer was Harry Jackson, a twenty-four-year-old former marine who had first encountered Pollock's work in the pages of *Dyn* while recuperating from combat wounds suffered in the assault on Tarawa —only days before Pollock's first show at Art of This Century. By that time,

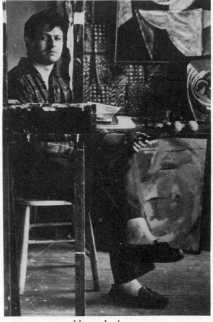

Harry Jackson

the war had worn Harry "down to the very goddamn nub," and he found in Pollock's *She-Wolf* something "totally authentic, honest, down to earth and real." "This man felt deep and straight," Harry said later. "He painted tough, not from the fingertips. Pollock's painting had what I felt in combat. It was visceral." Five years later, as a young art student studying with Rufino Tamayo at the Brooklyn Museum and living on the Lower East Side of Manhattan, Harry experienced a similar epiphany at Pollock's first showing of drip paintings at Betty Parsons in January 1948. He and his girlfriend, the painter Grace Hartigan, were among the few who found Pollock's controversial new style "fascinating," and they returned to the show again and again. Again, Pollock's art seemed to satisfy Harry's search for "something very profound and very straight." When he heard from Sonja Sekula, a gallery-mate of Pollock's, that "Peggy Guggenheim had abandoned him and he was very unhappy and lonely and no younger artists had ever said that they like his work because it's so controversial," Harry called Springs. Pollock's response was "Well, shit, come on out, goddamn it. What the fuck are you waiting for?" Harry left immediately, hitchhiked through the night and arrived at the Pollocks' doorstep at seven the next morning. Undoubtedly aroused from sleep, Pollock came to the screen door "wearing bib overalls and a kind of farmer's blue-jean jacket," Harry recalls. "I looked at him, he looked at me, and we just 'howdied.' We walked outside and hunkered down in the grass outside the back door like two yokels scratching the dirt . . . We had a love affair immediately."

For a man who insisted on authenticity in his art, Harry Jackson had shown remarkably little of it in his life. Born Harry Shapiro to a Jewish father who left home before Harry was born, and a midwestern farm woman who ran a diner near the Chicago stockyards, Harry had gone to extravagant lengths to deny his own past. Like Stella Pollock, Harry's doting Aunt Doris harbored strong cultural aspirations for her nephew, taking him on frequent trips to the Chicago Art Institute. But little Harry was also captivated by the "cowboys" who frequented his mother's diner after delivering their cattle to the stockyards.

Harry spent his first few teenage years trying to reconcile his aunt's artistic longings with his own cowboy fantasies. For a while he worked in a Chicago riding stable, taking care of saddle horses. But he yearned for the real West. Not long after seeing a photo-essay in *Life* magazine on the 300,000-acre Pitchfork Ranch in Wyoming, he left Chicago and headed west. At the age of fourteen, he signed on as a hand at the Pitchfork Ranch and learned to "ride and rope." By the time he turned twenty and volunteered for the marines, Harry's "personality transference" (as Paul Brach called it) was complete. A "nice Jewish boy" had become "a son of the plains." Years later, he brought his mother to Wyoming and instructed her: "This is where you gave birth to me."

Harry wore his new identity well. Square-jawed, ruggedly built, and darkly handsome, he looked and talked like a dime-store novel come to life. Describing his first encounter with Pollock, he slips easily into the loping rhythms, casual profanity, and bunkhouse hyperbole of his adopted identity: "[Pollock] was the old man. I treated him with great respect, gave him lots of goddamn space to move around in. 'Take all the room you want, it's your place.' He was like, 'If you want to fuck with me I'll knock the shit out of you.' But that's friendly, you see. That was the dance. That was Pollock's and my dance when we first met. It was just exactly like I was out in cow country. We just did it exactly like that. It's a ritual."

Not surprisingly, Pollock was instantly won. With his cowboy posturing and stocky good looks, Harry was the spitting image of brother Sande. For almost a week, the two men "scratched in the dirt," reinforcing each other's fantasies. Pollock regaled his young admirer with all the old untruths about *his* western past—a childhood in Wyoming and the drudgery of milking cows—to which Harry responded with his own backdated nostalgia. During the days, they sat in the yard chewing grass and pulling the legs off grasshoppers. Once or twice they tackled odd jobs around the house, like replacing an old toilet (jobs at which Pollock proved only "half-handy"). In the evenings, they would head to Dan Miller's store to stock up on beer, then stay up all night drinking and "analyzing works of art in magazines and old books." Inevitably, Pollock invoked the spirit of Tom Benton, the model on which Harry, knowingly or not, had fashioned himself. "He talked my goddamn ear off," Harry recalled. "[He] brought out *Cahiers d'art* and analyzed Tintoretto in great detail, explaining the composition of this and that; what he was doing was bringing me pure Tom Benton: Venetian Renaissance to Tom Benton. Tom to Jack, Jack to Harry."

Lee, who undoubtedly saw the farcical side to their exaggerated camaraderie, "got fed up early," Harry recalls. "She didn't like to have [Pollock]
fiddle-fucking around with me. . . . She tried to be civil, but if looks could kill,
I would have been dead many times over." To impress Harry, however, Pollock
made a show of chaffing under her bridle. "When Lee came down late at night
to suggest going to bed," Harry remembers, "he would say, 'Ah, shut up, you
goddamn cunt, go fix some coffee.' He was very vulgar with her." It was a Tom
Benton show of misogyny and abuse staged for Harry's benefit. "But she fucks
like a mink," Pollock would say by way of apology when Harry commented on
Lee's homeliness. He called her "you goddamn slut" and "you fuckin' slut."
"You ain't good for nothing but fuckin'," he would say with a sidelong glance
at Harry. "She's good stickin', Harry, I'll tell you that.' " The two men would
laugh and, according to Harry, "Lee loved all that in her own kind of half-
assed masochistic way. She liked being knocked around by Pollock."

In her own way, Lee probably did. She had, after all, been weaned on abuse
and humiliation. But there was another side to the Pollocks' relationship, a side
that Pollock tried to hide from friends like Harry. Other visitors saw *Lee* as the
abuser and Jackson as the victim. "She was always picking on him," recalls
Janet Hauck, "telling him what to do and what not to do. She'd say, 'You
haven't taken the garbage out yet, Jackson.' " Whether it was the garbage, his
behavior around company, the importance of keeping a schedule, how much
money he spent, or how loudly he played the phonograph, "she was always
riding him tough," Charlotte Park remembers. When Sam and Edys Hunter
visited that summer, Lee appeared to them "like a lion tamer," shouting "*Jackson!*" when she wanted to bring him to heel.

These were the two faces of their relationship. One day, Lee would take
command—"She couldn't *not* give directions," according to Ernestine Lassaw
—and Jackson would submit; the next day, Jackson would explode and Lee
would submit. One day at the dinner table she would press him hard to clarify
his ideas; the next day she would "cover" for his ignorance, supplying names
and definitions to save him from embarassment. One day he would plot with
Harry to travel to Wyoming; the next day he would admit, "Lee probably won't
let me go." One day Lee was "a mouse," Sam Hunter recalls, and Jackson
"was a big bear," and they "played scenes from 'The Honeymooners' "; the
next day "she dominated him completely in a matriarchal way." "It was almost
like a game," says Harry Jackson, describing the daily give-and-take. "He'd
needle the hell out of her and she'd love it; then she'd needle the hell out of
him and he'd love it." Gone was the one-sided adulation that had marked the
first years of their relationship. In its place was a creative tension, a mutually
beneficial back-and-forth over the vast no-man's-land of everyday living that
seemed to satisfy both Lee's need to possess and Jackson's need to be possessed
without seeming so. It was love, of a kind, and even those who witnessed their
collisions sensed the devotion behind the histrionics. "Jackson and Lee were
completely bound together," says Harry Jackson. "They were definitely in love."

But it was ultimately a love of attrition, and the costs on both sides could not be sustained forever.

In the meantime, Jackson transformed the steady flow of emotional support into a cascade of paintings. The summer and fall of 1948 were the most productive seasons of his life so far. In two years, he had refined the drip technique into a tool of astonishing power and range: from the ascetic, Miró-like elegance of *The Wooden Horse*, one of the last paintings from 1948, in which he attached the wooden head of a rocking horse (excavated from the rubble under John Little's new house) to a canvas of red-brown cotton duck mounted on board, and added only a few shapes in ochre and a tracing of fine, halting lines in red, white, and black; to the starburst of *Number 1, 1948*, a dazzling 5½-by-8½-foot canvas of phosphorescent white interlaced with Jackson's finest black web and proudly inprinted across the top with his repeated handprints, an echo perhaps of the Indian ruins he had explored with his father in Arizona, and certainly a sign of his growing confidence.

Another sign of confidence, misguided perhaps, was his decision to abandon traditional names and number his paintings instead. The theory (on which more than a few of Jackson's friends detected Greenberg's handprint) was that numbers would distance the images even further from outdated notions of content. Paintings were, after all, just color on canvas, and evocative names, like *Cathedral* and *Night Sounds*, with their suggestions of subjective or emotional content, only biased the viewer's true perception. In practice, however, the numbers created greater confusion all around: for artist, dealer, and collectors. Since numbers were assigned more or less randomly, not chronologically, not even Jackson could keep numbers and images straight. Inevitably, he resorted to informal designations, usually relating to a work's dominant colors (*Number 4, 1948: Gray and Red*; *Number 12A, 1948: Yellow, Gray, Black*) or primary feature (*The Wooden Horse, White Cockatoo*), some of which became attached to the paintings permanently. Numbers also implied a homogeneity that was belied by the images themselves. *Number 26, 1948*, for example, is a grisaille vision in which ribbons of black and gray, some loosely brushed, some poured, weave around ghost-like ribbons of silver on a white ground. Over their soft interplay is dribbled a latticework of fine black lines. *Number 5, 1948*, on the other hand, is dense with life and color. Beneath a pulverized skein of aluminum lie layers of gray-blue, turquoise, teal green, almost obscured, and beneath them, showing only at the edges, a sumptuous rust ground. Across the aluminum nebula Jackson has flung streaks of brilliant yellow and red and sprays of white.

To preserve the edge of accident that was jeopardized by his improved control, Jackson varied not only color but size, shape, and materials as well. He worked on composition board, metal, and cardboard. During the first half of the year, when money was desperately short, he often replaced canvas with

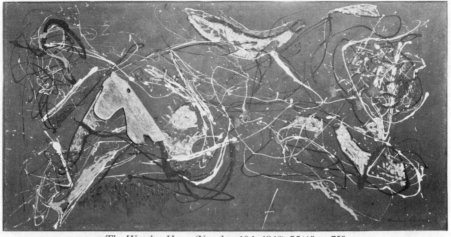

The Wooden Horse (Number 10A, 1948), 35½" × 75"

paper, stiffened with gesso, tacked to Masonite or mounted on board. He varied the density of the web, from the gorgeous multicolored coat of *Number 5, 1948,* to the transparent arabesques of *Black, White and Grey.* He could stretch the paint to the thinness of thread and swirl it into vast tangles, or pool it in great reservoirs of color, or do both at once, as in *Silver over Black, White, Yellow and Red,* where thick floats of white are overtracked by darting and looping silver lines. He worked in dark colors on light ground and, to arresting effect, in light colors on dark ground. In *Arabesque,* a dark rust ground, complicated by an open skein of black and green-gray, provides the backdrop for a stunning display of bravura white, spinning and curling across the big reddish canvas like tracings of sparks against a fire. *Arabesque* was also one of several works in which Jackson experimented with extravagant sizes and shapes. In addition to a tondo (the second and last round canvas he painted), there were several long, horizontal scrolls: from *White Cockatoo,* a playful 3-by-9½-foot dark-ground canvas with fragments of red, white, and blue caught in a black web, to the exuberant *Summertime,* a sliver of canvas less than three feet wide and eighteen feet long, in which black lines tumble from end to end like Mardi Gras revelers, decked in festive bits of red, blue, and yellow and surrounded by the silver hiss of sparklers.

As he approached his second show at the Parsons gallery in January 1949, Jackson had every reason to feel festive and exuberant. The jagged fragments of his life were finally fitting together. For the first time, key relationships—with Lee, Stella, Greenberg, and a handful of surrogate brothers—seemed to satisfy his vast needs for attention and approval. Lee's continuing devotion had quelled, for the moment at least, the fears of sexual inadequacy, and every day in the studio, little by little, the great tangled knot of his past was unwinding onto canvas.

■　■　■

Even in the midst of success, however, there were warning signs. Professionally, Greenberg's praise had made Jackson more enemies than friends, while at the Parsons gallery, sales continued to lag. Whatever confidence Jackson managed to generate in the studio was quickly dissipated in unpaid bills and bounced checks. Meanwhile, old colleagues were moving ahead. Nineteen forty-eight was not only the year of Willem de Kooning's first show, it was also the year Bill Baziotes won Alfred Barr's Abstract Surrealist Purchase Prize at the Museum of Modern Art.

But most galling of all was the continuing—and, to Jackson, inexplicable— success of Philip Guston. Only one year after Jackson's application for a Guggenheim Fellowship was rejected, Guston was awarded a Prix de Rome for a year of study in Italy. Since their V-E Day confrontation in 1945, Guston had won a Guggenheim Fellowship, a Carnegie competition, a position at Washington University, and an adulatory article in *Life* magazine. He had also begun to abandon the saccharine, illusionistic style that had made him the darling of traditionalists. While in Italy, he would embrace abstraction "as if he was being reborn," recalls Milton Resnick. It was a late and, to some, unconvincing conversion, but even as an abstractionist, Guston continued to attract the kind of establishment approval that had always been denied Jackson. H. W. Janson, a colleague of Guston's at Washington University, called the new paintings "[what] Mondrian would have done if he had been looking at the Impressionists instead of the Cubists."

Closer to home, Jackson was also being denied more and more of Stella's attentions. On January 26, 1948, two days before Jackson's thirty-sixth birthday, Arloie gave birth to a boy, Jay Conaway McCoy (later Jason). He was a beautiful baby, everyone agreed, and Stella immediately claimed him. "A darling little boy," she wrote Frank, ". . . [he] favors Jack a lot." Between babysitting and bouts of chicken pox, months separated Stella's visits to Springs. Sande, working overtime to support his enlarged family, was lucky to make one trip a year.

Without Stella's stabilizing influence, the "creative tension" between Jackson and Lee was more likely to run amok. Lee was already brooding over rumors (baseless) that Jackson was having an affair with Mercedes Matter or Vita Peterson, or both, during the summer of 1948. "The very *idea* of an affair made her crazy," says Harry Jackson. "She hated my guts because I took so much of Jackson's attention and we weren't embracing in bed for chrissake." There was fodder aplenty for Lee's paranoia. Both Peter Peterson and Herbert Matter were gone much of the summer, and Lee spent at least one day every week in town visiting Dr. Hubbard. Lee also knew her old friend Mercedes's reputation for "wanting to taste everything, smell everything, try everything." Besides, says Fritz Bultman, "Vita and Mercedes were glorious, gorgeous young women—which you certainly couldn't say about Lee at the time." Flattered by Lee's suspicions, Jackson took a perverse pleasure in encouraging them. At a dinner party, in Lee's view, he would grab a woman and proclaim

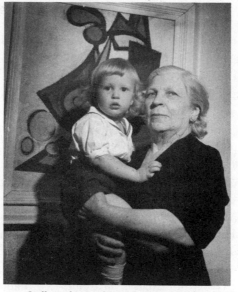

Stella with grandson Jay (Jason) McCoy

loudly, "I love *all* women," May Rosenberg recalls. "It was like he was playing a game with Lee, only she didn't see it was a game." Other times, late at night, he would stand outside neighbors' windows—when the husbands were away —and scream sexual threats. Reports of every such incident, of course, made their way back to Lee.

Toward the end of the summer, at a dinner party, the "game" turned vicious. "We were playing cards," Ruth Stein recalls, "and this one woman there liked Jackson very much and did not mind letting Lee know it. And Lee and this woman really went at each other. Jackson got up and staggered out on the porch and sat down. Then Lee came out and sat down next to him. He was flailing his arms, saying, 'Get out of here, you bitch. I hate your guts.' But she sat there with her arms around him, kissing him until all that anger dissipated."

The summer of 1948 *did* arouse dormant passions in Jackson, but they had nothing to do with either Mercedes Matter or Vita Peterson.

Another guest at the Pollocks' house that summer was Igor Pantuhoff, who arrived unannounced after several years on the society circuit in California. Time had not been kind to Igor's eccentricities. What in the thirties had seemed smart and urbane now seemed fatuous and dissipated. Far from being charmed by Igor's grand manner, Vita Peterson found him "enormously effeminate, foppish, and physically incapable. We thought he was homosexual but Lee said not." The Petersons weren't the only ones who were unmoved by Igor's "Oriental charm." May Rosenberg remembers that Jackson greeted his arrival "like a stone." "The longer he was there," May recalls, "the darker Jackson's mood got." Other guests observed that Igor could "drive Jackson into an absolute frenzy" without even saying a word. One evening on the beach, Vita Peterson noticed that Jackson "was building up a rage all evening long." Suddenly, without warning, he lunged at Pantuhoff. The two men grappled in the sand for a moment until Peter Peterson pulled them apart. Igor emerged from the melee with a split lip but, strangely, remained at the Pollock house.

A few days later, at a dinner party with John Little and Ward Bennett, Jackson went on a drunken rampage, throwing plates and furniture and toppling a tall cupboard filled with dishes. ("When the dishes crashed," Bennett recalls, "that's when John said, 'Let's get out of here.'") While Lee watched in horror, Jackson chased Igor through the house and out into the front yard where a day-long pouring rain had turned the lawn to mud. There Igor turned and confronted Jackson. "They started rolling in the mud," Bennett remembers, "but it was very bizarre. They weren't really fighting, they were sort of wrestling and sort of kissing each other at the same time."

The summer of 1948 also marked Lee's return to painting. For the first two years in Springs, she had virtually stopped, allowing months to go by between brief periods of work. At first there were practical reasons: only enough heat for one room and Jackson had a show to prepare; too much fixing-up to do around the house. When old excuses gave out, Lee made up new ones: she couldn't paint in the living room because "it was open . . . you know, no privacy, you can't close the door." When Jackson moved his studio to the barn, Lee didn't take over the larger and ideally lighted southwest bedroom where he had worked. She made that their bedroom and took for her studio a smaller, poorly lit room on the northeast side. In the summers, there were guests to be entertained, collectors and dealers to be wooed. It was a rare visitor in the summers of 1946 and 1947 who caught Lee at her easel and none of her paintings hung on the walls. (During the financially dire months of early 1948, Jackson painted over many of the works that she had brought from New York.) As late as the summer of 1948, Vita Peterson recalls, "Lee had given up painting altogether for [Jackson's] sake to avoid the possible competition."

As long as Lee showed no interest in returning to work, Jackson felt free to encourage her. Roger Wilcox remembers him saying, "Hey, I put together three canvases for you. I cut off the ends of this big roll; I don't want it that big. And so I had the stretcher bars, so I made them your size." According to Wilcox, Lee thanked him and took the canvases up to her studio, but later, when Jackson asked, "Are you working on any of those paintings?" she replied listlessly, "Nah, maybe I'll start next week, I don't know." It was Jackson who suggested that Lee "try a mosaic" and helped her assemble two tabletops—the house was short of furniture—using tesserae left over from one of his WPA projects: pieces of broken glass and tile with keys, coins, shells, pebbles, and jewelry thrown in, set in concrete. "He practically had to force her to do it," according to one friend. "He found the wagon wheel, provided the pieces, showed her how to lay the tile upside down, and poured the concrete."

Once Lee did begin to paint again in earnest, sometime in the spring or summer of 1948, Jackson's enthusiasm evaporated. Lee liked to say that she and Jackson visited each other's studios "by polite invitation." In fact, while

Lee always responded to Jackson's invitations instantly, she had to invite him "three or four times" before he responded to hers. "My enthusiasm for his work," she once admitted, "was far greater than his for mine." When he did come, he did so "grudgingly," friends noticed, and usually confined himself to a few terse Greenbergian comments: "That works" or "That doesn't work" or "Just continue painting and stop hanging yourself up." "He encouraged her, but he was disdainful," recalls Harry Jackson. "He had that 'little woman' attitude toward her. He took me up to look at her paintings and said something like 'That's Lee's little painting.' He wasted almost no time with her and considered almost everything he did in that area as sort of encouraging the little lady." According to Lisa Fonssagrives, wife of photographer Irving Penn and a friend of Lee's, "His attitude was almost as debilitating as outright criticism."

Lee, apparently, got the message. To avoid a confrontation, she worked only in the morning while Jackson was asleep. "She had to get up terribly early in order to work at all," says Fonssagrives. "The slightest change in her husband's mood could change her work."

Late in the summer, Lee invited Bertha Schaefer, an interior decorator and gallery owner, to visit the house in Springs. Schaefer was particularly impressed by one of the mosaic tables (Lee had given the other to Valentine and Happy Macy to thank them for a much-needed truckload of furniture) and asked to include it in an exhibition she was planning on room decorations based on modern painting and sculpture. When "The Modern House Comes Alive" opened at Schaefer's gallery in September, Lee's table was singled out for special praise by reviewers in the *World-Telegram*, the *Herald Tribune*, the *New York Times*, and the magazine *Architectural Forum*. Only the *Times* referred to Lee as the "wife of the painter J. Pollack [*sic*]." To celebrate Lee's triumph, Schaefer invited the Pollocks to dinner at her elegant, antique-filled New York apartment.

The result was disaster. Over Schaefer's objection, Jackson opened a third bottle of wine and gulped it down. When Schaefer, a prim, proud southern lady in her fifties, protested and tried to take the bottle from him, Jackson lashed back, demanding, "What does an old lady like you do for sex?" Then he turned his fury on the furniture, demolishing every precious antique within reach, including a rare Chinese screen. By the time Schaefer went to call the police, Jackson had passed out.

Incidents like the fight with Igor and the rampage at Bertha Schaefer's house signaled the most ominous development of all. Even in the midst of success, Jackson was drinking too much again.

In the summers, preoccupied with guests and work, he tended to drink less; in the winters, cold and bored, more; but, except during Stella's visits, hardly a week went by without a high of some kind. During the day, it was beer—Lee often bought several cases herself to ensure that he drank under her watchful eye. At night, it was whiskey with Roger Wilcox at Jungle Pete's. "He would start very fast," Wilcox remembers. "He'd have three drinks to my one, then five to my three. At a certain point, there was no stopping him. He'd just keep going until he fell down." Lee had learned to endure these passing storms stoically: to invent an explanation when Jackson missed an in-town appointment after a particularly debilitating binge, or to withdraw a weekend invitation at the last minute because "Jackson wasn't feeling well." On arriving at a party or dinner, she would routinely slip to the bar, cast a worried glance over the line of bottles, and whisper "Go slow" in the host's ear. And when Jackson stormed out of the room or passed out on a couch, she made the apologies. Such incidents may have been inconvenient and sometimes embarrassing, but they were nothing like the wild, week-long binges she had witnessed in New York.

By the fall of 1948, however, that edge of self-destruction had returned. Jackson's new car was partly to blame. With ninety dollars of Demarest money, he had bought a run-down Model A Ford like the one he and Sande drove in Riverside. It ran rough—when it ran at all—but it gave him mobility. For the first time since moving to Springs, he didn't need to rely on friends for a ride to the East Hampton bars or to walk to Jungle Pete's on a frigid night. Suddenly Lee had to worry about his safety as well as his sobriety. When he was gone all night, it was no longer just a question of where he had passed out or who was taking care of him. "[Jack] has a Ford Coupe," Stella announced darkly in a letter to Frank, "and he should not drive & drink [or] he will kill himself or someone."

But Jackson didn't need a car when he was bent on self-destruction. At a party in early July 1948, he picked a fight with William Phillips, the editor of *Partisan Review*. Herbert Ferber, who was sitting nearby, remembers that "William went very pale when he realized Pollock was ready to jump on him. He was very drunk and very violent. Before dinner, Pollock reached across the floor and grabbed a shoe from Sue Mitchell, the woman that Greenberg had brought—she had the most expensive-looking shoe in that gathering. And Pollock just tore it apart." While the rest of the guests stared at the broken shoe, Jackson ran to an open window and started to jump to the street far below. Phillips and Mark Rothko lunged after him and eventually wrestled him inside. Throughout the commotion, Arshile Gorky stood impassively by, moodily fingering his whittling knife. He wore a neck brace as the result of an automobile accident in which his neck was broken and his painting arm temporarily paralyzed.

A few weeks later, at the age of forty-four, Gorky hanged himself in his studio.

In the fall of 1948, after the debacle with Bertha Schaefer, Jackson looked as if he might follow Gorky down the path of self-obliteration. Yet, within a few months, he would begin the most productive two years of his life—two years in which, for the first and only time in his adulthood, alcohol played virtually no part; two years in which his art finally bodied forth the full power of his imagination. The reversal began inauspiciously enough on a late autumn day on the way back from Dan Miller's store. The Model A had refused to start, and Jackson, tipsy on beer, was trying to pedal his bike while carrying a case of beer under his arm. The bike hit a patch of gravel in the road and slid out from under him. He fell backwards and sideways, landing on the case of beer. Bottles exploded and shards of glass flew in every direction. When he stood up, cursing and shouting and kicking the bike, his arm was dripping blood. A few minutes later, he was sitting in the East Hampton Medical Clinic, being bandaged by a new doctor in town named Edwin Heller. To Jackson's surprise, Heller knew all about his drinking problem.

And he said he had a cure.

35

CELEBRITY

By 1948, the art world was ready for a star.

The market was ready. The postwar tidal wave of consumer spending that put two cars in every garage and meat at every meal had finally reached Fifty-seventh Street. Between 1940 and 1946, the number of private galleries in Manhattan nearly quadrupled. After 1944, sales at many galleries doubled and tripled every year. Art was no longer an indulgence for the rich only—the Mellons, Fricks, Baches, and Wideners—it was a consumer good, as available to the middle class as canned beer, nylon stockings, and golf balls. "For the first time in history," writes Marxist historian Serge Guilbaut, "art became a part of everyday life, a part of the environment, a decoration in middle-class homes." In 1942, when Gimbel's department store offered for sale items from William Randolph Hearst's collection of old master paintings, Gimbel's rival, Macy's, countered with its own "sale," announced in the *New York Times:* "authenticated paintings by Rembrandt, Rubens, etc. . . . A $130,000 collection of paintings at our lowest prices. . . . Pay only one third down on Macy's cash time, take months to pay, plus the service charge." When Macy's sold Rembrandt's *Portrait of an Old Man* for $6,894, Gimbel's countered with his *Portrait of a Child* at the "amazingly low price" of only $9,999.

America was ready. In 1946, with Europe still half buried in the rubble of war, Walter Lippmann announced the dawn of "the American century." "Fate has willed it," he proclaimed in a Paris magazine, "that America is from now on to be at the center of Western civilization rather than on the periphery." The year before, *View* magazine had bragged that "New York is now the artistic and intellectual center of the world," to which the critic Germain Bazin replied with prescient derision: "Will the Paris School become the New York School?" Some Europeans saw the future more clearly. "American painting . . . is developing rapidly," warned critic Léon Degand in 1946. "Young painters are throwing themselves into their work with such intensity that it is impossible that [America] . . . will not one day achieve an original style of its own. . . . I am convinced that the Americans are on the way toward a period of greatness in art."

The media were ready. The vast armies of new consumer-collectors needed advice on what to buy. They knew they wanted art; they wanted American art (wartime patriotism was still in vogue); and some even wanted avant-garde art (because that's what the Rockefellers and Blisses wanted). But within those broad parameters, many of the new collectors lacked the confidence to make their own distinctions. Only a handful could attend the gallery shows, like Bertha Schaefer's "The Modern Home Comes Alive" and Samuel Kootz's "Modern Painting for a Country Estate: Important Paintings for Spacious Living," which were mounted to help educate (and sell) them on the new art. Instead, most turned for advice on how to buy art to where they turned for advice on how to buy everything else: the media—especially the magazines. And the magazine of choice was *Life.* "The magazines defined taste," writes Guilbaut; "[and] *Life* became the buyer's *arbiter elegantiae.*"

In October 1948, *Life* convened a "round table" of sixteen critics in the penthouse of the Museum of Modern Art and asked them to comment on various works by French and American painters. For hours, the sixteen experts solemnly traded pronouncements while tape recorders hummed and shutters clicked. Their remarks, heavily edited, were published along with reproductions of the works in the October 11 issue. When Jackson's *Cathedral* came up for consideration, Greenberg called it "a first-class example of Pollock's work, and one of the best paintings recently produced in this country." Meyer Schapiro of Columbia University, James Johnson Sweeney, and, more surprisingly, Francis Henry Taylor, the director of the Metropolitan, agreed. But Aldous Huxley, Theodore Greene, a professor of philosophy at Yale, and, also surprisingly, Alfred Frankfurter, the editor and publisher of *Art News,* disagreed. Sir Leigh Ashton, director of the Victoria and Albert Museum in London, quipped: "It would make a most enchanting printed silk. But I cannot see why it is called the *Cathedral.*" It may have been responsible art criticism, but it was inconclusive advice and, worse still, boring journalism.

The problem was that the needs of magazines were not the needs of art. Experts could give them the veneer of expertise, but expertise wasn't enough. In art, as in everything else, the media cared about only "the story": Was it visual? Did it have impact? What was the "human interest" angle? They were looking not for ideas or movements, but for people—or, better yet, personalities: good looks, charm, charisma, or, in a pinch, idiosyncrasy. They were looking for controversy. Artists as different as Salvador Dali and Thomas Hart Benton had discovered that, and had commanded media attention not because of what they said but because of how they said it, not for their views but for their gall. Better to elicit anger, shock, or outrage from the reader than nothing at all. The media were looking for the romance of art—the outcast genius, the tortured soul, the artistic (and visual) equivalent of James Dean or Ernest Hemingway. And, as Clement Greenberg understood, they were looking for winners—not pluggers, not exemplars, not team players, but winners. Any excuse for superlatives. Anything to satisfy an ambitious nation's appetite for invidious comparison. Whether rookies-of-the-year, Nobel laureates, or Academy Award winners, they wanted the number one—the best, the first, and the only. "Everyone was *waiting* for the great American painter," says Budd Hopkins, an artist who was beginning his career in 1948. "It was just a matter of time."

To have his chance at the spotlight, however, Jackson would have to stop drinking.

The incident at Bertha Schaefer's apartment had sounded an alarm. Lee could no longer pretend—for Jackson's benefit or her own—that he was under control. Not that she didn't try. Soon after returning to Springs, she prompted Jackson to write a note of apology: "Thank you so much for being so nice to us while we were in New York. I hope you will forgive me for my inconsiderate behavior and for the inconvenience I caused." But, unlike so many others, Schaefer wasn't about to forgive. Within weeks, she descended on East Hampton like an avenging angel, hurling accusations (later retracted) that Jackson had assaulted her, threatening to have him arrested and thrown in jail, and vowing to sue for damages (a prospect almost as terrifying to Lee as jail). It wasn't long before exaggerated reports of the incident and of Schaefer's fury spread through the art community, confirming what dealers like Sam Kootz had been saying for years: Jackson was a drunk and more trouble than he was worth.

Eventually, after days of pleading by Clement Greenberg, Betty Parsons, Roger Wilcox, and Lee, Schaefer relented and dropped the charges. But the trauma had alerted Lee and others to the new reality. Jackson's drinking was no longer just a threat to his sobriety and safety, nor was it any longer just Lee's personal cross. Suddenly, it was an imminent threat to his productivity, his reputation, and his very real chance for celebrity.

Faced with a crisis, Lee finally loosened her grip enough to seek outside help. On a routine visit to the East Hampton Medical Center, she confided in her young doctor, Edwin H. Heller, that Jackson was, "just then, drinking heavily," she recounted later. "He suggested I try to send Jackson over to see him." Lee explained that "one didn't tell Jackson to do these things but that a moment would come . . ." It came not long afterward when Jackson fell off his bike and ended up on Dr. Heller's examining table. Heller was a local boy from Sag Harbor who had only recently graduated from Cornell Medical School and returned to the South Fork of Long Island to practice. Never having treated an alcoholic before, he took an interest in Jackson's problem that was more than medical but less than psychoanalytic. In simple, matter-of-fact terms, he explained that alcohol was Jackson's "personal poison." "Some people can't eat spinach," he said, "and you can't drink booze." He explained that Jackson wasn't addicted to alcohol, he was addicted to the *feeling* that alcohol induced. To help him achieve the same feeling without alcohol, Heller gave him a prescription for tranquilizers—phenobarbitol and Dilantin, according to Roger Wilcox—and told him to "take these whenever you feel the need for a drink and they'll calm you down. But under no circumstances should you combine them with alcohol." He arranged for Jackson to return to the clinic every week so that Heller could monitor his progress, adjust the dosage if necessary, and "just talk about his problem." Finally, he told Jackson: "Whenever the urge to drink gets too strong, just pick up the phone and call me."

To Lee's amazement, the prescription seemed to work. Jackson reported feeling calmer than he had in years. Soon afterward, he called Sande in Deep River and announced that he had "quit for good." "When Sande heard that," Arloie remembers, "he hung up the phone and said, 'If Jack can do it, I can do it.' And he did." (Jackson neglected to tell Sande or anyone else in the family about the tranquilizers.) By the time Jackson and Lee arrived in Deep River for the Christmas holidays three weeks later, "Jack's new leaf" had become the Pollock family *cause célèbre*—"The best news of all," Stella called it. "Jack and Lee were here and we had a very nice Christmas," she reported to Charles.

> And there was no drinking. We were all so happy. Jack has been going to a Dr. in Hampton and hadn't drank anything for over three weeks at Christmas hope he will stay with it he says he wants to quit and went to the Dr. on his own, the Dr. told him he would have to leave it alone everything wine to beer for they were poison to him. . . . The Dr. says it is up to him.

But Jackson had yet to be tested. The late fall and early winter had been unusually kind. With the show largely ready, he had spent most of his time preoccupied with the renovations on John Little's new house. When Little broke his arm and work was suspended, Jackson turned his attention to his own house, tearing out the partitions between the dining room and the kitchen and the hall and the stairs, to create a spacious area for entertaining—something that Lee was doing more of every summer. Nor was the Christmas with Stella a real test. In all the years Lee had known him, Jackson had never lost control in Stella's presence.

The real test would come in January. Even Stella, for all her optimism, was apprehensive: "When he has his show will be a test and a hard one for Jack," she wrote Charles. "If he can go through that without drinking will be something I hope he can and will."

For the first three weeks of January, Jackson busied himself with last-minute preparations. On Friday morning, January 21, he drove into the city with Lee, carrying a bundle of laths for making stretchers and the last of the paintings rolled up in the back of a borrowed station wagon. That night, Sande and Arloie arrived from Deep River. It was Sande's first vacation in two years, but he stuck to his pledge of abstinence, as did Jackson. Lee had arranged for them to stay at Grace Hartigan's small apartment on Thirty-third Street near the East River (Hartigan had moved in with Harry Jackson for the duration of the Pollocks' visit), but Jackson spent most of the weekend at the gallery, working long hours with Tony Smith and a crew of fellow artists to finish stretching and hanging the show in time for the Monday opening. When Parsons stopped by to check on their progress, Jackson tried to persuade her to hang the pictures unstretched by simply stapling them to the wall (the way he did in the studio), a procedure that would have halved the hanging time. But Parsons, whose look of cultivated indifference concealed an adamantine will, "put her foot down," recalls Herbert Ferber, one of the artists on Jackson's crew, "and said they *had* to be stretched." Despite their disagreement, Parsons came away impressed by Jackson's calm, professional—and sober—attitude.

The opening, coming in the middle of a spell of "lovely winter weather," attracted an unusually large crowd into Betty's already claustrophobic gallery. According to Harry Jackson, who shadowed him before the show, Jackson "was very nervous, very, very antsy, the opposite of the bucolic, quiet, straw-chewing fella I knew." Jackson must have taken one or more of Dr. Heller's tranquilizers just before the crowd arrived, because Herbert Ferber remembers seeing him standing "stone sober" in the middle of the crowded gallery a few minutes later, looking surprisingly "calm and detached." "All the other people who had openings at Betty's would keep a bottle in the back room," says Ferber. "But not Jackson." Even after the crowd left and he accompanied a group of friends, including Harry and Grace, to dinner, there was no drinking, as there had been after every previous show. It helped, of course, that the public response—despite complaints about the use of numbers instead of names—was unusually favorable. (Eventually, eleven of the show's fifteen paintings sold.) There was no denying that Jackson had passed the test. "Jack had a wonderful show best yet," Stella exulted in a letter to Frank, "[and] best of all he hasn't touched a drop of liquor since the first of Dec. he feels so much better and seems so much happier, we were all so glad he had such good luck."

No one was happier than Lee. Eager to rehabilitate Jackson's reputation before the rumors of drunkenness and the related jokes about peeing on the canvas crippled it irreparably, she immediately launched a campaign to spread the good news: Jackson Pollock was, at last, securely on the wagon. At every opportunity, she planted the story of Heller's "miracle cure." "He was the first man who was really able to help Jackson stop drinking," she said, insisting that Jackson hadn't "touched" alcohol since their first meeting. (Like Jackson, Lee always omitted any reference to tranquilizers.) To dramatize the new regime, she stopped serving liquor of any kind, even to guests—a revolutionary move in a social circle heavily dependent on alcohol. "Promptly the gloomy prognosis spread," wrote May Rosenberg of a dinner party at the Pollocks', "that [Lee] intended to serve no liquor this night. The thought settled like smog on parched throats." The campaign succeeded brilliantly. Before long, Jackson's abstinence had attained mythic status. Years later, people who had barely known him would talk authoritatively about the "dry years" during which Jackson's art flourished because he "never took a single drink."

Lee must have known from the beginning that it wasn't true. She had been up and down on Jackson's roller coaster too many times to believe in miracle cures. The myth was, at best, a convenient oversimplification, a screen behind which she could hide the more complicated and less flattering truth.

In fact, according to an account Lee gave years later, Jackson *never* quit drinking. It was true that, during the dry years, he could go weeks between drinks, withdrawn in tranquilized serenity, and that when he did sneak a drink —he later admitted that he kept a bottle of cooking sherry buried in the backyard throughout this period—it seldom led to the kind of uncontrollable binge that Lee feared most. When it did, the binge tended to be a private affair rather than a public display. "He would go up to the guest bedroom," Lee later confided to a friend, "and just sit there and have fits, be completely crazed for a while." "All that stuff that people try to say about two-year periods without drinking was bullshit," says John Lee, an intimate of Lee's after Jackson's death, recounting her revised story of the "dry years." "She said he was always a binge drinker. Given a couple of weeks of normal existence he would just go off the deep end . . . and he was always that way."

Nor was Dr. Edwin Heller, thoughtful and supportive as he was, the lone miracle worker Lee painted him to be. As Lee knew all too well, other competent, conscientious doctors—Wall, de Lazslo, Hubbard—had told Jackson not to drink and would again. Clearly, there was something else, a motivational element that made Jackson *want* to reach for pills instead of the bottle, that made him *want* to keep his frequent appointments with Heller, and, when he fell off the wagon, made him *want* to hide his binges in an upstairs bedroom.

Roger Wilcox, like Lee, had been awakened to the danger of Jackson's drinking by Bertha Schaefer's threats. He had played a decisive role in negotiating with Schaefer and ultimately placating her. "I realized then that he was really an alcoholic," says Wilcox, "and that I was hurting him by drinking with him, that his work and his health were suffering and it would kill him eventually if he didn't stop." In the past, when Wilcox had tried to warn him about the dangers of alcoholism, Jackson had always snapped back: "Oh, that's a lot of crap. If I feel like drinking, I'll drink, goddammit." But Jackson, too, was sobered by the Schaefer incident. This time, he came to Wilcox for help. "He asked me to find out what was wrong with him," Wilcox remembers. "He said, 'I want to work but I can't. I've got this need to get drunk. It's something I can't explain. Tell me what's wrong.'" Wilcox, an overt, self-reliant man who considered psychoanalysis "stupid mystical bullshit" and believed most people's problems were their own fault, was unsympathetic at first. "I said, 'Why can't you work? You've got paint, you've got canvas. Who's stopping you? Go ahead. So you're a drunk. The only person who can stop you from being a drunk is yourself.' " According to Wilcox, Jackson "felt bad about his lack of control over himself. He didn't want to be that way. He believed he needed to stop drinking in order to continue his work." Convinced that Jackson's career was at stake, Wilcox finally softened. For the next two years, he would act as Jackson's therapist. Characteristically, he couched the task in its most pragmatic terms: "I wanted to know why the hell this guy, who had all this talent and capability, and was really a very nice person, why he was so troubled. Why was he getting this reputation for being a horrible person, a drunk, a wildman?"

With no idea how to proceed—"I had never questioned people before," he admits—Wilcox turned for help to the back pages of his favorite magazine, *Astounding Science Fiction*, where he had seen an announcement of a forthcoming book by one of the magazine's frequent contributors, L. Ron Hubbard. The book, called *Dianetics*, promised "to reduce psychotherapy to a simple set of principles, which were corollaries to engineering principles." For Wilcox, the engineer, the appeal was obvious. "There was no mysticism, no bullshit," he recalls. "Just a few straightforward principles that anyone could apply." Hypnosis (Hubbard called it "reverie") was a key part of the therapy. Through hypnosis, one could delve into the past and discover critical, long-suppressed, and often painful events that prevented the full realization of the self. Only by dragging those events into the light of consciousness and overcoming them, only by discovering "*what* caused those dark and unknown fears which came in nightmares as a child" could a person make true progress toward self-knowledge and ultimate enlightenment.

Wilcox had successfully tried Hubbard's methods on other friends before, but only as a kind of parlor game. With Jackson, he was deadly earnest. "I would pose a mental problem," Wilcox remembers, "then tell him to count backwards from one hundred. That required some concentration and focused his attention on the problem. Then I would say, in a soft voice, 'When you reach such and such a number, you will be asleep, and you will sleep very calmly and very soundly, but you will still be able to hear my voice.' " Jackson resisted at first—"the first time we did it, he told me he wasn't *really* in a trance," Wilcox recalls. Gradually, however, as Jackson relaxed, the trances grew deeper and longer, and the memories that surfaced during them reached further and further into his past. He recalled the bullies in high school who had taunted him for his long hair and his refusal to play football. "He said it hurt when they called him a coward," Wilcox remembers. "If he had been small, like his brothers, they wouldn't have expected him to turn out a big macho man. But he was the biggest one in the family. He had to become what he was told to be, big and tough."

At each revelation, Wilcox took Jackson back another step. "You're seven years old now," he would say, "what does it feel like?"

"I was always walking along, looking at this and looking at that," Jackson said. "But the other guys thought that was sissy."

Year by year, each one more traumatic than the last, Wilcox guided Jackson back through his turbulent childhood. "He had a lot of traumatic experiences when he was a child," Wilcox concluded early in their sessions, "and he never got over them. He was scared to death, he was afraid of people—particularly afraid of men—and the only way he could escape from that fear was to drink."

The last and earliest memory Wilcox uncovered was by far the most traumatic. It was Jackson's memory of riding in his mother's wagon.

I said, "You're five now, Jackson. What do you remember?" And he told me about riding in his mother's wagon on the way into town to sell vegetables in Arizona. They were going along the road and there was a bull in the field, rushing toward the wagon, and a man on horseback coming at an angle, trying to intercept the bull. Jackson saw the bull coming, but there was nothing he could do about it. When the bull got close, the horse reared up and the wagon turned over and Jackson and his mother were thrown clear. He looked up and saw his mother lying there on the ground. At that moment, the man came up and got off his horse, picked Jackson up by his shirt with one hand and slapped him with the other, and said, "Why were you lying there crying? Boys aren't supposed to cry." He repeated that story several times under hypnosis. It had stuck in his mind forever, and as he was telling it to me, he started to really relive it. He was so terrified he actually started crying with me, big tears. I promised him that as long as he lived, I would never tell anybody this story because he didn't want anyone to know.

The long, cathartic sessions with Wilcox undoubtedly appeased Jackson's demons, but by spring 1949, his store of traumatic memories had been exhausted and neither man had any interest in the remainder of Hubbard's glib self-help philosophy. "Neither of us really believed in it," Wilcox recalls, "so Jackson said, 'Let's just forget that shit.'" In its place, Wilcox proposed a methodology even more suited to his pragmatic bent. He referred to it simply as "keeping Jackson occupied." "I said, 'Jackson, whenever something is bothering you and you really feel like going on a bender, just come and see me.'"

Throughout the spring and summer, Jackson took advantage of Wilcox's offer. Several times a week at least, sometimes once a day, he walked or drove the two and a half miles to the Wilcox house, where Lucia greeted him with lavish hospitality and Wilcox dropped whatever he was doing. From there the two men would head into the woods or to the beach, walking absently and talking. "We went exploring all the beaches from here to Montauk Point, all the remote beaches," Wilcox remembers. "He didn't like to be around people when he was in that kind of mood." Each time, they wandered farther and farther down the shore, past the bluffs at Barnes Landing, past the noisome, weather-bleached fish factories that rimmed the "Promised Land" basin, and out onto the spit of heavy sand that had once been open sea but now connected Long Island to the former island of Montauk. They spent weeks on the east side of Napeague Harbor, meandering through the "walking" dunes and the

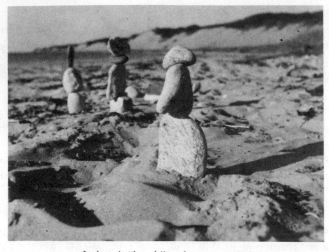

Jackson's "beach" sculptures, c. 1949

saltwater marshes of spartina grass and blossoming wildflowers. But Jackson's favorite spot was farther still, where the shore turned in and the bluffs of Montauk began to rise from the sea and the beach turned rocky. "Where the rocks were," Wilcox remembers, "that's where we used to go any time he wanted to get calmed down."

A trip could last the whole day. Lucia packed a picnic lunch, and the two men would sit on the beach till close to sundown. Wilcox did most of the talking, regaling Jackson with stories about his eerily similar childhood of paternal strife and high school rebellion. Jackson listened and played with beach rocks, making small sculptures in the sand. "Many times, we would carry a cooler with four or five beers all the way down to this beach that he liked," Wilcox recalls, "but we wouldn't drink them. We'd have our lunch and talk, and then we'd come all the way back, still carrying this damn cooler." After the third round trip, Wilcox packed orange juice instead of beer. "Aren't you going to take any beers?" Jackson asked as they set out. "Hell, no," said Wilcox. "Every time I do, we bring them all back, so what the hell's the point?" To Wilcox's astonishment, Jackson agreed. "You're right," he said, "we can do without it."

The long afternoons with Wilcox allowed Jackson to "do without it" for the first time in his life. On trips into the city or in the evenings when Roger was unavailable, tranquilizers filled the gaps. Lee, who distrusted Wilcox, clung to a mystical faith in doctors and pushed the pills on Jackson at every opportunity. "She would hold them out to him and say, 'Take these and everything will be all right,' " Wilcox remembers. " '[Heller] is a great doctor, he'll take care of you.' " But it was largely Wilcox's brotherly support, unqualified and uncorrupting, that for almost two years kept Jackson from being overwhelmed by the onrushing tide of celebrity.

■   ■   ■

The summer of 1949 began slowly, deceptively slowly, with the usual visits from Stella and Clement Greenberg. There had been nothing new in Greenberg's effusive praise of the January show—except perhaps the overtly self-congratulatory tone. The big white painting, *Number 1*, he wrote, "quieted any doubts this reviewer may have felt—and he does not in all honesty remember having felt many—as to the justness of the superlatives with which he had praised Pollock's art in the past." What *was* new was the degree to which other reviewers were beginning to echo Greenberg's formalist rhetoric. "Of the Hieroglyphics School, this is an exciting display," wrote Margaret Lowengrund in *Art Digest.* "It seems to strive to eliminate spatial form in favor of line and surface interest alone." Willem de Kooning's wife, Elaine, reviewing the show for *Art News,* showed her Greenbergian colors by admiring how "planes separate from the original flat surface of the canvas are not suggested."

The "popular" press was proving more resistant to Greenberg's ideas. In the *World-Telegram,* Emily Genauer reacted with exasperation. "Most of Jackson Pollock's paintings at the Betty Parsons Gallery resemble nothing so much as a mop of tangled hair I have an irresistible urge to comb out." She even complimented several paintings because "their less 'accidental' development and their spatial depth suggest how good a painter Pollock could really be." In the *Times,* Sam Hunter complained about "the disintegration of the modern painting" and "a disappointing absence of resolution in an image or pictorial incident"—complaints that Greenberg would have considered compliments. But even skeptics like Hunter admitted that the paintings had an impact. "What does emerge is the large scale of Pollock's operations, his highly personal rhythm and finally something like pure calligraphic metaphor for a ravaging, aggressive virility."

A short review in the February 7, 1949, issue of *Time* opened with a broad swipe: "A Jackson Pollock painting is apt to resemble a child's contour map of the Battle of Gettysburg." As proof, the editors included an impenetrable black-and-white reproduction of *Number 11, 1948.* "Nevertheless," the review continued, "he is the darling of a highbrow cult which considers him 'the most powerful painter in America.' " Unwilling, or unable, to dignify the show with its own review, *Time* took advantage of the opportunity to lambast avant-garde critics as well as avant-garde artists by quoting, at length, Sam Hunter's equally impenetrable review in the *Times,* pulling out a particularly abstruse phrase, "cathartic disintegration," to caption the painting.

Stella's visit in late March—her first since the birth of grandson Jay—coincided with spring planting. "[Jack and Lee] were getting ready to put in a garden," she reported to Charles, "they have good soil Lee loves to dig in the dirt and she has green fingers." During her stay, Stella took special pleasure in meeting Jackson's cultured friends, like Clement Greenberg. "Whenever I started to say anything about art or culture," Greenberg remembers, "Stella would tell everyone in the room to shush." To Stella's delight, Jackson was still on the wagon, although he had to drink "tons of coffee" to counter the effects of Heller's tranquilizers. By her report, Jackson and Lee seemed prepared for the onslaught of summer. "So nice to be there and see them so happy and no drinking," she wrote. "He can serve liquor to others. He feels so much better says so."

By late May, the house on Fireplace Road was filled every weekend with people from Lee's growing list of artists, critics, museum directors, dealers, and collectors who had been—or might prove to be—helpful to Jackson's career. Among the first of the guests was a wealthy young Philippino collector and artist, Alfonso Ossorio, who came with his companion, Ted Dragon. Ossorio, who also showed at Betty Parsons, had bought *Number 5, 1948* from the January show but postponed delivery until he moved into his new house at 9 MacDougal Alley in April. When the painting was badly damaged in delivery, Jackson agreed to do the necessary "repair" work if Ossorio would return the painting to his studio. The following month, Ossorio and Dragon drove to Springs with the painting and stayed the night at the Pollock house. Dragon, a twenty-seven-year-old ballet dancer whom Ossorio had met the previous year, thought the town looked like his native New England and "fell in love with it instantly." A month later, when they returned to pick up the repaired canvas and look for a house to rent, they were surprised to find that Jackson had radically altered the painting with a layer of red paint.

After moving into the large Hellmuth house on Jericho Lane, Ossorio and Dragon continued to see the Pollocks "two or three times a week," often bringing big boxes of food and other gifts, mistaking the Pollocks' Spartan country life-style for genuine poverty. Lee accepted such handouts gratefully and even encouraged the impression—no longer accurate—that she and Jackson were living on the financial edge. Ossorio was also welcome in Jackson's studio, where his admiration for artists and his patrician bearing combined in a ritual of flattery. "When Alfonso came to look at your paintings," recalls another artist's wife, "he did it with such grace and style. Instead of coming in like a shopper and just looking for something to buy, he made you feel like he was a patron who considered it a privilege to acquire one of your paintings." Jackson expressed his gratitude by taking the newcomers exploring along the beaches and, occasionally, spending an evening at the Hellmuth house. Shy and tranquilized, he made a poor guest. "He would say maybe three words all evening," Ted Dragon remembers. "He would sit there like a mummy the whole time." More enjoyable were the weekly trips, Ossorio's treat, to the movie house in East Hampton, where Jackson "loved the westerns and science fiction," Dragon recalls.

Ossorio and Dragon were merely the first in a long line of collectors who made it a point to visit "the darling of a highbrow cult" that summer. The guest list included established local lights like Valentine and Happy Macy and Roseanne Larkin, the sponsors of avant-garde art at Guild Hall, as well as newcomers like Jeffrey and Penny Potter. Potter, the aloof and aristocratic scion of a blue-blooded family, was looking to quit his job as a Broadway stage manager and move to East Hampton to get back in touch with nature, and to write. Around the beginning of the new year, while maneuvering to buy the Stony Hill Farm in Amagansett from the recalcitrant widow Hamlin, he had met Jackson cruising the farm's back roads in his Model A and was intrigued. "His mouth was half open," he later wrote, "his long heavy forearms hung from a soiled T-shirt, and his glassy look straight ahead was for something far from the Stony Hill Farm woods." To Potter, Jackson embodied the elusive blend of artistic sensibility and hands-on, masculine efficacy (he could fix a car and wield a hammer) that Potter himself, the would-be writer-engineer, aspired to. By summer, intrigue had turned to infatuation. Potter began making notes of his encounters with Jackson, recording every "wry half-smile" and every awkward silence for use in a planned novel to be called *The Outsider*, and then, when he abandoned the novel, in an oral biography that would chronicle the two men's "personality equivalents." To Jackson, Potter's Lincoln convertible, patrician bearing, and beautiful wife bespoke only one thing, money, and he spent the rest of the summer cultivating Potter's breathless attentions in the hope of a sale.

Reginald Isaacs, then a professor of city and regional planning at Harvard, was visiting in East Hampton when friends brought him to the Pollocks' house for a clamming expedition into Accabonac Harbor. Isaacs thought Jackson was just "a hired hand or some local fisherman just hanging around." It wasn't until afterward, sitting in the kitchen, that he caught a glimpse of Jackson's paintings in the dining room and exclaimed, "My God! Who made those?" For both men, it was a serendipitous encounter. Isaacs, who was equally taken with Jackson and with his art, bought a painting that very afternoon—the first of three—and went home touting Pollock as "the greatest painter of the century."

Not every visitor was so enthusiastic. When Clement Greenberg brought Peter and Chloe Scott, an eager young couple, and Robert Motherwell to a daytime gathering with several other couples, Jackson reluctantly agreed to lead the crowd through his studio. After an awkward silence and a few perfunctory "They're terrifics," Chloe Scott was heard to mutter ambiguously, "Oh dear, it's just too much to absorb in one afternoon."

That was rousing praise compared to the indignant comments that ricocheted through Guild Hall when three of Jackson's paintings appeared there in July. The event was "17 Eastern Long Island Artists," a show of local artists' work organized by John Little and sponsored, against bitter resistance from "the Maidstone Club Irregulars," by Roseanne Larkin and Enez Whipple, the director. "That was a breakthrough show, and a near breakdown of Guild Hall," said Gina Knee. The show included works by James Brooks, Alexander Brook, John Little, Wilfrid Zogbaum, Balcomb Greene, the Soyer brothers, Julien Levy, Ibram Lassaw, and Lee, but Jackson and his "incomprehensible drippings" were the center of attention. "White-gloved hostesses pouring tea and serving punch" recoiled at the sight of Jackson's paintings, embedded with cigarette butts and other debris. Compared to Guild Hall's usual fare of water-colors, seascapes, and still lifes, the show seemed a "horror chamber" and the artists in it, "barbarians and radicals." (One patron ran to the rest room to wash after shaking hands with an artist.) Jackson hardly looked like a barbarian or a radical, standing in front of his paintings in a tweed coat, tie, and polished loafers, looking thinner than he had in years. Few people dared approach him. Most stood at a safe distance and pointed surreptitiously, whispering, "That's him. He's the one." But Jackson seemed imperturbable, standing for hours in a cigarette fog, studying the floor in an effort to avoid the curious and often angry stares of regular patrons like Mrs. Harry Hamlin who, upon seeing one of his paintings, huffed that artists like that must live in trees. The most venomous comments came from the more traditional local artists for whom Guild Hall had long been a closed shop. They accused Jackson of being a fraud or, worse, a jokester—charges that sparked more than one fistfight during the show's three-week run. Jackson had the last laugh, however. By the time the show was over, all three of his paintings had sold.

It was a summer of fragments—professionally and socially—as the encroachments of celebrity fractured Jackson's life into smaller and smaller pieces. There were still moments of genuine pleasure: working on John Little's house, helping Jim Brooks buy a used car, walking on the beach with Roger Wilcox. In March, Jackson proudly hosted the wedding of Harry Jackson and Grace Hartigan at the house on Fireplace Road. It was an intimate affair; Jackson acted as best man, Lee as matron of honor, and the Pollocks' neighbor, Judge William Schellinger, "did the knot tying." But, more and more, such moments were crowded apart by obligations, introductions, and the minutiae of business. Just since the January show, there had been an exhibition at the University of Illinois and two showings of Peggy Guggenheim's collection (in Florence and Milan). In May, Jackson shingled the studio; in June, he negotiated a new contract with Betty Parsons for another two and a half years. The same month, he prepared a submission for the "Sculpture by Painters" show that opened in August at the Museum of Modern Art: a tiny terra-cotta piece, not unlike the WPA bronze he had cast on the sly in 1935. In August, he lent *Number 10, 1949*, another long, scroll-like canvas mounted on wood, to Sidney Janis for his "Man and Wife" show (Lee lent her *Junk Dump Fair*) and in the same month shipped an untitled work to Sam Kootz's gallery to join works by Gorky, Hofmann, Tobey, Motherwell, de Kooning, and Rothko in an ambitious show mounted by Kootz and Harold Rosenberg. The show's goal was nothing less than to identify the dynamic but muddled state of abstract art in America, both in words and in images. Despite the impressive array of artists, the show fell far short of its ambitions, due partly to Rosenberg's opaque catalogue essay ("When the spectator recognizes the nothingness copied by the modern painter, the latter's work becomes just as intelligible as . . . earlier painting") and partly to Kootz's unfortunate choice of a name for the new movement: "the Intrasubjectives."

If there was one theme that ran through the summer, that brought some coherence to Jackson's increasingly fragmented efforts, it was money. Whether it meant wooing potential collectors or braving the stares of Guild Hall hostesses, finding new buyers had become the summer's overriding mandate. One reason Peggy's Italian shows (and her failure to organize a show in Paris) had so little impact in Springs was that Jackson and Lee stood to gain nothing from the sales they generated. By not including any of Jackson's recent works, Peggy made it clear that she was more interested in reducing her own inventory than in advancing Jackson's career.

Nevertheless, the possibility of foreign sales continued to intrigue Jackson and Lee. Increasing exposure—thanks to Peggy—and favorable word-of-mouth indicated that European collectors were less resistant to his revolutionary art than Americans like Chloe Scott, who were still locked into what John Little called "the Guild Hall mentality." One person who agreed was Alfonso Ossorio, who had had some experience in buying and selling works of art abroad. After a number of conversations, Ossorio agreed to explore the possibility of mounting a show in Paris when he went to Europe in the fall. Meanwhile, Jackson searched for other new markets closer to home.

For years, Greenberg had been saying "the easel picture [was] a dying form" that would eventually be replaced by "the wall picture or mural." While Jackson didn't necessarily accept Greenberg's rhetoric as a description of commercial reality (he continued to paint scores of small, "sellable" works throughout his career), he (or Lee) did grasp its marketing implications. With Tony Smith, who was designing several homes that summer, he began to talk about doing large, commissioned paintings, like the Guggenheim mural, that would act as integral parts of a building's design. Smith even brought several of his clients to the studio in Springs in an effort, apparently unsuccessful, to direct a mural commission Jackson's way. The two men spent hours together, Smith reciting passages from Joyce and talking in poetic abstractions about the marriage of art and architecture, and Jackson offering the usual litany of half-truths about his western roots: milking cows, roping cattle, and learning poetry "first-hand" from southwestern Indians. "He knew the West as it really was," said Smith, who had spent some of his sickly childhood in the Southwest, "whereas he considered that I had been there as a dude. . . . [H]e obviously thought that life in those areas was more authentic than life is here." Jackson also apparently thought that collectors out west would better appreciate the western scale of the murals he wanted to paint. Sometime in June, he and Smith hatched plans to drive to California—with Lee, presumably—before the end of the year.

Not long afterward, Jackson's mural plans were given an unexpected boost by another architect eager to explore the common ground of architecture and art. At the remarkably early age of twenty-six, Peter Blake had gone almost directly from the Pratt Institute, where he studied with Louis Kahn, to a position as curator of architecture at the Museum of Modern Art. Bright, personable, and ambitious, Blake made a point of meeting Jackson at an East

Hampton party that summer and eagerly accepted an invitation to his studio. He found the experience "absolutely overwhelming." "It was a very sunny day," Blake recalls, "and the sun was shining in on the paintings. I felt like I was standing in the Hall of Mirrors at Versailles. It was a dazzling, incredible sight."

The analogy to Versailles suggested to Blake an idea for a museum using glass and mirrors to "create a sense of paintings defining the space, not the other way around." The design that began to take shape in his mind was based on a plan by Mies Van Der Rohe for an "ideal museum" that had appeared in an issue of *Architectural Forum*. Mies's plan was characteristically simple: a floor plane, a roof plane, and a few columns to suggest supporting structure. The paintings wouldn't hang on walls, they would *be* the walls, freestanding or simply hanging in space without visible support. Blake proposed building a model of the museum and filling it with miniature reproductions of Jackson's big paintings. The idea thrilled Jackson, who undoubtedly saw it as yet another way to promote mural commissions. When Blake suggested that "it would be nice to have some pieces of [miniature] sculpture to provide contrast," however, Jackson balked. "What do you think I am," he sputtered, "just a decorator?" But he did eventually produce the sculptures, bending and looping metal wire, then dipping it into wet plaster. "It was as if he took a painting from that period," says Blake, "and turned it into three dimensions." Sometime in July, Jackson and Lee persuaded Alfonso Ossorio to provide $1,000 for materials, and Blake began work on the model. Jackson wanted to have it ready in time for the November show.

Inevitably, Jackson's preoccupation with new buyers and marketing strategies followed him into the studio. There, despite Greenberg's rhetoric and Tony Smith's encouragement, he eschewed mural-size projects like *Pasiphaë* (5' by 8') and *Lucifer* (3½' by 9') and concentrated instead on producing a number of smaller, more accessible works. It was a marketing lesson first learned from Howard Putzel, who had constantly badgered his artists to produce "smaller works for timid collectors." Peggy herself had often complained about the difficulty of selling Jackson's giant canvases. In 1949, Jackson produced only one painting on that scale, the 5-by-8½-foot *Number 1, 1949*, an impenetrable tangle of black, yellow, white, aluminum, and pink with a strand or two of blue caught in a vortex so dense and furious that it seems to suck the paint inward, away from the edges of the canvas. There were other canvases that equalled *Number 1* in density and impact, if not in scale: *Number 8, 1949*, with its turbulent, open subweb of black and gray-green overlaid with heavy pourings of aluminum—by now a signature feature of Jackson's work; *Number 13, 1949*, with its jumble of matchstick brush strokes caught in an exquisitely fine tracery of eggshell white; and *Number 3, 1949*, with its fathomless layers of earthy green, yellow, and orange and its remarkable "whisks" of white—hundreds of tiny lines speeding in close rank through and around the twists of color. Beyond this handful of full-throated, symphonic works, Jackson focused his efforts on

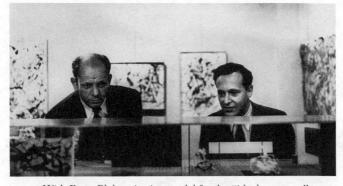

With Peter Blake, viewing model for the "ideal museum"

producing a number of smaller, simpler, and more affordable pieces, most of them on paper mounted on composition board. Even within these self-imposed constraints, however, he was capable of producing gorgeous images. In *Number 31, 1949,* he turned the icy hardness of the unabsorbent paper to his advantage, showering it with incandescent blues and reds and a flash of yellow. In places, he allowed the wet colors to mix, forming clouds of lavender, orange, and green. Elsewhere, wet colors fell on dry, creating rivers of cerulean blue on glacial whites, blood-red rivulets on blue-black fields, and yellow veins criss-crossed by threads of white as fine as silk. It was a ravishing—and accessible—display of color, no less so because Jackson may have painted it with a price tag in mind.

As the show approached, he produced a third set of paintings, even smaller and simpler than the first two. On canvases no bigger than one by two feet, mounted on Masonite to avoid the expense and trouble of stretching, he painted a series of bold, calligraphic images using a limited palette—seldom more than three colors—and a minimum of motion. Instead of piling paint in layers, he stripped the web to its fundamental forms—loops, puddles, and spatters—and isolated them like tiny unicellular organisms fixed on microscope slides.

The need to produce a quantity of identifiable and sellable works quickly—often with just a flick or two of the wrist—forced him to explore an entirely new dimension of the drip technique. For the first time, he ventured out from behind the veils of size and complexity and, in a series of bravely simple and exquisitely assured little canvases, confronted directly the fundamentals of form and line that in the past had always unnerved him.

Even as he explored the boundaries of the drip technique, however, Jackson showed signs of restlessness. It had become, perhaps, a little too easy, too predictable, too mechanical. New materials and commercial imperatives offered some fresh challenges, but he seemed to be quickly approaching the limits. More and more, new paintings evoked old ones: the viscous, string-like ridges of *Number 9, 1949*; the pebbles that punctuate the yellow, black, and aluminum maze of *Number 4, 1949.* In some paintings, even brush strokes

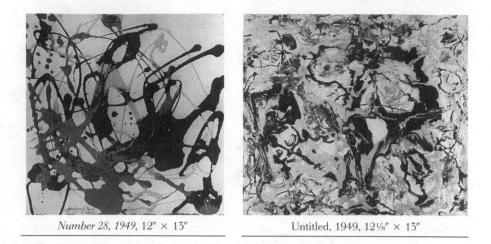

Number 28, 1949, 12″ × 13″   Untitled, 1949, 12⅛″ × 13″

reappeared. In one small composition from 1949 (untitled) he experimented with a pouring technique that produced a radically different, sharper image than the nebulae of colors in *Number 31, 1949*. The surest sign of his borning frustration, however, was *Out of the Web*, a large drip painting of black, white, gray, red, and yellow underlain by heavy brush strokes on the rough side of a Masonite panel. After letting the many layers of paint dry, he took a knife and cut Miró-like biomorphic shapes into the image and peeled away the paint within the cutouts to reveal the Masonite beneath. Even as his abstract skeins were about to achieve their fullest expression, somewhere in Jackson's subconscious, familiar figures struggled to break out of the web.

When, in July, *Life* magazine proposed doing a feature story on Jackson and his art, marketing imperatives again carried the day. "We went back and forth on the decision to 'chance' the *Life* article," Lee Krasner recalled later. "We discussed the advantages and the disadvantages." The primary advantage was obvious: "A favorable piece would help sell some paintings." The disadvantages were more complicated. The previous December, *Life* had run an article on the French artist Jean Dubuffet, including a full-page reproduction of *Smoky Black (Lili)* and a commentary that turned out to be a blistering pan. Entitled "Dead End Art: A Frenchman's Mud-and-Rubble Paintings Reduce Modernism to a Joke," it accused Dubuffet's work of "feebly mixed" intentions and "low" technical skill, and compared its "amusement value" to that of "juvenile finger painting." "There is more dignity in Al Capp's Dogpatch," it concluded, "than in the whole of Dubuffet's gaga cosmos." Lee, who drolly dubbed the Dubuffet review the ultimate "thumbs down," worried that Jackson might fare as badly. "You didn't know in advance what *Life* would do," she complained. On the other hand, the day after the article appeared, Dubuffet's dealer, Pierre Matisse, offered to buy back *Smoky Black (Lili)* for twice the amount he had sold it for only days before. The lesson was clear: publicity, good or bad, had a value all its own. It may have been as a reminder of that lesson that Lee kept a copy of the *Life* reproduction of *Smoky Black* tacked to the back of the bathroom door on Fireplace Road.

A little of the terror still showed when Jackson and Lee arrived at the Time-Life Building in Rockefeller Center on July 18, 1949. Dorothy Seiberling, the young writer who had been assigned to interview them, remembers Jackson dressed in his tweed coat and shiny loafers and "all kind of knotted up inside." Lee, on the other hand, was self-possessed and articulate. "She would step forward and speak for him," Seiberling recalls, "kind of amplify what he said. She didn't try to dominate or talk for him, just to make it easier for him and sometimes to explain. They were a very good combination." The story they told (it's impossible to tell from Seiberling's notes who is speaking) was a curious mix of personal fantasy, promotional hype, and political gesture that touched on the truth only coincidentally. Jackson claimed to be the first artist in his family. Charles and Sande, he said, followed in *his* footsteps. The years of study with Benton had been a "complete loss." He claimed that before coming to New York, while still out west, he had worked extensively with abstract forms, "both in sculpture and in painting"—referring, perhaps, to the experiments in Schwankovsky's class. The troubled years between 1935 and 1944, the years of Bloomingdale's, Henderson, and Bellevue, he referred to obliquely as "a kind of seclusion."

On the subject of his paintings, Jackson was equally elusive, often repeating, almost verbatim, previous recorded statements. On technique: "A real painter has to come through with something of his own—to say something individual. . . . A student should pay less attention to technique and concentrate on saying something. . . . If an artist is interested in a typewriter, he should be able to draw it." On his working habits: "When Pollock starts a picture he 'goes through' it completely," Seiberling noted, "carrying it as far as he can at one session. While he is painting, he knows when a picture is 'working,' but afterwards, when the inspiration is somewhat remote, he has to get [re]acquainted with his pictures." On the subject of abstraction, Greenberg would have been pleased with Jackson's statement: "I try to stay away from any recognizable image; if it creeps in, I try to do away with it . . . to let the painting come through. I don't let the image carry the painting. . . . It's extra cargo—and unnecessary." Greenberg would not have been pleased, however, with Jackson's admission that "Recognizable images are always there in the end."

When asked to name his favorite artists, Jackson offered only de Kooning and Kandinsky among twentieth-century painters—not Picasso or Matisse—and El Greco, Goya, and Rembrandt among the old masters. His mention of Goya, the first on record, was to some degree a bone to his patron Alfonso Ossorio, who had just given him a book on Goya. The bone to Greenberg was an unelaborated reference to his most recent reviews: "Pollock feels that he is a natural development from the Cubists," Seiberling wrote in her notes. Finally, when asked how he would respond to his many critics, Jackson offered: "If they'd leave most of their stuff (preconceived notions) at home and just look at the painting, they'd have no trouble enjoying it. It's just like looking at a bed of flowers. You don't tear your hair out over what it means."

On the way out of the Time-Life Building that day, it was Lee and Jackson's turn to tear their hair. They wouldn't know until the article appeared in August if it was thumbs up or thumbs down.

Not long afterward, Jackson finally accepted Dan Miller's invitation to take a ride in his tiny single-engine plane. From a grassy strip off Daniels Hole Road they lifted into the summer sky, and within seconds the curved shoulder of the Atlantic filled the horizon. On the right, across the shrinking expanse of Gardiners Bay, Jackson could see the North Fork, Plum Island, and, beyond, the Connecticut shore; to the right, a fine white line of sand stretching from Montauk Point back toward New York, separating the green island from the sail-specked sea. Jackson had never flown before, and he trembled with a mix of thrill and dread. "I could feel his knee banging against mine," Miller later recalled. They flew all the way to Block Island, a biomorphic cutout of land in the all-over ocean, before turning around. It was a view of the world that Jackson had never seen before, a view both terrifying and exhilarating.

Before the end of the year, he would soar to heights of a different kind, but the mix of feelings would always be the same.

36

BREAKING THE ICE

I s Jackson Pollock a threat to the American way of life? That was the question percolating through the offices of *Life* magazine as the deadline for the August 8 issue approached. Margit Varga, the longtime editor of the art department, responded with an emphatic yes. George Hunt, who had joined the staff only the year before as assistant editor, was inclined to agree. A painter himself who had studied with Guy Pène duBois, Hunt viewed the color proof of Jackson's *Number 12, 1948* with a disdainfully arched eyebrow. "He was a deeply conservative man," recalls a co-worker, "so of course he didn't really understand it." In fact, the only person at *Life* who did understand it, or thought he did, was Daniel Longwell, chairman of the magazine's Board of Editors. A "very enthusiastic, exuberant, curious person," Longwell had been to Jackson's January show and walked away with a painting. "It had a fly in it and [Dan] thought that was adventurous," Dorothy Seiberling recalls. Not too long afterward, Longwell ignited the furor in *Life*'s art department by suggesting: "Maybe we should do a piece on this fella Pollock." It was Longwell's editorial eye, looking over their shoulders, that kept Varga and Hunt's disdain in check as the article on Pollock took shape in early drafts.

But other eyes were watching as well: those of Henry Luce, owner and editorial czar of both *Time* and *Life*. With the aid of his chief editorial "hit man," Jack Jessup, Luce had been known to undercut his own art department by issuing anti–modern art blasts on the editor's page, his personal preserve. Rosalind Constable was another force to be reckoned with. Luce had given her a broad mandate to "keep abreast of all new avant-garde movements in all areas—culture, science, literature, et cetera," according to Seiberling, "so she would periodically write something about what was far out in the art world." Nothing, of course, was further out than Clement Greenberg and his outrageous claim that this wild, unknown painter, Jackson Pollock, was the greatest painter in America. Finally, there was *Time*'s formidable Alexander Eliot, an arrogant, conservative iconoclast who "took perverse pleasure in demolishing new things," according to Seiberling. Eliot was the man behind *Time*'s two previous snickering references to Jackson's work. "He thought it was something to make fun of," Seiberling recalls. Finally, there was Seiberling herself, who "didn't really understand what was going on in the Abstract Expressionist world" but, as a conscientious researcher, had been to gallery openings, had accompanied Arnold Newman to Jackson's house in Springs for a photo session, and was convinced that Pollock "had *some* substance."

The article that appeared on newsstands in the first week of August didn't so much resolve the intra-staff dispute as air it in public. The headline, spread across the page beneath a picture of Jackson, turned Greenberg's controversial claim into a question—"Is he the greatest living painter in the United States?" *Life* was inviting all of America to choose sides.

Beneath a picture of Jackson looking particularly cocky, the article opened with surprising evenhandedness:

> Recently a formidably high-brow New York critic hailed the brooding, puzzled-looking man shown above as a major artist of our time and a fine candidate to become 'the greatest American painter of the 20th century.' Others believe that Jackson Pollock produces nothing more than interesting, if inexplicable decoration. Still others condemn his pictures as degenerate and find them as unpalatable as yesterday's macaroni.

Hunt and Varga did get in their licks. "Critics have wondered why Pollock happened to stop this painting where he did," reads the caption under a reproduction of the eighteen-foot *Summertime*. "The answer: his studio is only 22 feet long." Another caption refers to Jackson "drooling" paint. A sidebar, entitled "How Pollock Paints (with enamel, sand and a trowel)," slyly questions whether "his pictures can be said to have a top, a bottom or a side." The article quotes Jackson's standard line—"When I am *in* my painting I'm not aware of what I'm doing"—then adds archly: "To find out what he has been doing he stops and contemplates the picture during what he calls his 'get acquainted' period. . . . Finally, after days of brooding and doodling, Pollock decides the painting is finished, a deduction few others are equipped to make." "Most of [the article] was straightforward," Seiberling recalls, "but we also had a little fun with it because we ourselves didn't know quite what to make of it."

But the article was less about the art than it was about Jackson. Except for a brief, disparaging allusion to Benton, there was no mention of his training, his antecedents, his relation to European modernism, or even his place in the abstract movement. It was a profile of a man—a troubled, attractive, and lonely man (no one else is pictured, even in the background). Long after the visual jokes and sly word choices had played out, it was the image of Jackson standing in front of *Summertime,* arms crossed defiantly, cigarette dangling seductively, not the painting, that lingered in the public imagination. There was something quintessentially American about this anti-artist, this handsome, rough-hewn

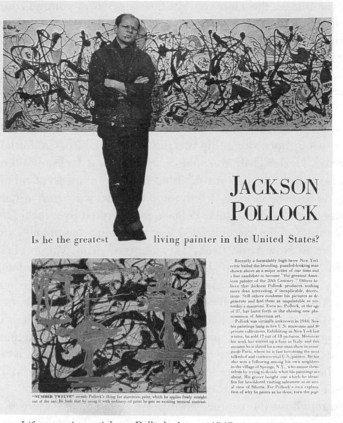

Life magazine article on Pollock, August 1949. © Arnold Newman

figure from the American West, living in the country not the big city, working in dungarees instead of a smock, in a barn instead of an atelier, painting with sticks and house paint instead of sable brushes and oil. "Look at him standing there," said Willem de Kooning when he saw the article, "he looks like some guy who works at a service station pumping gas." "He had everything," recalls Budd Hopkins. "He *was* the great American painter. If you conceive of such a person, first of all, he has to be a real American, *not* a transplanted European. And he should have the big macho American virtues—he should be rough-and-tumble American—taciturn, ideally—and if he is a cowboy, so much the better. Certainly not an easterner, not someone who went to Harvard. He shouldn't be influenced by the Europeans so much as he should be influenced by our own—the Mexicans, and American Indians, and so on. He should come out of the native soil, not out of Picasso and Matisse. He should be an inventor, in a funny way—a man who comes up with his own thing. And he should be allowed the great American vice, the Hemingway vice, of being a drunk. It's no wonder that he had the popular *Life* magazine success, because he was so American and unique, and quirky, and he had this great American face. Everything about him was right."

It was the *image*, the Hemingwayesque persona of contradictions that the *Life* article celebrated. "Pollock, at the age of 37," it asserted, "has burst forth as the shining new phenomenon of American art." Even if it hadn't been true before, it was now.

In Mount Pocono, Pennsylvania, Ettabelle Storm Horgan, who hadn't seen Jackson since the summer he spent in Devil's Hole in 1933, looked up from her copy of *Life* and said to her husband, "Look, Jack Pollock's famous now." In Phoenix, Arizona, Charles Porter examined the pictures closely to see if he could see "where Jack's fingertip was missing." In Chico, California, Charles's old girlfriend, Hester Grimm, couldn't believe it was Jackson and not Charles who had become "a famous artist." In Cody, Wyoming, skeptical townspeople launched an investigation to determine if Jackson was *really* a native son. In Deep River, Connecticut, Stella Pollock, when asked by a local paper for her reaction to the *Life* article, admitted that she didn't "completely understand" her son's art. In New York, Becky Tarwater (now Mrs. Mason Hicks) saw the article and "felt good for him" but didn't dare send her congratulations for fear of opening up old wounds. Other figures from the past were less reticent. Drs. Wall and Allen wrote from Bloomingdale's, gently inquiring about "what sort of an adjustment" Jackson had made since leaving the hospital, but adding that "the question asked at the beginning of the article can definitely be answered in the positive." Reginald Isaacs couldn't wait for a letter. "In my opinion," he wired *Life*, "Jackson Pollock *is* the greatest painter in the U.S. My enthusiastic opinion is shared by my wife, mother and children."

From throughout the country and overseas, fan mail—there was no other name for it—arrived at the house on Fireplace Road. Utter strangers wrote to thank Jackson for his work—"You [have] mastered the ease and graciousness which is the essence of real art," Daniel McFarland wrote from Durham, North Carolina—and to offer personal commentary: "I like your #12 the best." Some asked for autographs—or more. "Would you please write your name on one of the enclosed cards," asked H. M. Brehm of New London, Wisconsin, "(and maybe dribble a few drops of ink or paint or aluminium on another card) and mail them back to me?" "Would you be good enough to contribute a drawing to my collection of miniatures?" wrote Norman McGrath from Ireland. "The medium may be anything you wish . . . if you can give it a little title so much the better."

The biggest fan of all was Stella Pollock, who wrote batches of letters to family and friends proudly announcing *Life*'s "fabulous write-up" with the "picture that is just swell of him so be sure & get it." For months, however, only Sande openly acknowledged Jackson's newfound fame. Frank, Charles, and Jay remained conspicuously silent.

In Springs, people stopped Jackson in the street to congratulate him. Friends came to the house with copies of the magazine under their arms. For weeks, the article was the touchstone of local conversation. "Everyone in town was talking about the article in *Life*," recalls James Brooks. "They acted differently around [Jackson] after that, they were self-conscious with him." There were, of course, more than a few Bonackers who "weren't ready to admit to themselves that they were wrong," according to Dan Miller. "[They] made peace with themselves by figuring that *Life* magazine was crazier than Pollock."

Publicly, Jackson squirmed becomingly in the spotlight. Visitors to the house in the weeks after the article appeared found him "self-conscious," "nervous," "embarrassed," and "a little ashamed." But privately, he reveled in the attention. "He was delighted to be in print," John Little recalls. Dan Miller described him as "proud." Wilfrid Zogbaum was "willing to bet that Jackson didn't mind having his name linked to the phrase 'greatest living painter.' " When James Brooks and Bradley Tomlin brought a copy of *Life* to the house, Jackson was "so embarrassed that he couldn't read it while we were there," Brooks recalls. But as soon as they left, he arranged to have a hundred copies delivered to his door.

But the *Life* article was merely prelude. The best was yet to come.

Jackson's November 1949 show was both a public and a private triumph. The private one began a week before the opening when Jackson and Lee moved into Alfonso Ossorio's house in MacDougal Alley. Ossorio had gone to the Philippines to paint a mural for a chapel his family was erecting and, in a gracious parting gesture, offered the house to the Pollocks for the winter. Ted Dragon stayed behind, but spent most of every day rehearsing for his debut in Stravinsky's *Orpheus* with George Balanchine at the New York City Ballet. It was a comfortable home, a former coach house for one of the mansions on Washington Square, with a brick and wood interior painted white and filled with potted plants. Upstairs, a large, sun-filled studio with a sleeping loft gave out onto a balcony that Dragon filled with flowers every spring and summer. (When Jackson visited for the first time, he exclaimed, "It's like being in the country.") The downstairs walls were hung with Dubuffets, Ossorio's own sumptuous watercolors and encaustics, and works by Jean Fautrier and Wols (of which Jackson reportedly said, "I don't know where painting is going, but it certainly isn't going that way"). In the living room was a Giacometti sculpture. Ensconced in this casual, countrified elegance (Fritz Bultman called it "Village opulence"), Jackson immediately invited his family to visit. In the week preceding the show, Stella, Sande, and Jay all made the pilgrimage to 9 MacDougal Alley to see Jackson, offer yet another round of compliments on the *Life* article, and assure him that they would attend the opening.

The public triumph was no less gratifying. The *Life* article had created a wave of anticipation, and on the night of November 21, it crested. The crowd filled both rooms of Parsons's little gallery and spilled out into the hallway. Gossamer clouds of cigarette smoke filled the upper reaches of the windowless space. Glasses glinted and clinked and the babble of conversation seemed especially dense and breathless. It wasn't the usual crowd. These were not the friends and fellow artists who normally drifted from one opening to the next in

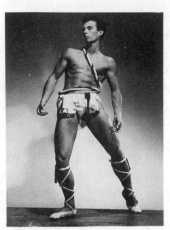

Ted Dragon as Orpheus in a 1950
production of Stravinsky's *Orpheus*

a show of solidarity. These were distinguished-looking men and women—most of them strangers—in tailored suits and designer-label dresses. Milton Resnick, who came with Willem de Kooning, remembers the odd, new feeling that permeated the Parsons gallery that night. "The first thing I noticed when I came in the door was that people all around me were shaking hands," Resnick remembers. "Most of the time you went to an opening, all you saw were other people that you knew, but there were a lot of people there I'd never seen before. I said to Bill, 'What's all this shaking about?' And he said, 'Look around. These are the big shots. Jackson has finally broken the ice.' "

Among the "big shots" was Roy Neuberger, the collector and financier, who stood uncertainly beside Sam Kootz all night; Burton Tremaine, a collector; and Edgar Kaufmann, Jr., the director of design at the Museum of Modern Art. Alexey Brodovitch, the art director of *Harper's Bazaar*, milled around Blake's model of "The Ideal Exhibit," and Dwight Ripley, a wealthy painter-poet-botanist-linguist, hovered around two paintings for a long time, unable to decide between them. (He eventually bought both.) Edward Root, a patrician friend and principle patron of Betty Parsons, spent most of the night talking with Happy and Valentine Macy, two of his social equals in the crowd. Even Alfred Barr was there—the surest sign that the ice had been broken. Only a few months before, Barr had chastised Peter Blake for his enthusiastic support of Jackson in a catalogue introduction he wrote for Bertha Schaefer. "He said he had read my piece and found it 'interesting.' " Blake recalls. "Then he said, 'But I don't think Pollock's work is something we should be supporting.' " Since then Barr had seen the *Life* article and softened his position. "He decided that Pollock was, after all, part of the family tree of modern art."

Jackson stood in the midst of the distinguished crowd, sober and sedated, dressed in a jacket and tie and shiny shoes. "He acted like a businessman," recalls Reuben Kadish. "When a collector would walk in, Jack would pay attention to him." With uncharacteristic aggressiveness, Betty Parsons moved through the crowd, offering special discounts under her breath to "the right names" and anyone else who seemed on the verge of buying. (Even with prodding from Kootz and a price break from Parsons, however, Roy Neuberger resisted paying $1,000 for *Number 8.*) Throughout the evening, Lee sat at the receptionist's desk, handing out reprints of the *Life* article. "She didn't let on she was Mrs. Pollock," recalls one guest. "That way she could get a better sense of people's reactions."

With few exceptions, the critics echoed the enthusiasm of the opening-night crowd. In the *New Yorker,* Robert Coates called the new works "better controlled" and "less strident," with "a depth of feeling and a sense of stricter organization that add greatly to [their] appeal. . . . They seem to me the best painting he has yet done." Amy Robinson struck the same conciliatory tone in *Art News:* "[Pollock] expresses a more intense emotion than ever in his newest pictures," she wrote. "While the closely woven layers of different colored lines appear at first to represent impulsive snapping of all restrictive bonds, including form, it is apparent that there is a definite pattern and feeling in each canvas." Coates and Robinson weren't the only reviewers who, for the first time, felt compelled to explain the *appeal* of Jackson's paintings. Carlyle Burrows, writing in the *Herald Tribune,* attributed their "fascination" to "the simple interplay of their color, combined with line of rhythmic intensity." Stuart Preston argued in the *Times* that color was "Pollock's forte." Where once the critics had joked about Jackson's drip technique, comparing it to "baked macaroni" or "a mass of tangled hair," now they competed with each other to find the most eloquent words to describe it. "Tightly woven webs of paint handled with a sweeping movement of the arm," wrote Robinson. Preston admired the "myriad tiny climaxes of paint and color," each one as "elegant as a Chinese character." Coates complimented the "overlapping swirls and skeins of brilliant color." Since the *Life* article, it seemed, almost every critic had undergone a similar conversion. In his review of the Whitney's "Annual Exhibition of Contemporary American Painting" that began a week after Jackson's show closed, Henry McBride had the courage to confess his reversal straight out. "Previous works by [Pollock] which I had seen looked as though the paint had been flung at the canvas from a distance, not all of it making happy landings. Even the present one has a spattered technic, but the spattering is handsome and organized and therefore I like it."

Not all the commentary was positive. Burrows accused the show of being "repetitious." "Mr. Pollock," he concluded, "is finding it difficult to extend his range in the method of painting he has so confidently developed." Stuart Preston thought the dense webs in the largest works "fail[ed] to add up to an over-all design," and suggested that Jackson work on a smaller scale. And Henry McBride couldn't resist comparing the painting in the Whitney show to a picture of "a flat, war-shattered city, possibly Hiroshima, as seen from a great height in moonlight." But even in criticism, the tone was now respectful; suggestions were offered to be helpful, never abusive. In fact, by the end of 1949, only one publication still held out against the rising tide of Jackson's celebrity. In the December 26 issue of *Time*, Alexander Eliot lashed out at Pollock, Greenberg, and the entire "fashionable and blank" world of avant-garde art. Reviewing the Whitney Annual, he labeled Jackson's *Number 14* a "non-objective snarl of tar and confetti" and warned: "If [his] sort of painting represented the most vital force in contemporary U.S. art, as some critics had contended, art was in a bad way."

But *Time*'s lone voice was barely audible above the congratulatory din. By the time the show closed on December 10, more paintings had been sold than in any of Jackson's previous shows. In addition to the small band of usual patrons (Tony Smith, Ossorio, Dragon, and the Macys), Parsons's sales book recorded a number of new names: Tremaine, Kaufmann, Kimball, Root, Ripley, Price (Vincent Price, a rising star of horror movies and an avid collector). Jackson's strategy of painting large numbers of small works for the timid first-time collector had succeeded almost too well. As one of the opening-night guests commented: "Who wouldn't have been willing to pay a few hundred dollars to have a painting by 'that artist who was profiled in *Life*'?" Even Mrs. John D. Rockefeller, under Alfred Barr's guiding eye, bought one of the small works (*Number 23, 1949*) for her collection—another first. Altogether, eighteen of the twenty-seven works in the show were sold, most of them in the first week, many on the first night. "[Jack] had the best show he has ever had," Stella wrote Frank soon after the show closed. "Eighteen paintings [sold] and prospects of others."

Despite the theatrical enticement of Peter Blake's model showing Jackson's mural-size paintings *in situ*, only two of the show's biggest canvases sold. In early December, however, Blake brought Marcel Breuer to Parsons's gallery, knowing that the Hungarian architect needed a painting for the dining room of a house he was designing for Bertram Geller in Lawrence, Long Island. "Breuer was so impressed," Blake recalls, "that he called the Gellers immediately and secured the commission for Jackson to do a mural" (on the condition that the ground be as close as possible to the commercial rust-colored ground of the 1948 painting, *Arabesque*). Suddenly, everything seemed to be breaking Jackson's way.

The show left Jackson and Lee in such a state of euphoria that they refused to return to the winter drudgery of Springs. Instead, they lingered at the MacDougal Alley house, entertaining friends, touring the gallery shows (Gorky, Buffie Johnson, Richard Pousette-Dart, Herbert Ferber, James Brooks, Mary Callery), and generally reacquainting themselves with city life. Lee wrote Ossorio: "We attended several openings, an educational reception at the museum, an insane dinner party given by a Mr. & Mrs. Lockwood, whom we didn't know, and who weren't there." With Ted Dragon as a guide, Jackson saw his first opera, *Tosca*, his first ballet, *Orpheus*, and his first modern dance performance, by Nick and Merle Marsicano. With the exception of modern dance, which, curiously, he thought "had no sense of progression or style,"

Jackson professed enthusiasm for everything. "If it had to do with music," recalls Dragon, "he loved it. I got him into a rehearsal of the Stravinsky *Orpheus* and he *adored* that. He was absolutely fascinated by the opera." Given such exaggerated, indiscriminate enthusiasm, one wonders which Jackson enjoyed more, the culture itself or the new role of culture *enthousiaste*. He was, after all, *part* of that culture now—a great painter, perhaps the greatest in America. And it became a great painter to appreciate great musicians and perhaps even great dancers. "He used to say, 'I don't know what the hell you're doing out there,' " Dragon remembers, " 'but you know I like it.' " He would listen for hours while Dragon played Chopin, Bach, Beethoven, and Schumann on the piano at MacDougal Alley, and loved to hear Dragon compare Schumann's stormy life as an unappreciated genius to his own. "Schumann was a very difficult man," says Dragon, "and his music, the later pieces, are difficult to like. It was the same with Jackson's art, and when I talked about similarities like that, he just beamed."

Jackson so enjoyed the city high life that he decided to skip the ritual trip to Deep River for Christmas. Lee, who had slipped easily back into the frenetic social pace of the Village, was only too happy to oblige. Never fond of the Pollock relatives, she undoubtedly considered it something of a triumph for her that Jackson no longer needed Stella. In Deep River, Stella took the news stoically, apparently accepting Jackson's explanation that he and Lee were "so tired from being in the City—just worn out." But others in the family suspected a darker explanation: that after the *Life* article and the triumphant show, Jackson no longer had time for his family.

The celebration went on at MacDougal Alley through the holidays and into the new year. Between the new pleasures of celebrity and the constant supply of tranquilizers, Jackson stayed relatively sober and subdued. Ted Dragon remembers the months of house-sharing as "very ordered." "Jackson had very, very little to say," Dragon recalls. "He would be so quiet and then every once in a while he would just come out with these very quiet statements." So confident was Lee of Jackson's new leaf that she didn't seem concerned about the consequences when the news came in March that Dr. Edwin Heller had been killed in an automobile accident in East Hampton. Jackson, too, seemed strangely unmoved at the news. He was on top of the world, and from there, Dr. Heller, like Stella, no longer seemed necessary.

Jackson had not only crossed into a new decade, he had broken through into a new dimension of success. Since the *Life* article, his reputation had taken on a momentum of its own, sustained less by reaction to his current work, or any work, than by the fact of past recognition. Fame had begun to feed on itself. He had become "the *Life* painter," an unignorable presence in the world of avant-garde art, regardless of how or what or whether he painted at all. After years on the social margin, and only months after the debacle at Bertha Schaefer's, invitations poured in, to dinners, parties, openings, symposia, and lectures. Within a relatively short time, he had moved from the periphery to the center of the increasingly fractious avant-garde community. Fellow artists like Robert Motherwell, who for years had dismissed Jackson as, at best, an eccentric, illiterate rustic in the high drama of modern art—the former Benton student in cowboy boots—were suddenly forced not just to acknowledge Jackson, not just to include him in their grand visions, but to seek him out to give those visions legitimacy.

In April 1950, Motherwell, along with Robert Goodnough, Richard Lippold, and Alfred Barr, presided over a three-day closed panel discussion at Studio 35. Jackson, who had returned to Springs in March to begin work on the mural for the Geller house, didn't attend. At the close of the sessions, however, when Adolph Gottlieb suggested that the group protest an upcoming juried competition at the Metropolitan Museum for its anti-abstract bias, Jackson's name quickly surfaced. "He was the only one who had gotten any real attention in the media," recalls John Little. "It was obvious that any protest would mean more if [Jackson] was involved." Gottlieb apparently agreed. From Gottlieb's apartment in Brooklyn, where a meeting was held soon afterward to draft a letter of protest, Barnett Newman called Jackson and asked him to come into the city immediately to sign the letter. Jackson declined the trip but sent a supporting telegram the same day:

I ENDORSED [*sic*] THE LETTER OPPOSING THE METROPOLITAN MUSEUM OF ART 1950 JURIED SHOW STOP JACKSON POLLOCK

The letter, which was sent to Roland L. Redmond, president of the Metropolitan, accused the museum's director, Francis Henry Taylor, of "contempt for modern painting" and claimed that the choice of jurors "does not warrant any hope that a just proportion of advanced art will be included." On May 22, the letter appeared on the front page of the *Times* under the headline "18 Painters Boycott Metropolitan: Charge 'Hostility to Advanced Art.' " The next day, the *Herald Tribune* denounced the protest in an editorial headlined "The Irascible Eighteen." But it wasn't until six months later, when *Life* decided to cover the story, that the group—since dubbed "the Irascibles"—was immortalized. On November 24, 1950, Jackson made a special trip with James Brooks to join fourteen of the eighteen to sit for *Life* photographer Nina Leen at the magazine's studio on West Forty-fourth Street. (*Life* had wanted them to pose, paintings in hand, on the steps of the Metropolitan, but Gottlieb refused, arguing they would look like supplicants rather than protesters. "They were very surprised at this," said Gottlieb, "because nobody refuses anything to *Life*.") It was the second time in two years Jackson had posed for *Life*'s cameras.

The picture of fourteen grave-faced, well-dressed men and one woman, with Jackson roughly in the center looking angry and self-assured, appeared in *Life*'s January 15, 1951, issue, soon after the offending exhibition, "American Painting Today 1950," opened at the Met. Leen's stark, full-page group portrait followed a lavishly illustrated report on the show. The caption was noncom-

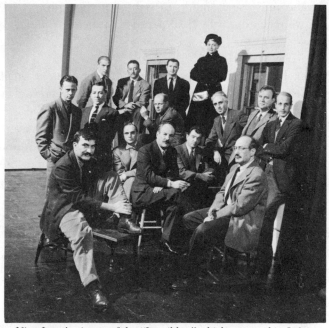

Nina Leen's picture of the "Irascibles," which appeared in *Life* in January 1951. Left to right, front row: Theodore Stamos, Jimmy Ernst, Barnett Newman, James Brooks, Mark Rothko; second row: Richard Pousette-Dart, William Baziotes, Pollock, Clyfford Still, Robert Motherwell, Bradley Walker Tomlin; back row: Willem de Kooning, Adolph Gottlieb, Ad Reinhardt, and Hedda Sterne.

mittal: "Irascible Group of Advanced Artists Led Fight Against Show," but the story, invoking specifics that would be familiar to readers, mentioned "the dribblings of Pollock" in the first paragraph. Even the protesters were surprised by the attention. "All we did was sign this letter," recalls Hedda Sterne, the lone female in the photograph. "Then somebody gave us a name. It was all blown out of proportion." At least one of the eighteen suspected that *Life* saw the story as just "the next installment in the continuing saga of Jackson Pollock, the cowboy painter."

Everywhere the ice of skepticism was breaking up. In the March 1950 issue of *Magazine of Art*, five years after comparing Jackson's work to baked macaroni, Parker Tyler publicly recanted. "[An] impregnable language of image," Tyler now called it, "as well as beautiful and subtle patterns of pure form." Impregnable and pretentious, Tyler's article, "The Infinite Labyrinth," set the tone for much of the woolly, pseudo-poetic criticism that would haunt Pollock's puzzling new images in the years to come.

Pollock's paint flies through space like the elongating bodies of comets and, striking the blind alley of the flat canvas, bursts into frozen visibilities. What are his dense and spangled works but the viscera of an endless nonbeing of the universe? Something which cannot be recognized as any part of the universe is made to represent the universe in totality of being. So we reach the truly final paradox of these paintings: being in non-being.

Not long after Tyler's article appeared, another prominent skeptic, Alfred Barr, chose Jackson as one of six avant-garde artists to represent America at the twenty-fifth Venice Biennale in June. Of course, half of the U.S. Pavilion would still be reserved for John Marin (Barr's conversion was never complete), but the honor was accompanied by a glowing tribute in the summer issue of *Art News*—Barr's first public commendation of Jackson's work. "Perhaps the most original art among the painters of his generation," he called it, ". . . an energetic adventure for the eyes, a *luna park* full of fireworks, pitfalls, surprises, and delights." The encomiums were accompanied by a reception in the MOMA penthouse attended by five of the chosen artists—Pollock, de Kooning, Hyman Bloom, Lee Gatch, and Rico Lebrun (Gorky, dead for two years, was the sixth)—and the eighty-year-old Marin. There, caught in a photograph amid trays of hors d'oeuvres and empty wineglasses (Jackson ostentatiously refused to drink), two artistic eras met: from the past, the cadaverous Marin in long locks and flowing cravat, looking every inch the eccentric *artiste peintre;* from the present, Jackson Pollock, with his square, plebeian jaw and close-cropped hair, looking professorial in tweed jacket, white shirt, black tie, gray flannel slacks, and polished loafers, indistinguishable from the gallery officials and patrons hovering around him. Far from being intimidated by Marin's presence, Jackson seems almost disdainful, while Marin eyes the next generation with a furtive, doubtful glance.

Marin wasn't the only one who still harbored doubts. In a preview of the Biennale for the New York *Herald Tribune*, Emily Genauer lamented that, except for works by Marin, visitors would see "not one single painting by any of the artists who have been recognized by our leading museums, critics, collectors, and connoisseurs as the most creative and accomplished talents in America." Although grossly exaggerated—works by Pollock, de Kooning, and Gorky had been in MOMA's collection for years—such comments alerted European critics to the disarray in the American art community. At a time when it was becoming increasingly difficult to deny New York's postwar artistic eclipse of Paris, European commentators eagerly pounced on the irresolute Americans. Writing in the *Listener,* London critic Douglas Cooper accused the six young American painters represented in the U.S. Pavilion of "mostly imitat[ing] well-known Europeans, with a singular lack of conviction and competence though on a very large scale." Cooper singled out Jackson for special criticism, calling him, with calculated ambiguity, "undeniably an American phenomenon." After summarizing the drip technique, he described the result as "an elaborate if meaningless tangle of cordage and smears, abstract and shapeless," and dismissed Barr's description of the work ("an energetic adventure for the eyes") as "merely silly." Others derided Jackson's paintings as "melted Picasso." A month later, *Time*'s Alexander Eliot gleefully reported the European reaction. "U.S. Painting did not seem to be making much of a hit abroad," he wrote in an unsigned article. "At Venice's 'Biennale,' the U.S. pavilion (featuring the wild and wooly abstractions of Arshile Gorky and Jackson Pollock) was getting silent treatment from the critics."

In fact, while the critics traded obituaries, the paintings themselves touched off an explosion of interest among European painters. Catherine Viviano, a dealer, remembers that scores of young Italian painters returned again and again to the U.S. pavilion, "tremendously excited" by Jackson's three paintings, especially *Number 1, 1948*, the big white canvas with lush purple accents and a row of handprints. "They loved his work," recalls Viviano. "They recognized immediately what a great artist he was." Touring the pavilion with several other Italian painters, Giorgio Morandi said, "They're interesting, these Americans. They jump into the water before they learn to swim." Looking at de Kooning's *Excavation*, he commented, "A little forced. Too much will." The Gorkys on the opposite wall elicited only the remark, "This guy is a little French. *Un po' sordo.* He's a little tone deaf." But when Morandi turned and looked into the second gallery and saw a huge Pollock, he gasped, "Now *this* is new. Such vitality, such energy!" In July, while the Biennale continued nearby, Peggy Guggenheim opened an exhibition of her entire collection of Pollock paintings at the Correr Museum across from San Marco Cathedral. The same painters who had been tantalized by *Number 1, 1948* now had a rare opportunity to see Jackson's work in depth. Arrayed around the paneled walls of the Sala Napoleonica were twenty-three works—twenty oils, including *Number 12, 1949* and *Number 23, 1949*, two gouaches, and one drawing. At night, the illuminated paintings were visible from the crowded piazza and the sight "sent all the Venetian painters mad with excitement," according to Peggy. A commentary by Bruno Alfieri, which had appeared originally in *L'Arte Moderna* with an Italian translation of Jackson's *Possibilities* statement, was reprinted as an introduction in the show's catalogue. At once agitated, indignant and ambivalent, it expressed the challenge that European artists saw in abstract art in general and Pollock's work in particular. "Jackson Pollock's paintings represent absolutely nothing: no facts, no ideas, no geometrical forms. . . . No picture is more thoroughly abstract than a picture by Pollock: abstract from everything . . . no picture is more automatic, involuntary, surrealistic, introverted and pure." It was that very purity, Alfieri complained, that made Jackson's work impervious to traditional criticism. After all, what could a critic say about paintings that were marked by:

- chaos
- absolute lack of harmony
- complete lack of structural organization
- total absence of technique, however rudimentary
- once again, chaos

What emerged from the chaos, Alfieri claimed, was not the art, but the *artist.* "Pollock has broken all barriers between his picture and himself: his picture is the most immediate and spontaneous painting. Each one of his pictures is part of himself." But how is a critic supposed to judge an artist? "What is his inner world worth? Is it worth knowing, or is it totally undistinguished? Damn it, if I must judge a painting by the artist, it is no longer a painting that I am interested in, I no longer care about the formal values contained in it. . . . That is, I start from the picture and discover the man."

From this turmoil of anger and doubt, Alfieri pulled a stunning conclusion: "Jackson Pollock is the modern painter who sits at the extreme apex of the most advanced and unprejudiced avant-garde of modern art. You might say that his position is too advanced, but you may not say that his pictures are ugly. . . . Compared to Pollock, Picasso, poor Pablo Picasso, the little gentleman who, since a few decades, troubles the sleep of his colleagues with the everlasting nightmare of his destructive undertakings, becomes a quiet conformist, a painter of the past."

In Europe, at least, the whispers had begun. Picasso finally had an heir.

Meanwhile, on Long Island, as farmers turned the green ryegrass and the dogwood threatened to bloom early in an unusually warm spring, Jackson continued to ride the tide of celebrity. From Switzerland, Bill Davis sent a ringing tribute: "Of the live painters still working in Europe (the well known ones and figuring Matisse as ½ dead) it has seemed to me during the past three years that very little if any of their stuff is in a class with your work." Even more welcome was the hint of a sale in the same letter ("We're still in the market for additions to the collection"), although Davis seemed to rule out the purchase of a major painting—increasingly the only kind of sale that stirred Jackson's interest. Igor Pantuhoff, passing through on one of his seasonal migrations in pursuit of high society, stopped at Fireplace Road to have dinner and pay homage. In a characteristically extravagant gesture, he pulled a platinum Cartier watch from his pocket and handed it to Jackson. "I want you to have this," he said, "because you're the greatest painter I know."

Everywhere Jackson turned that spring, he heard the same message. Peter Blake, Barr's eager young protégé, came by the studio often to check on the progress of the Geller mural and talk, always in adulatory tones, about the model museum which, since the November show, had languished in a storage room. "I felt very close to him when I was there," Blake recalls. "I was young and naive and he was a great artist making time for me, listening to what I had to say." Although Jackson seldom responded with more than a grunt, Blake, who felt Jackson's work was "spatially wedded" to the Accabonac landscape, was sure those grunts indicated a profound understanding of the "pendant relationship of art to architecture." It may have been Blake who, in an effort to spare Jackson from an awkward confrontation, suggested that he send someone else to the Geller house in Lawrence, Long Island, to install the finished mural in July. The artist who agreed to do the job, Giorgio Cavallon, recalls that Phyllis Geller was "mad as hell. She said, 'This is such a piece of junk and I spent a lot of money.' " It took a week to iron out the creases ("It came folded up like wrapping paper") and attach the 72-by-96-inch canvas to the back of a set of kitchen cabinets facing the dining room. (Years later, when the property was sold, the painting was worth more than the house.)

Another visitor during the pre-summer lull was Tony Smith. With the Geller mural finished and no new works yet begun, Jackson had ample time to indulge Smith's Irish charm and vaguely sexual blandishments. After the collapse of his latest effort to arrange a mural commission, Smith wasted no time in finding some new way to insert himself into Jackson's career. He revived the plans, abandoned the previous summer, for a car trip west to drum up sales. Between recitations from *Finnegans Wake*, musings on Catholic theology, and monologues on art and architecture, he urged Jackson to "do some really big paintings," to return to the scale of the Guggenheim mural, with or without commissions, as a way of showing collectors the potential of mural-size works.

It wasn't until Alfonso Ossorio returned from the Philippines in May, however, that Smith found the opening he was looking for. Having spent the winter with his devoutly Roman Catholic family, Ossorio found the return to secular New York unusually wrenching. At a dinner party hosted by Gerald Sykes and Buffie Johnson, his indignation boiled over. "Can you imagine?" he shouted, pounding the table. "There isn't a single private chapel in all the Hamptons! Not one!" The outburst led to a meeting with Tony Smith, another devout Catholic, at which Ossorio commissioned a design for a private chapel to be built "somewhere on Long Island." Smith urged that Jackson be commissioned to paint murals for the project, and Ossorio, who was always eager to help the Pollocks, enthusiastically agreed. "I was very excited by the enormous possibilities inherent in mural decoration," Ossorio recalls, "and I knew it was one of Jackson's interests, too." For the time being, no one talked about siting or cost or sponsorship. "It was not a specific building for a specific spot," says Ossorio, "it was a brilliantly symbolic idea that could be produced very simply or very grandly. It was a kernel, an acorn, from which trees would grow."

It was a spring of grand visions—an ideal museum, a symbolic chapel, mural commissions out west—to which Jackson added one of his own. Peering through the Plexiglas walls of Peter Blake's model museum at the tiny wire and plaster pieces set amid scaled reproductions of his paintings, Jackson had begun to harbor a new ambition. Soon after arriving in Springs in March, he arranged to use Roseanne Larkin's pottery studio in East Hampton. There, hunched over the little wheel and wearing an apron, he produced a series of small, receptacle-like sculptures in terra-cotta. "They were an attempt to make abstractions in pottery," recalled Lawrence Larkin, "an attempt to get two-dimensional painting into a three-dimensional piece." Larkin remembered that Jackson's hands were "very delicate, but so *big*," working the clay. "He had wonderful control." After only a few sessions, Larkin pronounced him a "great artist."

But after six months of celebrity, being merely a great artist or a great sculptor wasn't enough. Jackson had set his sights higher. He wanted David Smith's title, also conferred by Greenberg, of the *greatest* sculptor in America. "From the start, Jackson's idea was to do sculpture that was going to be greater than David Smith's," recalls Reuben Kadish, "that was going to raise him up that other notch so that he could be both the greatest painter and the greatest sculptor." Whether he was dissatisfied with the results at Larkin's studio or, perhaps, intimidated by David Smith's one-man show at Marion Willard's gallery in April, Jackson abandoned the effort after only a few sessions. Like the other grand visions of the spring, however, the ambition to make his mark as a sculptor continued to haunt him.

Jackson was still having trouble "getting into painting again" when the first summer people began to arrive in mid-April. "The first signs of spring are here," Lee wrote Ossorio, "[and] I don't mean the many things breaking through the earth, or the frogs, or birds, but the early comers." Since the previous summer, the *Life* article and the triumphant November show had moved Jackson from the social margins to the "A" guest list. Old friends eagerly reasserted old claims; mere acquaintances scrambled for a place on Lee's crowded calendar; and the East Hampton elite—most of whom had been, at best, cordial in previous summers—vied for the honor of introducing "the *Life* painter" in their respective circles. In July, even the board of Guild Hall relented and, despite the fisticuffs of the previous summer, mounted an exhibition, "10 East Hampton Abstractionists." Although the show included first-time appearances by Robert Motherwell and James Brooks, all eyes were on Jackson, whose "incomprehensible drippings" had, according to one account, "just emerged in all their threatening glory." Soon afterward, Eloise Spaeth, a prominent East Hampton art patron, organized a "field trip" to Jackson's studio. "We went in a huge bus," recalls one of the guests, Betsy Zogbaum. "The Spaeths invited us to come down because they wanted us introduced to Jackson and his work." On Fireplace Road, Lee, with growing confidence in Jackson's sobriety, threw a cocktail party for the busload of visitors.

On Sunday afternoons throughout the unusually hot and sultry summer, guests chosen from Lee's extensive lists would gather on the aluminum lawn chairs behind the Pollock house for clams and beer. Jackson would lead a small party out into the shallows of Accabonac Creek to dig for lunch while Lee circulated among the guests quoting from the latest reviews and fishing for sales. Returning with a tubful of clams, Jackson would treat the crowd to a display of knifesmanship. "As [we] sat around," one guest later recorded, "Jackson knifed open several dozen clams (with what seemed to be superhuman speed) and placed them in fine order on plates. The movement of knife into shell never faltered. He seemed to open each mollusk with a single jab and slice." Surrounded by admirers, Jackson delighted in such occasions when the roles of celebrity and host merged. "He wasn't a smiler as a rule," recalls Betsy Zogbaum, "but that summer it seemed like he was smiling every time I saw him."

The most prized invitations that summer were to Lee's dinner parties. They were small gatherings, seldom more than eight, a size that allowed Lee to control the conversation and keep an eye on Jackson. The guest lists were a careful mix of painters, potential collectors, and critics, including regulars from previous summers (Clement Greenberg, Peter and Vita Peterson, John and Josephine Little, Gerald Sykes and Buffie Johnson, Valentine and Happy Macy) and relative newcomers (Saul Steinberg and Hedda Sterne, Gina and Alexander Brook, Wilfrid and Betsy Zogbaum, Constantino and Ruth Nivola, Clyfford and Patricia Still, and a young painter from Texas, Joe Glasco). Old friends often brought guests of their own, eager to leapfrog into Jackson's orbit. John and Josephine Little brought Lillian Olaney and Alice Hodges from the Hans Hofmann school. Olaney's earlier hostility toward Jackson, like that of so many other critics, had mysteriously melted since their last meeting. "We were very warm toward each other on that visit," she recalls fondly. Greenberg brought his latest female companion, a young painter named Helen Frankenthaler who had graduated from Bennington the year before. John Myers, an ambitious young writer—whose presence confirmed the Pollocks' new social acceptability—brought Tibor de Nagy, a Hungarian émigré who ran a "professional" marionette theater. The Pollocks were won by de Nagy's European reserve (a perfect foil for Myer's gossipy flamboyance) and, over the summer, arranged a performance for his troupe at a church in Bridgehampton. Jackson also made a marionette—cut out of wood, covered with canvas, and "gaily painted." He also contributed a story about a Pueblo Indian boy called "The Fireboy" that de Nagy adapted into a play. "Jackson loved to tell this story about a little boy who wanted to be initiated into a famous clan," de Nagy remembers, "but he had to do three heroic things before he could become famous."

Despite the rush of socializing, not everyone saw more of Jackson than before. Some old friends were conspicuously missing from Lee's guest lists: Harold and May Rosenberg, Reuben and Barbara Kadish, Roger and Lucia Wilcox, James and Charlotte Brooks—in short, anyone who had known the *other* Jackson Pollock: the pre-1948, pre-tranquilized, pre-celebrated, pre-*Life* Jackson Pollock. "Lee was very full of entertaining and having the *right* people in," says Charlotte Brooks, "so we saw less and less of them." There were exceptions: John Little, whose icy propriety could be trusted and who had a past of his own to hide; Clement Greenberg, who had as much at stake in Jackson's reputation as Lee did. But otherwise, almost all the visitors to Fireplace Road in the summer of 1950 came to see a star.

Inevitably, they saw what they came to see.

"Entering his studio was like entering a shrine," said one of the many admirers who filled the house and studio in an unbroken procession that summer. "There was such concentration. He was there like a monk in his cell. You felt the energy and concentration in the place. You wanted to whisper." They came away talking about Jackson's "aura," describing him as "mystical," "poetic," "awe-inspiring," "illuminating," "other-worldly," and "sparkling." Lillian Olaney thought he had "the intensity of a lover," while another visitor said, "It was as if he were glowing." To Donald Kennedy, a local boy, Jackson was "gentle and imposing like a Brahmin." Almost everyone felt "honored" to be in his presence. One visitor compared him to "some sort of noble animal. Like you went into a cage and you could pet that tiger and look at it and be honored to be with it." Wilfrid Zogbaum approached Jackson "like a student approaching a teacher," and Joe Glasco, the young painter, "talked to him as an older artist and with great respect, nearly a reverence." The spring of grand visions had become a summer of flattery.

Suddenly, everything Jackson said had new meaning, levels of weightiness and perceptivity previously unrecognized. Marta Vivas thought his few contributions to any conversation—"maybe a 'yes,' 'I think so,' or 'I agree' "—were "grounded in another world" and were "the most interesting and profound things said all evening long." So strong and self-confirming was the aura of celebrity that even Jackson's long, tranquilized silences flattered him. "You could tell by the look in his eyes that he was not just following the conversation but furthering it in his mind," says Buffie Johnson. "Not that he came up with any telling remarks really. . . . A sentence or two was about as far as he would go . . . [but] he had a very alive face. He participated without saying a word."

Into Jackson's silences, his admirers eagerly poured themselves, attributing to him at various times a knowledge of Roman mythology, James Joyce's *Finnegan's Wake*, the poetry of William Blake and T. S. Eliot, Joseph Campbell's *Hero with a Thousand Faces*, Freud's *Man and the Unconscious*, the writings of Pico della Mirandola and Alfred North Whitehead, and American literature in general. Some would say he listened to Bach and Vivaldi, others that he cared only for jazz, still others that his special passion was Gregorian chant. Like his paintings, Jackson had become a mirror into which people peered and saw only their own reflections. To the Harvard-educated Ossorio, Pollock was an intellectual; to Jeffrey Potter, a car buff; to Tony Smith, a lapsed Catholic; to Harry Jackson, a true son of the West; to Clement Greenberg, a formalist champion; to Harold Rosenberg, an existential hero. To Leslie Fiedler, a professor of literature from the University of Montana who visited Springs that summer, Jackson seemed "a kind of artistic Mark Twain."

In this process of self-confirmation, Jackson was a willing accomplice; he wanted to be what others wanted him to be. Intuitive, attentive, and hungry for approval, he absorbed just enough from the conversations around him to create the illusion of familiarity: from Tony Smith, a few passages of Joyce; from Ted

Dragon, the names of composers and their works; from Harold Rosenberg and Ralph Manheim, names of philosophers and fragments of metaphysics. Just as he had done in the early forties with Freudian and Jungian psychoanalytic theories, just as he had done more recently with Greenberg's formalist rhetoric, Jackson developed a repertoire of words and phrases and all-purpose generalities that, when framed in long stretches of thoughtful silence, passed for genuine understanding.

In the world beyond Fireplace Road, Lee was his voice—standing at his elbow at parties, smiling, supplying conversation to fill his silences, summarizing the latest review for the huddle of awkward onlookers that invariably gathered around him. "Have you seen Jackson's new work?" she would ask. "It's such a marvelous thing." "Lee always took the initiative in talking to people about Jackson's work," recalls Roger Wilcox. "He would just stand by and listen, taking it all in." At backyard clam picnics, dinner parties, and openings, she exhorted guests to "buy a Pollock drawing; they'll be valuable one of these days." She could be charming and sociable, but business, Jackson's business, always took precedence. "When Jackson had a work in one of my shows, Lee would be very, very friendly," recalls Eloise Spaeth. "But if not, then she wouldn't give me the time of day." On one occasion, seeing a dinner guest admiring a large painting in the living room, she announced firmly: "It's been waiting here, and it's not going to leave until we get ten thousand for it." The guest gasped. On the telephone table, she kept copies of magazines with articles about Jackson. "She had everything arranged," recalls Buffie Johnson. "You always had to get an operator in those days, so you did a lot of waiting on the phone. Meanwhile she had things arranged there, his write-ups, and the magazines would flip open to the exact page. She left nothing to chance, no stone unturned, in publicizing Jackson."

Out of the public eye, Lee guarded Jackson's privacy and protected him from the past with increasing ferocity. Her task was made easier by the proliferating details of his career: the more people who clamored to see him, to come for dinner or visit the studio, the more ruthlessly she screened them. Only Lee issued invitations, and when the telephone rang, only Lee answered it. "She was keeping people away," recalls Vita Peterson. "Only a few could get into his studio where he worked." On the increasingly rare occasions when old friends like Roger Wilcox and Harold Rosenberg came to the door, Lee turned them away perfunctorily. "It would be impossible to create a master," said May Rosenberg, "as long as [Jackson] was also 'one of the boys.' "

If the studio was a shrine, Lee was its high priestess. Even in Jackson's presence, she spoke of him in the third person and always took care to call him "Pollock," not "Jackson," and never "Jack." In the evenings, when he would take out paper and draw for guests, "he would crumple up a piece of this marvelous handmade paper and throw it on the floor," recalls one frequent visitor. "Whence Lee would pick it up, unwad it, press it out, fix it all up, preserve every little effort." For Lee, nothing Jackson did warranted reproach.

"No matter what, she never apologized for him," recalls a friend. If dinner guests arrived and he was still at work, she would announce, "Pollock's in the studio. I'm sorry, but we'll just have to dine alone." If he spent an entire dinner party in embarrassing silence, she would explain: "He doesn't believe in talking, he believes in *doing*." If his insults or profanity offended a guest, she would concede only that he was "being difficult." If he took too many tranquilizers and passed out at a neighbor's house, he was entitled to stay where he was. On one such occasion, he urinated on May Rosenberg's new mattress, but Lee steadfastly refused to apologize. "He can do anything he wants," she insisted. "He's a genius."

When Berton Roueché, an East Hampton neighbor, came to interview Jackson for the *New Yorker* in June, it was Lee who met him at the door and, as she did all visitors, ushered him into Jackson's presence. The two men, both displaced westerners who had already met through Peter Blake, warmed to each other instantly. Ostensibly preoccupied with a boiling pot of currant jelly, Lee hovered around the kitchen table while Jackson "breakfasted" on a cigarette and a cup of coffee. At specific questions about dates and names (when had he moved to Springs?) Jackson invariably turned to her for answers. In a thin show of deference, she would "laugh merrily" before supplying them. "She's a native New Yorker," Jackson bragged, "but she's turned into a hell of a good gardener, and she's always up by nine." Lee, in turn, kept the conversation focused on art ("Jackson's art is full of the West," she said. "That's what gives it that feeling of spaciousness. It's what makes it so American") and on business ("Jackson showed thirty pictures last fall and sold all but five [and] his collectors are nibbling at those"). Later, she shadowed them into the dining room where Jackson showed Roueché some of his paintings. When he couldn't remember the title of a work, she supplied it (*Number 2, 1949*) along with a lengthy explanation ("Jackson used to give his pictures conventional titles . . . but now he simply numbers them. Numbers are neutral. They make people look at a picture for what it is—pure painting"). At the end of the interview, it was Lee, not Jackson, who attempted to summarize Jackson's art: borrowing a phrase from Peter Blake that Roueché would eventually use as the title for the *New Yorker* piece, she described it as "sort of unframed space."

Through the interviews, entertaining, and other distractions of celebrity, the studio had remained quiet since the previous fall. "I've been out to so many parties," Jackson complained to a friend, "I don't feel like a painter any more." For Jackson, whose art always followed closely the ups and downs of his life, the delay was a source of increasing frustration: the triumphs of the previous year had yet to find their way onto canvas. Finally, in late May, still riding the crest of Lee's support, friends' adulation, and public attention, he began to paint again.

37

RECOLLECTIONS OF EARLY CHILDHOOD

When the vast reservoir of ambition and confidence that had been slowly accumulating in the ten months since the *Life* article finally burst onto canvas, the explosion was so powerful that small canvases could no longer contain it. Jackson had to have space.

Tony Smith had exhorted him repeatedly to "think big," arguing that "great art demands an appropriate scale." Peter Blake's model museum sat conspicuously on a worktable in the corner of the studio, its miniature murals and mirrored walls a continual reminder of the possibilities of scale. There was persistent talk of mural commissions in California. (Howard Putzel had been wrong about large paintings: great art on a grand scale *could* be commercially viable. The Geller mural was proof of that.) Meanwhile, Greenberg continued to prophesy the death of the easel picture, and Lee repeated her Wild West rhetoric about the "spaciousness" of Jackson's paintings. Surrounded by talk of size—both of paintings and of reputations—Jackson rolled his bolts of white cotton duck further and further across the studio floor, testing his new confidence in the expanding void.

The first big painting of the summer was *Number 28, 1950*, a dense latticework of aluminum and white over blushes of rose and yellow with thin loops of black meandering across the rigorously all-over field, puddling and smudging, doubling back, thinning almost to nothing, leaving an erratic trail, like explorers lost on a glacier of silver and white. At 5'8" by 8'9", it was the largest canvas Jackson had created since the Guggenheim mural six years earlier. But it was only the beginning. While *Number 28* was still drying, he began another, larger work. Despite the size (7'3" by 9'10"), he worked slowly, close to the surface, spreading thin layers of tan, teal, silver, and white on the unsized canvas, stringing tiny lines and sprays of small drops over a few square feet at a time, then moving on, stepping around the edges, straddling the corners to reach toward the center, until the all-over image began to accumulate in a

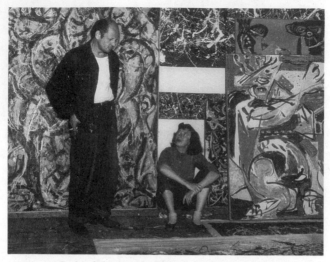

Gothic, left, *Arabesque*, top right, *The Key*, right

series of fine-mesh layers. There were some grand gestures—great thorough-fares of black through the hazy complexity of colors—but after each gesture would come more complexity, showers of blue and ticker tapes of white, dabs of green and cream-colored nebulae barely distinguishable from the raw canvas. As the colors crossed and blended and obscured one another—green into tan across a line of black, white into black with a speck of blue, often mixing wet in wet—new colors emerged: gray-green, pink, and deep purple. In week-long cycles of painting and drying that continued through most of June, the huge image grew both denser and lighter as the skeleton of black lines almost disappeared behind a luminous pastel cloud. Jackson called it simply *Number 1, 1950*, but Clement Greenberg, seeing the painting from a distance, was struck by its lavender glow—the result of the interplay of pink and blue-black—and suggested calling it "Lavender Mist."

Lavender Mist proved that Jackson could work on a *size* canvas commensurate with his new ambitions. Yet, for all its glorious effusive energy and exquisite detail, it was in one way still unsatisfying. Seen even from just across the studio, the delicate lines and loops and sprays of paint he had labored over were obscured in a cloud, the interwoven colors lost in their own halations. More than a single "great" painting, he had created a wall of little ones. Only the size of his canvas had changed, not the scale of his vision. He remained obsessed with concealment, with filling space instead of opening it. For years, he had been obscuring his imagery, abhorring the void: reluctant, except in rare instances, to leave canvas untouched. Always another layer of paint, a few more flicks or lines or puddles or drops to calm the fear that his imagery, his lack of draftsmanship, his demons, any part of himself, would be left exposed. That fear, as deeply rooted in the past as his ambitions, now posed the final obstacle to those ambitions. To make the leap to large-scale paintings—his own measure of greatness—he would have to loosen the veil.

In the next painting, he did just that. With only a broad housepainting brush and a bucket of black enamel, he hurled himself at a 8'10"-by-15' expanse of unsized, unforgiving canvas. Instead of sprays and filagrees, he poured great ropes of black as thick as fists, winding them into dense knots, then out again, across the stark white field to form new knots. Instead of working from one small area to the next, he roamed over the canvas all at once, his arm sweeping behind him as he giant-stepped from one side to the other. On his knees, arm outstretched toward the center, hands black to the wrists, he unfurled thick ribbons of paint in a single gesture, tipping the can of paint as he passed to quicken or slow the flow. The lines rose and fell, twisted and coiled, dividing like arteries or ending abruptly in bursts of black. Where there had been delicate webs, he wound dense, taut, capillary tangles; where there had been pastel clouds, he flooded the line with turbulent pools; even the droplets, flung from a heavily laden brush, fell full, round, and final on the canvas, each one distinct from across the room. This was the calligraphy of arrogance. Not since the Guggenheim mural had he worked so quickly or so confidently, combining —in what became known as *Number 32, 1950*—the calligraphic nuance of earlier, smaller works like *Number 23, 1949* and *Number 26, 1949*, works that explored the drip technique in blown-up detail, with the bravura compositional control of complex paintings like *Number 1, 1948.*

Finally, the vision matched the scale.

In late summer, with that vision firmly in his eye, Jackson completed in quick succession the two largest and, by consensus, greatest paintings of his career. *Number 31, 1950*, later called *One*, was, like each masterpiece of the summer of 1950, bigger than the last. At 8'10" by 17'6", *One* marked both a return to color and a retreat from the black-and-white brinksmanship of *Number 32*. Like *Lavender Mist*, it was a soft web of tan, blue, lavender, and white spinning around a black calligraphic skeleton like the one laid bare in *Number 32*. As in *Lavender Mist*, Jackson created the image through accumulation: layers of paint in infinite variations of line and puddle and interpenetration. Every corner of the vast canvas displays his virtuoso control of the drip technique: thick rivulets of black bordered by thin stains of gray-green and pink, islands of bright blue and teal overlain with threads and specks of pure white, each color and form, to the tiniest fleck, miraculously distinct and assured. Yet, for all the similarities of color and style, the scale is radically changed. The deep skeins in *One* don't merge into solids as they do in *Lavender Mist*; the colors don't dissolve into pastel clouds. The skeleton of great dancing loops beneath the web remains clearly visible, tying the vast image together in a single long-winded calligraphic statement.

But it wasn't until the next, and last, major painting of the summer, *Number 30, 1950*, later called *Autumn Rhythm*, that Jackson was able to combine the naked simplicity of *Number 32* with the reassuring complexity of *Lavender Mist*, his aspirations to greatness—and the scale appropriate to them—with his need to conceal. Like the miniature murals in Peter Blake's model museum, which

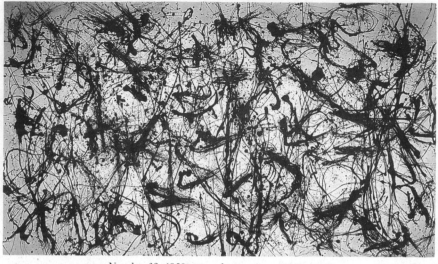

Number 32, 1950, enamel on canvas, 8'10" × 15'

he gazed at for hours, *Autumn Rhythm* looks as though it had been conceived and executed all at once by some giant hand. A cat's cradle of black stretches across the entire 17'8" expanse of unsized canvas; heavy lines run in unbroken arcs from top to bottom, almost nine feet, while smaller lines fling themselves halfway across the canvas in great aerial loops. Wisps of white and tan float through the loose fabric of black without obscuring it. Sprays of teal blue, only a few, insinuate themselves at the margins. Raw canvas breaks through everywhere. Jackson had finally found a new handwriting, one with the scale and openness to serve his grand ambitions even as it continued to conceal the inspired unspooling of memories that gave each larger-than-life loop its pitch and moment.

In achieving scale, however, Jackson had lost much else. The bilious yellow of the Guggenheim mural, the acidic green of *Full Fathom Five*, and the harsh orange of *Tiger* had been replaced by the easy pinks and creams and blues of *Lavender Mist*; the jarring rhythms of *Circumcision* and *White Cockatoo* by the assured balance of *Number 32*; the fiery insistence of *Number 5, 1948* by the unmitigated loveliness of *One*; the dark Ryderesque tangle of *Alchemy* and *Lucifer* by the lucidity of *Autumn Rhythm*. At the moment of its greatest triumph, Jackson's art had betrayed its greatest weakness. In reaching for scale and control, he had lost the unruliness of his vision, the critical core of torment that had propelled his art for two decades. After three years, pouring, dripping, and flinging paint had become too easy: the paint submitted too readily, the lariats landed where they were flung, the lines thickened and thinned, ebbed and flowed too obediently.

As early as the previous summer Jackson had shown signs of uneasiness with the drip technique. In paintings like *Out of the Web, Number 13, 1949, Number 6, 1949,* and *Small Composition,* he had begun to explore new directions, escape

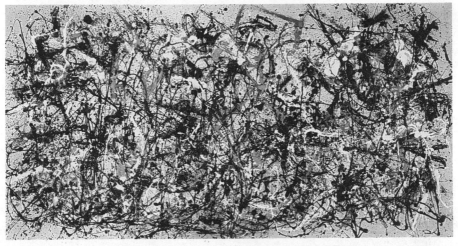

Autumn Rhythm (Number 30, 1950), 8'10½" × 17'8"

routes from what was often, even then, an exercise in composition and color. Rough biomorphic shapes, brushwork, and texture reappeared. He experimented with materials. But the *Life* article and the success that followed had cut off escape. Instead of moving on, he was drawn back into an easy style that increasingly threatened to turn into a rote exercise. As early as 1940, Bill Baziotes had warned Jackson about just such a trap, and the word that he used, "phony," was more and more in Jackson's conversations, its full implications muzzled only temporarily by the celebrity-driven obsession with scale.

Outside the studio, the gifts of success proved equally ambiguous. The tide of celebrity was too strong for Jackson to resist, his roots in reality too shallow, his childhood needs too deep. Beset by admirers, protected from criticism, and cut off from the past, he soon succumbed to the adulation that swirled around him. Years of insecurity and self-doubt dissolved, leaving only a spoiled child eager to claim center stage. When David Smith came to visit in midsummer, Jackson announced confidently: "Look, Dave, you're the best sculptor and I'm the best painter." To Grace Hartigan he bragged, "Everyone's shit but de Kooning and me." Some thought even the references to Smith and de Kooning were only a pretense of modesty. "At bottom, [Jackson] thought everybody stank but him," Betty Parsons later recalled. "He thought he was the greatest artist ever."

As the greatest, he owed debts to no one. He gave up going to museums to see the old masters because, according to Clement Greenberg, "he didn't want to repeat their mistakes." "I showed Jackson a book of colored reproductions of Rubens landscapes," Greenberg recalled. "He looked through it and said, 'I can paint better than this guy.' " Greenberg was "pissed and appalled." So was Peggy Guggenheim when Jackson stopped sending her announcements and reviews. "I gathered Pollock was becoming very important in America," she

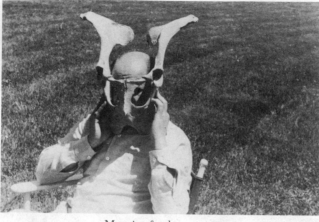

Mugging for the camera

wrote, ". . . but he is so ungrateful that they never even answer letters or thot [*sic*] to send me *Life* magazine." (In fact, in preparation for the *Life* article, Jackson had specifically requested that Peggy's early support not be mentioned.) When, in May 1950, Sam Kootz offered to show paintings by the Irascible Eighteen, Jackson led the refusal. Tony Smith had convinced him that his works deserved to be seen "in large scale," that for them to be framed and treated merely as art objects in Kootz's small gallery would diminish them and reduce his stature as a great artist. The message was clear: just as he no longer needed Rubens or Picasso, Jackson no longer needed Guggenheim, Kootz, or even Parsons. More and more, he left dealing with them to Lee. "He didn't want to stoop to such things," says Hedda Sterne. "They bored him."

It was in the midst of this deepening obsession with his image as a great artist that Jackson met a young photographer named Hans Namuth. A refugee from Germany whose reaction to the November Parsons show had been "hostile," Namuth, too, was more interested in Jackson's image than in his art. It was only because Alexey Brodovitch, his teacher at the New School and art director at *Harper's Bazaar,* called Pollock "the most important artist around today" that Namuth approached Jackson at the opening of "10 East Hampton Abstractionists" at Guild Hall on July 1. Namuth's family had rented a house in nearby Water Mill, and he needed a photographic project for the summer. "I thought it might be a good idea," he suggested to Jackson, "if you let me come and photograph you while you are painting." Jackson not only agreed but promised to start a new painting especially for Namuth's visit.

One weekend soon afterward, Namuth arrived at the Fireplace Road house with two loaded Rolleiflexes. Lee and an exhausted-looking Jackson met him at the door. "I'm sorry, Hans," Jackson said, "there's nothing to photograph because the painting is finished." Crestfallen, Namuth followed them to the studio where a freshly painted canvas covered the floor. After a few moments of silence, according to Namuth's story, Jackson picked up a can of paint and began to work again—"as if he suddenly realized the painting was not finished." For the next half-hour, Jackson flung paint on the canvas while Namuth's camera clicked, pausing only once every two rolls for reloading. When Jackson finished, Lee, who had watched the entire performance approvingly, flattered the young photographer with a bold lie: "[She] told me that until that moment," Namuth wrote, "she had been the only person who ever watched him paint."

In fact, the Pollocks were courting Namuth. For Lee, the promotional value of his dramatic shots of Jackson at work seemed worth the "annoyance" of his unwelcome intrusions and Teutonic hauteur. (As usual, she was right: within a year, Namuth's pictures would appear in *Portfolio*, a glossy, large-format "annual of the graphic arts.") After reviewing the contact sheets from the first session, she granted Namuth virtually unlimited access to the studio—an unprecedented privilege. In July and August, he returned several times, taking more than five hundred photographs over the course of the summer, working "whenever Pollock was in the mood."

For Jackson, these sessions and the photographs they produced were yet further proof of his claim to greatness. Only two summers before, he had watched as Herbert Matter, another photographer, made a film about Alexander Calder. "At that time he was reluctant to be photographed," Matter recalls, "but he followed the whole development of the Calder film and was very excited by it." Now it was Jackson's turn in the viewfinder. Far from ignoring the camera, as Namuth and others later claimed, he reveled in it. As Namuth moved around the studio, lying on the floor, standing on a ladder, dangling from the loft door, kneeling beside the canvas while Jackson worked, the solitary creative act became a historic event. In the narrow alleys of uncluttered floor around the huge canvas, Namuth jockeyed to find the right angle, the right light, and to avoid the flying lariats of paint. Unimpressed by the art, he focused his camera on the artist instead. Jackson's motions were, as always, "careful and deliberate," but by slowing the exposure to 1/25 of 1/50 of a second, Namuth could create the illusion of speed and impetuous energy—a simple flick of the wrist to stop the flow of paint from a stick could be transformed into an urgent blur; a step onto the canvas into an inspired lunge; an awkward sidestep into a spontaneous jig; a momentary glance into a trance-like glare. Namuth, whose childhood ambition was to be a stage director, didn't have to direct; Jackson was an intuitive, compliant actor. He and Lee had reviewed every picture and understood the illusion Namuth was trying to create. "The proofs," said Namuth, "then as today, reveal a collaboration."

Outside the studio, away from the props of paint and brushes, Namuth took a series of portraits. In all of them, the mood was set and the image dominated by Jackson's face. "His face was the reason I learned to like him sooner than I learned to appreciate his work," Namuth later wrote. It was a weathered, melancholy face—handsome once—with the look of a local gray-shingled farmhouse too long exposed to the ravages of the South Fork's sea winds and winter storms: permanently knotted brow; deeply creased and drooping jowls;

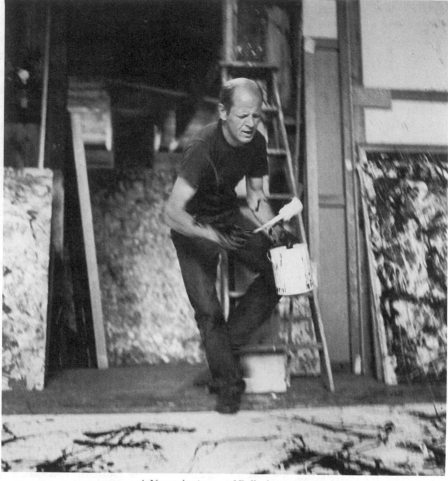

A Namuth picture of Pollock at work

sunken cheeks and a sinewy neck that betrayed the wasting effects of tranquilizers, cigarettes, and endless cups of coffee. Jackson's poses, arranged by Namuth, underscored the twin themes of distress and dissipation: sitting on the
running board of the battered Model A staring broodingly into the middle
distance, leaning against the weathered wall and peeling paint of the studio,
lying in the uncut grass staring into the sky, or turning over to gaze at the
ground. This was the other half of the image Namuth and Pollock were creating together: the great artist paying the price of greatness. A later commentator
called them portraits of "a tormented, agonized man, torn by self-doubt, the
victim of an inner *Sturm-und-Drang* nakedly revealed in his contorted face.
. . . The picture of the romantic Genius, possessed by demonic *terribilità.*" This
was the other side, equally contrived, of the blur of motion around the canvas,
the trance-like dance, the lunges and parries of Jackson at work as choreographed by Namuth's camera. Their air of postcoital lassitude, of exhaustion
and withdrawal, only complemented the illusion of "superhuman energy" and

cathartic outpouring. Here was the artist caught in rare repose, cooling like a burned-out crater between creative explosions.

It was by no means the first time Jackson had posed for the camera. From the day he first put on Charles's cap and work shirt, or grew his hair long like Krishnamurti, or dressed up in vest and cane, or stood for a camera in buckskin jacket and cowboy hat, Jackson had been creating images of himself, posturing earnestly for a posterity that he must have believed would someday take note. Now, under Namuth's direction, he was creating the role of the great American artist. The cowboy boots and ten-gallon hats he had shared with Sande at the Art Students League were gone, but the exaggerated masculinity and western ethos of the "Wyoming Kids" remained. "He loved to be the macho kid," recalls Ted Dragon. "It was always the blue dungarees, work shirt, rough and tumble—anything to offset the idea of the effete artist, with the flowing ties and the smock and the beret."

Inspired by his sessions with Namuth, Jackson became obsessed with the subject of the artist as actor. Frequently during the summer of 1950, he quizzed friends like John Little, Clement Greenberg, and Harold Rosenberg on the "persona" of the modern artist, collecting fragments of a portrait like pieces of a puzzle to be assembled at the next session before Namuth's lens. Penny Potter, a patron of theatrical companies and sometime actress, remembers "long, complicated conversations" in which Jackson asked about "creating a character role." "He was interested in what it was to be an actor," Potter recalls. Out of camera range, Jackson spent much of the summer rehearsing his new role: grumbling borrowed profundities and Bentonesque profanities; torturing guests with long silences and enigmatic stares; lacing his rare comments with references to sheep ranchers, cattle rustling, city slickers, and Indian lore; ridiculing the privileged eastern backgrounds and refined sensibilities of fans like Tony Smith, Jeffrey Potter, and Peter Blake; roaming the country roads around Springs in his Model A as if he were back in the sagebrush hills around Riverside with Sande, acting out—on a new, far grander stage—the old, irreconcilable fantasies of fence-post cowboy and sensitive artist.

For Jackson, fame was a second childhood, a chance to replay his past to a larger, more attentive, and far more indulgent audience.

Roger Wilcox remembers driving down Georgica Road with Jackson that summer and stopping in front of a house owned by William Seligson, a rich East Hampton businessman. It was a formal mansion, set on a vast, unbroken expanse of lawn. "Ten acres of flat perfection," according to Roger Wilcox, "no trees, no shrubbery, just perfect, flat lawn." "Did you ever see such a lawn?" Jackson gasped, gazing at the immaculate swath of green. "It's a god-damn green canvas. God, I'd like to paint on that." Later the same summer, after several days of rain and drizzle, he drove back to the Seligson house and onto the lawn. The Model A's tires sank deep in the soggy grass, leaving long

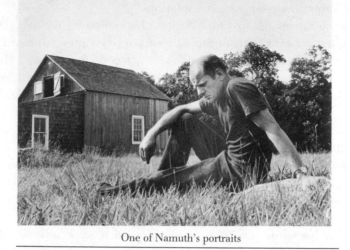

One of Namuth's portraits

mud ruts in the green perfection. "He drove all over that lawn and made his marks," Wilcox recalls. By the time he was finished and drove away, the lawn was crisscrossed with swirling black lines beginning to silver with rainwater.

When the police identified Jackson as the likely vandal, Seligson, a "stern, serious man with a big-shot look," drove to Fireplace Road for a confrontation. To his astonishment, Jackson blithely confessed. "He simply told him it was the world's biggest painting," says Wilcox, recounting the story Jackson told him. When Seligson complained that it would cost $10,000 to repair the damage and insisted Jackson pay for it, Jackson suggested that he leave it as a work of art. He even offered to return and sign it, adding, "then you can pay *me*." (When Seligson saw that Jackson couldn't possibly raise the money, he dropped the charges.) Lee, like Stella, dismissed the incident and others like it, calling them merely signs of Jackson's growing "assuredness."

At his critics, Jackson lashed out with petulant fury. In June, when Emily Genauer's article on the Venice Biennale appeared in the New York *Herald Tribune*, he stewed for days. John Little found him on the beach "agonizing" over a crumpled copy of the paper. "He was trying to decide what to do," Little recalls. "He had all sorts of nasty things he wanted to say in response, but all he said was 'I'll have to do something for her.'" A week later, Jackson bragged that he had sent the prim, rectitudinous Genauer a pair of lace panties with a note that suggested she needed "a good lay." Several months later, when *Time* reproduced a few unflattering fragments from Bruno Alfieri's Italian review under the headline, "Chaos, Damn It!" Jackson again reacted with exaggerated indignation, firing off a blistering reply to *Time* and complaining to a friend, "It isn't just me they're after. What they want is to stop modern art."

Jackson had always had a taste for the best, even in the worst of financial times, but now, as a celebrity, he *deserved* the best. On a trip to New York with

Tony Smith, he suggested dinner at the Stork Club. "Come on, Jackson, we can't get in there," Smith protested. "You don't have a tie. They won't let you in." But Jackson insisted, "I can get in." "On what basis?" Smith asked. "On the basis of my reputation," Jackson shot back. On the next visit, he set his sights on the "21 Club." Whether or not he succeeded in these attempts is not recorded, but on many similar occasions he was unceremoniously ejected.

Another regular stop on Jackson's increasingly frequent trips into the city was the row of expensive men's stores along lower Sixth Avenue. Lionel Abel remembers seeing him there "looking very dapper. He dragged me into the store with him," Abel recalls. "I didn't have any money at all at the time, and I had to watch him try on three or four suits, one after the other—and buy them all." Friends like Willem de Kooning noticed that Jackson "began to dress with a great style" about this time, favoring especially fine Scottish tweeds. By the time of the November show, choosing clothes had become a "ritual," according to Ted Dragon. "My God," says Dragon, "he had to have the right sport coat with the right cut and the correct tie and the right chino pants and the perfect loafers. And everything had to be the best quality."

The same was true of everything from kitchen implements to canned goods to cuts of meat for Sunday barbecues (Porterhouse only). Jackson even complained to Betty Parsons about the poor quality of most exhibition catalogues and insisted that his own be "printed on paper coated on one side (photo side) and soft on the reverse," because "it makes a very pleasant shape and size." For his own materials, he abandoned the cheap house paints he had been buying from Dan Miller and began ordering advanced acrylics from the New York paint maker Leonard Bocour, a pioneer in the development of acrylic paint. "It was expensive," Bocour remembers, "like forty or fifty dollars in the cadmium reds. He'd buy a gallon of this and a gallon of that. Seven or eight colors would come to three or four hundred dollars. But he never seemed to be concerned about the cost." He never was—whether playing poker, grabbing checks, paying for cabs, leaving tips, or lending money to friends. "Jackson was a good poker player because he didn't give a shit," recalls a friend. "Money meant nothing to him."

Soon after the *Life* article appeared, Jackson looked at the battered Model A parked in his driveway and asked Tony Smith if a great artist didn't deserve a better car. "What the hell kind of car do you want?" Smith asked. "Oh, I don't know," Jackson mused, "maybe a Cadillac or something."

Yet to the outside world, Jackson and Lee continued to maintain the pretense of poverty. Lee knew that for patrons like Alfonso Ossorio, who enjoyed seeing themselves as all that stood between the Pollocks and destitution and who served as a reliable safety net for Jackson's excesses, the appearance of impoverishment was a crucial asset. To offset Jackson's fine tweeds and chinos, she eschewed new clothes entirely, ostentatiously wearing the same "pathetic cloth coat" for several years. And even as Jackson consulted Peter Peterson on "how he should invest all his money," she continued to accept gifts of food brought by Ossorio out of sympathy for the "lamentable borderline existence" of a great artist.

Other than Lee, the only person who knew the full extent of Jackson's secret extravagance was Betty Parsons. By the end of the 1949–50 gallery season, she had sent the Pollocks checks totaling $3,174.89 on sales of $4,750. In June, the total jumped to $4,741.55 with a payment from the Museum of Modern Art for *Number 1, 1948* and, in July, to $5,841.55 with the final payment for the Geller mural. Sometime that same summer, Sam Kootz finally persuaded Roy Neuberger to pay the full asking price of $1,000 for *Number 8, 1949* and the total reached $6,508.23. (Ironically, it was Kootz's harping on the Pollocks' supposed poverty that clinched the sale.) At a time when the average blue-collar worker earned $2,800 in a year and the average white-collar worker only $3,500, and the mortgage payment on the Fireplace Road house was only about $20 a month, $6,500 was a solid, even bourgeois, annual income, and gross sales of over $10,000 put Jackson among the most profitable artists in America—certainly the most profitable avant-garde artist. In addition, as Parsons well knew, the Pollocks routinely supplemented their income and avoided paying commissions by bartering paintings for everything from kitchen appliances to dental services. Nevertheless, Jackson continued to plead poverty and badger Parsons to raise his prices. When Andrew Ritchie offered $1,000 for *Lucifer* (1947), Jackson defied Parsons and held out for $1,600, arguing, "I'm very fond of this painting—and this price is nearer to the price on my later work." The sale fell through.

In June, the battle broke into the open. "I am going to try and get some mural commissions thru an agent where I will pay a commission and that I feel it would be unfair for me to pay *two* commissions," Jackson wrote Parsons. "I feel it important for me to broaden my possibilities in this line of development. But any painting shown in your gallery and mural commission gotten by you —you will receive *your* commission. I hope you will find this satisfactory—I feel it is the only hope for me to get out of my financial mess, and also to develop in this direction." Parsons, in fact, did *not* find the proposal satisfactory and said so in unequivocal terms by return mail.

> I want, as you know, to be fair, as I am sure you want to be with me. Also, my experience has been that any artist that undertakes his own business, is inevitably taken advantage of. . . . As for a commission, I have discussed this kind of problem with a number of dealers and they all unanimously agree that as I pay all of your expenses, have built you up, as the market is limited, and since I am the only gallery that can show big pictures related to murals, I must take a commission.

Strapped for money herself, Parsons accused Jackson of being "extravagant" and living virtually "rent-free" off her predecessor Peggy Guggenheim's largesse.

But even Parsons didn't know what had happened to the thousands of dollars she sent to the Pollocks during 1949 and 1950. Harris tweeds, Porterhouse steaks, and penny-ante poker could account for only a fraction of it. All she knew was that somehow, somewhere, Jackson had found a way to spend money, an unseen hole down which he had poured thousands of dollars in less than a year.

The hole was his house. Between the winter of 1948–49 and the summer of 1950, almost every dollar that Jackson earned went into repairing, remodeling, furnishing, and decorating the Fireplace Road property. At first, there were old debts to pay off. He had started the work long before he could afford it. As early as the summer of 1948, Grace Hartigan remembers how he would "take Harry [Jackson] around the property and talk about all the plans he had for the place and what he wanted to do with it." When neighbors like John Little and Betsy Zogbaum opened up their old houses, Jackson couldn't resist any longer. In early 1949, still destitute, he began tearing out partitions between the dining room and the kitchen and the hall and stairs with the help of a local handyman and retired circus clown, George Loper. Jackson approached the job with childlike relish. "If you ran into a beam or something," recalls another local workman, "you'd say, 'Hey, Jackson, there's something in my way,' and he'd get a sledgehammer and knock it out of there." Before long, Jackson's enthusiasm outran his judgment. A workman arrived at the house one morning to find the second floor sagging ominously. "If we'd had a strong wind," he recalls, "the whole second floor would have been in the living room."

The following summer, only a few months after the white paint had dried and Lee's begonias and ferns had begun to thrive in the bright new open space, Jackson returned with his sledgehammer to install heating and plumbing. The Pollocks had suffered the discomforts of cold water and the vagaries of coal stoves for four years, and that, Jackson had decided—despite the continuing lack of funds—was long enough. With Ed Hults and Dick Talmage, two Bonackers who had worked on John Little's house, he laid plans for a new full bathroom upstairs with all new fixtures and white tile, new fixtures in the bathroom downstairs, new pipes, new radiators, and a new boiler. Hults and Talmage, who had just opened their business, were excited by the potentially lucrative job and willing to work cheap, especially in winter when work was scarce, but skeptical of Jackson's solvency. "I told him I'd be glad to advance the labor," recalls Hults, "if he came up with the couple of thousand for materials. I didn't want to get stuck." By now the *Life* article had appeared, however, and with it, the first signs of prosperity. Within a few days, Jackson produced the "couple of thousand" and, over the next few months, another thousand or more for the labor.

Even before the old debts were paid off, however, Jackson began work on the studio: shingling and roofing, running a new cold-water line from the house, replacing the old wiring so he could run his new motorized paint mixer, and hanging fluorescent lights with the help of Elwyn Harris, a local electri-

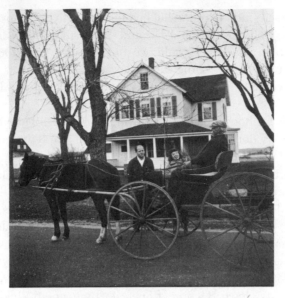

The Pollocks in front of their house in Springs, c. 1949

cian. As always, Jackson contacted, negotiated with, and supervised the workmen himself. Few of them ever saw Lee. Jackson left the dealers, collectors,
and the art to her; and, except for the plants and a few decorative touches, she
left the house to him.

Outside, he planted shrubs and new flower beds, enlarged the garden, secured a small tractor to mow the lawn, and installed a pump in the garden to
make watering easier. He also began to look with his newly acquisitive eye at
the surrounding property. "He wanted to build a good studio, to add to the
house, to get more land," said Tony Smith. "He was talking about substantial
additions, real investments." When he discovered that a small wooded lot
abutting his property had recently changed hands, he flew into a rage. "He
came into my office and lit into me and called me all the fuckin' this and
fuckin' that," recalls Ed Cook, the local real estate agent who had bought the
land. "I had this old-lady bookkeeper, seventy-five years old, and here he was
shouting all these uncouth things, giving it to me right and left. Finally I got so
mad I said, 'You get the hell out of here and don't you ever come back.' "
(Cook eventually conveyed half the land to Jackson in exchange for a painting
that his mother-in-law wouldn't allow in the house because she "couldn't sleep
under the same roof with it.")

Inside, Jackson repainted all the walls—white downstairs, yellow and white
in the guest room—and began to edit the eclectic array of furniture that had
accumulated in ten years of hard times, including everything from battered
wicker chairs brought from the Eighth Street apartment to a huge round
kitchen table donated by the Macys. Through the summer, he frequented local
stores and flea markets in search of acquisitions. Jane Graves, who had opened
an antique shop in East Hampton, recalls how he admired an expensive French

Provincial sideboard in her window. "He came inside to ask how much it was," Graves remembers, "and I got the feeling he would have bought it no matter what the price, but it wasn't for sale." He did, however, buy twin beds for the guest room, along with a wooden chest for blankets, a mirror, dresser, and chairs. Whenever furniture arrived at the house, he would spend hours arranging and rearranging, moving and surveying, until every detail was just as he wanted it. "He did it all himself," recalls Roger Wilcox, "and he made a beautiful house out of it."

Fame and prosperity had allowed Jackson the ultimate fantasy: to play Stella Pollock. Like Stella, he lavished attention on his house, making it his own, as if by decorating he could pile up a barricade of identity against a lifetime of emptiness and impermanence. For Jackson, the house was a way, as effective as distance or speed, to keep the demons at bay, to escape the noisy fear that his success was somehow a mistake—at best a fluke, at worst a fraud; that the spring of grand visions and summer of flattery would turn out to be as cruel an illusion as Stella's mothering; that his fans would prove ultimately as uncaring as his family, his fellow artists, beneath their deference, as resentful; and that his second childhood would end, like his first, in betrayal and abandonment.

In October, Jackson finally got the car he deserved: a dark blue 1947 Cadillac convertible. "Oh, how he gloried in that secondhand Cadillac!" said Berton Roueché. "It was a status thing. . . . [He] didn't want to maintain the Model A humility." With its fish-tail rear lights and lance-like bumpers, the Cadillac was every bit as gaudy, noisy, and distracting as the fame that had made it possible—and, in Jackson's hands, every bit as dangerous.

38

A CLAM WITHOUT A SHELL

The East Hampton dump lay about two and a half miles north of town at the end of a gravel spur off Accabonac Highway. It commanded the crest of a hill with a spectacular view of Gardiners Bay. From the edge of the dump, on a clear evening, one could see as far as the Connecticut coastline, and the breeze off the bay blew the overripe smells southeast, toward the potato fields and away from the road. It was a lonely, unexpected place with an oblique charm few summer people appreciated. Except on weekend afternoons, when most locals did their dumping, visitors were rare. Late on a summer night in 1950, not even the gulls, who scavenged there during the day, were around to watch as a Model A pulled off the highway and crunched to a stop at the end of the gravel spur. Inside were Jackson Pollock and Clement Greenberg.

They had left the party together. Without a word, by an unspoken understanding, they had recognized a mutual need to get away. "I didn't tell him I was depressed," Greenberg remembers. "I didn't have to—he sensed it." And Greenberg sensed that Jackson was terrified. He had seen Jackson in gatherings before, especially since the *Life* article appeared, gatherings of flatterers and admirers, sycophants and skeptics, gatherings in which he "looked like he wanted to crawl into a corner somewhere." He had heard him complain, eyes lowered, "I feel like a clam without a shell." "They didn't see the man or the genius," Greenberg remembers. "They saw only a freak." Jackson confided in Penny Potter that "sometimes he felt as if his skin had been taken off." It was the *Life* article that was at the root of his fears. Jane Graves recalls him in a moment of panic wishing it had never appeared. It had satisfied his old craving for approval and attention, but it had also stirred an even older fear. "They only want me on top of the heap," he told Denise Hare, "so they can push me off."

That night, the fear had driven him to the town dump with Clement Greenberg. "He said he'd had a terrible nightmare," Greenberg later told a friend about that night. "He was at the edge of this cliff and his brothers were trying to push him off."

That same summer in Iowa City, Iowa, less than two hundred miles from Tingley, the huge mural Jackson had painted for Peggy Guggenheim's apartment entrance hung in the mural studio at the University of Iowa. Peggy had tried to give it to Yale before returning to Europe, but the offer was spurned. Now it was suspended high up near the ceiling of the cavernous studio, poorly lit, noticed only by art students like Cile Downs who gave it an occasional, derisive glance. The rafters above it were also home to a covey of sparrows that "let go their droppings all over it," Downs remembers. "We thought that was appropriate. In fact, we laughed about how it was getting better and better with every plop." In Washington, D.C., a young painter named Gene Davis decided he couldn't afford the Pollock painting he had bought at Parsons's gallery and took it to the mailroom at the office where he worked to be wrapped and returned. "The attendants laughed when they saw it," Davis recalls. "They said it looked like bird droppings." And at the Betty Parsons Gallery in New York, an anonymous visitor left an angry note in the guest book: "Parsons must be nuts to insult the great name of art with crap. It isn't funny any more. This is the stupidest crap I have ever seen. Shit to Pollock."

Far from converting Jackson's critics, the parade of publicity following the *Life* article had driven most of them either to open ridicule or to clandestine resentment. It was easier to cope with the former: the letters to *Life* suggesting that a child could do better; a letter from a man in West Palm Beach, Florida, who claimed he created better abstract paintings by cleaning his brushes on the garage door; another from a would-be master in Arlington, Virginia, who claimed that he could out-Pollock Pollock "at the rate of one every five minutes." The article's lead question had triggered a deluge of derisive mail, which *Life* gleefully published:

Sirs:
Is Jackson Pollock the greatest living U.S. painter? No!
　　　　Frank Carselli, Holley, N.Y.

Sirs:
. . . Is he a painter?
　　　　Fred Boshaven, Jr., Grand Rapids, Mich.

Sirs:
Why use the word "living" so loosely?
　　　　Peggy Dobbratz Abernethy, Vergennes, Vt.

Jeannette Rattray, the editor of the East Hampton *Star*, openly defying the celebrity madness that had swept Jackson into social acceptability among the Guild Hall set, wrote in a 1950 editorial that her five-year-old niece "had spilled a bucket of paint over a piece of canvas and that the result was hailed as 'one of Pollock's best.' " When Jackson read the article, Roger Wilcox remembers, his only comment was "Well, the world is full of worms pretending to be people." But the criticism definitely "stirred him up," according to Wilcox. "All this stuff came down to Jackson's work being a deliberate sham, a put-on, and he was always sensitive about being called a phony."

Behind closed doors, dealers and reviewers who were reluctant to criticize Jackson openly contributed to the undercurrent of ridicule. Alfred Barr, who had praised Jackson's paintings in print and supported the museum's purchase of *She-Wolf*, continued to snipe in private, criticizing "the decorative qualities of the internecine all-over pattern" and dismissing those of his colleagues who claimed to find more serious meanings in Pollock's work. Curt Valentin stood by his earlier assessment that if Pollock was good, *he* was blind, and Charlie Egan took Clement Greenberg aside to ask: "You don't really take Pollock seriously, do you?" Others favored the more circumspect approach of William Shawn, editor of the *New Yorker*, who rejected Berton Roueché's proposal to turn his interview with Jackson into a full-fledged profile, saying, "Let's wait and see what happens to his reputation."

It was inevitable that the ridicule and resentment would eventually penetrate the cordon Lee had thrown around Jackson. She couldn't protect him from plain-spoken Bonackers like Ed Cook who, along with many locals, subscribed to the theory that Jackson painted with a broom. "People around here were always making jokes about his paintings," says Cook. The plumber Ed Hults thought it "crazy" that anyone paid good money for "one of those messed up road maps." Harder to dismiss was the cold reception among local art patrons. Jackson may never have heard Phyllis Geller call his mural for her dining room "a piece of junk," but the message was the same whenever a collector came through the studio that summer and left conspicuously empty-handed. Donald and Harriet Peters, who bought avant-garde paintings by the dozen, "wouldn't touch a Pollock. I was an innocent," recalls Harriet Peters (later Mrs. Esteban Vicente), "brought up, shall I say, a middle-class girl, and Pollock frightened me so intensely." Joe Liss resisted repeated inducements from both Lee and Jackson to buy a painting, adding a room onto his house instead. He did, however, bring his brother-in-law, Harold Kovner, a Manhattan real estate investor, to the studio. "Jackson was at work on the floor," Liss recalls, "and was polite. When we left the barn I said [to Harry], 'You ought to buy that painting.' And he said, 'I'm not going to buy the painting of some idiot who paints on the floor!' " Jackson offered a drawing to Stewart Klonis, a former schoolmate at the Art Students League who visited that summer, but Klonis, now the League's executive director, wouldn't take it. "I didn't see anything in his work," Klonis recalls. "I thought it was terrible." Leonard Bocour refused to accept two of Jackson's paintings in payment of a paint bill. (For someone as sensitive as Jackson, such personal, firsthand slights always stung, regardless of critical accolades or gallery sales.) Even those few patrons like Lawrence

Larkin who supported Jackson felt the backwash of skepticism and scorn. "Maidstone Club friends and even Guild Hall patrons thought we had our Pollock painting as a joke or to be kind," Larkin recalled. Jackson may have been a media phenomenon, a conversation piece at lawn parties, the summer's sensation, but to many his art was still at best a charity, at worst a joke.

But the real terror in Jackson's nightmares didn't come from abusive letters, subversive critics, bemused Bonackers, or chary collectors. It came from his fellow artists. In the interplay of past and present that was Jackson's emotional life, they were the brothers who spoiled and envied him, pampered and flattered him, even as they pushed him closer to the edge. "He was uncomfortable with other artists," says Conrad Marca-Relli. "He felt that they were either envious of him, or they hated his work, or they thought he was a phony, and all that made him distrust them."

Jackson's fears were justified. At a time when most avant-garde artists still worked in obscurity and held jobs to support themselves, his isolated, conspicuous success—both critical and financial—triggered a backstage storm of jealousy and rancor. "The myth of the great artist," says Paul Brach, "somehow diminished the rest of us. He is the sun and we are the black hole." Fellow artists who were friendly, even flattering, in public, privately derided him as "that wildman," or "the freak," or simply dimissed him as "irrelevant." Hans Hofmann, who was particularly "embittered" by Jackson's ascendancy, accused him of stealing the drip method, while others repudiated the method entirely, calling it "brash and heartless." "Those pictures that we think are so marvelous today," recalls Nick Carone, "then everybody thought were wild and overindulgent." Like many artists, Reginald Marsh expressed his contempt for Jackson's art by parodying it, creating his own drip painting and entering it in a show in Burlington, Vermont, as a joke. An old classmate from Manual Arts composed a poem: "He's a follower of Glop, the god of drip and drop . . ." At a party in Chilmark, Martha's Vineyard, the same summer, Thomas Craven accused Jackson of drinking a gallon of paint, then standing on a ladder and urinating. Tom Benton laughed appreciatively and wrote much the same thing in the second edition of his autobiography the following year. Phil Guston, furious at being eclipsed by his old high school classmate, called Jackson a "non-artist." "Guston felt *he* was the painter," recalls Carone. "He felt *he* was so accomplished and Jackson was inept and untalented, that he couldn't draw, that he was trying to be shocking. Then suddenly the art world is adulating this person that he considered a hanger-on and nobody cares much about him." Nobody, it seemed, cared much about Robert Motherwell, either. For years Motherwell had been "bragging that Jackson Pollock couldn't draw" and predicting confidently that "within five years he [Motherwell] would be hailed as America's foremost painter." By the summer of 1950, Jackson's success had forced Motherwell to rethink those ambitions.

The *Life* article had given artists something to fight about. "There had been such a dearth in American art for so long," says Herman Cherry. "Nobody had a chance. Then, suddenly, there was an opening, and everybody wanted to make it through that small opening, and they were all pushing and crawling over each other. There were tremendous egos. It was *raw*, really raw. Everybody was fighting for their place, and ambition was flying high."

But there was another reason, besides frustrated ambition, that so many of Jackson's fellow artists resented his success; another person who shared responsibility for the jealousies that fueled his paranoia, haunted his social encounters, and propelled him into the night to find solace at the edge of a garbage dump. That other person was sitting next to Jackson in the car that night.

Clement Greenberg once observed that people only contracted the diseases they deserved. "I never met a person with cancer," he said, "who didn't ask for it." The theory was typically Greenbergian: simple, muscular, symmetrical, seductive. It also helps explain why, by the summer of 1950, many avant-garde artists held him in such contempt. Despite his early championing of their cause, despite his future as the most influential art critic of the twentieth century, Clement Greenberg had nothing but contempt for artists.

"To be an artist is to be pompous," Greenberg would later declare with characteristic certitude. "Painters are less cultivated than writers and therefore pretentious in ways writers know enough to avoid." He was fond of the phrase "as stupid as a painter," and frequently lamented that "all artists are bores." When asked why he spent much of his career in their company, he answered: "Before analysis, I had a faculty for hanging around people I didn't like." His judgments of individual artists, even those whose work he supported, were curt and supercilious. Mark Rothko was "a clinical paranoid . . . pompous and dumb"; Jacques Lipchitz, "a south Balkan work *maître*"; Marc Chagall, "a Yiddish theater version of genius"; Adolph Gottlieb, "a pantspresser"; Arshile Gorky, a "violent anti-Semite"; Franz Kline, "a bore." Hans Hofmann was "tiresome"; Clyfford Still, "pretentious"; Fairfield Porter, "uncommonly obtuse"; Barnett Newman, "boring"; and Willem de Kooning, "tedious beyond belief."

Greenberg had been the intellectual bully of the art world ever since moving from the tougher neighborhood of literary criticism about 1941. As early as 1944, he had assailed "the extreme eclecticism" of the American art scene, calling it "unhealthy" and suggesting darkly that "it should be counteracted even at the risk of dogmatism and intolerance." Over the next few years he followed his own advice, championing abstract art, espousing a new critical agenda—color, surface, line, paint quality, flatness—and waging a fierce guerrilla war against the still dominant influence of the Surrealists, whom he accused of trying "to restore 'outside' subject matter" and of "confus[ing] literature with painting." At a time when few critics took avant-garde art seriously, most artists were willing to overlook such dogmatic excesses. Greenberg alone seemed to appreciate their "ferocious struggle." "[The artist's] isolation is inconceivable, crushing, unbroken, damning," he wrote in 1947. "That any-one can produce art on a respectable level in this situation is highly improbable. What can fifty do against a hundred and forty million?"

By 1950, however, both Greenberg and the art world had changed. Due largely to Greenberg's efforts and Jackson's media success, the legitimacy of abstract art had been established. Uneasy in victory, Greenberg withdrew to an even narrower and more dogmatic claim: what American abstract painters were doing "was not merely another interesting experiment; it was the right and historically inevitable—right because historically inevitable—direction in which painting must now move." In other words, abstract art, as defined by Greenberg, was "the *only* significant style for this time and place." The fierce, Talmudic zeal that had been directed toward the defense of abstract art was now turned on the artists themselves.

A self-described "child prodigy," Greenberg had once dreamed of becoming an artist himself. When his ambitions were frustrated by a disapproving father, he sought vindication of his own creativity in the creativity of others. He treated artists as wayward children to be remolded and "set right." "For Clem, all of these artists were sort of *tabula rasa*," says Miriam Schapiro. "In other words, *he* on some level was the genius." Disdainful of their intelligence, he felt free to ignore the artists' own representations as to what their art "meant," forcing the paintings to conform to the criticism rather than the reverse. Many artists suspected that he would have preferred to do away with artists altogether. "He pushed his theories to the point where gradually the artist would disappear from the painting," says Herbert Ferber, "and the painting would be nothing but paint and a support for the paint." On studio visits he was blunt and dismissive—"like an impatient parent," according to one artist. His eyes moved rapidly from painting to painting as he pronounced his verdicts: "That one's a mistake!" or, even more devastating, "That's really good," thereby negating everything else in the studio. He proffered not just specific criticisms but gen-eral advice on types of images, palettes, brushwork, and styles. He told Adolph Gottlieb to abandon the black-and-white images he had borrowed from Miró and "lead from his strength, which was color." According to one story, when he discovered a telephone book on which Franz Kline had cleaned his brushes, creating a series of oil sketches in heavy black strokes, he announced, "That's what you should do." (Years later, as executor, he would allow the paint to be stripped from the sculptures in David Smith's estate because "Smith was no colorist.") Even outside the studio, "Clem wanted to control everything," says Hilton Kramer, "from picking out who your girlfriends were going to be to what contracts you were going to sign."

In a community as fractious and verbal as the community of avant-garde artists, Greenberg's power and increasingly dictatorial style bred resentment and ridicule. While kowtowing in public, in private, artists referred to him derisively as "the grand pooh-bah," "Pope Clement," and "God." "Any time you take a mediocrity with an education," says May Rosenberg, whose husband would soon challenge Greenberg's hegemony, "inevitably they want to take charge of the world. They want to tell you how to tie your shoelaces. I never saw a mediocrity with power who was modest."

But it was Greenberg's open and largely exclusive alliance with Jackson that really ignited the fire-storm. Greenberg had thrown the golden apple into the crowd, and Jackson, unthinkingly, had rushed to pick it up. "Once Greenberg said [Pollock] was the greatest American artist," recalls Lillian Olaney, "the whole place exploded."

Beneath their anger and envy, many artists struggled with darker fears: fears that their world was changing; fears that media attention had given media figures like Greenberg an inordinate amount of power over insecure collectors, status-conscious museum officials, and careerist dealers, "most of whom came from making sweaters and shirts"; fears that the art world was passing out of their hands. Like Norman Bluhm, they remembered a day "when you would walk in to see a show and the dealer would come out and ask you what you thought," and they feared those days were gone. They feared that Greenberg's ascendancy was creating "a priest class" of critics and curators to whom words were more important than pictures, who "looked with their ears." They feared the appearance of what Adolph Gottlieb called "manufactured artists"—artists who were "full of dialectics" but who couldn't paint. Already there was a corrosive suspicion in the air that "people were getting publicity or notoriety for reasons other than their work," recalls Conrad Marca-Relli, "that it was all contrived." They feared that a lifetime of creative struggle no longer counted as much as public relations—"novelty" and "promotability." They feared that Greenberg was only the beginning, the opening wedge of a commercial imperative that to a generation of artists weaned on the Depression, the WPA projects, the Artists Union, and May Day parades was profoundly alien and disturbing. But most of all, they feared what commercialism would do to them: how they would respond to an art marketplace in which success was a genuine possibility; whether they would become, as Nathan Katz predicted, "like three dogs fighting over one bone."

In the late fall of 1949, soon after the article on Jackson appeared in *Life*, their rising fears coalesced into an organization. Meeting in Ibram Lassaw's studio at the corner of Sixth Avenue and Twelfth Street, a group of about twenty artists, including Willem de Kooning, Franz Kline, Milton Resnick, Philip Pavia, Conrad Marca-Relli, and Giorgio Cavallon, formed a club and contributed ten dollars apiece to rent a loft at 39 East Eighth Street near University Place. Unable to agree on a name—an ominous hint of things to come—they called themselves simply "The Club."

Ostensibly, the Club was a social organization, born out of the artists' frustrated need for a place to meet and talk, to "escape the loneliness of their studios [and] meet their peers to exchange ideas of every sort," according to Irving Sandler, the Club's foremost historian. In fact, the camaraderie was more like that of shipwreck survivors adrift in a crowded lifeboat. "It wasn't a congenial group at all," recalls Herman Cherry. "Hell, an outsider would have thought they hated each other. But, like marriage, instead of separating, they sort of stuck it out." As a visitor, Hedda Sterne found Club members "unbelievably hostile." "Insults flew back and forth, and they called that intellectual discussion," says Sterne. "But it was really fear."

Fearing the new art world, the Club clung desperately to the old. Its roots were firmly planted in the cafeteria culture of the Project when artists, flush with WPA money and free time, argued into the early morning at restaurants like Sam Johnson's, Romany Marie's, the San Remo, and the Waldorf cafeteria. The Waldorf on Sixth Avenue off Eighth Street had for the previous few years served as the group's informal clubhouse, a direct link with the past where, among the "Village bums, delinquents and cops," artists could smoke, drink coffee (the food was better and cheaper elsewhere), and table-hop from argument to argument—just like in the old days. At one table, Landes Lewitin dictated his views on a broad range of topics; at another, Aristodemos Kaldis held forth on the superiority of Greek culture; at another, John Graham held his nose against the smoke. Many of the Club's founding members had met on the Project, in the halcyon days of the Artists Union and the American Abstract Artists—before the war, before the galleries, before Greenberg. In the decade since, their agenda had hardly changed. Pure abstractionists like Ad Reinhardt, Harry Holtzman, and George McNeil, remnants of the AAA, took up their old feud with the "push-pull" disciples of Hans Hofmann. "Reinhardt would say he couldn't stand wiggly brushstrokes," Philip Pavia recalled, while Hofmann's followers derided the Mondrian lovers as "puritans" or "the hygienic school." Even the old antagonism toward European modernism, largely mooted by the war, survived at the Club as efforts to defend Matisse were shouted down with angry cries of "Decorative! Decorative!"

Like artists on the Project, Club members fancied themselves "rebels" and "outcasts," shunned by a reactionary art establishment and an unappreciative public. "We were the *salon des refusés*," says Conrad Marca-Relli. But it wasn't the past that they felt alienated from; it was the future. The hostility to Greenberg and his ideas was palpable, and Club discussions studiously avoided the formal issues that he had pushed to the top of the critical agenda. "Greenberg was a thousand miles away from us," says Philip Pavia, the Club's founder and organizer. "We were in a different world entirely." Instead of addressing current critical questions, evenings at the Club invariably degenerated into ferocious philosophical debates about "why an artist involves himself in painting," "the function of art," "the nature of the artist's moral commitment," and the artist's "existential role." (Out of one such discussion, the term "Abstract Expressionism" emerged.) Even charter members like Milton Resnick found themselves "choking" on the polemics. "Ideas got ritualized and positions got rigidified very early on," says Resnick. Willem de Kooning fled one interminable late-night argument crying, "They're a bunch of baboons!"

Talk of dealers, commissions, and money was tacitly forbidden. Group exhibitions were specifically banned because "we didn't want to introduce that kind of destructive competition," says Conrad Marca-Relli. With the exception of de Kooning, who kept tactfully quiet on the subject, few members had dealers and none was selling. "People in the Club didn't give a shit about what the dealers or critics or collectors or anybody was saying," recalls Herman Cherry, "because nobody was selling shit anyway." As in the Project days, talk of money was confined to tips on studios and bargains in art materials. Club members frequently exchanged self-congratulatory tales of their economic plight and passed the hat when one of their number was threatened with eviction. In such acts of solidarity, Club members found solace and, even more, dignity. "If anybody sold anything," recalls Jock Truman, "the rumor went around that the quality of his work was going down."

At times, it was as if the forties had never happened; as if Peggy Guggenheim had never opened Art of This Century; as if the new galleries with their opportunist dealers had never opened; as if Greenberg had never written a review; as if Jackson Pollock had never sold a painting.

From the beginning, Jackson felt the hostility. On his first visit to the Club on New Year's Eve 1949, the sculptor Peter Grippe, drunk and belligerent, confronted him. After a few angry words, Grippe threw a punch. "It was basically jealousy," recalls Ibram Lassaw, who witnessed the fight, "because Jackson's name was everywhere." In less dramatic ways, the same animosity permeated every aspect of the Club: from the clannish admission policy (nonmembers had to be accompanied by a member or have a note from a member) enforced at the door by the mean-spirited Lewitin, to the blackball system for electing new members. "No institution could have been less suited to Jackson," says Conrad Marca-Relli. "He never felt welcome there." The combative debates only underscored his inarticulateness; the crowd only reinforced his reticence. The pedantic dialogues only threatened to expose the vast gaps in his artistic education.

Robert Motherwell's arrival made a bad situation worse. Since the collapse of his plot with Matta to wrest control of the American Surrealist movement away from Breton, Motherwell had led a series of similar unsuccessful efforts to create the elusive "manifestation" that would catapult him to preeminence in American art. In 1948, with William Baziotes, Mark Rothko, David Hare, and Barnett Newman, he had established a school for young artists, called the Subjects of the Artist. The awkward name betrayed the school's anti-Greenberg (and anti-Pollock) agenda: "It was meant to emphasize that our painting was not abstract," said Motherwell, "that it was full of subject matter." When the school folded, a group of artists organized by Tony Smith continued the Friday night seminars under the name Studio 35 (the meetings were held in a studio at 35 East Eighth Street). Motherwell acted as "Master of Ceremonies," leading discussions on such topics as subject matter, finish, titles, self-expression, community relations, museum patronage, and public awareness. In 1950, he brought his intellectual bent, his scholarly pretensions, his frustrated ambitions, and his envious disdain for Jackson to the Club. "Motherwell was the first of another kind of artist," says Conrad Marca-Relli. "They were the uptown boys, people who had already made a name, already had a gallery uptown before they joined. With their arrival came panel discussions and guest speakers, and everything became more public, more formal." And, for Jackson, more intimidating.

Even at weekend dances—when the wooden chairs were cleared away, the philosophical wrangling was suspended temporarily, and Philip Pavia played his records of Italian folk music and jazz—the Club was still, for Jackson, an alien, hostile world. An awkward dancer, he could never master the two-step, not to mention the tarantella introduced by Pavia, and, sober, was too embarrassed to try. Nor could he enjoy the "crackling sexuality" that ran through the old building on dance nights—another throwback to the Artists Union days of the thirties. "If you were a pretty girl, you could write your ticket," recalls Phyllis Fleiss. "You could reign supreme at those events." Mercedes Matter, the only woman among the Club's early members, was one of those who gave the dances a sharp edge of sexuality. May Rosenberg compared the Club's sexual underlife to a country square dance in which "partners were passed to and fro" in ever-changing combinations. Fifteen years earlier, with liquor to embolden him and Sande to rescue him, Jackson would have tried, however unsuccessfully, to join in the misogynist game. But now, sober and alone, it only frightened him. The teeming sexuality, the sideline bragging of other artists about "all the women they had 'stuck,' " and the flirtatious attentions of Mercedes Matter and others only pushed him further into his shell. Conrad Marca-Relli remembers seeing him leaning against the wall at a Club dance, arms folded, eyes averted. "He looked like a big rough boy in the barn," recalls Marca-Relli. "The women were like strange creatures to him. He never fit in." Hedda Sterne saw him there, too, "gentle and quiet, but on the outside looking in."

Occasionally, in halting conversation, Jackson would try to distance himself from Greenberg, vehemently denying that Greenberg knew "what his pictures were about," and joining Franz Kline in "shrug[ging] at the big abstractions about historical necessity." He insisted to Barnett Newman, "I don't discuss paintings with critics," and on one of Greenberg's rare visits to the Club, purposefully incited a confrontation. "They called each other all sorts of names," recalls Conrad Marca-Relli. "Then they let it go and went on to something else." Such halfhearted efforts to win his way back into favor were to no avail, however. By 1950, it must have seemed to Jackson that his fellow artists had closed ranks against him—pushed him to the edge of the cliff where, for the first time in years, he could feel himself beginning to fall.

No artist had more reason to resent Jackson's success than Lee Krasner. Where other artists' careers had been eclipsed by Jackson's, hers had been virtually extinguished. The brief flare of productivity in the summer of 1948 that produced the "Little Image" paintings had been brought to an abrupt end by the debacle at Bertha Schaefer's apartment. In a single outburst, Jackson had reasserted the primacy of his emotional needs and alienated the first outsider in years who showed an interest in Lee's work. Then came the long struggle back to sobriety, then the fragile truce of tranquilizers and weekly "therapy" with Dr. Heller. At some point, Lee apparently accepted the ominous logic: Jackson's drinking and her artistic ambitions were inextricably linked. "During the time Jackson was on the wagon," says Ted Dragon, "Lee didn't want to do anything to unbalance that." "Lee gave up painting altogether at that point for his sake," recalls Vita Peterson, "to avoid the possible competition." Grace Hartigan remembers Lee telling her, "He doesn't want anyone painting around him."

After the *Life* article appeared in the fall of 1949, Lee had a new excuse for not painting. "Pollock was breaking through," she said. "We had our hands full." Between preparations for the November show and the extended stay at MacDougal Alley, the upstairs studio in Springs sat idle for weeks, then months, at a time. According to friends, it was "the best period of their relationship"—which meant it was the worst period for Lee's art. Only in the mornings, when Jackson was asleep and the phone was off the hook, did she feel it was "safe" to work. The rest of the day was consumed by his needs, from canning fruit to courting collectors. Ted Dragon saw Lee as "Jackson's Clara Schumann. She was a great artist in her own right, but she was determined to take that husband and make him. It was her obsession. Then, when he made it, living through him wasn't enough. She wanted it for herself."

Publicly, Lee would always deny envying Jackson's success. "I wasn't saying, 'Why are you getting ahead and I'm not?' " she later told an interviewer. Although she admitted "resenting being in the shadow of Jackson Pollock," she insisted that "it was never so sharp a thing to deal with that it interfered with my work." Privately, however, the inequity rankled. "That bastard Pollock," she complained to Lawrence Alloway after Jackson's death, "he had that big studio out there and I had the bedroom." "She felt put upon, put down," says Alloway. And not just by Jackson. When Barnett Newman called to enlist Jackson in the protest group that eventually became known as "the Irascibles," it was Lee who answered the phone. "Lee, get Jackson, it's very important," Newman said. "I must speak to him." "I was never asked to sign," she recalled bitterly. "Barney didn't even bother to tell me what it was about." By 1950, such slights had become commonplace. "There were," she complained, "very few painters in that so-called circle who acknowledged that I painted at all."

Paul Brach recalls a scene that was replayed often when fellow artists came to visit:

They're all in the living room. Greenberg's there and there's a lively discussion going on. They like Lee. She's smart. They say Lee has a real eye.
. . . Everyone is listening to her. But mainly her role is backup to Jackson.
It's hard for him to take the floor with these guys. He's not articulate, he's
very shy, he doesn't have it. But she does. She's his mouthpiece, and she
can handle it beautifully. *But nobody looks at her pictures.* Nobody is giving
her any kind of obeisance in terms of her own work. And the years go on
that way, and a certain kind of inner sadness accumulates.

Among the legions of admirers who made the pilgrimage to Jackson's barn,
almost none ventured upstairs to see Lee's little studio. Even old friends like
George Mercer "showed no interest in what she was doing." Only Jackson's
pictures hung on the long walls downstairs; hers were relegated to dark corners
and leftover spaces. After dinner, when Jackson hauled his latest paintings
from the studio to show guests, no one, including Jackson, asked Lee to fetch
hers from upstairs. No dealers called about her next show, no interviewers
asked questions about her past, no photographers lingered about her studio to
catch the blurred movement of her brush or the shifting moods of her face.

It was a subordinate role that stirred old resentments. Once again, Lee was
back in the house on Jerome Street, watching her brother Irving go off to the
library to study Pushkin and Tolstoy. She could share Jackson's celebrity, she
could share his money (unlike most artists' wives, she didn't have to support
him), she could even have the power, as his mouthpiece and manager, over
Jackson's art, but, she would later complain bitterly, "What I couldn't have was
a career."

As always, her envy first took the form of emulation. After years of what
Miriam Schapiro describes as "small, copable works—things that could be
done in your lap," she began to paint like Jackson, to work more boldly, to
"take chances," according to her biographer Barbara Rose, "and break new
ground, pushing herself to become more spontaneous and free, both in subject
matter as well as form." Although no one knows the exact chronology of Lee's
paintings, even the few that survive betray her childlike yearning to follow in
Jackson's footsteps. (To close friends, she later talked about her need to "work
through Pollock.") In *Continuum* and other Little Image paintings, she borrowed both his pouring technique and the all-over format of *Eyes in the Heat*
and *Shimmering Substance*, paintings she had often heard Greenberg praise.
In *Lava*, she forsook the lucid colors of Matisse and Hofmann for the dark
palette of Jackson's *Sea Change* and *Alchemy*. In *Gothic Frieze*—a title that
echoed through Jackson's oeuvre as well as Greenberg's criticism—she abandoned the cloisonnist curves of Picasso for the threatening Orozcoesque angu-
larity of *Night Ceremony* and *Night Mist*. In *Promenade*, she painted a
procession of "personages" closely resembling in mood and surface Jackson's
Guggenheim mural, another painting Greenberg admired. She worked on the

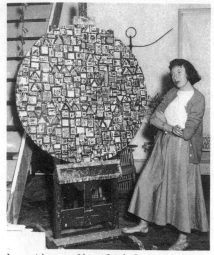

Lee with one of her "Little Image" paintings

rough side of Masonite, as she had seen Jackson do so often. In *Ochre Rhythm*, after years of "gray slabs" and heavy impasto, she applied paint thinly to the canvas for the first time, long after Jackson's *Tea Cup*. After years of resisting Surrealist theories, she began to experiment with automatism, finding in Jackson's example a sudden respect for "the unconscious as a source of psychological content," according to Rose, even if "she was not yet prepared to expose the contents of her psyche to public scrutiny." After years of constructing her paintings according to Mondrian's grid or Hofmann's rhetoric, she attempted for the first time fully automatic drawing directly in paint—the technique that had first brought Jackson notoriety in *She-Wolf* and *Guardians of the Secret*. She even abandoned her decade-old allegiance to abstraction, painting quasi-figurative stick figures like those in Jackson's *Male and Female* and *Stenographic Figure*.

As her ambition grew, so did her canvases, from the portrait-size Little Image paintings to the wall-sized *Blue and Black*. Physically and psychologically, she was straining at the boundaries of her tiny studio. "Her early works [in Springs] were very introverted," recalls Ethel Baziotes. "Then suddenly they became more extroverted. There was that split in Lee, like she didn't know which way to go." Ted Dragon noticed that Lee began to "come into her own" in early 1950. Jackson, too, noticed but, preoccupied with his own grand visions that summer, reacted at first with patronizing indulgence. "He seemed to take the attitude that 'Oh, well, the little woman is painting again,' " recalls Harry Jackson, "like he didn't think much of it." To Roger Wilcox, Jackson expressed only mild irritation: "Lee keeps copying me and I wish she'd stop."

But Lee's new assertiveness soon spilled over from art into life. No longer content to be ignored, she openly pressed herself on Jackson's visitors, cajoling them up the stairs to visit her studio. "She wanted me to see her work, even though she didn't care for me very much," Harry Jackson remembers of a visit

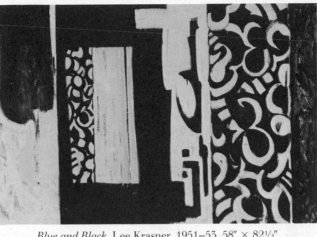

Blue and Black, Lee Krasner, 1951–53, 58″ × 82½″

in the summer of 1950. "She had always been a little jealous that I was out in his studio and never went to see hers, even though I slept right next to it." Harry kept his opinion of Lee's work—"a pastiche, devoid of artistic conviction"—tactfully to himself, but the polite, admiring reactions of friends like Ted Dragon, John Myers, John Little, Linda Lindeberg, and Bradley Tomlin gave her conviction of another sort. Greenberg, resorting to his favorite culinary metaphors, commented, "That's hot. It's cooking," which Lee took as a compliment. In July, one of her paintings won second prize in the "10 East Hampton Abstractionists" show at Guild Hall. Jackson's placed third.

Each new success for Lee sent tremors through Jackson's fragile world. "She wasn't pushing Pollock as much anymore," says Harry Jackson. "She was pushing Lee now."

Soon after Hans Namuth began photographing Jackson, Lee insisted that he come to her studio as well. "I should have made more of a fuss over her from the start," says Namuth. "As it was, we had unpleasant scenes together, so I came to take her picture, too."

That left only Jackson's family.

The idea of a Pollock family reunion had been in the air for years, ever since Stella's move to Deep River in 1944. With Sande in Connecticut, Jay in New York, Jackson in Springs, and Frank frequently in town on business, only Charles was missing. But a Pollock family reunion without Charles was unthinkable. It wasn't until 1950, when Charles moved back to New York and rented a summer house in Sag Harbor, only twelve miles from Springs, that plans were laid. Within a month, Frank Pollock loaded his wife Marie and his eight-year-old son Jonathan into a 1950 Pontiac in Los Angeles and struck out across the country with typical Pollock abandon ("My dad drove eighty or a hundred miles an hour the whole way," Jonathan recalls); Jay and Alma left their apartment in the city, and Sande brought his family and Stella from Deep

River. On a sunny weekend in July, they converged at the farmhouse on Fireplace Road. It had been seventeen years since they were last together.

For Jackson, the reunion was the culmination of a year of celebrity, the last stop on the backward path that fame had allowed him to retrace and rechart; a chance to coax from his family the attention he had sought and won in the larger world; a chance, finally, to win the approval of the only audience that ultimately mattered.

The prospect terrified him. As the weekend approached, he couldn't sleep or work. Lee watched with mounting concern as he laid and relaid elaborate plans, one minute dreaming of a "triumph over his family," the next minute plagued by nightmares "that it would be a bust."

Saturday, the first and only full day of the reunion, began with introductions. Charles, Elizabeth, and Marie met Lee for the first time. The scattered grandchildren discovered one another. For Charles's ten-year-old daughter, Jeremy, "it was being part of a huge family for the first time." While the children explored the house (they were more fascinated by Lee's mosaic table than by Jackson's paintings) and Accabonac Creek, Jackson took his brothers on a tour of the studio. In the afternoon, all five brothers led the grandchildren into the backyard for a game of baseball. Over Jonathan's objection that baseball was "a boys' game," Sande's daughter Karen, a "husky" nine-year-old, took the field alongside her father. Two-year-old Jay (who later renamed himself Jason), too young to play, spent the afternoon on Stella's knee, where he remained most of the weekend. The daughters-in-law took advantage of a flawless summer day and drove to a nearby beach. When the groups reunited that evening at the tables that had been pulled together in the center of the big room, Stella and Lee served a "Christmas feast in July" crowned by a massive roast. The table talk was far more animated than it had been seventeen years before. "There was a lot of laughter and jesting and reminiscing about boyhood events," recalls Elizabeth. Except for the paintings on the walls—many of which Jackson had hung especially for the occasion—and the conspicuous absence of alcohol, it was a typical family reunion. "There wasn't any bickering or anything," recalls Jeremy. "Everyone seemed to get along pretty well." After dinner, the tables were cleared and pushed back in place and a wrought-iron settee pulled out in front of Jackson's *Arabesque* for picture-taking: first the entire family, with Stella in the center holding Jason and Charles beside her; then Stella with just the daughters-in-law; then Stella with just her sons; then Stella with just her grandchildren. Sitting proud and rock-like in her black lace dress while the others shifted seats around her, even Stella smiled for the camera.

Behind the Rockwellian tableau of smiling faces and family unity, however, was a tangle of emotions as deep and dense as any of Jackson's painted skeins.

Despite her girlish grin, Alma Pollock had almost refused to attend. She had never forgiven Jackson for his drunken cruelties or Lee for her arrogance on

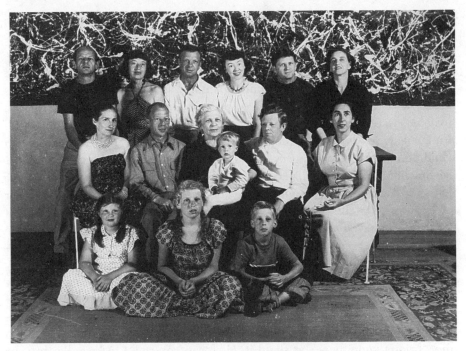

The Pollock family reunion, 1950. Left to right, top row: Jackson, Lee, Jay, Alma, Sande, Elizabeth; middle row: Arloie, Frank, Stella with Jason, Charles, Marie; front row: Karen, Jeremy, and Jonathan.

their trips into New York in the late forties. "When they stayed over at the apartment for one of his openings, Lee would borrow clothes from Alma and then just keep them," recalls Jay—in much the same way Jackson had "just kept" the collection of Indian blankets. Neither Jay nor Alma said anything, of course, but they had stopped visiting Springs long ago and, at Alma's insistence, spent the reunion weekend with Charles in Sag Harbor to avoid staying an unnecessary moment in Jackson's house.

Behind his tentative, go-along smile, Frank Pollock had a lot of worries on his mind. His son Jonathan had been pronounced "seriously ill" by doctors just before the trip east; his job at a nursery was producing pitifully little income and even less fulfillment; and, partly as a result, his marriage was showing signs of strain. Marie Pollock had made no secret of her disappointment when Frank quit school in 1933, effectively abandoning his dreams of being a writer. "He wrote like Ernie Pyle," says Marie, "only better. But he didn't have the drive." She had tried to push him into journalism, "but he would have had to start at the bottom," she recalls, "and he was too proud for that." Since then, Frank's life had been a series of bootless compromises—not unlike Roy Pollock's. "Frank looked the most like his father," says Marie, "but they were alike in other ways. They both ended up disappointed men."

Like Frank, Sande had surrendered his artistic aspirations for a life of family and job. Almost ten years later, neither had brought the promised rewards. At forty, he was still the tautly strung teenager, "obsessed with being a he-man"; a scrapper who awoke every morning to a strict regimen of push-ups and chin-ups. "It wasn't for the exercise," says one family member. "He was just tense, filled with aggression and strain from the moment he got up." In his eyes, however, and in the deep lines around them, the strain had begun to show. His secret defense work at the Pratt-Reed plant in Deep River left him exhausted, irritable, vulnerable to alcohol, and, for inexplicable reasons, persistently ill. Financially, his lot had improved little since the Project days. Between two children and Stella's profligacy, he still couldn't afford a house for his family. Meanwhile, Stella and Arloie continued to wage their subterranean war. In her letters to family, Stella fulminated against her daughter-in-law, accusing her of expropriating the money sent by the other brothers to help with Stella's upkeep—money that Stella considered her own. She suspected that Arloie tolerated her presence only because of these supplements to the family's mea-ger income. "I[t's] not me, [it's] *the money*," she complained to Charles. "They have borrowed till I am down to my last dollar. No money comeing in so they have to feed the kids [with] the money you sent." At the beach the Saturday of the reunion, the other daughters-in-law commiserated with Arloie. "Some-thing was said about Mother Pollock," Arloie remembers, "and they all said to me, 'I don't know how you stand it. How can you stand to have her in your home all the time?' "

Preoccupied with Sande and working to earn extra money, Arloie had vir-tually abandoned her children to Stella's care—with troubling results. Sande had wanted Karen to be "his precious little girl," the sister he never had. Instead, she had turned out to be a precocious, overweight tomboy who, by her own account, "wasn't pretty enough." Jason, on the other hand, was too pretty: an "exquisitely beautiful little boy" everyone agreed, so pretty that when Stella let his hair grow into long golden curls, people mistook him for a girl. From birth, he had been Stella's baby: he called his grandmother "Mommie" and his mother "Loie." Sande had wanted a cowboy for a son, but Stella had already determined that Jason would be a musician when he grew up.

The seventeen intervening years had been particularly unkind to Charles. At forty-eight, he looked and moved like a man twenty years older. Behind the fleshy, unsmiling mask, unseen by his still-admiring brothers, he was already wrestling with an old man's regrets. Under Benton's influence, he had clung to Social Realism too long. Out of misguided pride and the need to support his family, he had avoided the Project, missing the central social and creative experience of the decade. Finally, at the very moment when the New York art world began to explode, he had left for Michigan to teach calligraphy to college students. "He had missed out on the big movement," says Frank, "and he knew it. He bewailed the fact that if he hadn't settled for security, his work would have become more important. He would have developed along with the rest of the New York School. He would have become an abstract painter sooner." As early as the early forties, Charles was already beginning to feel the cumulative effect of so many wrong turns. In 1942, he suffered an artistic and emotional "breakdown." Abandoning his teaching position, he embraced non-objective painting and returned to the site of his childhood triumphs, Arizona. "I spent months in the desert painting," he recalls, "trying to erase all those years of Social Realism."

In New York, seven years later, he was still trying to reverse the mistakes of the previous decades. He had rented a studio on Third Avenue and arranged a show at the Circle Gallery. But now there were new obstacles to overcome: a disintegrating marriage to an increasingly embittered and shrewish wife; an unfamiliar, competitive art world; and the new burden of celebrity attached to the name Pollock. On his arrival in New York in the midst of Jackson's triumphs, Charles had decided not to show under his own name. One Pollock in the art world was enough. So he called himself "Charles Pima," after the tribe of Arizona Indians. At the reunion, he said nothing about the past or about his new identity, but, according to a friend, "inside, he boiled. It didn't show outwardly, but he boiled inside from a sort of injustice done to him."

In the midst of so many failed lives, Jackson's success stood out in galling contrast. Everywhere his brothers looked, they saw its fruits: in the cut of the dinner roast, in the freshly painted guest room, in the elegant Herter Brothers carpet in the living room, in the new furnishings, bathroom fixtures, and garden plantings. On every table Jackson had stacked copies of magazines—*Life, Art News, Art Digest*—with articles about him and reviews of his work carefully marked. "Must be great to be talked about in the newspapers and magazines," Jay commented. The walls were covered with his paintings, including two of his favorites, *Gothic* and *Arabesque*. What signs of prosperity his brothers couldn't see, Jackson eagerly reported. He led them around the property and shared his plans for buying the adjoining lots. In the studio he talked prices and galleries and reputation, at one point bragging: "I'm the only painter worth looking at in America. There really isn't anybody else." Pointing to *Lavender Mist* on the studio wall, he said to Frank, "Buy that painting for 15,000 and one day it will be worth 100,000." (Frank's wife, Marie, remembers that "at that time I can assure you we did not have 15,000 *cents*, let alone dollars.") To his hard-pressed brothers, Jackson's eagerness smacked of arrogance. "I think the fact that we were there didn't make a damned bit of difference to him," recalls Frank. "He was still *Jackson Pollock*, you know."

Where Jackson's self-promotional campaign left off, Lee's began. She slipped easily from her role as "gracious hostess" to that of salesman, quoting reviews and prices, and incongruously urging purchases on Jackson's strapped brothers as if they were well-heeled collectors. If a family member stared too long at a painting on the wall, she would sidle up and whisper its price. "One of the things that bothered us," recalls Jay, "was Lee's attitude: *We* hadn't produced anything, but Jackson had, and our only purpose in life was to buy his paintings so he could live. We ought to sacrifice so he could create. *That* was her attitude." The brothers also sensed, beneath the facade of hostess and promoter, Lee's deep antagonism. In the reunion portrait, she stands in her smart summer dress, disconnected from those around her, her lips pursed in impatience, her eyes filled with ennui. "She had Jackson under her control," recalls Frank, "and she wanted no interference from his side—from his brothers or his mother. She just put up with us. Her attitude was 'It's only a matter of time and they'll be gone and we'll be back to normal.' " Soon, the family's initial skepticism—"They didn't know what to think of her," Jeremy recalls— turned to cordial hostility.

Even more rankling to the brothers than Jackson's arrogance or Lee's disdain was the sight of Stella "sitting in silent adoration" of Jackson's success. Had she forgotten the endless family crises, the crossfire of distraught letters, the public displays, the hospitalizations, the family embarrassments? *They* hadn't forgotten. Nor had they forgotten that for all his talk of hundred-thousand-dollar sales, Jackson had never contributed to Stella's support. For an entire decade, he had lived off his family, never holding a job for long, never showing any gratitude, taking money and food and giving in return only headaches and sleepless nights and scenes in the gutter. And now that he had money, he was spending it on reshingling his studio, "opening up" the living room, and refurbishing the guest bath while Sande struggled in a tiny apartment to maintain solvency and domestic peace with occasional help from his older brothers. "Jack was making more money than any of us," says Frank, "and I don't think he had ever sent a dime to Stella or Sande."

At age forty, Jackson was still the favored child—Stella's baby—and, as on the Phoenix ranch, his brothers hardened against him. Their resentment found an easy target in Jackson's art. "The family thought he was pulling everybody's leg," recalls Jeremy. "They didn't take him seriously as an artist." "I was never able to turn any somersaults about any of Jack's paintings," says Frank. Following Jackson through the studio, Jay just smoked his pipe and shook his head. "It was something entirely new, and I couldn't recognize it," he recalls. "It didn't seem to fit what I thought art was." To the Pollocks, Charles was still the painter in the family. The fact that he chose to hide his resentment behind a mask of affability and quiet drinking only made them more sympathetic. Whatever the magazines said about Jackson, his brothers still shared Elizabeth's conviction that "when posterity finally judges value, Charles is the one who's going to be seen as the great artist of his time."

On Saturday night, in a last, desperate bid for his family's approval, Jackson pulled out a copy of Bruno Alfieri's article in *L'Arte Moderna*, which had just arrived in the mail and, with Lee at his side, tried to translate it for his guests. "Do you know any Italian?" he asked as he began, knowing, of course, that no one did. "That was the center of interest as far as Jack and Lee were concerned, and I guess they assumed the rest of us would find it fascinating," recalls Marie Pollock. "They made telephone calls to see if they could find anybody who spoke Italian and could translate it all the way through. They were reading it aloud and trying to figure out what it said." The battle line was drawn when the rest of the family turned to a game of anagrams on the other side of the room. Most, like Frank, resented that this obscure Italian article "was of paramount importance to Jack, rather than the fact that his family was gathering for the first time in seventeen years." But Jackson continued to repeat fragments of the review in broken Italian as if a crowd were listening. "He was determined to make us hear," says Frank—especially the part that compared him to Picasso. "Several times throughout the evening I heard a repeated refrain of *'povero Picasso, povero Picasso,'*" recalls Marie. I thought that was very funny. It was written in the article and I kept hearing it in the background. He was clearly gloating over the expression, and he kept repeating it all night." But the family was no longer listening. At one point, Alma turned to Jackson in exasperation and asked, "Is Picasso more important than your family?"

The triumph Jackson so desperately wanted had turned into a debacle. Instead of reshaping the past, he was reliving it. In the family portrait taken the same night, Jackson stands at the far edge of the group, farthest from Stella, his head drawn back stiffly, his mouth slack, his eyes filled with fear. Seventeen years earlier, he had caught the same look in a self-portrait: the look of a frightened, emaciated, hollow-eyed child, struggling to conceal his terror as he stares in the mirror, confronts the void, and feels himself falling into it.

Jackson never recovered from the reunion. He spent the rest of the summer "terribly withdrawn," Peter Blake remembers, convinced that his fellow artists, family, and even Lee had abandoned him. Increasingly, all that mattered to him were the affects of celebrity—the house, the flatterers, the grand visions. More so than ever, he became obsessed with his reputation, with his *image* as a great artist. When Berton Roueché's piece appeared in the August *New Yorker*, he gloated for days and insisted that Lee send a copy to each of his brothers. The family may have scattered, but Jackson was still locked in battle, still determined to show them that he was not just the greatest artist in America but the greatest artist in the Pollock family as well. The energy of that obsession propelled him through *One* and, in August, *Autumn Rhythm*. For a while, it even displaced alcohol—the lifeline he had always reached for in the past. But if the means was different, the end was the same: self-obliteration.

In August, Hans Namuth suggested making a movie of Jackson painting. "[It] was the next logical step," he argued. "Pollock's method of painting suggested a moving picture—the dance around the canvas, the continuous movement, the drama." By now, Jackson, too, was more interested in drama than in art and eagerly agreed. The result was a crude, seven-minute, black-and-white film taken with Namuth's wife's hand-held Bell & Howell. The best Namuth could say about it afterward was that it "reveal[ed] the continuity of Pollock's method of working"—in short, it moved.

But the film did whet both men's appetite for a grander, more ambitious effort. After securing the collaboration of Paul Falkenberg, a film editor who had worked with Fritz Lang and Georg Wilhelm Pabst (and who provided $2,000 of working capital), Namuth returned to Jackson's studio with plans for a longer film in color. With Lee's concurrence, Jackson agreed unhesitatingly. He had something to prove, and Namuth would help him prove it. If he had apprehensions about the project's artistic integrity—what Namuth called "the voyeuristic element"—they didn't deter him. The old fears of phoniness had been replaced by far greater fears.

From the first weekend of filming in September, Jackson surrendered himself completely to Namuth's direction. "He knew that Hans knew a lot more about it from the point of view of showmanship," recalls Conrad Marca-Relli, "and he knew that would make for a better film." When, despite the oncoming winter, Namuth insisted that the filming be done outside to avoid the expense of lighting the studio, Jackson agreed. Namuth chose the spot, a concrete foundation slab, dressed the set—a long canvas, a small stool, several pots of paint—and directed the action. From eyewitness accounts and the finished film, the process can be reconstructed. Jackson enters from off-camera dressed in blue denim pants and denim jacket, sits on the stool, and changes from his shiny loafers into laceless, paint-spattered shoes. He sets the loafers aside and walks to the canvas. He looks at it thoughtfully for a moment, then picks up a brush. Cut. Because of a cloud, an intruding shadow, a gust of wind, the scene has to be repeated. Jackson puts down the brush, changes back into the loafers, and retreats to the side to wait for Namuth's instructions: enter sooner, change shoes more slowly, look longer at the canvas before picking up the brush. Standing in the September breeze waiting for the film to be reloaded or the light to change, Jackson listens intently. Unsure of his cue, he asks Namuth, "Should I do it now, Hans?" Reshoots are followed by re-reshoots.

Once the painting begins, there are stretches of genuine creativity; paint can't be called back into the can. But the film runs out in mid-lariat and darkness interrupts even the most eloquent gestures. With reloadings and technical delays, a few minutes of painting stretches into a day, a weekend. The next weekend, Namuth returns with a list of fill-in shots suggested by Falkenberg: close-ups of "Pollock's shoes, paint-spattered and unforgettable, the pebbles shaken out of them, the cigarette thrown away as the intensity of painting increases." By the end of September, the filming disintegrates into bits and pieces of action. A can of paint has to be stirred again; a cigarette thrown away again; the shoes changed again. Namuth has decided on a close-up of Jackson signing his name to the painting. The simple act is shot and reshot.

But Namuth still wasn't satisfied. As he reviewed the rushes with Falkenberg, he sensed "somehow a main ingredient was missing." That ingredient was Jackson. "I realized that I wanted to show the artist at work with his face in full view," he later wrote, "becoming part of the canvas, so to speak—coming at the viewer—through the painting itself. How could this be done?" Namuth's solution, which came to him in a dream, he claimed, was to use glass instead of canvas. By photographing the painting process from underneath the glass, he could capture the most important element: Jackson's face. The art would be used only to frame the artist. Jackson approved of the idea—he had come this far; there was no turning back. Besides, during their conversations about the ideal museum, he and Peter Blake had already discussed doing "a painting that wouldn't just be supported in midair but that was transparent, that you could see landscape through and beyond."

Jackson spent the next few weeks constructing the sawhorse supports for the glass, and a scaffold sturdy enough for him to stand on and high enough for Namuth and his camera to fit underneath. In the meantime, Blake secured from Pittsburgh Plate Glass a four-by-six-foot piece of Herculite, a strong, shatterproof glass used in automobile windshields. From the time shooting began, on a chilly day in late October, the project seemed jinxed. Namuth squirmed in the cramped space under the glass lying on his back, searching for a comfortable position in which to hold the camera. When the camera was right, the light was wrong. With the lens pointing directly up into the sky, the image was always in danger of burning out. When the sun came out, Jackson was in silhouette; when it went away, in darkness.

Jackson contributed his share of "false starts," according to Namuth. If it wasn't the small group of onlookers milling around—more intent on movie-making than art-making—that distracted him, it was the wind off Gardiners Bay playing havoc with his delicate lariats of paint. From six feet in the air, the sight of Namuth sprawled on the ground directly beneath him, struggling with the camera on his chest and shouting out directions, made concentrating even more difficult. The wind muffled his voice. "Now?" Jackson called out, unsure if the film was rolling. Several times, he "lost contact" with the painting and had to start again. Unlike canvas, however, glass could be wiped clean and reused. (With the money almost gone, Namuth couldn't afford to buy another sheet.) One of Jackson's false starts appears in the film's final cut. After a minute and a half of arranging pebbles and wire mesh and lacing them together with paint, he suddenly stops and, looking exasperated, starts to wipe the plate clean. In the film, the glass is clear and he is painting again in a few seconds. In reality, it was a long, frustrating wait in the November cold, one of many starts and stops as the filming dragged deeper into winter.

Between Namuth's weekend visits—increasingly his only contact with the "real" world—Jackson withdrew further into himself, languishing in the studio, barricaded behind the huge canvases of summer, producing only an occasional small, convictionless work for the show that opened on November 28 at Parsons. His mood vacillated wildly between the arrogance of the previous year and the dark self-doubts conjured up by the family reunion. On one occasion, he pulled Lee into the studio and, pointing at *Lavender Mist*, asked, "Is this a painting?" ("Can you imagine?" says Lee, still marveling thirty years later. "Not 'Is it a *good* painting,' but 'Is it a painting?' ")

At a time of such vulnerability, *Time*'s review of the Venice Biennale in the November 20 issue hit particularly hard. "Jackson Pollock's abstractions stump

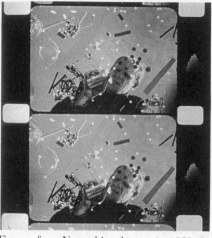

Frames from Namuth's color movie, 1950–51

experts as well as laymen," it began. "Laymen wonder what to look for in the labyrinths which Pollock achieves by dripping paint onto canvases laid flat on the floor; experts wonder what on earth to say about the artist." The review went on to claim that Jackson had "followed his canvases to Italy" and that the Italians had "tended to shrug off his shows," neither of which was true. Most infuriating, however, was the extensive excerpt from Bruno Alfieri's essay, which included the disparaging reference to "chaos" but omitted the flattering comparison to Picasso. Stung, Jackson fired off a telegram to *Time*:

NO CHAOS DAMN IT. DAMNED BUSY PAINTING AS YOU CAN SEE BY MY SHOW COMING UP NOV. 28. I'VE NEVER BEEN TO EUROPE. THINK YOU LEFT OUT MOST EXCITING PART OF MR. ALFIERI'S PIECE.

The fury of Jackson's reply surprised his friends. "It wasn't like Jackson to be defensive about cracks like that," says John Little. "He had let far worse go by without getting worked up." Gina Knee, who thought the review "wasn't that bad," saw Jackson on the street in Amagansett soon afterwards "*very* upset" and inconsolable. She remembered thinking, "There's more than that churning inside of him."

On a weekend in November, Clement Greenberg came to Springs to view the pictures for the coming show. Sunday evening, Jackson drove him to the East Hampton station where the two men waited for the train together in the car, trading silences and talking about the future. Jackson was unusually subdued, Greenberg remembers. "He sensed something was coming." The subject turned to the upcoming show, now only weeks away. "I told him I thought it would be his best show ever," Greenberg recalls, "but I also said I didn't think it was going to sell. He didn't want to hear that." When the train pulled in and Greenberg turned to say good-bye, he avoided looking Jackson in the eye. "I knew something was wrong, but I didn't want to think about it."

■　■　■

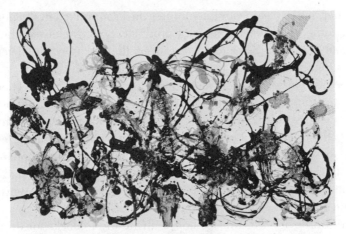

Number 29, 1950, the painting created for Namuth's color movie,
oil, enamel, and aluminum paint; mesh; string; colored glass; agates;
and marbles on glass, 48⅛″ × 72″

By Thanksgiving, Jackson had reached the breaking point. Time, money, patience, and fair weather had all run out. But Namuth insisted on one last shoot. The Saturday after Thanksgiving, November 25, was a clear, blustery day with a wind out of the northwest so strong that it distorted Jackson's face as he leaned over the glass and so "bloody cold" that his hand went numb around the brush. Namuth lay in the damp, leaf-covered grass, coaxing Jackson from one "final shot" to the next, through a mine field of "technical delays." Standing alone on the platform, shivering in the biting wind, Jackson waited, smoking a cigarette against the cold while the anger, frustration, and self-loathing that had been accumulating over the last three months slowly boiled toward the surface. Namuth noticed that Jackson was "full of tension [and] it was not just the cold." Finally, at about four-thirty, after the last rays of usable light had disappeared, Namuth announced, "We are done! It's great, it's marvelous." As Jackson climbed down from the scaffold, Namuth tried awkwardly to embrace him, but Jackson headed straight for the house.

Lee was in the kitchen preparing the turkey for a belated Thanksgiving feast. To celebrate the holiday and the last day of filming, she had invited a score of friends to an eight-o'clock dinner and recruited Peter Blake and Ted Dragon to help with last-minute preparations before the other guests arrived. When Jackson stalked in, followed closely by Namuth, he was "very blue," according to Blake, "frozen from the hideous cold." Without a word, he went straight to the kitchen sink, reached into the cabinet underneath, and pulled out a bottle of bourbon they kept for guests. Lee "went white." The room went silent. Blake, who was standing at the set table, "tried to speak," but couldn't think of anything to say. Namuth, trying to brush it off, walked into the next room to warm himself by the fire. Dragon, who had never seen Jackson drunk, leaned over and whispered to Lee, "Why are you so upset?" Between clenched teeth, Lee whispered back, "You just don't know. You don't realize what you're in for." To her, it was clear from the moment Jackson walked in the door that the end had come; that the two years of productivity and relative calm since the catastrophe at Bertha Schaefer's were over; that Jackson was determined to end them tonight—publicly, pathetically, spectacularly.

He filled two large tumblers and downed one in a few gulps. Then he filled it again and summoned Namuth from the living room. He announced loudly, "This is the first drink I've had in two years." Namuth broke the stunned silence. "Don't be a fool," he said. But Jackson wasn't listening. He had been listening to Namuth's directions for three months and that, apparently, was long enough. He downed the second tumblerful. By now Lee had recovered her composure enough to hurry Namuth out of the house, ostensibly to go home and change for dinner. Soon after he left, the phone rang and Jackson answered: Buffie Johnson was calling to invite the Pollocks for drinks. When she mentioned that Violet de Laszlo, Jackson's analyst in the early forties, was her houseguest for the weekend, "you could see his face light up even over the phone," Johnson recalls. "He said he'd love to come." They would have to come early, she told him, because she and de Laszlo were going to the Macys' for dinner. Jackson agreed eagerly. A few minutes later, however, Lee called back. "Jackson can't come," she told Johnson curtly. "He's got to help me with dinner; we have guests coming." Johnson had seen Jackson occasionally peeling vegetables for Lee's dinner parties, but couldn't help thinking, "he could have come if she would have let him off."

Lee's effort to contain the damage backfired. He filled and emptied another tumbler. By the time the other guests started to arrive—the Namuths, the Potters, the Zogbaums, John Little, Alfonso Ossorio—Jackson was reeling. Everyone, especially Namuth, tried to ignore him; most had never seen him drunk. But Jackson was impossible to ignore. In a rage, he tore a belt of sleigh bells from the living room door and swung it at Namuth. "Jackson, put those back!" Namuth ordered.

It was the wrong thing to say. At the sound of yet another "direction" from Namuth, Jackson imploded. All the repressed anger and self-hatred—from months of standing in the cold, waiting for the next shot, the next angle, painting on cue, stopping on cue, repeating on cue; the months of "Where do I stand?" "When do I come in?" and "Should I do it now?"—flooded back. All the phoniness and self-deception seemed suddenly, excruciatingly obvious. "Maybe those natives who figure they're being robbed of their souls by having their images taken have something," Jackson later told a friend. His brothers had been right. His desperate effort to prove them wrong by striking a Faustian bargain with Namuth—celluloid immortality for artistic integrity—by clinging to the *image* of the great artist, had only confirmed it: he *was* a fraud. Celebrity had betrayed him, just as his family had.

Jackson fought the recognition with rage. "You're a phony," he sputtered at Namuth, pointing his blunted finger. "I'm not a phony, you're a phony." Lee tried to dispel the gathering storm by calling everyone to the table, but Jackson and Namuth brought their argument with them, carried on in ferocious whispers. They sat down, oblivious to the other guests, Jackson at the head of the table, Namuth at his right. The whispering grew more intense. "I'm not a phony, but you're a phony," Jackson repeated—they were the "tiresome, awful repetitions of a drunk," recalls one witness—"You know I'm not a phony. I'm not a phony, but you're a phony." Suddenly, Jackson stood up, breathing heavily and glaring at Namuth. He clutched the end of the table with both hands. "Should I do it now?" he demanded in fierce self-mockery. "Jackson —no!" Namuth commanded. Yet another direction. One guest remembered wanting to throw something at Namuth or to shout, " 'Shut up, Hans.' He was being so pompous and authoritarian." Jackson never took his eyes off Namuth. There was a long pause before he repeated, louder this time, "Now?" Immediately, Namuth shouted, "Jackson—this you must not do!" One last time, in a roar, Jackson demanded, "*Now?*" but before Namuth could answer, he heaved the heavy table into the air.

For a split second, no one spoke and nothing moved. Then suddenly dishes began to hit the floor. Dozens of plates, cups, saucers, forks and knives, gravy boats and serving bowls slid in slow motion down the length of the long table and crashed onto the floor. Some guests sat in disbelief, others reared back to dodge the turkey, dressing, gravy, wine, salad, and creamed onions that flew in every direction. For a minute it looked as if the table might upend on top of Lee who was sitting at the end opposite Jackson. Instead, it tilted to the right like a listing ship and fell on its side.

When the last of the dishes stopped spinning, there was a long, anxious silence. It was broken by the crack of the back door slamming as Jackson left.

"Coffee," said Lee, "will be served in the living room."

Jackson must have been outside—in the cold again—before he realized that he had no place to go. Dr. Heller was dead. Roger Wilcox had left for a year in Mexico. Lee was inside. This time, there would be no reassuring office visits, no calming walks on the beach. He was falling, and no one was there to catch him. From a nearby bar, he called the Macys' where Violet de Laszlo and Buffie Johnson had just sat down to dinner. "Violet got on the phone," Johnson recalls, "and all we heard were shrieks and shocked laughter. 'Oh, Jackson, no. Oh, Jackson, you didn't.' But knowing Violet, I had a sense of how serious it was." Minutes later, Jackson appeared at the door, "lurching and very drunk indeed," according to Johnson. "He just headed for Violet like a bird heading for its nest." De Laszlo left the table and ushered him into another room. While the other guests listened to the muffled sounds through the door, Jackson poured out his agony in a tangled mass of words. "He was always inarticulate," says de Laszlo, "but when he was drunk like that he was incomprehensible." She tried to comfort him but sensed the futility of it. "There was nothing I could do," she recalls. "I had a feeling this depression was permanent. It was like he was at the end of his life."

39

THE UNRAVELING

The storm descended with unexpected speed and fury. The filming had ended just in time. Within days, great black clouds rolled in from the Atlantic, turning day into night. Cars were flipped like toys, fallen power lines danced in the streets, old trees bent into impossible curves. On Fireplace Road, 108-mile-per-hour winds rattled the studio and uprooted two giant elms. Gray sheets of rain and snow lashed the abandoned scaffold in the backyard and blotted out the view of Accabonac Harbor beyond. Inside, Lee cowered behind a bed, as she had since childhood at the sound of thunder, convinced, like her mother, that storms were omens of impending disaster.

Delayed by the bad weather, the Pollocks arrived in New York the day before the opening of Jackson's show on November 28, 1950. None of the show's thirty-two works had been stretched or hung—a process that normally took several days. With help from Giorgio Cavallon, Alfonso Ossorio, and Ted Dragon, Jackson stayed up all night unrolling the canvases from the huge drum that he used to transport them, and wrestling them onto stretchers. "They had never been stretched before," recalls Cavallon, "so they were a bitch to work on." Lee and Ray Eames watched while Parsons, smoking and pacing nervously, complained about the size of the paintings. "All you people," she said, wringing her slender hands, "all you people are painting such big pictures and they're so difficult to sell." (Gerome Kamrowski, who stopped by the gallery that night, thought she sounded "like the Baroness Rebay.") Miraculously, by the afternoon of the 28th, all the works were up, including the huge quartet from the summer: *Lavender Mist, Autumn Rhythm, Number 32,* and *One.* In Parsons's close, windowless gallery, they covered the walls from floor to ceiling, corner to corner, overwhelming the viewer with images. "It was more than an exhibition," said Lee, "it was an environment."

A few hours after the last painting was hung, the crowd arrived. "It was bigger than ever this year," wrote Jay, the only family member to attend, "and many important people in the art world [were] present." A few succeeded in elbowing their way back from the walls to view the paintings from a distance, but most gave up trying, muttering under their breaths that the works were "too big or too strong." Lee stood near the doorway, one eye always on Jackson, greeting guests "with a big smile," tenaciously upbeat despite the ominous events of the previous week. Many guests, ignoring the paintings altogether, stood in line just to shake hands with "the *Life* painter." Betsy Zogbaum's companion, an editor at *Harper's Bazaar*, was one of many who insisted on an introduction. "Like everybody else, she treated Jackson like some exotic animal in a zoo," recalls Zogbaum. "I was embarrassed for him." Jackson stood dutifully in the center of the crowd, dressed in tie and coat, looking, according to one witness, "absolutely ashen and hideously sober." There hadn't been time to get drunk before the show. Now and then he would glance toward the entrance to see if Stella or Sande had decided at the last minute to attend. Neither did. The anonymous admirers continued to squeeze in.

Jackson, as the critic Thomas Hess noted, held nothing in reserve. His collapse, when it finally came, was total. There was no gradual slide back to the self-destructiveness of the forties, no buffer of slow deterioration that would have given him, or Lee, or somebody, a chance to effect a rescue. By the time most people saw him slip, he had already hit bottom. Even as fans crowded the Parsons Gallery to see the grand visions of summer, Jackson was stumbling through the dark, familiar streets of the Village haranguing strangers and howling at the moon. It was like the old days, only he drank bourbon now instead of beer—fewer drinks in fewer bars to get drunker and sicker. There were also fewer old friends to besiege. Joe Meert, one of Benton's original Kansas City boys, and his wife, Margaret, lived on Cooper Square, and Jackson soon found his way there. "He would yell up at the window, 'Take me in. Take me in, Joe. I've got no place to stay,' " Herman Cherry remembers. When it was too late for yelling, he would collapse in the phone booth at a bar and call old friends, insisting in a quavering, plaintive voice, "I *am* a great artist. This is Jackson Pollock and I *am* a great artist." One startled wife replied, "I don't care if you're Rembrandt, you don't call up people in the middle of the night."

At first, Lee tried to look the other way. Comfortably settled in the MacDougal Alley house (Ossorio and Dragon left for Paris soon after the opening), she threw herself into the usual round of gallery-going and holiday parties as if Jackson's agony were a passing storm that, given time, would spend itself. Maintaining the appearance of normalcy, she coaxed him to shows: Buffie Johnson, Richard Pousette-Dart, James Brooks, Mary Callery. But the sight of his contemporaries being productive only depressed him further. A Picasso exhibition aroused old rivalries and a Gorky memorial retrospective at the Whitney only made him think of death. "More than 90 percent of the work I'd never seen before," he wrote Ossorio. "[Gorky] was on the beam the last few years of his life." Jackson apparently knew he needed help, but was afraid to accept it. In a drunken stupor, he barged into Violet de Laszlo's office while she was seeing another patient. At Lee's urging, he spent several sessions with the crusty, inflexible homeopath, Elizabeth Wright Hubbard, but after each session he would detour to a bar and not return to MacDougal Alley until the next morning, drunk and reeking of the gutter.

Desperate to prevent another public imbroglio like the one at Bertha Schaefer's, Lee kept such incidents to herself. In a letter to Ossorio, she referred only obliquely to the "drunken howlers" that kept her awake at night. At Christmas time, she breathed a sigh of relief when Jackson refused to join his family in Deep River.

As quickly as it had come together, Jackson's world began to fall apart.

Greenberg had been right: the show didn't sell. "People came to see a famous painter," says Betsy Zogbaum, "but no one dreamt of buying anything." Perhaps the big paintings were too intimidating, as Parsons complained, or the gallery was "overhung," as Greenberg argued. Perhaps the asking prices were too high: $4,000 for *Lavender Mist*; $5,000 for the black-and-white *Number 32*; $7,500 each for *One* and *Autumn Rhythm*, although even the little ones, the "mementos," most of them priced at $300, were passed over. Whatever the reason, the result, Parsons later admitted, was a disaster. Out of thirty-two works, only one, *Lavender Mist*, sold—to Alfonso Ossorio for a humiliating $1,500 "spread over a considerable period." "For me it was heartbreaking," said Parsons. "For Jackson it was ghastly." Greenberg called it "a terrible down," although he himself had failed to appear at the opening. Despite the warning signs, Jackson seemed surprised by the turn of fortune. Friends described him as alternately "deeply bitter" and "furious." He phoned Greenberg late at night to complain, "All you've written about me hasn't done me any fucking good, and I was foolish enough to believe it," and when he heard that Sidney Janis had complimented the show, he called him at three in the morning and screamed, "This is Jackson Pollock and I hear you like my work. Why don't you buy one?"

Unfortunately, the show stirred no such passions among reviewers. Most ignored it completely—a silence even more devastating than scorn. "The downtown people came up, and they thought the show was a dud," recalls Greenberg, who didn't write a review that year. "That was the consensus. Even though I suspected it, I was flabbergasted." In the *Times*, Howard Devree raised the old accusation of fraud. "More than ever before," he wrote, "it seems to me that Pollock's work is well over toward automatic writing and that its content . . . is almost negligible." Only Robert Goodnough, writing in *Art News*, managed to generate some enthusiasm for Jackson's "enormous" canvases. "Pollock has found a discipline that releases tremendous emotive energy combined with a sensitive statement that, if to some overpowering, can not be absorbed in one viewing—one must return." Goodnough singled out the black-and-white *Number 32* for special praise, describing how its "open black rhythms . . . dance in disturbing degrees of intensity, ecstatically energizing the powerful image in an almost hypnotic way."

One by one, the grand visions of the summer began to unravel.

When Ossorio left for Paris, the plans for a chapel decorated with Pollock murals fell into the enthusiastic but dilatory hands of Tony Smith. Ossorio offered to have a model built in Paris if Smith sent the necessary drawings, but warned Jackson of the need to "prod Tony from time to time." Meanwhile, Peter Blake's ideal museum remained just that, an unrealized ideal. Except for *Lavender Mist*, the show's big paintings had failed to sell, and not a single mural commission had materialized—from California or anywhere else—since the one for the Geller house. All the great expectations of the previous summer, encouraged by Tony Smith, had come to nothing—although no one, especially Jackson, was yet willing to admit it. In February, he turned down a commission to illustrate a book for Alexey Brodovitch, lamely explaining to Ossorio that "the concentration here is toward wall painting." And he continued to insist that there was still a great, untapped interest in his work "out there"—if not out west, then in Chicago. In anticipation of a show at the Chicago Arts Club set for the following October, he wrote Ossorio: "It is a new gallery designed by Mies Vanderoie [*sic*]—I think there might be some good reaction to my stuff out there."

Betty Parsons was another of Jackson's troubles. The shotgun wedding between farmboy and socialite had always been rocky, even in the best of times. Now that the paintings were no longer selling themselves, Betty's inadequacies rankled. Both Jackson and Lee complained bitterly that she took on too many artists, especially from among her amateur friends; that she didn't push sales, had no long-range plans, treated artists cavalierly, kept slipshod records, and ultimately cared more about her own art than about selling. Lee later called her a "gallery dabbler" and accused her of mounting "ego trip shows." By the end of the 1950–51 season, a year before his contract with Parsons expired, Jackson was already secretly sounding out other dealers and directing his friends away from "Betty's bins." "There is a lot of unrest among the painters in her gallery," he wrote Ossorio. "I don't know what, if anything, is the solution. . . . There is an enormous amount of interest and excitement for modern painting there—it's too damned bad Betty doesn't know how to get at it."

The critical backlash following the November show gave new license to Jackson's old enemies. Critics and fellow artists who had been stewing privately ever since the *Life* article could now vent their resentments openly. His paintings were conspicuously missing from the Art Students League's seventy-fifth anniversary exhibition at the Metropolitan Museum. His name was included in a list of lesser-known artists associated with the League, but the hostility directed his way at the opening in March was "palpable," according to Peter Busa. "He might have been more offended by the way they treated him," says Busa, "but he was too drunk to notice."

Nowhere were the insults more obvious than at the Club. Seeing the power that had accrued to Greenberg and eager to make a name for himself, Thomas Hess, the new editor of *Art News*, had begun championing Willem de Kooning, declaring him, in a bold swipe at both Greenberg and Pollock, "the best artist of the group." "Hess was playing a power game," recalls Conrad Marca-Relli, "pushing de Kooning and trying to get rid of Jackson in the number one spot." By early 1951, he had rallied many Club members, still resentful of Jackson's success, to what was being called "the de Kooning camp." The few times Jackson showed his face in the smoky loft on Eighth Street, he "became a target," recalls Philip Pavia. "He came into so much ridicule." After one particularly drunken, profanity-laden altercation, he stormed out the door, roaring, "I don't need a club."

The final insult came when Jackson attended a talk by Hess at the Club. The subject was Hess's recently published book, *Abstract Painting: Background and American Phase.* To Jackson, drunk and defensive, everything about the book seemed a slap in the face: the jacket, endpapers, and frontispiece all featured Gorky's *The Betrothal II;* the order of illustrations and text put Pollock last—out of alphabetical order. One witness remembers how Jackson "sat clutching the book as if he wanted to crush it." Several times during the discussion, he jumped to his feet, let out a string of obscenities, then succumbed to the jeering and sat down again, shifting in his chair and continuing his protest in an angry mumble. Finally, unable to bear it any longer, he stood up and hurled the book at de Kooning. "Why'd you do that?" de Kooning asked. "It's a good book." "It's a rotten book," Jackson replied. "He treats you better than me."

By mid-January 1951, Lee could no longer hide the truth—either from herself or from the outside world. Jackson was out of control. In his rare lucid moments, even Jackson admitted it. "I really hit an all-time low—with depression and drinking," he confessed in a letter to Ossorio. "NYC is brutal. . . . Last year I thought at last I am above water from now on in—but things don't work that easily I guess." In the same letter, he insisted that Elizabeth Wright Hubbard had been "extremely helpful" and generally indicated that the problem was safely behind him. But Lee knew otherwise. At the opening of the "Abstract Painting and Sculpture in America" show at the Museum of Modern Art penthouse in late January, Jackson drank so much champagne that he fell out of his chair several times and, when asked to say a few words to the assembled artists, panicked and fled the building. For Lee, it was a nightmare come true, exactly the kind of public spectacle she was desperate to avoid. Chasing him through the exhibit and out onto the street, she prevented him from driving off in the Cadillac only when Linda Lindeberg, who happened to be passing by, agreed to drive them home—all the way to Springs. Jackson was too drunk to protest, but forced Lindeberg to stop at practically every bar on the ride across Long Island. In his letter to Ossorio, Jackson admitted that he "couldn't get any idea of the [MOMA] show," but didn't explain why.

More and more, Lee was torn between New York, where liquor was accessible, and Springs, where the car was accessible. Fearing for her own life as well as Jackson's, she canceled her plans to accompany him on a car trip to Chicago in February. A group of Chicago artists who called themselves "Momentum" had invited him to serve on a panel of jurors that would select works for the group's annual exhibition. Despite his objections to the idea of a "contest," Jackson accepted the offer, which included an all-expenses-paid trip to Chicago. "I think seeing Chicago and the experience might do me good," he wrote Ossorio, "at any rate I'll try it." When Lee pulled out, he decided to fly.

Without Lee for the first time in a decade, Jackson lost all control. On the flight out, he drank until the stewardesses refused to serve him any more. From there the trip descended into one prolonged binge. According to Greenberg, who had recommended Jackson for the jury duty, "He was drunk all the time he was there." The jurying quickly turned into a farce as Jackson, drunk and belligerent, squared off against James Lechay, a hard-nosed "middle-of-the-road Romantic" who held the title of visiting artist at the school where Phil Guston had taught, the University of Iowa. (The third judge, seventy-year-old Max Weber, stayed out of the fracas.) "Between the two of them [Jackson and Lechay], they threw out most of the submissions," recalls Greenberg, who later heard of the debacle from participants. Out of 850 submissions, the jury rejected all but 47, despite the fact that the exhibition could have accommodated as many as 200 admissions. The sponsors were infuriated. "By rights a jury should fill every available spot," says Greenberg, who had judged the show the previous year. Jackson later described the competition as "disappointing and depressing" because "nothing original [was] being done." But most participants saw it differently. "Jackson and this other guy were competing," says Greenberg, "competing to see who could be the most rigorous—who could be the least charitable." Despite nonstop drinking, Jackson did manage to meet a few important collectors during his short stay, including Maurice Culberg, a prominent patron of Dubuffet. He also paid a reciprocal visit to Reginald Isaacs's apartment where *Number 2, 1950* hung in the place of honor. But mostly he drank. Bombed and restless during the pre-dinner speeches at the awards banquet on February 10, he lunged at his neighbors, muttered obscenities, and yawned ostentatiously. As the speeches droned on, he began playing with the heavy, gold-embossed plate on the table in front of him. He held it up to his face as if examining it closely, fanned himself with it, spun it like a top. Finally, he heaved it over his shoulder, turning back to the speaker with a look of deep concentration just as the plate crashed to the floor behind him.

By March, Lee was desperate. Hubbard's stern, grandmotherly advice and homeopathic remedies had proven inadequate. Jackson didn't need herbs or sympathy; he needed to stop drinking—soon. On Hubbard's recommendation,

Lee consulted Ruth Fox, a fifty-six-year-old psychiatrist who specialized in the treatment of alcoholism. Fox's approach involved a combination of intensive psychotherapy (two or three sessions a week of "depth analysis"), and group support through Alcoholics Anonymous.

Fox, who knew of Jackson through the *Life* article, responded quickly, believing that "the motivation to seek help for a drinking problem often evaporates within 24 hours." She arranged an initial interview and invited Lee, as part of "the treating team," to sit in on part of it. For two hours, Fox, a handsome, self-possessed woman, questioned Jackson, alternately sympathetic and firm, respectful and chastening. It couldn't have been long before she realized how closely he conformed to the alcoholic profile she had developed: egocentric, masochistic, withdrawn, impulsive, dependent, with a low tolerance for tension, low self-esteem, "longings for omnipotence," and "problems in the sexual area." His recent preoccupations with his image as a great artist confirmed another of Fox's theories: that the alcoholic tends to build

> an unconscious fantasy that he *is* whatever he *wishes* to be. . . . Then, regarding himself as unique and special, he thinks he is entitled to preferential treatment. The arrogant pride, the inordinate claims for special and unlimited privileges, the feeling of being entitled to unconditional happiness and love, the conviction that he should be free of responsibility for his actions—all these elements operate unconsciously, for the most part, [even] when the individual is not drinking.

Like her predecessors, Wall, Henderson, de Laszlo, and Hubbard, Fox considered such traits "vestigial traces of infancy" and sought their roots in childhood. She also believed that alcoholism had a genetic component, that an inability to metabolize alcohol could be inherited, so she undoubtedly probed into Roy Pollock's history of drinking. But the most important factor, Fox believed, the one that allowed the alcoholic traits to "completely dominate the personality," was the pharmacological property of the drug itself. "The predisposing traits urge the individual to the use of alcohol," she wrote, "alcohol emphasizes and enhances the traits themselves, and so the individual has recurrent recourse to the magical substance."

For Fox, chemistry was at the root of the problem, and therefore chemistry was the place to begin treatment. She insisted unequivocally that the first step toward recovery was abstinence. Unlike her predecessors, she considered analyzing a drunk "a waste of the analyst's time and the patient's money." Too often, she had seen patients who thought that simply by recognizing the source of their alcoholism—whether psychological, domestic, financial, or occupational—they had done their part. "The alcoholic then feels perfectly justified," she wrote, "in postponing the start of abstinence, that first, all-important step toward recovery, until the physician or other therapist has magically removed or solved the problems." For those patients who had trouble abstaining, Fox prescribed Antabuse, a brand of disulfiram, a new drug that, when taken in combination with alcohol, caused nausea and vomiting—chemistry to fight chemistry.

It was straight talk and Jackson seemed, at least temporarily, sobered by it.

Not so Lee. Despite Fox's reassuring manner and no-nonsense approach, Lee wasn't sure the treatment would work or, even if it did, that it would work in time to save Jackson from himself. In early March, she "forced him"—her own words—to draw up a will. Not surprisingly, the three-page document left everything in Lee's hands. She would be sole beneficiary and sole executor. When Jackson was forced to contemplate what would happen if Lee "failed to survive him," however, old animosities began to move behind the veil of legalese. Sande, the only brother who "understood" his art, was his second choice for executor, then Greenberg, then Ossorio. Sande was also named as contingent beneficiary. If both Sande and Lee predeceased him, Charles, Frank, and Jay were to divide the estate equally—but *not* the paintings. Jackson knew too well what his older brothers thought of his art. In an accompanying letter of request, he instructed the executor "to dispose of my paintings rather than distribute them to my brothers. Give them the proceeds of the sale. Try to maintain the paintings as intact as possible." The wounds reopened at the family reunion were not yet healed.

Meanwhile, the engine of celebrity rumbled ahead unattended. In Westerly, Rhode Island, listeners to station WERI heard Jackson's flat, slightly nasal voice coming over their radios, expounding on "the meaning of modern art." "Modern art to me is nothing more than the expression of contemporary aims of the age that we're living in," he said in response to a question from William Wright, an East Hampton neighbor who had recorded the interview in the last days of 1950. When asked how the public "should look at a Pollock painting," Jackson suggested that people "look passively" and "not bring a subject matter or preconceived idea of what they are to be looking for. . . . I think it should be enjoyed just as music is enjoyed." Most of Wright's questions were leading ("Would it be possible to say that the classical artist expressed his world by representing the objects, whereas the modern artist expresses his world by representing the *effects* the objects have upon him?"), and most of Jackson's answers were familiar ("the direction that painting seems to be taking here is away from the easel . . . into some kind of wall painting"). Occasionally, the exchange degenerated into blather:

WRIGHT: Well, isn't [a stick] more difficult to control than a brush? I mean, isn't there more a possibility of getting too much paint or splattering or any number of things? . . .

POLLOCK: No, I don't think so. I don't—ah—with experience—it seems to be possible to control the flow of the paint, to a great extent, and I don't use—I don't use the accident—'cause I deny the accident.

WRIGHT: I believe it was Freud who said there's no such thing as an accident. Is that what you mean?

POLLOCK: I suppose that's generally what I mean.

On January 15, Nina Leen's picture of the "Irascibles" appeared in *Life.* As far away as Mexico, where Robert Beverly Hale and his wife Barbara were vacationing, readers saw Jackson, looking like a "dour son of a bitch." In the same month, Hans Namuth's still pictures from the previous summer appeared in *Portfolio.* In its January issue, *Art News* named Jackson's November show at Betty Parsons one of the three best shows of the year, after John Marin's and before Alberto Giacometti's. In March, *Lavender Mist* and *Autumn Rhythm* appeared in *Vogue* as backdrops for full-page pictures by Cecil Beaton of models wearing "The New Soft Look." Breezily equivocating, the accompanying text called them "dazzling and curious paintings." In May, the Brooklyn Museum included Jackson's ink drawing, *Number 3, 1951,* in its sixteenth biennial "International Water Color Exhibition." The same month, Namuth's pictures appeared again in *Art News,* this time with an extensive article by Robert Goodnough called "Pollock Paints a Picture," in which the drip method was described in loving detail. ("Pollock uses metallic paint much in the same sense that earlier painters applied gold leaf, to add a feeling of mystery and adornment.") Also in May, Leo Castelli chose *Number 1, 1949* to be included in the famous Ninth Street Show beside paintings by members of the Club, and plans were laid for an October show at the Arts Club of Chicago, featuring Pollock, Ben Shahn, and Willem de Kooning. Everywhere, Jackson's paintings were being seen: from Austria, where a Viennese critic wrote Jackson for help on a book about "automatic painting"; to Japan, where two Pollock paintings were included in the Third Tokyo Independent Art Exhibition; to Mount Pleasant, Iowa, where a teacher at Iowa Wesleyan College wrote to find out more about Jackson's technique. In Europe, nineteen of Peggy Guggenheim's Pollocks toured Amsterdam, Brussels, and Zurich, while in America, the Museum of Modern Art's Department of Circulating Exhibitions took *Number 31, 1949* (later replaced by *Number 12A, 1948*) to twenty-five cities in three and a half years, from Fargo, North Dakota, to Fort Worth, Texas. In Paris, a Pollock, chosen by Michel Tapié, was shown in the "Véhémences Confrontées" exhibition at the Galerie Nina Dausset, and a Soviet critic took news of Jackson's "decadent bourgeois" art home from the Venice Biennale.

To Jackson, such delayed bursts of celebrity must have seemed unreal, as if happening in someone else's life, or in a movie. He had become alienated from his own image. The celebrated Jackson Pollock, the one he saw pictured and read about in the magazines, was confident, creative, prolific, and sober. In early 1951, the real Jackson Pollock was none of those things. Since falling off the wagon, he had produced only a few ink drawings on Japanese paper. He thought so little of the drawings that he quickly cannibalized them to make two collages and a papier-mâché sculpture for the "Sculpture by Painters" show at

Peridot Gallery in March; and so little of the sculpture that he left it outside, where it quickly disintegrated.

Nothing brought the feelings of emptiness and alienation into sharper focus than Namuth's movie. Like everything else that winter, it moved ahead on its own, blithe to Jackson's paralysis. Namuth and Falkenberg edited the months of film, prepared a final cut, and pasted together a script from bits and pieces of Jackson's previously published statements. (Jackson scribbled a few editorial changes in the margins.) To give the movie "authenticity," they asked Jackson to read it:

> My home is in Springs, East Hampton, Long Island. I was born in Cody, Wyoming, thirty-nine years ago. In New York I spent two years at the Art Students League with Tom Benton. He was a strong personality to react *against.* This was in 1929 [*sic*]. I don't work from drawings or color sketches. My painting is direct. I usually paint on the floor. I enjoy working on a large canvas.

On and on it droned in the same Dick-and-Jane style, Jackson's wooden monotone leavened only slightly by nervous haste:

> Sometimes I use a brush, but often prefer using a stick. Sometimes I pour the paint straight out of the can. . . . When I am painting I have a general notion as to what I am about. I *can* control the flow of the paint; there is no accident, just as there is no beginning and no end.

When the tape was played back, Jackson was appalled at the sound of his voice, but didn't complain. It wasn't his project anymore, if it ever was. Only when Falkenberg created a "music-effects" track, using recordings of Balinese folk music, did he finally balk. "But, Paul," he said, "this is exotic music. I am an American painter." Namuth and Falkenberg responded that there wasn't enough money in the shoestring budget for an original score. To break the impasse, Lee, who didn't like anything about the film but wanted to avoid an embarrassment, approached John Cage, the experimental composer. Cage was deeply immersed in the preparation of a piece for twelve randomly tuned radios but turned the job down for personal reasons: "I couldn't abide Pollock's work because I couldn't stand the man." He did, however, introduce Lee to a young composer friend, Morton Feldman, who was willing to do the job in return for an ink drawing. "[I] wrote the score as if I were writing music for choreography," said Feldman.

By the time the film premiered at the Museum of Modern Art on June 14, Jackson had lost interest in everything about it except Feldman's music, which he thought "might be great." As he sat in the darkened gallery, watching the familiar scenes of the previous fall being replayed in flickering light—putting on his shoes, contemplating the canvas, stirring the paint, wiping the glass— Jackson undoubtedly felt the worm of phoniness twisting inside him again. Like all the disembodied triumphs that winter, the film was both a painful reminder of his current creative block and additional proof that his brothers had been right: that his celebrity, like the film, had been a sham all along.

In the bleakest days of a bleak winter, Jackson took up pen and paper and began drawing again. During all of 1950, he had hardly touched a sketch pad. His ambitions demanded a far grander "arena" (his word). The results of these first tentative, chastened efforts after the Thanksgiving debacle must have surprised even Jackson. Nothing remained of the previous summer. The grand scale, the lyrical loops, the delicate webs, the elegant compositions, the gorgeous palette of pinks and tans—all vanished. In their place were small, spare visions in black and white, cryptic dots and stuttering lines, splatters and dashes in dry arrangements, all in relentlessly black ink. It was as if he were denying the recent past, punishing himself for the excesses of celebrity with a hardtack of imagery. Lee was shocked and baffled. The leap to canvas early in 1951 brought more surprises. Jackson did not, as Lee had expected, capitulate to color. The scale enlarged, but the imagery hardly changed—Jackson called his new paintings "drawing on canvas in black." He began using a brush occasionally. But the biggest shock came when Lee walked into the studio in the spring of 1951 and saw, in the black-and-white painting laid out on the floor, a recognizable shape. For the first time in five years, figures were emerging from behind the veil. Jackson had abandoned abstraction. "Some of my early images [are] coming thru," he wrote Ossorio. "[I] think the non-objectivists will find them disturbing—and the kids who think it simple to splash a Pollock out."

Where did these images come from? Why did Jackson, over the course of a few short months in the winter of 1950–51, abandon the palette, the technique, and the theories that had made him famous? Other than Jackson, the only person who knew the answers, the only person who wasn't surprised by these new, nightmarish visions was Tony Smith.

Smith was one of the few friends who didn't desert Jackson after the drinking started again. Unlike most of Lee's summer guests, who had never seen Jackson drunk, who knew only the icon, Smith found Jackson as attractive drunk as sober. During the winter, their bond, which up to then had been fond but casual, became the guiding force in Jackson's life. Partly, it was the camaraderie of a fellow alcoholic: Smith was always ready to share "a beer and a beef." Partly, it was Smith's intellectual banter—even if, as Roger Wilcox claims, Jackson "didn't know what the Sam Hill Tony was talking about." Partly, it was Smith's relentless flattery and the undercurrent of sexuality in his attentions. Partly, it was his sensitivity to Jackson's volatile moods. "Tony had antennae," says his wife, Jane. "He knew what Jackson's problems were." And how to respond. At times, Smith would entertain Jackson with recitations from Joyce or philosophical soliloquies; other times, the two men could sit for hours in utter silence. In many ways, Jackson's increasingly dark vision mirrored Smith's own Irish gloom. "Tony and Jackson were made for each other," says

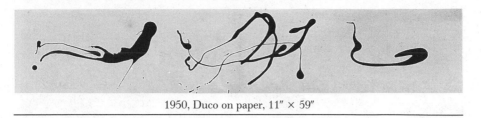

1950, Duco on paper, 11″ × 59″

Fritz Bultman. "They were both tormented souls, fellow travelers on the road to hell."

Whatever the reasons, Jackson quickly developed a desperate devotion to his young admirer. "He became Tony's biggest fan," recalls James Brooks, whom Jackson introduced to Smith. "He was so proud of his friendship with Tony," says Harry Jackson. "He said to me, 'Shit, Harry, he's got to know all kinds of stuff to be an architect.' " His letters to Ossorio in Paris brimmed with an adulation that not even Smith's delinquency on the chapel project could shake. After Smith's wife, Jane, left for Europe with Tennessee Williams in late 1950, Tony and Jackson became nearly inseparable. First at the house in MacDougal Alley, then on Fireplace Road, where Smith visited almost every weekend during the spring, they spent dozens of evenings together, drinking, smoking, riding through the countryside, and talking about everything from Oriental philosophy to Jackson's latest dream. "[I had a] constructive dream," Jackson wrote Ossorio, "([and] happily Tony was here to interpret it for me)."

Not since John Graham had anyone held such power over Jackson or his art —and Smith, unlike Graham, was eager to use it. "Tony loved to dominate you creatively," recalls Buffie Johnson. "He loved to make suggestions, tell you how to paint. He always wanted to get into the act, and I know he did with Jackson."

Out of these hours together, many of them in the studio, many of them in a drunken reverie, Jackson's new imagery emerged.

Smith urged him to "try something new." Jackson had felt constrained by the all-over composition and rigorous abstraction of his dripped images for some time and, as early as 1948, had experimented with various means— cutouts, montage, brush strokes, biomorphic shapes, and scale—to recapture the electricity of risk. He had even flirted on and off with figuration, in works like *Triad* and *White Cockatoo*, trying to tap into the psychic energy of core memories. If Smith hadn't pushed him toward larger and larger canvases the year before, Jackson might have abandoned the familiar territory of *Autumn Rhythm* and *One* sooner.

But that was last year. Now Smith wanted to know what was *next*. "Tony really tortured Jackson, even if he didn't realize it," says Buffie Johnson, whose house on Fifty-eighth Street was designed by Smith and who often saw the two men together. "Tony said, 'Well, what you did was great, Jackson, but what are you going to do next? What is this leading to? What is the *development?*'

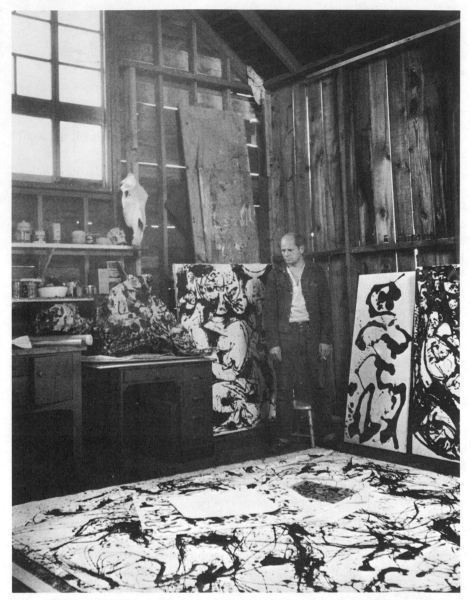

Number 22, 1951, left; *Image of Man (Number 3, 1951)* and *Number 15, 1951,* at right; *Number 32, 1950* on floor; and papier-mâché sculpture on desk.

He made Jackson very nervous by telling him he ought to change. Everybody did that to some extent, but Tony was the worst offender." Specifically, Smith pushed Jackson toward figuration, encouraging him both by example when the two men sketched together, and by suggestion, giving him a copy of *On Growth and Form,* a book filled with illustrations of *things:* cells, shells, scales, snow-flakes, and so forth. "Jackson's return to realistic images was a result of pres-sure from Tony," says Johnson flatly. "It was a classic example of Tony trying to paint through other people."

Smith also put Jackson back in touch with the imagery of his past, the imagery of José Clemente Orozco. (The two men discovered their common admiration for Orozco when Smith asked Jackson what he thought was the greatest work of art in North America and Jackson replied without hesitation, "the Orozco fresco at Pomona College.") The figures that Lee saw when she walked into the studio that spring were mostly refugees from Orozco: huge women with pendulous breasts, strange beasts and distorted faces bursting from the picture frame. Orozco's jagged, tenebrous world had always attracted Jackson, especially at times of emotional turmoil, when its grotesque forms and dark palette perfectly suited his own nightmarish vision. As late as 1949, he kept that imagery alive in his drawings, as well as in the genesis of his drip paintings. Even without Smith, Jackson might have turned to that imagery during the bleak, troubled winter of 1950–51. But Smith's enthusiasm gave Orozco's dark world new legitimacy and new appeal. On a trip to Smith's family home in South Orange, New Jersey, Jackson met Tony's brother Joseph, a Greek scholar, who had helped transfer the cartoons for Orozco's mural at Dartmouth.

Smith even gave Jackson his new medium—literally—by presenting him with a pad of rice paper and a bottle of black ink in late 1950. When Jackson emerged from his month-long binge following the November show, Smith used the gift as a way of luring his friend back to work: drawing was an easy transition; paper and ink were well suited to the confines of the MacDougal Alley house and to Jackson's alcohol-shortened attention span. Working in a miniature version of the drip technique, he followed Smith's advice and began experimenting with the paper's unusual texture and absorbency. The medium felt strange and clumsy at first: the ink far thinner and the paper far more absorbent than the paint and canvas he was used to. An image poured onto the top sheet would bleed through to the sheet beneath, creating a second ghost image that he would rework separately with ink, gouache, watercolor, or even paint. He used inks of various colors, but returned again and again to black. Even without Smith's endorsement, the black and white of ink on paper un- doubtedly suited his dark urges and jarring mood changes. (Violet de Laszlo called them "a very clear expression of depression.") From his Art Students League notebooks to *Number 32*, he had always associated black and white with drawing, and drawing with self-doubt. Without color, he was left alone with his oldest insecurities—the artist who couldn't draw. Black-and-white was like drinking: a form of self-abuse. (At a birthday party for Clement Greenberg on January 16, Jackson tried for the first time in years to combine the two. "It was pathetic," Greenberg recalls. "It was the only time I saw him try to draw while he was drunk. I don't think he ever tried it again.")

Smith may have provided the impetus for change, the link to Orozco, and the appropriate materials, but the images that began appearing in late spring belonged entirely to Jackson; the demons were his alone. From beneath the tangles of poured black lines, anatomies emerged: arms, legs, hands, eyes,

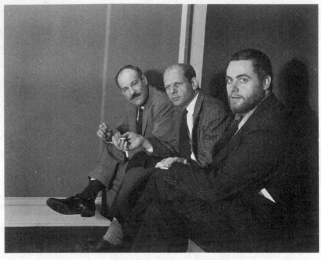

With Barnett Newman (left) and Tony Smith

sometimes in confused piles, sometimes in ominous isolation. There were strange animals—two- and four-footed—totemic figures, reclining figures, a crucifixion; hulking females with huge dry breasts and blank faces. Faces were everywhere: some almost identifiable, rendered like portraits, some all but obliterated in a vandalizing fury. Sometimes the images overpowered him, fighting their way out from behind the veil with a will of their own: a child on its mother's lap; a bull in a field; a stone-faced woman with her skeletal family. Some of the images he let come through; some he tried to conceal at the last minute by turning the image on its side or upside down when he signed it. He worked on long rolls of cotton duck, remnants from upholsterers and sailmakers, painting one image after another without stopping or cutting. When it came time to cut and sign, old fears took over. "He'd ask, 'Should I cut it here? Should this be the bottom?'" Lee recounted. "He'd have long sessions of cutting and editing. . . . Those were difficult sessions. His signing the canvases was even worse. I'd think everything was settled—tops, bottoms, margins— and then he'd have last-minute thoughts and doubts. He hated signing. There's something so final about a signature." With practice, Jackson learned to pour an image exactly as he wanted it: from cryptic to explicit; from abstract to "Rubensesque;" from the harsh compression of *November 14, 1951* to the open lyricism of *Echo*. To enhance his control, he started using glass basting syringes instead of sticks or hardened brushes. With them he could flood a line without reloading. "His control was amazing," Lee marveled. "Using a stick was difficult enough, but the basting syringe was like a giant fountain pen." And the canvas was like rice paper, bleeding and soaking to form intricate interplays of matte (where the paint soaked through) and glossy (where it accumulated) on the cream-colored surface. Jackson had turned drawing into painting, bringing old risks, old energies, and old insecurities to a medium that just a year before had seen his most self-assured triumphs. "He came over and wasn't too certain

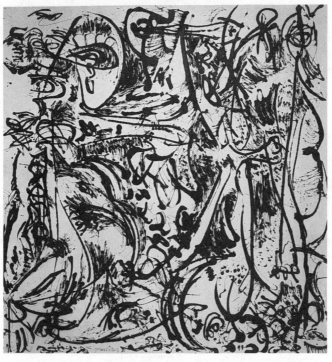

Echo (Number 25, 1951), enamel on canvas, 91⅞″ × 86″

about what he had made," recalls John Little (who didn't like the stark new images as much as Jackson's "regular colors"). Carol Braider remembered how Jackson "was worried about the image having come back," and Ibram Lassaw thought "he seemed terribly unsure of himself."

But painting wasn't enough. Throughout the summer, between spasms of work, Jackson continued to drink. A binge could last two or three weeks, during which the studio sat empty and idle in the summer heat. It would start with beer, a six-pack or two bought at Dan Miller's store and tossed into the back seat of the Cadillac. The beer fortified him for the bars. "He would sit in the car and drink the beers by himself," recalls Roger Wilcox, who had returned from Mexico in May to find Jackson recuperating from a two-week binge. "By the time he had six beers, he was ready to face people." Jackson quickly rediscovered the local spots that had sustained him in the past: Jungle Pete's, where Nina Federico fed him stuffed striped bass and coffee to sober him up; Joe Lori's bar in the East Hampton Hotel, where the hard-nosed management was likely to bring out Jackson's abusive streak ("He didn't like for anyone to tell him he'd had enough," says Wilcox. "Boy, that set him off"); and the Elm Tree Inn, where the bartenders were so indulgent that he usually just "slumped over and fell asleep." The manic energy with which Jackson threw himself back into the self-destructive cycle alarmed even the hardened Bonackers who shared the bar stools at Jungle Pete's. One day when Elwyn Harris, the electrician, and Dick Talmage, the plumber, saw Jackson coming, they tried to hide their bottle of gin. "But Pollock got there first," Harris recalled, "and drank it straight . . . about a half an hour later, I had a call from Jungle Pete's to come pick up Pollock." According to Ed Hults, another Springs resident, "He just couldn't get it down fast enough."

Nothing, it seemed, could slow the fall. At Ruth Fox's insistence, he attended several meetings of Alcoholics Anonymous in Southampton, but that effort was doomed from the start. The confessional format was wildly ill-suited to Jackson's reticent, suspicious nature. He derided his fellow alcoholics as "blabbermouths" and "lonelyhearts," and boasted defensively, "They *got* to drink; me, I only drink if I feel like it." One friend described Jackson as "too red-hot for AA." He visited Fox occasionally for the ego massage of analysis, but resisted taking the Antabuse she prescribed. Without *both* psychological and chemical therapy, Fox knew that meaningful progress was impossible. ("Without Antabuse, alcoholics frequently cannot tolerate the frustrations of analysis," she wrote, "and are apt to revert to drinking during difficult periods of the treatment.") Finally, after a particularly alarming binge in June, Fox persuaded Lee to commit Jackson to a private clinic in Manhattan, the Regent Hospital, for detoxification. At least twice during the summer, Jackson pretended to "dry out" in the clinic's East Sixty-first Street facilities, but kept a bottle of scotch hidden in the lavatory. After one such stay, Valentine and Happy Macy sent a consoling note: "Dear Jackson, Happy & I love you and believe in you, and in what you have done & what you will do—so we want to help you in as many ways as we can in getting over the temporary rough spots, like now."

Not everyone was so understanding. By midsummer, Jackson's social life had come to a virtual standstill. Invitations to cocktail parties and dinners no longer poured into the house on Fireplace Road. Lee no longer wanted to risk having guests in. Larry Rivers, a young painter, and Helen Frankenthaler, came by to pay homage and dedicate themselves "even more determinedly and forever to ART," but compared to the previous year, the house seemed deserted. "This has been a very quiet summer," Jackson lamented in a letter to Ossorio, "no parties . . ." Stories of Jackson's latest antics circulated around East Hampton: how he had insulted Mrs. John Hall Wheelock, wife of the Boston poet and grand dame, at the Guild Hall show ("She said how much she liked his work," recalls Buffie Johnson, "and he turned to her and said, 'Bullshit' "); how he had burst into the Zogbaums' house "absolutely roaring drunk and going on about how he was the greatest painter in the history of the world." He was the worst kind of guest, alternately pathetic and menacing. "People didn't want to touch him," says Gerome Kamrowski, "because they never knew which way he would spring." The stories dismayed some and pleased others, especially the Maidstone Club set, who found in them proof of their long-held suspicions. Locals, who had never stopped thinking his art was crazy—regardless of what *Life* said—now began to think that *he* was crazy. Friends who had welcomed him the previous summer pretended not to be

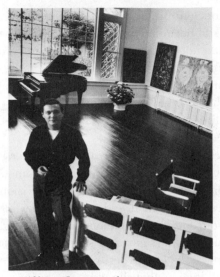

Alfonso Ossorio in the music room at
The Creeks

home when they heard the roar of the Cadillac approaching. "Jeffrey would turn all the lights out," recalled Penny Potter, "hoping he'd go away. And sometimes I'd turn them back on and Jeffrey would go upstairs in a snit—very angry. He thought [Jackson] was going to rape me, or pee on the floor." At Roger Wilcox's house, he did pee, not on the floor, but in the bed, after a night of carousing. The next morning, an enraged Lucia Wilcox chased him out of the house with a broom, calling him a "phony cowboy." "She laid down the law," recalls Wilcox. "She said, 'I will not have you come to my house. You're not welcome here when you're drunk.' " Between Lucia's banishment and Lee's indignation ("She didn't think Lucia had the right to treat Jackson that way," says Wilcox), the two men seldom saw each other again, and when they did, "it just wasn't the same."

About the only positive achievement of the summer was locating a house for Alfonso Ossorio. Before leaving for Europe, Ossorio had asked Lee and Jackson to reconnoiter East Hampton for a suitable property, but for most of the summer, Jackson was too busy drinking and Lee was too busy watching Jackson to do much looking. In early August, Jackson wrote apologetically: "I think the house idea had better wait until you are here." Soon afterward, Lee heard that "The Creeks," a large, secluded estate on sixty acres of waterfront land had become available. The house, a picturesque if dilapidated Italianate villa, had been built for the painter Albert Herter in 1899 at the end of a spit of land between two creeks that emptied into Georgica Pond. Its unusual U-shape brought light and water views into almost every room. The estate included a boat house, a huge, bright studio, terraces, and a garden. After a series of transatlantic calls and cables, Ossorio flew back to complete the sale. To secure the necessary funding from his father, a "formidable sugar magnate" and the ultimate source of money in the family, Ossorio invited him to East Hampton to inspect the house and have lunch with the Pollocks. The plan, like so many that involved Jackson, ended in chaos. On the appointed day, Alfonso missed the train to East Hampton. Jackson, not finding him at the station, said, "Well, fuck it," and, according to Lee, "went off to a bar and disappeared for the rest of the day." When Miguel José Ossorio arrived at the house on Fireplace Road in a big chauffeured limousine, only Lee was there to greet him.

In the midst of Jackson's darkest year, Lee had never been stronger. After they returned to Springs in May, her paintings blossomed into large gestural abstractions. While Jackson etched out his demonic visions in black between self-destructive binges, Lee worked and reworked her big colorful canvases, strangely liberated from the claustrophobia that had plagued her work for a decade. It was as if his weakness gave her strength. The contrast didn't escape Jackson: "Lee is doing some of her best painting," he wrote Ossorio in June, "it has a freshness and bigness that she didn't get before . . . [while] I've had a period of drawing on canvas in black."

If he hadn't been so preoccupied with his own celebrity, Jackson would have seen the confrontation coming sooner. Lee had been gathering confidence for some time, first at the 1950 Guild Hall show, then, in May, at the Ninth Street Show where she showed alongside him. By the summer of 1951, she was no longer "the little lady who paints"; he could no longer save his smaller scraps of canvas to make stretchers "her size." Her paintings were almost as big as his now. Pressing her advantage, Lee persuaded Jackson to invite Betty Parsons to Springs to see her work. Parsons was impressed but left without offering a show. Lee pressed again. "[Jackson] telephoned me and asked me to give [Lee] a show," Parsons recalled. "I said I never showed husbands and wives but he insisted." It was a victory for Lee—Parsons scheduled a show for the following October—but a costly one. Soon after Parsons's visit, Jackson launched into a two-week bender that ended in the Regent Hospital. At first, it looked like a replay of the debacle at Bertha Schaefer's. Except this time, Lee didn't capitulate. Problems or no problems, she continued to paint.

Jackson struck next where he knew Lee was most vulnerable.

On a trip to New York, he left her at the MacDougal Alley house and disappeared on a bar-hopping expedition, only to return a few hours later with a woman on his arm. "This was some woman he had picked up," recalls Annalee Newman who, with her husband Barnett, had stopped by while Jackson was gone. "He was embarrassed because he didn't expect to see Barney and me there, *not* because of Lee. He *wanted* Lee to see them together. He was really trying to hurt her. . . . Of course, Lee was humiliated."

About the same time, rumors began to float back to Lee about Jackson and a young woman who had long been a member of the artists' community in New York. They were credible rumors. She was a svelte, seductive, and stunningly beautiful woman, "at her best in languid poses of silent disdain." Men considered her "untouchable," according to Nicholas Carone, "so beautiful you dared not go near her." Many did, however, including Hans Hofmann, Willem de Kooning, Wilfrid Zogbaum, Morton Feldman, and Jackson's old rival, Phil Guston. "An affair with [her] came to be almost an initiatory rite into a society of the famous," wrote the wife of one of the woman's lovers, "a New York equivalent of the ceremonies of the French Academy." Whether prowling Club meetings in the city and cocktail parties in East Hampton, she "could not wait," recalled May Rosenberg. "She had to fall in love immediately." One of the many men who caught her errant eye was Jackson Pollock.

But Jackson was no match for such "knockout" looks and adhesive sexuality. As much as he would have liked to "play with the other boys," to "count the notches on his belt" along with Guston and de Kooning, he was always either too drunk or too scared, and her fleeting attentions came to nothing.

But that didn't stop Jackson from using the rumors (and the woman's reputation) to torture Lee. "He would say, 'Boy, was she terrific,' just to upset [Lee]," recalls Conrad Marca-Relli. "It was his way of playing a game. He had found her point of vulnerability, and he worked it mercilessly." Betsy Zogbaum found Lee in the kitchen one day "in an absolute fury" over the same woman. Jackson had played on her paranoia before, flirting with other women in her presence, but this time a meanness had crept into the adolescent taunting and innuendo. He wanted to hurt her. Returning late one night from the city, he pulled into the driveway of the house that May and Harold Rosenberg had rented temporarily. He banged at the door and called for May in a drunken bellow. "He said terrible, terrible things," May remembers, "threatening what he was going to do to me, using the foulest language, saying that I'd never have it so good." She came to the window—Harold was in New York—and tried to hush him. "I told him he would wake Patia, that he should go home and get some sleep, but he just kept yelling. Then I saw Lee sitting in the car, obviously petrified, and I knew he was only saying it because she was there. He was taunting her and she was just taking it—Lee who was always so fierce. I realized that she was *afraid.* I had never seen him hit her, but she was obviously afraid that he would."

Just then, May heard a noise on the stairs. When she turned around, she saw seven-year-old Patia coming down in her nightgown, crying hysterically and carrying a huge kitchen knife. "Don't you hurt my mother," she called out to Jackson between sobs. "He had said he was going to lay me," says May, "and Patia thought that meant he was going to hurt me."

By fall, Lee was willing to try anything.

She had always had a "penchant for charlatans," recalls John Myers, "a taste for daffy doctors that would send her to a Gypsy down the road for a special recipe for some kind of new sassafras elixir." Jackson was no better. A summer of Ruth Fox's trenchant analysis and hard choices had left him desperate for something more mystical—and easier. To friends, he continued to insist that he wasn't an alcoholic, that he could "turn it on and off like a beer tap." So when Elizabeth Wright Hubbard made a recommendation that Jackson consult a "biochemist" with a regimen that would "drive his thirst for drink away" by adjusting his body chemistry, both Jackson and Lee pounced on it.

Certainly, only desperation and self-delusion could have brought them, in September, to the swank Park Avenue offices of Dr. Grant Mark.

For someone who promised a longer and healthier life, Dr. Mark looked distressingly ill. With his anorexically thin six-foot-two-inch frame, blanched, gaunt face, albino-blond hair, and long fingernails curved grotesquely over the tips of his red, swollen fingers, he looked "like something out of a horror movie," according to Alfonso Ossorio. Nor was he, in fact, a medical doctor, although he had on his staff six M.D.'s—at one time including Hubbard—who made out prescriptions according to his directions. He may have been a Ph.D., but in his correspondence, he carefully avoided using "Dr." and described himself merely as the "Business Manager" of a company called "Psychological-Chemistry, Inc." Both at the office and on trips to East Hampton, he was frequently accompanied by his elderly mother, whom he described as his "best living advertisement" and to whom he assiduously fed biochemical drops and hot water with lemon juice.

Mark may not have been a doctor, but he had the requisite "Svengali air," and Jackson quickly fell under his spell. He told Jackson exactly what he wanted to hear: that he wasn't an alcoholic at all, he was merely the victim of "chemical derangement," an imbalance of "metals" in the body that could be corrected with the proper diet: no milk products and vast quantities of fresh vegetables, fruit juice, and eggs. The only meat permitted was fowl, but it had to be wild ("eat no bird that can't take off at fifty miles an hour") and it had to have been shot within the previous two hours. ("Where the hell are you going to find wild turkey in the Hamptons?" asked Ted Dragon.) In addition, Mark prescribed daily baths in a solution of kosher rock salt, presumably to leach out harmful mineral deposits. The most important element of the treatment, however, was the soy-based "emulsion" that, coincidentally, Mark sold. The mysterious health juice (Ted Dragon called it "crazy milk") came in quart bottles that had to be kept refrigerated "lest it lose its potency." Mark provided an ungainly refrigerated box for transporting a week's supply of the elixir, but getting Jackson and the container safely to and from New York once a week was, according to Ossorio who often drove, "a nightmare." "The box would promptly get lost at the Cedar Bar or left in a taxi." If Jackson stuck to the regimen and drank a quart of emulsion a day, according to Mark, liquor could no longer hurt him: the alcohol in his body would "find its own level." Unfortunately, in Jackson's wishful calculus, this came to mean that the more emulsion he drank the more liquor he could consume without ill effects. "He felt that a quart of liquor was equal to a quart of emulsion," says Ossorio. Finally, Mark instructed him to return every week to the Park Avenue offices for "analysis"—not psychological but chemical. One of the staff doctors would take blood and urine samples, and inject Jackson with tiny amounts of copper and zinc. "Oh, dear God," cried Roger Wilcox when he heard the news. "The treatment is worse than the illness."

Through the fall, Jackson visited "Dr. Mark" once a week and continued to drink (alternately liquor and emulsion), while Lee visited Dr. Hubbard and prepared furiously for her show. Between Parsons's visit in the spring and the show's opening on October 15, Lee's painting had suffered a curious reversal. Instead of continuing the free experiments with gestural abstraction, she had sought safety in her Hofmann school models, Mondrian and Matisse, covering large canvases with bands of color in cramped, calculated arrangements. Even Stella noticed the difference: "[Lee's] work has changed so much," she wrote Frank. Old friends, including Sande and Arloie, crowded into the opening and complimented her, but the show was a flop. Not a single work sold. Stuart Preston offered a mildly enthusiastic review in the *Times*, but earned Lee's ire with a patronizing reference to her "feminine acuteness."

Jackson's show, in late November 1951, didn't fare much better. At some level, Jackson may have hoped to upstage Lee. He was unusually meticulous about stretching and hanging his paintings; he insisted on a catalogue—his first since coming to Parsons—and he recruited Alfonso Ossorio to write a suitably impenetrable introduction exploring the show's dark themes:

> His painting confronts us with a visual concept organically evolved from a belief in the unity that underlies the phenomena among which we live. . . . An ocean's tides and a personal nightmare, the bursting of a bubble and the communal clamor for a victim are as inextricably meshed in the coruscation and darkness of his work as they are in actuality.

At Tony Smith's suggestion, Jackson had persuaded Parsons to underwrite a portfolio of six prints, photographically reproduced from six paintings in the show and silk-screened in editions of twenty-five at Sande's workshop in Essex, Connecticut. Even with the extra care, the catalogue, the handsome portfolio of prints, and the advantage of Parsons's prime, pre-Christmas slot, however, the show fizzled. In contrast to previous years, the opening was perfunctorily attended and throughout the three-week run, visitors were rare. Although sober the first night—Stella was there—Jackson set the tone for the show when he bolted afterward for the Village. "Jesus," Lee sighed. "We're in for another night." Jackson had anticipated public skepticism. ("Those black-and-whites were an easy target," says painter Paul Jenkins. "[People could say,] 'Only Franz Kline can do black and white, only de Kooning can do figures.' ") He even suspected that they wouldn't sell. He was right on both counts. After the opening, he often dropped by the gallery, often drunk, and stood in dolorous solitude among the stark black-and-white images. When Charles came by, the two went to a bar near the old Eighth Street apartment. "We sat down and Jack pulled out the catalogue," Charles remembers. "He said, 'I want you to see this. I'm a goddamn good painter.' " The words had a strange "finality,"

Charles thought. When Violet de Laszlo ventured into Parsons's gallery, she was struck immediately by a "foreboding of death."

As Christmas approached, death was indeed on Jackson's mind. More than one person had warned him about the noxious effects of the Devolac he had been using for the black paintings. "That stuff was so toxic they had to discontinue it," recalls Alfonso Ossorio. "Even Jackson complained about it. He had to keep the windows open when he used it." With winter approaching, he had to close the windows, but he still needed the barn—both as a place to paint and, more and more, as a place to get away from Lee, and to drink. Finally, he bought a Salamander kerosene stove, a black metal oven with a tall chimney that spit fire. It was a diabolical engine that "terrified" Lee. "A wooden barn, full of pigment and all sorts of flammable stuff, heated by one of those kerosene pot bellies," she complained. "[It was] very frightening."

Even more frightening, though, was Jackson's mood. For reasons that were unclear, the Pollock clan didn't gather in Deep River for Thanksgiving that year, nor did they make plans for Christmas. Jackson sat at the bar at Jungle Pete's or in the barn and waited for the "Santa shit" to pass. He cursed Jeffrey Potter for blocking off one of his favorite escape routes, an old logging road, to prevent out-of-towners from stripping the holly trees. He spent most of the holiday week drunk, at various bars, but decided to return home around eight o'clock on Friday night, December 28.

It was a clear, moonless night, and the road was dry as Jackson pushed the Cadillac, the last remnant of his celebrity, faster and faster down the Springs-Amagansett Road. Approaching the intersection of Old Stone Highway, the big car suddenly veered to the right, into the opposite lane, then off the road into the dark triangle of brush in the middle of the intersection. The lance-like bumpers caught three mailboxes in a row and spun them into the air. Still going sixty, the car hurtled across Old Stone Highway and into the grassy void on the opposite side. Jackson, finally alert, jerked the wheel sharply to the left, back toward the Springs Road. Instantly, the left two tires lost contact while the right two plowed deeper into the frozen ground, spitting up debris as the car careened sideways back onto the pavement, then off again on the other side, where it clung to the edge of the road, bottoming hard on driveway embankments, its wheels spinning furiously in the slick grass. Nothing could stop the long, low-slung Caddy, not even a telephone pole, hit a crunching glance. Trees and bushes flew by, strange shapes in the darkness, their branches clawing at the canvas roof. Fifty feet farther down the road, it hit a tree dead on. In an instant, the broad hood accordioned, the engine punched through the dashboard, the steering wheel pinned Jackson in the chest, and the big car—"his dreamboat"—jolted to a stop.

After a few minutes of dazed silence, Jackson climbed from the wreckage and staggered off into the darkness to search for help.

40

MIRACLE CURES

On one side of the big, airy studio, Betty Parsons shifted nervously in her chair, one hand entwined around a cigarette, the other draped over a bony knee. Across the room, facing her like a firing squad, sat seven men: Clyfford Still, characteristically grave and disapproving; Mark Rothko, looking like an accountant behind thick glasses and anxious eyes; Barnett Newman, with his walrus mustache and forced laugh; Ad Reinhardt, his gentle disposition concealed by a stern gaze; Herbert Ferber and Seymour Lipton, the "dentist" sculptors; and Alfonso Ossorio, whose first show at Parsons's gallery had just closed. Jackson was there, too, quiet and, for a change, sober, his chest still sore where it had been hit by the steering wheel.

They had called this meeting to give Parsons one last chance. They were tired of being neglected. They were tired of being crowded out by the scores of unknown artists—many of them amateurs, most of them women—whose works Parsons insisted on showing. They were tired of her bad record-keeping, her careless policy of lending paintings, and her infuriating habit of disappearing in moments of crisis. They were tired of no catalogues, no publicity, no support, no sales, and, worst of all, no money. "They simply said to Betty, 'Look here, you can't go on like this,' " recalls Ossorio.

First, they offered a carrot: if Parsons dropped all but twelve artists (the seven of them, plus five of her choosing), "they would make [her] the most famous dealer in the world." When she balked at that, they brandished the stick: "If you don't cut down on the frequency of shows and guarantee us some income," they threatened, "we'll have to leave you."

Parsons sat passively through the recital of grievances, her double-jointed legs—one in a flesh-colored stocking, the other in gray—winding tighter and tighter around each other, her sad eyes darting back and forth among the seven glowering figures in front of her. Finally, she looked "these powerhouses" in the eye and said, "Sorry. I have to be true to my conscience." She told them "it was *her* gallery," recalled Ossorio, "and if they didn't like the way she ran it, they could go." What she didn't tell them was that many of the female artists they wanted her to drop were both close friends and financial backers. "She felt committed to these women," according to Ossorio, "so she just twisted her legs together and said no."

For Jackson, it was the last straw. He had conceded the battle over mural commissions, although her "officious meddling" still rankled. He had over-looked it when she lost paintings or put off potential patrons. He could under-stand that Lee's show hadn't sold. He could understand why Ossorio's first show, which followed Lee's, had attracted so little attention. But the failure of the black-and-white show was more than he could forgive. Only two out of sixteen paintings had sold—virtually nothing: not the large works, not the medium-size works, not even the limited edition of signed prints for $200. She couldn't blame the reviews; they had been uniformly supportive. In the *Partisan Review*, Greenberg had called the show "a newer and loftier triumph." "If Pollock were a Frenchman," he wrote, "people would already be calling him 'maître' and speculating in his pictures. Here in this country the museum directors, the collectors, and the newspaper critics will go on for a long time— out of fear if not out of incompetence—refusing to believe that we have at last produced the best painter of a whole generation." (Greenberg had told Lee privately: "At last I see what you see. Jackson has learned to draw—like an *angel*.") Even the crotchety Howard Devree, writing in the *Times*, had agreed that the new works "gained immeasurably" from the reintroduction of figura-tion, and *Art Digest* called them Jackson's "most ambitious and complex [paint-ings] to date."

The critical reaction to the Arts Club show in Chicago in October had been less enthusiastic, but at least there had *been* a show. Unlike most artists, Jack-son was being seen around the world. His paintings had been illustrated in *Life* and *Time* and *Harper's Bazaar*. One had even appeared on television when Vincent Price showed it to Jack Paar on "The Tonight Show." In April the Museum of Modern Art would give him an entire room in its "15 Americans" show. With so much publicity, why wasn't Parsons able to sell more? Why weren't the prices higher? Jackson wasn't the only one asking such questions. From Chicago, Reginald Isaacs wrote to say he was "surprised to hear that the fine publicity that you have received during this last year has not increased your sales." And Bill Davis sent a note from Spain, admiring the November show's "magnificent" catalogue (which Parsons had resisted printing). "Let me know some prices," he added, ". . . I think your prices ought to be higher than ever."

By the time his contract expired on the first day of 1952, Jackson was fuming. He told Parsons not only that he was leaving her gallery but that he wanted to remove his paintings from the premises immediately. Parsons was flabber-gasted. She had taken him on when no one else in New York would risk it; she had spent four years developing his reputation; she had looked the other way when he took money directly from patrons like Ossorio and when he bartered paintings; she had, on occasion, forgone her own commission; and, on top of everything, she had put up with his temperament, his drinking, and his black-and-white mood swings. Barely concealing her own anger behind a steely, businesslike reserve, she fired back a response:

Dear Jack:

I am anxious to make clear to you what I feel concerning the removal of your work at this time from the gallery. As you know, all artists remain with me for a year after their show, so that it gives me the possibility to realize some business on their work—and do not forget, I pay your expenses. I always thought this was understood between us. However, I will understand perfectly if you wish to take your pictures out at the end of May. . . . As ever, Betty

Without much choice, Jackson backed down. He agreed to leave the paintings with her until the end of the season and to "keep an open mind" about renewing his contract, "if she succeeded in doing some business." In fact, he had no intention of renewing. Privately, he dissociated himself from Parsons completely, instructing Ossorio to omit any mention of her from the catalogue for his upcoming show in Paris. Later, Parsons would claim that she felt no resentment over Jackson's departure, only "hurt" and "disappointment." At the time, however, she summarily dropped Lee Krasner from the gallery. "It has nothing to do with your painting," she told Lee. "I still respect you as an artist but it is impossible for me to look at you and not think of Jackson and it is an association that I cannot have in here."

Beneath the cordial compromise, Parsons, too, saw that Jackson's decision was final. In his endless search for easy solutions, for someone (like Grant Mark) to make his problems disappear without pain or effort, Jackson had convinced himself that the reversals of the previous year had been Parsons's fault. Reclaiming his lost celebrity was simply a matter of changing dealers. The right dealer, like the right doctor, would make everything right again.

The right dealer—the only dealer, in Jackson's opinion—was Pierre Matisse. "Jackson thought he deserved the best," recalls John Little, "and Matisse was the best. All during the thirties and forties, he represented the giants: Picasso, Braque, and his father, Henri." In 1947, when Peggy Guggenheim announced her plans to close Art of This Century and return to Europe, Jackson had visited Matisse's gallery on Fifty-seventh Street just to sit and fantasize. By the summer of 1951, Jackson was bolder, although still not bold enough to confront Matisse directly. Instead, he asked Joe Glasco to approach Matisse's former assistant, Catherine Viviano. "[Joe] asked Viviano if she thought Matisse would handle me," Jackson bragged to Ossorio in June, "[and] she definitely thought he would." She was wrong. When Jackson made a more formal approach later that year, Matisse politely declined, saying he "didn't show Americans." In fact, as Jackson probably knew, he did show several Americans

(Loren MacIver and Theodore Roszak) and one Canadian (Jean-Paul Rio-pelle). What he didn't know was that before turning Jackson down, Matisse had consulted Marcel Duchamp. "What do you think of this Jackson Pollock?" he reportedly asked. "He's up for grabs." When the laconic Duchamp shrugged his shoulders dismissively, that was the end of it.

By the time Matisse said no, Jackson didn't care any longer. He had found an even better dealer: Grant Mark.

It hadn't taken Mark long to appreciate that Jackson was no ordinary patient. After several trips to Ossorio's opulent new house and several gifts of major paintings (including *Lucifer* and *Number 7, 1950*), his entrepreneurial instincts had been aroused. When Jackson told him about the discontent among Par-sons's artists and their ultimatum, he saw an opening. "Mark was a wheeler-dealer," recalls Ossorio, "always looking for a chance to run a scam." In January 1952, he presented his scheme to a pliant, gullible Jackson. Instead of the "confusing arrangement of dealers, museums, collectors, all withholding from the public in their private sanctuaries," he argued, what the art world needed was someone to "put art directly before the public." The same person could act as an "umbrella agent" for all major artists, marketing their works en masse to public institutions, especially corporations and hotels.

That person, of course, was Mark. "He wanted all the Abstract Expression-ists to sell their works through him," recalls Ossorio. "He was going to become the mastermind of the U.S. art market." Mark's ambitious plan and carnival barker's rhetoric undoubtedly reminded Jackson of Tom Benton's populist call to arms a decade before. It also appealed to his resentment against Benton's "precious fairies" and "museum boys," with whom he, too, had been battling so long for acceptance. "Pollock was caught up in the idea of getting art out of the 'arty' circles," recalled Barnett Newman. Acting as Mark's "salesman," Jackson tried to bring his fellow malcontents at Parsons into Mark's stable. Rothko, Still, Newman, and Tomlin all attended meetings in Mark's Park Avenue offices to hear the pitch. Of the four, only Newman expressed skepti-cism. "I used to be in business with my father and I know [Mark's] type," he said: " 'Here's a telegram from the President,' and he shows you the telegram (which he sent to himself), and there's a big deal coming up but he can't tell you about it." At their first meeting, Newman asked impertinent questions like "Who would pay for the paintings?" and was never invited back.

With Mark as his "agent," assuring him of financial success, Jackson de-cided he no longer needed a dealer. In February, he called Reginald Isaacs to announce that henceforth he would be "handling [his] own painting and pub-licity." Knowing Jackson's reticent, reclusive nature, Isaacs was skeptical but supportive. In return for a promise of yet another painting, he agreed to act as Jackson's agent in Chicago. "Since we now have four of your paintings," he wrote two days later, "we are well on our way to becoming a Chicago gallery for you. Certainly we would only be too pleased to show our Pollock paintings to anyone whom you sent to us. . . . We estimate that 400 people have seen [your paintings] since [they] were installed; and I think that compares favorably with a public gallery."

Ossorio also offered to help, although his record in marketing Jackson's work, as opposed to buying it, had thus far been less than sterling. During his brief return to the United States at the beginning of the year—to move into The Creeks—he had arranged a meeting with a group of prominent Catholics including James Johnson Sweeney, Maurice Lavannoux, the editor of *Liturgical Arts*, Father Ford of Columbia University, Rosalind Constable of Time/Life, and Otto and Eloise Spaeth to present formally the chapel project for which Tony Smith had finally completed the sketches and model. The design called for a series of "suspended hexagons" in a "honeycomb" arrangement with the altar at the center. Originally, the plan included wall space for murals, but after seeing the Namuth film and the painting on glass, Smith had replaced virtually all the walls with windows on which Jackson would execute similar works. At the meeting in MacDougal Alley, the assembled dignitaries greeted Smith's unconventional design "with practically total incomprehension," Ossorio recalled. "They were shocked, they were tongue-tied." They questioned both the "Christian ethos" of Jackson's work, and their own ability to raise the money—a project for which, said Ossorio, "there was not one iota of enthusiasm." Mortified, Tony Smith "stomped out the room."

A more important test of Jackson's new policy of self-sufficiency would be the upcoming show in Paris. Parsons had played no part in it. While in Paris, Ossorio had acted as Jackson's agent, organizing and financing the show in collaboration with Michel Tapié, a French critic who had mounted a show for Ossorio the previous year. The first signs were auspicious. In early March 1952, Jackson received an enthusiastic letter from Tapié: "I am both happy and honored to be able to expose your works in Paris. . . . I believe the occasion is good, as a great curiosity for American painting prevails in Paris at the moment." Although furious at Hans Namuth for overcharging for prints of his photographs, Jackson was impressed by the elaborate catalogue, which included a fatuous forward by Tapié, Namuth's pictures, and a translation of Ossorio's introduction of the black-and-white show (retitled "Mon Ami, Jackson Pollock"). When Jean Dubuffet dropped by the MacDougal Alley house to return a painting, Jackson pressed him to translate Tapié's forward. ("[He] couldn't do too well," Jackson complained.) The show opened at the Studio Paul Facchetti on March 7, and the initial reports from Ossorio, who had returned to Europe, thrilled Jackson. "The exhibition has been incredibly well attended," he wrote, "with young painters and critics coming back again and again and much animated discussion." But the best news of all was the early report of sales: five out of fifteen works had already sold, according to Ossorio, and more were likely. Barely able to contain himself, Jackson wrote back: "The sales are out of this world—certainly not expected by me, and everything around the sales are of course satisfactory."

Nothing remained satisfactory for long. First the critics weighed in. "The newspapers, alas, haven't been too cooperative," Ossorio reported, "and the official art world is as suspicious and hostile as one might imagine." Then the truth about sales began to emerge. In fact, Tapié had sold only two paintings: *Number 14, 1951* to a Swiss collector named Pollak for $1,200; and *Number 19, 1951* to the great Milanese collector, Carlo Frua de Angeli, for $750. Both were small works (due to a mix-up, there wasn't enough space to exhibit the big paintings Jackson had sent). Tapié himself had bought two additional small paintings (including *Number 17A, 1949*, one of those reproduced in *Life*) but insisted on a discount of fifty percent. Then there were the expenses: the elegant brochure, the translation, the photographs, the publicity, transportation, crating, stretchers, and so forth. By the time the expenses and Tapié's standard thirty percent commission were deducted, Jackson had made, on paper, only $1,066. And that was only the beginning of the complications. Due to a change in French import laws, the show had to be packed and out of the country by the end of April, creating an enormous logistical problem and discouraging follow-up sales. In addition, the Swiss collector Pollak was interested in buying *Number 27, 1950*, but wanted a special, deep discount for the double purchase. For the first time, Jackson found himself, with Ossorio, buried in the mountain of paperwork and details that he had always left to Parsons. Between the difficulties of transatlantic communication and the vagaries of French law (and perhaps the chicanery of European dealers), Jackson never saw the $1,066, and the paintings were "misplaced" in transit.

Not long after the full dimensions of the debacle in Paris became known, Grant Mark's scheme collapsed. In typically tight-lipped fashion, Jackson said only that "my experience with Dr. Mark . . . got more involved each week until a crisis last week." The combined blows left Jackson in shock. "This getting settled in a new gallery isn't easy to solve personally," he wrote Ossorio in March. "I feel like I have been skinned alive. . . . I'm still a little dazed by the whole experience." (Dazed, perhaps, but not disillusioned. Despite the embarrassment, he continued Mark's biochemical treatments for another year.)

When the "15 Americans" show opened at the Museum of Modern Art on April 9, 1952, Jackson was still without a dealer. With only a month left before Parsons, feeling scorned, was likely to throw his paintings on the street, he began to trawl Fifty-seventh Street in search of a replacement. Sam Kootz, who represented Dubuffet and Motherwell, would have been a likely candidate except for two problems: he didn't like Jackson's art and he didn't like Jackson. During the black-and-white show, he had infuriated Lee with his snide remark: "Good show, Jackson, but could you do it in color?" Only a few weeks before the Museum of Modern Art show, Jackson had staggered into Kootz's gallery and roared, "I'm better than all the fucking painters on these walls!" Kootz had asked him to leave then and wasn't about to ask him back. (Kootz had turned down David Smith for the same combination of reasons, calling Smith's art "just a lot of rusty iron," and Smith "a drunkard.")

Jackson tried Charlie Egan's gallery on Fifty-seventh Street where Willem de Kooning and Franz Kline had exhibited. Egan had no problem with Jackson's drinking—he was a drinker himself—and he liked Jackson's work, but the space was impossible. Egan's gallery occupied a tiny fifteen-by-fifteen-foot room on the top floor of a brownstone with a storage area that had been a bathroom and an office that had been a closet. Egan was apologetic, telling Jackson, "I wish you had come in ten years earlier." (When Harry Jackson came looking for a dealer only a few days later, Egan told him, "Come back in ten years.")

There were other possibilities. John Myers, who worked at the Tibor de Nagy Gallery, wrote a gushing fan letter ("[Your work] hit me like a ton of bricks. . . . moved me tremendously. . . . Thank you for a gorgeous experience") in which he hinted heavily that Jackson deserved "a much larger public." Through Ossorio, Michel Tapié offered a contract "for all or part of [Jackson's] work," promising to come to New York in the fall and open a gallery. Reves Lewenthal of the Associated American Artists Gallery had been courting him since the previous summer. Catherine Viviano had made it clear through Joe Glasco that he "might be better off in her gallery." When Grace Borgenicht opened her gallery, Jackson invited her to Springs, where he drove her around in his Model A and complained pointedly about not being adequately recognized.

But none of these had the standing or the distinguished stable of artists that Jackson was looking for. "He felt he was the best painter in America," recalls Leo Castelli, "and therefore deserved to be in the company of the best painters in the world." The AAA gallery he dismissed as "a Department store of painting (most of it junk)." The debacle in Paris had soured him on Tapié, and Tibor de Nagy, although a friend, had been in business for less than two years. He thought seriously about Viviano, Pierre Matisse's longtime assistant, and even visited her gallery with Lee. "I had heard that he would have liked showing with me," Viviano recalls, "but he just sat there and never talked to me about it."

The search was growing increasingly desperate. Whether out of spite, incompetence, or circumstance, Parsons had sold virtually nothing during the second half of the season. In a last-ditch effort to prevent other artists from bolting, she had borrowed $5,000 from a childhood friend and bought three Rothkos and three Stills—but no Pollocks. At $200 a month, Dr. Mark's emulsion was quickly depleting the meager savings Lee had managed to squirrel away in better days. For the first time since the forties, Jackson considered designing textiles to supplement his income. He talked vaguely about finding a teaching job and asked Jeffrey Potter if he needed an extra hand around the farm. For a while, he even toyed with an offer from the Armstrong Rubber Company to create designs for a new line of linoleum. The combination of uncertainty over a dealer and perilous finances left him, according to one of his few guests that spring, "exhausted and fatigued." And obsessed. Galleries and dealers were all he could think about. Tony Smith, who still visited occasionally, complained that "Jackson spent the whole damn day talking about galleries. . . . 'Which one would be the best one for me?' and 'What are they doing?' and so on and so on like he was making a shopping list. . . . It was just a lot of ambitious, self-serving nonsense."

Sometime in April, fed up with Jackson's indecision, Lee took matters into her own hands. She marched into the Sidney Janis Gallery just across the hall from Betty Parsons and announced, "Pollock is available." Janis was leery at first. "Don't you think, Lee, that the market is rather saturated with Pollock's work?" he asked. Lee looked at him with her sagacious squint. "Sidney," she said, "the surface hasn't even been scratched." Janis respected Lee's "sharp business sense," but agreed only to meet with Jackson. He admired the man's work, but, like his colleagues, was concerned about his character—"always drunk, rambunctious, and hard to handle." For Jackson, Janis was an ideal choice. Unlike many of the new dealers, he enjoyed impeccable credentials extending back to the early forties when his book, *Abstract and Surrealist Art in America*, first appeared. Since starting his gallery in 1948, Janis had shown "only the best": "His collection was never less than first class," according to John Gruen. In the early years, that meant only Europeans: Picasso, Léger, Mondrian, Giocometti. Jackson had visited Janis's gallery in its first year, during preparations for a Léger show. "[He] came in and he sat on a chair," Janis recalled, "and he sat, sat, and sat all afternoon. At the time he was showing with Betty Parsons, so I didn't say anything. Finally he left." Gradually, Janis, with Leo Castelli's help, had taken on a few of "the best" Americans, including Kline, Gorky, Baziotes, and de Kooning, who had deserted Charlie Egan only a few months before (which may explain why Jackson didn't approach Janis sooner). With only a few good artists, Janis could put extra thought and care into his shows, like "American Vanguard Art," which opened in Paris to rave reviews just days before Jackson's show at Paul Facchetti. With good artists came good collectors, a group that Janis coddled and cultivated with preternatural skill.

Janis was unlike Parsons in another way. Although an art lover with a distinguished pedigree, he was in the business not just for love; he intended to make a living. Not only was he eager to sell; like any good businessman, he was willing to spend money to make money. If that meant better shows, better catalogues, even subsidies to artists, he was willing. Although Jackson never cared much for Janis's cool formality (another reason, perhaps, for putting his gallery at the bottom of the list), after so many setbacks, he could no longer afford the luxury of being picky.

Janis didn't care much for Jackson either, so neither man looked forward to their meeting in late April. With so few options remaining, Jackson came as supplicant, a position he deeply resented. Why should the greatest artist in America have trouble finding a dealer? Why should he have to dress up in a gray pinstripe suit and submit to an interview? In the cab with Harry Jackson

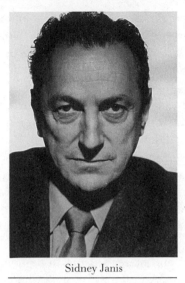

Sidney Janis

on the way to the gallery, the months of rejection and frustration—the unappreciated black-and-whites, the wrecked Cadillac, the Grant Mark fiasco, the bungled Paris show, the moribund sales, the inexplicable money bind—all the indignities caught up with him. When the cab stopped at a light alongside a limousine, he flew into a rage. "Goddamn sons of bitches, dirty sons of bitches!" he screamed out the window at the dark figures behind the limousine's tinted glass. "Goddammit, I can wear a pinstripe suit, too." Says Harry Jackson, "It was just a goddamn old banging-your-head-against-the-wall rage. Pollock wanted to know why these Connecticut WASPs, Harvard and Yale's gifts to the world, these smug, well-heeled sons of bitches lost in the bowels of some corporation or bank, why *they* should be doing so well and be so respected by society when *he*, Jackson, even at his stage of notoriety, was still essentially impoverished." "Who the fuck are *they?*" Jackson roared again and again. "They're nobody, they're nobody. *I'm* somebody." Harry thought the rage was directed at Sidney Janis as "a symbol of money being the only thing that's worth shit in this country." More probably, like most of Jackson's rages, it was directed at himself. He, after all, had left Parsons in search of more sales, more recognition, more money. He was too much *like* Janis. Even in the best of times, art had never been enough. He had enjoyed celebrity too much, missed it too desperately.

By the time they reached Janis's gallery, the rage had subsided. After that, "it was a kind of cat-and-mouse game," Harry recalls. "Pollock fancied himself a hell of a goddamn negotiator, but he couldn't pack Janis's socks." Convinced, apparently, that he (and Lee) could control Jackson, Janis offered him a contract, which Jackson quickly accepted. When he returned to Springs, he boasted to Jeffrey Potter, "This is *the* guy, they don't come any bigger."

■ ■ ■

If Jackson thought settling into a new gallery would miraculously reverse the long decline, he was wrong. The self-destructive binges continued unabated into the summer of 1952. As usual, Lee bore the brunt of the abuse. Twice during the summer, Jackson almost set the house on fire: once when he staggered in drunk and collapsed on the sofa with a cigarette in his mouth, another time when Lee awoke to flames in the bed. "I arrived and the mattress was still smoldering," recalls Roger Wilcox, who answered Lee's call for help. "We took it outside and turned the garden hose on it."

No one was safe. Neighbors like Dr. Raphael Gribitz often saw Jackson stumbling by the roadside or loading up on beer at Dan Miller's Store (a bender usually began with at least twenty or thirty bottles). Julien Levy watched in disbelief as Jackson stormed into his studio and tore the frame off a stretcher, railing against Levy's teaching position at the Art Students League: "Painters should paint and not teach, goddamn it!" he roared. Many followed the example of Jeffrey Potter and pretended not to be home when they heard the clatter of Jackson's Model A in the driveway. It didn't matter if he was sober. They dreaded his abject apologies as much as his rages. On a trip into the city, he barged into a dinner party being given by Dorothy Miller, organizer of the "15 Americans" show. When one of the guests, a psychoanalyst, heard that *the* Jackson Pollock was at the door, she begged Miller to let her talk to him. After nearly an hour sequestered in the front room with Jackson, she returned to the table. "Oh, God," she sighed. "I'd give my soul to work with him." At least once during the summer, such antics landed Jackson in the Regent Hospital again, where he was unable to pay his bills.

Incredibly, just as the binges began to hit new heights of intensity, just when he most needed help, Jackson stopped seeing Ruth Fox.

Fox could not have been surprised. Jackson's attendance at AA meetings had been brief and desultory at best. He had taken Antabuse only once or twice, and certainly never made the "commitment to a life of sobriety" that Fox considered the essential first step toward genuine recovery.

At the time, both Lee and Jackson told friends that Fox was at fault, that she was overly dogmatic and uncooperative. They especially objected to her criticism of Grant Mark's biochemical treatment. The truth, however, was that for the first time in his long history of psychotherapy, Jackson had met his match: an analyst whom he could not charm or manipulate.

First, the straight-talking Fox undoubtedly insisted that Jackson *was* an alcoholic, a label that, with the help of indulgent friends, he had so far managed to avoid. She no doubt saw through his litany of complaints about being depressed and unappreciated to the "alcoholic arrogance" at its core. From her writings, it's clear that she saw the rages and pouts and long, awkward silences of patients like Jackson not as the wages of genius but as "maneuvers"—tricks used by every alcoholic "to seem to deserve the care and concern and regard of others." She understood how an alcoholic like Jackson could be one minute "ingratiating, charming, even fawning," at the next, "hostile, grudging, even cruel," then "withdraw into himself, becoming aloof, cold and seeming to need no one." She saw through the manipulations to the fear of desertion, the low self-esteem, and the childlike fury that underlay so much of the alcoholic's "egocentricity"—the intense self-involvement that, according to Fox, would prevent him from ever "loving another person in a mature sense." The alcoholic "often has a burning desire for vengeance on a world that he feels has treated him shabbily," Fox later wrote. "Those nearest him—the ones he needs most—are usually the chief targets for his venom." For Jackson, who had come to think of therapy as just another forum for exercising his ego or venting his rage, Fox's insights cast long beams of cold, unwelcome light. Nine months of intermittent sessions had more than exhausted his capacity for truth.

Fox's fatal mistake, however, was implicating Lee Krasner. From the beginning, Fox had tried to include Lee in the treatment, sympathizing with her daily ordeal as the wife of an alcoholic and working through her to arrange for Jackson to attend AA meetings and therapy sessions. But Fox's firm views on what she called "the alcoholic spouse" put the two women on a collision course. Lee may have conceded that she married Jackson "knowing he was an alcoholic," that, like many wives of alcoholics, she "took pleasure in pain" and "chose to suffer." She may even have accepted Fox's description of the typical alcoholic couple's troubled relationship: isolation from friends, resentment, endless quarreling, threats, deteriorating sexual relations, rejection, and frigidity. But Lee could never have sat still for Fox's conclusions.

According to Fox, the alcoholic wasn't the only one in the relationship with "personality disturbances." In fact, Fox's studies of the alcoholic spouse would have led her to believe that Lee's problems might be "even more serious" than her husband's and that she was at least "equally in need of psychotherapy or counseling." In addition, despite her protests, Lee didn't *really* want Jackson to recover. Like most alcoholic spouses, she *needed* "to dominate a weaker man." His recovery was, in fact, "a threat to her neurotic demand that he be weak, inferior, helpless, dependent." Worst of all, Fox's research indicated that Lee actually *caused* Jackson's binges, that "she derive[d] pleasure from the pain she [was] able to inflict by precipitating the argument, the quarrel, the tension which unconsciously she [knew would] land her husband in another drinking bout." In Jackson's hands, such exculpating notions were lethal weapons, and in his increasingly frequent arguments with Lee, he must have used them to devastating effect: the drinking wasn't his fault, it was *her* fault; *she* was the one with the problem; *she* was the one who needed help; his only problem was *her*.

Nothing, however, could have frightened Lee as much as the implications of Fox's research for the future. For Lee, the next stage would be fear: fear that Jackson would "beat her up" and "fear of [losing] her own sanity." As his self-control deteriorated, she would assume more responsibility for the two of them and grow more self-reliant; both changes that would only aggravate Jackson's misbehavior. Gradually, he would become "more violent, more withdrawn,"

until finally, in the final stage, she would leave him, either "from some immediate and catastrophic quarrel or simply from accumulated tension." It was a
chilling scenario that Lee refused to accept.

In June, certainly with Lee's endorsement and probably at her insistence,
Jackson informed Fox that he wasn't coming back.

It was Jackson's last chance at genuine recovery. As bad as the drinking had
become, neither Jackson nor Lee was ready to face the harsh truths that could
have turned the decline around. Neither had the mettle to accept the confessions and compromises of rehabilitation. Instead, they turned with renewed
determination to easier, less threatening solutions. Lee clung to Dr. Hubbard's
quasi-mystical potions and the delusion that she and she alone could make
Jackson better. "He was headed toward disaster," recalls Ted Dragon, "and to
be of any help, Lee would have had to be tougher with him." But to be tougher
with Jackson, she first had to be tougher with herself. And for all her acid and
grit, that apparently was something Lee couldn't do. So she "watched his diet
and fed him vitamin pills more assiduously than ever," according to a friend,
and hoped for yet another miraculous turnaround.

Jackson, too, grasped at every ephemeral solution that floated by, beginning
with Dr. Mark's magic emulsion. Mysticism, with its vague etiology and magical solutions, provided an easy refuge. That summer, he began visiting the
nearby summer house of N. Vashti, an Indian dance instructor, and his wife
Pravina. "He spent a great deal of time with them," recalls John Little, "or
Lee would have them over for dinner. They talked a lot about mystical things."
The Hindu notion of Atman-Brahman, or pantheism, began to make its way
into Jackson's pronouncements. "You know, everything has a soul," he told
Miriam Schapiro. "Even a stone has a soul." He talked about "the universal
energy" and "the reality . . . in the trees." He read all or parts of Kahlil Gi-
bran's *The Prophet* and Ferdinand Osindowsky's *Beast Men and Gods*, a diary
of the author's mystical journey through Asia. In the latter, he was especially
captivated by the story of a tribal chieftain who cut off a man's head and then
magically replaced it. He flirted with astrology, telling a neighbor, "Goddamn
it, of course heavenly bodies influence our psyche!" He quizzed Tony Smith on
Oriental philosophies and relived his earlier flirtations with Krishnamurti and
Jung. For a while, he tantalized Smith by suggesting that he might convert to
Catholicism, even telling him, erroneously, that his father's family, the Mc-
Coys, had been Catholic.

Jackson sought refuge in new friends as well. Profoundly suggestible and
desperately in need of easy answers, he was inevitably drawn to those who
offered them. In the fall of 1952, he was drawn to Barnett Newman and
Clyfford Still.

Most of Jackson's fellow artists regarded Newman affectionately as something of a comic figure, a genial blowhard in a tailored tweed suit, Sherlock
Holmes hat, and monocle. He reminded John Myers of Major Hoople, a

character from the twenties comic strip "Our Boarding House": a "bumptious guy and opulent dresser who was all bravado and brag," according to Gerome Kamrowski. By 1952, Newman's hulking figure, walrus mustache, pliant face, and easy laugh had won him considerable affection but little respect among artists and collectors. The artists of his generation considered him an interloper and latecomer (he didn't begin painting seriously until 1945) and, like Motherwell, too much in love with words, especially his own, to be a true artist. (Subsequent generations of artists and collectors would substantially revise this view of Newman's worth.) His niche in the community, such as it was, resulted from his close association with Betty Parsons, to whom he had introduced Jackson in 1947. His shows of vertical stripes (he called them "zips") in 1950 and 1951 at the Parsons Gallery had been ridiculed by both critics and fellow artists, and his writings on "aesthetic philosophy" were dismissed by all but a few as pretentious even by the standards of the day. When, in the spring of 1952, Dorothy Miller failed to include him in her "15 Americans" show at the Museum of Modern Art, Newman was devastated. "He had this childlike expectation that with one or two shows he'd be famous and sell," recalls Clement Greenberg. "But nothing happened. Everybody hated the shows." Crestfallen and bitter, Newman withdrew his pictures from Parsons's gallery and vowed never to show in New York again. He also decided that he didn't really want to be successful after all, that "it didn't matter if anything sold." The only thing that mattered was the act of painting. "It was the artist's lot to go against the world," he told a friend. "Anonymity is the truest heroism."

In this state of self-imposed martyrdom, Newman had much in common with Jackson Pollock. Both felt underappreciated by the public and alienated from their fellow artists. To Jackson, the forty-seven-year-old Newman was an indulgent older brother, an attentive Charles who wrestled with him, took him to movies (especially fight movies), and, like Tony Smith, beguiled him with words. Although he often retrieved Jackson from drunken binges, Newman never encouraged him to stop drinking or even to drink less. Unlike Ruth Fox, he accepted at face value, even admired, Jackson's blustering machismo and, like many before him, mistook Jackson's attentive silence for comprehension, calling him, in one wildly off-base observation, "more mature than any of the guys that were my age." In turn, Jackson admired Newman's "authentic flair for conversation," his size, his erudition, and his amiable eccentricities. He envied Newman's relationship with his wife, Annalee, who earned much of the money that allowed Newman to buy his fine suits and devote his time to painting and writing, but remained uncomplainingly in his shadow. Newman was also, like Jackson, an incorrigible dandy, once boasting that he and Al Capone shared the same tailor.

Jackson was also drawn to Newman's quasi-mystical ruminations on art. He would beam when Newman rhapsodized on "the largeness of the concept" or described an image as "a contained thing, held, sort of trembling there." Newman told Jackson that he had reinvigorated American art in the same way

Faulkner and Hemingway had reinvigorated American literature. He had led "the fight against ritual, against empty forms instead of real emotions." He compared Jackson favorably to Mondrian, saying the Dutchman's "geometry (perfection) swallows up his metaphysics (his exultation)." Painting wasn't about perfection, Newman argued; it wasn't about paint or surface or color; it was about "the taste for the infinite." "Anyone can construct a good-English-sentence kind of picture," he said; the true artist is interested in "painting with a capital 'P.' "

Like Jackson, Newman could draw only passably from life and therefore, according to Clement Greenberg, grasped at profundities to justify his simple art. "With so little on the canvas," said Greenberg, "Barney had to generate a vast content for his art that [Thomas] Hess could write about." His signature image, the stripe, for example, wasn't merely a stripe, it was a representation of "his transcendental self." The pictures themselves weren't pictures but "experienced moment[s] of total reality." He claimed to find "clues to the highest uses of art" in the rituals of the American Indians of the Pacific Northwest like the Kwakiutl. In Newman's world, art wasn't art, it was ritual—a "ceremonial performance"; painting wasn't painting, it was metaphysics—"a mystic situation." And, most reassuring to Jackson, failure wasn't failure; it was heroism.

By one account, at least, Jackson was never entirely convinced either by Newman's ideas or by his art. "I don't give a damn about Barney's painting," he told Roger Wilcox. "He's just a nice guy, I like him." But at a time of increasing tension and frustration in the real world, Newman's lofty rhetoric offered Jackson easy, if temporary, refuge.

Clyfford Still provided a different kind of escape. Raised in small towns in Canada and the American Northwest, he brought a combination of Presbyterian high-mindedness and evangelical zeal to what he saw as a profoundly immoral and errant art world. Stern and humorless as a frontier preacher, he considered art not merely an occupation but a moral calling of the highest order. "Any fool can put color on canvas," he said; true painting is a "matter of conscience," and the true artist "can make a picture out of the truth." With his thin, bony, unsmiling face, fierce, protruding teeth, and Captain Ahab shock of black-and-white hair, he looked the part of art's avenging angel, smiting his numerous enemies in a series of blistering letters—"terrible, cutting letters," recalls Nicholas Carone, "letters so bad that people didn't want to talk about them because they were so personal." In them, Still spoke darkly of "the enemy" and battle lines and conspiracies, and lashed out with cruel superciliousness. A gifted polemicist, he reveled in the war of words, gloried in his battle scars, and took chilling pride in his readiness to sacrifice friendships over even the most minute infractions of his moral code.

No one was safe from Still's righteous wrath. "He was mad about everything," recalls Nicholas Carone. He denounced the public as senseless and inattentive, "the contemporary social ethic" as "a totalitarian trap." The art world he accused of being "controlled by merchants" who cared nothing about the welfare or integrity of artists. Critics were "the butchers who make hamburger of us for the public gut," and scholars were simply deadweight. ("The scholar will only defeat us if we allow him ascendancy.") Dealers were either manipulative, money-grubbing hacks (like Sidney Janis) or dupes of the system (like Betty Parsons). The work of most of his fellow artists was merely "an exercise in degradation." In Still's gospel, artists who profaned their sacred calling were "the most contemptible enemies of man." He objected to the "collectivism" of group shows and, although he claimed to be the original Abstract Expressionist, decried such labels as infringements on every artist's moral autonomy. Friends were not spared the sting of his venomous letters. When Betty Parsons complained because Still had left her gallery without informing her first, Still fired back a furiously indignant reply to the effect of "How dare you, a mere dealer, question the actions of an artist?" The two didn't speak for years. In fact, no one lived up to Still's dizzyingly high moral standards except Still. He was "the lonely pioneer," alone on the moral and artistic frontier.

What did Jackson see in the inflexible, self-regarding, and fiercely self-righteous Still? First, an ally. As vicious and relentless as he could be in opposition, Still could also be a fast and devoted friend, a lone companion against the conspiracy without. By the alchemy of words, he was able to transform Jackson's torment into a triumph of artistic integrity. Like Newman, he showered Jackson with flattery at a time when most other sources of esteem had dried up. He told Jackson that he (along with Newman and Still) had "changed the nature of painting." For Still, Jackson's fall from grace since 1950 only proved his moral fiber. He hadn't succumbed to the blandishments of commercialism; he was still his own man. The fact that he had radically altered his style at the height of his celebrity, moving from dripped abstractions to figurative black pourings, particularly impressed Still. He lavished praise on the black-and-white paintings and relished the criticism and incomprehension with which they were greeted by those of less acute moral insight. "Your show was a real blockbuster to the gutter-club vermin," he wrote Jackson. "It was amusing to see the confusion of their swarming."

Still saw Jackson as a victim of all that was wrong with the art world, even more so because he was unable to defend himself. In response to an article that impugned Jackson's work (as well as his own), Still penned a broadside to the author, Harold Rosenberg, calling him a "salon raconteur," "an intellectual lout," and a "front man for the mass assault on the individual," and proudly sent a copy of the letter to Jackson. "Two paragraphs in [Rosenberg's] article indulge in some very pointed insults to your work and mine," he wrote in an accompanying note. "Because of the unique circumstances I have found it pleasantly relaxing to unhook my slingshot in the form of the enclosed letter copy. I hope you will also find it at least exhilarating to know that those Bloated Presumptions are being vented." He closed by reassuring Jackson that "for the moment the air is clear."

Jackson welcomed Still's support. He admired the way Still could "handle himself" in the contentious community of artists and yet remain strangely aloof. He was intrigued, if not persuaded, by Still's sawtoothed, encrusted abstractions. "That guy's got something," he told Conrad Marca-Relli. For a while, he considered himself one of a triumvirate—Pollock, Newman, and Still—that represented the last best hope of American painting. "Jackson succumbed to Still," recalls Clement Greenberg. "It was the first time that he had ever joined up with a group. The first time he became one of the boys." For Still's benefit, Jackson even pretended to be a baseball fan, accompanying him to Ebbets Field to root for the Brooklyn Dodgers.

Another visitor to Springs in the summer of 1952 was Harry Jackson, who had his own cure for what ailed Pollock: a potent blend of alcohol and fantasy. The two men caroused from bar to bar, punching each other playfully and swapping boisterous stories of the West between beers. At Jackson's insistence, they called Tom Benton in Kansas City late one night. When Rita answered, Jackson slurred into the phone, "Goddamn, Rita, honey, I got my friend Harry here and he and Tom have *got* to meet." "Jack, I'm not gonna disturb Tom at this hour," Rita responded, her Italian accent still perfectly intact. "Call up when you're sober and you ought to be ashamed of yourself."

One night at the Elm Tree Inn, Jackson pushed his way onto the piano bench and "started banging away with his elbows," Harry remembers, "like a kid showing off." When the manager yelled, "Get your goddamn drunk ass out of here or I'll throw you out," Jackson got up and staggered out the door. "It wasn't because he was a good boy," says Harry. "It was because he knew the owner had a goddamn baseball bat behind the bar." Sitting on the porch, with a case of beer between them, Jackson begged Harry, "Tell me what it's like in Wyoming. Do you ride all day?" Harry, in turn, begged Jackson to come with him on his next trip west—"to knock some of that New York crap out of him." As long as he drank, Jackson was "rarin' to go," but when the next morning came, reality intruded, usually in the form of Lee Krasner. "She was very anti-Harry," says Harry. "She was against him going anywhere with me. She felt threatened by that." Even when they went down the road to Jungle Pete's, Harry felt "like a goddamn pre-teenage kid sneaking out of the house."

When Jackson and Harry finally did hit the road together, late one summer night, they headed east, not west, out over the Napeague strip where the land was so narrow they could see the moonlit water on both sides of the road, past Hither Woods where startled deer peered back from the scrub, past Fort Pond and Lake Montauk and up onto the grassy plateau of Indian Field. On this treeless pasture jutting into the Atlantic, the Montauk Indians had made their last stand against the encroachments of the white man (in court, not in combat). Now it was the improbable site of the Deep Hollow Dude Ranch. The Model A rattled over the dirt tracks, in and out of hollows where, in the spring, swift brooks ran. Jackson and Harry covered the last few hundred feet on foot so as not to alarm the horses or arouse the caretaker who, everyone knew, was well armed. They sat on the fence of the round corral while the horses milled and tossed and whinnied softly in the darkness. "Pollock would get me to jump on one of those horses, bareback and without any goddamn bridle," Harry recalls, "so I'd take the belt off my trousers and put it around the horse's neck and just ride him." When Harry tried to coax Jackson to join him, he refused. "He'd never been on a horse in his life," says Harry, "and he wasn't gonna start. . . . He seemed perfectly content just to sit there on the fence and watch me."

With or without Harry's companionship, booze continued to be Jackson's remedy of choice. In the right company, it put him into a deep, impenetrable reverie, a state that alternated between incoherent babbling and long, vacant silences. At The Creeks, to which Ossorio had given him virtually unlimited access, he listened for hours to Ted Dragon playing his beautiful, white Pleyel grand piano, a gift from a "music lover" in Paris. "When I was away, he would come and plink away at it himself," recalls Dragon, "or just bang out the same chord over and over." While friends like Dragon tolerated such fits of moodiness, Tony Smith outright admired them, telling Jackson that his alcohol-induced reveries were, in fact, therapeutic, perhaps even essential to his creativity.

But the rages were a different matter. They came on unexpectedly, like summer storms. He would get "very heavy and black, like a goddamn cur dog," according to Harry Jackson. He would start yelling, hurling insults at fellow painters—"cheap lousy fakes," "frauds and fools"—shadowboxing with imaginary enemies, and proclaiming himself "the only giant among artists," "the only painter alive," "the only damn painter who has a thing to say." Not even Ossorio and Dragon were exempt from such explosions. "Sometimes it took just one drink," says Ted Dragon, "and you saw this monster come out." One night he chased a terrified Rosalind Constable through the elegant rooms of The Creeks, with "a kind of vicious humor" in his eyes, according to Ossorio. Another night, Dragon found him in the ballroom pounding on the keys of the Pleyel with an ice pick.

Lee did what she could to control the damage, calling hostesses in advance to urge them to serve nonalcoholic punches, keeping a sharp eye on the bar at parties, appointing friends to watch over Jackson in her absence. She even began to buy liquor for him, bringing home a quart of whiskey every day—"to keep him off the road," she said. But when trouble came, as it invariably did, she no longer leapt to Jackson's rescue. By the winter of 1952, she had learned to "dissociate herself from [Jackson] when he became too troublesome," according to a friend, "appearing only when it was necessary to commandeer forces to put him to bed."

Lee's primary concern was no longer Jackson; it was his art. After an unproductive summer and a drunken fall, with only a few months remaining before his first show at the new gallery, Jackson had virtually nothing to show. She had stalled Janis by promising him his pick of the paintings, old and new, but soon he would insist on visiting the studio to see for himself. She knew, even if Jackson didn't, that the upcoming show was crucial to his faltering reputation. "She tried everything to get him painting again," recalls Clement Greenberg. "She ran around saying, 'Jackson's not painting!' as if that was all that mattered, and to hell with everything else, like his drinking. The whole effort was so misguided."

Friends noticed the change in Lee. Gone was the unreserved support, the selfless debasement of previous years. She was "increasingly hard" on her charge. Some even thought they saw in her new approach "an attempt to establish some separation." "She nursed him with an iron hand," observed Betty Parsons. The *art*, Lee seemed to have decided, was the only thing that made the reveries and rages tolerable. When Jackson and Lee came to her house for dinner that fall, Dorothy Miller remembered seeing Jackson covering his face "in agony" every time Lee looked at him. "Don't look at me like that," he begged her, "don't look at me like that!" "I think she hated him," said Miller.

Lee was no longer part of the solution, she was part of the problem— perhaps, Jackson must have wanted to believe, the *whole* problem. Perhaps Ruth Fox had been right after all. Hadn't Tony Smith been telling him that "Lee wasn't the best person for him"? Hadn't Gerald Sykes said that "he would have to drink twice as much if *he* were married to Lee." Even Ted Dragon, one of Lee's allies, believed the Pollocks "saw too much of each other," comparing them to the lovebirds he once kept. "They killed each other off," says Dragon. "And when I asked the aviaries in New York what to do, they said, 'Well, of course, they're lovebirds; they're famous for that. They're too much together.' "

Jackson had a more direct solution. He would abandon her before she abandoned him. Probably not consciously, but with all the grim determination and resourcefulness of a willful act, he set out to drive Lee from his life.

Their relationship, which had been in turmoil for the past year, now turned into open warfare. After years of hiding their differences (with uneven success), Jackson began to lash out at Lee in public, telling her, "Go fuck yourself woman, I'll do what I goddamn well please" when she corrected him, and calling her "whore," "slut," and "an ugly goddamn woman" in front of friends. On the rare occasions when guests visited, Jackson would walk with them out to the porch "in order to have some time alone, to carry on his own special little relationship without Lee," according to one friend. "He was doing little things like that all the time to Lee." Without telling her, he gave away to visitors the little found objects from the beach that she set out around the house. Lee would have to call the next day and ask for them back. Anything to hurt her. When the guests were gone, the real fireworks began. Neighbor Elwyn Harris recalled hearing screams coming from the house late into the night. Ruth Stein, Lee's sister, was astonished to find the domestic scene on Fireplace Road transformed into "a championship fight." And when Ruth's son, Ronald, asked to visit, Lee told him forthrightly: "You won't be able to take it." Convinced she was exaggerating, Ronald came anyway. "She was right," he remembers. "I couldn't take it. Day and night, continuous abusiveness. I never realized arguing could achieve that level. From the moment you woke up, twenty-four hours of tremendous, abusive, yelling fights." Where four years earlier he had seen good-humored ribbing, Harry Jackson now found "tremendous hate, all kinds of deep, deep resentments, a Milky Way of pros and cons." Eventually, even a disagreement over cigarette brands could spark a conflagration. When Jackson ran out of his Camels, even in the middle of the night, he would drive to the store rather than smoke Lee's Chesterfields.

Then he began to hit her.

Lee always denied that Jackson, even at his wildest and most drunken, ever abused her physically. The most she admitted was that "his feelings toward me became somewhat ambiguous." "There was never any physical violence," she avowed years later. "He would just use more four-letter words than usual. Or he would take it out on the furniture." At the time, however, no one who knew them was surprised when it finally came to blows. She had been afraid of him, afraid of his anger, for years. He had probably hit her occasionally in the past with the back of his hand, in a passing fury, roaring drunk. In the fall of 1952, however, she began appearing with black eyes and bruises. Houseguests remember seeing her in the morning, after a night of screamed recriminations and strange noises, with bruises on her face and arms. Harry Jackson, who thought Lee had "asked for it" many times, saw Jackson "get fed up and drunk and knock the old woman into the next room. Oh, shit," says Harry, "he kicked the piss out of her two or three different times when I was there."

One stormy night, in the middle of a dinner party, the lights blinked out, whereupon Jackson, already drunk and in an incendiary mood, "lost his temper and threw everybody out of the house." With a bottle of bourbon in one hand and a candle in the other, he stalked through the darkened house to the kitchen and returned with a six-inch butcher knife. "I'm gonna kill you," he roared at Lee. "I'm gonna kill you." It was the ultimate solution, the miracle cure that would solve all his problems.

After that night, or another like it, Lee decided she could no longer handle Jackson by herself. If he was ever to paint again, she needed help from the only person who might still be able to control him, the person whose mistakes she had inherited, the only person whose abandonment he still feared: Stella Pollock. Not long afterward, she called Stella in Deep River. "You did it to him," she fumed, "now *you* come and take care of him."

Stella arrived in mid-October, still suffering from the rheumatism and bursitis that had plagued her all year. She found Jackson and Lee in a state of utter exhaustion—the months of fighting had taken their toll. "They both have colds," she reported to Charles, ". . . and Lee has an infected eye." With Stella watching him, Jackson quit drinking and began to work. It was too late for the luxury of inspiration, even if he was confident it would come. He needed paintings for the November show, now less than a month away, and he needed them immediately. He began by cannibalizing the past, taking an old all-over painting that had been "finished" for almost a year and adding a few calligraphic swirls in black; covering a year-old, black-and-white figurative painting with quickly applied layers of red, yellow, blue, and white to evoke the intricate skeins of previous years. Retreating from the psychological brinksmanship of the black-and-white show, he turned again to the safety of color—"He has some nice paintings lots of color this year," Stella wrote Frank. There was no time—and perhaps no energy—for innovation. Even the handful of entirely new paintings, like *Number 12, 1952*, betray Jackson's haste, exhaustion, and faltering self-confidence. He agonized over a mammoth canvas that he had begun the previous spring with Tony Smith and worked on intermittently since (once with an additional assist from Barnett Newman). He entered and re-entered it "many, many times," according to Lee. "[He] just kept saying, 'This won't come through.' " Finally, desperate to rescue the image (and the expensive Belgian linen), he added eight vertical blue poles evenly spaced across the length of the dense, encrusted, overwrought surface, using a six-foot length of two-by-four as a guide. With the addition of several small stained canvases and at least five black pourings from the previous year (with the dates altered), Jackson had just enough paintings, twelve, for the show that opened at Janis's gallery on November 10.

No one knew better than Jackson how short he had fallen. As the opening approached, he was increasingly nervous and apprehensive. A quick trip to Deep River in early November did little to calm him. Only days before he was due in town to finish hanging the show, he arranged for friends to drive him because "he was so nervous he didn't trust himself behind the wheel," John Cole remembers. When he finally did arrive, he disappeared almost immediately, showing up later that night at Janis's gallery, drunk, defensive, and barely able to hold a hammer. The hanging dragged on until four the next morning. The next day at the opening, everyone seemed to agree the show was "good-looking." Janis played the collectors "like a fine musician," according to one observer, telling them "you'd better buy now if you want to buy a painting you want." Not everyone admired his tactics—Reuben Kadish called him "a sharp-shooter"—but almost everyone admired his results. Stella couldn't come to the opening, so Lee arranged for Elizabeth Wright Hubbard to take her place, standing over Jackson to ensure his sobriety. Halfway through the evening, however, Franz Kline suggested, "Jackson, let's get out of this place and have a drink," and no one saw them again for the rest of the night.

Much more important, if less publicized, than the Janis show was the retrospective that opened a week later at Bennington College in Vermont.

Jackson and Lee drove through the gray November landscape of western Massachusetts in Alfonso Ossorio's station wagon. When they arrived at Bennington, they were directed to an old carriage house that had been converted

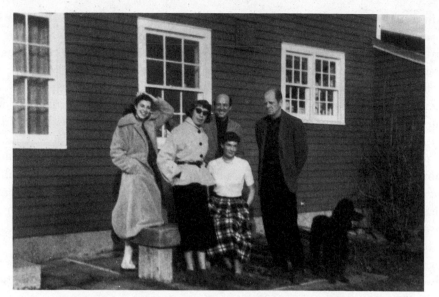

Lee and Jackson with Helen Frankenthaler (far left), Clement Greenberg (center), and Helen Wheelwright (seated) in Bennington, Vermont, 1952

into a dance studio. Inside, lined up against the weathered tongue-in-groove paneling, were eight of Jackson's greatest paintings, exhibited together for the first time: *Pasiphaë* and *Totem II*, from the days on Eighth Street before they were married; *The Key*, from a time when he was still struggling with a brush and the electric images from his past; *Number 2, 1949*, sixteen feet of dazzling white swirls; the huge loops and sumptuous simplicity of *Autumn Rhythm*; the uneasiness of *Number 9, 1950*; the figures emerging in *Number 2, 1951*; and finally the exquisite drawing of *Echo*. It was Jackson's first retrospective, but the effect was more than that of a backward glance over the shoulder. To Jackson, after a year of creative impoverishment, the demeaning search for a gallery, and the last-minute scramble to fill the Janis show, it was a long, elegiac gaze into a past that must have seemed as distant as the Phoenix ranch.

Paul Feeley, who had arranged the show with the help of Tony Smith and Gene Goossen, and his wife Helen hosted a party after the opening. Clement Greenberg and Helen Frankenthaler attended, along with most of the Bennington faculty. Jackson, dressed in black suit and tie—"like an undertaker" —stood apart from the crowd, "virtually motionless," in a trance, his elbow propped on the mantelpiece throughout the evening. When Goossen tried to engage him in conversation, he responded with monosyllables. But this time alcohol wasn't to blame—Helen Feeley had put Lee in charge of the bar. When a stranger unthinkingly offered him a drink, Clement Greenberg intervened: "Jackson, lay off." "Nothing doing," Jackson said, then added, "You fool." At that moment, Greenberg felt the same foreboding he had felt in the car outside the East Hampton train station; he heard the same bitter resignation in Jackson's voice: "Only fools won't accept the inevitable." This time, however, he felt no pity, only outrage. "When he called me a fool I was furious," Greenberg recalls, "and I was off of him for a couple of years. I didn't say it, but Jackson sensed it. . . . Besides, he had become, if not famous, at least notorious, and I suppose the battle had been won."

The retrospective, Greenberg's anger, even the grim November weather, all seemed to convey the same ominous message. Earlier, Greenberg had put it into words when he said he thought the Janis show was "wobbly," that all artists "have their run" and Jackson's "ten-year run was over." Even Lee had said it. "When you were off booze in '49 and '50, *look* what you did!" she told him. "But since then, back on booze, do you do *real* pictures?" Worst of all, Jackson knew it was true. According to Greenberg, "He knew it was over, that he'd lost his inspiration." He even knew that *Blue Poles*, for all his agony, "wasn't a success."

In the weeks before the show, Jackson had gone to The Creeks and stared for hours at *Lavender Mist*, "as if trying to find something," according to Ted Dragon. At Bennington, surrounded by the *"real* pictures" from his past, he must have wondered if it was lost for good.

41

AGAINST THE WORLD

Jackson spent the rest of the winter in a petulant funk: drunk, despondent, and mad at the world. Work was out of the question. He could tell himself it was because of the weather, or because of a head cold that lingered for months, or because George Loper, the retired circus clown, was shingling and insulating his studio and the infernal pounding made it impossible to concentrate. Whatever the reason, his art had come to a dead stop.

If Jackson couldn't work, nobody could. In January 1953, he stormed into Phil Guston's show at the Egan Gallery and ripped paintings from the wall, ranting incoherently about "easel pictures" and "embroidery." Guston, still bent on "topping everybody," had recently switched from the romantic realist work at which he excelled to delicate, painterly abstractions based, he claimed, on Monet. Many artists dismissed them as halfhearted and derivative at best, opportunistic at worst. "Guston was floundering," says Nicholas Carone, who attended these early shows. "He didn't understand the Abstract Expressionist movement. He just wanted success and to be included in the roster of the avant-garde." Later that spring, Jackson repeated the performance, barging into the opening of James Brooks's show at Grace Borgenicht, drunk and raving and, according to Borgenicht, "probably jealous."

Jackson refused to be cheered by the reviews of the Janis show—reviews that only two years before would have thrilled him. Robert Goodnough called the new paintings "tantalizing" and "ecstatic." "[They] make the gallery seethe with energy." He praised "the pure sensuousness of the paint" and "the transcendence of the materials." *Art Digest* hailed the "quite magnificent new canvases" and found *Number 12*, in particular, "tremendously exciting." In the *Times*, Howard Devree compared Jackson to Kandinsky and praised the new works as "far more packed with suggestion than anything I have hitherto seen." After all the accusations of "chaos," Jackson must have been pleased by Robert Coates's comment in the *New Yorker*: "I've always felt, underneath the surface exuberance of his work, a strong strain of careful consideration in the formulation of ideas." But even in the most fulsome review, Jackson could find support for his claim to being misunderstood and unappreciated. Two reviewers had singled out *November 12* for special praise, but both identified it as a landscape. Several others congratulated him on his decision to return to color, implicitly rejecting the "excursion" into black and white of the previous year.

Collectors, who voted with their wallets, virtually boycotted the show. Only one painting sold—the much praised *Number 12*, to the scion of the Rockefeller family, Nelson. Jackson's fellow artists criticized him for repeating himself and for "borrowing" from his contemporaries: the large areas of sensuous color in *Number 12* from Mark Rothko; the verticals in *Blue Poles* from Barnett Newman. The consensus seemed to be that he had slipped from his former heights. While Jackson may have quarreled with the reasoning, he accepted the judgment—it was the same one Greenberg and Lee had rendered. It was his own. "He didn't hold it against us that we didn't like the show," Greenberg recalls. "He didn't make excuses [or] try to fool himself. He knew it wasn't what it should have been."

At every turn, Jackson fought the praise and savored the criticism. Fan mail —an inquiry about prints and reproductions, an invitation to give a speech at the Cooper Union, a request for an interview from a Harvard undergraduate —could only have reminded him of better days. When Dorothy Miller wrote to inform him that Peggy Guggenheim had given *Full Fathom Five* to the Museum of Modern Art, he could only complain about how dealers and collectors had ignored and mistreated him in recent years. Where, for example, were the fifteen paintings he had sent to Paris? Where were the proceeds from the sales? Even the news in January that his show had been voted the second best one-man show of 1952 by the editorial staff of *Art News* failed to penetrate his self-pity. John Little recalls his reaction: "Aw, hell, what the fuck do they know?"

Jackson wanted Stella. In January, he called her in Deep River and, as much as his Pollock reticence would allow, begged her to come to Springs. She suggested that on her next trip into New York for her regular cortisone injections, she would try to arrange it. When a month passed and she failed to appear, Jackson again sought out Elizabeth Wright Hubbard. In the willfully naive belief that Hubbard might still do some good, Lee let Jackson come into the city unaccompanied one day a week for therapy. As always in the past, he made a beeline from Hubbard's office to a bar, usually the Cedar Tavern, and drank until closing time. After a night recovering on a friend's couch, he would return home the next morning.

In the spring, he demanded Stella again. He called repeatedly, more urgent each time. He offered to come into the city to meet her so she wouldn't have to travel alone. But each time Stella had an excuse: her knees were too stiff, her rheumatism had flared up again, Sande was working too hard. "It was either rain or snow or too cold," she wrote Charles. But Jackson must have sensed there was something else, something unsaid, holding her back, keeping them apart.

If, as the summer of 1953 approached, Jackson felt increasingly isolated and embattled, he blamed it on one man: Harold Rosenberg.

The trouble had begun almost a year before on a late summer evening at the Rosenbergs' quaint, brown-shingled house on Neck Path. Normally, Lee would have refused the invitation, especially at a time when Jackson's behavior was unpredictable, but the Rosenbergs had invited not artists this time but writers, friends from Harold's literary circle at the *Partisan Review*, and Lee may have hoped to enlist some fresh critical support for Jackson's faltering cause. Whatever her calculation, she must have regretted it. The conversation, loftily moderated by Rosenberg, quickly turned to dense abstractions and, just as quickly, lost Jackson. Drinking sullenly in a corner, he began to punctuate the discussion with "What a lot of shit," and "horse piss." Finally, after ostentatiously ignoring him for a while, Harold turned to Jackson and said in his most patronizing voice, "Listen, Jackson. Don't you think you've had enough to drink? What you need now is to stop interrupting and go upstairs and take a nice nap."

As soon as Jackson, too drunk to take offense, left the room, Lee erupted in a blinding rage. The whole evening had been a trap, she concluded. Rosenberg had deliberately invited Jackson that night in order to humiliate him. She had seem him do it before: pump Jackson full of liquor, then wait for him to make a fool of himself. She leapt to her feet and tore into the snickering Rosenberg. "How *dare* you!" she roared. "How *dare* you? He's a famous man and you speak as if he was just anybody." Rosenberg stood up, rising to his full six feet four inches in exaggerated indignation. "Don't tell me who's famous," he said in his high, raspy voice. "But if there's going to be anyone famous here, it's me and not that drunk upstairs." The other guests broke into laughter. Lee stormed out of the room.

Soon afterward, Rosenberg set out to make good on his threat.

He had been frustrated and disillusioned with developments in the art world for some time. The artists he had long advocated, Baziotes and Hofmann, were still mired in relative anonymity. His writings on the subject had been ignored by all but a few. The "Intrasubjectives" show had come and gone and hardly left a mark. As a frequent guest of Robert Motherwell, he had partaken of Motherwell's general disenchantment with the direction of the art world (away from him) and with Jackson's ascendancy in particular.

Nothing galled Rosenberg more, however, than the rise of Clement Greenberg. Rosenberg felt he knew, more than most, what a charlatan Greenberg really was. He had known him in the thirties, when, still a very blank slate, Greenberg had accompanied Igor Pantuhoff, that White Russian pretender, to Hofmann's school and to galleries and museums for a quick education. May Rosenberg, who had first sent Greenberg to Lee Krasner "to take him around

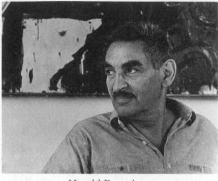

Harold Rosenberg

and tell him about art," thought even less of him. Now they were confronted with the sorry spectacle of the same Clement Greenberg—"that mediocrity," May called him—wielding definitive power in the world of avant-garde art, dictating who was great and who wasn't, ignoring good artists and deifying drunks with half-baked Kant and flabby theories on the historical inevitability of abstract art. (Rosenberg later described Greenberg as "a tipster on masterpieces, current and future.") He had undoubtedly heard the horror stories from artists like Willem de Kooning, at whose dinner table Rosenberg was a frequent guest and from whom he learned much of what he knew about art. Greenberg had come to de Kooning's studio and, pointing at various pictures, announced, "You can't do that, and you can't do that." De Kooning had thrown him out, but many artists were not so brave. Meanwhile, Rosenberg—the breathtaking intellect, the "glittering phrasemaker," poet, polemicist, philosopher—labored in relative obscurity. To May, who adored her husband despite his philandering, it was infuriating; to Harold, deeply mortifying. On a trip between New York and East Hampton that summer, a friend recalled him "lamenting, with great humor, his own lack of success." By the end of the summer, the humor was gone. He was determined to topple Greenberg and, by association, "that drunk upstairs," Jackson Pollock.

Although a lawyer by training and better known for his poetry and literary criticism, Rosenberg, like Greenberg, had done some painting himself, once submitting a "respectable" sketch of Pilgrims and Indians for a WPA post office mural. Also like Greenberg, he enjoyed the notoriety that came so easily to him in the largely unintellectual artists' community—so much so that even after moving to Washington, D.C., to edit the WPA's American Guide Series, he returned to New York every weekend. A lifelong Francophile, he exulted in the arrival of the Surrealists, especially Breton, whom he considered one of his few intellectual equals. But Rosenberg was too smart not to see the fundamental contradiction between the Surrealists' view of art as the ultimate expression of the artist's individual consciousness and his own Trotskyite view of art as a political tool, a contradiction that evoked the much larger confrontation between existentialism and Marxism. To Rosenberg, these two worldviews represented "two dogs barking up the same metaphysical tree"—namely "the situation of the individual protagonist in a historical drama." After the war, Rosenberg converted to anti-Communism and dropped his Marxist rhetoric but his obsession remained basically unchanged: how could an individual survive and not be overwhelmed by the homogenizing tide of the mass media? How could an artist create independently of mass culture? Robert Motherwell, another admirer of Breton, was asking similar questions, although he phrased them in a more overtly ambitious way: "The artist's problem is *with what to identify himself.*" As early as 1944, Motherwell had used what was essentially an existentialist argument ("Painting is therefore the mind realizing itself in color and space") to defend a formalist view of art. About the same time, Rosenberg saw an article on Dada by Richard Huelsenbeck, a militant leader of the German Dadaist movement, arguing that "literature should be action . . . made with a gun in the hand." According to Motherwell, Harold "fell in love with" Huelsenbeck's article and decided to include it in the lone issue of *Possibilities.*

In the same issue (which also included a public statement by Jackson), Motherwell and Rosenberg joined in an introduction that posited the artist's existential ecstasy as the ultimate political statement. "If one is to continue to paint or to write as the political trap seems to close upon him he must perhaps have the extremest faith in sheer possibility." In 1948, Rosenberg took the argument another step more explicit. The artist, because he "work[ed] directly with the materials of his own experience," was the only unalienated worker in America: the new revolutionary hero. And in order to "free himself from the past," as Marx required, he was called upon to "mak[e] a new self through his actions." Rosenberg had announced this new theory to the art world in his introduction to the "Intrasubjectives" show at Sam Kootz's gallery in 1949 ("The modern painter . . . begins with nothingness. That is the only thing he copies. The rest he invents") but, weighed down by Kootz's deadly title, the show—and Rosenberg's theories—quickly sank out of sight.

By the early 1950s, such ideas had filtered down from the philosophical heights into the hands of polemicists like Barnett Newman and Clyfford Still where they were transformed into radical dicta about the importance of the act of painting and the artist's responsibility to resist mass culture and commercialism. Newman especially, furious over the fate of his shows, had tried to transform the sour grapes of failure into the wine of philosophy: "It doesn't matter if anything sells," he told anyone who would listen. "It only matters that you paint. The act of painting is everything." By this route, and in this greatly simplified form, the ideas had even reached the ear of Jackson Pollock. In fact, Jackson and Rosenberg had discussed the issue at least once prior to the winter of 1952. Parroting Newman and Still, Jackson offered a garbled version of the importance of the "act of painting" on a train trip across Long Island.

Whatever Rosenberg's sources, the result would be his own: a product of his unique, if paradoxical, gifts for synthesis and obfuscation.

That fall, as he labored over successive drafts of an article for *Art News*, Rosenberg must have soon realized his dilemma. His long-evolving theory of the artist as existential hero, American pioneer, man of action, and political revolutionary led inexorably to one artist: Jackson Pollock. Who else but Pollock the westerner, Pollock the ice-breaker, the risk-taker, hurling himself at the canvas, Pollock as immortalized in Namuth's blurred "action" photos— who else could Rosenberg cast in his central role? Pollock, in fact, had already nominated himself in his *Possibilities* statement (which Rosenberg had a heavy hand in editing): "When I am *in* my painting, I'm not aware of what I'm doing. It is only after a sort of 'get acquainted' period that I see what I have been about. . . . [T]he painting has a life of its own. I try to let it come through." The other candidates for the part—de Kooning, Motherwell, Baziotes, Gorky— were either too cerebral and considered in their technique, too tied to European precedents, or simply too European. *But*—and here was the heart of the dilemma—*Rosenberg didn't like Jackson's paintings.* Not only that, he despised his drunken antics, dismissed his intelligence (later calling him "incapable of sustained mental effort"), and deeply resented his celebrity.

A lesser mind—or, some would say, a more honest one—would have recoiled at such a contradiction. But Rosenberg saw it as a challenge worthy of his supreme intellect: to define a new movement in art without endorsing, or even naming, its primary exemplar; to impugn Jackson's celebrity while applauding his methods; and finally, to topple Greenberg's critical regime without undermining the art it had brought to prominence. Only a critic who, like Breton, cared more about ideas than about paintings would have attempted it. Rosenberg relished it.

"The American Action Painters" appeared in the December 1952 issue of *Art News* just days after Jackson's Janis show closed. The argument opens with a bold, memorable stroke:

> At a certain moment the canvas began to appear to one American painter after another as an arena in which to act—rather than as a space in which to reproduce, re-design, analyze or "express" an object, actual or imagined. What was to go on the canvas was not a picture but an event.
>
> The painter no longer approached his easel with an image in his mind; he went up to it with material in his hand to do something to that other piece of material in front of him. The image would be the result of this encounter.

But directness and clarity soon give way to Rosenberg's contradictory agenda. Without naming names, he refers to Jackson as "one of the leaders of this [new] mode," and even describes "action painting" in such a way that it clearly evokes Namuth's pictures of Jackson at work: "Since the painter has become an actor, the spectator has to think in a vocabulary of action: its inception, duration, direction—psychic state, concentration and relaxation of the will, passivity, alert waiting." *But*, adds Rosenberg, there is more to action painting than just action. To be truly vanguard, the action must arise from a "personal revolt"—a liberation not only from the object but from art itself, from society, *and* from the past: in short, a personal and political revolution. Each painting reenacts the drama of liberation; each is an act of self-creation. Here again, as Rosenberg must have realized, no artist met the criteria more persuasively than Pollock. No artist had poured out his inner world, his "private myths," more convincingly. No artist's work was more "inseparable from [his] biography." No artist had risked more. No artist had cut his ties to the past, to inherited "Value" of any kind, with such anguished finality.

But there was yet another hurdle: "The test of any of the new paintings is its seriousness," writes Rosenberg, "and the test of its seriousness is the degree to which the act on the canvas is an extension of the artist's total effort to make over his experience." Even if an artist "took to the white expanse of canvas as Melville's Ishmael took to the sea," even if he arrived at his style after a wrenching personal/political revolt and reenacted that revolt each time he painted, he still *had to be serious.* Existential angst wasn't enough; *sincerity* was the key.

According to Rosenberg, this was the test that Jackson failed. Still without using names, the article ridicules Jackson's recent turn to mysticism, saying such a turn produces "*easy* painting[s]" and "unearned masterpieces." If an artist is merely a mouthpiece for the "Mystical," says Rosenberg—pulling Still and Newman into his net—if the artist's personal struggle is no longer a part of the dramatic dialogue on canvas, then the artist's life (his "daily annihilation") becomes merely decoration and the art, merely "apocalyptic wallpaper." He assails the "megalomania" inherent in the artist's claim that the Mystical speaks through him. Such an artist confuses the "sensation of having acted" with the true artistic act and therefore his art communicates nothing except a signature. His paintings cease to be "the emblem of a personal struggle," and the painter ceases to be a true artist. He becomes instead "a ghost inhabiting the Art World." The implications for Pollock are unmistakable. "The man who started to remake himself," Rosenberg concludes, "has made himself into a commodity with a trademark."

By comparison, Greenberg proves easy to dispose of. Because the new painting "has broken down every distinction between art and life," says Rosenberg, "it follows that anything is relevant to it. Anything that has to do with action— psychology, philosophy, history, mythology, hero worship. Anything but art criticism. . . . The critic who goes on judging in terms of schools, styles, form, as if the painter were still concerned with producing a certain kind of object (the work of art), instead of living on the canvas, is bound to seem a stranger." Elsewhere, in ever more thinly veiled references, Rosenberg calls Greenberg "a professional enlightener of the masses" and a member of the "taste bureaucracy." He has betrayed vanguard art, says Rosenberg, joining forces with a commercial establishment that *uses* vanguard artists, but neither appreciates nor, ultimately, wants them.

What is needed, of course, is "a new kind of criticism," Rosenberg maintains, one that recognizes "in the painting the assumptions inherent in its mode
of creation," one that counterbalances the "obtuseness, venality, and aimless-
ness of the Art World." What is needed is "a genuine audience—not just a
market . . . understanding—not just publicity." Enlightened criticism and an
understanding audience, of course, can come only from "the tiny circle of
poets, musicians, theoreticians, men of letters, who have sensed in their own
work the presence of the new creative principle." In short, from Harold Rosenberg.

Fortunately for Rosenberg, few artists bothered to read the article closely
and even fewer understood it. When Paul Brach confronted him with the truth
—"I think you wrote that article just to tear down Jackson"—Rosenberg replied, with an inscrutable smile and a gangster-like snarl, "You're a smart kid."
Others may have missed the grand strategy, but they understood the article
well enough to know that it had almost nothing to do with painting. Gerome
Kamrowski considered it "so full of bullshit that you didn't know if he was
talking about painting or some social event." "It was all such a lie," Nicholas
Carone lamented. "At least Greenberg had an eye." In the process of gerry-
mandering his theory to exclude Jackson, Rosenberg had created a definition
of action painting so abstract, so abstruse that it no longer had any relationship
to what artists—any artists—were actually doing. Was it realistic to expect
critics to begin judging art as action, looking over artists' shoulders from inception to completion? How was it possible to distinguish between "the automatic,
the spontaneous, the evoked," and the merely accomplished? Who would
grade an artist's "seriousness?" Had Rosenberg merely replaced the hated
"good or bad" test of Greenberg with his own equally arbitrary "sincere or
insincere" test, different only in that Harold Rosenberg would administer it?

Some of Rosenberg's fellow intellectuals at the *Partisan Review* saw the
article as a curious, slipshod excursion into irrelevance. William Barrett
warned: "It may not be the best thing in the world for the concrete mind of the
painter to drink too deeply of the waters of ideology, especially when dispensed
by so subtle a hand as Rosenberg," who, according to Barrett, "had the bewildering habit, even while he dazzled you, of leaving any subject more complicated and puzzling than when he took it up." Lionel Abel considered the article
"not only unclear, but wrong," especially in its definition of action. Just
as Rosenberg had accused modern art of being neither "modern" nor
"art," "action painting," it turned out, had nothing to do with either action or
painting.

What it did have was a catchy title.

As a polemic, as a crowd-pleaser, as an artifact of the very culture it castigated, "The American Action Painters" was, ironically, a roaring success. (Not
surprising given Rosenberg's twenty years of experience on the Advertising
Council inventing such icons of popular culture as Smokey the Bear.) The

phrase "action painting" buzzed through the December shows up and down Fifty-seventh Street and permeated holiday parties, provoking "numerous and inflammatory discussions and debates," according to one account. It may not have been exactly the reception Rosenberg anticipated, but he had certainly accomplished his primary goal. "He was determined to get noticed," recalls Roger Wilcox, an occasional visitor at the Rosenberg house in 1952, when the article took shape, "to do something sensational. He said he was just as happy if he got lots of praise for it or lots of criticism. Just as long as people were talking about it. He wanted attention."

On Fireplace Road, he got it. Lee Krasner's fury mounted as she listened to Bradley Walker Tomlin read the article out loud. Tomlin, a genteel man with an intellectual bent, undoubtedly helped her through Rosenberg's dense, elliptical, allusive argument, but Lee didn't need an interpreter to know that Jackson was being savaged. To her, the implication of lines like "the new painting has broken down every distinction between art and life," were all too clear: just as Jackson's life was going to hell, so was his art. Who else could Rosenberg be talking about when he referred to "private Dark Nights," "daily annihilation," "megalomania," and "easy painting"? After years of what Lee considered humiliations and slights from both Rosenberg and his wife, the article amounted to nothing less than a declaration of war—the opening salvo in a collision of epic dimensions.

If Harold Rosenberg wanted a fight, she would give him the fight of his life.

When Lee tried to rally her troops, however, she found the ranks distressingly thin. Tomlin, sympathetic but too sweet-tempered for combat, offered moral support but little else. Clyfford Still, who came by the house soon after the dispute erupted, wrote Rosenberg the usual blistering letter calling the article "an attack on painting," but successfully resisted a long-term enlistment in any cause other than his own. Clement Greenberg, Lee's most logical ally, was curiously silent at first. When she urged him to launch a quick counterattack, he balked, dismissing the whole notion of "action painting" as "a purely rhetorical fabrication." Besides, he explained, "You get in a fight only if you respect someone, and I don't respect Harold. He doesn't tell the truth." There were, of course, other reasons for Greenberg's uncharacteristic reticence. He had already begun to feel a rumble of discontent at the *Partisan Review* over his strident, dogmatic advocacy of a certain brand of abstract art. James Johnson Sweeney had recently been added to the *Review*'s editorial board in the full knowledge that he was no admirer of Greenberg's criticism. With his own power base threatened, Greenberg must have decided that it was hardly the time to engage Rosenberg, a well-respected and well-connected member of the same circle, in public combat. Especially over an article that, in Greenberg's opinion, was an attack not on him but on Jackson, an artist whose work he no longer respected at a time when he was increasingly preoccupied with his talented and attractive young protégée Helen Frankenthaler, who was proving far more receptive than Jackson to his formalist prescriptions. Besides, hadn't Jackson called him "a fool"?

At first, even Jackson proved a reluctant ally. According to Conrad Marca-Relli, who saw him soon after the article appeared, his initial reaction was more annoyance than anger. Like Lee, he never doubted that Rosenberg had used him as a model—he later referred to the article routinely as "Rosenberg's piece on me"—and he remembered his trainboard conversation with Rosenberg about "the act of painting." But to Jackson's unsubtle intellect, it appeared that Rosenberg had merely mangled his ideas. "How stupid," he remarked to Marca-Relli. "I talked about the act of painting, exposing the act of painting, not action painting. Harold got it all wrong." "It sounded to him completely absurd," says Marca-Relli. But at a time when the world seemed set against him, with money short and interest in his paintings flagging, Jackson readily accepted Lee's more paranoid view that he had, in fact, been deeply maligned, that "getting it wrong" was tantamount to being wronged. Soon his official reaction, as reported by Lee, changed from "annoyed" to "appalled," and the article became the focus of his antagonism toward an increasingly hostile world.

It wasn't long before the war escalated. Several days after the article appeared, Willem de Kooning and Philip Pavia stopped by Jackson's house and found Lee still venting her rage. Unthinkingly, de Kooning "announced his liking for the article" and proceeded to defend it and Rosenberg from Lee's withering assaults. The discussion "reached new heights" of rancor and vituperation, according to one account, until de Kooning and Pavia beat a hasty retreat under heavy fire. It might have been just another of the hundreds of arguments that Rosenberg's article sparked, but Lee refused to let it rest. In a hail of telephone calls, she accused de Kooning of "betraying her, betraying Jackson, betraying art."

In fact, Lee's list of grievances against de Kooning, both real and imagined, went back more than a decade, to the late thirties. She had "adored" him then. Strikingly handsome, Continental, gifted, the young Dutchman was everything Lena Krassner wanted in a man. Before meeting Jackson, she had considered de Kooning "the greatest painter in the world." Love—or at least infatuation—had followed inevitably. At a New Year's Eve party in the late thirties, she had thrown herself at him, sitting on his lap, playing the coquette. At the climactic moment, however, just as she was about to kiss him, he opened his knees and let her drop comically to the floor, humiliating her in front of friends and fellow artists. After drowning her shame in booze, she began to rail at him, calling him "a phony" and "a shit," until Fritz Bultman dragged her away and forced her into the shower with all her clothes on.

That night still ranked as one of the worst of Lee's life. In the years since, her scorned infatuation had turned to bile. She accused de Kooning of suborning Jackson's drinking, sabotaging his reputation, and, worst of all, "refusing

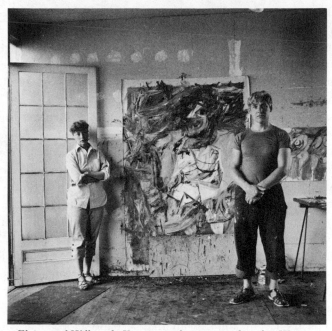

Elaine and Willem de Kooning with a painting from his *Women*
series, taken at the Castellis' house in East Hampton, August 1953

to acknowledge that [Jackson] was number one." For the same reasons, compounded by jealousy, Lee hated the woman de Kooning had married, Elaine
Fried, a smart, sociable, witty, vital, unpretentious, and—most galling—attractive young artist. Over the years, the two women had successfully gilded their
rivalry with a chilly cordiality that fooled no one except their husbands. Lee
suspected that Elaine, a close friend of Tom Hess, had been behind the second-
class treatment Jackson received in Hess's book, *Abstract Painting: Background
and American Phase*. She had forgiven Hess (she and Jackson asked him to
write a book on the black-and-white paintings), but both de Koonings had
remained high on her long list of enemies. De Kooning's defense of Rosenberg
catapulted him to the top of that list.

Lee had even more trouble recruiting Jackson for this new front in her
widening war. Jackson and Bill de Kooning had enjoyed a friendly, if not warm,
mutual respect since Lee introduced them in the early forties. When Lionel
Abel visited Springs in 1948, Jackson told him, "We've just had a painter here
who's better than me," Abel remembers. "He was talking about Bill de Kooning. They were competitive, but there was a lot of generosity lurking in that
competitiveness." The same summer, Jackson "bragged" to Harry Jackson and
Grace Hartigan about de Kooning and sent both young artists to see him at his
studio in New York. Reuben Kadish recalls that Jackson always considered de
Kooning "one of the top guys," a sentiment he shared with Dorothy Seiberling
when she interviewed him for the *Life* article in the summer of 1949. "Pollock's
taste in contemporary art," she wrote in her notes, "runs to similarly obscure

painters [like] de Kooning." The Club, Jackson's celebrity, and the rising tide of resentment it engendered among other artists had tested but not undermined the "lurking generosity" between the two men. To Lee's great mortification, they continued to drink together occasionally—more by coincidence than planning—to enjoy each other's company, and to admire each other's art, even as the battle lines were being drawn around them.

Unlike her allies, Lee's enemies coalesced against her with dreadnought efficiency. Rosenberg and de Kooning had enjoyed a casual friendship since the Project days. During the summer of 1952, when de Kooning set up a studio in the big house that Leo Castelli rented in East Hampton, the two men saw more of each other than they had in the previous decade. Both enjoyed the gamesmanship of intellectual discourse around the dinner table; both were used to being the center of attention: Rosenberg for his towering size and intellect, de Kooning for his looks. In conversation, both liked to play agent provocateur: Rosenberg by "saying things just to be contrary," de Kooning by dropping an incendiary remark then stepping back to watch others battle over it. They also shared a thoughtful, if not deep, philosophical streak. (When asked if he would rather be "a half-assed philosopher or a great painter," de Kooning replied, "Let me think about that.") To the subject of art, both brought what Leslie Fiedler called "a European eye" and an interest in ideas. If they differed, it was on the question of how those ideas related to painting: Rosenberg the radical ideologue; de Kooning the pragmatic, workmanlike Lowlander.

Ironically, the catalyst that transformed this casual friendship into a formidable alliance was Lee Krasner. Over the years, her dogged, single-minded promotion of Jackson had left deep reservoirs of ill will among those she had "elbowed out of Jackson's path." "She built this Chinese Wall around him," recalls Philip Pavia, "and everyone resented it." Both de Kooning and Rosenberg had felt Lee's protective coldness and her blazing temper. Not surprisingly, Rosenberg cast his antagonism in a political light: "Some people have been around Stalinists so long," he quipped, "they start acting like Stalin." Behind the enmity of both men, urging them on, lay the deeper, more bitter, and perhaps more manipulative anger of their wives, May Rosenberg and Elaine de Kooning, both of whom felt, for different reasons, that Jackson (and Lee) had monopolized the limelight for too long. At dinner parties, the two couples and their friends joked bitterly about Lee and the "life-and-death" passion she brought to her role as Jackson's shield and right arm. They took a certain furtive pleasure in her desperate, and increasingly unsuccessful, struggle to contain his self-destructive impulses and to conceal his peccadilloes from the world. To them, she was sometimes "Lady Macbeth," who would "gladly stab to make a king or get a lover," sometimes Medea, ready to "stab or choke *Jackson*" rather than see him delivered into the hands of his detractors. Whatever their other differences may have been, they were united in their hatred of Lee.

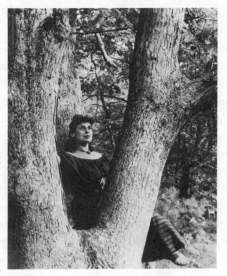

May Tabak Rosenberg

In this crossfire of personal antagonisms, ideas were the first casualty. Rosenberg liked de Kooning's paintings well enough—although not as much as those of Hofmann, Baziotes, and Gorky—but they bore little relationship to the theory of "action painting." Nor was de Kooning anything like the revolutionary hero portrayed in "The American Action Painters." In addition to being neither American nor, after 1952, nonfigurative, he was a thoughtful, controlled artist whose bravura brushwork belied the hours of preparation, execution, and evaluation that went into it. According to his wife, he "would sit and look for two hours for every five minutes of painting." Far from liberating himself from all aesthetic "Value," he openly carried on a dialogue with the European Beaux Arts tradition in which he was trained, and admired such unrevolutionary artists as Frederic Remington.

Fortunately, de Kooning considered Rosenberg's ideas as irrelevant as Rosenberg considered de Kooning's paintings. Herbert Ferber, who worked in a neighboring studio on Broadway, recalls that de Kooning dismissed Rosenberg's theories as "a lot of nonsense." One day he walked into de Kooning's studio and saw why. "There were fifty or seventy-five pounds of paint on the floor that he had just scraped off," recalls Ferber. "I said, 'What's that expensive stuff doing on the floor?' and he said, 'Well, you know, you have to think about what you do. I didn't like it, so I try this, and I scrape it off and try that.' That," says Ferber, "is not 'action painting.'"

But ideological consistency no longer mattered—if it ever did. At cocktail parties and openings, in artists' studios and East Hampton living rooms, at the Club and over the phone lines, the battle was joined.

Lee spread the story that Rosenberg had stolen the idea and the phrase "action painting" from Jackson. While acknowledging their conversation, Rosenberg indignantly denied the plagiarism charge. (To Lionel Abel, he admitted that Jackson had used the term "action painting" first but only because he, Rosenberg, "had put the idea in Jackson's mouth." Later, under fire, Rosenberg vehemently denied that he owed the idea *or* the phrase to anyone, least of all Jackson.) Rosenberg not only denied the charge, he denied that the article was even *about* Jackson. He accused Jackson of "painting like a monkey," invoking the stories that had been published in the wake of the *Life* article about a zookeeper and her precocious chimp. The comment quickly made the rounds. Lee and Jackson's partisans accused de Kooning of "craving recognition at Jackson's expense," and Rosenberg of "pushing Jackson out of the way to get de Kooning in." May Rosenberg accused Lee of "wanting to destroy everybody except for Jackson." Lee called May "paranoid," "psychotic," and "a madwoman," implying that only a madwoman could put up with Harold's cheating. May fired back accusations that Lee had "an aggravated case of dementia," implying that only a madwoman would put up with Jackson's drinking. May also charged that Lee only wanted to make money and had curried favor among rich collectors for years and greedily kept other artists away.

The dispute spread quickly. Lee launched counteroffensives not just against the Rosenbergs and the de Koonings but against anyone who defended them. She attacked the Club, as a hotbed of resistance to Jackson's reputation. The list of maligned artists grew longer and longer and soon included even old friends like Wilfrid Zogbaum. For whatever reason—perhaps because, having conquered Jackson, she craved new, more titanic collisions—Lee was determined to turn her attack on Rosenberg into a test of faith: a referendum on Jackson Pollock. Everyone in the art world would be forced to declare loyalties, to choose sides: either you were for Jackson or against him.

It was a disastrous miscalculation.

In the battle for hearts and minds, Rosenberg proved a formidable adversary. At the Club and the Cedar Tavern (an unofficial annex of the Club), his towering figure, fierce visage, and glib wit "made him an instant object of adoration." To many artists, he played the intellectual mentor who, like Breton, was among them if not of them. (At a concert of works by John Cage, Rosenberg stood up and announced to the overcrowded room: "This is for artists only. Everyone else can go home.") The artists liked the intellectuals he gathered around him: men like Tom Hess and Edwin Denby; and the nonstop intellectual conversation they generated. It made them feel good about themselves and the importance of what they were doing. When the article on "action painting" appeared, they didn't stop to ponder the details. As with so many of Rosenberg's other ideas, they knew they liked the *sound* of it. According to Leslie Fiedler, they reveled in the sheer masculinity of it. To the generation that had come through the Project, it justified the years of barroom antics, hard drinking, misogyny, and competitive cocksmanship. To the new generation of younger artists, it exploded the stereotype of the artist as foppish, worthless, and—worst of all in the can-do, postwar culture—ineffectual. At a time when anxiety about "making it" was just beginning to be felt, they took comfort in its defiant anticommercialism. They warmed to its antihistorical and pro-American prejudices. Although they made fun of it, they even liked Rosenberg's dense, indecipherable style. It made them feel that art was indeed a higher calling that touched on issues so profound and philosophical that it was impossible, even for an intellect as great as Rosenberg's, to communicate them clearly to ordinary minds.

But mostly they liked it because it wasn't Greenberg. Finally, someone had challenged Pope Clement; a gate-crasher had confronted the "bloody concierge" of avant-garde art. Finally, someone had found a different way of looking at abstract paintings; finally, someone was offering artists an escape from what they perceived as the yoke of Greenberg's caprice. They had had enough of his visiting their studios and "telling them what to paint" (a charge Greenberg would later vigorously deny); of his summarily dismissing young painters like Larry Rivers; of his deciding what was good, what was bad, who was great and who wasn't. In the Cedar Tavern, Milton Resnick heard Greenberg bragging "that he juried a show and gave somebody a prize on the condition that he turn the picture upside down because it looked better that way." "You son of a bitch," Resnick hissed as he got up from the table. "I'm never going to sit with you again." The other artists at the table followed him out the door. Everyone who heard the story applauded.

Neither Rosenberg's popularity nor Greenberg's disrepute, however, proved fatal to Lee's cause. If she had limited her attacks to Rosenberg, both she and Jackson might have emerged relatively unscathed from the usual round of name-calling and social trench warfare. It was by attacking Willem de Kooning that Lee doomed Jackson's cause to certain failure.

No artist was more respected or better liked. Far more convincingly than Rosenberg, de Kooning was "one of the boys." At the Club, he volunteered to wash glasses and sweep up after meetings. Unlike Jackson, he lived in the heart of the artists' community, a relatively small patch of New York City described by Irving Sandler as "centered in the studios on and around East Tenth Street, the Cedar Street Tavern, and the Club." At a time when Robert Motherwell was "living his haute bourgeois life" uptown and Clyfford Still maintained a monastic isolation, de Kooning was always available to younger artists. Sensitive and self-effacing, he brought to all his conversations enormous intensity, unpretentious intelligence and a dry, almost inadvertent sense of humor. (At a reception, he told Mrs. John D. Rockefeller, "You look like a million bucks.")

Unlike Jackson's celebrity, which many artists considered an invention of Clement Greenberg's, de Kooning's reputation derived from the only legitimate source: his fellow artists. He had worked his way up "through the ranks," earning their respect and support long before winning gallery recognition or media attention. Young artists especially, like Grace Hartigan, found him "a devastating experience because of his brilliant articulateness." They admired his thoughtful, persuasive art. Unlike Jackson's work—about which even his admirers often complained, "What the hell can you do with it?"—de Kooning's embraced them. "People could hook into the traditional in his paintings," says Nicholas Carone. "You know, a beautiful line, a nice passage." "De Kooning provided a language you could write your own sentences with," said Al Held. "Pollock didn't do that." Jackson may have been a force of nature, but de Kooning was the embodiment of culture. In fact, despite Rosenberg's require- ment that vanguard artists break with the past, most artists stood behind de Kooning (and, by association, Rosenberg) precisely *because* he, in turn, stood squarely in the *artiste peintre* tradition. He was "in the line": Cézanne, Matisse, Picasso, Hofmann, Matta, Gorky, de Kooning. "If you had a choice and you wanted to pick up on the whole grand tradition of Western art," recalls Irving Sandler, "you were against Jackson and with Bill." At the Club, a painter named Ari Stillman stood up and announced: "The young artists think de Kooning is Number One because he's interested in 'good' painting." Pollock he dismissed as a "primitive Breakthrough Boy," a "freak." "Jackson may have been the genius," says Sandler, "but the *painter* was Bill."

Finally, and perhaps most important, de Kooning reciprocated the respect his colleagues lavished on him. "When he came over for dinner," recalls Eleanor Hempstead, "it didn't matter if you had an El Greco or a Rubens or a Rembrandt on the wall, he went right for *your* work. Even if it was just some little watercolor, he would go and look at it and make a nice remark like 'Did you do this?' in an admiring way. He always commented."

For all Lee's efforts, for all the rising talk of "civil war" and the art world dividing into opposing camps, there was, as John Myers pointed out with a touch of sadness, "only one camp, really, and that was de Kooning's. . . . It was Jackson against the world."

Throughout the winter of Rosenberg's article, while Lee waged her war by telephone, Jackson felt increasingly isolated and besieged. "The whole art world was talking about de Kooning," recalls Nicholas Carone. "Jackson was all through. They were building up de Kooning and slaughtering Pollock." Friends described him as "hurt" and "bitter." "It was disastrous for him," says Carone, "because he loved painters and he loved paintings." On the few oc- casions when the two reluctant protagonists confronted each other in public, they tried to recapture the barroom camaraderie of earlier days. One night they were seen sitting on the curb outside the Cedar Tavern passing a bottle back and forth. "Jackson, you're the greatest painter in America," de Kooning would say, slapping Jackson on the back; to which Jackson would reply with another slap, "No Bill, *you're* the greatest painter in America." "They played a game," recalls Conrad Marca-Relli, "getting in some digs, trying to be playful." But beneath the surface, Marca-Relli and others noticed, the barbs now seemed "loaded," the game more serious, "as if they knew the stakes were higher."

On March 16, 1953, Jackson attended the opening of de Kooning's show at the Janis Gallery. Around the walls were five large paintings and several drawings, all of women: aggressive, tortured, vehemently brushed images; part Marilyn Monroe, part Medusa. "The turbulence," Elaine de Kooning later said, "came from his image of women, from his consciousness of their role—and it was not sweet." (Like Jackson, de Kooning had used his mother as a model. Cornelia de Kooning was an iron-willed woman who "could walk through a brick wall," according to Elaine, or serve as a figurehead "on the prow of a ship, breaking gigantic ice flows.") More perhaps than anyone else, Jackson recognized the power of de Kooning's women. They were, in a way, *his* paintings: *his* tortured vision of women, *his* turbulent sexuality, *his* emotionally charged figuration, painted with the power and conviction he had once possessed. Before Tom Hess declared his love for them, before Rosenberg pronounced them "acts of genius," before the Museum of Modern Art bought one, before the art journals proclaimed them "the final direction of the New York School," before *Time* magazine (Jackson's implacable enemy) roared its approval, Jackson knew they were masterpieces.

At the party afterward, Jackson tried to drink himself into obliviousness. Lee's friend George Mercer had seen him drunk before "but never this out of hand." At one point, Jackson yelled across the room to de Kooning, "Bill, you betrayed it. You're doing the figure, you're still doing the same goddamn thing. You know you never got out of being a figure painter." De Kooning, anxious to defuse the situation, yelled back good-naturedly, "Well, what are *you* doing, Jackson?" intending perhaps to remind Jackson of the figures that had appeared in his paintings two years before. But Jackson took it another way, apparently: as a cutting reference to his continuing work block. As de Kooning and everyone else knew, Jackson was no longer "doing" anything.

The drinks were not coming fast enough for Jackson, so he stormed out of the room in search of a bar. Mercer turned to Lee and asked, "Should I go with him?" "Lee said, 'There's nothing you can do,'" Mercer remembers, "'but it couldn't hurt to follow him and watch him.'" Jackson soon found a bar, but before he even sat down, "there was an electric hostility" in the room, according to Mercer. "He exchanged looks with a fellow at the bar, and they started to have a fight." Before it could develop, however, Jackson stalked out the door. Standing on the curb, he paused for a moment, waited for an approaching car, then, just as the car was about to speed by, stepped into its path. The car swerved wildly, missing him by inches.

The summer brought no peace. At Leo Castelli's big house on Jericho Lane, Willem and Elaine de Kooning again set up studios and entertained a steady stream of guests including the Rosenbergs, Conrad Marca-Relli, Philip Pavia, Wilfrid Zogbaum, Franz Kline, Robert Motherwell, and a changing cast of awestruck younger painters. With Rosenberg towering over them "like a scout master," they horsed around on the beach during the day (except for de Kooning who claimed "he would just get hot and sticky and sandy and sunburned") and crowded around the festive supper table in the evenings.

On Fireplace Road, the scene was very different. Depressed and embittered, Jackson passed the summer largely in solitude. For the first time in several years, he planted a garden, although, according to Ted Dragon, he "had no patience for it. If a plant wasn't doing well he'd just kick it up." George Loper moved from reshingling the studio to reshingling the house, although neither Jackson nor Lee knew where they would find the money to pay him. Despite his idleness—so unusual for the summer months—Jackson found painting a struggle. The three or four works he managed to finish reflected his mood: gray, sullen, elegiac. Even those that started out brightly with Jackson's favorite palette of yellows and reds, were soon transformed by the double prism of depression and retrospection. *Ocean Greyness,* with its multiple eyes and mask-like islands of color, invoked the troubled images of the early forties: Picasso's bestiary, Graham's African masks, Jung's archetypes. In *Greyed Rainbow,* he concealed the painting's colorful beginnings (confined to the lower half of the canvas) behind a heavy lattice of brushed and dripped black and white evocative of the great shimmering curtains of *Cathedral* and *Number 1, 1948.*

Interruptions that summer were rare, the Pollock's social circle having dwindled to a handful of regulars: the Littles, the Potters, Alfonso Ossorio, Ted Dragon, and the odd passing visitor. In August, Sidney Janis paid an obligatory call to review Jackson's latest work and to persuade him to give up the confusing numbering system and go back to conventional titles. It was a sign of his defeatism that Jackson acquiesced so readily. In the face of mounting debts, he was agreeable to anything that Janis thought might improve his dismal sales. High-minded talk about the neutrality of numbers and "pure painting" was the relic of an earlier, more idealistic time.

Jackson also urged Janis to recover the paintings from the Paris show (and the money from Tapié's elusive sales) but needed an advance in the meantime —"just a few dollars," Janis recalls, "to tide him over. It was the first of many times." Money was increasingly on Jackson's mind—perhaps as a symbol of fame's evanescence. (On a brief visit to the city that summer, Jackson saw Robert Motherwell at a Schrafft's men's bar and "talked angrily of how in America one never permanently 'makes it,' " Motherwell remembered, "that each new show is an absolute test, despite whatever one has done in the past.") One night at The Creeks—one of the few places outside the house where Lee felt Jackson was safe—Ossorio offered to give him ten thousand dollars "just so he could relax for a year." The next morning, more sober and lucid, Ossorio withdrew the offer.

Increasingly, Jackson found comfort in his unlikely friendship with Ted Dragon, whose deference and gentleness seemed to have a soothing effect on him. "He was like a great big shaggy dog," says Dragon. "He followed me everywhere. He gave me a small painting and named it *Dancing Head* for me." Jackson also gave the young dancer flowers and vegetables from his garden. (When Dragon told him just to put them on the table, Jackson seemed hurt. "Oh, no," he replied, "I raised these. I'm going to wash them and dry them

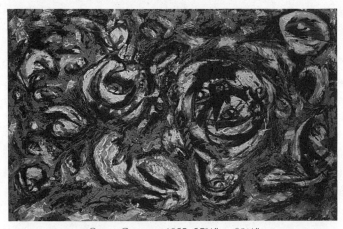

Ocean Greyness, 1953, 57¾″ × 90⅛″

and make an arrangement of them.") In the afternoons, the two men would sit on the terrace overlooking Georgica Pond and talk about gardening or cooking or music. "He wanted to know all about the great opera houses of Europe," Dragon remembers, "especially about all the behind-stage intrigues that went on." When Dragon carried on too long about Robert and Clara Schumann or Liszt, Jackson would cry out in mock exasperation, "Well, play the goddamn thing!" Chopin "bored the pants off him," Dragon recalls, but Liszt he found "fucking in'eresting."

Jackson's mood that summer brightened with the appearance of a new neighbor: Conrad Marca-Relli. A de Kooning partisan, Marca-Relli moved into the small house next to Jackson Pollock's place with considerable trepidation. Friends had warned him, "You're out of your mind. He'll destroy your house." Thus when Jackson stumbled in one day during a particularly delicate stage in the rebuilding of a fireplace, Marca-Relli went stiff with apprehension. "Let me help," Jackson offered. "I'm pretty good at that kind of stuff." "Oh, God, please don't," Marca-Relli snapped, motioning to his wife, Anita, to hurry and fetch Lee to take Jackson home. Moments later, when Jackson noticed Anita's absence, he turned to Marca-Relli with a baleful look. "She didn't go get Lee, did she? You didn't have to do that. I wasn't going to do anything wrong." Marca-Relli, who "felt like a heel," vowed that "from then on, I would treat him square, whether he was drunk or not." Not long afterward, in a gesture of reconciliation, Jackson rode over on the little tractor Jeffrey Potter had given him and offered to mow Marca-Relli's yard. "He started mowing in designs—all over the place! I mean, it was like his painting—he'd take it this way, that way." Marca-Relli shouted to him over the roar of the tractor, "How the hell do you expect to cut the grass that way?" Jackson shouted back, "Why? How would you do it?" Marca-Relli made right angles with his hands, but Jackson waved him off. "That's your way. *This* is my way." "By the time he got through," Marca-Relli recalls, "he had all the grass cut, no question about it. We were *mowed.*"

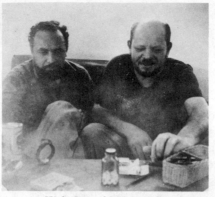

With Conrad Marca-Relli

Of the other guests whose appearance Jackson would have welcomed that summer, Lee turned most away. On several occasions Franz Kline, Philip Pavia, and even de Kooning himself drove over from East Hampton to extend an olive branch, but Lee "didn't want us in the same room with [Jackson]," says Pavia. She would either refuse to open the door or stand on the porch and say she didn't know where he was. Once, he appeared in the doorway behind her and there was "a big, awkward silence," Pavia recalls. "So we went home." Lee called them "the New York gangsters."

When Lee wasn't home, however, Jackson eagerly invited them in and, for just an evening, was back on the Phoenix Ranch with his brothers—"one of the boys" again. They drank, caroused, and played poker into the early morning hours. "Jackson started off sober as a judge," recalls Ronald Stein, who was visiting on one such occasion, "and played really good poker. But as he drank, his poker deteriorated and he got infuriated because other people were winning. He got more and more abusive until it wound up in this terrific, funny fight where they all tried to abuse each other." Around three in the morning, someone suggested going to the beach for a swim. The idea met with immediate drunken approval and they set out on bicycles for Louse Point. "You can imagine what it was like," says Stein. "Jackson could barely stand up, much less ride a bike. He crashed at least ten times within the first ten seconds."

At one point, he fell over and didn't get up. "He just lay there on his side and kept pedaling," Stein recalls. "He was wearing shorts, and his bare leg just ground against the road like sandpaper. He wouldn't let anybody touch him, and he was obviously just taking the skin off his legs and elbows. Finally they grabbed him and restrained him and dragged him into the house. He was walking around in bandages for about a month." After that, Lee redoubled her guard, and soon "the boys" stopped coming by.

Occasionally, fortified with enough liquor to defy Lee, Jackson would roar up to the Castellis', leave the Model A running in the driveway, and storm through the house "looking for de Kooning." "When he was in a mood like that," recalls Leo Castelli, "we all felt terrorized." Guests would scatter, Ileana

Castelli would hide the breakables, and de Kooning would disappear. Sometimes, when he didn't have the courage to stop, Jackson would just speed through the driveway in the Model A, honking his contempt. Once, he came tearing by blindly and almost destroyed a large, concrete sculpture that Castelli had commissioned from Larry Rivers.

One day that summer, Charles Boultenhouse returned from the movies to the little house he and Parker Tyler rented behind Dan Miller's store. "I found this note from Parker saying that Jackson had picked him up. Parker usually had this gorgeous handwriting, but this note was written in a horrible scrawl, which conveyed his absolute panic at having been taken to the Pollocks' place." When Boultenhouse came to rescue his friend, he found Jackson "in his cups" fulminating against action painting and Harold Rosenberg, and Tyler "in sheer terror." "Jackson had this huge kitchen knife," Boultenhouse recalls, "great for dicing and mincing, which he was playing with and muttering 'action painting' with utter hatred, and Lee was standing behind him, stroking his head and trying to soothe him, saying, 'Now, you know you've gotten over that, Jackson, you've gotten over that.' "

When Harry Jackson stopped by to announce that he was abandoning abstract art to "paint realistically and study painting technique," Jackson took it as a personal betrayal. "He got black," Harry recalled, "like [I] was after his goddam family jewels." He said, "Ah, shit, Harry. You can't go back to all that." "Who the fuck are you to tell me what I can or can't do!" Harry shot back. After a frosty farewell, Harry left for Europe to "study painting in a formal way" and "really look at the old masters." The two men would not see each other again for three years.

When Jane Smith returned from Europe for a few weeks, she and Tony drove their little Volkswagen to Springs for a weekend visit. Jackson took them on a scenic tour to Montauk and back—without the usual terror tactics—and afterward offered to give Jane the giant *Blue Poles*. (She politely refused the extravagant gift—"It was too big to belong to a private person," she told him, "it should belong to a city"—but accepted a black-and-white portrait instead.)

As soon as his wife was gone, Tony Smith could contain his long-simmering sexual desires no longer. After years of frustrating intimacy, of hinting to Jackson that "Lee wasn't right for him," of disguising his passion in poetic metaphors, of drawing Jackson out in discussions of "perverse sexuality," Smith finally made an outright pass—several passes, in fact. Or at least that was how Jackson interpreted them. Recoiling in horror, Jackson immediately sent a cable to Jane in Germany. "It said Tony was very depressed and missed me," recalls Jane Smith. "Jackson felt very strongly that Tony should come to Germany. So I made sure that Tony did come. And [Jackson] told me to destroy the cable after I read it. He must not have wanted Tony to know that he had sent it."

Bradley Walker Tomlin, a more recent friend, had been one of Jackson's staunchest, if least consequential, defenders in the days following the appearance of Rosenberg's article. Over the winter, he had allied himself closely with Lee, assisting in her campaign and admiring her paintings. That summer, when the house next door to the Pollocks' (the one Conrad Marca-Relli eventually bought) came up for sale, Jackson and Lee persuaded Tomlin to come out for a week and look it over. One night while he was there, Lee arranged a party—or the closest thing she could manage from her short list of safe guests. Giorgio and Linda Cavallon came, along with Marca-Relli. After dinner, Jackson drank too much, and what began as an "animated conversation" about action painting soon turned into "a heated, violent argument," according to Marca-Relli. At one point, infuriated at Lee, Jackson turned up the volume on his record player "until the house shook." Anticipating fireworks, Marca-Relli left early. The Cavallons, seeing that Tomlin was "quite tired" and "feeling sorry for him," said their good nights "hoping that would break the thing up," Giorgio Cavallon remembers. Instead, Jackson just went on, playing record after record at maximum volume until long after midnight while Tomlin, who had only recently recovered from a heart attack, sat on the couch that was supposed to be his bed, looking pale, sickly, and exhausted.

The next morning, after Tomlin, looking even worse, left to sign the papers on the house and while the Cavallons were preparing lunch, Jackson and Lee came down the stairs in full battle. "Lee got frantic and started yelling," Cavallon recalls, "and Jackson got so mad he took a butcher knife to her and said, 'You bitch, go upstairs.' Then Lee started screaming: 'Jackson, put that knife down!' " The Cavallons stood "frozen" until the ebb and flow of battle carried Jackson and Lee back upstairs. As soon as they had gone, Cavallon said to his wife, "I think we better get out of here." When Tomlin returned and heard the story, he asked to join them. That night they drove into the city and dropped Tomlin at his apartment on Third Street downtown where Wilfrid Zogbaum was staying. Two days later, Zogbaum called Cavallon to tell him that Tomlin was dead. "That night after you left, he got sick and went to the hospital. He had a heart attack."

When Marca-Relli heard the news, he was "sure the conversation at Jackson's did Tomlin in." Reluctantly, he brought the news to the Pollocks. "Gee, it's too bad about Tomlin dying," he offered. "What do you want him to do," Jackson snapped, "live for your convenience?"

By the fall of 1953, Jackson was virtually alone. He had even broken off with the miracle worker, Grant Mark—although not because of any personal epiphany. Elizabeth Wright Hubbard, the "final authority" on such matters, had undergone her own "crisis of realization" (including a genuine breakdown), packed her files, and left Mark's posh Park Avenue offices for good. (Not long afterward, Mark gave up his practice in New York.) With few friends, fewer visitors, little work, less money, and no easy cures to keep hope alive, Jackson began to talk openly of suicide. Several times he sought out Dr. Wayne Barker, a concerned, straight-talking psychiatrist who had rented a house on Fireplace

Road that summer. Although never formally Barker's patient, Jackson shared with him the urges that increasingly preoccupied him. "I'm no damn good," he told Barker. "What do you think of suicide?" Barker thought the question was just Jackson's "way of sizing you up."

Lee had already done her own "sizing up" and decided that, once again, the only person who could save Jackson from himself was Stella Pollock.

42

ABANDONED

For once, Lee and Jackson agreed. With the next show at the Janis Gallery scheduled for November and the studio almost bare, Jackson had to quit drinking and get to work. In August 1953, they invited Stella to Springs. But this time the invitation wasn't for a week or even a month. Desperate, exasperated, and shell-shocked by the long, harrowing summer, Lee yearned for a more permanent solution. She asked Stella to live with them.

In Deep River, Stella, now seventy-eight, stood poised in gloves and traveling veil, eager to accept the invitation. She was fed up with her grim, impoverished life in a small Connecticut town. Years of rheumatism and bursitis had left her weak, unable to walk long distances, and virtually imprisoned in the McCoys' tiny apartment. Her relationship with Arloie had deteriorated to the point where, according to Marie Pollock, "when Stella came to visit, it took her six weeks to get Arloie out of her system." In letters to other family members, she fumed over Arloie's "selfishness," accusing her of "wasting" money and stealing the checks the other brothers sent. The two women fought a fierce guerrilla war over the mail, racing each other to the mailbox to claim whatever contributions it might contain. The recriminations spread to every corner of their life together in stiflingly close quarters. "Stella didn't like the way Arloie raised her kids, the way she kept the kitchen, or the way she did the washing," recalls Marie Pollock. "Everything grated."

To Stella, Springs represented escape. The days she had spent on Fireplace Road and MacDougal Alley—sitting at the edge of parties, meeting Jackson's artist friends, listening to the high-flown talk, shopping in the mornings, gallery-going in the afternoons—had been among the best of her life. Clement Greenberg, who saw her often during that time, called her culture crazy, and commented that her idea of paradise was Greenwich Village. "Whenever anyone mentioned subjects like art or architecture, or anything cultural, she would move in and listen intently to every word." To Stella, Springs seemed to offer the life of refinement she had been searching for since leaving Tingley half a century before.

To Jackson's brothers, however, Springs represented something else entirely. When news of Stella's proposed move reached them, objections ricocheted around the country. Was Jackson in any condition? Did Lee really want Stella as a permanent houseguest? Could their relationship bear the strain? They had all heard the chilling stories of Jackson's recent downturn: the hospitalizations, the car wreck, the threats at knifepoint. Frank had recently visited and found "Jackson drinking beer and abusing Lee verbally, unmercifully, calling her a slut, a whore—all kinds of goddamned ugly things." In the three years since the family reunion, all the brothers except Sande had made the trek to Springs to "take Jackson under their wings and talk to him and get him to straighten up," according to Charles's daughter Jeremy, a high school student at the time.

Beneath the stated concern for Stella's welfare, however, were deeper, older, and more potent objections. Jackson *still* had made no contribution to the fund the brothers had set up to help Sande defray expenses and provide Stella with a small allowance. On several occasions, both Charles and Frank had made pleas on her behalf, and Jackson had promised to help, but the money never followed. Meanwhile, Jackson blindly pursued his campaign to impress his brothers with his affluence and importance. But the more he wanted to be seen as an adult and an equal, the more they saw him, in the words of one relative, as "a cantankerous child who, if he can't get his way, throws himself on the floor and kicks his heels." Lee was no better in their view. No one had forgotten her superciliousness at the family reunion. Far from encouraging Jackson to contribute to Stella's upkeep, like the other wives, Lee actively opposed it. "I tried to talk with him about his responsibilities toward his mother," Frank recalls, "but Lee wouldn't let me. She said, 'Jack's got his own responsibilities.'" When Lee discovered that Jackson had given Frank a painting, "her displeasure was perfectly clear," Frank recalls. (No one in the family yet knew about the terms of Jackson's will.)

The brothers also resented Stella's willful blindness. Even though they themselves had tried to protect her from the worst of Jackson's problems, they resented her refusal to acknowledge those problems and her Panglossian praise of his every effort at improvement, no matter how halfhearted or short-lived. She made excuses for his failure to contribute to her upkeep—"She talked about how he needed this special diet and how expensive it was," according to Marie—and reveled vicariously in his affluence. Even as she carped at Arloie for squandering Sande's meager earnings and misappropriating her allowance, she took perverse pleasure in Jackson's profligacy; the very fact that he was rich enough to waste money became a point of maternal pride. For Jackson's brothers, this was the story of Jackson and Stella in a nutshell. Whatever Jackson did, whatever lives he disrupted, whatever pain he inflicted, in Stella's eyes, he could do no wrong. For years Sande had sacrificed for her, endured poverty and domestic strife for her, yet, said Elizabeth Pollock, "the one she loved and adored, the one she always longed for, was Jackson." Now, after years of excusing his misbehavior, suffering his arrogance, and capitulating to his tantrums, they saw a chance to strike back. The fact that Stella wanted to go and Jackson wanted her to come so badly only made them all the more determined to prevent it.

On the other hand, something had to be done, and quickly, about the deteriorating situation in Deep River. In addition to domestic friction, the brothers worried about Stella's "old age quirks popping up" in a way that could be "unhealthy for Karen and Jay." Yet she couldn't live alone—on damp days, her arthritis left her virtually immobile—and none of the other brothers wanted to take her in.

Faced with such a "perplexing problem," they finally relented—at least temporarily. "Staying with Jack might be alright for a short time," Jay conceded in a letter to Charles, "provided it is during one of his sober periods, otherwise mother will be placed in a very awkward situation." Frank concurred. "In general," he wrote Charles at the end of August, "we do not believe that we ought to expect more than a temporary stay for Mother at Jack's." All parties agreed that two months was a fair trial. That, at least, would carry Jackson through preparations for the November show.

On Tuesday, September 1, Charles drove Stella to Springs. "[Jack] was in good shape," he reported to the family on his return. "We had a long private talk during the afternoon. My impression is that he is more ready than ever before to willingly assume some obligations towards Mother." But Charles had been through too many turns with Jackson not to harbor reservations. "I am fully aware," he wrote Jay in the cryptic circumlocutions typical of Pollock family correspondence, "that intangible events, seemingly beyond his control, may make a prolonged stay for Mother unpleasant or inadvisable." The next morning, before leaving, Charles had another "long talk," this time with Lee. He found her "cooperative and realistic." "She feels the decision to have Mother with them is Jack's," Charles wrote, "and that he may be ready to shoulder the responsibility."

For a while, Charles's reservations seemed misplaced. The weather turned fair and balmy, Stella's rheumatism disappeared, Jackson divided his time between harvesting the garden, painting, and tending to his mother's needs. Later, Stella would brag that Jackson and Lee "did more waiting on me than I ever got from [Arloie] in all the eleven years." Eager to put the family doubts to rest, Stella mailed a barrage of letters detailing her contentment and Jackson's good behavior. "I have just had my breakfast *cantelope* from Jack's garden very good," she wrote Charles. "It is a beautiful day. . . . Jack turned on the sprinkler and [the neighborhood children] got out there all bare even the little tike . . . then toasted hot dogs out in the yard Jack said how in the Devil did you ever raise five boys."

The paintings Jackson began under his mother's gaze reflected the same obsession with the past, both personal and artistic. In *Ritual*, he combined the

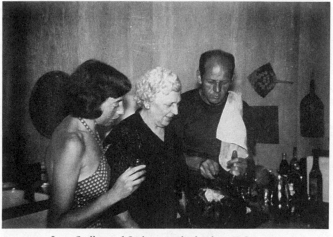

Lee, Stella, and Jackson in the kitchen at Springs

totemic figures, fractured anatomies, and personal nightmares of *Naked Man with Knife* (Stella's favorite painting) with a palette and a "spiralic" composition that echoed back to Benton's classroom. In *Sleeping Effort* and *Easter and the Totem*, old core memories resurfaced and assumed the same biomorphic, semifigurative form and dulcet coloring that they had in the mid-forties in paintings like *The Water Bull*, *The Tea Cup*, and *The Key*. In *Four Opposites*, the most fully abstract work of the winter, he concealed the figures in a lush tapestry of brushed color and aluminum paint evocative of the great drip paintings of the early fifties. Although some were decorative and derivative, others were as close as Jackson had come in years to the masterpieces of the past. Lee, who had yielded the kitchen to her mother-in-law for the duration, told a friend that the salutory effects of Stella's visit were "too good to be true."

She was right. In late September, the bubble burst. Details, of course, were never mentioned in family correspondence. Whether Jackson, in a drunken outburst, finally bared his darkest side to Stella or, like Roy Pollock, fled to the barn and drank himself furtively into unconsciousness once too often, no one in the Pollock family—least of all Stella—was willing to reveal. Perhaps a month of abstinence was more than Jackson could tolerate. In the past, Stella had never stayed for more than a week at a time. Whatever the reason, on Sunday, September 27, Charles arrived at the Fireplace Road house and, without explanation, returned Stella to Deep River.

After a series of frantic phone calls, Jackson and Lee succeeded in persuading Stella to return the following week. Once again, Charles accompanied her, ostensibly because "he wanted to see Jacks's work and Lee's too," but primarily to reassure himself that Jackson wouldn't make the same mistake, whatever it was, a second time. Once again, assurances were given all around. But the mood had changed. Even Stella, despite her determination to leave Deep River, now realized that Springs could never be a permanent solution. She treasured her illusions too much. If Jackson was truly self-destructing, she

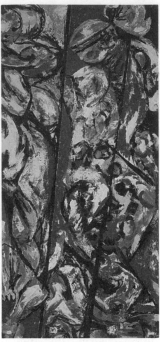

Ritual, 1953, 90½" × 42¼"

didn't want to witness it and, on her return, resisted his contrite entreaties to extend her stay beyond the end of October. "Jack had asked me to stay with them through Sept & Oct," she wrote Frank at the end of September, "now they want me to stay longer." To cover her hasty retreat, she offered lamely, "I think it is to damp here fore me and I have to get back to Deep River and get some clothes fixed nothing fits any more."

As soon as Stella left, Jackson plunged into another round of drinking, distinguishable from previous extravaganzas of self-abuse only in its supporting cast. This time, when Jackson disappeared or came home at three in the morning drunk and threatening, Lee called John Cole. The son of a "slightly down-at-the-heels society family" from East Hampton, who had gone to war and to Yale, Cole and his wife Cynthia had moved in 1951 into Berton Roueché's old place only three houses away on Fireplace Road. Neither could have imagined what life near the Pollocks would be like. Cole first earned Lee's confidence when she hired him to do some house painting. "I walked in every morning," says Cole, "so it was inevitable that I got involved in their lives." Soon he was being summoned on nights when Jackson disappeared to search the roads for his car "because Lee feared it might be overturned somewhere," or just to sit with her while she waited by the phone "for the cops calling to say that Jack had been killed." Sometimes the police called Cole directly, and he would go in his Model A to fetch Jackson out of a ditch. When he arrived at the house, Cole sensed "this tremendous tension," later comparing the experience to his wartime missions in a bomber over Germany. The few times he could coax a coherent sentence from Jackson, it was usually about his family, about his brothers—especially his "neurotically fraternal feeling" for brother Sande—and about his mother.

Jackson wanted Stella.

And he knew how to get her. With Lee in terrified pursuit, he would crash holiday parties "and make a pig of himself," according to one witness. "People would flee as soon as he appeared at the door." Only brave new friends, like the Coles, dared invite him to dinner anymore. "Then, of course, after we'd asked him, we'd spend the next two or three days wondering about whether he was going to be sober or not," says Cole. "Half the time he was and half the time he wasn't." At one such dinner, Jackson replayed the Thanksgiving debacle. "He just banged his hands down on the table and kept pushing," Cole recalls. "Everything slipped over towards him and off the edge, including all the lobster stew and white wine, which just about broke my heart."

Once, in a rare moment of sobriety, Jackson tried to explain his behavior in terms of "the effects of the moon." Lee nodded understandingly; "because the moon had quite an effect on me, too," she said. "It made me feel more emotional, more intense." But even Lee must have known that the moon had nothing to do with the intensity of Jackson's depression or the momentum of his drunken temper. He wanted Stella.

Because he couldn't work—or refused to work—his career, long in jeopardy, fell into irreparable shambles. So far he had sent only four works (*Ocean Greyness, Unformed Figure, Sleeping Effort,* and *Ritual*) to Sidney Janis for the November show, and even these he wasn't proud of. For two group exhibitions that season, Janis's "5th Anniversary Exhibition" and his "9 American Painters," Jackson chose paintings from the previous year (*Number 12, 1952* and *Blue Poles*) instead of current works. Looking back on the paintings of this period, he later told Elizabeth Wright Hubbard that "he wondered whether he was saying anything." By mid-October, Janis had no choice but to cancel the November show. This would be Jackson's first year without a show in a decade. The cancellation also forced him to borrow even more money from Janis to finish paying George Loper for the shingling job. Although the show was tentatively rescheduled for the following February to avoid the public humiliation of missing an entire season, no one, not even Lee, was confident Jackson would be ready, then or ever.

Jackson's plight attracted much attention and sympathy. No doubt recalling the enthusiasm he had always shown for renovating the house on Fireplace Road, Lee had the interior repainted. This time, however, Jackson ostentatiously ignored the entire project. Sidney Janis sent a series of supportive notes, complimenting the new works ("they are great!"), reporting the return of a few works from the ill-fated Paris show, relating some lukewarm praise from Clement Greenberg ("Clem reacted very nicely to your new things"), and generally trying to balance his concern for Jackson's spirits with his anxiety over the declining quantity and quality of his output. In one letter, he dangles the possibility of a sale ("we have at least one client who is most interested"), while at the same time explaining tersely why he hasn't sent any of the new paintings to the Whitney Annual ("it wouldn't do any good"). "We are keeping the 1953s for a grand coup, your one-man show," he wrote with patronizing cheeriness. "I have a hunch you are doing some painting. I am of course eager to see another bang-up Pollock show and I am sure I'll get my wish."

Clyfford Still, hearing of Jackson's depression and work block, tried to rally his spirits with a letter.

> Went up to Janis's gallery with Barney [Newman] the other day & took the liberty of pushing into the office to see some of the paintings you did this summer.
>
> What each work said, what it's position, what each achieved you must know. But above all, these details and attentions, the great thing, to see, came through. It was that here a *man* had been at work, at the profoundest work a man can do, facing up to what he is and aspires to.
>
> I left the room with the gratitude & renewal of courage that always comes at such moments. This is just my way of saying thanks, & with the hopes that some of my work has brought some of the same to you.
>
> Clyff Still

Jackson was too enamored of Still, too hungry for approval, apparently, to notice that the wordsmith Still had carefully avoided complimenting the new paintings. Instead, in gratitude, he rose from his creative inertia long enough to paint *The Deep*, a large, vertical canvas on which he transformed one of Still's jagged, paint-encrusted fragments of color into a dark, womb-like opening in the middle of an organic, sumptuously brushed white field. It was a tribute to Still—unlike anything else Jackson had done—yet, arguably, freer, surer, more evocative, more profound than anything Still had done. In late November, Still called Jackson to announce that he had joined the Janis gallery. Undisturbed by the apparent contradiction (the pioneer-artist of pure motives joining the most aggressively commercial gallery in New York), Jackson congratulated Janis: "it puts your gallery in the big league," he wrote, revealing just how incompletely he had absorbed Still's Puritan preachments.

Nothing Lee or Janis or Still or anyone did, however, could lift Jackson from his despair or put him back to work. Only one person could do that. By now, he was obsessed with her. If he couldn't work, he said, it was because "the idea, or the image, of his mother came over him so strongly that he'd see her." He complained of dreaming about her, of seeing her across a field and running toward her only to be cut off just short of her embrace. The months of dreaming and drinking and self-destruction, of railing and posturing across Long Island Sound for her attention, eventually found their way onto canvas. In the worst days of a stormy winter, both inside and outside, Jackson began work on a huge canvas. For the first time in two decades, he prepared sketches—the most telling sign of his faltering self-confidence. On the right side of a five-by-

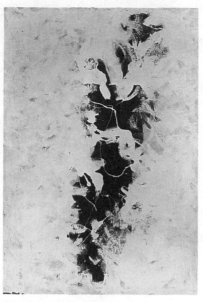

The Deep, 1953, oil and enamel on canvas,
86¾" × 59⅛"

eleven-foot expanse, he drew a giant Picassoid head in black outline; on the other side, a huge, limp-breasted woman, squatting on her haunches, a geyser of black paint shooting up from between her legs. It was the same terrifying female he had painted twenty years before surrounded by six skeletal males. The face, too, he had painted before. It was his own face, the face of a frightened young boy, one eye staring out from the Ryder-like gloom, the other obscured. Only now the face was a trembling outline of age and exhaustion, the staring eye a vacant, tearless tracing of resignation. Jackson called the painting *Portrait and a Dream.*

Throughout the early winter, between binges and hangovers, he worked and reworked both images: disguising the woman behind an angry veil of drips and splatters; adding color—his favorite yellows and reds—and detail to the face on the right. Obscuring one, exploring the other. "He fooled around with it a lot," recalls John Cole, who watched the painting evolve, "and it was up on the wall, up and down, up and down"—just like Jackson that winter, up and down, up and down. When Ruth Stein saw the painting, she suggested calling it *Man Against the World.* Lee quickly corrected her: "You mean, *The World Against the Man.*" To Parker Tyler and Charles Boultenhouse, who visited the studio, Jackson explained his own vision. "He indicated that it was a painting of great anguish," recalls Boultenhouse, "that it represented a terror of the void." The all-providing Stella, unreachable as ever, was all that stood between Jackson and the void. Or perhaps she was the void.

In December 1953, the plea went out again.

This time, however, Jackson's brothers hardened against him. The winter's

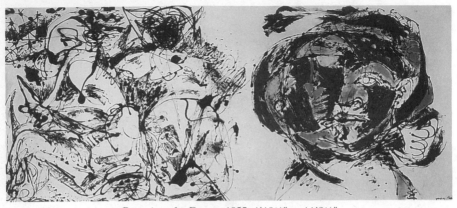

Portrait and a Dream, 1953, 4'10⅛" × 11'2½"

antics, including drunken and abusive phone calls to family members, had stiffened their resolve to deprive him of Stella. "Jackson's latest demonstration surely proves that we were foolish to even hope in that direction," Jay wrote Charles in December. In an apparent effort to outflank his brothers, Jackson and Lee boycotted Christmas in Deep River and arranged directly with Stella for her to come to Springs in January. When Charles got wind of the plan, he decided the time had come to put an end to the months of internecine warfare. He drove to Deep River and sat down with Stella, Sande, and Arloie. Soon afterward, he reported the meeting to Frank in California:

> Mother had planned to go to Springs soon after the holidays. I went up to persuade her not to go, but to stay on at Sande's instead.
> Jack is in one of his nasty moods and I'm convinced doesn't really want Mother there. I don't think we can count on him for any help. Also I don't think Mother ought to be exposed to his irrational behavior.
> Arloie and Sande both want Mother to remain. Of course there are difficulties, but I do not see how we can avoid them.

Jackson tried desperately to reverse the decision in a series of frantic phone calls, but it was hopeless. To the world, he may have been the *Life* painter, but in a confrontation within the family, Jackson was still Jackson and Charles was still Charles.

On every side, it was, at best, a temporary solution. Sande and Arloie protested that they were "glad to have mother back with them," but other family members suspected "they may be just accepting a condition just knowing that there is no other answer." With Arloie eight months pregnant, Stella apparently decided it was the wrong time to press her case further. "Mother's whole attitude has shown a marked change for the better," Sande wrote Charles when the holiday dust had cleared. "She seems more relaxed, at ease with the children and more nearly like herself." But in her letters to Charles, Stella resumed her vicious attacks on Arloie and shrill demands for more money.

"Loie is the one that is selfish I would be ashamed to ask for money if I was in her place. . . . I will need some *money this month*."

In Springs, Jackson managed to finish the last of the paintings he needed to fill the February show at Janis before falling apart. In a phone call to Stella, one of dozens that month, he told her that the new works had turned out "better than he expected." The rest of the month was lost. By February 1, the day of the opening, Lee was so desperate that she called Tony Smith in Germany and asked him what to do. Jackson was threatening suicide again. Smith, who had always minimized the dangers of Jackson's drinking, wrote back: "When I heard your voice, Lee . . . I was suddenly back on the track, with all its potential tragedy, but not despair." The solution, said Smith, was for both Jackson and Lee to visit him in Germany. "Jackson would be mad for the health food stores here," he joked, ". . . so you would feel right at home improving everyone's diet." Lee found nothing amusing in her plight. It was everything she could do to shepherd Jackson successfully through the opening where, according to Peter Blake, people were not interested in seeing "what kind of spectacle the pictures make, but what kind of spectacle the artist is going to make." Lee didn't trust Jackson long in New York. After only a week at MacDougal Alley, they retreated to the cold isolation of Springs where, at least, the Model A had the grace to freeze up occasionally and Jackson's rages could be confined to the kitchen. He did return to the city once, briefly, to meet Sande, who had decided, at the last minute, to see the show.

The reviews, although extremely generous, put Jackson in an untenable position: to accept the critics' comfort, he would have to embrace their rejection of his earlier work. In the *Herald Tribune*, Emily Genauer welcomed the show as "a real step forward in Pollock's development" ("they're really painted, not dripped!"), but dismissed the previous paintings as "empty and pretentious wall decorations." In an otherwise adulatory review in *Arts & Architecture*, James Fitzsimmons criticized Jackson's drip technique for being "limited" because "it excluded too many resources of the medium, too many levels of the mind and sensibility." Stuart Preston, in the *Times*, hailed "the happy advance over the impersonality of much of his early work." In *Art News*, Tom Hess expressed relief that Jackson had "return[ed] to some of his earlier statements" and emerged from the purifying fire of "his now-famous abstractions of poured and interlaced webs." Most galling of all, undoubtedly, was the *New Yorker*, which detected "touches of Motherwell" in *Easter and the Totem*.

Clement Greenberg, perhaps out of sympathy, chose not to review the Janis show that year. He did, however, tell Jackson privately that he thought the recent works were "soft," "forced," and disappointing; that he, Pollock, had "lost his stuff" and now, bereft of inspiration, was only repeating himself. Greenberg liked *Easter and the Totem* and *Greyed Rainbow*, and thought "he was onto something in *The Deep*, but just missed it." But overall, he stuck to his earlier assessment that Jackson had "had a phenomenal ten-year run, but it was over."

The collectors, it seemed, sided with Greenberg: not a single painting sold from the show.

By spring, Jackson had hit bottom—or what seemed liked bottom. He told Greenberg that "this time, he wasn't going to come out of his drunk." The battle over Stella had left his family shattered. Arloie's baby was stillborn. Sande, whose faltering print shop barely paid the bills, complained of "terrible headaches" from the chemicals he used, but, as always, kept working. Stella, who had gained weight during her long bout with arthritis, suddenly began to lose it at a perilous rate, alarming her doctors. Closer to home, Lee's colitis, which had flared up from time to time since the mid-forties, recurred with a vengeance, leaving her weak and gaunt and easy prey. One snowy night after they had gone to bed, John Cole and his wife heard a frantic knocking at their door. "It was Lee," Cynthia Cole recalls. "She was all agitated and excited saying, 'John, come, come, Jackson's dead! Jackson's dead!' " Cole threw on his clothes and drove Lee back to the house, where they found Jackson lying on the kitchen floor. Just when Cole began to think that he "had really done it," Jackson "popped up from the floor and burst out laughing. It was kind of cruel."

Crueler was yet to come.

The summer of 1954 brought no respite from the feelings of isolation and loneliness. The war with the Rosenbergs heated up immediately, although, on the all-important party circuit, Lee was at a disadvantage. She had virtually stopped giving parties, and Jackson had virtually stopped receiving invitations. At beach parties and open houses, even those hosted by May Rosenberg, she would appear just long enough to be noticed, then demonstrate her disdain with a conspicuous exit. "Lee was very cagey about that sort of thing," recalls Roger Wilcox. Jackson occasionally joined the battle, pulling up to the Rosenbergs' house late at night and roaring into the darkness: "I'm the best fucking painter in the world!"

Meanwhile, the stream of young painters continued to bypass Fireplace Road. On the rare occasions when they did show up—and Lee let them pass —Jackson offered little in the way of guidance or inspiration. If in a good mood, he might look at their work and say "very in'eresting." ("That was always his 'out,' " recalls Ted Dragon. "If you showed him a van Gogh, it was 'in'eresting.' ") If in a bad mood, he would try to intimidate them ("What the fuck is your involvement?") or turn them away with a terse "Fuck off." ("Why bother with those kids?" he once asked Clement Greenberg.) A few of "those kids," like Nicholas Carone, braved the chest-beating. "I wasn't going to take that shit from anybody," recalls Carone, "so I said, 'Who the hell do you think you are, talking to me like that? I'm a painter, too. You don't know my work, so what the hell are you talking about?' " For Jackson and Carone, it was the beginning of a fast friendship. But for most young artists, like Larry Rivers, Jackson's work was increasingly "impossible to separate from his social personality." The combination of his surliness and Lee's machinations produced an anti-Pollock backlash everywhere in the artists' community. On the party circuit and on the beach, "Jackson was being mauled," recalls Paul Jenkins. John Marquand, a young writer who rented a house on the dunes in Wainscott, "picked up the feeling a great deal that summer—'Jesus, look at Jackson, he's gone to hell.' They were all rooting for their man."

Their man, of course, was Willem de Kooning.

That summer, de Kooning moved from Leo Castelli's big house on Jericho Lane to considerably more modest quarters in a Victorian house in Bridgehampton called the "red house" or the "oxblood house" for its distinctive color. Together with his wife Elaine, Franz Kline, Nancy Ward, and Ludwig Sander, another painter, de Kooning set up his studio and quickly resumed the frantic social pace of the previous summer: drinking, roughhousing, talking, entertaining, and occasionally painting. "The house was just madness," Elaine de Kooning later recounted. "It attracted people like a little pile of honey attracts flies. . . . It was a kind of pleasant but nightmarish summer, parties every night, entertaining in the way a nightmare could be entertaining. . . . I mean a tremendous amount of social life. . . . There is such a thing as too many friends, too much talk, too much booze, too much of a good thing."

The party may have changed venue, but Jackson still wasn't invited. Chastened by their experiences the previous summer, de Kooning and Kline avoided the house on Fireplace Road, and Lee flew into a rage at the mere mention of de Kooning's name. But Jackson couldn't stay away. Rather than be left out of the party, he would defy Lee and drive the twelve miles from Springs to Bridgehampton, only to receive a gate-crasher's welcome: cordial but cool. According to Joan Ward, Nancy's sister and a frequent guest at the red house, the residents "would flee in all different directions when they heard the Model A approaching. *Nobody* wanted to see Jackson. He was too rough company. He was too demanding." In the evenings, if he hadn't had too much to drink, he would quietly slip upstairs and join them in front of the little black-and-white television set where de Kooning devoured old movie westerns and cowboy serials. More often, drunk and provocative, Jackson would grab two or three beers from the refrigerator, down them in seconds, then challenge someone, anyone, to a wrestling match. "If he got an arm lock on somebody and he felt he had the leverage, he could be really mean," recalls Ward. "He had a lot of anger inside looking for a way out."

Jackson had good reason to feel anger. At home, Lee was once again slipping from his grasp.

The drift had begun inconspicuously more than a year before when, in the heat of the battles over action painting, she began to build a small network of friends outside the art community. Jane Graves, John Cole's sister, the granddaughter of a Maidstone Club founder and proprietress of a small antiques shop in East Hampton, was the first of Lee's new circle. On one of the many evenings when Jackson deserted her, Lee had called Graves and asked her to

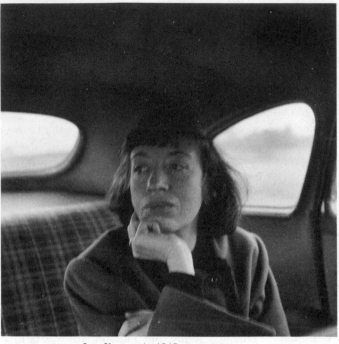

Lee Krasner in 1949. © Arnold Newman

spend the night. "She told me the dog was sick," Graves recalls, "and she didn't want to be in the house alone with him." The two women made supper and talked into the morning hours. Graves found her new friend "very smart and very sharp." After that, Lee used their friendship as a respite from the wars, both with the art community and with Jackson, a way of reconnecting with the larger world from which she had cut herself off. "We never talked about art or painting or Jackson," recalls Graves. "We talked about girls' things: clothes and people and gossip."

It was Graves who directed John Cole to Jackson to test his interest in a commercial fishing venture. The talks came to nothing, but Lee took advantage of the opening to add Cole's wife, Cynthia, to her circle. Pregnant for the first time and left alone for days during her husband's long fishing expeditions, Cynthia Cole needed Lee as much as Lee needed her. "John's whole vocabularly at the time consisted of ten words, all of which had to do with fishing," she recalls. "Lee was vibrant and interesting and eager to be friendly, although high strung." With Cole, Lee shared her apprehensions about Jackson's drinking and found, to her comfort, that Cole felt the same anxieties about her husband.

In the summer of 1953, Cole introduced Lee to Patsy Southgate, an extraordinarily attractive young woman—a "Grace Kelly, a real American beauty," according to Nick Carone—who had been Cole's best friend at Chatham Hall and a classmate at Smith. Their sons, Marshall and Luke, had been born only one day apart. Lee and Southgate, as different as they seemed, soon developed a special bond. To Lee, Southgate was New England, Protestant, patrician, and gorgeous, everything that Lena Krassner had always found so exotic and appealing. To Southgate, Lee was "a role model," whose competence and mettle contrasted sharply with her own mother's "inability to boil an egg." With such deep sympathies, Southgate quickly cast herself in the role of Lee's champion and defender. "I found Lee in a state of collapse," she says, "lusting for companionship." Pushing her son in a stroller down Fireplace Road, she visited Lee almost every day, offering comfort, admiration (when the two women went shopping together, Southgate complimented Lee's "really sexy body"), and exhortation. "I took Lee's side strongly from the point of view that This Woman Is Not Being Treated Fairly," she said later.

But Lee and Southgate shared another, deeper trait: masochism.

Like a number of young men in the early fifties, Southgate's husband, Peter Matthiessen, had come to the South Fork pursuing "images of courage and manhood," according to Cynthia Cole, "and to get in touch with fundamental things." Weaned on the writings and widely publicized exploits of Ernest Hemingway (*The Old Man and the Sea* appeared in 1952 and won the Pulitzer Prize the following year), Matthiessen had already followed Papa to Paris where he helped found the *Paris Review*, then to Spain where he "did all the Hemingway things," according to Cole. Now it was time to follow Santiago down to the sea and confront the elements. "Peter actually became a commercial fisherman to live up to the Hemingway machismo myth," says a close friend. With the machismo, inevitably, came Hemingway's chauvinism. Like Lee, Southgate, for all her beauty, had suffered her share of destructive competition at Matthiessen's hands and felt psychologically abused. When they drove together, he would tell her to crouch down in the car whenever they passed a group of Bonackers "so that he wouldn't be identified with this classy blonde," recalls a friend. To avoid competing with him directly, she renounced her ambition to be a writer; yet on those occasional mornings when she awoke with an idea for a story, she would come home that night to find he had already used it. When Southgate decided to try painting instead, "the following day Peter was painting something," according to Cynthia Cole. "There was a history of this kind of competition and her giving in to it."

Buoyed by Southgate's empathy and encouragement, Lee returned to her studio and began to work consistently for the first time in years. Since the ill-fated show at Betty Parsons in 1951, she had barely touched a brush, fearing perhaps that, as in the past, Jackson would retaliate with a week-long binge. Drawing was apparently safe, however, and during the long hours of waiting for him to return, she would draw on paper with brush and black ink, following the example of Jackson's black-and-white paintings. In 1953, soon after meeting Southgate, she began a series of collages, tearing her drawings into shreds and rearranging the pieces on canvas or Masonite to create intricate, black-and-white mosaics. Small, workman-like, and self-effacing, the new works fell far short of the broad, gestural abstractions she had created in 1950 and 1951, but at least she was working again. Over the winter, the collages grew in size and complexity. She introduced patches of color, brushwork applied over the collage elements, scraps of canvas, and even, in some of the larger vertical works, an insinuation of landscape. By the spring of 1954, when she exhibited in an all-women-artists show in Amagansett, she had cautiously reasserted herself as an artist, creating works that seemed to reflect her determination to reassemble the fragments of her past in a new, more satisfactory way, no matter how painstaking or jigsaw-like the solution.

On the eve of summer 1954, Southgate helped Lee arrange a solo exhibition of her new work at the House of Books and Music, an East Hampton book-store-gallery where Southgate worked. With memories of the debacle at Bertha Schaefer's apartment undoubtedly in her mind, Lee began final preparations for the June show.

One morning in mid-June, Jackson drove to Bridgehampton and found the red house nearly deserted. De Kooning, Kline, and Sander had gone to East Hampton to help Carol and Donald Braider, the owners of the House of Books and Music, settle in. Already "two sheets to the wind," Jackson helped himself to two or three more beers, then offered to carry boxes of books to the basement where the Braiders were storing them. Sensing trouble, Elaine de Kooning called her husband in East Hampton. When de Kooning and Kline arrived, "they threw their arms around Jackson," Elaine later recalled, "and began to horse around." Locking each other in a rigid embrace, Jackson and de Kooning staggered blindly around the yard until they stepped into the path that led from the back door to the garage and the outhouse. Worn down by years of use, the path had become a virtual "trench," recalls Philip Pavia, who was standing nearby, and it caught Jackson by surprise. He stumbled and fell heavily to the ground. De Kooning fell on top of him. Under their combined weight, Jackson's ankle snapped.

Kline and Pavia rushed to help as Jackson writhed inconsolably on the ground. "He was in *terrible* pain," recalls Pavia, "Jesus! Terrible pain." He was also "absolutely indignant," according to Elaine de Kooning. "He said, 'I've *never* broken a bone.' He felt it was insulting; his myth of invulnerability was shattered." With Jackson cursing and sputtering at every step, they loaded him into the Braiders' station wagon and rushed him to the East Hampton Clinic.

No one dared to face Lee. The accident only seemed to confirm what she had been saying for months, that the "New York gangsters" were out to kill her husband. Instead of taking Jackson home, they took him, in full cast and crutches, to Conrad Marca-Relli's place next door. "We were afraid to bring him to Lee," recalls Pavia. When the news finally reached her, Lee stormed the little house in a biblical rage, hurling accusations—they were "trying to beat him up"—and threatening to call the police. Only de Kooning had the courage to speak up. "[Jackson's] a big boy," he said. "If he wants to take some beer from the refrigerator, I'm not going to stop him."

By that afternoon, everyone in the art world had heard the news: de Kooning had broken Jackson's leg. The war had dragged on for a year and a half and now, at last, a palpable hit.

Jackson missed the opening of Lee's show. Confined to the upstairs bedroom for the rest of June and most of July, he languished in idleness and despondency, alternately feeling sorry for himself and lashing out at Lee. Unable to move around, he gained weight and grew a beard. Letters of sympathy from friends like James Johnson Sweeney and Reginald Isaacs failed to cheer him. Tony Smith, ever optimistic, wrote to suggest that Jackson market his paintings in Germany. "[There are] a great number of German millionaires right now," he effused, "and I think a showing might even lead to some sales." An offer of a teaching position at New York State College for Teachers not only failed to raise Jackson's spirits but probably triggered an outburst against artists who taught, a favorite target.

For all the expressions of sympathy, however, there were remarkably few visitors. Even Stella, despite the convenience of a ferry from Saybrook, Connecticut, directly to nearby Three Mile Harbor, failed to make an appearance. Sande came once, in early July, but returned home the next day. That left Lee alone most of the time to deal with Jackson's anger and self-pity. She tried encouraging him to draw to pass the time. Marca-Relli remembers her pep talks: "She'd say, 'Look at Matisse. He was in bed all the time he was making those beautiful collages. Why can't you at least keep drawing?' " But Jackson, perversely, refused to do work of any kind. He did occasionally look through art books, but mostly, it seemed, as an exercise in self-pity. One day Lee heard a crash and ran upstairs to find Jackson "sitting, staring," and fuming in bed, and her Picasso book on the floor on the other side of the room. "Goddamn it," he griped, "that guy has done everything. There's nothing left."

With Jackson safely confined upstairs, Lee moved her studio to the living room and resolutely continued painting. Over the summer, her collages grew larger. She used fewer and larger elements and introduced more color. Her brushwork opened up with "new bravura." If anything, convalescence only brought Jackson closer to the reality he seemed so desperate to deny. During the weeks of idleness, he knew Lee was working downstairs, and later, when he began testing his leg in mid-July, he passed her work every day in the living room. Conrad Marca-Relli remembers that, during this time, Jackson became "irritated" at the sight or mere mention of Lee's paintings.

With Jackson unable to leave, Lee no longer felt bound to the house—to be there "just in case" something terrible happened. Her friends noticed the change. At parties, she argued more forcefully and with more relish; she seemed more "lively and easily amused." For the first time in years, she joked about life with Jackson, about his mean pet crow, Caw-caw, and the goat who got drunk on fermented apples, doing, according to one friend, "a hilarious imitation of a drunken goat." When Marian Cook, the wife of a prominent local businessman, asked her to give a talk on the "new painting" to her church circle, Lee accepted eagerly. "She was poised and really quite interesting," recalls Ed Cook.

But the major step was learning to drive. For years Lee had relied on Jackson for almost every errand. No matter how drunk or vicious his mood, if she wanted to go to the store, she had to climb into the Model A next to him, close her eyes, and pray. "[She] was trapped in the house," said Patsy Southgate. "Jackson didn't want her to [drive], but *he* had mobility." Cynthia Cole had tried to teach her, but Lee had been hopelessly confused by Cole's lectures on "what happens when you step on the clutch," and the experiment ended in a "series of funny episodes." Now it was Southgate's turn. To overcome her student's "complete lack of self-confidence," she put Lee behind the wheel and her two children in the back seat. "That showed I had faith in her," says Southgate, "and it did the trick." By the end of August, Lee was confident enough to drive alone to John Marquand's little bungalow in Wainscott to demand payment for a drawing Jackson had given him while drunk. "I'll never forget the sight," recalls Marquand. "Coming through a potato field with dust flying, this old car pulls up and out steps Lee Krasner looking rather aggrieved and aggravated, and she says, 'Look, what do you think we do? We have to pay for groceries, too, you know!' I said, 'You've got a point,' and wrote a check."

Lee made herself pay a high price for her new freedom. Over the summer, her insides erupted again with ulcerous colitis. Strong and self-assertive in public, in private she suffered the relentless humiliating pain of cramps, constipation, and chronic bouts of blood-filled diarrhea. Drawings from the past were not the only things she was tearing up.

As the summer of 1954 came to an end, the mood on Fireplace Road was both ominous and melancholy. With his ankle still stiff, Jackson would hobble down the road to watch the red house gang play softball in Admiral Zogbaum's yard, or drive to the beach and watch the swimmers in the surf from a distance. Becky Reis saw him there. "Jackson, what's this I hear about you not painting these days?" she ventured cautiously. Jackson looked pained. "My wife's having a show," he said, half to himself. "At least someone in the family is working." He tried at least once to return to the red house, sneaking out of a dinner with Conrad Marca-Relli with the excuse of going to the store for more beer. "He wanted to see the boys," says Marca-Relli. "I tried to call and tell Lee where we were, but he wouldn't let me. He said, 'You can't let her know where I am.' " Hopping around in his cast in pursuit of de Kooning and Kline, Jackson tried to fit in, but they treated him "like an orphan," recalled Marca-Relli, "like an outsider. It was very sad to watch." Finally, he gave up and came home.

With his sore ankle, Jackson found the Model A's stiff clutch painful to use. So when Martha Jackson came by in search of new painters (and paintings) for her small gallery, Jackson gladly traded two black-and-white works for the dealer's green 1950 Oldsmobile convertible.

Then the storms began.

The first one, the one outside, arrived on August 31 when Hurricane Carol swept across Long Island. Winds of more than ninety miles an hour pushed tides to record highs, felled great elms on Main Street in East Hampton, ran ships aground, and blew the roofs off houses and motels.

Paradoxically, Carol's black clouds brought Jackson, after months of inactivity, a last chance to feel purposeful and needed. Neighbors flocked to the Pollocks' house on high ground, as rain downed power lines, lights flickered off, and the waters of Accabonac Creek rose ominously. James and Charlotte Brooks arrived early, escaping from Montauk just before the swollen sea cut it off from the rest of the island at Napeague Harbor. In anticipation of flooding, Jackson helped neighbors like Robert and Barbara Hale move appliances into upstairs rooms while Lee, struggling to control her dread of storms, prepared a vast pot of spaghetti. Their wet, cold guests huddled in the living room listening to the radio. Not since the great hurricane of 1938 had Barbara Hale seen the water higher or more trees uprooted. That year, her husband had looked out the window and remarked on "the boat going by," before realizing that it wasn't a boat at all but a neighbor's house. As bad as that was, she thought, this would be worse.

About noon, the rain stopped unexpectedly, the sky cleared, and the sun broke through. Just as the Pollocks' guests began returning to their houses, Wilfrid Zogbaum arrived with news that the storm had changed directions. "It's coming back again," he warned. Jackson ran to the Marca-Rellis' house, the one he considered most threatened by the rising waters and tried to convince Marca-Relli of the danger. But Conrad just pointed at the sky and said, "What are you worried about? The sun's out." Moments later, the storm returned. The creek flashed over its banks, raced across the low-lying marshland and into the Marca-Rellis' house. Suddenly, "the car was underwater, there was two feet of water in the house, and we were wading around in it," Marca-Relli remembers. The floodwaters spilled onto Fireplace Road, trapping people and cars in dark, cold, boot-high water. For hours, Jackson and "his crew" patrolled the neighborhood freeing cars stalled in the water or caught in the slime left behind. When the work ran out, Jackson rushed to Louse Point where Joe and Millie Liss, facing out to sea, had taken the worst of the storm's fury. "I've come to save you," Jackson announced. "Save what?" asked Joe Liss sardonically, gesturing toward the remains of his devastated home.

That night, while the cold rain and fierce winds lingered over Springs and most houses remained dark, Jackson sat around the big oak table in Nicholas Carone's kitchen enjoying the warmth of Carone's kerosene heater and the forbidden companionship of Kline, de Kooning, Carone, and his wife, Adele.

"They talked about painting and what was going on in the art world and where it was headed," recalls Adele Callaway. "It went on for hours and I remember wishing I had a tape recorder."

The next day, reality reasserted itself. On the trip back to Montauk with the Brookses, Jackson and Lee began to fight. "Lee wouldn't leave him alone," recalls James Brooks. "She yelled at him and nagged and nagged the whole way." Finally, Jackson turned on her. "If you don't shut up," he warned, "I'm going to hit you with a brick." At that, Charlotte Brooks, who had been sitting in the back seat growing increasingly distraught at the ugliness of the fight, burst into tears. When the car stopped on the bluff at Montauk overlooking the Brookses' house, they saw that the storm had swept the studio out to sea, carrying with it an entire summer's worth of paintings. "When Jackson saw that," James Brooks remembers, "he broke down and cried like a baby."

Even a year before, the sight of Jackson in tears would have moved Lee. But not anymore. Still stewing from the fight, she refused to get back in the car with him. Instead, she stayed with the Brookses, accompanied them into New York later that day, and spent the night in their apartment.

Jackson returned alone to Springs, where he joined Franz Kline in his just-bought 1937 Lincoln Roadster to survey the damage. Going south on Main Street, Kline pulled out to pass some slow-moving cars, not realizing that the road ahead was blocked by one of the trees felled in the storm. The Lincoln crashed through the tree and ran head on into a line of north-bound cars waiting on the other side. Jackson, with a cut lip, was the only one hurt.

In late November, Stella suffered a heart attack. Then another. Then a third. None was severe, but, as Jay wrote Charles, "that many attacks in a row is serious and at mother's age [it] could end very suddenly." Even in Deep River, where Sande was struggling to save his print shop from bankruptcy and Arloie had opened a small cleaning and alterations business to supplement the family income, Stella's attacks came as a surprise. Although immobilized, she had seemed strong and healthy up to the first stroke of pain.

When the news reached Springs, on the eve of Thanksgiving 1954, Jackson went on a rampage. At a holiday party given by Peter Scott, another "fisherman" like Peter Matthiessen, he stormed out of the house in a rage triggered, other guests thought, by Lee's instruction to "give him some milk" when he demanded a drink. A few minutes later, they heard a loud crash outside. Jackson had rammed his car through the blue-and-white lattice fence Scott had built for his wife. When the guests rushed outside to gape at the damage, Jackson put the car in reverse and drove back through the fence, destroying what little remained. Before speeding off, he stopped in front of the open-mouthed crowd and screamed, "Fuck you." "He said it to the whole group of us," recalls Millie Liss, "including Peter's mother, who had made this marvelous dinner. We couldn't believe it." As the guests wandered back into the house, Lee commented innocently: "All I said was give him some milk."

But Lee knew what the real problem was. Over her objections, Jackson had already sent a check for $25 to Stella, as well as checks to both of Sande's children. After a summer and fall strung out on the slim allowance Janis provided, Jackson finally saw the proceeds of a major sale: *Ocean Greyness* to the Guggenheim in early November. In Deep River, the money was received with a combination of gratitude and resentment—why had it taken so many years and such a dire turn of events to prick Jackson's conscience?

Once again, Jackson wanted Stella. And if, confined to bed, she couldn't come to him, he would go to her. Although in pain with colitis and opposed, as usual, to any plan that included her in-laws, Lee acquiesced—convinced, undoubtedly, that life alone with him in Springs would mean endless replays of the incident at Peter Scott's. They arrived in Deep River on Saturday, December 11. They came again at Christmas, bringing with them expensive presents—by Pollock standards—and relentless antagonisms. When Jackson gave Jason a bicycle, Lee insisted that Karen should "have a present as nice" and took her to Hartford to buy a coat. They came again in January and stayed almost two weeks on cots set up in the living room while Sande glumly arranged to liquidate his failing business and Arloie kept the family afloat with the meager earnings from her shop. Finally, Lee had had enough. In mid-January, she and Jackson returned to Springs, blaming their hasty departure on a forgotten dinner invitation in East Hampton. Jackson promised to return, but when the time came, Lee pled her colitis and the trip was canceled.

Besides, Lee had a better solution. Worn out, tired of caring, too sick to do anything but nag, involved with her own work again, fearful of Jackson and contemptuous of his family, she had decided that the time had come to give Jackson back. They had created this monster, now *they* should take care of him. In early February, she called Sande and asked once again for Stella to come to Springs—"East Hampton is where Stella should be," she said—*at least* for the rest of the winter. Emphasizing Jackson's recent generosity, she argued that he had finally accepted his responsibility to Stella and now she should accept her responsibility to him. If things went well, Lee suggested, the arrangement should be made permanent. The words were courteous, but the message was firm and unmistakable: Jackson's painting was the only worthwhile thing the Pollock family had produced and now, in return, they owed him Stella.

This time, it was Arloie who said no. After years of quiet suffering, recalling the nightmares she had seen in the Eighth Street apartment, for the first and only time in her long, adoring subservience to Sande, Arloie "put her foot down." "I think it was the only time I stood up and was very positive about my feelings," she recalls. "And I said absolutely not. I wouldn't let Stella go. This woman was eighty years old and had just had a heart attack. She didn't need to go and fight Jack's battles at this point in her life." Daughter Karen recalls that Arloie's stand sparked a conflagration at home and in Springs: "There were a lot of fights and a lot of anger, and Lee was furious with my father for letting this happen." But Arloie was unshakable. "[Stella] didn't need the aggravation or the strain—it would have been unbearable."

As Lee watched her last chance to avoid a catastrophe slip away, her fury knew no bounds. She had never forgiven Jackson's family for failing to appreciate his art; now, and for the rest of her life, she would fulminate against them for "leaving her alone with him," for not helping when he—and she—needed them most.

Jackson reacted in his own way. Only a few days later, when Sheridan and Francile Lord, friends of the Matthiessens, visited, he challenged Sherry Lord to a wrestling match. "Jackson was already drunk," recalls Cile Lord, "and he said, 'Come on, let's wrassle.' " Over Lee's protests, Sherry politely grappled with Jackson in the middle of the living room, "trying to keep him from falling down and yet not really engage him." Hoping to end the embarrassment quickly, Lord put his foot behind Jackson's leg and pushed him. Jackson fell backwards and hit the floor with a heavy "clunk." He came up clutching his ankle and crying out in pain, "I broke my ankle. I broke my ankle!" At first, no one believed him. "Oh, Jackson, come on, get up," they said. Furious, he yelled back, "Goddammit, I know I broke it. I heard it snap. I know when my ankle's broken." In fact, it was the same ankle he had broken eight months before at the red house. "How typical of Jackson," thought Cile Lord. "It was such a dumb thing to do, I wasn't even sorry for him."

The ensuing month in bed offered Jackson no rest, nor did the usual expressions of sympathy slow the seemingly inexorable ebbing of his support. In early March, Lee brought the latest bad news to his bedside. In the spring edition of *Partisan Review*, Clement Greenberg had repudiated him.

The break had been building for some time, beginning with Greenberg's conspicuous failure to review either the 1952 or the 1954 show. Since then, his visits to Springs had trailed off and his few encounters with Jackson had invariably ended with explosions like the one at Bennington. But no one, not even Lee, who had continued to nurture the relationship despite Greenberg's obvious disdain for her painting, expected the end to come so soon, so definitively, or so publicly. In the article, " 'American-Type' Painting," Greenberg—using words like "forced," "pumped," and "dressed up"—elaborated on the view he had already expressed to Jackson in private. The "peak of his achievement," according to the article, had been the 1951 show, "which included four or five huge canvases of monumental perfection." In his more recent shows, Jackson had become "an accomplished craftsman," but at the expense of energy and inspiration; a creative cul-de-sac at the furthermost reaches of Analytical Cubism who used color "pleasingly," Greenberg argued, only because "he was not sure of what he wanted to say with it."

The article not only formalized the break, it also named Jackson's successor in favor: Clyfford Still. In words that cruelly echoed his earlier praise of Jackson, Greenberg called Still "one of the most important and original painters of our time—perhaps the most original of all painters under fifty-five, if not the best." Still, said Greenberg, had "liberat[ed] abstract painting from value contrasts" and "as Pollock had not, from the quasi-geometrical faired drawing which Cubism had found to be the surest way to prevent the edges of forms from breaking through a picture surface." Behind Greenberg's elaborate effort to distinguish Pollock as a "late cubist" from Still as the leader among "post-cubists" (later dubbed "color-field" painters), many artists saw the article as a simple trade-in: Pollock for Still. Greenberg had decided that Jackson's American cowboy roots were, in his own words, "a lot of crap" and had found a new, *real* American hero. "He dropped the cowboy and picked up the old man of the mountain," says Budd Hopkins. "He went for a visionary screwball, like Ryder, somebody who could be seen as naive and American, like Pollock, someone who could be condescended to by the cultivated critic."

To Lee, the article represented not only a personal betrayal but also a failure of perception, a wanton misrepresentation of Jackson's art. Without the long history of personal antagonism that inflamed her reaction to Rosenberg's article, however, she was able to restrain her wrath. Realizing that Greenberg still exerted enormous influence in the art market, both she and Jackson were forced to express their displeasure in small, untraceable ways, like boycotting Greenberg's wedding and offering, as a present, only a small gouache on cardboard from WPA days. But Greenberg remained unapologetic. "I hear there's been a ruckus over my piece in Partisan," he wrote the Pollocks in May. "I hope that you two, at least, read the piece carefully; I weighed every word."

Jackson spent most of March 1955 confined to the upstairs bedroom, lashing out when Lee approached, knowing that she was at work downstairs, watching from his window as the trackless snow disappeared from around the studio. At some point, his anger over Stella's absence turned to despair. He stopped eating and turned away visitors. When he could move around again, instead of returning to the studio, he spent long afternoons at the movie theater in East Hampton or helped Robert and Barbara Hale renovate the old house they had bought. More than once, he drove all the way to Montauk and appeared unannounced on the doorstep of James and Charlotte Brooks. "He showed up in a rainstorm, soaking, and said his car broke down," recalls James Brooks. "He obviously had an impulse to get away from Lee."

That spring, people often saw Jackson wandering from house to house "like an abandoned child," according to Patsy Southgate. "He was patrolling the neighborhood looking for someone to visit," recalls Cile Lord. "He would come to your door in the middle of the day and just want to sit around, looking lonely and needy. You'd offer him a cup of tea and he'd want whiskey in it." Lee had given every neighbor instructions not to let Jackson have liquor, but, says Lord, "not letting Jackson do something was the neatest trick of the week." When friends like Lord grew impatient, Jackson would "get sort of hurt and we'd have to be sympathetic with him." He seemed especially drawn to friends with children: the Matthiessens, the Braiders, the Coles, the Carones, the Littles, the Talmages, the Gribitzes. He would spend hours wistfully watching their kids at play, bemoaning his own childlessness, and, at times it seemed, reenacting his own childhood. The Carones brought their twin sons, Christian and Claude, for Jackson to baby-sit. "He would take them upstairs and put them in his bed," Adele [Carone] Calloway remembers, "and he tucked them in and made everybody shush so no noise would bother them. . . . When he saw them drinking milk, he had a sudden craving for milk and he drank up all the milk in the house. Then he felt so bad he insisted that we jump in the car and he drove ninety miles an hour to Miller's store to buy them some more milk." At the Matthiessens' house half a mile north on Fireplace Road (and later in a converted barn on Jeffrey Potter's farm), Patsy Southgate found him "charming . . . like a little boy . . . very young, very threatened and vulnerable all the time." He visited Donald and Carol Braider so often they named their next baby Jackson. "With children," said Carol Braider, "he would be as gentle and lovely as a mother."

If children brought out Jackson's longing for Stella, Lee brought out his rage at her. By May, their battle had reached an unprecedented pitch. Convinced that Lee, like Stella, was abandoning him, increasingly resentful of her productivity, Jackson fought his fears with anger. Convinced that Jackson still needed her, increasingly addicted to the daily collisions, Lee satisfied her needs with anger. The result was a fierce, round-the-clock battle royal that neither one could win but neither was willing to lose. Fights no longer stopped and started, they merely passed from phase to phase, from screaming bouts to sputtering rages to bitter silence to random sniping and back again. Jackson was "crazed," recalls Ronald Stein, who had witnessed many fights over the years. "He was reaching into a part of his psyche that was not even rational or even human. He would shout, 'Bitch, bitch, bitch, bitch, bitch!' until the house shook." Lee would wait until the storm had passed to retaliate. "When he wasn't in a rage, she would pick at him," a friend recalls. " 'Jackson, do this; Jackson, do that.' " She would put food in front of him and he would refuse to eat it. "Now, Jackson," she would say, "it's good for you. Eat it." "I don't want food, I want tea," he would say. But when Lee brewed the tea and put it in front of him, he would say, "I don't want tea," and pour a shot of whiskey instead. Lee did manage to coax him into several "marriage counseling" sessions with Elizabeth Wright Hubbard, but she offered only herbs and platitudes.

On Friday, the thirteenth of May, Sam and Edys Hunter arrived in Springs for a weekend stay and were immediately plunged into the thick of battle. "Jackson played the hi-fi at decibels that would give you an earache," recalls Edys Hunter, "and Lee screamed at decibels that would give you an earache. That was the family scene." Sam Hunter thought Lee treated Jackson "like a lion tamer approaching a lion." Edys, who was pregnant at the time, made the mistake of getting in the car with Jackson. "It was a wild ride, and he would watch to see if you flinched," says Sam, who later called Jackson "a real psychopath." But Edys saw the method in his madness. "He wasn't reckless. He meant *me* no harm. He knew what he was doing. He only wanted to hurt Lee, not the rest of us." When the Hunters returned to New York, Edys wrote a tactful thank-you note describing the weekend as "memorable" and canceling plans for a return visit.

By summer, Jackson and Lee's life together had become an endless round of thrust and counterthrust, rage and retaliation. On a trip into the city with the Lords, Jackson vanished from the parking lot across from the Museum of Modern Art. "He just said, 'I'm going to see somebody,' and walked off down the block," recalls Cile Lord. "Lee knew anything she asked him to do, he'd do the opposite, so she implored us to get him to come back. But he just walked off. We came back without him." When Lee made arrangements for them to have dinner with the Hunters in New York, Jackson simply didn't appear. "He didn't want to spend the time with Lee," says Edys Hunter. But the next morning, he came around with orchids (and without Lee) to apologize. When Lee demanded more money for clothes and a larger share of the allowance from Janis, Jackson responded by lending $100 to Paul Brach and Miriam Schapiro for the deposit on a barn adjacent to The Creeks. Rebuffed by Lee in the bedroom, Jackson "went around asking various women he knew if they would have his baby," recalls a friend.

No opportunity to inflict pain, no matter how remote or fleeting, went unseized. When the catalogue for the "New Decades" show at the Whitney in May mistakenly reported that he had studied with Hans Hofmann, Lee's former mentor, Jackson flew into a calculated rage, indignantly demanding an apology from the museum and a correction in subsequent printings. In June, he threatened to desert her and go to Paris, following in the footsteps of de Kooning, who was scheduled to leave in July. Lee undoubtedly understood the dark insinuation: de Kooning's marriage to Elaine, as everyone knew, was teetering on the edge of collapse. As if to make good on his threat, Jackson drove to Riverhead and applied for a passport.

The summer, an unusually hot one, offered little relief from the heat of domestic combat. David Budd, a worshipful young painter from Florida who was spending the summer at The Creeks, came to the house one day on what he later described as a "pilgrimage." He found Lee "sitting on top of the store," but Jackson warm and welcoming. "That was a turning point in my life," says Budd. "He was a hero to me." Budd in turn introduced Jackson to his former teacher, Syd Solomon, on the beach one day. Forewarned of Pollock's volatile temperament, Solomon expected the worst but instead was "moved" by "the strong sense of tragedy that surrounded him." Roaming over the summer landscape, Jackson would drop in on young painters like Brach and Schapiro who were busy painting at the Bossey farm near the Green River Cemetery (they didn't begin renovating the barn that Jackson had helped them buy until the following summer). After passing Jackson's "shit test" ("He'd say 'shit,' and if you couldn't stand 'shit,' then you didn't pass the test"), Schapiro warmed to him, while Brach, who was uncomfortable around heavy drinkers, kept his distance. Jackson still visited The Creeks occasionally, although not as often as before. Over the winter, before the sale of *Ocean Greyness*, he had proposed to Ossorio that he and Lee sell their place and move into the big house with Alfonso and Ted. Ossorio had politely turned him down. "Our relationship wasn't quite the same after that," he later lamented.

In the meantime, someone else *had* moved into The Creeks: Clyfford Still. Supplanting Jackson in yet another way, Still had taken a small cottage near the main house for the summer and set up his studio in an adjacent barn. When Jackson came to visit, however, Still was usually too busy painting or tinkering under his cherished Jaguar to entertain company. Jackson had no way of knowing that Still, like Greenberg, had already turned against him. Earlier that year, he had written Ossorio expressing his disappointment in Jackson and accusing him of cowardice, wretchedness, and destructive self-hatred "second only to that of Mark Rothko." What prompted Still to send such a backbiting outburst to Jackson's long-standing patron isn't clear, although, as Still's friend Jon Schueler notes, "there wasn't a soul on earth who didn't get on his shit list at some point." According to Jane Smith, whose husband, Tony, was snubbed by Still for no apparent reason upon his return from Europe, "Still didn't approve of the fact that Jackson was accepting the help of certain New York dealers. He thought that was a sellout." While it was true that Jackson had toyed briefly with the idea of abandoning Janis and moving to Martha Jackson's gallery (as de Kooning had done), their secret correspondence had come to nothing. More likely, Still's reversal was based on artistic—that is, moral—grounds. "He was determined to create a new American art," recalls Jon Schueler, "an art that was absolutely American. He thought we had to get rid of, to lacerate, to cut out European influences like a cancer. What was left would be an American art." The primary cancer, according to Schueler, was Jackson Pollock, whose art Still had concluded represented "nothing but tired Impressionism."

Whatever his private reasoning, in public Still continued to curry Jackson's favor. Soon after Greenberg's article appeared, he wrote a mollifying note, giving Jackson and Lee "major credit" for Greenberg's "interest and favorable attitude" toward his work and taking care to note how uneasily Jackson's old crown sat on his rebel head: "May I add that I wish [Greenberg] had never seen my work or heard of it?" It would be another few months before Jackson learned of Still's true feelings.

In July, the battle with Lee came to a head when Clement Greenberg arrived in Springs to see his new psychoanalyst in Barnes Landing and stay the weekend with the Pollocks. Convinced apparently that Greenberg could still be useful to Jackson's career—and possibly to her own—Lee stifled her outrage at the recent article and played the dutiful hostess. Jackson, however, saw a clear provocation in the appearance of Lee's longtime ally. While Greenberg sat in the kitchen and watched with horror, the fighting reached new heights of ferocity. "Jackson was in a rage at her from morning till night," Greenberg recalls. "He had a sharp sense of how to find someone's sore spot and he was out to wreck her." When Greenberg began to take Lee's side in the running battles, Jackson sensed a conspiracy and lashed out even more desperately. He called her a "Jewish cunt" and announced that he had "never loved her." At every insult, Lee "howled" back in wild indignation. Finally, unable to bear another minute of the emotional fire-storm, convinced that "the marriage was killing both of them," Greenberg insisted that Lee see an analyst immediately and recommended Jane Pearce, a member of a group of analysts who summered in Barnes Landing.

The next day, Lee appeared in Pearce's office. "Clem pushed her to do this because he saw that Jackson was killing her," recalls Pearce. "Or allowing her to kill herself. It was a moment of absolute crisis." Pearce recommended that Lee seek therapy immediately. Lee agreed. Short of divorce, it was the ultimate act of independence, made easier, no doubt, by the fact that Patsy Southgate had entered analysis earlier that year. Jackson railed against it, but when Lee persisted, he quickly followed her to Pearce's office, confessed to being "seriously ill," and volunteered to reenter analysis. "Jackson couldn't stand the idea of Lee and me in therapy without him," recalls Greenberg. "He didn't want to be left out."

In September 1955, Jackson began formal therapy for the fifth time in his life. The weekly sessions with Pearce's associate, Dr. Ralph Klein, a young psychologist, brought him once again into the city, where he soon retraced old routes to the bars in and around Greenwich Village and, in particular, to the Cedar Tavern.

43

THE LAST ACT

It was just another nondescript neighborhood bar: a long narrow room with a bar in front and brass-studded leatherette booths in the back, a place of perpetual twilight, filled with smoke and the stale smell of beer. Most of the other bars along University Place near Eighth Street made some effort, however pathetic, to distinguish themselves: a jukebox, a television set, good food. Some even offered live entertainment and called themselves nightclubs. But not the Cedar. There were no paintings on the walls, no travel posters, no "arty emblems of Greenwich Village bohemia." Just "interrogation green" plaster, flaking imperceptibly in the fluorescent glare. If the Cedar had any distinction at all, other than its artistic clientele, it was the clock on the back wall that every now and then ran backwards.

Onto this invitingly neutral backdrop, patrons could project their private dramas. To Norman Bluhm, one of the many young artists who congregated there, the Cedar was "the cathedral of American culture in the fifties"; to Mercedes Matter, who for two years spent virtually every night there, it was "the most wonderful place and best time of my life." To Clement Greenberg, who rarely visited, it was "awful and sordid," a place where "washouts" and "doomed artists" herded against the tide of obscurity. To Jackson Pollock, who came every Tuesday after his appointment with Ralph Klein, it was yet another stage on which to play out, in ever shorter and more self-destructive cycles, the central drama of his life, a place to recreate his family and relive the past, trying, one last time, beneath the backward-running clock, to make it right.

He did it with a display of drunken antics that surpassed anything in his past; a weekly display that combined, in typical Pollock fashion, belligerence, petulance, profanity, pathos, self-destruction, self-deprecation, cowboy machismo, and even, occasionally, charm; a display so exaggerated, so singular, that people began coming on Tuesday nights just to see it; a display so memorable, so widely witnessed and reported, that for decades afterward, Jackson's reputation rested almost entirely on the wild tales emanating from the Cedar Bar. "Jackson would come in as though he were an outlaw coming in with two pistols," recalls Mercedes Matter. "You know, he'd say, 'You fucking whores, you think you're painters, do you?' " One night, he would sweep a dozen glasses off the table, a week later dump food on fellow patrons—friends or strangers, it didn't matter. He pulled tables from the wall, lunged at passing women, and shouted insults indiscriminately, his vocabulary sinking deeper and deeper into obscenity as the evening wore on. "He just *had* to provoke *someone*," recalls Conrad Marca-Relli. To John Myers, he made licking motions with his tongue and asked, "Sucked any good cock lately?" To Larry Rivers, he bared his arm and pantomimed shooting up. To a female painter, he snarled, "You may be a great lay, but you can't paint worth a damn." To a black man: "How do you like your skin color?" To any one of the dozens of young painters who frequented the Cedar: "What the fuck are you involved with?" or "What the fuck do you do?" or, in one strangely benign twist, "What are you doing to bring notoriety to your name?" To Jackson, gays were always "fags," women—and men— always "whores" (pronounced "whoors"), and fellow artists always "worms"— his nastiest epithet. "Every night Jackson was there," says Herman Cherry, "it was a contest of *cojones*." More than once, after breaking a table full of glasses and china, he would sit conspicuously in a corner booth and play with the sharp fragments, casually making designs as his fingers dripped blood onto the tabletop.

For Jackson, it was a weekly trip back in time, back to the rim of the Grand Canyon to entertain the road crew with his drunken stumblings, back to the Artists Union parties in the thirties where, in cowboy hat and boots, he had picked fights and passed out with Sande at his side. Like the road crew, friends at the Cedar fed him drinks "just to see what he would do next," recalls Milton Resnick. "Then they loaded him up with more whiskey to get rid of him." When "Sam" DiLiberto, the bartender, got fed up with his desperate antics and ordered him to leave, Jackson would linger outside the door, his liquor-swollen nose pressed against the window. "There'd be this bear's head outside looking in the little panes in the door," recalled Sam, "wanting in with his buddies."

Jackson's "buddies" were the young artists and writers who congregated at the Cedar to find support, to talk art (often returning from the nearby Club), or increasingly, to be entertained by Jackson. Among them were Lionel Abel, Norman Bluhm, Paul Brach, David Budd, Herbert Ferber, Budd Hopkins, Paul Jenkins, Conrad Marca-Relli, George McNeil, Milton Resnick, Irving Sandler, Jon Schueler, Syd Solomon, and Herman Somberg. But if they were all his brothers, Franz Kline was his Sande. Much more than Jackson, Kline was a Cedar regular, "one of those people who always got there before you did and was still there after you left," according to Larry Rivers. Tormented, like Jackson, by an unhappy childhood and a disintegrating marriage (his wife had recently entered an insane asylum), Kline, too, came to the Cedar to escape into the buzz and blur of alcohol and barroom camaraderie. Only occasionally would he disappear from the bar for a week-long "working binge" of twenty-four-hour days in the studio, slashing out the bold calligraphic canvases that had, so far at least, brought him only slightly more notoriety than his prodigious capacity for beer.

Every Tuesday night, Jackson would roar in and, first thing, scan the room for Kline's big, rough-hewn face and Bentonesque mustache. Friends remember him as being "hungry" for Kline's comradely, if indiscriminate, affection. "Jackson liked to be near him," recalls Syd Solomon, and he showed it in all the ways he had perfected with Sande: baiting, challenging, teasing, tormenting, scrapping, and conspiring in a running parody of sibling rivalry. When Jackson broke his plastic swizzle stick into little pieces and began to chew it, Kline did the same. They stared at each other "like they were playing *High Noon*," recalls Esteban Vicente, "while crunching on these plastic sticks." One night, finding Kline deep into a baseball story, Jackson elbowed him roughly. "Be right with you," Kline shot back impatiently in his truck-driver New Yorkese. When the story dragged on, Jackson elbowed him again. "Do that once more," Kline warned, "and I'll knock your clock off." When the story dragged on still further, Jackson snatched Kline's cap, threw it onto a shelf high up behind the bar, and ran out the door. (The next week, by way of apology, he came in and, in front of Kline, flung his own hat onto the shelf.) On other occasions when Kline tried to ignore him, Jackson poured soup on his head or threatened to throw beer mugs at him. In return, when Jackson's mood turned black, Kline could always defuse him. "Franz would say something amusing," recalls Mercedes Matter, "and this grin would come on Jackson's face, this adorable grin, and all the menace would disappear."

As the winter of 1955 approached, however, such salutary moments were increasingly rare.

While Jackson's studio sat idle, Lee prepared furiously for her October show at Eleanor Ward's Stable Gallery. The upstairs room overflowed with big vertical canvases, many over six feet tall. Since the previous summer, her images had grown even bolder, looser, more colorful, and self-assured. The little mosaic-like collage elements had evolved into larger, more linear fragments: pieces from her own previous work, jagged shards of heavy black paper, and, for the first time, scraps from Jackson's discarded paintings. Clement Greenberg, no fan of Lee's work, considered them "the best paintings that she had ever done." Also for the first time, she began to sign her full name, substituting a stylish script for the small block-letter initials she had been using. When Constantine Nivola brought Le Corbusier to Fireplace Road to meet Jackson, the French architect came away more impressed by Lee. "Pollock is like a hunter who shoots before he aims," he told Nivola afterward. "But his wife has talent. Women always have too much talent."

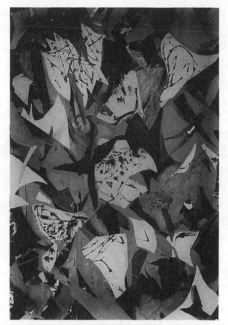

Bald Eagle, Lee Krasner, 1955, oil, paper,
and canvas on linen, 77″ × 51½″; among the
collage elements are fragments from a
black-and-white Pollock painting.

Not long afterward, Lee broached with Jackson a subject that had been on her mind for some time: a bigger studio. She already had one picked out—a little two-room shack set back from Fireplace Road just north of the house. Neither one said what both must have been thinking: Jackson already had a beautiful studio that he wasn't using.

In thinly veiled retaliation, Jackson berated collage as a medium, contending that he had done all there was to do with it in his single attempt in the early forties. He accused Lee of mimicking their neighbor Conrad Marca-Relli, who had begun experimenting with collage at about the same time. "Jackson didn't pay Lee's work much mind or respect," according to Cile Lord, and never missed an opportunity to demonstrate his contempt. When Eleanor Ward came to Springs to help Lee select the paintings for her show, Jackson asked her—within Lee's hearing—"Can you imagine being married to that face?" One night when Cile and Sherry Lord were visiting Jackson, Lee, who had been upstairs finishing the last canvases for the show, came down with an empty jar of Sobo glue in her hand and asked Jackson, in a plaintive voice, to please get her a refill from his studio. She was dressed for bed, pale and gaunt from yet another flare-up of colitis, and in no condition to brave the cold. As Lee must have expected, he refused to go. Lord thought, "He doesn't want her to be an artist."

In October 1955, Lee's show opened at the former horse stables on Fifty-eighth Street and Seventh Avenue that Eleanor Ward had converted into a gallery. Except for Betty Parsons, few in the opening night crowd bought pictures, but the reception was, even by Jackson's telling, favorable. Lee, who undoubtedly feared the worst, must have been surprised when Jackson appeared well dressed, completely sober, and, by one account, "glowing." All heads turned to look and marvel. "He was wearing a pin-striped suit and bench-made shoes, and he looked even taller than usual," recalls Ronald Stein. "I looked at him and thought, 'Wow, what a feeling that must be.' Women gravitated toward him, and everybody wanted to shake his hand." But Lee, like Stein, must have realized what Jackson was doing. "After Jackson walked in like that, it wasn't Lee's show any longer. He knew that's what would happen, and that's why he did it. Coming in sober, no breaking things up, no punching people in the nose, taking control away from Lee—it was the most sonofabitch thing he could have done."

Later, Jackson wreaked his revenge on Eleanor Ward in a more predictable way. Staggering into her gallery, he approached one of Ward's best clients, Kay Ordway, a "wraithlike, genteel spinster," and blurted out, "What you need is a good fuck." Ordway "fled in terror," Ward recalled. "It was ghastly."

The vigor and freshness of Lee's show must have haunted Jackson the next month when his own show opened at the Janis Gallery. Partly to defuse Jackson's rage and partly to keep his name before the art-buying public, Lee and Janis had pressed ahead with the show despite Jackson's apprehensions and despite the fact that he had virtually nothing new to show. Of the sixteen paintings exhibited (some of them on the ceiling due to lack of space), fourteen had been shown before and the other two—*White Light*, a heavy icing of white paint evoking the all-over canvases of 1946; and *Search*, a disjointed amalgam of soaked-in black, brushwork, and spattered color—had been painted long before. (*Search* may have been an old painting merely turned on its side and redated.) Janis called the show "15 Years of Jackson Pollock," trying perhaps to avoid the dread term "retrospective," but no one was fooled. Supported by rumors from the Cedar Bar, the truth was everywhere now: Jackson had stopped working—or at least stopped creating. Respectful in public, friends privately lamented his eclipse. "There was a lot of feeling that the work was falling apart," recalls Budd Hopkins. "I think everyone shared my feeling that Pollock was physically, psychologically, personally in terrible shape and that the art as art was in terrible shape, too."

The reviewers were not so discreet. In the *New York Times*, Stuart Preston threw up his hands in exasperation at the "gruff, turgid, sporadically vital reelings and writhings of Pollock's inner-directed art," concluding that it would remain incomprehensible "until psychology digs deeper into the workings of the creative act." *Art News* and *Arts Magazine* made similar apologies ("A Pollock painting, charged with his personal mythology, remains meaningless to him for whom Pollock himself is not a tangible reality"), but the tone was unmistakably elegiac; none of the reviews mentioned either of Jackson's new works. Hearing the news of Jackson's plight and smelling blood, *Time*'s Alexander Eliot wasted no time in attacking. "The bush-bearded heavyweight champion of abstract expressionism, shuffled into the ring at Manhattan's Sidney Janis Gallery, and flexed his muscles for the crowd," wrote Eliot in an article titled "The Champ" in the December 19, 1955, issue. Dismissing the earliest work, inaccurately, as "imitating imitations of Picasso" and describing the famous drip paintings as "Pollock's one big contribution to the shlosh-and-spatter school of postwar art," Eliot gloated shamelessly over Jackson's fall and mocked those reviewers who were still making excuses for his "gaudy drippings." Two months later, Eliot returned to print to give Jackson one last kick, dubbing him "Jack the Dripper," a phrase that, according to Jeffrey Potter, "caused Jackson to spend days of saying 'shit' and Lee to utter outraged shrieks."

Despite their battles, Lee took no joy in Jackson's defeats and carefully avoided displays of her own modest success. Although, clearly, she no longer loved him in any tender sense, she still considered him a great artist, clung to his cause, and bewailed his creative block as a waste, an injustice, and a tragedy for art. But she was no longer willing to throw herself on his pyre. "Lee had been to the shrink and had gotten some improvement," recalls Cile Lord, "and for the first time was able to detach herself from Jackson. His childish tantrums designed to keep her on the hook were not working the way they had." Now, instead of confronting him, she would simply retreat, assuming a defensive posture designed to placate, not provoke, and to preserve what little energy she had left for her art. Fed up with his troubled sleep, bedwetting, and setting fire to the mattress, she moved the double bed out of the master bedroom and replaced it with twin beds. When he flew into a rage, she would simply leave the house, taking Ted Dragon's advice to "remember the Russians." "I told her they never shot a gun at Napoleon," says Dragon, "they simply went north. And many a night she did just that and left him in his rages."

For the first time, both Jackson and Lee began to talk seriously to outsiders about divorce. After a year of surreptitious visits to psychiatrists ("People started going to New York for dentist appointments, which turned out to be psychiatric appointments," recalls Cynthia Cole), many of Lee's friends were, according to Cole, euphoric with a new feeling of "I've got to take care of me." More than a few were already "one foot into divorce court." Among Jackson's friends, Willem de Kooning had split with Elaine and brother Charles had announced his separation from Elizabeth after more than twenty years. For Jackson, however, talk of divorce was still only talk. He was less able than ever to care for himself, more firmly bound than ever by what Ronald Stein called "the grim pact of mutual assured destruction" that had kept them together for more than a decade. "Without Lee," he told a friend in a rare moment of honesty, "I wouldn't have survived [this] long."

For Lee, on the other hand, talk of "dissolving the marriage" was more plausible, and therefore more chilling. Although increasingly confident that she could live without Jackson, she knew, as he did, that he couldn't live long without her. Increasingly, the choice seemed to be to live without him or die with him. Years later, she would recount a dream that haunted her during the long winter of 1955. "Jackson and I were standing on top of the world. The earth was a sphere with a pole going through the center, I was holding the pole with my right hand, and I was holding Jackson's hand with my left hand. Suddenly I let go of the pole, but I kept holding on to Jackson, and we both went floating off into outer space."

Two days before Christmas 1955, while the Janis show was still running, Lee and Jackson left the Earle Hotel in the Oldsmobile convertible to return to Springs. On the way out of the city, they picked up Ronald Stein outside his apartment on East Seventy-ninth Street. Unknown to Jackson, who was drunk and in a black holiday mood, Lee had instructed Stein to talk Jackson out of driving. But Jackson had other ideas. Before Lee was settled in the back seat, he jammed the accelerator to the floor and the V-8 Oldsmobile screamed away from the curb "like a bat out of hell," Stein recalls. "Lights meant nothing to him. He just put his foot right down on the floor and we crossed Park Avenue like a bullet." Everywhere cars braked and honked and skidded to avoid him. He veered from lane to lane, around slow-moving vehicles, into oncoming traffic, always accelerating. Cars drove onto the sidewalk to avoid a head-on collision. "It was like a chase scene in a Hollywood movie," Stein recalls. Jackson turned onto the East River Drive and headed north, "tear-assing" toward the Triborough Bridge through heavy midday traffic, even passing a police car. Seeing the bridge ahead, Stein thought, "He'll never make it through the tollbooths. He'll never get through those narrow openings. We'll go off the bridge and into the river for sure." Stein was convinced Jackson "was trying to kill himself, and me, just to spite Lee. This was real serious madness. The guy should have been in a mental institution." Stein tried to grab the wheel, "but Jackson was strong and I couldn't get it away from him." Finally, just as the car was flying onto the approach ramp to the bridge, Stein lunged across the seat and turned the ignition key.

When the car finally coasted to a stop, Lee was the first to speak. "Jackson," she said evenly, "let Ronnie drive." Jackson shook his head no. "Then I'm getting out right here," she said. Jackson apparently didn't believe her. Why should he? Hadn't she always stayed in the car, no matter how drunk or how reckless he was? But this time she meant it. Without another word, she got out and started walking down the shoulder of the busy roadway, looking for a place to cross. Stein watched her disappear. "Are you coming or going?" Jackson asked gruffly. "I'll go with you," Stein said, "but if you do that again, I'm going to take the key again." "After that he drove like a perfect gentleman all the rest of the way," Stein recalls. "He was a little drunk, but there was no more madness."

The next day, however, when Lee arrived on the train, "all hell broke loose.

It was like a bomb had exploded." Stein, exhausted by the screaming fights, left later the same day. That night, loaded on liquor from every bar in the surrounding area (most refused to serve him more than two drinks), Jackson stumbled into Sam's, a bar in East Hampton. "He was having trouble with his wife," recalled George Schaefer who was sitting at the bar that night, "and was probably lonely." (On Christmas Eve, he may also have been thinking about his distant family, about Stella, and about how *she* had killed her husband.) When Jackson tried to start a fight, the bartender ordered him out; then, when he resisted, threw him out. Enraged, Jackson turned and put his fist through the glass in the door. By the time the police arrived, he had passed out on the sidewalk. He spent the rest of the night, Christmas Eve, in the East Hampton jail.

Creatively, physically, emotionally, Jackson was falling apart. He had often said that life and art were inseparable. "You cannot separate me from my paintings—they are one and the same," he told Lee, who refused to be convinced. "A man's life *is* his work; his work *is* his life," he mused to a friend about this time, locking his hands together to show what he meant. Now, as 1956 began, he seemed determined to prove it. In retrospect, Lee said later, "he seemed to be setting the stage for the last act."

Every morning throughout January and February, he trudged through the snow to the studio and lit the Salamander kerosene stove. The sound of it— "like a jet taking off"—would roar through the cold barn, smoke and flames would shoot from the exhaust pipe, and the frost on the windows would begin to melt, but Jackson never picked up a brush. Most mornings he would simply trudge back to the kitchen for another cup of coffee, or maybe a beer, and stare at the studio from the back door window. When Conrad Marca-Relli asked him why he continued to fire up the heater every morning, Jackson replied, "So the studio will be warm in case this is the day I can start to paint again." But that day never came. When Sidney Janis saw the fearsome Salamander shooting flames in the "tinderbox" barn, he urged Jackson to move the paintings to a fireproof warehouse. But Marca-Relli advised against it. "Let them burn," he said. "What do you care? You can paint some more, can't you? Don't let anybody take them. You need those paintings with you." In the end, fearing the empty space they would leave behind more than fire, Jackson kept the paintings with him.

Friends tried everything—pleading, consoling, cajoling—to start Jackson painting again. Marca-Relli asked him, "What's the biggest painting you've ever done?" "Oh, eight by twenty-two, something like that," Jackson replied. "You call that big?" Marca-Relli taunted. "Why don't you do a *really* big one? What about forty by sixty?" For a moment, he could see "a sparkle of challenge" come over Jackson's face. "I'm gonna do it," he said. "I'm gonna do a big one." He remembered the gymnasium at Tony Smith's house in South Orange, and began to make plans to work there. But the next time Marca-Relli saw him, he was drinking scotch and didn't remember a thing. Cile Lord suggested that she and Jackson set up a print shop together, like the one at the University of Iowa where she had worked. It was "all part of trying to get him working again," said Lord. But the plans "were forgotten almost as soon as they were laid." Reuben Kadish tried to interest him in working with clay, and Lee, knowing of his on-again-off-again interest in sculpture, would point to the large pile of junk iron in the backyard and suggest that maybe now was the time to start experimenting. Ron Gorchov remembers how many visitors to Fireplace Road "would come into the studio to talk about painting and end up making marks on his canvas." In what must have been the ultimate degradation, even Lee had tried to prompt him by starting a canvas or two. (By the time of his death, so many people had done the same thing that the paintings in his studio had to be divided into three categories: those done by Jackson, those done by others, and "collaborations.")

On those rare mornings when he stayed in the studio and tried to work, the drawings and paintings he produced were nothing like the great dripped visions of previous years. Continuing a review of the past that had begun with *Ocean Greyness* and *Ritual*, he made figurative oil sketches that evoked the Mexican muralists, especially Orozco. "They were real throwbacks," recalls Roger Wilcox, "really figurative, much more than the black-and-whites, and brushed, not dripped." Another visitor to the studio described the figures as "sort of the outlines of the figures in *Guardians of the Secret*, done in black with a brush, but not yet filled in with color." According to Wilcox, Lee was "appalled" by these retrogressive images, but Jackson apparently continued to work on them. Later that winter, Conrad Marca-Relli saw the same paintings "with the figures filled in with a multitude of colors." (Other visitors saw them in the studio as late as summer, but by the following fall, someone had destroyed them.)

Jackson's health seemed to follow the fortunes of his art. Years of self-abuse had finally broken him. In the desperate effort to avoid hard liquor, he had gained almost fifty pounds from hundreds of gallons of beer. Knowing that both Stella and Sande despised obesity, he tried to hide his condition from his family. But big coats and baggy pants couldn't conceal his swollen face, his sunken eyes, or his coarse, inflamed skin. His nerves were shot. At any loud noise—a truck backfiring, a tray falling, a crack of lightning—he would jump from his chair and pace the room in utter distraction for fifteen minutes or more. Somehow he had contracted hepatitis, which left him even more fatigued, irritable, listless, and despondent. And, in what was left of his liver, the slow scarring of cirrhosis was gradually killing him.

But it was the deterioration of his mind, not his body, that posed the most immediate threat. When he brought home a hunting bow and began shooting arrows in the house, Lee was convinced *she* was the target. One day he barricaded himself in the studio with a bottle of scotch and a stack of Jimmy Yancy and Fats Waller records. Locking the doors and blocking the windows with canvases, he turned the volume on the phonograph as high as it would go—

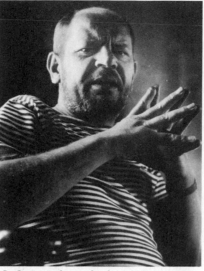

In Springs, during his last summer, 1956

"obviously experimenting with his psyche full blast." Panic-stricken, Lee called Ossorio and pleaded with him: "For God's sake, you've got to come over and help me get Jackson out of there." Even scarier were the days when he sat on the back porch or stood at the kitchen window "and just stared and stared and stared for hours," Ted Dragon recalls. "At the end, he was turning into a very weird personality." On a trip into New York, he ran out into the midday traffic on Madison Avenue as Budd Hopkins watched in horror. "He walked straight down the middle of the street," Hopkins remembers, "down the white line between lanes, car horns blowing. I didn't want to look, because I knew he was going to be dead in two seconds. It was a Russian roulette thing." On another trip, he tried to jump out of a fast-moving taxi. When informed of the incident, Lee was sure it was a suicide attempt, but Jackson denied it.

If Lee believed him, it was because there was never any doubt in her mind, or anyone else's, how Jackson would die. She had spent too many nights "not knowing where he was, who he was with, if he was alive or dead"—half in a rage, wishing him dead, wanting to kill him herself, half in torment that he might be killed, that she would hear the wailing of an ambulance in the distance or see a policeman at the door bearing the inevitable news. After the drive out from New York at Christmas time, she knew: the car was Jackson's weapon of choice. She insured the Oldsmobile "up to the eyebrows," according to Paul Jenkins. But Jackson still refused to slow down, even after being sentenced to two years' probation after the incident at Sam's. One night he returned, pale with fright, from a near-accident in which his car had spun completely around on a deserted road. "God, I was scared to death," he told Lee. But the next night he was back out on the road with a case of beer on the seat beside him. Of all his insanities, it was, in its own prosaic way, the most insane.

■ ■ ■

At the Cedar Tavern, meanwhile, he was a star again. The crowds waiting outside under the round neon sign, many of whom had come just to see "Old Grizzly" in action, would greet him by name when he arrived. Inside, people at the bar, two and three deep, would part to make room for him, slap him on the back, punch his arm, offer to buy him drinks, touch him for luck. When he got up, they would announce his movements in excited whispers: "There's Jackson!" or "Jackson just went to the john!" Among them were respectful admirers, "trying to get close to their king," David Budd recalls, as well as mere spectators, filled with the delicious anxiety that maybe tonight he would do something truly outrageous so that tomorrow they could tell their friends, "You should have been at the Cedar last night. You should have seen Jackson." To some, their attention looked like honest deference; to others, bear-baiting; to others, "nauseating sycophantic shit." Whatever it was, Jackson devoured it. He would ask the crowd, "Who's the greatest painter in the world?" and they would answer back, "You are," and he would echo, "It's me. They know it's me." "It was Jackson's bar," recalls Gerome Kamrowski. "He was the main attraction."

Like his art, Jackson's agony had become an act. In his desperation to regain his celebrity, to please the crowds, he had become a parody of himself. When he came to the bar in the middle of the day, he would sit so quietly among the secretaries and businessmen that "you wouldn't know he was there," according to Sam the bartender. Later in the evening, he would come by and peek in the window to check the size of the crowd. "If the audience wasn't big enough for his big dramatic entrance," Franz Kline recalled, "he would come back later, loaded slightly more." Now, instead of the good clothes he used to wear into the city, he often wore jean jackets and T-shirts to enhance the cowboy image. For the first time since the early thirties, he bought a pair of cowboy boots. He began affecting a drawl and a cowboy walk for his "Tuesday-night shoot-outs at the Cedar saloon."

The booze was still real, the language still incendiary, the self-abuse still deadly serious, but the rages had turned into histrionics, the fights into spectator sport. Willem de Kooning found that out when he slugged Jackson for insulting Joan Ward, who had just given birth to his child. Instead of returning the punch, as those around him urged, Jackson shook his head and said indignantly, "What? Me hit an artist?" The next day, Jackson called Nicholas Carone and complained: "That son of a bitch doesn't understand. I love him."

One night, Franz Kline scolded Jackson for berating Philip Guston. "You shouldn't have laid into Guston that way; you really hurt his feelings." Unrepentant, Jackson began to arrange the half-empty mugs on his table as if preparing to use them as ammunition. Before he could finish, however, Kline tipped the table up and the glasses tumbled into Jackson's lap. Jackson let out "a bellow" and retreated behind the swinging door that led to the kitchen and the men's room, where he wiped himself off. A minute later, he appeared in the doorway, his face flushed with what looked like rage. Tearing the swinging door off its hinges, he flung it across the room and stalked toward Kline. "Everybody stands up, it's like the O.K. Corral, a showdown," recalls Budd Hopkins, an eyewitness. "Jackson grabs Kline in a wrestling hold. Kline gives him a huge shove, pushing him back against the bar. Jackson lets out another roar and comes at Kline again. They grapple and fall to the floor." Just when Kline, the more agile and sober of the two, had Jackson pinned, Jackson whispered in his ear: "Not so hard, Franz."

Even the sale of *Blue Poles* to Fred Olsen for $6,000—a spectacular success at the time—was reduced to just another pretext for barroom braggadocio. The Tuesday after the deal was completed, Jackson wheeled into the Cedar and slapped his wallet down on the bar. It was a brand-new one with the letters "JP" embossed on it in gold. He ran his thick fingers over it and announced to the crowd, "J.P. Those are the initials to have if you're a painter."

Once again, Jackson was trapped in his own celebrity—as in Namuth's film, playing a role; feeling, week by week, more like a fraud, more like the phony that his brothers had always accused him of being. Jackson "stormed" the Cedar Bar and tried to be "one of the boys," said Clement Greenberg. "That can be killing, [trying to be] one of the boys."

But stardom at the Cedar Bar, despite its high cost, couldn't begin to satisfy Jackson's demons. The Cedar, after all, took up only one day of seven, even if the recoveries sometimes lasted until Thursday or Friday. "He was in a whole lot of pain," recalls Nancy Smith, a friend of Clement Greenberg's, "and he was kind of pleading all the time for someone to be sensitive to him and take him out of his miseries or to at least soothe him. The bumbling, bear-like act was just a cover-up for being so wounded." Conrad Marca-Relli described him as "like a little boy, on the verge of tears all the time and afraid to be alone."

Yet more and more Jackson *was* alone. In the afternoons, he would go to the Edwards Theater in East Hampton and sit among the empty seats to watch Humphrey Bogart in *The Desperate Hours* or James Dean in *Rebel Without a Cause*. Other days he would drive to Montauk, pausing to look at the skeletal ruins of an abandoned power station, or wander the familiar back roads around Jeffrey Potter's farm. A year before, he would have stopped along the way to visit friends. But by now most friends had made it clear he wasn't welcome. Peter Blake, fearful that Jackson would harm his pregnant wife, had cut off all contact. So had Lawrence and Roseanne Larkin and Joe and Millie Liss. Barbara Hale had barred him from the house that he helped renovate. Eleanor Hempstead had moved and pointedly kept her new address a secret from him.

One of the few places where he was still welcome was Nick and Adele Carone's old farmhouse in Three Mile Harbor—a house that Jackson had found for them. Carone was a handsome, earnest, familiar man with penetrating eyes—"If you painted with the intensity of those eyes," Jackson had told him when they first met, "that would be something"—and the two could talk

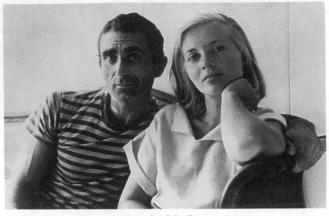

Nick and Adele Carone

endlessly about *paint*—not theory, not history, not politics—just paint: the
sheer material thrill of it. Jackson admired Carone's gutsy articulateness—"Say
that again," he would demand, "say that again"—and Carone loved the way
Jackson looked at his pictures. "My work was being *judged* by somebody very
meaningful," Carone recalls. "He would say marvelous things to me, like 'You
got it, got it good.' " Jackson raised his usual objections to Carone's teaching
(Carone's response: "I don't teach art, I teach a language"), but admired his
work enough to offer to trade paintings.

On Fireplace Road, the phone seldom rang. "He certainly wasn't the toast
of the town," recalls Conrad Marca-Relli. "No one was calling him up or
inviting him to anything, and he was bitter about it. He didn't seem to understand that he had brought it on himself. He would complain to me, 'What's
the matter? Why don't they want me over? Maybe they think I'm a phony as
an artist.' Lee must have told him a hundred times, 'Jackson you behave in
such a way that people are afraid to have you over; it's as simple as that.' " On
the rare occasions when he was invited out, Marca-Relli recalls, he felt obliged
to "make a scandal," as he did at Paul Wiener's house when he urinated in a
potted plant. The phone didn't ring for weeks after that.

When he went into New York to visit galleries, Lee no longer went along.
Friends saw him there—at the Alan Davie show, mumbling to himself about
his influence on English painters; at Mark Tobey's show, looking desperate; at
Joe Glasco's show, looking lost—but most kept their distance. Nell Blaine saw
him wander drunkenly into a shoe store near Eighth Street "looking bloated
and disfigured by alcohol." Thinking he was "just another Bowery bum," the
manager threw him out. "I went up to the manager and said, 'Do you know
who that was?' " Blaine recalls. "But the name Jackson Pollock meant nothing
to him. It was heartbreaking." Another night while in town, Jackson made the
mistake of showing up, sober and uninvited, at a party given by Robert Motherwell for Phil Guston. Drunk and sensing Jackson's vulnerability, Bill de
Kooning and Franz Kline set upon him, calling him a "has been" and even-

tually hounding him out of the party. "He had every right to get drunk or to slug them," Motherwell recalled, "but in fact he just took it."

On Thanksgiving, the Marca-Rellis and Carones brought their records to Jackson's house for a night of music and dancing—Lee joined in; Jackson only watched. But laughter and conviviality were largely a thing of the past on Fireplace Road. Few of the old circle came by anymore. The split with Clement Greenberg, now two years old, had never really mended. At dinner one night, Carone asked Jackson, "Who understands your pictures? How about Clement Greenberg? He's made a career on you. Does he understand?" Jackson thought for a moment before answering, with a touch of bitterness, "Not a fucking thing." Far more painful to Jackson was the continuing (and, to Jackson, inexplicable) chill in his relationship with Clyfford Still. Furious over Jackson's complicity in the Janis retrospective—which he considered a moral outrage—Still seized on Janis's failure to send him an invitation as an excuse to deliver a blistering attack on Jackson's integrity. On December 3, he wrote:

> Dear Jack,
>
> I did not receive an invitation to your show. This makes me somewhat curious. Is it that you are ashamed of it? Or are you ashamed of what you are willing to take from those who know how to use you to express their contempt for the artist as a man? It's a hell of a price to pay, isn't it?
>
> Yours most sincerely, Clyfford S.

The day it came, Jackson sat up until one in the morning, crying. He called a friend in New York City and read it, "but was beyond being comforted." "I'm in a terrible state," he finally said, and hung up.

On January 28, Jackson threw himself a birthday party. Despite miserable weather conditions and Lee's lack of interest, he called Barnett Newman, whose birthday was January 29, and insisted on a joint celebration. Newman, who saw Jackson almost every week on his trips into the city, tried to talk his way out of it, but Jackson pleaded, "You have to come." The Newmans brought a recording of *The Magic Flute* as a present, and, eager for their approval, Jackson spent most of the evening sitting quietly and listening to Mozart's opera of trial and redemption. He joked about "getting away from it all"—an increasingly common topic—either "back to the west" or perhaps to Spain, following Hemingway's trail. Newman went along with the plans, mostly to humor Jackson. "It was just a dream," he later admitted.

Jackson also managed to lure Tony and Jane Smith to Springs that weekend (Jane's birthday fell in early February). Since the Smiths' return from Europe in the spring of 1955, the two men had quietly resumed their friendship, carefully avoiding any mention of past indiscretions. The reconciliation was helped along no doubt by Smith's role in the sale of *Blue Poles* to Dr. Fred Olsen, for whom he was designing a house, and, in a less obvious way, by the birth of the Smiths' twin girls in July 1955. ("[Jackson] couldn't imagine our having them," Smith admitted.) Also, while in Europe, Smith had designed a tent-like structure to house three mural-size paintings of Jackson's—the last incarnation of Ossorio's ill-fated chapel project. On his return, he presented the drawings to Jackson. "He thought the light under the canvas would be wonderful for the paintings," Jane Smith recalls. Smith undoubtedly meant it, and Jackson took it, as an apology, even though this structure, like the others, was never built.

During the birthday weekend, Smith and Newman dragged Jackson out to his studio and "threw a little paint around" in a transparent (and unsuccessful) effort to strike a creative spark. No one was more obsessed with getting Jackson back to work than Smith. Later that winter, Jackson drove—without Lee—to the Smiths' house in South Orange, New Jersey, and spent most of the week-end in the small gymnasium that Smith used as a studio, experimenting on a larger scale with the tiny wire-and-plaster sculptures he had created for Peter Blake's model museum. Jane Smith remembers Jackson's sensitivity in these final encounters. "He was an exposed wire," she recalls, "just like Tennessee Williams. He seemed detached, but he never missed a comma."

If old friends no longer stopped by or called, if they avoided him on the street, it was because, at times, Jackson seemed determined to drive them away; determined to abandon them, as he had tried to abandon Lee, before they abandoned him. One night at the home of Joe and Margaret Meert, who had taken him in on innumerable nights after the Cedar closed, he set fire to the mattress and, in a drunken stupor, tried to put it out by urinating on it. After that, the Meerts understandably cooled to their late-night guest. He visited Phil Guston's studio and, admiring his recent large-scale works, helped persuade Sidney Janis to give him a show; but at the party after the opening, he tried to throw Guston out a window. When John Graham reentered his life briefly in 1954 or 1955, Jackson welcomed him "like a great-uncle he hadn't seen for years," recalls Nick Carone. "There is only one man who understands my pictures," Jackson told Carone, "and that's John Graham." But later, at a party in Leo Castelli's Manhattan town house, Jackson invaded Graham's studio in the basement and, with a crowd egging him on—demanding to see "the great Jackson Pollock splash out a masterpiece"—wreaked havoc on Graham's me-ticulously arranged paints and brushes. When Graham returned, he was "very irate," recalls Ron Gorchov. "How dare you use artists' brushes to do this frivolous thing!" he raged when Jackson came to apologize, and afterward complained bitterly that he had been "betrayed by his friend."

In early spring, when Harry Jackson returned to Springs after a two-year absence, arriving grandly in a friend's Rolls-Royce, Jackson treated him "very mean and small and petty," Harry remembers. He suspected that Pollock had still not forgiven him for taking up figurative painting again; but, more likely, it was the news that *Life* magazine, seizing gleefully on the story of an abstrac-tionist who had "returned" to realism, was planning to do a long feature story on Harry. Whatever the reasons, the two men never saw each other again.

More and more, Jackson brought to his encounters a desperate needfulness, a self-pitying vulnerability that made both tenderness and honesty impossible. He would say, "I'm a fucking phony," and wait for someone to disagree. When he wept—as he did with increasing frequency—"they were sort of crocodile tears," thought Patsy Southgate, "he'd be peeking through his fingers to see if you noticed him." He would point to one of his pictures and ask in a plaintive voice, "Isn't that a great painting?" "What could I say to that?" asks Lionel Abel. "It's not the kind of thing that encourages you to be honest." In March, Paul Jenkins came to pay his respects with the English painter Alan Davie and Friedel Dzubas. They found Jackson morose and paranoid—"like King Lear," according to Jenkins. "There was an awful lot of self-condemnation because he wasn't working. He clearly felt it was all over for him." Later that night, he lamented to Jenkins, "If five people appreciate your painting in your lifetime, that's really the most an artist can hope for."

For the second time in Jackson's life, the art world was being rocked by cataclysmic change. Record prices, proliferating galleries, media coverage, and postwar prosperity were producing a new generation of young collectors and reshaping the art market into something rich and strange and unrecognizable. In December 1955, *Fortune* magazine announced that artworks had become much more than mere status symbols; they were now first-rate investments. As a service to its readers, *Fortune* listed the available offerings: "gilt-edged" (old masters); "blue-chip" (Impressionists, Post-Impressionists, perhaps Picasso); and "speculative or 'growth' issues" (contemporary). The last of these, the works of living artists, were by far the best buy—"investments for the future," *Fortune* called them. For a mere $500 to $3,500, a "tyro collector" could buy the paintings of artists like de Kooning, Rothko, and Pollock, and get in on the ground floor of the international boom.

For the next decade, inspired by such bullish projections, the new collectors fanned out across Bohemia in search of shrewd investments as well as new, more colorful identities, while the artists tried to cope with the psychic dislocations of sudden prosperity. The success of the avant-garde "revolution" left the old Bolsheviks without direction and the new ones disinherited. Egoism and infighting followed inevitably. Artists accused one another of "selling out" even as they bargained with dealers and courted collectors. Charges of plagiarism became common currency. Mark Rothko attacked Barnett Newman for "stealing his ideas" even as he privately began referring to his own one-a-day works as "merchandise"; Clyfford Still attacked Rothko (and everybody else) for betraying "the fellowship of artists" and issued jeremiads against the exploitation of art by "crass young collectors-on-the-make" even as he backdated his paintings to prove their precedence. Clement Greenberg became a dealer, and de Kooning became a millionaire. Mercedes Matter wasn't the only one who lamented: "The minute success entered into the art world and it became a business, everything changed. It was all ruined."

Although he had a hand in making this new world, Jackson would never see it or share in its unimaginable spoils. It did, however, provide him, as a kind of parting gift, with his last and most indulgent audience.

Ben Heller, a jersey manufacturer and young collector, had known Jackson since 1953, when Paul Brach introduced them, but it wasn't until the summer of 1955 that he really began to take a serious interest in American painting in general and Pollock in particular. Two things had happened in the interim to change his mind. First, he had been to a show at the Museum of Modern Art that included artists from the Post-Impressionists to Gorky. What impressed him most about the show wasn't the art, however; it was the patrons. "You saw Payson, Whitney, Rockefeller, and Burden," he recalls. "You saw who was collecting, and it became very clear: no longer were you going to have three or four houses and umpteen servants. The new chic—the real ultimate expression of a cultivated, cultured, wealthy person—was art. Crystalline clear. That was it. The handwriting was on the wall." The other event was David Rockefeller's purchase in 1955 of Cézanne's *Boy in the Red Vest* "for $500,000." By his own account, that sale "set the world on fire" for Ben Heller.

When Heller first tried to reestablish contact, Jackson dismissed him as a "Johnny-come-lately" and an "operator" and left it to Lee to deal with him. By mid-winter 1956, however, he desperately needed what Heller had to offer. He began calling him late Tuesday nights after the Cedar had closed, and the two men would go to Ryker's or Nedick's for coffee and husky, intimate conversation. Despite their different backgrounds, Heller brought to this friendship with Jackson the same repressed creative longings as Jeffrey Potter. Like Potter, he considered the company of artists "more interesting than the conventional social life." Like Potter, he had a frustrated "artistic side"—a passion for music—and later brought recordings of Schoenberg, Bartók, Debussy, Stravinsky, and Renaissance music to Fireplace Road for Jackson to listen to. (At one point, Jackson told Heller that "he would have liked to be a composer rather than a painter.") Like Potter, Heller quickly succumbed to Jackson's rough charms and the aura of creative energy that surrounded him even in decline. Hopelessly infatuated, he extolled Jackson's genius, attributed to him great analytical powers and musical acumen, and even grew a beard in imitation of him. On December 20, 1955, he sent Jackson a holiday greeting:

My real purpose in writing . . . is to do something I've wanted to do for some time, and that is to say "thank you" for your paintings. They are very meaningful to me. Merry Christmas and Happy New Year.

To seal their bond, and to share in the art boom he sensed coming—"The Impressionists have reached their peak," he told a friend. "The Cubists are high. What's left? Miró? Giacometti? Dubuffet? The Americans are the most underpriced"—Heller wanted a Pollock. He had tried to buy *Echo* out of the Janis show, but the negotiations collapsed over price. Heller quickly apologized for the "mixup," explaining to Jackson that he found it "rather difficult to talk to you about your paintings as I respect too much your desires concerning them and can't really push very hard for what I want." Undaunted, he came to Springs in early January to try again, looking through the canvases in Jackson's studio, most of which had only recently returned from the Janis show.

Heller knew one thing: he wanted a big one. He had seem most of the big canvases the previous spring on a trip with Paul Brach. "Wow," he reported afterward, "they hit me in the gut." At that time, Brach had discouraged him from buying *Blue Poles*, and Jackson was reluctant to sell the others. But much had changed in the intervening year.

The big painting he wanted was *Number 31, 1950*, one of the four giant canvases from the summer of 1950, measuring 8'7½'' by 18'—or, as Heller calculated "twelve squares, twelve big paintings." (To Heller, art was like real estate. He always looked at the back of a painting and counted the squares, like acres, formed by the stretcher supports. The bigger the stretcher, the more squares there were. Years later, he would be able to recall their exact number on many of the pictures he had purchased. "It was astonishing to see all those squares," he recalls of his first sight of a big Pollock painting.) Heller asked Lee first if Jackson would sell. "*I* wouldn't," she said, "but ask him." This time Jackson was willing to sell, but he wanted $10,000. Lee conducted the negotiations. When the dust cleared, the price had dropped to $8,000—still the highest price a Pollock had ever brought and "a gigantic price at the time," according to Budd Hopkins. It was to be paid out over four years, and Heller would receive, in addition, a black-and-white painting "in recognition of his commitment to Pollock's work."

Even after the painting was hung, with considerable difficulty, in Heller's apartment on Riverside Drive and 100th Street (it was too tall for the room and had to be curved at the top and bottom), Heller still had a problem: he didn't like the title. "I really don't like number whatever-have-you," he told Jackson bluntly. Clement Greenberg had suggested *Lowering Weather*, but this, too, Heller found prosaic—"I didn't understand its relation to the painting"—and he asked Jackson to try again. Finally, after a brainstorming session in which Jackson shared with Heller his stories about riding the rails and his "oneness" with nature, the new title emerged: *One*. Satisfied, Heller wired Jackson on February 11:

> Have been looking at our picture for hours. It's too late to call. It has so much to do with my life and feelings, with life itself, with painting with a capital P that I almost cried. Great God it is a thing for the ages. Whatever the struggle keep after it. Love Ben

Heller competed for Jackson's affections with another young collector, B. H. (Bernard Harper) Friedman. A twenty-eight-year-old executive in his family's successful real-estate firm, Friedman described himself as "torn between the excitement of New York's postwar building boom and a continuing desire to write." In fact, there was never any doubt where his true allegiance lay. Like so many of the new collectors and patrons, Friedman was a gray flannel suit filled with creative yearnings, a businessman whose heroes were Wallace Stevens and Charles Ives, and to whom the world of action painters seemed, in May Rosenberg's phrase, "full of dizzying promise." Even before Heller brought Jackson to the Friedmans' New York apartment in the spring of 1955, Freidman considered him "a truly heroic figure . . . whose name was synonymous with the expression of freedom."

The reality proved somewhat less grand. Jackson arrived drunk and tense. "Don't offer him anything hard," Lee whispered while Jackson lumbered around the room looking at Friedman's collection—"a visual history of my own search for freedom," he called it—including Jackson's *Number 11, 1949*, a four-by-four-foot dripped work from 1949. After calling Friedman's Mondrian gouache "shit," Jackson fell asleep on the couch, took a shower, then accompanied the group to a steak house, where he gradually worked his way back to an inebriated state. The stop-start conversation centered on an article Friedman had written for *Arts Digest* the previous fall, "The New Baroque," in which he described Pollock as "one of the best and most influential" Abstract Expressionists—a "Rubens of our time." "That [article]," Friedman recalls, "paved the way for our friendship."

It was, in fact, much more than a simple friendship. Although more of a genuine connoisseur than most of the new collectors—he and his wife Abby had "trained" under Curt Valentin, the legendary dealer—Friedman approached Jackson not with a collector's eye for value, but with a novelist's eye for character and dilemma. Over the year and a half of their relationship, he gave Jackson the most unalloyed approval, the most ungrudging attention, that he had experienced since the early years with Lee. "I felt how much everyone . . . loved him," Friedman later wrote in *Almost a Life*, a thinly veiled novelization of his year with Jackson. "There were times when I felt jealous of those who knew him better and longer than I had." Eager to make up for the lost time, Friedman wrote Jackson, only a few months after meeting him, about "the necessity of doing a full length biography." He offered to spend "two years" on a book that would "relate [Jackson] not only to the history of modern art, but to the American generation which matured immediately during and after the Depression. . . . If I were successful, the book would have something like the texture of Boswell's *Johnson*," he reassured Jackson. By December 1955, Friedman had settled for a biographical article (not until fifteen years later, after he had left the family business and begun writing full-time, would he complete the biography). Jackson allowed himself to be interviewed at length on the condition that Friedman use no direct quotes and reveal nothing about the Pollocks' calamitous private life. More so than previous admirers, Friedman was realistic about his subject's intellectual limitations—"I doubt that he ever read more than just bits of *Moby-Dick*"—but Jackson's larger-than-life angst proved irresistible to Friedman's empathetic nature. He noted the way Jackson stared at the surf, studied the interplay of sand and water on

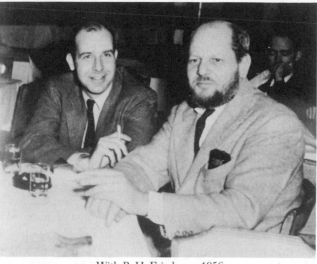

With B. H. Friedman, 1956

the beach, or sifted sand through his fingers. Two years after their first meeting, Friedman named his son Jackson.

From the start, Pollock treated Friedman more like a friend than a collector, introducing him and Abby to other friends, cavorting in the surf on Coast Guard Beach, proudly taking them to The Creeks to view *Lavender Mist*. Although he occasionally referred to his new protégé as a "young dilettante," he treasured Friedman's comments in "The New Baroque"—"he treated it like it was bordered in gold," recalls a friend—and increasingly sought his company on trips into New York. By the spring of 1956, the two men were seeing each other every week, escaping to bars and jazz clubs together, Jackson leading, performing, Friedman following with Boswellian ardor.

Nothing betrayed Jackson's endgame desperation more clearly or more ominously than his "love affair" with Ralph Klein. "He adored his shrink," recalls Patsy Southgate, who rode the train with him into the city. (It was her job to keep him from detouring into the bar at Pennsylvania Station.) "On the train he kept talking about how much he loved Ralph Klein. There was a lot of transference going on. He thought Klein was the only person who understood him." All winter long, Jackson never missed a Tuesday appointment, taking the long train ride in and then a subway to Klein's office-apartment on West Eighty-sixth Street. During the rest of the week, he called at least once a day to ask a question or rehash the last session. In conversation, he attributed to Klein "god-like powers" and, when asked what form he would want to take if reincarnated, responded without hesitation: "a psychiatrist." When Clement Greenberg, who had recommended Klein in the first place (and still saw him), asked Jackson how he liked therapy, Jackson responded, "I'm overjoyed."

As well he might have been, considering what Klein was telling him.

Klein belonged to the Barnes Landing Group, a small circle of analysts well known for their unconventional notions of "therapy," who summered in the South Fork. The group looked to Jane Pearce and Saul Newton for theoretical guidance—as well as referrals like Jackson. Pearce and Newton were still two years away from founding the Sullivan Institute for Research and Psychoanalysis, but the theories that led to their break with traditional Freudian analysis were already well-developed and deeply ingrained in disciples like Ralph Klein. Pearce and Newton claimed that their ideas were based on the work of Harry Stack Sullivan, an important psychoanalytic theoretician with whom Pearce had worked before his death in 1949 (although, according to one of Klein's associates, "Sullivan would have been horrified at the uses to which they put his name.")

Their basic dispute with Freud was over the nature of man. Where Freud saw human nature as essentially predatory and in need of control, Pearce and Newton argued that human nature was essentially beneficent and creative and in need of freer expression, not more repression. They preferred the word "dissociation" to "repression." "We believe that what is dissociated in most people, infants and adults, is their energy," says Pearce. "Their spontaneity, their creativity, their capacity for tenderness get repressed, and this frustration leads to a certain amount of hostility." To alleviate the hostility, it was only necessary to remove the repression. Within a decade, "Sullivanian" theories would be used to rationalize free love, sexual communes, and other more exaggerated forms of "association." ("Everyone was encouraged to have babies," recalls one former patient. "Saul Newton had some kind of bee in his bonnet that the world should be full of children—his children.") But even as early as 1955, when Jackson began seeing Klein, the message was already clear: "If it feels good, do it."

In therapy, Klein hewed to Pearce's theories with the tenacity of youth and inexperience. "I think that he probably saw the doctrinaire principles more clearly than he saw the person in front of him," says a colleague. Although he routinely took detailed psychological histories, Klein didn't believe in the significance of traumatic incidents and undoubtedly dismissed most of Jackson's oft-told memories out of hand. He must have quickly identified Jackson's troubled relationship with his mother, however, for soon friends were startled to hear Jackson "letting out his hostility" toward Stella, calling her "that old womb with a built-in tomb," and speculating that "maybe I paint because I want to sleep with my mother." (Lionel Abel's response: "You want to sleep with somebody, Jackson, but I don't think it's your mother.") He told Clement Greenberg straight out that he "hated his mother," and Lee saw in his continuing refusal to eat—typical of advanced alcoholism—a silent protest against Stella's most potent instrument of control.

Nothing felt better, of course, than drinking, and Jackson took Klein's injunction to "express himself" as a carte blanche at the bar. "He would say, 'What the fuck, everybody should always do what they want to do,'" Ted

Dragon recalls, " 'and if I want to dump Lee at home and sit with the guys down at the bar, so what?' " In fact, Klein complained to Pearce privately when Jackson began showing up drunk for sessions, but Pearce, no teetotaler herself, advised him that Jackson's drinking was beyond his purview; that he could only "put up with it, pray and hope that Jackson will come to therapy and deal with his anxieties in a better way." By Jackson's account, Klein never mentioned drinking again, never counseled against driving when drunk, and never suggested that Jackson seek help from other sources, such as Alcoholics Anonymous. When Conrad Marca-Relli asked, "Did you tell Klein you have a drinking problem?" Jackson replied, "Yes, but he says, 'That's your problem.' "

By the spring of 1956, as Jackson's health deteriorated and the drinking binges grew impossibly longer and wilder, Marca-Relli wasn't the only friend who began to question Klein's competence. Patsy Southgate called him a "pipsqueak." She wondered why somebody didn't say, "Hey, wait a minute—how about a second opinion?" Ben Heller was stunned when he called Klein to complain that Jackson *still* wasn't eating well and Klein responded glibly, "Look at the stuff that's in beer, the grain and so forth."

But Jackson clung to Klein—if anything, more desperately as the rest of his life disintegrated. At one point, at Marca-Relli's urging, he tried to break off the relationship; he even called Klein and told him, "Go screw. I'm not coming any more." But the next week at the appointed hour, he disappeared, and Marca-Relli knew where he had gone. "Maybe he was scared of not going in or maybe he just wanted a drink, but he couldn't break free." "Jackson was so desperately insecure," says Patsy Southgate, "he needed someone who was bowled over, someone who was nothing but supportive. That's what he found in Ralph Klein."

Jackson's problem, according to Klein, was that he hadn't *lived* enough. He was too focused on the past, especially the destructive relationship with Lee (with whom, Jackson said, he had not had sex in three years.) The solution? He needed to stop repressing his feeling and "act out his sexual impulses," to get back in touch with his creative energy. In other words, he needed a woman.

Soon Jackson began regaling his friends, male and female, with the wonders of the opposite sex and how much he loved them. He told Cile Lord that he had "discovered" women's bodies. "They're so beautiful," he said, "their breasts, their shoulders, their ears, their ankles, their noses, their wrists," and on and on until Lord couldn't help but laugh. He told Jeffrey Potter, "A lot of times I'd rather quietly hold a woman, just lying there by her, than screwing." When he and Tony Smith passed Greta Garbo walking on the Upper East Side, he turned to Smith and swooned, "I don't know about love . . . I've only experienced it three times. . . . one of them was when we passed that woman."

For practice, he took Joan Ward to dinner at a romantic Italian restaurant on Thompson Street. But "he had no small talk," Ward remembers, and the silence was so awkward that he finally retreated to some friends across the room and stayed so long that Ward got up and walked out. (He called later to apologize.) At a party, he begged Budd Hopkins to introduce him to a young, attractive female friend, Josie Wilkinson. "Jackson, she doesn't know anything about art," Hopkins warned. "I don't care," said Jackson. "I've got to meet her." When Hopkins made the introductions, Jackson, who had been wheeling through the party grabbing breasts as usual, was suddenly very polite. "He sort of shifted gears and was calling her 'Miss Wilkinson,' " Hopkins recalls. Soon afterward, however, Jackson turned away from the conversation, unzipped his pants, and relieved himself in a nearby potted plant. "Then he zipped himself up and resumed the conversation," says Hopkins. "The girl was totally stunned."

So were Elinor Poindexter and her daughter Christie when they met Jackson, drunk, coming out of an opening and he invited nineteen-year-old Christie to dinner at the Cedar Bar. "She didn't even really accept," recalls Poindexter. "He just said, 'Let's go, come on.' What could she do?" At the Cedar, with the elder Poindexter acting as chaperon, Jackson tried to "express his romantic feelings toward women." But all that came out was self-pity. Budd Hopkins remembers seeing Jackson sitting in a booth with the two women, tears running down his face, "telling them what a fraud he was, that he had never done the things he wanted to do, that he felt helpless."

He propositioned Jane Smith "any number of times," made passes at Patsy Southgate, and terrified Marisol Escobar in an effort to kiss her. When he grabbed Joan Ward at a party, Budd Hopkins remembers, Ward "just wrenched his hand off her while she was still talking to me." Drunk at Jungle Pete's one night, he stumbled around the crowded dance floor with Miriam Schapiro, pawing her roughly until, just as the music stopped, she shouted, "Cut it out, Jackson, or I'll kick you in the balls!" David Budd saw him walk up to a girl at the Cedar and say, "You got great tits—let's fuck." When she fled in disgust, he called after her, "What's the hurry?" One night in the Cedar Bar, he made a "beeline" for Audrey Flack, a rambunctious young art student in a bomber jacket and tight jeans. Although no "babe in the woods," Flack was terrified. "This huge man tried to grab me, pinched me in the behind, and burped in my face. He wanted to kiss me, but I took one look at him and I realized that this man whom everybody idolized was sick—sick, debauched, and desperate. I couldn't imagine kissing him. It would be like kissing a derelict on the Bowery."

Frustrated in the real world, Jackson turned increasingly to fantasy. He bragged to B. H. Friedman that he had "fucked Rita Benton." With others, he added Mercedes Matter and Vita Peterson to the list of fictitious conquests. To Jeffrey Potter: "Dames got their hooks out for us and if they've got dough, watch out . . . they're all over me, always were." He called Sande to titillate him with stories, mostly innuendo, all false, about "being involved with a lot of women." He told Reuben Kadish that he wasn't interested in painting anymore, only in women. Concerned that some might question the virility of a man married ten years and still without children, he insinuated Lee was infertile. The stories came so suddenly, so torrentially, that even admirers like Friedman thought perhaps Jackson protested too much.

According to one story emanating from the Cedar Bar, Franz Kline and some friends grew so tired of Jackson's drunken advances and sexual braggadocio that they hired a call girl and set her within his range. When he approached her with the inevitable "Wanna fuck?" the woman jumped up, grabbed her coat, and offered, "Let's go." According to the story, Jackson collapsed instantly. When David Budd brought to the Cedar a young female friend from Idaho—"a real dish, a real tomato, she looked like Daisy Mae in 'Dogpatch' "—Jackson, "who was as famous as a movie star then," says Budd, turned to her and growled, "Let's go to my place and *fuck*." "She didn't bat an eye," Budd recalls. "She just calmly said, 'No, not now. I don't have the time,' and went on talking. Jackson got up and said, 'Well, I don't either!' and walked off in a huff."

As Kline and Budd discovered, it was all an act: a desperate fantasy as false as the stories Jackson told. "I could have been a cow," says Terry Liss of Jackson's groping. "The way he reached out to touch was not touching. It had no relationship to feeling." The girls he lunged after in the street would just laugh, Clement Greenberg recalls. "He was drunk, so they didn't feel threatened." Which was exactly the point. Drunk, he never ran the risk of success. The brutish grappling, the childlike weeping, the grossness, the menace, were all forms of protection, ways of insulating himself from the very intimacy he professed to crave. Paul Brach wasn't the only friend who thought Jackson's approach was intended, at some level, to "assure that there would be no sexual action. To *guarantee* it." Drunk was an excuse for not being able to perform. Drunk was a way to forget the questions that his inability to perform always raised. The more he drank, the less likely success; the less likely success, the greater his anxiety; the greater his anxiety, the more he drank.

But if drink protected him from the anxiety of sex with women, what would protect him from the even greater anxiety of sex without them?—an anxiety that increasingly overtook him in the darkness outside of bars, especially in East Hampton, when he found himself in the company of strangers.

Around two o'clock in the morning on a frigid night in early 1956, Nick Carone was awakened by a telephone call from Lee Krasner. "Nick, you've got to come over," she said in the choked, stoic voice she always used to cover her near panic. Carone protested, "I'm asleep," but Lee insisted. "Nick, you've got to make an effort. Jackson has been gone all day."

"Where did he go?"

"That's what I'm worried about," she said with an inflection that Carone thought signaled a special dread, not just the usual anxiety over Jackson's drinking. "Some guys came around, some rednecks, and they came by and took him away. He hasn't come back. Please come and stay with me. I'm worried."

When Carone arrived at the Pollock house, he found Lee sitting in the ice-cold kitchen drinking coffee. He asked her again what had happened. "These guys came around and took him," she repeated with the same tone of dread. When he pressed—"Well, what's so unusual about that?"—she muttered something about "what they might do to him." Carone recalls: "She never came right out and said it, but it was clear she was frightened that they were going to rape him. I sensed that this was triggered by something in the past. . . . There was something strange there, something hidden." What Lee was afraid to say, no doubt, was that this was not the first time Jackson had disappeared under similarly bizarre circumstances. On several previous occasions, a group of strange men had taken him away, only to return in the middle of the night to "dump him on the doorstep"—bruised and shaken in ways that alcohol alone couldn't explain—then speed away.

Without taking off his coat and muffler, Carone joined Lee's vigil in the freezing kitchen, sipping coffee, rarely talking, waiting. "Every now and then, Lee would get up and look out a window and ask, 'Where is he?' Every time a car passed, she would say, 'Maybe that's him.' She was obviously terrified that they had done something awful to him."

Suddenly the kitchen door flew open and Jackson came in "like a wild animal." He looked at Carone and demanded, "What the fuck are you doing here?" "Waiting for you, Jackson," Carone replied, thinking, "He's going to kill me." Lee tried to calm him. "Jackson, are you okay?" she asked. "Would you like a glass of hot milk?" Jackson responded with rage. "Fuck you, you fucking cunt, what the fuck do you want from me anyway?" Rage. Rage. Rage. "This was going on with the greatest profanity I had ever heard in my life," Carone remembers. " 'You motherfucking cunt bitch' and on and on and on. And all I could think was, 'Jesus, I hope he's not going to kill me.' " Lee retreated across the kitchen, "silent and receptive, rather than fighting back," careful not to provoke, deaf to the hail of insults. Then he went slack for a few minutes, walked to the window, sat at the table, stood up. "He couldn't stay still," says Carone. Seeing an opening, Lee advanced cautiously. "Would you like that glass of hot milk now?" she asked. Something tripped the detonator and the tirade began again. "I've done it! Fuck! I did it!" Jackson roared. "What the fuck do they want from me anyway? What the fuck do they want from me? What the fuck! I've done it! What *more* do they want?"

Just when the rage should have begun to dissipate, it intensified. "Lee was getting seriously worried," Carone recalls. As Jackson stumbled toward the stairs, she moved in close with stunning fearlessness. "She did it to protect him from himself," says Carone, but he pushed her away as though he couldn't stand to be touched. "What the fuck are you doing to me?" he screamed over and over. "What the fuck are you doing to me?" "He was going like a madman. He got so angry, screaming and screaming. It was like he was losing his mind right there." Suddenly, he reached up and grabbed a chandelier that hung in the hallway at the foot of the stairs. Carone rose to stop him, but Lee motioned him to stay back. "*No*," she commanded. "Don't go near him. He might attack you." With a great heave, Jackson yanked the chandelier from the ceiling. It came off too easily, sending him tumbling over backwards into the corner of the room, where he landed on a big flowerpot, which exploded underneath him.

For a moment he lay so still that Lee thought he might be dead. "He was sprawled out and bleeding," says Carone, "and Lee didn't know what the hell had happened." Then he began to moan. Lee knelt down beside him and started again. "Are you all right, Jackson? Can I get you something?" The rage broken, he began to whimper, "It hurts. It hurts." "Where does it hurt?" Lee asked. Jackson rubbed his buttocks. "That got her worried again about what they had done to him," Carone recalls. "Was he sore from that?" "Come on, Jackson," she finally said. "I'll take you upstairs." She turned to Carone. "It's all right, let me take care of it," and she shouldered Jackson up to bed.

Not long afterward, Jackson was brooding in a booth at the Cedar Bar when a pretty young brunette sat down beside him. Her name was Ruth Kligman.

44

ESCAPE VELOCITY

By early spring 1956, Jackson and Lee both knew it had to end. The only question was how: Who would break? Who would let go first? Lee had grown strong enough to conceive of leaving. Jackson had grown self-destructive enough. They hurled challenges at each other. He beat her. She called the police. He threatened to leave her. She threatened to have him committed to a mental institution. He screamed, "I'll kill you." She screamed, "You're killing me." But still they clung to each other: unable, unwilling, afraid to escape; lashing out, Clement Greenberg recalls. "like a wounded animal tearing at its own entrails"; addicted to abuse and abusing; circling each other in ever tighter, more self-destructive orbits; preparing themselves for the inevitable collision that would end it all—or the miracle that would set them free.

No one wondered why Jackson was attracted to Ruth Kligman. She was, everyone agreed, a voluptuous twenty-five-year-old-woman: porcelain skin, big breasts, sensuous lips, lustrous brown hair, a warm, seductive voice and a flattering girlish way with men. The harder question was why was *she* attracted to *him*? Why wasn't she, like Audrey Flack and a dozen other young women who had felt Jackson's grope, disgusted by his swollen face, blotchy skin, and Bowery breath? It wasn't enough to say, as Ruth herself did later, that she was a young painter and he was simply "the great master." Flack and the others were also young painters, no less worldly than Ruth, no less ambitious, no less aware of Jackson's stature. ("He was like a movie star to me," says Flack.) Yet they had fled his debauched advances, the menace, and the pain that "radiated" from him. Why did Ruth Kligman, sitting close to him in the booth that night in the unflattering glare of the Cedar Bar, move even closer?

Like Lee Krasner, Ruth Kligman had come from a family in which abuse was often mistaken for love. Her father, a handsome local con man whom she

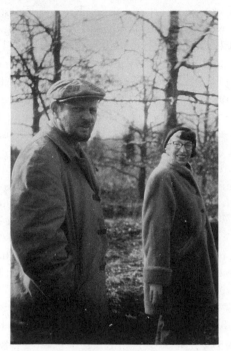

The last picture of Jackson and Lee together,
Springs, 1956

knew by his professional name, "Bootie," had married her mother when she was eighteen and promptly abandoned her. "My father didn't come to the house," says Ruth. "He came in my mother and that was it." Disowned by her well-to-do Russian Jewish parents over Bootie, Mary Kligman raised her twin daughters, Ruth and Iris, alone, always on the edge of poverty and paranoia. "My mother was always crying," Ruth later wrote. "She cried, I cried, and my twin sister cried, we all cried in a kind of horrible unison. I never knew what was wrong. But the outside world represented terror." Their only escape was the little movie house in Newark, New Jersey, where Ruth developed an obsession with fame, stardom, fantasy love, and distant, celluloid men. At one point, Mary Kligman dressed up her two dark-haired, brown-eyed little daughters and took them to a local Shirley Temple look-alike contest. She was "convinced we would win," Ruth recalls, "but they wouldn't even let us enter. No brunettes allowed." Most days were spent "waiting for Daddy." On the rare occasions when he appeared in his fancy clothes, Ruth felt a strange, electrifying mixture of terror, disgust, and ecstasy—"Daddy was always the desirable one," she would later admit.

At the age of five, Ruthie, as she was called, had her first nervous breakdown. She went into a catatonic state, refused to eat or sleep, heard strange noises, and saw "monsters with green fluorescent eyes" around her bed at night. The spell was broken only when an aunt took her into the bathroom, forced her to urinate in her own hands, then threw the urine in her face.

Ruth found her escape in art and men. The connection was made early, at the age of seven, when she fell madly in love with a drawing of Beethoven. "His eyes were wild, his forehead high, full of energy. I decided I would be similarly artistic—and if not, the wife or mistress of a genius. Or better yet, both," she later wrote. At thirteen, she went alone to the Metropolitan Museum and gazed in rapture at Rodin sculptures and a painting by Vermeer in which "the light was so clear and bright," she recalled, "that I looked behind the picture to see if there was a lightbulb." In school, she found real boys tiresome and frightening. Like Lee Krasner, she longed to get away from home, to flee to the city. She dreamed of "going into the backyard and jumping over the fence into a beautiful country with hills and green and sunlight and a man was there." Out of high school, she found a job modeling in the garment district on Seventh Avenue where her cigar-chewing bosses used to say, "Ruthie has class." When people asked about her past, she would tell them about her wealthy family, especially her rich, adoring father. She had a series of affairs with older men, but her real loves remained safely distant figures: "Baudelaire, Apollinaire, Rimbaud." "Men were such frightening people to me," she recalls, "that I could only manipulate them." At twenty, she met an older, married man who could afford her expensive fantasies—"my rich daddy," she called him. They went to the races in a limousine, to the Copacabana and the 21 Club, and Ruth "forgot about art for a while." "I took advantage," she later admitted. "I had him wrapped around my adorable little waist, I cried, got drunk when I didn't get my way, he spoiled me."

The fantasy ended abruptly two years later with another nervous breakdown. She took up art again, enrolling in a painting class at the New School and taking a job at the Collectors Gallery where "she had such a persuasive way of talking about art," recalls Audrey Flack, "that she could have been a great art salesperson." She devoured movie magazines and *Vogue*, spent hours at beauty parlors and in front of the mirror, and started seeing a Jungian analyst. When she told her father, who materialized briefly in a milk-white Cadillac convertible, about the analysis, he flew into a rage. His face "went white" and he started screaming. "That's for crazy people. . . . What the hell is wrong with you? Can't you control yourself with men? What kind of a creep are you? Are you a lesbian or something?" Sobbing hysterically, Ruth pleaded, "I need help," but Bootie was crazy beyond listening. "What are you, some kind of whore or queer?" he screamed as he opened the car door. "Get out of this car, you TRAMP." Then he pushed her out into the gutter and sped away.

Not long afterward, Jackson Pollock entered her life.

Like Beethoven, he arrived first in the abstract. In her newfound obsession with painting, she had asked Audrey Flack to introduce her to important artists. "You want to know artists," Flack said, "I'll introduce you to artists." Flack gave her three names: Pollock, de Kooning, and Kline. Ruth didn't recognize any of the names, but she carefully wrote them down. Then she pressed, "Which one is *the* greatest?"

"Pollock," said Flack.

She told Ruth about the Cedar Bar and wrote down the address, but refused to accompany her there—"I never wanted to go back to the place," she said. Ruth later claimed that she met Jackson on her first visit to the Cedar, but others remember her coming often and sitting in the smoky light, almost always dressed in pink, waiting for him to come in. She went to see his paintings at the Janis Gallery where, she recalls, "the energy poured into me and I understood them totally on every level." She may even have traveled to the bars of East Hampton and suffered the leers of locals in the hope of catching his eye. Terry Liss at the Elm Tree Inn remembers seeing her often the previous summer. Roger Wilcox saw her at the beach with her sister Iris. "Identical twins, like a surrealist event," says Wilcox, "and they were both on the make for artists." Long before she met him, Jackson was Ruth's "hero," an abstraction she adored "as other girls adored Brando or Elvis," by her account.

Finally, sometime in February 1956, she summoned her courage and "made a beeline" for him.

She later claimed that "the first moment we looked at each other, I fell in love with him and he fell in love with me." The reality, however, fell far short of the fantasy. Like Lee, Ruth found Jackson, for all his drunken advances and machismo bluster, a reluctant lover. After their first encounter, she waited breathlessly for his call. A week or more passed. Finally, she started calling the Cedar—"I couldn't take being treated casually," she said. When she reached him, drunk and distant on the other end of the line, he barely remembered her. She had to refresh his memory: Ruth Kligman, the "dark-haired girl" at the Cedar. But Ruth was "very persistent and aggressive," according to a friend, "and she just wore him out." It took almost two months, but her persistence paid off. One night she coaxed him, undoubtedly drunk, to her apartment on Sixteenth Street. By the next morning, Jackson was convinced that they had had sex.

The rest was easy.

Finally Jackson had something *real* to brag about, something to appease Ralph Klein and the boys at the Cedar. The next week, he paraded her in front of them. When David Budd saw her, dressed in a scarlet coat with a silver fox collar and "woozy with drink," he thought, "I can see how that would drive anybody off the wall. She's some cookie." "Why, Jackson," cried Willem de Kooning in astonishment, "do you have a *girl?*" Jackson waved him away with a warning: "Keep your hands off of her." When they left that night, de Kooning ran after them, calling, "Can I see her, can I see her?" Jackson had their picture taken by the photo girl in another bar and proudly passed it around among his friends in Springs. "He showed off this snapshot of her and wanted to know what I thought," Nick Carone recalls. "He was like a child." He boasted to Jeffrey Potter, the car buff, about his "late model cream puff . . . barely broken in [and] loaded with extras."

Ruth had a very different vision. To her, they were "Brando and Monroe," or "Bacall and Bogart." Jackson served her fantasies well, taking her to night-clubs like El Chico and Eddie Condon's, restaurants, and Broadway shows. They would enter and exit "like stars," Ruth wrote. People "bowed in front of us. . . . We were very tall." He treated her to taxi rides—"This is what women do in the real world," she exulted—bought her presents, and dressed in his "rich-looking" clothes so she could feel "glamorous." He bragged about the money he had made on the sales of *Blue Poles* and *One.* She talked about traveling together to exotic places and buying a pied-à-terre, preferably on Park Avenue, "instead of staying in some uncomfortable little room at the Hotel Earle when he came to town."

In return, Ruth served Jackson's fantasy. In public, she flattered him, clung coyly to his arm, and played lovers' games: finger games, eye games, jealousy games. At a club one night, he danced with another woman, so she danced with another man. Jackson slapped her and she swooned. On the rare occasions when they were alone, she avoided talking about art or his career—it invariably made him weep. That left Jungian analysis (they decided that he was the archetypal "Old Wise Man" and she, the archetypal "Lover") and previous affairs, real or imagined. "He talked a lot of Rita [Benton]," Ruth recalls. "He said, 'You remind me of her,' and I thought, 'Oh, she's *old.*' " He insisted that she was a virgin when they met and she didn't disagree. She said, in public, "I love you, Jackson," and he said, in public, "I love you, Ruth," and, according to Ruth, they both "loved the love."

Despite Jackson's boasts and Ruth's later claims, there was little, if any, sex. When they were alone, Jackson still made sure to be drunk, or wept profusely. (Tears, he had discovered, turned any woman into a mother.) Ruth probably preferred it that way. The best sex, she had concluded, was "metaphorical"—everything else diminished the fantasy. For her, power was consummation enough. "I wanted everyone to pay attention to me," she says, "and when I was with Jackson, they did." For Jackson, apparently, the strange, delicious thrill of having a desirable woman at his side was enough.

Far from hiding his relationship with Ruth, Jackson flaunted it, parading her in public places and professing his love for her on train rides with Patsy South-gate. At the house in Springs, he called her almost every day and talked for hours, with Lee in the next room. On the few occasions when he appeared with Lee in public, he dropped heavy, hurtful hints in rooms filled with know-ing ears. "Just how old *are* you, Lee?" he shouted to her from across the room at a dinner party. In conversations with Lee's friends, he talked about making "permanent arrangements" for Ruth and tested the waters of divorce, in the certainty that such hints would find their way back to Lee. "He viewed the whole thing as an amazing adventure," Patsy Southgate recalled. "Like a little boy, his dream was to have both."

To some extent, such callous talk may have been simply Jackson's clumsy effort to "express himself without guilt," as Ralph Klein had urged him to do —or, as Clement Greenberg succinctly put it, to "fuck appearances." According to Klein's philosophy, Lee should have been pleased that Jackson was "expressing himself and enjoying the company of another person," even if that other person was Ruth Kligman. But Jackson surely knew better. He knew Lee's special vulnerability too well. He had tracked it through a whole series of fabricated affairs: Rita Benton, Maria Motherwell, Vita Peterson, Mercedes Matter. Now he had something *real* with which to hurt her. Says Greenberg: "He was out after Lee's face."

Lee tried for as long as she could to ignore it, a response that only infuriated Jackson more and brought him more daringly into the open. Her friends were sympathetic. They avoided Jackson when they could and, when they couldn't, ignored Ruth. To Jackson's protests that "Lee doesn't understand me," most responded as Carol Braider did: "Oh, fuck off, Jackson." When they brought reports of Jackson's plans for divorce, Lee hardened against him. Where only a few months before she had been considering it herself, now she told friends: "I will *never* give Jackson a divorce." In an effort at conciliation, she proposed that they take a trip to Europe, visit Peggy Guggenheim, and see the Venice Biennale, but Jackson refused. He couldn't miss his weekly visit to Ralph Klein, he claimed, visits that now sometimes stretched to two or three days. It was clearly a standoff that could not last forever.

In June, Ruth moved to Sag Harbor, only twelve miles from Springs. She claimed that she didn't realize when she took the summer job as a monitor at the Abraham Rattner School of Art that it would bring her so close to Jackson, but in fact she was tiring of the life of a mistress: the indignities, the furtive phone calls, the condescending looks of Jackson's friends. Where Lee struggled to avoid a confrontation and Jackson talked of "having both," Ruth clearly understood that her only hope lay in confrontation. The very day she arrived, with a suitcase full of pink clothes—"in case someone invited me to a fancy-dress ball or to go yachting"—Jackson drove from Springs and took her to dinner at the Elm Tree Inn in Amagansett, just a few turns away from Fireplace Road. In the following weeks, he called every day and visited two or three nights a week. He displayed her at the crowded Coast Guard Beach where Ibram Lassaw and scores of others "stared at this *zaftig* chick with a curvaceous body walking next to Jackson." He drove her over to the Stony Hill Farm where Jeffrey Potter remembers "his grin, his arm around her, and the finger with the missing tip caressing her shoulder, bare above the halter." He even introduced her to Lee's closest friends like Cile Lord. "I think he had come to assume that we were sympathetic to him in *all* things," says Lord, who was not at all sympathetic in this. Soon he began spending nights away, no longer bothering with the pretense of visits to the analyst. Sometimes he spent them in Sag Harbor and, according to Ruth, would wake up "frightened-looking and nervous about the consequences" when he returned to Lee. Other nights he simply disappeared.

But Lee refused to give him the satisfaction of her rage, and that, in turn, infuriated him more. He began to drink more heavily than ever—from morning to night when he was home, "juggling whiskey and beer as if they were two different drugs," according to B. H. Friedman, "as if one counteracted the other." Reginald Isaacs arrived in Springs in June and found him drinking White Horse so fast "he couldn't keep up." The plan had been for Jackson to paint a "lifelike" family portrait of the Isaacses, but he was "too involved with the bottle" for any coherent activity, especially painting. He said he expected to be "in shape to paint" by the fall and invited Isaacs to return then.

Jackson began appearing for his appointments at Ralph Klein's office drunk and belligerent—a revelation for Klein—raging against Lee and how she had "trapped" him, and demanding to know what he should do. According to Patsy Southgate, Klein told him, "You don't have to do anything," or simply asked more questions: "Why don't you live with Ruth?" Privately, Klein and his colleagues (including Lee's analyst) "talked about Jackson's case a lot," recalls a former patient of the Barnes Landing group, "but they didn't know what the hell to do with him. He was overwhelming."

Meanwhile, Ruth Kligman was growing more impatient by the day, with both Jackson and Lee. She was beginning to think that perhaps her analyst, who had left for the summer, had been right when he told her to break off the relationship. It was going nowhere. Every time she broached the subject of their future to Jackson, he said that he hoped she would "understand," that he owed Lee "something," that he needed more time to resolve the impasse. But it wasn't a matter of time, Ruth now realized; it was a matter of will. Without some prodding, Jackson would never leave Lee. He was too deeply involved in their destructive game, too tied to her in thousands of unarticulated, impervious ways. It was time for Ruth to take matters into her own hands.

A few days later, Jackson announced that Ruth was pregnant.

Bursting with pride, he boasted to friends like Greenberg and Heller that "he wasn't shooting blanks" and grilled Ruth about her "family stock." But the initial elation soon wore off, and he saw his dilemma straight on. The prospect of a baby shattered his vague dreams of keeping Ruth "on the side" while continuing to live with Lee. Sooner or later, he would have to confront Lee directly. He had threatened it, promised it, and avoided it as long as he could. Now he would have to face the reality of divorcing her.

But Ruth had underestimated Lee's grip. "Jackson was absolutely terrified of Lee," she says, and even believing that a child was on the way, "he couldn't face her with the truth." Instead, he began to entertain alcoholic delusions of a life with *both* women: Ruth would move into the big house, and Lee would live in the shack out back that had already been designated as her studio. He suggested that they could "go to the house and talk about it with Lee," Ruth recalls, "the three of us, like grown-ups. He said, 'I know she'll like you.' Like Noel Coward or something, he thought we were all going to smoke and talk about it." The idea horrified Ruth. She wanted a confrontation, but not that way. She wanted it safely offstage and accused Jackson of lacking the courage —or maybe the will—to confront Lee alone. To appease her, he asked her to marry him—another desperate fantasy. Ruth was "thrilled with the idea of being Mrs. Jackson Pollock," but pressed again about what he planned for the current Mrs. Pollock. "She'll be well taken care of," he answered vaguely.

That wasn't good enough for Ruth. Caught between Jackson's reticence and the inevitable revelation that she *wasn't*, in fact, pregnant, she couldn't wait. One night in July, she and Jackson found themselves in Jackson's studio, drunk and giggling and trying, Ruth claimed, not to wake Lee, who was sleeping in the main house. The next morning when they emerged from the studio, Lee was standing at the back door, wrapped in a bathrobe and a towering indignation. "She was white with rage," Ruth later recounted. "Her face distorted with anger, her body shaking. She stared at me, trying to utter something coherent, stuttering and finally screaming at us, calling out, 'Get that woman off my property before I call the police!' "

When Jackson returned from Sag Harbor, Lee hurled her ultimatum: If you don't stop seeing Ruth, I'll leave you. Bursting with deluded confidence and White Horse, Jackson flung it back in her face: Go ahead, leave. If she left, she warned, she wouldn't return. But, for Jackson, there was no going back; too many lines had been drawn. Get out! he screamed.

They had been through these scenes before, usually over Jackson's drinking, but somehow had always found each other again. Jackson would sleep off the booze and wake up tame and needful. Lee would fix his drink of orange juice and raw eggs in the Waring blender and watch him drink it. She had learned to survive on such crumbs. But this time was different. Days passed and he didn't come around for the usual measure of maternal sympathy and forgiveness. Panic-stricken, Lee searched for a last-minute, face-saving compromise. She didn't have to leave for good, she decided; she could take the trip to Europe that she had long hoped they would take together. Her family supported the idea. "She was very sick with ulcerated colitis," Ruth Stein recalls, "and he was killing her. She desperately needed to breathe. Getting away was like oxygen for her." Instead of protesting, Jackson drove into town and bought Lee a ticket on the next ship. Despite the urging of friends, who were "anxious for the whole thing to come to an end," she was easily dissuaded from filing divorce papers before leaving. "She sat here on the terrace and talked about finalizing everything before she left," Ted Dragon remembers, "but I *strongly* advised against it. I told her, 'You're going away and you're going to think about this whole thing.' " After consulting her analyst, Len Siegel, she stopped talking about divorce altogether and began referring instead to "a trial separation" and telling her friends, "We've been fighting so much, we just need to back away." (When Jackson spoke to Ralph Klein, Klein said simply, "Let her go.")

As the departure day approached, in a final fit of masochistic fantasy, Lee begged Jackson to join her on the trip. When he refused, she offered to come back and "work something out": no questions, no apologies, complete capitulation. She must have known it was too late, but apparently needed to reassure herself that she was indeed the victim, that what happened after she left would not be her fault.

The night before the boat sailed, she dreamed of Jackson's death. He appeared to her as Jesus Christ, dying on the cross, his hands covered with mold. The next day, July 12, Barney and Annalee Newman and Day Schnabel took her to the pier to board the *Queen Elizabeth.* Annalee Newman remembers how "devastated" she was "that Jackson had thrown her out." On her way to the gangplank, she had a sudden change of heart. "I can't go," she cried, "Jackson needs me," and ran to a phone to call him. When he answered, she pretended she had left her passport at the house. They talked haltingly for a minute or two before she gave up. "Oh, I just found my passport," she said and hung up. After boarding, she went to the telephones and tried Jackson again, ship to shore. Unable to get through, she called her sister, Ruth Stein. "She was heartsick," Stein remembers. "Then in the middle of the conversation, a call came through on another phone. She said, 'Maybe it's him,' and hung up. A few minutes later, after talking to him, she called me back. 'Oh, God, I can't get him to come, I feel so . . .' I said, 'Well, what can you *do*? You have to survive.' "

The following Tuesday, Alfonso Ossorio ran into Jackson at Penn Station. He had just come from his last session with Ralph Klein before Klein's summer vacation, and he was trying to get down the steps to the tracks to catch the 4:19 for East Hampton. "He could hardly walk," Ossorio remembers. "He had to hold Patsy Southgate's hand. It was an appalling sight. He was half-blotted, extremely depressed and physically ill, body bloated, ankles swollen, face all red and blotchy." Jackson looked at Ossorio and called out in a feeble voice, "My doctor's on vacation and Lee's gone. At last, I'm free."

Lee didn't know it, but even as she made her last desperate phone calls to Jackson, Ruth Kligman had already moved into the house on Fireplace Road and unpacked her suitcase full of pink clothes. Like Jackson, she had gotten what she wanted—or what she thought she wanted.

They slept late and ignored knocks at the door. Clad perpetually in panties, Ruth fluttered about the house, exploring every room, admiring the copper pots in the kitchen, the abundant plants, the white walls, and everywhere Jackson's "awesome" paintings. "In my twenty-one years of middle class living and sharing crummy apartments," she later wrote (understating her age), "this was really new to me." She thrilled with excitement when Jackson called other "famous" artists like Barnett Newman and Mark Rothko, or they called him. During the day, they drove around the South Fork so Jackson could show her off, introducing her to those few friends who were willing to meet her and hadn't already. At night, they cooked elaborate meals, went to the movies in East Hampton, watched television on the big red velvet couch in the living room, and drank. By bedtime, Jackson had either passed out or fallen to weeping. He talked of escaping with her and traveling the country "where nobody knows me." In such moments of what seemed to Ruth emotional undress, she found him "very touching"—"He was wonderful as far as being able to cry and let out his emotions," she recalls. To Terry Liss, Jackson bragged about "how he got rid of Lee and how nice it was to have somebody in the home who really was making him feel good."

The honeymoon lasted a week. Where before, Ruth had been his escape from Lee, now she *was* Lee, a target for the same abuse, the same loathing, the same fears, and the same insatiable needs. Ruth would spend hours preparing for a party only to have Jackson decide at the last minute not to go or, if they did go, drag her away in the middle of it. He cursed her little kitten, Blanche. He yelled at her for overdressing and wearing makeup. When she woke up in a particularly blithe mood, he would brood. When she wanted to play her jazz records, he barked, "I don't like that kind of music." When she became sick, he grew short-tempered and irritable. When she wanted to be affectionate, he would complain about the prying eyes of neighbors and push her away. When they went to the beach, he insisted on sitting far away from the ogling crowd. He snapped at her inexplicably in the presence of visitors like Friedel Dzubas, bullied her friends when they came to visit, and fought with her openly when James Brooks stopped by. When she tried to paint in Lee's studio, Jackson snapped, "Why the hell do you want to be a painter?" He drank more than ever and started going to bed early in the evening.

He wanted Lee.

One day, about a week after Ruth's arrival, he slipped off to East Hampton and arranged to send a dozen red roses to Lee's hotel in Paris.

When the flowers arrived at the Hôtel Quai Voltaire, Lee was out. Despite the beautiful view of the Seine and the Louvre from her balcony, she avoided being alone in her room as much as possible. She toured the museums and the Left Bank galleries ("the painting here is unbelievably bad," she said), walked the parks and gardens, browsed the flea market, and spent the evenings going from nightclub to nightclub, "dancing like mad" with the legions of friends who by some kind coincidence were passing through Paris at the same time. In just one week, she had already seen Paul and Esther Jenkins (who had recently moved to Paris and acted as unofficial hosts), Betty Parsons, Ben Heller (who gave her some traveler's checks in partial payment for *Echo*, which he had recently bought), Helen Frankenthaler, Sidney Geist, René Drouin, Michel Tapié, Rodolph Stadler, Charles and Kay Gimpel, Norman Bluhm, and John Graham. Although she rarely spoke of Jackson, it was clear that her thoughts never left him. She saw some rolls of canvas in Jenkins's studio and muttered to herself, "As poor as Jackson and I were, we always had plenty of art supplies." When she saw John Graham—acting very arch, very White Russian—"she was glad to see him because he brought a proximity to Jackson," Jenkins recalls. At a small gathering, surrounded by quiet, sophisticated chatter, she turned to Jenkins suddenly. "My God!" she said with a marveling smile, "at this point, Jackson would do something utterly outrageous, like break a chair." As unimaginable as it must have seemed, she missed him. "She lived and breathed and ate Jackson Pollock," recalls Jenkins, "and only seemed happy when she was doing something that pertained to him."

Then the flowers came.

On July 22 she wrote Jackson a postcard, ostensibly to inform him of a change in her itinerary: the Gimpels had invited her to their house in Menerbes in the south of France. She would stop there on her way to see Peggy Guggenheim, delaying her arrival in Venice until early August. The real purpose of the postcard, however, was to acknowledge the flowers and their implicit message, and to send one in return. "I miss you & wish you were sharing this with me," she wrote, "—the roses were the most beautiful deep red. . . . It would be wonderful to get a note from you. Love Lee." At the bottom, she added a short postscript in parentheses: "How are you Jackson?"

Ruth knew something was wrong. Although unaware of the flowers and Lee's letters, she could sense the fantasy ending and what she called "the devilish game" beginning. She had come to Springs, according to B. H. Friedman, "thinking she was going to have a wonderful time and take over." By the second week, however, she was often bored, sometimes miserable, occasionally frightened, and Lee's hold on Jackson had, if anything, grown stronger. More and more, she found herself resenting him, resenting his fame, resenting his tantrums, and most of all resenting his hold on her. She resented the way he talked on the phone so much, especially to his mother. "He talked to her the way he talked to me," she recalls, "very slow, very tentative. And I thought, 'He doesn't have another mistress, does he?' " She resented the way he treated her in front of company, the way he acted as if she wasn't there, or apologized for her, or hemmed and hawed when talking about her on the phone. She resented the way he drove around endlessly, recklessly, just to avoid stopping somewhere and being seen with her. On a visit to Nick Carone's house, he simply left her in the car. When she complained—"Why have you turned against me, Jackson?"—he snapped back, "Are you a psychotic?"

But most of all, she resented the way his friends treated her. She knew, of course, that many of them refused to see her at all. Out of loyalty to Lee, the "wives' organization," as Paul Brach called it, made it clear that they didn't want Jackson bringing her around. Some of his friends, out of sympathy for Jackson's plight, tried to be cordial. Conrad Marca-Relli and his wife paid a house call but found Jackson drunk and Ruth "hostile" and left after ten minutes. Sherry and Cile Lord came to Fireplace Road for dinner one night and found his meanness toward Ruth almost unbearable. Even for the well intentioned, the sight of Jackson, bloated and hurting, consorting with a woman half his age, was hard to bear. "It was a strain when they came to visit," recalls James Brooks, "so we got them out as quickly as we could." When Jackson took her to meet Paul Brach and Miriam Schapiro, Ruth pointed out that Schapiro's palette "wasn't laid out right," Schapiro recalls. "We were furious . . . the absolute gall." The word quickly spread that "Jackson's girl" was "rather earthy and coarse," "not East Hampton." The judgment was conveyed to Ruth in sidelong glances, overlooked invitations, and whispered comments. "His friends obviously thought I was nothing," she wrote, "which was the way I felt underneath my prettiness and clothes and makeup."

No one was crueler than Clement Greenberg, who with his new wife, Jenny, had rented a house in Springs for the summer. When Jackson and Ruth came for dinner, Jenny's Bennington classmates, who were dressed in jeans, snubbed Ruth in her white linen dress and gold sandals, and Jackson treated her "like a piece of furniture." Greenberg turned an abstract discussion of friendship into a pointed inquiry on a subject that no one else had dared bring up: Lee. "[Clem] asked [Jackson] his plans about me," Ruth recalled, "and what his intentions were toward his wife." Ruth was affronted by Greenberg's accusatory tone—"[He] treated us as if we had done something bad, as if we were guilty of some sin." Jackson broke down. Afterward, when Ruth demanded to know why Jackson hadn't defended her, he could only say, "It's very complicated."

It had become very complicated indeed. Unable to drive, Ruth felt increasingly trapped by Jackson's unpredictable moods—especially his anger. Everything she did now seemed to anger him. Whole days would pass in mutual sulking. She would fix elaborate meals, big roasts, and he would refuse to eat them. Even more worrisome, he no longer talked of marriage. When Ruth did, Jackson would grow suddenly evasive—"I owe the woman something"—or rehash old fantasies: "We will all live together." He had made no effort to change his will. ("He wasn't that nutty," says Alfonso Ossorio.) She thought more and more about what would happen when Lee returned, and feared being "cast aside and thrown away."

In fact, as Ruth must have sensed at the time and later told a friend, Jackson was already "bored to death" with her. On July 27, he arranged a party to celebrate B. H. Friedman's thirtieth birthday—and, undoubtedly, to avoid another long weekend alone with Ruth. The Friedmans, the Brookses, and the Greenbergs gathered on Fireplace Road that night, and Jackson hid among the revelers, drinking at his new, furious rate of one case of beer a day. The Friedmans found Ruth "coquettish and affectionate" but couldn't hide their surprise "that Jackson could have taken up with a woman like this." At one point during the evening, he exploded at Ruth, "Fuck you," and the party fell silent. "Don't brag," she cooed back. Yet, later that night when the celebration moved to the studio and Jackson gave Friedman his choice among a portfolio of drawings, he also gave Ruth a painting—one of the recent ones that Greenberg had condemned earlier in the evening. (The painting disappeared from the studio after Jackson's death.)

He must have meant it as a parting gift, because the next night, at a party given by Dorothy Norman, he humiliated her with a cruel determination that other guests took as final. After the party, Ruth—"in a white rage" and far drunker than Jackson—threw a furious tantrum. Between great swigs of scotch, she smashed glasses on the kitchen floor until the cupboards were bare, screamed and raved and sobbed until Jackson slapped her hard across the face and she fell at his feet "like a broken doll."

Jackson had slapped her before, often, and she had liked it. But this was different. Not long after the party at Dorothy Norman's, Ruth called Terry Liss at the Elm Tree Inn and told her, in a desperate voice, how Jackson had "beat her up." "She said there was real violence," Liss remembers, "that Jackson had really knocked her around. And I said, 'Look, I have a room in my house. Don't be an ass. Stay with me. What do you need that for?' "

But Ruth never came. Instead, she told Jackson that she had an appointment with her analyst—a lie—and, on Thursday, August 2, took the train to New York. She had been with him less than three weeks.

For the first time in his life, Jackson Pollock was alone. From Stella to Charles to Sande to Lee to Ruth, the chain had remained virtually unbroken for forty-four years. Now he was "free," and the strangeness of it seemed to overwhelm him. Friends saw him that week wandering on the beach, walking by the roadside, driving aimlessly around the dry-grass summerscape, or parked in front of familiar houses, searching for the courage to knock on a door. When they stopped to talk, the response was always the same: "He said he was very lonely," recalls Millie Liss, "and he hadn't been working." "It was a very bad time for him," according to Nick Carone. "I never saw him so sad." At night, he clung to the phone as to a lifeline, talking for hours, shoulders hunched against the empty house, dialing anyone he thought might talk to him —even old, long-silent friends like Roger Wilcox. He called Tony Smith and eagerly accepted an invitation to New Jersey the following weekend, August 11. One day, soon after Ruth left, a dog appeared around the studio, lost and hungry. Jackson wanted to take it in, but it ran from him. Later that day, he saw the same dog lying by the Montauk road where it had been hit by a car and left to die. Tenderly, he loaded it in his car and rushed it to an animal hospital where he called Nick Carone. "He said he had found the most beautiful dog and asked would we want it if it pulled through. I said yes." Two days later, he came to Carone's house looking "like the walking dead, so, so low." "The dog died," he told Carone. "I've got to go home." "He was unspeakably sad about this dog he didn't even know—literally, so unhappy that he couldn't even talk, he missed it so."

What he missed was Lee. Clearly, he knew he had wronged her. When Carone visited soon after Ruth's departure, he found Jackson "disillusioned with Ruth." He realized the affair was "shit," according to Carone, "that he'd made a horrendous mistake and he *needed* Lee back." He laid plans to join her in Europe at the end of the month so they could come home together. But when he tried to call her in Paris, he was told she had left already for the south of France.

Unknown to Jackson, Lee's plans had changed once again. After spending a week with the Gimpels in the Midi, where she saw a Cézanne show, van Gogh's last landscapes, and the Roman ruins at Arles, she had called Peggy in Venice, only to be spurned. Bitter over what she perceived as efforts to minimize or erase from the record "everything I had done for Pollock" and, undoubtedly, infuriated by reports of the sale of *One* for $8,000 (she had already given away eight of her eleven drip paintings), Peggy not only refused to extend an invitation to Lee, she refused to find a room for her anywhere in Venice. Flabbergasted, Lee returned to Paris in early August and stayed in Paul Jenkins's apartment until she could find a hotel room.

When he couldn't reach Lee, Jackson called her friends, Betsy Zogbaum, Cile Lord, and Patsy Southgate. He took care not to call too late or too drunk. One afternoon, he wandered into the garden of Clement Greenberg's summer house looking "lost" and found Nancy Smith. "He rumbled for a while and twitched around," Smith recalls. "He just looked so miserable. Finally I said, 'Look, what's wrong?'" Jackson lowered his head and looked at her with baleful eyes. "Lee always cuts my fingernails," he said, "and she's away." "The reason he was so miserable," says Smith, "was that his fingernails were driving him crazy and he couldn't cut them himself. He needed Lee for that. So I said, 'If that's all that's bothering you, *I'll* cut them. And I did. And he cried." In a kind of apologetic offering, Jackson tried to stop drinking, or at least not drink as much. From a case of beer a day, he dropped to one or two cans on some days, and even these he occasionally left half full. When Lee came back, he must have told himself, she would be pleased to see how much better he was. And for all his hours of telephoning that week, he never called Ruth Kligman.

He walked the property on Fireplace Road, perhaps thinking about the wall he had planned to build to protect himself from the public eye. He had wanted a high earth barrier, like a dam, but Tony Smith had scoffed, "My God, it would take up half the lawn." He had settled for a post-and-rail fence that Jeffrey Potter and his crew put up. Around back, he sat on the pile of boulders that Potter had dug up with his big tractor shovel and hauled there. James Brooks found him sitting in the grass and gazing at the empty studio, in anguish over "the work left undone." He had said to Ruth, "You know I'm a painter and must get to work very soon now." But he never did. And the sense of worthlessness and failure consumed him. "I'm no good," he would cry out. "I'm no good. I'm a shit." At times like that, staring at the studio, pacing the land, obsessed with moving earth and piling boulders, condemning himself for the months, now years, of idleness, he must have heard his father's voice: "*Your case is sure a problem to me,*" Roy had written him thirty years ago. Roy Pollock had always known that his fifth son was a slacker, a ne'er-do-well: "*the thing to do is to go to work at something where you can gain knowledge and training by practical experience."* Now it must have seemed, by a long circuitous route, Roy had been proven right. Certainly Jackson had never felt more slack, more useless: *"I sometimes feel that my life has been a failure."* Only a few days before, Jackson had climbed to the top of the big pile of boulders and, facing the sunset, urinated on the rocks below, just as his father had done on a hot, bright summer day in the Arizona mountains while Sande's feet played in the transparent stream. Memories arrested in space. *"In this life, we can't undo the things that are past. . . ."* As if, even now, he could, Jackson ran into the house and called Ibram Lassaw, a metal sculptor. "He wanted to learn how to weld," Lassaw remembers, "to work with metal. He didn't talk about sculpture or anything, he just wanted me to teach him the skill."

Thoughts of the past, of Roy, stern and disapproving, must have mingled with thoughts of the present, of Clyfford Still, stern and disapproving. Why else would Jackson have been drawn to the kitchen drawer where he kept Still's letter from the previous December? He read it again, for the hundredth time, and sobbed uncontrollably: *"Is it that you are ashamed of [your show]? Or are you ashamed of what you are willing to take from those who know how to use you to express their contempt for the artist as a man? It's a hell of a price to pay, isn't it?"* He called Nick Carone and begged him to come over. To be alone with this letter, it was clear, was more than he could bear. Carone arrived to find Jackson "devastated." "He was in an absolute state about this thing," Carone remembers. "This touched his *core.* . . . I never saw such weeping."

On Thursday night, August 9, Ruth called. She was coming for the weekend and bringing a friend. Would Jackson meet them at the train station on Saturday morning? Sounding "sullen" and "lost" on the phone, Jackson accepted the news passively; he had been alone long enough. He called Tony Smith to cancel their Friday rendezvous at Luchow's, but Smith was out, taking a friend to the train station. Sensing Jackson's desperation, Jane Smith held him on the phone. "We talked volumes," she remembers. When conversation lagged, she sang to him in her warm, operatic soprano: *"Du meine Liebe, du mein Herz, du meine Wonne, du mein Schmerz . . ."* ("My love, my heart, my delight, my pain . . .") By the time Smith returned, it was after midnight, but Jackson wouldn't let go. "We talked on the phone for a long time . . . very late," Smith said later, describing Jackson as "very tired and depressed." Convinced that only work could reverse his friend's despair, Smith urged him to "get into portraits." "Do a lot of portraits of yourself," he suggested, like van Gogh. "But do *something!*"

The next day, Jackson drove to Stony Hill Farm to return some tools Jeffrey Potter had lent him. Caught on his way out, Potter said not to bother and Jackson mumbled to himself gratefully, "Good. That'll give me an excuse to come again." Even so, he delayed his leaving as long as possible, watching Penny Potter cook and playing with her six-year-old son, Job. Although "obviously miserable," Jackson seemed oddly sober. When he returned to Fireplace Road, however, something—the thought of Ruth's return, perhaps, or just the emptiness—propelled him to El Harris's store for four cases of beer. By the time Sherry and Cile Lord arrived for dinner, he was "drunk and babbling on." After they left, he tried to sleep, but the world was spinning too fast. He stumbled through the clear summer darkness toward the lights in Conrad Marca-Relli's house. Except for the aborted visit during Ruth's stay, the two friends hadn't seen each other in weeks. Marca-Relli was shocked by Jackson's condition. "Now that Jackson really needs help," Marca-Relli thought, "that damn doctor is on vacation." Jackson ran his swollen hands gently over one of Marca-Relli's paintings, barely touching the surface, feeling the texture, as if it were a strange new object just arrived on earth. "God, that's a great feel," he said with a combination of admiration and envy. Then he turned to leave. The last thing Marca-Relli heard him say as he faded into the darkness, looking up into the night sky with wide-open eyes: "Life is beautiful, the trees are beautiful, the sky is beautiful. Why is it that all I can think about is death?"

Ruth's train arrived the next morning about nine. Jackson had slept fitfully, if at all, and had already fought with Jeffrey Potter over a building jack (to level up Lee's new studio?) when Ruth stepped off the train with her friend, Edith Metzger. Ruth could tell instantly that Jackson was in a black mood. He had dressed in dirty clothes and looked "disheveled" next to the two women in their starched summer dresses. The campaign of sabotage began immediately. When Ruth tried to introduce Edith, Jackson merely grunted and walked away. "I hated the impression he was making," she wrote. She wanted to go directly to the house, but Jackson stopped at Cavagnaro's for an "eye-opener." He seemed to take a perverse pleasure in telling her that Blanche, her kitten, had "disappeared." Ruth was crushed. "Maybe Blanche will find her way home," she offered hopefully. "Don't count on it," he countered.

In the bar, Jackson barely looked at Edith, a pretty, petite girl, twenty-five years old, with wide blue eyes, full lips, and short black hair in a feathery cut. A German Jew who had fled with her family from the Nazis before the war, Metzger had, like Ruth, survived a troubled childhood. That was their bond. Her father had died when she was a girl, and she, too, was attracted to older, married men, the most recent being the manager of the beauty salon where she worked as a manicurist and receptionist. That relationship, like Ruth's with Jackson, had recently soured, sending Edith into a tailspin of depression and self-reproach from which she had yet to recover. (Ruth's advice on the train coming out: "Let your fantasy take over, make your wildest dreams come true.") If Jackson had bothered to ask, he might have heard Edith tell her story about "meeting" Hermann Goering. After a Nazi rally in Berlin, Goering had singled her out from the crowd, picked her up, and kissed her. In return, Edith bit him—so hard she could still remember the taste. But Jackson wasn't interested in Edith Metzger.

The house, when they finally arrived, was a mess. Dishes from the previous

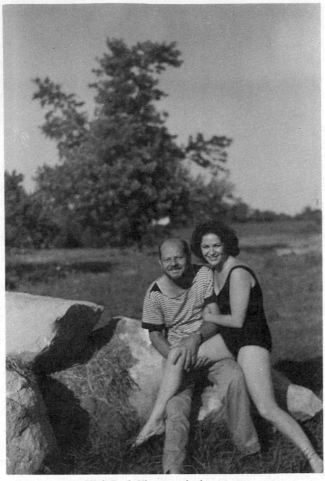

With Ruth Kligman, the last picture

night's dinner with the Lords still sat in the sink. Despite Jackson's pessimism, Ruth spent a few frantic hours looking for the missing kitten while he interrogated the dogs, Gyp and Ahab, as to Blanche's whereabouts. When she finally gave up and prepared lunch, Jackson waved it away and, instead, pulled a bottle of gin from the cupboard. He seemed to be raising the stakes; she had never seen him drink gin before. Ruth wanted to spend the afternoon at the beach and she and Edith changed into bathing suits. The momentary rush of hard liquor and Ruth's determined affections loosened Jackson enough for a photo session in the backyard. With Ruth's bare leg draped suggestively over his knee, he smiled for Edith and the camera, his face so swollen by now that his eyes were mere slits. Then they drove off—but not to the beach. Jackson took them instead to Montauk where they visited James and Charlotte Brooks briefly. "He was really a mess," Charlotte Brooks recalls. "He was sad and very drunk, and he didn't seem to have much feeling for life at all, or for her. We were anxious for them to leave as soon as they could. We didn't know how to cope with him." Coming back, Ruth and Edith expected to stop at the beach, but Jackson drove by without even slowing. As soon as they arrived back on Fireplace Road, he stalked up the stairs to bed, leaving Ruth and Edith alone. They never would get to the beach.

Jackson grilled steaks for dinner again, but mostly he drank—more gin. Ruth made coffee, but he refused it. They fought over plans for the evening. Jackson had been invited to a benefit concert at The Creeks. The idea of a party, especially a society gala, thrilled Ruth. Jackson complained about the cost—three dollars per person—and called Clement Greenberg to ask if he was going. "He never talked about money before," Greenberg says. "It was out of character. Then he said he wasn't dressed well enough. I think he was just looking for an excuse." The argument went back and forth for more than an hour: Ruth thought "maybe it would be fun"; he "didn't want to face a couple of hundred people." When she acquiesced, he changed his mind. They dressed —Ruth in her best white linen dress with "a lovely scoop neckline and back," Edith in a blue print dress, Jackson in a black velvet shirt—and sped off toward East Hampton still bickering about whether to go or not.

By now, the gin and the sleepless night were beginning to show. The car accelerated and slowed as Jackson's head bobbed up and down in a struggle to stay awake. The Oldsmobile, its top open to the muggy evening air, weaved back and forth on the road. Edith and Ruth exchanged worried glances as they lurched through the town and turned right onto the Montauk Highway. Edith whispered, "Ruth, he's drunk. Let's go home." Finally, just across from the entrance to The Creeks, at the intersection of Airport Road, Jackson pulled off the highway and slumped behind the wheel. Soon a policeman appeared. "Good evening, Mr. Pollock. Is there anything the matter?" he asked. Jackson replied, suddenly alert, "Nothing's wrong; we were just talking." The policeman left, but moments later Roger Wilcox stopped on his way to the concert, which was scheduled to begin at nine. Alarmed by Jackson's "pasty" look, Wilcox got out of the car while Lucia and their guest, Frederick Kiesler, waited. "Hey, Jackson," he called. "What are you doing? Aren't you going to this musical thing?" "I don't feel so well," Jackson replied faintly. "I feel kinda sick, I feel terrible. I'm not sure I'm going to the party." At that, Wilcox noticed, Ruth and Edith squirmed. "They wanted to go to that party," he remembers. "They were all dolled up, and they didn't want to go back and be stranded with a dull evening." By now, Ruth must have felt frustrated. She hadn't brought Edith all the way to East Hampton to spend the night in front of the television set.

This time, apparently, Ruth prevailed. They would go to the concert. But first Jackson needed to recover; even by his standards, he was in no condition for company. Hoping that some food might sober him up, they drove to a nearby bar where Jackson, barely able to walk, found a telephone and called The Creeks.

Alfonso Ossorio was already in the music room introducing Leonard Hambro, a concert pianist, when the phone rang. The maid took the message: Mr. Pollock would be late.

But now there was a new problem: Edith Metzger wouldn't get back in the car. Jackson's day-long campaign of terror had succeeded too well, with Edith at least. "I'm going to call for help, call a cab; I must do something," she told Ruth, her voice shrill and disapproving—like Lee's. The argument threatened to explode into a scene until Jackson, finally overcome, passed out.

But in that sleep, he must have continued to hear Lee's voice—fierce, mocking, independent—for he awoke in a blinding rage. He ordered the two women into the car and announced that they were going home. Edith again refused. "She was crying because she was so nervous and scared to death," Ruth remembers. Her fear only infuriated Jackson. "Get her back in here," he ordered Ruth, "or we're not going anywhere." Obediently, Ruth tried to coax Edith into the car. "But, Ruth," Edith protested, "he's drunk. I don't want to drive with him." "No, he's not; he's fine," Ruth lied. "I promise you we're going home. Come on! Get in!" When Edith finally relented and climbed into the back seat—as far away from Jackson as possible—he jammed the accelerator to the floor and the V-8 Oldsmobile rocketed into the street.

Edith began screaming almost immediately.

Within minutes, they skidded onto Fireplace Road, heading north, through the darkness, toward home. Edith screamed, "Stop the car, let me out!" But the screaming only seemed to make Jackson stronger, to make the car go faster. Ruth tried to calm her—"Edith, stop making a fuss. He's fine"—but she, too, felt a rush of terror as the car accelerated onto the long stretch of straight, deserted road between North Main and Gardiner Avenue. Ruth had been in the car before when Jackson lost his senses, when he jettisoned the world and existed, for a moment, only in the furious forward motion of speed, bent, it seemed, on some destination in midair. She shouted, "Please. Jackson, stop! Jackson, don't do this," but she knew he was out of reach. Gripping the wheel in his big hands, he leaned forward and hunched his shoulders against the winds that roared around them, roared so loud that even Edith's screaming seemed strangely diminished. In the hurling pandemonium, Ruth stared at Jackson in disbelief: his mouth drawn up in what looked like a laugh, but could have been terror, his eyes staring wide-open at the road ahead "as if he expected to lift off at any minute." Edith screamed again and again, "Let me out. LET ME OUT." She tried to stand up, as if to leap from the car, arms flailing, screaming—"LET ME OUT"—but the wind threw her back into the seat. Suddenly the road began to curve, just slightly, to the left, and the dark gray ribbon of concrete that whistled beneath them turned to oil-black asphalt. Locals knew that this innocent-looking bend in the road and the shift in road surface packed a "whomp" for any car that ignored it. Jackson himself had slowed down hundreds of times when approaching it. But not this time. The heavy Oldsmobile bottomed hard and jumped the high crown in the middle of the road. Once on the other side of that crown, nothing Jackson did could prevent the car from veering right. The right tires, front and rear, hit the soft shoulder in an explosion of gravel and dirt. Edith screamed. Jackson yanked the wheel to the left, too hard. The car careened across the road, leapt the crown again, and lunged sidelong into the brush on the left shoulder. For the next 172 feet, the big car danced at the edge of the roadway, on and off, brushing past big trees at sixty or seventy miles an hour. Edith buried her head behind the seat. Ruth thought, "This is it, it's happening. It's my death." Jackson clutched the wheel and watched, frozen, as the world hurtled past him in the darkness, beyond control. Finally the car lost its tenuous grip on the pavement and plunged into the underbrush. About seventeen feet from the road, the left front fender caught two resolute young elms, and the car spun wildly counterclockwise. Still speeding, but backwards now, it lurched another twenty feet before flipping end over end, front end over back, like a tossed coin. Jackson and Ruth were catapulted out of the front seat and into the woods, where Ruth landed safely. Edith clung to the car and it fell, upside down, on top of her.

For an instant, everything was silent—except the air rushing by. Escape velocity: he had finally reached it. The car was gone, Ruth was gone, Edith was gone, Lee was gone, Stella was gone. He was free: not falling, flying; flung from the tumbling car in a straight trajectory fifty feet long and ten feet off the ground. He covered it in less than a second, but, according to the coroner's report, was fully conscious, arrested in space, until he hit the tree.

It was nine o'clock the next morning in Paris when the phone rang in Paul Jenkins's apartment. Clement Greenberg was on the line, his voice distant and hoarse from a night of grieving and explaining. Jenkins answered the phone. Lee was across the room, sitting near the door to the balcony. When Jenkins heard the news, he turned to her and started to speak. But Lee knew already. The message had flown across the Atlantic by another, faster route. "Jackson is dead," she told him. Jenkins would never forget what followed. Lee started to scream—great, piercing, primitive screams, like the howling of a wounded animal, as if nothing so fine or so limited as human could contain her titanic grief. She "threw herself against the wall," Jenkins remembers, "she wanted to hurt herself." For a second, he feared she would fling herself off the balcony, to join him. "No, Jackson," she wailed again and again, "Jackson, Jackson, *Jackson*," as if to demand him back from the dead. How *dare* he go without her? How *dare* he leave her? Or had she left him? Jenkins grabbed her and pulled her onto the couch where the screaming, the heart-stopping screaming, went on—"Jackson, Jackson, Jackson"—until it was finally drowned out in a cascade of tears.

EPILOGUE

GLACIAL ERRATIC

A funeral service was held for Jackson Pollock at the Springs Chapel on Wednesday, August 15, 1956. Due to the extent of his injuries, the casket remained closed, although Hans Namuth tried to get a picture of the body while it was still in the funeral parlor. Lee, who had flown back from Paris on the first available flight, sat by herself in the front pew. She refused to sit with the Pollock family. Earlier that week, when Stella had tried to embrace her, Lee pushed her away, saying, "Where were you when he needed you?"

So the Pollock family sat in the second pew, leaving Lee alone in the spotlight. The other mourners were surprised at how little emotion she showed. One described her expression as "enigmatic." "It made me think I must be feeling worse than she did," recalled Gina Knee. "I decided she must be holding something back: relief." Lee had asked Clement Greenberg to give the eulogy, but when Greenberg insisted on saying a few words about Edith Metzger—"the girl Jackson killed"—Lee turned instead to the Reverend George Nicholson, pastor of the Amagansett Presbyterian Church, who read a passage from Romans 8 which many of the mourners found awkwardly irrelevant. In the middle of the service, someone in the jammed, sweltering chapel let out a long, plaintive wail. Those in the back and at the windows thought it was Lee. But it was Reuben Kadish.

A smaller group of mourners gathered after the service at the Green River Cemetery where Lee had bought three adjacent plots on the high ground at the far end of the cemetery under some trees. At the graveside, Lee once again chose to stand alone. Charles, Frank, Sande, Reginald Isaacs, Ben Heller, and James Brooks (wearing Jackson's dark suit) served as pallbearers. By the end of the short service, many were in tears. Sande and Reuben Kadish, who were standing near Jackson's whimpering dogs, wept uncontrollably. Willem de

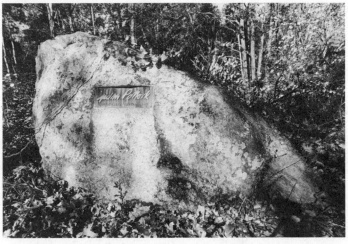

Pollock's gravestone. © Susan Wood

Kooning and a few others lingered until the gravediggers uncovered the mound of sandy soil and began shoveling it into the hole.

A few days later, Jeffrey Potter hauled the biggest stone from the pile in Jackson's backyard and placed it on the grave as a marker. But Lee didn't think it was big enough. After days of searching, John Little finally found one that was—a huge forty-ton boulder that lay mostly buried near the East Hampton town dump. It was one of the "glacial erratics" that studded the area, a chunk of granite brought from far away by some ancient ice sheet and deposited here, incongruously, in the potato fields of Long Island: a monument to timeless, ineffable forces of nature. Jeffrey Potter dutifully dug it out and, with a giant winch and a team of men, wrestled it onto Jackson's grave, taking care not to crush the coffin.

Soon after the funeral, Stella Pollock left Deep River and returned to Tingley, Iowa, to care for her brother Les—the task she had left off sixty years before. "I just had to do something for a change," she wrote a relative. "After Jackson was killed it was such a schock. . . . He is gone and we cant bring him back his work is over and he is at rest but we cant forget him." Not quite two years later, on April 20, 1958, Stella Pollock died in a hospital in Creston, Iowa. The cause of death was listed as "circulatory problems in her legs," but when the four surviving Pollock brothers gathered in Tingley for her funeral, they learned that Stella had killed herself by refusing to eat. "She made a decision, a conscious decision that she wasn't going to live any more," says Charles. "After Jack died, she just stopped wanting to live."

Five years later, in December 1963, Sande lay dying of leukemia in a Boston hospital. Years of working with chemicals in a secret government defense plant and a lifetime of duty and frustration had taken their toll. But "he was a fighter right up to the end," according to Charles, who sat by his bedside during the final days. On the last night before they turned off the life-support machines, in a reverie, Sande thanked Charles for sending the copies of the *Dial* to Orland. "He said they meant a lot to him and Jack," Charles remembers.

Arloie was at his bedside, too, and when the end finally came, she breathed a sigh of relief, then slipped quietly out the door. In the privacy of her room, she uncoiled her extravagant hair, letting it fall to her waist, removed all of her clothes, closed herself in the shower, and wept inconsolably.

Lee Krasner lived for another twenty years, during which she produced the biggest, boldest, most brilliantly colored works of her career, many of them derived from Jackson's *Easter and the Totem,* and most of them painted in Jackson's studio. To the end, she continued to collide with family and friends and with the art world, looking in vain for another match. On June 20, 1984, at the age of seventy-five, riddled with arthritis and almost completely alienated from the world, she lost her energy for more collisions and died. The death certificate cited "natural causes."

ACKNOWLEDGMENTS

Two writers working for seven years each on the same book can run up more debts than the Federal Government. In those years, we have spoken to more than eight hundred people—many of them three or four times, often for hours, sometimes for days at a time. Their words fill more than eighteen thousand pages of transcripts. For those who choose to calculate such things, that puts us approximately ten million words in their debt, of which we have repaid on the preceding pages a scant quarter million or so. In a woefully inadequate but well-meaning effort to make up the shortfall, we would like to list the names of all those who made this book possible and deserve to share the credit—but not the blame—for its contents.

First, of course, is Lee Krasner Pollock. Despite deteriorating health and a general intolerance for writers, she spoke with us seven times before her death in 1984, providing many insights into facets of Jackson's life to which she alone could bear witness. In addition, her nephew, Ronald Stein, gave us access to a cache of Lee's papers never before seen by researchers. To supplement our interviews with Lee, we sought out those few friends in whom she confided, both before and after Jackson's death. We also discovered, to our surprise, that while she rarely spoke with candor to interviewers from newspapers and magazines based in New York, she could be surprisingly frank with out-of-town journalists—the result, apparently, of a lifelong New York provincialism.

Jackson's brothers, Charles, Jay, and Frank, spent many days with us and provided the most enjoyable moments of the last seven years. (Frank even joined us on a road trip to visit some of the Pollocks' childhood homes.) It cannot have been altogether pleasant for them to have two more writers interviewing them about their youngest brother—a brother who, even in success, was not notably generous toward them. Still, they were exceedingly generous and kind to us, as were their wives: Sylvia (Charles), Alma (Jay), Marie (Frank), and Arloie (Sande), as well as Charles's first wife, Elizabeth. Jackson's nieces and nephews were also very helpful: Jeremy Capillé, Karen Del Pilar, Francesca Pollock, Jonathan Pollock, and Jason McCoy. (Jason, who later became a close associate of Lee's, was especially generous with his profound knowledge and understanding of the works of both his aunt and his uncle.) We join all the Pollock family in mourning the recent deaths of Jay and Charles.

Lee's sister, Ruth Stein, though not as contentious as Lee, proved equally articulate and had a remarkable ability, while relating family stories, to call her sister back to life. Our thanks also to Ruth's son, Ronald Stein; Lee's niece, Rena Kanokogi; Lee's sister, Esther Gersing; and Esther's son, Seymour Glickman.

Several close friends of Jackson's, at various times in his life, were of inestimable assistance, notably Peter Busa, Nicholas Carone, Reuben Kadish, and Roger Wilcox.

The other interviewees who were generous with their time and recollections, who provided us with information, or who supported us in other important ways, were Mary Abbott, Lionel Abel, William Abel, Gretchen Adams, Ann Allen, Sam Allen, Lawrence Alloway, Delores Ambrose, Ruth Ann Applehof, Pamela Arceneaux, Margaret Louise Archbold, R. L. Archbold, Dore Ashton, Susan Ball, Susan Barker, Sally Bartolotta, Carey Bartram, John I. H. Baur, Ethel Baziotes, Eleanor Becker, Madelon Bedell, Mimi Behrfeld, Leland Bell, Charles Bennett, Ward Bennett, T. P. Benton, Thomas Floyd Benton, Bill Berkson, Paul Biber, Catharina Biddle, Livingston Biddle, Pat Bigler, Leroy Birch, Nell Blaine, Peter Blake, Gabe Bloomenthal, Norman Bluhm, Leonard Bocour, Mary Lincoln Bonnell, Grace Borgenicht, Nicole Bouche, Charles Boultenhouse, Margaret Bouton, Finley Bown, Ruby Boyd, Paul Brach, Ramona Bradley, Walter Brandes, Myrtle Branstetter, Billy Breckenridge, Ernest Briggs, Ruth Brine, Alexander Bacon Brook, Charlotte Park Brooks, James Brooks, Lee Bryant, David Budd, Fritz Bultman, Jeanne Bultman, Eda Bunce, John Bunce, Olga Burroughs, Polly Burroughs, Marietta Bushnell, Marie Butler, Reginald Cabral, Nicolas Calas, Adele Callaway, John Callison, Lawrence Campbell, Stephen Campbell, Fred Cannastra, Lynn Cannastra, Pat Carlton-Ramakrishnan, Mary Carey, Catherine Carlin, Matthew Carone, Caroll Carr, Blanche Carstensen, Cecil Carstensen, Peg Cassidy, Leo Castelli, Donnelly Leo Casto, Alvi Cavagnaro, Giorgio Cavallon, Herman Cherry, Pari Choate, Paul Christopher, Terry Citarella, Bill Clark, Betty Clausen, Stuart Cleek, Margaret Coe, Cynthia Waterbury Cole, John Cole, Mary Coles, Oscar Collier, Mike Collins, Joseph Conlon, Shirley Connell, Edward Cook, John Cook, Lois Anderson Cook, Marjorie Cook, Marie Cooley, Clare Cooter, Edith Cooter, Robert Cooter, Steve Cotherman, Irene Crippen, Alexandra Cromwell, Gilbert Crowell, Alan Curl, Anne Cybowski, Michael Dalton, Sr., Whitney Darrow, Jr., Gene Davis, Glenda Davis, Hazel Finch Davis, Deborah Daw, Fielding Dawson, James Dawson, Martha Anderson Dawson, Emile de Antonio, Elizabeth de Cuevas, Sylvia de Cuevas, Kay Deering, Dorothy Dehner, Joseph Delaney, Josephine Del Deo, Salvatore Del Deo, Joseph DeMeio, Tibor de Nagy, Christie Dennis, Violet Staub de Laszlo, Rudy De Santi, Hester Diamond, Thomas Dillon, Dane Dixon, Mary Louise Dodge, David Dozier, Marjel Dozier, Ted Dragon, Elizabeth Duncan, Anita Duquette, Ray Eames, Anne Edgerton, Norma Edwards, Tamaria Eichelburg, Josephine Eighme, Margaret Eighme, Marietta Eighme, Betty Ellison, Ruth Van Cleve Emerson, Mary Ellen Engle, Werner Engel, Tom Enman, Jimmy Ernst, Julie Espinoza, Lisa Farrington, Mary Ann Fast, Richard Fast, Nina Federico, Morton Feldman, William C. Fellersen, Herbert Ferber, Ira Ferguson, Thomas Hornsby Feril, Marie Ferre, Rae Ferren, Margaret Fetty, Leslie Fiedler, Lyman Field, Jeffrey Figley, Daisy Finch, Helen Finch, Randall Finch, Sylvia Fink, Louis Finkelstein, Minnie Fitzgerald, Sara Fitzsimmons, Audrey Flack, Phyllis Fleiss, Christopher Fluhr, Lisa Fonssagrives, Xavier Fourcade, Muriel Francis, Abby Friedman, B. H. Friedman, Sanford Friedman, Gottlieb Friesinger, Louis Fusari,

Edward Garza, Jerome Garza, Emmanuel Ghent, David Gibbs, Joe Glasco, Arnold Glimcher, Grace Glueck, Augustus Goertz, Julia Goldsmith, Bertram Goodman, Cynthia Goodman, Robert Goodnough, Eugene C. Goossen, Ron Gorchov, Fred Gorstein, David Graham, Jane Graves, Clement Greenberg, Balcomb Greene, Pamela Grettinger, Joel Gribetz, Chaim Gross, Renee Gross, Isidore Grossman, John Gruen, Robert Gwathmey, Barbara Hale, Niki Hale, Robert Beverly Hale, Richard Hall, Catherine Halleman, Marion Halperin, Helen Halverson, Fowler Hamilton, Milo Hamilton, Mildred Hanney, Grace Hartigan, Jane Hartsook, Lois Hartzler, Gary Hassell, Janet Hauck, Francis Hayden, Christine Heag, Ben Heller, Dora Heller, Eleanor Hempstead, Joseph Henderson, Allan Herrick, Clair Heyer, Hazel Heyer, Rebecca Hicks, Dorothy Hitt, Sheila Hoban, Kristin Hoermann, Renoda Hoffman, Harry Holtzman, Budd Hopkins, Carolyn Hopping, Ettabelle Horgan, Axel Horn, Ora Horton, Zetta McCoy Houston, Richard Howard, Elizabeth Wright Hubbard II, Merle Hubbard, Robert Hughes, Vivienne Allbright Hughes, Estelle Hulse, Edward Hults, Ted Hults, Roger Humphries, Edys Hunter, Kermit Hunter, Sam Hunter, Laurence Hurlburt, Mary Anne Hurley, Jill Hutchinson, Max Hutchinson, Reginald Isaacs, Harry Jackson, Ken Jackson, Mary Jackson, Ralph Jackson, Sr., Ward Jackson, Larry James, Sidney Janis, Paul Jenkins, Earl Johnsmeyer, Buffie Johnson, Joyce Johnson, Keith Johnson, Philip Johnson, Wesley Johnson, Jr., Wesley Johnson, Sr., Wilbur Johnson, Emily Jones, Mervin Jules, Barbara Kadish, Thomas Kadomato, Jacob Kainen, Gerome Kamrowski, Shizuko Kato, Edgar Kaufmann, Jr., Nathaniel Kaz, Marjorie Keene, Chris Keller, Carlton Kelsey, Barbara Kiburz, John Kiburz, Lillian Olaney Kiesler, Ari Kiev, Lincoln Kirstein, Ruth Kligman, Stewart Klonis, Esther Klotz, Craig Klyver, Carolyn Knute, George Koerner, Hilton Kramer, Mary McClure Kreuzer, Maria Piacenza Kron, Patsy Jean La Bay, Lilly Kuida, Melvin Lader, Ellen Landau, Doug Langdon, Ernestine Lassaw, Ibram Lassaw, Minnabelle Laughlin, Margie Lawrence, Berthe Pacifico Laxineta, John Lee, Mark Lee, Harold Lehman, Adele Lerner, Joe LeSueur, Gail Levin, Carl Lightner, Donald Lightner, Helen Lightner, Joseph Liss, Millie Liss, Terry Liss, Jacqueline Little, John Little, Josephine Little, Mildred Lowe, George Long, Cile Downs Lord, Iris Lord, Sheridan Lord (confirmation only), Eleanor Lynch, Donna Mack, Irma Macon, Dale Maddux, Ron Magliozzi, Beatrice Ribak Mandelman, Conrad Marca-Relli, Charlie Marder, Karleen Marienthal, Edna Martin, Irving Markowitz, John Marquand, Maria-Gaetana Matisse, Roberto Matta, Peter Matthiessen (confirmation only), Herbert Matter, Mercedes Matter, Charlie Mattox, Patricia Maye, Jack Mayer, Barbara McCandless, Dean McClure, Donald McClure, Margaret Ann McClure, Paul McClure, Robert McDaniel, Joseph McGie, Marie McGilvrey, Evelyn Minsch McGinn, Dudley McGovern, Eleanor McKee, William McKim, Hazel Guggenheim McKinley, Donald McKinney, Gordon McMurphy, William McNaught, George McNeil, Kynaston McShine, Norman Mead, Joseph Meert, George Mercer, Ted Meriam, Janet Michaelieu, Robert Michels, Wallace Milam, Dorothy Miller, E. Roger Miller, George Sid Miller, Howard Miller, Sheldon Miller, Sylvia Miller, William Miller, Arthur Millier, Jr., Sarah Millier, John Millwater, Al Minnick, Miki Minsch, Akinobu Mori, Carol Mori, Laverne Mori, Atsuko Moriuchi, Gunji Moriuchi, Gilbert Morrill, Vince Moses, Elizabeth Mudgett, Rose Muliere, Lee Mullican, Lucia Hurtado Mullican, Lewis Mumford, Sophia Mumford, Franklin Murphy, Jean Murray, Eva Myer, John Bernard Myers, Sam Naifeh, Hans Namuth, Steven Nash, Elizabeth Nelson, Terence Netter, Annalee Newman (interviewed by David Peretz), Constantine Nivola, Linda Nochlin, John Nopel, Barbara Novak, Lorraine O'Dell,

Margaret Oglesby, Douglas Ohlson, Gordon Onslow-Ford, Frank Orser, Nicole O'Shea, Alfonso Ossorio, Frances Overholtzer, Wayne Overholtzer, Marina Pacini, Martin Pajeck, Raymond Parker, Hester Grimm Patrick, Tom Patterson, Philip Pavia, Jane Pearce, Lori Pellissero, David Peretz, Cula Perry, Gustaf Peterson, Olga Peterson, Vita Peterson, Kay Pettit, Eleanor Piacenza, Santo Piacenza, Elinor Poindexter, Charles Porter, David Porter, Neal Primm, Jay Pullins, Tim Purdy, John Queenan, Arthur Railton, Harry Rand, Peggi Randolph, William Rayner, Becky Reis, Milton Resnick, Merrill Rueppel, Francis Riddell, Ellen Schreck Rifley, Joyce Ritter, Ed Robertson, Selden Rodman, Patricia Rolf, Dorothy Rosamond, May Tabak Rosenberg, Patia Rosenberg, Charles Rozaire, Harriet Rubin, Grant Rusk, John Russell, David Ryffe, Lucia Autorino Salemme, Irving Sandler, Martica Sawin, George Schaefer, Miriam Schapiro, Nene Schardt, Abraham Schlemowitz, Arlene Schnitzer, Lucile Schoppe, Jon Schueler, Charloma Schwankovsky, Nancy Schwartz, Rachel Scott, Dorothy Seiberling, Mary Kay Simkhovitch, Edwin Sharp, Jim Shepperd, Gertrude Shibley, Kathleen Shorthall, Stefa Siegel, Jim Sleeper, David Slivka, Graziella Smith, Jane Smith, Marvin Smith, Nancy Smith, Thomas Smith, Joseph Solman, Ruth Solyer, Herman Somberg, Syd Solomon, Wayne Somes, Stephanie Sonora, Carol Southern, Patricia Southgate, Eloise Spaeth, Christopher Spingarn, Marshall Sprague, Saul Steinberg, James Stephenson, Hedda Sterne, Margot Stewart, Bayrd Still, Frances Stinchfield, Michael Stolbach, Cathy Stover, Wally Strautin, William Swafford, Gladys Swearingen, James Johnson Sweeney, Russ Sweet, Margaret Taft, Allene Talmage, Roy Tarbt, Tom Tarwater, Judy Throm, Janet Tidrick, Clayton Tirking, Araks Tolegian, Aram Tolegian, Michael Tolegian, Jane Tomassian, Abigail Little Tooker, E. Fuller Torrey, W. Lester Trauch, Evelyn Porter Trowbridge, Jock Truman, LeRoy Tucker, Marcia Tucker, Karl Turnquist, Ralph Turnquist, Wally Tworkov, Lee Tyson, John Van Alstine, Esteban Vicente, Harriet Vicente, Marta Vivas, Catherine Viviano, Margaret Viviano, Jean Volkmer, Lucy Voulgaris, Lee Vrooman, Elsie Wackerman, Otto Wackerman, Ellen Waggoner, Doris Wagner, Samuel Wagstaff, Theodore Wahl, James Wall, Lillian Wahrow, Helen Walker, Eleanor Ward, Joan Ward, Sandra Weiner, Karen Weiss, Wendy Weld, Hazel Hawthorne Werner, Steve Wheeler, Helen Wheelwright, Enez Whipple, Jane Wickiser, Lowell Wilbur, Donna Jean Williams, Dorothy Williams, Helen Finch Wilson, Reginald Wilson, Cathy Wirtala, Judith Wolfe, Shirley Wood, Susan Wood, Mary Woods, Irene Worth, Barbara Woytowicz, C. L. Wysuph, Athos Zacharias, Leonard Zick, Jr., Elizabeth Zogbaum.

We want also to express our appreciation to those Pollock scholars who made our work so much easier. Without the fine catalogue raisonné by Francis V. O'Connor and Eugene V. Thaw, our research task would have been infinitely more complicated and burdensome. O'Connor's Ph.D. dissertation on Jackson's early years, "The Genesis of Jackson Pollock," and his catalogue for the Museum of Modern Art were also extremely helpful. (Our gratitude, too, to Mr. Thaw—president of the Pollock-Krasner foundation as well as a Pollock scholar—for giving us access to the restricted Pollock-Krasner archives at the Archives of American Art and for his generous permission to reproduce Jackson's paintings and to quote from unpublished writings by Pollock and Krasner.) Jeffrey Potter's oral biography of Pollock, *To a Violent Grave*, not only provided important material, it directed us to key sources from whom we were able to secure similar material for our own use. Also helpful were the interviews in "Who Was Jackson Pollock?" by Francine du Plessix and Cleve Gray as well as those in *The*

Party's Over Now by John Gruen. Deborah Solomon's recent biography—begun after we began ours—added some documentary items that eluded us. *Love Affair*, Ruth Kligman's memoir of her relationship with Pollock, remains an important source, despite occasional romantic excesses. William Rubin's many articles on Pollock are probably the most enlightening body of critical writings on his art.

Most important of all, undoubtedly, was B. H. Friedman's biography, *Jackson Pollock: Energy Made Visible*. It was the road map that gave us our bearings in many initially unfamiliar areas of Pollock's life. Friedman himself, despite disagreeing with us on some points, provided us with gracious and valuable assistance. For Lee Krasner, the two principal scholarly sources were Ellen Gross Landau's Ph.D. dissertation on Krasner's early years and Barbara Rose's catalogue for the retrospective exhibition that she curated for the Houston Museum of Fine Arts. Lee's dealer and friend, Robert Miller, was also extremely generous with his time, support, and valuable insights.

Paul Brach, Giovanni Favretti, Leslie Fiedler, and S. Frederick Starr all very graciously agreed to read the manuscript for us, no small favor given its length. They caught numerous errors and offered many valuable suggestions. Dr. David Peretz worked with us from the beginning of the project, helping to refine some of the psychological concepts which inform the book, especially regarding Pollock's childhood and his relationship to Lee Krasner. Donald McKinney, who became a close friend of Lee's during the many years he represented the Pollock estate at the Marlborough Gallery, helped us understand Lee's complex relationship to Jackson's art and, in the process, became a friend of ours.

Over the course of several years, a number of people have helped shoulder the enormous burdens of transcribing interviews and collecting research materials from various libraries. In particular, we should thank Ennis Bengul, Jim Biester, Jan Ellis, Avon Fair, Mari Hoashi, Ted Hults, Mike Jacula, Derek Janssen, Robert Kurilla, Miriam Kuznets, Diana Lemchak, Edmund Levin, Martha Shopmyer, Rosemary Sneeringer, and Robert Taylor.

Our agent Connie Clausen deserves a special award for her patience and friendship through what seemed to her an endless ordeal. Our editor at Clarkson N. Potter, Carol Southern, gave the manuscript both conscientious editorial scrutiny and loving support, a rare and marvelous combination from which the book has benefited in innumerable ways. Designer Barbara Richer and production supervisor Teresa Nicholas have produced a handsome volume, despite formidable obstacles. The copy editors, Donna Ryan and Mark McCauslin, performed a similar miracle on a vast, unwieldy manuscript. Finally, our gratitude goes to the many people at Crown Publishers who have given us their support over the years, including Phyllis Fleiss, Bruce Harris, Nancy Kahan, Susan Magrino, Alan Mirken, Michelle Sidrane, Gael Towey, and, more recently, S. I. Newhouse, Jr.

SELECTED BIBLIOGRAPHY

Abel, Lionel. *The Intellectual Follies: A Memoir of the Literary Venture in New York and Paris.* New York: Norton, 1984.

Adams, James Truslow. *The Epic of America.* Boston: Little, Brown, 1931.

Ades, Dawn. *Dada and Surrealism,* 1974. Reprint. London, Thames & Hudson, 1974.

Allen, Frederick Lewis. *Since Yesterday: The 1930s in America, September 3, 1929–September 3, 1939,* 1939. Reprint. New York: Harper & Row, 1972.

Alloway, Lawrence. Exhibition catalogue. *Jackson Pollock: Paintings, Drawings and Watercolors from the Collection of Lee Krasner Pollock.* London: Marlborough Fine Art, June 1961.

———, and Mary Davis MacNaughton. *Adolph Gottlieb: A Retrospective.* New York: The Arts, 1981.

Art of This Century. Exhibition catalogue. *Jackson Pollock.* Introduction by James Johnson Sweeney. New York: Art of This Century, 1943.

Ashton, Dore. *The New York School: A Cultural Reckoning,* 1973. Reprint. New York: Penguin, 1979.

———. *Yes, but ... A Critical Study of Philip Guston.* New York: Viking, 1976.

Baigell, Matthew. *Thomas Hart Benton.* New York: Abrams, 1975.

Barrett, William. *The Truants: Adventures Among the Intellectuals.* Garden City, N.Y.: Doubleday, 1982.

Barr, Alfred H., Jr. Exhibition catalogue. *Cubism and Abstract Art.* New York: Museum of Modern Art, 1936.

———. *Matisse: His Art and His Public.* New York: Museum of Modern Art, 1951.

Benton, Thomas Hart. *An American in Art: A Professional and Technical Autobiography.* Lawrence: The University Press of Kansas, 1969.

———. *An Artist in America.* 4th rev. ed. Columbia: University of Missouri Press, 1983.

Bernstein, Irving. *The Lean Years.* Boston: Houghton Mifflin, 1960.

Biddle, George. *An American Artist's Story.* Boston: Little, Brown, 1939.

Blavatsky, Helena P. *The Secret Doctrine: The Synthesis of Science, Religion, and Philosophy.* Vol. 1. Pasadena: Theosophical University Press, 1974.

Bourne, Peter G., and Ruth Fox, eds. *Alcoholism: Progress in Research and Treatment.* New York: Academic Press, 1973.

Branstetter, Myrtle. *Pioneer Hunters of the Rim.* Mesa, Ariz.: Norm's Publishing House, 1976.

Braun, Emily, and Thomas Branchick. *Thomas Hart Benton: The America Today Murals.* New York: The Equitable, 1985.

Brittain, Vera. *Thrice a Stranger.* New York: Macmillan, 1938.

Brodovitch, Alexey. "Jackson Pollock," *Portfolio.* Cincinnati: Zebra Press, 1951.

Brown, Milton W. *American Painting from the Armory Show to the Depression.* Princeton, N.J.: Princeton University Press, 1955.

Burke, John. *Buffalo Bill: The Noblest Whiteskin.* New York: Putnam, 1973.

Burroughs, Polly. *Thomas Hart Benton: A Portrait.* Garden City, N.Y.: Doubleday, 1981.

Bychowski, Gustav, and J. Louise Despert, eds. *Specialized Technniques in Psychotherapy.* New York: Basic Books, 1952.

Campbell, Bruce F. *Ancient Wisdom Revived: A History of the Theosophical Movement.* Berkeley: University of California Press, 1980.

Carmean, A. E., and Eliza E. Rathbone. Exhibition catalogue. *American Art at Mid-Century: The Subjects of the Artist.* Washington, D.C.: National Gallery of Art, 1978.

Carruth, Hayden. *The Bloomingdale Papers.* Athens: The University of Georgia Press, 1975.

Cennini, Cennino. *The Book of the Art of Cennino Cennini: A Contemporary Practical Treatise on Quatrocento Painting.* Edited and translated by Christiana J. Herringham. London: Allen & Unwin, 1899.

———. *A Treatise on Painting.* Translated by Mrs. Merrifield. London: Lumley, 1844.

Centre Georges Pompidou. Exhibition catalogue. *Jackson Pollock.* Paris: Centre Georges Pompidou, Musée National d'Art Moderne, 1982.

Chase, W. Parker. *New York: The Wonder City, 1932.* Reprint. New York: New York Bound, 1983.

Chipp, Herschel B., ed. *Theories of Modern Art: A Source Book by Artists and Critics.* Berkeley: University of California Press, 1968.

Coe, Ralph T. Exhibition catalogue. *Sacred Circles: Two Thousand Years of North American Indian Art.* Kansas City, Mo.: Nelson Gallery of Art–Atkins Museum of Fine Arts, 1976.

Cohen, Sol. *Notable American Women, 1607–1950: A Biographical Dictionary.* Cambridge, Mass.: Harvard University Press, 1971.

Collins, Mabel. *Light on the Path.* Pasadena: Theosophical University Press, 1971.

Congdon, Don, ed. *The Thirties: A Time to Remember.* New York: Simon & Schuster, 1962.

Conn, Howard F., ed. *Current Therapy: 1954: Latest Approved Methods of Treatment for the Practicing Physician.* Philadelphia: Saunders, 1954.

Cowley, Malcolm. *Exile's Return: A Narrative of Ideas.* New York: Norton, 1934.

Craven, Thomas. *Modern Art.* Rev. ed. Garden City, N.Y.: Halcyon House, 1950.

———. *Thomas Hart Benton.* New York: Associated American Artists, 1939.

Crunden, Robert M. *Ministers of Reform: The Progressives'*

Achievement in American Civilization, 1889–1920. New York: Basic Books, 1982.

Dawson, Fielding. *An Emotional Memoir of Franz Kline.* New York: Pantheon Books, 1967.

Diamonstein, Barbaralee, ed. *The Art World: A Seventy-Five Year Treasury of Artnews.* New York: Artnews Books, 1977.

———, ed. *Inside New York's Art World.* New York: Rizzoli, 1979.

Douglas, Ann. *The Feminization of American Culture.* New York: Knopf, 1977.

Dreier, Mary E. *Margaret Dreier Robins: Her Life, Letters and Work.* New York: Island Press Cooperative, 1950.

Eisenstein, Victor W., ed. *Neurotic Interaction in Marriage.* New York: Basic Books, 1956.

Ellis, Edward Robb. *The Epic of New York City.* New York: Coward, McCann, 1966.

Encyclopedia Americana. Danbury, Conn.: Grolier, 1984.

Epstein, Jason, and Elizabeth Barlow. *East Hampton: A History and Guide.* 3d rev. ed. New York: Random House, 1985.

Ernst, Jimmy. *A Not-So-Still Life: A Child of Europe's Pre-World War II Art World and His Remarkable Homecoming to America.* New York: St. Martin's Press, 1985.

Falk, Peter Hastings, ed. *Who Was Who in American Art.* Madison, Conn.: Sound View Press, 1985.

Feingold, Henry L. *Zion in America: The Jewish Experience from Colonial Times to the Present.* New York: Twayne, 1974.

Feldstein, Stanley. *The Land That I Show You: Three Centuries of Jewish Life in America.* Garden City, N.Y.: Anchor/Doubleday, 1978.

Fermi, Laura. *Illustrious Immigrants.* Chicago: University of Chicago Press, 1968.

Fiedler, Leslie. *What Was Literature? Class Culture and Mass Society.* New York: Simon & Schuster, 1982.

Fox, Ruth, ed. *Alcoholism: Behavioral Research, Therapeutic Approaches.* New York: Springer, n.d.

———, and Peter Lyon. *Alcoholism: Its Scope, Cause and Treatment.* New York: Random House, 1955.

Frank, Elizabeth. *Jackson Pollock.* New York: Abbeville Press, Modern Masters Series, 1983.

Frascina, Francis. *Pollock and After: The Critical Debate.* New York: Harper & Row, 1985.

Fried, Michael. Exhibition catalogue. *Three American Painters: Kenneth Noland, Jules Olitski, Frank Stella.* Cambridge, Mass.: Fogg Art Museum–Harvard University, 1965.

Friedman, B. H. *Almost a Life.* New York: Viking, 1975.

———. *Jackson Pollock: Energy Made Visible,* 1972. Reprint. New York: McGraw-Hill, 1974.

Fry, Edward F. Exhibition catalogue. *David Smith.* New York: Guggenheim Museum, 1969.

Gaugh, Henry. *Willem de Kooning.* New York: Abbeville Press, Modern Masters Series, 1983.

Golding, John. *Cubism: A History and an Analysis: 1907–1914.* New York: Harper & Row, 1959.

Goldman, Shifra M. *Contemporary Mexican Painting in a Time of Change.* Austin: University of Texas Press, 1977.

Goldmark, Josephine Clara. *Impatient Crusader: Florence Kelley's Life Story,* Urbana: University of Illinois Press, 1953.

Goodman, Cynthia. *Hans Hofmann.* New York: Abbeville Press, Modern Masters Series, 1986.

Graham, John. *System and Dialectics of Art.* Baltimore: Johns Hopkins Press, 1971.

Green, Eleanor. *John Graham: Artist and Avatar.* Washington, D.C.: The Phillips Collection, 1987.

Greenberg, Clement. *Art and Culture: Critical Essays,* 1961. Reprint. Boston: Beacon Press, 1965.

Greer, Germaine. *The Obstacle Course: The Fortunes of Women Painters and Their Work.* New York: Farrar, Straus & Giroux, 1979.

Gruen, John. *The Party's Over Now: Reminiscences of the Fifties —New York's Artists, Writers, Musicians, and Their Friends.* New York: Viking, 1967.

Guggenheim, Peggy. *Art of This Century.* New York: Art of This Century, 1942.

———. *Out of This Century: Confessions of an Art Addict.* New York: Universe Books, 1979.

Guilbaut, Serge. *How New York Stole the Idea of Modern Art:*

Abstract Expressionism, Freedom, and the Cold War. Translated by Arthur Goldhammer. Chicago: University of Chicago Press, 1983.

Guild Hall. Exhibition catalogue. *Artists and East Hampton.* East Hampton, N.Y.: Guild Hall Museum, 1976.

———. Exhibition catalogue. *Crosscurrents: An Exchange Between Guild Hall Museum and the Provincetown Art Association and Museum.* East Hampton, N.Y.: Guild Hall Museum, 1986.

Hall, Radclyffe. *The Well of Loneliness,* 1928. Reprint. New York: Avon Books, 1981.

Harvard Law School. *Alumni Directory of the Harvard Law School: 1973.* Cambridge, Mass.: Harvard Law School, 1973.

Haslam, Malcolm. *The Real World of the Surrealists.* New York: Galley Press, 1978.

Head, Joseph, and S. L. Cranston, eds. *Reincarnation in World Thought.* New York: Julian Press, 1967.

Hefner, Robert J., ed. *East Hampton's Heritage.* Essays by Clay Lancaster and Robert A. M. Stern. New York: W. W. Norton, 1982.

Helm, MacKinley. *Modern Mexican Painters.* New York: Harper & Brothers, 1941.

Henderson, Joseph L. *Thresholds of Initiation.* Middletown, Conn.: Wesleyan University Press, 1967.

Henstell, Bruce. *Sunshine and Wealth: Los Angeles in the Twenties and Thirties.* San Francisco: Chronicle Books, n.d.

Hess, Thomas. *Abstract Painting: Background and American Phase.* New York: Viking, 1951.

Hibbard, Howard. *Michelangelo: Painter, Sculptor, Architect.* New York: Vendome Press, 1974.

History of Cass and Bates Counties. St. Joseph, Mo.: Steam Press, 1884.

Honeyman, Lois. *The Willson Family Tree.* Photocopy in possession of Irene Crippen and Dean McClure.

Howe, Irving. *World of Our Fathers.* New York: Simon & Schuster, 1976.

Hubbard, L. Ron. *Dianetics: The Modern Science of Mental Health: A Handbook of Dianetic Procedure,* 1950. Reprint. Los Angeles: Bridge Publications, 1978.

Hunter, Sam. *Hans Hofmann.* New York: Abrams, 1963.

Hymns of the Church of Jesus Christ of the Latter-Day Saints. Salt Lake City: Deseret Book for the Church, 1948.

Janis, Sidney. *Abstract and Surrealist Art in America.* New York: Reynal & Hitchcock, 1944.

———. Exhibition catalogue. *Abtract and Surrealist Art in the United States.* San Francisco: San Francisco Museum of Art, Jan. 1944.

Jewell, Edward Alden. *Have We an American Art?* New York: Longman, Green, 1939.

Johnson, Alvin. *Pioneer's Progress.* New York: Viking, 1952.

Johnson, G. Wesley, Jr. *Phoenix: Valley of the Sun.* Tulsa, Okla.: Continental Heritage Press, 1982.

Jung, C. G. *Contributions to Analytical Psychology.* New York: Harcourt Brace, 1928.

———. *Memories, Dreams, Reflections.* New York: Pantheon Books, 1961.

———. *Modern Man in Search of a Soul.* New York: Harcourt Brace, 1933.

———. *Two Essays on Analytical Psychology.* New York: Meridian Books, 1956.

C. G. Jung Institute of San Francisco: *The Shaman from Elko.* San Francisco: Jung Institute, 1978.

Kandinsky, Wassily. *Concerning the Spiritual in Art.* New York: Wittenborn, 1947.

Karp, Walter. *The Center: A History and Guide to Rockefeller Center.* New York: American Heritage, 1982.

Kazin, Alfred. *Starting Out in the Thirties.* Boston: Little, Brown, 1962.

Keppel, Frederick A., and R. L. Duffus. *The Arts in American Life.* New York: McGraw-Hill, 1933.

Keun, Odette. *Abroad in America.* London: Green, 1939.

Kligman, Ruth. *Love Affair.* New York: Morrow, 1974.

Klotz, Esther. *The Mission Inn: Its History and Artifacts.* Riverside, Calif.: Rubidoux Printing, 1981.

Kootz, Samuel M. *New Frontiers in American Painting.* New York: Hastings House, 1943.

Samuel M. Kootz Gallery. Exhibition catalogue. *The Intrasubjectives.* New York: Samuel M. Kootz Gallery, 1949.

Kozloff, Max. *Renderings: Critical Essays on a Century of Modern Art.* New York: Simon & Schuster, 1971.

Kramer, Hilton. *The Revenge of the Philistines: Art and Culture, 1972–1984.* New York: Free Press, 1985.

Krishnamurti, J. *Life in Freedom.* New York: Horace Liveright, 1928.

Kunitz, Stanley J., ed. *Twentieth Century Authors: First Supplement.* New York: Wilson, 1955.

Lader, Melvin P. *Arshile Gorky.* New York: Abbeville Press, Modern Masters Series, 1985.

Landgren, Marchal E. *Years of Art: The Story of the Art Students League of New York.* New York: McBride, 1940.

Lane, John R., and Susan C. Larsen, eds. Exhibition catalogue. *Abstract Painting and Sculpture in America, 1927–1944.* Pittsburgh: Museum of Art, Carnegie Institute, 1983.

Leason, B. M. *Early History of Ringgold County, 1847–1937.* Privately published, 1937.

Levy, Julien. *Memoir of an Art Gallery.* New York: Putnam, 1977.

Lomask, Milton. *Seed Money: The Guggenheim Story.* New York: Farrar, Straus, 1964.

Lukach, Joan M. *Hilla Rebay: In Search of the Spirit in Art.* New York: Braziller, 1983.

Lutyens, Emily. *Candles in the Sun.* London: Hart-Davis, 1957.

Lutyens, Mary. *Krishnamurti: The Years of Awakening.* New York: Farrar, Straus & Giroux, 1975.

Lynes, Russell. *Good Old Modern: An Intimate Portrait of the Museum of Modern Art.* New York: Atheneum, 1973.

Manual Arts High School. *The Artisan: Winter, 1929; Summer, 1929; Winter, 1930; Summer, 1930.* Los Angeles: Manual Arts High School, 1929.

Marlborough-Gerson Gallery. Exhibition catalogue. *Jackson Pollock: Black and White.* B. H. Friedman, "An Interview with Lee Krasner." New York: Marlborough-Gerson Gallery, 1969.

Marling, Karal Ann. *Tom Benton and His Drawings: A Biographical Essay and a Collection of His Sketches, Studies, and Mural Cartoons.* Columbia: University of Missouri Press, 1985.

Masserman, Jules H. *Current Psychiatric Therapies.* Vol. 5. New York: Grune & Stratton, 1965.

Maurer, Evan M., and Jennifer L. Bayles. Exhibition catalogue. *Gerome Kamrowski: A Retrospective Exhibition.* Ann Arbor: University of Michigan Museum of Art, 1983.

Mayhew, Eleanor R., ed. *Martha's Vineyard: A Short History.* Edgartown, Mass.: Duke County Historical Society, 1956.

McChesney, Mary Fuller. *A Period of Exploration, 1945–1950.* Oakland, Calif.: Oakland Museum Art Department, 1973.

McCoy, Garnett, ed. *David Smith.* New York: Praeger, 1973.

McCullough, David W. *Brooklyn . . . And How It Got That Way.* New York: Dial Press, 1983.

McElvaine, Robert S. *The Great Depression: America, 1929–41.* New York: Times Books, 1984.

McGie, Joseph F. *History of Butte County.* Butte County, Calif.: Butte County Board of Education, 1982.

McKinzie, Richard D. *The New Deal for Artists.* Princeton, N.J.: Princeton University Press, 1973.

McWilliams, Carey. *Southern California Country: An Island on the Land.* New York: Duell, Sloan & Pearce, 1946.

Melville, Herman: *Moby-Dick, or the Whale,* 1851. Reprint. Evanston and Chicago: Northwestern University Press and the Newberry Library, 1988.

Merritt, H. Houston, and Lawrence C. Kolb. *The Medical Clinics of North America: May 1958: Clinical Problems in Neurology and Psychiatry.* Philadelphia: Saunders, 1958.

Metropolitan Museum of Art. Exhibition catalogue. *Monet's Years at Giverny: Beyond Impressionism.* New York: Metropolitan Museum of Art, 1978.

Midtown Galleries. Exhibition catalogue. *Philip Guston.* New York: Midtown Galleries, 1945.

Missouri the Center State. Vol. 4. St. Louis: S. J. Clarke, 1915.

Moak, Peter V., ed. Exhibition catalogue. *The Robert Laurent Memorial Exhibition: 1972–1973.* Durham: University of New Hampshire, 1972.

Moffett, Ross. *Art in Narrow Streets: The First Thirty-Three Years of the Provincetown Art Association.* Falmouth, Mass.: Kendall, 1964.

Morison, Samuel Eliot. *The Oxford History of the American People.* New York: Oxford University Press, 1965.

Mumford, Lewis. *The Early Years.* New York: Dial Press, 1982.

———. *Sketches from Life: The Autobiography of Lewis Mumford: The Early Years.* New York: Dial Press, 1982.

Munro, Eleanor. *Originals: American Women Artists.* New York: Simon & Schuster, 1979.

Murphet, Howard. *When Daylight Comes: A Biography of Helena Petrovna Blavatsky.* Wheaton, Ill.: Theosophical Publishing House, 1975.

Museum of Fine Arts. Exhibition catalogue. *Fairfield Porter: Realist Painter in an Age of Abstraction.* Boston: Museum of Fine Arts, 1982.

Museum of Modern Art: *Museum of Modern Art, New York: The History and the Collection.* New York: Harry N. Abrams, 1984.

Myers, John Bernard. *Tracking the Marvelous: A Life in the New York Art World.* New York: Random House, 1983.

Naifeh, Steven W. *Culture Making: Money, Success, and the New York Art World.* Princeton, N.J.: Princeton University Press, 1976.

Namuth, Hans. *Pollock Painting.* Rev. ed. Edited by Barbara Rose. New York: Agrinde Publications, 1980.

Nemser, Cindy. *Art Talk: Conversations with 12 Women Artists.* New York: Scribner's, 1975.

New York Panorama: A Companion Guide to the WPA Guide to New York City, 1938. Reprint. New York: Pantheon Books, 1984.

Noun, Louise R. *Strong-Minded Women: The Emergence of the Woman-Suffrage Movement in Iowa.* Ames: Iowa State University Press, 1969.

O'Connor, Francis V. Exhibition catalogue. *Jackson Pollock.* New York: Museum of Modern Art, 1967.

———. Exhibition catalogue. *Jackson Pollock: The Black Pourings.* Boston: Institute of Contemporary Art, 1980.

———. ed. *The New Deal Art Projects: An Anthology of Memoirs.* Washington, D.C.: Smithsonian Institution Press, 1972.

———, and Eugene V. Thaw, eds. *Jackson Pollock: Catalogue Raisonné of Paintings, Drawings, and Other Works.* New Haven, Conn.: Yale University Press, 1978.

O'Doherty, Brian. *American Masters: The Voice and the Myth.* New York: Ridge Press/Random House, 1973.

O'Hara, Frank. *Jackson Pollock.* New York: Braziller, 1959.

Olcott, Henry S. *Old Diary Leaves: The History of the Theosophical Society.* Vol. 1. Adyar, India: Theosophical Publishing House, 1975.

O'Neill, John P., ed. Exhibition catalogue. *Clyfford Still.* New York: Metropolitan Museum of Art, 1979.

Ossorio, Alfonso. *Fourteen Paintings.* London: Thomas Gibson Fine Art, n.d.

Betty Parsons Gallery. Exhibition catalogue. *Jackson Pollock: 1950.* New York: Betty Parsons Gallery, 1950.

Betty Parsons Gallery. Exhibition catalogue. *Jackson Pollock: 1951.* New York: Betty Parsons Gallery, 1951.

Patrick, Lucille Nichols. *The Best Little Town by a Dam Site or Cody's First 20 Years.* Cheyenne, Wyo.: Flintlock, 1968.

Patterson, Tom. *A Colony for California: Riverside's First Hundred Years.* Riverside: Press-Enterprise, 1971.

Peabody, R.R. *The Common Sense of Drinking.* Boston: Little, Brown, 1931.

Philipson, Morris. *Outline of Jungian Aesthetics.* Evanston, Ill.: Northwestern University Press, 1963.

Phillips, William. *A Partisan View: Five Decades of the Literary Life.* New York: Stein & Day, 1983.

Picon, Gaetan. *Surrealists and Surrealism: 1919–1939.* New York: Rizzoli, 1977.

Pointer, Larry, and Donald Goddard. *Harry Jackson.* New York: Abrams, 1981.

Polytechnic High School, Riverside, California: *The Orange and Green: 1928: Year Book of Polytechnic High School.* Riverside, Calif., 1928.

Potter, Jeffrey. *To a Violent Grave: An Oral Biography of Jackson Pollock.* New York: Putnam, 1985.

Powell, W. E., ed. *Publications of the Bureau of Ethnology.* Vol. 1. Washington, D.C.: Smithsonian Institution, 1881.

Pratt, Caroline. *I Learn from Children: An Adventure in Progressive Education.* New York: Simon & Schuster, 1948.

Price, Frederic Newlin. Exhibition catalogue. *Ryder: A Study of Appreciation.* New York: Ferargil Gallery, 1932.

Prown, Jules David, and Barbara Rose. *American Painting:*

From the Colonial Period to the Present. Updated ed. New York: Rizzoli International, 1977.

Purcell, Ralph. *Government and Art.* Washington, D.C.: Public Affairs Press, 1956.

Putz, Ekkehard. *Jackson Pollock: Theorie und Bild.* Hildesheim: Georg Olms Verlag, 1975.

Raskin, Neil H., and Otto Appenzeller. *Headache.* Vol. 19 in series: Major Problems in Internal Medicine. Philadelphia: Saunders, 1980.

Rattray, Edward T. *The South Fork: The Land and the People of Eastern Long Island.* New York: Random House, 1979.

Robbins, Daniel, and Roy R. Neuberger. Exhibition catalogue. *An American Collection.* Providence: Museum of Art, Rhode Island School of Design, 1968.

Robertson, Bryan. *Jackson Pollock.* New York: Abrams, 1960.

Robinson, Cervin, and Rosemary Haag Bletter. *Skyscraper Style.* New York: Oxford University Press, 1975.

Rodman, Selden. *Conversations with Artists.* New York: Capricorn Books, 1961.

Rodriguez, Antonio. *A History of Mexican Mural Painting.* New York: Putnam, 1969.

Roosevelt, Theodore. *Thomas Hart Benton,* 1887. Reprint. New York: Haskell House, 1968.

Rose, Barbara. Exhibition catalogue. *Lee Krasner: A Retrospective.* Houston: Museum of Fine Arts, 1983.

———. Exhibition catalogue. *Krasner/Pollock: A Working Relationship.* New York: Grey Art Gallery, 1981.

Rose, Bernice. Exhibition catalogue. *Jackson Pollock: Works on Paper.* New York: Museum of Modern Art, 1969.

Rose, F. Clifford, and M. Gawel. *Migraine: The Facts.* Oxford, England: Oxford University Press, 1979.

Rosenberg, Harold. *The Anxious Object.* Chicago: University of Chicago Press, 1964.

———. *Barnett Newman.* New York: Abrams, 1977.

Rubin, William S. *Dada and Surrealist Art.* New York: Abrams, 1968.

———. Exhibition catalogue. *Dada, Surrealism, and Their Heritage.* New York: Museum of Modern Art, 1968.

———, ed. Exhibition catalogue. *Pablo Picasso: A Retrospective.* New York: Museum of Modern Art, 1980.

Russell, Gene H. *Orland's Colorful Past.* Orland, Calif.: Orland Community Scholarship Association, 1977.

Russell, William Logie. *The New York Hospital: A History of the Psychiatric Service, 1771–1936.* New York: Columbia University Press, 1945.

Ryan, Robert E., Sr., and Robert E. Ryan, Jr. *Headache and Head Pain: Diagnosis and Treatment.* St. Louis: Mosby, 1978.

Sage, Leland. *A History of Iowa.* Ames: Iowa State University Press, 1974.

Sandler, Irving. *The New York School: The Painters and Sculptors of the Fifties.* New York: Icon / Harper & Row, 1978.

———. *The Triumph of American Painting: A History of Abstract Expressionism.* New York: Praeger, 1970.

Saper, Joel R. *Headache Disorders: Current Concepts and Treatment Strategies.* Boston: John Wright / PSG, 1983.

Saroyan, William. *The Daring Young Man on the Flying Trapeze and other stories.* New York: Random House, 1934.

Schlesinger, Arthur M., Jr. *The Coming of the New Deal.* Boston: Houghton Mifflin, 1959.

———. *The Crisis of the Old Order: 1919–1933.* Boston: Houghton Mifflin, 1957.

Schneiderman, Rose. *All for One.* New York: Paul S. Eriksson, 1967.

Schwankovsky, Frederick J. *Art Appreciation Essays.* Los Angeles: Los Angeles City School District, 1927.

Seldes, Lee. *The Legacy of Mark Rothko: An Exposé of the Greatest Art Scandal of Our Century.* New York: Holt, Rinehart & Winston, 1978.

Sevareid, Eric. *Not So Wild a Dream.* New York: Knopf, 1946.

Simkhovitch, Mary Kingsbury. *Neighborhood: My Story of Greenwich House.* New York: Norton, 1938.

Sinnett, A. P. *Incidents in the Life of Madame Blavatsky.* London: Redway, 1886.

Sloan, John. *Gist of Art: Principles and Practice Expounded in the Classroom and Studio.* New York: American Artists Group, 1939.

Solomon, Deborah. *Jackson Pollock: A Biography.* New York: Simon & Schuster, 1987.

Speck, Isaac G. *The Genealogy of the Speck and Benjamin Reed Families: From 1754 to 1900.* Dupont, Ohio: C. L. Speck, 1900.

Spoto, Donald. *The Kindness of Strangers: The Life of Tennessee Williams.* Boston: Little, Brown, 1985.

Sprenger, Florence. *The Spirit of the Toilers: An Intimate History of Manual Arts High School.* Dallas: Taylor Publishing, 1977.

Still, Bayrd. *Mirror for Gotham: New York as Seen by Contemporaries from Dutch Days to the Present.* New York: New York University Press, 1956.

Tabak, May Natalie. *But Not for Love.* New York: Horizon Press, 1960.

Thompson, D'arcy Wentworth. *On Growth and Form.* Cambridge, England: Cambridge University Press, 1942.

Tingley Centennial History Committee. *A History of Tingley, Iowa, 1883–1983.* Tingley, Iowa: Tingley Centennial History Committee, 1983.

Trilling, Lionel. *The Liberal Imagination.* New York: Viking, 1950.

Tuchman, Maurice. Exhibition catalogue. *New York School: The First Generation: Paintings of the 1940s and 1950s.* Greenwich, Conn.: New York Graphic Society, 1977.

The WPA Guide to California: The Federal Writers' Project Guide to 1930s California, 1939. Reprint. New York: Pantheon Books, 1984.

The WPA Guide to New Orleans: The Federal Writers' Project Guide to 1930s New Orleans, 1938. Reprint. New York: Pantheon Books, 1983.

The WPA Guide to New York City: The Federal Writers' Project Guide to 1930s New York, 1939. Reprint. New York: Pantheon Books, 1982.

Waldberg, Patrick. *Max Ernst.* Paris: Jean-Jacques Pauvert, 1958.

Wall, Joseph Frazier. *Iowa: A History.* New York: Norton, 1978.

Warhol, Andy, and Pat Hackett. *POPism: The Warhol 60's.* New York: Harcourt Brace Jovanovich, 1980.

Weaver, John D. *Los Angeles: The Enormous Village.* Santa Barbara, Calif.: Capra Press, 1980.

Weeks, Sarah T., and Bartlett H. Hayes, eds. *Search for the Real and Other Essays.* Andover, Mass.: Addison Gallery of American Art, 1948.

Weld, Jacqueline Bograd. *Peggy: The Wayward Guggenheim.* New York: Dutton, 1986.

Whitechapel Gallery. Exhibition catalogue. *Lee Krasner: Paintings, Drawings, and Collages.* London: Whitechapel Gallery, 1965.

Whitney Museum of American Art. Exhibition catalogue. *200 Years of American Sculpture.* Boston: David R. Godine, 1976.

Wigmore, L. W. *The Story of the Land of Orland.* Orland, Calif.: Orland Register, 1955.

Williams, Gertrude M. *The Passionate Pilgrims: A Life of Annie Besant.* London: John Hamilton, 1931.

Williams, Tennessee. *Dragon Country: A Book of Plays.* New York: New Directions, 1970.

———. *Memoirs.* Garden City, N.Y.: Doubleday, 1972.

World Almanac: 1985. New York: Newspaper Enterprise Association, 1984.

Wyoming State Archives Museums and Historical Department. *More Buffalo Bones.* Cheyenne: Wyoming State Archives Museums and Historical Department, 1982.

Wysuph, C. L. Exhibition catalogue. *Jackson Pollock: Psychoanalytic Drawings.* New York: Horizon Press, 1970.

Yee, Chiang. *The Silent Traveller, a Chinese Artist in Lakeland.* New York: Scribner's, 1938.

Yeo, Wilma, and Helen K. Cook. *Maverick with a Paintbrush.* Garden City, N.Y.: Doubleday, 1977.

NOTES

ABBREVIATIONS

JP	Jackson Pollock
LK	Lee Krasner
ABP	Alma Brown Pollock (wife of Marvin Jay)
ACM	Arloie Conaway McCoy (wife of Sanford)
CCP	Charles Cecil Pollock
EFP	Elizabeth Feinberg Pollock (first wife of Charles)
FLP	Frank Leslie Pollock
LRP	LeRoy Pollock
MJP	Marvin Jay Pollock
MLP	Marie Levitt Pollock (wife of Frank)
SLM	Sanford Lee McCoy
SMP	Stella McClure Pollock
SWP	Sylvia Winter Pollock (second wife of Charles)

AAA	Archives of American Art
CG	Clement Greenberg
DP&G	Francine du Plessix and Cleve Gray
int.	interviewed
FVOC	Francis V. O'Connor
NYT	*New York Times*
OC&T	Francis V. O'Connor and Eugene V. Thaw
PG	Peggy Guggenheim
q.	quoted
THB	Thomas Hart Benton

PROLOGUE: DEMONS

SOURCES

Books, articles, records, and transcripts

Friedman, *JP*; Gruen, *The Party's Over*; Marlborough-Gerson Gallery, *JP*; OC&T, *JP*; Potter, *To a Violent Grave.*

Bruno Alfieri, "Piccolo discorso sui quadri di JP," *L'Arte Moderna*, 1950 (English typescript in MOMA file); DP&G, "Who Was JP?" *Art in America*, May–June 1967; Stanley P. Friedman, "Last Years of a Tormented Genius," *New York*, Oct. 29, 1973; R[obert] G[oodnough], *Art News*, Dec. 1950; CG, "The Present Prospects of American Painting and Sculpture," *Horizon* (London), Oct. 1947; "JP: Is He the Greatest Living Painter in the United States?" *Life*, Aug. 8, 1949; B[elle] K[rasne], *Art Digest*, Dec. 1, 1950; B. H. Friedman, interviews with LK, in Marlborough-Gerson Gallery, *JP*; [Berton Roueché], "Talk of the Town," *New Yorker*, Aug. 5, 1959; James T. Vallière, "Daniel T. Miller," *Provincetown Review*, Fall 1968; James T. Vallière, "De Kooning on Pollock," *Provincetown Review*, Fall 1967; "Words," *Time*, Feb. 7, 1949.

"Art Buy Sensation," Sydney *Daily Mirror*, Oct. 23, 1973; "Expert Defends 'Blue Poles': JP work 'authentic,' " *Sydney Morning Herald*, Oct. 25, 1973; "JP, Artist, Wrecks Car, Escapes Injury No Holiday Fatalities," *East Hampton Star*, Jan. 3, 1952; Aline B. Loucheim, *NYT*, Sept. 10, 1950; Israel Shenker, "A Pollock Sold for $2-Million, Record for American Painting," *NYT*, Sept. 22, 1973.

East Hampton Town Police, Police Log, Dec. 28, 1951, p. 571.

CG, Barnett Newman, and Betty Parsons, int. by Kathleen Shorthall for *Life*, 1959, Time/Life Archives.

Interviews

Peter Blake; Paul Brach; Peter Busa; Nicholas Carone; Herman Cherry; John Cole; Robert Cooter; Violet de Laszlo; Karen Del Pilar; Sanford Friedman; David Gibbs; CG; Merle Hubbard; Edys Hunter; Sam Hunter; Harry Jackson; Paul Jenkins; Buffie Johnson; Reuben Kadish; Gerome Kamrowski; Ruth Kligman; LK; Millie Liss; Conrad Marca-Relli; Mercedes Matter; ACM; Akinabu Mori; Annalee Newman (int. by David Peretz); Constantine Nivola; Doug Ohlson; CCP; CCP (int. by David Peretz); FLP; MLP; MJP; Charles Porter; Miriam Schapiro; Nene Schardt; Jon Schueler; Jim Shepperd; Jane Smith; Patsy Southgate; Ronald Stein; Ruth Stein; Milton Resnick; May Tabak Rosenberg; Araks Tolegian; Evelyn Porter Trowbridge; Roger Wilcox.

NOTES

"I'm going to kill myself": Jane Smith. Although Lee Krasner was infuriated when the story of the painting of *Blue Poles*—based on an interview with Tony Smith—appeared in *New York* magazine in October 1973 (Stanley P. Friedman, "Last Years"), she never denied its accuracy. In a typically legalistic manner, she denied only that Smith, and later Barnett Newman, had helped paint the final work. OC&T (II p. 193) carefully record Lee's position on the matter: "Lee Krasner Pollock denied that any other artist participated in the creation of the painting as it looks today." Lee was, of course, speaking the literal truth: JP had scraped off all of the paint dripped onto the canvas by anyone else long before he completed the work that now hangs in the Australian National Gallery. From extensive interviews with the people who knew Tony Smith best, it is clear that he was not a man to tell lies or to take credit where credit was not his due, and the story he told Friedman in 1973 was identical in all major points with the story that he had told his wife, students, and friends (Jane Smith, Johnson, Ohlson, Shepperd, and others) in the years since the fatal evening, twenty years before, when he drove out to Springs to be with his suicidal friend.

Talk of suicide: Wilcox. Smith alarmed: "[I] felt that

something was wrong," Smith told a staff correspondent of the *Sydney Morning Herald*; q. in "Expert Defends 'Blue Poles,' " Oct. 25, 1973. **"Hold on":** Q. by Shepperd. **Critics dazzled:** See G[oodnough], *Art News*, p. 47; K[rasne], *Art Digest*, p. 16. **"The most powerful":** "The Present Prospects of American Painting and Sculpture," *Horizon*, pp. 25–26. *Life* **magazine:** "JP," *Life*, pp. 42ff. **Drive taking four hours:** Shepperd.

Cooking sherry: Wilcox. **"An alcoholic** *in excelsis***":** Int. by Shorthall, 1959. **From beer to bourbon:** Wilcox. **Drinking since junior high school:** ACM. **Alcoholic father:** MJP; MLP. **"A way out":** Q. by Wilcox. **"How the hell":** Wilcox. **Wrecking Cadillac:** On Dec. 28, 1951; police log, East Hampton Town Police, p. 571; "JP, Artist," *East Hampton Star*, Jan. 3, 1953.

Smith arriving in Springs: Jane Smith; Stanley P. Friedman, "Last Years," p. 48. **"I was afraid":** Q. in Stanley P. Friedman, "Last Years," p. 48. **Looking fit:** Jenkins. **Solution of rock salt:** B. H. Friedman, p. 192. **Guano and ground beets:** MLP. **"A proper balance":** B. H. Friedman, p. 172. **Pollock's smile and dimples:** Cherry; Matter. **Smith's physical attraction to Pollock:** Johnson; Wilcox. **Lee's fear of storms:** Ruth Stein. **LK:** When JP talked to her about his drunken binges, he would say, "Think of it as a storm that will pass." **Trying to become invisible:** Carone. **Lee cradling Jackson's head:** Carone; Rosenberg.

Both Jackson Pollocks: See Vallière, "Daniel T. Miller." **"I can't do anything"; "the pictures just come":** Q. by friend, name withheld by request. **Smith drinking with Pollock:** Kamrowski. **"What the fuck":** Q. by Carone in a similar situation. **"Cowboy painter":** See de Kooning, q. in Vallière, "De Kooning on Pollock," pp. 603–05. **"People have always frightened and bored me":** JP to CCP and FLP, Oct. 22, 1929. **Jackson at parties:** Wilcox. **"Stripped of his skin":** Wilcox, recalling JP. **"Pained, painful person"; "awkward, long silences":** Brach; Schapiro. LK, q. in Gruen, p. 233: "Jackson had a mistrust of words. Words were never his thing. They made him feel uncomfortable. And people made him uncomfortable." **Working up courage with beers:** Wilcox. **"Ugly-touch Hemingway":** Southgate. **Company of neighborhood girls; "house":** Trowbridge. **Estranged from father:** FLP. **Tests of manhood:** CCP; FLP; MJP. **Jackson's ambiguous sexual urges:** Busa; Carone; de Laszlo; Sanford Friedman; Gibbs; Johnson; Kadish; Marca-Relli, etc.

Sparse correspondence: In the course of researching this book, we have discovered only three unknown letters and eight unknown notes from JP. Several more letters, written by JP to Manuel Tolegian in California, were burned in 1951. **Late night phone calls:** Benton; Jane Smith; Newman, int. by Peretz. **Pollock's telephone style:** Kligman. **Lending money:** Brach: JP lent him and Miriam Schapiro the deposit for their house in East Hampton. **Remodeling houses:** Little. JP offered help to still others, including Marca-Relli. **Painting bike:** Nivola. JP also painted a bike and presented it as a gift to his nephew, Jason McCoy (Del Pilar), probably remembering that his father had done the same as a birthday gift for his brother Frank. **Teaching archery:** Hubbard. **Beguiling smile:** Cherry. **"Renowned twinkle":** Schueler. **Apology:** Cherry.

Painting of *Blue Poles***:** Ohlson; Shepperd; Jane Smith; Stanley P. Friedman, "Last Years." **"For Chrissakes"; "When a painter"; unwrapping linen and searching for paints:** Stanley P. Friedman, "Last Years," p. 48. **"I can't start a painting":** Q. by Smith in Stanley P. Friedman, "Last Years," p. 48. **"I come from Orange":** Q. by Shepperd, recalling Smith. **Walking on waxed paper:** "Art Buy Sensation," *Sydney Daily Mirror*, Oct. 23, 1973. **"So that's the way":** Q. by Smith in Stanley P. Friedman, "Last Years," p. 50. **Paw-like hands:** Hopkins. **"Forget the hand":** Int. by Shorthall, 1959.

Distant father: FLP. **Granite-faced mother:** Tony Smith, q. in DP&G, "Who was JP?" p. 53. **"Cry-baby"; "mama's boy":** Mori. **Accident-prone:** Charles Porter, for childhood accident. For constant needfulness, see ACM; CCP; FLP; Schardt. **Drinking at an early age:** ACM. Del Pilar: "As long as I can remember, the whole family would spend their time talking about what could be done about Jackson and his problems. There were all these late night phone calls across the country, and it was always about Jackson. He was always the center of attention." **"I'll show them someday":** Q. by CCP, int. by Peretz. **"That fucking Picasso":** Q. by

LK, int. by B. H. Friedman, in Marlborough-Gerson Gallery, "JP," n.p. **Assaulting policemen:** Araks Tolegian, recalling her husband Manuel. **Driving insanely:** Edys Hunter; Liss; Ronald Stein, etc. **Destroying property:** Araks Tolegian, recalling Manuel. **Carried home:** Kadish; ACM. **Turning up phonograph:** Sam Hunter. **Upending dinner table:** Blake; Cole. **Flaunting mistress:** Kligman.

"Bilious green"; "it looks like vomit"; "laying it on": Smith, q. in Stanley P. Friedman, "Last Years," p. 50. **"Splashed and drooled.":** Tony Smith, q. in "Expert Defends 'Blue Poles,' " *Sydney Morning Herald*, Oct. 25, 1973. **Painting and use of syringes:** Ohlson; Shepperd; Jane Smith; "Art Buy Sensation," *Sydney Daily Mirror*, Oct. 23, 1973; "Expert Defends 'Blue Poles,' " *Sydney Morning Herald*, Oct. 25, 1973; Stanley P. Friedman, "Last Years." **Abstract painting":** Q. in [Roueché], "Talk of the Town," Aug. 5, 1950, p. 16. **"Caused a kind of havoc"; "violent arguments":** Loucheim, *NYT*, Sept. 10, 1950. **"Compared to Pollock":** Alfieri, "Piccolo dicorso sui quadri di JP," n.p. **No early proficiency; competing with brothers:** FLP; MJP; Cooter: Charles was always considered the family artist. **"Always in transition":** Int. by Shorthall, 1959.

"We spent a long time": Smith, q. in Stanley P. Friedman, "Last Years," p. 50. **Scraping off canvas and completing** *Blue Poles*: OC&T II, pp. 193, 196. **Sale of** *Blue Poles*: Shenker, "A Pollock Sold for $2-Million." In America, in Europe, and especially in Australia, there was an outpouring of articles on the sale of the painting. Before *Blue Poles*, the highest price paid for an American painting had been $250,000, for *Steelworkers at Noontime* by Thomas Anshutz. **Rembrandt, Velázquez, and da Vinci:** Twelve years earlier, the Metropolitan Museum of Art had paid $2,300,000 for *Aristotle Contemplating the Bust of Homer* by Rembrandt; more recently, the Metropolitan had paid $4,100,000 for a portrait, *Juan de Pareja*, by Velázquez; and the National Gallery of Art in Washington, D.C., had paid an unreported price, rumored to be about $5,000,000, for the portrait of Ginevra da Benci by da Vinci. **Picasso:** The National Gallery of Art in Washington, D.C., had paid $1,000,000 within the previous year for a Cubist painting of a nude by Picasso.

1. STRONG-MINDED WOMEN

SOURCES

Books, articles, manuscripts, brochures, documents, and transcripts

Crunden, *Ministers of Reform*; *History of Cass and Bates Counties*; Honeyman, *The Willson Family Tree*; Leason, *Early History of Ringgold County*; Noun, *Strong-Minded Women*; Sage, *A History of Iowa*; Solomon, *JP*; Speck, *The Genealogy of the Speck and Benjamin Reed Families*; Tingley Centennial History Committee (TCHC), *A History of Tingley, Iowa*; Wall, *Iowa*.

Arts & Architecture, Feb. 1944; Murdock Pemberton, "A Memoir of Three Decades," *Art*, Oct. 1955.

"Died, March 13, 1880—Matt Pollock's little boy" (newspaper clipping in possession of Clair Heyer); "Obituary—Mrs. Jennie McClure," *Tingley Vindicator*, July 1941; "Obituary—J. R. McClure," *Tingley Vindicator*, Apr. 1917; "Obituary—J. M. Pollock," *Tingley Vindicator*, Dec. 2, 1909; Marriage notice, *Tingley Vindicator*, Jan. 29, 1903.

Edna Alcorn Belzer, "Emeline" (unpub. ms.), Alexandria, Va., 1952; Ella Conner Cornwall, "Some Recollections of Ella Conner Cornwall" (unpub. ms.), Ellston, Iowa, n.d.; Herbert F. Cornwall, "Some of the Recollections and History of Herbert F. Cornwall" (unpub. ms.), Ellston, Iowa, n.d.; Clair B. Heyer, "Hometown before Pollution" (unpub. ms.), 1982; Clair B. Heyer, "How Reliable Is Census Data? An Evaluation of Manuscript Census Reports as Source Material for Historical Research in a Study of One Iowa Township" (M.A. thesis), De Kalb: Northern Illinois University, 1966; Stella Lorimor, autograph book, in possession of Dean McClure; FVOC, "The Genesis of JP: 1912 to 1943" (Ph.D. thesis), Baltimore: Johns Hopkins University, 1965.

"Home Culture Club," Tingley, Iowa, 1907–08 (pamphlet in possession of Clair Heyer); Ringgold County Tour Bulletin, 39th Annual Reunion, July 27, 1975.

Bates County, Mo., marriage certificate, Recorder's Office,

July 22, 1881; Box Butte County, Nebr., marriage license and certificate, Recorder's Office, Jan. 13, 1903; record book of the justice of peace, Tingley, Iowa, 1899; Ringgold County, Iowa, Agricultural Census, 1880; Ringgold County, Iowa, Census, 1880, vol. 28, sheet 21, line 26; Ringgold County, Iowa, Recorder's Office, book 14 of Misely, p. 594.

ACM, int. by James T. Vallière, n.d., AAA; SLM, int. by Kathleen Shorthall for *Life*, 1959, Time/Life Archives; SLM, int. by CG, c. 1956.

Interviews

Margaret Louise Archbold; R. L. Archbold; Madelon Bedell; Charles Bennett; Jeremy Capillé; John Cook; Lois Cook; Marjorie Cook; Robert Cooter; Irene Crippen; James Dawson; Martha Dawson; Karen Del Pilar; Josephine Eighme; Margaret Eighme; Marietta Eighme; Marie Ferre; B. H. Friedman; Gary Hassell; Allan Herrick; Clair Heyer; Hazel Heyer; Dorothy Hitt; Zetta Houston; Harry Jackson; Wilbur Johnson; Reuben Kadish; John Kiburz; Barbara Kiburz; LK; Carl Lightner; Helen Lightner; Eleanor Lynch; Dean McClure; Donald McClure; Margaret Ann McClure; Paul McClure; Elizabeth Nelson; Frances Overholtzer; Wayne Overholtzer; CCP; CCP (int. by SWP); EFP; FLP; Jonathan Pollock; MLP; MJP; SWP; Ed Robertson; Patricia Rolf; Lucile Schoppe; Marvin Smith; Patsy Southgate; Janet Tidrick; Helen Walker; Leonard Zick, Jr.

NOTES

"Scotch and Irish": *Arts & Architecture*, Feb. 1944. **Godfrey Augustus Speck:** Speck, p. 1. **Marriage to Sarah Townsend:** Speck, pp. 2–3. **Samuel and Jane Speck:** Speck, pp. 72–73. **"Weaver of woolens":** SMP to Crippen, Jan. 6, 1957. **Archibald and Eliza Jane:** Speck, p. 73. **Lettie Boyd:** Crippen. **Pushing into continent:** Clair Heyer. **Reasons for immigration:** Wall, pp. 55, 13. **Specks leaving Ohio:** Speck, p. 73. **"He who paints pictures":** Wall, p. 14. **"Beautiful land":** Sage, p. 3. Also interpreted as "drowsy ones"; Wall, p. 14. **Capture of Indians:** Wall, p. 12. **"Grand rolling prairie":** Albert M. Lea, *Notes on the Wisconsin Territory* (Philadelphia: H. S. Tanner, 1836), p. 14, q. in Wall, pp. 13–14. **Some 200,000 settlers:** Wall, p. 49. **Probable Speck route:** See Wall, p. 49. **Land prices:** Wall, pp. 118, 123. **"Blue stem"; "higher than a horse's":** Cornwall, "Some of the Recollections and History of Herbert F. Cornwall," n.p. **Land preparation; prairie breakers:** Wall, pp. 123–25. **"Freeze chickens":** Belzer, "Emeline," p. 6. **Diseases; plagues; grain prices:** Wall, p. 124. **Indian uprisings:** Wall, p. 60. **"To get land":** Wall, pp. 64–65. **"Do-less":** Belzer, "Emeline," p. 4.

Women's determination: Capillé: "The history of the United States is built on people like my grandmother. I mean, you don't *react*. You watch your children and your husband being shot down by the Indians in the wagon train and you pick up the rifle and you go on. That was her idea of how a competent, strong woman functions." **Tale of unhitched wagon:** Belzer, "Emeline," p. 4: The two people were Francis and Martha Cornwall. **Barclay Cappoc; Iowans with John Brown:** Wall, p. 99. **Some 70,000 Iowa men:** Wall, p. 108. **"Liberty Pole":** Belzer, "Emeline," p. 8. **Death of Elizabeth Speck:** Speck, p. 73.

Jennie's unpredictability: SMP to CCP, EFP, and Jeremy, 1939. **Changes in Jennie:** Margaret Eighme. **Severe side of Jennie:** Crippen. **"Stricter than the Methodists":** Wayne Overholtzer. **"Almost Sabbath":** Margaret Eighme. The Eighmes, longtime residents of Tingley, knew both Jennie McClure and Lizzie Pollock and their families. **Forbidden to play baseball:** FLP. **Only "p'sams" allowed:** Margaret Eighme. **Dancing "the last straw":** Frances Overholtzer, who once boarded with Jennie McClure. **Jennie proud of handiwork:** Crippen; Clair Heyer. **The "40 yards of blankets":** SMP to Crippen. **"Talking about":** Herbert Cornwall, q. in Belzer, "Emeline," p. 10. **"Busy hands":** CCP. Leonard Zick noticed the same characteristic in his mother, Stella's sister Nell.

Effects of Civil War on Iowa women: Wall, p. 114; Noun, p. 23. **"Any woman":** Lizzie Bunnell, Peru, Ind., *Mayflower*, Aug. 1, 1861, q. in Noun, p. 24. **Girls disguising themselves:** Wall, p. 113. **"Spirit of equality"; "the first state":** Tilton, lecture, Dec. 1866–Jan. 1867, q. in Noun, p. 72. **"Women were classed":** Anna Dickinson, "Women and

Idiots" (lecture), 1868, q. in Noun, p. 90. **Iowa women's rights bill:** Noun, p. 222. **Marriage of Jennie Speck:** Speck, p. 73.

John Robinson McClure's ancestry: Donald McClure; see Honeyman, p. 60. SMP to Crippen, Jan. 6, 1957: "Great Grand Pa Boyd was born in Ireland. a linene weaver My Grand Mother & Dad on my Mothers side of the houses Great Grand Mother McClure wove first piece of linen when 16. 40 yards of blankets 107 yards of carpet There house burned 1 a.m. 1-9-1870 loom was burned to married October 7, 1873 had a hard time getting Uncle out he was upstairs." **McClures' route to Iowa:** Dean McClure.

McKee McClure: Dean McClure; Crippen. The closest name in the cemetery is James McKee McClure, but this may have been his uncle; Crippen notes that there is some "confusion in the graveyard." Ann Reid McClure was a cousin of Whitelaw Reid, prominent owner of the New York *Tribune*, ambassador to the Court of St. James's, and Republican vice-presidental candidate in 1892. **"Exposed to cholery";** Jennie McClure to Crippen, 1933. The letter proceeds: "Your Uncle John Father & Mother come around from Ohio on the Ohio river was expecting to go to Morning Sun left the boat at Burlington & was going across crountry & his Father had been exposed to cholery on the rivery & he died before they got to Morning Sun. your Uncle John was only about 2 years old then his Mother didnt marry again till your uncle was 5 years old & she married a man by the name of Willson. am tiard will have to rest takes me so long to tell a little From your Aunt Jennie Mc." **Death of McKee McClure:** Honeyman, p. 60: The family got off the boat at Keokuk, and he died at Fort Madison. Jennie McClure to Crippen, 1933: They got off at Burlington, and he died before getting to Morning Sun. Having discovered other inaccuracies in stories assembled by Honeyman, we have accepted Jennie McClure as the more reliable source.

Marriage to Adam Willson: Crippen; Dean McClure; Honeyman, p. 60. **Move to Sharon, Iowa:** "Obituary—J. R. McClure," *Tingley Vindicator*, Apr. 1917. **"McClure Trait":** Bennett: J. R. McClure "was more or less of a quiet sort—a hardworking, quiet sort of person." He must have been studious as well. Bennett: "The McClures were pretty tight-lipped. They didn't talk freely." **Further travels of J. R. McClure:** "Obituary—J. R. McClure," *Tingley Vindicator*, Apr. 1917. **Log house:** Bennett. **Stella Pollock born:** Honeyman, p. 60.

Small farm: J. R. McClure's farm consisted of 80 acres; the average was 160 acres. **Son more welcome:** Clair Heyer. **Numbing routine:** Ethyl Smith Romans to Heyer, 1965, in TCHC, p. 72. **Sunday supper:** Mary Irving Link, "Childhood Days in Tingley, 1916–1922," in TCHC, p. 71. **"They wouldn't even hardly":** Wayne Overholtzer. **Fruit butter:** Leason, p. 146. **Molasses:** Leason, p. 24. **Hominy:** Leason, p. 190. **Preparations for winter:** Daisy Smith Heyer to Clair Heyer, 1965, in TCHC, p. 72; Ethyl Smith Romans to Clair Heyer, 1965, in TCHC, p. 73. **Pie:** Leason, p. 232.

Stella as a child: Del Pilar; Dean McClure. **"A strong individual":** Del Pilar. **Description of Stella:** Crippen and others. **Anna quiet and thoughtful:** Mary effervescent: Margaret Eighme. **Member of Presbyterian Church:** Crippen; "Obituary—Cordelia Jane Speck McClure," *Tingley Vindicator*, July 1941. **"To heaven by short cut":** Tidrick. **"Hellbound":** Clair Heyer. **"Hardshelled":** Clair Heyer; see "Tingley United Presbyterian Church," in TCHC, pp. 66–68. **Birth of Samuel Cameron and David Leslie:** Speck, p. 61. **Best land taken:** Sage, p. 100. **"Heartbreak deals":** Bennett. **Grasshopper plague:** Leason, n.p. in photocopy. **Hog cholera:** TCHC, p. 101. **Corn prices; heavy rains:** TCHC, pp. 9–10.

Railroad coming to Tingley: O. C. House, "Early History," Mount Ayr *Record-News*, Aug. 27, 1931, in TCHC, p. 8. **Humeston and Shenandoah:** Wayne Overholtzer. **Thomas Jefferson:** Wall, p. 118: Jefferson "liked classical symmetry in his buildings, semantic precision in his laws, and geometric accuracy on his maps." **Land Ordinance of 1785:** TCHC, p. 101. **McClures moving to section 18:** Crippen. **Buildings and businesses:** O. C. House, "Early History," Mount Ayr *Record-News*, Aug. 27, 1931, in TCHC, p. 8. **Calling it a village:** Clair Heyer. **Plans for opera house:** O. C. House, "Early History," Mount Ayr *Record-News*, Aug. 27, 1931, in TCHC, p. 8.

Euphonia Isabell: Also called Fronia Isabelle and Euphronia in family records. **Stella acting as mother:** Dean

McClure. **Kate Peckham:** Clair Heyer. **Reliance on Stella:** Dean McClure. **Euphonia's death:** Walker; Dean McClure. **"A little flower":** The message on the tombstone of Roy's sister Nina.

Move to Tingley: Crippen. **For Stella a liberation:** MJP. **Ladies' clubs:** TCHC, p. 67. **Raphael to Lord Byron:** "Home Culture Club." Women who belonged to the club would meet monthly to present reports on topics assigned the previous month. In April 1908, the general topic was the fine arts, with talks on Raphael and Rosa Bonheur; TCHC, p. 67; see also Bennett. **"Art and art consciousness":** Pemberton, "Memoir of Three Decades." **Nearest library:** In Fairfield, Iowa; see Wall, pp. 194–95. Clair Heyer: Like most farm families, the McClures would have kept only a few books of poetry and a copy of Meredith's *Lucile* in addition to the Bible. **Lecture series:** Wall, p. 195; Bedell. **Female domain; "intellectual and artistic":** Clair Heyer. **Piano and art teachers; the Castle at Chillon:** Clair Heyer; Crippen. **"When I was young":** Q. by ACM.

Stella's resemblance to Aunt Stella: Marietta Eighme. Josephine Eighme: Her nickname was "Aunt Stell." **"When you are in a distant land":** Aug. 13, 1889; Stella Lorimor, autograph book in possession of Dean McClure. **Fine dresses; linen napkins:** Crippen. **Sealed invitations:** Josephine Eighme. **Victorian decor; strolling into town:** Schoppe. **White collar; "I sat":** Frances Overholtzer. **"She was correct":** Marietta Eighme. **Description of Stella Lorimor:** Crippen; Margaret Eighme; Marietta Eighme; Josephine Eighme; Wayne Overholtzer; Schoppe; see "Obituary—Cordelia Jane Speck McClure," *Tingley Vindicator*, July 1941. Crippen: Stella Lorimor was "solid. Yes she was *solid.* She had a sense of humor, she had it, but I'll tell you, the Specks, they didn't go around with a smile on their face. No, they were very serious people. They really and truly were. Aunt Stella was the same way as Stella [Pollock], quiet and tall and heavy featured but very *stylish.*" Wayne Overholtzer: Stella Lorimor was a "stern woman, *very* stern." **World beyond Iowa:** Stella Lorimor, autograph book. **"She was a big woman":** Frances Overholtzer. **"It was kind of hard":** Josephine Eighme.

Stella watching Aunt Stella: Crippen. **More a model than Jennie McClure:** Margaret Eighme; Marietta Eighme. **"Kind of short and loud":** Josephine Eighme. **"She knew what she wanted":** CCP. **Playing with Cam and Les:** Clair Heyer. **"Devilment" with Cam and Les:** Wayne Overholtzer. **Landing before justice of the peace:** Clair Heyer; record book of the justice of the peace, Tingley, 1899: Les was arrested and charged with mischief, destroying property, and disturbing the peace. He pled guilty to "unlawful assembly" and was fined $3.00 plus $.60 and given a suspended sentence of ten days. **Les falling behind in school:** FLP. **Sandlot baseball:** Dean McClure. **Roughhousing with Cam and Les:** Cooter describes Stella roughhousing in a similar manner with her sons many years later; see also ACM. **Anna's illness; Stella Lorimor's marriage:** Margaret Eighme.

2. SENSITIVE MEN

SOURCES

See chapter 1.

NOTES

Jackson not talking about father: Busa: "Jackson always talked about his mother. Never said a goddamned word about his father." **Roy's reticence about past:** ACM; CCP; FLP. **Beliefs about adoption:** Crippen; MJP. **McCoy family Bible:** Martha Dawson, a distant relative who finally penciled the name "Le Roy" into the Bible on Oct. 14, 1983, during an interview with the authors.

Alexander from County Donegal: Marjorie Cook; Houston. **Arriving in 1774:** Houston. **Chaplain in army:** Martha Dawson. **Dickinson College:** Marjorie Cook; Ferre. **Later career:** Marjorie Cook. In 1799, in a sectarian dispute between the church's conservative faction, called Old Lights, and liberal reformers, New Lights, Alexander McCoy's name was stricken from the Presbyterian rolls and he established a renegade presbytery more in conformity with his conservative views. **Presbyterian legacy:** Crunden, p. 15: "From its birth

in the Middle West, a generation of intelligent youth, though remaining devoted to their parents, resisted efforts to compel them into the ministry or missionary work. . . . Over the long term, their goal was an educated democracy that would create laws that would, in turn, produce a moral democracy. The place for Christianity was in this world." Roy's brother John became a minister after graduating from Sterling College, a Presbyterian school in Kansas; Nelson. See also George Davis Herron, q. in Crunden, p. 49.

Alexander and Martha Pattison McCoy; stopping in Knox, Ohio: Marjorie Cook. **Jackson County, Missouri:** Now called Cass County. **Description of Alexander and Rebecca McCoy:** Josephine Eighme. **Marriage:** Crippen. **Family moving:** Josephine Eighme. Wall, p. 160: There was a precipitous drop in farm prices in 1870. **McCoys losing effects:** Margaret Eighme; Josephine Eighme. **Bottom of ladder:** Bennett. **Birth of Nina and Roy:** Crippen. **Tuberculosis:** Nelson; Houston. **Death of Nina and Becky:** Crippen; Crippen to FLP, Apr. 26, 1983; May 1, 1983.

Census of 1880: Vol. 28, sheet 21, line 26. **Story that both of Roy's parents died:** MJP to Crippen, Aug. 30, 1978. **Formally adopted:** ACM. **McCoys and Pollocks related:** Crippen. **Deathbed declaration:** R. L. Archbold; Crippen. "I can't give my son away," Rebecca said; q. by Nelson. **Act of compassion:** Clair Heyer; Ringgold County Tour bulletin, July 27, 1975. **"A bit on the scruffy side":** Clair Heyer. Soon after Nina showed symptoms of tuberculosis, Becky may have sent LeRoy to the Pollocks' house as a precaution. Lizzie Pollock was a logical choice: she had only a single, adopted child in the house (Crippen), lived near the McCoy farm (Crippen), and knew Becky well (R. L. Archbold). At the time, she was forty-three years old and pregnant, in what must have been her last try at a child of her own. A severe but loving woman, Lizzie adored LeRoy from the time he came into her home in 1878. By the time Becky died a year later, she had become fiercely attached to him. Instead of demanding his son back immediately upon Becky's death, Alexander yielded to the current of events, allowing LeRoy to stay with the Pollocks while Elizabeth McClelland, exhausted from caring for her daughter and grieving at her loss, recovered in his house. When Lizzie Pollock's infant son died in March of 1880 ("Died, March 13, 1880—Matt Pollock's little boy," newspaper clipping in possession of Clair Heyer), her frustrated maternal love closed around young LeRoy.

Description of Matt Pollock: "Obituary—J. M. Pollock," *Tingley Vindicator*, Dec. 2, 1909. The Pollock family was originally from Nova Scotia, then moved to Marysville, Ohio, and finally in 1853 to Mercer County, Illinois. At age twenty-six, Matt enlisted in Company C of the 36th Regiment, Illinois Veteran Volunteers, and served until the last day of the Civil War. Upon discharge, he returned to Marysville and, on January 8, 1865, married Elizabeth Lewis, whom he hadn't seen in twelve years. **Adoption of Frank:** 1880 Iowa census, vol. 28, sheet 21, line 26. Frank, who was born in Ohio, probably the orphan of settlers who had died on the trip west, was adopted about 1870. **Wheelbarrow:** MJP to Crippen, Aug. 30, 1978. Lizzie was born Elizabeth Lewis. She and Matt left Illinois for Ringgold County, Iowa, in 1871, settling in Eugene, where, after five years, he saved up enough to make a downpayment on a small farm of his own, close to the little cluster of homesteads around which the town of Tingley would soon coalesce. **Further description of Matt Pollock:** "Obituary—J. M. Pollock," *Tingley Vindicator*, Dec. 2, 1909. Matt's mother was from Virginia; Crippen to FLP, May 1, 1983. **Matt's holdings:** Ringgold County Agricultural Census, 1880, in possession of Clair Heyer. Pollock owned 60 improved acres and 21 unimproved acres, valued at $1,500, with $50 worth of implements and machinery and $300 worth of livestock. In the same year, Alexander McCoy owned only 32 improved acres and 8 unimproved acres, valued at $700, with $30 worth of implements and machinery and $180 worth of livestock. Heyer, "Hometown before Pollution": "Total valuations placed [McCoy] sixth from the very lowest among the township's 96 farmers." **Matt unpopular:** Clair Heyer, recalling Ethyl Smith Romans.

Lizzie doing "God's work": R. L. Archbold. **"Strong and courageous":** Marietta Eighme. **"A religious fanatic":** MJP. **President of WCTU:** Listed first in meeting of Apr. 22, 1909; TCHC, p. 76. **Description of Lizzie:** Marietta Eighme: "Now, Mrs. Pollock, she was angular in every way, the beaky nose and deep-set eyes, kind of gnarled hands." **"She was very strong":** MJP. **"Made everybody toe the mark"; "didn't approve of everybody": R. L. Archbold. **Mouse story:** Josephine Eighme, the woman in the story. According to Jay, when Lizzie's grandsons wanted to play on Sunday afternoons, she railed at them. "You might have to work on Sunday, feed the cattle and things like that, but if you wanted to go out and play baseball in the back yard, that was out. She would sit in the chair and read the goddamned Bible all day. That kind of woman must have made life miserable for a young boy like him." **"She had a very loyal":** Marietta Eighme: Just before her death, Lizzie Pollock confided in a friend, "I love them boys more than life itself." **Image of small boy:** ACM. **"To an unnatural":** SLM, int. by Shorthall, 1959. **Death of Alexander McCoy:** Martha Dawson. Soon after his return to Missouri on April 26, 1881, he married Mary Jane Thompson; Martha Dawson; marriage certificate, Bates County, Mo., Recorder's Office, July 22, 1881. Henderson Clark (Martha Dawson; *The History of Cass and Bates Counties,* pp. 365–68), Mary Jane's first husband, was murdered by Richard T. Isaacs on August 26, 1978, for the cattle he was driving to St. Louis. Isaacs proceeded to St. Louis and, three days later, sold the cattle for $955.20. Isaacs seems to have stolen the cattle because his fiancée, a Miss Chilson, had rejected his previous proposal, saying that he could not support her adequately. Isaacs was captured on September 5, sentenced on September 25, and hanged on October 25. "This case presented one of the most remarkable known in the history of the county for cold-blooded cruelty and atrocity." Clark's death left Thompson with two small sons and 360 acres of prime Missouri land; Martha Dawson; Lynch; Robertson. Under Missouri law, the land automatically became Alexander's property when he married her in 1881. During the three years of their marriage, Alexander and Mary Jane had two children, Mabel Edith and Mary Zenetta, the second born after Alexander's death in an outbreak of dyptheria that also killed Mary Jane's two sons by Henderson Clark. Mary Jane had one child by her third husband, a tyrant named Andrew Jackson Dugan who is alleged to have murdered her. **Roy receiving nothing:** FLP. **Walter Edie:** Ringgold County Tour Bulletin, July 27, 1927. Walter Edie's farm was located in section 17. **Strong for his size:** ACM. **Package deal:** SLM, int. by Shorthall, 1959. **Farming boys out:** Wayne Overholtzer. **Orphans:** Crippen. **"Sometimes a kid wouldn't get along":** Clair Heyer. **Gangs working farms:** SLM, int. by Shorthall, 1959. **Panoramic photo:** ACM **Roy running away:** SLM, int. by Shorthall, 1959; O'Connor ("The Genesis of JP," p. 2), incorrectly cites this interview as evidence that Roy moved to Arkansas. There is, in fact, no evidence of such a flight. Solomon (p. 18) writes that Roy ran away to Missouri and returned home after two weeks starving. Although we were told the story of such a flight (by Arloie McCoy, JP's sister-in-law), we found no further evidence of it. **"Horses straining":** TCHC, p. 102. **"A craftsman of the soil":** CCP. **"Liquor difficult to obtain:** Wayne Overholtzer. **Iowa Prohibition: "We promise to abstain":** TCHC, p. 76. Lizzie was a member of the Tingley chapter; TCHC, p. 76. **Cheering for Weaver:** CCP. **Iowa Grange membership:** Sage, p. 189. **Farmers at mercy of bankers:** Sage, p. 212. **Iowa farmers resisting Populism:** Wall, p. 143. **Voting Republican:** Wall, p. 154. **LeRoy embracing socialism; Roy's politics; celebrating Russian Revolution:** FLP: Roy "was very much interested in the Russian Revolution, in the idea of the workers taking over a state." **Only 25 percent graduating:** Clair Heyer: As of 1890.

Inspiration for raft trip: FLP to Crippen, Apr. 26, 1983: "Mark Twain's stories were doubtless the compelling force behind this adventure." **Roy and Ralph setting out:** Tidrick, "Ralph Tidrick," in TCHC, p. 294. **Stopping to earn money:** CCP. **Work at a hotel:** Tidrick, recalling letter from Aunt Etta Foster. **Learning French:** Tidrick. **Tidrick falling ill; boys returning:** Tidrick enlisting: Tidrick, "Ralph Tidrick," in TCHC, p. 394; Tidrick. **Adoption:** Ringgold County, Iowa, Recorder's Office, book 14 of Misely, p. 594. **Tingley attitude toward adoption:** Crippen. **Adoption for control:** SLM, int. by CG, c. 1956: It was done "in order to control him." **"Throw his suitcase":** Tidrick.

McClures disappointed: Bennett, recalling Stella's brother Les McClure. **Social pecking order; "ne'er-do-well":** Bennett. **"On the trashy side":** Clair Heyer, recalling his mother, Daisy Smith Heyer. **McClures warming to Roy:** Bennett. **"A very quiet man":** ACM, int. by Vallière, n.d.

"People were able": Clair Heyer. **John McClure training Roy:** Bennett. **"Lone Socialist":** Q. by SMP, q. by MLP. **Anna almost dying:** Margaret Eighme. **Mary a nurse:** Frances Overholtzer. **Mary accompanying Anna; Anna returning to die:** Margaret Eighme. **John Keicher; death of Anna; Mary's marriage:** Honeyman, p. 61. **Keicher a conductor:** Solomon, p. 16. But Margaret Eighme says he was a rancher. **Stella finding work; becoming engaged:** Josephine Eighme. **Stella's pregnancy and marriage:** Marriage license and certificate, Box Butte County, Nebr., Recorder's Office, Jan. 13, 1903. The marriage took place on January 14; *Tingley Vindicator,* Jan. 29, 1903: "Word has been received by Tingley relatives of the marriage of Mr. Roy Pollock and Miss Stella McClure, which took place January 13 [sic] at Alliance Nebraska. They are now living in Wyoming."

This sequence of events was unknown to JP and his brothers, who always assumed that Roy moved to Denver to join Stella and that they were married there in January 1902. On the marriage certificate, Roy is listed as residing in Tingley, not Denver. Clearly, the family story was fabricated, presumably by Stella, to cover an awkward situation.

3. STELLA'S BOYS

SOURCES

Books, articles, documents, and transcript

Burke, *Buffalo Bill; Encyclopedia Americana: 1985;* Honeyman, *The Willson Family Tree;* McWilliams, *Southern California Country;* Morison, *The Oxford History of the American People;* OC&T, *JP;* Patrick, *The Best Little Town by a Dam Site;* Solomon, *JP;* Wyoming State Archives Museums and Historical Department, *More Buffalo Bones.*

Park County Enterprise, Jan. 31, 1912; *Park County Enterprise,* Nov. 16, 1912; "The Big Store that Sells Everything," *Cody Enterprise,* July 1, 1972; "Fruit Cost $54,000,000," *NYT,* Jan. 13, 1913; "Obituary—J. M. Pollock," *Tingley Vindicator,* Dec. 2, 1909.

Maricopa County, Ariz., warranty deed, Sept. 15, 1913; Wyoming State Board of Health Bureau of Vital Statistics, Cheyenne, certificate of birth, file no. 1912, registered no. 2656, May 31, 1938.

SLM, int. by Kathleen Shorthall for *Life,* 1959, Time/Life Archives.

Interviews

Sam Allen; Margaret Louise Archbold; R. L. Archbold; T. P. Benton; Catherine Carlin; Steve Cotherman; Mary Ellen Engle; Gottlieb Friesinger; Francis Hayden; Doug Langdon; Donna Mack; ACM; ABP; CCP; CCP (int. by SWP); FLP; MJP; MLP: Charles Porter; John Queenan; Nene Schardt; Lucile Schoppe; John Van Alstine; Ellen Waggoner.

NOTES

Buffalo Bill: See Burke. Charles and Jay remember meeting Buffalo Bill: "We didn't know him," says Jay, "but we played marbles with him." **Wealthy landowners:** Patrick, p. 10. **Description of Cody in 1905:** Photo in possession of ACM; Patrick, p. 73. **Recruiting Buffalo Bill:** Patrick, p. 16. **"Look out for wild Indians"; smelling salts:** Patrick, p. 27. **Indians:** Patrick, p. 5. **Mountain lion:** Patrick, p. 81, extracted from the *Cody Enterprise,* Feb. 1905. Paddy McGinnis, a miner who was in the shop at the time, grabbed the lion by the throat, threw it across the shop, then killed it with a steel bar. **"Occupations":** *Cody Enterprise,* Dec. 1902, q. in Patrick, p. 57. **"Enterprise, energy":** *Cody Enterprise,* Dec. 1902, q. in Patrick, p. 57. **Canal and dam:** Patrick, p. 69. **Irma Hotel:** Patrick, pp. 45, 56, extracted from the *Cody Enterprise,* July 1901 and Dec. 1902. **Cherrywood bar:** Van Alstine. **Film companies:** In June 1912, a "Kinemacolor man from London, England," came to make a "natural moving picture film of Cody"; *Cody Enterprise,* q. in Patrick, p. 160. **"Eastern gentlemen":** Patrick, p. 136, extracted from the *Cody Enterprise,* Apr. 1909. **Remington:** In May 1907, R. F. Elwell, an artist from New York, told the *Cody Enterprise,* "that one would find a $500 Remington (of Wm. F. Cody, scout) hanging on the wall of a store so far from the big centers is certainly convincing proof of the townsmen's artistic tastes." **"School marm" tours: Patrick, p. 139, extracted from the *Cody Enterprise*, July 1909. **"Dear Sir":** "Girl Wants a Cowboy," *Northern Wyoming Herald*, Dec. 1910, q. in Patrick, p. 150.

Bank killing: "Murder Most Foul Committed at Cody," *Meeteetse News*, Nov. 2, 1904, q. in Patrick, p. 78. **First movie house:** The Electric Theatre; Patrick, p. 136, extracted from the *Cody Enterprise*, Apr. 1909.

Roy working at hotel: CCP. **Salsbury Avenue house:** Hayden; MJP. For the 1901 town plat, drawn by Bronson Rumsey, see Patrick, p. 22. **View of river:** CCP. **Marvin Jay:** Honeyman, p. 60. Marvin Jay was born on May 27, 1904, and called "Mart" until his wife, Alma, decided that she preferred the name "Jay." As a boy, Charles was called "Chas." **Sunlight Copper Mining Company:** Patrick, p. 73, extracted from the *Cody Enterprise*, Mar. 1904; in this article, "Pollock" was misspelled "Pollack," an error that fills the Pollock literature to this day.

Rock-crushing plant: CCP. **Roy part owner:** CCP; FLP; MJP. Charles and Jay say Gideon Hayes owned it; Frank says Tom Archbold. **Aunt's house:** Schoppe. **Description of parlor:** CCP; photos in possession of ACM. **Ladies' Home Journal:** FLP. **Cody Trading Company:** "The Big Store that Sells Everything," *Cody Enterprise*, July, 1, 1972. Jay says he and Charles traded gunny sacks for penny candy at the store.

Ladies' Emporium; small diamond; "Poker Nell": Patrick, p. 63, extracted from the *Cody Enterprise*, July 1903. The paper explained the diamond as "a flashy eye-catcher, something that could be a distinct advantage for a card dealer." **Stella following fashions:** CCP. **Photo of family:** In possession of MJP. **Hierarchy of privileges; refusing to speak to Roy; tantrum:** MJP.

Roy cutting hair: MJP. **Photo of Charles and Marvin:** In possession of MJP. **Buggy ride:** CCP. **Orange Athletic Club:** Patrick, p. 112, extracted from the *Cody Enterprise*, Feb. 1907. Sometime during this period, a large, "unsociable" bull buffalo escaped from Colonel Cody's corral and "ran berserk up and down Sheridan Avenue." After trying unsuccessfully to rope it, the cowboys opened a corral gate near the center of town and baited it with several domesticated cows. "The idea may have had some merit," a local historian observed, "but neither the cattle nor the buffalo could see it. The fence was strained at both sides of the corral as the cattle tried to leave in one direction while the bull tried the other," Patrick, p. 85, extracted from the *Cody Enterprise*, Aug. 1905; CCP. The commotion brought out all the townspeople to watch, including Roy and Charles. From the high vantage of his father's shoulders, the sight of the penned animal—eighteen hands high—made an indelible impression. In the next few years, Charles would recount the story to each of his brothers as they became old enough to admire and envy him; CCP, int. by Shorthall, 1959. The sight must also have come back to Roy, time after time, as he began to feel his family moving in one direction while he tried the other. **Frank born:** Honeyman, p. 60: Frank Leslie was born on August 9, 1907.

Sant Watkins ranch: Hayden. A second section of the ranch—with a house and sheds for handling the sheep and a lambing shed—was located about three and a half miles south of Cody. **Hart Mountain:** Solomon, p. 19. **About $400 a year; alfalfa:** Hayden. **Johnson County War; "hired killers":** Morison, p. 759. **Five people killed:** *Encyclopedia Americana: 1985*, 29, p. 587. **Linn's Sheep Ranch raided; "blasted him":** Patrick, p. 118, extracted from the *Cody Enterprise*, May 1907. **Similar raid; "ran the herder off":** Patrick, p. 130, extracted from the *Cody Enterprise*, May 1908.

Description of Sanford Watkins: Hayden. **Sanford Pollock born:** Sanford LeRoy was born on May 26, 1909; Honeyman, p. 60; see FLP. **Camp herders' life:** Hayden. **With 10,000 sheep:** FLP. **JP's tales of the West:** Benton. **Images of frontier life:** E.g., *Going West*, c. 1934-38, OC&T 16, I, p. 16.

Roy beginning to drink: MJP. **Number of bars:** Hayden. **"Boys buying whiskey":** *Northern Wyoming Herald*, Nov. 1911, q. in Patrick, p. 147. **"Shooting up the town":** A.C. Thomas, editor, *Meeteetse News*, Apr. 1906, q. in Patrick, p. 98. **"An overdose":** *Meeteetse News*; June 1908, q. in Patrick, p. 132. **"Ladies of the town":** Patrick, p. 94, extracted from the *Cody Enterprise*, Feb. 1906. **"Let's Trample Evil":** James Hook, editor, *Cody Enterprise*, Feb. 1906, q. in Patrick, p. 94. **Primary cause of death:** Patrick, p. 134, extracted from the *Cody Enterprise*, Nov. 1908. **Hunting trips:** CCP.

Roy rarely caught drinking: CCP; MJP. FLP: "Dad very probably did drink when he was away." **Winter of 1910-11:** R. L. Archbold. **Roy short of breath:** FLP. **Tom Archbold ill:** R. L. Archbold. **Health designated reason:** FLP. Charles disagrees that Roy's health led to their departure from Cody, but Dr. Friesinger says his endocarditis would have been affected by the cold. **Lower Sage School:** Hayden. **Stella initiating move:** CCP. **Death of Tom Archbold:** R. L. Archbold: He died of tuberculosis. **Pollocks wanting girl:** MJP.

Roy going for Dr. Waples: Solomon, p. 19. **January 28, 1912:** Certificate of birth, Wyoming State Board of Health Bureau of Vital Statistics, Cheyenne, File No. 1912, Registered No. 2656. **Annie Howath:** Hayden; ABP. Jay and Alma later visited Cody and met Annie Howath, who remembered midwifing three Pollock boys. But Alma remembers Stella telling her that, because of the difficulty of JP's birth, the doctor had to be called in.

Description of Dr. Waples: Hayden. **"That's nothing new":** SMP and CCP, q. by ABP. **"Black as a stove":** SMP, q. by ABP. In births with this kind of complication, there is a high incidence of oxygenation and minimum brain damage, which can lead to difficulties in impulse control, irritability, and concentration—all problems that plagued JP in later years. Dr. John Queenan: "The baby may turn from a head-first to a rear-end position and may get the cord wrapped loosely around the neck. Usually, this doesn't make any difference in the uterus, but when the baby starts to descend in the birth canal during labor, then commonly the cord tightens. It would be just like somebody putting their hands around your neck and squeezing. It cuts off the blood flow—the oxygen supply—to the brain. The baby's head would be cyanotic—blue to purple." See also interview with Dr. Mary Ellen Engle. **Jackson's birthweight:** "A fine son, weighing twelve pounds and a quarter, was born Sunday morning to Mr. and Mrs. Roy Pollock of this city. This makes five sons that have come to live in this happy family and the Pollocks are quite the envy of the whole community"; *Park County Enterprise*, Jan. 31, 1912. **Stella never bearing another child:** ABP, recalling SMP. **Roy going hunting; called "Jack":** FLP. **Roy leaving Cody:** "Mrs. L. R. Pollock and five sons expect to leave in about two weeks for San Diego, California, where they would make their home. Mr. Pollock went out to San Diego about a month ago, where he is now at work at his trade. He has purchased a lot in the city and expects to build in a short time"; *Park County Enterprise*, Nov. 16, 1912. This was typical of the newspaper stories fabricated by Stella to enhance her image in a community she was joining or leaving. **Trip to Tingley:** CCP; MJP. **Met by sleigh:** MJP. **"For Sale":** *Park County Enterprise*, Nov. 1912, q. in Steve Cotherman, "Ten Months in Cody," p. 8.

National City a fruit-growing town: Solomon, p. 22. **Leaving Cody on November 28, 1912:** SMP to CCP and SWP, Feb. 6, 1958: "Jackson was born 28-1912. He wasnt a year old when we went to San Diego. Dad and all you kids had the mump & measles in Jan we went to Phoenix in August Frank went with Mrs edelman as her husband was in Phoenix they went Aug 9th Franks birthday six year old and the rest of the family the next week I don't remember the year he went to New York. we left Cody on Thanksgiving day *1912*." **Trip to National City; across Puget Sound; Stella not breastfeeding in public; veil:** CCP.

Roy unable to find work: CCP, FLP, and MJP. **Plasterer; farm worker:** MJP. **Staying with Mrs. Edelmann:** FLP; SMP to CCP and SWP, Feb. 6, 1958. **Sixth Street:** Solomon, p. 22. **Jackson the most beautiful baby:** Margaret Louise Archbold. **Mother's face:** FLP. **Mother's mouth:** ACM. **Epidemic:** SMP to CCP and SWP, Feb. 6, 1958; CCP.

Iowa farmers going to California: McWilliams, pp. 162-64. **Roy dreaming of farm:** FLP; MJP. **Only scraps remaining; freeze:** FLP. "Fruit Cost $34,000,000," *NYT*, Jan. 13, 1913: The fruit growers alone lost $19,169,880 as "the result of the recent cold wave." **Leonard Porter; contact with Porter; distant relative:** FLP. Porter: They were related through Roy's maternal grandmother, Elizabeth McClelland. **Porter moving to Phoenix:** Charles Porter. **Roy visiting Phoenix:** CCP; FLP. **Frank sent ahead; family following:** SMP to CCP and SWP, Feb. 6, 1958. **Plot of land:** Warranty deed, Maricopa County, Ariz., Sept. 15, 1913. Excluding the streets that bounded the plot, it was closer to eighteen acres. **Distance from town:** Solomon (p. 27) incorrectly states the size of the plot as forty acres. **Rooming house:** FLP. **Arriving at house:** CCP.

4. SENSITIVE TO AN UNNATURAL DEGREE

SOURCES

The chapters on the Phoenix years could not have been written without the help of Arloie Conaway McCoy's (Loie Conaway's) unpublished children's story, "The High Steps and the Low Steps," which she lovingly assembled during the late 1930s from Sande's stories about his youth in Arizona. Some fictional elements were added by Arloie—for example, a young girl named Rosemary who comes to live with the Pollock family—but for the most part the stories are careful retellings of Sande's memories of actual events, and we have verified with Arloie the stories that we extracted from her manuscript for use in these chapters. We have also verified the material in the chapters with Charles, Frank, and Jay Pollock.

Some of the names in "The High Steps and the Low Steps" were taken directly from the Pollock family: Sande, for example, remains Sande, and the dog Gyp remains Gyp. Some of the names are only slightly changed: the Moris, for example, became the Moros and the Pollocks became the McKays—a slight variation on the original family name McCoy. However, some name changes are more significant: Charles becomes Michael and Jackson becomes Peter; Jay and Frank have been collapsed into a single character named Tom. For clarity, we have substituted the real names for the fictitious ones in all quotations from Arloie's manuscript.

Books, articles, manuscripts, documents, and transcript
Barr, Jr., *Matisse*; Diamonstein, *The Art World*; Friedman, *JP*; Golding, *Cubism*; Johnson, Jr., *Phoenix*; Metropolitan Museum of Art, *Monet's Years at Giverny*; FVOC, *JP*; OC&T, *JP*; Solomon, *JP*.

"Charles Pollock in Conversation with Terence Maloon, Peter Rippon, and Sylvia Pollock," *Artscribe*, Sept. 1977; Axel Horn, "JP: The Hollow and the Bump," *Carlton Miscellany*, Summer 1966; William Rubin, "JP and the Modern Tradition, Part I:1. The Myths and the Paintings," *Artforum*, Feb. 1967; William Rubin, "Pollock as Jungian Illustrator: The Limits of Psychological Criticism, Part I," *Art in America*, Nov. 1979; Charles Stuckey, "Another Side of JP," *Art in America*, Nov.–Dec. 1977.

Des Moines *Register*, Jan. 14, 1957.
Donnelly Lee Casto, "JP: A Biographical Study of the Man and a Critical Evaluation of His Work" (M.A. thesis), Tempe: Arizona State University, 1964; FVOC, "The Genesis of JP: 1912 to 1943" (Ph.D thesis), Baltimore: Johns Hopkins University, 1965.
Maricopa County, Ariz., warranty deed, Sept. 15, 1913.
SLM, int. by Kathleen Shorthall for *Life*, 1959, Time/Life Archives.

Interviews
Paul Brach; Peter Busa; Jeremy Capillé; Nicholas Carone; Donnelly Lee Casto; Irene Crippen; Karen Del Pillar; Sylvia Fink; Dorothy Hitt; Edward Hults; Sam Hunter; Reuben Kadish; Ruth Kligman; Joe LeSueur; Donald McClure; ACM; Evelyn Minsch McGinn; Shizuko Mori Kato; Akinabu Mori; CCP; CCP (int. by SWP); EFP; FLP; Jonathan Pollock; MLP; MJP; SWP; Charles Porter; Ellen Schreck Rifley; Nene Schardt; Araks Tolegian; Evelyn Porter Trowbridge; Lee Vrooman; Samuel Wagstaff.

NOTES

"Shrieks of laughter"; "Chamber of Horrors": L. Merrick, "Chamber of Horrors," *Art News*, Mar. 1, 1913, in Diamonstein, p. 25. **Picasso:** Golding, p. 122. **Matisse:** Barr, Jr., p. 160. The critic was Marcel Sembat. **"I tend":** Q. in Barr, Jr., p. 160. **Monet:** Metropolitan Museum of Art, p. 32. **New home:** Warranty deed, Maricopa County, Ariz., Sept. 15, 1913. **Jackson seeing with retina:** Brach: "When Matta returned to the U.S. in the mid-1950s, he put down the new American painting as being 'merely retinal.' " **"To an unnatural degree":** SLM, int. by Shorthall, 1959. **Bookcase:** FLP. **Grass rug:** Conaway, p. 30. **Falling**

asleep: Conaway, p. 90. **Retreat from midday sun:** Conaway, pp. 29–30. **Dad reading; Mother clipping:** FLP. **Stella never touching books:** MJP. **Crochet basket:** Del Pillar; FLP. **Doilies:** FLP. **Pillowcases:** Jonathan Pollock. **Rugs; curtains; bedroom; sleeping arrangements:** FLP. **Sleeping nude:** FLP; MJP. **Teddy bear; "For some time":** Conaway, p. 87. **Lace:** MJP. **Pants and shirts:** FLP. **Socks and jeans:** Conaway, p. 42. **"They'll never stay":** Q. in Conaway, p. 42. **Everything made by Stella:** ACM.

Umbrella trees and blackbirds: FLP. **Sparse grass:** Conaway, p. 47. **Dinner on hot nights:** Conaway, p. 123. **Sleeping in yard:** MJP; Conaway, p. 123. **Protection from mosquitoes; "It'd be so hot":** Mori. **Cottonwood trees:** Johnson, Jr., p. 29. **Waiting for mailman:** Conaway, p. 33. **Stove:** FLP. **Not allowed near stove:** CCP. **Kettle:** CCP. **Stella washing clothes:** FLP. **Bathing:** CCP. **Christmas candy; walnuts, popcorn; "from corner to corner"; flypaper:** FLP. **Cellarway:** Conaway, p. 62. **Crocks of buttermilk; butter jar; apple barrel:** Conaway, p. 64. **Sweet milk:** Conaway, p. 63. **Skimming cream:** FLP.

Standing at screen door: FLP. **Stella priming pump; flume and trellis:** FLP. **Outhouse:** CCP. **Can of lye:** FLP. **Brothers urinating:** MJP. **Jackson urinating from seated position:** LeSueur and Wagstaff, recalling Kligman. **Description of barnyard:** Photos in possession of AAA. **Patchwork drinking milk:** Conaway, p. 45.

Description of Gyp: FLP. **Gyp's pedigree:** Conaway, p. 9. **"Great companion"; "member of the family":** FLP. **Collecting eggs; horses:** CCP. **"Getting too familiar":** FLP. **Hogs:** Conaway, p. 52. **Cows:** CCP says eight; FLP says twelve. **Milking cows:** Conaway, pp. 104, 106. **"Softened":** Conaway, p. 106. **Hayloft:** Conaway, p. 45. **Jackson fork:** FLP.

Size of farm: Mori; FLP; warranty deed, Maricopa County, Ariz., Sept. 15, 1913. **Low embankment:** Conaway, p. 46. **Adobe house:** CCP. **Surrounding mountains:** Porter. **Irrigation ditch:** Porter; Conaway, p. 46. **Water:** FLP. **Zanjero:** FLP. **"How many feet":** Q. by FLP. **Swimming in canal:** Conaway, p. 47. **Receding puddles:** Rifley. **Green "borders":** FLP; Conaway, p. 47. **Watermelon:** CCP. **Strawberries:** Porter. **Tomatoes:** FLP. **Cucumbers; cantaloupes; corn:** CCP. **Sweet potatoes, yams, okra; Phoenix farmers' market; alfalfa:** FLP.

Sand, rocks, and sagebrush: Conaway, p. 4. **Gravel banks:** Conaway, p. 17. **Gully:** Conaway, p. 20. **"Bare, rainwashed earth":** Conaway, p. 17. **Wooden bridge:** Conaway, p. 18. **"Here and there":** Conaway, p. 17. **Arroyo:** Conaway, p. 4. **Cacti; stillness:** Conaway, p. 20. **"Mother wouldn't like it":** Q. in Conaway, p. 16. **"Stay on the road":** Q. in Conaway, p. 18. **"If the brush rustled":** Conaway, p. 20. **Location of sanitarium:** Conaway, p. 3: A little more than two miles from the Pollock farm. **Description of sanitarium:** FLP. **Unnatural quiet:** Conaway, p. 7. **Jackson never saw sanitarium; "sick people":** Conaway, p. 18.

Location of Porter farm: FLP; Porter. **Sharecroppers:** Trowbridge. **"Lower class":** Rifley. **Friendly:** MJP. **Summer Sundays:** Porter. **Description of Schreck farm:** Rifley. **Description of Minsches:** McGinn. **Mr. Wyncoop; "retired prospector":** FLP. **Wyncoop owning Porter farm:** Trowbridge. **Inventions:** CCP. **Location of Mori farm; Yoshiro Mori a houseboy:** Mori: "For a while, my father was a very successful farmer. He was kind of a hustler, I guess. He was the first Japanese to buy a truck and the first to buy land in Phoenix, Arizona. He died at the age of forty-four [in 1921] and my mother remarried." Santa Cruz: Kato. **Ayame Hamasaki:** Mori. **Kumamoto; arriving in 1913:** Kato. **Local missionary:** Mori: The missionary was named Thornton. **Description of Mori house:** FLP. **Mori's truck:** Photo in possession of Mori. **Making bread:** Kato. **White dress:** Photo in possession of Mori. **Japanese food; Japanese newspaper:** Kato. **Calligraphy:** Message on back of postcard in possession of Mori. **Never attending church:** MJP: "When we were in Cody, I remember going to church a couple of times with my Father and Mother. But when we lived on the ranch, we never went to church so far as I know. And when we moved to Phoenix, we never went to church." Although Roy was an agnostic, Frank recalls that he permitted his wife to hang a portrait of Christ on a wall in their Phoenix home. **"Hayride picnic":** CCP. **The Hohokam:** Johnson, Jr., p. 18: The actual dates were 300 B.C., when the Hohokam migrated from present-day Mexico, to A.D. 1100, when the civi-

lization reached its peak. The population of its network of cities is estimated at 50,000 to 100,000. Without beasts of burden, the Hohokam built adobe homes that may have been several stories high and, using sharp rock axes, dug miles of canals to water their productive fields. The Hohokam art forms included pottery figures of humans and animals. **"The most complex"; Salt River valley:** Johnson, Jr., p. 18. **Accompanying Roy to Phoenix:** CCP; FLP. **Restaurant:** FLP. **Walking along tracks; "IWW":** CCP. The Wobblies, members of the IWW (International Workers of the World), were active in Phoenix during the years that the Pollocks lived there. Especially after World War I, the Phoenix local secretariat tried to unify all workers into a single large union, recruiting heavily from discharged soldiers and sailors; Johnson, Jr., pp. 87–88. **Roy explaining labor movement:** FLP; MJP.
Visitors: Conaway, p. 60. **Only 646 cars:** Johnson, Jr., p. 89. **Waiting for mailman: "I think":** Q. in Conaway, p. 34. **Selling melons to Indians:** FLP. **Apache wars:** Johnson, Jr., p. 49: During the 1890s, the citizens of Phoenix organized a group called the Phoenix Guards to "do battle with Apache marauders." Only when the boundaries of the Papago reservation were adjusted did the troubles with the Apaches end. **Seeing peaceful Indians:** CCP. **Old buggy:** Conaway, p. 5. **Brown Jim:** Conaway, p. 48. **Going to Goldwater's:** FLP. **Description of Goldwater's:** Johnson, Jr., p. 71. **Blacksmith; Pancho Villa:** CCP. **Chinese peddlers' "village":** Mori. **Baskets:** FLP. **Pots:** CCP to Rubin, q. in Rubin, "JP and the Modern Tradition, Part I: 1," p. 22 n. 9. **Silverware:** FLP; CCP to Rubin, q. in Rubin, "JP and the Modern Tradition," p. 22 n. 9. **Beads:** FLP. **Blankets:** CCP to Rubin, q. in Rubin, "JP and the Modern Tradition," p. 22 n. 9. **Jewelry:** FLP. **Saturdays:** Johnson, Jr., p. 74.

5. AN ORDINARY FAMILY

SOURCES

See Chapter 4.

NOTES

"An Ordinary Family": Manuel Tolegian, q. by Araks: On the surface, the Pollocks "*seemed* like an ordinary family" (our emphasis). **Pigs and cows:** FLP: "He was a very able craftsman. If he built a gate, it was absolutely level and the hinges hung just right. And if he made a fence, which he did with barbed wire that he bought in big rolls, every strand—whether it was three-strand or four-strand—was absolutely parallel." **Blue ribbons:** Solomon, p. 23. **Melons and alfalfa:** Conaway, p. 98. **Louisiana yams:** CCP. **Inviting Lizzie to Phoenix:** FLP. **Watermelon photo:** In possession of Hitt. **Sandy soil:** Mori: The Pollocks' land was even sandier than the land immediately surrounding it. **"A very quiet type":** FLP. **Only Frank committed:** FLP. **Charles delivering papers; family kitty:** CCP. **Stella refusing to help; insisting on choice vegetables:** FLP.
Reading to Charles and Jay: MJP; FLP: "With the younger sons he didn't have that much contact." **Kerosene lamp:** FLP. **Talk of Mississippi trip:** CCP. **Talk of adoption:** MJP. **Belief in the "higher power"; slingshots forbidden:** FLP. **Scolded for destroying eggs:** Conaway, p. 128. **"Look up from his plow":** MJP. **Readings becoming rarer:** FLP. **Jackson crying for Roy:** Conaway, p. 54. **"The kind without":** Conaway, p. 59. **Shooting at nine:** Conaway, p. 19. **Driving team at ten:** MJP. **Charles driving to sanitarium:** CCP. **Choicest jobs:** CCP; FLP; MJP. **Walking in order of age:** Conaway, p. 57. **"Tagging along":** Conaway, p. 56.
"Low Steps, High Steps": Conaway, p. 1. **Footraces:** Conaway, p. 3. **"The High Steps were awakened":** Conaway, p. 1. **School arrangements:** Casto, p. 12. **Spoiling Jackson:** MJP: "We didn't ask him to help out around the house. We worked, and he did whatever he wanted to." MLP: "Maybe the whole family conspired not to let Jack work because they worked so damned hard." Kadish: "You might say he was just a spoiled little brat, the way everybody took care of him, provided for him." **Jackson waiting for trivial tasks:** Conaway, p. 47. **"I will too":** Conaway, p. 76. **"As I ran":** Conaway, pp. 57–59. **"Busy running":** Conaway, p. 131. **Jackson referred to as "the baby":** FLP. MLP: "They used

to refer to him as baby up until his teenage years." **Jackson's recurrent dream:** Hunter, recalling dream recounted to Greenberg. **"His trips":** Conaway, p. 131. **Fabricating presence at birth of Brown Jim:** Conaway, p. 121. **"'Remember the time'":** Conaway, p. 18.
"Making mischief": Kato, q. by FLP. **Telling Sande about "playing doctor":** Kadish and Schardt, recalling SLM. Schardt: "He was caught playing doctor once and very severely reprimanded by his parents or by the girl's parents."
"Charles read the funnies": Conaway, p. 30. **Marbles, gum, bubbles:** MJP. **Jackson and Sande trying to whistle:** Conaway, p. 16. **Prince; *Republican*; movies and circus; velodrome; "Model T Polo":** CCP. **"Just like Grandma":** EFP. **Cody papers:** Notably the *Cody Enterprise* and the *Meeteetse News*. **Cartoons; artistic epiphany:** CCP. See CCP to FVOC, Nov. 17, 1963, q. in FVOC, "The Genesis of JP," pp. 8–9. **Mrs. Warner:** CCP. Sande thought her name was Mrs. Bidwell, which is why O'Connor calls her that in FVOC, p. 9. **Charles cutting out illustrations; "library of art":** CCP. **"And learned to make":** "Charles Pollock in Conversation," p. 12. **Wilson School; Ginsu Matsudo; drawing of submarine:** CCP. **"Charles started":** SLM, int. by Shorthall, 1959. **"When Jackson was a little boy":** Jan. 14, 1957.
Sande shooting birds: FLP. **Old enough to hunt:** Nine was the required age; SLM, int. by Shorthall, 1959. **Sande wanting to go hunting:** FLP. **Jackson consigned to Sande:** Kadish, recalling SLM: "Sande took care of Jack from the time they were toddlers. There could have been some animosity." EFP (Charles's first wife, who is very protective of him): "For the first ten or twelve years of Jackson's life, Charles was like his father and his mother in caring for him in the family." But all of the evidence suggests that it was Sande who played these roles. **Stella holding Sande back:** FLP.
Date of finger incident: Porter. OC&T (IV p. 205) mistakenly assigns the incident to 1923. **Roy with zanjero; Stella with Lizzie:** MJP. **Sande near chopping block:** SLM, int. by Shorthall, 1959. The chopping block is visible in photo in possession of AAA; see FVOC, p. 12. **Charles Porter present:** Porter; Trowbridge. Porter (born Sept. 8, 1908) was eight years old at the time of the incident. **Jackson fetching piece of wood:** SLM, int. by Shorthall, 1959. **Chopping block:** CCP. **"Porter saw Jack":** SLM, int. by Shorthall, 1959.
Rooster swallowing fingertip; "almost a pet": SLM, int. by Shorthall, 1959. **No one saw rooster swallow it:** SLM, int. by Shorthall, 1959; Porter. **Searching for fingertip:** CCP. **Porter running home; Jackson led to Stella; Stella reacting calmly and treating wound:** SLM, int. by Shorthall, 1959. **Stella commandeering horse and buggy:** MJP. **Dr. Monacle:** FLP; Porter. The only other doctor in the area was Dr. Coit Hughes, the Porter family doctor. FLP: "The finger healed. There was some root still there, and the nail grew out—sort of curved over the end of it."
"The one who got sick": SLM, int. by Shorthall, 1959. **"Laid his finger":** McGinn to FVOC, May 17, 1964, q. in FVOC, "The Genesis of JP," p. 6. The story that Porter dared his friends to put their finger on the block and let him cut it off and that JP took the dare is reported in Horn ("JP," p. 82), but Porter and Trowbridge persuasively deny this. **"Were bored":** Horn, "JP," p. 82. **Sande wielding ax:** Hults. By punishing himself, was JP trying to punish Sande for abandoning him in favor of Porter? In letting Porter cut off his finger, was he imagining himself in the opposite role, wielding the ax at Porter—like his father castrating a pig, perhaps, or his mother beheading a chicken—instead of daring Porter to wield it at him? Many years later, when frustrated or angry, he often fantasized beheading or castrating people.
Stella seldom visiting: CCP; Mori; Porter. **"Low-down drudgery":** SMP, q. in Solomon, p. 26. **Poring over printed matter; Henry Field catalogue:** FLP: "In that catalogue, Field always told the history of the family and showed pictures of them." **Writing letters:** Crippen. **Stella staying indoors; garden:** FLP; MLP. **Best ingredients:** FLP. **Trying new recipes:** MLP. **Neglecting everyday chores:** FLP. **"An exquisite seamstress":** EFP. **"My mother despised":** "Charles Pollock in Conversation," p. 12.
Pollock boys eating every meal at home: CCP. **Medical care in Phoenix:** Johnson, Jr., p. 87. **Avoiding medical care:** FLP: She didn't even take Frank to the doctor when he cut his elbow "to the bone." **Avoiding school events:** CCP.

Boys kept from church: FLP. "Independent and adventurous": SLM, int. by Shorthall, 1959. "Ran for his life": FLP. "Made Mother nervous": FLP. "Did you miss me": Q. in Conaway, p. 72. Bull attacking buggy; Stella and JP thrown: Wilcox. Frank Pollock remembers that Stella experienced a "runaway" in Phoenix, but he doesn't recall it was caused by a bull or that JP was in the buggy at the time. Stella with Jackson: McClure; Schardt. Jeremy Capillé (Stella's grandaughter): "I used to have the feeling that Grandma was angry. Afterwards, as I got older, I realized that was just the way she was." On one occasion, JP ran into the kitchen to tell his mother about a dogfight he had just seen. Stella asked, "You weren't bitten, were you?" When JP said no and started to explain, she dismissed him abruptly. "All right—wash yourself"; story in Conaway, p. 28. "[Mother] wanted me": Q. in Conaway, p. 79. "A very timid child"; "Evie": Trowbridge.
Sande playing "house": Conaway, pp. 126–27. Scene recreated for camera: Photo in possession of Trowbridge. In 1946, JP painted a man and a woman—or a boy and a girl—sitting at a table drinking tea, and called it The Tea Cup: OC&T 150, I, p. 142. Ten years after leaving Phoenix, when Laxinetta asked him how he lost the tip of his finger, JP claimed he accidentally chopped it off himself while killing chickens; and in 1942, when his mother visited him in New York, he gave her a painting of a huge figure wielding a knife: Naked Man with Knife (OC&T 60, I, p. 47). ACM: Stella later claimed it was her favorite of his pictures. "Lee Krasner Pollock . . . always considered these pictures [Naked Man and Bird] related"; Rubin, "Pollock as Jungian Illustrator, Part I," p. 123.
"A glutted market": CCP to FVOC, Nov. 17, 1963, q. in FVOC, "The Genesis of JP," p. 5. Development of long staple hybrid; demand: Johnson, Jr., p. 82. "Cottoncrazy"; small farmers squeezed out: SLM, int. by Shorthall, 1959. At about this time, the Goodyear Tire and Rubber Company began setting up test farms to develop hybrid long staple cotton. "Cotton grew well in the rich alluvial soils of the valley," says Johnson, Jr. (p. 82), "and many farming fortunes were made on a scale never before seen in Phoenix." "Hopelessly extravagant": "Charles Pollock in Conversation," p. 12. Argument: CCP. Talk of sending Frank to agricultural school; Stella sending for brochures: FLP. "Something different": MJP. Possible ultimatum: CCP. Roy uninvolved: FLP; Schardt. Auction: FLP. Date of auction: Jan. 1918, according to Maricopa County, Ariz., land deed, cited in Solomon, pp. 26–27. Stella passing out watermelon; "it was the end": FLP.

6. ABANDONED

SOURCES

Books, articles, manuscript, brochure, and documents

McAlester and McAlester, A Field Guide to American Houses; McElvain, The Great Depression; McGie, The History of Butte County; Morison, The Oxford History of the American People.
William S. Evans, Jr., "Ethnographic Notes on the Honey Lake Maidu," Part I, Nev. State Occasional Papers, no. 3, Carson City: Nevada State Museum, May 1978; Francis A. Riddell, "Honey Lake Paiute Ethnography," Part II, Nev. State Occasional Papers, no. 3, Carson City: Nevada State Museum, May 1978.
Susanville Lassen Advocate, June 24, 1921.
Loie Conaway, "The High Steps and the Low Steps," (unpub. ms.), n.d.
Brochure for Diamond Mountain Inn, c. 1913, printed by B. R. Holmes.
Butte County Records, Feb. 11, 1918, p. 287; Butte County Records, Dec. 31, 1919, p. 442; Great Register of Lassen County, General Election, Nov. 3, 1920; Lassen County Deeds, Jan. 30, 1920, Book 6, p. 73; Lassen County Deeds, July 11, 1921, Book 8, p. 339.

Inteviews

Patricia Bigler; Jeremy Capillé; David Dozier; Marjel Dozier; Margaret Eighme; Mary Ann Fast; Richard Fast; Edward Garza; Jerome Garza; Marjorie Keene; Joseph McGie; Evelyn Minsch McGinn; Donald McKinney; Gordon McMurphy;

Ted Meriam; Hester Grimm Patrick; CCP; FLP; MJP; SWP; Jay Pullins; Tim Purdy; Francis Riddell; Wayne Somes; Gladys Swearingen; Araks Tolegian.

NOTES

"Something better": FLP. Rise in Chico population; farming: Meriam. Churchgoing: Pullins. Diamond Match Company: Meriam. Trees and flowers: McGie, I, pp. 222, 224. Life of John Bidwell: McGie, I, pp. 33–35. Bidwell's widow: McGie, I, p. 35. Her name was Annie Kennedy. Mrs. Bidwell's treatment of Indians; funeral: Keene. Sacramento Avenue farm: The Pollocks purchased the farm on February 11, 1918, for about $4,000 (inferred from the $4 in revenue stamps) from W. S. Kilpatric and Irene H. Kilpatric; Butte County Records, Feb. 11, 1918, p. 287. Stella's decision: FLP. Built at turn of century: Richard Fast. Craftsman movement: McAlester and McAlester, pp. 453–55. Description of house; failure to inspect property: FLP.
"The dirty seven": Patrick. "Charles looked like an artist": Somes. Charles in rumpled jeans: Photo in possession of Patrick. Charles as dandy: CCP. Gray dress vest: CCP. "Charles always had": SWP. Obsessed with breasts: Based on dozens of hours of interviews with Charles, Frank, and Jay. "Lovely ornamental borders": Patrick. Photo of Jackson: In possession of McGinn. Stella hanging Charles's art: FLP: "In Chico, Charles's art was all around the house, paintings and things. Landscapes mostly." Charles has no such recollection.
Jay enlisting: MJP. Jay the athlete: FLP; MJP. "Pollock Tore Up Campus": MJP. "Punk"; "squirt"; Jackson watching Jay box: FLP. "I was pretty competitive," Jay recalls, anticipating JP's later attitude toward his success as an artist, "and I was getting all this credit because I was a good football player or boxer, and yet I always had the feeling that it was somehow false."
Agricultural demonstrations: FLP. Growers' cooperative: CCP. Alkaline strip: FLP. The land has since been made usable. "The water used to drain through here," says Somes, a Pollock neighbor who still owns the adjoining property, "and it brought alkalies and salts up to the surface. In 1918 or 1920, they diverted the run-off to Mud Creek and that solved the problem." FLP: Before buying the property, Roy hadn't even taken the simple precaution of "checking with the neighbors, who could have warned him about the problem." Pumpkins: McGie, II, p. 10. Roy's job in rice fields: CCP; FLP.
"I heard her say": FLP: I never heard of Jews before that time. I thought, who the hell are the Jews?" Although Stella seems to have brought a typical nineteenth-century anti-Semitism with her to northern California ("she was actually anti-Semitic in a sense," says Frank), it was not a deep-seated prejudice—"she really didn't know much about them." She showed no antagonism when three of her five sons married Jewish women. Northerners: McGie: These winds passed through Chico from the Sacramento Valley to the San Joaquin Valley; they would last about three days, and then the winds would reverse, bringing rain.
Jackson attending school: Bigler, attendance data technician, Chico Unified School District, to authors, Mar. 5, 1984. Description of Sacramento Avenue School: Somes; photo in possession of Patrick. "The Tartar": Somes. Phelan Ranch: Phelan was a California state senator; Somes. Banana cream cake; jumping from trees: FLP; Somes. Ball games: Somes. Slingshots: FLP. Dragonflies forbidden target: Somes. "Once in a great while": Meriam.
Agriculture and war's end: McElvain, p. 11; McGie, I, p. 210: "When wartime Food Administrator Herbert Hoover allowed the price of wheat to be set at $2.20 a bushel, farmers increased wheat acreage by nearly 40 percent and output by almost 50 percent. This in turn meant chronic 'overproduction' in the 1920s, a massive agricultural depression during America's 'prosperity decade,' and a further dislocation in the world economic structure." Farm mortgages doubling: McElvain, p. 36: The figure was $3.3 billion in 1910; $6.7 billion in 1920. Decrease in farm income: McElvain, p. 21. Roy losing money: FLP.
Roy unhappy in Chico; looking for new property: FLP. Sale of Chico farm: Butte County Records, Dec. 31, 1919, p. 442. The Pollocks sold the farm to Frank V. Wienner. Purchase of Janesville Hotel: Purdy to authors, Oct. 28,

1983; Lassen County Deeds, Book 6, p. 73. **Collateral agreement with Rice:** Purdy to authors, Oct. 28, 1983. **Cherry trees:** FLP. **Sheep:** FLP.

Janesville population: McMurphy. **Failed second trip for look at hotel:** FLP; MJP. **Hotel room rate:** David Dozier. **Weather in Janesville:** Jerome Garza.

Snow; trip to Janesville: FLP. **Description of escarpment and Honey Lake:** Jerome Garza: Honey Lake was all that remained of a huge inland sea called Lake Lahontan, which covered all of the valley in prehistoric times. **General store:** FLP. **Post office; Odd Fellows Hall:** McMurphy. **Bank:** Jerome Garza. **Burl tree:** McMurphy. **Highway:** Marjel Dozier: The highway ran from Doyle to Susanville. **Houses cut off from each other:** McMurphy. **"We had very little communication":** Marjel Dozier.

Sierra Nevadas, a barrier; town's founding: Jerome Garza: The area was first settled by Isaac Roop in 1854. **Janesville population:** McMurphy and others regularly gossip about the town's many maimings and murders. Marjel Dozier: The town was founded about 1860 and named after an early settler, Jane Christie Decious. **Visit from neighbor family:** FLP. **"That was a family":** McMurphy. **High fence:** FLP, McMurphy: The steps were called a "style" and were used either to keep the children from climbing through the gate or to provide access during a heavy snow. **Mrs. Drake and Miss Smith:** FLP.

Diamond Mountain Inn: Purdy: The hotel was built by Dennis Tanner. Even during the winter, JP could be trapped in the hotel for long periods if school was closed because of harsh snowfalls. McMurphy: "In February [1919], it cut loose with four feet of snow here. We were stranded on our home ranch and we didn't go back to school for about three weeks." **Black Bart:** McGie, I, p. 234. For details of Black Bart's career, see McGie, I, pp. 223–38. **Occasional salesmen:** CCP; FLP. **Permanent guests:** FLP. **Baxter Creek Irrigation Project:** Purdy to authors, Oct. 28, 1983. **Description of hotel:** Purdy to authors, Oct. 28 1983; advertising brochure of about 1913. **Elm leaves:** Photo in possession of Purdy. **Location of bar:** CCP. **Prohibition:** Eighteenth Amendment, Prohibition, ratified Jan. 1919, went into effect Jan. 1920. **Kitchen, dining room, and bedroom for "the help":** CCP. **Guest rooms:** Frank says there were fifteen to twenty rooms; Purdy says there were twenty-two. **Mélange of furnishings:** FLP.

Time of Bear Dance: Swearingen. **Indians appearing in front of the hotel:** FLP. **Wadatkut:** Riddell, p. 21. **White man settling in valley:** Riddell, p. 26: The man was Isaac Roop. **Babakukua ridiculing shaman:** Riddell, p. 24. **Servants and farmhands:** Jerome Garza. Marjel Dozier: "My grandmother was absolutely terrified of the Indians because they were very stealthy when they came to kill the whites." In fact, the Wadatkut were largely peaceful. Jerome Garza: There had been a "massacre" (Pearson's Massacre) in 1860 in which a white family was killed on the other side of Honey Lake, but that had been carried out by Indians from Nevada, not the local tribes. **Location of Bear Dance:** McMurphy. **Number of participants:** Swearingen, who is a Maidu princess and the granddaughter of the Maidu chief, or Hele, Joaquin, who officiated at the Bear Dance witnessed by the Pollock boys. **Kasawinaid:** Riddell, p. 39. The village name means "Takes his pants off" and refers to the actions of a local rancher who chased two Indians girls; the name is recent but the village probably had been inhabited since prehistory. **Granite boulders:** McKinney notes the similarity of these boulders in the Janesville burial ground and the boulders that JP would later try to sculpt in Los Angeles and pile in his backyard in Springs. **Pollocks watching:** FLP. **Bear Dance:** Swearingen; Evans, Jr., pp. 23–24, 33–39. **Stella cutting herself:** FLP: "She damn near lost her life." **Nora Jack:** FLP. **Legends:** Riddell, p. 91. She told them how Diamond Mountain had been much taller once, and on top was a spring where old people could bathe and regain their youth. One day the Coyote god suggested that old people should die. The Wolf god, who wanted to keep the spring open, objected. A terrible argument ensued during which the Coyote god became angry and kicked the side of the mountain so hard that the top half toppled over, forming nearby Bald Mountain, and the water from the spring spilled out into the valley, forming Honey Lake. The spring was gone and the last of its water soon dried up. Death became inevitable. **"Feasting, dancing":** McGie, p. 23. **Pollock church attendance:** CCP; FLP; MJP.

Jay's job in Altebertus; stopping in Janesville: MJP. **"Cat" Grimm:** Patrick: His given name was Quentin. **Charles's job in Westwood; not stopping in Janesville:** CCP. **Frank's job with Dr. May; "dropped in from somewhere";** Roy isolated and irritable; daily schedule; Stella's daily schedule:** FLP. **Guthrie's business proposition;** Roy spending time with surveyors:** FLP.

Dining room's local following: FLP. **Mortgage payments:** The Pollocks purchased the hotel with a $6,000 mortgage (Lassen County Deeds, Jan. 30, 1920, Book 6, p. 73) and sold it with a $5,890 mortage; Lassen County Deeds, July 21, 1921, Book 8, p. 339. **Automotive revolution:** McElvain, p. 18: From 1919 to 1929, the number of automobiles in the U.S. rose from less than 7 million to more than 23 million. **Fate of Diamond Mountain Inn:** Purdy: The hotel closed down in the late 1920s and was abandoned by the time it burned down in 1931. **Uncle Frank and family arriving:** CCP; FLP; MJP. **Roy admiring brother:** FLP. **Description of Rose Fivecoats:** FLP. She may have been of Indian origin. **Charles's arrival:** Susanville *Lassen Advocate*, June 24, 1921: "Three of L. R. Pollock's boys came home from Chico where they attended school." **Charles in Westwood:** CCP. **Description of Betty Nelson:** MJP. **"A conspicuous nose":** FLP. **Betty's breasts:** CCP; FLP; MJP: She was of either Swedish or Norwegian descent. FLP: Uncle Frank had adopted her as a homeless six-year-old in order to rescue her from an alcoholic and ne'er-do-well father; see also Les McClure to Miss Queree, n.d.

Roy caught drinking; Roy's time not accounted for; Political discussion at hotel: CCP. **Presidential contest:** Morison, pp. 880–83. **Roy's support for Debs:** CCP. **Sheep incident:** FLP: "Mother would have sided with her boys. She would have accepted our story that we had nothing to do with the sheep. And even if we had, it wouldn't justify giving us a beating." **Roy joining surveyors:** FLP. **Stella registering for Roy:** Great Register of Lassen County, General Election, Nov. 3, 1920.

7. LOST IN THE DESERT

SOURCES

Books, articles, manuscripts, brochure, documents, and transcript

Branstetter, *Pioneer Hunters of the Rim*; McGie, *History of Butte County*; OC&T, JP; Russell, *Orland's Colorful Past*; Wigmore, *The Story of The Land of Orland*.

"Arizona: Apache Trail," *Tonto Trails*, Summer 1983–Winter 1984; "Charles Pollock in Conversation with Terence Maloon, Peter Rippon, and Sylvia Pollock," *Artscribe*, Sept. 1977; *Dial*, July–Dec. 1922; Arthur M. Hind, "Some Remarks on Recent English Painting by Arthur M. Hind," *International Studio*, Jan. 1925; Norman Mead, "Kohl's Ranch," *Tonto Trails*, Summer 1983–Winter 1984; Norman Mead, "Welcome to Tonto Country," *Tonto Trails*, Summer 1983–Winter 1984; Tracy Mead, "The Salado: Mysterious Cliff Dwellers of the Tonto Basin," *Tonto Trails*, Summer 1983–Winter 1984.

"Boy Was Faithful to his Canine Companion," *Orland Unit*, Sept. 6, 1921; *Orland Unit*, Aug. 23, 1921; *Lassen Advocate*, July 15, 1921; *Lassen Advocate*, Aug. 26, 1921; *Lassen Advocate*, Sept. 2, 1921.

Donnelly Lee Casto, "JP: A Biographical Study of the Man and a Critical Evaluation of His Work" (M.A. thesis), Tempe: Arizona State University, 1964; Loie Conaway, "The High Steps and the Low Steps" (unpub. ms.), n.d.

Frederick Stansbury Clough, *The Stansbury House, Chico, California*, Chico: Appelman Press, 1976.

Glenn County Records, July 11, 1921, p. 414; Glenn County Records, Jan. 6, 1923, p. 76; Lassen County Deeds, July 11, 1921, Book 8, p. 339; Phoenix Public School Records, 1923–24; Walnut Grove Elementary School Teacher's Register, Sept. 4, 1922–May 23, 1923.

SLM, int. by Kathleen Shorthall for *Life*, 1959, Time/Life Archives.

Interviews

Myrtle Branstetter; Peter Busa; Carroll Carr; Stuart Cleek; Robert Cooter, William Fellersen; Helen Finch; Dorothy Hitt; Wesley Johnson, Sr.; Wesley Johnson, Jr.; Reuben Kadish; Marjorie Keene; Ruth Kligman; Minabelle Laughlin; Conrad

Marca-Relli; ACM; Evelyn Minsch McGinn; John Bernard Myers; CCP; FLP; MJP; MLP; Charles Porter; Patsy Southgate; LeRoy Tucker; Evelyn Porter Trowbridge; Otto Wackerman; Roger Wilcox.

NOTES

"L. R. Pollock traded": *Lassen Advocate,* July 15, 1921. On August 26, 1921, the *Advocate* reported, "Mr. Gearhart, new proprietor of the hotel property has taken possession of that place" and, on September 2, 1921, that "The Pollocks, former proprietors of the hotel, left Tuesday (August 30th) for Orland, their new home." **Sale of Janesville property:** Lassen County Deeds, July 11, 1921, Book 8, p. 339: The Pollocks bought the Orland farm from A. R. and Rose B. Gearhart for ten dollars and sold them the Janesville hotel for the same amount. **Trip to Orland:** FLP. **"F. Pollock":** *Orland Unit,* Sept. 6, 1921.
Location of Orland farm: Today the farm is on the northeast corner of the intersection of Route 32 and Road P. **Handsome house:** Fellersen. **Barn, windmill, orchard:** FLP. **Eighteen acres:** Glenn County Records, July 11, 1921, p. 414. The Pollocks purchased the south lot of number 5, subdivision number 14, which consisted of 17.5775 acres. **"One of the better houses":** Fellersen. **Once active; Frank tending farm; "hay for sale"; monthly check:** FLP.
Land around Orland: Keene: "You wouldn't believe how barren and vacant this land was." **Water from mountains:** Russell, p. 32: In 1906, local farmers requested the construction of a project under the Reclamation Act of 1903. The secretary of the interior approved the project on December 18, and a location was chosen about three miles north of the confluence of Stony Creek and Little Stony Creek. "Irrigation water from the project, one of the oldest federal reclamation projects in the country, began on April, 8, 1911." **Dry winters:** Wigmore, p. 55. **Paving Streets:** Wigmore, p. 54. **"Blocks of ice":** Keene. **Swimming pool:** Keene; Wigmore, p. 51. **Farmers talking:** Wigmore, p. 51. **Birch family:** Cleek. **Petersen:** Fellersen. Petersen, who employed Frank occasionally, died after the Pollocks left Orland.
"Storm after storm": Wigmore, p. 51: "During one week of that storm, 3.16 inches of rain fell here and Stony Creek went on its greatest rampage since 1915." **Talk of wells and dams:** Wigmore, p. 56. **Second jobs:** Keene. **Russian pickers:** Finch. **Pearce & Frank's; People's Store:** Keene. **Stella's illness:** FLP. **Details of illness unknown:** Frank later assumed it was a boil on her thigh that had to be lanced. He may be confusing this medical problem with a similar one in Janesville when a sore caused by a rusty can had to be lanced. **Charles visiting Orland:** CCP. **Date of visit:** New Year's weekend indicated in *Orland Unit,* Jan. 3, 1922. Wigmore, p. 57: New Year's Day 1922, "bitter cold." **Charles quitting school:** CCP: "I began to realize that I wasn't going to get much of a grade and maybe wouldn't graduate at all." **"Get involved":** CCP, q. by MJP. **Reasons for leaving:** CCP: Not only because of his poor grades but because "I had fights with the academic overseers, who objected to the things I wanted to do on the *Caduceus.*" **"Get all of it"; "the educated professions":** Q. by FLP. Only much later did her son recognize the irony of Stella's position: encouraging her sons to get a good education while "putting a lot of hazards in the way"; FLP. **"Isolated"; "something that seemed more important"; Jay's surveying job:** MJP. **Frank outwardly submissive:** FLP. **Frank attending Chico High:** FLP. B. W. Shaper, principal of Chico High School, confirms that Frank attended for one year, beginning in September 1922. **Homer:** FLP. **Roy held blameless:** FLP: "The only thing I have to stop to think about, and I've only done that recently, is why he didn't get a job in the community, closer to where we lived, so we could all be together."
Less and less money: FLP; Cleek: "Times was pretty tough. Folks was awful hard up. As I recall, it doesn't seem like the Pollocks boys was very flush with money either. They were poor just like the rest of us." **No electricity:** Finch. **Gauthiers:** FLP. **Drucks:** Finch. **Sharps; Stella's activities on Orland farm; Mortgage; selling farm:** FLP. **Sale of Orland farm:** Sold to George E. Wright of Orland on January 6, 1923; Glenn County Records. "As far as I can determine, our equity in the Orland farm was sold for a 1920 Studebaker Special 6 and two residential lots, one in the hills above Oakland and another in Half Moon Bay, which is below

San Francisco." Soon after the sale, the Pollocks sold the two properties—sight unseen—through realtors. **Possessions lashed to car; Gyp on trip:** FLP. **Jay along on trip:** MJP.
Arriving in Phoenix: FLP: The family left Chico in June but began living with the Minsches in September. The summer may have been spent in Phoenix looking for a home. "I don't think my mother had arranged to live with the Minsches before we got there." **Job in Tonto National Forest:** Frank is not clear if Roy was fired from the survey crew, if the work just ended, or if the same crew was transferred to Arizona. **Hearing of Mrs. Minsch's death:** CCP; FLP. **Minsch farm:** McGinn. Jacob owned forty acres; but his niece and nephew, whom he "looked out for," owned eighty more acres. **"Raw-boned"; raucous laugh:** FLP. **Minsch family origins; sharing bunkhouse with Minsch boys:** McGinn. **Walnut Grove School photo:** In possession of FLP, who says it was taken February 14, 1922. **Photo of outing with Minsches:** In possession of McGinn. **"The sexiest thing":** LK, q. by Myers. **Last picture:** In possession of Kligman. **Trowbridge and Sabelman:** Trowbridge taught JP and Sande in 1921–22; Sabelman taught school the next year, 1922–23, during which the Pollocks left in midyear; Teacher's Register for Walnut Grove Elmentary School, Sept. 4, 1922, to May 23, 1923. **"Hand-e-over":** Cleek: "We'd throw the ball and holler 'hand-e-over.' Whoever had the ball had to touch somebody on the other side. We drew a little circle—that was the jail—and if you touched anybody, why, they waited in the jail." **"Took a dim view":** Cleek. **Birds and animals:** McGie, I, p. 220.
Hiking along Salt River: McGinn; Orville Minsch, q. in Casto, p. 14: "We did the things that all boys do. . . . Jack loved the desert." **Swimming:** McGinn; Orville Minsch, q. in Casto, p. 14. **Digging caves:** FLP. **"Whacked":** McGinn. **Stella indifferent:** McGinn: "To my knowledge, she was never angry or upset." **Daredevil reputation:** McGinn, q. by Casto, incorrectly says it was during this stay in Phoenix that JP lost the tip of his finger, and that JP cut it off himself. **Birthday swim; Jackson killing cat:** McGinn. **Peck's bad boy:** Phrase used by Marca-Relli to describe JP as an adult. **Jackson refusing to skip school:** Phoenix Public School Records show that JP was present 162 days in the school year 1923–24, Sande only 79½. JP was admitted to Monroe School on September 17, 1923.
No contact with Indian culture: The earliest known contact with Indians was with the Wadatkut who, except for "a few fringes, beads and some beautful baskets" (Swearingen), had largely adopted the culture of their employers. **Shinn and Williams:** McMurphy. **"Diggers":** McGie, I, p. 223. The term applied to the local Janesville Indians because they had once subsisted on nuts dug from the ground; other regions had other epithets. **Shinn kicked to death; Williams dying in fight:** McMurphy, recalling Theresa Peterson Carmen Ross. **Monteze LeMaster:** Cleek; Finch. **Monteze's age:** Walnut Grove Elementary School Teacher's Register, Sept. 4, 1922– May 23, 1923. **"That girl was sure handy":** Cleek. **Art class:** Walnut Grove Elementary School Teacher's Register, Sept. 4, 1922–May 23, 1923: Much of Friday was devoted to cultural subjects. In addition to art class, the students recited poems from 11:05 until 12:00 and worked on their penmanship from 1:30 until 1:50.
Jackson going to Chico with Frank: FLP; MJP. **Charles drawing for school paper:** FLP. **"Awful"; "filthy"; Charles clipping reproductions:** CCP. *Studio:* "A Magazine of Fine and Applied Art," it devoted itself to defending English art from the encroachments of "fetish worship," a thinly veiled reference to the critical popularity of the new French painting among "turncoat" English critics like Roger Fry and Clive Bell; Hind, "Some Remarks," p. 3. **"I couldn't resist":** First sentence from our interview; second sentence from "Charles Pollock in Conversation," p. 12. **Stansbury encouraging Charles:** CCP; FLP; Tolegian. **Victorian house:** Clough, pp. 5–11. **Description of Stansbury:** Patrick; see Clough, pp. 15–16. **"She would always encourage":** Patrick. It was Stansbury who deduced that Charles was cutting reproductions from the library magazines, and urged him to confess his crime and, by working in the rice fields one summer, to reimburse the library; CCP. **Otis Art Institute:** CCP. Twenty-four years later, still teaching, she wrote: "I enjoy the students as much if not more than ever. There are always a few who thrill with their work"; Angeline Stansbury to CCP, Dec. 28, 1944.
"A revelation": CCP. **Articles in *Dial*:** Lawrence, "The

Fox," July, pp. 75–87, Aug., pp. 184–98; Mann, "Tristan," Dec., pp. 593–610; Russell, "The Aroma of Evanescence," Nov., pp. 559–62, and "What Is Morality," Dec., pp. 677–79; Pound, "Paris Letter," Sept., pp. 332–37, Nov., pp. 549–54; Williams, "When Fresh, It Was Sweet," Dec., pp. 617–19; Stevens, "Bantams in Pine Woods," July, pp. 89–93, and others; and Eliot, "The Waste Land," Nov., pp. 473–85. **Art reproductions in** *Dial:* Picasso, "Two Drawings," Oct.; de Fiori, "Bather," "Standing Figure," "Walking Figure," Aug.; Brancusi, *The Golden Bird,* Nov.; Marc, *Horses,* Sept.; Severini, *Fresco,* Oct. **Criticism:** Fry, "M Jean Marchand," Sept., pp. 388–91, and Purrmann, "From the Workshop of Matisse," July, pp. 32–40. *Les Capucines:* July. **Sande's artistic aspirations:** FLP; ACM; Cooter; Kadish. **Sande speaking of** *Dial* **on deathbed:** CCP.

Phoenix Union High School: McGinn. **Frank cutting classes:** FLP. **Sande cutting classes:** Phoenix Public School Records, 1923–24. **Frank drinking in desert:** FLP. He stopped drinking entirely in 1962; MLP. **Date of Minsch's marriage to Dowdle:** May 1924; McGinn. **Trip to Carr Ranch:** OC&T IV (p. 205) incorrectly states that "The family moved back to Chico in the spring." The error originated with Orville Minsch who was quoted by Casto (p. 13) as saying the Pollocks moved back to Chico in early spring of 1924. The error was repeated in OC&T along with the additional error that the Pollocks moved to Riverside from Chico when, in fact, they drove directly from the Carr Ranch to Riverside in early September 1924. **Warehouse burned to ground:** FLP. **Returning to California in fall:** FLP. **Location of Ranch:** Some 15–20 miles north of the intersection of Routes 88 and 288; FLP to authors, Nov. 30, 1985; Tucker. **Description of Ranch; "all the cowboys"; "housekeeping cabins"; "native" costumes:** FLP. **Mogollon Rim:** Pronounced "Muggie-own" and named after an early Spanish governor of the Territory of New Mexico. Zane Grey: Branstetter, p. 77: Grey saw his cabin for the first time on September 14, 1922. **Team of surveyors:** FLP: Roy "wasn't a surveyor. He was a roadman, or a chainman, or whatever." **Roy visiting Ranch:** FLP.

Day hike to Indian ruins: SLM, int. by Shorthall, 1959; Mead, "Welcome to Tonto Country," pp. 18–21; Conaway, pp. 157–79. Given Sande's description of the hike, the Cherry Creek cliff dwellings must have been the ruins the Pollocks visited. We have used a variation on one particularly felicitous phrase in Arloie's account: "Gradually the clouds below them were sucked up by the sun, disclosing a vista of unbelievable grandeur"; Conaway, p. 168. **Urinating on flat rock:** Southgate. Frank says the incident must have occurred during this hike.

Women doing masonry: Laughlin: Roy was correct. Although the men did the heavy construction work, the women prepared the mud for the bricks and plaster and often did much of the plastering as well, so the handprints JP saw probably were women's. In retelling the story, Sande guessed that the dwellings they visited had been built by the same Pueblo Indians whose extensive cliff dwellings in Colorado and New Mexico had become national parks; Conaway, pp. 174–76. In fact, the villages of the Tonto Basin were constructed by the Salado Indians between 1300 and 1400 as a defensive measure against marauding Apaches from the north; Mead, "The Salado," pp. 42–43.

8. JACK AND SANDE

SOURCES

Books, articles, manuscripts, brochures, documents, and transcripts

Conn, ed., *Current Therapy: 1954;* Friedman, *JP;* Klotz, *The Mission Inn;* Merritt and Kolb, eds., *The Medical Clinics of North America: May 1958; World Almanac 1985;* OC&T, *JP;* McWilliams, *Southern California Country;* Patterson, *A Colony for California;* Southern Calif. Panama Expositions Commission, *Southern California;* Polytechnic Hich School, Riverside, Calif., *The Orange and Green: 1928;* Robertson, *JP;* Tingley Centennial History Committee, *A History of Tingley, Iowa;* Wysuph, *JP.*

William Rubin, "JP and the Modern Tradition, Part I: 1. The Myths and the Paintings," *Artforum,* Feb. 1967; James H. Wall, "Psychotherapy of Alcohol Addiction in a Private Men-

tal Hospital," *Quarterly Journal of Studies on Alcohol,* Mar. 1945.

Donnelly Lee Casto, "JP: A Biographical Study of the Man and a Critical Evaluation of His Work" (M.A. thesis), Tempe: Arizona State University, 1964; Loie Conaway, "The High Steps and the Low Steps" (unpub. ms.), n.d.; FVOC, "The Genesis of JP: 1912 to 1943" (Ph.D. thesis), Baltimore: Johns Hopkins University, 1965.

Riverside Cultural Heritage Board Item, meeting date, Sept. 15, 1982: "Nomination of the JP House, 4196 Chestnut Street, as a Structure of Merit of the City of Riverside"; "Sherman (Institute) Indian High School," n.d.

Grant Elementary School Records, Riverside Unified School District, 1926–27.

JP, int. by Dorothy Seiberling, for *Life,* July 18, 1949, Time/Life Archives; SLM int. by CG, c. 1956; SLM int. by Kathleen Shorthall for *Life,* 1959, Time/Life Archives.

Interviews

Margaret Louise Archbold; Peter Busa; Tony Citarella; Clare Peterson Cooter; Robert Cooter; Gilbert Crowell; Violet de Laszlo; Harry Jackson; Esther Klotz; ACM; Gordon McMurphy; Vincent Moses; Tom Patterson; CCP; FLP; MJP; MLP; Russ Sweet; May Tabak Rosenberg; Araks Tolegian; E. Fuller Torrey; Roger Wilcox; C. L. Wysuph.

NOTES

Pollocks' belated move: Patterson. **Twenty-five years:** McWilliams, p. 163. **"The Iowa immigration to Southern California started about 1900, momentarily abated during the First World War, and then sharply increased from 1920 to 1930." Some 160,000 Iowans:** McWilliams, p. 163. Between 1920 and 1930, the population only rose from 2,404,021 to 2,470,939; *World Almanac 1985,* p. 249. **Skyrocketing land prices:** Farmlands purchased in 1880 for $5 were selling for $75 an acre in 1905; McWilliams, p. 163. **All-Year Club:** McWilliams, pp. 136–37.

Typical cars: Klotz. **"The first great migration":** McWilliams, p. 135, recalling Edwin Bates. **"Hog and hominy":** McWilliams, p. 168. By 1930, a third of all those who had been born in Iowa were living in some other state; McWilliams, p. 24. **"What part of Iowa":** McWilliams, p. 170. **"On the road":** McWilliams, p. 165. **Hot days:** FLP. **Date of arrival:** FLP gives the date as soon after Labor Day 1924; OC&T (IV p. 205) gives it as "late 1924 or early 1925," perhaps based on the lack of school records for the Pollock boys at Riverside Polytechnic High School. **Parade of cars:** McWilliams, p. 161.

Colony settlement; "people of intelligence": McWilliams, p. 215. **English citrus farms:** The Riverside Trust Company and the San Jacinto Land Company Limited; Patterson. **Tennis and Polo Clubs:** Klotz; Patterson. **Victoria placenames:** Moses. **First orange trees:** McWilliams, p. 209. **Development of orange industry:** McWilliams, p. 210. **"To own a well-stocked":** McWilliams, p. 207, recalling Charles Fletcher Lummis.

Premier winter resort: Patterson. Riverside later surrendered this reputation to Palm Springs. **Naming and enlargement of Mission Inn:** Klotz, pp. 6ff. **Cultivated and conservative community:** Moses. **Stella locating home:** FLP. The house, numbered 1196 when the Pollocks lived there, still stands, but the address has been changed to 4196. **"I never thought":** Robert Cooter. **Description of Pollock home:** Riverside Cultural Heritage Board Item, Sept. 15, 1982. **Stella's appetite for distinction:** FLP: "It was a *fine* house, and Mother took good care of it." To help pay the high rent, Stella started serving meals to people like Augusta Weeks, a nurse, and boarding people like Charlie Brockway, a classmate of Frank's. **Frank in Riverside:** FLP.

"The cowboy painter": Rubin, "JP and the Modern Tradition," p. 14. For the notion of JP as the "man out of the West," Rubin cites, in particular, Pierre Restany, "America for the Americans," *Ring des arts,* 1960. **"Lariats":** Rubin, "JP and the Modern Tradition," p. 14, citing Rudi Blesh, *Modern Art, U.S.A.,* New York: 1956, p. 253. **"Cattle range":** Rubin, "JP and the Modern Tradition," p. 14, citing Robertson, p. 35, who wrote that JP painted "in the way that a cow-hand wields a lariat." **"Into rapture":** Rubin, "JP and the Modern Tradition," p. 14: Among young Europeans, especially Frenchmen, "The very virtue of 'the American' is that he is supposedly naive, unconscious of, or outside, any traditions of art, and hence 'styleless'—a kind of Noble Savage. Pollock as cowboy not only fits into the French myth of an *école du pacifique* (which reaches east to the Badlands as well as west to Japan), but sorts well with the cult of Hollywood westerns celebrated by the young critics of the *Cahiers du cinéma.*" **"Saddles and horses":** Int. by Shorthall, 1959. **Jackson afraid of horses:** Jackson. **Single-shot .22s; avoiding large animals:** Robert Cooter: They did go deer hunting, but never killed a deer. **"The cowboys would get bored":** Int. by Shorthall, 1959. None of SLM's classmates remembers the cowboys; McMurphy. **"All the old codgers":** Int by Shorthall, 1959. **Jackson and Sande's relative sizes:** FLP. **Jackson and Sande wrestling:** Robert Cooter; ACM. **"The runt":** FLP. **Punching bag:** Robert Cooter. **Description of Riverside:** See Patterson, pp. 251-60. **Water scarce:** McWilliams, p. 5. **Santa Ana River:** The other two "driest rivers" are the Los Angeles and the San Gabriel: McWilliams, p. 6. **"Come out all dusty":** Q. in McWilliams, p. 6. **"The land does not":** McWilliams, p. 8, recalling Frank Fenton, author of *A Place in the Sun.* **Air and light:** McWilliams, pp. 6-7. **Description of Jackson and Sande:** Photo in possession of ACM. **Trips into mountains:** Robert Cooter. **Hunting in school clothes:** FLP. **More than 16,000 acres of groves:** McWilliams, p. 216. **Roaming in groves:** Moses. **Animals hunted:** Robert Cooter.

Sande emulating Charles: ACM: "I think he [Sande] began to get interested in art probably when he was thirteen or fourteen because Charles was interested in it. The younger brothers, particularly the younger two, were interested in what Charles did and were very proud of him. . . . I think that sparked them." **"I thought Sande":** See also Evelyn Minsch McGinn, q. in Casto, p. 14: "I would have thought that Sandy [*sic*] would have been the artist of the family because I remember he was the artistic one." **Clare Peterson:** Later married to Leon Cooter.

"Jack got inspired"; visiting Mission Inn; Robert Cooter. **Macaws:** Klotz, pp. 127-28. **Cloister Court:** Klotz, p. 28. **Spanish Art Gallery:** *Old Darby* and *Roman Warriors:* Klotz, p. 37. *Old Darby* was painted in 1884. **California Alps:** Klotz, p. 49. **Lola Montez's furniture:** Klotz, p. 47. Lola Montez was the stage name of Marie Dolores Eliza Rosanna Gilbert (1818-61), a "Spanish" dancer from Ireland who captured the eye of Louis I during a performance in Munich and, by encouraging political liberalism, brought about her own expulsion and his abdication. **Buddha:** Klotz, p. 65. **Ceramic cupid:** Klotz, p. 47. **"Catacombs":** Moses: The Riverside writer Helen Hunt Jackson had done much to "romanticize our Indian and Spanish pasts" after the city had rejected these pasts in the 1880s and 1890s. Along with a new respect for the missions and for Indians as "the noble savage," the "wealthy began collecting Indian artifacts." Conferences and colloquia on American Indians were also held at the Mission Inn during the 1920s. While in Riverside, JP could have seen Indian art at the Sherman Indian Institute (founded in 1892 at Perris, California, as the Perris Indian School, and later transferred to Riverside), a school for the "training of reservation Indians from all over the United States. It was an attempt to Americanize these Indians but by the same token to preserve their artifacts." During the 1920s, schoolchildren were regularly taken to the institute on field trips; see "Sherman (Intitute) Indian High School," n.p. **Description of Cooter:** Photo in **The Orange and Green:** 1928. **Joint activities in Riverside:** Robert Cooter. **Description of Leon Cooter:** Clare Cooter. **Date car acquired:** Robert Cooter: They had the car by 1926 and could not have had it before Sande's sixteenth birthday in 1925. **Description of car:** Robert Cooter; FLP: The tires were called cornhuskers because they were manufactured in Nebraska. **Livery stable:** Robert Cooter. **Fields of filaree:** Patterson, p. 36. **Weekend trips; tobacco:** FLP. **Quail; deer:** Robert Cooter. **Respite from heat and dust:** FLP. **Edge of Wrightwood:** Robert Cooter: The ridge is called Sulfur Slide. **Lone Pine Canyon Road camp:** Robert Cooter. **"Tent-shacks":** Robert Cooter; Conaway, p. 135. **Work of road crews:** Robert Cooter. **Pitching tent:** Conaway, p. 135. **Eating with workers:** Robert Cooter. **Stove:** Robert Cooter; McCoy, p. 136.

Little known of Roy: Neither the federal road-building authorities nor the state agencies bothered to preserve employment records from the twenties. **Roy foreman:** Robert Cooter. **Cabin:** FLP; Archbold. The camp had to exist by the spring of 1927 because that is when the Pollocks had to sell it

to pay the hospital charges for Sande's appendicitis. **Digging space for car:** FLP. **Roy at cabin:** MLP. **Roy visiting on holidays:** Robert Cooter: JP, Sande, and their father "didn't do things together. He didn't go on camping trips with us. He never was home enough. We seen him at the road camp more than we ever saw him at home and he'd only be home on Thanksgiving and Christmas"; confirmed by FLP. **Meeting men on Roy's crew:** Robert Cooter. **Description of Louis Jay:** FLP. **Jay working with Roy before:** Robert Cooter. **Jay visiting Pollock home:** FLP. **Spinning tales:** Conaway, p. 156. **Jay smoking pipe:** Conaway, p. 137. **Fred Wiese a Texan:** Robert Cooter. **Description of Jay and Wiese:** Photos in possession of ACM. **Jay and Wiese going to Grand Canyon; Jackson and Sande going to Bryce National Monument:** Robert Cooter. The monument was created in 1923, the national park in 1928. **Exploring Zion Canyon:** Robert Cooter. Zion National Park was established in 1919. **Markagunt Plateau; trip to Kaibab; "reclining mountain"; mustang hunt; introduced to "Red"; "better than an Indian":** Robert Cooter. **"How'd you guys":** Red, q. by Robert Cooter. **"Processing":** Robert Cooter.

Jackson graduating from Grant: Grant Elementary School records, 1926-27. **Two family moves:** An address of 1194 North Street appears on JP's school records from Manual Training School, indicating that the family had moved by September of 1926. The Pollocks rented the house at 4138 Mulberry for a short period prior to September 1926 and then moved to 3184 North Street (a later renumbering) by the beginning of the school year. Both the Mulberry Street and the North Street houses were destroyed when California State Route 91 was built; FLP; Cultural Heritage Board Item, Sept. 15, 1982. **"Soccer ball":** Robert Cooter. **Description of Sande:** ACM. **Sande finding "girlfriend":** FLP. **Sande a "ladies' man":** Crowell. **Still a small town:** Robert Cooter. **Conservative Calvinist:** Moses. **"Kissing and petting":** Robert Cooter. **D Street in San Bernardino:** FLP. **"Weenie bakes"; "button, button"; Sande "was never without a girl"; Jackson "puttering" and drawing; continuing to see Leon:** Robert Cooter. **Never dating:** FLP: "I don't remember him [Jackson] ever with a girl in Riverside." **Description of Arloie:** Photo in Polytechnic High School, Riverside, Calif., p. 26. **"Made you want":** Robert Cooter. **Sande watching Arloie; Cooter telling Sande about joint date:** Robert Cooter. **Arloie:** Also called Loie; ACM. **Jack and Sande passing Conaway home; trips with Arloie to mountains; Jackson staying home; drawing:** Robert Cooter. **Putting Gyp to sleep:** FLP. **Sande collapsing during run:** Robert Cooter. **No one calling Arloie:** ACM. **Cabin sold:** FLP; Robert Cooter. **Roy arranging jobs:** FLP. **Trip to Grand Canyon:** ACM; SLM, int. by Shorthall, 1959. **Seeing wheel roll by:** FLP; ACM.

"He always talked about it": LK: "I do remember he [Jackson] described that trip to the North Rim with fondness." **"Reconnaisance truck":** SLM, int, by Shorthall, 1959. **Jackson with main party:** FLP. **Transit man:** The transit man manipulated the repeating theodolite, also called the American transit, a device for measuring horizontal and vertical angles. **Chain man:** The chain man handled the Gunter's chain, a 66-foot chain made up of 100 links or short sections of wire connected to the next link by a loop; 80 chains equaled 1 mile; the Gunter's chain has since been largely replaced by the steel tape.

Roy on different crew: FLP. **Calabash pipes:** Photos in possession of FLP and ACM. Robert Cooter: Louis Jay smoked a pipe. **Louis Jay's fondness for Pollock boys:** FLP. **"Chemical vulnerability":** See Fox, "Treatment of Chronic Alcoholism," in Merritt and Kolb, eds., p. 808. Dr. Fox—one of the country's preeminent authorities on alcoholism—was briefly JP's own physician during the 1950s. **Friends noting Jackson's lack of tolerance for alcohol:** Rosenberg, etc. **Road workers amused:** Araks Tolegian, recalling Manuel. Most sources have isolated the trip to the Grand Canyon as the start of JP's drinking problem; see OC&T IV, p. 205, and Friedman, p. 7. CCP: "Jackson had been drinking since he was fifteen. He started on the North Rim of the Grand Canyon." It is likely that JP was drinking before this, and certainly Sande was. As for Louis Jay's role, Frank disagrees that he was in any way "responsible."

Hatchet accident: ACM. **Possibility of broken bone:** ACM: She wasn't sure if JP's leg was broken, but if it was, he wouldn't have been able to come home as he did. **Walking**

to Riverside High: Robert Cooter. **Furniture:** JP made a lamp and Sande a table, both now in possession of ACM. **Reputations as roughnecks:** ACM. **"The Gold Dust Twins"; Jackson no longer invited:** Robert Cooter. **Jackson's grades falling:** Grant Elementary School Records, 1926–27. **Slipping further:** SLM, int, by Shorthall, 1959. **Size of high school:** There were 1,115 students in the 1927–28 school year. **School sports relatively brutal:** Robert Cooter. **Sports or ROTC:** FLP. **ROTC:** Sweet, an ROTC officer during JP's year at Poly High. **Brothers disappointed in Jackson as athlete:** FLP. "The High Steps and the Low Steps" indicates that Sande knew JP had a "yellow streak" in him from childhood, despite Sande's later comments to the press about their adolescence. **Story of fight:** JP later recounted the story to Wilcox. Since Sande and Cooter often got into fights, such a confrontation seems likely. **Reputation for scrapping:** FLP; Robert Cooter. **"Mix it up":** Robert Cooter. **"Yellow":** Q. by Wilcox, recalling JP.

Liquor hard to come by: Moses. **ROTC incident:** Nowhere firmly dated, it must have happened soon after JP joined the ROTC in early fall. Although Sande told Greenberg, c. 1956, that JP was "kicked out for calling ROTC officer SOB," Sande's interview with Shorthall in 1959 indicates the incident alone did not cause JP to leave. If it was even contributory, however, it must have taken place before he decided to leave the school, no later than early December 1927, in time for word to get to his father by December 11, when Roy wrote to him. Thus a date of October or November. In "The Genesis of JP" (p. 11 n. 36), O'Connor quotes Mr. Robert Clyde, director of counseling and guidance for the Riverside Schools in a letter of May 7, 1964: "[JP's] records do not show him being enrolled in a ROTC unit," although Clyde conceded that "early records are relatively limited." Robert Cooter: "I never heard of that incident. . . . I am sure I would have heard of that if there had been anything to it." Given Sande's certainty, however, we believe the incident took place. The incident is mentioned in OC&T (IV p. 206) as well as in several other accounts, and has been wrongly cited to indicate that JP was kicked out of school, rather than out of ROTC.

"Leggings": Int. by Shorthall, 1959. **"You're a god damned":** Q. by SLM, int. by Shorthall, 1959. **"Kicked out":** SLM, int. by Shorthall, 1959. **Leon quitting school:** Peterson. **Jackson thinking about quitting; letter from Roy:** LRP to JP, Dec. 11, 1927. **Jackson quitting school:** In "The Genesis of JP," O'Connor quotes Robert Clyde, in a letter of May 7, 1964, as saying that "[Pollock] moved to Arizona on March 8, 1928." **Jackson going to Arizona:** Roy may have left for summer work in the Kaibab Forest in March 1928. He was there by summer and the break between summer and winter work usually came in March. It is still unlikely that JP traveled with him, since we know that JP worked at Crestline, not far from Riverside, during the summer. If he had gone with his father to Arizona in March, he would have stayed through the summer. **Sande going to Los Angeles: Frank going to New York:** FLP. **Summer job at Crestline:** LRP to JP, Sept. 19, 1928.

9. LIGHT ON THE PATH

SOURCES

Books, articles, catalogue, manuscripts, documents, and transcripts

Ashton, *Yes, but . . .* ; THB, *An Artist in America*; Blavatsky, *The Secret Doctrine*; Campbell, *Ancient Wisdom Revived*; Collins, *Light on the Path*; Friedman, *JP*; Goldman, *Contemporary Mexican Painting in a Time of Change*; Head and Cranston, eds., *Reincarnation in World Thought*; Helm, *Man of Fire*; Henstell, *Sunshine and Wealth*; Kandinsky, *Concerning the Spiritual in Art*; Krishnamurti, *Life in Freedom (LIF)*; Lutyens, *Krishnamurti*; McWilliams, *Southern California Country*; Manual Arts High School (MAHS), *The Artisan: Winter, 1929*; MAHS, *The Artisan: Summer, 1929*; MAHS, *The Artisan: Winter, 1930*; MAHS, *The Artisan: Summer, 1930*; McElvaine, *The Great Depression*; Murphet, *When Daylight Comes*; OC&T, *JP*; Olcott, *Old Diary Leaves*; Sinnett, *Incidents in the Life of Madame Blavatsky*; Solomon, *JP*; Sprenger, *Spirit of the Toilers*; Weaver, *Los Angeles*; Williams, *The Passionate Pilgrim*.

Articles in *Manual Arts Weekly (MAW)*; "Glimpses of the

Ojai Camp," *International Star Bulletin (ISB)*, July 1929; J., "Before the Ojai Camp: Krishnaji's Talks," *ISB*, July 1929; J., "Krishnaji in America," *ISB*, Apr. 1930; Krishnamurti, "The Noble Life," *ISB*, June 1930; Krishnamurti, "Some Questions and Answers," *ISB*, July 1929; Krishnamurti, "A Talk to Teachers at Los Angeles," *ISB*, June 1930; "Ojai Star Camp," *ISB*, Jan. 1929; "Charles Pollock in Conversation with Terence Maloon, Peter Rippon, and Sylvia Pollock," *Artscribe*, Sept. 1977; Yadunandan Prasad, "News Letter from America," *ISB*, July 1930; "Reports of Talks by J. Krishnamurti," *ISB*, July 1930; A. P. Sinnett, "H.P.B.," *Review of Reviews*, June 1891.

Des Moines *Register*, Jan. 14, 1957; *Manual Arts Weekly (MAW)*, Sept. 11, 1928–June 23, 1930.

Pennsylvania Academy of the Fine Arts, *Catalogue*, Philadelphia: Pennsylvania Academy of the Fine Arts, 1908–09.

FVOC, "The Genesis of JP: 1912 to 1943" (Ph.D. thesis), Baltimore: Johns Hopkins University, 1965; Laxmi P. Sihare, "Oriental Influence on Wassily Kandinsky and Piet Mondrian, 1909–1917" (Ph.D. thesis), New York: New York University, 1967.

CCP Papers, AAA; Chronology prepared by CCP for EFP, Feb. 1975, AAA; Krishnamurti Foundation of America Archives; L.A. Unified School District Records, Sept. 11, 1928, to June 5, 1930; Pennsylvania Academy of the Fine Arts Records, 1909–10; JP Papers, AAA.

SLM, int. by Kathleen Shorthall for *Life*, 1959, Time/Life Archives; Reuben Kadish, int. by James T. Vallière, n.d., AAA; Manuel Tolegian, int. by Betty Hoag, Feb. 12, 1965, AAA.

Interviews

Peter Busa; Marietta Bushnell; Herman Cherry; Paul Christopher; Robert Cooter; Elizabeth Schwankovsky Duncan; George Gosse; Ora Horton; Sam Hunter; Carolyn Schwankovsky Knute; Maria Piacenza Kron; Ernestine Lassaw; Berthe Pacifico Laxineta; Mark Lee; Harold Lehman; Paul McClure; ACM; Karleen Marienthal; Wes Meyers; Arthur Millier, Jr.; ABP; CCP; EFP; FLP; MJP; MLP; May Tabak Rosenberg; Grant Rusk; David Slivka; Araks Tolegian; Aram Tolegian; Ralph Turnquist; Roger Wilcox.

NOTES

Bungalow on West Fiftieth: 1056 West Fiftieth; L.A. Unified School District Records, Sept. 11, 1928, to June 5, 1930. **Drive from Riverside:** FLP. **"They were the first things":** McClure. **Stella window shopping:** ACM: Her favorite stores were Bullock's and Robinson's, still two of the leading department stores in Los Angeles. **Maternal duties discharged:** McClure. **Sande anxious for Los Angeles:** Cooter; ACM. **Arloie's anemia; Sande sleeping on couch; weekends in Riverside:** ACM. **Manual Arts:** See Marienthal; Sprenger. Destroyed in the earthquake of 1933, the original buildings were replaced by structures in a more streamlined style. **Double-time schedule:** Each class was in fact two classes, winter and summer, "A's" and "B's," each with its own yearbook, graduation ceremonies, officers, mascot, and class color. **3,200 students:** Actual number, 3,204; "Los Angeles High Leads List of Schools at Present," *MAW*, Sept. 18, 1928. **"The Land of enchantment":** Q. in Henstell, p. 17. The author of *The Wizard of Oz* continues: "[We had] passed a winter on the Nile, another at beautiful Taormina, had wintered at Sorrento, at Nice, and, in America, at the Florida and Gulf coast resorts. But it is only after we discovered Hollywood . . . that we wandered no more." Baum was paid by real-estate brokers for his glowing assessment. **Most students white:** See MAHS, *The Artisan: Winter, 1929*, pp. 17–46. The number of Oriental students was more impressive. **Students' clothing; "school is a business":** Duncan; Lehman. **Editorial about "cords":** "Boys Wash Your Cords," *MAW*, Feb. 25, 1930. **"Desist" from wearing makeup:** "Girls' Dress Rules," *MAW*, Feb. 4, 1929. **Demerits:** Laxineta. **Jackson's first day:** L.A. Unified School District Records, Sept. 11, 1928, to June 5, 1930. **"Schwany":** Duncan. **Schwankovsky handsome:** Duncan; Lehman. **"Kook":** Laxineta. **"Extremist":** Manuel Tolegian to Hoag, Feb. 12, 1965. **"He was on one side":** Lehman. **Bringing nudes to Manual Arts:** Duncan; Lehman. JP to CCP and FLP, Oct. 22, 1929: "We are very fortunate in that this is the only school in the city that have models. Altho it is difficult to have a nude and get by the board, Schwankavsky [*sic*] is brave enough to have them." **Schwankovsky's ancestry:** Duncan. **"An unhappy young man":** Duncan. **Pennsylvania Academy:** Knute; Pennsylvania Academy of the Fine Arts school records, 1909–10. Schwankovksy studied with Thomas P. Anshutz and William Merritt Chase; Pennsylvania Academy of the Fine Arts, pp. 4–5. **Art Students League:** Knute; FVOC, "The Genesis of JP," p. 13. **Goucher; séances and spirits:** Duncan. **Dickens "their guiding spirit":** Knute. **"The practical one"; tea leaves; Ouija board; "out-of-body experiments":** Duncan.

Schwankovsky set designer: Knute. **Silent movies;** Duncan. **Schwankovsky going to Manual Arts:** Duncan. **Merely competent:** Lehman. **Thirty-two years:** Schwankovsky to FVOC, Mar. 16, 1964, q. in FVOC, "The Genesis of JP," pp. 13, 33 n. 45: He was there for "some thirty-two years." Duncan says her father spent thirty-six or thirty-seven years at Manual Arts. **Schwankovsky's subject matter:** Knute. Lorser Feitelson to FVOC, June 3, 1964, q. in FVOC, "The Genesis of JP," p. 33 n. 47.

Stage sets: See Frances Jones, "Maid of France," in MAHS, *The Artisan: Winter, 1930*, p. 139. **Fencing team:** Duncan. **"Color week":** Louise Oliver, "School Life," in MAHS, *The Artisan: Summer, 1930*, p. 159. **Occasional solo:** Duncan. **Schwankovsky seldom teaching:** Laxineta. **Shirtsleeves:** Lehman. **Baritone:** Duncan; Laxineta. **Velvet cape; musical soirees:** Araks Tolegian, recalling Manuel. **Dark rumors:** Laxineta; Lehman. **Phrenocosmian:** Louise Oliver, "School Life," in MAHS, *The Artisan: Summer, 1930*, p. 165.

Lehman: Although Schwankovsky spent little time in the classroom, he often invited students into his office for "gabfests." Ashton, p. 14: "Guston and Pollock were Schwankovsky's star pupils." But neither Knute nor Duncan can remember him commenting on JP until late in life when a television crew in Los Angeles producing a short film on JP sought him out. The only student Schwankovsky remembered fondly according to Duncan was Gus Ariola, a cartoonist famous for the comic strip "Gordo." At Manual Arts, JP adopted the nickname "Hugo"; MJP; Araks Tolegian, recalling Manuel. JP used "Hugo" when he signed Tolegian's copy of the 1930 Manual Arts yearbook; Araks Tolegian. Schwankovsky was an admirer of Victor Hugo; Duncan.

"Artists with no firm base": Duncan: Her brother, Frederick Schwankovsky III, and his wife taught their pet "parakeet to say, 'Grandpa says down with modern art.'" **"Expand their consciousnesses":** Schwankovsky to FVOC, Mar. 16, 1964, q. in FVOC, "The Genesis of JP," p. 195 n. 45, **Poetry and music; painting dreams:** Duncan. **Schwankovsky's technical experiments:** Lehman; Araks Tolegian, recalling Manuel. Manuel Tolegian, int. by Hoag, Feb. 12, 1965: "We just poured paint on a piece of paper, you see, and we put watercolor with alcohol and turpentine." **"Crazed looking":** Araks Tolegian. **Schwankovsky borrowing from stage design; "He did a lot":** Duncan. **"[Jack] couldn't":** SLM, int. by Shorthall, 1959.

Goldstein and Guston: Throughout this period, Guston continued to use his family name, Goldstein, although he must already have contemplated changing it: He signed all of his cartoons in the *MAW* "Phil Goldstein" except one signed "Phil Goldy"; *MAW*, June 4, 1929. **"Drawing seriously";** Goldstein born in Montreal: Ashton, p. 12. **Goldstein dapper:** Ashton, p. 16. **Gathering in Schwankovsky's office:** Lehman. OC&T IV, p. 206: In 1928, JP's "acquaintances included Philip Guston, Reuben Kadish, Manuel Tolegian, Harold Lehman, Leonard Stark, Donald Brown, and Jules Langsner." In fact, JP didn't meet Lehman until Lehman moved to Los Angeles in February 1930. JP didn't meet Kadish, Langsner, or Stark until summer 1931 when JP returned to Los Angeles from New York. **Hodges banished:** Laxineta; Horton: Hodges, who met Mrs. Pacifico on a ship voyage from New York, boarded at her home. **Hodges's effeminate manner:** Horton. **Hodges's talent:** Laxineta. **Description of Brown; Brown's reading:** ABP; Friedman, p. 10; Ashton, p. 15.

Tolegian's birth date: Tolegian, int. by Hoag, Feb. 12, 1965: "Until I went into the Army, I thought I was born October 8, 1912." **"Jeriar Tolegian":** Aram Tolegian: Manuel was called Jeriar or Jeryar—the spellings were interchangeable—within the family. **Construction and farm work;**

grocery store; father getting cancer; dying; Manuel taking father's name: Aram Tolegian. **Manuel's tales of his father:** Araks Tolegian, recalling Manuel. Aram Tolegian: His father was a woodcarver, so he obviously had some artistic inclinations. **Chicken coop "studio":** Araks Tolegian, recalling Manuel; Aram Tolegian. **Sketches after masters:** Solomon, p. 40. **"He worked hard":** Q. by Araks Tolegian. **Pollock teaching others to smoke; Mrs. Tolegian's attitude:** Araks Tolegian, recalling Manuel: His mother's name was Haiganoush. **Sight of coop:** Aram Tolegian. **Alma marrying Jay; Brown's books:** ABP. **"Jack's mother":** Q. by Araks Tolegian. **Boys received by Stella:** Araks Tolegian, recalling Manuel. Jules Langsner to FVOC, Mar. 18, 1964, q. in FVOC, "The Genesis of JP," p. 23. **Goldstein sleeping over:** Ashton, p. 13.

"Philosophy of religion": LRP to JP, Sept. 19, 1928. **Painting of Jesus:** FLP. **Cooters devout:** Cooter. **"I think your philosophy":** LRP to JP, Sept. 19, 1928. **"The most celebrated":** John Steven McGroarty, 1921, q. in McWilliams, p. 249. **"Shrine of fakers":** Austin F. Cross, in Ottawa, Canada, *Evening Citizen*, q. in McWilliams, p. 248. **"Every religion":** Hoffman Birney, q. in McWilliams, p. 250. **Population of elderly:** Of the ten largest cities in the United States in 1950, Los Angeles had the second lowest percentage under age twenty and the highest percentage age forty-five and over; McWilliams, p. 229. **Cults with curative powers:** McWilliams, p. 257: "Invalidism and transiency have certainly been important factors stimulating cultism in the region." **"I am told":** Mrs. Charles Steward Daggett, 1895, q. in McWilliams, p. 249. **"Ranked as a leading industry":** Louis Adamic, q. in Weaver, p. 94.

Schwankovsky raised Episcopalian: Duncan. **Buddhist:** Kadish. **Hindu; Rosicrucian:** Lehman. **Friend of Blavatsky:** Lehman. **"Diffus[ing] information":** Henry Steel Olcott, Sept. 7, 1875, q. in Campbell, p. 27. **Description of Blavatsky:** Campbell, pp. 4–6. Sinnett, "H.P.B.," p. 554: She filled her stories "with expletives of all sorts, some witty and amusing, some unnecessarily violent." **Blavatsky's imagination:** Sinnett, p. 24: According to her sister, "at a young age," Blavatsky could tell the "most incredible tales" with the "cool assurance and conviction of an eyewitness." **Nineteenth-century enthusiasms:** Among these were Mesmerism, Swedenborgianism, Freemasonry, and Rosicrucianism; Campbell, p. 20. **"The unity"; "single, primitive":** Campbell, p. 36. **"Universal Over-Soul":** Blavatsky, *The Secret Doctrine*, pp. 14–17. **Blavatsky borrowing material:** Blavatsky claimed books such as *Isis Unveiled* were dictated by "somebody who knows all . . . My *Master*"; q. in Olcott, p. 214. William Emmette Coleman proved by textual analysis that the book was borrowed from more earthly sources: some one hundred early books on the occult; Campbell, p. 33. **"Cycle of incarnation":** (1) The Body, or *Rupa;* (2) Vitality, or *Prana-Jiva;* (3) Astral Body, or *Linga Sarira;* (4) Animal Soul, or *Kama-Rupa;* (5) Human Soul, or *Manas;* (6) Spiritual Soul, or *Buddhi;* and (7) Spirit, or *Atma;* Campbell, p. 66. **"Masters"; "Adepts":** Campbell, p. 24.

Séance hoax: In Bennares, Blavatsky placed a wooden shrine, or "cabinet," in the window that looked from her bedroom into an adjacent audience room; Campbell, p. 85. According to a press statement, "If letters, addressed to the Mahatmas, be placed in here and the doors closed for a few moments, the letters will be found to have disappeared, and replies written upon Chinese or Tibetan paper to have come mysteriously from the addressed Adepts"; q. in Murphet, p. 141. When Emma Coulomb, a dissatisfied assistant to Blavatsky, charged that the back of the cabinet could be opened and that the answers were written in Blavatsky's hand on rice paper resembling her personal note paper (Campbell, pp. 57–58), the cabinet was destroyed; Campbell, p. 90.

Annie Besant: Lutyens, pp. 13–14. As a young woman, Besant had fought for womens' rights (Williams, p. 30) and against the divinity of Christ, later taking up such causes as birth control and fair working conditions; Lutyens, p. 14; Campbell, p. 102. Asked to write a review of Blavatsky's tome, *The Secret Doctrine*, she found in Theosophy the direction and purpose for which she had been searching. **Leadbeater's pederasty:** Among Leadbeater's more controversial views was a belief in masturbation as a cure for rampant sexuality and a precaution against sexual diseases. When he was discovered imparting his philosophy to several adolescents—with demonstrations—a major scandal ensued; Campbell, pp. 115–18; Lutyens, p. 13. Besant reluctantly agreed that Leadbeater be removed from the society, but within two years of becoming president, she reinstated him; Campbell, p. 118; Lutyens, p. 19. **Membership of 45,000:** Lutyens, p. 50. Many wealthy dilettantes joined Lady Emily Lutyens, wife of the architect, in all but abandoning their families to follow Krishnamurti; Lutyens, p. 80. Blavatsky also briefly enlisted the support of Thomas Edison, William Butler Yeats, James Joyce (Campbell, pp. 168–69), and both Kandinsky and Mondrian.

As a young man, Wassily Kandinsky was enormously impressed with both *Theosophy* by Rudolf Steiner and *Thought Forms* by Annie Besant and Charles W. Leadbeater (Campbell, p. 169) as "a theoretical framework, an ideology, for carrying painting beyond the realm of representation"; Hilton Kramer, in Head and Cranston, p. 353. The solution—incorporated in Kandinsky's own book, *Concerning the Spiritual in Art,* published in 1910—was a joining of mysticism and art; Campbell, p. 169. Kandinsky was impressed by the society's eagerness "to approach the problem of the spirit by way of an *inner* knowledge," based on procedures derived from "ancient wisdom," especially Oriental religions; Kandinsky, p. 32. He learned from Blavatsky's *Secret Doctrine,* along with the books by Steiner, Besant, and Leadbeater, about correspondences between colors and sound and about the evolution of the universe from the intrinsic to the extrinsic as a model for the creation of art. "Technically," he wrote, "every masterpiece is created as the cosmos was"; q. in Sihare, "Oriental Influence," p. 85.

Mondrian, too, was fascinated by Theosophy. Sihare, "Oriental Influence," p. 249: "From 1914 onwards, Mondrian's primary concern was the ideal representation of Spirit and Matter in his paintings. . . . Mostly guided by Oriental and Theosophical symbolism and the basic concept of duality in unity, he coined his own formulas." Working both from the Theosophical appreciation of geometric shapes as religious symbols and from the notion that the artist, as a repository of both the male and the female, is in an ideal position to establish unity, Mondrian determined that vertical lines, black and white, and space symbolized the spirit; while horizontal lines, the primary colors, and form symbolized matter; Campbell, p. 171. By combining them in his de Stijl paintings, he created a material analogue for religious unity, a "harmonious representation of Spirit and Matter, the two aspects of the One"; Mondrian, q. in Sihare, "Oriental Influence," p. 260.

Magazine predicating "a new sixth sub-race"; "Theosophists all over": Q. in McWilliams, pp. 255–56. **"A great flying fish":** McWilliams, p. 255. The society was active in Southern California as early as 1900, when Katherine Tingley, a New England convert, established the Point Loma Theosophical Community near San Diego; Campbell, pp. 131–40. **"The new Messiah":** Lutyens, p. 254. **"The Divine Spirit"; "the Literally Perfect":** *Theosophist,* Jan. 1926, q. in Lutyens, p. 259. **Predicting "World Teacher":** Lutyens, pp. 11–12. **Description of young Krishnamurti:** Lutyens, pp. 3, 7, 22. **"Most wonderful":** *Clairvoyant Investigations by C. W. Leadbeater and "The Lives of Alcyone,"* some facts described by Ernest Wood; with notes by C. Jinaradasa (Adyar: privately printed, 1947), q. in Lutyens, p. 22. **"The definite consecration":** *Herald,* Mar. 1926, q. in Lutyens, p. 242. On December 28, 1925, in an address to the Star Congress at Adyar, at 8:00 A.M., standing under a large banyan tree, Krishnamurti first spoke as the World Teacher. **"Happiness through Liberation":** Lecture, May 15, 1928, Hollywood Bowl; Lutyens, p. 276.

Krishnamurti's message: See Krishnamurti. **Schwankovsky and Krishnamurti:** Schwankovsky to FVOC, Mar. 16, 1964: "Krishnamurti . . . was a personal friend"; q. in FVOC, "The Genesis of JP," p. 15. **World Teacher at Laguna Beach:** Duncan. **"The mouthpiece":** "Krishnamurti Relates Personal Ideas and Doctrines to Group of Young Philosophers," *MAW,* May, 20, 1930; see also Lehman; Friedman, p. 10; FVOC, "The Genesis of JP," pp. 15, 17. **Jackson relying on others for information:** Manuel Tolegian, int. by Hoag, Feb. 12, 1965: "He did very little reading. Between you and me, he couldn't read too well, or write. He never had the training."

"Was looking as a youngster": Elizabeth Wright Hubbard to FVOC, May 14, 1964, q. in FVOC, "The Genesis of JP," p. 33 n. 49. **"Often speaking of Schwankovsky":** FVOC, "The Genesis of JP," pp. 33–34 n. 53, recalling inter-

view with LK, Jan. 21, 1964. Kadish, int. by Vallière, n.d.: "Schwankovsky . . . both Jack and Phil [Guston] spoke of him. He touched both of them with a bit of mysticism." **Jackson writing Charles:** An undated letter from Charles to JP establishes that JP discussed the issue in earlier letters to Charles. **"Every thing it has to say":** JP to CCP, Jan. 31, 1930. JP used only lowercase letters in typing this letter to Charles. Friedman (p. 14) explains this as an imitation of e.e. cummings, to whose poetry he may have been introduced by Don Brown. But given the haphazardness of the margins, spacing, and punctuation, the complete absence of capitalization, the uniqueness of this letter (it is the only document JP is known to have typed), and the fact that JP clearly did not work from a draft, it seems far more likely that he simply had not mastered the use of the typewriter's shift key.

"If you make yourself": Krishnamurti, "A Talk to Teachers at L.A.," p. 6. In describing JP's reaction to Theosophy and Krishnamurti, we haven't limited ourselves to the two written sources that he mentioned in his letter to Charles: His awareness developed throughout his two years in Los Angeles and he learned far less from written sources than from what he heard from his teacher and friends as well as directly from Krishnamurti himself at Ojai. Where Krishnamurti's ideas quoted in the text do not derive from *Life in Freedom (LIF),* yet find parallels in that 1928 book, this is noted. Krishnamurti, *LIF,* p. 60: "I have painted my picture on the canvas and I want you to examine it critically, not blindly. I want you to create because of that picture a new picture for yourself. I want you to fall in love with the picture, not the painter, to fall in love with Truth and not with him who brings the Truth. Fall in love with yourself and then you will fall in love with every one."

"Through all time": Collins, p. 77. **"The moment you are really struggling":** Krishnamurti, "A Talk to Teachers at L.A.," p. 8. Krishnamurti, *LIF,* pp. 41–42: "Because you have no true purpose in life there is chaos within you; there is misery without understanding, strife without purpose, struggle in ignorance. But when you have established the goal of the Beloved [Truth] in your heart and mind there is understanding in your life. . . . When you have established the Beloved in your heart, you are ready to face the open seas, where there are great storms, and the strong breezes which quicken life." Also, p. 86: "Through contentment you do not find happiness, but a state of stagnation. If you would know true happiness there must first be that inward conflict, which will bring forth in you the flower of life."

"Which plows through mud": Q. in J., "Krishnaji in America," p. 17. **"The appreciation":** Q. in "Reports of Talks by J. Krishnamurti," p. 21. Krishnamurti, *LIF,* p. 56: "When my brother died, the experience it brought me was great, not the sorrow—sorrow is momentary and passes away, but the joy of experience remains"; and (p. 67) "If you would find that Truth you must put aside all those things upon which you have leaned for support and look within for that everlasting spring. It cannot be brought to you through any outward channel."

"I have often": Krishnamurti, "The Noble Life," *ISB,* June 1930, p. 20. **"It is indeed":** J., "Krishnaji in America," p. 17. Krishnamurti, *LIF,* p. 39: "Revolt is essential in order to escape from the narrowness of tradition, from the binding influences of belief, of theories. If you would understand the Truth, you must be in revolt so that you may escape from all these—from books, from theories, from gods, from superstitions—from everything which is not of your own."

"Each one": Krishnamurti, "The Noble Life," p. 22. Krishnamurti, *LIF,* p. 34: "As every human being is divine, so every individual in the world should be his own master, his own absolute ruler and guide." **"Self-perfection":** Krishnamurti, "A Talk to Teachers at L.A.," p. 12. **"To myself":** JP to CCP, Jan. 31, 1930. **"The swift knowledge":** Krishnamurti, "The Noble Life," p. 14. **"Intellect"; "make a living link"; "does it flow":** Q. in "Reports of Talks by J. Krishnamurti," pp. 7–8. **Need to rebel:** Krishnamurti, *LIF,* p. 48: "I have long been in revolt against all things, from the authority of others, from the instruction of others, from the knowledge of others."

10. A ROTTEN REBEL

SOURCES

See Chapter 9.

NOTES

"An heroic idealism": "Krishnamurti Relates Personal Ideas and Doctrines to Group of Philosophers," *MAW*, May 20, 1930. **Intellectual left:** Schwankovsky grew more conservative with time and ended up a rabid anti-Communist, much like Thomas Hart Benton. **Theosophy's political voice:** Campbell, p. 119. **"Not fit for heathen China":** Q. in Henstell, p. 50. **Upton Sinclair:** Henstell, p. 49; McWilliams, p. 290. The event took place in 1915. After Sinclair's arrest, a man read from the Declaration of Independence, and was arrested. A man then said, "We have not come here to incite violence," and was arrested; q. in McWilliams, p. 290. **The *Nation* removed; teachers labeled Bolsheviks; paid spies:** McWilliams, p. 291. **Criminal Syndicalism Act:** Between 1919 and 1924, under the Act, 531 men were indicted, 264 tried, 164 convicted, and 128 sentenced to San Quentin Prison for terms of one to fourteen years; McWilliams, pp. 290–91. **Meetings broken up; "shove days":** McWilliams, pp. 290–92. **"Unemployment is a crime":** Louis Adamic, q. in McWilliams, p. 292. **More than 12,000 arrests:** McWilliams, p. 292; actually, 12, 202. McWilliams, pp. 292–93: "It was not the climate or the sunshine of Southern California that developed a strong undercurrent of liberradical thought in the community, but rather the extraordinarily short-sighted and stupid activities of the power-drunk tycoons who ruled the city." **"Respect Upper-classmen":** *MAW*, Feb. 19, 1929. **Brown's poems:** Don Brown, "More Truth Than Poetry: II. The Junior," in "Manual Poets Display their Skill in Interesting Poems," *MAW*, Sept. 18, 1928. **Knute Rockne; Red Grange:** Henstell, p. 118. **"Week before big game":** " 'Beat Poly Week' Started at Manual This Term," *MAW*, Oct. 23, 1928. The school was L.A. Polytechnic High. **"Student Body Overconfidence":** *MAW*, Nov. 6, 1928. **Hiding under bleachers:** Araks Tolegian, recalling Manuel. **"Musical assembly":** "First Musical Assembly of Term Is Held," *MAW*, Oct. 16, 1928. **"High school slackers":** "Successful Rally in Auditorium Last Wed.," *MAW*, Nov. 13, 1928. The assembly took place Nov. 7, 1928. **Brochure February or March:** Based on references in the brochures: to a former student president admired for his preference of art over athletics (this could only be David Dingle, president the previous term); to forefathers and a Constitution Day competition (there was a citywide competition for speakers to commemorate Constitution Day); to students who had been at Manual for only one term (JP had by this time attended Manual Arts for only one complete term); and to school elections (held at the beginning of each term). **Small brochure:** Variously called a brochure, a leaflet, and a pamphlet. MLP: It was a brochure, meaning that it consisted of a single page folded over. **Early one morning:** MLP. **Lockers and mailboxes:** Araks Tolegian, recalling Manuel; Kadish; Ashton, p. 14. **"STUDENTS ... We present":** OC&T IV, pp. 206–07. The course offerings were far from biased against art: In the fall semester, 1928–29, the school offered twenty-five art courses, sixteen phys. ed. courses, thirty-nine music courses, sixteen mechanical drawing courses. To graduate, the school required no fewer than forty periods of art appreciation (roughly two semesters) and no fewer than forty periods of music, *plus* no less than one-half year of practical art; *MAW*, Sept. 11, 1928. **Goldstein the writer:** Ashton, p. 14. **Brown the writer:** Confirmed as likely by ABP. **Schwankovsky the writer:** Suggested as likely by Kadish. The wording would argue for Brown as the principle writer—his hand is notable in phrases like "unreasonable elevation," "consequent degradation," and "animated examples of physical prowess." Schwankovsky is unlikely to have penned the line that attributes a school's success to "adminstrative reputation." **Janitor pointing to Jackson:** Solomon, p. 42. **"STUDENTS ... There is":** OC&T IV, p. 207. **Jackson's spelling errors:** JP always had trouble with words ending in "ue"

("vouge" for "vogue," "physic" for "physique" and, as an adult, "technic" for "technique"); he also had trouble with the compounding of words (such as "inrespect"); and he was an inveterate misspeller of words such as "honerable," "answers," and "gaint." **Debate on sports craze:** "Interscholastic Athletics Is Forum Topic," *MAW*, Nov. 11, 1928. The topic for debate on November 5, 1928: "Resolved: That interscholastic athletics are injurious to the student body as a whole." **"Biased and unjust":** Roku Sugahara, "Darts and Dashes," *MAW*, Feb. 26, 1929.

Pollock expelled: By the standards of the day, the Manual Arts student government was extraordinarily democratic and independent of faculty interference. Except for the auditor and treasurer, all officers were selected from the student body. When charges were brought—by a teacher or fellow student —courts were held, student counsel represented both accused and accuser, and a student jury determined the verdict. The principal could overturn jury determinations but seldom did. The school's unusual system was considered a model by liberal educators around the country and was often cited in contemporary textbooks on civics and government; "Manual Cited as Fine Type of Self Govt.," *MAW*, May 7, 1929. Manuel Tolegian, int. by Hoag, Feb. 12, 1965: "He was a kind of rebellion against the order of the day, you know, in high school. [He] rebelled against teachers, rebelled against classes, until he was finally expelled from high school because he just wouldn't attend any classes." **Reports of Goldstein's expulsion:** Ashton, p. 14. **Goldstein continuing to provide illustrations:** Cartoons appeared on Feb. 4, 19; Mar. 12; Apr. 2, 16, 30; May 7, 21, 28; and June 4, 1929. **Brown's departure:** "Don Brown, Popular Spectator Editor, Leaves Manual," *MAW*, June 11, 1929. **Lindbergh:** *MAW*, May 7, 1929. **Von Hindenburg:** *MAW*, May 21, 1929; **Hoover:** *MAW*, June 4, 1929. **"I wanted":** Q. in Solomon, p. 42. **Roy making trip to Los Angeles:** LRP to CCP, Apr. 30, 1929. **Roy's attitude toward schooling:** CCP. **"The secret":** LRP to JP, Sept. 19, 1928. **"If you are well satisfied":** LRP to JP, Dec. 11, 1927.

Pollock at Communist meetings: JP to CCP and FLP, Oct. 10, 1929; MJP. **Jewish Community Center:** Solomon, pp. 42–43. **Pollock and Mexican muralists:** JP to CCP and FLP, Oct. 22, 1929. **Mexican artists agitating for revolution:** The artists wanted "to make their production of ideological value to the people," to make the "goal of art, which now is an expression of individualistic masturbation ... one of beauty for all, of education and of battle"; manifesto, 1923, of the Syndicate of Revolutionary Painters, Sculptors, and Engravers of Mexico, q. in Goldman, p. 4. **Trip to Ojai:** Lehman; Araks Tolegian, recalling Manuel; Ashton, p. 14. **Description of campground:** Photo in possession of Krishnamurti Foundation of America. **Two thousand followers:** In fact, some twelve hundred participants showed up for the camp; J., "Before the Ojai Camp," p. 35. **Air at Ojai:** Lutyens, p. 158. **"Imagine Italy":** Q. in Lutyens, p. 257. **Organization of camp; "sheets, blankets":** "Ojai Star Camp," pp. 30–31. **Light-flecked ground:** J., "Before the Ojai Camp," p. 35. **"Divine Spirit"; "World Teacher":** Annie Besant, q. in the *Theosophist*, Jan. 1927, q. in Lutyens, p. 259. **"Overwhelmed"; "it reminded one":** Charles W. Leadbeater to Fabrizio Ruspoli, in the *Australian Theosophist*, Oct. 1928, q. in Lutyens, p. 59. **"An odd figure":** Emily Lutyens, *Candles in the Sun*, pp. 30–35. **Krishnamurti's clothing:** Lutyens, p. 100. **"Like many":** Campbell, p. 128. **"Isn't the theory":** Krishnamurti, "Some Questions and Answers," p. 18. **Wandering through countryside:** Prasad, "News Letter from America," p. 38. **Bach:** "Glimpses of the Ojai Camp," p. 20: performed June 2 by the Bach singers. **Oriental music:** "Glimpses of the Ojai Camp," p. 11: performed May 28 by Mrs. Henry Eichem. **Plays:** Shaw's *Dark Lady of the Sonnets* and Barrie's *Rosalind*, along with an adaptation of Tolstoy's *Michael*, performed June 1. "Glimpses of the Ojai Camp," p. 19. **Dance:** "Glimpses of the Ojai Camp," p. 21: performed June 2 by Ruth St. Denis. **Eating at long tables:** Photo in possession of Krishnamurti Foundation of America. **Krishnamurti reciting poem:** "Glimpses of the Ojai Camp," p. 16. **"Ah, come":** Krishnamurti, *ISB*, June 1930, p. 13. **Meeting Krishnamurti:** Lehman: Others from Manual Arts did meet him. **"Vague and dreamy":** Lutyens, p. 4. **"Be rather":** Krishnamurti, *Life the Goal* (Ommen, Holland: Star Publishing Trust, 1928), q. in Lutyens, pp. 279–80. A similar statement was recorded at the 1929 Ojai camp: "You have come here to find out how to live. . . . Before you can discover that, you will have to go through the process of rejection. . . . I say this not that I may have followers. I do not want anything from anyone"; "Glimpses of the Ojai Camp," p. 7. **Follow the Occult**: JP to CCP and FLP, Oct. 22, 1919. **Refusing meat**: ACM; Laxineta.

Jackson going to Santa Ynez; "**cooking and washing**": LRP to CCP and FLP, July 20, 1929. **Visit lasting a month**: Laxineta. "**Batching together**": LRP to CCP and FLP, July 20, 1929. "**Wanted to come back**": Q. by Laxineta. "**[Jack] is a very good**": LRP to CCP and FLP, July 20, 1929. **Fight the summer of 1929**: Busa: The fight took place when JP was working with his father; this was the only time they worked together without others in the family. Laxineta: JP returned earlier than expected, disgruntled, from his summer stint. **Fistfight**: Busa, recalling JP; Wilcox, recalling JP. **Desire to return home**: Busa, recalling JP; Laxineta. "**I do not think**"; "**the secret of success**": LRP to JP, Sept. 19, 1928. **Jackson refusing to work with father again**: Roy would have expected JP to take a summer job along with Frank, who came back home from New York for that purpose; FLP.

Manual Arts gang dispersed: Guston was staying with his mother in Ocean Park, Lehman was now living at West Lake Park, and Tolegian was still living near Jefferson Boulevard in south Los Angeles; Lehman. **Schwankovsky at Laguna**: Although Schwankovsky occasionally taught summer school courses in Los Angeles, he tended to spend school vacations with his family in Laguna Beach; Duncan. **Sande's expensive suits**: Kadish: SLM spent $180 on a suit and $30 on a pair of shoes. **Sande's square friends; Arloie hinting about marriage; roadster coupe**: ACM. **Loan to Cooter**: Cooter.

Jackson's letter to Charles: Although lost, the contents can be inferred from Charles's response. **Charles not seen in four years**: The last time he visited was probably Christmas 1925. **First letter in eight years**: CCP. "**[Jack] held Charles**": Kadish. **Charles drafting reply**: The final copy of the letter no longer exists, only the amended first draft, and the first paragraph of a tentative final draft. It was Charles's practice to draft letters and then prepare a final copy in calligraphic script; he later taught courses in calligraphy at Michigan State University; CCP. "**With clearer understanding**": JP to CCP, Oct. 22, 1929. "**Your letter has confounded me**": CCP to JP, n.d. "**The possibilities of architecture**": Charles later wanted his daughter Jeremy to become an architect. **Charles's closing**: Krishnamurti, *LIF*, p. 34: "As every human being is divine, so every individual in the world should be his own master, his own absolute ruler and guide."

September 10: "Purple Portals Open Today; Initial Grind Commences," *MAW*, Sept. 10, 1929. **Surveyor's boots**; "**ham actor**"; "**I really think**"; "**seclusive**": Int. by Hoag, Feb. 12, 1965. "**In the background**": ABP. **Flouting course requirements**: Araks Tolegian, recalling Manuel. **Los Angeles high school rules**: *MAW*, Sept. 10, 1929. **Jackson taking English classes**: JP to CCP and FLP, Oct. 22, 1929: "I am now taking American Literature, Contemporary Literature, Clay Modeling and the life class." Based on class schedules, the literature teacher had to be either Blanche Freeman or Lucy Hifle. "**Rotten**"; "**cold and lifeless**"; "**[when I had] to talk**": JP to CCP and FLP, Oct. 22, 1929. "**He just wouldn't attend**": Int. by Hoag, Feb. 12, 1965.

"**Prospective gridiron heroes**"; **looking for "beefers"**: Bob McGraw, "Poly, L.A. High, Lincoln and Franklin Have Championship Contenders, Hollywood's Line Experienced and Plunge-Proof," *MAW*, Sept. 17, 1929. "**The battle of the ages**"; "**slackers**": Bob McGraw, "Poly, L.A. High," *MAW*, Sept. 17, 1929. "**Purple and grey hoghiders**" **favored**: "Football Prospects Bright as Manual and Poly Favored by Local Newspaper Writers," *MAW*, Sept. 10, 1929. "**It's a ghastly**": Bob McGraw, "Tanbark Talk," *MAW*, Sept. 24, 1929. **Jackson ambushed by football players**: Araks Tolegian, recalling Manuel; Wilcox, recalling JP. **Jackson's appearance**: Araks Tolegian, recalling Manuel: "They didn't like him at all—he wore surveyor boots and dressed funny." Manuel Tolegian, int. by Hoag, Feb. 12, 1965: "He was dressed eccentrically. I can see why he didn't have too many friends among football players in high school."

"**Mean, short-tempered**": Turnquist. "**Came to blows**"; **principal's office**: JP to CCP and FLP, Oct. 22, 1929. "**The Czar**": Sprenger, p. 18. **Wilson's background**; "**no alibi**": Sprenger, pp. 17–19. "**He was too thick**"; "**I have a number**": JP to CCP and FLP, Oct. 22, 1929. **Teachers defend-**

ing Pollock: Araks Tolegian, recalling Manuel. **Stella meeting with Wilson**: FLP. "**If I get back**"; "**another fellow**"; "**we were ignorant**": JP to CCP and FLP, Oct. 22, 1929.

"**Ladies' man**": Rosenberg. **Goldstein demoted to "assistant**": Although Goldstein's name continued to be listed on the masthead through December, none of his cartoons or marginal illustrations appeared in the paper; see *MAW* from Sept. 10, 1929 to Jan. 28, 1930. **Jackson withdrawing**: McClure, recalling SMP. **Jackson's nightmares**: JP to CCP, Jan. 31, 1930. "**If there is**"; "**a new outlook**": JP to CCP and FLP, Oct. 22, 1929.

Hungry scavenging for garbage: Weaver, p. 110. **Soup kitchens denied**: Weaver, p. 109: "The situation is not alarming," Mayor John R. Porter said in response to the Depression. "We do not find it necessary to feed our unemployed men here. In San Francisco I saw free soup kitchens. There are none here." "**Suicide Bridge**": McWilliams, p. 246. From October to December, industrial production dropped more than 9 percent; from September to December, imports dropped 20 percent; McElvaine, p. 48. By 1933, there was a drop of 29 percent in GNP, 78 percent in construction, and an astonishing 98 percent in investments. Unemployment rose from 3.2 percent to 24.9 percent; McElvaine, p. 75. "**Lift the city**": *Los Angeles Times*, q. in Weaver, p. 110. **Pollock readmitted**: Probably after the Christmas vacation, but before the end of the first semester. "**This so called happy part**": JP to CCP, Jan. 31, 1930. JP used only lowercase letters in typing this letter to Charles.

"**Choosy about girls**": Q. anonymously in Ashton, p. 16. Cooter, too, wondered "why Jack's not interested in girls." **Jackson receiving word through Stella**: JP to CCP, Jan. 31, 1930: "[I] suppose mother keeps you posted on family matters." **Charles meeting Elizabeth**: Chronology prepared by CCP for EFP, Feb. 1975. By this time, Elizabeth Feinberg had begun using her pen name, Elizabeth England; EFP. **Frank courting Marie**: FLP. Although they did not meet until June 15, 1930 (MLP), Frank was by now clearly eager for a relationship. **Meeting Berthe**: Laxineta. **Place where Hodges boarded**: 1900 West Forty-second Street, says Lehman, who later boarded there; but Horton, who owned the house, says it was 4017 West Forty-third. "**Musical jam**": Laxineta; Solomon, p. 44.

Severe dress: Lehman. **Long hair**: Laxineta. **Authoritative touch; stiff demeanor**: Lehman. **Berthe's reaction to Jackson**; "**clean**": Laxineta. **Berthe not attracting good-looking boys**: Horton: Her previous boyfriend was Al Linde, "a big, big bruiser"—"six feet six inches tall and about just as wide." **Bertha changed to Berthe**; "**Holy cow, no!**": Laxineta. "**In fact, she was overly serious**": Lehman. **Recognizing Pollock; curtailing practice**: Laxineta: She had been giving recitals since she was twelve. **Pollock earning money**: JP, along with his friends, could conceivably have earned some money by firing ceramics: "We have gotten up a group and have arranged a furnace where we can have our stuff fired. we will give the owner a commission for the firing and glazing. there is a chance of my making a little book money"; JP to CCP, Jan. 21, 1930. Also, he could have borrowed the money from Sande, who apparently was doing well in his job with the *Times*. **Gifts**: Laxineta.

Victorian house: Lehman. **Location of Pacifico home**: Horton. **Jackson winning over Pacificos**: Horton; Laxineta. **Jackson driving Pacifico car; rolling cigarettes, Kranich & Bach**; "**all he was interested in**"; **Berthe allowing a kiss; Beethoven, Chopin, and Gershwin**: Laxineta. **Bungalow court**: Precisely when the Pollocks moved to their new home and its precise location are not known. **Berthe not shown drawings**: Laxineta. **Pollock working furiously**: Horton.

"**I am doubtful**"; "**architecture interests me**": JP to CCP and FLP, Oct. 22, 1929. **Pollock never in watercolor class**: No mention in JP to CCP, Oct. 22, 1929. "**[I] have started**": JP to CCP, Jan. 1, 1930. **Martin not accomplished**; "**group of figures**": Lehman, who remembers JP's student works as relief sculptures. "**Some of his work**": Kadish. "**My drawing [I] will tell you**": JP to CCP, Jan. 1, 1930. Tolegian, int. by Hoag, Feb. 12, 1965: "He was not too successful in classic art. He didn't quite master it." Yet his work did have a certain energy and control over color, and his friends later claimed to have recognized this at the time. Even Tolegian admitted that he "had a great feeling for color, you know, and there is no doubt about it, he was a natural born painter, artist, you know." Kadish: "I remember some of his drawings. They had a lot of energy. We all admired it. Now, Phil was very slick. There's no question about it. And Harold Lehman the same way. But Jack came along with all the energy, and you felt that he had it, the command. Even in the relationship between Tolegian and Phil Guston and Jack in the high school days, there was always this thing—'Wait till you see this guy, boy's he's a terrific guy, no matter, anything and everything he does.' "

February 3: *MAW*, Feb. 3, 1930. **Pollock reenrolling:** JP to CCP, Jan. 1, 1930. **Ungraded basis:** Los Angeles Unified School District Records: His courses were "UNG"—ungraded. **Lehman moving to Los Angeles; casting studio:** Lehman. **"A great genius"; "unbelievable talent":** Cherry. **"As though I was"; Jackson's athletic body; Pollock admiring Lehman; browsing in bookstores:** Lehman. McWilliams, p. 231: "As a community at the end of a long trail of migration, Los Angeles became the junkyard for a continent." **Stanley Rose's bookshop:** Lehman: He bought Théodore Duret on the Impressionists and Ezra Pound on Gaudier-Brzeska, along with old copies of *Creative Art, The Studio, The Arts, Burlington,* and *Connoisseur.* Like Charles, Lehman liked to tear pictures out of magazines: "I always looked up *Vanity Fair* and tore out the art pages." **Daltzell-Hatfield and Stendhal galleries:** The two best private galleries in town; Daltzell-Hatfield also showed western watercolorists and some other modern American paintings imported from New York; Lehman. **"Picturesque"; "didn't like to draw":** Lehman.

Monologues; Lehman and Goldstein at L.A. High: Lehman. **Goldstein's scholarship:** "M.A. Art Students Receive Several Scholarships," *MAW*, June 23, 1930. **Playing records:** Lehman. **Discussing filmmaking:** Ashton, p. 16. **Reporting on tracts:** Lehman. On May 18, 1930, JP traveled to Schwankovsky's Laguna Beach studio, "The Little Art Theater"—Araks Tolegian, recalling Manuel, called it nothing but "a gas station with a view"—to hear Krishnamurti speak. More than five hundred enthusiasts crammed into the small garden to hear the former "Master," who had by now disavowed the Theosophists and the divinity they had conferred on him; "Krishnamurti Relates Personal Ideas and Doctrines to Group of Young Philosophers," *MAW*, May 20, 1930. Afterward, Schwankovsky wrote about Krishnamurti for the *Weekly:* "Krishnamurti's heroic point of view will appeal to the youth of today who lives in an age when . . . it is usually hard to find heroes to worship;" q. in "Krishnamurti Relates Personal Ideas and Doctrines to Group of Young Philosophers," *MAW*, May 20, 1930.

In a 1924 Buick: FLP. Kadish: "When Charles came back to Los Angeles, he came back like a patriarch." **Charles visiting Phoenix; return to Los Angeles:** CCP: In Phoenix, Charles found work illustrating a fledgling magazine called *Arizona.* **Charles introduced to Arthur Millier:** CCP. Millier, who also contributed to national publications, such as *Time* and the *Christian Science Monitor,* wrote for the Los Angeles *Herald Express* after his retirement from the *Times;* Millier, Jr.: His father "prized his abilities as a journalist above being an artist." More dispassionate observers have confirmed his son's estimation that, "in those days, he was the premier critic in the western United States." *Times* **copyboy; "layout, fancy lettering":** CCP.

Enrolling at Otis; moving to Echo Park; student activities: CCP. Grant Rusk of the Los Angeles County Museum of Art to authors, Dec. 2, 1985: "Checked all exhibitions taking place from 1922 to 1926 and could come up with only one that had something to do with Mexican artists." This was the "First Pan-American Exhibition of Oil Paintings," held at the Museum from November 27, 1925, to February 28, 1926, and included one painting by Rivera, *Día de Flores,* but none by either Orozco or Siqueiros. **Charles buying magazines:** CCP. **Millier suggesting League:** Kadish.

Charles arriving in New York; "received with open arms": CCP. **Charles studying with Benton:** Charles studied first, briefly, with Boardman Robinson and Max Weber, the other two American artists whose work he had seen at the Exposition Park show in L.A.; CCP. **Bentons finding apartment:** CCP; chronology prepared by CCP for EFP, Feb. 1975. The address was 36 Eighth Avenue; FLP. **Charles invited to Martha's Vineyard:** THB to CCP, July 14, 1928. **Charles baby-sitting:** FLP. **Charles's work in New York:** CCP.

Art women's work: Discussed by many of the artists or former artists we interviewed—especially Kron, Lassaw, and Slivka. **Art a manly exercise:** Benton (p. 265) had nothing but the most articulate disdain for art and artists who created under the influence of "nervous whim and under the sway of . . . overdelicate sensibilities" and "Our New York aberrants . . . of the gentle feminine type with predilections for the curving wrist and outthrust hip." **Spats and vests:** CCP. **Shirts and suspenders:** Photo in possession of AAA.

Frank leaving for Big Pines: FLP. **Trip to Pomona:** CCP. **Prometheus:** Helm, pp. 49–51. **Articles recommended by Charles:** JP to CCP and FLP, Oct. 22, 1929. **Charles leaving for Wrightwood; Stella's acceptance of Sande and Arloie:** CCP. **Jackson remaining in Los Angeles:** FLP. Laxineta says his father wanted him to come to work but he refused. She claims this was because JP didn't want to leave her, but according to McClure, JP didn't see much of her over the summer. **Paul McClure:** Son of Stella's brother Cameron McClure. **Jackson sketching furiously; "Jack idolized Charles":** McClure. **Jackson urged to go to New York:** CCP to authors, Sept. 1983. **Proposing to Berthe:** Laxineta: "He was going to go east and he didn't want to lose me." **"We would live":** Q. by Laxineta. **"She thought we were too young":** Laxineta. **"You're so naive":** Q. in Solomon, p. 46. Laxineta: She was practicing for a performance with the L.A. Philharmonic Orchestra.

Trip to New York: FLP: The only mishap took place in New Jersey, where "some troopers stopped us because we had some guns in the car. And we had a dirty car, and we probably had some dirty hats on and western gear of some sort. We had the top down, and there we were, three wild men, unshaven." **"Too long"; "didn't sound very interesting":** CCP. Friedman (p. 8) notes incorrectly that JP had been called Paul until this time. When interviewed by Hoag (Feb. 12, 1965), Tolegian incorrectly said that he and JP went to New York together.

---

11. THE BEST PAINTER IN THE FAMILY

SOURCES

Books, articles, manuscripts, records, and transcripts

Allen, *Since Yesterday;* Ashton, *The New York School;* Baigell, *THB;* THB, *An American in Art (American); An Artist in America (Artist);* Brown, *American Painting from the Armory Show to the Depression;* Burroughs, *THB;* Cennini, *The Book of the Art of Cennino Cennini; A Treatise on Painting;* Chase, *New York;* Cowley, *Exiles Return;* Craven, *Modern Art;* Ellis, *The Epic of New York City;* Friedman, *JP;* Gruen, *The Party's Over Now;* Johnson, *Pioneer's Progress;* Kazin, *Starting Out in the Thirties;* Kramer, *The Revenge of the Philistines;* Keun, *Abroad in America;* Landgren, *Years of Art;* McKinzie, *The New Deal for Artists;* Museum of Fine Arts, *Fairfield Porter;* New York Panorama;* OC&T, *JP;* Potter, *To a Violent Grave;* Robinson and Bletter, *Skyscraper Style;* Simkhovitch, *Neighborhood;* Solomon, *JP;* Still, *Mirror for Gotham; The WPA Guide to California; The WPA Guide to New York City;* Yee, *The Silent Traveller.*

Walter Abell, "The Limits of Abstraction," *Magazine of Art,* Dec. 1935; THB, "America and/or Alfred Stieglitz," *Common Sense,* Jan. 1935; "Form and the Subject," *Arts,* June 1924; "Mechanics of Form Organization in Painting, Part V," *Arts,* Mar. 1927; Milton Bracker, "Three New Yorkers," *NYT Magazine,* Mar. 31, 1940; "Benton," *Time,* Jan. 5, 1931; Thomas Craven, "THB," *Scribner's,* Oct. 1937; Axel Horn, "JP: The Hollow and the Bump," *Carleton Miscellany,* Summer 1966; William A. McWhirter, "Tom Benton: At 80: Still at War with Bores and Boobs," *Life,* Oct. 3, 1969; Lewis Mumford, "THB," *Creative Art,* Dec. 1928; Stephen Polcari, "JP and THB," *Arts,* Mar. 1979; Barbara Rose, "Arshile Gorky and John Graham," *Arts,* Mar. 1976; "Painters of a Flaming Vision," *Vogue,* Dec. 1981; James T. Vallière, "The El Greco Influence on JP's Early Works," *Art Journal,* Fall 1964.

Edward Alden Jewell, "Orozco and Benton Paint Murals for New York," *NYT,* Nov. 23, 1930.

THB, "The Intimate Story" (*Intimate*), unpub. ms. in possession of the Benton Testamentary Trust; FVOC, "The Genesis of JP: 1912 to 1943" (Ph.D thesis), Baltimore: Johns Hopkins University, 1965.

THB Classbooks, 1929–30, 1930–31, 1931–32, Art Students League Archives; registration cards for James D. Brooks, Pete Busa, Herman Cherry, Whitney Darrow, Jr., Joseph Delaney, Mervin Jules, Nathan Katz, Bruce Mitchell, Archie Musick, Philip Pavia, CCP, JP, Fairfield Porter, Bernard Steffen, Manuel Tolegian, Reginald Wilson, Art Students League Archives.

THB, int. by Kathleen Shorthall, Nov. 9, 1959, for *Life*, Time/Life Archives; SLM, int. by CG, c. 1956.

Interviews

T. P Benton; Thomas Branchick; James Brooks; Peter Busa; Lawrence Campbell; Jeremy Capillé; Blanche Carstensen; Herman Cherry; Whitney Darrow, Jr.; Joseph Delaney; Ruth Emerson; Lyman Field; Margo Henderson; Harry Holtzman; Axel Horn; Harry Jackson; Mervin Jules; Reuben Kadish; Gerome Kamrowski; Nathaniel Kaz; Stewart Klonis; Rosalind Krauss; Maria Piacenza Kron; Terence Mahon; William McKim; George McNeil; Philip Pavia; Eleanor Piacenza; Santos Piacenza; CCP; EFP; FLP; MLP; Harry Rand; Nene Schardt; Gertrude Shibley; Jim Sleeper; Marshall Sprague; Bayrd Still; Araks Tolegian; Reginald Wilson; Mark Witkin.

NOTES

Empire State Building: Officially opened May 1, 1931; Ellis, p. 552. **New York towers:** Chase, p. 151. **Schist:** *New York Panorama*, p. 24. **Terms for sails:** *New York Panorama*, p. 9. **"Dynamic immobility":** Cowley, p. 210. **"Amplitude":** *New York Panorama*, p. 15. **Burlesque houses:** Kazin, pp. 87–88. **Fair:** Keun, p. 59. **Cabs:** Ellis, p. 532. **"Eddy and mill":** Still, p. 323. **Broadway neon:** Keun, p. 52; Chiang Yee, q. in Still, p. 311. **"Like dried figs":** Chiang Yee, q. in Still, p. 312: Subway passengers also compared to "plaster poured into a mould." **"Licorice ribbon":** Still, p. 311. **Tenements:** Still, p. 310. **Mindless intoxication:** *New York Panorama*, p. 13. **"Full of people":** *New York Panorama*, p. 17. Thomas Wolfe, speaking as Eugene Gant, q. in *New York Panorama*, p. 17: "Proud, cruel, everchanging and ephemeral city, to whom we came once when our hearts were high." Sleeper, a historian of New York: "What fascinates me is the fertility of the soil here, the depth and richness of associations. . . . It's very unnerving to some people and stimulating to others." Clifford Odets, q. in Bracker, "Three New Yorkers," p. 7: It was the center of the world, "not because of anything we've consciously done, but because of the ceaseless flow here of talent from elsewhere." **Sleeping on couch; eating meals:** CCP. **"Out-Benton Benton":** Rita Benton, q. by FLP. **"Very suave":** Name withheld by request. **Bequeathed apartment and paintings:** CCP; Cherry. Charles inherited the Benton Sychromist paintings when his teacher left them behind in the closet of the apartment that Charles also inherited. **Invitations to the Vineyard:** CCP. **Fractious art world:** Brown, p. 81: "After the war American art was in a state of chaos; not the chaos of disintegration, but of uninhibited exploration. . . . America was open to influence and counterinfluence, to experiment and theory, and now even current European art innovations found immediate echo here." **Civil war brewing:** Stieglitz spoke for the modernists, touting an art "by the few and for the few . . . it would lose its subtlest, most intimate charm, if it were shared by the diffident crowd" (S[adakichi] H[artmann], "That Toulouse-Lautrec Print!" *Camera Work*, no. 29, pp. 36–38, q. in Brown, p. 41), while Benton, a one-time frequenter of 291, now claimed that "no place in the world ever produced more idiotic gabble" and that "the contagion of intellectual idiocy there rose to unbelievable heights"; THB, "America and/or Alfred Stieglitz," p. 22. **"The disease":** John Sloan, *Gist of Art; Principles and Practice Expounded in the Classroom and Studio*, recorded with the assistance of H. Farr, New York, American Artists Group (c. 1939), p. 44, q. in Brown, p. 62. **Changes sweeping the art world:** Brown, p. 196: "By 1929 the doctrine of art-for-art's sake had already begun to lose its hold on American art. . . . The social realists were making social statements and Thomas Benton wanted walls upon which to paint his 'Epic'. . . . The depression clarified such ideological directions." **Benton a modernist:** Benton considered "the representation of objective forms and the presentation of abstract ideas of form to be of equal artistic value"; *The Forum Exhibition of Modern American Paintings*, n.p., q. in Brown, p. 65. **"Country-wide revival":** THB, q. in McKinzie, p. 106. **"Not heroics":** Q. in Allen, p. 35. **"Amer-**

ican Wave": Baigell, pp. 87–89. The term "was coined for this drive for an art that reflected the new search for American roots and a pride in the American past." **"There can be little doubt":** Abell, "The Limits of Abstraction," p. 735. **Barr on paucity of articles:** Ashton, p. 100. **"The way of George":** *American*, p. 147. Brown, p. 192: "Modernism had dominated American art for almost two decades, during which time the long-standing American tradition of realism continued as an undercurrent. As the twenties advanced, the realist current accumulated strength until, after 1929, it burst into prominence again. An early major crystallization of the new realistic tendencies was the mural series painted by Thomas Hart Benton in the New School for Social Research in 1930." **Admission to the League:** FLP: "Charles was instrumental in getting Jack into the Art Students League." But admission to the League was so liberal no special influence was needed. Charles *did* provide the necessary example, advice, and encouragement. **Greenwich House:** 46 Barrow Street. **Class with Ben-Shmuel:** OC&T IV, p. 209. **Art-related activities:** CCP to FVOC, n.d.; see Simkhovitch. **Greenwich House annex:** 16 Jones Street. **Charles's advice:** Cherry: Charles was "very quiet, very formal." Charles admits he rarely talked to JP about his art—"I didn't think any comments of mine would help"—or his personal life—"I wasn't paying any attention to whom he saw." **"Youth, dimples":** EFP. **"When Jackson first got":** Capillé. CCP characteristically denies any competitiveness with JP: "I don't feel there was any conflict between Jack and me, and between my position at that moment and his."

Jackson's new apartment: 240 West Fourteenth Street; EFP; FLP. There is some confusion about whether JP lived with Tolegian at this point. Frank thinks JP *later* moved to an apartment on Tenth Avenue with Tolegian. **Jackson at the League:** JP signed up for Benton's Life Drawing, Painting and Composition course, which met five days a week from 7:00 to 10:00 P.M., ostensibly with two criticisms a week from Benton, for a tuition of $12 a month. By February 16 of the new year, Benton had arranged financial assistance for him, and JP remained in the class through May. In October 1931, JP registered in Benton's Mural Painting class and, a year later, on October 3, 1932, in Benton's Life Drawing, Painting, and Mural Composition class, where he served as monitor. In December, he was elected an official member of the League. In January 1933, JP joined John Sloan's Life Drawing, Painting, and Composition class. In February or March 1933, he also registered in the sculpture class of Robert Laurent. Although classmates recall JP taking drawing classes with George Bridgman, there is no record of his enrollment; THB Classbooks, 1930–1931, 1931–1932; registration card for JP. **"Wonderfully loose":** Emerson. **Wilmarth:** Landgren, p. 17. The founding of the League was precipitated by the National Academy's refusal to open its doors for a season. **League address in 1875:** Fifth Avenue at Sixteenth Street. **"Alcove" system rejected:** Landgren, p. 102. **"Parisian ateliers":** Landgren, p. 19. **Hardenbergh:** Campbell. At the time, Hardenbergh was best known for his design of the mammoth car barn at Third Avenue and Sixty-sixth Street, also a French Second Empire "palace." **League policies:** Campbell; FVOC, "The Genesis of JP," p. 38. **Inviting artists to the League:** Emerson. **Artists on the faculty:** Landgren, pp. 112–14. **"One reason":** Q. in Landgren, pp. 90–91. In 1907 some conservative teachers gained control of the school's governing board and forced the League to adopt more academic methods, but their initiatives were soon reversed; Landren, p. 102. **Studio 9:** Klonis; but Landgren (p. 63) notes *four* studios on the fifth floor. **"They were all"; "monitor":** Horn, "JP," p. 80. **Benton appearing on Tuesday:** Holtzman. **"Anybody want criticism":** Friedman, p. 20. **"He wouldn't go near":** Horn. *Artist*, p. 333: "I never gave direct criticisms unless they were asked for and even then only when the asker specified what was occasioning difficulty." **Weeks without word:** Cherry. **"The rhythm"; "the nature":** CCP. **"Correction":** Jules. **Lectures:** FVOC, "The Genesis of JP," p. 37. **"To be able"; "the hollow":** Horn, "JP," p. 81. **Baroque rhythms":** *American*, p. 37. **Models:** Emerson. **"To identify":** Horn, "JP," p. 80. **Ticklish models:** Friedman, p. 25.

Michelangelo: Friedman, p. 21. **Tintoretto:** Horn, "JP," p. 84; Friedman, p. 21; Cherry. **Rubens:** Friedman, p. 21. **Rembrandt:** Friedman, p. 21; Busa; Jules. **Dürer, Schön, Cambiaso:** *Artist*, p. 333. **Signorelli, Massaccio, Mantegna, Brueghel, Assyrian bas-reliefs; El Greco:** Horn, "JP,"

p. 84; FVOC, "The Genesis of JP," p. 136; Busa; Cherry. **Sketchbooks:** Vallière, p. 6: Fifty-two pages of sketches include over sixty compositions after El Greco, twenty after Rubens, three after Michelangelo, and one after Rembrandt's *Night Watch*. Three principal sketchbooks still exist. Vallière (p. 6) dates the first two "between 1936 and 1938," arguing that the sketchbooks, Grumbacher "Leonardo," were in production only from 1936 to 1951. But FVOC says the sketchbooks were "probably on the market as early as 1932"; OC&T III, p. 13, citing Grumbacher to FVOC, Nov. 26, 1975.

Despite this new information, and despite the reasonable assumption that the first two sketchbooks and their Bentonesque formal analyses were made during JP's tenure in Benton's class at the League, O'Connor (OC&T III, pp. 13–14) argues for a later date. Benton, on seeing reproductions of the sketchbooks in October 1973, wrote that the works showed two or three years' experience, that his students did not use fine sketchbooks in the classroom, and that in his opinion the drawings, especially those from life, were not done until Benton had stopped teaching at the League, sometime in 1933. O'Connor also writes that the life drawings seem to have been done during JP's visits to the League after he was no longer formally associated with it and that internal evidence suggests that the drawings from El Greco were done from a copy of the Hyperion edition of that artist's works, published in 1937, still in JP's library in 1956. He equivocates by dating the sketchbook c. 1933–38, but writes that the drawings from El Greco, in particular, could not have been done until "1937 or after."

Benton, however, was never a terribly good source on his students' work. He wrote (THB to FVOC, May 31, 1964) that JP never made clay models when in fact he did, both in Laurent's class (Pavia) and on Martha's Vineyard (Emerson). As to the quality of the page, JP could easily have "borrowed" one of Charles's sketchbooks, or even been given it. The drawings could have been done outside of class—either at the League itself, since students were encouraged by Benton to visit the small library to make copies from the masters, or at home, since students at the time were permitted to borrow League books; Jules. Too much has been made of the books in JP's library at the time of his death. Most were given to him, not purchased; moreover, he had access to other books.

O'Connor is clearer on the dating of the second sketchbook, c. 1937–38, but again, these dates seem too late. Although the second sketchbook shows a more mature grasp of Benton's methods, we would argue that the drawings were done no later than 1935–36, certainly well before JP's admission to Bloomingdale's. O'Connor's dates for the third sketchbook, c. 1938–39, seem more plausible, since the drawings have similarities in subject with the drawings that JP made for Dr. Henderson during this period.

JP's sketches from this early period show an anxious attempt to master Benton's methods. An interesting sheet contains studies of four works by Signorelli. Although Benton had prescribed an orderly progression of study—"It is advisable to seek, in analysis, first the main linear and then the main cubic movements and to go into the minor rhythms of the details only after these have been satisfactorily determined" (THB, "Mechanics of Form Organization in Painting," p. 145)—JP impatiently darts from one style to another, as from one Signorelli painting to another. At the top, he draws the "main linear movements" of a leg from *Martyrdom of St. Catherine*. At the bottom, he makes a crude assessment of the cubic movements in *Lamentation over Christ*. In the middle of the sheet, he makes a more careful study of the angels from *Crowning of the Elects*. To simplify the composition, and to stress the pyramidal structure, he eliminates one of the five angels in the original and the wings from the two principal angels. Although intending a cubistic analysis, in drawing the leg of the angel on the right JP drifts into a linear analysis and, from this, to a rough chiaroscuro sketch of that figure. He then shifts back to a straightforward cubistic analysis of the foreshortened heads ot some of the elects in Signorelli's painting, who are straining to see the vision of the angels. At top center, JP draws a turbaned head from yet another Signorelli painting, *Feast in the House of Simon*, a drawing so crude it might have been made back in Los Angeles or even in Riverside. Perhaps in frustration, JP fills some of the empty spaces left on the paper with abstract designs of interlocked swirls resembling the contour lines on a geological map; OC&T 402, III, p. 17; see FVOC, "The Genesis of JP," pp. 135–36.

There are some direct copies of paintings, notably an exaggerated copy of the figure of Jonah from Michelangelo's Sis-

tine Chapel. Although proportionally crude, these copies are more exact than JP's drawings from the live model, which are strained to the point of distortion. In a series of drawings of a nude woman, JP fails to connect the woman's arms to her torso in a plausible way, he tacks the breasts onto the chest and provides so little sense of bone structure and musculature that the folded arms in one drawing twist like ropes of raw dough; OC&T 426–27, III, pp. 37–39. Although the lines are forceful—OC&T (III, p. 14) note that JP has pressed the pencil down so hard that he leaves an indentation in the paper and creates a graphite sheen—they are extremely rough. The strength of these early drawings is in their forcefulness and intensity, not in their assurance or verisimilitude.

From the second sketchbook, it is clear that JP did make some progress; that even for this artist who drew his strength from spontaneity, conscientious effort and study produced results. The copies from the old masters are more accomplished, as can be seen in the study of Michelangelo's Adam from the *Creation of Man*; OC&T 428, III, p. 20. His grasp of compositional space is surer, as can be seen in the cubistic analysis of a complex group of equestrian and pedestrian figures in Rubens's *Christ Entering Jerusalem*; OC&T 446, III, p. 50. Even at this relatively late date, JP is engaging in some of Benton's most basic exercises, including a study of the recession of forms in space (OC&T 445, III, p. 49) and the disposition of volumes in space around a central axis; OC&T 434, III, p. 44. But perhaps the most interesting development in this second sketchbook is the concentration of patterned lights and darks that achieve, in their prescient abstraction, something of his mature force; see especially OC&T 432, III, p. 42, in which he isolates the drapery of the figure of Christ in El Greco's *Coronation of the Virgin* and develops it with remarkable strength.

Block forms: Benton later called this form of figure analysis, based on Cambiosi, "spiralic countering" and defined it as the "arrangement of cubic forms about an axis [in such a way that] forms counter one another"; THB to FVOC, Apr. 4, 1964. **"Benton demanded":** Jules. **"[Jackson] was out":** THB, int. by Shorthall, Nov. 9, 1959. **Tracing; "horror":** Busa. **"Hairy scribble-scrabble":** Horn, "JP," p. 83. **Hip or thigh:** OC&T 450, III, p. 52. **Drapery; faces and hands:** OC&T 421, III, p. 33. **"Jackson's drawings":** Horn, "JP," p. 83: "with the possible exception of those of Deyo Jacobs." **League a touchstone:** Campbell, Holtzman, and many others say it was *the* center. **"Just going along":** Kaz. **"We were all":** Cherry.

Porter and Trotsky: Kramer, p. 162. He made the trip in 1927, during his junior year at college; Witkin. **Holtzman:** Holtzman. **Brooks; "too much rolly":** Brooks. **"Missouri gang":** Cherry; Sprague; Musick had lived for some time in Colorado Springs and would retire there from New York. **Meert close to Charles:** Busa; Wilson. **Meert gentle, reticent:** Cherry. **"A dreamer":** Shibley. **"Poetic":** Schardt. **Meert and Charles favorites:** Cherry; Wilson. Cherry: Meert and Benton would later break up "because of politics. Meert was inclined towards the left—may have been a Communist—and by this time, Benton had become very reactionary." **Katz:** Kaz: "They used to take bets on whether I was a midget or just a young kid. It was a standing joke, especially when I was the monitor of a class."

Busboy: Wilson. **Gorky always with women:** Araks Tolegian, recalling Manuel. **Wolfhounds:** Pavia, q. in Gruen, p. 264. **Gorky at League classes:** Rand: Gorky was a monitor in a League class that included Barnett Newman, who was at the League from 1922–1926. **"Towering":** Rose, "Arshile Gorky and John Graham," p. 63. **Gorky's height and erudition:** Rand. **Fox and de George:** Kaz.

Tolegian and Pollock living together: CCP. **"Joking"; "they would insult":** Horn. **"Very dapper"; "aloof":** Kaz. **Tolegian in cafeteria:** Araks Tolegian, recalling Manuel. Hauteur, **"outlandish jargon":** Rand. Manuel later told Araks he discovered that Gorky was Armenian when he accidentally spilled coffee on him in the lunchroom and Gorky began swearing in Armenian. Gorky was born Vosdanig Manoog Adoian. He arrived in America in 1920 and changed his name to Archele, then Arshele, before settling on Arshile; Rand. **Tolegian writing poetry:** CCP. **Pollock shy:** Kaz. **"With his high heel":** Wilson. **"The smile":** Horn, "JP," p. 81. **"Stupefied"; "just plain dense"; "Jackson always seemed":** Kaz. Resnick: When you talked to him, "it was as if he didn't understand you."

Grosz: Grosz was nominated to teach at the League on March 25, 1932. Despite "his real prejudice against any foreigners" (Emerson), Sloan supported the appointment of George Grosz, calling him "the only modern German painter of whom the French critics think anything." When only one of the twelve board members voted for Grosz, Sloan resigned in fury. Grosz eventually was invited to join the faculty; Landgren, pp. 102–04. Campbell: Sloan used the Grosz affair as a pretext for a referendum in his losing battle for autocratic rule of the democratic League. **Sloan and Lie:** See Landgren, pp. 102–04; Campbell; Emerson; Holtzman; Klonis: Sloan simply wanted to be able to dictate faculty selections. **"Specific"; "I do everything":** Kaz. **"He developed":** *Artist*, p. 336. **Unmailed letters:** JP to SMP, Sept. 20, 1932. **Charles saving drawings:** CCP. **Fifty-eighth Street speakeasy; "just knock"; League collections; gin with English labels:** Kaz. **Delaney:** Delaney. **Mitchell:** Campbell; Delaney; Kadish. Mitchell was from Cornwall-on-Hudson. **Widespread drinking:** Cherry; Kaz. **"Joe, you know":** Q. by Delaney.

12. BENTON

SOURCES

Books, articles, manuscripts, brochure, records, and transcript

Baigell, *THB*: THB, *An American in Art (American); An Artist in America (Artist);* Braun and Branchick, *THB;* Burroughs, *THB;* Centre Georges Pompidou, *JP;* Craven, *THB,* Douglas, *The Feminization of American Culture;* Fiedler, *What Was Literature?;* Roosevelt, *THB;* Yeo and Cook, *Maverick with a Paintbrush.*

Matthew Baigell, "THB in the 1920s," *Art Journal,* Summer 1970; Thomas Craven, "THB," *Scribner's,* Oct. 1937.

Maecenas Benton, "Benton Chronology," July 22, 1915; THB, "The Intimate Story" *(Intimate),* (unpub. ms. in possession of the Benton Testamentary Trust).

Western Military Academy: Catalogue and Register, 1906–1907, Upper Alton, Ill.: Western Military Academy, 1907.

Newton County, Mo., census, 1900.

Betty Parsons, int. by Kathleen Shorthall for *Life,* 1959, Time/Life Archives.

Interviews

Herman Cherry; Lyman Field; Harry Jackson; Larry James; Rosalind Krauss; Ernestine Lassaw; Ibram Lassaw; Dudley McGovern; Wallace Milam; CCP; FLP; May Tabak Rosenberg; Syd Solomon.

NOTES

Incident at Coast Guard Beach: Solomon. **Victorian world shaped by women:** Douglas, pp. 4–7: Victorian sentimentalism, more prevalent in America even than in England itself, stemmed from "the drive of nineteenth-century American women to gain power through the exploitation of their feminine identity as their society defined it. . . . Increasingly exempt from the responsibilities of domestic industry, they were in a state of sociological transition. . . . They were becoming the prime consumers of American culture." Sentimentalism became a political tool for redressing the balance in favor of men that had been further distorted by the industrial revolution, for endowing society with the very sensibilities that were seen as limiting women's worth; see Douglas, p. 12. **Artists unproductive or homosexual:** Cherry. **Impact of industrialization on women and art:** Douglas: In the Northeast, this sociological transformation of women from serious-minded, hardworking producers into frivolous, relatively inactive consumers was a result of the industrial revolution. Douglas (p. 55) writes of the transformation of the American home wrought by the industrial revolution: "Formerly an important part of a communal productive process under her direction, it had become a place where her children stayed before they began to work and where her husband rested after the strain of labor. Once her family had looked to her quite literally to clothe and feed them; now they expected a complex blend of nurture and escape from her 'voluntary' care." With a loss of productive capacity came a loss of power.

Changes in market for literature and art: Douglas, p. 9: These changes in the market "debased" art from the serious to the light, from the noble to the frivolous: "The well-edu-

cated intellectual minister of the eighteenth century read omnivorously, but the dense argumentative tracts he tackled forced him to think. . . . His mid-nineteenth-century descendant was likely to show a love of fiction and poetry and a distaste for polemical theology; he preferred 'light' to 'heavy' reading. By the same token, numerous observers remarked on the fact that countless young Victorian women spent much of their middle-class girlhoods prostrate on chaise longues with their heads buried in 'worthless' novels. Their grandmothers, the critics insinuated, had spent their time studying the Bible and performing useful household chores." **"American culture":** Douglas, p. 5. **"Enormous need":** Douglas p. 73. *Uncle Tom's Cabin* and *Moby-Dick:* Douglas, p. 367: "Melville specifically warned women away from *Moby-Dick;"* see Fiedler, p. 28. **"Mass culture":** Douglas, p. 3. **Exclusion of female artists:** Ernestine Lassaw; Ibram Lassaw. Harry Jackson, Ernestine Lassaw, and others have noted that several women artists of the period felt compelled to "masculinize" their names; e.g., Grace Hartigan briefly taking the name George Hartigan. **Exchanging women:** Rosenberg.

"A pack of precious ninnies": *Artist,* p. 281. **Epic mural cycle:** Baigell, "THB in the 1920s," p. 425: THB intended a completed cycle of sixty murals. **Fight with Ives; "Just about bashed":** Jackson. **"Leftists attacked him":** *Artist,* p. ix. **No one more of a man:** FLP: "Among dogs, Benton was the bulldog." **Going to whorehouses:** Cherry, who later clarified: "Benton went to these places to make drawings. He was completely intent on his work. As an assistant on a mural, my inflamed youth made up what I guess would be called fantasies. Today my ideas of masculinity are different." **Benton's profaneness and pugnacity:** Jackson. **Benton's vulgarity:** *Artist,* p. 145. **Benton's misogyny:** Burroughs, p. 113: "He was inclined to ignore his female students completely." When Burroughs asked him about the place of women in the art world of the 1930s, he said, "You never heard of any female Rembrandts or El Grecos—interesting, isn't it?" **Jackson a willing student:** "On retrouvera encore Benton dans le côté cowboy, dans le rôle homme de l'ouest, dans ces déguisements qui jusqu'à la fin de sa vie accompagneront Pollock"; "Pollock, Jung et Picasso," entretien avec Claire Stoullig, in Centre Georges Pompidou, p. 46. See also, Burroughs, p. 114: "Although seemingly quite different personalities, they also had much in common: the Midwesterners' pride and distrust of the Easterners and Academics; the need to shock people with their behavior and statements; parents divided over their careers; and the crude, obscene language when drinking." Burroughs could have added that they both had strikingly similar love-hate relationships with their mothers; both rode the freights and worked as surveyors; both risked becoming dandies at a young age, and had to fight to prove their manhood; both struggled against a natural lack of technical facility; both boasted of their successes with women but felt awkward around them and demonstrated little need for their company; both had become artists to the displeasure of their fathers and to the inordinate pride of their mothers; both would steal supplies when poor and desperate—Benton, from Macy's (Burroughs, p. 47), JP from the WPA storeroom; Krauss, recalling LK.

Founding of Neosho: 1839; James. **Wood and stone house:** James: Benton called it a stone house, but in the only photo of the building, taken after it burned down in 1917, it seems to be a structure largely of wood. **"Marvels" of the Benton home:** *Intimate,* pp. 3–6. **Birth date:** Burroughs, p. 29. **"Southern hill people"; "frontiersmen"; "tidewater aristocrats":** *Intimate,* pp. 42–43. **"Old Bullion Benton":** Burroughs, p. 31. **Thomas Hart in every generation:** McGovern. **Welsh blood; physique and disposition:** *Intimate,* p. 43. THB uses the word "phlegmatic," but he seems to have meant "choleric." **"From obscurity":** *Intimate,* p. 2. **Lizzie choosing M.E.:** *Intimate,* p. 8. **"Was not in any sense":** *Intimate,* p. 21. **"A tall, willowy"; "sang and tinkled":** *Intimate,* p. 8. **Lizzie a spoiled baby:** *Intimate,* p. 24. **Waxahachie:** Burroughs, p. 29. **"Celtic"-looking:** *Intimate,* p. 44. **"Electness:** *Intimate,* p. 45: "The Wises saw themselves as superior to and separate from other people and rarely let down the barriers protecting that elevation." **"Found themselves":** *Intimate,* p. 16. **Lizzie's different goal:** *Intimate,* p. 17. **"Pictures on the wall":** *Intimate,* p. 65. **St. Louis gowns; "brunette handsomeness":** *Intimate,* p. 24. **Lizzie a political asset:** *Intimate,* pp. 25–26. **Bonhomie:** *Intimate,* p. 26. **M.E.'s populism:** *Intimate,* p. 31. **"Lizzie Wise may**

have been": *Intimate*, p. 8. "Plain men": *Intimate*, p. 3. Lizzie's efforts to control M.E.: *Intimate*, pp. 54–55. Indignant screams; Tom frightened; "I was aware": *Intimate*, p. 20. "A plain manifestation": *Intimate*, p. 23.

"I was conditioned": *Intimate*, p. 3. Douglas, p. 8: "Middle-class literary women lacked power of any crudely tangible kind and they were careful not to lay claim to it. Instead they wished to exert 'influence,' which they eulogized as a religous force. . . . This was the suasion of moral and psychic nature, and it had a good deal less to do with the faith of the past and a good deal more to do with the advertising industry of the future than its proponents would have liked to believe." "Influence" was to be asserted through psychological insight and manipulation. Horace Bushnell said of a wife's role: "[Hers] is not an ambitious noisy power; it is silent, calm, persuasive, and often so deep as to have its hold deeper than consciousness itself;" q. in Mary Bushnell Cheney, *Life and Letters of Horace Bushnell*, New York: 1880, p. 111, q. in Douglas, pp. 61–62.

Tom advising on choice of dresses: *Intimate*, pp. 66, 105. Embroidery and crewelwork: Burroughs, p. 31. Lizzie's flowers: *Intimate*, p. 95. "More in the spirit": *Intimate*, pp. 95–96. "Unusual interest": Burroughs, p. 31. Preparation for parties: *Intimate*, p. 105. "Her taste": *Intimate*, p. 66. "Rid[ing] in a high": *Intimate*, p. 13. Packed lunch: *Intimate*, p. 125. Bringing flowers: *Intimate*, p. 34. "The mooncalf age": *Artist*, p. 12. Parties: *Intimate*, p. 112.

Two worlds: *Intimate*, p. 32: "As it is with most boys, I tended to regard my father as a more interesting person than my mother and to see his activities in a more glamorous light than hers." M.E.'s cronies: *Artist*, p. 7. M.E.'s jokes and stories: *Intimate*, p. 20. "Expository men": *Artist*, p. 5. Man's world: *Intimate*, p. 19: "a world of men." "Always reeking": *Intimate*, p. 49. "Erecting and mending": *Intimate*, pp. 18–19. "An addiction"; M.E. talking to himself: *Artist*, p. 5. M.E. working with figures; "in moody silence": *Intimate*, p. 26.

Tom asked to kill woodpeckers; *Intimate*, p. 36. "The worst game-shy": *Intimate*, p. 37. "Visions": *Intimate*, p. 47. "The homeliest man": Craven, p. 9. Lobbying for better address; "keep his Washington": *Intimate*, p. 54. "After hearing": *Intimate*, pp. 54–55. "A socially proper address": *Intimate*, p. 55.

Lizzie convinced Tom a genius: Burroughs, p. 31. "Drawing pencils"; Lizzie keeping Tom's pictures; "were saying": *Intimate*, p. 64. Art tutors: *Intimate*, p. 73. Corcoran lessons; Western High School: *Intimate*, p. 84. Tom attended art classes at the Corcoran Gallery, and then, in 1903–04, at Western High School in Georgetown; Yeo and Cook, pp. 11, 22. Drawing trains and ships; "parading behind": *Intimate*, p. 51. Books on Indians: *Intimate*, p. 81: Tom still had these reports of the U.S. Bureau of Ethnology when JP met him in 1930. "Bitter disappointment"; "as a depictor": *Intimate*, p. 73.

"Something like a Puritan": *Intimate*, p. 65. Burroughs, p. 37: "In spite of an early intimacy between father and son, the father later tried his best to prevent the boy from becoming an artist; he was profoundly prejudiced against all artists." M.E.'s attitude turned "from indifference to active opposition . . . when we moved to Q Street"; *Intimate*, p. 67. But regardless of his reservations, even though he assuredly would have preferred to see his son follow him into the law, M.E. continued to subsidize Tom's art far into his adult years. "I knew that there was money at home for my education and I set myself to get it. With my mother's backing, I finally succeeded and set out, when I was nineteen years old, for Paris"; *Artist*, p. 33. It may have been his mother's backing, but it was also his father's consent. In later years, even after his wife had deserted him to join Tom in New York, the colonel would send Lizzie an extra twenty dollars for Christmas expenses and even some meal and flour for corn bread, knowing how fond his son was of it; Burroughs, p. 54. "The boy": *Intimate*, p. 64. "Were sorry": *Artist*, p. 25.

Lizzie introduced to President; "Overwhelmed"; "seventh heaven"; "probably the happiest": *Intimate*, p. 69. "To teach the home folks"; Washington-style dinners: *Intimate*, p. 85. "Set all the food": *Intimate*, pp. 85–86. "Mighty uppity"; "[My father] constantly admonished": *Intimate*, p. 86. Promenades; "Mother outshone": *Intimate*, p. 87. "Went into hysterics"; M.E.'s explanation for defeat: *Intimate*, p. 102. "You can't take": Q. in *Intimate*, p. 102. "[She] leaned": Burroughs, p. 34, q. from the journal of Ellen Maury Slayden, wife of a Virginia congressman. Sisters

coming to care for Lizzie: *Intimate*, p. 121. End of career: *Artist*, p. 15. "Moody spells"; adding numbers: *Intimate*, p. 26.

Abandoning art: *Intimate*, p. 105. Picking fights; "scoundrelly Republicans": *Intimate*, p. 115. Complaints about "quarrelsome" Benton; *Intimate*, pp. 116–17. Chores: *Intimate*, p. 89. "Where we added": *Artist*, p. 9. Athletic hopes dashed: *Intimate*, p. 110. Football team: Burroughs, p. 34: Tom was competitive in swimming, boxing, football, and baseball. We have evidence only of wrestling, football, and boxing, although, by Tom's own admission, he wasn't very good at football or boxing. Being cut from the squad: *Intimate*, p. 124. "A hero worship": *Intimate*, p. 127.

Boxing: *Intimate*, p. 110. Burlesque shows; Wagner; drawing opera scenes: *Intimate*, p. 111. "Picture-making": *Intimate*, p. 108. "Saddle-maker"; "violin-maker": *Intimate*, p. 80. Another way to prove that an artist could also be a man was to treat it merely as a pastime, an entertainment, like whittling or juggling. Working in the fields, young Tom "drew comic pictures to amuse his companions;" *Intimate*, p. 88. At other times, he claimed that drawing "excused him from chores" (*Intimate*), and later, in military school, that it "relieved me of boresome military drills"; *Intimate*, p. 137. A few years later, Tom would sidle into the art world as a cartoonist, just as JP entered with thoughts of becoming a mason. Mr. Calhoun: "a big city man"; "a little puffy"; "a great talker"; "We could hardly": *Intimate*, p. 122. "He was most enthusiastic"; Paris and *"La vie de Bohème"*: *Intimate*, p. 128. Benton (*Intimate*, p. 128) remembers his father saying " 'Something is wrong with that man,' but he wouldn't say what." "[His] stories": *Intimate*, p. 129. Surveying crew: *Intimate*, p. 132. "A wild boomtown": *Intimate*, p. 131. "That irrepressible itch": *Artist*, p. 17. "On Saturday nights": *Artist*, p. 18. Relatives; "respectable people": *Intimate*, pp. 131–32. "The right kind": *Intimate*, p. 132. With Calhoun in hotel; "and see what a city"; "became excited"; "I caught"; "embarrassed": *Intimate*, p. 133. No more contact with Calhoun: Still, Tom asked for Calhoun's help in arranging a Joplin exhibition for the works that he had painted as a student in Paris; THB to M.E. and Elizabeth Benton, n.d. "Remembered for years": *Intimate*, pp. 133–34: "I almost felt sorry for him. Years later, losing caution with age, he carried his homosexual activities too far for the Joplin area to stomach and was run out for corrupting young boys. Vice was an accepted part of Joplin life but not Mr. Calhoun's kind."

Official account of career choice; "grinning fellows"; "they laid"; "how it was done"; " 'so' ": *Artist*, p. 19. "I don't think": *Artist*, p. 20. "Rehabilitation": *Intimate*, p. 129. "Huge masculine figures": Unidentified source, q. by Burroughs, p. 48. Arrival in Chicago; "genius outfit"; scuffles: *Artist*, p. 32. "He bought himself": Burroughs, p. 42. "Notoriously drunk": Craven, "THB," p. 35: "Most of the time, fighting in cafés and quarreling with girls."

Lizzie abandoning M.E.: Burroughs, p. 48: Lizzie helping Tom avoid combat: *Artist*, p. 43; Baigell, pp. 48, 53; Burroughs, p. 52. Lizzie went to Washington to see Secretary of War Daniels to make sure that he got into the comparatively safe navy; Burroughs, pp. 52–53. Honeymoon at Lizzie's: Burroughs, p. 64. Lizzie invited to Vineyard: Burroughs, p. 72. Permanent house: Burroughs, p. 78. Designs for embroidery and crewelwork: Burroughs, p. 31. "As the last"; Tom drawing train incident: *Intimate*, p. 52.

13. JACK SASS

SOURCES

See Chapter 11.

NOTES

"[Jackson] had no": *Artist*, p. 332. "Some strange irregularity": Craven, p. 340. "Jack's talents": *Artist*, p. 332. "He had great": Benton to FVOC, March 31, 1964. "Halting"; "badly"; "crude": Craven, pp. 341, 58–59. "[Tom] made his": Craven, p. 340. "Lack of technical": Burroughs, p. 42. "They were all": *Artist*, p. 34. "Great talents"; "intense interests": *Artist*, p. 332. "I [liked] the idea": *Artist*, p. 32. "We agreed": *Artist*, p. 36. Craven, p. 341: Benton's "most gracious defender was Macdonald-Wright who steadfastly maintained that buried in his halting, badly imitative, and crude performances were the seeds of genius." **"I had seen":** *Artist,* p. 332. **Benton a student of different movements:** Burroughs, pp. 51–52. **"Casting around":** *American,* p. 102. **"With every whiff":** *Artist,* p. 38. **Benton and Weichsel** *American,* pp. 35–36. **Benton and Dewey:** *American,* pp. 167–68.

"Lurking uneasiness": *Artist,* p. 36. **Becoming violent with alcohol:** Burroughs, p. 191. Both Benton and JP were heavy drinkers: "It was obvious from the very beginning that Pollock was a born artist," Benton told Leonard Lyons. "The only thing I taught him was how to drink a fifth a day"; q. in the *Lyon's Den,* October 15, 1965, q. in Burroughs, p. 118. When drinking, each also had the same unusual urge to relieve himself in public. Burroughs (p. 97) quotes a friend: "I never saw him use a bathroom in my life. . . . At any party, he'd just walk to the door or stand in the doorway to relieve himself."

Attracted to unsophisticated boys: John Rixey, son of a Virginia tidewater aristocrat, and Benton's best friend in Washington, D.C., was the exception; *Intimate,* p. 83. **"Un-cultivated":** *Artist,* p. 45. **"Thrown among boys":** *Artist,* p. 45. **Disappearing:** See Burroughs. **Hayden; "A very young":** *Artist,* p. 80. **"Fixed up":** *Artist,* p. 134; see *American,* p. 61. **Westerners Benton's favorites:** Whitney Darrow, Jr., who graduated from Princeton, and whose father worked for Scribner's in New York: "Mine was not a background that interested him." **"He was inclined to ignore":** Burroughs, p. 113. **"Benton didn't think":** Edith Symonds, q. in Potter, p. 37. **"Tom hated women":** Q. in Burroughs, p. 79.

Benton growing circumspect: T. P. Benton: "Careless." **"Beauty" of Italian boys; "who wouldn't":** Q. by Emerson. **Rage against "pansies":** *Artist,* p. 266: "A very real danger to the cultured institutions of the country lies in the homosexuals' control of policy." **Recoiling at contact with men:** McKim: "Tom could hardly stand to have another man touch him." **Virulent attacks:** "For the most part, the fairies are so deeply involved in their own peculiar sensibilities, so intent on their own jealousies, hysterical animosities, and nursed preferences that they cannot appreciate contemporary forces until these have been consecrated by general acceptance"; *Artist,* p. 265. Benton distinguished between homosexuality—the persuasion—and homosexualism—the culture, damning the latter; *Artist,* p. 266. In fact, he claimed to admire a man so overwhelmed by lust that he was "ready to jump anything from a steer to a kitchen mechanic"; *Artist,* p. 265. **"Tom, you're protesting":** Mildred Small, q. by Burroughs.

Friends: Asked about the rumors that Benton had homosexual leanings, Blanche Carstensen said, "Well, some of us wondered about that, yes." **Son:** T. P Benton: "I guess eventually my father is going to be established as a man of homosexual leanings. There's no way to stop it." **Biographer:** Burroughs: "Tom was bisexual." An anonymous family friend, q. in Burroughs, p. 192: Benton's father always feared that " 'there was something wrong with him, that he must be a homosexual if he wanted to become an artist.' . . . [Tom] was always afraid people would think this because of his size and his profession."

Pollock and Benton's relationship: See also Friedman, p. 19. **"Down to the last":** Kaz. **"Tailed after Benton":** Holtzman, q. in Solomon, p. 56. **"A western artist":** *Artist,* p. 261. **"Frontier family":** Q. by Darrow. **Milking cows:** Jackson. **Wild stallions, wolves:** Rose, "Painters of a Flaming Vision," p. 334. **Buffalo:** CCP. **"High-heel boots"; "it was no costume":** Wilson. **"Jackson always walked":** Pavia, q. in Gruen, p. 262. **"Only California":** THB to FVOC, Mar. 31, 1964: "Jack was a brooder, so he undoubtedly had partially mystical tendencies. Don't all young artists? But I never saw any evidence of this attachment to a mystical cult. Of course he would have known that I might ridicule such an attachment. But he was too open, too frank a young man to play any kind of double personality game." **"He was highly":** Kamrowski. **"Egos were not":** *Artist,* p. 45. **Benton's introspection:** Craven, p. 7: In Paris, "The brash Missourian lost his assurance and drifted toward despondency," and later (p. 20) was "quiet [and] contemplative." **Making art masculine:** See Symonds, q. in Potter, p. 37.

Progressive educators: Historian Charles Beard, philosophers Thorstein Veblen, John Dewey, and James Harvard Robinson, and economist Alvin Johnson; see Johnson, *Pi-*

oneer's Progress. **Home of the New School:** Although Frank Lloyd Wright was considered as the architect for the building (Johnson, p. 320), the design was awarded to Joseph Urban, an immigrant to New York from Vienna and the Secession movement (see Robinson and Bletter, p. 19) who had designed palaces for the Khedive of Egypt (Johnson, p. 320) but had made his living and his reputation in this country designing sets for the Boston and Metropolitan opera companies as well as the Ziegfeld Follies; Braun and Branchick, p. 16. In his hands, the New School attempted to convey, like Benton's murals, the force of technology; Dr. Johnson would call its streamlined facade, with its alternating bands of brick and glass, "straightforward, rational and unafraid" and pronounce it fully within "the spirit of the New School"; *Prospectus for The New School for Social Research, 66–72 West Twelfth Street, New York City,* q. in Braun and Branchick, p. 17.

Orozco appointment protested: Notably by Ralph Pierson, who argued that the school should not commission a foreign artist without also commissioning an American, and Lewis Mumford, a longtime Benton friend and supporter (see Johnson, p. 328); Mumford had long championed Benton as a muralist; Mumford, "THB." **"An authentic American":** Johnson, p. 328. **Boardroom:** The recessed lights circling the entire boardroom ensured an even illumination while the streamlined yet rich Art Deco design promised an appropriate setting for the colorful mural that Benton had in mind; Braun and Branchick, p. 17. **Dining room:** Burroughs, p. 103.

Benton's methods: Braun and Branchick, p. 69: "[Benton's] methods were elaborate, time-consuming, and self-consciously disciplined, in a deliberate emulation of Renaissance methods." Painting was, in Benton's view, not a matter of spontaneity: "Real form demands an obvious imposition of will on the elements of mind"; "Form and the Subject," pp. 303–08. In adapting his "rolly-polly" style to the painting of murals, of course, Benton was denying not just the European abstraction of his youth, but the prevailing notion—derived largely from the thinly painted, softly colored, simply composed, and elegiac murals of Puvis de Chavannes (Braun and Branchick, p. 31)—that a mural should defer to its surrounding architecture.

"He had a bureau": Jules. **"Walking tours" into the "hinterland":** *American,* p. 60: The states visited were Virginia, North Carolina, Tennessee, Missouri, Texas, Kansas, and California. "I learned to produce them with great rapidity and I often ended a trip with three or four sketch books. Not every drawing was successful, nor was this important, for the very making of it would cut a memory impression and thus help build up the general image of America which I was now searching for"; *American,* p. 60. **"General image":** *American,* p. 60.

Changing West **panel:** Braun and Branchick, p. 46. The primary challenge was to bring this disparate imagery, encompassing a whole continent and a whole nation, into a single mural cycle. Benton, *American,* p. 63: "This was solved by composing each subject so that some parts of the periphery of its design were left open. . . . In some areas of the mural where these differences [between pictorial units] were so great that peripheral jointures were too difficult to make, sections of the moulding that framed the mural were injected into the mural design itself. Separations such as this are often found in the illustrated pages of nineteenth-century magazines and books." In separating some of his images this way, Benton arranged the strips of architectural molding, using both curved and straight pieces, into a variety of pleasing shapes, often formally related to the shapes they frame.

Trip to Bethlehem Steel: Johnson, p. 329. **Rita, T.P., and Caroline Pratt:** Braun and Branchick, p. 21, citing Deborah Solomon. **Elizabeth:** Braun and Branchick, p. 21, citing CCP to Emily Braun, Dec. 14, 1984. **Max Eastman, Peggy Reynolds, Alvin Johnson, and Benton:** "Benton," *Time,* Jan. 5, 1931, p. 32. **Jackson's "action posing":** THB to FVOC, Mar. 31, 1964.

Tintoretto-like bas-reliefs: *American,* p. 46: Benton had read in 1919 of Tintoretto's use of bas-reliefs for his *Last Supper* in Santa Maria della Salute. **A 400-year-old text:** Cennini, *The Book of the Art of Cennino Cennini or A Treatise on Painting; American,* p. 64. **Advantages of tempera:** Branchick; Braun and Branchick, p. 68. Other users of tempera were Reginald Marsh, Boardman Robinson, and Denys Wortman; Braun and Branchick, p. 68. **Demands of tempera:** It requires a relatively smooth, white surface, and Benton didn't

prepare his surface as carefully as he should have. He picked the number of coats of gesso (seven) out of his head, didn't wait long enough for each coat to dry, and didn't sand between each coat; Branchick. **Assisted by Cherry:** Cherry isn't certain this was the mural cycle he worked on, but, given the dates of his time in New York, this is the only one he could have worked on. **Preparations:** *American*, p. 64; Branchick. **Without assistance:** THB to FVOC, Mar. 31, 1964: "I had *no* assistance on the mural except for moving the panels about." **Use of distemper:** *American*, p. 42. Benton (*American*, p. 58) used distemper poorly: "I made the mistake of using too heavy a glue solution, with the consequence that most of the paintings cracked so badly that they were not worth preserving."
"Incalculable energy": Craven, p. 19, who called Benton's art "fundamentally an intellectual performance." **"Big-boned":** Braun and Branchick, p. 46. **"Master designer":** Craven, p. 19. Matthew Baigell, p. 87: Benton "clearly ran the risk of stereotyping behavior patterns, types of activity, and landscapes. His paintings could become a kind of impressionistic journalism, savoring the typical features of the subject being painted but not exploring the individual psychology, motivation, or even context in which it occurred." Stephen Polcari, "JP and THB," p. 120: "Despite the American Culture subject matter, the three-dimensional space, modeled forms, and his often-stated antagonism to modern European art, Benton shared modern painting's emphasis on abstract two-dimensional patterning and all-over design." Polcari (p. 121) compares the overlapping images in *America Today*—the way "they spill over into one another at a portion of their boundaries"—to Analytical Cubist *passage*. CCP: "The influence [on JP's work] has nothing to do with [Benton's] subject matter, or with Benton's color. It has altogether to do with Benton's method of diagramming the underlying structure of western painting." **Jackson uncomfortable with concentrated work:** Elizabeth Pollock, noting Charles's laborious process, says the Benton-derived process "took hours of *work*. You couldn't imagine Jackson doing anything like that."
"I was given": *Artist*, p. 332. THB to FVOC, Mar. 31, 1964: "I made friends with my students at the League. They came to our apartment. My wife met most of them." **Jackson's unique access:** Darrow; Delaney; CCP. THB to FVOC, Mar. 31, 1964: "Jack became somewhat closer than the rest because he used to 'baby sit' for our young son." Tolegian sometimes accompanied JP to the Bentons', but the hospitality extended to him was at first largely derivative. **T.P. pensive:** Field: Although introspective, T.P. was also athletic and performed well on his high school football and track teams. **Pollock taciturn:** Schardt: JP was "extremely shy and troubled, and he was torn when he was working with Benton." **Telling stories to T.P.; "the spooky mythology":** *Artist*, p. 338. **Boy's idol:** *Artist*, p. 332.
Jackson working for Rita: Kron; Eleanor Piacenza. **"Little tasks":** Kron. **Fifty cents a night:** SLM, int. by CG, c. 1956. **Five dollars a day:** Kron. **Rita taking advantage:** Eleanor Piacenza: "Rita used people to her advantage. She would use these kids to baby-sit, wash the kitchen floor, come down to the Vineyard and open up the house." But Rita could be very generous to her surrogate children. Araks Tolegian recalls that Manuel received anonymous gifts of milk outside his door every morning during his early years in New York. Later he discovered that Rita had arranged to have the milk delivered to him. **Rita's Italian background:** Eleanor Piacenza; Santos Piacenza: Their father, Ettore, returned to Italy "after about twenty years because he wanted to die in the old country." Burroughs, p. 4: Rita arrived in America with her two brothers in 1912. **Loose clothes:** FLP. **Hair:** Kron. **Hair bouncing, hips swinging:** Emerson. **"Beam-shaking":** McWhirter, "Tom Benton," p. 66. **Spaghetti for fifty:** Jules; Santos Piacenza. **"Mother of the world":** Emerson.
Benton teaching Rita; "slim"; "wore a red hat": *Artist*, p. 48. **Lizzie's prejudice against Rita's background:** Burroughs, p. 4. Burroughs, p. 64: "According to relatives, his mother didn't want or expect him to marry." In 1912, Lizzie Benton became so ill that Tom was forced to travel to her bedside in Neosho. This precipitated an almost instant recovery, whereupon she joined Tom on his return to New York, leaving M.E. behind. Burroughs, pp. 47–48: "Even if she told some friends that she left the Colonel because he was so 'lazy,' others were clearly of the opinion that she left him because her children, especially Tom, had moved to the East." **"Were**

certain": *Artist*, p. 48. **Marriage; honeymoon:** Burroughs, p. 64. **"Mommie":** Q. in Burroughs, p. 145. **"Mama":** Q. in Burroughs, p. 25; correspondence between THB and Elizabeth Benton.
Verbal skirmishes between Tom and Rita: Jackson. Most of these arguments centered around Benton's refusal to play the family man. The fact that he took his marital duties lightly—"The bonds of marriage did not lay [*sic*] very heavily on my back," he later wrote (*Artist*, p. 75)—didn't seem to bother her terribly. Kron: "I think Rita liked the idea of being Mrs. Thomas Hart Benton. The satisfaction she got out of that was more than she got out of the relationship." But she couldn't forgive her husband for giving their children the same short shrift: "He's the worst husband and worst father that ever lived," Rita complained to one Vineyard neighbor (q. in Burroughs, p. 95) about Benton's long sketching trips, which left her stranded with a small child. Emerson: As an adult, Rita was constantly torn between her devotion to Benton and her devotion to the children. **"Goddammit, woman":** Q. by Jackson. **"Don't be vulgar"; "Italian men":** Q. by Kron.
"Tom was Rita's man": Q. in Burroughs, p. 172. **"Put everything in Rita's hands":** Jackson. **Rita's bargaining:** Burroughs, p. 79. **Designing hats and posing:** Burroughs, p. 64. **Doing Tom's chores:** Burroughs, p. 108. **Promoting Tom:** Kron: "She was very instrumental in promoting and pushing Tom. He wouldn't have done it himself." Emerson: "Rita is largely responsible for Tom's success." Craven, "THB," p. 37: Rita was not only "one of the few women of my acquaintance who understands paintings" but one who proved "clever at selling paintings." When Benton made a generous slip, promising some friend a gift of his own work, Rita quickly became his "watchdog, determined Tom would not give it away"; Mary Manners, q. in Burroughs, p. 97. **"In a business":** Emerson. **Boy hero named "Jack Sass"; "wild stallions"; "we received"; "explored"; "Jack Sass" was Jackson Pollock:** *Artist*, pp. 338–39.

14. THE OLD LOVE

SOURCES

Books, articles, manuscript, brochures, documents, records, and transcripts

Allen, *Since Yesterday*; Ashton, *Yes, But . . .* ; THB, *An American in Art (American)*; *An Artist in America (Artist)*; Braun and Branchick, *THB*; Burroughs, *THB*; Congdon, *The Thirties*; Craven, *THB*; Friedman, *JP*; Hall, *The Well of Loneliness*; Honeyman, *The Willson Family Tree*; OC&T, *JP*; Potter, *To a Violent Grave*; Powell, *Publications of the Bureau of Ethnology*, vol. I; Wall, *Iowa*; Sevareid, *Not So Wild a Dream*.

Gerald Clarke, "The Miracle of '32," *Time*, Oct. 17, 1983; Robert Goodnough, "Pollock Paints a Picture," *Art News*, May 1951; Axel Horn, "JP: The Hollow and the Bump," *Carleton Miscellany*, Summer 1966; "No One Has Starved," *Fortune*, Sept. 1932; William Rubin, "JP and the Modern Tradition, Part I: 1. The Myths and the Paintings," *Artforum*, Feb. 1967.

FVOC, "The Genesis of JP: 1912 to 1943 (Ph.D. thesis), Baltimore: Johns Hopkins University, 1965.

Los Angeles Museum Catalogues of Art Exhibits, A–Z, 1931–32, Los Angeles: Los Angeles Museum, 1921–32; *Southwest Museum Handbook, 1931*, Los Angeles: Southwest Museum, 1931.

Chronology prepared by CCP for EFP, Feb. 1975, AAA.

THB Classbooks, 1929–30, 1930–31, 1931–32, Art Students League Archives; registration cards for Whitney Darrow, Jr., JP, and Manuel Tolegian, Art Students League Archives.

THB, int. by Kathleen Shorthall, Nov. 9, 1959, for *Life*, Time/Life Archives; Manuel Tolegian, int. by Betty Hoag, Feb. 12, 1965, AAA.

Interviews

Ward Bennett; Fritz Bultman; Peter Busa; Reginald Cabral; Lawrence Campbell; Jeremy Capillé; Nicholas Carone; Herman Cherry; Whitney Darrow, Jr.; Joseph Delaney; Sanford Friedman; Violet de Laszlo; Ruth Emerson; Sanford Friedman; David Gibbs; Axel Horn; Ora Horton; Buffie Johnson; Mervin Jules; Reuben Kadish; Gerome Kamrowski; Nathaniel Kaz; Craig Klyver; LK; Maria Piacenza Kron; Berthe Pacifico Laxineta; Harold Lehman; Conrad Marca-Relli; ACM; John

Bernard Myers; Philip Pavia; David Peretz; Eleanor Piacenza; ABP; CCP; EFP; FLP; MLP; Neal Primm; Harry Rand; Charles Rozaire; Grant Rusk; Araks Tolegian; Steve Wheeler; Roger Wilcox; Reginald Wilson.

NOTES

Desire for Rita: JP may have accompanied Rita to Martha's Vineyard to help prepare the Benton's summer house at Chilmark. **"Inherent restlessness":** Burroughs, p. 95. **"The Bonds":** *Artist,* p. 75. **Students urged to travel:** THB to FVOC, Apr. 26, 1965, q. in FVOC, "The Genesis of JP," p. 40. **Pennsylvania truck; "I just went":** Manuel Tolegian, int. by Hoag, Feb. 12, 1965. **Cleveland streetcar:** Araks Tolegian, recalling Manuel. **Two million on the roads:** Congdon, p. 102. **"In search":** "No One Has Starved," p. 28. **Tolegian "terrified" of robbery:** Araks Tolegian, recalling Manuel. **People murdered for little:** Sevareid, p. 45. **Remainder of Tolegian's trip:** Araks Tolegian, recalling Manuel; JP to CCP and FLP, n.d. **"I got thrown":** JP to CCP and FLP, n.d. **"Experienced the most marvelous":** JP to CCP, June 10, 1931. JP, int. by Goodnough ("Pollock Paints a Picture," p. 38): "You get a wonderful view of the country from the top of a freight car."

"Miners and prostitutes": JP to CCP and FLP, n.d. **Jail:** JP must have been arrested at this point in his trip, because Manuel didn't know anything about it and it had already happened by the time JP arrived in St. Louis. **"Hooverville":** Primm. **"Spavined Fords":** "No One Has Starved," p. 28. **"Where the curvature":** Sevareid. **Great exodus to come:** See Allen, pp. 157-72. **"Black blizzards":** See Allen, pp. 157-72. **"A new social dimension":** Sevareid, p. 41. **"Cutthroats":** JP to CCP and FLP, n.d. **"Tex-KT":** Sevareid, p. 42. **Criminals and derelicts:** Sevareid, p. 42. *Changing West:* Braun and Branchick, p. 46. **Pilfered ice:** Sevareid, p. 46. **Bread a dime; meal a quarter; "boes":** Delaney. **Racing to the A&P; coffee shops and soup lines:** Busa. **"You didn't have to":** Delaney. **Railway "deeks":** Sevareid, p. 41. **Indulgent train operators:** Sevareid, p. 43. **"Hotshots":** Delaney. **"[I] rather imagined"; "well-built":** Sevareid, p. 44. **"Terrible"; "scary":** Araks Tolegian, recalling Manuel.

League classmate: Busa. **Jackson's homosexual experiences:** Busa, to our knowledge, was the only male friend to whom JP opened up about his homosexual desires; he was certainly one of the few people close enough to JP to have elicited such candor. But Busa was by no means our only source on the issue of JP's confused sexuality. Reuben Kadish, perhaps JP's closest friend outside his family and a close friend of Sande's, admits that he and Sande both assumed that JP had homosexual tendencies and experiences: "There is no question about it. And I know it was painful to Sande." "I don't think I should comment, or judge anybody morally or amorally or immorally," Kadish says. "The big thing that is made about Proust and his homosexuality, for instance, is that if the mores of the time didn't permit that kind of honesty, that kind of declaration, I'm not sure he would have done it any other way. Gide, the same thing. There are a lot of people in that particular area. It comes out in the end, I suppose, but what effect does it have on the work?"

According to Buffie Johnson: "Tony Smith told me about the time when Jackson was with some buddy of his, who was not a practicing homosexual. Well, let's call him John. They were kind of at the reeling stage and somebody suggested doing something and Jackson said, 'Oh, hell, John, let's go home and fuck.' " See also "Fruits and Nuts," Chapter 30, for material from Bennett and Cabral on JP's participation in the homosexual subculture of Provincetown in 1944. See also "The Last Act," Chapter 43, for material from Carone on JP's possible homosexual activities in Springs.

Others, like Conrad Marca-Relli, who did not know of specific homosexual experiences, would later say, "I think he may have had doubts about his being homosexual." "Certainly there was a dormant gay quality and he resented it in himself—he didn't know how to handle it," said Fritz Bultman; q. in Potter, p. 214. "Jackson was very up-front with Lee about his homosexual instincts and about his fear of them," says David Gibbs. According to Sanford Friedman, Jackson's bisexual inclinations "was a subject she was not averse to referring to and discussing briefly."

Violet de Laszlo, one of JP's psychiatrists, says that anxiety over homosexual feelings may have been at the root of JP's

problems. Dr. David Peretz, a psychoanalyst on the faculty of Columbia who has read many of our research materials, says that JP was much too unresolved for labels of any kind but that his sexual trauma, if not his sexual inclinations, is crucial to understanding JP's psychological makeup.

"He looked": Horton. **"[Jack] looks":** SMP to CCP and FLP, n.d. **"My trip":** JP to CCP and FLP, n.d. **"Grim misery":** Primm, professor of history at the University of Missouri at St. Louis: "I have never seen a description either in private papers or in the press or anywhere else implying that it was anything other than grim and miserable. To present this as a kind of colorful thing would be a terrible distortion." **"Gave swell color":** JP to CCP and FLP, n.d. **Brown and Sande roommates:** ABP. **Letters to Pacifico:** Laxineta. **Pacifico dating another man:** Horton; Laxineta: The man was Jack Laxineta, whom Berthe eventually married. Berthe claims that while JP was in New York they wrote each other "just about every day" and that JP's "letters from New York were love letters." It is hard to imagine JP writing regularly, let alone daily. **Visit to Jackson; Crude mural:** Horton; Laxineta.

Drive to Wrightwood: JP to CCP and FLP, n.d.; see also LRP to FLP, July 12, 1931. **Roy laid off; federal road job; job for Jay:** LRP to FLP, July 12, 1931. **"Raw food":** JP to CCP and FLP, n.d. **"[Jay] and I":** LRP to CCP and EFP, Sept. 27, 1931. **"Hope [Jack] finds":** LRP to FLP, July 12, 1931. **Old friends form new community:** Also included: Jules Langsner, a young poet, and Leonard Stark, a photographer; Kadish. **Feitelson and Macdonald-Wright:** Cherry. **"A combination":** Fletcher Martin to Dore Ashton, Oct. 21, 1974, q. in Ashton, p. 18. **Arensberg home:** Ashton, p. 20. **Goldstein leaving Otis; new style:** Ashton, p. 21; see *Mother and Child,* Ashton, p. 9. **Musical trips and records; weekly reports:** Lehman. **"The old bunch":** JP to CCP, n.d.

Kadish material: Kadish. **"You don't need:"** Q. by Kadish. **Description of Kadish:** Photo in possession of Kadish. **Vilna:** Now called Vilnius. **Samuel Shuster:** Kadish: Samuel came to this country "around 1911, 1912." "Kadish" was Samuel's given name. **Kadish an intellectual artist:** Lehman. **"Imaging power":** Kadish. **Record-setting heat:** Clarke, "The Miracle of '32," p. 77: The record heat spell of August 1931 worried the organizers of the 1932 Olympics. **Visiting museums and galleries; evenings over beer:** Kadish. **Southwest Museum:** Klyver: The summer of 1931 was a time of considerable transition for the museum. From 1930 to 1932, the northwest coast objects were moved from the lobby to the auditorium to a permanent northwest coast hall. After opening in 1914 with an undefined collection, from natural history to the fine arts, the Southwest Museum took on a new director in 1926 who limited its focus to Native American art. Today it is "the major collection west of the Mississippi." **Southwestern and Plains artifacts; Pacific Coast baskets:** *Southwest Museum Handbook, 1931,* pp. 6-13.

Trips to Los Angeles County Museum: Kadish. **Old masters and local art:** Rusk: There were constant shows of local art during this period, including "Artists of Southern California," 1930-31, and a one-woman show by Grace Clements, July 1-15, 1931; *Los Angeles Museum Catalogues of Art Exhibits, A-Z, 1931-32.* **South Pacific exhibits:** Kadish; Rozaire. **Tapa cloths:** Made by pounding mulberry bark.

Roy finding Jackson a job: Araks Tolegian, recalling Manuel. **Tolegian invited along:** JP to CCP and FLP, n.d.; SMP to FLP, n.d. **Sawing:** Araks Tolegian, recalling Manuel. **"Jack and Tolegian":** SMP to FLP, n.d. **Continued heat:** SMP to FLP, n.d. **Arguments between Jackson and Tolegian:** Araks Tolegian, recalling Manuel. **Manuel accusing supervisor; Jackson threatening Tolegian:** Araks Tolegian, recalling Manuel; Manuel Tolegian, q. in Potter, p. 40. **"Cut my throat":** Araks Tolegian, recalling Manuel. **"I have finished":** JP to CCP, n.d. JP didn't join Sande and Arloie on their trip to San Francisco to see the Rivera mural, which they didn't get to see because it was "in a private meeting room for the Stock Exchange members. They also saw [Bill] Hayden for a moment—Sande as usual was in a hell of a hurry so did no good there. After we left last year Sande did some interesting water colors—but did not do anything through the winter"; JP to CCP, n.d. **"I haven't done":** JP to CCP, n.d.

Roy depressed and ill: LRP to CCP and EFP, Sept. 27, 1931: "I am feeling rotten today have a cold on my bronchol tube . . . I haven't any kick coming I feel like I might be good this summer for several years yet." **"I wish":** LRP to FLP, July 12, 1931. **"The most unfatherly":** Manuel Tolegian, q. by Araks. **"I don't know":** JP to CCP, n.d. **Jackson driving to Oklahoma City:** LRP to CCP and EFP, Sept. 27, 1931. **"Dad thinks":** JP to CCP, n.d. **Charles and Elizabeth:** They convinced the family they were married that summer. One family tree (Honeyman), probably prepared with Stella's help, listed the marriage as July 15, 1932. **Jackson stealing Benton's favor:** CCP; q. in Potter, p. 32. **Elizabeth furious at Charles:** EFP: "Charles is the must unenvying man, entirely lacking in jealousy." **Tenth Street studio:** 49 East Tenth Street. EFP: It was Charles's studio; Frank and Marie say they visited JP there prior to May 1932. **Meals prepared at 47 Horatio Street:** Potter (p. 40) says that JP moved with Charles to the Horatio Street apartment, but Frank and Marie say he did not.

Registration: JP registered on October 12, 1931; registration card for JP. **Mural Painting:** Registration card for JP. **No course in murals:** THB to FVOC, Mar. 31, 1964. **Jackson receiving private tutoring:** Manuel Tolegian, q. in Potter, p. 34. Benton, visiting Tolegian in the late 1960s, saw his copy of Bryan Robertson's book on JP, pointed to one of the drawings, and exclaimed, "I did that! That's not Pollock's work"; q. by Araks Tolegian, recalling Manuel. **"Great heavy X":** Jules. **"I used one":** THB to FVOC, Mar. 31, 1964.

Discussions between Gorky and Davis: Pavia. **Darrow at League:** Registration card for Darrow. **Ethnology publication:** CCP, q. in Rubin, "JP and the Modern Tradition, Part I: 2," p. 22 n. 9. **Editor's argument:** Powell, p. 20. **"Man starts":** Q. in OC&T III, p. 2. **"Barbed-wire" handwriting:** Araks Tolegian. **"His mind was absolutely":** THB, int. by Shorthall, Nov. 9, 1959. "Jack did not have a logical mind"; THB to FVOC, Mar. 31, 1964. **"The deep wellsprings":** *Artist,* p. 336.

"Continuous running"; "Jack fought": Horn, "JP," p. 83. **"Damn fine colorist":** Q. in Burroughs, p. 118. **Benton considered poor colorist:** Jules; Darrow, q. in Potter, p. 43; Manuel Tolegian, q. in Potter, p. 34. **"The human element":** Q. in Burroughs, p. 118. This was all the more damning since most of his contemporaries considered Benton's work lacking in "the human element"; see Craven, p. 19: "His depth of thinking is not to be disputed; all that his art requires is greater depth of feeling." **Charles's paintings:** CCP, q. in Potter, p. 38. **Jackson's works turned to the wall:** FLP. **Washington Square Show:** The show began in 1931, organized by Vernon Porter; Campbell. **Date of show:** Campbell. **Jackson on MacDougal Alley; posing:** Delaney. **Five to ten dollars:** Kaz; Manuel Tolegian, int. by Hoag, Feb. 25, 1965. **No one bought:** Delaney.

Jackson's visits to Bentons: MLP. **Benton discovering harmonica:** *Artist,* p.. 256: It was given to T.P. by Tolegian. Both O'Connor (p. 51) and Friedman (p. 33) say the musicales began in the fall of 1933. In *Artist* (p. 256), Benton dates them from the work slump following completion of the New School murals in early 1931. By winter 1931–32, JP was practicing the mouth harp every night; JP to LRP, Feb. 1932. Benton became so involved in his new hobby that he invented a new system of musical notation for the harmonica, replacing traditional musical notes with numbers and using arrows to indicate when to blow (pointing up) and when to suck (pointing down); Burroughs, p. 120. **"A revelation":** *Artist,* p. 256. **Composers; "we commenced":** *Artist,* p. 257. **Benton's group playing:** Busa; photo in Burroughs, p. 120. **Mandatory attendance at musicales:** Busa. **Charles on mouth harp; "I was":** CCP. **Steffen on dulcimer:** Kadish: Sande eventually played the harmonica, too. **Jackson playing harmonica at Wrightwood:** FLP. **Jackson smashing violin:** CCP, q. in Potter, p. 38; LK. **"[I] can't play":** JP to LRP, Feb. 1932. **"Enthusiastically":** Q. in Burroughs, p. 119.

Typhoid fever; "the grip": JP to LRP, Feb. 1932. **Whitney murals:** *American,* p. 67. **"Hard luck":** JP to LRP, Feb. 1932. **Jackson assuming Tom's duties:** There is no direct evidence, but Frank says he assumed them when he occupied a similar position in the Benton family. **"From the beginning":** Kron. **Cooing in sultry voice:** CCP. **Smoothing frustrations:** Piacenza. **"She was a very flirtatious":** Kadish. Emerson: "She was often flirtatious with other men . . . even with my husband, and he was crazy about her." **Jackson's seduction:** Gibbs, recalling LK: JP later told Lee Krasner that "Mrs. Benton played with him and titillated him and got him all excited." **Frank's arrival; "she had winning ways":** FLP. **Rita thirty-seven:** Kron: Rita was born about

1895; her brother Santos, in 1890. **Frank's trip to Harlem club with Rita; her hand on his knee:** FLP.
Tales of sexual adventure: In a conversation about the past between Charles and Frank in October 1985, the only topic that sparked deep enthusiasm was their tales of visits to red-light districts, Charles's in New Orleans in 1934, Frank's in the Panama Canal Zone in 1928. **"You know how dogs":** Q. in Burroughs, p. 95. **Rabelaisian fantasy:** Benton used the word "Rabelaisian" in *Artist,* p. 96. **"Liked sexy women":** Rand. **Tolegian corresponding with future wife:** Araks Tolegian. **Tolegian scouting New York:** Kron. **Katz fifteen:** Kaz was born March 9, 1917; Kaz. **Katz a regular at parties:** Kaz. By the end of the decade this precinct had been divided into the Midtown South Precinct and the Midtown North Precinct. **Paddy wagons:** Kaz. Although far from prudish, the thirties were not years of unrestrained sexuality, partly because the Depression affected romance: "How could a guy go after a girl if he didn't have any money to take her out," says Kaz. Kamrowski: "In those days, there was no sexual revolution and marriage was very expensive."

"'Blocs,' psychic obstructions": THB to FVOC, March 31, 1964. **Rumors of Jackson's "affair":** Wheeler, recalling Morris Kantor. **"I could see":** Horn. **"Of course, feeling":** Q. in Burroughs, p. 118. **"Rita Benton played":** JP, q. by LK, q. by Gibbs. **Jackson's binges:** Delaney; Kaz. **Katz's studio; Lincoln Square Arcade:** Kaz. It was on the site of the current Lincoln Center. **Jackson at League dances:** Kaz; Pavia. **Penthouse parties:** Kaz. **Money from Stella:** JP to LRP, Feb. 1952, mentions a "token" sent from home. **Jack Frost; corn whiskey; Sterno:** Kaz.

Christmas Eve incident: Araks Tolegian, recalling Manuel. **Church of the Nativity:** Given Tolegian's directions, this is the only church it could have been. The old Greek Revival building was torn down in 1970. **"Jack walked":** Manuel Tolegian, q. by Araks. See CCP, q. in Friedman, p. 26. **Scuffles and brawls:** Delaney. **Saturday night bouts:** McNeil. **Hudson River incident:** Araks Tolegian, recalling Manuel. **"Angry"; "I had to jump":** Manuel Tolegian, q. by Araks. **Jackson working himself up:** Pavia. **"He'd look you over":** Wilson. **"Pugnacious and ornery":** Jules. **"He'd walk up":** Busa. **"He bragged":** Jules.

Family rarely saw misbehavior: CCP; EFP. **Visit to Jackson's apartment:** MLP. It took place in 1931. But the return address on his letters shows JP was still in Charles's studio in February 1932. Since the incident precipitated JP's departure, either it occurred after February or JP was still using Charles's address for mail. **"No particular interest";** **Rose taking a liking:** MLP. **Quizzical squint:** Horn. **Jackson cutting wood; Marie's hat destroyed:** MLP: It was "the most disorganized party I'd ever been to." **Jackson aggressive with Rose:** FLP; MLP. **Ax incident:** MLP. **"You're a nice girl":** Q. by MLP. **Charles's painting already sold:** MLP. **Charles unemotional:** EFP; Capillé. **Jackson evicted:** MLP. **Jackson and Frank sharing apartment:** FLP: He thinks it was near the corner of Thirty-fourth Street and Eighth Avenue. **Description of room:** MLP. **Rose "attractive"; "reserved":** FLP. **Independent; Marie meeting Rose:** MLP. **Seducing Jackson:** FLP: "I imagine Rose was employed. She probably had the only money between the two of them." **No dates:** MLP.

15. INTO THE PAST

SOURCES

Books, articles, manuscripts, film, document, and records

Adams, *The Epic of America;* Allen, *Since Yesterday;* Baigell, *THB;* Baigell, ed., *A THB Miscellany;* THB, *An American in Art (American);* THB, *An Artist in America (Artist);* Braun and Branchick, *THB;* Burroughs, *THB;* Congdon, *The Thirties;* Friedman, *JP;* Helm, *Modern Mexican Painters;* *Hymns of the Church of Jesus Christ of Latter-Day Saints;* Jewell, *Have We an American Art?;* Kootz, *New Frontiers in American Painting;* Lane and Larsen, eds., *Abstract Painting and Sculpture in America, 1927–1944;* Marling, *Tom Benton and His Drawings;* OC&T, *JP;* Potter, *To a Violent Grave;* Schlesinger, *The Crisis of the Old Order;* Weaver, *Los Angeles.*

THB, "Art and Nationalism," *Modern Monthly,* May 1934;

THB, "Art vs. the Mellon Gallery," *Common Sense*, June 1941; THB, "Form and the Subject," *Arts*, June 1924; Thomas Craven, "THB," *Scribner's*, Oct. 1937; Axel Horn, "JP: The Hollow and the Bump," *Carleton Miscellany*, Summer 1966; Edward Alden Jewell, "American Painting," *Creative Art*, Nov. 1931; "U.S. Scene," *Time*, Dec. 24, 1934.

Edward Alden Jewell, "Orozco and Benton Paint Murals for New York," *NYT*, Nov. 23, 1930.

Ellen Gross Landau, "LK: A Study of Her Early Career (1926–1949)" (Ph.D. thesis), Newark: University of Delaware, 1981; FVOC, "The Genesis of JP: 1912–1943" (Ph.D. thesis), Baltimore: Johns Hopkins University, 1965.

Strokes of Genius: JP (film), Court Productions, 1984.

Chronology prepared by CCP for EFP, Feb. 1975, AAA.

Registration cards for Whitney Darrow, Jr., JP, and Manuel Tolegian, Art Students League Archives; THB Classbooks, 1930–31, 1931–32, Art Students League Archives.

Interviews

Peter Busa; Lawrence Campbell; Jeremy Capillé; Herman Cherry; Betty Clausen; Whitney Darrow, Jr.; Joseph Delaney; Gottlieb Friesinger; Axel Horn; Mervin Jules; Reuben Kadish; Stewart Klonis; ACM; George McNeil; Philip Pavia; ABP; CCP; EFP; FLP; MJP; MLP; Milton Resnick.

NOTES

Letters to Jackson: Some inferred from JP's return letters, notably JP to LRP, Feb. 1932; JP to SMP, May 1932; others as indicated. **Frank in debt:** MLP. **Twelve dollar coat:** FLP. **Brockway visit:** JP to LRP, Feb. 1932, and JP to SMP, May 1932; Brockway referred to as "Charlie B." **"Growing up" problems:** CCP. **"The usual stress":** SLM to CCP, July 1941. **Kadish:** "Sure, they were difficult years, they were difficult years for a lot of young people." **Million jobless:** There were 1,160,000 in New York City ("No One Has Starved," p. 25) and 12,000,000 jobless in the country; Schlesinger, p. 248. **Janitorial work:** Darrow.

April: Dating based on JP to LRP, Feb. 1932, and JP to SMP, May 1932; in the first letter, mailed probably in mid-April, Charles is still waiting to hear; in the second, written only weeks before he left, Charles is no longer included. **Charles helping arrange trip:** Darrow, in "Strokes of Genius." **Darrow; "getting away":** Darrow. **Expenses would be "$25 to $30":** Q. by Darrow: He got $35 for a cartoon in those days and had saved about $300 from sales. **Schoppe wanting ride home:** MLP. **Date of trip; Packard:** MLP. **Putting car in order:** JP to SMP, May 1932. **Trip to Nebraska; visit to Marie's uncle; Marie's uncle shocked:** MLP: "The next morning, Uncle Elijah was going to take us all to breakfast in the hotel dining room, but when he saw these four unshaven, really grungy looking guys in the daylight, he took us to a little café off the main drag instead where not too many people would see us." **"Looking very wild"; storm; Bryce Canyon; changing tire; Wrightwood:** MLP.

Summer on Montecito Drive; sleeping arrangements: ACM: On visits from Riverside, Arloie slept with Stella. **Sitting in kitchen with Kadish:** Kadish. **Stella packing preserves:** Kadish; MLP. **Kadish working with Siqueiros:** Kadish. **Siqueiros jailed:** Helm, pp. 91–92: He had been director general of all trade unions in the state of Jalisco, then general secretary of the national confederation of Mexican syndicates. **Siqueiros experimenting with media:** Helm, p. 93. **Subject of mural:** Kadish. **"Syndicate of painters":** Kadish; see Helm, p. 91: There had been a Syndicate of Technical Workers, Painters, Sculptors & Engravers in Mexico, which had fallen apart due to internal rivalries. In this instance, the Spanish word for "syndicate" was used to mean "union." **Kadish signing mural:** Kadish, q. in Potter, p. 49. Phil Guston and Sande assisted on it. **Kadish introducing Jackson and Siqueiros; trip to Chouinard; Jackson reacted coolly:** Kadish.

Bentonesque refinement: Kadish. **Doodle filling page:** OC&T 389, III, p. 6; 391, III, p. 7. **Orozco-like lights and darks:** OC&T 421, III, p. 33. **Swirling lines:** OC&T 402, III, p. 17. **Trip to Ensenada:** Darrow. **Olympiad:** July 30–Aug. 14, 1932; Weaver, pp. 118–19. **Clattering old Ford:** Darrow. **Sleeping in open:** Darrow, in "Strokes of Genius." **Boots on dashboard; playing mouth harp:** Friedman, p. 28. **"Until the coyotes":** Darrow, in Potter, p. 43. **Tobacco;**

Diamond matches: Friedman, p. 28. **Eggs and bacon; beans:** Darrow. **Never stopping long:** Darrow. **Pad, ink sticks:** Darrow, q. in Potter, p. 43. **"He did a desert":** Darrow, in "Strokes of Genius." **"Liberally":** Darrow, q. in FVOC, "The Genesis of JP," pp. 42–43. **Oil derricks:** JP's painting, *Camp with Oil Rig*, may have been inspired in part by JP's visit to Texas that summer; but it was more directly a copy of a drawing by Benton, *Oil Field, Texas Panhandle*, dated 1926–27, in Marling; 1928, by Benton himself; Marling, fig. 4-1, p. 69. **Plantation workers:** Friedman, p. 28. **Unloading bananas; "the negro":** JP to SMP, Sept. 1932. **Glimpsing Benton sketches:** JP to SMP, Sept. 1932: "... saw plenty of interesting country people and things. Arkansas and Tennessee I liked especially well." JP may have confused Alabama and Arkansas —Darrow is not sure—as he did Indianapolis and Minneapolis on a previous trip.

Ten dollars left: Darrow, q. in Potter, p. 43. **"He was a very likeable":** Darrow, q. in FVOC, "The Genesis of JP," pp. 42–43. **Cold reception from Elizabeth:** JP to SMP, Sept. 17: "I'm starting out badly again." Then JP recounts a dinner with Elizabeth but without Charles, clearly implying a skirmish, then reports positive news about the trip and the coming year. **"A happy Italian":** JP to SMP, Sept. 17, 1932. **Real-estate agency:** EFP. **"A stinking relic"; Charles and Elizabeth's summer:** Near Rockaway Beach; chronology prepared by CCP for EFP, Feb. 1975. **Jackson regaining room:** CCP. **Spaghetti and wine; too poor for electricity:** EFP.

New term: Registration card for JP. **Benton returning:** JP to SMP, Sept. 17, 1932. **Jackson monitor:** Registration card for JP. **"Pleased smile":** Horn. **Males and females alternating:** Horn. **Standard group of models:** Jules. **"Tiger" Ed Bates:** Horn calls him "Ed," Jules calls him "Tiger *Jack* Bates." **"A beautifully"; Bates's brother:** Jules. **Hank Clausen:** Cherry; Clausen. **Jackson posing models:** Darrow, q. in Potter, p. 41. **Holding same pose:** Darrow, in "Strokes of Genius." **"The Arts of Life":** *American*, pp. 67–69. **Publicity:** For articles, see Braun and Branchick, pp. 36–37 n. 124. **"I improved":** *Artist*, p. 249. **Paying off debts:** *Artist*, pp. 249–50. **Rita exploiting market:** Craven, "THB," p. 37: Rita was "one of the few women of my acquaintance who understands paintings" and was "clever at selling pictures."

"Babbitts, Rotarians": Allen, p. 201. **Relief from Depression:** Malcolm Cowley, "A Farewell to the Thirties," *The New Republic*, Nov. 8, 1939, q. in Congdon, p. 499. **American writers:** Allen, p. 207. *The Epic of America*: Allen, p. 206; Adams, *The Epic of America*. **"Much wider":** *American*, p. 156. **"We were psychologically":** *American*, p. 164. **"The most virile":** "U.S. Scene," p. 25. **Wood in Iowa:** "U.S. Scene," p. 26. **Benton and Wood unacquainted:** *American*, p. 152. **Curry in Connecticut:** "U.S. Scene," p. 25; Curry's most famous works were two turbulent paintings, *Tornado* and *Baptism in Kansas*.

"Neither Wood": *American*, p. 148. The movement probably derived its name from the fact that its three leaders all came from the same largely ignored region west of the Appalachians (*American*, p. 147); yet the three artists "made their discoveries and came to their conclusions separately," according to Benton; *American*, p. 151. "What distinguished us from so many other American painters of our time was not a difference in training or aesthetic background but a desire to redirect what we had found in the art of Europe toward an art specifically representative of America"; *American*, p. 151. This search led the Regionalists to the same time period of European art history: Benton to the Italian Renaissance, Wood to the northern Renaissance; see Baigell, *THB*, p. 91.

"American Wave" coined: Actually coined in 1931; Baigell, *THB*, p. 88. **"A standardized":** Allen, p. 201. **"His father took":** Burroughs, p. 46. **"I cannot honestly":** *Artist*, pp. 76–77. **Benton's search for his past:** *Artist*, p. 84: The travels began in the mountains of "Virginia, West Virginia, Kentucky, Tennessee, Georgia, the Carolinas, Missouri, and Arkansas." **"It is high time":** "Form and the Subject," p. 308. *American*, p. 155. **"Poised and quick":** Burroughs, p. 113. **"The most genuinely American":** Edward Alden Jewell, "Orozco and Benton Paint Murals for New York"; Jewell, "American Painting," p. 367. **Benton's defense:** *American*, pp. 150, 156. **"The arts of our pioneers":** *Artist*, pp. 26–27. **"We can afford":** THB, "Form and the Subject," p. 303. **"Still-lifes":** THB, "Form and the Subject," pp. 303, 307–08;

"When the creative life is barren or starved, the mind tends to dignify insignificant actions with high-sounding and impressive nomenclature." **Demagogic essence:** THB, "Art and Nationalism," pp. 233–34: "Those of us who have read much aesthetics realize finally that the verbal plays about the subject are undertaken only by philosophers who have nothing to say —also, that they are attended to only by those little professors and critics whose empty minds find their level in the subject." **"If it were left":** Interview with New York *World-Telegram*, excerpted in *Art Digest*, Apr. 15, 1941, p. 6, q. in Baigell, ed., p. 79. **"There is hope":** THB, "Art vs. the Mellon Gallery," p. 172. Benton would go on to condemn the "hothouses of international aesthetics" and even Picasso himself as a "high priest" of the "cult of art," "rehasher of dead procedures," and "the most luxuriant of the hothouse flowers"; THB, "Art and Nationalism," pp. 233–34. **"Incipient Fascism":** Baigell, "Beginnings," pp. 59–61. **McNeil helping found AAA:** Susan C. Larsen, "The Quest for an American Abstract Tradition, 1927–1944," in Lane and Larsen, eds., p. 36. **"Poor art":** Q. by McNeil. **"By a curious":** Kootz, p. 13. **"While most rejected":** Kainen, int. by Landau, Jan. 22, 1979, q. in Landau, p. 5. **Gellert or Lozowick:** THB, "Art and Nationalism," pp. 35–36. **"Couldn't paint anything":** *American*, p. 171. See THB, "Art and Nationalism," pp. 35–36. **"The Social Viewpoint":** Monroe, *Art in America*, p. 65. **Social realism an alternative:** Landau, p. 51.

Craven **Benton's "hatchet man":** Pavia. **Benton good copy:** Burroughs, p. 99. **"There are no artists":** Q. by McNeil. **"Narrow-minded":** McNeil. Father Coughlin, a Catholic priest and radio evangelist, used the pulpit of the airwaves to voice his conservative political views. Martin Dies, congressman from Texas, was chairman of the House Committee to Investigate Un-American Activities, formed May 26, 1938. **"Far be it":** *Artist*, p. 265. **"That son-of-a-bitch":** *Artist*, p. 258. **Jackson attacking Picasso:** Pavia, q. in Potter, p. 36. **"A very primitive":** Horn. **"Oh, yeah?":** Q. by Jules. **"Wop culture":** Pavia. **"Outlandish statements":** Jules. **"Yelling shambles"; "enraged Commie":** *American*, p. 171.

Drop in enrollment: THB Classbooks, 1930–31, 1931–32, Art Students League Archives. **"Menopause crowd"; enrollment near minimum; "faithful Bentonites":** Jules: Jules and Benton later had a falling-out over the portrayal of blacks in the latter's murals. Klonis: Some drop-off in enrollment from the beginning of the month to the end was common. **"New, naive":** Jules.

"We had many ardent": THB to FVOC, Mar. 31, 1964. **Jackson still posing:** There is a portrait of him "low in the corner" of the Whitney mural, *The Arts of the West*; Horn, "JP," p. 82. **"He followed"; "he did not have":** THB to FVOC, Mar. 31, 1964. **Preparing panels:** Jules. **Another commission:** Benton signed the contract in early December 1932. *American*, pp. 68–69: It was offered to him when his brushes were barely dry from the Whitney commission, completed in September. **Pollock hoping to work on murals:** Inferred from JP to LRP, Feb. 1932. **"Jack would not":** THB to FVOC, Mar. 31, 1964. **Pollock making models:** Darrow, q. in Potter, p. 37. Pavia: JP made these models in Laurent's class. **Indiana commission:** *American*, p. 69. **Pollock made member of League:** Registration card for JP.

Photograph of Roy: In possession of FLP (misdated in OC&T IV, p. 215). **Blue Eyes:** MLP. **"Too many cold":** Q. by FLP. Friesinger, a leading heart specialist at the Vanderbilt University Hospital, confirms the adverse effects of cold weather on endocarditis. **Roy returning to camp; symptoms returning:** MJP to CCP, Jan. 30, 1933. **Stella visiting friend:** MLP. **Contacting Stella; recognizing seriousness; "it seemed":** MLP. **French Hospital:** 531 College Street; MLP. **Roy deteriorating:** MLP. **"Los Angeles has sure been hard hit":** SMP to JP, CCP, and EFP, Jan. 1933. **Marie informing Frank:** MLP. **102 degree temperature; Roy taken to hospital:** 1200 North State Street; MLP. **Dr. Rynin:** MLP. **"Malignant Anaconditis":** MJP to CCP, Jan. 30, 1933. **Jackson writing Roy; "damned hard work":** JP to LRP, Feb. 3, 1933. **Tests:** The laboratory tests at Los Angeles County General Hospital were made by Dr. Rynin's wife, a laboratory technician; MLP. **"Malignant endocarditis":** Friesinger: "Malignant" means "infectious" or "bacterial" endocarditis. The word has spawned the false rumor that Roy died of cancer; MLP; Potter, p. 46. **"Leaking heart valve":** FLP. **Causes:** Friesinger. **"It is a case"; "it is fatal":** MJP to CCP, 1933.

Appropriateness in Roy's illness: MJP to CCP, FLP, JP, and EFP, Mar. 6, 1933: "His unbounded strength became his weakness and downfall—an overtaxed and developed heart." **"My father died":** FLP. **Inherent defect:** Called subacute, or chronic, endocarditis. **"I sometimes feel":** LRP to JP, Dec. 11, 1927. **"We have not told Dad":** MJP to CCP, 1933. **Summer arrangements:** MJP to CPP, n.d. **Roy planning to meet daughter-in-law:** SMP to CCP, EFP, FLP, and JP, Mar. 17, 1933: "He wanted to see Elizabeth so much." **"The beautiful golden"; "sunshine fresh"; "drenching nightsweats":** SMP to CCP, EFP, FLP, and JP, Mar. 17, 1933. **"Without a murmur"; "he enjoyed having":** MJP to CCP, FLP, JP, and EFP, Mar. 6, 1933. **Inaugural; "what Roosevelt's answer"; "the synthetic"; "President Hoover"; "the rules"; "The money changers":** Allen, p. 84. **Roy searching airwaves; choir broadcast:** SMP to CCP, EFP, FLP, and JP, Mar. 17, 1933. **"Come, come":** Lyrics by William Clayton, old English tune, *Hymns of the Church of Jesus Christ of Latter-Day Saints*, p. 13. **Roy complaining:** SMP to CCP, EFP, FLP, and JP, Mar. 17, 1933. **"Great pain":** MJP to CCP, FLP, JP, and EFP, Mar. 6, 1933. **"[Was] the only thing"; Jay getting doctor; Stella holding Roy:** SMP to CCP, EFP, FLP, and JP, Mar. 17, 1933. **"Her parents had made fun":** SMP, q. by MLP. **Stella not wanting Roy to live with disease; Roy in Stella's arms; eight-thirty; Jay just arriving; "Mother"; Roy wanting to say more:** SMP to CCP, EFP, FLP, and JP, Mar. 17, 1933. **Stella not crying:** MLP. **"He passed away":** SMP to CCP, EFP, FLP, and JP, Mar. 17, 1933. **"Dad passed":** MJP to CCP, FLP, JP, and EFP, Mar. 6, 1933.

16. OUT OF THE VOID

SOURCES

Books, articles, manuscript, records, and transcripts

Alloway and MacNaughton, *Adolph Gottlieb*; Brown, *American Painting from the Armory Show to the Depression*; Burroughs, *THB*; Falk, ed., *Who Was Who in American Art*; Friedman, *JP*; Gruen, *The Party's Over Now*; Hibbard, *Michelangelo*; Karp, *The Center*; McWilliams, *Southern California Country*; Melville, *Moby-Dick*; Moak, *The Robert Laurent Memorial Exhibition*; OC&T; JP; Potter, *To a Violent Grave*; Price, *Ryder*; Sloan, *Gist of Art*; Solomon, *JP*; Whitney Museum of American Art, *200 Years of American Sculpture*.

Ahron Ben-Shmuel, "Carving: A Sculptor's Creed," *American Magazine of Art*, 1938–39; Horace Brodsky, "Concerning Sculpture and Robert Laurent," *The Arts*, May 1921; Rosamund Frost, "Laurent: Frames to Figures, Brittany to Brooklyn," *Art News*, Apr. 1–14, 1941; Walter Gutman, "News and Gossip," *Creative Art*, Jan. 1933; Axel Horn, "JP: The Hollow and the Bump," *Carleton Miscellany*, Summer 1966; Sam Hunter, "JP," *Museum of Modern Art Bulletin*, 1956–57.

David Hale, "Ex-Fresnan, artist Manuel Tolegian, dead at age 72," *Fresno Bee*, Sept. 4, 1983.

FVOC, "The Genesis of JP: 1912 to 1943" (Ph.D. thesis), Baltimore: Johns Hopkins University, 1965.

Box Butte County, Nebr., marriage license and certificate, Recorder's Office, Jan. 13, 1903; Chronology prepared by CCP for EFP, Feb. 1975, AAA; registration card for JP, Art Students League Archives.

Tony Smith, int. by James T. Vallière, Aug. 1965, AAA; Manuel Tolegian, int. by Betty Hoag, Feb. 12, 1965, AAA.

Interviews

Margaret Louise Archbold; Paul Brach; Peter Busa; Joseph Delaney; Joseph DeMeio; Chaim Gross; Renee Gross; Isidore Grossman; William Homer; Ettabelle Horgan; Axel Horn; Mervin Jules; Reuben Kadish; Nathaniel Kaz; Stewart Klonis; Maria Piacenza Kron; George McNeil; E. Roger Miller; Alfonso Ossorio; Philip Pavia; CCP; EFP; FLP; MLP; SWP; Milton Resnick; Abraham Schlemowitz; David Slivka; Christopher Spingarn; Ralph Turnquist; Doris Wagner; Reginald Wilson.

NOTES

Law librarian: The librarian was Rita Benton's brother, Louis Piacenza. **"Tell Frank":** Louis Piacenza, q. by FLP.

Reading telegram: CCP. "Moment of silence": FLP. Telephoning and travel costly: CCP; FLP. Frank lamely suggests that they didn't phone "because we didn't have a phone." Writing letters: CCP. "I really can't": JP to SMP, SLM, and MJP, Mar. 8, 1933. Cemetery: 1712 South Glendale Avenue. Archbolds at funeral: Archbold. Stella unshaken: MLP. Frank, asked about Stella's reaction to JP's death: It was "the first tragedy in her life." Earthquake: At 5:55 P.M. Buildings collapsing: Weaver, p. 203. Manual Arts a victim: Turnquist. Extra eggs; lame walking: Weaver, p. 203. Hill feeling jolt: SMP to CCP, EFP, FLP, and JP, Mar. 17, 1933. CCP: No one in the family visited Roy's crypt again. FLP: "He's in a crypt, he's not in the ground—not that he should be. And I'm ashamed to say I never visited it. Not that I could help at all." But the boys didn't have to wait until their father died to go home; they could have left as soon as they knew he had a fatal disease, when the banks were still open and loans could still be arranged.
No money for travel: FLP to MLP, Apr. 12, 1933. Frank visiting Marie: FLP. Charles going to Chicago: CCP. "I can only wish": JP to SMP, Mar. 25, 1933. Jackson refusing ride; "[Mother] still had": FLP. "I'm going to school": JP to LRP, Feb. 1932. Painting "jobs"; "struggle with the elements": JP to LRP, Feb. 3, 1933. "Bad habits": Pavia; Pavia, q. in Gruen, p. 264: "The big point about Jackson and the Art Students League was that he wanted to be a teacher there. But they wouldn't let him because of his bad habits." Kaz: "He was an intense guy, and he wanted to be Benton's number one, right-hand man. But he just didn't have the discipline." Klonis: JP didn't receive the teaching position because "his work was so unlike anything else done there that he was told he would not be able to attract students." But at this time JP's work was still faithfully Bentonesque. Klonis may be referring to a later application. "Just a bum": JP to CCP, summer 1932.
Sloan's class: JP enrolled January 3; registration card. Sloan anecdotal: Brown, p. 18. Sloan teaching Cubism: Alloway and MacNaughton, p. 14; see Sloan, Gist of Art. Preoccupation with methodology: Alloway and MacNaughton, p. 13. Sloan's reaction to modern art so diminished the quality of his own work that Brown (p. 63) calls it "one of the tragedies of American art. . . . Sloan, set loose in a field where he was neither emotionally nor intellectually acclimated, was destroyed as an artistic personality." "Benton tolerated": Manuel Tolegian, q. by Araks. Sloan's clothing: Manuel Tolegian, q. in Potter, p. 44.
"Mason": Marriage license and certificate, Box Butte County, Nebr., Recorder's Office, Jan. 13, 1903. Fascination with earth-moving: Potter, p. 17. "Do what is best": LRP to JP, Dec. 11, 1927. "A method": JP to CCP, summer 1932. "That's the new"; "sculptoring I think": JP to LRP, Feb. 1932: JP also tried to appeal to his father on the issue of politics: "Suppose you still get the Nation there. I thought the article by Ernest was very good the best of the bunch—'If I were Constitutional Dictator' I think—the one by Chase was good I think—It's looking as tho we're going to have to be enlisting for the capitalist government—the Manchurian business is begging to be envolved."
Martin's modeling class: JP to CCP and FLP, Oct. 22, 1929. "Found a bit": JP to CCP, Jan. 31, 1930. Block of stone: Aram Tolegian. "He originally": Int. by Vallière, Aug. 1965: "I can remember very clearly his telling me that he came to New York to learn to sculpt like Michelangelo." Kadish becoming a sculptor: Kadish: About 1950. Book on Michelangelo: Stark, int. by FVOC, Mar. 30, 1964, q. in FVOC, "The Genesis of JP," p. 173 n. 7: JP said he sent Stark a book on photography in return but Stark never got it. Joining class at Greenwich House: JP may have gone to a formal class at the Greenwich House annex on Jones Street or just to Ben-Shmuel's studio on Jane Street and served as his studio boy. "I have joined": JP to LRP, Feb. 3, 1933. Description of Ben-Shmuel: Chaim Gross. Archie Levitt: Brach. Carving wooden forms: Ben-Shmuel, "Carving," p. 502. "Monumental carver": Ben-Shmuel, "Carving," p. 504. Assisting Zorach: Chaim Gross. One work, Mother and Child, was carved 1927-30 from Spanish Florida Rosa marble. "Angry": Chaim Gross; Grossman; Kaz. "Not a teacher": Resnick: "Ben-Shmuel would dismiss the whole idea that he was a teacher. To him, teaching was ridiculous."
Ben-Shmuel opinionated: Schlemowitz. Exhibitionistic: Pavia. Ben-Shmuel not drinker: Grossman. "Gentle

eccentric": Kaz. "Lots of personality": Pavia. "Outlandish": Kaz. "Weird"; "nuts"; "crazy": Grossman. Brutish to women: Resnick. Humiliating to women; "to him they were"; Impotence: Grossman: "Morris Levine told me Ben-Shmuel was impotent. And he was probably the best friend [Ben-Shmuel] had." Latent homosexuality: Grossman: "That was my feeling about him later on, when I got to know a little more about life. That was his problem—he was a latent homosexual."
Ben-Shmuel working alfresco; Browne's studio; Katz an apprentice: Kaz. Ben-Shmuel undisciplined: Renee Gross. Ben-Shmuel haphazard: Grossman. Ben-Shmuel articulate: Kadish. "It he liked you": Schlemowitz. From marble to rubbish: Ben-Shmuel, "Carving," p. 503. "Sixth sense": Ben-Shmuel, "Carving," p. 502. Fired clay: Mexican Madonna (1927), carved in fired clay to resemble the sculptures of Gauguin. Bronze: Saint Sebastian (1932), both attenuated and vertical in the manner of the German sculptor Wilhelm Lehmbruck. Near-abstraction: Torso of a Young Boy (1929), in black granite, with the simplicity of a classical Cambodian temple carving. Monumentalism: Portrait of a Young Woman (1929), in Scotch granite.
Ben-Shmuel proud: Resnick. Hammer and chisel to compressed air: Brodsky, p. 13. Carving vs. sculpting: Grossman. Michelangelo: Although carving was "the technique Michelangelo used and advocated all his life" (Hibbard, p. 15), he did occasionally make wax models for some works, including the David (Hibbard, p. 34), and used assistants for at least some of the rough carving; Hibbard, pp. 97, 101, 109-110, 112, 172. Late Greeks first carvers: The Egyptians apparently had used enlarging and transferring devices, but the purposes were structural and architectural, not plastic.
Zorach: One of the new breed was William Zorach, a Lithuanian immigrant to Cleveland, who returned briefly to Europe to study art in Paris. He exhibited in both the 1911 Salon d'Automne in Paris and the 1913 Armory Show in New York. It wasn't until 1917 that he made his first sculpture as an adult, a relief carved from wood, and by 1922 he was committed both to sculpture and to direct carving. Zorach preferred archetypal subjects—"the relationships between man and woman, woman and child and child and animal"—and conferred on them a primitive monumentality; Whitney Museum of American Art, p. 323.
Flannagan: The greatest sculptor of the new movement, John Flannagan, was attracted to direct carving, not for reasons of monumentality, but of intimate mysticism. In a tragic life marked by alcoholism, nervous breakdowns, a severe automobile accident, and suicide, he, too, began sculpting in 1922, turning, five years later, from wood to stone. He preferred working natural field stones which he collected on long trips. He usually derived his subjects—an elephant, a duck, a bird hatching from an egg—from the original shape of the stone, creating images so true that they seem to have emerged from the material rather than from his imagination. An admirer of Eastern art, especially that of India, he called his works "occult fossils." Like JP, he was especially interested in images of transformation, epitomized by the later work, Triumph of the Egg, catching the chick at the moment of its emergence from the shell; Whitney Museum of American Art, pp. 271-72. "A sea of marble": Brodsky, "Concerning Sculpture and Robert Laurent," pp. 13-14.
Pollock quitting Sloan for Laurent: Feb. 3, 1933; registration card. "A native": Paraphrased from Frost, "Laurent," p. 10. Laurent was born in France on June 29, 1890, to a fisherman's daughter and a weaver's son on the same French coast to which Gauguin was drawn about the same time. Under the sponsorship of Hamilton Easter Field, a wealthy American painter, Laurent came to America for nearly three years, then continued his education in Paris where he was particularly impressed by the rounded bronze women of Aristide Maillol. In 1907, he joined Field on a grand tour of Europe and three years later moved to the United States to begin his career as a sculptor; Moak, pp. 13, 15, 17.
"Quite delicious": Q. in Moak, p. 17. Pavia: Laurent introduced his students to Cubism. Laurent preferring carving: Laurent (q. in Moak, p. 18) said he "always preferred cutting directly in materials" and that he usually started "cutting without a preconceived idea" because this kept him "more alert and open to surprises." Works cast from plaster: Laurent wrote in the early 1930s (q. in Moak, p. 20): "Working in plaster is a combination of modelling and direct cutting."

Laurent's inheritance: Laurent was the childless Field's only heir; Moak, p. 17.

Laurent's career was not completely free of controversy. Only months before JP enrolled in his class, his *Goose Girl*, based on the myth of Leda and the Swan, was exhibited at Radio City Music Hall. The statue of a nude girl with an amorous goose instantly ignited a fury of Puritan outrage; Karp, p. 67. "Just *what* is the Goose Girl doing?" reporters demanded; q. in Frost, "Laurent," p. 11. Despite rumors that the brouhaha had been stirred up by the Music Hall's director as an opening-night publicity stunt (Frost, "Laurent," pp. 11, 37), an "art expert," DeWolf Hopper, was called in to quell the rising public outcry. Hopper's response (q. in Gutman, p. 77) was inconclusive—"Well, I've had six wives, but none of them looked like that"—but the statue was removed nevertheless, causing some outrage at the nearby League. Despite its removal, Laurent was and continued to be a favorite among the Rockefellers, especially Mrs. John D., Jr., Mrs. Nelson, and Abby Rockefeller Milton; Frost, "Laurent," p. 37.

Laurent's basement studio; Pavia's father: Pavia: "My father thought sculptors were rich people, because he worked for sculptors and they made those lousy monuments you see all over Italy." "Well, you might": Frost, "Laurent," p. 37. **Laurent's parties; trips to speakeasy:** Pavia: "I had many things": JP to SMP, SLM, and MJP, Mar. 8, 1933. "I always feel"; "cutting in stone"; "it holds my interest": JP to SMP, SLM, and MJP, Mar. 25, 1933. **Pollock doing janitorial work:** Horn, q. in Potter, p. 45. **"Persistently searching":** Ben-Shmuel, "Carving," p. 508. **Pollock abandoning stones:** Horn. **Stone head:** OC&T 1042, IV, p. 121.

Pollock going to Ben-Shmuel's summer place: FLP to MLP, Apr. 12, 1933; Pavia. Thirty miles northeast of Philadelphia. **Stone yard:** Pavia. **Various granites:** Ben-Shmuel, "Carving," pp. 502, 505, 508. **Davis:** Kaz; photo in possession of AAA. **Davis a student of Ben-Shmuel; wealthy; cosmopolitan:** Kaz. **Davis drinking with Pollock:** Horgan. **Jackson not traveling with Frank:** FLP. **Or with Tolegian:** Tolegian, int. by Hoag, Feb. 12, 1965. **"[The apprenticeship]":** FLP to MLP, Apr. 12, 1933. **Jackson moving:** Chronology prepared by CCP for EFP, Feb. 1975. **East Eighth Street:** EFP.

Ben-Shmuel's violence: Resnick. **The Devil's Hole; Davis's house and studio:** Horgan: Built by her father-in-law. Horgan, our primary source for JP's association with Davis, lost track of JP until 1949, when she saw her second husband reading *Life* magazine: "I just happened to walk by him and look over his shoulder and see a picture of Jack. 'I know him,' I said. 'That's Jack Pollock.' I said I'd known him when I was just a young kid." Horgan's information is confirmed by DeMeio, her employer many years ago, and by Wagner, whose family lived in one of three other houses on the same isolated road as Davis's cabin, and who remembers JP as a "blond Polish boy." **Dark:** DeMeio. **Squirrels, deer, and pheasant:** Miller. **Wild turkey; "Going into that hollow":** DeMeio. **"Houseboy":** Q. by Horgan. **Horgan doing housecleaning:** DeMeio; Horgan. **Having models come in; sketching and modeling:** Horgan; Wagner. **Going to Storm's house; lamb stew; square dances; Pollock going into New York with Davis:** Horgan. **Continuing to see Davis:** Horgan. **Never speaking of Davis:** There is no mention of JP's association with Davis in the official record, nor is there any memory of it among his family and close friends. **Pollock renting room:** Busa. **Pollock failing to register:** Registration card. **Pollock visiting the League:** Busa. **Seen in Bridgman's class:** Delaney; Kaz. The school records don't show him officially enrolled in the class; registration card. But the skull that appeared in JP's room at this time (Busa) and Bridgman's interest in skeletal analysis indicate that this could be the time he studied with Bridgman. **Pollock seen arguing with Gorky:** Pavia. **No longer bragging about Charles:** Horn.

Pollock still eager for Rita; hinting about an affair: Busa. **Jackson's silence:** Kron. **Alcohol legal:** The Twenty-first Amendment was ratified on February 2, 1933. **"A dog in spring":** Busa. **"Roaring like a Satyr":** Horn, "JP," p. 83. **"Wild Indian":** Resnick. **"A maniac":** EFP. **"Mr. Hyde":** Horn, "JP," p. 83. **Fight in Harlem:** Busa: **"If Americans":** Q. by Busa.

Springarns: Springarn: J. E. Springarn was also a founder of the NAACP. **Formal affair:** Kron. The Springarns lived at 9 West Seventy-third Street. **Amy Springarn:** Born in 1883,

making her fifty at the time. **Amy a student of Benton:** Springarn. **Jackson and friends playing at Springarn party; "sophisticated"; "the maids"; Pollock heading for bar; Pollock and Tolegian drifting apart:** Kron. **Tolegian's one-man show:** Hale, "Ex-Fresnan." **"I don't give":** Q. by Delaney. **Tolegian denying knife incident:** Q. in Potter, p. 41. **Knife incident:** Burroughs, p. 119; Darrow, q. in Friedman, p. 26.

Busa's background: Busa. **Fifty-eighth Street rooms; Busa telling Jackson about time on rails:** Busa. Although they were tireless in their exchange of sexual stories, the Pollock brothers surrounded the subject of homosexuality with a cordon of silence. JP knew nothing of Charles's encounter soon after arriving in Los Angeles in 1922 with a fellow artist who, misconstruing Charles's long hair and Edwardian clothing, promptly propositioned him. Nor did Frank speak of an incident during his "dandy days" in New York: "I was standing on Fifth Avenue, out by myself with a goddamned cane, and some guy came up to me and said, 'Where should we go?' Jesus Christ! I said, 'You hit on the wrong guy.' I hightailed it out of there and never carried a cane again." Both came away from their experiences disgusted, distrustful, and portentously silent. SWP: "Charles is the most liberal man in the world. The only thing he won't tolerate is homosexuality. Sande, too."

Coaxing Jackson home "upright": Jules. **"Run me over":** Resnick. **Punching out store windows:** Karl Fortress, q. in Potter, p. 54. **"Comatose" silence:** Wilson. **Ending in the gutter:** Kaz. **Night boat:** Kaz; Pavia. Pavia says it was the Albany Night Boat. **Unscrewing light bulbs:** Pavia. **Threatening to jump overboard:** Kaz.

Ten years' absence from sculpture: Kadish. **Skull "borrowed" from Bridgman:** Busa: JP was kicked out of the rooming house on Fifty-eighth Street when the landlady discovered the skull sitting on his bed and thought it was a bad omen. (The skull was still in JP's studio at the time of his death.) **Woman with five figures:** OC&T 10, I, p. 9. **Woman with crowd:** OC&T 59, I, p. 46. **Style not Benton's:** CCP: In 1933, JP was doing small experimental works in a style unlike Benton's; CCP to FVOC, Dec. 17, 1963, q. in FVOC, "The Genesis of JP," p. 50. **Ryder's show:** Solomon, p. 56, citing Busa. **Pollock studying Ryder monograph:** Price, *Ryder*. *Sentimental Journey* **and** *Going West:* Solomon, pp. 56–57. **Pollock and** *Death Rides the Wind:* OC&T 5 and 6, I, p. 5; see FVOC, "The Genesis of JP," p. 163. **Forgery:** Ryder scholar (name withheld by request). *Going West:* OC&T 16, I, p. 16; see FVOC, "The Genesis of JP," p. 166. *The Wagon:* OC&T 2, I, p. 3; see FVOC, "The Genesis of JP," pp. 165–66. **Painting of farm family:** Unpublished painting in possession of Robert Miller. **"'All visible objects'":** Melville, p. 164. **Poker games and three-card monte:** Busa. **Pollock's doodles:** OC&T 391, III, p. 7. **Self-portrait:** OC&T 9, I, p. 8. **Ryderesque gloom:** FVOC, "The Genesis of JP," pp. 167–68: This self-portrait may have been patterned after Ryder's own early mature self-portrait, which JP could have seen. Both are small, and just as the work by JP is isolated on a white ground with an edge of raw canvas showing, the work by Ryder is thinly painted at the bottom. The work by Ryder was not in the 1932 catalogue by Price (*Ryder*) but was exhibited at the Kleeman Galleries in New York in October and early November 1935 and published in *Art Digest* on November 15, 1935, p. 10. The Kleeman Galleries were at 38 East Fifty-seventh Street, the Ferargil Galleries at 63 East Fifty-seventh Street; since JP was associated with the Ferargil Galleries through Rita Benton, it is almost certain that he would have seen the Ryder exhibition. Hunter, "JP," p. 6: JP's works of this period "showed many of the mannerisms and captured something of the emotional atmosphere of Ryder's dream landscapes."

17. THE DARING YOUNG MAN ON THE FLYING TRAPEZE

SOURCES

Books, articles, manuscript, document, and transcript

Allen, *Since Yesterday*; THB, *An Artist in America* (*Artist*); Bernstein, *The Lean Years*; Brittain, *Thrice a Stranger*; Burroughs, *THB*; Congdon, *The Thirties*; Ellis, *The Epic of New York City*; Friedman, *JP*; Hamilton, *In America Today*; Josephson, *Infidel in the Temple*; Kazin, *Starting Out in the Thirties*; Marling, *Tom Benton and His Drawings*; Mayhew, ed., *Martha's Vineyard*; McElvaine, *The Great Depression*; McKinzie, *The New Deal for Artists*; Mumford, *The Early Years*; *New York Panorama*; OC&T, *JP*; Potter, *To a Violent Grave*; Saroyan, *The Daring Young Man on the Flying Trapeze*; Solomon, *JP*; Still, *Mirror for Gotham*; *The WPA Guide to New Orleans*.

"No One Has Starved," *Fortune*, Sept. 1932; William Rubin, "JP and the Modern Tradition, Part I: 1. The Myths and the Paintings," *Artforum*, Feb. 1967; Mary Heaton Vorse, "A School for Bums," *The New Republic*, April 29, 1931.

FVOC, "The Genesis of JP: 1912 to 1943" (Ph.D. thesis), Baltimore: Johns Hopkins University, 1965.

Chronology prepared by CCP for EFP, Feb. 1975, AAA.

SLM, int. by Kathleen Shorthall, Nov. 9, 1959, for *Life*, Time/Life Archives.

Interviews

Pamela Arceneaux; T. P. Benton; James Brooks; Polly Burroughs; Peter Busa; Robert Cooter; Whitney Darrow, Jr.; Karen Del Pilar; Axel Horn; Reuben Kadish; Gerome Kamrowski; Maria Piacenza Kron; ACM; Charles Mattox; Sophia Mumford; Eleanor Piacenza; CCP; EFP; MJP; MLP; Rachel Scott; Jim Sleeper; Araks Tolegian; Steve Wheeler; Reginald Wilson.

NOTES

Mitchell appearing: CCP. **Darrow appearing; Jackson being held:** Darrow. The jail at the corner of Tenth Street and Sixth Avenue was torn down in 1974. **Wrecking nightclub:** EFP. **"Something minor":** CCP. **Howe:** CCP; EFP; Darrow. He was a colleague of Elizabeth's on the New York *World*. Probably because of his patrician background and Princeton deportment, Darrow was also once asked to go to court in JP's behalf; Potter, p. 48. **Howe; "severe admonishment":** EFP.

"I had hoped": FLP to CCP, Oct. 10, 1933. **Charles's vigil; "ask to see"; Greenwich House murals:** CCP: He doesn't know how the idea originated. **Charles's entry:** Political subject matter was apparently typical of Charles's paintings of the time. In November 1934, he exhibited a painting at the John Reed Club called *A Chicken in Every Pot*, described by the *New York Times* as showing "three outcasts preparing their scanty meal in the open"; Nov. 10, 1934; FVOC, "The Genesis of JP," p. 145. **Jackson's entry:** OC&T 8, I, pp. 6–7; O'Connor ("The Genesis of JP," p. 142) identifies the instruments as a banjo, a clarinet, an accordian, and two harmonicas, although the painting is difficult to decipher; according to O'Connor ("The Genesis of JP," pp. 143–44), JP's choice of mural subjects was appropriate because the Greenwich House was noted for its school of music for more than six decades. But JP had been in Ben-Shmuel's Greenwich House workshop only briefly, and it is unlikely that he, or Charles, was familiar with Greenwich House history. **Rita hearing about drinking:** Kron. **Duration of Vineyard stay:** CCP; Busa. **"Without alcohol":** THB to FVOC, Mar. 31, 1964. **Blueberries:** CCP. **Learning to sail from T.P.:** Araks Tolegian, recalling Manuel. **Helping with chores:** *Artist*, p. 334. **"Strike out":** Burroughs, p. 116. **Beach picnics:** Burroughs, p. 83. **Sunbathing:** Burroughs, p. 116: Nude swimming was "one activity . . . which the Island residents would never share." **Sketching or painting:** OC&T 24–30, I, pp. 21–30; Busa: He brought back "a lot of interesting landscapes from Martha's Vineyard." **Gay Head lighthouse:** Mayhew, ed., frontis. **Squid-spaghetti; vermicelli with clams:** Burroughs, p. 82. **Lobster; fresh fish:** CCP. **"Jack's Shack":** Burroughs, p. 116. Although Benton makes a great deal of fixing up the chicken coop for JP (Burroughs, p. 116; Friedman, p. 26; *Artist*, p. 334), it had been made livable by 1928 or 1929 when Charles visited; CCP. The shack may have been further improved during one of JP's early visits. **No radio, cards, or phonograph:** CCP. **Regular 4:00 A.M.:** Burroughs, p. 116.

"He was mostly": Q. in Friedman, p. 25. **Cross-country trip:** OC&T (IV, p. 218) and Friedman (p. 33) say 8,000 miles. CCP to Rubin (q. in "JP and the Modern Tradition," p. 22) also gives the 8,000-mile figure. Chronology prepared by CCP for EFP, 1975, gives the figure as 6,000 miles, but given the route, 8,000 appears to be accurate. **Preparations for trip:**

CCP. **Price and production of coal:** Congdon, p. 49. **Mining town conditions:** "No One Has Starved," p. 27. **"Eating days":** Congdon, p. 49.

Harlan County battle; Harlan County draws intelligentsia: Bernstein, *The Lean Years*, excerpted in Congdon, pp. 51–52. **Intellectual pilgrimage:** The results of the Dreiser-chaired National Committee for the Defense of Political Prisoners were published in a book, *Harlan Miners Speak*; Wilson and Cowley came separately as part of a delegation of New York writers; later, a committee of prominent attorneys came under the sponsorship of the ACLU. Bernstein, *The Lean Years*, excerpted in Congdon, p. 53: "It seemed that a writer or an intellectual who failed to reach Harlan in 1931–32 was hardly worth his salt." **Union movement failing:** Bernstein, excerpted in Congdon, p. 54.

"Home of the blues": Marling, p. 50. **Street scenes:** Marling, p. 55, fig. 2–5. **Legalized prostitution:** Storyville enjoyed a legal existence from 1897 to 1917; *The WPA Guide to New Orleans*, p. 216. **"Palaces"; "cribs":** *The WPA Guide to New Orleans*, p. 216. **Legend lingers:** Mae West's movie, *Belle of the Nineties*, was originally to have been called *Belle of New Orleans*; *The WPA Guide to New Orleans*, p. 217. **Procuresses:** *The WPA Guide to New Orleans*, p. 219. **French Quarter revives:** Arceneaux. **"Everything goes":** Q. in *The WPA Guide to New Orleans*, p. 217. **Elizabeth on Jackson's sex life:** EFP: "I never did see him with a woman. No. Never. Never."

"The new Sahara": Allen, p. 160. **Dust Bowl:** Allen, pp. 157–58. **"Black blizzard":** Allen, p. 158. **Farmhouses deserted:** Allen, pp. 160–61: A survey in 1936 of a seven-county area in southeastern Colorado showed 2,878 houses still occupied, 2,811 abandoned. **"Deeper than":** R. D. Lusk, "The Life and Death of 470 Acres," *The Saturday Evening Post*, Aug. 13, 1938, q. in Congdon, p. 386. **Road clogged; "square-shouldered":** Allen, p. 160. **"It was the year":** Chronology prepared by CCP for EFP, Feb. 1975. **Arrival in Los Angeles:** SMP to CCP and JP, Aug. 30, 1934: She thanks them for stopping on their way back east at Tingley to visit her relatives. Allowing for the visit to Martha's Vineyard at the beginning of the summer, for at least a few weeks in Los Angeles, and for news of the boys' visit to get back to Stella from Tingley, they probably left New York in late June or early July, spent about two weeks on the road, arrived in Los Angeles around the third week of July and left in mid-August. **Power plant work:** MJP to CCP, Apr. 23, 1934. **Frank and Sande try CWA:** SMP to JP, CCP, and EFP, Jan. **Financial retrenchment; "we are eating":** MJP to CCP, Apr. 23, 1934.

Sande continuing to work: Sande's job ended in late 1932, after having become part-time in the spring of that year. **Sande's clothing:** In the summer of 1931 (dated internally in OC&T IV, p. 211), JP wrote Charles: "Mart [Jay] is wearing a suit he bought in Chico—and Sande wears them out as fast as he gets them." **Commuting to Riverside:** ACM; MLP. **"Jams"; "most of [them]":** Jay accused one of Sande's friends of having "sticky fingers." The friend spent a weekend at the Pollock home, and "several articles disappeared when they left," Jay wrote Frank. "My mershum cigarette holder was seen in his apartment and I went over after it. Didn't get it, but gave him a good scare"; MJP to FLP, n.d. **Sande's resorting to self-abuse:** Del Pilar: "My father was suicidal. I know that, although I don't know why. My father was also alcoholic, although my mother would like to say he wasn't.'" **"He missed":** MLP. **Ascot Speedway:** Kadish. **Sande not drawing:** MJP to CCP: "[Sande] has done very little drawing, if any." **Vicarious artist:** ACM. **Urged by Kadish to join class:** Kadish; JP to SMP, n.d. (dated Oct. 1, 1932, by FVOC in OC&T IV, p. 214). **Sande assisting Siqueiros:** Kadish; Lehman. On their last project together, a mural for the Workers Cultural Center in the spring of 1934, Sande himself painted one of the central figures, an old woman; Kadish; Lehman.

"While your out": JP to SMP, SLM, and MJP, Mar. 25, 1933. **Sande living through others:** Del Pilar, a psychiatric nurse. **"We sure missed":** SMP to CCP and JP, Aug. 30, 1934. **October arrival:** FVOC, "The Genesis of JP," p. 52. **"With 34 cents":** SLM, int. by Shorthall, Nov. 9, 1959. Potter (p. 50) writes that Sande drove back with JP in the fall of 1934, but Sande told Shorthall that he arrived in New York and "looked up Jack." Stella wrote Charles and JP (Aug. 30, 1934) telling them how Sande had "cried" when they left Los Angeles.

"The proud unsinkable": Mumford, p. 469. "Stringency": Brittain, p. 276. Sixteen million jobless: Kazin, p. 4. Strikes: McElvaine, p. 225. Class warfare: The cities were Minneapolis and San Francisco; McElvaine, pp. 224–29. "Among New York": Sleeper: Edmund Wilson's book, *The American Jitters,* captured the sense of disintegration. "Wobblies": Kazin, p. 33. Paper bags: Kazin, introduction to *New York Panorama,* p. xiv. Sidewalks blocked: Hamilton, p. 19. Coffee wagon: Hamilton, p. 22. Butts and newspapers; odd jobs: Josephson, p. 79. Thousands coming to city: Josephson, p. 80. Makeshift dwellings: Ellis, p. 532. Emergency shelter: Kazin, introduction to *New York Panorama,* p. xiv. "Less sweet": Josephson, p. 79. "Serried rows": Hamilton, p. 19. "'Nowadays'": Josephson, p. 75. Location of shanties: Hamilton, p. 22. "Depression shanties": CCP. Palpable despair: Hamilton, p. 24. People dying: Josephson, p. 75. "Going on Relief"; "picketing": Ellis, p. 552. "Do you want": Ellis, pp. 533–34: "A total of 1,595 New Yorkers killed themselves in 1932—the highest number since 1900."

One of four jobless: Ellis, p. 533. Top floor apartment: Kron says the building was between eight and thirteen stories high, but it must have been shorter; she would throw rocks at the windows to announce her arrival. Commercial building: Kron. The first floor apparently was used to store lumber; Friedman, p. 54. Alone among rubble: Kron. Depression shanties: Chronology prepared by CCP for EFP, Feb. 1975. Barn-like: Wilson. Other visitors: Including CCP, Busa, Tolegian, and Wilson. Bringing cookware; "pornographic murals": Kron. Bentons, Pratt, and Marot: Mumford; Scott. "Swabbing it down"; five dollars a week: SLM, int. by Shorthall, Nov. 9, 1959. Pay at Klein's: $10.80; Ellis, p. 532.

"Jack was a very": Rita Benton to FVOC, Mar. 1, 1965, q. in FVOC, "The Genesis of JP," p. 54. Milk deliveries: Piacenza; Araks Tolegian, recalling Manuel. Bentons hard up: THB to FVOC, Mar. 31, 1964: "He never tried to borrow money. But, of course, he knew we didn't have any to spare in those days." Market for large works: Benton did receive a mural commission in 1934 from the Treasury Department for a mural in the new Federal Post Office, but his relationship with the department deteriorated so badly that he never completed the mural; *Artist,* p. 383. Only ceramics selling: CCP to FVOC, May 1, 1964, q. in FVOC, "The Genesis of JP," p. 54.

Rita prompting Jackson: Rita to FVOC, Mar. 1, 1965 (q. in FVOC, "The Genesis of JP," p. 55): "Jack and I went to a place where these ceramics were bought ready to be painted and fired. We bought the china." Rita says Tom suggested the idea, but she clearly prompted Tom to suggest it. Ceramics workshop: Busa. Tutoring from Benton; "quickly successful": *Artist,* p. 334. Rita selling Jackson's work; "we opened": Rita Benton to FVOC, Mar. 1, 1965, q. in FVOC, "The Genesis of JP," p. 55. Gifts to Rita: THB to FVOC, Mar. 31, 1964; OC&T 916–21, IV, pp. 3–6. Rita insisting on payments: Rita Benton to FVOC, Mar. 1, 1965; Rita continued to display the gifts proudly on her mantel in the Vineyard until JP's death and in the house in Kansas City thereafter; Edith Symonds, q. in Potter, p. 48.

Government aid: McKinzie, p. 76. "A general increase"; "so overcrowded"; starvation: "No One Has Starved," p. 22: In New York City, twenty people died of starvation in 1932; another twenty-five died of malnutrition. "The form": Saroyan, p. 17. "The trivial": Saroyan, p. 19. "The tiny": Saroyan, p. 18. "Starvation": Kazin, p. 14. Relief payments: "No One Has Starved," p. 22: The amounts varied on what William Hodson, executive director of the New York Welfare Council, called "a disaster basis," from a box of groceries to sixty dollars a month per family. Coffee and bread: Araks Tolegian, recalling Manuel. Twenty-five-cent meal: Kazin, introduction to *New York Panorama,* p. xiv. The 81,000 in breadline: Vorse, p. 293. Tin bowl: Josephson, p. 78. Fifth Avenue: Solomon, p. 67. "I started": Q. by T. P. Benton. Police calling Rita: Solomon, pp. 67–68. "Trying to wring": SLM to Kadish, n.d.

"Sometimes people stole": Wheeler. Sending money to Frank: SMP to CCP and JP, n.d. Kadish: "I don't think they were stealing food from the streets." Sande's cowboy outfit: Kamrowski. "Tighter than": Q. by Brooks. "The real problem": Q. by Araks Tolegian. Palm Garden benefit; Sande on Jackson's shoulders; "looked for the tallest": Busa. Sande not stopping Jackson: FLP; Kadish.

18. A GREAT HOPE FOR AMERICAN PAINTING

SOURCES

Books, articles, manuscripts, document, and transcripts

Ashton, *The New York School;* THB, *An Artist in America (Artist);* Biddle, *An American Artist's Story;* Burroughs, *THB;* Craven, *THB;* Diamonstein, *The Art World;* Ellis, *The Epic of New York City;* Friedman, *JP;* Gaugh, *Willem de Kooning;* Josephson, *Infidel in the Temple;* Keppel and Duffus, *The Arts in American Life;* McElvaine, *The Great Depression;* McKinzie, *The New Deal for Artists;* FVOC, ed., *The New Deal Art Projects;* OC&T, *JP;* Potter, *To a Violent Grave;* Purcell, *Government and Art;* Schlesinger, Jr., *The Coming of the New Deal.*

"For Bread Alone," *Time,* May 13, 1966; Bruce Glaser, "JP: An Interview with LK," *Arts,* Apr. 1967; "Look Down That Road," *Art Digest,* May 1, 1935; Gerald M. Monroe, "The '30s: Art, Ideology and the WPA," *Art in America,* Nov.–Dec. 1975; FVOC, "The Genesis of JP: 1912–1943," *Artforum,* May 1967; "South Carolina Harvest," *Architectural Record,* Jan. 1937.

"Benton to Quit Hectic City for Missouri Calm," New York *Herald Tribune,* Apr. 2, 1935; "Job Goodman, 58, Abstract Painter," Obituary, *NYT,* Dec. 24, 1955; "Mrs. T. H. Benton Collection One of Several in Which High Standard is Reached," *NYT,* Dec. 1, 1934.

FVOC, "The Genesis of JP: 1912 to 1943" (Ph.D. thesis), Baltimore: Johns Hopkins University, 1965; May Natalie Tabak, "A Collage" (unpub. ms., n.d.).

Chronology prepared by CCP for EFP, Feb. 1975, AAA.

LK, int. by Barbara Rose, June 1966, AAA; Charles Mattox, int. by Dorothy Dehner, LK, Jason McCoy, and Robert Miller, Mar. 1, 1972, AAA; SLM, int. by Kathleen Shorthall for *Life,* 1959, Time/Life Archives; Manuel Tolegian, int. by Betty Hoag, Feb. 12, 1965, AAA.

Interviews

James Brooks; Peter Busa; Herman Cherry; Dorothy Dehner; Harry Holtzman; Harry Jackson; Reuben Kadish; Gerome Kamrowski; Nathaniel Kaz; Stewart Klonis; LK; Maria Piacenza Kron; Ibram Lassaw; Harold Lehman; John Little; Conrad Marca-Relli; Mercedes Matter; Charles Mattox; ACM; George McNeil; Sophia Mumford; Philip Pavia; CCP; EFP; SWP; Beatrice Ribak; May Tabak Rosenberg; Rachel Scott; Wally Strautin; Theodore Wahl; Roger Wilcox.

NOTES

"They're hiring": Tabak, "Art Project," in "Collage," p. 194. "They were shouting": Tabak, "Art Project," in "Collage," pp. 194–95. "Exhilarating"; "one had to": Tabak, "Art Project," in "Collage," p. 195. Years of destitution: Josephson, p. 385, quoting Julien Levy on artists as the "Forgotten Men" of the Depression. Empty galleries: FVOC, "The Genesis of JP," p. 53. Two hundred artists and students: Josephson, p. 386. "It was like winning": Cherry.

Prices, imports, and production: McKinzie, p. 4. Artist unemployment: Josephson, p. 374. Market for commercial art: Kamrowski. Stone work prohibited: Biddle, pp. 271–72. Private support limited: FVOC, "The Genesis of JP," p. 53, citing the *NYT Index* for 1933, pp. 180–81, concerning items about plight of unemployed artists in New York City and the emerging relief and exhibition measures. "Anything reasonable": Ashton, p. 45. "Out of habit": Josephson, p. 386. "For the overwhelming": Q. in Keppel and Duffus, p. 122. Cashing checks; "then a scout"; "the government couldn't": Tabak, "Art Project," in "Collage," p. 203. Dental work, tickets, meals, and liquor: Josephson, p. 386. Weekly checks: Busa. "Began to seem": Tabak, "Art Project," in "Collage," p. 210. De Kooning making displays: Rosenberg; Gaugh, p. 7. De Kooning, q. by Rosenberg: "You mean, for $23 I can paint all the time?" "I decided": Q. by friend, name withheld by request. "Really had a field day": Tabak, "Art Project," in "Collage," pp. 210–11. New partners: Josephson, p. 386.

Date of work relief: Dec. 1932; see Purcell, *Governme*

and Art, p. 47. **New York program; a hundred artists; art classes:** McKinzie, pp. 5–6. **Ben-Shmuel's workshop:** There is no direct evidence that Ben-Shmuel's class was sponsored by this program, although many similar ones were. **Biddle letter:** Dated May 9, 1933; McKinzie, p. 5. **Continued funding for "teachers' project":** McKinzie, p. 77. **PWAP funded:** "Federal Art Plan to Provide Funds for Needy Artists," *Art News*, Dec. 16, 1933, in Diamonstein, ed., p. 121. **"Of the best":** Q. in Treasury Department Order PWB No. 2-c Organization, Oct. 16, 1934 RG/121-118, q. in McKinzie, p. 37. Although the CWA was administered by Roosevelt's old lieutenant, Harry Hopkins, the PWAP was placed under the authority of the Treasury Department for no better reason than that the Treasury secretary's wife, Elinor Morgenthau, had expressed an interest in the arts. **Efforts modest:** PWAP was authorized to receive enough money to support 1,500 artists at $35 to $45 weekly, 1,000 artists at $20 to $30 weekly, and 500 laborers at $15 weekly; Edward Bruce, "Preliminary Plan on Public Works of Art Project" (unpub. paper), Nov. 1933, cited in McKinzie, p. 10. **"The first applicant":** McKinzie, p. 13. **Cleaning statues:** McKinzie, p. 29. The project was arranged by Juliana Force with Mayor Fiorello La Guardia. **Artistic debate paralleled; "historic social revolution":** Josephson, p. 374. McKinzie, p. 5: Biddle's "inspiration, clearly, was the experiment in the 1920s, sponsored by Mexican President Álvaro Obregón, in which young artists covered public buildings in Mexico City with murals expressing the ideas of the Mexican revolution," which produced "what some critics, then and since, have considered the greatest national school of painting since the Italian Renaissance." About four hundred murals were completed under the auspices of the WPA; *Report of the Assistant Secretary of the Treasury to Federal Emergency Relief Administrator—Public Works of Art Project: Dec. 8, 1933, to June 30, 1934* (Washington, D.C.: Department of the Treasury, 1934), p. 7, cited in McKinzie, p. 27. **Traditionalists:** They "saw art as noble and scholarly, and, if it were good, slightly mystical"; McKinzie, p. 7. **"Identified with"; "a very small percentage":** *NYT*, Dec. 13, 1933, cited in McKinzie, p. 12: Among the eight societies that lodged charges against her were the National Sculptors Society, the Society of Mural Painters, the Architectural League, and the American Artists Professional League. **"There is a woman":** SLM to Kadish, n.d. **"The natural results":** Q. in *NYT*, Mar. 11, 1934, q. in McKinzie, p. 13. **One percent for "embellishments":** Edward Bruce, "Suggested Plan for Continuance of the Government Fine Arts Activities Inaugurated Under the Public Works of Art Project" (unpub. paper), Apr. 20, 1934, cited in McKinzie, p. 36; see also Ashton, p. 46. **"Ending the dole"; "adequate for":** Harry Hopkins to Franklin D. Roosevelt, Dec. 14, 1934, cited in McKinzie, p. 76. **More than 3,700 artists:** In May 1934, Roosevelt authorized money for Bruce's revised Treasury plan to be implemented, but only for one month; see McKinzie, pp. 35–36. After that, the battle resumed. **Union membership doubling:** Monroe, "The '30s," p. 66. **PWAP projects abandoned:** Ann Cranton, "Public Works of Art Project Report Covering Its Activities and Liquidation" (unpub. paper), 1935, RG121/105, cited in McKinzie, p. 32. **Transfer of projects:** FVOC, "The Genesis of JP," p. 18. **Goodman class:** Strautin. **Goodman:** "Job Goodman": Director of Instruction at Greenwich House. Born 1897 in Russia; immigrated to U.S. 1905; studied at ASL; died 1955. **Jackson off relief:** FVOC, "The Genesis of JP," p. 90: JP's WPA employment records were supplied to FVOC by the Federal Record Center of General Services Administration in St. Louis, Mo.; see also OC&T IV, p. 219. **Firemen's Memorial:** OC&T IV, p. 219. **Statue of Washington:** Carved 1856 by H. K. Brown after an original by Houdon. **Joined by Sande:** Kadish. **Jackson demoted:** FVOC, "The Genesis of JP," p. 62. **Statue of Peter Cooper:** OC&T IV, p. 219; FVOC, "The Genesis of JP," p. 62: Kadish, int. by FVOC, Jan. 7, 1964: In later years, when passing through Cooper Square, JP often recalled cleaning the Cooper statue. **"That the government":** Josephson, p. 374. **"Hell, [artists]":** Q. in Schlesinger, Jr., pp. 263–81. **"Put to work"; "that is all":** Q. in Josephson, p. 381. **"Piss pot"; "conditions here":** SLM to Kadish, July 16, 1935, q. in Ashton, pp. 33–34. **Both proposals approved:** The Treasury program began in July 1935; the FAP in August. **Percentage of non-relief artists:** About 25 percent; "Final Report of Treasury Relief

Art Project" (unpub. paper), RG121, cited in McKinzie, p. 39. **Aspirations:** "Federal Support of Fine Arts" (unpub. memorandum), George Biddle to Edward Bruce, Nov. 16, 1933, Bruce to Biddle, Nov. 22, 1933, Biddle Papers, q. in McKinzie, p. 10. **"The Ritz":** Dubbed by *Time*, q. in McKinzie, p. 39. **Tolegian TRAP artist:** Tolegian, int. by Hoag, Feb. 12, 1965. **FAP figures:** McKinzie, p. 75. **Creation of WPA:** Josephson, p. 373. **"Those who are forced":** Q. in McElvaine, p. 266. **WPA figures:** Josephson, p. 375. **Raking leaves:** McElvaine, p. 265. **Airfields:** Ultimately, more than 20,000 playgrounds, schools, hospitals, and airfields were improved or constructed; McElvaine, p. 265. **Only 5 percent of WPA funds; 2 percent of WPA employees:** Josephson, p. 375. **Two hundred artists on WPA:** Ashton, p. 47. **Two hundred serious artists:** Josephson, p. 386; figure for 1932. **One thousand signing up; six thousand employed:** Ashton, p. 47; the figure is given as 5,500 in Josephson, p. 382. **Screening procedures:** State Final Report file, especially California, Connecticut, New York City, RG59/651.3115, cited in McKinzie, p. 86. **Anyone with framed painting:** Rosenberg. There were other ways to get on the project, including a recommendation from an art school, or proof of having been paid for art-related skills; see McKinzie, pp. 86–87.
McMahon: Audrey McMahon, int. by Richard D. McKinzie, Mar. 31, 1970, cited in McKinzie, p. 77. **Cahill:** "The Reminiscences of Holger Cahill," Columbia Oral History Collection, Columbia University, New York, cited in McKinzie, pp. 75, 78. **"Two people":** Kadish. **"I have changed":** SLM to Kadish, July 16, 1935. Stories later circulated that Roy had tried to change his name back to McCoy but found the procedure too expensive and that Sande had promised his dying father that he would adopt the family's true name; ACM. But of all the Pollock brothers, Sande was the most pragmatic, and $23.86 a week was more than adequate compensation for a name that had been borrowed in the first place. The legal change didn't come until 1942; ACM. **Jackson joining mural division:** OC&T IV, p. 219; FVOC, "The Genesis of JP," p. 63. **Asked to assist Goodman:** Mattox. **"Force account":** "The Reminiscences of Holger Cahill," pp. 355–58, cited in McKinzie, pp. 84. **Individual standards:** Kamrowski: "If you were an assistant you had to check into the project supervisor. It was like punching a time-card." McNeil: "We were each assigned a mural and left alone, which was simply magnificent." **"Kind of a martinet":** Mattox, int. by Dehner, LK, McCoy, and Miller, Mar. 1, 1972: JP, George Cox, Oliver Kerwood, and the others held this view of Goodman. **Sixteenth Street studio:** Mattox, int. by Dehner, LK, McCoy, and Miller, Mar. 1, 1972; it was near Sixth Avenue, on Sixteenth or Seventeenth Street, according to Mattox. **"Inspections"; "some evidence":** Mattox. **"Unskilled, intermediate":** McKinzie, p. 85. **Objective works encouraged:** Olin Dows to Frederic Knight, Sept. 1, 1936, RG121/119, cited in McKinzie, p. 42; Artists learned to "paint section"; Erica Beckh Rubenstein, "The Tax Payers' Murals" (Ph.D. thesis, Cambridge, Mass.: Harvard University, 1944), cited in McKinzie, p. 55. **Diller and Holtzman:** Holtzman; McNeil.
Sponsors required: JP was not alone in failing to secure a mural commission for one of his own designs. LK, q. in Bruce Glaser, "JP," p. 36: "In order to get a work of art for some public building, somebody from the public had to say we want a painting of a certain kind. Unfortunately, art doesn't work well when subjected to democratic processes. Predictably, the abstract artists were not much in demand." Busa: "Every damn one of [Jackson's] presentations was rejected. He never did get a mural to do." **"The story of Costume":** SLM to Kadish, July 16, 1935. **History of aviation:** Butler Air Terminal, La Guardia Airport, by James Brooks, assisted by Sande and others; Brooks. **Goodman's mural:** FVOC, "The Genesis of JP," p. 142. Mattox, int. by Dehner, LK, McCoy, and Miller, Mar. 1, 1972: The original destination was Erasmus Hall High School in Brooklyn. **One thousand murals begun:** Josephson, p. 382. **Few abstract murals:** McNeil: Only Gorky's Newark Airport mural, Stuart Davis's mural for WNYC, Ilya Bolotowsky's mural for the Williamsburg housing project, and one by Byron Browne were completed. Because abstract artists knew nothing would ever come of their efforts, they diverted most of their time to their "own work." **"If and when":** SLM to Kadish, July 16, 1935. McKinzie, p. 27: Murals "comprised less

than 3 percent of the items produced, but they commanded disproportionate attention. Government art became chiefly mural art in the public mind." **Concealing income:** McNeil. Some artists assigned to the mural division showed up for work, then spent the day playing cards while the person to whom they were assigned did all the work; see Tabak, "Art Project," in "Collage," p. 28. **Pilfering:** Cherry. **Mattox:** When Smith went to Europe in 1935, Mattox took over his position; Dehner. **Mattox at distribution center; "a lot of the artists"; "we took"; "mileage":** Mattox.

"Force account" abolished: "The Reminiscences of Holger Cahill" pp. 355–58, cited in McKinzie, p. 84: "Finding the relief chief [Hopkins] at a cocktail party sitting on the floor and leaning against the host's fireplace, Cahill told him the decision was 'perfectly silly.' " **New regulations:** FVOC, "The Genesis of JP," p. 64, citing interview with Ahron Ben-Shmuel, Dec. 2, 1965; letters from Jack Tworkov, Apr. 17, 1964; Louis Block, May 20, 1964; Dorothy Miller, June 22, 1964; Jacob Kainen, Sept. 3, 1965. Ashton, p. 48: The system "permitted artists to work at their own speed."

Impact of WPA: LK, int. by Rose, July 31, 1966. **Socializing at WPA offices:** Cherry. **Sense of community:** Marca-Relli: "It brought all the artists together so we met each other and came to know each other." **Shielding others from rules:** Ashton, p. 48. **"There was a wonderful feeling":** Name withheld by request. **"Like one big":** Ribak; see also McKinzie, p. 178. **"Not unlike payday":** Friedman, p. 36. Those not on the project were marked with a stigma that would linger for decades. Afraid of being ostracized, John Little kept his well-paying job as a fabric designer secret throughout the period; Little. Barnett Newman confessed years later (q. in Ashton, p. 44): "I paid a severe price for not being on the project with the other guys; in their eyes I wasn't a painter."

"Symbol [of] people's"; "[bring] to the artist": Edward Bruce, q. in William F. McDonald, *Federal Relief Administration and the Arts* (Columbus: Ohio State University Press, 1969), q. in Ashton, p. 46. **Other pay scales; sleeping in parks and subways:** Ellis, p. 532. **Works disappearing:** Mattox: When paintings were sold, it was usually in bulk for about ten dollars a piece. **Only $60 a month:** McKinzie, p. 87. **World-owes-me:** Busa. **Unemployed Artists Group:** McKinzie, p. 14. **Artists Union founded:** Actually, PWAP was established in December 1933; the Artists Union adopted that name in February 1934; see Monroe, "The '30s," p. 66. **Bureaucratic enemy:** McKinzie, p. 85: "WPA's inability to adjust to the habits of artists had something to do with the decision of many artists to organize unions to deal with the WPA." **"Deprived workers":** McKinzie, p. 86. **Union popular:** Mattox. **No mere windfall:** See Darrow, q. in Potter, p. 52.

Benton offered job: Craven, p. 16; Burroughs, p. 123. **Mural commission:** *Artist,* p. 258. **Authorized $16,000:** Craven, p. 16. **"I began to feel":** *Artist,* p. 261. SLM to Kadish, July 16, 1935: "There is a definate movement among artists to get out of New York into the midwest and west to develop regional art. (Wood-Iowa, Benton-Missouri, Curry-Kansas, ect.)" **Rhetorical jousting:** Burroughs, p. 123. **Friends questioning Benton's art:** Mumford; Scott. **Benton sulking:** Burroughs, p. 10. **Benton leaving:** "Benton to Quit Hectic City for Missouri Calm." **"Had lost all":** Q. in New York *Sun,* Apr. 12, 1935, q. in Burroughs, p. 124.

Resettlement Administration: CCP; McElvaine, p. 301. **Benton wanting Charles:** CCP. **Charles's work exhibited:** "Mrs. T. H. Benton Collection One of Several in Which High Standard is Reached." **Reproduced:** *Look Down that Road,* p. 17; *South Carolina Harvest,* p. 5. **Mentioned:** "Mrs. T. H. Benton Collection One of Several in Which High Standard is Reached"; notice of exhibition at the Ferargil Galleries. Works by Joseph Meert and Reginald Wilson, among others, were also listed, but not works by JP, even though he was represented in the exhibition. **Elizabeth promoting Charles:** SWP: "Elizabeth has always tried to market Charles's work—as Charles says, 'unsuccessfully.' " **Stella's talk of selling quilts:** SMP to JP, CCP, and EFP, Jan. **Eighth Street apartment handed over:** Chronology prepared by CCP for EFP, Feb. 1975. **Leaving Houston Street:** Alone among JP's friends, Peter Busa recalls that JP and Sande lived for a while prior to moving to Eighth Street in a cold-water flat on Greene Street. **Allocating spaces at Eighth Street:** ACM. EFP: "Sande gave up his own life. He,

too, wanted to paint, but he spent all his time, when he wasn't earning a living, acting as Jackson's nursemaid." **Jackson thriving:** Kamrowski: "Jackson's life represents a remarkable series of contingencies, and having a brother who would keep the pad warm and still be there when he got back was crucial."

Making lithographs with Wahl; "just to get rid": Wahl. OC&T, p. 132: JP made lithographs at the Art Students League between 1932 and 1935, when, as a member, he had access to the lithographic studio. In early 1933, however, he became involved with sculpture, first with Ben-Shmuel and Robert Laurent, then with Davis, and he would not have used the League facilities until the following fall, by which time he had stopped taking courses and visited the League only intermittently, preferring to spend his weekends at Davis's place in the Poconos; O'Connor relies heavily on Klonis's unreliable memory of these events. **Pollock's lithographs:** OC&T 1055 IV, pp. 132–41. **Martha's Vineyard sketches:** OC&T 385–86, III, p. 3. **Watercolors:** OC&T 932, 934, IV, pp. 18–19. **Mississippi cotton pickers:** *The Cotton Pickers,* OC&T 12, I, pp. 12–13; FVOC, "The Genesis of JP," pp. 62, 154–57. **Vineyard Sound:** OC&T 30, I, p. 25. **Bather:** OC&T, 919, IV, p. 5.

Brooklyn Museum exhibition: FVOC, "The Genesis of JP," p. 62; the show was the Eighth Exhibition of Watercolors, Pastels and Drawings by American and Foreign Artists, Feb. 1–28, 1935. The work is OC&T 935, IV, p. 20, size and medium not certain; no longer extant. The exhibition listed JP as represented by Ferargil Galleries; Curator, Department of Painting and Sculpture, Brooklyn Museum, to FVOC, July 21, 1964, q. in FVOC, "The Genesis of JP," p. 62. **Lewd mural:** Kron. **Ryder exhibition:** Twenty-six oils on exhibition in October and November. We disagree with O'Connor's conclusion ("The Genesis of JP," p. 169) that JP's best Ryderesque works were painted after seeing this exhibition. **Visits to Museum of the American Indian:** Kadish; Lehman. **Eight-inch bowl:** OC&T 916, IV, p. 3. **Nine-inch platter:** OC&T 917, IV, p. 3. **Ashtray:** OC&T 920, IV, p. 6. **Eighteen-inch plate:** OC&T 918, IV, p. 4; Benton always believed that this constituted JP's first use of the drip. THB to FVOC, Mar. 31, 1964: The plate "has dripped pigment all over. Jack simply found, I suggest, that dripping produced a lively and spontaneous effect. It could well have been the result of an accidental drip of paint off the brush which 'looked good' and was followed up." **Seventeen-inch bowl:** OC&T 919, IV, p. 5.

Lehman in New York: Lehman. **Frick:** The Frick Collection opened to the public on December 14, 1935; Alfred M. Frankfurter, "Frick Art Gallery to Open to Public," *Art News,* Dec. 14, 1935, in Diamonstein, ed., pp. 137–40. *Expulsion from the Temple:* See OC&T 409, III, p. 23; 436, III, p. 45. **Sande urging Kadish:** SLM to Kadish, July 16, 1935, q. in Ashton, pp. 33–34. **Kadish and Goldstein arrive:** During the winter of 1935–36; Ashton, p. 34. **Camping out:** Ashton, p. 34. **Reaction to Mexicans:** Despite their youthful disdain for the "much heralded Mexican Renaissance" (Ashton, p. 31), especially the work of Rivera, they could not hide their admiration for certain of the Mexican painters, Siqueiros, in particular. **Orozcoesque mural proposals:** Busa.

WPA office: 110 King Street. **Cafés and cafeterias:** Village cafeterias, like the Waldorf and Stewart's, and cafés, like the Jumble Shop; LK; Matter; SLM, int. by Shorthall, 1959. **Gorky holding forth:** Pavia; Pavia, q. by Potter, p. 61. **Wax maquettes for Goodman:** Mattox. **"Making these Renaissance"; "things which were":** Mattox, int. by Dehner, LK, McCoy, and Miller, Mar. 1, 1972. **Sessions of unknown number:** Dehner. **Small foundry:** It was adjacent to the Tivoli movie theater; Dehner; Mattox, int. by Dehner, LK, McCoy, and Miller, Mar. 1, 1972: "I don't remember that piece, but I would very much judge that that was one of the pieces [Jackson did], because it looks like similar things I saw there in the studio when I visited it." **Small, complex bronze piece:** OC&T S/1, IV, p. 158. **Later Orozcoesque experiments:** Wilcox; confirmed in part by Harry Jackson.

"I think the little": THB to JP, n.d. **"A genius":** Q. by Kron. **"By 1934":** THB to FVOC, Apr. 4, 1964, q. in FVOC, "The Genesis of JP," p. 153. *Cotton Pickers:* OC&T 936, IV, p. 20; exhibition dates: Feb. 3–21, 1937; this may be the same work as *Threshers* being exhibited under a new title. *Cody, Wyoming:* Potter, p. 50. **"Had something":** CCP **"[He] told me":** Tworkov to FVOC, Apr. 17, 1964, q. in FVOC, "The Genesis of JP," p. 78. Joseph Solman, q. in FVOC, ed., p. 118: John Lonergan (Diller's colleague, a p ect supervisor) also admired JP's work: "I recall Lonergan going out of his way to show me an early emotional abstraction, an oil on paper, of Jackson Pollock. He was truly excited by it."

19. AN ANTIDOTE TO REGIONALISM

SOURCES

Books, articles, manuscripts, film, and transcript

THB, *An Artist in America (Artist)*; Goldman, *Contemporary Mexican Painting in a Time of Change*; Helm, *Modern Mexican Painters*; Kazin, *Starting Out in the Thirties*; O'Hara, JP; Rodriguez, *A History of Mexican Mural Painting.*
Axel Horn, "JP: The Hollow and the Bump," *Carleton Miscellany*, Summer 1966; Laurence P. Hurlburt, "The Siqueiros Experimental Workshop: New York 1936," *Art Journal*, Spring 1976.
"40,000 March Here in May Day Parade, Quietest in Years," *NYT*, May 2, 1936.
FVOC, "The Genesis of JP: 1912–1943" (Ph.D. thesis), Baltimore: Johns Hopkins University, 1965; Harold Lehman, "The Siqueiros Experimental Workshop" (lecture), Artists Union, N.Y.C., c. 1936.
Man on Fire (PBS film), 1984.
SLM, int. by CG, c. 1956.

Interviews

Peter Busa; August Goertz; Axel Horn; Mervin Jules; Reuben Kadish; Harold Lehman; ACM; CCP; Irving Sandler; Nene Schardt; Reginald Wilson.

NOTES

Dynamism and fecundity; Unimpressed by first meeting: Kadish. **Trip to Buenos Aires:** Helm, p. 92. Siqueiros had been barred from returning to Mexico. On May 1, 1929, he had participated in a violent workers' demonstration and was thrown into jail. Having already been jailed in 1918 for military misconduct (Rodriguez, p. 373), he now served a second year in jail. On his release he was expelled from Mexico; Helm, p. 92. **Buenos Aires stay:** Helm, p. 93. **Manifesto:** Helm, p. 93. **American Artists Congress; sponsored by Gershwin:** *Man on Fire*, 1984. **New "workshop":** Hurlburt, "The Siqueiros Experimental Workshop," p. 238. **"A laboratory":** The Siqueiros Experimental Workshop. **"The naughty boy":** Horn, "JP," p. 85. **"Throw down":** Helm, p. 91. **Siqueiros's childhood; jailed at thirteen:** Helm, p. 89. **Revolutionary at fourteen:** Helm, p. 90. **"The ideal goal":** Manifesto issued by Syndicate of Revolutionary Painters, Sculptors, and Engravers of Mexico, 1923, q. in Goldman, p. 4. **Not a heavy drinker; "Uncontrollable excesses":** Helm, p. 91. **"A man on fire":** *Man on Fire*, 1984. **Siqueiros disarming:** Horn. **"The class war":** Siqueiros, q. by Busa. **Charisma:** Kadish: The word is Kadish's. **"Extremely *simpático*":** Lehman; Siqueiros, in *Man on Fire*, 1984: "He was a very talented young man." **Arm wrestling; "twisting":** Busa.
Siqueiros's loft: CCP. **Address of loft:** OC&T IV, p. 219. **Early boil:** Kazin, pp. 32–33. **Dozen artists:** Hurlburt, "The Siqueiros Experimental Workshop," p. 238. **Young sculptors:** Morris Schulman, Harold Ambellen, and Bernard Woltz; Lehman. **"Core":** Hurlburt, "The Siqueiros Experimental Workshop," p. 239. **Hispanic artists:** Luis Arenal, Antonio Pujol, Conrado Vasquez, José Gutiérrez, and Roberto Berdecio; Hurlburt, "The Siqueiros Experimental Workshop," p. 238. **"Comrade":** Siqueiros to JP, SLM, and Lehman, Dec. 1936. **"Practicing artists"; workshop:** Horn. **"Outlandish":** CCP to FVOC, Nov. 10, 1966, q. in FVOC, "The Genesis of JP," p. 23. **"Torrential flow":** Horn, "JP," p. 85. **Duco:** Specifically, pyroxilin, and first used by Siqueiros in 1933; Goldman, p. 11. **"Il Duco":** Sandler. **Art belonging to workers:** Diego Rivera, q. in O'Hara, p. 14: Art should express "the new order of things . . . the logical place for this art, . . . belonging to the populace, was on the walls of public buildings." **"Lacquer had"; "it was like"; "failed experi-**

ments"; **"almost instantly":** Horn, "JP," p. 86. **Industrial surfaces:** Lehman.
Painters like workers: Kadish. **Silk-screening frame:** The first recorded noncommercial use of the silk-screening process was in 1938 on a FAP; WPA workers soon formed the National Serigraph Society. **Siqueiros portraits:** Hurlburt, "The Siqueiros Experimental Workshop," pp. 240–41. **Siqueiros not working from drawings:** Lehman. **"Liberated" lazy Susan:** Horn. **"Striking halations":** Horn, "JP," p. 86. **Siqueiros "seizing" the image:** A pattern of dripped paint was used to create the kinky hair, "heavily incrusted with pigment," in a four-foot-high portrait of James Ford, the 1936 vice-presidential candidate of the U.S. Communist party; Lehman; see Hurlburt, "The Siqueiros Experimental Workshop," pp. 240–41. **August Goertz:** It was a follower of Siqueiros named Conrado Vasquez who initiated the drip technique in the Siqueiros workshop. **Dripping paint in Horn's apartment:** Horn, who shared the apartment with Mervin Jules. **"Aesthetic orthodoxies"; "conformist":** *Artist*, p. 267. **Siqueiros's modern tools; "putting out to pasture":** Horn, "JP," p. 85. **"Violation"; "accidental"; "scale"; "the whole ambience":** CCP to FVOC, Nov. 10, 1966, q. in FVOC, "The Genesis of JP," p. 23. **"Fairies":** *Artist*, p. 265. **Jackson's letter to Roy; "composition":** JP to LRP, Feb. 1932. **"Lifted art":** JP to LRP, Feb. 3, 1933.
Float: Horn. **"As far as the working class":** Lehman. **Description of float:** Lehman; Hurlburt, "The Siqueiros Experimental Workshop," p. 239. **"An essay":** Q. in Hurlburt, "The Siqueiros Experimental Workshop," p. 239.
Gift of Model A Ford: OC&T IV, p. 220. **Differences put aside during parade:** "40,000 March Here in May Day Parade": The parade lasted for two and a half hours. The head of the parade left the starting point on the lower West Side a little after 9:00 A.M. and arrived at the reviewing stand at the north end of Union Square at 11:40 A.M. "As a special peace gesture ordered by Police Commissioner Valentine, the police guarded the route without their nightsticks." **Hitler lookalike; "shuffling line"; "all grades":** "40,000 March Here in May Day Parade." **Listening to speeches:** Lehman. **Photograph with Siqueiros:** In possession of AAA.
"He was always working": Q. in Hurlburt, "The Siqueiros Experimental Workshop," p. 239. **At workshop less than two months:** SLM, int. by CG, c. 1956. **"I am at more unrest":** Siqueiros to JP, SLM, and Lehman, Dec. 1936. **Trip to coal country:** Kadish. **"God damn":** Q. by Schardt. **WPA artists leaving city:** Wilson. **Taking farmhouse:** ACM; Wilson. **"Dutch":** Pennsylvania Dutch—in other words, German. **Arloie arriving:** ACM.

20. THIS UNNATURAL MASS OF HUMAN EMOTIONS

SOURCES

Books, articles, manuscript, document, and records

Ashton, *The New York School*; Ashton, *Yes, but . . .*; THB, *An Artist in America (Artist)*; Burroughs, *THB*; Friedman, *JP*; Gruen, *The Party's Over Now*; Mayhew, ed., *Martha's Vineyard*; FVOC, ed., *The New Deal Art Projects*; OC&T, JP; Potter, *To a Violent Grave*; Solomon, *JP.*
Axel Horn, "JP: The Hollow and the Bump," *Carleton Miscellany*, Summer 1966; Gerald M. Monroe, "Artists as Militant Trade Union Workers During the Great Depression," *AAA Journal*, 1974.
FVOC, "The Genesis of JP: 1912 to 1943" (Ph.D. thesis), Baltimore: Johns Hopkins University, 1965.
Chronology prepared by CCP for EFP, Feb. 1975.
Dockets Nos. 6414 and 6415, District Court 35, Dukes County, Mass.

Interviews

T. P. Benton; Peter Busa; Blanche Carstensen; Cecil Carstensen; Herman Cherry; Karen Del Pilar; B. H. Friedman; Ron Gorchov; Isidore Grossman; Joseph Henderson; Rebecca Hicks; Axel Horn; Reuben Kadish; Gerome Kamrowski; Nathaniel Kaz; Maria Piacenza Kron; Harold Lehman; Beatrice Ribak Mandelman; ACM; Jason McCoy; William McKim; Dale Maddux; Mercedes Matter; Charles Mattox; ABP; CCP; EFP; MLP; May Tabak Rosenberg; Nene Schardt; Araks Tolegian; Lester Trauch; Theodore Wahl; Steve Wheeler; Roger Wilcox; Reginald Wilson.

NOTES

Bucks County house: Wilson; photo in possession of ACM. **Bank foreclosures; Spartan accommodations; New York writers:** Trauch. **Painting on porch:** Wilson. **Kadish visiting:** Kadish. **Country range:** Wilson. **Drive to Erwinna; Williams's store:** Maddux. **Canal barges; behavior of canalers; coal and grain:** Trauch. **Description of Revere:** Maddux: The hotel, a frame building, burned down twenty-five years ago. **Jackson driving; trips into New York:** Wilson: They went to the city "every week or two weeks." **"You goddamn":** Q. by Wilson. **Sande's marriage date; hot, humid day:** ACM. **Sande insisting on black minister:** ACM. **Masochistic courtship:** Del Pilar. **Arloie's search for minister:** ACM. Sande apparently made little or no effort to assist Arloie in her search. He had already been in New York for two years, and he already had several black friends, including JP's former classmate, Joe Delaney, and the Art Students League model, Tiger Ed Bates. **Wedding:** ACM. **Wrought-iron bed:** Hicks. **Sande clearing section of closet:** ACM. **Arloie's hair:** Hicks. **Sewing and cooking:** ACM. **Arloie a good cook:** Hicks. **Attracting visitors:** ACM; Lehman. **Three or four times a week; "too expensive":** ACM. **Sketching trip:** SLM to Samuel Wagstaff, Feb. 14, 1962.

Frank's marriage date: Apr. 2, 1935; MLP. **"His brothers":** Rosenberg. **Marriage thinkable now:** Kamrowski. **Goldstein bunking with Pollocks:** Ashton, *Yes, but* . . . , p. 34. **Cherry's broken love:** Cherry. **Mitchell married:** Lehman; Kadish. **Schardts meeting:** Schardt. **Telegian on prowl:** Ruth Stone to MLP, Nov. 9, 1936. **Telegian talking marriage:** Araks Telegian. **Tutelage of Ben-Shmuel:** Grossman; Kaz. **"He liked to humiliate":** Grossman. **Party; "vacuuming up the wine":** EFP. **"You are the ugliest":** Q. by EFP. **"Scuffling"; "a girl's":** EFP.

Jackson no longer fabricating affairs: Busa; Lehman. **"Sexually, Jackson"; "dating" unaffordable:** Kamrowski. **Dance-floor and barroom antics:** Busa; Lehman. **Jackson not dating:** When a friend of Marie's came to New York in late 1936 with an introduction to JP, she received a polite but unimpassioned reception: "When I arrived on the scene he was fast asleep on the couch. Upon being awakened he stared at me vaguely—mumbled—shook his head—almost fell asleep again—made a great effort and rambled on—something on this order—'Sure—sure—I remember you, Ruthie! sure—Manual Arts—hate reminiscences—old school days—Let's talk about school days—remember those pamphlets I distributed?' . . . Then he suggested that when she returned to Los Angeles she look up his mother and fell back asleep. 'Romantic—what?' " Ruth Stone to MLP, Nov. 9, 1936.

Sylvia: Horn; Wilson; Arloie remembers the name as Shirley, but says "it could have been Sylvia." **Height and hair:** Horn; Wilson; ACM: The hair was light brown and "kind of fuzzy." **Last name unknown; Jackson joining Schardt and Wilson; farmhouse:** ACM. **Near Frenchtown; five dollars a month:** SLM to CCP, Oct. 29, 1936; Arloie says JP paid only five or ten dollars for the entire winter. **Description of farmhouse; talk of staying the winter:** ACM. **Accident while drunk; "Jack had"; bill for eighty dollars:** SLM to CCP, Oct. 29, 1936: JP had to pay for the other person's damage, which indicates the accident was his fault. **November return:** ACM; Ruth Stone to MLP, Nov. 9, 1936. **"Too cold":** Q. by ACM. **Sylvia dropped:** ACM.

Nightly forays; turned away or thrown out; rounds of drinks: Kadish. **Jackson given coffee; sudden violence:** ACM. **"I remember Sande":** Schardt. **Tears:** Wilson. **Held by Sande:** See ACM, q. in Potter, p. 53. **Arloie's professions of affection:** ACM: "He was very sweet, and I remember him as a very loving, kind brother." **Dances:** Held at the Artists Union loft on Sixteenth Street and Sixth Avenue; Mattox. **Jackson's belligerence and abuse; checking for periods:** Busa: When JP later visited one of his classes at Cooper Union, he said, "Pete, at least six of your women here have periods." **Dance-floor behavior:** Busa; Kadish. **Christmas party:** Busa. **Jackson cutting in:** Busa; Gruen, p. 230. **"Do you like":** Q. by Friedman; see Gorchov, who, recalling Lee Kras-

ner, describes the same incident: "This is all from Lee. This I got from Lee. She told me directly." **"Dog gets on your leg":** Busa. **Jackson apologizing:** Gorchov. **"He started":** LK, q. by Gorchov.

"Much heralded": Ashton, *Yes, but* . . . , p. 31 Rivera's **"crudities"; Siqueiros's "shitty" painting; "dominated":** Goldstein to Lehman, July 14, 1934, q. in Ashton, *Yes, but* . . . , p. 31. **Christ panel in Dartmouth mural:** Entitled *Modern Migration of the Spirit.* **Sketching on the Vineyard:** SLM to Samuel Wagstaff, Feb. 14, 1962. **Experimenting with Orozco's style:** See especially the ceramic bowls, e.g., OC&T 920, IV, p. 6. **Dating of Orozcoesque works:** As with all JP's early works, there is great confusion. O'Connor (in "The Genesis of JP") concludes that they were generally done after 1938, citing (pp. 176–77) SLM to CCP, July 1941, in which Sande writes that JP had "thrown off the yoke of Benton completely and is doing work . . . related to that of men like Beckman [sic], Orozco and Picasso" and (p. 177 n. 1) a remark by Motherwell that, in the winter of 1941–42, Pollock was moving from Orozco to Picasso."

Yet Sande dated a sequence of similarly Orozcoesque drawings c. 1937; OC&T 482–85, III, pp. 70–71. Moreover, Bryan Robertson—presumably with Lee Krasner's advice—dated a related drawing c. 1934; OC&T 486, III, p. 72. O'Connor himself dates the related drawings c. 1933–39; OC&T 479–86, III, pp. 68–72. He dates some of the Orozcoesque paintings c. 1934–38 (OC&T 31–56 I, pp. 27–41) and others 1938–41 (OC&T 57–62, I, pp. 44–49) even though one of the latter (OC&T 58, I, p. 45) was inscribed "Jackson Pollock 1937" by an unknown hand on a photo taken of it by Lehman about 1941–42.

We believe JP's primary Orozcoesque period began during the middle thirties and lasted through his stay at White Plains, as indicated by the bowls, which have an Orozcoesque quality, and by the reference to Thomas Dillon, a fellow patient at that hospital, on one page of a sketchbook (OC&T 478, III, p. 67). We think JP turned away from Orozco toward Picasso and primitive art about 1939, primarily as a result of his exposure to *Guernica* in 1939 and to the exhibition "Picasso: Forty Years of His Art," held that year at MOMA; of Henderson's characterization of native American art as spiritually valuable; and of the lessons of John Graham (see chapter 23, "Intimations of Immortality").

O'Connor (pp. 177–78) notes JP's early exposure to Orozco, beginning in 1930, and allows that JP could have seen the Dartmouth murals (although he had "no evidence that he saw them in the original") but chooses to emphasize instead the general resurgence of interest in Orozco among New Yorkers in 1939. He quotes (p. 179) SLM to CCP, Jan.–Feb. 1939, noting that Sande "saw some photos of Orozco's Guadalajara frescoes. Christ what a brutal, powerful piece of painting. I think it would be safe to say that he is the only really vital living painter. . . ." O'Connor ("The Genesis of JP" pp. 179–80) also cites an Orozco exhibition at the Hudson D. Walker Galleries in the fall of 1939 and a fresco, *Tank and Dive Bomber,* painted by Orozco in 1940 in full public view at MOMA, then argues that these two events accounted for JP's own resurgence of interest in the Mexican painter.

Aside from the early trips to Pomona, and JP's early and repeated references to the Orozco fresco as the greatest painting in America, it is now known that JP *did* go to Dartmouth to see the murals in 1936; Wilson. It is also known that Guston arrived in New York in 1935 from a trip to Mexico bringing with him a very considerable enthusiasm for Orozco, and touting Orozco's fresco in Buenos Aires. As for Motherwell's comments, his association with JP was too late and too superficial to contradict the testimony of more knowledgeable sources such as Busa. As for Sande's letter to Charles, it seems likely that he was noting primarily that, as late as 1941, JP had finally and "*completely*" [our emphasis] left Benton behind. We don't think Sande meant to imply that JP was responding to additional artists—Beckmann, Orozco, and Picasso—for the first time; otherwise, why would he have given JP's Orozcoesque drawings a date of 1937?

Skeletal beasts: OC&T 467–68, III, p. 62; 470, III, p. 63; 473, III, p. 65; 482, III, p. 70; 484, III, p. 71. **Pregnant women:** OC&T 460, III, p. 58; 462, III, p. 59; 470–71, III, pp. 63–64; 475–76, III, p. 66. **Skeletal animals in wombs:** OC&T 473, III, p. 65; 483 III, p. 70. **Crosses:** OC&T 475–77, III, pp. 66–67; see also OC&T 50, I, pp. 36–37. **Chains:** OC&T 476, III, p. 66; 481, III, p. 69. **Skulls:** OC&T 483, III,

p. 71. **Flayed skin:** OC&T 467–68, III, p. 62; 470, III, p. 63; 475, III, p. 66; 484, III, p. 71; 486, III, p. 72. **Infants nailed to cross:** OC&T 475, III, p. 66; 477, III, p. 67. **Infants chained to cross:** OC&T 476, III, p. 66. **Infant carcasses:** OC&T 477, p. 67. **Academicians and kneeling figure:** OC&T 49, I, pp. 36–37. **Nightmare tableau:** OC&T 59, I, p. 46.

Portraits of Stella: See especially OC&T 59, I, p. 46. **Faceless females:** OC&T 59, I, p. 46; 475–76, III, p. 66. **Horses:** OC&T 51–53, I, pp. 38–39; 55, I, p. 40. **Horse skeletons:** OC&T 482–83, III, p. 70. **Horse humans:** OC&T 59, I, p. 46; 61, I, p. 49. **Horse birds:** OC&T 468, III, p. 62; 477, III, p. 67. **Horse bulls:** OC&T 467, III, p. 62.

Project pictures: The early paintings that JP kept for himself—such as the Ryderesque *Seascape*, dated 1934 (OC&T 30, I, p. 25), or gave to friends, mainly the Bentons, such as *Going West*, with its cowboy subject and Ryderesque style (OC&T 16, I, p. 16)—are his more innovative and risky works: comparatively abstract and dreamy in content, thickly painted, extremely somber, and very strong, especially for this early date. The paintings that JP painted for the WPA allotment, on the other hand, tend to be clearly representational, thinly painted, lackluster in style, banal in subject matter: a horse grazing in a field (OC&T 17, I, p. 17), a farmer plowing a field (OC&T 15, I, p. 15), women picking cotton (OC&T 12, I, pp. 12–13), simple landscapes (OC&T 22, I, p. 20) and seascapes (OC&T 25, I, p. 23). The same is true of the feathery landscapes that JP apparently made while in Kansas City (OC&T 18–21, I, pp. 18–19), which were clearly done for sale to earn traveling money; see letter from THB to FVOC, describing the sale of one painting to Frank Paxton, q. in OC&T I, p. 19. The painting from this series that JP gave the Bentons, *Red Barn*, was probably a leftover.

For all his disapproval of "phoniness," JP was apparently willing, when essential, to paint on demand. This must have been torture for him, however, and may help explain his running battle with the WPA (see JP to CCP, [Thursday], in which JP noted that the WPA had rejected a painting because "they didn't like the form in the water," adding that he didn't mind because it hadn't been "a good picture" anyway.)

Turkey and recording; "not having much": JP to CCP, "Thursday." OC&T IV, p. 221: The painting may be OC&T 14, I, pp. 14–15. **"Whose scatological":** Horn, "JP," p. 87. **Jackson lunging at Siqueiros:** Horn. **"Horsed around":** Kadish. **"He was killing":** Horn, "JP," p. 87. **"With a deft":** Horn. **Taking Jackson home:** Horn, "JP," p. 87. **Sande refusing Stella:** SLM to CCP, Oct. 29, 1936. **Confusion over government commitment:** Monroe, "Artists as Militant Trade Union Workers," p. 8. **"Would be fatal":** SLM, q. by CCP. **"A succession"; "mentally sick"; "as you know"; "help [Jackson]":** SLM to CCP, July 27, 1937. **Cary Baynes:** Henderson. **Sande impressed by credentials:** SLM to CCP, July 27, 1937.

Rita's party: Kadish. Hicks recalls that she met JP first, not at 46 East Eighth, but at a party given by a friend, Nancy Knight, at her "little studio down on Eighteenth Street." **Municipal Art Galleries exhibition:** Marchal E. Landgren, "A Memoir of the New York City Municipal Art Galleries, 1936–1939," in FVOC, ed., p. 286: The following artists were included in the exhibition: JP, Philip Goldstein, George R. Cox, Millicent Cox, Bertram Goodman, Lehman, Guy Maccoy, SLM, Genoi Grace Pettit, Bernard Schardt, J. B. Steffen, Manuel Tolegian, and Wilson. **"Slim and pretty"; Becky's brown hair:** Kadish. **Sitting near window:** Kadish. **Banjo:** Hicks; Kadish says she played the guitar, but it was in fact the banjo. **"A lovely girl":** ACM.

Becky Tarwater's background; "the theater bug": Hicks. **Meeting Charles:** CCP. **Introduced to Steffen:** ACM. Hicks says it wasn't Steffen who made the introduction, but rather Nancy Knight. Arloie's memory seems more secure on this point. **Jackson drinking at party:** Hicks; Kadish. **"Jack, I don't":** Hicks. The Allerton is at Lexington and Fifty-seventh Street. **"All I'm able":** JP to CCP, Jan. 30, 1937. **Dinners on Eighth Street; "a tortured"; never shown paintings or museums:** Hicks; **Never introduced to friends:** Lehman; Wilson. Kadish: He met her once or twice at parties. **Telephone calls; conversation; No visits to** *Naughty Naught;* **Mason Hicks:** Hicks. Mason lived in Tudor City at the time. **Jackson could be charming; "a great big"; kisses:** Hicks. **"Slight improvement":** SLM to CCP, July 27, 1937. **Charles's move to Detroit:** Chronology prepared by CCP for EFP, Feb. 1975; see also FVOC, "The

Genesis of JP," p. 65. **"Without giving":** SLM to CCP, July 27, 1937. **Meeting at White Castle Restaurant:** Hicks; Arloie remembers it as being on Sixth Avenue. **Good-bye; gardenia; proposal; refusal:** Hicks: "What he needed was a mother, not a wife."

"Went berserk": Q. in Potter, p. 48. **Week-long binge:** Araks Tolegian, recalling Manuel. **Sande and Arloie in country:** ACM. **Visits from Kadish:** Kadish. **Mid-July:** Wilson: JP went to Bucks County before, not after, the trip to Martha's Vineyard; he was in the Vineyard by July 21. **Stay brief and uneasy:** Wilson.

Boat trip: Benton. **Description of boat trip:** Burroughs, p. 5. **Furtive letter:** Hicks; JP to Becky Tarwater, Aug. 21, 1937. **Date of Vineyard incident:** Dockets Nos. 6414 and 6415, District Court 35, Dukes County, Mass. **Oak Bluffs:** See Mayhew, ed., pp. 99–113. **Arrival unexpected; no one to welcome him:** *Artist,* p. 335. **Sending message to Rita:** THB to FVOC, Apr. 4, 1964, q. in FVOC, "The Genesis of JP," p. 67. **Buying gin as present:** *Artist,* p. 335. **"Opened the bottle":** THB to FVOC, Apr. 4, 1964, q. in FVOC, "The Genesis of JP," p. 67. **Stutz:** Benton. **Rita trying to fetch Jackson; second call:** *Artist,* p. 335. **Getting to Chilmark on own:** THB to FVOC, Apr. 4, 1964, q. in FVOC, "The Genesis of JP," p. 67. **Renting bicycle:** *Artist,* pp. 335–36. **"Take hold":** THB to FVOC, Apr. 4, 1964, q. in FVOC, "The Genesis of JP," p. 67. **Seeing girls; "he promptly":** *Artist,* p. 336.

"When [Tom] heard": Burroughs, p. 117. **Falling and gashing face:** *Artist,* p. 336. **Arrested:** Dockets Nos. 6414 and 6415, District Court 35, Dukes County, Mass. JP was not arrested for "disorderly conduct" as reported in *Artist,* p. 335; Burroughs, p. 117; and Potter, p. 55. **Pleading guilty:** Dockets Nos. 6414 and 6415, District Court 35, Dukes County, Mass. **Unable to pay fine; empty jail:** THB to FVOC, Apr. 4, 1964, q. in FVOC, "The Genesis of JP," p. 68. Potter (p. 55) claims that JP was held in an outhouse with a locked chain around it because a cell was not available, but Edgartown did have a jail (with indoor plumbing) and, according to Benton, JP was the only one in it. **Sheriff calling Chilmark:** Burroughs, p. 117. **Night in jail:** THB to FVOC, q. in FVOC, "The Genesis of JP," p. 68: "The jailer fed him, after he sobered up, and finding Jack a good boy took him to the movies after supper." **"A matter of fun":** THB to FVOC, Mar. 31, 1964.

Vineyard activities: Burroughs, p. 10. **Walks to Atlantic:** Burroughs, p. 11; JP to Becky Tarwater, Aug. 21, 1937. **Oval picture; going to the pond,** OC&T 28, I, p. 24. **Gift to Tom's nephew:** OC&T I, p. 24. **Letter from Becky:** Hicks. **"Darling Becky":** JP to Becky Tarwater, Aug. 21, 1937, in possession of Hicks. **Sande and Arloie return:** About the same time that Sande and Arloie returned from Bucks County, Charles scolded JP for neglecting their mother: "Whatever other responsibilities we may or may not have, we certainly owe Mother the courtesy of regular letters. . . . good intentions are not enough. . . . [T]his is a serious matter Jack and I hope you will take it seriously"; CCP to JP, Sept. 13, 1937.

"Wet nurse": EFP. **Violence:** Kadish. **Fistfights:** Kadish; Wahl. **"Filthy"; sleeping in gutter; refused service in bars:** Kadish. **Found passed out by strangers:** Ribak. **Bowery stray:** Kadish. **"Worried":** SLM to CCP, Feb. 1938, referring to "the first part of the winter." **Tablecloth shredded:** Solomon, p. 85. **No children while living with Jackson:** ACM. **Periods of withdrawal; "horrendous feelings":** Kadish. **Head in hands; never painting just after binges:** ACM: "I never saw him paint during those periods." **Going to kitchen; good periods:** Kadish. **"Calm sea":** Busa. **Federal Art Gallery:** 225 West Fifty-seventh Street; OC&T IV, p. 223.

Visit from Benton: SLM to CCP, Dec. 13, 1937, cited in FVOC, "The Genesis of JP," p. 68. **Tolegian and Sande pulling out; Jackson leaving for Kansas City:** SLM to CCP, Dec. 21, 1937. **Valentine Road house:** McKim. **Benton harder and cooler:** Cecil Carstensen. **Upheaval at art institute:** Benton. **"He wouldn't be":** Blanche Carstensen. **Two-week stay:** SLM to CCP, Dec. 21, 1937; JP to CCP, Jan. 6, 1938. **T.P. unable to recall trip:** Benton. **Four landscapes:** OC&T 18, I, p. 18; OC&T 20–21, I, p. 19. One was given to the WPA but appears stylistically to have been painted in Kansas City. **Sold to friends:** One (OC&T 21, I, p. 19) was sold to Frank Paxton; THB to James T. Vallière, July 13, 1964. **Round of parties:** Lawrence Adams to FVOC, Aug. 11,

1964, q. in FVOC, "The Genesis of JP," p. 68. **"Stag affairs":** Cecil Carstensen. **"There was considerable"; "feats"; "the usual":** Lawrence Adams to FVOC, Aug. 11, 1964, q. in FVOC, "The Genesis of JP," p. 68. THB to FVOC, Mar. 31, 1964: "He could be a little wild when he went out on the town, but there was so much wildness in [Democratic party boss] Tom Pendergast's Kansas City at the time that the wildness of an undeveloped genius was not even noticible." **King's Beach:** Benton. **Confrontation with Rita:** Wheeler, recalling Morris Kantor. **"She was his ideal":** Artist, p. 241: Rita apparently told Benton something about this event, although probably not all; Benton here implies that he had heard similar professions of love. **Proposing to Rita:** Wheeler, recalling Morris Kantor.

"She turned him down": Wheeler. So visible was JP's infatuation for Rita that, when viewed against the limitations of the Bentons' marriage, it generated outrageous rumors not only of a torrid affair but even of an illegitimate child; Burroughs. **"After [Rita] turned him down":** Morris Kantor, q. by Wheeler. **Kansas City binge; "so sick"; taken to doctor; "disease":** THB to FVOC, Mar. 31, 1964: "We had had some amusing experiences with Jack when he got high but never thought of them as reflective of a serious condition." **"The doctor told me":** THB to FVOC, Mar. 31, 1964.

"Our plans": SLM to CCP, Feb. **Six-week trip:** OC&T IV, p. 223. **May 28:** SMP to CCP, May 19, 1938. **Running through streets:** Solomon, p. 80, citing 1984 interview with Jacob Kainen. **"Horrendously sick":** Kadish. **Diller "covering" for JP:** Friedman, p. 55. Ashton, p. 48: "Burgoyne Diller, one of the most diplomatic and sympathetic supervisors, personally visited artists who had not checked in to cajole and persuade them to meet their minimum obligation." Dorothy Miller, int. by FVOC, Jan. 16, 1964, q. in FVOC, "The Genesis of JP," p. 94: When "Pollock tried to leave the Easel Division because his work was not acceptable . . . Diller went after him and made him come back and accept his check."

Jackson applying for leave: SMP to CCP and EFP, May 19, 1938. **Request denied:** FVOC, "The Genesis of JP," p. 70: JP was told that there could be no assurance that the job would be there when he got back. **Four-day binge; "sherry wine and rotgut"; urine; Bellevue:** Kadish. **Jackson's objections:** Wilcox. **Sande arranging commitment:** SLM to Clarence O. Chaney, June 1, 1938. **"Continued absence":** OC&T IV, p. 223. **June 12:** SLM to Clarence O. Chaney, June 1, 1938; OC&T IV, p. 223, note that it was June 11.

21. RETREAT

SOURCES

Books, articles, manuscripts, and transcripts

Carruth, *The Bloomingdale Papers;* Cohen, *Notable American Women;* Conn, ed., *Current Therapy;* Dreier, *Margaret Dreier Robins;* Goldmark, *Impatient Crusader;* C. G. Jung Institute of San Francisco, *The Shaman from Elko;* McKinzie, *The New Deal for Artists;* Mumford, *Sketches from Life;* OC&T, *JP;* Potter, *To a Violent Grave;* Pratt, *I Learn from Children;* Russell, *The New York Hospital;* Schneiderman, *All for One.*

"The Bloomingdale Asylum: 1821–1894," *New York Hospital–Cornell Medical Center Newsletter,* Summer 1976; "Bloomingdale Hospital," *New York Hospital–Cornell Medical Center Newsletter,* Fall 1976; Donald M. Hamilton, Hewitt I. Varney, and James H. Wall, "Hospital Treatment of Patients with Psychoneurotic Disorders," *American Journal of Psychiatry,* Sept. 1942; Donald M. Hamilton and James H. Wall, "Hospital Treatment of Patients with Psychoneurotic Disorders," *American Journal of Psychiatry,* Jan. 1942; "How a Disturbed Genius Talked to His Analyst with Art," *Medical World News,* Feb. 5, 1971; "More History . . . Construction 1922–Now," *New York Hospital–Cornell Medical Center Newsletter,* Winter 1977; Lewis Mumford, "Life on the Dial," *New York Review of Books,* Feb. 20, 1964; "The New York Hospital: 1771–1976," *New York Hospital–Cornell Medical Center Newsletter,* Spring 1976; James H. Wall, "The Evaluation of Treatment," *Psychiatric Quarterly,* no. 1, 1953; James H. Wall, "The Psychoses: Schizophrenia," in Conn, ed., *Current Therapy;* James H. Wall, "Psychotherapy of Alcohol Addiction in a Private Mental Hospital," *Quarterly Journal of Studies on Alcohol,* Mar. 1945; James Hardin Wall, "A Study of Alcoholism in Men," *American Journal of Psychiatry,* July 1935; James

H. Wall and Edward B. Allen, "Results of Hospital Treatment of Alcoholism," *American Journal of Psychiatry,* Jan. 1944; Judith Wolfe, "Jungian Aspects of JP's Imagery," *Artforum,* Nov. 1972; C. L. Wysuph, "Behind the Veil," *Art News* Oct. 1970.

"Labor Unions: A Friendly Explanation of Their Point of View," *NYT,* Oct. 4, 1914; Helen Marot, "Conquering Time" (letter to the editor), *NYT,* Mar. 7, 1916; "Helen Marot," *NYT,* June 4, 1940; "Organized 150,000 Women: Trade Union Leaguer's Ten Years of Work Reviewed by Secretary," *NYT,* May 10, 1914; "A Woman's View of Labor: Helen Marot Discusses in Manly Fashion Pending Questions Between Wage Earners and Wage Players," *NYT,* Oct. 1, 1916.

Joseph L. Henderson, "JP: A Psychological Commentary" (lecture); Helen Marot, "Oneself: A Story of Arrested Growth and Development" (unpub. ms.); FVOC, "The Genesis of JP: 1912 to 1943" (Ph.D. thesis), Baltimore: Johns Hopkins University, 1965.

SLM, int. by CG, c. 1956; SLM, int. by James T. Vallière, Aug. 1963, AAA.

Interviews

Peter Busa; Pat Carlton; Tamaria Eichelberg; Janet Hauck; Joseph Henderson; Axel Horn; Mervin Jules; Reuben Kadish; LK; Harold Lehman; Adele Lerner; ACM; Lewis Mumford; Sophia Mumford; Lucia Salemme; Rachel Scott; Patsy Southgate; Wally Strautin; James Wall; Steve Wheeler; Roger Wilcox.

NOTES

"Huge old asylum": Carruth, p. vii. **Details of admission; physical examination, neurological exam, X rays; specialists:** Wall, "Psychotherapy," p. 550. **Nurses:** Carruth, p. vii. **Tenseness, depression"; "outstanding mental symptoms"; "suicidal preoccupation":** Hamilton, Varney, Wall, "Hospital Treatment," p. 244.

"Voluntary patient": See Wysuph, "Behind the Veil", p. 52; Potter, p. 57. **Inebriate certification"; "an inebriate"; "for a period":** Wall, "Psychotherapy," p. 549. The state law was intended to short-circuit the grueling involuntary commitment process while ensuring that voluntary patients, like JP, remained at the hospital long enough for treatment to be effective. **"Centered around"; alcohol banned, put to bed:** Wall, "A Study," p. 1399. **Prolonged baths:** Carruth, p. vii. **Steam cabinet; wet packs:** Wall, "Psychotherapy," p. 550. **Ultraviolet light; massage:** Wall and Allen, "Results," p. 478. **Preferable to drugs; "rich in calories"; "abundant fluid"; proper elimination; "colonic irrigations":** Wall, "A Study," p. 1399. **Free to roam:** Wall. **Mail checked:** JP to SLM, June 21, 1938. **Forced and tube feeding:** Wall, "The Psychoses," p. 717. **"Impulsive, stuporous"; shock treatment:** Wall, "The Evaluation," p. 240; Carruth, p. vii: Wall, "The Psychoses," pp. 717–18: "Shuffleboard, handicrafts, and tepid baths . . . together with occasional consultations with a doctor, were still regarded as good enough treatment even for deep psychosis, and when these failed the usual recourse was to shock and sometimes to isolation." The typical treatment was "a series of from 8 to 12 electric shock treatments, one being administered every other day." After five years of unsuccessful treatment, "prefrontal lobotomy must be considered." **Founding of hospital:** See "The Bloomingdale Asylum;" "Bloomingdale Hospital;" "More History;" "The New York Hospital." It was actually founded in 1771, making it the second oldest in the country, but the separate mental hospital didn't come into being until 1821, when the first building was built on the present site of Columbia University; "The New York Hospital," p. 1; "The Bloomingdale Asylum," p. 2. **Shackles and bars:** Lerner. **Bloodletting:** "The New York Hospital," p. 2. **"Moral management"; humanitarian treatment; "as rational beings":** "The Bloomingdale Asylum," pp. 1–2. **New York's richest families:** Newsletter, "Bloomingdale Hospital," pp. 5–6; "More History," p. 4. **Luxurious facilities:** Russell, p. 428. **Exercise and dance classes; age of men:** Russell, p. 405: In some years, a third of those admitted were under thirty. **"Competitive games"; "sweating out":** Wall, "A Study," p. 1399. **Clothing:** Carruth, p. vii. **Entertainments:** Russell, p. 425. **Plays and operettas:** Wall and Allen, "Results," p. 478. **Olmsted:** Eichelberg: There is some dispute now whether Olmsted himself or members of his staff designed the grounds. **"Guest villas"; "for the insane":** Russell, p. 351. **Evening events:** Wall, "A Study," p. 1400. **"A substitute":** Wall and Allen,

"Results," p. 478. **Charity case:** ACM. **"Breezy, affable":** Wall, "Psychotherapy," p. 551. **McCoys in Bucks County:** ACM. **"Imagine you are getting":** JP to SLM, June 21, 1958. **"[He] was rather":** Wall, q. in Potter, p. 57.

Dr. Allen; working with Wall; Wall's residency: Wall. **Interest in "alcoholic psychosis":** Wall, "Psychotherapy," p. 550–51. **Long-term study:** Wall, "A Study." Wall and Allen ("Results," p. 474) describe a study of 100 alcoholic patients in which there was "1 sculptor." Since Wall would have seen JP at the time not as a painter but as a sculptor, he could easily have been referring to JP. The 100 patients were studied from 1934 to 1940; follow-up studies conducted three to eight years after discharge "revealed that 23 were recovered and 19 were managing better"; Wall, "The Evaluation," p. 243. **Wall a Freudian:** Wall: He was analyzed by Dr. Bertram Lewin. **"Unburden himself":** Wall, "Psychotherapy," p. 550. **"The patient must be convinced":** Wall, "The Psychoses," p. 716. **Jackson's silence:** Wall, "Psychotherapy," p. 553: "The shy, sensitive or schizoid person is usually passive in his adjustment to hospital treatment. He has used alcohol to overcome his shyness and often, in his social and professional adjustments, he has beeen able to give the impression of being a jovial extrovert. Beneath the submissive and passive exterior the patient is frequently seething with resentment. . . . Patients of this type are frequently those who have accomplished much in the fields of art, literature, music and science." **Turning to Sande:** Wall, "The Psychoses," p. 716: "Families . . . can help much in creating special environments for the unusually sensitive person." SLM to CCP, July 1941, makes it clear that Wall briefed him on JP's problems. **Wall breaking down defenses:** We can assume this on the basis of Sande's letter, which demonstrates how clearly Wall identified JP's problems, and of the therapy that Wall recommended, discussed later in the chapter, which was carefully adapted to JP's problems.

Wall's sessions confidential: Wall. Although Wall has occasionally divulged small details of his interaction with JP to various people (cf. letter to LK, Sept. 12, 1963), he has refused to discuss the main points of their therapeutic sessions. **Family drinking problem:** It seems unlikey that either JP or Sande talked about their father's alcoholism; Charles, Frank, and Jay still deny that he was an alcoholic, even while providing evidence of it. **No hereditary factor:** The genetic component of alcoholism had not yet been established at the time; see Wall, "Psychotherapy," p. 551. **"The example":** Wall, "Psychotherapy," p. 551. **"Aggressive [women]":** Hamilton and Wall, "Hospital Treatment," p. 551. **"In the case":** Wall, "Psychotherapy," p. 551. **"Took no part":** Hamilton and Wall, "Hospital Treatment," p. 551. "The security of the family was disturbed in 29 [of 68] patients, who before the age of six lost one of their parents by death, desertion, or divorce"; Hamilton, Varney, and Wall, "Hospital Treatment," p. 243. **"A weak individual":** Hamilton and Wall, "Hospital Treatment," p. 551. **"Pathological but ambivalent":** Wall and Allen, "Results," p. 474. **"Close to their mothers":** Wall, "Psychotherapy," p. 552. **"A source of growing":** Hamilton and Wall, "Hospital Treatment," p. 551. **Adolescent drinking; "when drinking begins"; "fundamentally afraid":** Wall and Allen, "Results," pp. 474–75. **"Overt homosexuality":** Hamilton, Varney, and Wall, "Hospital Treatment," p. 243. **"Effeminate approach":** Wall and Allen, "Results," p. 474. **Reasons for therapy:** In a sample group of one hundred patients, precipitating factors were: childbirth, six; marriage of a near relative, six; serious illness of a relative, thirty-five; death of a member of the family, six; trouble with in-laws, six; change in work or economic circumstances, six; concern over some physical defect, five; disappointment in love, twelve; conflict over homosexuality, fourteen; other, sixteen; Hamilton, Varney, and Wall, "Hospital Treatment," p. 243.

Gardening detail: Hauck; see also Russell, p. 422. **Occupational diversions:** Russell, pp. 422–23. **"Metal work":** Wall, "A Study," p. 1400. **Copper bowl:** OC&T 1045, IV. p. 123. **Plaque:** OC&T 1047, IV. p. 123. **Working from drawings:** Wall to LK, Sept. 12, 1963. **"Attached great importance":** SLM, int. by James T. Vallière, second weekend in Aug. 1963, AAA. **"He spoke":** Wall to FVOC, Mar. 28, 1974, q. in OC&T IV, p. 125.

Jackson restless: JP to SLM, Sept. 1938. **Six months:** Wall, "Psychotherapy," p. 549. **Nine months:** Hamilton, Varney, and Wall, "Hospital Treatment," p. 245. **"An intelligent":** Potter, p. 57. **Tentative release date:** JP to SLM,

Sept. 1938. **Brief visit home:** Wall, "Psychotherapy," p. 554. **"My time here":** JP to SLM, Sept. 1938. **"Interest and curiosity":** Wall, "A Study," p. 1400. **"It was obvious":** Q. in Potter, p. 58. **Date of release:** JP to SLM, Sept. 1938: "The end of Sept. . . . around the 1st." Most releases were scheduled for Fridays, so September 30 was the likely date, although Sande may not have picked him up until the next day, October 1. **Jackson released:** See Wall and Allen, "Results," p. 478.

Doctors falling under Jackson's spell: One doctor, Henderson, in "JP," p. 23, later admitted succumbing to "countertransference." **"My recollection":** Q. in Potter, p. 57; see also Allen to Vallière, Sept. 2, 1963, showing that Allen felt the same way. **"I remember you":** Wall to JP, Nov. 22, 1949, AAA. **"A waste":** Wilcox. **Summer seldom mentioned:** There is one exception; JP looked up a friend he made at the hospital, a jeweler from New York named Thomas A. Dillon, and gave him a bowl similar to the one he had given Wall; see OC&T IV, p. 9. **"Really furious":** Wheeler. **Salemme institutionalized:** Salemme; Wheeler. **Jackson storming out:** Wheeler. **"I am very strongly":** THB to JP, Oct. 3, 1938. **"I was worried":** Rita Benton to JP, Oct. 3, 1938; emphasis in the original. **Busa and Horn:** Busa; Horn. Kadish was one of the few who heard the full story; Kadish. **"Had gone away":** Busa. Lehman, for example, knew nothing of the stay at Bloomingdale's; Lehman. **"Will you let Sande":** JP to "Willy or Walter," June 21, 1938.

Stella's first grandchild: Jeremy Eleanor, born 1938. **Date of application to WPA:** JP to SLM, Sept. 1938: "Now what I want to try and do is come down and see how I stand with the project. If I can get back on I will stay up here and come down a day or two each week, until around the 1st [of October]." **Dies Committee:** McKinzie, p. 158. **"A hotbed"; "one more link":** McKinzie, p. 155. **Midterm elections:** McKinzie, p. 158; in the November elections, the Republicans gained eighty-one House seats and eight Senate seats. **Cut in pay:** From $23.86 per week to $91.00 every four weeks; FVOC, "The Genesis of JP," p. 72. **Hopkins resigning:** McKinzie, p. 150. **"From all appearances":** SLM to CCP, 1939, q. in FVOC, "The Genesis of JP," pp. 72–73.

Follow-up visits: "During the last weeks of treatment they are encouraged to visit their homes and resume their work"; Wall, "Psychotherapy,'" p. 554. **Shying away from painting; concentration on sculpture:** Strautin. **Lithography:** JP sent a lithograph to the Bentons for Christmas, 1938; OC&T IV, p. 224. **"Story of my life":** OC&T 925, IV, p. 9. **Bowl presented to Wall:** OC&T 924, IV, p. 8. **"The flight of man":** Wall to FVOC, Mar. 28, 1974, q. in OC&T IV, p. 8. **Wall's commentary:** Wall to LK, Sept. 12, 1963. **Bowl sent to Bentons:** OC&T 922, IV, p. 7; see SLM, int. by CG, c. 1956: After Bloomingdale's, JP went abstract for the first time. **Sande and Arloie hopeful:** SLM to CCP, July 1941. **Strautin:** Kadish.

Jackson meeting Marot: It is possible that they knew each other earlier, since Marot was friendly with the Bentons, especially Rita, long before JP arrived in New York. **Talks with Marot:** See SLM, int. by CG, c. 1956, in which Sande reports that JP used to go talk with Marot and Pratt "c. 1936." Kadish: "I know that he would often be going to see her." **Marot's clothes and spectacles:** Cohen, "Helen Marot," in *Notable American Women*, vol. 2, p. 500. **"Didn't pay much attention":** Sophia Mumford. **"Strong-bottomed":** The word is Sophia Mumford's for Caroline Pratt, but applies equally well to Stella. **Marot's build:** Sophia Mumford. **Marot's birth:** June 9, 1865; Cohen, "Helen Marot," in *Notable American Women*, vol. 2, p. 499. **"I want you":** Q. in Cohen, "Helen Marot," in *Notable American Women*, vol. 2, p. 499. **Tracts:** For example, *Handbook of Labor Literature* (1898), *American Trade Unions* (1913), *Creative Impulse in Industry* (1918); for general history, see Cohen, "Helen Marot," in *Notable American Women*, vol. 2, pp. 501–02. See also Dreier, n.p.; Goldmark, pp. 81–82, 155; "Labor Unions," *NYT*, Oct. 4, 1914; Helen Marot, "Conquering Time" (letter to editor), *NYT*, Mar. 7, 1916; "Helen Marot," *NYT*, June 4, 1940; "Organized 150,000 Women," *NYT*, May 10, 1914; Pratt, pp. 18–19; Schneiderman, pp. 80, 92, 96; "A Woman's View of Labor," *NYT*, Oct. 1, 1916.

Grudging respect for Marot: Especially from Gompers; Sophia Mumford. **Fellow reformers:** Sophia Mumford. **"[She] dropped":** Mumford, p. 247. **Living with Pratt:** Scott: Marot and Pratt owned separate brownstones on Twelfth Street, but Marot rented hers out and moved into Pratt's house at 165 West Twelfth.

Interest in psychology: Mumford, p. 247. Interest in anthropology: Cohen, "Helen Marot," in *Notable American Women*, vol. 2, p. 500. "She had seen": Mumford to FVOC, May 6, 1964, q. in FVOC, "The Genesis of JP," p. 93 n. 33, A lifetime without marriage or children had left Marot vulnerable to JP's wayward-boy charms. Scott: "Helen felt that she had missed something by not marrying and made up for it by mothering everybody. Unlike the cool, dictatorial Pratt (Scott) —who disapproved of lullabies (Sophia Mumford)—Marot warmed quickly to strangers and, says Scott, "was always briefing her friends on what they should do."
Marot's relaxed appreciation: Sophia Mumford: She was far more relaxed than Pratt. "Swift insights": Mumford to FVOC, May 6, 1964, q. in FVOC, "The Genesis of JP," p. 93 n. 33, Sophia Mumford: "Caroline was interested in people as students. Helen was much more interested in people as people." Carlton: "Caroline Pratt was enveloped in ignorance about sex." When Sophia Mumford contemplated having a second child, Pratt said, "If you really care about education," Pratt said, "you won't have another child. There are plenty of children in the world to educate," at which point Marot broke in and said, "Oh, shut up, Caroline! It's a biological urge and you don't understand it"; q. by Sophia Mumford. Playing with Parrish: Also Jessie Wilcox Smith; Cohen, "Helen Marot," in *Notable American Women*, vol. 2, p. 499. Marot on the *Dial:* For Marot's involvement with the *Dial*, both the fortnightly *Dial* and its successor, see Mumford, p. 217, and Mumford, "Life on the Dial," p. 4. Creative impulse": Carlton.
Interest in Sherrington and Herrick: Mumford; see also Mumford to FVOC, May 6, 1964, q. in FVOC, "The Genesis of JP," p. 93 n. 33. Mumford, p. 247: She considered Sherrington's 1906 book on reflexes, *The Integrative Action of the Nervous System*, "her bible." Despite the sometimes extravagant claims of Jungian critics (e.g., Wolfe, "Jungian Aspects of JP's Imagery," p. 65), there is *no* evidence that Marot was interested in Jungian analysis. "Growth and development": Marot's last manuscript, which summarized her ideas on psychology, was called "Oneself: A Story of Arrested Growth and Development"; Cohen, "Helen Marot," in *Notable American Women*, vol. 2, p. 501. Jackson's openness with Marot: Busa; Scott. Friend and confidante: Lewis Mumford. Complaints about therapy: LK, Kadish, Southgate, Wilcox, etc. "[Therapy] never grew him": Q. in Potter, p. 63.
Cary Baynes: Wysuph, "Behind the Veil," p. 52; C. G. Jung Institute of San Francisco, pp. 14-19. Although Marot's friend Baynes was a Jungian, and therefore would naturally have attempted to locate a Jungian analyst for Jackson, there is no evidence that Marot specified a Jungian analyst; see "How a Disturbed Genius Talked to His Analyst with Art," p. 25. Baynes recommending Henderson: Henderson to B. H. Friedman, Jan. 1, 1970, in Friedman files. Henderson's address: East Seventy-third Street between Park and Lexington; Henderson.

22. ARCHETYPES AND ALCHEMY

SOURCES

Books, articles, manuscripts, and transcript

Ashton, *The New York School;* Coe, *Sacred Circles;* Fermi, *Illustrious Immigrants;* Friedman, *JP;* Green, *John Graham;* Henderson, *Thresholds of Initiation;* Jung, *Contributions to Analytical Psychology;* Jung, *Memories, Dreams, Reflections;* Jung, *Modern Man in Search of a Soul;* Jung, *Two Essays on Analytical Psychology;* C. G. Jung Institute of San Francisco, *The Shaman from Elko;* Philipson, *Outline of a Jungian Aesthetics;* Potter, *To a Violent Grave;* Trilling, *The Liberal Imagination;* Wysuph, *JP.*
David Freke, "JP: A Symbolic Self-Portrait," *Studio International*, Dec. 1973; Donald E. Gordon, "Department of Jungian Amplification, Part I: Pollock's 'Bird,' or How Jung Did Not Offer Much Help in Myth-Making," *Art in America*, Oct. 1980; Gareth S. Hill, "J.L.H.: His Life and His Work," in C. G. Jung Institute of San Francisco, *The Shaman from Elko*, ("J.L.H."); "How a Disturbed Genius Talked to His Analyst with Art," *Medical World News*, Feb. 5, 1971; Rosalind Krauss, "JP's Drawings," *Artforum*, Jan. 1971; Elizabeth Langhorne, "JP's 'The Moon Woman Cuts the Circle,'" *Arts*, Mar. 1979; William Rubin, "Pollock as Jungian Illustrator:

The Limits of Psychological Criticism, Part I," *Art in America*, Nov. 1979; William Rubin, "Pollock as Jungian Illustrator: The Limits of Psychological Criticism, Part II," *Art in America*, Dec. 1979; Irving Sandler, David Rubin, Elizabeth Langhorne, and William Rubin, "Department of Jungian Amplification, Part II: More on Rubin on Pollock," *Art in America*, Oct. 1980; Judith Wolfe, "Jungian Aspects of JP's Imagery," *Artforum*, Nov. 1972; C. L. Wysuph, "Behind the Veil," *Art News*, Oct. 1970.
Joseph L. Henderson, "JP: A Psychological Commentary" (lecture); FVOC, "The Genesis of JP: 1912 to 1943" (Ph.D. thesis), Baltimore: Johns Hopkins University, 1965. SLM, int. by James T. Vallière, Aug. 1963, AAA.

Interviews
Peter Busa; Violet de Laszlo; Joseph Henderson; LK; George McNeil; Sam Naifeh; Nene Schardt; Judith Wolfe; C. L. Wysuph.

NOTES

Many Freudian analysts: Fermi (p. 142) estimates that about two-thirds of all European psychoanalysts eventually fled to the United States. **Henderson intrigued by artists:** Naifeh, a Jungian analyst in San Francisco, a colleague of Dr. Henderson's, and, coincidentally, a cousin of one of the authors; Wysuph. **Seeing Jackson gratis:** Wysuph. **Henderson's birth:** Aug. 31, 1903. **Henderson's origins:** "J.L.H.," pp. 10–12. **Relationship with Wilder:** "J.L.H.," p. 12. **Princeton:** "J.L.H.," p. 13. **"At sea"; meeting Bayneses:** "J.L.H.," p. 14. **"I decided":** Q. in "J.L.H.," pp. 14–15. **Jung's home:** Henderson: An institute in town housed the library and secretariat. **Dream of becoming an analyst:** "J.L.H.," pp. 15–16. **"Asking his dreams":** "J.L.H.," p. 21. **"If you're really":** Jung, q. by Henderson, q. by Naifeh. **University of London; "white horse":** "J.L.H.," pp. 15–16. **Another dream:** A red-headed snake killing a "ray-like, black fish"; "J.L.H.," pp. 15–16. **Marriage to Cornford:** "J.L.H.," pp. 17–19: They were introduced by Mrs. Cary Baynes. **"Swallowed Jung":** Naifeh. **Analyzed by Jung:** "J.L.H.," pp. 15–16.
Earlier arrival of Rank and Ferenczi: Ashton, p. 122. **Freud dominating New York:** See Freke, "JP," p. 217. **"A puritanical reluctance"; more favorable climate elsewhere:** Ashton, p. 123. **Onset of Jackson's therapy:** Henderson to B. H. Friedman, Jan. 1, 1970, in Friedman files: He was never sure exactly when JP started therapy except that it was "early 1939." **"Large, self-contained man":** Q. in Potter, p. 58, which refers to Henderson as "The Source."
Jung and "imaginal mind": Naifeh. **"For him, Pollock":** Name withheld by request. **Focus on the future; "innermost self":** Naifeh. **Ignoring history:** Q. in Potter, p. 59. **No look at records; never spoke with others; "[Jackson] was taken"; "[Jackson] explained"; "saw to it":** Q. in Potter, pp. 58–59. **Jung and alcoholism; "managed"; "the emergence":** Naifeh. **"Managing" job Sande's:** Henderson, "JP," p. 21: Sande carried the burden of Jackson's reality function. **"Drinking was necessary":** Q. in Potter, p. 59. **Jackson saying little:** Friedman, p. 41. **"He seemed preoccupied":** Q. in "How a Disturbed Genius Talked to His Analyst with Art," p. 25. **"Talk about himself":** Wysuph, p. 10. **"This was not even":** Q. in Potter, p. 59.
"Embryonic germ-plasm"; "individuation": Jung, *Two Essays on Analytical Psychology*, p. 108. **Accumulated psychic experience:** Jung (*Contributions to Analytical Psychology*, p. 246) called them "the psychic residua" of "countless typical experiences of our ancestors." **"The creative process":** Jung, *Contributions to Analytical Psychology*, p. 248; emphasis in the original. **"Visionary mode":** Philipson, p. 104. **"The artist reaches out":** Jung, *Contributions to Analytical Psychology*, p. 248. **"We are astonished"; "genuine, primordial":** Jung, *Modern Man in Search of a Soul*, p. 184. **"Synthesis of the individual":** Jung, *Two Essays on Analytical Psychology*, p. 299. **"Substitute gratification":** "Art and Neurosis," in Trilling, p. 161. **"Genetic fallacy":** Philipson, p. 91. **Personal conditions: psychic significance:** Philipson, pp. 100–01. **"It is art":** Jung, *Modern Man in Search of a Soul*, p. 196.
Symbols that lead to health: Jung, *Modern Man in Search of a Soul*, p. 193: "It was conceivable that a work of art, no less than a neurosis, might be traced back to those knots in the psychic life we call the complexes. . . . No objection can be

raised if it is admitted this approach amounts to nothing more than the elucidation of those personal determinants without which a work of art is unthinkable. But should the claim be made that such an analysis *accounts for the work of art itself*, then a categorical denial is called for." **"Dream the myth":** Jung, *Two Essays on Analytical Psychology*, p. 299. **"What is essential":** Jung, *Modern Man in Search of a Soul*, p. 194.

One or two works: Henderson. **"Human figures":** Q. in Friedman, p. 42; see, e.g., OC&T 545–49, III, pp. 112–13; see also OC&T 507, III, p. 87; 557, III, p. 118; 495, III, p. 80; 536, III, p. 106. **Gouache brought to early session:** Henderson, "JP," pp. 14–15; OC&T 940 IV, p. 23. **Jackson taking notes:** See OC&T 556, III, p. 118. This drawing has traditionally been considered a "study" for the gouache; we believe it is a schematic done after the gouache. **Violence and distortion:** Henderson, "JP," p. 14. **"[Pollock's] own highly developed":** Q. by Langhorne, in Sandler et al., "Department of Jungian Amplification," p. 59. **"Ordering symbols":** Henderson, "JP," p. 15.

"The analyst (out of knowledge)": Henderson, pp. 17–18; this is from a supposedly anonymous case study but the subject is clearly JP. **"He did not have free":** Q. in Friedman, p. 41. **Drawing of tree with snake:** Not identified in *Thresholds of Initiation*, but it is OC&T 555, III, p. 117. **"Would normally seek"; "a movement of regression":** Henderson, p. 39. **Showing illustration of snake; "a simple form":** Henderson. **"A psychic birth-death-rebirth":** Gordon, "Department of Jungian Amplification," p. 44; see Henderson, "JP," pp. 2, 17. **Curved lines, straight lines:** Wysuph, p. 14.

Henderson becoming uneasy: Henderson, "JP," pp. 2, 20. **"A genuine, primordial"; "something derived":** Jung, *Modern Man in Search of a Soul*, p. 184. **Previous profiles:** Philipson, p. 121. **"True symbolic";** Jung, *Modern Man in Search of a Soul*, p. 184. When JP brought in an elaborate drawing of a mandala, Henderson acknowledged that JP could have seen a reproduction of one in Jung's *Secret of the Golden Flower* or some other Jungian text, and that JP might have made the drawing to get Henderson's approval, but decided to overlook this possibility because JP's honesty as an artist would not have allowed him to create an image that he "did not feel"; Henderson, "JP," p. 2.

The need to preserve spontaneity, or at least the appearance of spontaneity, clearly obsessed Henderson, both at the time and for years afterward; Henderson, "JP," p. 12. In subsequent accounts of JP's therapy, he frequently revised his description of the circumstances under which the drawings were submitted. According to one version (Krauss, "JP's Drawings," p. 58, citing a conversation with Henderson), the drawings were "dream representations which Pollock produced specifically for his analytic sessions—rather than drawings made independently of the therapy." According to Rubin ("Pollock as Jungian Illustrator, Part II," p. 86, citing Henderson, "JP"), Henderson "actively exhorted [Jackson] to produce symmetrical, mandala-like images" and, when he met resistance, fought "tooth and nail" until JP acquiesced. But in a letter to Lee Krasner (Oct. 16, 1970, in Friedman files), Henderson claimed that he never asked JP to make drawings, that JP had brought them in unprompted. Elsewhere (q. in Friedman, p. 41), he said that JP "was already drawing them, and when I found out, I asked for them." The extent to which Henderson educated JP to Jungian theories once the analysis began—and thereby risked "leading" his imagery—was also the subject of frequent revisions. "I did not consciously discuss Jung or Jungian theories with Jackson," Henderson claimed in 1980 (q. in Gordon, "Department of Jungian Amplification," p. 44), although he allowed that he had pointed out to JP "those characteristics in his work which seemed to represent 'healthy' or 'unhealthy' signs" (q. in Wysuph, p. 13) and elsewhere (Wysuph, pp. 21, 16) admitted that he discussed with JP "the Jungian faith in a 'psychic birth-death-rebirth cycle' as well as the 'symbol-ordering' device of the circular mandala." At various times, he claimed that JP said virtually nothing during their sessions ("I commented upon them spontaneously," q. in Friedman, p. 410); that JP was already familiar with Jungian theories and supplied the analyses that JP brought ("According to Henderson, Jackson Pollock was already familiar at the time [of therapy] . . . with the principles of Jungian psychology"; Wysuph, p. 19); and finally that he couldn't remember anything about the sessions (He had lost all "recall [as] to what extent he may have entered into detailed analytical discussions of the drawings"; Wysuph, "Behind the Veil," p. 53). Wysuph,

who has studied the issue closely with Henderson himself, says JP "got that kind of jargon from his discussions with Henderson." Even Langhorne ("JP's 'The Moon Woman Cuts the Circle.' " p. 131)—in arguing that the most likely "explanation for the archetypal nature of Pollock's imagery around 1941 is saturation in Jungian thought while under Jungian analysis" —implies that Henderson was JP's instructor in Jungian lore.

Jackson untutored in Jung: Those who would like to think that JP brought some knowledge of Jung's ideas into his relationship with Henderson assume that he learned about Jung from Helen Marot; see Wolfe, "Jungian Aspects of JP's Imagery," p. 65; see also Krauss, "JP's Drawings," p. 61. In fact, Marot, was far more interested in Sherrington than in Jung throughout the period of her friendship with JP. **Henderson a father figure:** Henderson himself claims ("JP," p. 20) that he became a father figure to JP. **Jackson never reading Jung:** Busa; see also Langhorne, "JP's 'The Moon Woman Cuts the Circle,' " p. 131, and Rubin, "Pollock as Jungian Illustrator, Part I," p. 116. **Jung in English:** *Contributions to Analytical Psychology* and *Modern Man in Search of a Soul*. **Jackson writing about "anima" and "animus":** Busa.

Symbols become leitmotifs: See OC&T 516–27, III, pp. 92–100; 533–39, III, pp. 103–09; 550–55, III, pp. 114–17. **Circular Chinese Tao:** OC&T 521v, III, p. 96; 522r, III, p. 97; 527, III, p. 100; 533r, III, p. 103; 534v, III, p. 104. **"Axis mundi":** OC&T 519r, III, p. 94; 525, III, p. 99; 531, III, p. 102; 534r, III, p. 104; 534v, III, p. 104; 549, III, p. 114. **Crescent moon:** OC&T 518v, III, p. 93, 521v, III, p. 96; 523, III, p. 98; 525, III, p. 99. **Snake:** OC&T 519r, III, p. 94; 520r, III, p. 95; 521v, III, p. 96; 524–25, III, pp. 98–99; 527, III, p. 100; 530–31, III, pp. 101–02; 533r–34r, III, pp. 103–04; 550, III, p. 114. **Crossed lines:** OC&T 518v, III, p. 93; 520r, III, p. 95; 521v, III, p. 96; 522v–23, III, pp. 97–98; 534v, III, p. 104; 537r, III, p. 107. **Pelvic basin:** OC&T 522r, III, p. 97; 523, III, p. 98; 538v, III, p. 108. **Mandala:** OC&T 520r, III, p. 95; 524–25, III, pp. 98–99; 527, III, p. 100; 533v, III, p. 103; 535r, III, p. 105; 537r, III, p. 107; also note evidence that Henderson had introduced Jackson to Native American symbology: OC&T 520r, III, p. 95; 521r, III, p. 96; 552–54, III, p. 116. **Images repeated, more finished:** See OC&T 534v, III, p. 104; 537r, III, p. 107. **Angular figures:** OC&T 541, III, p. 110; 544, III, p. 111, **Jagged lines:** OC&T 542–43, III, pp. 110–11.

Drawing that provided synopsis of case: OC&T 555, III, p. 117. **Teaching tool:** Henderson, "JP," pp. 15–17. **Schematic female:** Q. in Wysuph, p. 17. **Not a phallus:** Henderson, p. 109. **Axis mundi; reorganizing psychic life:** Henderson, "JP," pp. 15–16. **"Reality function":** Q. in Wysuph, p. 17. **Pelvic basin; opposites:** Henderson, "JP," pp. 15–16. **"The principal":** Q. in Wysuph, p. 16. Henderson ("JP," pp. 15–16) added a caveat to this diagnosis: The only troubling sign that remained in the drawing was the existence of the horse and the bull in the background, denoting the instinctual aspects required to produce JP's integration on a conscious level. While the drawing indicated that such integration had already occurred on the unconscious or semiconscious level, as represented by the snake and plant symbols, integration had yet to take place in the conscious world—that is, in reality. **Same image seven times:** OC&T 525–26, III, p. 99; 531, III, p. 102; 533v, III, p. 103; 538r, III, p. 108; and especially 552, III, p. 115; for closely related symbols see 523, III, p. 98; 535r, III, p. 105; 537v, III, p. 107; 556, III, p. 118. **Continuing value:** Later Henderson (p. 110) would claim: "By allowing the symbols expressive of his inner experience to emerge and by giving them form in his paintings, he began to be cured." In the most important of the drawings that Jackson had brought, Henderson argued, "The pole had a centering effect upon his disorganized psychic life, restoring a sense of structure. In the same way, his representation of the plant with its enigmatic leaves or fruit was placed in the very center, from which it seemed to exert an ordering, nurturant effect."

Jackson reluctant to discuss Jung: Schardt. **Incapable of discussing Jung:** See LK, int. by Rubin, Apr. 1967, q. in Rubin, "Pollock as Jungian Illustrator, Part I," pp. 117, 120: JP called the dog in *Guardians of the Secret* a "father-figure"; as Rubin notes, in Jungian terms a dog is a female symbol, not a male one: "On the lone occasion when Pollock identified the psychological significance of one of his early images, he attributed to it precisely the opposite symbolism . . . than we would be led to expect from Jung's references." **Jung, artists,**

and the unconscious: As at least one art historian (Freke, "Jackson Pollock," p. 218) has suggested: "A theory which asserts that the unconscious is mythopoetic and that the arts are its mouthpiece naturally commends itself to those involved in artistic activity."

"To help [Jackson]": Q. in Friedman, p. 43. "Adequately": Henderson, "JP," pp. 20–21. "Reality function": Q. in Wysuph, "Behind the Veil," p. 17. Jackson sober at sessions; "astonished"; "how little"; "unorthodox analysis"; "my duty": Henderson, "How a Disturbed Genius Talked to His Analyst with Art," p. 28: Henderson also claimed that he failed to treat Jackson's alcoholism because "his symbolic drawings brought me strongly into a state of counter-transference to the archetypal material he produced." "The lives of artists"; natural balance always upset: C. G. Jung, *Modern Man in Search of a Soul*, p. 195. "Schizophrenic group": Also that Picasso's pictures "immediately reveal their alienation from feeling": Jung, *The Spirit in Man, Art and Literature*, translated by R.F.C. Hull (Princeton, N.J.: Princeton University Press, 1966), pp. 135–41. q. in Rubin, "Pollock as Jungian Illustrator, Part II," p. 87: Rubin notes that, in a clarifying note (p. 137 n.3) to the 1934 edition of the text (added after considerable controversy in the press), Jung backtracked and said he had not meant to say that Picasso was literally a schizophrenic but merely that he had a "disposition" to the disease: "Thus Picasso is not 'psychotic'; he simply has a 'habitus' which leads him 'to react to a profound psychic disturbance not with an ordinary psychoneurosis but with a schizoid syndrome.' " "Everything in the unconscious": Jung, *Memories, Dreams, and Reflections*, prologue, p. 3. Henderson raised by Navajo: Hill, "J.L.H.," p. 10. "Obsessed": Q. in Hill, "J.L.H.," p. 10. Visits to the Zuni and Sia tribes: Hill, "J.L.H.," p. 10. Lecture on rituals: Hill, "J.L.H.," p. 19. Racial memory: According to Jung (Wolfe, "Jungian Aspects of JP's Imagery," p. 70), "Americans are all possessed by an Indian soul. . . . It is noteworthy that Pollock has chosen images from Jung that were originally produced on the American continent." See also C. G. Jung Institute, p. 56. When Henderson himself allegedly disputed Jung's notion that "Americans are all possessed by an Indian soul," Jung asked him about his most recent dream. Henderson's associations included the image of some Indian women in his childhood home of Elko, Nevada, carrying their papooses. "Jung's laughter in response," writes the Jungian scholar, "convinced him that Jung was right, that the American psyche does contain an Indian component," Hill, "J.L.H.," pp. 9–10. Two penciled doodles: OC&T 950, IV, pp. 32–33; it was at this time that snakes and arrows entered JP's artistic vocabulary for the first time, more likely a result of his contact with Henderson than of his familiarity with Orozco, as inferred by FVOC, "The Genesis of JP," p. 191. Gouaches with Indian motifs: OC&T 946–49, IV, pp. 28–31; see also OC&T 554, III, p. 116, which incorporates a tableau painted in an Indian-like geometric style and filled with Indian motifs, and *Circle* (OC&T 64, I, pp. 50–51), a circular work on Masonite approximately eleven inches in diameter, incorporating a number of intertwined snakes, painted in red, yellow, blue, and green with some black. In OC&T 65, I, pp. 50–51, JP incorporates both the enriched Indian palette (with areas of bright yellow, red, and blue with green and black) and a number of seemingly Indian motifs—a chaotic grouping of horses, snakes, arrows, feathers, and lightning bolts—all presided over by a woman, seen in profile and depicted with Stella-like implacability. These Indian gouaches are related to a series of paintings by John Graham. See, for example, *Interior*, c. 1939–40, cat. 29, in Green, p. 105. Shamanistic masks: Compare with OC&T 946, IV, p. 28; see also OC&T 70, I, p. 55; 77, I, p. 60; 78, I, p. 61; and 79, I, p. 62. "Alarming aspect": Coe, p. 128. Conversation with Wingert: Busa. Celebrating mythological past: Coe, p. 125. Associations with animals: Coe, p. 127. Carvings: Coe, p. 126. Jackson's reaction to Indian art: SLM, int. by Vallière, Aug. 1963: "Jackson disliked innate objects," adding that what he liked about the Indian objects they saw together was "Two heads in one." Bull attacking woman: OC&T 507, III, p. 87. Bull transforming into man: OC&T 557, III, p. 118. Horse transforming into snake: OC&T 534, III, p. 104. Snake in womb: OC&T 531, III, p. 102; also: a bull, OC&T 495, III, p. 80; a horse and bull, OC&T 536, III, p. 106; snakes, bulls, and birds, OC&T 561, III, p. 120, and 563, III, p. 121; a bizarre image divided into three strict horizontal parts: human lying down on top, horse standing in middle, snake uncoiled along the bottom,

OC&T 550, III, p. 114; animals struggling with men, OC&T 545–48, pp. 112–13.

23. INTIMATIONS OF IMMORTALITY

SOURCES

Books, articles, manuscripts, and transcripts

Allen, *Since Yesterday*; Alloway and MacNaughton, *Adolph Gottlieb*; Ashton, *The New York School*; Centre Georges Pompidou, *JP*; Diamonstein, ed., *The Art World*; Diamonstein, ed., *Inside New York's Art World*; Graham, *System and Dialectics of Art*; Green, *John Graham*; C. G. Jung Institute, *The Shaman from Elko*; Lukach, *Hilla Rebay*; McElvaine, *The Great Depression*; McKinzie, *The New Deal for Artists*; *New York Panorama*; OC&T, *JP*; Potter, *To a Violent Grave*; Rose, *LK*; Schwankovsky, *Art Appreciation Essays*; Solomon, *JP*.

Alfred M. Frankfurter, "Picasso in Retrospect: 1939–1900: The Comprehensive Exhibition in New York and Chicago," *Art News*, Nov. 18, 1939; John Graham, "Primitive Art and Picasso," *Magazine of Art*, Apr. 1937; CG, "New York Painting Only Yesterday," *Art News*, Summer 1957; Hayden Herrera, "John Graham: Modernist Turns Magus," *Arts*, Oct. 1976; Gareth S. Hill, "J.L.H.: His Life and His Work," in C. G. Jung Institute; Eila Kokkinen, "John Graham During the 1940s," *Arts*, Nov. 1976; Elizabeth Langhorne, "Department of Jungian Amplification, Part II: More on Rubin on Pollock, *Art in America*, Oct. 1980; Gerald M. Monroe, "Artists as Militant Trade Union Workers During the Great Depression," *AAA Journal* 1964; Gerald M. Monroe, "The '30s: Art, Ideology and the WPA," *Art in America*, Nov.–Dec. 1975; "Reports of Talks by J. Kirshnamurti," *International Star Bulletin*, July 1930; Barbara Rose, "Arshile Gorky and John Graham: Eastern Exiles in a Western World," *Arts*, Mar. 1976; William Rubin, "Pollock as Jungian Illustrator: The Limits of Psychological Criticism, Part I," *Art in America*, Dec. 1979; Irving Sandler, "Department of Jungian Amplification, Part II: More on Rubin on Pollock," *Art in America*, Oct. 1980; Irving Sandler, "John D. Graham: The Painter as Esthetician and Connoisseur," *Artforum*, Oct. 1968; Sidney Tillim, "The Alloway International," *Arts*, Mar. 1964; Judith Wolfe, "Jungian Aspects of JP's Imagery," *Artforum*, Nov. 1972.

Ellen Gross Landau, "LK: A Study of Her Early Career (1926–1949)" (Ph.D. thesis), Newark: University of Delaware, 1981; FVOC, "The Genesis of JP: 1912 to 1943" (Ph.D. thesis), Baltimore: Johns Hopkins University, 1965.

Fritz Bultman, int. by Irving Sandler, Jan. 1, 1968, AAA; LK, int. by Barbara Rose, July 31, 1966, AAA.

Interviews

Lionel Abel; Fritz Bultman; Eda Bunce; Peter Busa; Nicholas Carone; Dorothy Dehner; Anne Edgerton; Ron Gorchov; Eleanor Green; CG; Reuben Kadish; Gerome Kamrowski; Lillian Olaney Kiesler; Ruth Kligman; LK; Harold Lehman; ACM; Jack Mayer; David Porter; May Tabak Rosenberg; Nene Schardt; Herman Somberg; Hedda Sterne; Wally Strautin; Roger Wilcox.

NOTES

Unemployment figures: Allen, p. 266. World's Fair: *New York Panorama*, pp. 487–500. Jackson going to Ferndale: SLM to CCP, June 3, 1939. Quarry: Schardt. Trips to town: Bunce. Garden; fruit trees; "the farming": Schardt. No lights; butter and beer: Bunce. Jay, Alma, and Meerts visiting: Schardt. Strautins and Goldsteins: Strautin. Trips into New York: Schardt. "Everyone was drinking": Bunce. Cut 1,500 artists: FVOC, "The Genesis of JP," p. 72. "We have been investigated"; "my pack of lies": SLM to CCP, March 1939. More than 775,000 lost jobs: McElvaine, p. 308. Loyalty oath: McKinzie, p. 163. WPA Art Program: FVOC, "The Genesis of JP," p. 73, citing "The United States Government Art Projects, A Brief Summary," excerpted by the Department of Circulating Exhibitions, MOMA, from annual articles on painting and sculpture prepared by Dorothy C. Miller for *Collier's* Yearbook (1935–43). State and local control: McKinzie, p. 149. "Force account": McKinzie, p. 116.

Artists' demonstrations: See Monroe, "Artists as Militant Trade Union Workers," pp. 7–10, and Monroe, "The '30s," pp. 64–67. **"We are defeated":** Rose, pp. 39–40. **"[He said,] one person"; "force and vitality"; "one knew exactly":** LK, int. by Rose, July 31, 1966. **"He has painted everything":** John Graham, q. in Herrera, "John Graham," p. 104. **"Little bit":** Q. in Greenberg, "New York Painting Only Yesterday," p. 85. **"Picasso is the greatest":** John Graham, q. in Herrera, "John Graham," p. 102.

Description of Graham: Graham. **Eyes:** Solomon, p. 101. **"You always knew":** Q. in Herrera, "John Graham," p. 104. **Receiving friends in the nude; acrobatic tricks:** Wilcox. **Clothing:** Gorchov. **Monocle:** Rose, "Arshile Gorky and John Graham," p. 63. **Bought on Third Avenue:** Solomon, p. 101. **Posture:** Busa. **Graham's intellect;** Herrera, "John Graham," p. 105. **"We want bread!"** De Kooning recalling Graham, q. in Herrera, "John Graham," p. 105. **"A universal genius":** Q. in Rose, "Arshile Gorky and John Graham," p. 64. **"Any repetitive act":** Kokkinen, "John Graham During the 1940s," p. 101. **Smoking "primitive"; "the proliferation":** Graham, q. by Wilcox. **Interest in rich women:** Rosenberg. **Staring at women's feet on the beach:** Porter. **"Women should be wounded":** Q. by Dehner. **"Utterly charming":** Dehner. **"Extremely elegant":** Sterne. **"Very sophisticated":** Kligman.

Intimate of Imperial family: See Dehner, foreword to Graham, p. xvi; Kokkinen, "John Graham During the 1940s," p. 100; Dehner. **Portrait of Czar Nicholas:** Dehner; Sterne. It was typical of his eccentricity that he also displayed portraits of Saint Nicholas and Nicholas Lenin. **"When I grew up":** Q. in Herrera, "John Graham," p. 103. **Graham's age:** Wilcox; Kligman.

Graham born in 1887: According to a certified copy of Graham's baptismal records, he was born on December 27, 1886, by the Julian calendar then in use in Poland and Russia, or on January 8 or 9, 1887, by the Gregorian calendar; Green, p. 133. **Versions of ancestry:** Rose, "Arshile Gorky and John Graham," p. 64. **Nobility in his blood:** Green, p. 133. **Baptized in Kiev:** On Dec. 1, 1891, in a Roman Catholic church; Green, p. 133. **Imperial Lyceum:** Enrolled in 1899; Green, p. 133. **Law degree:** Dehner, forword to Graham, p. xvi. He received the equivalent of a J.D. from the University of St. Vladimir in 1913; Green, p. 134. Despite his later claims, Graham never held a judgeship. **Two children:** Kyril (Green, p. 134) and Maria; Edgerton. **Cavalry experience:** Kokkinen, "John Graham During the 1940s," p. 100. **Coronet:** Contrary to Graham's later claims, a relatively low rank; Green, p. 134. **St. George Cross:** Allentuck, introduction to Graham, p. 10; Green, p. 134. **Three crosses:** Obituary, *Art News*, Sept. 1961, p. 46, cited in FVOC, "The Genesis of JP," p. 79. **Joining counterrevolution:** Allentuck, introduction to Graham, p. 11. **Imprisoned with czar:** Green (p. 134) concludes "this story cannot be supported." **Second wife:** Married to twenty-three-year-old Vera Aleksandrovna Sept. 24, 1918, in Moscow; Green, p. 135. **Southhampton to New York:** Arrived in New York Nov. 28, 1920; Green, pp. 135–36. **Studied with John Sloan:** Allentuck, introduction to Graham, p. 12. Graham studied at the League from 1922 to 1924; Kokkinen, "John Graham During the 1940s," p. 100. **Presenting himself as Continental:** Allentuck, introduction to Graham, p. 12. **Exponent of Cubism:** Dehner, foreword to Graham, p. xiv; Dehner; Edgerton. **Meeting Picasso; frequent trips to Paris:** Dehner. **Doubts about claims to European travel:** Green. **"A connoisseur":** Rose, "Arshile Gorky and John Graham," p. 62. **"The best young painter":** Q. by David Smith in "Notes on My Work," *Arts*, Feb. 1960, q. in Landau, "LK," p. 192. **"His annual trips":** Smith in "Notes on My Work," *Arts*, Feb. 1960, q. in Landau, "LK," p. 192. **"A missionary":** CG. **Third wife:** Married to Elinor Gibson Jan. 9, 1924; Green, pp. 137–38. **Imitating Cloisonnism:** Allentuck, introduction to Graham, p. 20; see *Abstraction*, 1931, in the Phillips Collection, Washington, D.C. Kamrowski: "The Art Students League was a conservative bastion, and the only modernists on the New York scene were Graham and Hofmann, Gorky and Stuart Davis. No one else had the intellectual discipline to do a cubist picture." **Stopped painting:** Herrera, "John Graham," p. 104. **"The monastery"; "a suffering"; "to freshen the air":** Dehner, foreword to Graham, p. xvii. **"[Graham's] introduction":** "Notes on My Work," *Arts*, Feb. 1960, q. in Landau, "LK," p. 192. **Graham's book:** On its publication in 1937, *Art Digest* (May 15, 1937, p. 31) called it "a catechism of art, covering every angle in hundreds of

questions and answers. Necessarily dogmatic, provocative, and stimulating, by an artist in the movement"; q. in Allentuck, introduction to Graham, p. 43. **"Young outstanding"; "some are just as good":** Graham, p. 154. **Graham hired by Rebay:** Green, p. 141. Edgerton, archivist at the Solomon R. Guggenheim Museum: Graham never worked at the museum itself although both he and his fourth wife, Constance Wellman, worked for Rebay prior to the museum's opening in 1939. Lukach (p. 153) and Kamrowski say Graham worked as an assistant to Rebay in her capacity as curator. **Eighth Street apartment:** MJP and ABP were also in the apartment that summer. **Schardts becoming neighbors of Graham; Graham and JP meeting soon afterward:** Schardt. Arloie recalls that the Schardts introduced JP and Graham, but Schardt denies this. **Graham at Waldorf Cafeteria:** Gorchov, recalling Graham. **Graham's afternoon teas:** Kokkinen, "John Graham During the 1940s," p. 99.

The date and circumstances of JP's first encounter with Graham are unclear. By one account (which Green, p. 141, accepts), JP was so impressed by the "insight" in Graham, "Primitive Art and Picasso," that he wrote and tried to get in touch with him soon after it appeared in 1937; LK, int. by Ellen Landau, Feb. 28, 1979, q. in Landau, "LK," p. 178. But Krasner never said that JP and Graham actually became friends at this point. Sterne: JP "would have had to have met him soon after the article appeared." Gorchov puts the date even earlier: "He did reminisce a lot about Jackson Pollock after he died. He said that in the '30s—around '35, '36, '37, '38—they always got together at the Waldorf Cafeteria." O'Connor (OC&T IV, p. 221) assumes JP met him "in April, May or June of 1937 after reading his article," an assumption based on information provided him by William Lieberman to the effect that Graham considered putting JP's name in the second edition of *System and Dialectics of Art*, of which there was no lifetime second edition. But Graham presumably could have been rethinking that list any time after 1937.

JP himself described his first meeting with Graham (to Carone): "I went to see Graham because he knew something about art and I had to know him. I knocked on his door, and I told him I had read the article and that he *knew*. Graham looked at me and looked at me, then said, 'Come in.' " A dramatic story, perhaps, but an unlikely one. In the spring of 1937, while JP slouched toward Bloomingdale's, Graham was still in an out-of-the-way Brooklyn garret (Edgerton: Graham's address was One Sidney Place) surrounded by a coterie of young artists (Kokkinen, "John Graham During the 1940s," p. 99), none of whom knew JP until the 1940s; Dehner. That summer, JP embarked on the long journey from Pennsylvania to Martha's Vineyard to Kansas City that would end the following summer in White Plains. Moreover, it is highly possible that JP failed to see the article when it first appeared. Bunce: "Jack didn't discuss the magazines much in those days because none of us was affluent enough. I suppose he would get ahold of the art magazines somewhere, somehow, but it wasn't a major part of his life."

"Jackson had a unique place": Mayer. Graham (q. by Bultman) later said "that 'Jackson was a good boy—a good character—despite his shenanigans." **"Really crazy":** Constance Graham, q. in Solomon, p. 101. **"Who the hell":** Q. in Allentuck, introduction to Graham, p. 22. **Franklin stove:** Busa. **"Theorizing":** Kokkinen, "John Graham During the 1940s," p. 99. **Copy of *System and Dialectics*:** Graham inscribed the copy (no. 503 of the Delphic Studios limited edition) "To Jackson Pollock from Graham"; Landau, "LK," p. 194. **Taking works to Graham:** Kadish. **"The greatest of all arts":** Dehner, foreword to Graham, p. xiv. **Yoruba, Gouro, and Gabonese works:** Allentuck, introduction to Graham, p. 79. **Crowninshield collection:** Edgerton: Graham actually assembled the collection for Condé Nast, the company that owned *Vanity Fair*. Green, p. 140: He began buying for Crowninshield as early as 1933. **Graham displaying collection:** Schardt. **"Lyric"; "majestic"; "awesome";** Graham, p. 131. **"Wholly different principles"; "spiritual emotions":** Graham, preface to "Exhibition of Sculptures of Old African Collections . . . Organized by John Graham" (New York: Jacques Seligmann Gallery, 1936), q. by Allentuck, introduction to Graham, p. 77. **Primitive races:** Q. in Sandler, "John D. Graham," p. 52. **"It should be understood":** Q. in Sandler, "John D. Graham," p. 52. **"Into the canyons":** Herrera, "John Graham," p. 104; see Allentuck, introduction to Graham, p. 42. **"Bring

to our consciousness": Q. in Sandler, "John D. Graham," p. 52. **Pulled from "inside":** Busa.
Color the essence: Hofmann; see Rose, p. 46. Sandler ("John D. Graham," p. 51), however, argues that Hofmann considered line more important than color. **"Gesture, like voice":** Graham, p. 165. **Admiration for draftsmen:** Graham, p. 105; also Mondrian. **"Automatic":** Graham, p. 135. **"Authentic":** Graham, p. 165. **"Imitation of nature":** Q. in Herrera, "John Graham," p. 102. **"No technical perfection":** Graham, p. 134. **"Clear up":** JP to CCP, n.d. **"Neither faithful nor distorted":** Graham, p. 134.

Introduction to Picasso: Several writers have noted the coincidence that "Pollock's analysis [with Henderson] was situated in the context of the arrival of the most influential of Picasso's works in the United States"; Marcelin Pleynet, "Pollock, Jung et Picasso," interview with Claire Stoullig, in Centre Georges Pompidou, p. 46. Sandler ("Department of Jungian Amplification, Part II," pp. 57–58) also notes that "Graham's linking of primitive art, Picasso's painting, and 'the deepest recesses of the Unconscious' (where Graham said Picasso delved) may have prompted Jackson Pollock to enter Jungian analysis or at least may have allayed possible doubts about his Jungian psychiatrist, Dr. Joseph Henderson."

Trip to Arensberg home: Lehman. **Seeing *Three Musicians;* trips to see *Guernica:*** Busa. ***Guernica*-inspired sketches:** See OC&T 607, III, p. 148; OC&T 490, III, p. 77; OC&T 500, p. 82; OC&T 521, III, p. 96; OC&T 540, p. 109. **"Step outside":** Somberg. **Picasso retrospective:** "Picasso: Forty Years of his Art," mounted by Barr at MOMA, Nov. 15, 1939–Jan. 7, 1940. **"The master"; "the painter"; "the most fertile"; "an accepted classic":** Frankfurter, "Picasso in Retrospect," excerpted in Diamonstein, ed., *Art World,* p. 152.

"Picasso drops": Graham, p. 169. **Graham's admiration for cloisonnism:** As exhibited in Graham's 1931 painting, *Abstraction,* now in the Phillips Collection in Washington, D.C.; see Kokkinen, "John Graham During the 1940s," p. 100. **"The period of the greatest":** Q. in Sandler, "John D. Graham," p. 51. **"Refute modeling":** Q. in Allentuck, introduction to Graham, p. 79; see Graham, p. 181. **Assailing obsession with hygiene:** Rose, p. 46: "In Graham's view, accidents should be cultivated, not avoided, and a dramatic, emotional painterly style was preferable to pristine surfaces and hard edges." **Limitations of mediums:** Graham, q. in Sandler, "John D. Graham," p. 51: "The difference between the arts arises because of the difference in the nature of the mediums of expression."

"Terribly important": LK, int. by Rubin. **"Picasso's painting":** Q. in Sandler, "Department of Jungian Amplification, Part II," p. 57. **Rejection of facility:** Sterne: "Picasso had tremendous talent all his life, and he fought it. If you look at his early work, he could easily have been a 'pretty' artist, but he went against his facility." **Using Picasso's sketches:** The drawings had been published in *Cahiers d'art,* vol. 12, no. 4–5, 1937; see Langhorne, "Department of Jungian Amplification, Part II," p. 61, citing interview with Bultman. **Sure, lyrical, expressive works:** For example, OC&T 607, III, p. 148. **Woman throwing back her head:** OC&T 507, III, p. 87. **Horses rearing:** OC&T 490, III, p. 77; 500, III, p. 82; 521, III, p. 96; 540, III, p. 109. **Bull pawing ground:** OC&T 495, III, p. 80; 507, III, p. 87. **Heads transforming into masks:** See OC&T 70, I, p. 55; 77, I, p. 60; 78, I, p. 61; and 79, I, p. 62. See also the drawings given to Henderson: OC&T 503, III, pp. 84–85 and OC&T 544, III, p. 111. *Reclining Woman:* OC&T 69, I, p. 54. Decorative geometric forms, clearly Picassoid in origin (note diamond patterns in *Girl before a Mirror*), serve as the background to the main figure.

Picasso's drawings and gouaches: *Composition with Minotaur (Curtain for Le 14 Juillet)* of Romain Rolland, May 28, 1936; see also *Minotaur, Horse, and Bird,* Aug. 5, 1936. Rubin, "Pollock as Jungian Illustrator," p. 110: "The Cretan Minotaur of the Theseus legend—half-man, half-bull—became Picasso's 'alter-ego.' " **JP looking at *Cahiers d'art:*** Busa; see also Rubin, "Pollock as Jungian Illustrator," p. 110. **"As symbols of Eros"; Picasso's bull different from Jackson's:** Rubin, "Pollock as Jungian Illustrator," p. 110: That Picasso's bull also carried a political message—his bull was, in many of these images, a symbol of the hated Franco as well as of "irrational impulses and undirected libido"—did not make the image any the less powerful for Jackson.

Le Maître: Dehner. **Jackson integrating Picasso:** Tillim, "The Alloway International," p. 59, "Pollock had more success with Picasso than any of his contemporaries because

his ambivalence ruled out any likelihood of complete subservience to any artistic authority." **Grotesque man-beasts:** OC&T 71, I, p. 56; 77, I, p. 60; 79, I, p. 62; 80, I, p. 63. **Terrorizing harpies:** OC&T 68, I, p. 53; 508, III, p. 88. *Bird:* OC&T 72, I, pp. 56–57.

24. THE WAGES OF GENIUS

SOURCES

Books, articles, manuscripts, document, and transcripts

Ashton, *The New York School;* Ashton, *Yes, But . . . ;* Barr, *Matisse;* Cohen, *Notable American Women;* Friedman, *JP;* Graham, *System and Dialectics of Art;* Henderson, *Thresholds of Initiation;* Josephson, *Infidel in the Temple;* C. G. Jung Institute, *The Shaman from Elko;* McElvaine, *The Great Depression;* McKinzie, *The New Deal for Artists;* FVOC, ed., *The New Deal Art Projects;* Peabody, *The Common Sense of Drinking;* Potter, *To a Violent Grave;* Rubin, ed., *Pablo Picasso;* Solomon, *JP;* Weld, *Peggy;* Wysuph, *JP.*

Bruce Glaser, "JP: An Interview with LK," *Arts,* Apr. 1967; Donald E. Gordon, "Department of Jungian Amplification, Part I: Pollock's 'Bird,' or How Jung Did Not Offer Much Help in Myth-Making," *Art in America,* Oct. 1980; Hayden Herrera, "John Graham: Modernist Turns Magus," *Arts,* Oct. 1976; Gareth S. Hill, "J.L.H.: His Life and His Work," in C. G. Jung Institute; "How a Disturbed Genius Talked to His Analyst with Art," *Medical World News,* Feb. 5, 1971; Eila Kokkinen, "John Graham During the 1940s," *Arts,* Nov. 1976; Carter Ratcliffe, "New York Today: Some Artists Comment," *Art in America,* Sept.–Oct., 1977; William Rubin, "Pollock as Jungian Illustrator: The Limits of Psychological Criticism, Part I," *Art in America,* Dec. 1979.

David Hale, "Ex-Fresnan, artist Manuel Tolegian, dead at age 72," *Fresno Bee,* Sept. 4, 1983.

Joseph L. Henderson, "JP: A Psychological Commentary" (lecture); Ellen Gross Landau, "LK: A Study of Her Early Career (1926–1949)" (Ph.D. thesis, Newark: University of Delaware, 1981; FVOC, "The Genesis of JP: 1912 to 1943" (Ph.D. thesis), Baltimore: Johns Hopkins University, 1965.

Chronology prepared by CCP for EFP, Feb. 1975, AAA. Reuben Kadish, int. by James T. Vallière, AAA; Manuel Tolegian, int. by Betty Hoag, Feb. 12, 1965, AAA.

Interviews

Lionel Abel; Paul Brach; Eda Bunce; Peter Busa; Dorothy Dehner; Violet de Laszlo; Ron Gorchov; Janet Hauck; Joseph Henderson; Reuben Kadish; Gerome Kamrowski; LK; Maria Piacenza Kron; Harold Lehman; ACM; George McNeil; Eleanor Ribak Mandelman; Sam Naifeh; CCP; Harry Rand; Miriam Schapiro; Nene Schardt; Rachel Scott; Gertrude Shibley; Hedda Sterne; Wally Strautin; Araks Tolegian; Steve Wheeler; Roger Wilcox; C. L. Wysuph.

NOTES

Charles at Michigan State: CCP. **Sande looking for job:** Schardt; Strautin. Schardt: "It was as if Sande was removing himself psychically in order not to interfere with Jackson's development." Strautin: "He didn't want to be in a competition with Jackson." **Avant-garde:** See Ashton, *The New York School,* p. 31; see also Glaser, "JP," p. 36. **Graham making introductions:** Dehner, preface to Graham, p. xviii: "Graham was a generous friend in so many ways, generous with his knowledge, his praise, and his friends. It was through him that we met Avery, Stuart Davis, Gorky, Xceron, Friedrick Kiesler, and others in the early days of our friendship. He delighted in bringing people together who he thought might enjoy one another." **"[He] preferred":** Kokkinen, "John Graham During the 1940s," p. 100. **"The best sculptor":** Q. in Kokkinen, "John Graham During the 1940s," p. 99. **Dehner:** Dehner. **"Young outstanding American painters":** Q. in Allentuck, introduction to Graham, p. 12; listed in the holograph revisions of *System and Dialectics.* **Sterne:** Sterne. **De Kooning:** Gorchov. **"One knew who was painting":** LK, q. in Glaser, "JP," p. 36. **Waldorf and Stewart's:** Kron; Landau, "LK," p. 46. **Ratner's:** At 138 Delancey Street; Brach; Schapiro. **Romany Marie's:** At 55 Grove Street; Busa. **Jumble Shop:** Eighth and MacDougal streets; Ratcliffe, "New York Today," p. 82. **"Gra-**

ham's latest account": Ashton, *The New York School,* p. 31. "The years": Q. in Friedman, p. 69.

Wilson, Edie, and Musick departing; patronizing German bar: Kadish. **"Trying to get a foot":** Bunce. **Schardt:** Schardt. **Ribak:** Mandelman, who called him "Sloan's favorite student." **"Went ape":** Hauck: "That's why he liked us so much, because we liked his work." **At ease with Kadish:** Kadish: From 1930 until September 1938, he came to New York "every chance I got"; moved there for good in 1944–45. JP was also at ease with Meert; Shibley.

Graham's erudition and memory: Wilcox. **"A couple of ales":** Kadish. **Visits to museums:** Kadish; Lehman. In a visit to the Seligmann gallery, JP and Sande (to Kadish, n.d.) saw "about twelve El Grecos—most of which are heads but one crucifixion of outstanding quality." **"Flamelike vibrancy"; "a horse sniffing":** Kadish, int. by Vallière, n.d.: JP saw the work in reproduction in a book at the Frick Collection library. **Visiting "Indian Art" exhibition:** FVOC, "The Genesis of JP," pp. 190–91; de Laszlo, q. in Gordon, "Department of Jungian Amplification," p. 53. The exhibition lasted from January 22 to April 27, 1941. **Graham accompanying him:** Constance Graham, q. in Solomon, p. 102. **Graham educating Jackson:** Gorchov; Schardt. **Klee and Kandinsky exhibitions:** Michael Loew, q. in Potter, p. 61. **Beckmann exhibition:** Weld, p. 302. **"[Jack's] thinking":** SLM to CCP, July 1941. **Awareness of Miró:** The Gallery of Living Art had six paintings by Miró (FVOC, "The Genesis of JP," p. 196), and MOMA held a major Miró retrospective, Nov. 19, 1941–Jan. 11, 1942. **"He had an aesthetic":** Q. in Potter, p. 59. **"Highly intelligent":** De Laszlo. **"No interest in Cubism":** Wheeler.

"Jack is doing": SLM to CCP, May 1940. **Date of Marot's phone call:** Henderson, "JP," p. 22: The phone call was about a week prior to Marot's death on June 3, 1940. **Marot's visit to studio:** Scott. **" 'I saw Jackson' ":** Q. in Friedman, p. 43. **Marot's death:** Cohen, p. 502. **Binge:** Henderson. **Jackson destroying his own work:** De Laszlo; Kadish. **"A truly glorious wake":** Q. in Friedman, p. 43. Henderson ("JP," p. 22) later claimed that JP "became" a chronic alcoholic several years *after* he left Henderson's care; "JP," p. 3. **Henderson admitting ineffectiveness; "Thence forward [I] dwelt":** Q. in Friedman, p. 44. *The Common Sense of Drinking:* By R. R. Peabody, Boston: Little, Brown, 1931. JP noted the book on a drawing, OC&T 439, III, p. 46.

"Discovered": Wysuph, p. 17. **"Human deprivation":** Henderson, p. 111: In the light of his analytic findings, Henderson revamped some of his earlier assessments of JP's drawings—and discovered "the state of human deprivation" that still existed "on the personal level of his life," with "pathetic limbs reaching up toward an unfeeling, abstract kind of feminine image most probably denot[ing] the problem which remained to be solved." **"Need for the 'all-giving mother' ":** Wysuph, p. 17. **"Violent agitation"; "paralysis or withdrawal":** Q. in Wysuph, p. 14. Henderson repeatedly asserted ("How a Disturbed Genius Talked to His Analyst with Art," p. 28) the schizophrenic nature of JP's illness (his "schizoid tendency") only to contradict himself repeatedly and say that he was not schizophrenic, although he was often close to it; "JP," p. 14. Wysuph says Henderson told him that "Pollock was the most schizoid artist he ever knew." De Laszlo referred to his "rather schizoid isolation" but said she preferred "to speak of syndromes, meaning a group of symptoms, rather than of the illness"; q. in Potter, p. 66. She agrees that he was manic-depressive and says that, all the time they were acquainted, he was in a sustained depressive phase. Sam Naifeh, a colleague of Henderson's, says the confusion of terminology is understandable: "It is easy to confuse manic-depression and schizophrenia in their acute forms, especially among alcoholics." The difference is that the manic-depressive has the ability to rebound from manic and depressive episodes—"particularly if the person is supported and helped. If they are, then between episodes they are very normal. In the schizophrenic, the process is so constant that you sometimes find a deterioration of personality, and thus you see the low affect and the emptied-out human being." Henderson cited drawings to prove each of the conditions he diagnosed; see Wysuph, pp. 14–15. For his "violent agitation," see Wysuph, plates nos. 2 and 3; for his "state of withdrawal," see Wysuph, plates nos. 16 and 64; for his "introversion," see Wysuph, plate no. 10. William Rubin has addressed some of Henderson's diagnoses based on an analysis of JP's art. In particular, Rubin notes that the "ambiguity of line"—that is, lines and shapes serving several functions" ("How a Disturbed Genius Talked to His Analyst with Art," p. 15)—is a stylistic device that was the "stock-in-trade of Miró and Masson in their hybrid personages and had also occasionally been employed by Picasso." Two other stylistic elements—a "claustrophobic compaction of forms within a specified area" and a "thin white line surround[ing] an agitated rendering of confused human and animal forms" —are also typical stylistic elements used by artists whose sanity has not been called into question; "Pollock as Jungian Illustrator," pp. 107–08.

"Novice in a tribal initiation rite": Q. in "How a Disturbed Genius Talked to His Analyst with Art," p. 25. **"Wild paroxysms":** Henderson, p. 110. **"Ritual death"; "ritual rebirth":** Henderson, p. 108. **"He had in fact suffered":** Henderson, p. 111. In Henderson's view, until Marot died, JP had managed to keep an unbalanced personality in some sort of artificial balance by resorting to others to complement his own strong intuitive function: he had relied on Marot "for his need to give and receive feeling," on Henderson himself "to help structure his thinking function toward achieving a more rational and objective view of his life and art," and on Sande for carrying "much of his reality function"; Wysuph, p. 17. With Marot gone, his four functions were once again out of balance. **"Wanted to paint"; "lashing out at competitors":** De Laszlo. **Descending on Gorky's apartment:** Busa. **Gorky's height; "immensely strong":** Rand. **"Nothing but shit":** Q. by Abel, recalling Gorky. Busa: JP said, "Why don't you get some shit in your work?" **Gorky threatening him:** Abel, recalling Gorky. **Tearing down Tolegian's paintings:** Araks Tolegian, recalling Manuel. **Tolegian selling work to White House:** Tolegian, int. by Hoag, Feb. 12, 1965; the painting was called *Cheyenne* and was purchased for one of the executive office buildings; see McKinzie, pp. 31–32, for description of White House purchase of thirty-two paintings from Corcoran exhibition. **Ferargil Galleries:** Between 1934 and 1941, Tolegian had a dozen one-man shows; Hale, "Ex-Fresnan, artist Manuel Tolegian, dead at age 72." **Jackson laying siege to Vandam Street building:** Araks Tolegian, recalling Manuel.

Time **article on Goldstein:** Kadish. **Goldstein having little WPA success:** Ashton, *Yes, But . . . ,* p. 34. **Goldstein winning competitions:** Lehman, citing a *P.M.* magazine illustration contest. **Mural for World's Fair:** McKinzie, p. 113. *Maintaining America's Skills* **winning prize:** Ashton, *Yes, But . . . ,* pp. 43–44: There was a rave review by Ruth Green Harris in the *NYT.* **"I haven't been up":** JP to CCP, n.d. **Jackson recovering in studio:** ACM. **"I haven't much to say":** JP to CCP, summer 1940. **"Hanging by a cord":** De Laszlo. **"Hint of suicide":** De Laszlo, q. in Potter, p. 68. **"Regrets, sorrow":** Q. in Herrera, "John Graham," p. 104. **Graham aware of Jackson's problems:** Sterne. **"Freud was on the right track":** Q. by Gorchov. **"Lay analyst":** Sterne; Wilcox. **Graham rejecting title; "nothing but listening":** Gorchov, speaking of similar sessions with Graham: "I would talk for hours and he would do nothing but listen. Once he said, 'This is the psychoanalytic method—just listening. Just meditating on what somebody says for a long time.' Sometimes I would be talking and he'd say, 'Do you mind if I just listen impassively?' And we would go on like that sometimes for an hour or two."

Henderson's dreams: Hill, "J.L.H.," in C. G. Jung Institute, pp. 21–22: The dreams were repeated images of train trips back and forth across the continent and names of midwestern places. **"Too stifling":** Hill, "J.L.H.," in C. G. Jung Institute, p. 21. **Henderson founding Jung Institute:** Naifeh. **Henderson's departure not traumatic:** Friedman, p. 43.

De Laszlo in New York: De Laszlo. **"It is frequently efficacious":** Henderson, p. 46: "One might assume that such a youth would need to work with a sympathetic older man with whom he might establish a positive homosexual transference and thereby win freedom from the regressive tendency to return to the mother for support. Yet this very good idea is frequently untenable because the feeling which could invest such a transference with the power of an initiation experience is still too bound in the original mother fixation. Only she or her surrogate can free him . . . " Henderson, p. 38: "Re-education in a psychological sense seems to require a recapitulation of the whole life history, a reactivation of the mother's image together with the childhood pattern of behavior all the way back to infancy. From there it may stretch into the depths of the collective unconscious, where the return is to the archetypal rather than to the personal mother." **De Laszlo's age:** She was twelve years older than Jackson. **Frequency of sessions; de Laszlo's living arrangements:** De Laszlo.

Minimum of Jung from de Laszlo: De Laszlo: "Dr. Henderson's approach was much more interpretive than mine." **Graham helping with de Laszlo's fee:** Sterne. **Bringing Graham to session:** Gordon, "Department of Jungian Amplification, Part I," p. 51: Graham gave her a copy of "Primitive Art and Picasso" at this time.

"Dear Sir": De Laszlo to Examining Medical Officer, Selective Service System, Local Board 17, May 3, 1941. **Examination at Beth Israel; statement from de Laszlo:** On May 26, de Laszlo wrote: "Dear Sir, Further to my letter to you with reference to Jackson Pollock, Order no. 867, Pollock has reported to me that he has undergone a special psychiatric interview at Beth Israel Hospital on May 22. On that occasion he was told to obtain from me a statement to the effect that he has been admitted to the Westchester Division of the New York Hospital on June 11, 1938. I have had occasion to see a letter from the then attending M.O., Dr. Wall, in which it was stated that Pollock would be dismissed in September of that same year.

"I can therefore testify that Jackson Pollock has been a resident free patient at the Westchester Division of the New York Hospital during four months in 1938. As far as I am aware he was admitted under the diagnosis of acute alcoholism."

Classified IV-F: De Laszlo to Examining Medical Officer, Selective Service System, Local Board 17, May 3, 1941. Pollock registered on Oct. 16, 1940. His order number was 867. For additional details, see FVOC, "The Genesis of JP," p. 75. **"Rejected"; "neurotic":** Q. by Ahron Ben-Shmuel, int. by FVOC, Dec. 2, 1963, q. in FVOC, "The Genesis of JP," p. 75. **Reinstatement on WPA:** FVOC, "The Genesis of JP," p. 21: His salary was cut to $87.60 per month. **Discovering Packard:** Bunce.

"Did you do this?"; "No. You did": Q. in Rubin, ed., p. 350. **Matisse in Nice:** Barr, p. 257. **Numbers of WPA works:** McKinzie, p. 105. **Furor over "communist infiltration":** See McKinzie, p. 165; see also Audrey McMahon, q. in FVOC, ed., p. 74. **"Bohemian chiselers":** Q. in Josephson, p. 384. **"Consumed the precious":** McCullough, p. 117. **"Ingrates":** McKinzie, p. 89; see Josephson, p. 384. **"A winter of ups and downs":** SLM to CCP, Oct. 22, 1940. **Loyalty oaths:** The new law in question was the Hatch Act; see McElvaine, p. 308. **Congressional mandate concerning Communists:** McKinzie, p. 165. **"They're dropping people":** SLM to CCP, Oct. 22, 1940. **Stella moving to Tingley:** MJP to CCP, Jan. 31, 1939; SMP to CCP, EFP, and Jeremy, 1939. She was still there in 1941; chronology prepared by CCP for EFP, Feb. 1975. **Letter to Charles: "definite neurosis"; "depressive mania"; "self-destruction"; "since part of [Jackson's] trouble":** SLM to CCP, July 1941. **Date of meeting Lee again:** ACM.

25. LENA KRASSNER

SOURCES

Books, articles, manuscripts, lectures, and transcripts

Ashton, *The New York School*; Chipp, ed., *Theories of Modern Art*; Feingold, *Zion in America*; Feldstein, *The Land That I Show You*; Friedman, *JP*; CG, *Art and Culture*; PG, *Out of This Century*; Howe, *World of Our Fathers*; Josephson, *Infidel in the Temple*; Kazin, *Starting Out in the Thirties*; McCullough, *Brooklyn*; Munro, *Originals*; Nemser, *Art Talk*; Potter, *To a Violent Grave*; Rose, *LK*; Solomon, *JP*; Weeks and Hayes, eds., *Search for the Real and Other Essays*; Whitechapel Gallery, *LK*.

Lawrence Campbell, "Of Lilith and Lettuce," *Art News*, Mar. 1968; Cynthia Goodman, "Hans Hofmann as a Teacher," *Arts*, Apr. 1979; CG, "Influences of Matisse," *Art International*, Nov. 1973; Elizabeth Pollett, "Hans Hofmann," *Arts*, May 1957; Louise Elliott Rago, "We Interview LK," *School Arts*, Sept. 1960; Barbara Rose, "LK and the Origins of Abstract Expressionism," *Arts*, Feb. 1977; Emily Wasserman, "LK in Mid-Career," *Artforum*, Mar. 1968.

David Bourdon, "LK: I'm Embracing the Past," *Village Voice*, Mar. 1977; Roberta Brandes Gratz, "Daily Closeup: After Pollock," *New York Post*, Dec. 1, 1973.

Ellen Gross Landau, "LK: A Study of Her Early Career (1926–1949)" (Ph.D. thesis), Newark: University of Delaware,

1981; FVOC, "The Genesis of JP: 1912 to 1943" (Ph.D. thesis), Baltimore: Johns Hopkins University, 1965; May Natalie Tabak, "A Collage" (unpub. ms.), n.d.

Fritz Bultman, "Hans Hofmann" (lecture), Hirshhorn Museum and Sculpture Garden, Washington, D.C., Nov. 1976, in Bultman files; LK (lecture), International Affairs Building, Columbia University, New York, Oct. 5, 1983.

Fritz Bultman, int. by Irving Sandler, Jan. 6, 1968, AAA; Lillian Kiesler, int. by Ellen Landau, Feb. 27, 1979; LK, int. by Barbara Rose, July 31, 1966, AAA: LK, int. by Dorothy Seckler, Dec. 14, 1967; Apr. 11, 1968; and Nov. 2, 1964, AAA.

Interviews

Peter Blake; Paul Brach; Fritz Bultman; Jeanne Bultman; Giorgio Cavallon; Herman Cherry; Deborah Daw; Ted Dragon; Ray Eames; Muriel Francis; B. H. Friedman; Esther Gersing; David Gibbs; Seymour Glickman; CG; Janet Hauck; Harry Holtzman; Richard Howard; Gerome Kamrowski; Rusty Kanokogi; Lillian Olaney Kiesler; LK; Maria Piacenza Kron; Ellen Landau; Ernestine Lassaw; Ibram Lassaw; John Lee; John Little; Beatrice Ribak Mandelman; Mercedes Matter; Donald McKinney; George McNeil; George Mercer; John Bernard Myers; May Tabak Rosenberg; Ronald Stein; Ruth Stein; Michael Stolbach; Steve Wheeler.

NOTES

Date of arrival and legend of conception: Ruth Stein; see also Landau, "LK," p. 19, citing LK files. **Shpikov:** Gersing. **Typical station departure:** Howe, p. 35. **"A person gone":** Marcus Ravage, q. in Howe, p. 35. **Financial problems and malnutrition:** Feingold, p. 115. **Steerage tickets:** Steerage from Bremen to New York in 1903 cost $33.50; the cost of getting to Bremen "perhaps half again as much"; Howe, p. 33.

Pogroms: Feingold, p. 117. **Kishinev incident:** Feldstein, p. 110. **Impact of Russo-Japanese War:** Feingold, p. 119. **Joseph a tobacco peddler:** Ruth Stein. **Shuka:** B. H. Friedman, introduction to Whitechapel Gallery, "LK," p. 5. **"Troublesome trifling":** Howe, p. 11. **"Tall and slender":** Abraham Cahan, q. in Feingold, p. 122. **Ellis Island:** Jewish immigrants called it the Isle of Tears; Feingold, p. 122; the Krassners arrived in a Dutch ship, the *Ryndam*; Landau, "LK," p. 19. **Jerome Street:** The address was 546 Jerome Street. **Fish and produce market:** LK later referred to it as a "food shop," but as Ruth says, "they were in the fish business." **"Nasty, little slum":** Q. in McCullough, p. 201; Riis was referring specifically to neighboring Brownsville.

Scale of emigration: Feingold, p. 120: 1,562,800 between 1881 and 1910. **Bringing the shtetl along; paternal role among Jews:** See Howe, pp. 172–73. **Character of Joseph Krassner:** Ruth Stein. **"Whom one did not speak to":** Paraphrase of Elizabeth Stern, q. in Howe, p. 173. **Moody and introspective:** Ronald Stein. **"Assert the moral right"; "if we needed":** Ruth Stein. **Father remaining in synagogue:** Rose, p. 13: "The Krassner family followed the classic pattern: Father Joseph was an introspective, sensitive man rooted in the Talmudic tradition of critical inquiry and philosophical debate. He owned a small produce store in Brooklyn, which was essentially run by his wife Anna, a practical, outgoing woman of strong character and constitution. Typically in such families, the women took care of the business and worldly affairs"; see Howe, pp. 8–11.

"She was all business": Ruth Stein. **Anna married at eleven:** Ruth Stein: "My mother says she doesn't think she was twelve when she was married. It was not so unusual— getting married very young, often at eight or nine years." **One child died:** Named Riva. **Lifting heavy boxes; "doing all the things":** Kanokogi. **Irving at home:** B. H. Friedman, introduction to Whitechapel Gallery, p. 5. **Strain of mysticism in family:** See Munro, p. 104. **Pesa:** Solomon, p. 112. **Storms:** Solomon, p. 111.

Longing for Russia: "The shock of transplantation and the sheer ugliness of the new environment lent to Old World life a golden glow," writes Feingold (p. 123). **Oedipal triangle:** According to Howe (p.176), "the Oedipal romance was peculiarly Jewish, perhaps even a Jewish invention." **"Any member of the family":** LK, q. in Nemser, p. 83; see Gibbs. **"A smattering of English":** LK, q. by Gibbs. **"Like living in some little ghetto":** Q. by Gibbs. **"An oddball"; "an outcast":** Q. by Dragon. **Early desire to leave home:** Gibbs, recalling LK. **Ruth's name changes:** Ruth Stein.

Photo of Lee and Ruth: In possession of Ruth Stein. **"Work-until-you-drop":** Kanokogi. **Relatives showing off Ruth:** Kanokogi; Ruth Stein.

Lee promenading as child; "a social call"; Lehmans, Granvilles: LK. **Irving dominating home:** Ruth Stein: "Our father was very passive. He just allowed Irving to take over. And believe me, Irving *enjoyed* it." **Lee reading fairy tales:** LK. **Coaxing friends to read to her:** Friedman; Howard. **Listening to Caruso recordings:** LK. **Irving and Lee both "tough":** Decades later, in the course of analysis, Ruth discovered that a pathological fear of horses ("If my mother knew there was a horse within two miles, she was inconsolable," says Ruth's son, Ronald), dating from childhood, was actually a legacy of her life with Lee and Irving. "I was afraid to walk into a strange room because I thought there might be a horse in there," she recalls. "At night, I would be terrified that a horse was following me up the stairs. Then the analyst found out who my horses were. The horses were Daddy, Irving, and Lee. I had three horses that were killing me." **The immovable object":** Ronald Stein. **"I crashed":** Q. in Nemser, p. 83.

"Jesus Christ [was] the Lord"; "he just wasn't mine": Q. in Gratz, "After Pollock." **"Condition of slavery":** Josephson, p. 25. **Neighbors considered mundane:** McKinney, recalling LK; see Josephson, p. 17. **"Colliding":** LK. **Copying advertisements:** Solomon, p. 111. **"Haphazard":** LK. **"Sounded more alive":** Friedman, p. 67. **Painting of Queen Isabella:** LK. **Graduating from P.S. 72; rejected by Washington Irving:** Landau, "LK," p. 21.

Urge to security: Josephson, pp. 17–18: "We might be of mixed English, German, Irish and French ancestry, or . . . Jewish, yet the prevailing 'Protestant Ethic' of middle-class America seemed to possess all our parents alike. They were anxious and mainly preoccupied with all that was material and useful in 'getting ahead.' " **Capital of Jewish culture; "Paris of the East":** Ibram Lassaw. **"The graphic arts":** Q. in Howe, p. 574. **Objects used in worship:** Howe, p. 578. **"Outside the boundaries":** Howe, p. 574. **Families against career in art:** The sculptor Jo Davidson heard from his father that to be an artist was to be "a loafer, a perpetual pauper, an absolutely useless person;" q. in Howe, p. 574. When Lassaw told his father of his plans to become an artist, "he thought I was crazy. He said, 'You'll starve to death.' He thought I was ruining my life." Cherry, who grew up in a Jewish family in Philadelphia, heard from his parents, "over and over, 'How will you make a living?' " Guston's parents, according to Cherry, "wanted him to become a furrier, because his whole family was furriers. They were dead set against him becoming an artist." In 1915, Tom Benton's old friend John Weichsel established an essentially Jewish People's Art Guild; Howe, p. 581. In 1917, the Educational Alliance reopened art classes after a twelve-year hiatus, and it soon attracted such future luminaries as Ben Shahn, Adolf Gottlieb, Louise Nevelson, Barnett Newman, and Mark Rothko; Howe, p. 577. Eventually, some Jewish artists—Shahn, Weber, the Soyer brothers —also turned their attention to Jewish subjects, but only after having immersed themselves in the styles of French art, many of them in Paris itself; Howe, p. 580. Even if Weber painted *Hasidic Dancers* or *The Rabbi,* even if Shahn did illustrations for the Haggadah (Howe, p. 581), the artistic vocabulary used to depict these Jewish subjects was never precisely Jewish. And as Harold Rosenberg was later to write, "Style, not subject matter or theme, will determine whether or not paintings should be considered 'Jewish' or placed in some other category"; q. in Howe, p. 582. The most that Howe and others have been able to find was "Some tonality of 'Jewishness' " in the paintings of Raphael Soyer and others (Howe, p. 584)— nothing more than an "aura," "tone," "posture," "inflection." And even this was to be lost as a younger generation, struggling to come up with original styles, managed to create art that no longer imitated European styles but that, in its originality, no longer reflected the aspiration toward Jewish styles; Howe, p. 584. **"Into the gentile unknown":** Howe, p. 574.

"A combination": Howe, p. 265. **"Quiet and modest":** Howe, p. 268. **Shopgirl or teacher:** Howe, p. 266. **Not allowed any opinions:** Paraphrased from Rebecca Kohut, q. in Howe, p. 265. **"The progression"; "came to value"; "some were even drawn"; "a niche of privacy":** Howe, p. 266. **"A woman alone":** Anzia Yezierska, q. in Howe, p. 269. **Family hardly noticing Lee:** LK: "[Art] meant nothing to them. Art only severed me further from my family;" see LK, q. in Nemser, p. 83. **Name changes:** Rose, p. 33; the change

took place about 1935. LK: "It just seemed one more letter to sign when you made your signature." But family members like Ruth viewed the change as "a symbolic divorce from the past." **"A mauve sweater":** Q. by Stolbach.

Decorating lampshades: Landau, "LK," p. 21. Lee flunked every course that year; Nemser, p. 83. **Admitted to Washington Irving:** LK, int. by Dorothy Seckler, Nov. 2, 1964. **"I am going to pass":** Q. by LK, q. in Nemser, p. 83; LK, int. by Dorothy Seckler, Nov. 2, 1964. **Giving small paintings away:** LK; John Lee. **"Terrible rush":** Kazin, p. 4. **"[It] revealed a style":** Josephson, p. 26. **Moving to Manhattan:** There was one false start. For a few months in 1926, Lee returned to Brooklyn and lived with Ruth and her new husband at their home at 557 Jerome Street; Landau, "LK," pp. 21–22. Lee's next oldest sister, Rose, had died, and according to Jewish custom, it was up to one of her unmarried sisters to marry her widowed husband and care for her two daughters. When Lee, the obvious choice, refused to marry her brother-in-law, fifteen-year-old Ruth dutifully stepped forward. When Lee returned to Manhattan for good, it was to an apartment near Fifth Avenue and Fifteenth Street; Landau, "LK," p. 25. **"Coming over the bridge":** Q. by Gibbs. **Alcove system:** LK, q. in Nemser, p. 83. **Hinton finding Lee's work "messy" and promoting her:** LK, int. by Landau, Feb. 21, 1980, q. in Landau, "LK," pp. 22–23. **"In utter disappointment":** LK, int. by Seckler, Nov. 2, 1964. **"I'm going to promote":** Hinton, q. by LK, int. by Seckler, Nov. 2, 1964. **Perard; hired by Perard to make drawings:** Landau, "LK," p. 23. **"Victor Perard was the first one":** LK. **Class at the Art Students League:** Rose, p. 18. **"Disdainful of her work":** LK. **"Infuriated"; "drew strength":** Mercer. **Modeling for Dykaar:** (1886–1933); his most famous sculptures were of Calvin Coolidge and Eugene V. Debs; see Landau, "LK," p. 39. **"Was no place for a young artist":** LK. **Academy accepting Lee:** Landau, "LK," p. 25.

Arriving at the academy: Landau, "LK," p. 25. **Description of academy:** Cavallon. **"We looked at each other":** LK, int. by Seckler, Apr. 11, 1968. **"I was very busy":** LK, int. by Seckler, Nov. 2, 1964. Cavallon, a fellow student at the academy, generously says "everybody was an average student there." **Probation:** Solomon, p. 112. **"Rarely got along":** Cavallon. **"A nuisance"; "impossible":** Rago, "We Interview LK," p. 31. **"Smart-alecky"; "too sure of herself":** Landau, "LK," p. 28, citing LK, int. by Landau, Jan. 15, 1979. Many of Lee's "offenses" seem trivial in retrospect, and indicate that the academy was even more stubborn than Lee. On December 7, 1929, for example, she was suspended for two days for substituting, without permission, a painting of a still life of a fish for the mandatory drawing in Charles Courtney Curran's life drawing class; Barbara S. Krulik to Landau, Sept. 26, 1979, q. in Landau, "LK," p. 28. **"This student":** Note by teacher in National Academy of Design file, q. in Solomon, p. 112.

Summer in Long Island: LK. **Nielsen's reaction to Lee's work:** LK. **"That's a dirty trick":** Q. by LK, q. in Nemser, p. 84; see Campbell, "Of Lilith and Lettuce," p. 63. **Judges skeptical:** Rose, p. 15. **"His reaction":** Q. in Nemser, p. 84; see Lawrence Campbell, "Of Lilith and Lettuce," p. 63. **"Painting figures":** Solomon, p. 112; Landau, "LK," p. 28. **Trip to the Heckscher Building:** Landau, "LK," p. 31, citing LK, int. by Landau, Feb. 21, 1980. **"Painting in Paris":** Jan. 19–Feb. 16, 1930. **"Really hit":** LK, int. by Seckler, Nov. 2, 1964: "The experience came through directly, not through an intellectual source. Nothing was said, but the aftereffects were automatic." **Incident at the academy; "brightly-checkered"; "No!"; "I can't do anything":** Q. in Campbell, "Of Lilith and Lettuce," p. 63. Lee Krasner described another such incident when a new female model applied for work: "She was wild. Her face was white, her hair was orange, she had purple eyelids and black around the eyes." As class monitor, Lee booked her immediately—"even though she wasn't exactly Academy stock." When the instructor, Leon Kroll—one of the more open-minded teachers on the faculty—saw the model, he demanded loudly, "Which one of you is the monitor?" Lee defiantly raised her hand. Kroll stalked to her easel, took one look at her painting, and screamed, "Young lady! Go home and take a mental bath!" "By now I suppose I must have seemed to [them] like some smart-aleck kid," she later said, "trying to imitate the French and show them all up"; q. in Campbell, "Of Lilith and Lettuce," p. 63.

The fact is that there was no consistent antagonism toward

Impressionist painting at the National Academy of Design in 1929. Several members of the faculty, including Lee's drawing instructor, Charles Curran, had adapted its lessons in their own landscapes of the period; Landau, "LK," p. 40 n. 31, referring specifically to Curran's *Rose Bower* of 1923 and Ivan Olinsky's *The Bathers* of 1928. Thus Lee's protests that her portrait owed nothing to the French painters she so admired —"I had simply tried to paint what I saw" (q. in Campbell, "Of Lilith and Lettuce," p. 63)—are difficult to accept. When it was pointed out that one of her own teachers, Curran, had adapted the new style in his paintings of the same period, she insisted that she had never seen Curran's paintings; Landau, "LK," p. 40 n. 31.

Relationship with Pantuhoff: It must have begun by early 1930, says Ronald Stein, because Igor painted a portrait of Joseph Krassner at that time. **Prix de Rome:** According to one academy official, it was only the "equivalent of a Prix de Rome"; letter from Barbara S. Krulik to Landau, Sept. 26, 1979, q. in Landau, "LK," p. 34. But Busa, Cavallon, Rosenberg, and Lee called it a Prix de Rome. Because of the turn in his style, Lee later said, "Igor's work was all right, but I didn't have enormous admiration for him." At the time, however, friends such as Cavallon remember, she was wildly impressed with his talents.

People puzzled by Pantuhoff's stories: Fritz Bultman. **Description of Pantuhoff:** Fritz Bultman; Jeanne Bultman; Francis; Rosenberg; Ronald Stein; Ruth Stein. **"Without a cent":** Kiesler. **Photo with Lake:** Ronald Stein; Sterne. **Claims to noble blood:** Rosenberg; Landau, "LK," p. 35, citing Barbara S. Krulik to Landau, Sept. 26, 1979, and interviews. **Seven years old:** Born Sept. 22, 1911. **Fleeing to Turkey; studying in Paris:** Fritz Bultman. **Florida businessman:** Francis: The man was Woody Kaylor. **Lincoln:** Ronald Stein. **Description of Pantuhoff:** Busa. **"[She] said only a man":** Rosenberg; see also LK. **Moving in with Pantuhoff:** Rosenberg. Among young male artists, having a wife or lover on the city payroll as a teacher was considered "a bonus miracle"; Rosenberg, "Art Project," in "A Collage," p. 188. CG: "Barney Newman, Adolph Gottlieb, and William Phillips, the editor of the *Partisan Review*, all had teachers for wives. High school teachers in those days made good money." Busa recalls a joke from the 1930s: "How do you become an artist? First, you marry a teacher."

"Withdraw from the field": LK. **Decision to become a teacher:** "I decided I would teach in the New York City high school system. So I went to CCNY to get my pedagogic credits"; q. in Nemser, p. 84. **Bright stockings; evening dress; nun's habit; makeup; feathers; wig:** Little. **Sparkle and gaiety:** Bultman. **"A kind of arrogance":** Kiesler, int. by Landau, Feb. 27, 1979. **"Animal energy":** Kiesler. **Books on Picasso:** At least one of the books on Picasso was Henri Mihaut's *Picasso* (Paris, 1930); Landau, "LK," p. 35, citing Mercer, int. by Landau, Oct. 30, 1979. He also gave her a copy of Jean René's *Raoul Dufy* (Paris, 1931). **Introducing Lee to Gorky and de Kooning:** Rosenberg; Bultman, int. by Sandler, Jan. 1, 1968. **"Igor sort of struggled":** Mercedes Matter. **"How much you get paid":** Q. by Little. **Amorous adventures:** In the midst of their relationship, Pantuhoff was busy making conquests among many different women, including a Cape Cod barkeeper; Little. **Complaints of snobbery:** Ibram Lassaw: "He thought of himself as closer to the nobility than he was, and therefore as socially superior to most of the clods that were around him." **Drunken insults; moral lassitude:** Cavallon recalls that Pantuhoff offered to help Gorky sell his work and persuaded him to do a sketch, then persuaded Cavallon to make a frame for it: "When he came to pick it up, he liked it, but when I told him it would cost five dollars, he said, 'Oh, jeez, I forgot my pocketbook.' I never did get paid, and Gorky—who never got his sketch back—didn't either. Pantuhoff was that type of person—very low, very disgusting."

"I like being": Q. by Bultman in Potter, p. 65. **Sharing apartment with Rosenbergs:** Rosenberg; the single man was a pharmacist whose name no one recalls. **Visits to Greenlawn:** Ronald Stein; Ruth Stein. **Entire neighborhood entranced:** Ronald Stein. **Family believing they were married:** Ronald Stein; Ruth Stein. We couldn't locate records of such a marriage, or of a dissolution. It is hard to believe, however, that Lee would never have disabused her relatives of the notion in the many years that followed, long after they would have ceased being shocked. Ronald Stein (probably closer to Lee over a longer period of time than any-

one in her life after JP's death): "I think that it lasted an extremely short time, and it was a formal marriage, and [there was] some sort of a formal dissolution of the marriage." Some acquaintances, such as Abel, also assumed they were married, when there was no reason to try to create such an impression; McNeil: "People didn't pay any attention to private lives." **Studying at CCNY; waitressing:** LK, lecture, Columbia University, Oct. 5, 1983. **"No part of teaching":** LK, int. by Landau, Feb. 21, 1880, q. in Landau, "LK," p. 44. **Lee at front of line for PWAP:** LK.

Hofmann "school" address: McNeil. **Description of class:** Mercer. **Lee's outfit:** Kiesler. **Hofmann school still life:** Eames. **Cellophane and raking light:** Goodman, "Hans Hofmann as a Teacher," pp. 121–22. **"Animal magnetism"; "voluptuousness"; "a unique student"; Hofmann agreeing:** Kiesler, int. by Landau, Feb. 27, 1979. **Lee pushy toward women:** Hauck. **"Hanging around":** Harold Rosenberg, q. in Friedman, p. 69. **Lee's lack of reading:** CG: "Lee was not particularly well educated, and she hadn't read much." **"This was a prestate":** Int. by Rose, July 31, 1966. **"And then the minister":** LK. **"It looks like":** Little. **"Too bad":** Q. by Little. **"A painter's painter":** McNeil, int. by Landau, Mar. 1, 1979, q. in Landau, "LK," p. 111. **"Nobody took Lee Krasner seriously":** Mandelman.

Hofmann's early history: Pollett, "Hans Hofmann," p. 31. **Hofmann and modernist masters; studying alongside Matisse:** Pollett, "Hans Hofmann," p. 31; Ashton, p. 81. **Matisse's school:** The school was aborted after two months because the master was inundated with commissions; Kiesler. **Hofmann becoming a teacher:** See Goodman, "Hans Hofmann as a Teacher," p. 120. **"Cher maître":** Holtzman. **"As strong as a mountain":** Mercer. **"Good German ego":** Kamrowski. **Hofmann's personality:** Bultman, int. by Sandler, Jan. 6, 1968. **Hofmann's permanent mark:** Goodman, "Hans Hofmann as a Teacher," p. 120. **"He brought Paris":** Matter. **Flatness; inertness:** Bultman, "Hans Hofmann," pp. 4–5. **Denis on flatness:** Chipp, ed., p. 94. **Gauguin on color:** Chipp, ed., p. 61

"Put a spot"; "activate the surface": Q. in Landau, "LK," p. 110, citing "Hofmann," *Brooklyn Museum Annual*, 1967–68. **"Equilibrium":** Bultman, int. by Sandler, Jan. 6, 1968. **Twice-weekly rounds:** Goodman, "Hans Hofmann as a Teacher," p. 122. **"Keep the picture"; "make the colors":** Q. by Wheeler. **"Give the most":** Q. in Ashton, p. 82. **"Lacked sufficient"; "had a hole"; "how to handle color"; "why colors worked":** Wheeler. **"This is wrong":** Q. by McNeil. **"The mythical perfect picture":** Wheeler. **"Pompous, blustering":** Larry Rivers, q. in Goodman, "Hans Hofmann as a Teacher," p. 120, citing "Hans Hofmann Students' Dossier," compiled by William Seitz, 1963, in MOMA Library: Rivers's overall assessment of Hofmann was positive. **"Do not make it flat!":** Q. in Goodman, "Hans Hofmann as a Teacher," p. 123. **Gibberish:** Wheeler: "Someday I'm going to get up a glossary of all the bullshit things Hofmann used to talk about." **Hofmann dissolving into German:** Goodman, "Hans Hofmann as a Teacher," pp. 121–22. **"Beefed up the timid hearts":** Q. in Goodman, "Hans Hofmann as a Teacher," p. 120, citing "Hans Hofmann Students' Dossier," compiled by William Seitz, 1963, in MOMA Library.

"Would come up"; "what did this man say": Q. in Nemser, p. 85. **"This is so good":** Q. by LK. **"A number of times":** LK. On two occasions, Kiesler saw Hofmann draw arrows on a sketch of LK's, ostensibly to show how the composition might be improved. LK was infuriated. **Lee's drawing complimented:** Kiesler, int. by Landau, Feb. 27, 1979. **Hofmann tearing drawing; "this is tension":** Incident based on LK; Kiesler, int. by Landau, Feb. 27, 1979; Goodman, "Hans Hofmann as a Teacher," p. 124. **"I had a total fit":** LK. "But not in his presence. I bottled that up inside me until he had left." **"This has got"; "keep the picture":** LK, q. by Wheeler. **Lee's work at the Hofmann school:** Landau, "LK," p. 129.

Hofmann hiding his paintings; "he did not want": Bultman: Later, some students realized his real purpose was "to avoid any critical confrontation." **Hofmann worshiping Matisse:** Bultman, int. by Sandler, Jan. 6, 1968; CG, "Influences of Matisse," p. 28: Hofmann insisted on Matisse's greatness "as he insisted on little else." CG, p. 232: Hofmann "could teach as much about Matisse's color as Matisse himself." **Using Matisse as model:** In fact, ever since she saw her first "live Matisse, not in reproduction" at MOMA in 1930;

Landau, "LK," p. 31, citing LK, int. by Emily Wasserman, Jan. 9, 1968, p. 4. Even before arriving at the Hofmann School, LK had tried to "do something that hit from Matisse"; LK, int. by Seckler, Dec. 14, 1967. **Borrowing from Matisse:** See *Still Life*, 1938, fig. 15, in Rose, p. 24. **Using pointillistic style:** Landau, "LK," p. 124. In *Bathroom Door*, Lee played with the Matissian subject of one space opening onto another space framed by a window, a door, a mirror, or a painting; see Landau, "LK," p. 62.
"One of the leading": LK, int. by Seckler, Nov. 2, 1964. **"Swing like a pendulum":** LK, q. in Wasserman, "LK in Mid-Career," p. 38. **Drawings based on Picasso:** Perhaps a specific drawing by Picasso in the Stieglitz collection that was on exhibition in "Cubism and Abstract Art" at MOMA in 1933 and that Stieglitz had given to the Metropolitan Museum of Art: Rose, "LK and the Origins of Abstract Expressionism," pp. 95–96; see Rose, p. 20. **Seeing Guernica; "it knocked me"; "four or five times":** LK, int. by Rose, July 31, 1966. **Exhibition with Picassoid works:** Exhibition sponsored by the American Abstract Artists at the Riverside Museum; LK, int. by Rose, Mar. 1972, q. in Landau, "LK," p. 149. **Description of Mondrian:** See PG, p. 159. **"Queasy":** LK, int. by Seckler, Dec. 14, 1967. **"Very strong"; "stay with it":** Q. by LK, int. by Secker, Dec. 14, 1967. **"Oh, it was beautiful":** Int. by Seckler, Dec. 14, 1967, slightly condensed. **Painting with Fine:** Landau, "LK," p. 142, citing interviews with Fine, July 19, 1979, and Aug. 4, 1979. **"Mondrian at that point":** Q. in Landau, "LK," p. 141, citing LK, int. by Emily Wasserman, Jan. 9, 1968, p. 5.
Moving to East Ninth Street: While Igor was in Europe, Lee lived at 51 East Ninth Street, across the street from the apartment she later shared with Pantuhoff. **"An intense"; "he was a real"; "I could hear":** Q. in Potter, p. 64. **"I'm not anti-Semitic":** Q. by Rosenberg. **"You son of a bitch":** Q. by Rosenberg. **Rumors of abortion:** Landau; Rosenberg. **"Someplace out west":** LK.
Portrait painter on ocean cruises: Michael Loew, q. in Potter, p. 64. **Lee attracting more attention:** Bultman agrees with Rosenberg that this was a problem. **Overlooking Igor:** CG: "All along we noticed her work more than Igor's." **Lee chastising Igor:** Landau, "LK," p. 35, citing Mercer, int. by Landau, Oct. 30, 1979. On one visit, Harold Rosenberg enthusiastically asked to see LK's work without mentioning Igor's. May immediately felt a chill in the room; Rosenberg. **Dating of Pantuhoff's departure:** Igor gave her a copy of John Cassou's *Paintings and Drawings of Matisse*, inscribed "To Lee with admiration from Igor"; Landau, "LK," p. 35. The book was published in 1939 and was inscribed that same year while Pantuhoff was still in New York. **Pantuhoff's departure:** Rosenberg. **Pantuhoff disappearing for at least a year:** Bultman (int. by Landau, Feb. 27, 1979) told Landau ("LK," p. 36) that Pantuhoff left New York soon after the invasion of Europe in 1939.
American Abstract Artists: Called the "Park Avenue Cubists," led by A. E. Gallatin and George L. K. Morris, and including Holtzman, Perle Fine, and Giorgio Cavallon; see Rose, p. 40. **Rejection of subject matter:** See Rose, p. 40. **Circle of homosexuals:** CG: "There were a lot of queers around Lee. I didn't see them around Lee again until Jackson died, and then the queers came back." **Mercer's Harvard years:** Mercer: "Devoted as I was to Lee, we were not having an affair." Cavallon and Greenberg, among other friends, incorrectly assumed they were having a sexual relationship. **Activities with Mercer:** Mercer.
Evening at Café Society: All details, except where noted, Bourdon, "LK," p. 57. **"Had a wonderful sense":** An anonymous partner, q. in Von Wiegand, "Memoir of His New York Period," pp. 59–60, q. in Landau, p. 147. **"I thought, 'Of course'"; "some movie actor":** Q. in Bourdon, "LK," p. 57. **Rimbaud's poem:** Friedman, p. 71: When Tennessee Williams, an intimate friend of Bultman's at the time, visited her studio and had the audacity to criticize the Rimbaud verses, Lee, infuriated, threw him out. **Mercer drafted:** Mercer.

26. LEGENDS

SOURCES

Books, articles, manuscripts, film, and transcripts

Diamonstein, ed., *Inside New York's Art World*; Friedman, *Almost a Life*; Friedman, *JP*; Greer, *The Obstacle Course*; Gruen, *The Party's Over Now*; McElvaine, *The Great Depression*; McKinzie, *The New Deal for Art*; Nemser, *Art Talk*; FVOC, *The New Deal Art Projects*; Potter, *To a Violent Grave*; Rose, *Krasner/Pollock*; Rose *LK*.
James Brooks et. al., "JP: An Artists' Symposium, Part I," *Art News*, Apr. 1967; DP&G, "Who Was JP?" *Art in America*, May–June 1967; Grace Glueck, "Krasner and Pollock: Scenes from a Marriage," *Art News*, Dec. 1981; CG, "New York Painting Only Yesterday," *Art News*, Summer 1957; James Lane, "Mélange," *Art News*, Jan. 15–31, 1942; Norbert Lynton, "London Letter," *Art International*, Nov. 1965; "Mrs. JP," *Time*, Mar. 17, 1958; Barbara Rose, "American Great: LK," *Vogue*, June 1972; Barbara Rose, "LK and the Origins of Abstract Expressionism," *Arts*, Feb. 1977; Harold Rosenberg, "The Art Establishment," *Esquire*, Jan. 1965; Amei Wallach, "Krasner's Triumph," *Vogue*, Nov. 1983.
Flora Lewis, "Two Paris Shows à la Pollock," *NYT*, Oct. 3, 1979; Amei Wallach, "LK: Out of JP's Shadow," *Newsday*, Aug. 23, 1981.
Ellen Gross Landau, "LK: A Study of Her Early Career (1926–1949)" (Ph.D. thesis), Newark: University of Delaware, 1981; FVOC, "The Genesis of JP: 1912 to 1943" (Ph.D. thesis), Baltimore: Johns Hopkins University, 1965.
"Strokes of Genius: JP" (film), Court Productions, 1984.
Fritz Bultman, int. by Irving Sandler, Jan. 6, 1968, AAA; Lillian Olaney Kiesler, int. by Ellen Landau, Feb. 27, 1979; LK, int. by Barbara Rose, July 31, 1966, AAA; LK, int. by Dorothy Seckler, Nov. 2, 1964, and Dec. 14, 1967, AAA; SLM int. by CG, c. 1956.

Interviews

Lionel Abel; Ethel Baziotes; Leland Bell; Peter Blake; James Brooks; Fritz Bultman; Edith Bunce; Peter Busa; Herman Cherry; Deborah Daw; Violet de Laszlo; Karen Del Pilar; Ray Eames; B. H. Friedman; CG; Grace Hartigan; Harry Holtzman; Axel Horn; Harry Jackson; Reuben Kadish; Gerome Kamrowski; Lillian Olaney Kiesler; Hilton Kramer; LK; Ellen Landau; Harold Lehman; John Little; Herbert Matter; Mercedes Matter; ACM; Jason McCoy; Donald McKinney; George Mercer; John Bernard Myers; David Peretz; EFP; FLP; Milton Resnick; May Tabak Rosenberg; Nene Schardt; Patsy Southgate; Ruth Stein; Margot Stewart; Wally Strautin; Samuel Wagstaff; Steve Wheeler; Betsy Zogbaum.

NOTES

"[Graham] looked at me: Int. by Landau, Feb. 28, 1979, q. in Landau, p. 175. **Penny postcard:** *Strokes of Genius*. **"I am arranging":** Q. in Landau, p. 178. **Overwhelmed; "this is big-time":** Q. in *Strokes of Genius*. **"I was astonished".** Q. in DP&G, "Who was JP?" p. 49. **"That might have broken":** LK, int. by Seckler, Nov. 2, 1964, q. in Landau, p. 179. **Canvassing Artists Union:** LK. **Canvassing AAA:** Landau, p. 170. **De Kooning shrugging shoulders:** LK. **Downtown Gallery:** Landau, p. 179. **"By the way":** Q. in Landau, p. 179. **"Sure".** Q. by LK.
"I was in a rage": Q. in DP&G, "Who Was JP?" p. 49. **"Something got into me":** Int. by Rose, July 31, 1966. **"Bounded":** LK. **"I found out later":** LK; see also DP&G, "Who Was JP?" p. 49; Glueck, "Krasner and Pollock," pp. 58–59. **"I knocked":** Q. in DP&G, "Who Was JP?" p. 49. **"I introduced myself":** Combined from DP&G, "Who Was JP?" p. 49 and *Strokes of Genius*. **"Actually, we had met":** LK; see also DP&G, "Who was JP?" p. 49; Diamonstein, p. 201. **"Impressed";** LK. **"Moved":** Q. in Glueck, "Krasner and Pollock," pp. 58–59. **"Overwhelmed":** Q. in DP&G, "Who was JP?" p. 49. **"Blasted":** Q. by Busa. **"Stunned":** Q. in Gruen, p. 230. **"Bowled [her] over":** Q. in DP&G, "Who Was JP?" p. 49. **"Felt the presence":** In *Strokes of Genius*. **"Felt as if the floor":** Q. in DP&G, "Who Was JP?" p. 49. **"Fully understood":** Rose, "LK and the Origins of Abstract Expressionism," p. 99. **"Almost died":** Q.

in "Mrs. JP," p. 64. **"My God":** Q. in Wallach, "Krasner's Triumph," p. 502. **"Oh, I'm not sure"; "don't touch it!":** Q. in DP&G, "Who Was JP?" p. 49. **"Arrangements for return visit:** Glueck, "Krasner and Pollock," pp. 58–59. **Krasner remembering earlier encounter:** Friedman; Rosenberg; see also B. H. Friedman, introduction to Whitechapel Gallery, p. 8, where Lee is quoted as saying she "barely remembered" Pollock from the Artists Union incident. **"The one who stepped all over":** LK; see also Diamonstein, ed., p. 201. **"No guy was ever"; "an old maid":** Q. in Friedman, *Almost a Life*, p. 162; this novel is a fictional account of JP and Lee Krasner by a friend, in which many of the details are taken from their lives. **Following Pollock's career:** See Rosenberg. McKinney (Lee's close friend and dealer in the 1960s): "It was very clear from things she said that she knew exactly who [Jackson] was during the period from 1936 to 1941." McKinney was also close to Mark Rothko and recalls Rothko saying that, although he wasn't friends with JP until later, he knew him by reputation as early as 1940: " 'It was a tiny art world,' Rothko said, 'and it's not as if Jackson was an unknown.' " **Pollock recovering from binge:** LK; ACM; see also DP&G, "Who Was JP?" p. 49. **Studio malodorous:** EFP. **Martinson coffee cans:** Wagstaff, recalling LK. **Wicker chairs:** Photo in possession of Kadish. **Works in Pollock's studio:** Landau, p. 182: Lee also remembered seeing *Birth* on her first visit. Lee later told Gruen (p. 230) that "One work—the painting later titled *Magic Mirror*—just about stunned me." **"She found him the most beautiful":** Myers. **"Met someone she liked":** Matter, in "Strokes of Genius." **"Fantastic, powerful hands":** Q. in DP&G, "Who Was JP?" p. 49. **"Terribly in love":** Myers; see Ruth Stein: "Lee would never go through what she went through, never subjugate herself to another person's art that way. She wasn't that magnanimous. It had to be *love* and it had to be *him*." **"When they first":** Horn. **"Living together":** LK, q. in Glueck, "Krasner and Pollock," p. 59. **Weeks before Pollock showed up:** LK, int. by Jeanne Wasserman, Jan. 9, 1968, cited in Landau, p. 184. **"I asked him":** LK; see also Wallach, "LK," *Newsday*, Sept. 23, 1981. **Lee never cooking:** Wallach, "LK," *Newsday*, Sept. 23, 1981. LK, int. by Jeanne Wasserman, Jan. 9, 1968, q. in Landau, p. 184: JP's comments on her work were "very generous." **Remembering earlier encounter:** LK, in Glueck, "Krasner and Pollock," p. 59: "When he came to my place, we both remembered we'd met several years before at an Artists Union loft party." **Going to opening together:** LK, int. by Jeanne Wasserman, Jan. 9, 1968, cited in Landau, p. 184. **"Wasn't really serious":** Lehman. **"Never went anywhere"; "if a guy interested me":** LK character, q. in Friedman, *Almost a Life*, p. 162.

"Like a goat": Name withheld by request. **Pneumatic breasts:** Asked why several of the Pollock brothers married Jewish women, Frank Pollock said, "[Jews] tend to be intelligent and educated and big-breasted. If you listen to them, it intrigues you, and the girls are bosomy and attractive." **"I thought of Jackson":** LK. **Seduction of de Kooning:** LK: Sometime during the 1930s—before she was forced to execute the Dutch artist's mural, as a result of a recently imposed Alien Rule that prevented de Kooning from executing it himself—a mutual friend had taken her to visit de Kooning's studio, where she found him with "an attractive little girl named Julie, who, as I remember, played the violin." **"Funny man"; "very warmly":** LK. **"This is Frederick Kiesler"; "And this":** Q. by LK; see also DP&G, "Who Was JP?" p. 51. **"Meshed"; "we knew":** LK character, q. in Friedman, *Almost a Life*, p. 162. Horn saw them together soon after they "took up with one another seriously. I had the feeling that they sought each other out because neither one of them had any alternatives." **"Psychologically embedded":** Int. by Landau, Feb. 21, 1980, q. in Landau, p. 202. **De Kooning only other American:** LK: "There was Pollock, there was de Kooning, and there was me." **Artists in McMillen show:** Landau, p. 184, citing McMillen catalogue. **"Resembles [Stanley William] Hayter":** Lane, "Mélange," p. 29. **"Walked off":** Q. in Friedman, *JP*, p. 53. **Between Matisse and Braque:** LK, int. by Seckler, Nov. 2, 1964. **"Just being in that show":** Int. by Landau, Feb. 28, 1979, q. in Landau, p. 185. **Matter modeling with Lee:** Blake. **Herbert's background:** Herbert Matter. **Matter town house:** The house, which was next door to the Tudor Hotel, no longer exists. **"Meeting place":** Bultman, int. by Irving

Sandler, Jan. 6, 1968. **Léger living with Matters; Calder's** *Circus:* Bultman, int. by Sandler, Jan. 6, 1968; Herbert Matter. **Matter guests:** Herbert Matter; Mercedes Matter. **"Talked a blue streak":** Mercedes Matter. **"Find their voices":** LK. **De Kooning's studio:** At 143 West Twenty-first Street. **Introduction to de Kooning:** LK. **"Probably at a bar":** Q. by Little. **Introduction to Greenberg:** CG; Lee Krasner, however, told the authors that she introduced JP to him at a party. **"In her uncouth way":** CG. His reaction may have been kinder than that of most because he considered himself an outsider like JP. Although he had attended a few Hofmann lectures with Lee and Pantuhoff, he was then an editor at *Partisan Review* and was, by his own account, "almost entirely out of touch with art life"; "New York Painting Only Yesterday," p. 58. **"Absolutely aghast":** Wagstaff. **"Hofmann school immaculate":** Q. by Wagstaff. **"An incredible mess":** LK. **"With this";** Q. by LK, q. in Landau, p. 210, citing LK, int. by Barbara Rose, n.d. **"That's the point":** Q. by LK, q. by Wagstaff. **"Hofmann, being a teacher":** Q. in D&PG, "Who Was JP?" p. 51. **"A silent-looking man":** Rosenberg. Betsy Zogbaum had a similar experience when she visited Lee in early 1942. "Lee and I had a dinner engagement. I went down to her studio and there was this very silent young man. He didn't say anything. Lee and I were just chatting away. Lee never looked his way. Finally, we got up to leave, and I still didn't know who he was. His name didn't even come up in the conversation. I learned later that it was Jackson." **Arloie waiting to have child:** McCoy: "She put her foot down and said she wouldn't live with Jackson when she had any children." **Jackson spending nights at Lee's:** Del Pilar: "He started to live with Lee because my mother [Arloie McCoy] had given him an ultimatum." **Rent raised; "the gouge is on":** SLM to CCP, July 1941. **Jackson planning to stay:** SMP to CCP, May 1941. **"I had a talk":** SLM to CCP, Mar. 10, 1942. **No more justification for WPA:** See McElvaine, p. 320. **Sande laid off:** SLM to CCP, July 1941. **Project rolls "shopping lists"; "employed in war production"; help from Hayden:** SLM to CCP, Mar. 28, 1942. **Job with Sperry Gyroscope:** ACM. Brooks: Sande used tools borrowed from him to demonstrate his qualifications for the job. Sande paid to have his name legally changed a week before reporting to work in mid-May; SMP to CCP, May 5, 1942. He didn't resign from the Project until August; FVOC, "The Genesis of JP," p. 77. **"He's at Bellevue"; "what the hell"; "put him"; "is this":** LK. **"It was my first meeting":** See LK, q. in Friedman, *JP*, pp. 56–57. **"Did you people":** LK. **Not connecting binge wih Stella's arrival:** DP&G, "Who Was JP?" p. 50: "It took a long time for me to realize why there was a problem between Jackson and his mother." **Jackson and Stella staying at Lee's:** SMP to CCP, May 5, 1942: JP staying at Lee's; Bultman: Stella was staying there. It's possible they switched off. **"Held audience":** Bultman. **Friends brought to meet Stella:** Bultman; Wheeler. **"Eccentric cowboy":** Kamrowski. **"[Sande] had devoted":** McCoy. **Sande "blighted":** Del Pilar: "Jackson and my father [Sande] were neurotically attached." **"Swallowed up":** Kiesler. **Lee subordinating herself:** See Greer, especially p. 103. **"Irrelevant"; "he was the important thing":** Q. in Gruen, p. 230. **"Keeping house":** LK. **Shopping for presents:** JP to SMP, summer 1943. **"A wonderful sense":** Int. by Landau, Feb. 21, 1980, q. in Landau, p. 201. **"Meshed well":** Baziotes. **Learning to cook:** LK. **"I wanted that role":** Q. in Wallach, "Krasner's Triumph," p. 501. **Dressing for Jackson:** Rose. **"Bohemian vamp":** Rosenberg. **"Peck & Peck girl":** Zogbaum. **Corresponding with Jackson's relatives:** E.g. LK to SMP, summer 1943. **Making Jackson's phone calls:** See, e.g., Sidney Janis to JP, Sept. 1943. **"She was always saying":** Rosenberg; see also Rosenberg, int. by Landau, Feb. 22, 1980, q. in Landau, p. 223.

Lee stopping work: Bultman; Busa; Hartigan; Holtzman; Kadish; Mercedes Matter; Resnick; Rosenberg; Strautin. **Not a single work completed:** Some paintings attributed to Rose, LK (figs. 29, p. 32; 37, p. 42; 43, p. 49; 44, p. 51), supposedly were painted during this period, but we strongly suspect backdating or forward-dating. Her paintings throughout this period were nothing but "Gray Slabs"; see Landau, p. 211. **"Blackout" period:** Q. in Nemser, p. 86. **Only Jackson's works hung:** Holtzman; Rosenberg. **Jackson held to blame:** Rosenberg: "Jackson said he didn't want her painting." Later critics have denied that Lee ever stopped painting; see, e.g., Rose, *LK*, p. 49: "Although it is popularly supposed that Krasner stopped painting and devoted herself solely to her relationship with Pollock, we find ample evidence that she continued to work and to exhibit in the early forties." Rose, *Krasner/Pollock*, n.p.: "One misconception this exhibition should correct is the idea that Krasner ever stopped painting." Wallach, "Krasner's Triumph," p. 445: "But what Lee Krasner, the artist, never did was stop painting." **WPA workers offered to War and Navy departments; War Services:** McKinzie, p. 169. **"Creative" projects scrapped:** Dorothy Miller, "The United States Government Art Projects, A Brief Summary," prepared by the Museum of Modern Art from articles prepared for *Collier's* Yearbook, 1935–43, pp. 17–18, q. in FVOC, "The Genesis of JP," p. 80. **Camouflage and propaganda posters:** Audrey McMahon, q. in FVOC, ed., pp. 74–75. **Lee's mural abandoned:** Rosalind Bengelsdorf Browne, q. in FVOC, ed., p. 238. **"The culture of this country":** Q. in FVOC, "The Genesis of JP," p. 81. **Lee choosing Jackson for project:** The team also included Ben Benn, Ray Klein (Eames), Jean Xceron, Frederick Hauck, Agostine, Frank Greco, and Ernest Truback. **Description of project:** FVOC, "The Genesis of JP," pp. 81–82, citing Pearl Bernstein, administrator, Board of Higher Education, City of New York, to Miss Audrey McMahon, general supervisor, City War Services Program, Oct. 1, 1942, and *NYT*, Sept. 28, 1942, and Sept. 29, 1942. **Jackson coming to work with Lee:** LK, int. by Landau, May 1, 1979, q. in Landau, p. 212. **Jackson loafing; "it was like":** Busa. **"Shedding" process:** LK. **De Laszlo sensing her role preempted:** De Laszlo, q. in Potter, p. 75; see de Laszlo. **"Systematically disengaging":** Cherry. **"Getting rid of anybody":** Rosenberg. Bultman: "We wouldn't see Jackson for long periods, but we saw Lee often, so we just assumed she was running things—she usually did." **Legend of the woman behind the man:** Peretz: "There is a paradox. Even though artists very often have a feeling that making art is women's work, women themselves were not emotionally free to do it. They were doing *real* women's work, housework, instead. Wasn't Lee in all likelihood giving Jackson the care she wished someone would have given her? That is common in the psychology of the Woman behind the Man." Greer, pp. 103, 133: "When art appears to a woman in the person of a loved male, her attitude to it necessarily partakes of the nature of her relationship to men. If male relatives exercise dominion over the hearts and minds of their womenfolk, unrelated males who are love objects exercise more destructive power still. Many women escaped the family pitfall only to be betrayed by sexual love. . . . Generally speaking, artistic women tend to marry not for support and comfort but for esteem. They marry 'upward.' A female artist almost always seeks love where she feels admiration." **"There would never have been":** Myers, int. by Rose, n.d., AAA, q. in Landau, p. 227. **"All of Pollock's":** Int by Landau, Oct. 30, 1979, q. in Landau, p. 227. **"Guided by an apparition":** Q. in Potter, p. 79. It was a view that not only elevated LK but also, indirectly, brought JP into Hofmann's modernist fold. **Hurrying home to fix dinner:** Busa. **"She gave in":** Q. in "Mrs. JP," p. 64. **Wanting Jackson to need her:** De Laszlo: "I don't think she discouraged him from seeing me. I think that his relationship with her became the paramount relationship in both their lives and she just absorbed his interests and energies. She was no more possessive or jealous than anyone in love might be." **"People who could be influential":** Schardt. **"Jackson insisted":** Kadish. **Lee clinging to paintings:** McKinney. **"Mrs. Jackson Pollock":** Rosenberg, "The Art Establishment," p. 114. **"Articulate and cool-headed":** Landau, p. 201. **"After looking":** LK, q. in DP&G, "Who Was JP," p. 51. **Matters arranging Calder visit:** Herbert Matter. **"You didn't talk":** Int. by Landau, Feb. 28, 1979, q. in Landau, p. 186. **Kadish bringing collectors:** Kadish. Despite Kadish's help, Lee continued to treat him with cold cordiality. Within a few years, she would cut him out of JP's life entirely. Clearly, careerism wasn't her only motivator. Kamrowski: "At some point, Jackson realized that here was an extremely good mouthpiece for him, a good storm trooper, a great salesman. He realized she could be extremely useful to him, and he used her." **"Lee's influence on Jackson":** Rose, *Krasner/Pollock*, n.p. **"Krasner put [Jackson] in touch":** Rose, *LK*, pp. 98, 100. **"She helped Pollock":** Int. by Paul Cummings, Mar. 24,

1968, q. in Landau, p. 227. **"Was immediately recognized":** Elaine de Kooning, q. in Brooks et. al., "JP," p. 64. **"[Pollock] was never a student":** Q. by Bultman. **"Any ultimate assessment":** Lynton, "London Letter," p. 33. **Efforts to "convert" Jackson:** Bunce: During this period, they were "constantly talking painting . . . very excitedly and very intensely." **"Not [being] abstract enough":** Q. by Busa. **Jackson not understanding Cubism:** Busa. **Jackson not caring for Cubism:** Wheeler. **Lee pooh-poohing Jung:** LK; see also LK, int. by Seckler, Dec. 14, 1967: She particularly distrusted Jung's ideas on art. **Lee revising works:** LK. **"Preferred a one-shot deal":** Busa. **Jackson not appreciating Matisse:** LK; Landau. **Jackson not appreciating Mondrian:** JP "made faces about Mondrian"; Bell, q. in Potter, p. 72. **Lee reviling Siqueiros:** Landau, p. 91: Lee remembered a violent argument with JP about Siqueiros. **"Could take [Benton] seriously":** LK: "I didn't hammer it in or anything. It wasn't like I said it every day at eleven o'clock." **"Just shut up and paint":** Q. by Wheeler. **Different attitudes toward *Guernica*:** Landau. **"A violent transition":** LK, int. by Seckler, Nov. 2, 1964.

Lee picking up Jackson's brush: Busa. **Months before relationship recovered; "shop talk":** LK. **"[Jackson] would . . . speak":** Int. by Seckler, Nov. 2, 1964. **"Shorthand":** Myers, int. by Landau, Jan. 18, 1979, q. in Landau, p. 228. **"Great painting!":** LK, q. in Landau, p. 228 n. 41. **"I practically had to hit him":** Q. in Lewis, "Two Paris Shows à la Pollock, *NYT*, Oct. 3, 1979. **"We didn't talk art":** Int. by Seckler, Nov. 2, 1964. **"From inside"; "the way Jackson did":** LK; see also LK, int. by Seckler, Dec. 14, 1967. **"Lose Cubism":** Rose, "American Great," p. 154. **"To jettison all":** Landau, p. 211. **Setting out to convert, being converted:** Wheeler. **"Pollock was too demanding":** Jackson. Kiesler, who was closer to Lee at the time than to JP: "For those first years, I always objected that Lee was being swallowed by Jackson when she was the real artist."

"I daresay": Int. by Holmes, q. in Landau, p. 207. **Shift in colors:** See Landau, p. 206. **Lee Jackson's editor:** Sande complimented Lee on her "good eye," and for "encouraging him to take chances"; SLM int. by CG, c. 1956. **"Jackson was a person":** Southgate. See also Donald Braider to Norman Kotker, Mar. 8, 1971, q. in Landau, p. 223 n. 4.

27. A WELLSPRING OF INSPIRATION

SOURCES

Books, articles, manuscripts, and transcripts

Ades, *Dada and Surrealism*; Ashton, *The New York School*; Barr, *Cubism and Abstract Art*; Diamonstein, ed., *The Art World*; Diamonstein, ed., *Inside New York's Art World*; Ernst, *A Not-So-Still Life*; Friedman, *JP*; PG, *Out of This Century*; Haslam, *The Real World of the Surrealists*; Lane and Larsen, *Abstract Painting and Sculpture in America*; McCoy, ed., *David Smith*; Myers, *Tracking the Marvelous*; *New York Panorama*; OC&T, *JP*; Picon, *Surrealists and Surrealism*; Potter, *To a Violent Grave*; Rubin, *Dada and Surrealist Art*; Rubin, *Dada, Surrealism and Their Heritage*; Sandler, *The Triumph of American Painting*; Tuchman, *New York School*; Weld, *Peggy*.

Arts & Architecture, Feb. 1944; Robert Alan Aurthur, "Hitting the Boiling Point, Freakwise, at East Hampton," *Esquire*, June 1972; George Biddle, "The Surrealists—Isolationists of Art," *New Republic*, Oct. 27, 1941; Blendon Reed Campbell, "Surrealism, New School of Native Art," *Literary Digest*, Dec. 15, 1934; Barbara Cavaliere and Richard C. Hobbs, "Against a Newer Laocoön," *Arts*, Apr. 1977; Thomas Craven, "Our Decadent Art Museums," *American Mercury*, Dec. 1941; "Dali's Display," *Time*, Mar. 27, 1939; Martha Davidson, "Surrealism from 1450 to Dada & Dali," *Art News*, Dec. 12, 1936; Jimmy Ernst, "The Artist Speaks," *Art in America*, Nov. 1968; B. H. Friedman, "The New Baroque," *Arts Digest*, Sept. 15, 1954; Matthew Josephson, "The Superrealists," *New Republic*, Feb. 3, 1932; Max Kozloff, "An Interview with Matta," *Artforum*, Sept. 1965; Lewis Mumford, "Surrealism and Civilization," *New Yorker*, Dec. 19, 1936; John Bernard Myers, "Surrealism and New York Painting, 1940–1948: A Reminiscence," *Artforum*, Apr. 1977; Gordon Onslow-Ford, "The Painter Looks Within Himself," *London Bulletin*, June 1940;

Wolfgang Paalen, "The New Image," trans. by Robert Motherwell, *Dyn*, Apr.–May 1942; David Rubin, "A Case for Content: JP's Subject Was the Automatic Gesture," *Arts*, Mar. 1979; William Rubin, "Notes on Masson and Pollock," *Arts*, Nov. 1959; William Rubin, "Toward a Critical Framework: 1. Notes on Surrealism and Fantasy Art," *Artforum*, Sept. 1966; Sibilla Skidelsky, "The Sham of It," *Art Digest*, Feb. 1, 1937; Sidney Simon, "Concerning the Beginnings of the New York School: 1939–1943, An Interview with Peter Busa and Matta" ("Busa and Matta"), *Art International*, Summer 1967; Sidney Simon, "Concerning the Beginnings of the New York School: 1939–1943, An Interview with Robert Motherwell" ("Motherwell"), *Art International*, Summer 1967; Amei Wallach, "Krasner's Triumph," *Vogue*, Nov. 1983; Simon Watson-Taylor, "Exquisite Corpses and Strange Apparitions," *Art and Artists*, Dec. 1967; Jeffrey Wechsler, "Surrealism's Automatic Painting Lesson" (Wechsler), *Art News*, Apr. 1977.

"Art Changed, Dali Goes on Rampage in Store, Crashes Through Window into Arms of Law," *NYT*, Mar. 17, 1939.

FVOC, "The Genesis of JP: 1912 to 1943" (Ph.D. thesis), Baltimore: Johns Hopkins University, 1965; Melvin Paul Lader, "PG's Art of This Century: The Surrealist Milieu and the American Avant-Garde, 1942–1947" (Lader) (Ph.D. thesis), Newark: University of Delaware, 1981; Ellen Gross Landau, "LK: A Study of Her Early Career (1926–1949)" (Ph.D. thesis), Newark: University of Delaware, 1981; May Natalie Tabak, "A Collage" (unpub. ms.), n.d.

Bultman, int. by Irving Sandler, Jan. 6, 1968, AAA; Robert Motherwell, int. by Paul Cummings, Nov. 24, 1971; Feb. 21, 1972; Mar. 30, 1972; May 1, 1974; AAA.

Interviews

Lionel Abel; Ethel Baziotes; James Brooks; Fritz Bultman; Peter Busa; Matthew Carone; Nicholas Carone; Giorgio Cavallon; Phyllis Fleiss; CG; Harry Holtzman; Reuben Kadish; Gerome Kamrowski; Hilton Kramer; LK; Ernestine Lassaw; Harold Lehman; Roberto Matta; Mercedes Matter; John Bernard Myers; Gordon Onslow-Ford; Becky Reis; May Tabak Rosenberg; Irving Sandler; Martika Sawin; Hedda Sterne; Steve Wheeler; Roger Wilcox.

NOTES

"Screwy": "Dali's Display," "Risqué": "Art Changed," *NYT*, Mar. 17, 1939. "Extreme"; "the World's No. 1 Surrealist": "Dali's Display," "It's not art": Busa. Arrival from Paris: "Art Changed," *NYT*, Mar. 17, 1939. Working all night; description of windows; "a stuffed trophy": "Dali's Display," "Water buffalo": "Art Changed," *NYT*, Mar. 17, 1939. "Decapitated head": Q. in "Dali's Display," Jackson and Busa present; "what work of art": Busa. Dali asleep at St. Moritz; Dali screamed and "stormed": "Art Changed," *NYT*, Mar. 17, 1939. "Sizzling": "Dali's Display," "Hired to do": Q. in "Art Changed," *NYT*, Mar. 17, 1939. Dali unappeased: "Art Changed," *NYT*, Mar. 17, 1939. "These are some": Magistrate Louis B. Brodsky, q. in "Dali's Display."

European émigrés: "One of the great war aims is to get to New York"; Yehudi Menuhin, q. in Alfred Kazin, Introduction to *New York Panorama*, p. xv. Other artists: Also, Josef Albers, Marc Chagall, Fritz Glarner, Jacques Lipchitz, Amédée Ozenfant, Pavel Tchelitchew, and Ossip Zadkine, among others; see Ashton, p. 118; Weld, p. 254.

Duchamp's *Mona Lisa*: Picon, p. 18. Picabia's "Portrait of Rembrandt": Haslam, p. 59. "ART does not exist": Q. in Ades, p. 6. Duchamp giving up "anti-art": Rubin, *Dada and Surrealist Art*, p. 113. Nothing coming of nothing: Hugo Ball (q. in Ades, p. 5) called Dada a "harlequinade made of nothingness" in his diary, *Flight out of Time*. "Dialectical transformation": Georges Hugnet, q. in Rubin, *Dada and Surrealist Art*, p. 115. "The most touching": Q. in Rubin, *Dada and Surrealist Art*, p. 116. Window on the inner world; "without too much respect": Ades, p. 31. Breton's ways to tap unconscious: Rubin, *Dada and Surrealist Art*, pp. 116, 121. "Dictated in the absence"; "outside"; "Psychic automatism"; "true function"; "superior reality": From the definition of Surrealism in the First Manifesto of 1924, q. in Ades, p. 33. "I believe": Q. in Ades, p. 32. The word "surrealism" had first been used by the poet Guillaume Apollinaire in 1917 in a program for *Parade*, the ballet by Erik Satie; Rubin, *Dada and Surrealist Art*, p. 115.

"Illustrated": Busa. Dali's artistic vocabulary: Picon, p.

138. Dali was the only Surrealist artist who truly interested Freud; see Freud to Stefan Zweig, July 20, 1939, cited in Picon, p. 158. "Hand-painted dream": Q. in Rubin, *Dada, Surrealism and Their Heritage*, p. 40. Dali and Magritte relying on literal images: In 1942, Wolfgang Paalen ("The New Image," p. 9) wrote: "Salvador Dali has . . . never made paintings which could be qualified as automatic. This point has to be clearly established, because his defenders pretend that his academic style does not matter since he uses it as a means to relate automatically experienced images [of dreams]. But it is precisely for this reason that his painting instead of being automatic is simply an academic copy of a previously terminated psychological experience."

Dominguez's process: Called *décalcomanie*; see Picon, 164, quoting *Dictionnaire abrégé du Surréalisme*, Paris, 1938. Frottage: Picon, p. 95. Fumage: Picon, p. 167. "Finessed mechanics": William Rubin, "Notes on Masson and Pollock," p. 39. Masson's background: See Picon, p. 226. "Let[ting] his hand": William Rubin, "Notes on Masson and Pollock," p. 39: Masson "occasionally clarified these nascent images but never allowed them to become literal." Glue technique: Rubin, "Notes on Masson and Pollock," p. 40: "Unlike the Surrealist techniques known as *décalcomanie* and *frottage*, this was not a trick discovered accidentally and subsequently exploited for artistic possibilities; it represented, rather, a solution called forth by a pressing painterly problem. Just such a need brought Pollock to his drip method." Squeezing paint from above: Ades, pp. 36–37. "The subconscious a wellspring": Q. in Weld, p. 274, citing "Answers to Questions," *Possibilities*, Winter 1947–48. Breton's preference for literature: Such Romantic-Symbolist figures as Charles Baudelaire, Gérard de Nerval, and Apollinaire were "resurrected" from Dada ignominy to join certain Dada heroes such as Jarry and Lautréamont; Rubin, *Dada and Surrealist Art*, p. 115. Breton's word games: Rubin, *Dada and Surrealist Art*, pp. 116, 121. "Lamentable expedient": William Rubin, "Toward a Critical Framework," p. 36. "Pictorial themes"; "transposable": Sandler, p. 34. Masson leaving movement; Dali replacing him: Lader, p. 69.

"Newer Super-Realism": Nov.–Dec., Wadsworth Athenaeum in Hartford, Conn.; Levy gallery, New York, Jan. 1932. "The return of trompe l'oeil": Lader, p. 66. For an example of a critic equating Surrealism with illusionistic painting, see Josephson, "The Superrealists," p. 76. "The artist sees": Campbell, "Surrealism," p. 19. Regionalist reaction to Surrealism: Biddle, "The Surrealists," p. 538: "There is no danger to the Republic from this band of weazened, sapless, and occasionally loudmouthed *homunculi*. Let them play with the melting watches."; see also Craven, "Our Decadent Art Museums," p. 686. Suggesting an American subject: Campbell, "Surrealism," p. 19; see Lader, pp. 67–68. Awareness of Surrealism's other side: Lader, p. 80.

"Done in a state": Barr, p. 179. Barr conferring legitimacy; largest Surrealist exhibition; "Every artist associated": Lader, pp. 70–71. Mumford an exception: Mumford, "Surrealism and Civilization," p. 79. "Sham": Skidelsky, "The Sham of It," p. 13. "Maelstrom": Davidson, "Surrealism from 1450 to Dada & Dali," in Diamonstein, ed., *The Art World*, p. 142. "A farce"; "a huge absurdity": Skidelsky, "The Sham of It," p. 13. "The supreme hoax": Leo S. Goslinger, unidentified clipping, Ferdinand Perret Library, National Collection of Fine Arts Library, Smithsonian Institution, Washington, D.C., q. in Lader, p. 72. "Bound to be amused": Davidson, "Surrealism from 1450 to Dada & Dali," in Diamonstein, ed., *The Art World*, p. 142.

Gorky the first: Tabak, "Tell Me More," in "A Collage," pp. 543–48. Kamrowski meeting Baziotes: Lader, p. 463: At Krasner's loft. Wechsler, p. 45: It was soon after his arrival. Kamrowski: When he met Baziotes, the latter was already interested in the Surrealists. "We considered Dali": Q. in Simon, "Busa and Matta," p. 18. "Automatism was the first": Q. in Simon, "Motherwell," p. 23. Baziotes taking Surrealism at its word: Busa, q. in Simon, "Busa and Matta," p. 19: "Among all of us, he was probably the most faithful adherent to orthodox Surrealism." Baziotes studying Miró and Arp: See Busa, q. in Simon, "Busa and Matta," p. 19. Baziotes experimenting with *coulage*: Baziotes; David Rubin, "A Case for Content," p. 107. Baziotes going to Columbia: Baziotes. Talking about Surrealism to Pollock: Baziotes; Kamrowski.

Dating of discussions with Baziotes: Kamrowski.

Wechsler (p. 45) gives date as 1941. Baziotes: "It must have been 'forty." Kamrowski: The incident took place in "the fall of 'thirty-nine or the winter of 'forty." **Kamrowski's studio:** at 241 Sullivan Street. **"Was bringing":** Kamrowski to B. H. Friedman, 1972, q. in Wechsler, p. 45. **"Wasn't going well":** Kamrowski. **Baziotes dribbling paint:** Wechsler, p. 45. **"Interpreted" as "bird's nest"; "declined to comment":** David Rubin, "A Case for Content," p. 107, citing interview with Kamrowski, June 26, 1978. **"Demonstration"; "very free":** Kamrowski, q. in Wechsler, pp. 45–46. **"Made his point"; "puzzling":** Q. in Wechsler, p. 46. **"Everything wells up":** Q. in Picon, pp. 12–13. **Gentle Baziotes** Fleiss: "The sweetest, gentlest, dearest, kindest, nicest man of them all was Baziotes." **Ex-boxer:** Kamrowski: "He was a lightweight at 125 pounds." **Boxing "psychologically useful"; selling newspapers and shining shoes:** Baziotes. **Bootleggers, hat factory, stained glass; Leon Kroll's class; always an umbrella:** Ernst, p. 187. **Ethel's "Byzantine" serenity:** Ernst, p. 186. **"Dressed like":** Ernst, pp. 186–87.

    Paalen exhibition: Apr. 9–22, 1940. **Paalen a Hofmann student:** Ashton, p. 124. **Miró exhibition:** Mar. 12–Apr. 16. **Marine Terminal mural; Brooks, admirer of Miró:** Brooks. An earlier exhibition, "Joan Miró, Recent Works," had been presented in 1938; Picon, p. 203. **Influence of Miró in Baziotes's work:** Busa. **Masson exhibition:** Feb. 17–Mar. 14. It is unlikely, given JP's friends and artistic development at the time, that he would have seen the Masson shows at Rosenberg and Matisse in 1932, at Matisse in 1935, and at Rosenberg in 1936. **"How much":** Myers. **"The only person":** Q. by Myers; see also Myers, "Surrealism and New York Painting," p. 56; confirmed by Wilcox. **Collaboration between Pollock and Baziotes:** Baziotes: Baziotes was also "a fan of *Moby-Dick*." Motherwell, q. in Simon, "Motherwell," p. 21: "I asked Baziotes who he thought to be the most talented of his friends. Baziotes thought probably Pollock." **"When I am away":** Unpub. version of statement by William Baziotes (1944), handwritten by Ethel Baziotes, AAA, q. in Cavaliere and Hobbs, "Against a Newer Laocoön," p. 112. **"What happens on the canvas":** Q. in Friedman, "The New Baroque," p. 12. **"To talk about art"; "phony"; "his own kingdom":** Q. by Baziotes.

    Onslow-Ford in New York: Sandler, p. 43 n. 26; Sawin, an expert on Onslow-Ford, is not certain that JP attended the lectures. Onslow-Ford was invited to America by Kay Sage and the Society for the Preservation of European Culture in 1940. **Jackson at Onslow-Ford lectures:** Lader, p. 187: "Onslow-Ford does not remember actually seeing Pollock there, nor had he met him by that time. Others who were present, however, have told him that Pollock was there." **"Look within himself":** Onslow-Ford, "The Painter Looks Within Himself," pp. 30–31. **Onslow-Ford's background:** Sawin. Onslow-Ford was in Paris from 1937 to 1939; Picon, p. 168. **"The person who introduced":** Onslow-Ford.

    "It was the challenge": Q. in Weld, p. 272. **Blackening name of Surrealism:** Nicholas Carone, a close friend of Matta's: "The Surrealist influence on Pollock is far vaster than critics have allowed. They don't want any allegiance to the European culture. It has to be something native American. There is an American Surrealism that the critics don't want to touch." To wit, CG: "The influence of the European painters on American art at midcentury is a convenient myth. Most of the Europeans who came were Surrealists." **Limited interaction with Surrealists:** Lader, pp. 76–77; Motherwell, int. by Cummings. **"Really enjoyed":** Bultman, int. by Sandler, Jan. 6, 1968. **Larré:** Weld, p. 270. **Free French Canteen:** Motherwell, int. by Cummings. **Surrealists' talk; "longing for the bistros":** Weld, p. 270. **Spending time with Reises:** See Motherwell, int. by Cummings; Lader, p. 95. Reis: "My husband could get the artists out of any difficulties, and find customers for them, and buy paintings from them." **Spending time with Murphys:** Wilcox; Aurthur, "Hitting the Boiling Point," p. 96. **"Kept away from everything"; "terrible snobs":** CG, q. in Weld, p. 273. **Duchamp and Seligmann more accessible:** Weld, p. 272. **Gorky favorite of Breton and Tanguy:** Abel. **French-speaking Americans preferred:** Bultman, int. by Sandler, Jan. 6, 1968. **"The Surrealists arrived":** Tabak, "Surrealists," in "Collage," p. 442.

    "Insisted in thinking": Q. by Weld, p. 270, citing "Eleven Europeans in America," *The Museum of Modern Art Bulletin*,

1946. **"Breton may have spoken":** Q. in Weld, p. 272. **"Autocratic":** Ernst, "The Artist Speaks," p. 58. **"It was amazing":** Q. in Weld, p. 257, citing interview, Feb. 12, 1979. **"He was full":** Q. in Weld, p. 269. **Breton refusing to learn English:** Weld, p. 270. **Abhorring eggs and gays:** Weld, p. 270, citing David Hare. **Calas ordered to marry:** CG. **"A form of psychoanalysis"; "gage"; "he got mortally offended"; "being brought blindfolded":** PG, p. 222.

    Surrealists seeming frivolous: See Friedman, p. 52. **"In this country":** Tabak, "Surrealists," in "Collage," p. 442. **Leaves and excrement:** Weld, p. 151. **Puritan sensibilities offended:** Ashton, p. 86. **Co-opting of American dealers:** Abel. **Co-opting of collectors and museums:** Lader, p. 77. **Levy taking orders from Breton:** Abel. **"The Museum of Modern Art people":** Motherwell, int. by Cummings, Nov. 24, 1971. **"Swallowed all Gallic":** Ashton, p. 86. **"[Reis's] only money":** Int. by Cummings.

    Hélion: A founder of the Abstraction-Création group in Paris; see Lane and Larsen, p. 167. **Prisoner-of-war camp:** In Poland; Lane and Larsen, p. 168. Hélion married Peggy's daughter Pegeen not long after; Weld, p. 320. **"One day I looked":** Q. by Abel. **Similar epiphanies:** Lehman: Léger also paid a visit to the mural that Lehman was painting at Riker's Island prison, with Sande as an assistant: "After looking quite a while at my full scale sketch, he said something in French to [George Boochever, Assistant Commissioner of Corrections,] who turned to me and translated, 'M. Léger would like to know how long it's going to take you to paint this.' I said, 'It should take me about a year and a half.' Which he then told to Léger, after which Léger responded, in French. The man turned to me and said, "M. Léger says he could do it in six months." Lehman explained the scheduling difficulties. "But the point is, here was a world-famous, established artist setting himself against a young painter in America. The competitive spirit was there." **"We have met them":** Int. by David Sylvester, in McCoy, ed., p 170. **"I don't see":** Questionnaire in *Arts & Architecture*, p. 14.

    "A diamond": Busa. **"Gorky is like a cow":** Q. by Cavallon. Sterne: "Gorky was always under the influence. He always understood from within. He *became* Modigliani. He didn't just paint like Modigliani, he became him. And he could do a quick drawing like Picasso, including the signature. Gorky also made some of the greatest Gorkys totally under the influence of Matta, and they're probably better than anything by Matta." **Baziotes deserving to be leader:** Busa, q. in Simon, "Busa and Matta," p. 19: "Among all of us, he was probably the most faithful adherent to orthodox Surrealism. . . . Bill was the one who would go out on the street and make the contacts. Even Kamrowski (who later had the blessing of Breton) was squeamish about it."

    Matta's background: Picon, p. 226. **Reputation as libertine:** Myers, p. 67. **"A loved son"; "the most energetic:** Motherwell, q. in Simon, "Motherwell," p. 21. **"Touched base":** Nicholas Carone. Busa, q. in Simon, "Busa and Matta," p. 17: "Surrealism was a fuse which lit up the American scene. But from where? It was [Matta's presence] that personalized Surrealism for us." **"A genius":** Nicholas Carone. **Matta as champion of automatism:** Kamrowski. **Date of Matta's planning:** Motherwell, q. in David Rubin, "A Case for Content," p. 105. This incident could be dated as late as the fall of 1942. **"He wanted to show"; "He realized":** Simon, "Motherwell," p. 21.

    Motherwell a disastrous choice: Motherwell, int. by Cummings: He appealed to the Surrealists because he was willing and able to be helpful to them.

    Gorky and Baziotes reading *Minotaure*: Rosenberg. **Motherwell's background; "the French milieu":** Q. in Simon, "Motherwell," p. 20. **Studies with Seligmann:** According to Motherwell (q. in Simon, "Motherwell," p. 20), this was arranged by Meyer Schapiro. But Wilcox says it was arranged by his wife, Lucia, who knew Seligmann well. **"In the three months":** Q. in Simon, "Motherwell," p. 20. **Ferrera:** Her name was given to us by Baziotes. **"A little capricious":** Kamrowski. **"Imbued":** Q. in Simon, "Motherwell," p. 21. **"I would talk":** Motherwell, int. by Cummings. **"You have a tremendous":** Q. by Motherwell, int. by Cummings. **"Ransacking":** Motherwell, q. in Diamonstein, ed., *Inside New York's Art World*, p. 247. **Motherwell's good looks:** Int. by Cummings. **Fired by Breton:** Lader, pp. 277–78. Myers, p. 35: "Motherwell's intellectual pretensions did not sit well on Breton's very high brow." The two men came to blows when Motherwell served for a few days as editor of Breton's magazine. Asked to translate an article from the French, Motherwell told Breton that he could not translate the term *conscience sociale* because the term "social consciousness" meant something different in America. "Breton . . . fired him on the spot, then later gave Matta hell for suggesting him"; Lader, pp. 277–78, citing David Hare, letter in "Communication," *Art News*, Dec. 1967, p. 10. **"He used to come"; "a joke":** Q. by Wilcox. **"Le petit philosophe":** Q. by Myers, p. 35. **"A windbag":** Q. by Wilcox.

"He had a tremendous": Q. in Simon, "Busa and Matta," p. 18. **"Revolution of the young":** Motherwell, q. in FVOC, "The Genesis of JP," p. 210, citing André Fermigier, "Paris/New York/1940–45," in *Art de France* (Paris, 1964), p. 252. **"To develop some sort":** Lader, p. 82. **"Show up"; "reliance":** Cavaliere and Hobbs, "Against a Newer Laocoön," p. 111. **"Annoyed because":** Q. in Simon, "Busa and Matta," p. 18. **Matta and Motherwell touring studios:** Motherwell: Matta did not accompany him on trips to Gorky's studio or de Kooning's; see Cavaliere and Hobbs, "Against a Newer Laocoön," p. 111. **Gorky bemused:** Tabak, "Tell Me More," in "Collage," pp. 543–48. **De Kooning indifferent:** Cavaliere and Hobbs, "Against a Newer Laocoön," p. 111. Busa doesn't agree with Motherwell's characterization. **"Exhilarated":** Kadish.

"Initiate"; "the Surrealist mysteries": Motherwell, int. by FVOC, Feb. 14, 1964, q. in FVOC, "The Genesis of JP," p. 210. When Motherwell tried to explain Surrealism to him, Gorky baited him repeatedly with the line, "Tell me more," then delighted his friends with the story; Tabak, "Tell Me More," in "Collage," pp. 543–48. Motherwell (q. in Simon, "Motherwell," p. 21) said he spent "four or five hours . . . explaining the whole Surrealist thing in general and the theory of automatism in particular" to JP. Motherwell would later say JP "listened intently" and "invited me to come back another afternoon" to provide more details. JP's friends "thought the claims of Bob hilarious"; Tabak, "Tell Me More," in "Collage," p. 546. Pavia: "Motherwell, nobody survives that guy's wrath. He's so terrible. His stories. I just laugh when I hear them!" Kamrowski: "Motherwell may very well be the Pope of the Abstract Expressionists, and certainly that movement couldn't have existed without him, but I think for him to claim everything, to claim everything for himself is *his* folly. When I first met Matta, with Bill [Baziotes] and Jackson and that group, Motherwell was just an art history student from whatever place."

"First Papers of Surrealism": Weld, pp. 287–88. **Superman and Father Divine:** Busa. It is often said that JP was asked to exhibit in this show but turned down the invitation because he didn't believe in group activities; see OC&T IV, p. 226; David Rubin, "A Case for Content," p. 104. There is no hard evidence for this. Nine months before the "First Papers" show, JP had shown in the McMillen show, a very similar show that included a number of Europeans and about the same number of Americans. He raised no objections then about being part of a group. It seems more likely that he dropped out of the group that Matta and Motherwell had put together, and may have dropped out of the "manifestation" they were planning (before it was scrapped), and that this withdrawal is being confused with a supposed withdrawal from the "First Papers" show.

Meetings on Twelfth Street: Baziotes: The meetings sometimes took place at Francis Lee's studio. Busa: They sometimes took place at Motherwell's apartment. **Description of Matta's apartment:** Kamrowski. **"The Exquisite Corpse" (game):** Lader, p. 160. **"The exquisite corpse" (sentence):** Watson-Taylor, "Exquisite Corpses and Strange Apparitions," p. 20. **"To locate a common":** Baziotes, int. by David Rubin, June 16, 1975, q. in "A Case for Content," p. 105. **"The effort of the dance":** Written c. 1943; OC&T 697, III, p. 206. **"What is a fox?":** Busa, int. by David Rubin, q. in "A Case for Content," p. 105 n. 32. **"One rainy night":** Motherwell, int. by Bryan Robertson, q. in Cavaliere and Hobbs, "Against a Newer Laocoön," p. 111. **"Fermé":** Q. in Kozloff, "An Interview with Matta," p. 26. **Jackson best at psychoanalysis:** See David Rubin, "A Case for Content," p. 105. **Attendance falling off:** Baziotes: Attendance was so sporadic that she and Lee both attended sessions, but never overlapped.

Ninth Street meetings: Busa. For address, see Simon, "Busa and Matta," p. 18. **Date of meetings:** Busa. Lee Krasner dismissed the impact of these evenings on the development of Abstract Expressionism as "overblown, to put it mildly"; LK to Landau, May 1, 1979, q. in Landau, "LK's Early Career," p. 234. **"Treated their wives":** Q. in Wallach, "Krasner's Triumph," p. 501. **"Resented most":** Q. in Simon, "Busa and Matta," p. 18. **Enthusiasm for Jackson's work:** Kadish. **"To find new":** Matta, q. in Kozloff, "An Interview with Matta," p. 25: "These things were like rain catching up with a man who is running." **"Natural elements"; "what it would be":** Busa. Later Matta would claim (q. in Weld, p. 274) that he used these sessions to lecture the Americans—who were "absolutely ignorant of European ideas"—on the principles of psychic automatism. In fact, Motherwell was the only one of the regular guests who had not been experimenting with automatism for several years.

"The hours of the day": See David Rubin, "A Case for Content," p. 105. **"Surrealism was largely":** Q. in David Rubin, "A Case for Content," p. 105. **Art subservient to metaphysics:** "To me, painting is a technique at the services of a certain consciousness"; Matta, q. in Kozloff, "An Interview with Matta," p. 26. **"What common images":** Baziotes, int. by David Rubin, June 16, 1976, elaborated on, May 25, 1977, q. in "A Case for Content," p. 105. **"Draw the hours":** LK, int. by David Rubin, Apr. 8, 1977, q. in "A Case for Content," p. 105. Busa: Krasner told Matta that she "liked his spirit, but thought his work was not plastic enough;" Busa, int. by Landau, Oct. 13, 1979, q. in Landau, "LK's Early Career," p. 215. **Matta's "dogmatism":** Busa. **"Too much like":** Q. by Bultman, int. by David Rubin, Nov. 22, 1976, q. in "A Case for Content," p. 105. **"Intense":** Bultman, int. by David Rubin, Nov. 22, 1976, q. in "A Case for Content," p. 105. **"I can do that":** Q. by Busa. **Jackson's belief in Motherwell's influence with Guggenheim:** LK.

Motherwell tracing images: Wilcox describes his arrival at Motherwell's East Hampton studio: "I got there a little early for a visit to his studio. He lived on the second floor of Buddy Katz's carriage house. I found the door open a little ways, so I knocked and went in. There his things were all spread out, and there he was assembling tracings of elements from Miró and other artists." **"He was a literary":** Name withheld by request.

Motherwell's background: Motherwell, int. by Cummings. **Resentment of Motherwell:** Kramer: "A lot of people in that generation and in every artistic generation since in New York have always very much resented the fact that Motherwell came from a family of money and had a university education and speaks well and has edited books and all of that. Strangely enough, I think it has acted as a barrier to a disinterested view of his art." **Motherwell's life-style:** Kamrowski; Lassaw. **Father ruined in crash:** Motherwell, int. by Cummings. **Sudsidies from mother:** Holtzman.

People intimidated by Motherwell: Abel. **Illusion of power:** Kamrowski. **Motherwell claiming introduction to Guggenheim:** Motherwell, int. by FVOC, Feb. 19, 1964, q. in FVOC, "The Genesis of JP," p. 84. Motherwell, q. in Simon, "Motherwell," pp. 21–22: "I think a lot of Pollock's interest in me was not altogether in what I was saying, but in the fact that I had a connection with Peggy Guggenheim." **Motherwell's visit, Lee's help:** Motherwell to Vallière, Aug. 31, 1964. **Motherwell's explanation of automatism to Hofmann:** See Simon, "Motherwell," p. 22; see also Motherwell's later version of the same story, q. in Potter, p. 70. **Carrying Jackson; "it was a helluva job":** Q. in Simon, "Motherwell," p. 22. **Meeting with de Kooning:** LK, see also Motherwell, q. in Potter, p. 70.

Jackson suggested; "he had been painting": Motherwell, q. in Simon, "Motherwell," p. 22. **"Attack on the material":** Motherwell, q. in Potter, p. 71. **Jackson tearing paper:** Motherwell, to FVOC, Feb. 14, 1964, q. in FVOC, "The Genesis of JP," p. 211. **Spitting on paper:** Motherwell, q. in Simon, "Motherwell," p. 22. **Burning edges with:** Motherwell to FVOC, Feb. 14, 1964, q. in FVOC, "The Genesis of JP," p. 211. **"Generally, he worked":** Q. in Simon, "Motherwell," p. 22. **"I can still remember":** Q. in Diamonstein, ed., *Inside New York's Art World*, p. 248. **Jackson's T-shirt:** Motherwell to FVOC, Feb. 19, 1964, q. in FVOC, "The Genesis of JP," p. 79. **"Left-handed"; "Marlon Brando"; "Brando was more controlled":** Motherwell, q. in Potter, p. 70.

28. EXCITING AS ALL HELL

SOURCES

Books, articles, manuscripts, and transcript

Ernst, *A Not-So-Still Life*; Friedman, *JP*; PG, ed., *Art of This Century*; PG, *Out of This Century*; Lane and Larsen, eds., *Abstract Painting and Sculpture in America*; Levy, *Memoir of an Art Gallery*; Lomask, *Seed Money*; Lukach, *Hilla Rebay*; McKinzie, *The New Deal for Artists*; Myers, *Tracking the Marvelous*; Nemser, *Art Talk*; FVOC, ed., *The New Deal Art Projects*; OC&T, *JP*; Potter, *To a Violent Grave*; Solomon, *JP*; Weld, *Peggy*.

Robert M. Coates, review, *New Yorker*, May 29, 1943; Jean Connolly, "Art," *Nation*, May 29, 1943; Josephine Gibbs, "End of the Project," clipping in Time/Life file; Grace Glueck, "Krasner and Pollock: Scenes from a Marriage," *Art News*, Dec. 1981; PG, "PG Replies," *Art Digest*, June 1943; "Isms Rampant: PG's Dream World Goes Abstract, Cubist, and Generally Non-Real," *Newsweek*, Nov. 2, 1942; [B]elle [K]rasne, "Fifty-Seventh Street in Review: Fritz Glarner," *Art Digest*, Feb. 15, 1951; Elizabeth Langhorne, "JP's 'The Moon Woman Cuts the Circle,'" *Arts*, Mar. 1979; Klaus Mann, "Surrealist Circus," *American Mercury*, Feb. 1943; William Rubin, "Pollock as Jungian Illustrator: The Limits of Psychological Criticism, Part I," *Art in America*, Nov. 1979; "Surrealists in Exile," *Time*, Apr. 20, 1942; Francis Henry Taylor, "National Art Week and the Museum," *Bulletin of the Metropolitan Museum of Art*, Nov. 1940.

Susan Heller Anderson, "For PG, A Lifetime of Knowing Her Own Mind," *NYT*, Apr. 17, 1979; Grace Glueck, "Art People: Dublin Climate Travels, Too," *NYT*, Oct. 14, 1977; Henry McBride, "New Gallery Ideas," New York *Sun*, Oct. 23, 1942; Israel Shenker, "PG Is Dead at 81; Known for Modern Art Collection," *NYT*, Dec. 24, 1979.

Melvin Paul Lader, "PG's Art of This Century: The Surrealist Milieu and the American Avant-Garde, 1942–1947" (Lader) (Ph.D. thesis), Newark: University of Delaware, 1981; Ellen Landau, "LK: A Study of Her Early Career (1926–1949)" (Ph.D. thesis), Newark: University of Delaware, 1981; FVOC, "The Genesis of JP: 1912 to 1943 (Ph.D. thesis), Baltimore, Johns Hopkins University, 1965.

LK, int. by Dorothy Seckler, Nov. 2, 1968, AAA.

Interviews

Lionel Abel; Ethel Baziotes; Leland Bell; Fritz Bultman; Peter Busa; Jimmy Ernst; CG; Richard Howard; Buffie Johnson; Reuben Kadish; Gerome Kamrowski; LK; Harry Holtzman; Harold Lehman; Herbert Matter; Alfonso Ossorio; David Porter; Lucia Salemme; Hedda Sterne; Michael Stolbach; James Johnson Sweeney; Steve Wheeler; Roger Wilcox.

NOTES

Perfunctory drawings: OC&T 643–64, III, pp. 174–86. **Last three months of 1942:** SMP to CCP, Feb. 10, 1944. *Stenographic Figure:* Rubin ("Pollock as Jungian Illustrator, Part I," p. 116) argues that there is only one figure in the painting, an interpretation with which both Lee Krasner and Eugene Thaw "agreed" (p. 123 n. 56). However, JP typically favored the subject of two figures seated across a table from one another, and the image clearly supports such a reading—the title notwithstanding. **Stella's visits:** SMP to CCP, Feb. 10, 1944. **"Arbitrary": "numbers":** Busa. **Holding a flower:** Langhorne, "JP's 'The Moon Woman Cuts the Circle,'" p. 133: The shape is a yellow flower, as in *The Secret of the Golden Flower*, a book translated by Helen Marot's friend, Cary Baynes. This was the primary book of the Tao, a "conscious way to unite what is separated. Its symbol is the Golden Flower. . . . the flower in Pollock's painting dramatizes that consciousness for which the moon woman so intently strives." While it is difficult to attribute any specific symbolic meaning to JP's use of the motif, Langhorne may well be correct in identifying the shape as the Golden Flower. **Ejaculation in *Male and Female*:** This is arguably the first painting in which JP made significant use of poured and spattered paint. **"An honorable discharge":** Landau, "LK," p. 174, citing FVOC, *The New Deal and Now*, 2d edition, (Greenwich,

Conn.: New York Graphic Society, 1971), p. 27. **Canvases auctioned:** Gibbs, "End of the Project," p. 7. **Murals covered:** McKinzie, p. 125. **Murals destroyed:** McKinzie (p. 165) gives an account of panels in Flatbush to which the Flatbush Chamber of Commerce and the American Legion objected; those panels were burned. **"Went home":** McKinzie, p. 125. **Jackson's paintings included:** *Man, Bull, Bird,* OC&T 57, I, p. 44; Glueck, "Art People: Dublin Climate Travels, Too." **"Pipe heat":** Glueck, "Art People: Dublin Climate Travels, Too." **Jackson reclaiming works:** Lehman. **Prices for WPA works:** McKinzie, p. 124.

Posters for navy: See Landau, "LK," pp. 173–74. **Sheet-metal training job:** On October 14, 1942, JP was reassigned as a "vocational trainee in aviation sheet metal" at the WPA Project Service Trade Center in Brooklyn at a salary of $52.80 a month. He was there only eight days before he was reassigned to the Art Program on October 21. **Lee's team:** Landau, "LK," p. 174, citing Busa, int. by Landau, Oct. 13, 1979. **"The most unregimented"; "The question"; training programs:** Busa. **Lee's salary:** SMP to CCP, Feb. 10, 1943. **Mechanical drafting course:** Landau, "LK," p. 212, citing documents in Lee's personal files and WPA Vocational Training record card. Busa: The teacher was Henry Dolle. **"Hunks of machinery":** Int. by Landau, Oct. 30, 1978, and Nov. 3, 1978, q. in Landau, "LK," p. 212. **Lettering to copy:** Busa.

Jackson assigned to course in Brooklyn: FVOC, "The Genesis of JP," p. 82. **"To take a course":** SMP to CCP, Feb. 10, 1944. **Liberating canvas:** Howard, recalling LK: "He had gone in, stolen a lot of canvas, wrapped it around his leg, and come home. Lee said, 'Jackson, what's the matter with you?' And he said, 'Just wait a minute,' then unbuckled his pants and took out the canvas." **Shoplifting paint:** Solomon, pp. 127–28. **"Dead broke":** JP, q. in Myers, p. 81.

Silk-screening job: LK, int. by Seckler, Nov. 2, 1968; Ralph Rosenborg, int. by FVOC, Nov. 10, 1964, q. in FVOC, "The Genesis of JP," p. 82; LK to FVOC, Sept. 10, 1966 (prepared by James T. Vallière); Friedman, p. 55. **"Squeegee man":** Creative Printmakers: Solomon, p. 128. **Sweatshop:** Busa. **"That was the end":** LK, int. by Seckler, Nov. 2, 1968. **Jackson not wanting Lee to work:** Glueck, "Krasner and Pollock," p. 60. **"Other artists"; "Jackson was totally":** LK, q. in Glueck, "Krasner and Pollock," p. 60: The others identified by Lee were Tony Smith, Barnett Newman, and Adolph Gottlieb. **Only 150 artists making living:** Taylor, "National Art Week and the Museum," pp. 3–4. **Gypsy Rose Lee; "She wouldn't look":** Bultman; see also Weld, p. 255.

"Filled with torments": PG, p. 7. **"Those stupid":** PG, q. in Weld, p. 33. **Guggenheim leaving for Paris:** Weld, p. 45; she left in 1920, at age twenty-two. **Appearance:** See Weld, p. 46. **Cigarette holder:** PG, p. 42. **"The place was crowded":** Levy, p. 34. **"Was more French":** Weld, p. 49. **"The King of Bohemia":** Q. in Weld, p. 51. **Attack on chandelier:** Weld, p. 56. **Relationship with Clotilde:** Weld, p. 55. Vail later became overtly incestuous with his daughters, especially Apple; Weld, pp. 229, 313. **"Thrilled her":** Weld, p. 75. **"He talked"; Holms's drinking:** PG, p. 70: "His capacity for drink was greater than anyone's I have ever known. He drank about five drinks to other people's one." **"Everyone I love":** Q. in Weld, p. 98.

Peggy turning to art: Laurence Vail, in particular, had "recommended that as Peggy had no brains and no talent, she should give her money away to writers, poets, and artists who did"; Weld, p. 70; see also Lader, p. 16. **Preference for old masters:** Lader, p. 22. **"Carried with it":** Weld, p. 108. **Guggenheim Jeune:** Weld, p. 131. **"Tanguy really loved":** PG, p. 157. **"Extremely uncomfortable":** PG, p. 160. Penrose, q. in Weld, p. 172: "[The affair] was never very serious. How could it be serious when she went to bed with everyone she met? She was very much in heat, one might say, anyone could jump into bed with her." **"Childish":** PG, p. 141. Although she claimed (p. 141) that "[Beckett] was in love with me as well," the evidence is to the contrary; see Weld, p. 162. **Beckett:** Sindbad, Peggy's son by Laurence Vail, doubted that there was a relationship; Weld, p. 162.

Financial losses: Lader, p. 31. **"I felt":** PG, p. 164. **Enlisting help:** Lader, pp. 31–35. **Buying a picture a day:** Her motto was "Buy a picture a day"; Shenker, "PG Is Dead at 81." **Wealth exaggerated:** Porter. Because her father had lost much of his inheritance in the years before his death, she

was what she called a "poor" Guggenheim (PG, p. 12); "from that time on I had a complex about no longer being a real Guggenheim. I felt like a poor relative and suffered great humiliation thinking how inferior I was to the rest of the family." Her inheritance from her father was "close to $450,000"; Weld, p. 31. She later inherited an additional $500,000, more or less, from her mother; Weld, p. 114. Porter: Her income during the early 1940s was $40,000 a year. **Buying strategy:** Shenker, "PG Is Dead at 81." **Generosity:** Mary McCarthy, q. in Weld, p. 70: She exhibited a "neat, precise generosity."
"They decided": Q. in Shenker, "PG Is Dead at 81." **Favorite sister:** Weld, p. 21: Benita was "the love of Peggy's childhood." **Vowing never to return:** "As a result of Benita's death I decided never again to go to America"; PG, p. 65. **"Household goods":** Weld, p. 211. **Last stand in Marseilles:** Lader, pp. 46–47; Weld, p. 214. **"Exquisitely-made"; "he had"; "and a handsome":** PG, p. 180. **"I did not like":** PG, p. 220.
Cork Street and Boulevard Montparnasse: Peggy frequented the bars along Boulevard Montparnasse while in Paris, where she lived mostly in hotels, and Guggenheim Jeune was on Cork Street in London. **Eye shadow:** Lehman. **Description of Guggenheim:** Weld, p. 255. **French talk of American food:** Rupert Barneby, q. in Weld, p. 255. **"Mephistophelean":** Johnson, q. in Weld, p. 253. **"Surrealism's headquarters"; "financial angel"; "she practically":** "Surrealists in exile," p. 50.
Kiesler: See Weld, p. 266. **Views banished:** Lader, p. 116. **Materials:** Weld, p. 286. **"Break down the physical":** Kiesler, q. in Weld, p. 285, citing Kiesler, "Design Correlation," p. 76. **"As thorough a sample":** Weld, pp. 266–67. **Read and van Doesburg's list; work by Ferren:** Weld, p. 267: Weld generously characterizes her interest in American art at this time as "cautious." **"Great physico-mental":** André Breton, "Genesis and Perspective of Surrealism," in PG, ed., p. 26. **Pictures of eyes:** Weld, p. 267. **Gallery name:** Peggy chose it because she liked it, not because the Baroness Hilla Rebay, director of her uncle Solomon's museum (four blocks away), was determined to prevent her from debasing the family name; see Ernst, pp. 224–25; Weld, p. 265.
"Drove people crazy": Weld, p. 288. **Opening night crowd; description of gallery:** Weld, p. 290. **"Surrealist Circus!":** Mann, "Surrealist Circus!" p. 174. **"Isms Rampant":** Isms Rampant," p. 66. **"A sort of blend":** "Art That's Modern and Mysterious," *New York Journal American,* clipping in the PG Papers, q. in Lader, p. 129. **"My eyes":** McBride, "New Gallery Ideas." **"She made a big":** Q. in Weld, p. 290. **"Research laboratory"; "serve the future":** "PG to Open Art Gallery—Art of This Century," press release, Oct. 1942, in Exhibition Catalogues Collection, AAA, q. in Lader, p. 126. **Earrings by Calder and Tanguy:** To show her impartiality toward abstraction and Surrealism.
Philandering father: Weld, p. 23. **"Dizzy" mother:** Weld, p. 18. **Nannies:** Weld, p. 20: They followed a regimen of cold baths, rigid sleeping positions, and plenty of discipline. "I once had a nurse who threatened to cut out my tongue if I dared to repeat the foul things she said to me"; PG, p. 7. **Dispute over advertisement in *VVV*:** Lader, pp. 204–05. **"Had sacrificed":** PG, p. 235. **"Mesquin":** Q. in PG, p. 235. *VVV* **cover show canceled:** Lader, p. 200. **Replacement show:** "15 Early 15 Late Paintings," by Braque, Chagall, Dali, de Chirico, Duchamp, Ernst, Gris, Kandinsky, Klee, Léger, Masson, Miró, Mondrian, Picasso, and Tanguy; Weld, p. 300. **Ernst in Amagansett:** Wilcox: Lucia Wilcox helped pay the rent. **Attempted seduction of Duchamp:** See Weld, pp. 278–79. **Joke about Tanning:** Weld, p. 294. **"Parlor anarchists":** Mann, "Surrealist Circus," p. 174. **"I am not":** PG, "PG Replies," p. 4.
Sweeney promoted to adviser: Weld, p. 300. **"Whipping boy":** Weld, p. 331. **Matta sole "European":** Lader, pp. 205–06. **Seeking out American Surrealists:** Lader, p. 194; e.g., Cornell, who was represented in the gallery's first temporary exhibition in December 1942; Lader, p. 193. Lader, p. 205: Peggy's "separation from Ernst had other, more far-reaching implications for the history of American art. The timing of this personal tragedy coincided exactly with her shift in allegiance away from the Surrealists to a group of younger, relatively unknown American artists."
"Shocking": Q. in Weld, p. 305. **Description of Putzel:** Myers; Lader, p. 145; Weld, p. 332. **Eye for quality:** Betty Parsons, q. in Weld, p. 330. **Cigarette holder and glasses:**

Charles Seliger, int. by Weld, Mar. 31, 1979, q. in Weld, p. 331. **Weakness for martinis:** Weld, p. 331. **"He paid twenty":** Levy, q. in Weld, p. 331. **"An insane":** Weld, p. 331. **"She treated him":** Q. in Weld, p. 331.
Putzel's background: Weld, p. 194. **Hollywood gallery:** Lader, pp. 146–49. **"Movie people":** Charles Seliger, int. by Weld, Mar. 31, 1979, q. in Weld, p. 194. **Letter to Onslow-Ford:** Q. in Lader, p. 166, citing Onslow-Ford to Hermine Benhaim: The letter arrived around Christmas time. Ronnie Rose Elliott, an artist, who was exhibiting at an adjacent gallery, recalled (int. by Lader, Feb. 11, 1976, q. in Lader, p. 166) Putzel inviting her up to see Jackson's work: "I want to show you someone whom I think is a very great artist. I found him, and we're going to exhibit him. To me, he's one of the best . . . This is going to be the major artist in this country." **"Artists for victory":** Dec. 7, 1941–Feb. 23, 1943. **Baziotes "approved":** PG, int. by Lader, Apr. 3, 1978, q. in Lader, p. 260.
Collage show: Apr. 16–May 15, 1943. **Collage from Gypsy Rose Lee:** Weld, p. 301. **Connolly a close friend:** See Lader, p. 210. **Rumors that Peggy "edited" entries:** Busa. Wheeler: "She put those that she wanted Sweeney to look at in one pile and those that she didn't even want Sweeney to see in another pile." **Voting system:** See Lader, pp. 210–11.
"Dreadful": Q. by Ernst. Ironically, PG (q. in Anderson, "For PG") later claimed, "Pollock was easily accepted by me. His art was so overwhelming and wonderful I loved it right away." **Guggenheim sure Pollock wouldn't make cut:** Weld, p. 305. **Mondrian wanting time:** Weld, p. 304. **Mondrian walking around:** Ernst, p. 241. **"Rooted":** Ernst, p. 241. **"Pretty awful"; "that's not painting"; "absolutely no discipline":** Q. in Ernst, p. 241; also q. in Weld, p. 305. **"I'm not so sure":** Q. by Ernst in Potter, p. 72. **"You must watch":** Q. by Krasner, q. in Weld, p. 305. **"You can't be serious"; "The way I paint":** Q. by Ernst, q. in Weld, p. 305.
"Look what": Q. by Ernst. **"Pollock was easily":** Q. in Anderson, "For PG." **"She was willing":** Q. in Weld, p. 305. **"Mondrian's nod":** LK. **Reason for Mondrian accepting jury duty; Holtzman and Mondrian:** Holtzman. "I would be dead": Q. by Holtzman. **"Master":** Glamer, q. in [B]elle [K]rasne, "Fifty-Seventh Street in Review," p. 20. **Holtzman's sculpture:** Holtzman: The work is now in the Yale art gallery in the Société Anonyme collection. **"Everybody assumes":** Q. in Ernst, p. 242: According to Ernst's account, Mondrian went on at some length in the same vein: "Just because it points in the opposite direction of my paintings . . . my writings . . . is no reason to declare it invalid. . . . I don't know enough about this painter to think of him as 'great.' But I do know that I was forced to stop and look. Where you see 'lack of discipline,' I get an impression of tremendous energy. It will have to go somewhere, to be sure." **Jury "respecting"** both Holtzman and Pollock: Holtzman; see also Lader, p. 378. **"For once the future":** Connolly, "Art," p. 643. **"Those twin branches":** Coates, p. 49. **"Things really broke":** JP to CCP, July 29, 1943. **Jackson hearing about Mondrian:** Kadish. **Sales from Spring Salon:** Lader, p. 211. **Job at museum:** Kamrowski: Fabean and De Niro got him the job. **"He would make pastiches":** Bell. **"Cosmic":** Bell. **"Nicht cosmic":** Q. by Bell. **Ingratiating note:** Lukach, p. 155: "Others who worked at the museum at the same time recall a certain fractiousness on Pollock's part, but his letters to Rebay are prefectly courteous." **"I have been":** JP to Hilla Rebay, Apr. 15, 1943, q. in Lukach, pp. 154–55; see fig. 50, following p. 240. **Another obsequious letter:** "May I take this moment to thank you for our interview on April 30, in regards to a possible job opening at the Museum of Non-objective art. And again may I stress the value received from your criticism of my work and for the material check received. Knowing you will find my services most dependable and trustworthy"; JP to Hilla Rebay, May 1, 1943, q. in Lukach, p. 155. **"Custodian":** Lukach, p. 155. There is no evidence to support Potter's claim (p. 72) that John Graham had any role in securing the job for JP, despite his earlier association with Rebay. **Began work:** Lukach, p. 155.
Guggenheim's improbable mistress: Rosalind Bengelsdorf Browne, q. in FVOC, ed., p. 230: "The Baroness was then curator of Mr. Guggenheim's collection, and, let it be said, probably of Mr. Guggenheim." The baroness ungratefully pooh-poohed the widespread talk that she was Guggenheim's mistress: "Why, when I knew him first, he was an old man;

old enough to be my father, and this he was exactly to the end"; q. in Lomask, p. 175. **"Bubbles Bauer";** Salemme. **Converted showroom:** Bell. **"About two visitors":** Salemme. *Modern Screen Romance:* Bell. **"Very well dressed":** Salemme. **Spitting orders:** Bell: "If you stood too close, you got a shower." **Description of Bauer:** Bell. **"Execrable":** Myers, p. 81. **"Baronial splendor":** Ernst, pp. 224–25. In a bizarre turn, the previous year, Bauer had rewarded the baroness for her largesse by falling in love with his housekeeper, which understandably infuriated the baroness, who accused the new Mrs. Bauer of being a "streetwalker and a spy." This resulted in a crossfire of libel suits and then a visit to Rebay by the FBI (instigated, no doubt, by the Bauers), who proceeded to lock up the baroness on the suspicion that *she* was a spy. The faithful Solomon arranged her release and the faithful baroness soon forgave her beloved Bauer; Weld, p. 110.
No visits to other galleries: Bell. **No marriages without permission:** Salemme. **Hiring spies:** Bell; Salemme. **"Write down":** Bell. **Feeling free to "improve" canvases:** Bell; see also Bell, q. in Potter, p. 73. **"We have another":** Q. by Salemme. **Bing Crosby record:** Bell; Salemme. **Jackson cleaning and hanging pictures:** Joe Meert to FVOC, June 12, 1964, q. in FVOC, "The Genesis of JP," p. 82. **Running elevator:** LK, int. by Landau, May 1, 1979, q. in Landau, "LK," p. 233. **Duties of De Niro and Xceron:** Bell: JP might also have had contact with I. Rice Pereira, Ralph Rosenborg, and Attilio Salemme. **Basement flooding:** Bell. **"For leaving the basement"; "drunk and wrecking":** Salemme.
Putzel staying for dinner: LK. **"He told Jackson":** Q. in Weld, p. 307. **"Jackson was thoroughly":** LK. **Date of Peggy's visit:** Datable because it was also the day Busa was married. **Lee wanting to skip wedding:** Busa. **Fifteenth Street house:** The house, at 212 West Fifteenth Street, belonged to Busa's bride's sister. **Lee discovering Jackson best man; other guests:** Busa. **"What a dumb thing":** Q. by Busa. **Lee handing Busa ring:** Busa. **"[Jackson] suggested"; "almost incoherent"** LK, q. in Nemser, p. 88. **Description of Peggy:** Sterne. **Peggy cursing stairs:** LK, q. in Nemser, p. 88. **Weak ankles:** Sterne: "She used to continuously twist or break her ankles." **Denouncing Putzel and Lee:** LK relinquishing studio; storing work at Jackson's:** Busa. **"L.K. L.K.":** Q. by LK. **"I didn't come":** Q. by LK, q. in Nemser, p. 88. LK: "That was really like a hard thrust. I thought, 'What a bitch.' " Johnson, q. in Weld, p. 256: "Peggy had . . . almost a mannerism of making it clear to others that they really didn't count for much."
Burning Landscape: Bought later that summer; see Putzel to JP, summer 1943; also LK to SMP, July–Aug., 1943. **Cornell show:** Nov. 30–Dec. 1942; see Lader, p. 368. **Hélion show:** Feb. 8–Mar. 6; see Lader, pp. 371–72. **Peggy preferring Baziotes:** Lader, p. 260, citing PG, int. by Lader, Apr. 3, 1978. **"The most beautiful":** Q. in LK to SMP, July–Aug. 1943. **Duchamp's reaction to *Stenographic Figure:*** Weld, p. 305. **"You know where":** Q. by Denise Hare, q. in Potter, p. 72. **Bell fired:** Bell. **"[Duchamp] didn't give a goddam":** Q. in Weld, p. 277. **"Didn't mind wearing":** Q. in Weld, p. 278. **"Pas mal":** See Weld, p. 305. LK: "Vail, and the whole outgoing group, were furious at her for taking on someone like Pollock."
Putzel handling details: LK. **"Work in peace":** PG, q. in Lader, p. 215, citing PG, *Confessions of an Art Addict* (New York: Macmillan, 1960), p. 105. **Financial arrangement:** Lader, p. 215, citing PG, p. 105. **"Whether a larger scale":** Weld, p. 306. **Unprecedented deal:** Abel: "Matta was one of the few painters who had a dealer who gave him money every month, Pierre Matisse." CG, q. in Weld, p. 306: "The contracts [with Guggenheim and Parsons] were utterly unique for that generation of artists. . . . [John] Marin, Milton Avery might have contracts. [But generally] it wasn't done and dealers wouldn't buy." André Breton, at the urging of Kay Sage, also received $200 a month from Peggy; Lader, p. 90.
"Have signed": JP to LK, July 1943. The letter is undated, but Lee was in Huntington Station, Long Island, the week of July 15 and returned on Saturday, July 17. **"Left and didn't":** Ossorio, recalling JP. **"Canned for talking":** Bell. **"Between the canned music":** Q. in Myers, p. 81. **"Quit my dreaming":** JP to SMP, March 8, 1933. **Wall 9 by 20 feet:** Exact proportions, 8'11½" by 19'9"; JP to CCP, July 1943. **"It looks pretty big":** JP to CCP, July 1943.

29. BEHIND THE VEIL

SOURCES

Books, articles, manuscripts, film, documents, and transcripts

Alloway, *JP*; *Art of This Century*, *JP*; Friedman, *JP*; PG, *Out of This Century*; Janis, *Abstract and Surrealist Art in America*; Janis, *Abstract and Surrealist Art in the United States*; Lane and Larsen, eds., *Abstract Painting and Sculpture in America*; FVOC, *JP*; OC&T, *JP*; Potter, *To a Violent Grave*; Weld, *Peggy*; Wysuph, *JP*.

Paul Brach, "Tandem Paint: Krasner/Pollock," *Art in America*, Mar. 1982; Robert M. Coates, review, *New Yorker*, Nov. 20, 1943; DP&G, "Who Was JP?" *Art in America*, May–June 1967; Manny Farber, "JP," *New Republic*, June 25, 1945; David Freke, "JP: A Psychological Self-Portrait," *Studio International*, Dec. 1973; CG, "Marc Chagall, Lyonel Feininger, JP," *Nation*, Nov. 27, 1943; Elizabeth Langhorne, "JP's 'The Moon Woman Cuts the Circle,' " *Arts*, Mar. 1979; Robert Motherwell, "Painters' Objects," *Partisan Review*, Winter 1944; Stephen Polcari, "JP and THB," *Arts*, Mar. 1979; Review, *Art News*, Nov. 15, 1943; Maude Riley, "Fifty-Seventh Street in Review," *Art Digest*, Nov. 15, 1943; William Rubin, "Notes on Masson and Pollock," *Arts*, Nov. 1959; William Rubin, "Pollock as Jungian Illustrator: The Limits of Psychological Criticism, Part I," *Art in America*, Nov. 1979; William Rubin, "Pollock as Jungian Illustrator: The Limits of Psychological Criticism, Part II," *Art in America*, Dec. 1979; Jonathan Welch, "JP's 'The White Angel' and the Origins of Alchemy," *Arts*, Mar. 1979; Judith Wolfe, "Jungian Aspects of JP's Imagery," *Artforum*, Nov. 1972. C. L. Wysuph, "Behind the Veil," *Art News*, Oct. 1970; "Young Man from Wyoming," *Art Digest*, Nov. 1, 1943.

Edward Alden Jewell, review, *NYT*, Nov. 14, 1943; Hilton Kramer, "The Inflation of JP," *NYT*, Apr. 9, 1967.

Melvin Paul Lader, "PG's Art of This Century: The Surrealist Milieu and the American Avant-Garde, 1942–1947" (Lader) (Ph.D. thesis), Newark: University of Delaware, 1981; Ellen Gross Landau, "LK: A Study of Her Early Career (1926–1949)" (Ph.D. thesis), Newark: University of Delaware, 1981.

Strokes of Genius: JP (film), Court Productions, 1984.

The William Baziotes Collection, AAA.

James Brooks, int. by James T. Vallière, n.d., AAA; CG, int. by Kathleen Shorthall, Nov. 9, 1959, Time/Life Archives; JP, int. by William Wright, 1951, for radio program, WERI, Westerly, Rhode Island.

Interviews

Ethel Baziotes; James Brooks; Peter Busa; Violet de Laszlo; Jimmy Ernst; CG; Balcomb Greene; Harry Holtzman; Axel Horn; Harry Jackson; Sidney Janis; Buffie Johnson; Reuben Kadish; Gerome Kamrowski; LK; Harold Lehman; John Little; Mercedes Matter; ACM; George Mercer; FLP; MJP; David Porter; Becky Reis; May Tabak Rosenberg; Herman Somberg; Hedda Sterne; James Johnson Sweeney; Roger Wilcox; Reginald Wilson; Betsy Zogbaum.

NOTES

Behind the Veil: The phrase was used by Wysuph as the title for his article in *Art News*. **Rate of production:** About twelve paintings in about eight weeks. **"Like somebody had knocked"; painting had looked finished:** Little. *Moon Woman Cuts the Circle:* Langhorne, "JP's 'The Moon Woman Cuts the Circle,' " pp. 128–29; Wolfe, "Jungian Aspects of JP's Imagery," pp. 65–73. **Jungian analysis of paintings:** During the 1970s, a host of Jungian scholars (Freke, Langhorne, Welch, Wolfe, Wysuph) turned to Jung's writings for help in interpreting JP's paintings, especially those from the 1942–43 period. Langhorne ("JP's 'The Moon Woman Cuts the Circle,' " p. 128) argues that the paintings lend themselves "to quite precise interpretation in the light of Jungian psychology." Freke ("JP," p. 221) maintains that JP undertook "a consciously Jungian programme for his work." "Such a position," writes Rubin ("Pollock as Jungian Illustrator, Part II," p. 86), "requires that Pollock be seen as consciously and deliberately elaborating an iconographic scheme —and this was not his way of working, either as he describes it or as we see it operating." Oddly, the same scholars who argue that JP was consciously aware of Jungian ideas also argue that the Jungian archetypes in his painting emerged from his unconscious. Langhorne, "JP's 'The Moon Woman Cuts the Circle,' " p. 131: "Though Pollock quit Jungian analysis in 1942, he in effect continues his autopsychoanalysis, mediated by the images of his art."

Of course, Rubin ("Pollock as Jungian Illustrator, Part I," p. 110) proposes an alternative subject matter—the Minotaur legend, pointing to its "ubiquitousness" in both Picasso and late Surrealism as "a more immediate and likely candidate for absorption in Pollock's personal mythology than many of the references—some very obscure—which Jungian critics deduce from books by Jung that Pollock almost certainly never read." JP does appear to be have been aware of Jung's writings. He appears to have attended a meeting of the Analytical Psychology Club of New York City and noted certain books, including *The Concept of the Collective Unconscious* by Jung and *Initiate History* by Henderson (undated note in JP Papers). But JP encountered those references—the tail-eating serpent, for example—not in Jungian writings, as some scholars have suggested (Langhorne, "JP's 'The Moon Woman Cuts the Circle,' " p. 133), but in his sessions with Henderson and de Laszlo. Langhorne (p. 128) admits that JP's "four years of Jungian psychotherapy" were "at the core of his involvement with Jung."

JP undoubtedly looked to Jungian theory as a source of subject matter. Holtzman, who had been reading Jung since he was eighteen (he describes himself as a "poor Jung man"), remembers visiting JP on Eighth Street and discussing their common "involvement with Jungian views." Bultman says, "Jackson was trying to dissociate himself from the past, trying to find a whole different vocabulary, and Jungian analysis was full of a new vocabulary." Kamrowski says JP was "using Jungian imagery as a *device*" to come up with an original style. Johnson, a friend of JP's and an avid Jungian who knew Jung personally, says the scholars who have looked to Jung's writings to interpret JP's paintings don't understand the kind of person JP was, even in Jungian terms: "Oh, my dear, the Jungians are awfully academic. Not Jung himself, but his followers. As an 'intuitive,' JP can't be fit into this kind of criticism. It's really not pertinent."

What JP derived from Jungian analysis—in addition to a few specific motifs, as opposed to elaborated myths—was permission to engage in his own myth-making. Alloway, n.p.: "Myth in Pollock's hands was never an exercise in classical allusion but kept that enigmatic center which it is the function of myth to preserve." Rubin, "Pollock as Jungian Illustrator, Part II," p. 86: "Pollock's pictures are mythopoetic in the truly creative sense; he did not paint Jungian glosses or paradigms but created his own private myths whose elusive meanings are inseparable from the pictorial language he invented to recount them. To attach their symbols to a study of Jung or even to the broader literature of mythology itself is to deprive them of their originality." De Laszlo says JP *had* to work from the unconscious: "He was *enormously* introverted. He was introverted to a pathological extent—meaning that he was in one way enormously unconscious."

The myths that JP created were extremely personal and obscure. Rubin, "Pollock as Jungian Illustrator, Part I," p. 117: "While I think Pollock considered all his images to have psychological content, their *precise* definition or identification— given how little we know of the artist's intimate life and thought—is a chancy if not impossible (and most likely wrongheaded) task, even if we do not misread the forms." Indeed, subjects can seldom be inferred from titles (see Rubin, "Pollock as Jungian Illustrator, Part II," p. 73), which were often later changed *(Pasiphaë)* or else are clearly unrelated *(She-Wolf).* To some extent, this was probably as JP wanted it. In one of his most famous statements on his paintings, especially applicable to works from this period, he said that "*She-Wolf* came into existence because I had to paint it. Any attempt on my part to say something about it, to attempt an explanation of the inexplicable, could only destroy it"; q. in Janis, p. 112. Freke ("JP," p. 220) notes that "this only means that Pollock was not prepared to explain it, not that it had no meaning nor that the meaning is too vague—it may indeed have been too precise for a man who is known to have been extremely reserved."

Occasional clues to JP's mythology can be found, however. On the margin of a drawing, he wrote, "The rock the fish was winged and split of two—so one could grow to be and was the son" (frame 256, from a Pollock drawing, 51B2, Marlborough period, in JP Papers). We can envision a rock being transformed into a fish, the fish sprouting wings, then splitting in two, as a way of giving birth to the son. Freke ("JP," p. 221) notes a myth in Jung of "monstrous fish and the sea journeys associated with them . . . they symbolize the all-devouring Mother, that is, the hero's 'anima.' To gain immortality the hero must go back to the Mother in her aspect of death and conquer her, and the fish is the symbol often chosen to represent her; the hero's eventual emergence from its belly symbolizes his rebirth as immortal."

On another drawing (c. 1943, OC&T 704, III, p. 211), JP wrote, "Thick / thin / / Chinese / Am. indian / / sun / snake / woman / life / / effort / reality / / total / / shoes / foot." He then added the numbers 13 (the unlucky number) and 46 (JP's lucky number) to the image. This does not seem to be so much a Jungian pairing of opposites as it is a set of personal associations: some obvious, as in "thick" and "thin," "shoes" and "foot"; some more personal, as in "Chinese" and "American Indian"; and some quite poignant, as in the equivalence of "effort" and "reality." A similar set of personal associations exists on an ink and gouache drawing on paper (c. 1943, OC&T 963, IV, p. 43): "Male / Woman / goat / deer / [illegible]."

Busa says, "I found it easy to hear him talk about his work, which he wouldn't do if there were more than four or five people, because he was terribly self-conscious—quite withdrawn and reserved. But when he talked about the work, he always talked about it in psychoanalytic terms. He would relate a story. He would say, 'This is the apex,' and 'here is the relationship of the id to the superego,' and 'this is what the sensor plays,' and 'this is the line of the orbit of the division. . . .' He would go into it like that. It wasn't all Jungian. He knew a lot about Freudian psychology, too." •

Only a "general notion": Alloway, n.p.: "The figurative works are not pre-planned but improvised." **"No, because it hasn't been":** JP, int. by Wright, 1951. **"Of course I did":** Q. in Weld, p. 323. **Jackson detesting titles:** LK. **"[Jackson's] unconscious"; "in a sense":** Brooks, int. by Vallière, n.d. Kadish: "Before he'd have a show scheduled, there would be this tremendous explosive kind of work period."

Three weeks begun late 1942: The evidence is that *Search for a Symbol* was painted around November or December 1942 and that *Pasiphaë* was completed after the Guggenheim show, although one report suggests that *Pasiphaë* was still wet when it was first exhibited at Art of This Century, from April 11 to April 30, 1944, in the "First Exhibition in America of Twenty Paintings"; see Lader, p. 242. *Search for a Symbol:* The original title, *Male and Female in Search of a Symbol*, was shortened for the 1945 showing at Art of This Century; see OC&T 89, I, pp. 78–79. We accept Freke's contention ("JP," p. 221, supported by OC&T 89, I, pp. 78–79) that this painting's "stylistic place is very early in 1943 or even 1942." **"Personage[s] over":** Janis to JP, Sept. 27, 1943. *Guardians of the Secret:* In a photo that Kadish took of JP (in Kadish's possession) while the painting was still in process, the table can be seen in perspective, as it is in *Search for a Symbol.*

Title of *Pasiphaë*: For some time, the title led scholars to assume that the painting depicted the myth of Pasiphaë, the queen of Crete, making love to her bull. Rubin, in particular, writing in 1959 ("Notes on Masson and Pollock," p. 42), compared JP's painting to an early painting called *Pasiphaë* by Masson, only to find that JP's painting was originally entitled *Moby-Dick.* Rubin ("Pollock as Jungian Illustrator, Part II," p. 74), writing twenty years later: "On a visit to Pollock's studio in the company of James Johnson Sweeney, PG expressed some dislike of the title *Moby-Dick*, and Pollock said he was willing to change it. After some discussion, Sweeney—who had that morning come upon a reference to the Minoan Queen in some work he was doing on Pound and Eliot— suggested the title *Pasiphaë*. According to his wife, Pollock said something to the effect of 'Who the hell is Pasiphaë?' Sweeney recounted the tale, which Pollock found very interesting because it concerned the mother of the Minotaur and dealt with a combination of eros and bestiality. (He later jotted down an outline of the story, which survives among his papers.)"

Putzel's address: 67 East Fifty-seventh Street; Lader, p. 171, citing postcard from Putzel to William Baziotes, Sept. 16, 1943. **Lee's perception of Putzel:** LK. **"Small pictures":** Putzel to JP, Oct. 2, 1943. **Jackson obliging:** Putzel to JP, Nov. 1, 1943. *Wounded Animal:* OC&T 97, I, p. 87. Both *Wounded Animal* and *Male and Female in Search of a Symbol* appear to have been added late, since they did not appear by name in the catalogue; see FVOC, "The Genesis of JP," p. 29. **Abstract exercises:** OC&T 92–94, I, pp. 82–85; see Putzel to JP, Nov. 1, 1943. **Paintings finished and delivered:** Putzel to JP, Oct. 2, 1943. **More small-scale works:** Lader, p. 225. **Gouaches:** OC&T 972–73, IV, pp. 50–51. **Drawings:** E.g., OC&T 697, III, p. 206. **Segovia concert:** Putzel to JP, Nov. 1, 1943: see also Landau, "LK," p. 237. **"She really flipped":** Q. in Weld, p. 310. **Macpherson married and homosexual:** See Weld, pp. 308–09. **"[He] came into my life":** PG, caption facing p. 197. **Sixty-first Street apartment:** 155 East Sixty-first Street; Weld, p. 313. **"Less as a lover":** Weld, p. 311. **"You can have an affair":** Q. in Weld, p. 311. **Divorce from Ernst:** On Macpherson's advice, she forced Ernst, who was continuing to paint at her residence, Hale House, while living elsewhere with Tanning, to vacate the premises altogether; Weld, p. 311. **"In a man/child":** Ernst. **Jackson making Peggy uncomfortable:** Weld, p. 323. **"A trapped animal":** Ernst, q. in Potter, p. 74. **Peggy speaking to Krasner:** Porter: "I had the impression that Lee did all of Jackson's talking for him, including with Peggy."
Lee calling from Cafeteria: Busa. **Keeping visitors to a minimum:** LK. **"I'm not working":** LK to SMP, summer 1943. **Frank and Sande visiting:** JP to CCP, July 29, 1943. **Baby-sitting:** LK. **"The wonderful things":** LK to SMP, summer 1943. **Losing shoes:** JP to SMP, summer 1943. **"People who found":** Weld, p. 388. **"Stood over a manhole":** Q. in Weld, p. 327. **"Dinner for a few people"; "two maids"; not catered":** LK, q. in Weld, p. 314. **"They would quarrel":** Q. in Weld, p. 325. **"Breasts to pop out":** Sterne. **"Kookie":** Q. in Weld, p. 314. **Lee thinking Peggy nymphomaniacal:** Weld, p. 314. **"Bitch":** Q. in Weld, p. 306. **"Too much money":** LK. **Guggenheim attitude toward Russian Jews:** See Weld, pp. 34ff. **"Holding a job":** Kiesler, int. by Landau. **"He was grateful":** Q. in Weld, p. 325.
"Cordon bleu chef": Putzel to JP, fall 1943. **"Mrs. Goodspeed":** Putzel to JP, Oct. 1943. **"[James Thrall] Soby":** Putzel to JP, Oct. 1943. **Artist-correspondent:** JP to SMP, summer 1943. **Reynal buying work:** Reynal to LK and JP, Aug. 4, 1943: She paid for the painting in five installments of $100 each. **Morley offering exhibition:** LK to SMP, summer 1943. **Morley wanting *Guardians*:** Kadish. **"I enjoyed very much":** Janis to JP, Sept. 27, 1943. **Reproduction of *Guardians*:** Janis, no. 64, p. 22. **Reproduction of *She-Wolf*:** Janis, color plate 80, p. 113. **Greenberg becoming a critic:** CG, int. by Shorthall, Nov. 9, 1959. **"I don't think he'll take it":** LK to SMP, summer 1943. **Pollock family withholding judgment:** If JP expected support, even purchases, from his family—which he did—none was to be found; FLP; MJP. **"My painting had him worried":** JP to CCP, July 29, 1943.
Showing Lehman paintings: On another occasion Lehman claimed he saw the paintings in JP's studio. **Lehman knowing Putzel in L.A.; moving to Woodstock:** Lehman, who, despite his early promise, had almost disappeared from the American art scene. **"These small pictures":** Putzel to JP, 1943. **Riley a friend of Putzel's:** Putzel to LK and JP, 1943, in which he refers to Riley as "a friend at court." **"Born in Wyoming":** Riley, "Fifty-Seventh Street in Review," p. 18. **Endorsement penned by Putzel:** Lader, pp. 225–26, citing PG, int. by Lader, Apr. 4, 1978: "[Putzel] was writing many, if not all, of the press releases for Art of This Century at the time." **"One of the strongest":** "Young Man from Wyoming," p. 11.
Introduction request by Peggy: Sweeney. **"Talent, will,":** Introduction to Art of This Century, n.p. **Jackson throwing catalogue; "undisciplined":** LK. **"He was furious":** See also LK, q. in DP&G, "Who was JP?" p. 51. **"Fine introduction":** LK, q. in DP&G, "Who was JP?" p. 51. **Sweeney on committee at MOMA:** Hunter, "Introduction, to MOMA, p. 22. **"Dear Sweeney":** JP to Sweeney, Nov. 3, 1943 (emphasis added). **Repainting *Search for a Symbol*:** A number of accounts say JP painted the work specifically for Sweeney after reading his introduction (DP&G, "Who was JP?" p. 51, and Friedman, p. 61), but it had already been

painted. He may well have done some repainting after reading the introduction. **"I want you to see":** Q. by LK.
Small crowd; warm night: Reis. *Conflict:* OC&T 91, I, p. 82: 12 by 15½ inches. **Prices:** Listed in *Art News*, Nov. 15, 1943, p. 23. **Uniforms in evidence:** Zogbaum. **Lassaw on leave:** Lane and Larsen, eds., p. 183. **Matter loan:** OC&T 92, I, pp. 82–83. The painting, a wedding gift to the Matters, was listed as "10. Untitled" in the catalogue. The Matters later lost the work, although it turned up in other hands; Matter; see OC&T I, p. 92. **"Sweeney did so much":** PG, p. 254. **Description of Jackson at opening:** Kadish. Reis says he was "terribly nervous." **"A little boy":** Reis. **"Sixty times":** LK. **"At least a quart":** Reis. **"Lee protesting party":** LK. **"A wild man":** Q. by Wilcox. **"Very Masson":** Q. in Simon, "Concerning the Beginnings of the New York School," p. 19. **"Burst a blood vessel":** Q. by Somberg. **Scribbled obscenities:** Weld, p. 324. **"Pollock unnerved me":** Ethel Schwabacher, q. in Weld, p. 324. **"A belch":** Greene.
Outpouring of publicity: Lader, pp. 230–31. **Reviews:** Coates, review, p. 49; CG, "Marc Chagall, Lyonel Feininger, JP," p. 621; Jewell, review, *NYT*; McB[ride], review, New York *Sun*, clipping in JP artist file, N.Y. Public Library, misdated in file, cited in Lader, p. 228; Motherwell, "Painters Objects," pp. 93–97; review, *Art News*, Nov. 15, 1943; Riley, "Fifty-Seventh Street in Review," p. 18. **"A kaleidoscope":** Clipping in JP artist file, N.Y. Public Library, misdated in file, cited in Lader, p. 228. **"An authentic discovery":** Coates, review, p. 49. **"We like all this":** Riley, review, p. 18. **"Among the strongest":** CG, "Marc Chagall, Lyonel Feininger, JP," p. 621. **"Mr. Pollock's forcefulness":** Coates, review, p. 49. **"Out a-questing":** Riley, "Fifty-Seventh Street in Review," p. 18. **"The first painter":** CG, "Marc Chagall, Lyonel Feininger, JP," p. 621.
"[Jackson's] abstractions"; "his work is personal": Review, *Art News*, p. 177. **"A young Western":** Coates, review, p. 49. **"A sense of history":** Kramer, "The Inflation of JP."
Lee at gallery every day: Weld, p. 293. **Macpherson not enthusiastic:** PG, p. 248: "I liked the mural but Kenneth couldn't bear it." **Position of mural:** Kamrowski: The painting was too tall to stand flat against the wall, and thus was set at an angle. **Jackson sitting and staring:** Little, recalling LK, q. in Potter, p. 75. Little says JP stared at the mural "for months," but this isn't possible. **"More and more depressed":** PG, p. 247. **"Made the leap":** Busa. **Bill and Ethel Baziotes to dinner:** Baziotes; see also JP to Bill Baziotes, Dec. 15, 1943. in the William Baziotes Collection: "Dear Bill Can we expect you and Ethel Thursday night about six thirty hope you can make it best Jack Wednesday." The "Thursday" in question was December 23.
Stipend in jeopardy: Little: "They needed the money." The mural itself involved no extra compensation beyond JP's monthly stipend of $150. If Little's story is correct—and he is very definite about it—the only financial coercion that Peggy could have exercised was withholding the stipend. **Holidays with Sande:** JP to SMP, Feb. 4, 1944. **Visits from Sande:** SLM visited New York in late July; JP to CCP, July 29, 1943. He also probably came down for the November show. **"Enduring"; "dump":** SLM to CCP, June 27, 1943. **Seventyeight-hour weeks:** JP to CCP, July 29, 1943.
Jackson locked in: LK. **"I don't know what":** Q. by Little. **Not disturbing Jackson:** Little, in *Strokes of Genius*. **"Could only wring her hands":** Little. **"I had a vision":** Q. by Jackson. JP described the same vision to Busa and Kadish on separate occasions. **Images obliterated:** Busa: "He told me that he obliterated specific references in that painting which came from his unconscious." **"Every animal":** Q. by Jackson. **Bentonesque lines:** See Polcari, "JP and THB," p. 124: "In *Mural* of 1943 Pollock took up Benton's challenge of creating a horizontally extended rhythmic pattern. In such a composition, Benton suggested, several poles would have to be disposed along the horizontal axis and rhythmic counterpoint disposed around them. Pollock's 'poles' are arbitrarily lengthened vertical contours, and around them are disposed myriad biomorphic forms." **Color in the Guggenheim mural:** Color seems to have been secondary to structure in JP's eyes: Mercer remembers JP telling him, "When I looked at the Guggenheim mural, I had to push color aside."
Fifteen hours: There is disagreement about how long the physical act took. Estimates range from three hours (PG, p. 247) to six hours (Kamrowski) to several days (Lehman). The most reliable and consistent story is that it took JP from about sundown to about sunup (Little), or "fifteen hours" (Wilcox).

"Became hysterical"; "knowing his weakness"; "come home": PG, p. 248. Calling Duchamp and Hare: PG (p. 248) says the second individual was "a workman," but Weld (p. 326) says it was Hare, quoting him as a source. "Wanted us to tack it up": Hare, int. by Weld, Feb. 26, 1979, q. in Weld, p. 326. Jackson incoherent: Wilcox. Jackson going to marble fireplace: Brach, "Tandem Paint," p. 92. Urinating: Friedman, p. 80; PG, pp. 247–48; Lader, p. 288; Weld, p. 326. All of Peggy's accounts say that JP was naked. But several eyewitnesses and other accounts disagree; Busa; Wilcox. In our opinion, stripping implies a degree of premeditation inconsistent with his state of inebriation and a degree of exhibitionism inconsistent with his character. Busa: Peggy told him that, later that same evening, "Jackson fell asleep and vomited all over my bed."

30. FRUITS AND NUTS

SOURCES

Books, articles, manuscripts, and transcripts

Abel, *The Intellectual Follies*; Ashton, *The New York School*; Friedman, *JP*; Harvard Law School, *Alumni Directory of the Harvard Law School*; Moffett, *Art in Narrow Streets*; MOMA, *Museum of Modern Art*; Cindy Nemser, *Art Talk*; FVOC, *JP*; OC&T; Potter, *To a Violent Grave*; Solomon, *JP*; Spoto, *The Kindness of Strangers*; Weld, *Peggy*; Williams, *Memoirs*.

Answers to questionnaire, *Arts & Architecture*, Feb. 1944; Bruce Glaser, "JP, an Interview with LK," *Arts*, Apr. 1967; Grace Glueck, "Krasner and Pollock: Scenes from a Marriage," *Art News*, Dec. 1981; Hayden Herrera, "John Graham: Modernist Turns Magus," *Arts*, Oct. 1976; "JP: An Artists' Symposium, Part I," *Art News*, Apr. 1967; Robert Motherwell, "Painters' Objects," *Partisan Review*, Winter 1944; Vivien Raynor, "JP—'He Broke the Ice,'" *NYT Magazine*, Apr. 2, 1967; Maude Riley, "Rejected Youth," *Art Digest*, May 15, 1944; Barbara Rose, "American Great: LK," *Vogue*, June 1972; Sidney Simon, "Concerning the Beginnings of the New York School: 1939–1943, An Interview with Peter Busa and Matta," *Art International*, Summer 1967; James Johnson Sweeney, "Five American Painters," *Harper's Bazaar*, Apr. 1944; Amei Wallach, "Krasner's Triumph," *Vogue*, Nov. 1983.

Samuel G. Freedman, "Julian Beck, 60, Is Dead; Founded Living Theater," *NYT*, Sept, 17, 1985; Robert Taylor, "LK: Artist in Her Own Right," *Boston Globe*, May 18, 1980; Amei Wallach, "Out of JP's Shadow," *Newsday*, Sept. 23, 1981.

Melvin Paul Lader, "PG's Art of This Century: The Surrealist Milieu and the American Avant-Garde, 1942–1947" (Lader) (Ph.D. thesis), Newark: University of Delaware, 1981; FVOC, "The Genesis of JP: 1912 to 1932" (Ph.D. thesis), Baltimore: Johns Hopkins University, 1965; May Natalie Tabak, "A Collage" (unpub. ms.), n.d.

Robert Motherwell, int. by Paul Cummings, Nov. 24, 1971; Feb. 21, 1972; Mar. 30, 1972; May 1, 1974, AAA.

Interviews

Lionel Abel; Emil de Antonio; Ethel Baziotes; Ward Bennett; Nell Blaine; Paul Brach; Charlotte Park Brooks; James Brooks; Fritz Bultman; Peter Busa; Reginald Cabral; Nicolas Calas; Lynn Cannastra; Nicholas Carone; Herman Cherry; Dorothy Dehner; Salvatore Del Deo; Muriel Francis; Sanford Friedman; David Gibbs; Cynthia Goodman; CG; Balcomb Greene; Chaim Gross; Ben Heller; Harry Holtzman; Axel Horn; Richard Howard; Elizabeth Wright Hubbard II; Merle Hubbard; Sam Hunter; Philip Johnson; Reuben Kadish; Gerome Kamrowski; Edgar Kaufmann, Jr.; Lillian Olaney Kiesler; Lincoln Kirstein; Maria Piacenza Kron; Ernestine Lassaw; John Little; Herbert Matter; ACM; Hazel Guggenheim McKinley; George McNeil; George Mercer; John Bernard Myers; Alfonso Ossorio; CCP; EFP; David Porter; Beatrice Ribak Mandelman; Becky Reis; May Tabak Rosenberg; Nene Schardt; Jane Smith; James Johnson Sweeney; Araks Tolegian; Samuel Wagstaff; Steve Wheeler; Betsy Zogbaum.

NOTES

"Jackson usually drank": LK; see also Raynor, "JP—'He Broke the Ice,'" p. 72. Chelsea Hotel lunch: McKinley: Some time later, McKinley returned to the Chelsea and suggested that they cut the piece out of the carpet and frame it.

Jackson kept away from gallery: Wagstaff: "I remember Peggy telling me that she tried to keep Pollock out of the gallery because he was always so drunk." "Perfectly nice": Q. by Wagstaff. Paintings dispersed: For exhibitions, see FVOC, "The Genesis of JP," p. 34; for sales, see Lader, pp. 229–30. "Nameless smaller work": Porter. FVOC, "The Genesis of JP," p. 35: There is no record of what works appeared in Porter's gallery. Among other painters in his 1944 show, "A Painting Prophecy 1950," were Richard Pousette-Dart, Mark Rothko, and Clyfford Still. Pinocatheca show: May 9–27, 1944. Sales: Mr. and Mrs. James Davidson Taylor bought some gouaches and drawings; Lader, p. 230, citing Davidson Taylor to Lader, July 5, 1978. Mrs. Lloyd buying *Male and Female*: Lader, p. 230, citing Eleanor B. Lloyd to Lader, July 24, 1978: Lloyd had bought it by the time it joined the show in Chicago (Mar. 5–31, 1945). "[Pollock] represents": Motherwell, "Painters' Objects," p. 97. Accepting Motherwell's help: Solomon, p. 146. Later, Lee claimed that Putzel, not Motherwell, assisted JP with this interview. OC&T, IV, p. 232. "Where were you born?": *Arts & Architecture*, Feb. 1944, p. 14. "American painters have generally": Emphasis added.

Barr detesting Jackson: "Detested" is de Antonio's word. Barr tweedy, cultured: Brach. Barr's background: Sam Hunter, "Introduction," to MOMA, pp. 10–11. The college was Wellesley. Shape of the Museum's collection: De Antonio: "Barr was really an enemy of Abstract Expressionism. He was totally hooked on French art, which was the appropriate place to be in 1929 when he started as the first director at MOMA. But as the world changed and it became apparent that what was taking place here in America was more interesting than what was left in France, Barr wasn't interested. He hated those guys personally and he detested their work. . . . At that point, official culture hated those people, and Barr stood for advanced, civilized, official culture." It was another four or five years before Barr was convinced, according to Philip Johnson, at which point "He introduced me to Pollock. He thought Jackson was the number one painter in the country. Of course, he was very generous to the other AbEx painters, too. He took me to Rothko's studio because I had to buy a painting of his for the museum [with my personal funds]. Barr said, 'Look, my damn trustees don't want to go for this and I've got to have it.' So I bought it. That's what I did with Rothko and Kline, too."

She-Wolf recommended and reserved: Lader, p. 229. Janis campaigning for purchase: Janis to JP, Sept. 27, 1943: Janis was promoting the purchase of *She-Wolf* even though it was *Male and Female in Search of a Symbol* that he considered "the most provocative painting by an American I've seen." Friedman, p. 64, says the museum debated the purchase from the November show through the May purchase. But according to Betsy Jones of MOMA (to James T. Vallière, Nov. 12, 1965), the purchase of *She-Wolf* was approved after the next scheduled meeting of the acquisitions committee after the November show. Museum's traveling show: Feb. 3–May 17; Sweeney. Frank saw the show and wrote JP: "*She-Wolf* is hung to excellent advantage in the galleries and catches the eye immediately upon entering the gallery a quarter of a block away. . . . it seemed more meaningful than when I saw it in the cramped space of your studio last year." National audience for *She-Wolf*: Cincinnati Museum of Art, Feb. 8–Mar. 12; Denver Art Museum, Mar. 26–Apr. 23; Seattle Art Museum, May 7–June 10; Santa Barbara Museum of Art, June–July; San Francisco Museum of Art, July. Janis asking for lower price; "they couldn't afford": LK, q. in Weld, p. 325. "Go tell them": PG, q. by LK, q. in Weld, p. 325. "He didn't say a word": Q. in Potter, p. 79. *Harper's Bazaar*: Sweeney, "Five American Painters"; see Glaser, "JP," p. 38: The other featured artists were Morris Graves, Gorky, Avery, and Matta. "Clinched the deal": LK; see also Weld, p. 325. "Not particularly": Sweeney. Purchase order issued: Betsy Jones, MOMA, to James T. Vallière, Nov. 12, 1965. Hunter, having seen the in-museum memoranda, recalls that "Sweeney was very pro-Pollock, but he met with resistance from Barr and Soby." "Very happy": Q. in Solomon, p. 146.

"Dedicated" herself: PG (p. 264) claims that she dedicated herself to JP starting in 1943 (a claim that does not comport with other accounts): "I worked hard to interest people in his work and never tired of doing so. . . . One day Mrs. Harry Winston, the famous Detroit collector, came to the gallery to buy a Masson. I persuaded her to buy a Pollock instead." But this work (OC&T 130, I, p. 129) is officially dated c. 1945 and was probably bought out of the 1946 show. **"Into the right hands":** Q. by Porter. **Giving drawings as gifts:** PG, p. 264.

"I am getting $150": JP to CCP, May 1944. **"Slight recognition"; "same low figure":** SLM to CCP, May 4, 1944. **"Didn't get any cash":** SMP to CCP, EFP, and Jeremy, May 24, 1944. **Jackson's complaints to Putzel:** Putzel to JP, May 1944. **Colored drawing; works in Spring Salon:** Lader, p. 392: There were also works by several minor artists. **"Attack on Peggy's integrity:** Riley, "Rejected Youth," p. 15. **"Detected a decline":** Lader, p. 169, citing Ethel Baziotes, int. by Lader, Nov. 4, 1976. **Rumors of Peggy's departure; "look out for themselves":** Lader, p. 169, citing Robert Motherwell to William Baziotes, n.d., the William Baziotes Collection. **Artists wooed by Kootz:** PG, p. 264; Weld, p. 334. **"Probably—possibly":** Putzel to JP, May 1944, p. 233.

"Rather wild": PG to Herbert Read, Nov. 12, 1945, Herbert Read Archives, q. in Weld, p. 337. **Unwieldy canvases:** She displayed the eight-foot *Pasiphaë* in the April 1944 "First Exhibition in America" show. **"Much weaker"; "much more readily":** PG to Herbert Read, Nov. 12, 1945, Herbert Read Archives, q. in Weld, p. 337: "My chief function seems to be to find and give unknown artists a chance, and I have quite a few who are really worthwhile. . . . [JP] is, I think, the best of all these new young people, and may sometime be as well known as Miró. I support him, and Sweeney and I have in a measure got him very well started. His painting is rather wild and frightening and difficult to tell. Motherwell, on the contrary, is much weaker, and his taste is so perfect that he sells much more readily." **"Devilish":** PG, p. 264. **"I did sell":** Q. in Weld, p. 325. **"I concentrated":** PG, p. 264. **"Go out and get a job":** Q. by Porter. **"Generally spartan":** Weld, p. 107. **"Too good to waste":** Q. by Weld, p. 107. **"She did not create":** Weld, p. 107. Soon after the gallery opened, she had imposed an unprecedented twenty-five-cent admission charge and sat by the door gleefully collecting quarters until persuaded that she was discouraging visitors; Weld, pp. 292–93.

Greene disliking Jackson's art: Greene. **Bultman's reaction:** Bultman. **"A kind of isolation":** Q. in Simon, "Concerning the Beginnings of the New York School," p. 19. **Graham feeling Jackson had betrayed modernism:** Bultman. **Graham's drift to mysticism:** See Herrera, "John Graham," pp. 100–05. **"Graham abandoned":** LK; see also Herrera, "John Graham," p. 105: "But Lee Krasner, Pollock's wife, says that Graham had always maintained that he lost interest in an artist once he had become recognized. . . . 'I saw this acted [out] with Pollock,' she affirmed." **"The web"; "ready to snare":** Baziotes. **Kadish returned from India:** FLP to JP, July 31, 1944. **Resentment of Jackson's success:** "We weren't in that circle," Ernestine Lassaw says of Motherwell and JP. "Those were people with a little more social savvy than we had." **Matta's hilarious stories:** Abel, pp. 91–92. **"One sometimes wondered":** Motherwell, q. in "JP," p. 30.

Peggy's lists of lovers: Porter. **"With practically every man":** Weld, p. 52. **"With the window-cleaner":** Tanya Stern, q. in Weld, p. 316. **Sex with dogs:** Rupert Barneby, q. in Weld, p. 316: It was rumored that when she met Macpherson, he asked to borrow her dog for a love session, and she said, "Not without me"; q. in Weld, p. 316. **"Anything in pants":** LK. **"She tried awfully hard":** Q. in Weld, p. 315. **"Middle-aged":** David Hare, q. in Weld, p. 315. **"Homosexual" approach to sex; "around them so much":** John Richardson, q. in Weld, p. 315. **Lee out of town:** PG, q. in Weld, p. 325. **Peggy wanting proof of gratitude:** LK, q. in Weld, p. 325. **Jackson falling asleep:** When Busa asked Peggy if she and JP ever slept together, she said JP fell asleep the one time they tried. **Jackson vomiting:** Busa. **Jackson urinating:** EFP. **"He threw his drawers"; "very unsuccessful":** PG, q. in Weld, p. 325. **Peggy's fabricated triumphs:** LK, q. in Weld, p. 316: "Affair after affair of hers is a Fantasyland. She had a fantasy of her sexiness." **"He probably did":** Matter. **"Put a towel over her head":** Q. by Busa and Matter.

"Athenians": Weld, p. 309. **"Pandemonium":** Julien Levy, q. in Weld, p. 315. **"No one else around":** Q. in Weld, p. 315. **Artists at war:** The navy: Little, Zogbaum (Ernestine Lassaw); the army: Brooks, Bultman (Muriel Francis), McNeil, Mercer. Axel Horn, and Clyfford Still did war-related

work. Charlotte Brooks: James was "deferred twice from the army" in order to finish his Butler Air Terminal mural. **"Those that were too old":** Q. in Weld, p. 315. **Motherwell draft board incident:** Heller, recalling Motherwell. Busa was deferred because of an "inner ear infection," and Tolegian, says Araks, for a "perforated eardrum." CG: James Agee and Cal Lowell were given conscientious objector status. **"Hairdressers":** Ashton, p. 147. **"Seen me in uniform":** Q. in Weld, p. 313. **Sailors dragged in by Tyler:** Tabak, "Parker Tyler," in "A Collage," p. 454. **Sailors dragged in by Peggy:** Weld, p. 317. **MOMA streaker's antics; "Used to frolic":** Busa.

Group at George's Tavern; "It wasn't really a homosexual hangout": Busa. **Williams a Bultman family friend:** Francis. **"The big lie":** Q. by Busa. **Little's apartment; "sandy-haired"; Bennett a Hofmann student:** Bennett. **"Was very attracted":** Busa. **Busa's veracity:** In nine hours of interviews with the authors, Busa demonstrated a startling, confessional openness and, unlike so many of JP's friends, modestly understated his role in the artist's life. **"Kissed" Jackson:** Name withheld in deference to the man's widow. **Later encounters:** Carone; see chapter 43, "The Last Act." **"[Jackson] liked men":** Q. by Gibbs. According to Sanford Friedman, Lee said similar things to him and Richard Howard. **"I'm gonna fuck":** Q. by Little.

Hubbard's background: Elizabeth Wright Hubbard II; Merle Hubbard. **Krasner persuaded Peggy to show Hofmann:** Goodman; Kiesler; Lader, p. 240; Weld, p. 332. **"She was convinced":** Q. in Weld, p. 332; see also Lader, p. 240. **Paint tube incident:** Zogbaum. **Lee taking her easel to Kadish's studio:** Kadish; Solomon, p. 137. **Setting up easel in Jackson's old bedroom:** LK. **"I gave up the model":** Q. in Rose, "American Great," p. 154. **"The Cubist grid":** Rose, "American Great," p. 154. **"From the inside out":** Wallach, "Krasner's Triumph," p. 502. **"Sitting on the easel"; "very frustrating":** Q. in Glueck, "Krasner and Pollock," p. 59. One issue that Lee Krasner lied about in interviews (e.g., in *Strokes of Genius*) was the level of JP's support for her work: "There must have been, right from the beginning, although never discussed, a mutual respect, because his ego wouldn't have taken it and mine wouldn't have. So the fact that we were together—I wasn't challenged by it, that's not the feeling I had, I was very exhilarated. He was terrific, you know. And I didn't feel threatened by him."

"I don't want you to paint": Q. in Rose, "American Great," p. 121. **Lee quitting:** Zogbaum. Rosenberg: "When Jackson married her, or even before, he said there was to be no painting by her, and she stuck to it, because she was afraid." But the evidence is that JP's injunction was rarely if ever verbalized because it never had to be. **"A good woman painter":** Q. by ACM. **"I didn't hide":** Q. in Rose, "American Great," p. 121. **"Nowhere in evidence":** Holtzman. Although no one seems to remember seeing Lee's work in evidence, two photos taken at the time show that at least one major painting of Lee's was hanging in the apartment, and grandly framed at that.

Date of Benton's visit: Dated in SMP to CCP, EFP, and Jeremy, June 16, 1944: "Benton dropped in a couple of weeks ago on his way to Martha's Vineyard." **"The bell rang":** Q. in Nemser, p. 87. **"Effusively":** Taylor, "LK." **Benton asking to see Lee's work:** Benton, q. by LK, q. in Wallach, "Out of JP's Shadow." **"I knew what"; "gray slabs":** Q. in Nemser, p. 87. **"I stood"; "The silence":** LK, q. in Taylor, "LK." **"A little awkward":** LK, q. in Nemser, p. 87. **"Having a beer"; "a rough time":** LK, q. in Wallach, "Out of JP's Shadow." **Jackson reworking Lee's canvas; "total page":** LK, int. by Emily Wasserman, Jan. 9, 1968, q. in Landau, "LK," p. 232 n. 58. LK, q. by Landau: The incident took place "early in their relationship"; see also Kadish's account of when and why she moved into his studio. **"At that time":** Q. in Glueck, "Krasner and Pollock," p. 59. **Lee moving back into Kadish's studio:** Kadish.

"He couldn't stand": Kadish. **Dating of vacation:** SMP to CCP, EFP, and Jeremy, June 16, 1944. Tennessee Williams, letter dated June 21, 1944, copy in possession of Bultman: They were in Provincetown by June 21. **Renting studio to Steffen:** SMP to CCP, EFP, and Jeremy, June 16, 1944. **Ride to Provincetown:** Little. See Solomon (p. 148) for conflicting account of the trip to Provincetown. **Hofmann's home:** Del Deo; Mercer: Hofmann lived in two houses: one on Miller Hill Road, the second on Commercial Street with his wife, Miz. The two houses were near each other on the outskirts of town. **Choosing works for Hofmann's show:** Little. **Jackson painting with Bennett:** The canvas is approximately six by thirty inches, in black enamel on a ground of red fading to orange. Although the paint in the work is brushed rather than dripped, it bears a strong resemblance—in color, format, and design—to some of JP's later drip paintings. **"Lee didn't think":** Q. in Solomon, p. 149. **Agreeing to move:** Little. **Description of new place:** Del Deo. **Location of new place:** Del Deo; Gross. **"Back road"; "only a sliver":** Del Deo. **New Beach:** Now called Herring Cove Beach; Del Deo. **"Crew cut":** JP to SLM, ACM, and SLM, summer 1944. **Description of fishermen:** Del Deo. **Few civilians:** Moffett, p. 94. **Ernst expelled:** Ossorio; see also Moffett, p. 94. Little: "The summer I was in Provincetown, the FBI came to Fritz [Bultman]'s house at four A.M. for questioning. It seems old Hans [Hofmann] liked to paint in certain locations on the beach and they thought he was spying for the Germans, even though he was an American citizen. They gave him a rough time. Once, on the beach, they got so angry they took his painting off the easel and walked on it." **Few cars:** Moffett, p. 94. **"To bring good luck":** Del Deo. **"Provincetown looks":** JP to SMP, ACM, and SLM, summer 1944. **"Sandwich boy":** Blaine, int. by Lader, q. in Lader, p. 249. **Peggy reportedly planning to close gallery:** JP to SMP, ACM, and SLM, summer 1944; Lader, pp. 248–49. **"Howard has quit":** JP to SMP, ACM, and SLM, summer 1944. **Lee helping Hofmann with Kootz:** Little. **Lee's studio in Hofmann's house:** Potter, p. 78. **"I am nature":** Q. by Bultman; Lee later contradicted the seeming arrogance of JP's statement: "People think he means he's God," she told Wallach in 1981 ("Out of JP's Shadow"). "He means he's total. He's undivided. He's one *with* nature, instead of 'That's nature over there, and I'm here." **"Repeat yourself":** Q. by LK. This incident is often misplaced during the first encounter between Hofmann and JP. Bultman's memory that it took place the summer of 1944 is very specific, Lee's memory that it took place earlier is muddled. **Jackson throwing easel:** Zogbaum, recalling Janet Hauck, whose husband, Fred, was standing next to Hofmann, in harm's way. **Miz's reaction:** Mercer: "I can feel her hostility brushing against me still. Miz's attitude toward Pollock was set from that day on." **"Dropped in"; "living out of a suitcase":** Myers. Bennett and others doubt that he actually lived at any time with JP and Lee. **Williams renting room:** Bennett. **Knaths:** Del Deo. **Biked over:** LK, q. in Friedman, p. 72. **Writing *The Glass Menagerie:*** Since Williams completed the play that fall (Williams, p. 83), he must have been working on it that summer. **"He used to carry me":** Williams, p. 56: Williams puts JP in Provincetown in the summer of 1940. In fact, there are a number of stories putting him there in summers other than 1944: Schardt says 1941, Bultman says 1943. Our research indicates that JP was there only once with Lee. JP did not know Lee in 1940 or 1941 and their whereabouts in the summer of 1943 are well documented. JP could have taken a brief vacation to Provincetown on his own in the summer of 1940 or 1941. But his unwillingness to go anywhere without Sande in those days makes such trips highly conjectural. Spoto (p. 109) notes that, in the first draft of his memoirs, Williams dated his meeting of Cannastra to the summer of 1945, but goes on to say that "by this time Cannastra had apparently moved to New York, and the evidence suggests that in fact their meeting took place . . . in 1941." Cannastra did not graduate from the Harvard Law School until 1945 (Harvard Law School, p. 98), so Williams's original dating was closer, although still off by one year. **"A little bit heavier":** Williams, p. 56. **Beck's background; Living Theater:** Freedman, "Julian Beck." **"Other activities"; sex in the balcony:** Bennett. **"Lunatic fringe"; "a collection":** Williams, letter dated June 21, 1944, copy in possession of Bultman. **"One of the aboriginal"; "beat":** Williams, p. 83. **Setting out:** Williams, p. 84. **Jackson in group:** Bennett. **"He had a map"; "carefully"; "rocks off":** Williams, p. 84. **Girl breaking leg in cemetery:** Cabral: The girl's name was Vivian. **"That gay bunch"; Jackson arrested:** Cabral. **"Beautiful":** Williams, p. 83. **"Poetic looking"; "extremely quiet":** Blaine. **Cannastra's stammer:** Williams, p. 83. **"Completely altered":** Blaine. **"Frustrated artist"; "sexual problems":** Q. by Blaine. **Provincetown bars:** Del Deo. **Jackson drinking heavily:** Bennett. **"Begging for a punch":** Bell. **Swimming with Lee:** SMP to CCP, EFP, and Jeremy, Aug. 18, 1944. **Rolls**

of canvas unopened: LK, q. in Friedman, p. 72: "It was not what you would call a productive summer. We had shipped up some rolls of canvas. In September they were still unpacked —all we had to do was change the FROM to TO." **Lee stopping in Deep River:** SMP to CCP, EFP, and Jeremy, Aug. 18, 1944. **Family descending:** JP to Wally and Ed Strautin, Aug. 25, 1944. **Williams returning to Harvard with Cannastra:** Williams, p. 83. **Stolen headstones:** Bennett. **"Damn swell swimming"; "a god-damned bit":** JP to Wally and Ed Strautin, Aug. 25, 1944. **Family rescue:** Sande presumably came to the Cape because he knew JP was in bad shape and probably encouraged their mother to come for the same reason, although, from her correspondence, it seems unlikely that she was fully aware of JP's problems. **A very strong woman":** Blaine: The woman was Jane Watrous. **"Second thoughts"; "and went away":** Blaine. **Cannastra beheaded:** Williams, p. 84. Lynn Cannastra: "He committed suicide."

31. ESCAPE

SOURCES

Books, articles, and film

Ashton, *Yes, but . . .;* Friedman, *JP;* Midtown Galleries, *Philip Guston;* Nemser, *Art Talk;* OC&T, *JP;* Potter, *To a Violent Grave;* Rose, *LK;* Weld, *Peggy.*
"Carnegie Awards Prizes for 1945," *Limited Edition,* Oct. 1945; DP&G, "Who was JP?" *Art in America,* May–June 1967, pp. 48–59; Grace Glueck, "Krasner and Pollock: Scenes from a Marriage," *Art News,* Dec. 1981; CG, "Art," *Nation,* Nov. 11, 1944; CG, "Art," *Nation,* Apr. 7, 1945; "Passing Shows," *Art News,* Apr. 1–14, 1945; Barbara Rose, "American Great: LK," *Vogue,* June 1972; Maude Riley, "Baziotes' Color," *Art Digest,* Oct. 1, 1944; Maude Riley, "JP," *Art Digest,* Apr. 1, 1945; William Rubin, "JP and the Modern Tradition, Part I: 2. The All-Over Compositions and the Drip Technique"; Parker Tyler, "Nature and Madness among the Younger Painters," *View,* May 1945; James T. Vallière, "Daniel T. Miller," *Provincetown Review,* fall 1968.
Howard Devree, "Among the New Exhibitions," *NYT,* Mar. 25, 1945; Alfred Frankenstein, "World of Art and Artists," *San Francisco Chronicle,* Aug. 12, 1945; Joseph Liss, "Memories of Bonac Painters," *East Hampton Star,* Aug. 18, 1983. *Strokes of Genius: JP* (film), Court Productions, 1984.

Interviews

Paul Brach; Charlotte Park Brooks; John Bunce; Peter Busa; Herman Cherry; Edward Cook; Dorothy Dehner; David Gibbs; CG; Axel Horn; Elizabeth Wright Hubbard II; Buffie Johnson; Barbara Kadish; Reuben Kadish; LK; Harold Lehman; John Little; ABP; FLP; MJP; MLP; May Tabak Rosenberg; David Slivka; Ruth Stein; Michael Stolbach.

NOTES

The season: See Friedman, p. 79. **Hofmann dinner:** Little; Friedman (p. 75) for dating. **"Filthy dirty":** Reuben Kadish. *There Were Seven in Eight:* OC&T 124, I, pp. 122–23 (43″ × 102″). **Begun in spring:** Little. **Making etchings:** Friedman, p. 75. **Mecca for European artists:** Hayter, q. in Potter, p. 79. Rose (p. 65 n. 39) claims that JP met Miró during the winter, citing interview with Miró in *Miró in America* (Houston: Museum of Fine Arts, 1982). But Kadish, who was extremely close to JP during this time, has no memory of such a meeting. **Kadish working with Hayter:** Reuben Kadish. **"Molotov cocktail":** Dehner. **"Filled with brio":** Johnson. **Hayter joining them:** Friedman, pp. 72–73. Friedman says JP met Hayter in 1943 when Kadish "returned from Mexico." Kadish was in India part of 1943 and in California for a while thereafter. He didn't return to New York until 1944. We have found no evidence to substantiate Friedman's assertion that Hayter and JP met regularly "by appointment" from 1943 until 1950. **White Horse Tavern:** Hayter, q. in Potter, p. 79. **Hotel Albert:** Friedman, p. 75. **Cedar Tavern:** Dehner. **"Source of inspiration"; "plumbed the depths":** Q. in Potter, p. 79. **"Lost":** Reuben Kadish. **"Spraying the stream":** Q. in Friedman, p. 80. **Calling out Lee's name:** CG. **Jackson slipping away:** Kadish was only too ready to accompany JP on his nightly forays and, by his own admission, never, in twenty-five years of friendship, ventured to suggest that he'd had enough: "It wasn't for me to tell him how to live his life." Little, in an obdurate insistence on southern hospitality, would offer JP a drink whenever he walked by the door. **Lee turning to Pollock family:** See SMP to CCP, EFP, and Jeremy, Nov. 21, 1944, and July 9, 1945. **Joseph Krassner ill:** Ruth Stein: He died in November 1944 at "close to ninety."

Lee encouraging therapy: Little. **"Thunderstorms"; "mother and father"; "enormous bosoms"; "Yes, sir":** Hubbard: "She said, 'You have to treat the patient, not the disease.' If three people had pneumonia, they might get three different remedies." **Hubbard's history:** Hubbard. **College of Physicians and Surgeons:** Class of 1921. **Homeopathy:** She later became president of the Homeopathic Society.

Exhibition-quality paintings: *Gothic*, OC&T 103, I, pp. 98–99; *Night Mist*, OC&T 104, I, pp. 100–01; *The Night Dancer*, OC&T 105, I, p. 102; *Night Ceremony*, OC&T 106, I, p. 103. **Etchings:** Except for trial proofs, the plates created by JP at Atelier 17 remained unprinted until 1967 when editions were made under the supervision of William Lieberman of MOMA; see Friedman, p. 73. Kadish says Hayter was seldom in the workshop when JP was there and, in any event, never commented on JP's efforts. This contradicts those commentators who claim that JP learned about composition or line from Hayter; see Friedman, pp. 73–74. **Frustration with etching medium:** Kadish: "Etching is not only reversed, but there's something about the line you put down that ends up being quite different. The acid takes over, and the metal has something to say, so he didn't have control, and that made him very impatient."

Baziotes exhibition: "Paintings and Drawings by William Baziotes: First One-Man Exhibition," Oct. 3–21, 1941; Weld, p. 395. **Postponed Giacometti exhibition:** Weld, pp. 264–66. **Motherwell exhibition:** Oct. 24–Nov. 11, 1944, including oils, tempera, papiers collés, etchings, colored drawings, and drawings; Weld, pp. 396–97. **"Spontaneously designed":** Riley, "Baziotes' Color," p. 12: She criticizes "a lack of workmanship" in the oil paintings. **"Unadulterated talent":** CG, "Art," p. 599: Greenberg writes that Baziotes's pictures "were marred by his anxiety to resolve them . . . [and] the sheer love of elaboration," while Motherwell lacked intensity and owed too much to Picasso. But the insistent balancing of the positive and the negative that marked Greenberg's review of JP's opening is gone. **Solid sellers:** Weld, p. 268. **Receipts below $2,800:** MJP to EFP and CCP, July 23, 1945.

Series of horses: OC&T 115, I, pp. 110–11; 116, I, pp. 110–11; 118, I, pp. 112–13; 119, I, p. 113; 120, I, p. 113. **Monochromatic background:** OC&T 107, I, p. 104. **Accents in pastels:** OC&T 109, I, p. 105; *Night Sounds*, OC&T 111, I, pp. 106–07. **Sgraffito:** OC&T 108, I, pp. 104–05; 110, I, p. 106; 112, I, p. 108; 113, I, p. 108. **Gangly horse:** OC&T 110, I, p. 106. *Totem Lesson 1:* OC&T 121, I, pp. 114–15. *Totem Lesson 2:* OC&T 122, I, pp. 118–19. *Two:* OC&T 123, I, pp. 120–21. *There Were Seven in Eight:* OC&T 124, I, pp. 122–23. These works are often described as part of an evolution from the 1943 Surrealist masterpieces to the classic drip paintings; see Rubin, "JP," p. 17. If there is such a thing as stylistic evolution in JP's career (and he was never that consistent in his approach to his work), it is hard not to see these works as a step backward from the Guggenheim mural. Rubin writes that "the drawing in those pictures, while still representational, becomes increasingly galvanic and begins to unlock itself from the description of the totemic forms which, as we shall see later, body forth Pollock's early dramas. The fragmentation of these forms, already quite advanced in *Night Ceremony* of 1944, leads to an almost autonomous rhythm of the line in certain gouaches and pastels of 1945 and early 1946. The larger paintings of that period, *Circumcision* (1946) and *The Blue Unconscious* (1946), though more descriptive in their forms, reveal a comparable progression toward compositional openness and linear autonomy. Though they retain an obvious hierarchy of larger and smaller forms, these paintings already tend to be distributed with considerably even density over the whole picture surface." Rather than following some simple line of evolution and development, JP seems to be taking the subject matter of the Surrealist totemic paintings and, instead of covering up the image with arabesques, fracturing and splaying it into abstract shapes across the surface of the canvas, more or less as he did in the Guggenheim mural. See Riley, "Baziotes' Color," p. 12: "His paintings have to be

taken one at a time. Complete readjustment must be made in turning from one to the next. So that the antagonism seems also to exist between paintings."

Portrait of H.M.: OC&T 126, I, pp. 124–25. **Slivka's visit:** Slivka. **Heat; crowd at show:** SMP to CCP, Apr. 5, 1945: "Was very hot in the City for March in the 80 most of the time and one day up to 84°." **Admiration for brushwork:** *Art News* ("Passing Shows," p. 6) was basically negative: JP "derives his style from that of Kandinsky though he lacks the airy freedom and imaginative color of the earlier master." **"Big, sprawling":** Devree, "Among the New Exhibitions," p. 8. **"Nervous, if rough":** The review was archly titled "Nature and Madness among the Younger Painters," p. 30. **"Belligerence":** Riley, "JP," p. 59.

Unequivocal praise: Frankenstein, "World of Art and Artists": "The flare and spatter and fury of his paintings are emotional rather than formal, and like the best jazz, one feels that much of it is the result of inspired improvisation rather than conscious planning." In the next breath, however, he called the mediocre woodcuts of an artist named Charles Smith "no less interesting." **"Jackson Pollock one-man show":** CG, "Art," p. 397. **Delayed reaction:** CG: "I wasn't bowled over at first. I didn't realize what I'd seen until later." **Baziotes and Motherwell going to Kootz:** Weld, p. 334.

Philip Guston: Brach. **Years in Iowa:** Ashton, p. 51. **Influenced by Regionalism:** Lehman, who says that although Guston "disliked intensely" the work of Grant Wood, "the artistic influences out there appealed to a side of Phil that was extremely sentimental, even schmaltzy, if you will." **Musa's taste for sentiment:** Horn. **Mother Goose story:** Ashton, p. 65. **Guston's transformation:** Those close to him could excuse the work, or even praise it, as Ashton later would (p. 66), as a masterpiece of "mood and atmosphere, of stillness and mystery, of sublimated ritual." **Provincial curiosities:** Reuben Kadish, whose son Daniel later married Guston's daughter Musa: "I think that hurt Guston, at least artistically, to be out in Iowa all those years." **Midtown Galleries exhibition:** Midtown Galleries, "Philip Guston." **"Place of honor":** Lehman. **"Living masters":** *Art News*, p. 194; among the others "headed for immortality" was Vincent Spagna. Guston won the first prize at the Carnegie Institute's annual exhibition, which opened on October 11, 1945; "Carnegie Awards Prizes for 1945," p. 7.

Guston competitive: Cherry: "When he left Marlborough Gallery, he said to me, 'I don't give a goddamn about being in a gallery any more, my name is in all the history books anyway.' That's a fabulous ego. History was apparently a big thing in his mind." **"Long-drawn-out fistfight":** Busa, recalling Guston. **"Broke down":** Reuben Kadish, q. by Cherry. **Guston abandoning sentimentalism:** Busa; Cherry; Reuben Kadish; Lehman. Brach disagrees with them.

"Absolutely against it": In *Strokes of Genius*. **"ultimatum":** Q. in Glueck, "Krasner and Pollock," p. 60; see also *Strokes of Genius:* "I gave him the ultimatum, either we get married or split." **"It just snapped":** Q. by Stolbach. She told Greenberg the same thing. **"I said [to Jackson]":** Q. in Nemser, p. 87; see also Gibbs; *Strokes of Genius;* Glueck, "Krasner and Pollock," p. 60. **"Cannonball":** Brooks. **"Shack":** SMP to CCP, EFP, and Jeremy, July 9, 1945. **From Hayter:** Reuben Kadish. **A month already gone; "cleaned up his brushes":** SMP to CCP, EFP, and Jeremy, July 9, 1945.

High tide: Liss. The Lisses rented the same house the following summer, and Millie Liss says that JP and Kadish used to leave garbage under the house to be carried away by the high tide, although sometimes the tide didn't reach high enough and the place "turned into a dump." **The Sound:** Block Island Sound. **Description of sight:** Slivka. **Description of shack:** Potter, p. 80. **Searching for clams; fishing; racing down road:** Barbara Kadish. **Doting on Patia:** Rosenberg. **Clam chowder:** S. W. Hayter, q. in Potter, p. 80. **Slivka's visit:** Slivka. **Putzel dying:** Weld, p. 336. **Receiving news of war:** Reuben Kadish. **Krasner on bike:** Barbara Kadish. **Jackson not working:** Reuben Kadish. **Falling into tar:** Barbara Kadish, q. in Potter, p. 80. **"Impossible"; "always found a way":** Reuben Kadish. **A weekend":** LK; LK (drafted by Vallière) to FVOC, Sept. 10, 1966; DP&G, "Who Was JP?" p. 50. **Pollock family threat of boycott:** FLP.

Inquiries about rentals: LK. **"What do you think":** LK; see similar version in Rose, "American Great," p. 154. **"Are you crazy?":** LK. **Few weeks later:** LK, cited in Rose, "American Great," p. 154: two or three weeks later; LK, cited in DP&G, "Who Was JP?" p. 50: three days later. Given LK's tendency to telescope time to heighten dramatic effect, the first estimate seems more likely. **"We're leaving":** LK. **Lee stunned:** Rose, "American Great," p. 154. **Brooks finding another apartment:** Potter, p. 80. **Frank moving to farm:** FLP to SMP, Oct. 23, 1945. **Jackson eager to be father:** Hubbard; Reuben Kadish. When news came that Frank's son Jonathan was "seriously ill," "Jack broke down and cried," SMP reported to CCP, EFP, and Jeremy, Nov. 5, 1945. **"Pollock didn't basically move":** Q. in Vallière, "Daniel T. Miller," p. 34. emphasis added. **Real-estate agent:** "Captain" Merton Edwards, according to LK, q. in Liss, "Memories of Bonac Painters." **House sold:** LK, q. in DP&G, "Who Was JP?" p. 50; but LK, q. in Liss, "Memories of Bonac Painters": The house was merely "taken off the market." **Motherwell recruiting:** See Weld, p. 276. In most of her later interviews, Lee incorrectly identified Dan Miller as the man who put them in touch with Ed Cook. **Cook:** Cook: "Motherwell was building his Quonset hut on a piece of property I found for him, and he brought Lee and Jackson Pollock in to see me and asked if there was anything available." **"A steal":** Cook. **"Didn't have forty dollars":** LK, q. in DP&G, "Who Was JP?" p. 50, emphasis in the original. See Potter, p. 86. The chronology of Peggy's financing of the house has been widely misstated. We think the error originated with Peggy, who thought she had lent JP and Lee the money in 1945 when, in fact, the papers lending them the money were drawn up and signed sometime in the first three months of 1946; see Weld, p. 343. Peggy's recollection put the loan even before JP and Lee went to East Hampton for the first time. A close reading of Lee's interviews confirms that they rented the house first, then subsequently persuaded Peggy to make the loan. Whether the loan was informally agreed to by the time the house was rented, long before the paperwork was completed, is unknown. **Deposit borrowed:** Cook. **"Non-practicing Jew":** LK. **"God will understand":** Q. by Rosenberg. **"Be very quiet":** LK, q. by Stolbach. **Guggenheim refusing to attend:** Peggy (see Weld, p. 344) later said she was still angry at Lee for borrowing the $2,000 for the Springs house, but at the time of the wedding, the transaction had not yet been finalized and probably had not yet been initiated. **May confused with another:** Rosenberg; Friedman, p. 82. **"If May isn't there":** Q. by Rosenberg: "He wanted somebody pure for his wedding." When Lee went back to Peggy, she said, "I already have a luncheon that day." **"It was a beautiful":** Q. in Weld, p. 343. **Jay in Flushing; disposition of rooms:** MJP. **No paintings moved to Springs:** See Friedman, p. 82. **Blankets and rugs:** MJP to James T. Vallière, Apr. 25, 1965. Reuben Kadish: In the 1930s JP and Kadish had admired the dozen brightly patterned blankets as exciting samples of primitive art. **Arrangement not honored:** MJP to James T. Vallière, Apr. 25, 1965. **Weekend of November 3:** SMP to CCP, EFP, and Jeremy, Nov. 5, 1945. **"Northeaster":** LK, q. in Rose, "American Great," p. 54. **Butcher's truck:** Liss, "Memories of Bonac Painters."

32. STARTING OVER

SOURCES

Books, articles, manuscripts, film, and transcripts

Barrett, *The Truants;* Epstein and Barlow, *East Hampton;* Frascina, ed., *Pollock and After;* Friedman, *JP;* Gruen, *The Party's Over Now;* Guild Hall, *Artists and East Hampton;* Guild Hall, *Crosscurrents;* PG, *Out of This Century;* Kligman, *Love Affair;* Kunitz, ed., *Twentieth Century Authors;* Namuth, *Pollock Painting;* Potter, *To a Violent Grave;* Rose, *LK;* Solomon, *JP;* Tabak, *But Not for Love;* Weld, *Peggy.*

Robert Alan Aurthur, "Hitting the Boiling Point, Freakwise, at East Hampton," *Esquire,* June 1972; DP&G, "Who Was JP?" *Art in America,* May–June 1967; Grace Glueck, "Krasner and Pollock: Scenes from a Marriage," *Art News,* Dec. 1981; CG, "Art," *Nation,* Apr. 7, 1945; CG, "Art," *Nation,* Apr. 13, 1946; CG, "Avant-Garde and Kitsch," *Partisan Review,* Fall 1939; CG, "Jean Dubuffet, JP," *Nation,* Feb. 1, 1947; CG, "Towards a Newer Laocoön," *Partisan Review,* July–Aug. 1940; "JP: An Artists' Symposium, Part I," *Art News,* Apr. 1967; Ellen Johnson, "JP and Nature," *Studio International,*

June 1973; Barbara M. Reise, "Greenberg and The Group: A Retrospective View," *Studio International,* May 1968; "Reviews and Previews," *Art News,* May 1946; Gaby Rodgers, "She Has Been There Once or Twice: A Talk with LK," *Women Artists Newsletter,* Dec. 1977; Barbara Rose, "American Great: LK," *Vogue,* June 1972; William Rubin, "JP and the Modern Tradition, Part III: Cubism and the Later Evolution of the All-Over Style," *Artforum,* Apr. 1967; "The Summer Place," *Time,* Aug. 14, 1964; "Unframed Space," *New Yorker,* Aug. 5, 1950; James T. Vallière, "Daniel T. Miller," *Provincetown Review,* Fall 1968; Ben Wolf, "Fifty-Seventh Street in Review," *Art Digest,* Apr. 15, 1946.

Florence Haxton Bullock, "Stripped Down to Sex," New York *Herald Tribune Weekly Book Review,* Apr. 28, 1946; Grace Glueck, "Met Acquires Early Pollock," *NYT,* Jan. 13, 1982; Joseph Liss, "Abstraction at Louse Point," *East Hampton Star,* Feb. 25, 1982; Amei Wallach, "LK: Out of JP's Shadow," *Newsday,* Aug. 23, 1981.

Melvin Paul Lader, "PG's Art of This Century: The Surrealist Milieu and the American Avant-Garde, 1942–47" (Lader) (Ph.D. thesis), Newark: University of Delaware, 1981; Ellen Gross Landau, "LK: A Study of Her Early Career (1926–1949)" (Ph.D. thesis), Newark: University of Delaware, 1981; May Natalie Tabak, "A Collage" (unpub. ms.), n.d.

Strokes of Genius: JP (film), Court Productions, 1984.

Elwyn Harris, int. by Kathleen Shorthall for *Life,* Nov. 9, 1959, Time/Life Archives; CG, int. by Kathleen Shorthall for *Life,* Nov. 9, 1959, Time/Life Archives; CG, int. by James T. Vallière, Mar. 20, 1968, AAA; Daniel T. Miller, int. by Kathleen Shorthall for *Life,* Nov. 9, 1959, Time/Life Archives; George Schaefer, int. by Kathleen Shorthall for *Life,* Nov. 9, 1959, Time/Life Archives; Richard and Allene Talmage, int. by Kathleen Shorthall for *Life,* Nov. 9, 1959, Time/Life Archives.

Interviews

Ethel Baziotes; Paul Brach; Charlotte Park Brooks; James Brooks; Fritz Bultman; Peter Busa; Nicholas Carone; Giorgio Cavallon; John Cole; Mike Collins; Edward Cook; Mary Louise Dodge; Nina Federico; Phyllis Fleiss; David Gibbs; Grace Glueck; CG; Balcomb Greene; Grace Hartigan; Eleanor Hempstead; Harry Holtzman; Edward Hults; Ted Hults; Harry Jackson; Reuben Kadish; Gerome Kamrowski; Hilton Kramer; LK; John Lee; Millie Liss; Terry Liss; John Little; Cile Downs Lord; Conrad Marca-Relli; Dorothy Miller; George Sid Miller; Lucia Mullican; John Bernard Myers; EFP; David Porter; May Tabak Rosenberg; Carol Southern; Ronald Stein; Ruth Stein; Allene Talmage; Esteban Vicente; Harriet Vicente; Steve Wheeler; Roger Wilcox.

NOTES

Miller one-eyed: George Sid Miller: "As a kid he shoved a knife in his eye, and at one time I think he was the only one-eyed licensed airplane pilot in the United States." **"Wildhide"; "didn't know much":** Miller, q. in Vallière, "Daniel T. Miller," p. 35. **"That old Pollock":** Reconstructed from Dan Miller, int. by Shorthall, Nov. 9, 1959, and Vallière, "Daniel T. Miller," p. 35. **Springs:** Population at the time about 360; Solomon, p. 161. **Hundred years:** Ever since the 1870s, when the Long Island Railroad opened eastern Long Island up to New Yorkers by extending the line to Bridgehampton; Helen A. Harrison, "Guild Hall and East Hampton: A History of Growth and Change," in Guild Hall, *Crosscurrents,* p. 42. **Tile Club:** Guild Hall, *Artists and East Hampton,* p. 7. **Guild Hall:** Guild Hall, *Crosscurrents,* p. 43. **Bathers; "almost English":** "The Summer Place," p. 46. **Clambakes:** See, e.g., *Seaside Sketches: A Clam Bake,* by Winslow Homer, in Guild Hall, *Artists and East Hampton,* p. 14. **Fishermen:** See, e.g., *Captain Bickford's Float* by John Twachtman, in Guild Hall, *Artists and East Hampton,* p. 17. **Bizarre games:** Tabak, "Surrealist Fun and Games," in "Collage," pp. 446–49: Like inviting friends to a party, then watching from the bushes as they arrived at an empty house. **"Parisian" sky:** Attributed to Lucia Wilcox in "The Summer Place," p. 46. **"Where can we find":** Paraphrased from Helen Phillips, q. in Potter, p. 86. **East Hampton and Springs:** Edward Hults; Talmage. **"Below the bridge":** Talmage. **Lionel Gardiner:** See Rattray, p. 86. **Springs families;** Ted Hults and (for Lester) Aurthur, "Hitting the Boiling Point," p. 94. **Bonacker phrases; Bonackers:** Edward Hults. **Impact of Roosevelt:** Talmage.

"She felt cast down"; "just to spruce"; offer refused: Glueck. "Bonackers are Bonackers": Q. in Potter, p. 88. Sleeping until noon: See "Unframed Space," p. 16; Little; LK, q. in DP&G, "Who Was JP?" p. 50. Big money: Cook. Story of arrival: Dodge. "The strange city couple": George Sid Miller. No car or coal: LK, cited in Landau, "LK," p. 221: War rationing was still in effect. "That crazy artist": Cook. Bicycling to Miller's: Edward Hults. Young boys: Collins. "Wears a rope": Millie Liss. "Never shaves": Name withheld by request. Buying booze: George Sid Miller. Jungle Pete's: Federico. "Uppity": Edward Hults. "Common as dirt": Name withheld by request. "Helloo": Edward Hults. "Drifts": Cook. "Unspoiled": Tabak, *But Not for Love*, p. 29. Drifts natural resources: Tabak, *But Not for Love*, p. 25. "I'm going to be a Bonacker": Q. by George Sid Miller, q. in Potter, p. 89. "You only got to wait": George Sid Miller, q. in Potter, p. 89.

"I opened the door": JP to Ed and Wally Strautin, Nov. 29, 1945. Kitchen stove: LK, cited in Landau, "LK," p. 221. Staying warm: Cavallon. "It was hell": In *Strokes of Genius*. "Stuffed with": LK, q. in Rose, "American Great," p. 154. Water pump giving out: Edward Hults. Porch floor: Wilcox. Barn: LK, q. in Namuth, n.p. Tool shed: Wilcox. "The work is endless": JP to Louis Bunce, June 2, 1946. Mile to Jungle Pete's: Talmage. Loan for bicycle: Federico, q. in Potter, p. 89. No one saying hello: Edward Hults. Jackson buying paint: Dorothy Miller. Hitching with Levy: Julien Levy, q. in Potter, p. 93. "On the books": Edward Hults.

"Strictly business": Wilcox, although there is testimony that he was also "kind-hearted"; Edward Hults. Spending time in office; "highflown": Daniel T. Miller, int. by Shorthall, Nov. 9, 1959. Miller was a master in the local Masonic lodge; Bultman. Jackson agreeing; Miller a drinker: Potter, p. 110. Lee going marketing: Dodge. Kadishes urged to come: Kadish. "Let's get away": Q. by Reuben Kadish. Not returning until funeral: Kadish. "When can we expect": JP to Reuben Kadish, Feb. 8, 1946. "Despite Lee": Charlotte Brooks; James Brooks. "Lee wasn't feeling well": Baziotes. Lee's family banished: Ruth Stein.

Description of Stella: EFP, q. in Potter, p. 20. "Bad boy": Jackson. "Pollock had a strong": Q. in DP&G, "Who was JP?" p. 53. One-night binge: See Bultman, q. in Potter, p. 67. "Holding himself in check": Wilcox. Lee's resentment of Stella: Rosenberg: "Lee and I both considered her mother-in-law a bore, ignorant—a woman who had nothing to talk about except her five sons and her sewing. She wasn't fond of Lee either, even though she sewed for her." Baking pies and cakes: Wilcox. Makeup incident; "speechless": Rosenberg. Jackson painting again: The last known painting before the move was *Water Figure* (OC&T 127, I, p. 126), which JP signed and dated "11-45" in the process of packing the studio for the move. Four or five canvases: Wilcox. Size of canvases: We agree with OC&T (I, p. 117) that the large paintings that have traditionally been dated 1945, especially *There Were Seven in Eight* and *Totem Lesson 2*, were probably begun in 1944. The Child Proceeds: OC&T 145, I, p. 135. *Sun-Scape*: OC&T 143, I, p. 136. *Circumcision*: OC&T 142, I, pp. 134–35; Wilcox for naming.

"Lee and I": JP to Louis Bunce, Jan. 5, 1946. "A city person": Q. in Rodgers, "She Has Been There Once or Twice," p. 3. Loan refused: Wilcox. "Mrs. Moneybags": Fleiss. Lee editing manuscript: See Weld, p. 345. Peggy distributing copies: Peggy "was encouraged in her writing by critic Clement Greenberg to whom she showed each chapter for editing"; Lader, p. 250, citing interview with CG Mar. 14, 1980. "Could have done better": LK, q. in Weld, p. 347. Book jacket: Lader, p. 251. JP used motifs from a black and red serigraph Christmas card of 1944 on the front and a photographically reversed black-on-white sketch for the back. "Go ask Sam Kootz": Q. by LK, q. in DP&G, "Who was JP?" p. 50. "I went to see Kootz": Q. in DP&G, "Who Was JP?" Friedman: Lee said that Kootz said he wouldn't take JP "because he was a drunk," indicating that Lee was referring to another appeal to Kootz, or that she fabricated the story. "How could you": Q by LK, q. in DP&G, "Who Was JP?" Porter, perhaps relying on misinformation from Peggy: "Peggy discussed with me the problem she had one time when Jackson threatened to leave the gallery if she didn't give him an extra $2,500." Advice from Davis and Porter: Porter. Visit to Springs: JP to Reuben Kadish, Feb. 8, 1946. "More happy": LK.

"Things couldn't have"; financial details: JP to Reuben Kadish, Feb. 8, 1946. Monthly deduction: Glueck, "Krasner and Pollock," p. 60; contrary to other accounts (Friedman, p. 81; PG, pp. 264–65; Potter, p. 86), the 1945 contract was negotiated almost a year before the loan for the house, not at the same time; the terms of the loan were *added* to the 1945 contract in 1946. Paintings as collateral: Wallach, "LK"; Glueck, "Met Acquires early Pollock": *Pasiphaë* was the only painting specifically mentioned in the agreement; the other two were apparently to be designated later. In an interview with the authors, Lee said that three paintings *in addition to Pasiphaë* were put up as collateral, but her earlier memory is more credible. Date of transaction: Weld, p. 343: Signed Feb. 19. "Hell of a lot": JP to Reuben Kadish, Feb. 8, 1946.

April show: The show ran at Art of This Century from April 2 to April 20. "Moving out"; "Joe Meert": JP to Louis Bunce, June 2, 1946. "Jackson Pollock is one": "Reviews and Previews," p. 63. "Surface virtuosity": Wolf, "Fifty-Seventh Street in Review," p. 16. "Transitional": CG, "Art," Apr. 13, 1946, p. 445. "Out of My Head": Aaron Bohrod, "Surrealism and Sex à la Guggenheim," Chicago *Sunday Tribune*, q. in Weld, p. 346. "An urge on wheels": Bullock, "Stripped Down to Sex." "Boudoir Bohemia"; book under every arm: "Boudoir Sex," *Art Digest*, Apr. 15, 1946, q. in Weld, p. 347. Friedman: Peggy's family bought up copies of the book and destroyed them.

Fauna and flora: Epstein and Barlow, pp. 76, 87, 94–95, 101. Ducks and terns: Ted Hults. Freshwater springs: Epstein and Barlow, p. 149. Marshlands: Epstein and Barlow, pp. 85, 88–89, 180. "Loved to go out": Q. in DP&G, "Who Was JP?" p. 51. Beaches rebuilt: Epstein and Barlow, p. 92. Bonac fishermen: Richard and Allene Talmage, int. by Shorthall, Nov. 9, 1959. Birds: Epstein and Barlow, p. 98. Beach plums: Epstein and Barlow, p. 183. Pitch pines; cranberry and blueberry patches: Epstein and Barlow, p. 86. Garden; Gyp: LK. "His farm": Wilcox. "[Jackson] was happy": Q. in DP&G, "Who Was JP?" p. 51. "I'd rant and rave"; "cozy, domestic": Q. in Glueck, "Krasner and Pollock," p. 60. Rooting in the garden: JP, q. by LK in DP&G, "Who Was JP?" p. 51: "I'll dig it and set it out if you'll water and weed." Lee's easel folded: Rosenberg. Cherry saplings: Epstein and Barlow, p. 152. Walks to marshes and dunes: LK. "Or we would sit": Q. in DP&G, "Who Was JP?" p. 51.

May 17: SMP to CCP, EFP, and Jeremy, June 13, 1946. Seventy-first birthday: SMP to CCP, EFP, and Jeremy, May 8, 1946; SMP to CCP, EFP, and Jeremy, June 13, 1946; Stella's birthday was May 20; Sande's thirty-seventh was on May 26.

The Water Bull: OC&T 149, I, pp. 141–42. *The Tea Cup*: OC&T 150, I, p. 142. *Bird Effort*: OC&T 153, I, p. 145. *Yellow Triangle*: OC&T 151, I, p. 143. *The Key*: OC&T 156, I, pp. 148–49. Pastels: See, e.g., *Constellation*, OC&T 154, I, p. 146. *The Magic Mirror*: OC&T 85, I, p. 68.

Painted bedrooms: JP to Ed and Wally Strautin, Oct. 2, 1945. Bathroom; porch; Wilcox. Hustek: Edward Hults: This happened in late fall 1946. Hustek put too much thinner in the paint and it peeled a year later. "Grand": JP to Ed and Wally Strautin, Oct. 2, 1945. View blocked: LK. Help from Wilcox: Wilcox. New site: Edward Hults.

"No, no, I don't want": Q. by LK, q. in Namuth, n.p. "He wanted his studio": Q. in Namuth, n.p. JP built cabinets and shelves and boarded up a window; Solomon, p. 168. Description of barn: Photos in Namuth, n.p.; Edward Hults; LK; Wilcox. *The Blue Unconscious*, a big canvas: OC&T 158, I, pp. 150–51: 84″ × 56.″ Images in *Something of the Past*: OC&T 160, I, p. 153.

The Key too big for bedroom: Wilcox. "[It] took up": Q. in Namuth, n.p. Jackson turning paintings around: LK. Fragmentation in *The Blue Unconscious*: OC&T 159, I. p. 150. Jackson's way of seeing: Carone. Motherwell made much the same point in "JP: An Artists' Symposium, Part I," p. 65: "Pollock was very interested that I, too, painted on the floor sometimes, and he had adopted the procedure for himself more consistently than I did. . . . [The procedure] allows one to crop, which in turn can lead ultimately to the allover picture."

"Dumb and boring": CG. Greenberg's background: CG; Kunitz, ed., pp. 386–87. Greenberg looking in other directions: Greenberg's goal was "to be remembered," and even if he considered art criticism "the most ungrateful form of 'elevated' writing I know of," at least there were very few people so far who had "done it well"; q. in Kunitz, ed., p. 387. **"As for [Greenberg] becoming":** Barrett, p. 137. **Session at the League:** With Richard Leahy; Wheeler. **Lectures at Hofmann school:** Rosenberg. **Gallery-going:** Bultman; Rosenberg. Bultman says Pantuhoff and Greenberg went to a WPA class together at "the Academy." **Lee contemptuous of critics:** Ronald Stein: "She was a mystic about art. Therefore she was contemptuous of anybody who would try to explain it in any way. Art was by definition inexplicable." **Skeptical about Greenberg's intelligence:** Bultman. **"He's helping us":** Q. by Myers. **Inviting Greenberg:** Wilcox says that it was Lee's decision to invite Greenberg.

"Lee and I would sit": CG, int. by Vallière, Mar. 20, 1968: Lee's strategy was to agree with Greenberg except "when I didn't like a picture enough—and usually she was right." **Description of Greenberg:** See Gruen, p. 179. **"She was damn significant":** CG. Myers: "Every one of his ideas for establishing his particular critical structure *all* came from Lee, every last one of them. I don't care what anybody says, I *know* this is true." **"Warmed-over Hofmann":** Myers.

Greenberg's certitude: For example, "The Chinese invented kitsch." **Immersion in Marxism:** Barrett, p. 151. **Revolutionary spirit:** See Reise, "Greenberg and The Group," p. 254. **"Content is a morass":** Q. by Brach. **"Picasso, Braque":** CG, "Avant-Garde and Kitsch," p. 37: "To the exclusion of whatever is not necessarily implicated in these factors." The following year (in "Towards a Newer Laocoön," p. 305), he added that "The arts lie safe, now, each within its 'legitimate' boundaries, and free trade has been replaced by autarchy. Purity consists in the acceptance, willing acceptance, of the limitations of the medium of the specific art." In 1947 ("Jean Dubuffet, JP," p. 137), he wrote, "As is the case with almost all post-cubist painting of any real originality, it is the tension inherent in the constructed, re-created flatness of the surface that produces the strength of his art." **"Ours was an age":** Barrett, p. 152. **"My generation":** CG.

Greenberg giving advice: Kramer: "In relation to the painters, he imagines himself in the role of Ezra Pound editing 'The Wasteland.'" **Late July:** Sometime between July 26 and 28. **Something of the Past:** Wilcox, who helped JP move the barn, recalls *Blue Unconscious* as already begun at that time; Lee recalls that *Something of the Past* was one of the first canvases JP started after the move to the barn. **"Squinting":** Friedman, p. 157. **"Jackson's best":** CG. **"Manifest destiny":** CG, "Art," Apr. 7, 1945, p. 397. **Reintroducing imagery:** CG. **Tense encounter:** Little, recalling JP. **"Do eight or ten":** In the mid-fifties, Greenberg would say, in a similar circumstance, "Paint me a show"; Jackson. **"Critical clichés":** Lord. **"Be nice to Clem":** Bultman, recalling JP. On another visit to Springs the same year (dating based on Greenberg's description of the painting technique JP was using at the time and the presence of Bill Davis in the studio; CG, int. by Shorthall, Nov. 9, 1959), while sitting around, talking, and having a few drinks in the studio (CG, int. by Shorthall, Nov. 9, 1959), Greenberg told JP that a certain painting was wrong somehow and challenged JP to fix it. Without a word of protest, JP put the painting on the floor, reached for a tube of white paint, and started moving around the canvas."

Janet Sobel's show: Lader, pp. 313–14: Greenberg said he and JP saw Sobel's work in 1944 at Peggy's gallery. Lader assumes that Greenberg got the gallery wrong and that he was referring to Sobel's April 1944 show at the Puma Gallery. Weld, p. 341: "Greenberg recalled how impressed Pollock had been by [Sobel's] show in 1946" at Art of This Century. Given the relationship between Greenberg and Pollock, we think Weld is correct and that Lader incorrectly "corrected" Greenberg's memory. In an effort to substantiate Greenberg's original recollection, Rubin refers to Sobel's paintings in a group show at Art of This Century in "early 1944" ("JP and the Modern Tradition, Part III," p. 30) although Lader's exhaustive review (pp. 387–92, 452) of the exhibition catalogues and other records does not reveal any Sobel paintings at Art of This Century until the 1946 solo show. **"Struck":** CG. **Sobel's career:** See Rubin, Part III, p. 30. **"Facial features":** Lader, p. 314. **"Overall design":** CG, int. by Shorthall, Nov. 9, 1959: Years later, Sobel would call Sidney Janis and say she, not Pollock, should have been considered the originator of Pollock's style. Rubin ("JP and the Modern Tradition, Part III," p. 30 n. 30) cites Greenberg in "American-Type painting" for the proposition that JP admitted that Sobel's pictures had made an impression on him. The references to Sobel were

incorporated into the revision of Greenberg's article for the publication of the 1961 *Art and Culture* (p. 218), but were not included in the original article (p. 187).

Earliest doodles: See, e.g., OC&T 389, III, p. 6; 391, III, p. 7; 400, III, p. 11; 420, III, p. 33; 441, III, p. 47; 456, III, p. 55; 457, III, p. 56; 465, III, p. 61. **Abstract motifs on ceramics:** OC&T 918, IV, p. 4; 920, IV, p. 6. **Prescient experiment:** OC&T 33, I. p. 28–29. **Henderson abstract doodles:** OC&T 505v, III, p. 86; 530, III, p. 101; 542, III, p. 110; 543, III, p. 111. **Henderson semi-abstract doodles:** OC&T 505r, III, p. 86; 512, III, p. 90; 518r, III, p. 93; 519v, III, p. 94; 522v, III, p. 97; 526, III, p. 99; 527, III, p. 100; 541, III, p. 110; 551, III, p. 115. For examples of the same type of drawing between roughly 1940 and 1944, see OC&T 575r, III, p. 126; 576r, III, p. 127; 576v, III, p. 127; 577r, III, p. 127; 577v, III, p. 127; 578r, III, p. 128; 579v, III, p. 129; 585v, III, p. 133; 586v, III, p. 133; 587r, III, p. 134; 601, III, p. 142; 603r, III, p. 144; 603v, III, p. 144; 604, III, p. 145; 606, III, p. 147; 609, III, p. 150; 612r, III, p. 152; 626, III, p. 160; 633, III, p. 165; 640, III, p. 171; 641, III, p. 172; 642, III, p. 172; 644r, III, p. 174; 646, III, p. 176; 648r, III, p. 177; 649, III, p. 178; 658r, III, p. 183; 660r, III, p. 184; 663, III, p. 186; 674, III, p. 193; 696, III, p. 205; 697, III, p. 206; 698, III, p. 207; 699, III, p. 208; 702, III, p. 210.

Jackson seeing Tobey's show: Busa. **"Exception":** JP to Louis Bunce, June 2, 1946; also Morris Graves. Both Greenberg and, later, William Rubin were determined to separate JP from Tobey. See CG, int. by Shorthall, Nov. 9, 1959: According to Greenberg, JP had never seen a work by Tobey when he began his drip paintings. Few artists were interested in Tobey's 1944 show in New York, Greenberg adds. When JP saw Tobey's *Tundra* for the first time, in reproduction, he supposedly said Sobel did the same thing better. See also Greenberg, "American-Type Painting," p. 187; and Rubin, "JP and the Modern Tradition, Part III," p. 29: "Pollock arrived at his all-over style quite without having seen the Tobeys we have been describing," and (p. 27) "Pollock himself did not see this white writing [of Tobey's] when it was shown in the Willard Gallery in 1944; the line of his integration of the all-over style—developing cues from Impressionism, Cubism and Surrealism—in no way presupposes contact with Tobey. Tobey arrived at his all-over pictures not via Surrealism but through Klee (his 'doodling' and Cubist-influenced grid compositions) and, more significantly, I believe, for his quality, through Oriental calligraphy." Rubin presumably derived his notion that JP was unaware of Tobey's work from Greenberg; both were unaware of JP's letter to Bunce, which did not come to light until 1984, the year of Bunce's death, and of Busa's testimony that he and JP attended the exhibition together. Both critics were too eager to deny Jackson's contact with Tobey, and thereby to deny his contact with a tradition (namely Oriental calligraphy) outside the modernist genealogy. Even more questionable is the effort to dismiss the "quality" of Tobey's work because of such contact.

Canvas worked on with Bennett: Bennett; painting in Bennett's possession, not included in OC&T. **Experiments toward all-over composition:** See OC&T 723–25, III, pp. 226–28. **Rest of the summer:** LK, q. in Rose, p. 53. **Eyes in the Heat:** OC&T 162, I, pp. 156–57. **Croaking Movement:** OC&T 161, I, pp. 154–55. **Earth Worms:** OC&T 163, I, p. 158. **Shimmering Substance:** OC&T 164, I, pp. 158–59. **Size of Croaking Movement:** Actually 53½" by 43¼". **Size of Shimmering Substance:** Actually 30⅛" by 24¼". **"That's for Clem":** Q. by CG. **"It is the tension":** CG, "Art," Feb. 1, 1947, pp. 137, 139.

Schaefer's taxi: Schaefer, int. by Shorthall, Nov. 9, 1959. **Flora and fauna:** Epstein and Barlow, pp. 86, 74; goldenrod: Southern. **June trip:** June 26. **Guggenheim closing gallery:** Friedman, pp. 93–94. **"Everything got to be":** PG, q. in Weld, p. 359. **Jackson squeezed in:** See Friedman, p. 94. **Nursery View Cabins; Elm Tree Inn; "only bar":** Wilcox. **Police driving Jackson home:** int. by Talmage. **"The kind of man"; "powerhouse":** Hempstead. **Carpet-sculpting machine:** Cole. **"Go to the mailbox":** Q. by Cole. **Wilcox history:** Wilcox. **Inventions:** From mixing cleaning powder in paint so it could be easily washed off grocery store windows (his first) to a machine that silkscreened labels onto curved bottles. **Neon light business:** Wilcox worked with the developer of neon lighting, Georges Claude.

"I wasn't about to have a child": Q. by Gibbs; John Lee: She may have known at the time about JP's brothers and thought his drinking ran in the family. Other friends admit that even if JP had been perfectly healthy, Lee probably would have refused. Gibbs: "She had absolutely no interest in motherhood." In the thirties, during her modeling days, Lee had refused to have a child by Igor Pantuhoff, supposedly on the grounds that it would ruin her figure; see Rosenberg and Ruth Stein. In public, Lee always argued that she and Pantuhoff or she and JP were too poor to have children; see Friedman. **"He was enough child":** Rosenberg.

Ride in MG: Potter, p. 185. **Supposed affair with Maria Motherwell:** Busa, John Cole, and Esteban and Harriet Vicente mistakenly assumed an affair took place. Wilcox, however, says it did not, that Maria was too devout a Catholic to have engaged in an affair. Her friend Mullican agrees and adds, "She took marriage very seriously. She was beautiful, and she enjoyed being beautiful, but she didn't sleep around." Holtzman, who knew her well, says, "I don't think she would have been at all interested in Jackson." **"Lee forbid me":** Paraphrased from Motherwell, q. in Potter, p. 211. Given Motherwell's account, this incident must have taken place in 1946. **Jackson not liking Motherwell's work:** Hartigan. **"Son of a bitch":** JP, q. by Kamrowski. **"Phony":** Marca-Relli, recalling JP: "A lot of people felt that way about Motherwell." **Jackson receiving women coolly:** Rosenberg: "He would come out of the house and carefully close the door behind him. Then we would sit on the steps in plain view of the road. There was not a single time I went in for a glass of water or anything. And it only happened when Lee wasn't there."

Series titles: These were JP's own, according to Lee (q. in Johnson, "JP and Nature," p. 259, citing interview with LK, Oct. 22, 1971). JP's idea may have been that grouping his paintings would help establish an "identifiable image" in the public eye. During his summer stay at Louse Point, Mark Rothko had talked a great deal about the need to establish an identifiable image; see Liss. "Abstraction at Louse Point."

Ride with Rosenbergs: Tabak, "War Games," in "Collage," p 434. **Thanksgiving; "[Jack and Lee]":** SMP to FLP, MLP, and Jonathan, Dec. 30, 1946. **Holiday cut short:** Tabak, "War Games," in "Collage," p. 434. **"Hobo coffee":** See Kligman, p. 105. **Clothing:** LK, q. in Friedman, p. 87: "An outfit the likes of which you've never seen." See also DP&G, "Who Was JP?" p. 51. **"Incredible white light":** Q. by Lee. **"But what he managed":** Q. in DP&G, "Who Was JP?" p. 51. **Stella's arrival:** SMP to FLP, MLP, and Jonathan, Dec. 30, 1946.

---

33. MEMORIES ARRESTED IN SPACE

SOURCES

Books, articles, manuscript, and transcripts

Burroughs, *THB*; Carmean and Rathbone, *American Art at Mid-Century*; Frank, *JP*; Friedman, JP; Goodman, *Hans Hofmann*; Hunter, *Hans Hofmann*; Kozloff, *Renderings*; Namuth, *Pollock Painting*; O'Doherty, *American Masters*; OC&T, *JP*; O'Hara, *JP*; Potter, *To a Violent Grave*; Prown and Rose, *American Painting*; Raskin and Appenzeller, *Headache*; Rodman, *Conversations with Artists*; Rose and Gawel, *Migraine*; Ryan, Sr., and Ryan, Jr., *Headache and Head Pain*; Saper, *Headache Disorders*; Waldberg, *Max Ernst*.

Charles D. Aring, "The Migrainous Scintillating Scotoma," *JAMA*, Apr. 24, 1972; Robert Alan Aurthur, "Hitting the Boiling Point, Freakwise, at East Hampton," *Esquire*, June 1972; Paul Brach, "Tandem Paint: Krasner/Pollock," *Art in America*, Mar. 1982; DP&G, "Who Was JP?" *Art in America*, May–June 1967; B. H. Friedman, "An Interview with LK Pollock," in Marlborough-Gerson Gallery, *JP: Black and White*; Robert Goodnough, "Pollock Paints a Picture," *Art News*, May 1951; CG, "Art," *Nation*, June 9, 1945; CG, "Art," *Nation*, Apr. 13, 1946; CG, "Towards a Newer Laocoön," *Partisan Review*, July–Aug. 1940; E. H. Hare, "Personal Observations on the Spectral March of Migraine," *Journal of the Neurological Sciences*, 1966; K. S. Lashley, "Patterns of Cerebral Integration Indicated by the Scotomas of Migraine," *Archives of Neurology and Psychiatry*, 1941; FVOC, "Hans Namuth's Photographs of JP as Art Historical Documentation," *Art Journal*, Fall 1979; Whitman Richards, "The Fortification Illusions of Migraine," *Scientific American*, May 1971; David S. Rubin, "A Case for

Content: JP's Subject Matter was Automatic Gesture," *Arts*, Mar. 1979; William Rubin, "JP and the Modern Tradition, Part I: 1. The Myths and the Paintings; 2. The All-Over Compositions and the Drip Technique," *Artforum*, Feb. 1967; William Rubin, "JP and the Modern Tradition, Part II: 3. Impressionism and the Classic Pollock; 4. Color and Scale; Affinities with the Late Monet," *Artforum*, Mar. 1967; William Rubin, "JP and the Modern Tradition, Part III: 5. Cubism and the Later Evolution of the All-Over Style," *Artforum*, Apr. 1967; William Rubin, "JP and the Modern Tradition, Part IV: 6. An Aspect of Automatism," *Artforum*, May 1967; Sidney Simon, "Concerning the Beginnings of the New York School: 1939–1943, An Interview with Peter Busa and Matta," *Art International*, Summer 1967; Charles F. Stuckey, "Another Side of JP," *Art in America*, Nov.–Dec. 1977; Sidney Tillim, "The Alloway International," *Arts*, Mar. 1964; Parker Tyler, "Nature and Madness Among the Younger Painters," *View*, May 1945; C. L. Wysuph, "Behind the Veil," *Art News*, Oct. 1970.

CG, "The Pollock Market Soars," *NYT Magazine*, Apr. 16, 1961; Vivien Raynor, "JP in Retrospect—'He Broke the Ice,' " *NYT Magazine*, Apr. 2, 1967; Amei Wallach, "LK: Out of JP's Shadow," *Newsday*, Aug. 23, 1981.

Frank A. Seixas, "JP: An Appreciation" (unpub. ms.).

CG, int. by Kathleen Shorthall for *Life*, Nov. 9, 1959, Time/Life Archives; CG, int. by James T. Vallière, Mar. 20, 1968, AAA; JP, int. by Dorothy Seiberling for *Life*, July 18, 1949, Time/Life Archives.

Interviews

T. P. Benton; Fritz Bultman; Peter Busa; Jeremy Capillé; Nicholas Carone; Dorothy Dehner; Audrey Flack; Cynthia Goodman; Ron Gorchov; Chaim Gross; Robert Beverly Hale; Ben Heller; Budd Hopkins; Paul Jenkins; Buffie Johnson; Reuben Kadish; Lillian Olaney Kiesler; Hilton Kramer; LK; Harold Lehman; Joe LeSueur; Herbert Matter; Mercedes Matter; George McNeil; John Millwater; Philip Pavia; Vita Peterson; FLP; MJP; Milton Resnick; May Tabak Rosenberg; Irving Sandler; Gertrude Shibley; Patsy Southgate; Michael Stolbach; Araks Tolegian; Samuel Wagstaff; Roger Wilcox.

NOTES

Description of painting process: Hale; LK; Mercedes Matter; Peterson; Wilcox; Friedman, p. 184; Goodnough, "Pollock Paints a Picture," p. 40; FVOC, "Hans Namuth's Photographs of JP," p. 49; O'Hara, p. 26. **Recalcitrant pen; "dribble and blob":** Wilcox. Beginning with William Rubin in 1967, there has been a campaign to delete the word "drip" from the vocabulary of Pollock criticism: "*Poured* pictures is a more apposite term," Rubin wrote in that year; "JP and the Modern Tradition, Part I," p. 19. O'Connor addressed the terminological problem at great length in "Hans Namuth's Photographs of JP," pp. 48–49. Rubin, O'Connor, and the critics following their lead consider the word "drip" demeaning (it did, after all, play into the hands of critics who dubbed Pollock "Jack the Dripper") and dismissive of the artistic intent in JP's working style. The term is in some ways inadequate—it by no means conveys the many different ways in which JP deposited paint on the canvas—but as a generic term there is none better: it is the term that JP himself used, and it had a psychological significance for him that no other term could have.

Stories of style by accident: Friedman, p. 97. **Pot kicked over:** Sandler. **Discovery while drunk:** Richard Talmage, q. in Potter, p. 103; see Rubin, "JP and the Modern Tradition, Part I," p. 17: "The critical tradition by which innovations in modern painting are derided as the products of drink goes back to the time of Courbet and the Impressionists." **Throwing paint:** Fuller Potter, q. in Potter, p. 99. **On-slow-Ford:** Carmean and Rathbone, p. 128 n. 7. **Baziotes:** Busa, q. in Simon, "Concerning the Beginnings," p. 17. **De Kooning; Resnick:** Resnick. **Kamrowski:** Bultman. **Gorky; Reznikoff:** Resnick: JP was also fascinated by an artist named Max Schnitzler who began painting all-over abstractions of "marks of paint" as early as 1937. "They were on the project together. They knew each other very well." During a trip into the city at this time, Schnitzler was apparently directed to JP's show at the Betty Parsons Gallery. "He stood around and looked at those paintings and said, 'That son of a bitch!' Not much later, Jackson came to the Waldorf Cafeteria and saw

Max. He said, 'I heard you called me a son of a bitch'—and smiled." **Others:** Rubin, "JP and the Modern Tradition, Part IV," p. 31: "[Pouring paint] was not at all uncommon as a marginal or 'coloristic' effect." Paul Jenkins notes, in particular, Gianni Dova and Enrico Donati. **"I did drip":** Smith, q. by Dehner.

Hofmann: Little, q. in Potter, p. 100. **Early Hofmanns:** Miz was referring especially to *Spring*, 1940, and *Fantasia*, 1943; see FVOC, "The Genesis of JP," p. 256 n. 18. Hunter (p. 20) called *Spring* "something of a 'sport' or maverick" in Hofmann's career, arguing that the technique was not used again for three years and was "never again to be given such exclusive attention." **Stealing from Hofmann:** Kiesler: "Miz said that Jackson had come up to his studio, had seen his first drip painting, and that that's how he first learned about drip painting. I never took it too seriously." See Johnson, q. in Potter, p. 100. Goodman, p. 45: "Evidence suggests that all of Hofmann's so-called dripped paintings may have been erroneously dated."

Dispute: See, e.g., Rubin, "JP and the Modern Tradition, Part II," p. 33; "Part IV," p. 28. Rubin, "Part II," p. 33: "Far too much emphasis tends to be placed upon the historical precedence in the invention of new techniques (the fuss about who invented dripping is a case in point) as opposed to what is done with them." **Shamanistic rituals:** Brach, "Tandem Paint," p. 95. **"Fundamental rhythms":** Kagan, "Improvisations," pp. 97–98. **"A different edge":** CG, int. by Shorthall, Nov. 9, 1959. **"Divisionist preoccupation":** Rose, p. 54. On the basis of statements from many people, we believe that Lee's all-over canvases are misdated; that they did not begin until after the mosaic table, which was created in 1947. **European tradition:** Rubin, "JP and the Modern Tradition, Part III," p. 20.

"I do not think it exaggerated": CG, "The Pollock Market Soars." In the pursuit of what Kramer calls a "fixed morphology"—"this, leading to this, leading to the next thing, in perfect relationship"—historians like William Rubin have focused on the modernist antecedents, with a bow to the Surrealists—but only the abstract Surrealists. Rubin, "Part IV," p. 28: "In the broadest sense, Pollock's drip paintings descend from a line within the modern tradition bent on increasingly loosening the fabric of the picture surface in a 'painterly' way." "Part III," p. 20: "Like Pollock's poetry, which shifted from an explicit to an implicit state, the Cubism had gone underground. *There, it gave his all-over drip pictures precisely that architectonic tautness of structure which had been missing from the Impressionism which, I believe, also profoundly—though even more indirectly—informed their style.*" [Emphasis in original.] **"Wagner's Ring":** Kramer. **"Flinging a pot":** Ruskin, q. in Prown, p. 107. **"Marginal or 'coloristic'":** Rubin, "Part IV," p. 31. **Ernst poking holes:** Waldberg, p. 388: When two paintings created by Ernst using the drip method—*The Mad Planet* and *Young Man Intrigued by the Flight of a Non-Euclidian Fly*—were exhibited by Betty Parsons at the Wakefield bookshop in 1942, JP and Motherwell "were astounded by the delicacy of their structures and begged Max Ernst to tell them their secret. It was a simple one: [that is, dripping paint from a can (with a hole pierced in the bottom) swung from a string]. Jackson Pollock later used this technique, called 'dripping'—or 'pouring'—most systematically and he was later credited with its invention." Rubin, "Part IV," p. 30: "Ernst told the French critic Françoise Choay that Pollock discovered the [drip] technique through his pictures."

Ernst's experiment: Waldberg, p. 388. **Schwankovsky's classroom:** Araks Tolegian, recalling Manuel. **Formal reasons:** See *Burning Landscape*, OC&T 95, I, p. 86; also *Composition with Pouring I*, OC&T 92, I, pp. 82–83. It is difficult to believe the two fully realized drip paintings dated 1943—*Water Birds* (OC&T 93, I, p. 84), and *Composition with Pouring II* (OC&T 94, I, p. 85)—were actually painted that year. The provenance for OC&T 92 does suggest that some version of the painting was completed in 1943, although JP may have taken a 1943 work and subsequently dripped paint on it. **"Painting is self-discovery":** Q. in Rodman, p. 82. **Reticence:** "The network of line serves as the protective shield which could be expected of an artist who has been characterized as private and nonverbal"; David S. Rubin, "A Case for Content," p. 108; see Bultman, q. in Potter, p. 204. **"Continue the flattening-out":** CG, "Art," June 9, 1945, p. 657. **"Purity in art":** CG, "Towards a Newer Laocoön," p. 305. **"A**

habit of discipline": CG, "Art," Apr. 13, 1946, p. 445. **"If there is anything":** Q. in Carmean, p. 38, citing interview of Mar. 1978. **"Heads, parts"; "'I choose to veil'":** Q. by LK, q. in Friedman, "An Interview with LK Pollock," n.p.

Veiling the image: In "Part II, p. 86," William Rubin writes that Lee told him in June 1979 that "Pollock made the remark about 'veiling' in reference to *There Were Seven in Eight*, and it doesn't necessarily apply to other paintings—certainly not to such pictures as *Autumn Rhythm, One*, etc." Rubin, "Part II, p. 84," describes *There Were Seven in Eight* as a painting in which JP painted a " 'frieze' of totemic forms," then "added the web of arabesqued drawing." Rubin, "II, p. 83": "There is only one poured canvas, *Galaxy*, 1947—one of the first Pollock painted—in which there is the unmistakable presence of figurative forms under the abstract web." But Lee's disdain for writers was well known. Stolbach notes that she would often tell a writer what he or she wanted to hear, usually assuming that that is what would end up being written anyway. On March 13, 1983, Lee told Elizabeth Frank (q. in Frank, p. 43) that her conversation with JP referred to *Guardians of the Secret*, not only a different painting, but a painting from an entirely different period. To Amei Wallach, one of the few writers with whom Lee spoke openly, she said (q. in "LK") that "Pollock never was a completely abstract painter." Stolbach remembers Lee saying that she "never determined that Pollock ever stopped being a figurative painter." She told Wysuph (recalled in "Behind the Veil," p. 55) that the drip paintings are "no less figurative" than his earlier ones and that "the figures and 'veils' are so integrated as to be indistinguishable." Many of JP's friends and colleagues echo these latter sentiments. Kadish: "His work always started with images. And I think it always maintained the particular force of those images. The paintings were never abstractions. Never, never, never abstractions." Tillim, "The Alloway International," p. 59: "I don't believe he ever conceived of a painting apart from some kind of subject matter." JP's own statement on the subject (q. in Rodman, p. 8) is remarkably clear: "I'm very representational some of the time, and a little all the time. But when you're painting out of your unconscious, figures are bound to emerge."

Galaxy: OC&T 169, I, pp. 166–67. **Images discernible:** Rubin, "Part II," p. 83; see also Bultman, q. in Potter, p. 204, to the effect that the dripped paint in *Shooting Star* (1947), also covers an earlier image. *Watery Paths:* OC&T 171, I, pp. 168–69. *Magic Lantern:* OC&T 172, I, p. 170. *The Nest:* OC&T 174, I, p. 172. *Vortex:* OC&T 178, I, p. 176. **New way of creating imagery:** See *Composition with Black Pouring* (OC&T 170, I, p. 168) probably the first work in which JP clearly used the drip technique to create a recognizable image. **"Crawl inside them":** MJP. **Jungian framework:** See David S. Rubin, "A Case for Content," p. 109: The "collective unconscious [was] conceived by the artist as energy in constant flux in an infinite space." See also p. 104.

Eye problem, including dating: Wilcox: "It had been going on for many years. He didn't know when it occurred for the first time." **"A temporary malfunction":** Wilcox. **"Nothing wrong":** Q. by Wilcox. **Journals:** Wilcox: There was a society of physiological optics which was commonly known as the Helmholtz Society in England." **Medical terminology:** For the current literature, see: Aring, "The Migrainous Scintillating Scotoma," pp. 519–22; Hare, "Personal Observations," 259–64; Lashley, "Patterns of Cerebral Integration," pp. 331–39; Raskin and Appenzeller, *Headache*; Richards, "The Fortification Illusions of Migraine," pp. 89–96; Rose and Gawel, *Migraine*; Ryan, Sr., and Ryan, Jr., *Headache and Head Pain*; Saper, *Headache Disorders*. Given Wilcox's description, Dr. Millwater, an eye expert at Vanderbilt University, said JP was "probably describing ocular migraine, which is the visual imagery or aura that occurs before you have a headache. The visual image results from an electrical discharge from the occipital cortex—from the posterior part of the visual pathway. Some people describe a flashing light. Some describe wavy lines. Some describe a little light that gets bigger and bigger. Or a fortification spectrum—a sawtoothed effect like the top edge of a saw. Some describe a gossamerlike veil."

Realization that the imagery had occurred in his paintings: Wilcox: "The drip paintings were totally like the electrical discharges he was experiencing. But he didn't try to *paint* the discharges. Curiously, it was only after he made several of the drip paintings that he recognized the connec-

tion." **Freedom from tools:** See Tillim, "The Alloway International," p. 56; Wilcox: "All I know absolutely for certain is that JP expressed to me enough ways and enough times that his purpose was to separate himself physically from the surface on which he was making the impression." Dripping vitiated the need to draw. JP, int. by Seiberling for *Life*, July 18, 1949: "He insists that it is only necessary to be a master of your own mode of expression—that there are no real ABCs that an artist has to learn other than those which facilitate his own expression. 'If an artist is interested in a typewriter,' Pollock remarks indifferently, 'he should be able to draw it.' " Dripping substituted for the traditional pencil or brush an entirely new kind of draftsmanship.
Line becomes lyrical: See William Rubin, "Part I," p. 15: "In the style that realized his full identity, the Expressionist element disappeared and the violence, frustration, and tension were largely transformed into a passionate lyricism." **Profile of head:** Wilcox: A head was one of the first images JP painted with the drip technique. **Automatism and control:** William Rubin, "Part II," p. 31: "The artist himself has said, 'I *can* control the flow of paint: there is no accident.' Yet even a cursory glance at a drip Pollock shows that on a *purely operational level* this was not entirely true despite the remarkable virtuosity he developed in his technique. There are numerous small spots and puddlings which were manifestly not one hundred percent controlled *as they happened.* But they are accidental only then; in the final work they have been transmuted into esthetic decision." See also O'Doherty, p. 105. **"He painted like a machine":** Q. in Friedman, p. 100. **"I don't know where":** Q. by CG.
Breakthrough: Wilcox: JP "discovered" the drip technique when "he was trying to draw a head without contacting the paper. And he did." Since JP had "discovered" the drip technique years before, Wilcox may be referring to the first instance when JP painted an image "in the air." **Carone's description:** Wilcox: "JP talked to Nick more than anybody else that I know of about his art, about painting." **"Working in the air":** Q. in Namuth, n.p. **"Aerial form[s]":** Int. by Barbara Rose, q. in Namuth, n.p. **"Take his stick":** Namuth, n.p.
"Alien code": Stuckey, "Another Side of JP," p. 82. **Figures emerging:** JP, q. in Rodman, p. 82. Wilcox argues persuasively that JP, for the first time, "discovered the truth of psychoanalysis while he was doing his drip paintings." **Always figurative:** LK, q. by Stolbach. **"Skins":** Carone: "Those are layered paintings, but they're skins of dimensions, they're *skins.* It's not overlaying like in a Cubist painting, it's like overlaying to synthesize and bring it to the surface again. It's like he's digging in by layers to bring it up to the surface. That's why it's so packed with energy. They could explode, those paintings." **A dimension away:** Jenkins: "He was not involved with the figure, but he transformed our notion of the figure. He took it out of or away from Cubism and was able to discover an astral possibility." **"Memories arrested in space":** JP, c. 1950, q. in OC&T IV, p. 253.
"Loveliness": See O'Doherty, p. 106. **Joseph Meyer's:** Lehman. **"Feeling for matière:** Tyler, "Nature and Madness Among the Younger Painters," p. 30. **"His feeling for the land":** Q. in DP&G, "Who Was JP?" p. 52. **"Popped into his head":** Wilcox. **Urinating from seated position:** Kligman, q. by Wagstaff: "It was very strange—he always sat down on the john to take a piss"; see also LeSueur, recalling Kligman. **"Peeing competitions":** FLP; MJP. **"I'm from the West":** JP, q. by Busa. **Urinating in Rosenberg's house:** Rosenberg. **In Wilcox's house:** Wilcox. **In Meert's house:** Shibley. **In Lee's bed:** Wilcox.
"How do you know": Q. in Seixas, "JP," n.p. But JP's view of lovemaking was a child's-eye view, part possession and part assault. When JP's twelve-year-old niece, Jeremy, visited the studio, she was struck by the violence of her uncle's relationship with the canvas. "It was almost as if what was in his hand wasn't a stick, it was a knife or a hatchet or weapon of some sort. I remember being made terribly uneasy by it." Another visitor thought JP "tore into a canvas the way Joe Louis destroyed Max Schmeling"; Aurthur, "Hitting the Boiling Point," p. 200. In the late forties, JP began to "abuse" his canvases, using knives and trowels instead of sticks and brushes, lacing the paint with nails, tacks, broken glass, and lit cigarettes; Friedman, p. 99. He kicked them, stepped on them, and loaded them for the trips to New York "as if they were so many bags of potatoes"; Raynor, "JP in Retrospect."
"Tchelitchew had it": Q. by Jenkins. **Rumors of urinat-**

ing: Benton; Gross. Busa: A similar fascination with feces is involved in the thickly pigmented canvases that preceded the drip paintings: "He was what you might call anal-erotic. . . . He could play with paint. He could make a painting called *Shimmering Substance* like you would make a mud pie." **Slapdash art":** Q. by Gorchov.
Always Stella: See O'Doherty, p. 106. Flack: "Part of what is so important about him is his maleness, his virility. And yet look what it comes from, and why it was so insisted upon—fragility, and the association with the female." Heller: "Jackson was one of the few painters that I know who was both masculine and feminine. When a painter has that power, but also that delicacy and exquisiteness, you've got to be in the presence of something great." **"Lifted the instrument":** Kozloff, p. 146.

34. A PERFECT MATCH

SOURCES

Books, articles, manuscripts, lecture, film, and transcripts

Ashton, *The New York School;* Ashton, *Yes, but . . . ;* Barrett, *The Truants;* Diamonstein, ed., *Inside New York's Art World;* Fried, *Three American Painters;* Friedman, *JP;* CG, *Art and Culture;* Gruen, *The Party's Over Now;* PG, *Out of This Century;* Kunitz, ed., *Twentieth Century Authors;* Lader, *Arshile Gorky;* Maurer and Bayles, *Gerome Kamrowski;* Nemser, *Art Talk;* OC&T, *JP;* O'Doherty, *American Masters;* Phillips, *A Partisan View;* Pointer and Goddard, *Harry Jackson;* Potter, *To a Violent Grave;* Rose, *LK;* Seldes, *The Legacy of Mark Rothko;* Tabak, *But Not for Love;* Weld, *Peggy.*
R[enée] A[rb], "Spotlight on: De Kooning," *Art News*, Apr. 1948; Robert Alan Aurthur, "Hitting and Boiling Point, Freakwise, at East Hampton," *Esquire*, June 1972; M[argaret] B[reuning], "Fifty-Seventh Street in Review," *Art Digest*, Jan. 15, 1948; "The Best," *Time*, Dec. 1, 1947; Robert Coates, "The Art Galleries," *New Yorker*, Jan. 17, 1948; Rosalind Constable, "The Betty Parsons Collection," *Art News*, Mar. 1968; DP&G, "Who Was JP?" *Art in America*, May–June 1967; Grace Glueck, "Krasner and Pollock: Scenes from a Marriage," *Art News*, Dec. 1981; CG, "Art," *Nation*, Jan. 24, 1948; CG, "Jean Dubuffet, JP," *Nation*, Feb. 1, 1947; CG, "The Present Prospects of American Painting and Sculpture," *Horizon*, Oct. 1947; "JP: An Artists' Symposium, Part I," *Art News*, Apr. 1967; Ken Kelley, "Betty Parsons Taught America to Appreciate What It Once Called 'Trash': Abstract Art," *People*, Feb. 29, 1978; Alonzo Lansford, "Fifty-Seventh Street in Review," *Art Digest*, Jan. 15, 1948; Grace Lichtenstein, "The Remarkable Betty Parsons," *Art News*, Mar. 1979; Aline B. Loucheim, "Betty Parsons: Her Gallery, Her Influence"; "The Moon-Woman Cuts the Circle," illustrated in *Dyn*, Nov. 1944; Cindy Nemser, "LK's Paintings," *Artforum*, Dec. 1973; JP, "My Painting," *Possibilities I*, Winter 1947–1948; "Reviews and Previews," *Art News*, Feb. 1947; "Reviews and Previews," *Art News*, Feb. 1948; [Berton Roueché], "Unframed Space," *New Yorker*, Aug. 5, 1950; William Rubin, "JP and the Modern Tradition, Part II," *Artforum*, Feb. 1967; Calvin Tomkins, "A Keeper of the Treasure" ("Keeper"), *New Yorker*, June 9. 1975; Emily Wasserman, "LK in Mid-Career," *Artforum*, Mar. 1968; B[en] W[olf], "Non-Objectives by Pollock," *Art Digest*, Jan. 15, 1947; Judith Wolfe, "Jungian Aspects of JP's Imagery," *Artforum*, Nov. 1972.
J. Hoberman, "Harold Rosenberg's Radical Cheek," New York *Voice Literary Supplement*, May 1986; Michael Kernan, "LK, Out of Pollock's Shadow," *Washington Post*, Oct. 23, 1983; Amei Wallach, "LK: Out of JP's Shadow," *Newsday*, Sept. 23, 1981.
Melvin Paul Lader, "PG's Art of This Century: The Surrealist Milieu and the American Avant-Garde, 1942–1947" (Lader) (Ph.D. thesis), Newark: University of Delaware, 1981; Ellen Gross Landau, "LK: A Study of Her Early Career (1926–1949)" (Ph.D. thesis), Newark: University of Delaware, 1981; May Natalie Tabak, "A Collage" (unpub. ms.).
LK (lecture), Columbia University, Oct. 5, 1983.
Strokes of Genius: JP (film), Court Productions, 1984.
CG, int. by Kathleen Shorthall for *Life*, Nov. 9. 1959, Time/ Life Archives; CG, int. by James T. Vallière, Mar. 20. 1968, AAA: LK, int. by Barbara Rose, July 31, 1966, AAA; LK, int. by Dorothy Seckler, Dec. 14, 1967, AAA; Daniel T. Miller,

int. by Kathleen Shorthall for *Life*, Nov. 9. 1959, Time/Life Archives; Barnett Newman, int. by Kathleen Shorthall for *Life*, Nov. 9, 1959, Time/Life Archives; Alfonso Ossorio, int. by Forrest Selvig, Nov. 19, 1968, AAA; Betty Parsons, int. by Kathleen Shorthall for *Life*, Nov. 9, 1959, Time/Life Archives JP, int. by Dorothy Seiberling for *Life*, July 18, 1949, Time/Life Archives.

Interviews

Ruth Ann Applehof; Ethel Baziotes; Ward Bennett; Norman Bluhm; Paul Brach; Charlotte Park Brooks; James Brooks; Fritz Bultman; Peter Busa; Herman Cherry; Dane Dixon; Ted Dragon; Herbert Ferber; Phyllis Fleiss; Lisa Fonssagrives; B. H. Friedman; Joe Glasco; CG; Grace Hartigan; Janet Hauck; Ben Heller; Elizabeth Wright Hubbard II; Merle Hubbard; Edward Hults; Ted Hults; Edys Hunter; Sam Hunter; Harry Jackson; Buffie Johnson; Reuben Kadish; Gerome Kamrowski; LK; Ernestine Lassaw; Millie Liss; John Little; Cile Downs Lord; Maria-Gaetana Matisse; Herbert Matter; Mercedes Matter; ACM; George Mercer; George Sid Miller; Annalee Newman (int. by David Peretz); Alfonso Ossorio; Gustaf Peterson; Vita Peterson; Becky Reis; Milton Resnick; May Tabak Rosenberg; Miriam Schapiro; Ronald Stein; Ruth Stein; Hedda Sterne; Michael Stolbach; Esteban Vicente; Marta Vivas; Steve Wheeler; Roger Wilcox; Eileen Wilhelm; Betsy Zogbaum.

NOTES

Lee's response to new work: Glueck, "Krasner and Pollock," p. 61: "Krasner doesn't remember her specific response when Pollock began to make his breakthrough 'drip' paintings in 1946." **"Everything I saw":** Q. in Glueck, "Krasner and Pollock," p. 61. **Sleeping twelve hours; Lee tiptoeing:** Tabak, p. 40. **"Major step":** CG, "Jean Dubuffet, JP," p. 139. **"Controlled yellows":** W[olf], "Non-Objectives by Pollock," p. 21. **"Latest pictures":** "Reviews and Previews," Feb. 1947, p. 45. **Mural:** OC&T 102, I, p. 95. **Show selling well:** At least six of the sixteen paintings exhibited were sold by the following September; OC&T IV, p. 240. JP's résumé listed only "important purchases," so the number of sales may well have been higher. **Davis's purchases:** Friedman, p. 95. **"Unreasonable dread":** Adapted from Tabak, p. 48. **"Wouldn't touch Americans":** Ossorio, int. by Selvig, Nov. 19. 1968. **"Going blind":** Q. by Parsons, in Tomkins, "A Keeper of the Treasure," pp. 51–52. **"It isn't my fish":** Q. by Maria-Gaetana Matisse. **Levy:** Weld, p. 356. **Kootz:** Friedman, p. 115; Weld, p. 356. **Former socialite:** Friedman, p. 115. **Parsons's new gallery:** Lader, p. 327. Gallery at 15 East Fifty-seventh Street; Sam Kootz had the other half, which Sidney Janis later took over; Gruen, pp. 236–37. She began the gallery with $1,000 of her own savings and $4,000 borrowed from friends. **"I'm crazy":** Q. in Weld, p. 356. **Passing on Jackson:** For story about Rothko, Pollock, Newman, and Still coming to Parsons and wanting to stay together as a group, see Tomkins, "Keeper," p. 51. Apparently, when Parsons took only three of them, their feelings of solidarity succumbed to commercial and career concerns. **Willard:** Lader, p. 327. **Realist galleries:** Friedman, p. 116.
Compromise: Friedman, p. 116. **Continued allowance:** Weld, p. 356. **Details of deal:** Friedman, pp. 115–16; Lader, p. 327; Weld, p. 356; Reis. The precise financial arrangement between Parsons and Guggenheim is not clear. Some sources say that Betty was to get any commissions over and above $300 per month; see Friedman, p. 116. The question seems to be about the method of accounting and what commission, if any, Parsons earned on the earlier paintings, for which Guggenheim set the price.
Early Parsons history: Tomkins, "Keeper," p. 47. **"Such heavy drinking":** Parsons, q. in Tomkins, p. 49. **Visit to Springs:** Parsons. q. in DP&G, "Who Was JP?" p. 55; Constable, "The Betty Parsons Collection," p. 58. **"Settled down":** LK. **Student and debutante:** Lichtenstein, "The Remarkable Betty Parsons," p. 55. **Family house:** Tomkins, "Keeper," p. 46. **Father:** Tomkins, "Keeper," p. 46. **Mother; "thank God":** Q. by Parsons in Tomkins, "Keeper," p. 46. **Class with Borglum:** Tomkins, "Keeper," p. 47. **Marriage:** Spring 1919; Tomkins, "Keeper," p. 47. **Divorce:** Tomkins, "Keeper," p. 46. **Schuyler alcoholic:** Tomkins, "Keeper, p. 47. **Homosexual:** Connors.
Armory Show: Tomkins, "Keeper," p. 47. **Paris:**

Tomkins, "Keeper," pp. 47–48. **Description of Parsons:** Tomkins, "Keeper," p. 48. **"Da Vinci forehead":** Saul Steinberg, q. in Tomkins, "Keeper," p. 46. **Mistaken for Garbo:** Tomkins, "Keeper," p. 48. **"You see the Sphinx":** Q. in Tomkins, "Keeper," p. 46. **Dietrich and Graham:** Tomkins, "Keeper," pp. 47–48. **Roosevelt:** Kelly, "Betty Parsons," p. 78. Ferber: "Betty was as uninterested in men as she was in making money." **"His whole rhythm":** Q. in DP&G, "Who Was JP?" p. 55. **"Loved his looks":** Parsons, q. in DP&G, "Who Was JP?" p. 55. **Introduction by Newman:** Tomkins, "Keeper," p. 52. **"Rapid-fire":** Lichtenstein, "The Remarkable Betty Parsons," p. 55. **Small truthful":** Friedman, p. 116. **Social Register background grating:** Potter, p. 109. **Lesbianism threatening:** Jackson. **Art reflecting the West:** Tomkins, "Keeper," p. 51. **Showing appreciation:** LK. Barnett Newman took Parsons to Springs for the weekend. At first things didn't go well: "After dinner we all sat on the floor, drawing with Japanese pens. [Jackson] broke three pens in a row. His first drawings were sensitive, then he went wild. He became hostile, you know. Next morning, he was absolutely fine"; Parsons. q. in DP&G, "Who Was JP?" p. 55.
Parsons and verbal contracts: Seldes, p. 23. **"Not as tolerant":** JP, q. by Wilcox. **"Dumped":** Parsons, q. in Kelley, "Betty Parsons," p. 78. **Sweeney asked to supervise:** Weld, p. 356. **Gallery dismantled:** Lader, p. 326. **Collection in storage:** PG, p. 268. **Phone off hook:** Tabak, p. 40. **"That's probably why":** Q. by Edys Hunter. **"Jackson was afraid":** Southgate. **"Trade was in her blood":** Tabak, p. 47: "Perhaps, to some extent, it was in the blood of most of the artists' wives." **Preserving foods:** Ruth Stein. **Stella visiting; "swell":** SMP to CCP, EFP, and Jeremy, late summer-fall of 1947. **"Heavy hocks":** Ronald Stein. **Jackson with children:** Elizabeth Wright Hubbard II; Merle Hubbard. **Jewish food:** Ruth Stein—pahrkas (cabbage rolls), knedler (dumplings), tsimis (carrots and sweet potatoes).
Lee nurturing Jackson: Ruth Stein: "She used to say, 'Let him be, let him be.' But she meant, 'Let him be *great*. Let him be a great artist.' " **Greenberg as houseguest:** In fact, Lee was shaping Greenberg into the most important arrow in her quiver. Not that she admired his criticism (she didn't), but as she herself said (int. by Rose, July 31, 1966), he was an art critic, and there were few critics at the time from which to choose. Wheeler: "Naturally, being very aggressive and very career-minded, Lee latched on to anyone who had some entrée that could be of value to her." **Beach and bike-riding:** CG. **Collection of Mirós:** Rose, p. 65. **"City development":** Ted Hults. **The direction":** Wilcox, although he insists that JP "wasn't about to go kissing Greenberg's ass." **"Clem likes this":** Q. by Sam Hunter. It was the simple but effective technique by which Greenberg had already rid JP's work of subject matter; O'Doherty, p. 110: "It must have been a happy surprise to Greenberg when Pollock, in 1947, began to paint pictures which absolved that quintessential formalist critic of the embarrassment of 'content.' "
Greenberg's speech pattern: Barrett, p. 138. **"Who in his right mind":** Virginia upbringing: CG. **"Looked like idleness":** Q. in Kunitz, p. 386. **Austere father:** Fleiss. **"Appetite for business":** Q. in Kunitz, p. 386. **"Sounding off":** Tabak, "Surrealists," in "Collage," p. 443. **"Clem leaped":** Tabak, "Surrealists," in "Collage," pp. 443–44. **"I was awed":** Fleiss: "I remember I was writing then, and I would give him something to read. He'd say, 'It looks like it was written by my fifteen-year-old sister.' And I'll tell you, after that, I didn't write for many, many years." **"To be attacked":** CG. **Contentiousness:** Ashton, p. 160: "[CG's] role as *agent provocateur* in relation to the general public was indispensable. When Greenberg said 'great,' the press replied 'heaven forbid', but Greenberg's consistency and his confidence could not be ignored." **Jackson's respect for book learning:** CG, q. in Potter, p. 182. **"Don't tell Clem":** Q. by Bultman. **"Listened intently":** Lord. **"Jackson was never a bore":** CG.
Guston's fellowship: Ashton, p. 76. **Jackson inquiring about application:** Myers to JP, Sept. 15, 1947. **"Historical death":** Barrett, p. 147. **Pollock points a way":** CG, "Jean Dubuffet, JP," p. 139. **"Large movable pictures":** JP, q. in OC&T IV, p. 238. **"My painting does not come":** Pollock, "My Painting," p. 78. **Hard-headed":** CG, "The Present Prospects," pp. 24–27. **The Best?":** p. 55. **Reproduction upside down:** For the story that the reproduction was printed upside down, see Friedman, p. 104; Potter, p. 92. We suspect that the source of this bit of apocrypha was Lee Krasner, who,

in her inventive way of speaking, may have used such a phrase to refer to the article's total failure to understand JP's art. **Thanksgiving visit:** SMP to FLP, MLP, and Jonathan, Dec. 11, 1947: "Sande & Jay both had to work." **"Jack was busy":** SMP to FLP, MLP, and Jonathan, Dec. 11. 1947; *Reflection of the Big Dipper:* OC&T 175, I, pp. 172–73. *Sea Change:* OC&T 177, I, pp. 174–75. *Vortex:* OC&T 178, I, p. 176. *Phosphorescence:* OC&T 183, I, pp. 182–83. *Shooting Star:* OC&T 182, I, p. 181. *Cathedral:* OC&T 184, I, pp. 184–85. **Gravel:** As in *Galaxy,* OC&T 169, I, pp. 166–67. **Other objects:** As in *Full Fathom Five,* OC&T 180, I, pp. 178–79. **Greenbergians on reflective paint:** CG, int. by Shorthall, Nov. 9. 1959. See also Fried (pp. 44–45) for the Greenbergian view of the use of reflective paint in Frank Stella's work.

Titles: Friedman, p. 94: JP's typical approach was to have close friends "free-associate verbally around the completed work. From their responses, from key words and phrases, he often, though not always chose his titles—typically, vague, metaphorical, or 'poetic.' " **Manheims helping with titles:** LK, q. in Wolfe, "Jungian Aspects of JP's Imagery," p. 72. **Pollock's paintings compared to Gothic cathedrals:** CG, "The Present Prospects," p. 25. **Manheim's titles:** See Friedman, pp. 119–20. **"Vetoing":** LK, q. in Wolfe, "Jungian Aspects of JP's Imagery," p. 72. **Staying with Ruth:** Stein.

Parsons's gallery: Loucheim, "Betty Parsons," p. 141. **"Communications break down":** Coates, "The Art Galleries," p. 57. **Handful of guests:** Friedman, p. 116. **Floors:** Tomkins, "Keeper," p. 52. **Hostility:** Parsons. q. in Potter. p. 92. **"All too Dionysiac":** Sterne. **"Radical":** Glasco. **"Protecting priestess":** Loucheim, "Betty Parsons," p. 141. **"I give them walls":** Q. in Tomkins, "Keeper," p. 52. **Jackson sober:** Parsons, q. in Potter, p. 92. **Tearing up hat:** Friedman, p. 116.

"Lightweight": "Reviews and Previews," Feb. 1948. pp. 58–59. **"Tremendous energy":** Coates, "The Art Galleries," p. 57. **"Pollock's current method":** Lansford, "Fifty-Seventh Street in Review," p. 19. **"[This show] signals":** CG, "Art," Jan. 24. 1948, p. 108. The seeds of Greenberg's modernist argument were planted in this article; the argument was later taken up and elaborated by William Rubin, in particular. "Where the Pollocks differ" from the 1913 Mondrians, Rubin wrote in 1967 ("JP and the Modern Tradition, Part II," p. 25), "is that they contain *no vestige at all of modeling.* . . . The very shallow optical space of his pictures is not a matter of illusion but of the actual overlapping of different color skeins and the tendency of certain colors to 'recede' or advance.' . . . Jackson worked to minimize any sense of spatial illusion by locking the warm colors literally inside the skeins of the non-hues, of which the aluminum in particular was used to dissolve any sense of discreteness the space of the web might have—in effect to 'confuse' it into a unified mass of light sensations." Rubin's error is not in describing what happens visually in one of JP's drip paintings, but in attributing to JP consciousness and purposefulness where clearly none existed.

Jackson and Analytical Cubism: Kadish. **Different source:** Barrett, pp. 148–49. "Pollock was not a painter in pursuit of strict form. . . . The impulse in Pollock's painting came from elsewhere; it did not operate within the convention of strict and controlled form; if anything, it was disruptive of form. Pollock is very much in the American grain, like the writers Walt Whitman or William Faulkner, who throw themselves on the vitality of their inspiration, trusting that its sheer vital flow will be sufficient to generate enough form to sustain the work." **Jackson's source:** Barrett, p. 149: "In Pollock this inspiration is not always sufficient to generate enough form, and the painting sags; when the vitality of his primary impulse carries him along, the effect is stunning." **"Didn't agree":** CG, int. by Shorthall, Nov. 9. 1959. Greenberg said this after his " 'American-Type' Painting" article had appeared, long after he had abandoned JP and Lee Krasner, and long after they had more or less written him off as a sponsor.

"Feeling that their dog": Weld, p. 358. **Walter Phillips:** M. B., "Fifty-Seventh Street in Review," *Art Digest,* Jan. 15, 1948, p. 19. **Two paintings sold:** Weld, p. 358. **Prearranged sale:** This accounts for the note in the Time-Life Archives saying that three paintings were sold. **Heating one floor:** Landau, "LK," p. 240. **At $21 a cord:** JP to Ed and Wally Strautin, Nov. 29. 1945. **Wood for stove:** Parsons, q. in Potter, p. 93. **Bounced check:** Int. by David Peretz. **A $56 grocery bill:** George Sid Miller has given several versions,

including "close to forty dollars" (q. in Potter, p. 103); the figure used here is the one he gave us. **Credit:** George Sid Miller, q. in Potter. p. 102. **Three more to choose from:** JP, int. by Seiberling, July 18, 1949. **Sold painting for $7,300:** George Sid Miller, q. in Potter, p. 103. Miller (int. by Shorthall, Nov. 9. 1959) said he got seven times what he paid for it, which would be only $592; but he also admitted that he didn't like to talk about the amount for fear that people would start asking for loans, and he said that the amount offered was "such a high price [he] couldn't resist." The figure of $7,300 is more credible. **"Wouldn't take his paintings":** Bluhm: "The guy who runs Home Sweet Home [transportation service] was here recently and was telling me about Jackson wanting to give him a painting when Jackson owed him something, and the guy said he wouldn't take that. Dumb asshole."

"Made a real issue": Q. in Solomon, p. 183. **"Because of his behavior":** Levy, q. in Potter, p. 92. **Little keeping money secret:** Little. **Trip with Wilcox:** Wilcox. Aurthur, "Hitting the Boiling Point," p. 200: Aurthur reports that both JP and Wilcox had old Fords when, in fact, JP didn't get his until later in 1948. **"Offering a discount":** Q. in Potter, p. 93. **Lee's campaign:** Porter. **Francis visiting Parsons:** Francis. **"Terrible financial condition":** Parsons to PG, Apr. 5, 1948. q. in OC&T, II, p. 66. **"[Peggy] just disappeared":** Parsons. q. in Weld, p. 359. **"[Peggy's] dedication":** Q. in Weld, p. 359. **Francis purchase:** Francis. **"We lived a year":** Q. in [Roueché], "Unframed Space," p. 16.

"A singular concentration": A[rb], "Spotlight on: De Kooning," p. 33. **Invective:** Elaine de Kooning in "JP: An Artists' Symposium, Part I," p. 64. **Knife nearer Jackson's throat:** Kamrowski. **"Pardon me":** Q. by Elaine de Kooning, in "JP," p. 64. **"Jackson, why the hell":** Q. by Ethel Baziotes. **"No reputations":** CG, "The Present Prospects," p. 29. **From "Modern" to "Contemporary":** Friedman, p. 124; statement made on Feb. 17, 1948. **"Obscurity and negation":** Plaut, q. in OC&T IV, p. 242. **Tomlin agitating:** Friedman, p. 124. **Demonstration:** Friedman, p. 124; Potter, p. 96.

Demarest trust: Ann Shiras, secretary, Eben Demarest Trust Fund, to JP, June 13, 1948. The first payment of $417.28 was made on October 21, 1948; Jerome P. Corcoran, Trust Officer, Mellon National Bank and Trust Co., to JP, October 1, 1948. **Terms of the trust:** Eileen Wilhelm, officer of the Mellon Bank in Pittsburgh, which administers the Demarest Trust. **John H. Sweeney:** When Parsons told Shorthall (Nov. 9, 1959) that Sweeney pried the grant out of "some Boston foundation," she was getting the facts confused. The Demarest Trust was a Pittsburgh foundation, but John Sweeney, one member of the trust's advisory committee, was in fact a resident of Boston, which supports the inference that he was James Johnson Sweeney's contact on the advisory committee and instrumental in securing the grant for JP. The coincidence of name is obvious. Further support comes from Friedman who notes (p. 121), presumably recalling Lee Krasner, that the fund was "connected with James Johnson Sweeney's family." **Lee's contact with Sweeney:** LK. She was also in contact with Sweeney's close friends, Herbert and Mercedes Matter, who had recently returned from California.

Little: Little. **Haucks:** Hauck. **Newman:** Newman, int. by Shorthall, Nov. 9, 1959. **Zogbaums:** Zogbaum. **Hunters:** Sam Hunter. **Brooks and Park:** Charlotte Brooks; James Brooks. **Mercer:** Mercer. **Greenberg:** CG. **Kirstein invited:** Davis to LK and JP, from Lisbon, Sept. 26. 1948: "Have you had Lincoln Kirstein for the weekend?" **Sykes:** Johnson. **Lisses:** Liss. **Jackson barbecuing:** Little. **Lee promoting Jackson:** Hartigan: "She went over everything. She showed us earlier paintings, things that Sweeney had written, and talked about their hopes of Jackson being able to get recognition. It was quite a presentation."

Mercedes and Vita with Lee: Vita Peterson. **Matter filming Calder:** Herbert Matter. **Beach sessions:** Vita Peterson. **Amagansett:** Little. **East Hampton:** Vita Peterson. **"Immensely American":** Gustaf Peterson. **Children:** Alex Matter and Andrea Peterson. **Stories about Gyp:** Vita Peterson. Peterson said the stories that JP told were about a wondrous dog named Ahab—the name of a black poodle that JP and Lee owned in the 1950s. But Ahab was acquired from Alfonso Ossorio and Ted Dragon, whom JP hadn't yet met. Peterson does say that JP was accompanied by Gyp at times, and any reference to an earlier dog with the same name must have been to Gyp.

Fishing with Little: They fished for "whiting" at dusk; see Friedman, p. 123. **Rarely talking:** Little. **Renovating Little's house:** Edward Hults; Little. **Whiskey banned by Lee:** Wilcox. **Matter's age:** Herbert Matter. JP, q. by Blake: "You know, I really love that guy. I really love Herbert Matter." **Filming on the beaches:** According to Friedman (p. 121), Matter wanted to relate the shapes and movements of the mobiles to the "white cliffs and gusty winds" of Montauk. **Jackson helping with film:** Herbert Matter. See also Friedman, pp. 121–22. **"Never have I known":** Q. in Hoberman, "Harold Rosenberg's Radical Cheek," p. 11. **"Doing boy things":** Q. in Friedman, p. 137. **"Pure chaos":** Kamrowski. **"Disaster":** Q. in Friedman, p. 88. **Jackson impressed by "floating" panels:** Kamrowski. Exhibition, Feb. 16–Mar. 6. 1948; see Maurer and Bayles. *Gerome Kamrowski.* **Smith asked for similar installation:** Smith's account of this incident in DP&G, "Who Was JP?" p. 53, is fraught with errors, presumably just the result of a faulty memory. **"Great"; "thrilling":** Q. in DP&G, "Who Was JP?" p. 53. **Dyn:** A magazine edited by Wolfgang Paalen and Kurt Seligmann. The work was *The Moon Woman Cuts the Circle,* and was illustrated following page 16 of the November 1944 issue. Harry Jackson incorrectly remembers the work as *She-Wolf.* **Assault on Tarawa:** Harry Jackson was one of 5,600 marines who stormed Betio Island, Tarawa, on November 20, 1943; Pointer and Goddard, pp. 34–35. **"Goddamn nub"; "totally authentic":** Jackson. **"Felt deep":** Harry Jackson, q. in Pointer and Goddard, p. 43: On March 18, Harry Jackson noted in his journal that the painting had "an incredible authority and certainty, a vitality. It was a very Plains Indian sort of thing, mixed with German Expressionism." **Studying with Tamayo:** Hartigan. He studied with Tamayo at the Brooklyn Museum under Public Law 16 for disabled veterans, and later, in 1948, at Hofmann's Eighth Street school; Pointer and Goddard, p. 45. **Residence on Lower East Side:** Harry Jackson: 3 Baruch Place—Cage and Feldman were "about a block away." **Jackson and Hartigan finding Pollock "fascinating":** Hartigan. **"Something very profound"; Sekula:** Harry Jackson. **"Peggy Guggenheim had abandoned":** Sekula q. by Hartigan. **"Well, shit":** Q. by Harry Jackson.

Harry Shapiro: Brach; Hartigan. **Father leaving home:** Pointer and Goddard, p. 23. **Mother running diner:** Hartigan. **Aunt encouraging trips to museum:** Harry Jackson. **Captivated by "cowboys":** Pointer and Goddard, p. 23: These men must have been surrogates for his father who, on sporadic visits home, took his son "for his first horseback ride and . . . to watch polo practices at the nearby 124th Field Artillery Armory." **Photo-essay in Life:** "Winter Comes to a Wyoming Ranch," by Charles Belden, *Life,* Feb. 8, 1937, cited in Pointer and Goddard, p. 26. **Working at Pitchfork Ranch:** Harry Jackson. **"Ride and rope":** Hartigan. **"Nice Jewish boy":** Brach. **"You gave birth":** Q. by Harry Jackson. Harry was painting during much of this time. His aunt Doris, who bought him a Hoot Gibson outfit, also took him to the Art Institute of Chicago to admire plaster casts of equestrian statues by Donatello and Verrocchio; Pointer and Goddard, p. 25. Like Benton, he tried to resolve the dichotomies by his choice of subject matter, filling his sketchbook with drawings of cowboys and Indians and soldiers; Pointer and Goddard, p. 23. Among the first works of art that he admired were Benton's Indiana murals, which were shown at the Chicago Art Institute during the 1933 world's fair. (Panels from the State of Indiana Exhibit at the Century of Progress International Exposition, Chicago, 1933–34.) **Jackson talking about childhood:** Harry Jackson, recalling JP. **Backdated nostalgia:** Harry Jackson refers to JP's "false nostalgia" about his childhood in the West. **Activities around the house; "half-handy"; "analyzing works":** Harry Jackson. **"You goddamn slut":** Q. by Harry Jackson. **"Like a lion tamer":** Sam Hunter. **Clarifying Jackson's ideas:** Charlotte Brooks: "Lee would make him clarify his thoughts. She was really tough. She wouldn't let him get away with anything, and he would get angry. She would force him into being articulate." **Covering for Jackson:** Resnick, q. in Potter, p. 174. **"Won't let me go":** Q. by Jackson. **"She dominated him":** Harry Jackson. **Sensing the devotion:** Hartigan: "They were really devoted to each other, on every level—including, obviously, a sexual one."

The Wooden Horse: Number 10A, 1948, OC&T 207, II, pp. 28–29. **Wooden head:** Little. *Number 1, 1948:* OC&T 186, II, pp. 2–3. **5½-by-8½-feet:** 68 by 104 inches. *Number*

4, 1948: Gray and Red: OC&T 202, II, pp. 22–23. *Number 12A, 1948: Yellow, Gray, Black:* OC&T 200, II, pp. 20–21. *Number 26, 1948: Black and White,* OC&T 187, II, p. 6. *Number 5, 1948:* OC&T 188, II, p. 7. **Composition board:** *White, Black, Blue, and Red on White,* OC&T 189, II, p. 8. **Metal:** *Tondo,* OC&T 208, II, p. 30. **Cardboard:** *Number 23, 1948,* OC&T 199, II, pp. 20–21. **Paper used for canvas:** *Number 15, 1948: Red, Gray, White, Yellow,* OC&T 196, II, p. 17. **Gesso:** *Number 12A, 1948: Yellow, Gray, Black,* OC&T 200, II, pp. 20–21. **Masonite:** *Number 3, 1948,* OC&T 195, II, p. 16. **Board:** *Triad,* OC&T 198, II, p. 19. Either at the time or later, he mounted some works on canvas *(Silver over Black, White, Yellow, and Red;* OC&T 192, II, pp. 11–12) or chipboard *(Number 20, 1948:* OC&T 191, II, p. 10). *Black, White and Gray: Number 11A, 1948,* OC&T 203, II, p. 24. See also *Number 23, 1948,* OC&T 199, II, pp. 20–21; *Number 22A, 1948,* OC&T 201, II, pp. 22–23; *Number 4, 1948: Gray and Red,* OC&T 202, II, pp. 22–23. **Vast tangles:** *Number 20, 1948,* OC&T 191, II, p. 10. **Great reservoirs:** *Number 12A, 1948: Yellow, Gray, Black,* OC&T 200, II, pp. 20–21. *Silver over Black, White, Yellow and Red:* OC&T 192, II, pp. 11–12. **Dark over light:** See, e.g., *Number 23, 1948,* OC&T 199, II, pp. 20–21; *Number 22A, 1948,* OC&T 201, II, pp. 22–23; *Number 4, 1948: Gray and Red,* OC&T 202, II, pp. 22–23; *Black, White and Gray: Number 11A, 1948,* OC&T 203, II, p. 24. **Arabesque:** *Number 13A, 1948,* OC&T 217, II, pp. 38–39 (37¼" x 116½"). See also *Number 15, 1948: Red, Gray, White, Yellow,* OC&T 196, II, p. 17; *Number 16A, 1948,* OC&T 197, II, p. 18; *Triad,* OC&T 198, II, p. 19. **Tondo:** *Circle,* OC&T 64, I, p. 50, dated 1938–41. **White Cockatoo:** *Number 24A, 1948,* OC&T 194, II, pp. 14–15 (35" x 114"). **Summertime:** *Number 9A, 1948,* OC&T 205, II, pp. 26–27 (33¼" x 218"). See also *Number 25A, 1948: Yellow Ochre Scroll,* OC&T 193, II, pp. 12–13 (35" x 112⅝"); *Number 7A, 1948,* OC&T 210, II, pp. 32–33 (36" x 135").

Baziotes winning prize: Baziotes. **Guston's Prix de Rome:** Cherry; Ashton, "Yes, but . . . ," p. 82. **Article in Life:** "Philip Guston," pp. 90–92. **New style conceived in Italy:** Cherry. Schapiro: Guston conceived his new signature image while sitting on an Italian beach. **Continued approval:** Resnick: "When [Guston] first became abstract . . . he immediately got attention that people who had been painting like that for years never got. They never got into the Whitney." **"[What] Mondrian would have done":** Q. by Brach. **Jason's birth:** ACM: Arloie liked to interpret the name "Jason" as a combination of Sande's two brothers' names, Jay and Jackson. **"A darling":** SMP to FLP, MLP, and Jonathan, Feb. 7, 1948. **Baby-sitting; chicken pox; Sande working overtime:** SMP to FLP, MLP, and Jonathan, Jan. 10. 1949. **Rumors (baseless) of affairs:** LK, q. to Friedman; Hauck; Sterne. **"Wanting to taste":** Rosenberg. Vita Peterson, who claims that JP and Mercedes were "highly attracted to one another," says they never had an affair: "I asked her and she said not." Esteban Vicente, another confidant of Matter, also denies any affair. Herbert Matter: "I think Jackson was quite attracted to Mercedes but there was never the slightest thing between them . . . that's my feeling."

Sexual threats: Rosenberg. **Arrival of Pantuhoff:** LK. **Society circuit; "Oriental charm":** Rosenberg. **"Drive Jackson":** Vita Peterson. **"No privacy":** LK, q. in Diamonstein, p. 210. **Poorly lit room:** Wilcox. **Lee rarely caught at easel:** Jackson; Vita Peterson; Wilcox, etc. Wilcox: The first year, he caught her there occasionally. **None of Lee's work hung:** Resnick. **Lee's canvases reused:** Stolbach: These were probably the so-called "gray slabs" or "slab paintings" from 1942 to 1944. **"Try a mosaic":** LK, q. in Diamonstein, ed., p. 210. **Mosaic tables:** See Landau, "LK," pp. 241–42; Diamonstein, p. 210; Wasserman, "LK in Mid-Career," p. 10; Nemser, "LK's Paintings 1946–49," p. 62. The accepted date for the tables is 1947, but visitors in the summer of 1948 (notably Harry Jackson) say she was working on the tables at that time. **"Had to force her":** Harry Jackson. Wilcox: "Jackson got her to work with him on the table. He didn't want to touch the project. She said, 'No, Jackson, you do it.' And he said, 'No, we're going to do it together.' It was his idea and he had to talk her into taking part." According to Lee, she used a scheme she had made for Hofmann as a basis for the design.

Lee painting again: Hartigan and Harry Jackson say that Lee had not yet begun at this time. Elsewhere, Harry talks about JP being disdainful of Lee's efforts—implying that there were efforts to be disdainful about, although, called on to be more specific, the only work he could remember was the mosaic table. But Stella wrote Frank in late 1947 (SMP to FLP, MLP, and Jonathan, Dec. 11, 1947) suggesting that Lee was already at least dabbling by that date and that she had not been working on prior visits. This would place her return to painting at the end of 1947. Lee herself was never firm about her dates. In some interviews (e.g., int. by Nemser, p. 88), she cited 1946 as the onset of her new style. Elsewhere (int. by Seckler, Dec. 14, 1967), she was less firm: "More or less in 1946." Landau, "LK," p. 242: "Krasner's tables constituted the first substantive work she was able to bring to a successful conclusion since her 'gray slabs' had begun to evolve almost four years before." This, also, would suggest a late 1947 date for her renewed career. Many people who knew Lee and were in and out of the house in the summer of 1948 say that she wasn't painting at all. Harry Jackson's statement about Lee's painting could date from October or November 1948 when he and Hartigan came, or to the summer of 1949, the summer of 1950, and so forth. Lee probably never stopped working completely, and always dabbled now and then. But she didn't really get back into it in any "consistent" (Bultman's term) or meaningful way until the summer of 1948 or afterward.

Jackson's enthusiasm evaporated: Wilcox maintains the idea that JP discouraged Lee's painting is "strictly a lie"; we believe that the encouragement was superficial and the discouragement strong, if subtle. **Jackson's invitations:** Actually, JP didn't invite Lee often. According to Applehof, a young art historian who later lived with Lee for part of a summer, JP preferred to bring the works into the living room and show them. **"Three or four times":** LK. **"My enthusiasm":** Q. in Kernan, "LK." For obvious reasons, Lee contradicted herself in print on this point; see LK, q. in Gruen, p. 232: "There was never any conflict or competition about our respective work. Jackson had the greatest interest in my painting—even enthusiasm." **"Grudgingly":** Dragon. **"That works":** Q. by LK, q. in Gruen, p. 232. **"Just continue":** Q. by LK, q. in Nemser, p. 92. **Jackson "disdainful":** Harry Jackson. Like many visitors, Harry, too, was disdainful: "Her paintings were, shit, pleasant to look at. Better than a bare wall but only slightly . . . the kind of stuff the schools produce by the tons. It's all *understood*, pat." There were, of course, exceptions like Wilcox and his wife Lucia who "liked her painting and . . . encouraged her to paint." **"'Little woman attitude'":** Harry Jackson.

Lee working mornings: LK, lecture, Columbia, Oct. 5, 1983. Charlotte Brooks: Lee would get started at 8:00 in the morning, which would leave her about three hours of painting before JP got up at 10:30 or 11:00. **Schaefer visit:** Wilcox: "She was an interior decorator who had a gallery as part of her shop." **Truckload of furniture:** Among the items that the Pollocks received from the Macys were a large Spanish table, a Jacobean chest, and a handwoven rug. "We'll have to give them something," JP said to Lee. "What about one of your mosaic tables?" LK answered, "What about one of your paintings?" "Have you seen them admire my paintings?" JP asked. "But every time they're here, they mention your table." All from Wallach, "LK." **Lee asked to participate in show:** Landau, "LK," p. 244, citing interview with LK, July 19, 1979. **Reaction to Lee's table:** Landau, "LK," p. 245. **"Wife of the painter":** Review by Aline B. Loucheim, q. in Landau, "LK," p. 245. **Schaefer dinner:** Wilcox, who heard about the event from both JP and Schaefer. **Description of Schaefer:** CG. **"What does an old lady":** CG: "Jackson sensed that that was where Schaefer was vulnerable. It was *not*."

Hardly a week: Ronald Stein. **Lee buying beer:** Wilcox. **Missing appointments:** JP to Wally and Ed Strautin, Oct. 2, 1946. **"Jackson wasn't feeling":** See JP to Louis Bunce, July 29, 1949, concerning a canceled visit by the Bunces to Springs. **"Go slow":** Q. by Ferber. **Ninety dollars:** Harry Jackson claims that he lent JP $250 for the car, but according to Hartigan, JP already had the car when she and Harry met him. Harry did lend him some money, although less than $250. Potter, p. 96: JP said it was $90, which JP returned soon thereafter but not, as Harry Jackson claims, when wired to do so from Mexico. Hartigan: Harry did wire for money from Mexico—but he wired his father, not JP, for the money. **"[Jack] has a Ford":** SMP to FLP, MLP, and Jonathan, Jan. 10, 1949. **Fight with Phillips:** Ferber; see Phillips, p. 88. Phillips claims he helped JP home; Ferber says it was Rothko. **Gorky's suicide:** The accident took place on June 26. Gorky hanged himself on July 21; Lader, p. 118.

35. CELEBRITY

SOURCES

Books, articles, manuscript, records, and transcripts

Epstein and Barlow, *East Hampton;* Friedman, *JP;* Gruen, *The Party's Over Now;* Guilbaut, *How New York Stole the Idea of Modern Art;* Hubbard, *Dianetics;* Kootz Gallery, *The Intra-subjectives;* Lynes, *Good Old Modern;* Naifeh, *Culture Making;* Potter, *To a Violent Grave;* Tabak, *But Not for Love.*

Robert Alan Aurthur, "Hitting the Boiling Point, Freakwise, at East Hampton," *Esquire,* June 1972; E[laine de] K[ooning], "Reviews and Previews," *Art News,* Mar. 1949; "Dead End Art: A Frenchman's Mud-and-Rubble Paintings Reduce Modernism to a Joke," *Life,* Dec. 20, 1948; Léon Degand. "Le retour d'un grand peintre, F. Léger," *Lettres françaises,* Apr. 13, 1946; DP&G, "Who Was JP?" *Art in America,* May–June 1967; CG, "Art," *Nation,* Feb. 19. 1949; "A *Life* Round Table on Modern Art," *Life,* Oct. 11, 1948; Walter Lippmann, "La destinée américaine," *Les études américaines,* Apr.–May 1946; Aline B. Loucheim, "Who Buys What in the Picture Boom?" *Art News,* July 1, 1944; M[argaret] L[owengrund], "Pollock Hieroglyphics," *Art Digest,* Feb. 1, 1949; Ludwig Mies Van Der Rohe, "Museum," *Architectural Forum,* May 1943; "Words," *Time,* Feb. 7, 1949; James T. Vallière, "Daniel T. Miller," *Provincetown Review,* Fall 1968.

Emily Genauer, "Ethel Edwards Proves Mature Artist," New York *World-Telegram,* Feb. 7, 1949; Sam Hunter, "Among the New Shows," *NYT,* Jan. 30, 1949; Paul Richard, "Two-Sided Pollock," *Washington Post,* Oct. 15, 1983; Edmund White, "Mythic Links," *Village Voice,* Oct. 4, 1983.

Judy Seixas, " My Journal: A Weekend in East Hampton" (unpub. ms.), Sept. 25, 1949, n.p.

Record of JP's sales, Time/Life Archives.

LK, int. by Dorothy Gees Seckler, AAA; Alfonso Ossorio, int. by Forrest Selvig, Nov. 19, 1968, AAA; Tony Smith, int. by James T. Vallière, Aug. 1965, AAA.

Interviews

Peter Blake; Charles Boultenhouse; Charlotte Park Brooks; James Brooks; David Budd; Ted Dragon; Herbert Ferber; B. H. Friedman; Jane Graves; CG, Grace Hartigan; Dora Heller; Budd Hopkins; Axel Horn; Edward Hults; Reginald Isaacs; Harry Jackson; LK; Ernestine Lassaw; John Lee; John Little; ACM; George Mercer; Alfonso Ossorio; Vita Peterson; May Tabak Rosenberg; Dorothy Seiberling; Marta Vivas; Enez Whipple; Roger Wilcox.

NOTES

Private galleries quadrupling: From 40 to 150; Guilbaut, p. 91, citing *Fortune,* Sept. 1946, p. 144. For different numbers, see Naifeh, p. 81: 73 in 1945; 97 in 1950; 123 in 1955; based on a review of the listings in *Art News* and *Art Gallery.* **Sales after 1944:** Guilbaut, p. 91, citing *Fortune,* Sept. 1946, p. 144. **Art not just for rich:** Guilbaut, p. 94, citing *Newsweek,* June 28, 1943, p. 82. **"Part of everyday life":** Guilbaut, p. 94. **"Authenticated paintings":** Q. in Guilbaut, p. 93, citing *Newsweek,* June 28, 1943, p. 82.

"The American century"; "fate": Lippmann, "La destinée américaine," p. 1. **"New York is now"; "will the Paris School":** Germain Bazin, *L'Amour de l'Art,* July 1945, p. 27. q. in Guilbaut, p. 127. **"American painting":** Degand, "Le retour d'un grand peintre," p. 1. The French were never completely convinced of the triumph of American painting. In April 4, 1947, issue of *Arts,* a French critic described his reaction to an exhibition of American paintings that had been sent to Paris, chiding the naiveté of Americans for thinking that there was something new or innovative in abstract art: "Is the purpose of this show to demonstrate to us that abstract art no longer holds any secrets for American artists? Or is it perhaps that they know no other aesthetic? Or is it merely that someone wanted to prove to us that the Yankees, always eager for novelty, are now at the cutting edge of modern art? . . . This kind of audacity has long been familiar in the art of western Europe. For us it could not cause either surprise or scandal. The only thing that can still attract us in a work is therefore its quality. This is not conspicuous in the painting of [Americans such as] Baziotes and Motherwell"; Denys Chevalier, "Introduction à

la peinture américaine," *Arts,* Apr. 4, 1947, q. in Guilbaut, p. 151.
Wartime patriotism: Loucheim, "Who Buys What in the Picture Boom?" p. 12: "It is considered 'patriotic.'" **Rockefellers and Blisses:** By moving into the domain of current art, they could stay ahead of the general public; see Guilbaut, p. 94. *Life:* Graves: "At that time, *Life* was *the* magazine. All the news was filtered through *Time, Life, Newsweek, Look,* and *The Saturday Evening Post.* But *Life* was the main one." **"The magazines defined taste":** Guilbaut, p. 94.
"Round table": "A *Life* Round Table on Modern Art," *Life,* Oct. 11, 1948, pp. 56–70, 75–79. **Sweeney:** Sweeney recalled the more positive remarks in his own introduction to the 1943 exhibition at Art of This Century, noting *Cathedral*'s "spontaneity," "freedom," "expression," "sense of textured surface," and "linear organization." **Huxley:** "It raises a question of why it stops when it does. The artist could go on forever. . . . It seems to me like a panel for a wallpaper which is repeated indefinitely around the wall." **Greene:** The work left him "completely cold . . . a pleasant design for a necktie." **Frankfurter:** He "thought this work remarkably good if compared with a lot of abstract painting that is being turned out nowadays." *Cathedral:* The same painting was later sent to San Francisco to appear in the Third Annual Exhibition of Contemporary Painting at the California Palace of the Legion of Honor; Friedman, p. 125. **Romance of art:** See White, "Mythic Links," p. 54.
Note of apology: JP to Bertha Schaefer, Oct. 11, 1948. **Schaefer's accusations:** Wilcox. **"Drinking heavily":** LK, q. in Gruen, pp. 231–32. **"One didn't tell Jackson":** Q. in Friedman, p. 126. **Jackson falling off bike:** Edward Hults. **Heller's background:** Heller. **First alcoholic treated:** LK, q. in DP&G, "Who Was JP?" p. 48. **"Personal poison":** Heller, q. by LK. **"Can't even spinach":** Q. by LK, q. by Mercer. **"You can't drink":** Q. by James Brooks. **"Take these":** Heller, q. by LK; see Friedman, p. 127. Friedman (p. 172) says Heller gave JP Antabuse, a relatively new drug at the time. JP was given Antabuse in the early 1950s, but there is no evidence that Heller gave it to him. Several people remember two different drug therapies, one with tranquilizers, one with Antabuse: Jackson, LK; Mercer; Wilcox. **"Just talk":** Rosenberg. **"Whenever the urge":** Q. by Rosenberg.
Feeling calmer: Friedman, p. 127. **"Quit for good":** JP, q. by ACM. **"Jack's new leaf":** ACM **"The best news":** SMP to FLP, MLP, and Jonathan, Jan. 1, 1949. **"Jack and Lee were here":** SMP to CCP, Jan. 10, 1949. **Tearing out partitions:** Potter, p. 103. **For entertaining; "show will be a test":** SMP to CCP, Jan. 10. 1949. See also SMP to FLP, MLP, and Jonathan the same day: "I hope he will say no to every offer of liquor and his show will be a test if he can turn it down I hope so." **Last-minute preparations:** SMP to FLP, MLP, and Jonathan, Jan. 10, 1949. **Driving into New York:** Potter, p. 110. **Borrowed station wagon:** Ferber. **McCoys' arrival; first vacation:** ACM to FLP, MLP, and Jonathan, Jan. 27, 1949. **No drinking:** ACM. **Staying at Hartigan's:** Hartigan. **Hanging the show:** During one of these sessions, Ferber and JP exchanged a sculpture for a painting: "I really fell in love with a small painting," says Ferber, "and asked him if he would swap a sculpture for it, and he did." **Parsons impressed:** Q. in Gruen, p. 238.
"Lovely winter": SMP to FLP, MLP, and Jonathan, Jan. 24, 1949. **Large crowd:** ACM to FLP, MLP, and Jonathan, Jan. 27, 1949. **Dinner:** Hartigan; Jackson. **Eleven works sold:** SMP to FLP, MLP, and Jonathan, Mar. 16, 1949. The same figure appears in a record in the archives of Time/Life. But given the poor records kept by Parsons and JP, Stella's figures remain, ironically, the best record of JP's sales. **"A wonderful show":** SMP to FLP, MLP, and Jonathan, Mar. 16. 1949. **Lee spreading news:** Rosenberg; Wilcox. **"He was the first":** Q. in DP&G, "Who Was JP?" p. 48; see also Friedman, p. 126, and Gruen, p. 54. **No reference to tranquilizers:** Lassaw: "In those days, nobody considered alcoholism bad. If you were taking drugs, they might have thought it was bad, but alcohol, they did it themselves." **The gloomy prognosis":** Tabak, p. 198. **"Never took":** Budd, who is only one of several dozen who repeated this myth to us.
Never quit drinking: This observation was confirmed by Boultenhouse, Horn, Lee (recalling LK), Peterson, Wilcox, etc. Wilcox, for example, says JP "was never completely off alcohol, but pretty much so." **Cooking sherry:** Horn. **"Be completely crazed":** LK, q. by Lee. **Jackson needing to stop:** Wilcox added, "Some people don't want to face their

problems, but you have a problem you want to face. Because you have important things to do." **Career at stake:** "Lucia and I decided that we were going to try to stop him because of that disastrous thing that happened [at Bertha Schaefer's house]. We decided to try to work on him." *Astounding Science Fiction:* Previously named simply *Astounding Stories.* **"Reduce psychotherapy":** Wilcox. **"Reverie":** Hubbard (p. 266) called his form of light hypnosis *"reverie,"* which, unlike true hypnosis, required the patient to remain at all times conscious. **Bringing events into the light:** Hubbard, p. 273, called the process of overcoming "erasing engrams." **"Unknown fears":** Hubbard, p. 1. **Parlor game:** Wilcox; he had already experimented on his wife Lucia, on Leo Castelli, and other friends. **Description of spit:** Epstein and Barlow, pp. 82–83. **Grass and wildflowers:** Epstein and Barlow, pp. 179–82. **Favorite spot; Lee's distrust:** Wilcox.
"Quieted any doubts": Greenberg, "Art," Feb. 19, 1949, p. 221. **"Of the Hieroglyphics":** L[owengrund], "Pollock Hieroglyphics," pp. 19–20. **"Planes separate":** [De] K[ooning], "Reviews and Previews," p. 44. The review misspells JP's name "Pollack." **"Mop of tangled hair":** Genauer, "Ethel Edwards Proves Mature Artist."**"The disintegration":** Hunter, "Among the New Shows." **"Contour map":** "Words," p. 51. **Stella's visit; "green fingers":** SMP to CCP, Apr. 1949. **"Tons of coffee":** Ossorio, int. by Selvig, Nov. 19. 1968. **"So nice":** SMP to CCP, Apr. 1949. **Meeting Ossorio:** Friedman, *Alfonso Ossorio,* pp. 32ff. **Number 5, 1948:** OC&T 188, II, p. 7. **Ossorio and Dragon in Springs:** Dragon. **Restoration of painting:** Dragon; Ossorio. **Picking up painting:** Friedman, *Alfonso Ossorio,* pp. 32ff. Thereafter, Dragon (q. by Ossorio) would joke, "Don't let Pollock do any restoration work on a painting unless you want it better." **"Two or three times":** Dragon. **"When Alfonso came":** Vivas. **Exploring beaches:** Ossorio, q. in DP&G, "Who Was JP?" p. 58.
Potter's background: He would drop hints of a grandmother rich enough to have a chauffeur (Potter, p. 121) and of a great-grandfather who, as Episcopal bishop of New York, refused John D. Rockefeller membership in his church, Saint John the Divine; Ossorio. **Potter wanting to quit job:** Potter, p. 114. **Wanting to write:** Potter, p. 126. **Widow Hamlin:** Mrs. Harry Hamlin. **Potter meeting Jackson:** Potter, p. 105. **"Mouth was half open"; "wry half-smile":** Potter, p. 105. **"Personality equivalents":** Potter, "Author's Note," n.p.; the book, not published until 1985, was *To a Violent Grave.* **Lincoln convertible:** Potter, p. 110. **Isaacs's background:** Isaacs. **Isaacs's visits:** SMP to FLP, MLP, and Jonathan, n.d., in which she mentions that JP is having "people from Chicago this weekend." We conclude that the visit probably took place on the weekend of Friday, July 22. **"My God!":** Q. in Richard, "Two-Sided Pollock." **Isaacs taken by the man and his art:** Isaacs, q. in Potter, p. 113. **Three acquisitions; "the greatest painter":** Isaacs, q. in Richard, "Two-Sided Pollock": In November 1973, Isaacs's seventh floor apartment in Cambridge was robbed of all three paintings. On July 1, 1975, the police received a telephone call from a woman who told them to search a hotel room in Newton, where they located *Number 7, 1951.* In October 1983, the painting was sold to the National Gallery of Art; the other two works remain missing.
"They're terrific": Q. in Seixas, "My Journal," n.p. **"Maidstone Club Irregulars":** Dragon. **Show organized by Larkin:** Aurthur, "Hitting the Boiling Point," pp. 201–02. **Whipple; "breakthrough show":** Q. in Potter, p. 111. **"Incomprehensible drippings":** Aurthur, "Hitting the Boiling Point," pp. 201–02. **"White-gloved hostesses"; "horror chamber"; "barbarians":** Gina Knee, q. in Potter, p. 111. **Washing hands:** Enez Whipple, q. in Potter, p. 111. **Jackson's clothing:** Potter, p. 112. **Hamlin's huffing:** Potter, p. 112. **Venomous artists; fistfight:** Aurthur, "Hitting the Boiling Point," pp. 201–02. **Three-week run:** July 7–26, 1949. **Three paintings sold:** SMP to FLP, MLP, and Jonathan, July 26, 1949.
Buying Brooks a car: Charlotte Brooks; James Brooks. **Wedding:** Hartigan. The reasons for the marriage were not exclusively romantic: "I could get a lot more money under Public Law 16, a kind of GI Bill for the combat disabled, if I was married." says Harry, "about thirty-five dollars more a month." **"Did the knot tying":** Jackson. **University of Illinois:** Friedman, p. 130. **Florence:** La Strozzina, Strozzi Palace, Florence, *La Collezione Guggenheim,* Feb. 19–Mar. 10. 1949. **Milan:** Palazzo Reale, under auspices of L'Associazione

Artisti Italiani, June, 1949. **Shingling:** SMP to CCP, Apr. 1949. **New contract:** It ran through Jan. 1, 1952. **Date sculpture submitted:** Barbara Dillman to JP, June 21, 1949, confirming that the sculpture was picked up by a representative of the museum on this date. **Terra-cotta piece:** OC&T 1053, IV, p. 129. **WPA bronze:** OC&T S/a, IV, p. 158, which OC&T include in "Problems for Study." *Number 10, 1949:* OC&T 240, II, pp. 62–63. **"Man and Wife":** Sidney Janis Gallery, Sept. 19–Oct. 8, 1949. **"When the spectator:** Rosenberg, Introduction to Samuel M. Kootz Gallery, *The Intrasubjectives,* n.p.

Word-of-mouth overseas: Ossorio. On a ride into New York, JP listened intently as Ossorio outlined the advantages of selling abroad. **"The easel picture":** JP, application for Guggenheim Fellowship, q. in OC&T IV, p. 238. **Smith bringing clients:** SMP to FLP, MLP, and Jonathan, June 26, 1949: "There were some people out the Sunday we were there to see about a mural in a modern home that is being built he is very much excited about it." O'Connor (in OC&T IV, p. 245) believes this reference is to the Gellers, for whom JP completed a mural in 1950. But Blake, who persuaded Marcel Breuer, the Gellers' architect, to commission the mural, did not show the paintings to Breuer until the November 1949 show. So this must refer to another mural commission that did not materialize. **Smith told about western roots; "he knew the west":** Int. by Vallière, Aug. 1965. **Drive to California:** SMP to FLP, MLP, and Jonathan, June 15, 1949. The plans for the trip west drifted into limbo to be revived periodically over the next seven years.

Meeting Blake: Friedman says they met in 1947, but Blake remembers specifically that it was after JP was on the wagon, which would put it in late 1948 at the earliest or, more likely, the summer of 1949. **Blake's background:** Blake; Lynes, p. 276. **"Absolutely overwhelming"; "create a sense":** Blake. **"Ideal museum":** Mies Van Der Rohe, "Museum," pp. 84–85. **Description of museum; Jackson thrilled; "it would be nice":** Blake. **"Just a decorator":** JP, q. by Blake.

Sizes: *Pasiphaë,* 56″ x 96″; *Lucifer,* 41″ x 105½″. *Number 1, 1949:* OC&T 252, II, pp. 74–75 (63″ x 104″). The other large painting was *Out of the Web: Number 7, 1949,* OC&T 251, II, pp. 72–73 (48″ x 96″). **Horizontal Composition:** OC&T 227, II, pp. 50–51 (10″ x 10′2″), was long but exceedingly narrow. JP gave it to the Larkins. *Number 8, 1949,* OC&T 239, II, pp. 60–61 (34″ x 71¼″), was also relatively large. *Number 8, 1949:* OC&T 239, II, pp. 60–61 (34″ x 71¼″). *Number 13, 1949:* OC&T 231, II, p. 54 (23″ x 31″). *Number 3, 1949: Tiger,* OC&T 250, II, p. 72 (62″ x 37″). **Symphonic works:** Also *Number 9, 1949,* OC&T 248, II, p. 70 (44¼″ x 34″); *Number 4, 1949,* OC&T 249, II, p. 71 (35½″ x 34½″); and *Number 11, 1949,* OC&T 246, II, pp. 68–69 (45″ x 47¼″). **Smaller pieces:** *Number 19, 1949,* OC&T 229, II, p. 52 (31″ x 22½″); *Number 12, 1949,* OC&T 233, II, p. 55; *Number 33, 1949,* OC&T 234, II, pp. 56–57 (22½″ x 31″); *Number 34, 1949,* OC&T 235, II, pp. 56–57 (22″ x 30½″); *Number 15, 1949,* OC&T 236, II, p. 58 (31″ x 22½″); *Number 30, 1949, "Birds of Paradise,"* OC&T 237, II, p. 59 (31″ x 22½″); *Number 17, 1949,* OC&T 243, II, p. 65 (22½″ x 28½″); *Number 16, 1949,* OC&T 244, II, p. 66 (31″ x 22¼″). *Number 31, 1949:* OC&T 242, II, p. 64 (30¼″ x 22″).

Works with limited palette: *Number 28, 1949,* OC&T 218, II, p. 42 (12¼″ x 13″); *Numbers 24, 25, 29, 1949 (Triptych),* OC&T 219–21, II, pp. 42–43 (27″ x 12″; 28″ x 11″; 17¼″ x 15″; *Number 23, 1949,* OC&T 223, II, p. 46 (26½″ x 12″); *Number 26, 1949,* OC&T 224, II, p. 47 (23″ x 14″); *Number 27, 1949,* OC&T 225, II, p. 48 (21″ x 12½″). *Number 9, 1949:* OC&T 248, II, p. 70 (44¼″ x 34″). *Number 4, 1949:* OC&T 249, II, p. 71 (35½″ x 34½″). **Brush strokes reappearing:** *Number 11, 1949,* OC&T 246, II, pp. 68–69 (45″ x 47¼″); *Number 3, 1949,* OC&T 250, II, p. 72 (62″ x 37″). **Small composition:** *Small Composition,* OC&T 241, II, p. 63. *Out of the Web: Number 6, 1949,* OC&T 247, II, pp. 68–69 (44″ x 54″). He had used a similar technique in several collages; see OC&T 1030, IV, pp. 104–05; OC&T 1031, IV, p. 105; OC&T 1032, IV, pp. 106–07; OC&T 1033, IV, pp. 106–07.

Date article proposed: Seiberling. **"Went back and forth":** LK, int. by Seckler. Ossorio: "Jackson and Lee were terrified of submitting to an interview because of what *Life* had done to poor Dubuffet." **"Feebly mixed":** "Dead End Art," p. 22. **"Thumbs down"; "you didn't know":** LK, int. by Seckler. **Matisse's offer; reproduction on door:** Ossorio. **Time-Life Building:** One West 49th Street. **Seiberling interview:** *Life,* July 18, 1949. **Book on Goya:** Ossorio. **"I could feel":** Vallière, "Daniel T. Miller," p. 36.

36. BREAKING THE ICE

SOURCES

Books, articles, manuscript, and transcripts

Alloway and MacNaughton, *Adolph Gottlieb;* Friedman, *JP;* Fry, *David Smith;* Guilbaut, *How New York Stole the Idea of Modern Art;* Myers, *Tracking the Marvelous;* Namuth, *Pollock Painting;* OC&T, *JP;* Potter, *To a Violent Grave;* Robbins and Neuberger, *An American Collection;* Rose, *LK;* Solomon, *JP;* Tabak, *But Not for Love.*

Robert Alan Aurthur, "Hitting the Boiling Point, Freakwise, in East Hampton," *Esquire,* June 1972; Alfred H. Barr, Jr., "Gorky, De Kooning, Pollock," *Art News,* June–July–Aug., 1950; Anthony Bianco, "When the Dow Took a Dive, Roy Neuberger Didn't Even Blink," *Business Week,* Oct. 6, 1986; E. A. Carmean, "The Church Project: Pollock's Passion Themes," *Art in America,* Summer 1982; Robert Coates, "The Art Galleries," *New Yorker,* Dec. 3, 1949; Douglas Cooper, "The Biennale Exhibition in Venice," London *Listener,* July 6, 1950; A[rthur] D[rexler], "Unframed Space: A Museum for JP's Paintings," *Interiors,* Jan. 1950; DP&G, "Who Was JP?" *Art in America,* May–June 1967; [Alexander Eliot], "Handful of Fire," *Time,* Dec. 26, 1949; [Alexander Eliot], "What's in Fashion: American Pavillion at Venice's 25th Biennial Show of Contemporary Art," *Time,* June 12, 1950; B. H. Friedman, "'The Irascibles': A Split Second in Art History," *Arts,* Sept. 1978; "JP: Is He the Greatest Living Painter in the United States?" *Life,* Aug. 8, 1949; "Letters to the Editors," *Life,* Aug. 29, 1949; "The Metropolitan and Modern Art," *Life,* Jan. 15, 1951; A[my] R[obinson], "Reviews and Previews," *Art News,* Dec. 1949; Harold Rosenberg, "The Search for JP," *Art News,* Feb. 1961; [Berton Roueché], "Unframed Space," *New Yorker,* Aug. 5, 1950; Irving Sandler, "The Club," *Artforum,* Sept. 1965; Jeffrey Schaire, ed., "Was JP Any Good?" *Arts and Antiques,* Oct. 1984; Parker Tyler, "JP: The Infinite Labyrinth," *Magazine of Art,* Mar. 1950; James T. Vallière, "Daniel T. Miller," *Provincetown Review,* fall 1968.

Carlyle Burrows, Review, New York *Herald Tribune,* Nov. 27, 1949; editorial, New York *Herald Tribune,* May 23, 1950; "18 Painters Boycott Metropolitan; Charge 'Hostility to Advanced Art.'" *NYT,* May 22, 1950; Emily Genauer, "Art and Artists: American Selection for the Venice Show; Does It Represent Us As It Should?" New York *Herald Tribune,* May 28, 1950; "The Irascible Eighteen," New York *Herald Tribune,* May 23, 1950; Henry McBride, New York *Sun,* "Abstract Painting: The Whitney Museum Annual Is Completely Inundated with It," Dec. 23, 1949; Stuart Preston, "Abstract Quartet: Late Work by Kandinsky, Pollock, and Others," *NYT,* Nov. 27, 1949.

Bruno Alfieri, "A Short Talk on the Pictures of JP," *L'Arte Moderna,* unpub. English typescript, MOMA files.

Alfonso Ossorio, int. by Forrest Selvig, Nov. 19, 1968, AAA; Alfonso Ossorio, int. by Kathleen Shorthall for *Life,* Nov. 9, 1959, Time/Life Archives.

Interviews

Lionel Abel; Peter Blake; Charlotte Park Brooks; James Brooks; Fritz Bultman; Nicholas Carone; Leo Castelli; Giorgio Cavallon; Tibor de Nagy; Dorothy Dehner; Ted Dragon; Leslie Fiedler; B. H. Friedman; Joe Glasco; Hester Grimm Patrick; Eleanor Hempstead; Rebecca Hicks; Budd Hopkins; Ettabelle Storm Horgan; Merle Hubbard; Harry Jackson; Buffie Johnson; Reuben Kadish; Lillian Olaney Kiesler; Hilton Kramer; LK; John Little; Cile Downs Lord; ACM; George Mercer; John Bernard Myers; Alfonso Ossorio; Vita Peterson; CCP; FLP; MJP; Charles Porter; Milton Resnick; May Tabak Rosenberg; Dorothy Seiberling; Eloise Spaeth; Ronald Stein; Hedda Sterne; Esteban Vicente; Harriet Vicente; Marta Vivas; Catherine Viviano; Roger Wilcox; Betsy Zogbaum.

NOTES

***Life* offices and the Pollock article; "deeply conservative"; "very enthusiastic":** Seiberling. **Number 12, 1948:** OC&T 200, II, pp. 20–21. **Not long afterward:** Seiberling says late spring 1949. **"Maybe we should":** Q. by Seiberling. **Jack Jessup:** Actual name, John Jessup. **Luce's blasts:** Seiberling: "We were constantly having to protest that undercut-ting. There was a clear division within the magazine." **"Didn't really understand"**: Seiberling. **"Is he the greatest"**: "JP," pp. 42-43, 45, **Quintessentially American**: See Friedman, p. 133. **"Look at him"**: De Kooning, q. by Resnick. **"Look, Jack Pollock's"**: Horgan. **"Where Jack's fingertip"**: Porter. **"A famous artist"**: Patrick. **Cody investigation**: Solomon, p. 194, citing the *Cody Enterprise*, Aug. 12, 1949. **"Completely understand"**: SMP, q. in the Deep River, Conn., *New Era*, Aug. 25, 1949, q. in Solomon, p. 194. **"Felt good"**: Hicks, **"What sort of an adjustment"**: Wall to JP, Aug. 23, 1949. **"In my opinion"**: Isaacs to editors of *Life*, Aug. 8, 1949; see "Letters to the Editors," p. 9. **"You [have] mastered"**: Daniel D. McFarland to JP, n.d. **"I like"; "would you please"**: H. M. Brehm to JP, Aug. 6, 1949. **"Contribute a drawing"**: Norman McGrath to JP, Sept. 13, 1949. **"Fabulous write-up"**: SMP to CCP, EFP, and Jeremy, n.d. **"Picture"**: SMP to FLP, MLP, and Jonathan, July 26, 1949. **Frank, Charles, and Jay silent**: FLP; CCP; MJP. **Stopped in street**: Potter, p. 114. **Copies under arms**: James Brooks. **"Weren't ready"**: Q. in Vallière, "Daniel T. Miller," p. 36. **"Self-conscious"**: Q. by Charlotte Brooks. **"Nervous"**: Parsons, q. in Potter, p. 114. **"Embarrassed"**: James Brooks. **"Proud"**: Miller, q. in Vallière, "Daniel T. Miller," p. 36. **"Willing to bet"**: Wilfrid Zogbaum, q. in Potter, p. 114. **Arranging for delivery**: Little, Friedman, q. in Potter, p. 115; During Friedman's first trip to Springs, JP had shown him a stack of copies of the *Life* article, handed him one, and told him that it was "a part of the story."

Ossorio's chapel: Designed by Anthony Ramon, a disciple of Frank Lloyd Wright; Ossorio, int. by Selvig, Nov. 19, 1968. **Dragon rehearsing with Ballet**: Dragon. Previous sources are incorrect in saying that Dragon went to the Philippines with Ossorio. **Description of house**: Dragon. **"It's like... the country"**: q. by Dragon. **"I don't know"**: JP, q. by Ossorio, q. in DP&G, "Who Was JP?" p. 58.

Not the usual crowd: Esteban Vicente; Harriet Vicente. **"Broken the ice"**: Resnick: This famous phrase was later used to describe the revolutionary impact of JP's art on the styles of other artists, but it was originally used to describe the commercial breakthrough his paintings achieved. "Jackson got the right people interested," Resnick says. **Neuberger**: Bianco, "When the Dow Took a Dive," pp. 76-78. See Robbins and Neuberger, *An American Collection.* **Brodovitch**: Namuth, *Pollock Painting*, n.p., for the fact that he was there. **Ripley**: De Nagy; Ossorio. **Ripley's purchases**: *Number 26, 1949*, OC&T 224, II, p. 47; *Number 18, 1949*, OC&T 226, II, pp. 48-49, since lost. **Barr chastising Blake**: Blake, q. in Potter, p. 96. **Brach**: "Barr's reversal may not have depended as heavily on the *Life* article as the timing would suggest." **"The right names"**: Neuberger resisting: Parsons, q. in Potter, p. 119. **"She didn't let on"**: Merle Hubbard. **"Better controlled"**: Coates, "The Art Galleries," Dec. 3, 1949, p. 95. **"[Pollock] expresses"**: R[obinson], "Reviews and Previews," p. 43. **"Fascination"**: Burrows, review, New York *Herald Tribune*, Nov. 27, 1949. **"Pollock's forte"**: Preston, "Abstract Quartet." **"Overlapping swirls"**: Coates, "The Art Galleries," Dec. 3, 1949, p. 95. **"Happy landings"**: McBride, "Abstract Painting." **"Repetitious"**: Burrows, review, New York *Herald Tribune*, Nov. 27, 1949, p. 48. **"Fail[ed] to add up"**: Preston, "Abstract Quartet." **"War-shattered city"**: McBride, "Abstract Painting." **"Fashionable and blank"**: [Eliot], "Handful of Fire," p. 26: Eliot's choice for "the country's most promising young painter" was a young realist named Henry Koerner.

Smith: *Number 9, 1949*, OC&T 248, II, p. 70. **Ossorio**: *Number 19, 1949*, OC&T 229, II, p. 52. **Dragon**: *Number 30, 1949 "Birds of Paradise"*, OC&T 237, II, p. 59. **Macys**: Triptych: *Numbers 24, 25, 29, 1949*, OC&T 219-21, II, pp. 42-43. **Tremaine**: Number 6, 1949, OC&T 247, II, pp. 68-69. **Kaufmann**: *Number 12, 1949*, OC&T 233, II, p. 55. **Kimball**: *Number 28, 1949*, OC&T 218, II, p. 42. **Root**: *Number 34, 1949*, OC&T 235, II, pp. 56-57. **Ripley**: *Number 26, 1949*, OC&T 224, II, p. 47; *Number 18, 1949*, OC&T 226, II, pp. 48-49, since lost; *Number 27, 1949*, OC&T 225, II, p. 48. **Price**: *Number 27, 1949*, OC&T 225, II, p. 48. **"Who wouldn't"**: Little. *Number 23, 1949*: OC&T 223, II, p. 46. **First-night sales**: Ossorio. **"[Jack] had the best"**: SMP to FLP, MLP, and Jonathan, Dec. 22, 1949.

Blake's model; Breuer's visit: Blake. **"We attended"**: LK to Ossorio, early spring 1950. **Dragon introducing Jackson to culture; "had no sense"**: Dragon. **"So tired"**: SMP to FLP, MLP, and Jonathan, Dec. 22, 1949. **Family's**

darker explanation: ACM; FLP; MJP. **Jackson unmoved by Heller's death**: Potter (p. 128) quotes JP soon after Heller's accident expressing something akin to anguish, but we don't give the quotation credence. The evidence indicates that JP was in New York when the accident happened, and, even if it is accurate, the quotation does not in our opinion betray any genuine sense of loss. Heller's death is still considered by many to have caused JP to start drinking again; Rosenberg: "After Heller died, JP began drinking at once. He was just lost. The doctor had given him a feeling of self-respect. He acted like a big brother to him." In fact, Heller died eight or nine months before JP fell off the wagon.

Letter drafted; call from Newman: Solomon, p. 203. **"I endorsed"**: Q. in Solomon, p. 203. **"Contempt for modern"**: Q. in "18 Painters Boycott Metropolitan; Charge 'Hostility to Advanced Art,'" *NYT*, May 22, 1950. *Life* **article**: "The Metropolitan and Modern Art," *Life*, Jan. 15, 1951, pp. 34-38. The term "irascible" first appeared in an unsigned editorial in the *Herald Tribune* on May 23, 1950; see Alloway and MacNaughton, p. 48: Eighteen painters originally signed the letter along with ten sculptors. See also Sandler, "The Club," p. 29. **November 24**: Alloway and MacNaughton, p. 49. **Driving in with Brooks**: Potter, p. 129. For a full account of the event, including a list of the other painters, see Friedman, **"The Irascibles,'"** *Arts*, Sept. 1978, pp. 96-102. **"They were very surprised"**: Q. in Alloway and MacNaughton, p. 49. **Picture in *Life***: "The Metropolitan and Modern Art," p. 34. **"The next installment"**: James Brooks; see also Little.

"[An] impregnable language": Tyler, "JP," pp. 92-93, 92. **"Most original art"**: Barr, "Gorky, De Kooning, Pollock," p. 60. **MOMA reception**: Friedman, p. 151. **Attendees**: Friedman, p. 156. **Jackson refusing to drink**: Friedman, p. 152. **Eras meeting**: We are indebted to Friedman (pp. 151-52) for this insight. **"Not one single"**: Genauer, "Art and Artists." **Eclipse of Paris**: See Guilbaut. **"Mostly imitat[ing]"**: Cooper, "The Biennale Exhibition in Venice," p. 14. **"Melted Picasso"**: Q. by Brach. **"U.S. Painting"**: [Eliot], "What's In Fashion," p. 50. **Other Italian painters**: Gino Severini, Lucio Fontana, Pericle Fazini. **"They're interesting, these Americans"; "A little forced"; "A little French"**: q. by Carone. **Correr Museum exhibition**: PG to CG, Feb. 12, 1958. *Number 12, 1949*: OC&T 233, II, p. 55. *Number 23, 1949*: OC&T 223, II, p. 46. **Works shown at Correr Museum**: Friedman, p. 157. **"Sent all the Venetian"**: PG to CG, Feb. 12, 1958. **Alfieri piece as catalogue**: Friedman, p. 157; Alfieri, "A Short Talk on the Pictures of JP." **"Jackson Pollock's paintings"**: Alfieri, "A Short Talk on the Pictures of JP."

"Of the live": [Bill Davis] to JP, n.d. **Cartier watch; "The greatest painter"**: Q. by Bultman. **"Spatially wedded"; "pendant relationship"**: Blake. **Geller mural**: OC&T 259 II, pp. 80-81. The final installment of the payment was dated July 10, 1950. We assume that it was held until soon after installation. See Mrs. Bert Geller to JP, July 10, 1950. **Painting worth more than house**: Blake, q. in Potter, p. 119. The painting was eventually sold to William Rubin and, still later, to the Museum of Contemporary Art in Tehran.

Smith visit: Potter, p. 123. **No new works**: JP to Ossorio, spring 1950: "The studio is untouched. . . . I am gradually getting into painting again." **"Really big paintings"**: Q. by LK. **Ossorio's return**: JP to Ossorio, spring 1950: JP apologizes for sending Ossorio the Tyler article in the March issue of *Magazine of Art* by regular mail and speculates that it will arrive "a week before you leave." Given JP's lack of promptness and international mail delays in 1950, Ossorio probably returned no earlier than mid-May. **"Can you imagine"**: Q. by Johnson. **Chapel; "somewhere on Long Island"**: Carmean, "The Church Project," p. 110. **Larkin's pottery studio; "abstractions in pottery"**: Q. in Potter, p. 107. **Greenberg's praise of Smith**: Dehner. **Smith's Willard Gallery show**: "David Smith," Apr. 18-May 15, 1950; Willard Gallery at 32 East Fifty-seventh Street; noted in catalogue for traveling exhibition; Fry, *David Smith*.

"Getting into painting": JP to Ossorio, spring 1950. **"The first signs"**: LK to Ossorio, spring 1950. **"Incomprehensible drippings"**: Aurthur, "Hitting the Boiling Point," p. 202. **Cocktail party**: Zogbaum. **Lee's guest lists**: Ossorio. **"Jackson knifed open"**: Myers, p. 101. **Small dinner parties**: Castelli. **Glasco**: He was born in Oklahoma but moved to Texas when he was six; Glasco. **De Nagy**: De Nagy. **Marionette "gaily painted"**: Myers, p. 105; Myers says that the puppet was later accidentally destroyed by the children of Larry Rivers. De Nagy: By the end of the summer, JP and Lee were urging de Nagy to open a gallery. "They said there was no outlet with Peggy gone, no outlet for the young generation of painters following them." By November, with financial backing from Jeanne Reynal and Dwight Ripley, de Nagy and Myers had rented a railroad flat on Fifty-third Street and opened the Tibor de Nagy Gallery. **Rosenbergs absent:** Rosenberg. **Kadishes absent:** Kadish. **Wilcoxes absent:** Wilcox. **Brookses absent:** Charlotte Brooks. **"Entering his studio":** Vita Peterson. **"Aura"; "mystical"; "poetic":** Kiesler. **"Awe-inspiring":** Vivas. **"Illuminating":** Vita Peterson. **"Other-worldly":** Vivas. **"Sparkling":** Johnson. **"Glowing"; "gentle":** Donald Kennedy, q. in Potter, p. 217. **"noble animal":** Ronald Stein. **"Like a student":** Johnson. **"Talked to him":** Glasco. **"Maybe a 'yes' ":** Johnson. Harold Rosenberg complained about the "intellectualization" of JP in "The Search for JP," p. 60: "What is to be gained by attributing to Pollock *literary discoveries* outside his range?" **Roman mythology:** Ossorio, int. by Shorthall, Nov. 9, 1959, recalling Frank O'Hara. **Finnegan's Wake:** Little. **William Blake:** Kiesler. **T. S. Eliot:** Jackson. **Hero with a Thousand Faces:** Ossorio, int. by Shorthall, Nov. 9, 1959. *Man and the Unconscious:* Vivas. **Pico della Mirandola:** Ossorio. **Alfred North Whitehead:** Abel. **American literature:** Fiedler. **Bach and Vivaldi:** Potter, p. 113. **Jazz:** Friedman. **Gregorian chant:** Ossorio. **An intellectual to Ossorio:** "You felt that he was in tune with the idea that one word could mean many things. You felt he thought on several levels. He loved the Joyce recordings of his collected works, the music of Joyce's voice"; Ossorio, q. in DP&G, "Who Was JP?" p. 58. **Existential hero to Rosenberg:** Rosenberg, introduction to Samuel M. Kootz Gallery, *The Intrasubjectives* **"Artistic Mark Twain":** Fiedler. "There is in Pollock some fundamentally American quality, so that I think of him along with Huckleberry Finn and Jay Gatsby, a 'heart-of-the-heart-of-the-country' American"; Fiedler, q. in Jeffrey Schaire, "Was JP Any Good?" *Arts and Antiques,* Oct. 1984, p. 85.

Jackson picking up bits of knowledge: Fiedler: "There was no doubt that American literature was of interest to him, although most of his understanding of literature and the mind came secondhand." Abel: "Jackson quoted Whitehead to me. I didn't know what he was talking about. Somebody had told him about it." Kramer: "Jackson sort of picked up diverse literary and intellectual notions from his friends."

"Buy a Pollock"; "it's been waiting": Q. by Mercer: "I sort of gasped. At the time, that was pretty high for his work. She seemed very much interested in its financial value." Mercer thinks the painting was either *Number 1, 1950* or *Number 5, 1950.* **Lee issuing invitations:** Castelli. **Lee answered phone:** Rose, p. 9. **"To create a master":** Tabak, p. 47. **Calling Jackson "Pollock":** Tabak, p. 47. **"He would crumple":** Lord. **Jackson above reproach:** Blake: "Anything he did was all right with her." **"Never apologized":** Hempstead. **"Pollock's in the studio":** Q. by Dragon. **"Believes in doing":** LK; see also LK, q. in DP&G, "Who Was JP?" p. 51. **"Being difficult":** Tabak, p. 47. **"He's a genius":** Q. by Rosenberg. **Lee greeting visitors:** LK. **Roueché introduced by Blake:** Blake. **Jackson and Roueché warming to each other:** Roueché, q. in Potter, p. 127. *Number 2, 1949:* OC&T 222, II, pp. 44–45 **Roueché's interview:** [Roueché], "Unframed Space," p. 16. **"So many parties":** Q. by Zogbaum.

---

37. RECOLLECTIONS OF EARLY CHILDHOOD

SOURCES

Books, articles, and transcripts

Friedman, *JP;* Myers, *Tracking the Marvelous;* Namuth, *Pollock Painting;* OC&T, *JP;* Ossorio, *Fourteen Paintings;* Potter, *To a Violent Grave;* Robertson, *JP;* Solomon, *JP.*

DP&G, "Who Was JP?" *Art in America,* May–June 1967; Grace Glueck, "Krasner and Pollock: Scenes from a Marriage," *Art News,* Dec. 1981: JP, "Letter to the Editor," *Time,* Dec. 11, 1950; Barbara Rose, "Hans Namuth's Photographs and the JP Myth; Part One: Media Impact and the Failure of

Criticism," *Arts,* Mar. 1979; James T. Vallière, "Daniel T. Miller," *Provincetown Review,* Fall 1968; James T. Vallière, "De Kooning on Pollock," *Partisan Review,* Fall 1967.

CG, "The Pollock Market Soars," *NYT Magazine,* Apr. 16, 1961; Joseph Liss, "Memories of Bonac Painters," *East Hampton Star,* Sept. 13, 1983.

CG, int. by James T. Vallière, Mar. 20, 1968, AAA; Elwyn Harris, int. by Kathleen Shorthall for *Life,* Nov. 9, 1959, Time/Life Archives; Betty Parsons, int. by Shorthall for *Life,* Nov. 9, 1959, Time/Life Archives; JP, int. by Dorothy Seiberling for *Life,* July 18, 1949, Time/Life Archives; Mr. and Mrs. Richard Talmage, int. by Shorthall for *Life,* Nov. 9, 1959, Time/Life Archives.

Interviews

Lionel Abel; Peter Blake; Leonard Bocour; Edward Cook; Dorothy Dehner; Ted Dragon; Herbert Ferber; B. H. Friedman; Jane Graves; CG; Grace Hartigan; Ben Heller; Edward Hults; Edys Hunter; Harry Jackson; Lillian Olaney Kiesler; Ruth Kligman; LK; John Little; Herbert Matter; Hans Namuth; Doug Ohlson; Alfonso Ossorio; Vita Peterson; May Tabak Rosenberg; Bill Smith; Hedda Sterne; Allene Talmage; Roger Wilcox.

NOTES

"Think big": Q. by LK. **Dating of the large drip paintings:** Friedman (p. 166) dates *Number 32, 1950,* July or August; *Number 31, 1950* and *Number 30, 1950,* September or October. But Namuth met JP on July 1, 1950, and, by his own account, visited the studio soon thereafter for his first photo session, at which JP painted *Number 31, 1950 (One).* Solomon, pp. 205–06: When Rudolph Burckhardt visited the studio in June, JP had just completed *Number 32.* That would put *Number 28, 1950* in May–June; *Number 32* in late June; *Number 31, 1950* in July; and *Autumn Rhythm* in July–Aug; see OC&T II, p. 79. This chronology also respects JP's preference for working in the summer.

Number 28, 1950: OC&T 260, II, pp. 82–83 (5'8" × 8'8"). **Largest canvas in six years:** It was only slightly bigger than the Geller mural and only two inches longer than *Number 1A, 1948* (OC&T 186, II, pp. 2–3); there were also several scroll canvases that were considerably longer. **Description of Lavender Mist:** OC&T 264, II, pp. 86–87; Ossorio, n.p.; Ossorio says the painting has grayed since it was painted. *Number 32, 1950:* OC&T 274, II, pp. 98–99. *Number 31, 1950:* OC&T 283, II, pp. 105–07. **Tiniest fleck:** See, e.g., detail from *One* in Robertson, plate 38, opposite page 71. *Number 30, 1950:* OC&T 297, II, pp. 116–19 (8'10" × 17'8"). **Gazing at miniatures:** LK. **"Phony" in conversations:** Wilcox. **"Look, Dave":** Q. by Dehner. **"Everyone's shit":** JP, q. by Hartigan. **"Everybody stank":** Int. by Shorthall, Nov. 9, 1959. **"Greatest artist ever":** Q. in Friedman, p. 181. **"Repeat their mistakes":** CG. **"Rubens landscapes":** Int. by Vallière, Mar. 20, 1968. **"Pissed":** CG. **"I gathered":** PG to Charles Seliger, Nov. 11, 1949, Charles Seliger Collection. **No mention of Peggy's support:** JP, int. by Seiberling, July 18, 1949. **Jackson refusing to show at Kootz:** Others who refused were Still, Rothko, and Newman; Friedman, p. 153. **Seen "In large scale":** Friedman, p. 153. **Namuth "hostile":** "My first reaction was hostile," Namuth later wrote in *Pollock Painting,* n.p. "The paintings seemed disorderly and violent. I could not tear myself away from my old loves: Vincent van Gogh, Franz Marc, Paul Klee." **"Most important artist":** Brodovitch, q. in Namuth, n.p. **Namuth approaching Jackson:** Namuth, n.p. Blake says he introduced Namuth to JP. **"A good idea":** Namuth, n.p. **Jackson agreeing:** JP couldn't have been too camera-shy, given the roster of prominent photographers he invited to photograph him, including Matter, Burckhardt, Newman, and Namuth.

"I'm sorry, Hans": Q. in Namuth, n.p. **Lee's approval:** "I suggested going into the studio so that I might at least see what he had been working on. He looked at his wife, who nodded"; Namuth, n.p. **"As if he suddenly"; "[she] told me":** Namuth, n.p. **"Annoyance":** "She sometimes became a little annoyed that I broke into their lives when it was not completely convenient, but in the end she allowed me to do what I wanted"; Namuth, n.p. *Portfolio;* **"Annual of the graphic":** [Brodovitch], "JP," n.p. **Return visits:** Namuth claims he visited the Pollocks almost every weekend that summer, but his published photographs indicate only three separate visits. **"Whenever Pollock":** Namuth, n.p. **Ignoring the camera:** See Rose, "Hans Namuth's Photographs . . . Part One," p. 112. **"Careful and deliberate":** CG, "The Pollock Market Soars," p. 135. JP's movements were described as "harmonious and quiet" by another studio witness, Herbert Matter: "He would do things, and then he looked, and then he went to the other side and looked again and did a few more things. It was never fanatical." **Slowing exposure:** Namuth, n.p. Matter: "Some of the pictures Namuth took, he used a really slow exposure, so Jackson seems to be moving much faster than he actually was." **Reviewing pictures.** Namuth, n.p. **"The proofs":** Namuth, n.p. Rose ("Hans Namuth's Photographs . . . Part One," p. 112) argues, incorrectly we think, that "Pollock, totally immersed in his own trance-like activity, was oblivious to the repeated click-click of high-speed film that permitted Namuth to capture Pollock's spontaneity in images that freeze the artist's motions into a blur of urgency."

Portraits: Namuth claimed he was prodded into taking these portraits by Edward Steichen who, when shown the earlier shots, had "dismissed the pictures, saying, 'You know, Namuth, this is not the way to photograph an artist. The nature and personality of such a complex human being are only partially revealed when you show him at work. Spend some time with the man, take pictures of him as he wakes up in the morning, brushes his teeth, talks to his wife, eats breakfast . . . follow him through his day'"; q. in Namuth, n.p. Namuth's staged portraits came no closer, of course, than the shots of JP at work to revealing JP's "complexity." **"His face":** Namuth, n.p. **Arranged by Namuth:** LK. **"A tormented":** Rose, "Hans Namuth's Photographs . . . Part One," p. 112. **"Super-human energy":** Rose, introduction to Namuth, n.p.

Quizzing Little: Little. **Quizzing Greenberg:** CG. **Quizzing Rosenberg:** Rosenberg. **"Long, complicated":** Q. in Potter, p. 137. **References to western lore:** See, e.g., Potter, pp. 125, 137. **Ridiculing Potter:** See, e.g., Potter, pp. 121, 124. **Ridiculing Blake:** Blake. **"Did you ever":** JP, q. by Wilcox. **"Stern, serious":** Wilcox, **"Then you can pay me":** Q. by Wilcox. It wsn't until JP took Seligson to the studio and showed him his paintings that Seligson's blood began to cool. "Now I understand why you did this," Seligson said (q. by Wilcox), promising not to file a complaint. (He must also have sensed that JP couldn't possibly have raised the money.) As a parting goodwill gesture, JP offered the bewildered businessman a painting, which Seligson refused. **"Assuredness":** LK, q. in Namuth, n.p. **"Agonizing":** Little. **"A good lay":** Q. by Little. **"Chaos, Damn It!":** *Time*, Nov. 20, 1950, pp. 70-71. **Blistering reply:** The telegram wasn't published in "Letters to the Editor" until the Dec. 11, 1950, issue of *Time*. **"It isn't just me":** Q. in Potter, p. 130.

"Come on, Jackson": Q. in Friedman, p. 134. Story confirmed by Ohlson. **"21 Club":** Ad Reinhardt, q. in Friedman, p. 134. **Unceremoniously ejected:** Friedman p. 134, citing "An Ad Reinhardt Monologue" (tape recorded by Mary Fuller on April 27, 1966), *Artforum*, October 1970, pp. 36-41. **"Began to dress":** Q. in Vallière, "De Kooning on Pollock," p. 605. **Kitchen implements:** Edys Hunter. **Canned goods:** Kligman. **Cuts of meat:** Kiesler. **"Printed on paper":** JP to Parsons, Oct. 17, 1949. **Bocour:** Bocour, who insists that beginning in 1952, JP was buying acrylic paints, even though no paintings in the catalogue raisonné are listed as being in this medium. **Poker; checks; cabs; tips:** Friedman. **Lending money:** Jackson. **"A good poker player":** Heller. **"What the hell":** Q. in Friedman, p. 134. **"Maybe a Cadillac":** Q. in Friedman, p. 134. **"Pathetic cloth coat":** Ossorio, q. in DP&G, "Who Was JP?" p. 58. **"How he should invest":** Vita Peterson. **"Lamentable":** Ossorio. "Certainly in those days it was a question of buying materials. The Pollocks lived up to the limit"; Ossorio, q. in DP&G, "Who Was JP?" p. 58.

Parsons knew of extravagance: Parsons, int. by Shorthall, Nov. 9, 1959. **Checks of $3,174.89; sales of $4,750:** Monica at Parsons Gallery to LK, Mar. 7, 1951. **June amounts:** JP, handwritten addendum to Monica to LK, Mar. 7, 1951. *Number 8, 1949:* OC&T 239, II, p. 61. **Kootz's harping:** Friedman, p. 142, **Average wages and costs:** Bill Smith, U.S. Bureau of Labor Statistics: Figures for 1950: A production worker in manufacturing made $56.53 a week; a bookkeeper in Atlanta made $65 a week; the cost of a new house averaged $10,905. **Kitchen appliances:** Edys Hunter. **Dental services:** Ferber. **Offer for *Lucifer*:** Parsons to JP, June 15, 1950. **"I'm very fond":** JP to Parsons, n.d.; inaccurately dated 1949 in OC&T IV, p. 245. **"I am going to try";**

JP to Parsons, n.d. **"I want, as you know":** Parsons to JP, June 25, 1950. **Parsons strapped:** "As you realize, my financial situation is no better than yours. I am continually in debt"; Parsons to JP, June 25, 1950. **"Extravagant"; "rent-free":** Int. by Shorthall, Nov. 9, 1959. **Dating of renovations:** SMP to CCP, Jan. 10, 1949. **Loper:** Hults; see Potter, p. 180. **"If you ran"; "If we'd had a strong wind":** Hults.

Following summer: Talmage: LK, q. in Liss, "Memories of Bonac Painters." **Begonias and ferns:** Myers, p. 104. **Cold water and coal stoves:** Glueck, "Krasner and Pollock," p. 60. **Hults and Talmage:** Hults. **Working cheap:** Talmage. **Payment:** Hults. Hults and the real estate agent. Ed Cook, sent JP an old ink-splattered blotter that reminded them of Jackson's paintings. "Jackson thought so much of it that he had it framed," Hults recalls, "and hung it in his kitchen for a few years. He got the biggest charge out of that."

Work on studio: See SMP to CCP, Jan. 10, 1949. **Water line; paint mixer:** Hults. **Fluorescent lights:** Harris, int. by Shorthall, Nov. 9, 1959. **Negotiating and supervising:** Hults, q. in Potter, p. 107. **Art transactions left to Lee:** Significantly, the details of sales were communicated, not by Parsons to JP, but by Parsons's gallery assistant, M. L. Monica, to Lee Krasner; Monica to LK, Mar. 15, 1951. **Plants:** "There was one very tall vase in the living room into which Lee put a single gigantic sunflower every summer. In the fall she combed the fields for flowers to dry. In the bay window was her indoor garden of magnificent hanging pots of begonias, ferns (the more exotic the better), Canary Island ivy, fuchsias, spider plants. On the floor below were spread stones picked up along the seashore, and on these were placed more pots of plants"; Myers, p. 104.

Garden and lawn: LK, q. in DP&G, "Who Was JP?" p. 51; Mr. and Mrs. Richard Talmage, int. by Shorthall, Nov. 9, 1959. **Pump:** Mr. and Mrs. Richard Talmage, int. by Shorthall, Nov. 9, 1959. **"He wanted to build":** Q. in DP&G, "Who Was JP?" p. 53. **"She couldn't sleep":** Q. by Cook. **Repainting:** Wilcox. **Colors:** Kligman, **Search for acquisitions:** Little. **Twin beds:** Kligman. **Date car purchased:** SMP to CCP, Oct. 1950. **Cadillac:** Acquired in exchange for a painting; Dan Miller, q. in Vallière, "Daniel T. Miller," p. 41. **"Oh, how he gloried";** Q. in Potter, p. 144. **Description of Cadillac:** Potter, p. 144.

---

38. A CLAM WITHOUT A SHELL

SOURCES

Books, articles, documents, and transcripts

Barrett, *The Truants*; THB, *An Artist in America*; Burroughs, *THB*; Friedman, *JP*; Gruen, *The Party's Over Now*; Kunitz, ed., *Twentieth Century Authors*; Namuth, *Pollock Painting*; Nemser, *Art Talk*; Potter, *To a Violent Grave*; Rose, *LK*; Sandler, *The New York School*; Solomon, *JP*.

Robert Alan Aurthur, "Hitting the Boiling Point, Freakwise, at East Hampton," *Esquire*, June 1972; Barbara Cavaliere, "An Interview with LK," *Flash Art*, Jan.-Feb. 1980; Barbara Cavaliere and Richard C. Hobbs, "Against a Newer Laocoön," *Arts*, Apr. 1977; "Chaos, Damn It!" *Time*, Nov. 20, 1950; "Charles Pollock in Conversation with Terence Maloon," Peter Rippon, and Sylvia Pollock," *Artscribe*, Sept. 1977; DP&G, "Who Was JP?" *Art in America*, May-June 1967; Grace Glueck, "Krasner and Pollock: Scenes from a Marriage," *Art News*, Dec. 1981; CG, "Art," *Nation*, June 10, 1944; CG, "Art," *Nation*, June 9, 1945; CG, "Avant-Garde and Kitsch," *Partisan Review*, Fall 1939; CG, "The Present Prospects of American Painting and Sculpture," Oct. 1947; CG, "Towards a Newer Laocoön," *Partisan Review*, July-Aug. 1940; Robert Hughes, "Arrogant Intrusion," *Time*, Sept. 30, 1974; Max Kozloff, "The Critical Reception of Abstract Expressionism," *Arts*, Dec. 1965; Max Kozloff, "An Interview with Robert Motherwell," *Artforum*, Sept. 1965; Rosalind Krauss, "Changing the Work of David Smith," *Art in America*, Sept.-Oct. 1974; "Letters" (from Joseph W. Henderson and Rosalind Krauss), *Art in America*, Apr.-May 1975; "Letters to the Editors," *Life*, Aug. 29, 1949; JP, "Letters to the Editor," *Time*, Dec. 11, 1950; Barbara M. Reise, "Greenberg and The Group: A Retrospective View, Part 1," *Studio International*, May 1968; Irving Sandler, "The Club," *Artforum*, Sept. 1965; James T. Vallière, "De Kooning on Pollock," *Partisan Review*, Fall 1967.

Hal Burston, "JP: He Paints as He Pleases," *Long Island Newsday*, Dec. 1, 1950; Barbara DeLatiner, "LK: Beyond Pollock," *NYT*, Aug. 8, 1981; Michael Kernan, "LK, Out of Pollock's Shadow," *Washington Post*, Oct. 23, 1983; Hilton Kramer, "Altering of Smith Work Stirs Dispute," *NYT*, Sept. 13, 1974; Hilton Kramer, "Questions Raised by Art Alterations," *NYT*, Sept. 14, 1974; Hilton Kramer, "Sculpture Reproduction, a Rising Battle," *NYT*, Oct. 21, 1974; Vivien Raynor, "JP in Retrospect—'He Broke the Ice,' " *NYT Magazine*; Amei Wallach, "LK: Angry Artist," *Long Island Newsday*, Nov. 12, 1973.

Motherwell Archives, AAA.

CG, int. by James T. Vallière, Mar. 20, 1968, AAA; Barnett Newman, int. by Kathleen Shorthall of *Life*, Nov. 9, 1959, Time/Life Archives.

Interviews

Lawrence Alloway; Ruth Ann Applehof; Ethel Baziotes; Peter Blake; Norman Bluhm; Leonard Bocour; Paul Brach; James Brooks; Jeremy Capillé; Nicholas Carone; Giorgio Cavallon; Herman Cherry; Edward Cook; Gene Davis; Violet de Laszlo; Dorothy Dehner; Karen Del Pilar; Dane Dixon; Ted Dragon; Jimmy Ernst; Herbert Ferber; Phyllis Fleiss; B. H. Friedman; Jane Graves; CG; Grace Hartigan; Ben Heller; Edward Hults, Ted Hults; Edys Hunter; Sam Hunter; Harry Jackson; Buffie Johnson; Reuben Kadish; Nathaniel Kaz; Lillian Olaney Kiesler; Stewart Klonis; Hilton Kramer; LK; Ernestine Lassaw; Ibram Lassaw; John Lee; Harold Lehman; Joe Liss; John Little; Cile Downs Lord; Beatrice Ribak Mandelman; Conrad Marca-Relli; Mercedes Matter; ACM; Jason McCoy; George Mercer; Mrs. George Mercer; Hans Namuth; Alfonso Ossorio; Philip Pavia; Vita Peterson; ABP; CCP; EFP; FLP; Jonathan Pollock; MJP; MLP; SWP; David Porter; Becky Reis; May Tabak Rosenberg; Irving Sandler; Miriam Schapiro; Jon Schueler; Carol Southern; Hedda Sterne; Jock Truman; Esteban Vicente; Harriet Vicente; Helen Wheelwright; Roger Wilcox; Betsy Zogbaum.

NOTES

Description of dump: Ted Hults. **Going to dump:** CG. JP apparently liked to go to the dump and sit and think and enjoy the view: Potter (p. 108) saw him there alone, sitting on the running board of his Model A, staring at the garbage. **Jackson terrified:** Parsons, q. in Friedman, p. 180: "He was either bored or terrified of society." See Brooks, q. in Potter, p. 114. **"Wanted to crawl":** Edward Hults. **"Clam without a shell":** Q. by CG; q. by LK, q. in Friedman, p. 140; q. by Penny Potter, in Potter, p. 114. **"Didn't see the man":** CG. **"As if his skin":** Penny Potter, q. in Potter, p. 156. **"Top of the heap":** Q. in Potter, p. 114. **"A terrible nightmare":** Q. by Sam Hunter. **Yale refusing mural:** Potter, p. 76. **"Parsons must be nuts":** In AAA. **Letters:** "Letters to the Editors," p. 9: child, Mrs. F. D. O'Sullivan, Jr.; garage door, P. B. Perrault; "at the rate," Preston W. Angell. **"Bucket of paint":** Burston, "JP."

"The decorative qualities": Q. by Ossorio. **Valentin's assessment:** Valentin, q. by Parsons, q. in Potter, p. 91. **"You don't really":** Q. by friend, name withheld by request. **"Let's wait":** Shawn, q. by Roueché, q. in Potter, p. 127. **"A piece of junk":** Q. by Cavallon. **Liss resisting pleas:** Joe Liss. **Klonis:** Executive Director from 1947 to 1980. **Klonis:** When Pollock donated a painting for a charity auction at the Art Students League, the painting fetched very little. **Bocour refusing trade:** Bocour. **"Maidstone Club friends":** Q. in Potter, p. 90.

Obscurity and odd jobs: Sandler: Philip Pearlstein painted a picture in exchange for a $15 recording of *The Magic Flute*. **"That wildman":** Carone. **"The freak":** Q. by friend, name withheld by request. **"Irrelevant":** Hans Hofmann, q. by CG. **"Embittered":** Kiesler. **"Brash and heartless":** Hofmann, q. by Schueler. **Marsh; Burlington show:** Klonis. **"He's a follower":** Name withheld by request. **Craven's accusation:** Burroughs, p. 118. **Benton's accusation:** JP (p. 317) "began pouring paint out of cans and buckets just to see what would happen." **"Non-artist":** Guston, q. by Carone. **"Bragging that Jackson":** Berton Roueché, q. in Potter, p. 127. **"Within five years":** Aurthur, "Hitting the Boiling Point," p. 200. **Rethinking of Motherwell's ambitions:** Aurthur, "Hitting the Boiling Point," p. 200: "Just about when the five years were up, and it was clear that Pollock would make it, Motherwell, having to settle for a little less, aban-

doned his Pierre Chareau–designed Quonset hut in East Hampton and departed forever." **Something to fight about:** Rosenberg. Jack Tworkov, q. by Brach: "The art world is a long line waiting to get through a narrow doorway. Most people die while still on line."

"I never met"; "pantspresser"; "boring": CG. **"Tedious beyond belief":** Q. in Gruen, p. 182. **Move from literary criticism:** Greenberg began writing regular art reviews for the *Nation* in 1941, but he had written on art before, in 1939 and 1940, notably, in the *Partisan Review* ("Avant-Garde and Kitsch" and "Towards a Newer Laocoön"). He became the *Nation's* regular art critic in 1944, although he also continued to write literary criticism; see Kunitz, ed., p. 587. **"Extreme eclecticism":** CG, "Art," June 10, 1944, p. 689. **New critical agenda:** In 1945, Greenberg castigated the lyrical tendency of abstract painters in "New Metamorphism," a show at Howard Putzel's short-lived Gallery 57. In the *Nation* (June 9, 1945, p. 657), Greenberg decried the "return of elements of representation, smudged contour lines and the third dimension." He urged (p. 658) the artist to explore "the means of his art in order to produce his new subject matter," not to "hunt about for new 'ideas' under which to cover up the failure to develop his means." **War against Surrealists:** Reise, "Greenberg and The Group . . . Part l," p. 256: "Greenberg did not like the Surrealists, who were French, differently-styled Marxists, Freudian-oriented, and concerned with 'content'; his aversion was so strong that he seldom mentioned their presence in New York in his accounts of immigrant artists." **"'Outside' subject matter":** CG, "Avant-Garde and Kitsch," p. 49 n. 2. **Confus[ing] literature":** CG, "Towards a Newer Laocoön," p. 309. **Ferocious Struggle"; "[the artist's] isolation":** CG, "The Present Prospects of American Painting and Sculpture," p. 30.

"Interesting experiment": Barrett p. 136. **"Child prodigy":** CG. **Treating artists as children:** Kozloff ("The Critical Reception of Abstract Expressionism," p. 30) called his work "both self-contradictory and authoritarian." **Ignoring artists:** See Cavaliere and Hobbs, "Against a Newer Laocoön," p. 114. **Paintings forced to conform:** Cavaliere and Hobbs, "Against a Newer Laocoön," p. 115: "Most of Greenberg's criticism is prescriptive. He assumes the role of coach. Standing on the sidelines he urges his favorites on to further tests. Rather than dealing with each painting individually and assessing their paintings in light of their intentions, he programmatically evaluates them according to his own standards and tries to persuade them to follow his own theories." **"Like an impatient":** Davis. **"That one's a mistake!":** Q. by Friedman. **"Lead from his strength":** CG. **What you should do":** Q. by Zogbaum: "Sam Kootz was putting on a show of eleven unknowns and Clement Greenberg was chosen to go down and pick out something from Kline. Those were the ones he chose." **"Smith was no colorist":** CG. See Hughes, "Arrogant Intrusion," p. 73; Kramer, "Altering of Smith Work Stirs Dispute"; Kramer, "Questions Raised by Art Alterations"; Kramer, "Sculpture Reproduction"; Krauss, "Changing the Work of David Smith," pp. 30–34; "Letters" (from Joseph W. Henderson and Krauss), p. 136. Dehner: "I was furious! I felt as bad as if somebody had painted out half of the Sistine Chapel. I just thought it was an outrageous act of arrogance." Although Greenberg couldn't compel obedience, he was quick to punish those, like Little, who defied him: "He came to my second show at Betty Parsons and made a show of standing in the door. He didn't come in, he just looked around quickly, then turned and left. Of course, everybody noticed."

"Grand pooh-bah": Wheelwright: "He became the big pooh-bah. He was the one to whom everybody kowtowed. Whatever Clem said, that was the word of God." **"Pope Clement":** Marca-Relli. **"God":** Kiesler. **"Making sweaters":** Bluhm. **"A priest class":** Pavia. **"Looked with their ears":** Heller. **"Manufactured artists":** Q. in Gruen, p. 259; Gottlieb says this about Barnett Newman. Wheelwright believes Greenberg ("the devil!") destroyed her first husband, artist Paul Feeley. Hofmann, q. by Mrs. George Mercer: "It takes three things to make a success in the art world. The first is good press. The second is a good critic. The third is talent. In that order."

The Club: See the definitive article on the Club, Sandler, "The Club," pp. 27–31. **Lassaw's studio:** Actually, 487 Sixth Avenue. **Twenty artists:** For a complete list, see Sandler, "The Club," p. 27. **Address of loft; unable to agree on name:** Vallière, "De Kooning on Pollock," p. 604. In arguing for an artists' club, Marca-Relli was inspired by his memory of a club in Rome: "They had a beautiful building, with a restaurant on the first floor, and were always hosting lunches and dinners. I thought, Jesus Christ, how do the Europeans manage these things? When I came back to New York I mentioned it many times. The idea was already in the air. Of course, I hoped we would do it with real style, but we didn't." **"Escape the loneliness":** Sandler, "The Club," p. 29. **Sam Johnson's:** Friedman, p. 108. **Other cafés:** Sandler, "The Club," p. 27. **Address of Waldorf:** Friedman, p. 108. **"Village bums"; food better elsewhere:** Sandler, "The Club," p. 27. **Lewitin; Kaldis:** Mercedes Matter. **Graham:** Pavia, q. in Gruen, p. 268. **Joint experience on work projects:** Friedman, p. 108. **"Reinhardt would say":** Q. in Gruen, p. 269. **"Puritans"; "the hygienic school":** Pavia, q. in Gruen, p. 269, **"Decorative":** Kadish.

"Rebels"; "outcasts": Marca-Relli. Sandler ("The Club," p. 29) accepts this self-image: "Reacting against a public, which, when not downright hostile to their work, was indifferent or misunderstanding, vanguard artists created their own audience, mostly of other artists—their own art world." **Avoiding formal issues:** Kozloff, "An Interview with Robert Motherwell," p. 37. **"Founder and organizer:** Barrett, p. 134; Sandler ("The Club," p. 29) calls Pavia "the dominant force in Club affairs . . . who made up any financial deficit and arranged the programs." Sandler, "The Club," p. 29: The early spur-of-the-moment character of the Club soon gave way to planned lectures and panels. **"A different world":** Pavia. **"Why an artist":** Sandler, "The Club," p. 30. **"Abstract Expressionism":** Pavia (q. in Gruen, p. 270) claims he invented the term. **Without consensus:** "Reinhardt refused to recognize the word 'expressionism'—he wanted to use the word 'abstraction' "; Pavia, q. in Gruen, p. 270. **"Baboons":** Q. by Resnick. **Exhibitions banned:** Cherry; Marca-Relli. **Talk of money:** Sandler, "The Club," p. 29. **Passing the hat:** Barrett, p. 133.

Admission policy: Ernestine Lassaw: "If you weren't in Lewitin's good graces, he wouldn't let you in." **Blackball system:** Sandler, "The Club," p. 29: "Two negative votes (it had to be two because Lewitin always voted no) and a candidate was rejected." **Gaps in education:** See Elaine de Kooning, q. in Friedman, p. 122. **Subjects of the Artist:** Friedman, p. 108; see also Cavaliere and Hobbs, "Against a Newer Laocoön," pp. 110–17. **"Our painting":** Motherwell, q. in Kozloff, "An Interview with Robert Motherwell," p. 37. **"Master of Ceremonies":** Cavaliere and Hobbs, "Against a Newer Laocoön," p. 110. See Sandler, "The Club," p. 29. **Jackson intimidated:** Elaine de Kooning, q. in Potter, p. 122.

Chairs cleared away: Porter. **Folk music:** Ibram Lassaw. A visiting architect was terrified that the building would collapse. "You could have lost the entire New York movement if the floor collapsed," says Matter. **Tarantella:** Ernestine Lassaw. **"Crackling sexuality":** Southern. **Pretty girls:** Matter: When a woman's name came before the membership committee, people would ask, "What does she look like?" **Matter only woman:** Matter; in "The Club," p. 27, Sandler says Matter was a later member. **Edge of sexuality:** Dixon; Rosenberg; Esteban Vicente; Harriet Vicente; Zogbaum. **Misogynist game:** Fleiss; Ribak. **Jackson frightened:** Harry Jackson. **"All the women":** Q. by Wilcox. **Jackson always alone:** Ernestine Lassaw. **"What his pictures":** Carone. **"Shrug[ging]":** Barrett, p. 140. **"I don't discuss":** Q. by Newman, int. by Shorthall, Nov. 9, 1959.

Lee not painting: Reis: "I think she held back because she didn't want to interfere with JP's career." **"Pollock was breaking through":** Q. in Nemser, p. 91. **"The best period":** Johnson. **"Safe" to work:** LK, q. by Dragon. **"I wasn't saying":** Q. in DeLatiner, "LK": "For me, it was quite enough to continue working, and his success, once he began to sell, gave us an income of sorts and made me ever so grateful because, unlike wives of the artists who had to go out and support them, I could continue painting myself." **"In the shadow":** DeLatiner, "LK." Reis: "Lee was very anxious for Jackson to succeed, but privately unhappy that she was not able to pursue her own career." **Not just by Jackson:** Brooks. **"Lee, get Jackson":** Q. by LK, q. in Kernan, "LK." **"Very few painters":** LK, q. in Glueck, "Krasner and Pollock," p. 58. **Few admirers:** Krasner insisted that the artists who were "hanging all over the place" did see her works, despite numerous accounts to the contrary; see Cavaliere, "An Interview with LK," p. 14. But this directly contradicts her later statement that few "acknowledged that I painted at all."

"Showed no interest": George Mercer. **Leftover spaces:** Johnson. **Jackson showing works:** Johnson: Sometimes he would bring in an entire show's worth of paintings. **No one asking to see Lee's:** Edys Hunter.

Sharing the money: LK, q. in DeLatiner, "LK." **"What I couldn't":** Q. in Wallach, "LK." **"Take chances":** Rose, p. 66. **Inexact chronology:** Applehof; Wilcox. **"Work through Pollock":** LK, q. by John Lee. "When the Guild Hall show was up," recalls John Lee, "I said, 'You know, most people like your paintings more than they like Pollock's.' She said, 'Of course they do.' Her implication was that her paintings were easier to get, or easier to like. But there was no implication—and I could read her pretty well—that she was a *better* artist than he was. She was an artist, and he was a genius. She may have gone along with the Barbara Rose thing [the thesis that Pollock and Krasner influenced each other's work in equal measure], but she never believed it. Her only qualification was, why should she not be allowed to be influenced by one of the geniuses, like everybody else, just because she was his wife?"

Continuum: Rose, fig. 52, p. 58. *Lava,* Rose, fig. 69, p. 74. *Gothic Frieze:* Rose, fig. 61, p. 63. *Promenade:* Rose, fig. 62, p. 64; for reasons stated above, we believe the date 1947 given by Rose is erroneous. **Masonite:** Rose, p. 65. *Ochre Rhythm:* Rose, fig. 65, p. 68. Rose speculates that Krasner began this canvas in 1950. **Painting thinly:** Rose, p. 68. **"The unconscious as a source:"** Rose, p. 66. **Automatic drawing:** Rose, p. 68. **Stick figures:** Rose, fig. 64, p. 68. **Canvases growing:** Rose, p. 68. **Portrait-sized Little Image paintings:** See, e.g., *Untitled,* Rose, fig. 60, p. 62 (38″ × 38″). *Blue and Black:* Rose, fig. 67, p. 71. **Cajoling visitors:** Dragon. **Dragon's admiration:** "I said wow! I loved it!" **Myers, Little, Lindeberg, Tomlin:** Nemser, p. 91. **"That's hot":** Q. by LK, q. in Nemser, p. 91.

Plans for reunion: MLP. **No sleep or work:** LK. **Lee's concern:** Dragon, q. in Potter, p. 159. **"Triumph"; "a bust":** LK. **Charles, Elizabeth, and Marie meeting Lee:** CCP, EFP; MLP. **Fascinated by table:** Jonathan Pollock. **Tour:** Jonathan Pollock: "I remember walking around in that barn. Jackson was showing Dad and the other brothers some of the canvases that were stacked up there." **Baseball; "a boy's game":** Jonathan Pollock, **Renaming of Jason; going to beach:** ACM. **"Christmas feast in July":** MJP. **No alcohol:** Capillé. **Family pictures:** In possession of MJP. **Alma not forgiving Jackson:** Capillé. Jackson "just keeping" blankets: After JP died, says Jay, Krasner "wouldn't listen to a word about it." **Jay and Alma stopped visiting:** MJP. **Jonathan "seriously ill":** Q. by MLP: Jonathan had ear, nose, and throat problems all his life; around the time of the family reunion, he underwent surgery to have his adenoids removed. **Frank's job at nursery:** MLP.

"Being a he-man": CG. **"Aggression and strain:** SWP. **Sande's illness:** ACM. Kadish: Sande died in 1963 of leukemia contracted from breathing chemical fumes in his windowless shop room. Stella's letters to her family from the mid-forties onward are full of references to Sande's inexplicable sore throats and, in at least one letter, pointed, without knowing it, to the cause; SMP to CCP, EFP, and Jonathan, Apr. 11, 1944: "Sanford has had a terrible sore throat for over two weeks had to go to the Dr. is better working in the plant doesn't help it any." **Stella and Arloie:** SWP. **"I[t's] not me":** SMP to CCP, Jan. 14, 1954. **Children cared for by Stella:** Capillé; Del Pilar, Jason McCoy. **"His precious":** Del Pilar. **"Exquisitely beautiful":** EFP. **Jason mistaken for girl:** Del Pilar. **"Mommie"; "Loie":** SMP to CCP, EFP, and Jonathan, Aug., n.d. **Stella wanting musician:** SMP to CCP, Feb. 21, 1950.

Charles's intervening years: CCP; EFP. **"Breakdown"; "three months in the desert":** "Charles Pollock in Conversation," p. 13. **Third Avenue studio:** Cherry. **Circle Gallery show:** CCP. **One Pollock was enough:** Charles never admitted this: "For some reason, I thought I didn't want to show under the name of Pollock." Charles used the name only for one exhibition at the Circle Gallery—"a momentary aberration," he called it. CCP: When JP heard about the name change, he called Charles and said, "What the hell did you do that for!" **"Charles Pima":** CCP. **Resentment not showing:** EFP: "He never showed any resentment toward Jackson. He was protective and helpful. There was never the slightest sign of envy. . . . *I* was the one who had that feeling." CCP: "In some ways, unfortunately, I always had too many strings to my bow. Jack had one string." **Charles boiling:** Cherry, who was not at the reunion, made this general comment about Charles in the early fifties. ABP: "He doesn't show it at all, but inside he must be bitter. How could he not be? Resentful of his brother and bitter towards the failure of history." CCP: He and his family spent parts of the summers of 1950 and 1951 in Sag Harbor. Capillé: Except for the one-day family reunion, Charles's family rarely saw JP and Krasner, even though they were living only twelve miles apart. **"Must be great":** MJP to MLP, FLP, and Jonathan, Dec. 3, 1950. *Gothic; Arabesque:* Photos in possession of MJP. **"The only painter"; "buy that":** Q. by FLP. Frank remembers the painting as *Autumn Rhythm,* which had not yet been painted at the time of the reunion. **"Gracious hostess":** EFP. **Lee whispering prices:** MJP. **Lee putting up with the family:** She told Dragon that any visit from a family member upset her, because it upset JP; LK, q. by Dragon, q. in Potter, p. 159. **"Silent adoration":** EFP. **Jackson's failure to help with Stella:** EFP; FLP; MJP; MLP. The family generally blamed Lee for JP's stinginess. **Charles's affability and quiet drinking:** Capillé. **"When posterity":** EFP. ABP: "Charles should have been the one who was a success. . . . That's what all the rest of the family thought. Certainly his mother did." **"Do you know":** Q. by ABP in Solomon, p. 204. **"Is Picasso":** Q. in Solomon, p. 204.

Gloating over *New Yorker:* LK. **"The next logical step"; black-and-white film; "Reveal[ed]"; Falkenberg:** Namuth, n.p. **Lee's encouragement:** Potter, p. 129. **"Voyeuristic element":** Namuth, n.p. **September dating:** Namuth insists the filming took place in September and October, but we believe that it continued into November and therefore probably began in mid- to late September. **Jackson agreeing to outdoor shooting:** Namuth, n.p. **Reconstruction of filming:** Raynor, "JP in Retrospect," p. 50; also LK; Little; Wilcox; Dragon; Marca-Relli; Namuth. **"Pollock's shoes":** Falkenberg, q. in Namuth, n.p. Namuth also "simulated" a "short transitional passage that shows JP's shadow flinging paint dramatically onto a canvas. . . . I periodically consider deleting it because it is not convincing"; Namuth, n.p. **"A main ingredient":** Namuth, n.p. **"Artist at work":** Namuth, q. in Friedman, p. 163. Blake says it was *his* idea to work on a piece of glass as a way of photographing Pollock. Namuth, n.p., claims the idea was his. **"A painting that . . . was transparent":** Blake. **Pittsburgh Plate Glass:** See Friedman, p. 163. **Herculite:** Blake. Namuth (n.p.) says it was glass (not true) and that it cost $10 (very unlikely). **Late October:** Namuth is the only one who believes the filming was finished by late October. **Namuth lying on back:** Namuth (n.p.) says it took "many unsuccessful attempts." **Jackson's "false starts":** Namuth (n.p.) says JP had "several" false starts. **"Now?":** Q. by LK. **Couldn't afford more glass:** Namuth, n.p. **Arranging pebbles:** Friedman, p. 163. **November cold:** LK. **Jackson withdrawing:** Blake describes him as "terribly withdrawn" during this period. **"Jackson Pollock's abstractions":** "Chaos, Damn It!" pp. 70–71. **"No chaos damn it":** JP, "Letters to the Editor," p. 10. **"Wasn't that bad"; "very upset"; "more churning":** Q. in Potter, p. 130. **Greenberg visit:** CG.

November 25 dating: Namuth insists that this incident occurred in October, but a November date is suggested by Potter (p. 130), Johnson, and Zogbaum. Johnson says that, when she talked to JP on the phone that day, he was particularly upset about the *Time* Biennale review, which didn't come out until November 20. **Mean day; "bloody cold":** Blake, q. in Potter, p. 131. **Hand going numb:** Namuth, n.p. **"Final shot"; "technical delays"; "full of tension"; four-thirty; "we are done!":** Namuth, n.p. **Turkey:** Blake, Dragon, and Namuth say the meal was turkey. Jeffrey and Penny Potter (Potter, p. 131) both say it was roast beef. The other guests aren't sure. **Friends invited:** Potter, p. 130: Hans and Carmen Namuth, Jeffrey and Penny Potter, Wilfrid and Betsy Zogbaum, Peter Blake, John Little, Ted Dragon, Alfonso Ossorio, Gina Knee, and her husband Alexander Brook. Betsy Zogbaum claims she wasn't there and that Knee and Brook declined the invitation. **Bourbon:** Blake, q. in Potter, p. 131. **"Went white":** Ossorio, q. in DP&G, "Who Was JP?" p. 58. **Silence; Blake standing at table:** Blake, q. in Potter, p. 131. **"Tried to speak"; Namuth trying to brush it off:** Blake. **"Why are you so upset?":** Dragon. **"You just don't know":** Q. by Dragon. **Summoning Namuth:** Namuth, n.p. **"The first drink":** Q. by Blake. **"Don't be a fool":** Q. in Friedman, p. 165. **Second tumblerful:** Namuth, n.p. **Namuth hurried out:**

LK. Changing before dinner: Namuth, n.p. **"Jackson can't come":** Q. by Johnson. **Zogbaums arriving:** Potter (p. 130) says that Betsy Zogbaum was there, but she denies it. **Trying to ignore Jackson:** Namuth, n.p. **Jackson swinging sleighbells:** Potter, p. 132; Namuth says only that JP threatened "playfully—and perhaps not completely playfully" to hit him with them. **"Maybe those natives":** Q. by Potter, p. 129. **"You're a phony":** Q. by Johnson. Johnson says she wasn't there, but "it was described to me so graphically." **Seating arrangements:** Potter, p. 132. **"I'm not a phony":** Q. by Johnson. **"Tiresome, awful":** Blake. **Jackson standing up:** Potter, p. 132. **"Jackson—no!":** Q. by Blake. **"Shut up, Hans":** Penny Potter, q. by Blake. **"Now?":** Q. by Blake. **Creamed onions:** Dragon, q. in Potter, p. 131. **Door slamming:** Potter, p. 132. **"Coffee":** Q. in DP&G, "Who Was JP?" p. 50.

Wilcox in Mexico: Wilcox: He had left for Mexico for a four-month research job with the Bigelow Sanford Carpet Company, studying primitive yarn-making and weaving techniques. "Lucia and I invited Jackson to go with us. I told him it wouldn't cost him anything. I told him I could support a family of four on the money the company was giving me. But Lee didn't want to leave." **Nearby bar:** De Laszlo. **Macys' dinner:** Johnson. De Laszlo: JP must have decided to ignore Krasner's antagonism toward de Laszlo, because he later invited her to his studio to see the photographs Namuth had taken and to look at the work that was there.

39. THE UNRAVELING

SOURCES

Books, articles, film, document, record, and transcripts

Bourne and Fox, eds., *Alcoholism;* Bychowski and Despert, eds., *Specialized Techniques in Psychotherapy;* Carmean and Rathbone, *American Art at Mid-Century;* Eisenstein, ed., *Neurotic Interaction in Marriage;* Fox. ed., *Alcoholism;* Fox and Lyon: *Alcoholism;* Friedman, *JP;* Gruen, *The Party's Over Now;* Hefner, ed., *East Hampton's Heritage;* Hess, *Abstract Painting;* Marlborough-Gerson Gallery, *JP;* Masserman, *Current Psychiatric Therapies; The Medical Clinics of North America;* Namuth, *Pollock Painting;* Nemser, *Art Talk;* FVOC, *JP;* OC&T, *JP;* Brodovitch, "*JP," Portfolio;* Betty Parsons Gallery, *JP: 1950;* Betty Parsons Gallery, *JP: 1951;* Potter, *To a Violent Grave;* Putz, *JP;* Barbara Rose, *LK;* Bernice Rose, *JP;* Seldes, *The Legacy of Mark Rothko;* Solomon, *JP;* Tabak, *But Not for Love;* Thompson, *On Growth and Form.*

Lawrence Alloway, "Pollock's Black Paintings," *Arts,* May, 1969; "American Fashion: The New Soft Look," *Vogue,* Mar. 1, 1951; [Alexey Brodovitch], "JP," in *Portfolio;* DP&G, "Who Was JP?" *Art in America,* May–June 1967; Ruth Fox, "The Alcoholic Spouse," in Eisenstein, ed., *Neurotic Interaction in Marriage;* Ruth Fox, "Disulfiram (Antabuse) as an Adjunct to the Treatment of Alcoholism," in Fox. ed., *Alcoholism;* Ruth Fox, "Modified Group Psychotherapy for Alcoholics," *Postgraduate Medicine,* Mar. 1966; Ruth Fox, "A Multidisciplinary Approach to the Treatment of Alcoholism," *International Journal of Psychiatry,* Jan. 1968; Ruth Fox, "Psychotherapeutics of Alcoholism," in Bychowski and Despert, eds., *Specialized Techniques in Psychotherapy;* Ruth Fox, "Treatment of Chronic Alcoholism," in Masserman, *Current Psychiatric Therapies;* Ruth Fox, "Treatment of Chronic Alcoholism," in *The Medical Clinics of North America;* Ruth Fox, "Treatment of the Problem Drinker," in Bourne and Fox, eds., *Alcoholism;* Robert Goodnough, "Pollock Paints a Picture," *Art News,* May 1951; Robert Goodnough, "Reviews and Previews," *Art News,* Dec. 1950; "JP: An Artists' Symposium, Part I," *Art News,* Apr. 1950?; Ken Kelley, "Betty Parsons Taught America to Appreciate What It Once Called 'Trash': Abstract Art," *People,* Feb. 29. 1978; "The Year's Best: 1950." *Art News,* Jan. 1951.

Lawrence Alloway, "The Art of JP: 1912–1956," *London Listener,* Nov. 27, 1958; p. 888; Howard Devree, review, *NYT,* Dec. 3, 1950; Flora Lewis, "Two Paris Shows à la Pollock," *NYT,* Oct. 3, 1979; Stuart Preston, "Among One-Man Shows," *NYT,* Oct. 21, 1951.

Jackson Pollock (film), produced by Hans Namuth and Paul Falkenberg, narration by JP, music by Morton Feldman, 1951.

JP, will and letter of request, Mar. 9, 1951; Police Log, East Hampton Town Police, Dec. 28, 1951.

CG, int. by Kathleen Shorthall for *Life*, Nov. 9. 1959, Time/Life Archives; Elwyn Harris, int. by Shorthall for *Life*, Nov. 9, 1959, Time/Life Archives; Alfonso Ossorio, int. by Shorthall for *Life*, Nov. 9, 1959, Time/Life Archives; JP, int. by William Wright, WERI, Westerly, R.I., 1951; Tony Smith, int. by James T. Vallière, Aug. 1965, AAA.

Interviews

James Brooks; Fritz Bultman; Peter Busa; Nicholas Carone; Giorgio Cavallon; Herman Cherry; Violet de Laszlo; Ted Dragon; Ray Kaiser Eames; Jimmy Ernst; Morton Feldman; Herbert Ferber; B. H. Friedman; David Gibbs; Joe Glasco; Grace Glueck; CG; Budd Hopkins; Edward Hults; Harry Jackson; Paul Jenkins; Buffie Johnson; Reuben Kadish; Gerome Kamrowski; LK; John Little; Conrad Marca-Relli; Herbert Matter; ACM; George Mercer; John Bernard Myers; Annalee Newman (int. by David Peretz); Constantine Nivola; Doug Ohlson; Alfonso Ossorio; Philip Pavia; Vita Peterson; CCP; Milton Resnick; May Tabak Rosenberg; Irving Sandler; Jim Shepperd; Jane Smith; Herman Somberg; Ruth Stein; Michael Stolbach; Allene Talmage; Esteban Vicente; Harriet Vicente; Joan Ward; Helen Wheelwright; Enez Whipple; Roger Wilcox; Betsy Zogbaum; Howard Zucker.

NOTES

Winds; elms: MJP to FLP and Jonathan, Dec. 3, 1950. **Lee terrified of storms:** Stein. **Hanging show:** Cavallon. **Lee and Eames watching:** Eames. **"All you people":** Q. by Kamrowski. **"It was more":** LK. See Allan Kaprow in "JP: An Artists' Symposium," p. 60. **"It was bigger":** MJP to FLP, MLP, and Jonathan, Dec. 3, 1950. **"Too big":** Q. by friend, name withheld by request. **"A big smile":** MJP to FLP, MLP, and Jonathan, Dec. 3, 1950. **"Absolutely ashen":** Zogbaum. **Nothing in reserve:** Hess, q. in Alloway. "The Art of JP," p. 888. **Drinking bourbon:** CG. **"I am a great artist"; "I don't care":** Q. by Feldman. **Gallery-going and parties:** LK to Ossorio, spring 1950. **Depression deepened:** Little. **"More than 90":** JP to Ossorio, Jan. 6, 1951. **Barging into de Laszlo's:** De Laszlo. **Sessions with Hubbard:** JP to Ossorio, Jan. 1951. **"Drunken howlers":** Ossorio to LK and JP, n.d.

Paintings intimidating: Kamrowski, recalling Parsons. **"Overhung":** CG. **Prices:** Catalogue for "JP," exhibition at Betty Parsons Gallery, Nov. 28–Dec.16, 1950. **Disaster:** Parsons, q. in Potter, p. 134. **"Spread over":** Friedman, p. 198; Parsons (q. in Potter, p. 134) says it was only $1,200. **"Heartbreaking"; "a terrible down":** Q. in Potter, p. 134. **Greenberg not there:** CG. **"Deeply bitter":** Jackson. **"Furious":** CG. **"All you've written":** Q. by CG. **"This is Jackson":** Q. by Motherwell, q. in Potter, p. 152. **"More than ever before":** Devree, review, *NYT*, Dec. 3, 1950. **"Found a discipline":** Goodnough, "Reviews and Previews," p. 47. In contrast, Greenberg considered *Number 32* the only "dud" in the show.

"Prod Tony": Ossorio to LK and JP, n.d. **"The concentration here":** JP to Ossorio and Dragon, Feb. 1951. **"A new gallery":** JP to Ossorio and Dragon, June 7, 1951. **Rocky relationship:** See Parsons, q. in DP&G, "Who Was JP?" p. 55; see also Parsons, q. in Potter, p. 109. **Complaints about too many artists:** Friedman; Ossorio; Stolbach, recalling LK. **Not pushing sales:** Parsons, q. in "Betty Parsons," p. 83: "I've never pushed sales very hard. Most dealers love the money. I love the painting." **No long-range plans:** Ossorio, q. in Potter, p. 142. **Cavalier treatment:** Ferber; Wheelwright. **Slipshod records:** See Seldes, p. 23. **Caring for her own art:** Ferber. **"Gallery dabbler"; "ego trip shows":** Q. by Stolbach. **"Betty's bins":** Tony Smith, q. by Jane Smith. **"A lot of unrest":** JP to Ossorio and Dragon, Feb. 1951.

List of lesser-knowns: See Potter, p. 137. **Hess's motivation:** Somberg. **Hess championing de Kooning:** Pavia, q. in Gruen, p. 272: "Tom Hess was building [de Kooning] up." **"So much ridicule":** Q. in Gruen, p. 272. **"The de Kooning camp":** Ernst. **"I don't need":** Q. by Ernst. *The Betrothal:* Friedman, p. 147. **"Sat clutching":** Pavia, q. in Friedman, p. 148. **"Why'd you do that?"; "a rotten book":** Q. in Friedman, p. 148. **"An all-time low":** JP to Ossorio, Jan. 1951. **"Abstract Painting and Sculpture":** Jan. 23–Mar. 25. JP's *Number 1, 1948* was shown. See Friedman, p. 170. **Jackson's behavior at MOMA; driven home by Lin-**

deberg: Cavallon. **"Couldn't get any idea":** JP to Ossorio, Jan. 1951.

Lee canceling trip: As late as late January, JP was still planning for Krasner to accompany him; see JP to Ossorio, Jan. 1951. **Objections to "contest":** In JP to Ossorio, Jan. 1951, JP referred to serving on a jury as "something I swore I'd never do." **Expenses paid:** SMP to FLP, MLP, and Jonathan, Mar. 10. 1951. **"I think seeing Chicago":** JP to Ossorio, Jan. 1951. **Hard-nosed:** CG. **"Middle-of-the-road":** Friedman, p. 171. **Disappointing":** JP to Ossorio and Dragon, Feb. 1951. **Culberg:** He owned seventeen Dubuffets, one of which he had recently given to the Art Institute; JP to Ossorio and Dragon, Feb. 1951. *Number 2, 1950:* OC&T 261, II, p. 84. **Place of honor:** Isaacs to JP, Feb. 22, 1952. **Awards dinner:** Hopkins.

Hubbard's recommendation: LK. **Fox's age:** Friedman, p. 172. Fox was born on June 21,1895, interned at Peking Union Medical College from 1925 to 1929 on a Rockefeller Foundation grant, and graduated from Rush Medical College in 1926. She was a resident at Colorado Psychopath Hospital in Denver from 1926 to 1927 and had been doing her groundbreaking research on disulfiram since 1949. **"Depth analysis" and group support:** See Fox, "Treatment of Chronic Alcoholism," p. 110. **"Motivation . . . evaporates":** Fox. "Treatment of the Problem Drinker by the Private Practitioner," p. 228. **"The treating team":** Fox, "Treatment of the Problem Drinker by the Private Practitioner," p. 229. **Two hours:** Fox, "Treatment of the Problem Drinker by the Private Practitioner," p. 231. **Sympathetic and firm:** Fox, "A Multidisciplinary Approach to the Treatment of Alcoholism," p. 37. **"Longings for omnipotence":** Fox, "A Multidisciplinary Approach to the Treatment of Alcoholism," p. 36. **"Problems in the sexual area":** Fox and Lyon, p. 82. **"An unconscious fantasy":** Fox and Lyon, p. 156.

"Vestigial traces": Fox and Lyon, p. 84. **"Completely dominate":** Fox and Lyon, p. 89. **"A waste of . . . time":** Fox, "A Multidisciplinary Approach to the Treatment of Alcoholism," p. 37. **"Postponing . . . abstinence":** Fox, "Treatment of the Problem Drinker by the Private Practitioner," p. 234. **Disulfiram:** See Fox, "Treatment of Chronic Alcoholism," p. 110. **"Forced him":** Q. by Newman, int. by Peretz. **Details of will:** JP, Will and Letter of Request, Mar. 9, 1951. **"Modern art to me":** Int. by William Wright, 1951.

"Dour son of a bitch": Barbara Hale to LK and JP, July 20, 1951. **Portfolio:** [Brodovitch], "JP," n.p. *Art News* citation: "The Year's Best," pp. 42–43, 58–59. **"The new soft look":** "American Fashion," pp. 156–59. *Number 3, 1951:* OC&T 818, III, p. 297. Friedman (p. 173) says that in March, a JP watercolor entitled *Number 1, 1951* appeared in the Whitney Annual. We have been unable to identify the work. It could have been *Number 7, 1951* (OC&T 815, III, p. 294), an ink drawing on rice paper, which appeared in the following year's Whitney "Annual Exhibition of Contemporary American Sculpture, Watercolors, and Drawings," Mar. 13–May 4, 1952. **"Pollock uses metallic paint":** Goodnough, "Pollock Paints a Picture," p. 41. **Ninth Street Show:** May 21–June 10, 1951. **Plans for October show:** Oct. 2–27, 1951; OC&T IV, p. 264. **"Automatic painting":** Arnaud Raynor to JP, Aug. 25, 1951. **Tokyo Exhibition:** Feb. 27–Mar. 18, 1951; see Friedman, p. 173. **Mount Pleasant letter:** S. Carl Fracassini, Art Department, Iowa Wesleyan College, to JP, Apr. 8, 1951. *Number 31, 1949:* OC&T 242, II, p. 64. *Number 12A, 1948:* OC&T 200, II, pp. 20–21; "Calligraphic and Geometric: Two Recent Linear Tendencies in American Painting"; see Friedman, p. 159, where, through a typographical error, the original painting in this exhibition is misidentified as *Number 13, 1949*. **Fargo:** Jan. 8–29, 1951. **Fort Worth:** Texas Christian University, June 2–23, 1952. **Galerie Nina Dausset:** Friedman, pp. 173–74. **"Decadent bourgeois":** Soviet journalist, q. in Friedman, p. 168, citing Thomas Hess's manuscript for *Abstract Painting*.

Drawings on Japanese paper: JP to Ossorio, Jan. 1951: "I have been making some drawings on Japanese paper." **Collages:** *Number 2, 1951.* OC&T 1039, IV, pp. 114–15; OC&T 1040, IV, pp. 116–17. **Sculpture:** OC&T 1054, IV, p. 130. **"Sculpture by Painters":** Mar. 27–Apr. 21, 1951. **Script for film:** See Putz, *JP*, pp. 108–09, which includes a facsimile. Namuth's claim (n.p.) that the script was a "communal effort" in which JP took part is, at best, an exaggeration. **"Authenticity":** Namuth, n.p. **"My home":** Narration to *JP*, produced by Hans Namuth and Paula Falkenberg, 1951. **Nervous haste:**

Potter, p. 139. **Jackson appalled by voice:** JP to Ossorio and Dragon, June 7, 1951. **"Music-effects":** Falkenberg. q. in Namuth, n.p. **Balinese folk music:** Solomon, p. 320: Gamelan music. **"But Paul":** Q. by Falkenberg, in Namuth, n.p. **No money for score:** Namuth, n.p. **Lee not liking film:** Nivola, q. in Potter, p. 140; Lewis, "Two Paris Shows à la Pollock." **Cage work:** *Imaginary Landscape No. 4,* 1951. **"I couldn't abide":** Q. by Sandler. **Cage introducing Feldman:** Feldman, q. in Potter, p. 139. **Feldman a young friend:** JP to Ossorio and Dragon, June 7, 1951. **Ink drawing as fee:** Feldman, q. in Potter, p. 139. **"[I] wrote the score":** Q. in Friedman, p. 173. Feldman's score for two cellos was recorded by Daniel Stern; Namuth, n.p.

"Might be great": JP to Ossorio and Dragon, June 7, 1951. **Film showing:** Several famous people who were invited didn't come, including Blanchette and Nelson Rockefeller; Blanchette Rockefeller to JP, June 11, 1951, and David D. [Boyer], secretary to Nelson Rockefeller, to JP, June 11, 1951. **Black ink drawings:** See, e.g., OC&T 787–96, III, pp. 272–77. **Lee shocked:** LK, int. by Friedman, in Marlborough-Gerson Gallery, n.p.: "I had no idea why figures reemerged in his work, or why he limited himself to black." **"Drawing on canvas":** JP to Ossorio and Dragon, June 7, 1951. **Using Brush:** See, e.g., *Number 11, 1951,* OC&T 341, II. pp. 160–62. **Lee seeing image:** Little. **"Early images":** JP to Ossorio and Dragon, June 7, 1951.

Smith's flattery: Jane Smith: "Tony would say, 'These are the artists: Newman, Pollock, Rothko, Still.' And he'd just say it over, and over, and over, and then you'd hear it played back." See also Myers. It helped that Smith wasn't (yet) a painter: He later said (q. by Shepperd) that he was able to get along with the painters because he "wasn't directly competing with them." **Sitting together in silence:** Ward. **Devotion to Smith:** Brooks; Bultman. **Letters to Ossorio:** JP to Ossorio and Dragon, Feb. 1951: "Tony has finally gotten two houses—one design is finished—really something terrific." **Jane leaving:** Smith. **Smith's weekend visits:** Johnson, q. in Potter, p. 123. **Evenings together:** Carmean and Rathbone, p. 148. **Oriental philosophy:** Tony Smith, q. in DP&G, "Who Was JP?" p. 54. **"Constructive dream":** JP to Ossorio, Jan. 1951.

"Try something new": Tony Smith, q. by Johnson, *Triad:* OC&T 198, II, p. 19. *White Cockatoo:* OC&T 194, II, p. 14. **Sketching together:** Ohlson. **"The Orozco":** Q. by Smith, int. by Vallière, Aug. 1965. **Refugees from Orozco:** For O'Connor's often misguided interpretations of these figures, see FVOC, *JP.* **Imagery kept alive:** See e.g., *War,* OC&T 765, III, pp. 254–55 (1947); 770–75, III, pp. 259–61 (1946–47); 783, III, p. 267 (1948–49). Smith's wife Jane recalls that "Tony and Jackson had this mutual feeling about [Orozco]. They loved his work and talked about it often." **Joseph Smith:** Jane Smith.

Gift of paper and ink: Carmean, in Carmean and Rathbone, p. 137: "Tony Smith recalls giving Pollock a booklet or pad of rice paper, in a long scroll-like format on September 26, 1950." But Jane Smith recalls buying the rice paper as a present for JP around Christmas time that year when JP and Lee Krasner were staying at Ossorio's house in MacDougal Alley: "We went to Chinatown with Barney [Newman] and Lee [Krasner]. Jackson did not go because he didn't feel well. I got the idea that we must take something back to him, so I bought rice paper for him in a Chinese store." **Jackson experimenting:** See OC&T 811–26, III, pp. 290–305. **Ghost image:** Carmean and Rathbone, p. 137. **Gouache:** OC&T 814, III, p. 293 (white gouache); OC&T 820, III, p. 299 (green gouache). **Watercolor:** OC&T 824, III, p. 303; *Number 18, 1951,* OC&T 826, III, p. 305. **Paint:** *Number 8, 1951,* OC&T 816, III, p. 295. **"A very clear":** De Laszlo.

Anatomies emerging in piles: *Number 16, 1951,* OC&T 337, II, p. 156 (totemic figures, heads, eyes, body parts, all mixed up); *Number 9, 1951.* OC&T 340, II, p. 159. **Animals:** *Number 23, 1951 "Frogman,"* OC&T 335, II, p. 153 (could be a bull, heavily obscured; O'Connor sees a female figure); *Number 21, 1951,* OC&T 334, II, p. 152 (figure on left side; O'Connor sees a monkey). **Totemic figures:** *Number 3, 1951 (Image of a Man),* OC&T 321, II, p. 134. **Reclining figures:** *Number 11, 1951,* OC&T 341, II, pp. 160–62 (O'Connor sees a reclining figure). **Crucifixion:** *[Black and White Painting III],* OC&T 332, II, p. 150 (Christ-like figure; O'Connor sees a figure taken from Orozco's mural, *The Trench,* 1952; FVOC, p. 13.) **Hulking females:** *Number 27, 1951,* OC&T 328, II, pp. 144–45 (head on right with "dream" over it; Orozcoesque

woman on left, undoubtedly painted as two pictures but left uncut). **Portraits:** *Number 24, 1951,* OC&T 331, II, p. 149 ("double" head, not so disguised). **All but obliterated:** *Number 4, 1951,* OC&T 316, II, p. 129, acquired by Ruth Fox. **Child on lap:** *Number 20, 1951,* OC&T 338, II, p. 157 (O'Connor sees a seated figure with a child in its lap). **Bull in field:** *Number 14, 1951,* OC&T 336, II, pp. 154–55 (bull or she-wolf type image). **Woman with skeletal family:** *Number 7, 1951,* OC&T 324, II, pp. 138–39 (an abstracted version, perhaps, of the early canvas of the horrifying woman with the pendulous breasts surrounded by six actual skeletons, one for each of the six men in Stella's life). **Upside down:** *[Black and White Painting II],* OC&T 330, II, p. 148. He also combined images, as in *Number 7, 1951,* OC&T 324, II, pp. 138–39. **Remnants:** LK, int. by Friedman, in Marlborough-Gerson Gallery, n.p. **One after another:** This process can be seen clearly in *[Black and White Polyptych],* OC&T 298, II, pp. 120–21. **"Should I cut it":** Int. by Friedman in Marlborough-Gerson Gallery, n.p. **"Rubensesque":** Tony Smith, int. by Vallière, Aug. 1965. *Number 14, 1951:* OC&T 336, II, pp. 154–55. **Echo:** OC&T 345, II, pp. 166–67. **"His control was amazing":** Friedman, introduction to Marlborough-Gerson Gallery, n.p. According to Alloway ("Pollock's Black Paintings," pp. 40–43), the paintings should be called "black" rather than "black and white," since no white paint was used. **Drawing into painting:** See Bernice Rose, *JP.* **"Was worried":** Q. in Potter, p. 204.

Binges: Wilcox. **Beer from Miller's:** Marca-Relli. **Federico sobering him up:** Talmage. **"Slumped over":** Wilcox. **"Pollock got there first":** Int. by Shorthall, Nov. 9, 1959. **AA meetings:** Potter, p. 218. **"Blabbermouths":** Q. by Busa. **"Lonelyhearts":** Q. by Potter, p. 218. **"They got to drink":** Q. by Potter, p. 218. **"Too red-hot":** Penny Potter, q. in Potter, p. 218. **"Without Antabuse":** Fox, "The Alcoholic Spouse," p. 166; Fox also wrote (Fox and Lyon, p. 175): "Antabuse alone can cure very few if any cases of alcoholism; taken in conjunction with psychotherapy, it can be of very real use." **Regent Hospital:** Zucker: Between Lexington and Park; not the hospital of the same name that currently exists. Dr. Zucker, who examined JP for Dr. Fox during one of his visits, was amazed by the "thick wads of firm tissue under Jackson's kneecaps." JP told him that he got them "because I paint on my knees." JP was forthcoming during the interview, refusing only to own up to having hidden the bottle of scotch during his last visit. **Scotch in lavatory:** Zucker. **"Dear Jackson":** Valentine Macy to JP, June 25, 1951.

"Even more determinedly": Larry Rivers, q. in "JP: An Artists' Symposium, Part I," p. 32. **"Very quiet summer":** JP to Ossorio and Dragon, Aug. 1951. **"Absolutely roaring":** Zogbaum. **Pathetic and menacing:** See Potter, p. 136. **Maidstone Club set:** See Enez Whipple, q. in Potter, p. 112. **Locals thinking him crazy:** Edward Hults; Talmage. **"Turn all the lights out":** Q. in Potter, p. 136. **"Phony cowboy":** Q. by Wilcox. **"It just wasn't the same":** Wilcox. **"I think the house":** JP to Ossorio and Dragon, Aug. 1951. **"The Creeks":** Ossorio; Hefner, ed., pp. 109–10. **"Formidable sugar magnate":** Gibbs, recalling LK. **"Well, fuck it":** Q. by LK, q. by Gibbs. **"Went off to a bar":** Q. by Gibbs.

Lee's work liberated: See Barbara Rose, pp. 66–69. **"Lee is doing":** JP to Ossorio and Dragon, June 7, 1951. **Ninth Street Show:** May 21–June 10, 1951. **"The little lady":** Henry Jackson. **Lee's work bigger:** She painted more than one 4'10"-x-6'10½" work—*Blue and Black,* 1951–53, and *Untitled,* 1951. **Lee insisting on Parsons visit:** Barbara Rose (p. 70) says it was in spring, but JP and LK didn't return to Springs until the second week in May; SMP to MLP, FLP, and Jonathan, June 4, 1951. **Jackson acquiescing:** Bultman. **"[Jackson] telephoned me":** Parsons, q. in DP&G. "Who Was JP?" pp. 48–59. See also Nemser (p. 92) where Krasner tries to use JP's phone call to refute the argument that he saw her as a competitor. **Ended in Regent Hospital:** Zucker.

"This was some woman": Int. by Peretz. **"Languid poses":** Tabak, p. 53. **Hofmann, de Kooning:** Esteban Vicente; Harriet Vicente. **Zogbaum:** Peterson. **Feldman:** Friedman. **Guston:** Esteban Vicente; Harriet Vicente. **An affair":** Tabak, p. 56. **"Could not wait":** Tabak, pp. 129–30. **"Knockout":** Carone. **"Play with":** Rosenberg. **"Count the notches":** Kadish. Glueck: "It was pure Mozart, pure Don Giovanni." **No affair:** Peterson; Esteban Vicente; Harriet Vicente. The woman's husband: "I never heard that, and she would have told me the truth. Lee believed it, but she was paranoid about these things." **Late one night:** LK. Rosen-

berg rental: The Rosenbergs had rented a house from Wilfrid Zogbaum to be used as a studio for Harold but had moved to it temporarily because it was better insulated than their own house on Neck Path. **"Don't you hurt":** Q. by May Rosenberg. **Jackson looking for mystical treatment:** See Potter, p. 146. **"Turn it on":** Q. in Potter, p. 146. **Hubbard recommending "biochemist":** Ossorio. **"Drive his thirst":** Dragon. **Park Avenue offices:** Ossorio. **Description of Mark:** Ossorio. **"Business Manager"; "Psychological-Chemistry, Inc.":** Mark to JP, Dec. 4, 1952. **"Best living advertisement":** Q. by Ossorio. **Treatment of mother:** Ossorio. **"Svengali air":** Potter, p. 145. **Jackson falling under spell:** Dragon. **"Chemical derangement":** JP, q. in Potter, p. 146. **No milk products:** CG, int. by Shorthall, Nov. 9, 1959. **"Eat no bird":** Ossorio. **Fowl shot within two hours:** Dragon. **Daily baths:** Friedman, q. in Potter, p. 145. **Soy-based "emulsion":** Potter, p. 145. **"Lest it lose":** Ossorio, int. by Shorthall, Nov. 9, 1959. **"The box would":** Ossorio, q. in DP&G, "Who was JP?" p. 58. Ossorio gave conflicting testimony on how many bottles constituted a week's supply, saying once (int. by Shorthall, Nov. 9, 1959) that it was four and once (q. in DP&G, "Who Was JP?" p. 58) that it was seven. **"Find its own level":** JP, q. by Ossorio. **Copper and zinc:** Raphael Gribitz, q. in Potter, p. 145. **"Oh, dear God":** Wilcox.

Lee visited Hubbard and working: Dragon, q. in Potter, p. 203. **Reversal in Lee's work:** Barbara Rose, p. 70. **"[Lee's] work":** SMP to FLP, MLP, and Jonathan, Nov. 30, 1951. **McCoys at opening:** SMP to CCP, Oct. 22, 1951. **Lee complimented:** Mercer. **Preston review:** Preston, "Among One-Man Shows." **Lee's reaction to review:** LK.

Jackson's show: Nov. 26–Dec. 15, 1951. **"His painting confronts":** Betty Parsons Gallery, n.p. Friedman (p. 185) says that Ossorio wrote this in August 1951 and originally conceived of it as an introduction for the upcoming Paris exhibition with Tapié. In fact, Ossorio wrote it for this show and it was used later in the Paris catalogue. **Smith's suggestion:** JP to Ossorio and Dragon, June 7, 1951. **Parsons underwriting prints:** Friedman (p. 185) says the funding of $400 came from Alexander Bing. **Prints:** OC&T 1091–96, IV, p. 154. **Reproduced from paintings:** *Number 7, 1951*, OC&T 324, II, pp. 138–39; *Number 8, 1951*, OC&T 327, II, pp. 142–43; *Number 9, 1951*, OC&T 340, II, p. 159; *Number 19, 1951*, OC&T 333, II, pp. 150–51; *Number 22, 1951*, OC&T 344, II, p. 165; *Number 27, 1951*, OC&T 528, II, pp. 144–45. **Pulled by Sande:** See Friedman, p. 185; Solomon, p. 226: JP visited the shop one day to see what Sande was doing. "All I want is five hundred dollars," he told Sande; q. by ACM. **Visitors rare:** LK. **"Jesus":** Q. by Blake. **Dropping by drunk:** Jenkins. In fact, JP was drunk at his show for the first time: Paul Jenkins came by and saw that JP had "tied one on that day and he was sensing outrage and tension." **"Finality":** CCP. **"Foreboding of death":** De Laszlo. **Kerosene stove; "terrified":** LK. **"A wooden barn":** Q. in Namuth, n.p. **No clan gathering:** SMP to FLP, MLP, and Jonathan, Nov. 30, 1951. **"Santa shit":** Q. by Potter, p. 149. **Potter blocking road:** Potter, p. 149. **Dating and timing of crash:** The *East Hampton Star* article and all subsequent references have given the date as Saturday, December 29. However, a copy of the police log for the East Hampton Town Police (p. 571) indicates that the accident was reported by Patrolman Jacobs at "2000" (8:00 P.M.) on Friday, December 28, 1951. **Description of crash:** Police log, East Hampton Town Police, Dec. 28, 1951, p. 571. **"His dreamboat":** Potter, p. 149.

40. MIRACLE CURES

SOURCES

Books, articles, and transcripts

Ashton, *The New York School;* THB, *An Artist in America;* Burroughs, *THB;* Epstein and Barlow, *East Hampton;* Fox and Lyon, *Alcoholism;* Friedman, *JP;* Gruen, *The Party's Over Now;* Marlborough-Gerson Gallery, *JP;* McChesney, *A Period of Exploration;* Myers, *Tracking the Marvelous;* Namuth, *Pollock Painting;* Nemser, *Art Talk;* OC&T, *JP;* O'Neill, ed., *Clyfford Still;* Potter, *To a Violent Grave;* Rattray, *The South Fork;*

Rodman, *Conversations with Artists;* Rosenberg, *Barnett Newman;* Solomon, *JP;* Tabak, *But Not for Love.*

E. A. Carmean, "The Church Project: Pollock's Passion Themes," *Art in America,* summer 1982; Rosalind Constable, "The Betty Parsons Collection," *Art News,* Mar. 1968; DP&G, "Who Was JP?" *Art in America,* May–June 1967; J[ames] F[itzsimmons], "Fifty-Seventh Street in Review," *Art Digest,* Dec. 15, 1951; Ruth Fox, "The Alcoholic Spouse," in Eisenstein, ed., *Neurotic Interaction in Marriage;* Ruth Fox, "Treatment of Chronic Alcoholism," in Masserman, ed., *Current Psychiatric Therapies;* Stanley P. Friedman, "Last Years of a Tormented Genius," *New York* magazine, Oct. 29, 1973; CG, "Art Chronicle: Feeling Is All," *Partisan Review,* Jan.–Feb. 1952; F[airfield] P[orter], "Reviews and Previews," *Art News,* Dec. 1951, p. 48; Kenneth B. Sawyer, "U.S. Collectors of Modern Art 3: Alfonso Ossorio," *Studio International,* Mar. 1965; Calvin Tomkins, "A Keeper of the Treasure," *New Yorker,* June 9, 1975; Judith Wolfe, "Jungian Aspects of JP's Imagery," *Artforum,* Nov. 1972.

E. A. Carmean, "The Puzzle of Pollock's Paintings," *Washington Post,* Mar. 21, 1982; Howard Devree, "By Contemporaries," *NYT,* Dec. 2, 1951; Vivien Raynor, "JP—'He Broke the Ice,' " *NYT Magazine,* Apr. 2, 1967.

CG, int. by James T. Vallière, Mar. 20, 1968, AAA; Elwyn Harris, int. by Kathleen Shorthall of *Life,* Nov. 9, 1959, Time/Life Archives; Barnett Newman, int. by Shorthall for *Life,* Nov. 9, 1959, Time/Life Archives; Alfonso Ossorio, int. by Forrest Selvig, Nov. 19, 1968, AAA; Alfonso Ossorio, int. by Shorthall for *Life,* Nov. 9, 1959, Time/Life Archives; Betty Parsons, int. by Shorthall for *Life,* Nov. 9, 1959, Time/Life Archives.

Interviews

Emile de Antonio; Grace Borgenicht; Paul Brach; Jeremy Capillé; Nicholas Carone; Leo Castelli; Cynthia Cole; John Cole; Ted Dragon; Herbert Ferber; Joe Glasco; E. C. Goossen; CG; Edys Hunter; Harry Jackson; Mary Jackson; Sidney Janis; Buffie Johnson; Reuben Kadish; Gerome Kamrowski; LK; John Lee; John Little; Cile Downs Lord; Conrad Marca-Relli; Maria-Gaetana Matisse; George Mercer; John Bernard Myers; Annalee Newman (int. by David Peretz); Alfonso Ossorio; Vita Peterson; FLP; Becky Reis; Miriam Schapiro; Jon Schueler; Jim Shepperd; Jane Smith; Eloise Spaeth; Ronald Stein; Ruth Stein; Margot Stewart; Catherine Viviano; Steve Wheeler; Roger Wilcox; Betsy Zogbaum.

NOTES

Parsons meeting with artists: Tomkins, "A Keeper of the Treasure," p. 54: Parsons says the meeting took place at her studio apartment at 143 East Fortieth Street. **Still:** Ossorio (q. in Potter, p. 147) denies that Still attended the meeting, but in two other interviews, one with the authors and one with Shorthall, Nov. 9, 1959, he says Still was there. Also, Parsons (in Tomkins, "A Keeper of the Treasure," p. 52) says that Still was there. **Reinhardt:** Hunter. **Jackson sore from accident:** See Potter, p. 150. **"Most famous dealer":** Tomkins, "A Keeper of the Treasure," p. 54. **"If you don't":** Q. by Ossorio. **"These powerhouses":** Ossorio. **"Sorry":** Q. by Ossorio. **"It was *her* gallery":** Int. by Shorthall, Nov. 9, 1959. **Parsons committed to women:** Ossorio: Among those women were Agnes Martin, Anne Ryan, and Chryssa. **"Officious meddling":** LK. **Lost paintings:** *Number 25, 1950,* sent to Hilltop Theatre Art Room in Lutherville, Maryland, and almost lost; see Potter, p. 143. **Put off patrons:** There is good reason to believe that Parsons was the reason the mural commission from the AAA never came off. JP to Ossorio and Dragon about the commission in August 1951: "The mural (AAA) isn't definitely out—but is a matter of waiting (how long I don't know) and it involves other things and people too damned involved to try and explain in a letter." **Ossorio's show given little attention:** Potter, p. 146. **Sales:** Solomon, p. 225. **"A newer and loftier":** CG "Art Chronicle," p. 102. **"Learned to draw":** CG. **"Gained immeasurably":** Devree, "By Contemporaries." **"Most ambitious":** F[itzsimmons], "Fifty-Seventh Street in Review," p. 19; see also P[orter], "Reviews and Previews," p. 48, for a generally positive review. **Work on "The Tonight Show":** See OC&T 225, II, p. 48; OC&T are uncertain about the date of the appearance, giving it as "1952?" **"Surprised to hear":** Isaacs to JP, Feb. 22, 1952. **"Magnificent catalogue":** Davis to LK and JP, Dec. 4, 1951.

"Dear Jack": Parsons to JP, Jan. 31, 1952. **"Keep an open**

mind": Friedman, p. 193. **Omitting Parsons from catalogue**: Ossorio to LK and JP, Mar. 6, 1952: "I hope you like the catalogue. I left B.P. off as you told me to." **Parsons claiming no resentment**: Ferber. **"Hurt"; "disappointment"**: Q. in Gruen, p. 238. **"It has nothing"**: Q. by LK in Nemser, p. 94. **Visit to Matisse's gallery**: Viviano; 41 East Fifty-seventh. **"[Joe] asked Viviano"**: JP to Ossorio and Dragon, June 7, 1951. **"Didn't show Americans"**: Q. by Viviano. **MacIver, Roszak, and Riopelle at Matisse**: Myers. **"What do you think"**: Q. by Myers. **Duchamp shrugging shoulders**: Myers.

Lucifer: OC&T 185, I, pp. 186–87. *Number 7, 1950*: OC&T 272, II, p. 96. **Jackson gullible**: Dragon: "Mark got Jackson more and more in his power." **"Confusing arrangement"**: Q. by Barnett Newman, int. by Shorthall, Nov. 9, 1959. **"Umbrella agent"**: Ossorio. **"Precious fairies"**: THB, p. 265. **"Museum boys"**: Q. in Burroughs, p. 164. **"Pollock was caught"**: Int. by Shorthall, Nov. 9, 1959. **"Salesman"**: Ossorio. **Jackson arguing for Mark; "I used to be"; "Who would pay"**: Newman, int. by Shorthall, Nov. 9, 1959. **"Handling [his] own"**: Isaacs to JP, Feb. 22, 1952, in response to JP's phone call of February 20. **"Since we now"**: Isaacs to JP, Feb. 22, 1952. **Ossorio marketing Jackson's work**: Ossorio: He had persuaded his brother Robert to buy several works. **Return to U.S.**: Dragon. **Meeting with Sweeney and Lavannoux**: Ossorio, int. by Selvig, Nov. 19, 1968. **Constable**: Carmean, "The Church Project," p. 122. **Spaeths**: Spaeth. **"Suspended hexagons"; "honeycomb"**: Ossorio, int. by Selvig, Nov. 19, 1968. **Windows replacing walls**: Tony Smith, q. in Carmean, "The Puzzle of Pollock's Paintings." **Meeting in MacDougal Alley**: Friedman, pp. 203–04. **"Incomprehension"; "Christian ethos"; "not one iota"; "stomped out"**: Ossorio, int. by Selvig, Nov. 19, 1968.

Ossorio arranging French show: Ossorio. **"I am both happy"**: Tapié to JP, Feb. 29, 1952. **Furious at Namuth**: JP to Ossorio and Dragon, Aug. 1951: "I would give him hell except he is terribly ill from a kidney operation." **Jackson impressed by catalogue**: JP to Ossorio, Mar. 30, 1952. **Ossorio's introduction translated**: Friedman, p. 191. **"Couldn't do too well"**: JP to Ossorio, Mar. 30, 1952. **"The exhibition"; five of fifteen sold**: Ossorio to JP, n.d. **"Out of this world"**: JP to Ossorio, Mar. 30, 1952. **"The newspapers"**: Ossorio to JP, n.d. **Really only two sales**: Friedman, pp. 191–92. There is some disagreement about prices. Friedman gives no prices; the ones quoted are from Ossorio's letter to JP at the time; a note in JP's files, dated Jan. 13, 1952, gives the prices as $750 and $500 respectively. **Not enough space**: Tapié to JP, Feb. 29, 1952. **Tapié bought two works at discount**: Ossorio to JP, n.d. **Expenses of show**: See Friedman, p. 192. **Import laws**: Ossorio's Byzantine solution (Ossorio to JP, n.d.) was "to have the crates sent to Switzerland, the pictures to be paid for in Swiss francs to be transferred to New York and the remaining paintings shipped in bond across France sealed in their crates and on to America." *Number 27, 1950*: OC&T 271, II, pp. 94–95. **Special, deep discount**: Ossorio to JP, n.d.: Pollak (the buyer) wanted both paintings for $2,700. **Jackson never saw money**: FVOC to E. V. Thaw, July 22, 1972. **"Misplaced"**: Ossorio. **"My experience"; "this getting settled"**: JP to Ossorio, Mar. 30, 1952. **Continued treatment**: Dragon; Ossorio.

MOMA's "15 Americans": Apr. 9–July 27, 1952. **Still no dealer**: CCP to SMP, Apr. 5, 1952. **"Good show"**: Q. by LK, int. by Friedman, in Marlborough-Gerson Gallery, n.p. We know it was Kootz from Ossorio, q. in DP&G, "Who Was JP?" p. 58. **"I'm better"**: Q. in Solomon, p. 173, citing interview with Joyce Kootz. **"Rusty iron"; "drunkard"**: Q. by Ferber. **Trying Egan's**: Harry Jackson; Stewart for location. **De Kooning and Kline at Egan's**: Mary Jackson of the Janis Gallery: De Kooning didn't begin to show with Janis until the "Man and Wife" show of 1949. **Egan a drinker**: Parsons, q. in Gruen, p. 240. **Description of Egan's gallery**: Stewart. **"Ten years earlier"; "come back"**: Q. by Harry Jackson. **"Ton of bricks"**: Myers to JP, Feb. 3, 1952. **"For all or part"**: Ossorio to JP, n.d. **Lewenthal courting him; "might be better"**: JP to Ossorio and Dragon, June 7, 1951. **Driving Borgenicht around**: Borgenicht, q. in Potter, p. 153. **"A Department store"**: JP to Ossorio and Dragon, June 7, 1951. **Parsons borrowing $5,000**: Constable, "The Betty Parsons Collection," p. 59. **At $200 a month**: Grant Mark to JP, Dec. 4, 1952. **Considering textiles**: Little. **Teaching job**: Julien Levy, q. in Potter, p. 109. **Asking Potter for work**: Potter,

p. 127. **Linoleum; "exhausted"**: Goosen. **"Talking about galleries"**: Q. by Kamrowski. **"Pollock is available"**: Q. by Janis. **"Don't you think"**: Q. in Gruen, p. 247. **"Sidney"**: Q. by Janis, q. in Gruen, p. 246; see also Friedman, p. 193. **"Sharp business sense"**: Janis. **"Always drunk"**: Janis, q. by Castelli. **Gallery started in 1948**: Janis. **"Only the best"; "his collection"**: Gruen, p. 243. Zogbaum: "He never made any pretenses about taking on any artist who wasn't recognized." **"[He] came in"**: Janis, q. in Gruen, p. 247. **Janis's artists**: Mary Jackson. **Castelli's help**: Brach. **De Kooning deserting Egan**: Castelli has a clear memory that de Kooning's move to Janis predated JP's. **Paris reviews**: Tapié to JP, Feb. 29, 1952. **Janis a businessman**: De Antonio. **Janis willing to spend**: Parsons, q. in Potter, p. 129. **Jackson not caring for Janis**: Harry Jackson; Little. **Jackson resenting interview**: Harry Jackson. **"Goddamn sons of bitches"; "who the fuck"**: Q. by Harry Jackson. **"This is *the* guy"**: Q. by Potter, p. 157. Antonio: Castelli claims to have put JP together with Janis; see Potter, p. 138. But de Antonio, based on interviews with Janis, believes such claims are unfounded. **Almost setting house on fire**: Wilcox. **Gribitz**: Raphael Gribitz, q. in Potter, p. 218. **Storming into Levy's studio**: Ossorio. **"Painters should paint"**: Q. by Levy, in Potter, p. 109; see also Friedman, p. 90. **Dreading apologies**: Raphael Gribitz, q. in Potter, p. 218. **"Oh, God"**; Psychoanalyst, q. by Miller, q. in Potter, p. 157. **Unable to pay bills**: Borgenicht, q. in Potter, p. 153.

"Commitment to a life": Fox, "Treatment of Chronic Alcoholism," p. 111. **Objecting to criticism of Mark**: Friedman, p. 172. **Meeting his match**: Wolfe, "Jungian Aspects of JP's Imagery," p. 65. **Label of alcoholic**: Marca-Relli: "Jackson would say, 'I don't drink because I'm an alcoholic. I drink because I have such depression. I've got to fight the depression.'" **"Alcoholic arrogance"**: Fox, "The Alcoholic Spouse," p. 155. **"Maneuvers"; "to seem to deserve"**: Fox and Lyon, p. 83. **"Ingratiating"; "hostile"**: Fox, "The Alcoholic Spouse," p. 155. **Fear of desertion**: Fox and Lyon, p. 86. **"Egocentricity"; "loving another"**: Fox, "The Alcoholic Spouse," p. 155. **"Desire for vengeance"**: Fox, "The Alcoholic Spouse," p. 156. **Including Lee in treatment; sympathizing with Lee's ordeal**: Fox, "The Alcoholic Spouse," p. 155. **"Knowing he was an alcoholic"**: Fox, "The Alcoholic Spouse," p. 160: Fox notes the "uncanny ability of the alcoholic to seek in marriage an equally immature and needful person." **Fox's description of the relationship**: Fox and Lyon, pp. 185–86.

"Personality disturbances"; "even more serious"; "equally in need": Fox, "The Alcoholic Spouse," p. 159. **"To dominate"; "a threat"; "she derive[d] pleasure"**: Fox and Lyon, p. 183. **"Beat her up"; "fear of [losing] her own"; "more violent"; "from some immediate"**: Fox and Lyon, p. 186. **"Watched his diet"**: Tabak, p. 48. **Vashtis**: CG; Little; Parsons, q. in DP&G, "Who Was JP?" p. 55; Friedman, p. 181. We were unable to ascertain the first name of N. Vashti. **"The universal energy"**: Q. by Potter, p. 154. **"The reality"**: Q. by Raphael Gribitz, q. in Potter, p. 115. *The Prophet; Beasts, Men and Gods*; **captivated by Osindowsky**: Wilcox. **"Goddamn it"**: Q. by Raphael Gribitz, q. in Potter, p. 115. **Jackson quizzing Smith**: Jane Smith. **Converting to Catholicism**: Friedman, p. 203; see also Ossorio. **McCoys Catholic**: Ossorio.

Newman as comic figure: Myers, p. 93. **Affection but not respect**: Ferber; CG. **Beginning to paint**: Newman, int. by Shorthall, Nov. 9, 1959. **Not a true artist**: Adolph Gottlieb, q. in Gruen, pp. 258–59: Barney "was never an artist. If he became an artist, he became a manufactured artist. He was something of a fake—full of dialectics that had nothing to do with anything." Greenberg was one of the first to take Newman seriously. Sandler, p. 13 (citing CG, "Art Chronicle," pp. 100–01): "In 1952 Greenberg came to the conclusion that any artist as widely disparaged as Newman could not be all bad." **Newman's position derived from Parsons**: Kamrowski. **"Aesthetic philosophy"**: Myers, p. 93. **Not included in Miller's show; removing paintings from Parsons and vowing not to show**: Tomkins, "A Keeper of the Treasure," p. 54. **"It didn't matter"; only act of painting mattered**: CG. **"The artist's lot"**: Goosen.

Newman wrestling: Wilcox. **Going to movies**: Newman, int. by Shorthall, Nov. 9, 1959: The fights themselves were too expensive. **Incessant talk**: Newman, int. by Shorthall, Nov. 9, 1959. **Retrieved Jackson from binges; never telling Jackson to stop drinking**: Annalee Newman, int.

by David Peretz. **Admiring Jackson's machismo:** Newman, int. by Shorthall, Nov. 9, 1959, called him "very manly." **"More mature":** Int. by Shorthall, Nov. 9, 1959. **"Authentic flair":** Myers, p. 93. **Size:** Wilcox. **Erudition:** Kadish. **Treatment of wife:** Edys Hunter. **Sharing Al Capone's tailor:** Myers, p. 93.

"The largeness"; "a contained thing"; "the fight against": Newman, int. by Shorthall, Nov. 9, 1959. **"Geometry (perfection)":** Newman, q. in Rosenberg, p. 41. **"The taste for":** Newman, q. in Rosenberg, p. 24. **"Anyone can construct":** Newman, int. by Shorthall, Nov. 9, 1959. **Difficulty drawing from life:** CG. **"Transcendental self":** Rosenberg, p. 51. **"Experienced moment[s]":** Newman, q. in Rosenberg, p. 75. Rosenberg, p. 62: These were embodiments of the Jewish mystical concept of *Makom* or Place—"the habitation of the invisible God and a synonym of his being." **"Clues":** Newman, q. in Rosenberg, p. 27. **"Ceremonial performance":** Rosenberg, p. 30. **"A mystic situation":** Newman, int. by Shorthall, Nov. 9, 1959. **"I don't give a damn":** Q. by Wilcox.

"Any fool"; "matter of conscience": Q. in Ashton, p. 34. **"Can make a picture":** Q. in McChesney, p. 46. **War of words:** See O'Neill, ed., p. 27. **Sacrificing friendships:** In a letter to Mark Rothko, dated Apr. 20, 1949 (q. in O'Neill, ed., pp. 26–27), for example, he bragged that "[Andrew] Ritchie does not like me anymore!" **"The contemporary"; "a totalitarian":** Q. in O'Neill, ed., p. 180. **"Controlled by merchants":** Q. by Carone. **"The butchers":** Still to Mark Rothko, Apr. 20, 1949, q. in O'Neill, ed., pp. 26–27. **"The scholar":** Still to a friend, July 1950, q. in O'Neill, ed., p. 29. **"An exercise"; "the most contemptible":** Q. by Still, q. in O'Neill, ed., p. 191. **Claims to be first Abstract Expressionist:** CG. **Reply to Parsons:** Tomkins, "A Keeper of the Treasure," p. 54. **"The lonely pioneer":** Ashton, p. 34. **"Changed the nature":** Q. by JP, q. in Rodman, p. 84. **"Your show":** Still to JP, Sept. 14, 1952. **"Salon raconteur":** Still to Rosenberg, Sept. 14, 1952. We were unable to find the article referred to by Still. He might have been referring to Rosenberg's "American Action Painters," which appeared in the December issue of *Art News.* **"Two paragraphs":** Still to JP, Sept, 14, 1952.

"Handle himself"; "that guy's": JP, q. by Marca-Relli. But Wilcox: "I can remember Jackson saying that his name is very appropriate to his art. There's not much happening in it." **"Jackson succumbed":** Int. by Vallière, Mar. 20, 1968. **Baseball:** Solomon, p. 176. Also for the benefit of Tony Smith, who, says Jane Smith, was crazy about baseball. **"Goddamn, Rita":** Q. by Harry Jackson. **"Jack, I'm not":** Rita Benton, q. by Harry Jackson. **Elm Tree Inn story:** Harry Jackson. **"Tell me":** Q. by Harry Jackson. **Napeague strip:** Epstein and Barlow, p. 212. **Indian Field:** Rattray, p. 132. **Walking last few feet:** Jackson, q. in Potter, p. 142.

Jackson's reverie: Dragon; Ossorio. **Access to The Creeks:** Glasco. **Smith saying alcohol was useful:** CG. **"Cheap lousy fakes"; "frauds and fools"; "the only giant"; "the only painter alive"; "the only damn painter":** Q. in Tabak, pp. 47–48. **Destroying piano; Lee urging nonalcoholic punch:** Dragon. **Asking friends to watch Jackson:** Mercer. **"Keep him off the road":** Q. by Lord. **"Dissociate herself":** Tabak, p. 48. **Janis promised his pick:** Janis, q. in Potter, p. 158. **"An attempt to establish":** Cynthia Cole. **"She nursed him":** Int. by Shorthall, Nov. 9, 1959. **"Don't look at me":** Q. by Dorothy Miller, q. in Potter, p. 157. **"I think she hated":** Q. in Potter, p. 157. **"Lee wasn't the best":** Q. by Kamrowski. **"He would have to drink":** Q. by Johnson.

Hiding differences: Rosenberg. **"Go fuck yourself":** Q. by Harry Jackson. **"Whore"; "slut":** Q. by FLP. **"Ugly goddamn woman":** Q. by Harry Jackson. **"Some time alone":** Lord. **Lee asking for return of objects:** Lord. **Harris hearing screams:** Harris, int. by Shorthall, Nov. 9, 1959. **"You won't be able":** Q. by Ronald Stein. **Cigarette brands:** John Lee, recalling Krasner, who dated this dispute "sometime around '52." **"His feelings toward me":** Q. in Gruen, p. 233. **"There was never":** LK, q. in DP&G, "Who Was JP?" p. 50. **Not surprised by blows:** Peterson, who didn't say she saw JP hit Krasner, only that she would be surprised if he didn't. **Houseguests seeing bruises:** Harry Jackson; also Harris, int. by Shorthall, Nov. 9, 1959. **"Lost his temper":** Applehof, recalling LK. **"I'm gonna kill you":** Q. by Tony Smith, q. by Shepperd. **"You did it to him":** Q. by Kadish, recalling Sande.

Stella's arrival: SMP to FLP, MLP, and Jonathan, Oct. 27, 1952. **Stella's illness:** SMP to Irene Crippen, Nov. 15, 1952: "I have been on the burn most of the summer neuralgia in my chest and Rheumatism in my knees so stiff I could hardly move or turn over in bed. . . . somedays quite stiff and depends on the weather." Capillé, for the fact that it was bursitis. **"Both have colds":** SMP to CCP, Nov. 10, 1952. **Adding swirls:** *Number 1, 1952,* OC&T 358, II, pp. 182–83; begun in 1951, finished in 1952; see OC&T IV, p. 261, fig. 68. **Figurative painting covered up:** *Convergence: Number 10, 1952,* OC&T 363, II, pp. 186–89; underpainting is typical black and white figurative: OC&T II, p. 171. **"Some nice paintings":** SMP to FLP, MLP, and Jonathan, Oct. 27, 1952. *Number 12, 1952:* OC&T 364, II, pp. 190–91. **Faltering confidence:** CG, q. in Potter, p. 191. **Painting begun with Smith:** *Blue Poles: Number 11, 1952,* OC&T 367, II, pp. 193–97. **"Many, many times":** LK, q. in Namuth, n.p. **Working at Blue Poles:** Friedman, "Last Years of a Tormented Genius." **Belgian linen:** Solomon, p. 234. **Small stained canvases:** *Number 2A, 1952, Number 2B, 1952, Number 2C, 1952;* OC&T 359–61, II, pp. 184–85. **Five with dates altered:** *Number 6, 1952,* OC&T 350, II, p. 172; *Number 3, 1952,* OC&T 351, II, p. 173; *Number 4, 1952,* OC&T 352, II, p. 174; *Number 5, 1952,* OC&T 353, II, p. 175; *Number 7, 1952,* OC&T 354, II, pp. 176–77; Wilcox, for the altering of dates.

Trip to Deep River: SMP to CCP, Nov. 10, 1952; Stella erroneously says, "they were up for Thanksgiving." **Hanging until four:** Parsons, int. by Shorthall, Nov. 9, 1959; see also Parsons, q. in DP&G, "Who Was JP?" p. 55. **"Good-looking":** Reis. **"Like a fine musician":** Little. **"You'd better buy":** Q. by Kadish. **"Sharp-shooter":** Kadish. **"Jackson, let's get out":** Q. by Reis. **Kline and Jackson not seen again:** Reis. **Bennington College show:** Nov. 17–30, 1952. **Station wagon; dance studio:** Goosen: JP didn't help hang the show, which makes sense given how recently the Janis show had opened. **Feeley with Smith and Goossen:** Wheelwright; also Raynor, "JP—'He Broke the Ice,' " p. 64. **"Like an undertaker":** Goossen. **"Virtually motionless":** Raynor, "JP—'He Broke the Ice,' " p. 64. **Monosyllables:** Goossen. **Lee in charge of bar:** Wheelwright. **"Jackson, lay off":** CG. **"Nothing doing":** Q. by CG. **"Only fools":** CG. **"Wobbly"; "have their run":** CG. **"When you were off booze":** Q. by CG, q. in Potter, p. 165. **"Wasn't a success":** Lee knew, too: CG, q. in Potter, p. 163. **Jackson staring at Lavender Mist:** Dragon, q. in Potter, p. 135.

41. AGAINST THE WORLD

SOURCES

Books, articles, manuscripts, and transcripts

Ashton, *The New York School;* Ashton, *Yes, but . . . ;* Barrett, *The Truants;* Centre Georges Pompidou, *JP;* Friedman, *JP;* Gruen, *The Party's Over Now;* Samuel M. Kootz Gallery, *The Intrasubjectives;* Myers, **Tracking the Marvelous;** Nemser, *Art Talk;* OC&T, *JP;* O'Doherty, *American Masters;* Picon, *Surrealists and Surrealism;* Potter, *To a Violent Grave;* Rosenberg, *The Anxious Object;* Sandler, *The New York School;* Solomon, *JP:* Tabak, *But Not for Love.*

Robert Alan Aurthur, "Hitting the Boiling Point, Freakwise, at East Hampton," *Esquire,* June 1972; "Big City Dames," *Time,* Apr. 6, 1953; Robert Coates, "The Art Galleries," *New Yorker,* Nov. 22, 1952; DP&G, "Who Was JP?" *Art in America,* May–June 1967; J[ames] F[itzsimmons], "Fifty-Seventh Street in Review," *Art Digest,* Nov. 15, 1952; R[obert] G[oodnough], "Reviews and Previews," *Art News,* Dec. 1952; "JP: An Artists' Symposium, Part I," *Art News,* Apr. 1967; Max Kozloff, "The Critical Reception of Abstract-Expressionism," *Arts,* Dec. 1965; Max Kozloff, "An Interview with Robert Motherwell," *Artforum,* Sept. 1965; Robert Motherwell and Harold Rosenberg, Editors' Preface, *Possibilities: An Occasional Review,* Winter 1947–48; Robert Motherwell, "The Modern Painter's World," *Dyn,* Nov. 1944; JP, "My Painting," *Possibilities 1,* Winter 1947–48; Barbara Rose, "Hans Namuth's Photographs and the JP Myth: Part Two: Number 29, 1950," *Arts,* Mar. 1979; Barbara Rose, "JP et l'Art Americain," in Centre Georges Pompidou, *JP;* Harold Rosenberg, "The American Action Painters," *Art News,* Dec. 1952; Harold Rosenberg, "The Herd of Independent Minds: Has the

Garde Its Own Mass Culture?" *Commentary*, Sept. 1948; Harold Rosenberg, "Introduction to Six American Painters," *Possibilities 1*, Winter 1947–48; Harold Rosenberg, "The Mythic Act," *New Yorker*, May 6, 1967; Harold Rosenberg, "The Search for JP," *Art News*, Feb. 1961; William Rubin, "Pollock as Jungian Illustrator: The Limits of Psychological Criticism, Part II," *Art in America*, Dec. 1979; Gabrielle Smith, "Helen Has a Show," *New York*, Feb. 17, 1969; "The Year's Best: 1952," *Art News*, Jan. 1953; James T. Vallière, "De Kooning on Pollock," *Partisan Review*, Fall 1967.

Howard Devree, "Ingres to Pollock—A French Master's Work—Abstract Painting," *NYT*, Nov. 16, 1952; J. Hoberman, "Harold Rosenberg's Radical Cheek," *Village Voice Literary Supplement*, May 1986; Joseph Liss, "Memories of Bonac Painters," *East Hampton Star*, Sept. 13, 1983; Curtis Bill Pepper, "The Indomitable Bill de Kooning," *NYT Magazine*, Nov. 20, 1983.

Donnelly Lee Casto, "JP: A Biographical Study of the Man and a Critical Evaluation of His Work" (M.A. thesis), Tempe: Arizona State University, 1964; Ellen Gross Landau, "LK: A Study of Her Early Career (1926–1949) (Ph.D. thesis), Newark: University of Delaware, 1981; May Natalie Tabak, "A Collage" (unpub. ms.).

CG, int. by Kathleen Shorthall for *Life*, Nov. 9, 1959, Time/Life Archives; CG, int. by James T. Vallière, Mar. 20, 1968, AAA; JP, int. by Dorothy Seiberling for *Life*, July 18, 1949, Time/Life Archives.

Interviews:
Lionel Abel; Susan Barker; Norman Bluhm; Grace Gorgenicht; Charles Boultenhouse; Paul Brach; David Budd; Fritz Bultman; Peter Busa; Jeremy Capillé; Nicholas Carone; Leo Castelli; Giorgio Cavallon; Herman Cherry; Dorothy Dehner; Ted Dragon; Herbert Ferber; Leslie Fiedler; Phyllis Fleiss; B. H. Friedman; Joe Glasco; CG; Grace Hartigan; Eleanor Hempstead; Harry Jackson; Mary Jackson; Sidney Janis; Buffie Johnson; Reuben Kadish; Gerome Kamrowski; Hilton Kramer; LK; Ellen Landau; Ernestine Lassaw; Ibram Lassaw; Joe LeSueur; John Little; Beatrice Ribak Mandelman; Conrad Marca-Relli; George Mercer; John Bernard Myers; Alfonso Ossorio; Philip Pavia; Milton Resnick; May Tabak Rosenberg; Irving Sandler; Jim Shepperd; David Slivka; Jane Smith; Stephanie Sonora; Patsy Southgate; Ronald Stein; Michael Stolbach; Esteban Vicente; Harriet Vicente; Marta Vivas; Joan Ward; Steve Wheeler; Helen Wheelwright; Roger Wilcox.

NOTES

Head cold: SMP to CCP, Jan. 29, 1953. **Loper a clown:** Potter, p. 180. **Renovating studio:** SMP to CCP, Jan. 29, 1953: The shingling was going on in the dead of winter, not in spring, as stated in OC&T IV, p. 271. **Impossible to concentrate:** Little. **Destroying Guston's show:** Friedman, p. 223. **"Easel pictures":** CG. **"Embroidery":** Esteban Vicente. **"Topping everybody":** Cherry. **Switch in styles:** About 1951. **New style based on Monet:** Ashton, *Yes, but...*, p. 103. **Halfhearted:** Kramer: "Guston always had very ambivalent feelings about abstract art." Busa, who considered Guston "opportunistic," thought his abstractions all came out of *Shimmering Substance*. Even Kadish, later Guston's in-law, says, "Guston felt that kind of Midtown Gallery American art was going downhill and that the art world was heading in the direction of American Abstract Expressionism. It may very well be that he was exploiting the new situation." **"Probably jealous":** Q. in Potter, p. 153.

"Tantalizing": G[oodnough], "Reviews and Previews," p. 42. **"Quite magnificent":** F[itzsimmons], "Fifty-Seventy Street in Review," p. 17. **"Far more packed":** Devree, "Ingres to Pollock." **"I've always felt":** Coates, "The Art Galleries," pp. 178–79. **Landscape:** Devree ("Ingres to Pollock") complimented JP for "getting away from the confusion of means and ends which has been all too prevalent in nonobjec...

[...]: F[itzsimmons], "Fifty-Seventh Street [...] ollock takes up from where he left off [...]er 12, 1952*: OC&T 364, II, pp. 190– [...] Rothko and Newman; work slip-[...]01. **Inquiry about prints:** Charlotte [...]953. **Speech invitation:** Elliot Wilen-[...]er Union Students Association, AIA, to [...]erview request:** Richard S. Field to JP, [...] letter:** Miller to JP, Feb. 10, 1953; she

also told him that Edgar Kaufmann had donated *Number 12, 1949* (OC&T 233, II, p. 55) a small painting on paper. **Complaining:** Little. **Art News citation:** "The Year's Best: 1952," pp. 42–43.

Begging Stella to come: SMP to CCP, Jan. 29, 1953. **Cortisone injections:** Capillé. **Stella saying she would try:** SMP to CCP, Jan. 29, 1953. **Jackson seeking out Hubbard; offering to meet Stella; "rain or snow":** SMP to CCP, May 18, 1953. **Guests from *Partisan Review:*** May Rosenberg. **"A lot of shit"; "Listen, Jackson":** Q. by May Rosenberg. **Evening a trap:** LK. See also Resnick, q. in Potter, p. 181. **"How dare you!":** Q. by May Rosenberg. **"Don't tell me":** Q. by May Rosenberg in Potter, p. 181. **Lee storming out:** May Rosenberg. **Greenberg learning from Pantuhoff:** Bultman. **"Take him around"; "that mediocrity":** May Rosenberg. **Half-baked Kant:** See Barrett, pp. 137ff. See also Tabak, "Our Pal," in "A Collage," p. 295. **"A tipster":** "Action Painting: Crisis and Distortion," in Rosenberg, *The Anxious Object*, p. 43. **Rosenberg learning from de Kooning:** Carone. **"You can't do that":** Q. by de Kooning, q. in Potter, p. 183. **"Glittering phrasemaker":** Barrett, p. 143. **"Lamenting":** Aurthur, "Hitting the Boiling Point," p. 205.

"Respectable" sketch: May Rosenberg, int. by Landau, Feb. 22, 1980, q. in Landau, "LK," p. 98 n. 17. Brach: Miriam Schapiro's father, who knew Rosenberg well, said, "He tried bullshitting everyone, then he found the artists. They were pushovers." **American Guide Series:** Harold Rosenberg, q. in Gruen, p. 173. **New York weekends:** May Rosenberg. **"Two dogs":** Harold Rosenberg, q. by May Rosenberg. **"Individual protagonist":** Hoberman, "Harold Rosenberg's Radical Cheek," p. 11. **"The artist's problem"; "painting is":** Motherwell, "The Modern Painter's World," *Dyn*, pp. 9–14. **Huelsenbeck:** Picon, p. 32. **"Literature should be action"; "fell in love":** Motherwell, q. in Kozloff, "An Interview with Robert Motherwell," p. 37: Motherwell believed that Rosenberg's notion of "action" derived directly from that piece. In "Introduction to Six American Painters" (p. 229), Rosenberg invoked Huelsenbeck's militancy: "An action is not a matter of taste. You don't let taste decide the firing of a pistol or the building of a maze."

"If one is to continue": Motherwell and Rosenberg, Editors' Preface, p. 1. **"Work[ed] directly":** Rosenberg, "The Herd of Independent Minds," p. 244. **"The modern painter":** Rosenberg, introduction to Samuel M. Kootz Gallery, n.p. **"It doesn't matter":** Q. by CG. **Jackson's garbled version:** CG, int. by Shorthall, Nov. 9, 1959. Wheeler claims that, in 1947, he was the first to use the term "action" in relation to painting in print.

Rosenberg laboring: Aurthur, "Hitting the Boiling Point," p. 205: Rosenberg was an agonizingly slow writer. **Jackson playing central role:** Rosenberg later conceded as much in "The Mythic Act," p. 164. **"When I am in":** JP, "My Painting," pp. 78 ff. Compare JP's original holograph (OC&T IV, p. 241) with the rewritten version that appeared in the magazine. The former includes very little of the statement. Rosenberg ("The Search for JP," p. 58) later acknowledged the role this statement had in his thinking (without acknowledging his role in editing it): "JP's chief public statement about his work, a three-paragraph note written in 1947, is devoted entirely to method," he wrote in 1961; "it contains no reference to the paintings or what he was trying to achieve through them. Apparently, he assumed the value of what he did lay in his way of doing it." Obviously, Rosenberg was unaware of JP's public statements on the issue. In the 1950 radio interview, JP was asked, "Isn't it true that your method of painting, your technique, is important and interesting only because of what you accomplish by it?" "I hope so," he said. "Naturally, the result is the thing—and—it doesn't make much difference how the paint is put on as long as something has been said. Technique is just a means of arriving at a statement." **Rosenberg not liking Jackson's paintings:** Bluhm; Carone; Wilcox. Carone: When JP confronted Rosenberg, telling him that he knew nothing about art, Rosenberg said he knew enough to know that JP painted "like a monkey," referring to the monkey whose paintings had been reproduced in newspapers. **"Incapable of sustained":** Rosenberg, "The Search for JP," p. 59.

Caring more about ideas: See Myers (p. 68), quoting his own journal from Mar. 1946: "Harold believes that the visual arts exist on a lower level of human expression." See also Kozloff, "The Critical Reception of Abstract Expressionism,"

p. 33: For Rosenberg, as for Benton, paintings existed only "to illustrate a rhetorical field theory." **Rosenberg's *Art News* essay:** "The American Action Painters," pp. 22–23, 48–50. **"I think you wrote"; "smart kid":** Brach. **"So full of bullshit":** Kamrowski. **"Such a lie":** Carone. **"Drink too deeply":** Barrett, pp. 143–44. **"Not only unclear":** Abel: "To have action, you must have some element of destructiveness. If a lifeguard jumps in the water and saves someone from drowning, that's really not action, that's routine—that's what he *does*. But if I do it and almost drown, that's an action. There's got to be a destructive, perilous element. When Picasso paints a cock as Christ in the arms of the Virgin, he's attacking the church; that's an act." However, Abel may not be sufficiently crediting the emphasis that Rosenberg places on "risk" in his definition of action. **Smokey the Bear:** Hoberman, "Harold Rosenberg's Radical Cheek," p. 11, quoting Irving Howe's memoirs: "The sheer deliciousness of it, this cuddly artifact of commercial culture as the creature of our most unyielding modernist!" **"Numerous and inflammatory":** Rose, "JP et l'Art Americain," p. 18. **Tomlin reading article:** LK; see also O'Doherty, p. 109, and Rose, "JP et l'Art Americain," p. 19, both of which rely on LK. **Rosenberg calling Jackson a megalomaniac:** May Rosenberg. **Lee perceiving slights by Rosenbergs:** Lassaw. **Tomlin sweet-tempered:** Friedman. **Still coming by:** O'Doherty, *American Masters*, p. 109; Rose, "JP et l'Art Americain," p. 19. **"An attack on painting":** As characterized by CG, int. by Shorthall, Nov. 9, 1959. **Lee recommending rebuttal by Greenberg:** CG. **"A purely rhetorical":** CG to Donnelly Lee Casto, q. in Casto, "JP," p. 99. **"You get in a fight":** CG. **Sweeney no admirer of Greenberg:** Barrett, pp. 145–47. **According to Greenberg an attack on Jackson:** Kramer. **In Greenberg's opinion:** At this time, Greenberg considered JP "profoundly unsure of himself"; Rose, "Hans Namuth's Photographs . . . Part Two," p. 118; Rose (incorrectly, we think) calls this opinion "one of the monumental critical errors of the twentieth century." **Frankenthaler more receptive:** Wheelwright, Budd: "Greenberg couldn't force Pollock to do what he wanted. In a way, it was easier to make someone else do it. He knew damn well he couldn't have someone else using a bunch of sticks dripping paint, but, being a pretty good painter himself, he could see that you could take canvas and stain it. So Frankenthaler does it. And the next thing you know, Dzubas is doing it, and Morris Louis, and pretty soon you could hardly tell one of Greenberg's painters from the other." Frankenthaler's new style dated from 1950, the year she met Greenberg and the year she saw Pollock's show at Betty Parsons; see Gabrielle Smith, "Helen Has a Show," p. 46. **Greenberg's changed attitude toward Pollock:** Marca-Relli: "Jackson would get very drunk, and there'd be this scene, and they would practically kill each other." Myers: "Clem would threaten Jackson, and Jackson would threaten him back—Jackson would tell Clem that he was going to beat him up and knock him out, and so on and so forth." Greenberg: He gave a talk at the Guggenheim Museum and noted that Dubuffet "lost his stuff after 1950." In the discussion period that followed, Greenberg added—at the height of de Kooning's new popularity—that "De Kooning is another case of an artist who has lost his stuff." Not long afterward, Greenberg was sitting at a bar called Dillon's when de Kooning came up to him. "I heard what you said," de Kooning said, angry. "You're riding on Pollock's back the way Tom Hess is riding on my back." Greenberg said, "You son of a bitch. I don't believe Pollock said that. What would I get out of 'riding on Pollock's back'?" At that, de Kooning took a swipe at Greenberg's face, and a fight was prevented only when others stepped in and held them back; story from Greenberg. Ward: "He punched Clem Greenberg pretty good." **Jackson's annoyance:** Marca-Relli. **"Rosenberg's piece on me":** Q. by Friedman. **"How stupid":** Q. by Marca-Relli. **"Appalled":** Lee later said JP was "appalled"; see Rubin, "Pollock as Jungian Illustrator," p. 91 n. 56. **Lee still raging; "announced his liking":** O'Doherty, p. 109. **De Kooning's defense:** Rose, "JP et l'Art Americain," p. 19. **"New heights":** O'Doherty, p. 109. **De Kooning's retreat:** LK; Rose, "JP et l'Art Americain," p. 19. **"Betraying her":** LK, q. by Little. **Lee's grievances against de Kooning:** Little. **"Adored":** May Rosenberg. **"The greatest":** LK, q. by May Rosenberg. **Lee sitting in de Kooning's lap:** LK. **Bultman dragging Lee to shower:** Bultman; LK; Landau. **De Koo-**

ning accused of encouraging Jackson to drink: Wilcox. **De Kooning accused of sabotage:** May Rosenberg. **"Refusing to acknowledge":** LK, q. by Pavia. **Lee hating Elaine de Kooning:** Pavia; Stolbach. **Description of Elaine:** Slivka; Gruen, p. 207. **Suspicion that Elaine influenced Hess:** Friedman. **Asking Hess to write book:** Friedman, p. 148.

Jackson and de Kooning: Resnick: "Jackson never cared for anybody really." **Abel's visit:** Abel is not sure of the date; he thinks it was " '46, '47, something like that," but 1948 was the first summer that de Kooning spent in Springs. **Feelings of generosity:** CG, int. by Vallière, Mar. 20, 1968. **Jackson "bragged" to Harry Jackson:** Jackson. **"One of the top":** JP told Kadish that "de Kooning has a lot on the ball, except that he never finishes a painting." **"Pollock's taste":** Seiberling, interview with JP, July 18, 1949.

Rosenberg, center of attention: Aurthur, "Hitting the Boiling Point," p. 205: Rosenberg was "always the dominant figure on the beach, the center of a swirling group of young painters and radical writers." **"Saying things":** Esteban Vicente. **"Half-assed":** Ward. **"Let me think":** Q. by Ward. **Lee catalyst for alliance:** Pavia: Krasner was constantly expanding her list of potential enemies: "Lee hated women, all women. And even among men, she only liked nonartists. The longer you had known Jackson, the worse it was." **"Elbowed out":** Kadish. **"Stalinists":** Q. by Kadish. **"Life-and-death" passion; "Lady Macbeth"; "gladly stab"; "stab or choke":** Pavia. **De Kooning's art unrelated to "action painting":** See O'Doherty, pp. 109–10: "In Rosenberg's discussion of Pollock, he seems to suffer irritation that the actor he has cast to play the leading role is not available, despite his denial, not unusual in such cases, that he wanted Pollock for the part." **Rosenberg on de Kooning's art:** Friedman, p. 146. **"Would sit":** Q. in Potter, p. 161; she also admitted that JP's method was more "kinetic." **Beaux Arts tradition:** O'Doherty, p. 109. **Admiration for Remington:** Hempstead.

Story of Rosenberg's theft: Bryan Robertson, cited in Rosenberg, "The Search for JP," p. 60; also CG, int. by Shorthall, Nov. 9, 1959. We can assume that Krasner was the source of both of these accounts. **Acknowledging conversation:** Rosenberg, "The Search for JP," p. 60. **"Had put the idea":** Abel. **Rosenberg denying debt:** See Rosenberg, "The Search for JP," p. 60. **"Painting like a monkey":** Harold Rosenberg, q. by Carone. **Craving recognition"; "pushing Jackson":** Marca-Relli. **"Wanting to destroy":** May Rosenberg. **"Paranoid"; "psychotic"; "a madwoman":** Q. by Ernestine Lassaw. **"An aggravated case":** Tabak, p. 46.

Attacks on Club: Pavia. **Maligning Zogbaum:** Vivas. See also Tabak, p. 46. **"An instant object":** Gruen, p. 172; see also Marca-Relli; Myers, p. 69. **"This is for artists":** Q. by Ward. **Intellectuals around Rosenberg:** Sandler. **Masculinity of the phrase:** Fiedler, who thought artists were attracted to its aggressive, masculine undertones. **Antihistorical, pro-American:** O'Doherty, p. 109. **Dense style:** O'Doherty, p. 109: "densely poetic mode of art writing." **"Bloody concierge":** Bluhm. **"Telling them what":** Johnson. He had even tried it with de Kooning, who had summarily thrown him out of his house; see de Kooning, q. in Potter, p. 183. **Greenberg's denial:** CG. **Dismissing Rivers:** Fleiss. Pavia, q. in Gruen, p. 270: Greenberg "put a railroad track in the middle of every gallery. He always said, this guy's good and this guy's bad; the right side is good and the left side is bad." The air soon filled with rumors of how Greenberg had influenced those he favored, especially David Smith and JP. Smith's wife, Dehner, would later refer to the sculptor's *Cubi* series as his "Greenberg series." **"Juried a show":** Resnick, q. by Marca-Relli.

Washing glasses: Ibram Lassaw. **Sweeping up:** Pavia, q. in Gruen, p. 272: Pavia called him "the most faithful [member] of all." **"Centered in the studios":** Sandler, p. 37. **"Haute bourgeois"; Still's isolation; de Kooning's availability:** Brach. **Intensity:** Sandler. **"Like a million bucks":** Q. by Ward. **"Through the ranks":** Ernestine Lassaw. **"What the hell":** Q. by Budd. Carone: "You couldn't copy Jackson's work. You had to get into it, you had to recreate the same dialectical process of working with the unconscious." Only on rare occasions could JP articulate his ideas in ways that were helpful to younger artists. Hartigan: "He came to my studio one time and saw a copy of the *Artists' Handbook* and told me to 'Toss it out the window.' **De Kooning provided":** Q. by Sandler. **"In the line":** Carone. **"The young**

artists": Q. by friend, name withheld by request. **"Civil war":** Pavia. **"Only one camp":** Q. by Sandler. **"Hurt":** Carone. **"Bitter":** Little. **"You're the greatest":** **"No, Bill":** Q. by Sidney Geist, q. in Solomon, p. 241. **De Kooning show:** Mary Jackson. **"The turbulence"; "could walk through"; "on the prow":** Elaine de Kooning, q. in Pepper. "The Indomitable Bill de Kooning," p. 70. **"Acts of genius":** Q. by May Rosenberg. **De Kooning purchased by MOMA:** *Woman I.* **"The final direction":** Ashton, *New York School;* p. 213. *Time's* **approval:** "Big City Dames," p. 80; see Ashton, *New York School,* p. 213. **"Out of hand":** Mercer. **"Bill, you betrayed":** Q. by Marca-Relli. **"Well, what":** Q. by Marca-Relli. **Stalking out of bar:** Mercer. **Castelli enclave:** Liss, "Memories of Bonac Painters." **Motherwell:** Motherwell, q. in Potter, p. 185. **"Like a scout":** May Rosenberg. **"Hot and sticky"; festive dinners:** Liss, "Memories of Bonac Painters."
Reshingling house: JP to Sidney Janis, Nov. 1953. **Change in palette:** See editors' note, OC&T II, p. 199: The paintings from 1953 "recapitulate and redefine his earlier styles and images." *Ocean Greyness:* OC&T 369, II, pp. 204–05. **Invoked images:** See *Birth* c. 1938–41, OC&T 77, I, p. 60; *Composition with Masked Forms,* 1941, OC&T 79, I, p. 62; *White Horizontal,* c. 1938–41, OC&T 82, I, p. 65. *Greyed Rainbow:* OC&T 370, II, pp. 206–07.
Janis visit: Janis. **"Talked angrily":** Motherwell, q. in "JP: An Artists' Symposium, Part I," p. 30. **Safe at The Creeks:** Glasco. **"Just so he could relax":** Ossorio. **"Oh, no"; "Well, play":** Q. by Dragon. **"Out of your mind":** Q. by Marca-Relli. **"Let me help":** Q. by Marca-Relli. **"Oh, God":** Marca-Relli. **"She didn't go":** Q. by Marca-Relli. **"Felt like a heel"; "from then on":** Marca-Relli. **Mowing incident:** Marca-Relli. **Lee refusing to open door:** May Rosenberg. **Denying knowledge of whereabouts:** Pavia; May Rosenberg. **"The New York gangsters":** Q. by Pavia. **Visits stopping:** May Rosenberg. **"Looking for de Kooning":** Castelli. **Ileana Castelli hiding things:** Castelli, q. in Potter, p. 184. **Almost destroying Rivers sculpture:** Castelli, q. in Potter, p. 184; see Rivers, q. in "JP: An Artists' Symposium, Part I," p. 33. It is widely believed that JP destroyed the sculpture, a legend that Castelli dismissed by noting that "it was made out of cement." **"He got black":** Q. in Potter, p. 204. **"Ah, shit, Harry":** Q. by Harry Jackson. **"Who the fuck"; "study painting":** Harry Jackson.
Scenic tour for Smiths: Tony Smith, q. in DP&G, "Who was JP?" p. 53. **Offer of** *Blue Poles;* **"it was too big":** Jane Smith. **Black-and-white portrait:** *Number 7, 1952,* OC&T 354, II, pp. 176–77. The next day, as the Smiths were getting into their car to begin the journey home, JP said, "Take your painting." But Lee said, "Not now, Jackson, not now." Jane Smith never did get her portrait, which eventually was acquired by the Metropolitan Museum of Art. **"Perverse sexuality":** Tony Smith, q. in DP&G, "Who Was JP?" p. 53. Smith also spread the rumor (q. by Johnson) that JP had been sitting and drinking with a male friend, one who was not actively homosexual. When they reached the "reeling stage, someone suggested doing something, and JP said, 'Oh, hell, let's go home and fuck.' " **Passes:** Wilcox: "Tony was a homosexual. He tried to make passes at Jackson a couple of times —at least that's what Jackson thought it was." In support of Smith's homosexual or bisexual inclinations: Bultman; Johnson; Myers. Where before the incident Smith could do no wrong, afterward he could do no right. JP even ridiculed the cantilevered house Smith designed for Theodoros Stamos on the North Fork: "Can you imagine a guy being so stupid to build a house that way?" he said to Wilcox. Smith, q. in DP&G, "Who Was JP?" p. 53: "There were real conflicts, partly due to the manner in which [Jackson] kept things apart in his mind." This statement must be read in light of Smith's statement to Friedman (p. 89) that "Jackson was puritanical. I've never known anyone who was more—I mean stern. On the other hand, I have heard that he was fascinated by all sorts of things which he considered perverse." Shepperd: "I was talking with Tony once, and he mentioned out of the blue that he thought Jackson was not homosexual, that, if anything, he was impotent rather than homosexual. The comment wasn't related to anything; he just sort of threw it out."
Tomlin admiring Lee's work: Nemser, p. 90. **Pitching house to Tomlin:** Slivka, who had turned down JP's suggestion that *he* buy the house. **"Animated conversation":** Marca-Relli. **Jackson infuriated:** Cavallon. **"Until the house shook":** LK; see also, Friedman, p. 88. **Tomlin's**

heart attack: Cavallon. **Tomlin looking worse:** Marca-Relli. **"Frozen"; "we better get out"; Tomlin's death:** Cavallon. **"That night"; "Gee":** Q. by Cavallon. **"What do you want":** Q. by Marca-Relli. **"Final authority":** Hempstead. **"Crisis of realization"; Hubbard breaking off with Mark:** Ossorio. **Talk of suicide:** Wilcox. **Seeking out Barker:** Susan Barker says her husband's cure for JP's persistent headaches was to "Stop drinking the night before." **Barker renting nearby; not formal patient:** Susan Barker. **"No damn good"; "what do you":** Q. by Wayne Barker, q. in Potter, pp. 179–80. **"Way of sizing you up":** Wayne Barker, q. in Potter, p. 180.

42. ABANDONED

SOURCES

Books, articles, and transcripts

Friedman, *JP;* Henderson, *Thresholds of Initiation;* Marlborough-Gerson Gallery, *JP: Black and White;* Namuth, *Pollock Painting;* FVOC, *JP: The Black Pourings;* OC&T, *JP;* O'Hara, *JP;* Potter, *To a Violent Grave;* Rose, *LK;* Sandler, *New York School;* Solomon, *JP.*

Robert Alan Aurthur, "Hitting the Boiling Point, Freakwise, at East Hampton," *Esquire,* June 1972; [Robert M. Coates], "The Art Galleries, American and International," *New Yorker,* Feb. 20, 1954; S. Lane Faison, Jr., "Ten Paintings by JP," *Nation,* Feb. 20, 1954; James Fitzsimmons, "Art," *Arts & Architecture,* Mar. 1954; Christopher E. Fremantle, "New York Commentary" *Studio,* June 1954; B. H. Friedman, "An Interview with Lee Krasner Pollock," in Marlborough-Gerson Gallery, *JP: Black and White,* n.p.; CG, " 'American-Type' Painting," *Partisan Review,* Spring 1955; T[homas] B. H[ess], "Reviews and Previews," *Art News,* Mar. 1954; "JP: An Artists' Symposium, Part I," *Art News,* Apr. 1967; James T. Vallière, "Daniel T. Miller," *Provincetown Review,* Fall 1968; Amei Wallach, "Krasner's Triumph," *Vogue,* Nov. 1983.

Emily Genauer, "Art and Artists: Reappraisal of the Avant-Garde," New York *Herald Tribune,* Feb. 7, 1954; "Hurricane Rips Eastern Seaboard; No Lives Lost Here," *East Hampton Star,* Nov. 2, 1954; "JP Injured," *East Hampton Star,* Sept. 2, 1954; Joseph Liss, "Memories of Bonac Painters," *East Hampton Star,* Aug. 18, 1983.

CG, int. by Kathleen Shorthall, for *Life,* Nov. 9, 1959, Time/Life Archives; CG, int. by James T. Vallière, Mar. 20, 1968, AAA.

Interviews

Lionel Abel; Ethel Baziotes; Peter Blake; Charles Boultenhouse; Paul Brach; Ernest Briggs; Charlotte Park Brooks; James Brooks; David Budd; Fritz Bultman; Adele Callaway; Jeremy Capillé; Nicholas Carone; Herman Cherry; Cynthia Cole; John Cole; Oscar Collier; Edward Cook; Karen Del Pilar; B. H. Friedman; Ron Gorchov; Jane Graves; CG; Barbara Hale; Budd Hopkins; Merle Hubbard; Ted Hults; Edys Hunter; Sam Hunter; Sidney Janis; Paul Jenkins; Reuben Kadish; Ruth Kligman; Joe LeSueur; Joe Liss; Millie Liss; John Little; Cile Downs Lord; Sheridan Lord (confirmation only); John Marquand; Peter Matthiessen (confirmation only); ACM; Terry Netter; Alfonso Ossorio; Philip Pavia; Jane Pearce; David Peretz; EFP; FLP; MLP; SWP; Becky Reis; Miriam Schapiro; Jon Schueler; David Slivka; Jane Smith; Syd Solomon; Carol Southern; Patsy Southgate; Ronald Stein; Ruth Stein; Marta Vivas; Samuel Wagstaff; Joan Ward; Steve Wheeler; Roger Wilcox; Betsy Zogbaum.

NOTES

Date of visit: The idea was already being discussed when Jay wrote to Charles, Aug. 31, 1953. **"Selfishness":** SMP to CCP, Jan. 14, 1954. **War over mail:** SMP to CCP, Nov. 16, 1955. SMP to CCP, Oct. 22, 1951: "[She and Sande] talk about getting a job but that is as far as it goes. If I was in Loie's place I would of had a job four months ago." This from a woman who had seldom held a job during the years of poverty with Roy. **Stella's enjoyment of Jackson's life-style:** ACM. **"Culture crazy":** CG. **"Whenever anyone":** Int. by Shorthall, Nov. 9, 1959.

"Jackson drinking beer": FLP. **Flaunting affluence:**

On one visit, JP played some new Count Basie records for his brother Frank and, when Frank told him he wasn't familiar with Basie's music, JP patronizingly told him he should be; FLP. MLP: "We heard again and again that the only painter worth looking at in America was him." **"Cantankerous child"**: Capillé. **Lee not encouraging contributions:** FLP, q. in Potter, p. 108. **Protecting Stella from problems:** ACM. **Resentment of Stella's praise:** MLP. **Jackson doing no wrong:** EFP. **Favoritism:** Karen Del Pilar, Stella's unfavored grandchild: "I was tremendously jealous," she admits. **Years of excuses:** Del Pilar.

"Old age quirks": MJP to CCP, Aug. 31, 1953. **Living alone impossible:** CCP to MJP, Sept. 5, 1953: "I do not think it wise for her to live alone. For one thing there is always the danger of a serious fall; also, unless she improves remarkably, which seems most unlikely, Mother is no longer able to walk out for groceries and the like. Even if she were able to live alone, $100.00 a month would hardly be enough for her needs." **"Perplexing"; "staying with Jack":** MJP to CCP, Aug. 31, 1953. **"A temporary stay":** FLP to CCP, Aug. 29, 1953. **September 1 drive; "[Jack] was in"; "fully aware"; "another long talk"; "cooperative":** CCP to MJP, Sept. 5, 1953. **Stella in Springs:** SMP to CCP, EFP, and Jeremy, Sept. 12, 1953. **"Waiting on me":** SMP to CCP, Jan. 14, 1954. **"Breakfast cantelope":** SMP to CCP, EFP, and Jeremy, Sept. 12, 1953. **Ritual:** OC&T 376, II, p. 217. **Stella's favorite painting:** ACM. **Sleeping Effort:** OC&T 373, II, pp. 212–13. **Easter and the Totem:** OC&T 374, II, pp. 214–15. **Four Opposites:** OC&T 377, II, pp. 218–19. **"Too good":** LK, q. by Little. **Return to Deep River; "wanted to see": "Jack had asked":** SMP to FLP, MLP, and Jonathan, Sept. 29, 1953.

"Slightly down-at-the-heels": Collier; see also John Cole, q. in Potter, p. 166. **Roueché's old place:** Potter, p. 176. **"Because Lee feared":** John Cole. **"For the cops":** Blake. **"Neurotically fraternal":** John Cole. **"Make a pig":** Blake. **"Effects of the moon":** JP, q. by LK. **"Because the moon":** Q. in Namuth, n.p.

Four works sent to Janis: JP to Janis, Sept. 28, 1953. **Paintings from previous year:** Janis; JP to Janis, Sept. 28, 1953; JP to Janis, n.d. **"He wondered":** JP, q. by Hubbard, recalling Elizabeth Wright Hubbard. **Cancellation:** For evidence that, even as late as early October, the show was scheduled originally for November, see Janis, q. in Potter, p. 187. **Borrowing more money:** JP to Janis, n.d. **Jackson ignoring repainting:** John Cole, q. in Potter, p. 166. **"They are great!"; "Clem reacted"; "one client":** Janis to JP, Oct. 20, 1953. **"Went up to Janis's":** Still to JP, Oct. 29, 1953. **No compliments from Still:** Years later, in a letter to B. H. Friedman, Still remained unwilling to express admiration for the works themselves. See Friedman, p. 223. **The Deep:** OC&T 372, II, pp. 210–11 (7'3" × 4'11"). **White field:** O'Hara, p. 31: "An abyss of glamor encroached upon by a flood of innocence." **Tribute to Still:** Carone; Wagstaff. CG: "He looked at what Clyff was doing and made a stab at it." When JP asked Krasner for her opinion of the work, she said (q. by Wagstaff), "I don't know what to say except I see you've done one of your crazies." **"The big league":** JP to Janis, n.d.

"The idea, or the image": LK, q. by Cile Downs (Lord), q. in Potter, p. 204. **Dreaming of Stella:** Henderson, pp. 44–45. Jackson gave a more detailed description of a similar dream to Roger Wilcox a few years earlier: "In this dream," Wilcox remembers, "he is in a place with very high grass, as high as your head, waving in the breeze. There is a path through this grass, and at the end of it, he sees a figure in flimsy veils coming toward him. It's a beautiful woman, but he can't really see her clearly. He stands there watching as she comes toward him, but she doesn't seem to be getting any closer. When he starts walking toward her, she disappears." **Sketches:** John Cole, who saw the work in progress. **Five by eleven:** Actually 4'10" by 11'2". **Earlier painting:** OC&T 10, I, p. 9. **Early self-portrait:** OC&T 9, I, p. 8. **Portrait and a Dream:** OC&T 368, II, pp. 200–03. JP told Elizabeth Wright Hubbard that it was a self-portrait of him "when I'm not sober"; Hubbard, int. by FVOC, Feb. 22, 1964, q. in Institute of Contemporary Art, JP: The Black Pourings, 1951–1953," p. 20. The name was originally Portrait with a Dream; OC&T II, p. 200. **"You mean":** Q. by Ruth Stein. **Stella the void:** JP described the upper right-hand corner of the panel to Lillian Kiesler and Alice Hodges as the "dark side of the moon"; JP, q. by LK, q. in Friedman, "An Interview with Lee

Krasner Pollock," in Marlborough-Gerson, n.p. He said the same thing to Lee Krasner, q. in Namuth, n.p.

Winter's antics: MJP to CCP, Dec. 4 or 14, 1953: "Surely Elizabeth can set him back on his heels or hang up when he calls in that condition." **"Jackson's latest":** MJP to CCP, Dec. 4 or 14, 1953. **Arrangements for January visit; "Mother had planned":** CCP to FLP, Jan. 2, 1954. **"Glad to have mother"; "no other answer":** MJP to CCP, Dec. 4 or 14, 1953. **"Mother's whole attitude":** SLM to CCP, Jan. 5, 1954. **"Loie is the one":** SMP to CCP, Jan. 14, 1954; emphasis in the original. **"New works better":** SMP to CCP, Jan. 14, 1954. The identity of the works is not clear. **Call to Tony Smith; "When I heard":** Smith to LK and JP, Feb. 8, 1954. **February opening:** One-man show, Sidney Janis Gallery, Feb. 1–27, 1954, ten works; JP was so nervous about the opening that he told John Cole, "I can't face the drive into New York," so they loaded the paintings into the back of Cole's car and Cole drove him in; Cole. **"What kind of spectacle":** Blake to JP, Feb. 4, 1954: "That head [in Portrait and a Dream] was wonderful. I thought it was better than any of the great, monumental Picassos that I've ever seen, and it was just as good as any of the Easter Island heads." **One week in New York:** SMP to CCP, Feb. 23, 1954. **Sande seeing show:** SMP to CCP, Feb. 27, 1954.

"A real step": Genauer, "Art and Artists." **"Limited":** Fitzsimmons, "Art," pp. 7, 30. **"The happy advance":** Stuart Preston, review, NYT, q. in Friedman, p. 206. **"Return[ed] to some":** H[ess], "Reviews and Previews," p. 40. In the same review, Hess says JP's new works create a visual space "of about 6 inches in depth" where "Pollock's usual energetic dramas are played—full of shouting, gesticulation and fury. But the space itself is a calm and stable medium." **"Touches of Motherwell":** [Coates], "The Art Galleries," p. 81. **"Disappointed":** CG; Friedman, p. 207. **"Soft"; "forced":** CG, int. by Shorthall, Nov. 9, 1959. **"Lost his stuff":** CG. **Greenberg liking two works:** CG, int. by Vallière, Mar. 20, 1968. **"Onto something"; "phenomenal":** CG.

"This time": CG. **Arloie's baby:** Arloie's baby was one of five newborns that died in the same week in the same small hospital. Given the amount of toxic waste generated by secret defense-industry plants in the area (the kind of waste that would later poison Sande), it is likely that a study of the Deep River area would have revealed high groundwater concentrations of carcinogens and other life-threatening toxins; see SMP to CCP, Feb. 27, 1954. **"Terrible headaches":** Kadish; see also SMP to CCP, Feb. 27, 1954. **Stella's weight loss:** SMP to CCP, Feb. 27, 1954. **Lee's colitis:** Southgate. **Snowy night:** Cynthia Cole. **Finding Jackson on the floor:** John Cole: "Lee was too close to his suicidal tendencies. I just thought he was a troublesome drunk." **"Had really done it"; "popped up":** Cynthia Cole.

No more parties: Zogbaum. **Beach parties:** Slivka, who recalls attending an after-dark beach party at Barnes Landing with the Pollocks, the de Koonings, the Brookses, Louis Shaker, Paul Brach, and others. **Exiting Rosenberg parties:** Wilcox. **"I'm the best":** Q. by Rosenberg. **"Very in'eresting":** Q. by Dragon. **"If you showed":** Dragon. **"What the fuck":** Q. by Carone. **"Fuck off":** Q. by de Kooning, in Vallière, "De Kooning on Pollock," p. 205. **"Why bother":** Q. by CG. According to Greenberg, this remark was made in New York. **Friendship with Carone:** Friedman. **"Impossible to separate":** Rivers, q. in "JP: An Artists' Symposium, Part I," p. 33. **Residents of "red house":** Friedman. **De Kooning's Studio:** Liss, "Memories of Bonac Painters." **"Just madness":** Q. in Liss, Memories of Bonac Painters. **Lee's rages:** See Cile Downs (Lord), q. in Potter, p. 202. **Twelve miles to Bridgehampton:** Ted Hults. **De Kooning's taste for westerns:** Pavia. **Wrestling challenges:** Ward.

Talks about joint fishing venture: John Cole, q. in Potter, p. 166. **Cynthia Cole and Lee sharing anxieties:** Cynthia Cole: Her husband John "would happily share beer with [Jackson]. And I think Lee may have felt that that might trigger off a big episode where Jackson would just disappear." **"A role model":** Southgate. **Southgate's daily visits:** Southgate, q. in Potter, p. 180. **"Really sexy body":** Q. by LeSueur. **"I took Lee's side":** Southgate, q. in Potter, p. 198. **Young men:** Joe Liss: "In East Hampton at the time, there were a number of people with sophisticated pasts who came to take on these yeoman jobs. But they lived on their charm, really." **Work for Paris Review:** Potter, p. 189. **"Peter became a commercial fisherman":** Name withheld by request. **"This classy blonde":** Southern.

Lee not painting: John Cole. "I never saw her painting." Southgate: "When I met her, Lee wasn't painting at all." The possible exception is *Blue and Black* (Rose, fig. 67, p. 70). Rose dates the painting 1951–53 and concedes that it "should have generated a series of 'big pictures.' As it stands, it is an exceptional prefiguration of works she would not feel free enough or sure enough to paint for a decade to come." We believe that *Blue and Black* was either a survivor from the large, formal, chromatic abstractions she showed at the Betty Parsons Gallery in 1951 or, more likely, a substantially later work backdated by the artist or misdated by others. **Lee drawing:** Rose, p. 79. She would tack drawings to her studio wall, then systematically tear them up. Still later, she would begin pasting the fragments back together; Wallach, "Krasner's Triumph," p. 502. **Black-and-white mosaics:** *Black and White Collage* (Rose, fig. 71, p. 76); *Untitled Collage* (Rose, fig. 72, p. 77); *Black and White Collage* (Rose, fig. 74, p. 79). **Small works:** 22″ × 30″, 22″ × 30″, and 29″ × 23″, respectively. **Patches of color:** *City Verticals* (Rose, fig. 75, p. 80); *Untitled* (Rose, fig. 76, p. 80). **Brushwork over collage:** *Porcelain* (Rose, fig. 80, p. 84). **Scraps of canvas:** *Shattered Light* (Rose, fig. 81, p. 84). **Landscape:** Rose, p. 82; *Forest No. 1* (Rose, fig. 78, p. 82); *Forest No. 2* (Rose, fig. 79, p. 83). **All-women-artists show:** Group Show—Eight Painters, Two Sculptors," at Hampton Gallery and Workshop, Amagansett; see Rose, p. 164. **Reassembling fragments of past:** See Rose, p. 83.

Exhibition at House of Books and Music: LK. **Bookstore-gallery:** Aurthur, "Hitting the Boiling Point," pp. 204–05. **Mid-June dating:** SMP to CCP, July 8, 1954: "Jack and Dekooning were scuffling one day three or four weeks ago and Jack fell and broke his ankle." The date was not July 15, as cited in OC&T IV, p. 273. **De Kooning and friends helping Braiders; Jackson offering to help; Elaine de Kooning calling husband; "they threw their arms":** Elaine de Kooning, q. in Potter, p. 201; this version is supported by Wilcox and by SMP to CCP, July 8, 1954. **Stepping into path; Jackson and de Kooning falling:** Pavia. **"Absolutely indignant":** Q. in Potter, p. 201. **Rushing to clinic:** Carol Braider, q. in Potter, p. 201. **Accused of attempted murder:** Potter, p. 201. **Cast and crutches:** John Cole. **"Trying to beat":** Pavia. **"A big boy":** Q. in Friedman, p. 209. **Rumors that de Kooning broke Jackson's leg:** Zogbaum.

Jackson missing opening: Schapiro. **Period of confinement:** SMP to CCP, July 8, 1954. **Feeling sorry for himself:** Potter, p. 201. **Weight and beard:** Friedman, p. 209. **Sweeney letter:** Sweeney to JP, July 15, 1954. **Isaacs letter:** Isaacs to JP and LK, Aug. 22, 1954. **"German millionaires":** Tony Smith to JP, Aug. 23, 1954. **Teaching position:** Stanley A. Czurles, director of art education, to JP, July 9, 1954. **Stella not visiting; Sande's visit:** SMP to CCP, July 8, 1954. **"Sitting, staring":** LK. **"Goddamn it":** Q. by LK. **"New bravura":** Wallach, "Krasner's Triumph," p. 502. **Testing leg:** SMP to CCP, July 8, 1954. **Passing Lee's work:** Gorchov: While convalescing, JP spent a lot of time "looking at Lee's work." **Lee arguing more forcefully:** Graves. **"Lively"; "a hilarious imitation":** Cile Lord.

Driving: When Krasner was feeling strong, she would harangue JP from the passenger seat. Ronald Stein: "It was a continuing run of very vocal criticisms." But when JP was feeling strong, any outing could become a paralyzing war of nerves. "He knew that if he got her in the car, he could really work her over. He had her captive and he terrorized her." Even JP's friends admired Krasner's courage. Dan Miller (q. in Vallière, "Daniel T. Miller," p. 38) had often seen them drive up to his gas pumps and thought to himself, " 'Well, Lee, I wouldn't drive with that son-of-a-gun—I'd get up and walk off.' But she didn't." (Punctuation altered slightly.) **"[She] was trapped":** Southgate, q. in Potter, p. 198. **"What happens"; "series of funny":** Cynthia Cole. **"Complete lack":** Southgate. **Dating of lessons:** SMP to CCP and Jeremy, Sept. 7, 1954. **Symptoms of colitis:** Peretz.

Ankle stiff: The ankle was "stiff" through early September; SMP to CCP and Jeremy, Sept. 7, 1954. **Softball games at Zogbaums':** John Cole; Pavia. **"What's this I hear":** Reis. **"My wife's":** Q. by Reis. **Black-and-white works traded:** *Number 5, 1951* (OC&T 323, II, pp. 136–37) and *Number 23, 1951* (OC&T 335, II, p. 153); see also OC&T, IV, p. 273; Marca-Relli, q. in Potter, p. 198. Aug. dating from SMP to CCP and Jeremy, Sept. 7, 1954. **Montauk cut off; hurricane:** "Hurricane Rips Eastern

Seaboard," Nov. 2, 1954. **Neighbors flocking to Pollocks'; Jackson helping neighbors; "the boat"; Barbara Hale's thoughts on storms:** Hale. **Pause in storm:** "Hurricane Rips Eastern Seaboard," Nov. 2, 1954. **"It's coming back":** Q. by Hale. **"The sun's out":** Marca-Relli. **Waters on Fireplace Road; "his crew":** Hale. **"I've come":** Q. by Joe Liss. **"Save what?":** Joe Liss. **Houses remaining dark:** Callaway. **"If you don't":** Q. by James Brooks. **Brooks studio swept to sea:** Aurthur, "Hitting the Boiling Point," p. 202. **Jackson returning to Springs alone:** Charlotte Brooks. **Car crash:** "JP Injured," Sept. 2, 1954. **"That many attacks":** MJP to CCP, Dec. 8, 1954. **Struggling against bankruptcy:** SMP to CCP and Jeremy, Sept. 7, 1954. In late January 1955, SLM had to give it up; SMP to CCP, Feb. 10, 1955. **Arloie opening business:** SMP to CCP, Nov. 11, 1954. **Stella seeming strong prior to attack:** ACM.

Thanksgiving: Nov. 25. **"Fishermen"; "give him some milk"; fence incident:** Millie Liss. **"Fuck you"; "All I said":** Q. by Millie Liss. **Lee's objections:** She routinely objected to JP sending money to his mother or to any member of his family and, after his death, refused to share her considerable income from JP's paintings with family members. Even when Sande was dying of cancer and needed money to pay medical expenses, Krasner wouldn't authorize him to print another edition of the silk-screen prints he and JP had made in 1951; Kadish; ACM. **Jackson's checks:** SMP to CCP, Dec. 7, 1954. **Slim allowance:** JP approached several people for part-time work, including John Cole, Peter Matthiessen, and Jeffrey Potter; see Potter, p. 196. JP even suggested selling the house and moving in with Ossorio (Ossorio, q. in Potter, p. 207), a plan that Ossorio rejected. In addition to Janis's allowance, JP received a check from Reginald Isaacs for $50 in late October (Isaacs to JP, Oct. 21, 1954) and another for the same amount on November 5 (Isaacs to JP, Nov. 5, 1954), apparently without informing Janis of either check. **Sale of Ocean Greyness:** Official word came to JP on Nov. 3, although the deal was no doubt made and JP informed before that; see James Johnson Sweeney to JP, Nov. 3, 1954. **Reaction to checks in Deep River:** ACM.

Arrival in Deep River: SMP to CCP, Dec. 7, 1954. **Christmas visit:** MJP and ABP were also there; MJP to CCP, Dec. 8, 1954. **"Have a present"; trip to Hartford:** Del Pilar. **January visit; return to Springs; promise of return to Deep River:** SMP to FLP, MLP, and Jonathan, Feb. 7, 1955. **Lee pleading colitis:** SMP to CCP, Jan. 15, 1955. **Lee afraid of Jackson:** Charlotte Brooks; James Brooks. **Lee contemptuous of family:** Del Pilar. **"East Hampton is where"; "put her foot"; "[Stella] didn't need":** ACM. **Lee never forgiving family:** Kadish. **"Leaving her alone":** CG.

Date of second ankle accident: Feb. dating: Martha Jackson to JP, Feb. 14, 1955: "I hear you have broken your leg again." **Lords came over:** In an earlier interview, Cile Lord said the incident took place at the Lords' house. **Sherry Lord pushing Jackson:** In essence, tripping him; confirmed by Sheridan Lord. **"Clunk":** Cile Lord. **"I broke":** Q. by Cile Lord. **"Oh, Jackson":** Cile Lord. **"Goddammit":** Q. by Cile Lord. **Same ankle:** Some people have maintained that JP's bones were brittle due to the year and a half of drinking Grant Mark's nondairy drink; Sam Hunter, recalling Ruth Fox; also Wilcox. **"How typical":** Q. in Potter, p. 215.

Lee bringing news to bedside: LK. **Explosion at Bennington:** Marca-Relli: JP "had to swallow his pride when Greenberg was around. . . . Clem used to come around and try to talk, but there would be explosions. Someone would say something, or Jackson would just boil over, and you would have to keep them apart." **Greenberg's disdain for Lee's work:** Bultman; Cile Downs (Lord) (q. in Potter, p. 139) remembers Greenberg looking at Krasner's paintings and rudely being more impressed with the splatterings of paint on the walls behind them than by the paintings themselves. Greenberg (q. in Potter, p. 139) later said he didn't think much of Krasner as an artist. **"Forced, pumped":** CG, " 'American-Type' Painting," p. 186. **"Peak of his achievement":** CG, " 'American-Type' Painting," p. 186. Greenberg may have misstated the year of the show. He later said the black-and-white paintings were JP's best, but he may have been revising his opinions. In citing "four or five huge canvases of monumental perfection," he probably meant the 1950 show, which included *Autumn Rhythm, One, Number 32, 1950,* and *Lavender Mist.* The 1951 show of mostly black-and-white paintings had only one or two large canvases. **"An accomplished"; "pleasingly"; "he was not sure":** CG, " 'American-Type' Painting," p. 186.

Still the new favorite: Like JP, Still did not feel any sustained gratitude for Greenberg's favor. Briggs: "Still and Greenberg were mostly on the outs from early on. I don't think he had much respect for Greenberg's understanding of the work, whether it was Pollock's or his own." **"One of the most"; "liberat[ed] abstract painting":** CG, " 'American-Type' Painting," p. 187. **"Late cubist" vs. "post-cubists":** The characterization of Greenberg's article is Greenberg's own; CG, int. by Shorthall, Nov. 9, 1959; see also Sandler, p. 13. **"A lot of crap":** Int. by Shorthall, Nov. 9, 1959. **Lee infuriated:** CG, q. in Potter, p. 221; see Bultman; Little. **Wanton misrepresentation:** CG, int. by Shorthall, Nov. 9, 1959. **Boycott of wedding:** CG to JP, May 21, 1955. **Wedding gift:** OC&T 952, IV, p. 35. **"A ruckus":** CG to JP, May 21, 1955.

Jackson not eating: Pearce. **Turning away visitors:** Marca-Relli. **Afternoons at movies:** Confirmed by Sheridan Lord. **Helping the Hales:** See Potter, pp. 196–97. **Lee forbidding neighbors to let Jackson have liquor:** Cile Lord. **"Get sort of hurt":** Cile Downs (Lord), q. in Potter, p. .215. **Watching kids:** Southgate, q. in Potter, p. 189. **"Charming":** Southgate. **"Like a little boy":** Southgate, q. in Potter, p. 218. **Braiders naming baby Jackson:** Cile Lord. **"Gentle and lovely":** Q. in Potter, p. 167. **"She would pick at him":** Name withheld by request. **"Now, Jackson":** Q. by Cile Lord; see Eleanor Ward, q. in Potter, p. 174. **"I don't want food":** Q. by Cile Lord, q. in Solomon, p. 245. **Marriage counseling:** LK. When JP gave Hubbard a bouquet of red and white flowers, she composed a poetic thank-you note that is almost pathetic in its dissociation from the reality of a marriage on the brink of collapse; Elizabeth Wright Hubbard to JP, Apr. 28, 1955.

May 13; "memorable weekend": Edys and Sam Hunter to LK and JP, May 18, 1955; Edys also talks about "the thrill of seeing all the paintings—the Pollocks and the Krasners." **Jackson coming with orchids:** Edys Hunter. **Lee demanding more money:** Southgate. **Lending $100:** Brach. **Lee refusing sex:** Kligman. **Jackson asking women to have his baby:** Name withheld by request. **Jackson demanding apology from Whitney:** John I. H. Baur, Whitney Museum of American Art, to JP, May 31, 1955. **Jackson threatening trip to Paris:** Martha Jackson to JP, Apr. 23, 1955. **Passport:** Issued July 21, 1955 (#738532). **Hot summer:** SMP (to CCP, Sept. 7, 1955) called it "sickening heat, like Iowa summers." **"Pilgrimage":** Budd. **"Sitting on top"; meeting Solomon; "moved"; "sense of tragedy":** Solomon. **Dropping in on Brach and Schapiro; barn; "shit test":** Schapiro. **Brach uncomfortable with drinkers:** Brach.

Still's Jaguar: Ossorio. **"Second only":** Still to Ossorio, Mar. 15, 1955, q. in Friedman, p. 224. **"There wasn't a soul":** Schueler. **Smith snubbed by Still:** Smith. **Correspondence with Martha Jackson:** Martha Jackson to JP, Feb. 14, 1955, in which Martha Jackson included a contract for JP to sign; and Apr. 23, 1955, in which she suggested that she could arrange a "full length show" of JP's work at the 1956 Venice Biennale and accused Janis of taking "some of Valentine's 'crap.' " De Kooning had only one show at Martha Jackson's gallery before returning to Janis in 1956. **"Major credit"; "interest"; "may I add":** Still to JP, Apr. 30, 1955. Between the two letters, apparently, Still had written Greenberg directly, accusing him of having based his characterizations of Still's art on conversations with JP and Krasner, among others. Greenberg wrote back on March 15 denying that the Pollocks had ever tried to explain Still's art to him and stating that they had expressed nothing more than admiration.

Lee stifling outrage at Greenberg: Marca-Relli. "Although she detested Clem personally, Lee was doing everything to keep Jackson and Clem together, to keep him in Jackson's camp." Steve Wheeler: "Lee had to keep Jackson at arm's length from Clem. She was really very concerned that Jackson was going to demolish Clem. Lee always was the peacemaker there, knowing how important Clem was for her and for him." **Greenberg taking Lee's side:** CG. **"Jewish cunt":** Q. by Vivas. **"Never loved her":** Q. by CG. **"Howled":** LK. **"The marriage":** CG. **Greenberg recommending Pearce:** CG; LK. **Jackson against seeing Pearce:** Krasner later claimed that JP "didn't say it was out of the question. But he didn't support it. Didn't say go, didn't

say don't go." **"Seriously ill":** Pearce. **Jackson volunteering to reenter analysis:** LK.

43. THE LAST ACT

SOURCES

Books, articles, manuscript, lecture, records, and transcripts

Dawson, *An Emotional Memoir of Franz Kline*; Friedman, *Almost a Life*; Friedman, *JP*; Graham, *Systems and Dialectics*; Gruen, *The Party's Over Now*; Kligman, *Love Affair*; Naifeh, *Culture Making*; OC&T, *JP*; Potter, *To a Violent Grave*; Rose, *LK*; Seldes, *The Legacy of Mark Rothko*; Solomon, *JP*; Warhol and Hackett, *POPism*.

Robert Alan Aurthur, "Hitting the Boiling Point, Freakwise, at East Hampton," *Esquire*, June 1972; Paul Brach, "Postscript: The Fifties," *Artforum*, Sept. 1965; DP&G, "Who Was JP?" *Art in America*, May–June 1967; [Alexander Eliot], "The Champ," *Time*, Dec. 19, 1954; [Alexander Eliot], "The Wild Ones," *Time*, Feb. 20, 1956; B. H. Friedman, "The New Baroque," *Arts Digest*, Sept. 15, 1954; B. H. Friedman, "Profile: JP," *Art in America*, Dec. 1955; Grace Glueck, "Krasner and Pollock: Scenes from a Marriage," *Art News*, Dec. 1981; Hayden Herrera, "John Graham: Modernist Turns Magus," *Arts Magazine*, Oct. 1976; Thomas Hess, "Pollock: The Art of a Myth," *Art News*, Jan. 1964; Eric Hodgins and Parker Lesley, "The Great International Art Market: I," *Fortune*, Dec. 1955; "JP: An Artists' Symposium, Part I," *Art News*, Apr. 1967; Eila Kokkinen, "John Graham During the 1940s," *Arts Magazine*, Nov. 1976; Frank O'Hara, "John Graham at the Stable Gallery," *Art News*, Apr. 1954; Rosalind Krauss, "Contra Carmean: The Abstract Pollock," *Art in America*, Summer 1982; Barbara Rose, "Arshile Gorky and John Graham: Eastern Exiles in a Western World," *Arts Magazine*, Mar. 1976; Irving Sandler, "The Club," *Artforum*, Sept. 1965; Leo Steinberg, "Month in Review," *Arts*, Dec. 1955; P[arker] T[yler], "Reviews and Previews," *Art News*, Dec. 1955; James T. Vallière, "De Kooning on Pollock," *Partisan Review*, Fall 1967.

Stuart Preston, "Among Current Shows: Museum of Modern Art Acquisitions—Americans and Europeans," *NYT*, Dec. 4, 1955.

May Natalie Tabak, "A Collage" (unpub. ms.), n.d.

LK (lecture), Columbia International Affairs Building, Oct. 5, 1983.

East Hampton Town Police, Police Log, Dec. 24, 1953.

Bartender of Sam's, int. by Kathleen Shorthall for *Life*, Nov. 9, 1959, in Time/Life Archives; CG, int. by Kathleen Shorthall for *Life*, Nov. 9, 1959, in Time/Life Archives; Elwyn Harris, int. by Shorthall for *Life*, Nov. 9, 1959, in Time/Life Archives; Barnett Newman, int. by Shorthall for *Life*, Nov. 9, 1959, in Time/Life Archives; Alfonso Ossorio, int. by Shorthall for *Life*, Nov. 9, 1959, in Time/Life Archives; George Schaefer, int. by Shorthall for *Life*, Nov. 9, 1959, in Time/Life Archives.

Interviews

Lionel Abel; Ruth Ann Applehof; Dore Ashton; Nell Blaine; Peter Blake; Norman Bluhm; Paul Brach; Ernest Briggs; James Brooks; David Budd; Fritz Bultman; Eda Bunce; Adele Callaway; Nicholas Carone; Leo Castelli; Alvi Cavagnaro; Herman Cherry; Cynthia Cole; Emil de Antonio; Tibor de Nagy; Karen Del Pilar; Christie Poindexter Dennis; Dane Dixon; Ted Dragon; Herbert Ferber; Audrey Flack; B. H. Friedman; Emmanuel Ghent; Grace Glueck; Ron Gorchov; CG; Robert Beverly Hale; Ben Heller; Eleanor Hempstead; Budd Hopkins; Edward Hults; Ted Hults; Harry Jackson; Sidney Janis; Paul Jenkins; Reuben Kadish; Gerome Kamrowski; Ruth Kligman; LK; Ibram Lassaw; Joe Liss; Millie Liss; Terry Liss; John Little; Cile Downs Lord; Sheridan Lord (confirmation only); Conrad Marca-Relli; Jason McCoy; George McNeil; Mercedes Matter; Jack Mayer; Jeffrey Meyers; Annalee Newman (int. by David Peretz); Constantine Nivola; Alfonso Ossorio; Martin Pajeck; Philip Pavia; Jane Pearce; Elinor Poindexter; David Porter; Milton Resnick; May Tabak Rosenberg; Irving Sandler; Bertha Saunders; Miriam Schapiro; Jon Schueler; Gertrude Shibley; David Slivka; Jane Smith; Nancy Smith; Syd Solomon; Herman Somberg; Patsy Southgate; Ronald Stein; Hedda Sterne; Allene Talmage; Esteban Vicente; Harriet Vicente; Catherine Viviano; Eleanor

Ward; Joan Ward; Steve Wheeler; Roger Wilcox; Betsy Zogbaum.

NOTES

Cedar Tavern: Located on University Place between Eighth and Ninth streets in the 1950s, later moved to its present location at University Place between Eleventh and Twelfth streets. **Other bars:** Kamrowski. **"Arty emblems"; flaking plaster:** Sandler, "The Club," p. 31. **"Interrogation green":** Budd; Sandler, "The Club," p. 31. **Clock:** Mercedes Matter. **Sweeping glass off table:** The proprietor, "Sam" DiLiberto (q. in Potter, p. 194), would add the broken items to his bill. **Dumping food:** Dawson, pp. 78–82. **Pulling tables:** Sam DiLiberto, q. in Potter, p. 194. **Obscenities:** Friedman, *JP*, p. xx. **"Sucked any":** Q. by Larry Rivers, q. in Potter, p. 195. **Pantomiming shooting up:** Larry Rivers, q. in Potter, p. 195. **"A great lay":** Q. in Hess, "JP," p. 39. **"How do you":** Q. by Larry Rivers, q. in Warhol and Hackett, p. 14. **"What the fuck":** Q. by Brach. "I'm a bag boy at the A&P," answered Brach. "I'm a baseball player," answered Schueler. "What do you do?" **"Fags":** Q. by Larry Rivers, q. in Potter, p. 195. **"To bring notoriety":** Q. by Hopkins. **"Whores":** Q. by Wilcox. Budd (q. in Potter, p. 195) noted that there was a lot of tearing of shirts and pushing and using the word "whore." **"Worms":** Q. by Wilcox: "To call someone a worm was Jackson's nastiest epithet. Somewhere he got the idea that worms have no nervous system at all, that they're the lowest form of life." Hess, "Pollock," p. 39: "He liked to blurt for blurting's sake. This made him seem picturesque and risky." **Playing with sharp fragments:** Sandler.

Picking fights: Cherry: "I told him, 'Look, if you don't stop swinging your arms like that, I'm really going to hurt you.' " Kadish: "He became absolutely irrationally abusive. Once he dragged me outside and started to punch me—a couple of real punches in the face—then I pushed him against a car and he started to cry." McNeil: JP reveled in the apprehensive hush that fell over a room when he entered. All he had to do was growl and a place would clear at the bar. CG: "I took to ducking under the table when Jackson approached, and sneaked out the back when his back was turned." Hopkins: "When Pollock was drunk, you did your best to avoid him. You didn't bring him over because you never knew what was going to happen."

Jackson wanting in: Barnett Newman was only one of many who advised JP to avoid the Cedar; int. by Shorthall, Nov. 9, 1959. **DiLiberto:** Real name wasn't Sam, last name DeLiberto; q. in Potter, p. 194. **"This bear's head":** Q. in Potter, p. 156. Marca-Relli: "You would see his nose pressed against the window trying to get in, like a poor dog. And he would call somebody out and say, 'Please tell them to let me in. I'll be good.' And finally they would let him in. Within two minutes, he would start that foul language, and everyone would say, 'Out, Jackson, get out!' It was like a game." **Coming from Club:** Somberg. **Kline his Sande:** Pavia (q. in Gruen, p. 271) called JP's relationship with Kline "brotherly." **"One of those people":** Rivers, q. in Warhol and Hackett, p. 14. **Kline's childhood:** Hopkins. **Kline's marriage:** Marca-Relli. **Kline's escape:** Cherry: Kline was "pleasantly drunk all the time," mostly on beer. **"Working binge":** Cherry. **Capacity for beer:** Sandler. **Kline's indiscriminate affection:** Rivers, q. in Warhol and Hackett, p. 14. **Cap incident:** Sam DiLiberto, q. in Potter, p. 199. **"Be right with you"; "Do that once more":** Q. by Sam DiLiberto, q. in Potter, p. 199. **Jackson pouring soup:** Wheeler.

Lee preparing for show: SMP to CCP, Oct. 17, 1955; see also Solomon, p. 244. **Big vertical canvases:** Rose, p. 89. **Work more self-assured:** See *Lame Shadow* (Rose, fig. 88, p. 89); *Stretched Yellow* (Rose, fig. 90, p. 91); *Shooting Gold* (Rose, fig, 89, p. 90). **Changed collage elements:** Friedman, *JP*, p. 220. **Scraps from Jackson's paintings:** Applehof; see *Bald Eagle* (Rose, fig. 87, p. 88). **"The best":** CG. **Full name now used:** See *Bird Talk* (Rose, fig. 86, p. 87) and *Shooting Gold* (Rose, fig. 89, p. 90); Rose, p. 89. **"Like a hunter":** Q. by Nivola.

New studio for Lee: Ronald Stein: This two-room shack, enlarged, eventually became Stein's house. See, to contrary, Rose, p. 100: "Until his death [Pollock] remained her greatest —virtually her only—supporter, always encouraging her to work and praising it to others." Although Krasner later condoned revisionist history of this sort, she never made the ar-

guments herself: "Although Lee Pollock had confidence in the quality of her own work, she never thought of it in the same terms as those in which she thought of Jackson's . . . she thought of Jackson as a genius"; Friedman, *JP*, pp. 220–21. **Berating collage:** Marca-Relli. **"Jackson didn't pay":** Q. in Potter, p. 202. **Eleanor Ward's visit:** Solomon, p. 245. There was a heated exchange between Ward and Krasner over who would select the paintings for the show; see Ward, q. in Potter, p. 202. **"Can you imagine":** JP, q. by Ward, q. in Potter, p. 174. **Lee asking for glue; "He doesn't want":** Cile Downs (Lord), q. in Potter, pp. 202–03. **Former horse stables:** Gruen, p. 42. **Favorable reception of Lee's show:** LK, lecture, Columbia International Affairs Building, Oct. 5, 1983; SMP to CCP, Oct. 17, 1955: "Lee's show is over Jack said it was very well received." **"Glowing":** Ronald Stein. Krasner's recollection of the incident was characteristically sanitized. Krasner (q. in Glueck, "Krasner and Pollock, p. 61) described JP as "proud as a peacock" at the Stable Gallery show. **"Wraithlike":** Ward, q. in Potter, p. 209. **"What you need":** Q. by Ward, q. in Potter, p. 209. **"Fled in terror":** Q. in Potter, p. 209. **Jackson's show:** "15 Years of JP," Nov. 28–Dec. 31. **Pressing ahead with show; Jackson's apprehensions:** Friedman, *JP*, p. 210; Potter, p. 226. **Paintings on ceiling:** JP and Krasner were apparently surprised, then amused, by this unorthodox mounting technique; Krauss, "Contra Carmean," p. 26. *White Light:* OC&T 380, II, pp. 222–23. *Search:* OC&T 382, II, pp. 226–27. *Search* possibly old painting: It was originally signed on the lower right side, indicating a vertical composition. JP later removed his first name and date and reinscribed the painting in the lower left corner. **"Gruff, turgid":** Preston, "Among Current Shows." *Art News:* T[yler], "Reviews and Previews," p. 53. **"A Pollock painting":** Leo Steinberg, "Month in Review," pp. 43–44. **"The bush-bearded"; "imitating":** [Eliot], "The Champ," p. 64. **"Pollock's one big":** [Eliot], "The Champ," p. 66. **"Jack the Dripper":** [Eliot], "The Wild Ones," pp. 70, 75. **"Caused Jackson":** Potter, p. 227.

Lee's modesty: Friedman, *JP*, pp. 220–21: She spoke defensively of her work to JP, when she spoke of it at all. **Tender love gone:** Brach. **Lee retreating:** See Cile Downs (Lord), q. in Potter, p. 202. **Twin beds:** Kligman; see Kligman, p. 106. **"Remember the Russians":** Dragon. **Talk of divorce:** LK, q. by Cile Lord. JP, q. by Friedman and CG. **"One foot":** Cynthia Cole. **Charles and Elizabeth separating:** They had to marry officially before they could divorce officially; McCoy. **"Without Lee":** Q. by Joan Ward, q. in Potter, p. 175. **"Dissolving the marriage":** LK, q. by Applehof. **"Jackson and I":** Q. in Rose, p. 98.

Car racing incident: Ronald Stein. **Refused more than two drinks:** Bartender of Sam's, int. by Shorthall, Nov. 9, 1959. **"He was having":** Int. by Shorthall, Nov. 9, 1959. **Christmas Eve in jail:** Bartender of Sam's, int. by Shorthall, Nov. 9, 1959. It is reported (by Edward Hults, q. in Potter, p. 144) that JP threw a brick through the window, but we choose instead to follow the reports of firsthand witnesses and participants to the *Life* interviewer four years after the event. **"You cannot":** Q. by LK, q. in Gruen, p. 232. **"A man's life":** Q. in Friedman, *JP*, p. xvi. In his last public statement, in June 1956, he reiterated his belief that "painting is a state of being. . . . Painting is self-discovery. Every good artist paints what he is"; OC&T IV, p. 275. **"Setting the stage":** LK. **"Like a jet":** Potter, p. 164. **"So the studio":** Q. by Marca-Relli, q. in Friedman, *JP*, p. 214. **Janis recommending removal of paintings:** Janis, q. in Potter, p. 164. **"Let them burn":** Marca-Relli. **Jackson fearing empty space:** Marca-Relli, recalling JP. **Paintings remaining:** Friedman, *JP*, pp. 214–15. When JP complained to Newman that people were bothering him by coming to the studio and wanting to see his work, Newman suggested that he get a lock. JP did so (they had to break it after his death), but rather than helping him get back to work, it may only have symbolized the end of his productivity; Newman, int. by Shorthall, Nov. 9, 1959.

Marca-Relli urging big painting: Marca-Relli. Heller tried to cheer JP up with the story of the composer Arnold Shoenberg; "I said, 'You aren't the only one, Jackson,' " Heller played two pieces by Shoenberg and then told JP that ten years had elapsed between them: "Ten years! Think of that. Ten fucking years." **"All part of trying"; "were forgotten":** Cile Downs (Lord), q. in Potter, p. 214. **Working with clay:** Kadish. **Lee pointing to pile of iron:** LK, q. in DP&G,

"Who Was JP?" p. 51. **Time for experimenting:** LK. **Lee starting his canvases:** Marca-Relli. **Three categories:** Cile Lord. In a way, the efforts to "get Jackson working again" (CG) only confirmed his worst fears: that his only purpose in life, his only value, was in his art. Only a few friends, like Carone, took the more sympathetic view that "Jackson's life had value outside his art. . . . He had already made his revolutionary statement. . . . He had no apologies to make." **"Sort of the outlines":** Harry Jackson. **"With the figures":** Marca-Relli. **Seen as late as summer:** Sterne. **Paintings destroyed:** None of the paintings are in OC&T, and no one has suggested a plausible explanation for their disappearance other than that they were destroyed—either during JP's lifetime or afterward. If they were destroyed after JP's death, it must have been with Krasner's approval. Given her loving protection of every doodle, no matter how inconsequential (see, e.g., OC&T 871–78, III, pp. 333–37), it seems far more likely that JP destroyed them himself. **Avoiding hard liquor:** CG. **Fifty pounds:** Estimate by LK. **Hiding condition from family:** Del Pilar; Kadish; see, e.g., SMP to FLP, MLP, and Jonathan, Nov. 30, 1951. **Description of Jackson:** De Nagy; Tony Smith, q. in DP&G, "Who Was JP?" p. 53. **Trucks and trays:** Friedman, JP, p. 227. **Lightning:** LK. **Unable to concentrate:** Little; see also Friedman, JP, p. xvii. **Hepatitis:** Pearce. **Cirrhosis:** Kligman: His family knew about the cirrhosis. **Lee feeling she was target for arrows:** Marca-Relli; Harris, int. by Shorthall, Nov. 9, 1959. **Barricaded in studio:** See Friedman, JP, p. 226. **"Obviously experimenting":** Ossorio, q. in Potter, p. 186. **"For God's sake":** Q. by Ossorio, q. in Potter, pp. 185–86. **Jumping out of taxi:** Friedman; see also Friedman, Almost a Life, p. 104. **"Not knowing":** Friedman, JP, p. 220. **Two years' probation:** East Hampton Town Police, Police Log, Dec. 24. 1953. **Near-accident:** Joe Liss: JP knocked down a row of mailboxes. **"God, I was scared":** Q. by Cile Lord. **"Old Grizzly":** Confirmed by Sheridan Lord. **Jackson greeted at Cedar:** Friedman, JP, p. xviii. **Making room:** Friedman, JP, p. xviii; Almost a Life, p. 28. **Buying him drinks:** Friedman, JP, p. xix. **Touching for luck:** Friedman, JP, pp. xvii, xix. **"There's Jackson!":** Larry Rivers, q. in Warhol and Hackett, p. 14. **"You should have been":** Q. by Lassaw. **Honest deference:** Friedman. **Bear-baiting:** CG. **"Nauseating":** Kligman, p. 45. **"Who's the greatest":** Bunce; see also Castelli; Cherry. Ibram Lassaw: "In our culture, drinking made you a hero. Fitzgerald did it. Hemingway did it." **"You wouldn't know":** Q. in Potter, p. 194. **"If the audience":** Q. by Zogbaum. **Playing to cowboy image; boots:** Brooks. **Histrionics:** Marca-Relli: "He came over and said, 'You call yourself a painter?' That was his usual approach. And I said, 'Jackson, I'm your friend,' and he said, 'That's right, that's right,' and went on to the next guy: 'You call yourself a painter?'" **"How do you know":** Q. by Carone. **Fight with de Kooning:** Gruen, pp. 228–29. **"Hit an artist?":** Q. in Gruen, p. 229. **"That son of a bitch":** Q. by Carone. **"You hurt his feelings":** Q. by Hopkins. **Sale of Blue Poles:** The date of the sale of Blue Poles—from which JP earned $4,000—has been reported as both 1954 and 1955. Because Tony Smith had a role in the sale, it must have occurred sometime after Smith's return from Europe in May 1955. Heller and Brach looked at the painting in JP's studio in early spring 1955. Therefore, the sale was probably made in summer or fall of that year. **"JP":** Q. by Heller. **"One of the boys":** Int. by Shorthall, Nov. 9, 1959. **Recoveries:** Marca-Relli. **Watching Bogart:** Marca-Relli. **Watching Dean:** Southgate. **Drive to power station:** Jane Smith. **Blake cutting off contact:** Blake, q. in Potter, p. 205. **Larkins cutting off contact:** Lawrence Larkin, q. in Potter, p. 205. **Lisses cutting off contact:** Millie Liss. **Barbara Hale barring him:** Robert Beverly Hale. **Hempstead keeping address secret:** Hempstead. **Finding Carone house:** Eleanor Ward, q. in Potter, p. 192. **Description of Carone:** Jenkins. **"If you painted":** Q. by Carone. **"Say that again":** Q. by Carone. **"I don't teach art":** Carone. **Offer of trade:** Carone's wife, Adele Callaway: "Nick didn't take him up on it, though. He thought it would be mercenary." **Jackson at Davie show:** Viviano. **Desperate:** Ashton, q. in Potter, p. 220. **Lost at Glasco show:** Viviano. **"Has been":** Q. by Motherwell, q. in Potter, p. 220. **"He just took it":** Q. in Potter, p. 220; see account of same incident in "JP: An Artists' Symposium, Part I," p. 29. **Carone asking about**

Greenberg: Carone. **"Dear Jack":** Still to JP, Dec. 3, 1955. **Jackson crying; "Beyond being comforted":** Friedman. **"A terrible state":** Q. by Friedman. After receiving the catalogue and the invitation, Still wrote JP, Dec. 21, 1955, not exactly apologizing, but trying to normalize relations. **Joint celebration with Newman:** Annalee Newman, int. by Peretz. **Newman seeing Jackson weekly:** Barnett Newman, int. by Shorthall, Nov. 9, 1959: The meetings were at the Cedar. **Newman arguing against celebration:** Annalee Newman, int. by Peretz: He said the car needed new points and it was too cold to get them. *The Magic Flute;* **"getting away"; "back to the west"; "just a dream":** Barnett Newman, int. by Shorthall, Nov. 9, 1959. **Smiths visiting Springs:** Jane Smith. **"[Jackson] couldn't imagine":** Q. in DP&G, "Who Was JP?" p. 54. **"Threw a little":** Annalee Newman, int. by Peretz. **Jackson's solo visit to Smiths:** Jane Smith. **Sculpture:** The sculpture, about two feet by two feet, was described by and is currently in the possession of Jane Smith.
Setting mattress on fire: Shibley. **Meerts cooling to Jackson:** Cherry. **Jackson at Guston's party:** Robert Motherwell, q. in "JP," p. 29. **Trying to throw Guston out window:** Ashton, who thinks the party was at Mercedes Matter's "stable garage on MacDougal Alley"; see also Potter, p. 226. **"Only one man":** Q. by Carone. **Castelli's town house:** 4 East Seventy-seventh Street. **"The great Jackson":** Gorchov. **Jackson abusing Graham's paint supplies:** Gorchov; Mayer; Wilcox. **"How dare you"; "betrayed":** Q. by Gorchov. **Visit by Harry Jackson; "very mean":** Jackson. *Life* feature about Harry Jackson: The article appeared on July 9, 1956. **"I'm a fucking phony":** Q. in Kligman, p. 129. **"Crocodile tears":** Q. in Potter, p. 223. **"Isn't that a great painting?":** Q. by Abel. **"If five people":** Q. by Jenkins.
Proliferating galleries: Naifeh, p. 81: The number of galleries nearly doubled between 1955 and 1965. **"Gilt-edged":** Hodgins and Lesley, "The Great International Art Market: I," p. 150. **"Investments for the future"; "tyro collector":** Hodgins and Lesley, "The Great International Art Martket: I," p. 152. **Success of "revolution":** Brach, on the second generation: "They may have worn workers' caps and peasant boots, but they were all the sons of Red Army generals and went to the best schools"; see Brach, "Postscript," p. 32. **"Selling out"; "stealing his ideas":** Ferber. **"Merchandise":** Rothko, q. by Bultman, who lived on the same Upper East Side block as Rothko. **"The fellowship"; "crass young":** Seldes, p. 36. **Still backdating works:** CG: "Both Newman and Still backdated their paintings to make themselves more important. That's how dumb they were. They thought they could get away with it." **Greenberg a dealer:** A consultant to French & Co; CG.
Heller's background: Friedman. **Heller meeting Jackson in 1953:** Heller. **Introduced by Brach:** Brach. Heller, however, says he called JP "cold" in 1953 at the suggestion of Ossorio. **Rockefeller purchase; "for $500,000":** Heller. In fact, *Garçon au Gilet Rouge* was bought by Rockefeller in 1955, but not at auction, not from the Beatty collection, and not for $500,000. Bertha Saunders, curator of David Rockefeller's collection, would say only that the actual figure was considerably less than Heller remembers. **"Johnny-come-lately"; "operator":** Q. by Kligman. **Lee left to deal with Heller:** Little. The Vicentes: "Pollock did not have much interest in Heller." **Conversation with Heller; "more interesting":** Heller. **Heller's passion for music:** See Heller, q. in Potter, p. 186. **"To be a composer":** JP, q. by Heller. **Heller infatuated:** Brach: "It was hero worship." **Growing beard in imitation:** Little; Ossorio, int. by Shorthall, Nov. 9, 1959. **"The Impressionists"; "the Cubists":** Q. by Friedman, JP, p. xiv. Friedman: "Ben saw values earlier, that is dollar values. I am not talking about real values. Ben was a bit behind in terms of what was going on in New York and a bit more interested in investment." **Negotiations for Echo collapsing:** LK. **"Mixup"; "rather difficult"; visit to Springs:** Heller to JP, Dec. 20, 1955. **"Wow":** Q. in Friedman, JP, p. xiv. **Brach discouraging Blue Poles:** Brach. **Jackson reluctant to sell others:** Friedman, JP, p. xiv.
Number 31, 1950: OC&T 283, II, pp. 105–07. **"Twelve squares":** Heller. **"I wouldn't":** Q. by Heller. **Jackson wanting $10,000; Lee negotiating:** LK. **"In recognition":** Friedman, JP, p. 198. **Painting having to be curved; "I really don't like":** Heller. **Title found prosaic; asking to try again:** CG, q. in Potter, p. 187. **"I didn't understand":** Heller. **"Have been looking":** Heller to JP, Feb. 11, 1956.

"Torn between": Friedman, *JP*, p. xi. **Stevens and Ives:** Friedman, *JP*, p. xvi. **"Full of dizzying promise":** Tabak, "Collage," p. 555. **"A truly heroic"; encounter with Jackson:** Friedman, *JP*, pp. xi–xx. *Number 11, 1949:* OC&T 246, II, pp. 68–69 (45″ × 47¼″). **"One of the best":** Friedman, "The New Baroque," p. 13. **"Trained" under Valentin:** Friedman. **"I felt how much":** Friedman, *Almost a Life*, p. 125. **"The necessity":** Friedman to JP, n.d. **Biographical article:** Friedman, "Profile," p. 59. **"I doubt he ever read":** Friedman. **Surf and sand:** Friedman, q. in Potter, p. 224. **Naming son:** Jackson Friedman, born Feb. 28, 1957. **Introducing Friedmans to friends:** Cile Lord. **Cavorting in surf:** See Friedman, q. in Potter, p. 224. **Viewing** *Lavender Mist:* Friedman. **"Young dilettante":** Q. in Kligman, p. 134. **"Bordered in gold":** Name withheld by request. **Friedman idolizing Jackson:** See, e.g., Friedman, *JP*, p. 98.

Klein's office-apartment: Ghent: The apartment was on the south side of Eighty-sixth Street between Riverside Drive and West End Avenue. **Daily calls:** Ossorio, int. by Shorthall, Nov. 9, 1959, recalling the Elwyn Harrises, who shared a party line with the Pollocks. **"God-like powers":** Southgate, q. in Potter, p. 232. **"A psychiatrist":** Q. in Kligman, p. 108. **"I'm overjoyed":** Q. by CG. **Barnes Landing Group:** Pearce. **"Sullivan would have":** Ghent. **"Encouraged to have babies":** Nancy Smith. **Klein taking histories; devaluing traumatic incidents:** Pearce. **"That old womb":** Q. in Potter, p. 203. **"Maybe I paint":** Q. by Abel. **"You want to sleep":** Abel. **"Hated his mother":** CG. **Refusal to eat:** LK.

"Express himself": Pearce. **Klein complaining to Pearce:** Pearce. **No teetotaler herself:** Nancy Smith. **"Put up with it":** Pearce: Pearce believed that alcoholism was based neither on genetics nor on a chemical deficiency but rather on "anxiety." While some of her patients attended AA, others did not, and she did not require it. Even later, when it became much more conventional for a therapist to demand that a patient stop drinking before beginning analysis, she did not make it a requirement. **Klein's lack of advice on drinking:** Southgate; LK, q. by Glueck. **"Did you tell":** Marca-Relli. **"Yes, but":** Q. by Marca-Relli. **"Pipsqueak":** Southgate. **"Hey, wait a minute":** Southgate. **"Look at the stuff":** Q. by JP, q. by Heller. **"Go screw":** Q. by Marca-Relli.

Jackson hadn't lived enough: CG: "According to what Jackson said himself. **"No sex in three years:** Kligman. **"Act out":** Ghent. Nancy Smith, another patient, says she was "encouraged to express myself. The idea was that if someone you loved was expressing themselves and enjoying the company of another person, you could only be happy for them." CG: "Jackson had always been a sexual dud, so Ralph encouraged him to make for women." **"They're so beautiful":** Q. by Cile Downs (Lord), q. in Potter, p. 211. **"A lot of times":** Q. in Potter, p. 212. **"I don't know":** Q. by Tony Smith, q. in DP&G, "Who Was JP?" p. 54. **Josie Wilkinson incident:** Hopkins. **Poindexter incident:** Elinor Poindexter; Christie Poindexter Dennis. **"Express his romantic":** CG.

"Any number": Jane Smith. **Passes at Southgate:** Southgate, q. in Potter, p. 211. **Terrifying Marisol:** Marisol, q. in Gruen, p. 205. **"Cut it out":** Q. by Brach. **"You got great"; "what's the hurry?":** Q. by Budd. **"Beeline"; Flack rambunctious; "babe"; "this huge man":** Flack. **"Fucked Rita":** Friedman. **Matter and Peterson:** Marca-Relli: JP said this in Krasner's presence, obviously for her ears. Krasner later told Friedman that JP had slept with them. As indicated earlier, JP was lying about his associations with both women. **"Dames got their":** JP, q. in Potter, p. 212. **"Being involved"; only interested in women:** Kadish. **Blaming Lee's infertility:** Bultman. **Friedman's reaction:** Friedman, q. in Potter, pp. 212–13. **Call girl story:** Brach. **"A real dish":** Budd. **"No sexual action":** Brach. **Excuse for non-performance:** Schapiro. On a trip to Gerard Point, JP and Slivka saw two women standing across the inlet on Louse Point beach. "Jackson said, 'Dave, why don't we swim over there and fuck 'em both?' I said, 'Jackson, I'll let you swim over, and even if you only fuck one, I'll wait for you.' He said, 'Well, I don't know. . . . Got to have help. . . . Maybe it's not such a good idea. . . . It's kind of cold.' I said, 'That's what I figured.' "

Two o'clock: Carone, q. in Potter, p. 192. **In early 1956:** Carone: "It was the year of Jackson's death and very cold." **Previous occasions; "dump him on the doorstep":** Dragon. **Remainder of story:** Except where noted, Carone.

---

44. ESCAPE VELOCITY

SOURCES

Books, articles, manuscript, records, and transcripts

Friedman, *JP*; PG, *Out of This Century*; Kligman, *Love Affair*; Namuth, *Pollock Painting*; Potter, *To a Violent Grave*; Solomon, *JP*; Weld, *Peggy*.

DP&G, "Who Was JP?" *Art in America*, May–June 1967.

"Toll of Ten Lives in Motor Crashes, Saturday in S'ampton, E. Hampton," *East Hampton Star*, Aug. 16, 1956.

Ruth Kligman, "Just Like a Woman" (unpub. ms.) n.d.

Police Accident Report, East Hampton Town Police, #914, Aug. 11, 1956, submitted by Patrolman Earl Finch.

Elwyn Harris, int. by Kathleen Shorthall for *Life*, Nov. 9, 1959, in Time/Life Archives; Alfonso Ossorio, int. by Shorthall for *Life*, Nov. 9, 1959, in Time/Life Archives; Richard and Allene Talmage, int. by Shorthall for *Life*, Nov. 9, 1959, in Time/Life Archives.

Interviews

Norman Bluhm; Paul Brach; Charlotte Park Brooks; James Brooks; David Budd; Peter Busa; Nicholas Carone; Ted Dragon; Morton Feldman; Audrey Flack; Abby Friedman; B. H. Friedman; CG; Ben Heller; Paul Jenkins; Reuben Kadish; Ruth Kligman; LK; Ibram Lassaw; Joe Liss; Millie Liss; Terry Liss; Cile Downs Lord; Iris Lord; Conrad Marca-Relli; John Bernard Myers; Annalee Newman (int. by David Peretz); Alfonso Ossorio; CCP; FLP; Milton Resnick; May Tabak Rosenberg; Miriam Schapiro; Jane Smith; Nancy Smith; Stephanie Sonora; Patsy Southgate; Ronald Stein; Ruth Stein; Michael Stolbach; Samuel Wagstaff; Eleanor Ward; Joan Ward; Roger Wilcox; Betsy Zogbaum.

NOTES

Jackson beating Lee; Lee calling police: Wheeler. **Jackson threatening to leave:** Kadish. **Threatened institutionalization:** CG; Ronald Stein; Wheeler. Ronald Stein: "She never had any doubt that it wasn't going to happen. She knew Jackson would never voluntarily go into a hospital. It was so apparent that he didn't want to be cured."

Twenty-five-year-old: Ruth at times claimed she was twenty-one at the time she met JP, but the police accident report lists her age as twenty-five. **"Radiated":** Flack. **Kligman meeting Jackson:** See Kligman, pp. 26–34. **Bootie; mother disowned over Bootie:** Kligman. **Mary:** Iris Lord. **"Always crying":** Kligman, p. 165. **"Convinced we would win":** Kligman, p. 141. **"No brunettes allowed"; "The desirable one"; "monsters"; aunt forcing her to urinate; "his eyes"; "the light"; "going into the backyard":** Kligman. **"Ruthie has class":** Kligman, p. 22. **Wealthy family:** Kligman, "Just Like a Woman," p. 128. **Older men:** Iris Lord: Ruth was "the darling of older men." Kligman, "When I was in a position to pick, I'd alway pick the Big Daddy type. Because I wanted a Big Daddy. I was very spoiled." **"Baudelaire, Apollinaire"; "My rich daddy":** Kligman. **"Forgot about art":** Kligman. **"I took advantage":** Kligman, "Just Like a Woman," p. 104. **Second breakdown:** Kligman: "I had another nervous breakdown at twenty-one." **Job at Collectors Gallery:** Flack. **Vogue; beauty parlors; mirrors:** Kligman, p. 65. **"Went white"; "I need help"; "what are you":** Kligman, pp. 214–15.

"You want to know artists": Flack. Kligman told the authors the list was given to her, not by Flack, but by a painting teacher from Scarsdale recommended to her by her Jungian analyst. We accept Flack's recollection. **Kligman writing names down:** Flack, q. in Potter, p. 228. **"Which one":** Q. by Flack. **"Pollock":** Flack. **Kligman claiming she met Jackson on first visit:** See Kligman, p. 30: When JP finally appeared, "It made going to the Cedar Bar all those dead nights worthwhile. Jackson Pollock had finally shown up." **"Hero"; "as other girls":** Kligman, p. 59.

February 1956: Friedman, p. 232. **"Made a beeline":** Flack. **"The first moment":** Kligman. **"I couldn't take":** Kligman, p. 39. **Jackson barely remembering her:** Kligman. **"Dark-haired girl":** See Kligman, p. 40; Kligman's reconstruction of this conversation is somewhat different. **"Very persistent":** Sonora. **Two months:** Terry Liss; see also

Friedman, p. 232: "Pollock's relationship with Ruth Kligman began casually in February 1956 and intensified in the spring." **Jackson drunk:** Kligman claims he was sober, even though he came from the Cedar—an impossible notion; see Kligman, pp. 42–45. **Jackson convinced he'd had sex:** Krasner once told Stolbach that Kligman should have called *Love Affair* " 'My Five Fucks with Jackson Pollock'—because that's all there were!" Myers says the affair was later called "the famous fuck"—meaning that JP and Ruth had made love, at most, one time; when Krasner overheard a group discussing that scenario, she turned to them and said, *"Once?"* Kligman later told Sonora that JP was too drunk to make love the whole time she was with him.
"Woozy with drink"; "I can see": Budd. **"Why, Jackson":** De Kooning, q. by Kligman. **"Keep your hands":** Q. by Kligman. **"Can I see her":** Q. by Kligman. **Picture taking:** Carone. **"Late model cream puff":** Q. in Potter, p. 228. **"Brando and Monroe":** Kligman. **El Chico:** Kligman, p. 57. **Eddie Condon's:** May 14, 1956; B. H. Friedman to authors, Feb. 27, 1984. **Broadway shows:** Kligman: E.g., *Waiting for Godot*. **"Like stars":** Kligman, p. 58. **"In the real world":** Kligman, p. 47. **"Rich-looking"; "glamorous":** Kligman, p. 58. **"Instead of staying":** B. H. Friedman, recalling Kligman.
Kligman flattering: B. H. Friedman. **Lovers' games:** Kligman, p. 81. **Jackson slapping her; swooning:** Kligman; see also Kligman, p. 152. **"Old Wise Man"; "Lover":** Kligman, p. 88. **A virgin; she didn't argue:** Kligman. **Little, if any, sex:** Sonora, recalling Kligman. **Ruth preferring it that way; "metaphorical":** Kligman: "Sexuality is for me a metaphor." **Having desirable woman enough for Jackson:** Terry Liss. **Professing love for Kligman to Southgate:** Southgate, q. in Potter, p. 231. **Lee there during calls:** Kligman; also Kligman, p. 54. **"Just how old":** Q. by B. H. Friedman. **"Permanent arrangements":** B. H. Friedman. **"An amazing adventure":** Q. in Potter, p. 231. **"Express himself":** CG, recalling JP. **"Fuck appearances":** CG. **"Expressing himself and enjoying":** Nancy Smith. **Jackson knowing Lee's vulnerability:** Marca-Relli.
Friends avoiding Jackson and Ruth: Friedman, p. 233. **"Oh, fuck off":** Braider, q. in Potter, p. 231. **"I will *never*":** Q. by Cile Downs (Lord), q. in Potter, p. 233. **Proposed trip to Europe:** LK. **Job at Rattner School; unaware this would bring them together:** Kligman, p. 72. This claim is difficult to take seriously, since Kligman had been to East Hampton often and had ridden the train, which stops in Sag Harbor. **Condescending looks:** Kligman. **"In case someone invited":** Kligman, p. 76. **Dinner at Elm Tree Inn:** Kligman, p. 79. **"*Zaftig* chick":** Ibram Lassaw. **"His grin":** Potter, p. 228. **"Frightened-looking":** Kligman, p. 84. **"Juggling whiskey":** Friedman, pp. 225–26. **Isaacs's visit:** Isaacs. **"Lifelike"; "too involved"; "in shape":** Isaacs, q. in Potter, p. 230. **"Trapped":** JP, q. by Kligman. **"Talked about Jackson's":** Nancy Smith. **Kligman told to sever relationship:** Kligman, p. 71. **"Understand"; owed Lee "something":** Q. in Kligman, p. 162. **Pregnancy:** Kligman. When Kligman was told, "Jackson told people he had impregnated a woman during the last year of his life," she responded, "No, he didn't. He thought it was me, but it wasn't."
Jackson boasting to Greenberg: CG: "He got someone pregnant that last year. He was so proud that he could." **"He wasn't shooting blanks":** Heller. **"Family stock":** See Kligman, pp. 86–87. **Life with both women; Ruth accusing Jackson of cowardice:** Kligman. **"Thrilled with the idea":** Kligman; see also Kligman, p. 87. **"She'll be well":** Q. in Kligman, p. 86. **"She was white":** Kligman, p. 95. **Always making up:** Jane Smith. **Lee fixing drink; buying Lee a ticket:** Southgate. **"Anxious for the whole":** Dragon. **"Trial separation":** Southgate. **"We've been fighting":** Q. by Southgate. **"Let her go":** Q. by JP, q. by Kligman. **Dream of Jackson as Jesus:** Jenkins, who heard it from Krasner in the Luxembourg Gardens on the day JP died. **July 12:** SMP to FLP, July 23, 1956. **Day Schnabel:** A sculptor. **"Devastated"; "that Jackson":** Newman, int. by Peretz. **"I can't go"; "oh, I just":** Q. by Carol Braider, q. in Solomon, p. 247. **"My doctor's":** Q. by Ossorio, int. by Shorthall, Nov. 9, 1959.
Kligman arriving in Springs: Contrary to the account in Kligman's book, Rosenberg and Wilcox remember that, even on her first trip, Kligman came to Springs with a friend or friends, and that she was never alone with JP. **Sleeping late:** Kligman, p. 185. **Panties:** Kligman, p. 132. **Kligman admiring house:** Kligman, p. 103. **"Awesome"; "in my twenty-**

one": Kligman, p. 104. **Calling "famous" artists:** Kligman. **Meals and movies:** Kligman, p. 147. **Watching television:** Kligman, pp. 109, 154. **"Where nobody":** Q. in Kligman, p. 111. **"Very touching"; "he was wonderful":** Kligman. **"Got rid of Lee":** Terry Liss.
"Effect of Lee's departure on relationship with Ruth: Terry Liss; B. H. Friedman: "It couldn't have helped his relationship with Ruth that Lee was out of the country, because Lee was not there to be hurt by this thing." **Jackson deciding not to attend parties:** B. H. Friedman. **Dragging Kligman away:** Friedman, p. 233. **Overdressing and makeup:** B. H. Friedman; Kligman, p. 107. **"I don't like":** Q. by Kligman. **Jackson irritable:** Kligman, p. 130. **Pushing her away:** Kligman. **Sitting far away:** CG; Kligman, p. 130. **Snapping at her:** Kligman, p. 116. **Bullying her friends:** See incident with Abe Glasser in Kligman, pp. 154–59. **Fighting with her:** James Brooks. **"Why the hell":** Q. in Kligman, p. 127. **Early to bed:** Kligman. **Roses:** LK to JP, July 21, 1956. **Lee out when roses arrived:** LK. **"The painting here"; gardens and flea markets; "dancing like mad":** LK to JP, July 22, 1956. **Jenkinses:** Jenkins. **Traveler's checks from Heller:** Heller. **Lee seeing friends:** All except Heller from LK to JP, July 22, 1956. **Gimpels:** LK, q. in Weld, p. 387. **Bluhm and Graham:** Bluhm. **Rarely speaking of Jackson:** Jenkins. **"As poor as Jackson":** Q. by Jenkins. **Seeing Graham:** Graham. **"I miss you":** LK to JP, July 22, 1956.
"Devilish game": Kligman, p. 117. **Resenting Jackson:** Kligman, p. 117. **Resenting his treatment in front of company:** See, e.g., Kligman, p. 116. **As if she wasn't there:** See, e.g., Kligman, p. 119. **The way he talked about her:** Friedman, p. 233. **Driving around:** See Potter, p. 235. **Leaving her in car at Carone's:** Eleanor Ward, q. in Potter, p. 235. **"Why have you":** Q. by Cile Downs (Lord), q. in Potter, p. 254. **"Are you a psychotic?":** Q. in Kligman, p. 169. **Friends refusing to see her:** Cile Lord. **"Hostile":** Marca-Relli; see also Marca-Relli, q. in Potter, p. 253. **Dinner with Lords:** Cile Lord. **Reaction to Jackson's meanness:** Cile Downs (Lord), q. in Potter, p. 253. **"Jackson's girl":** B. H. Friedman. **"Rather earthy":** Brach. **"Not East Hampton":** B. H. Friedman. **"His friends obviously":** Kligman, p. 137. **Bennington girls snubbing Ruth:** Kligman, p. 122; Nancy Smith. **"A piece of furniture":** Kligman, p. 122. **Discussion of friendship:** Nancy Smith. **"[Clem] asked [Jackson]":** Kligman, p. 122. **"[He] treated us":** Kligman, p. 123. **"It's very complicated":** Q. in Kligman, p. 123.
Elaborate meals uneaten: Kligman, p. 153. **"I owe the woman":** Q. in Kligman, p. 162. **"All live together":** Q. in Kligman, p. 161. **No effort to change will:** Ossorio. **"Cast aside":** Kligman, p. 152. **"Bored to death":** Wagstaff. **Friedman party:** B. H. Friedman. **"Coquettish":** Abby Friedman. **"A woman like this":** B. H. Friedman. **"Fuck you":** Kligman, q. by Wagstaff. **"Don't brag":** Q. in Namuth, n.p. **Friedman given choice of drawings:** B. H. Friedman. Friedman says he chose the smallest (OC&T 704, III, p. 211). **Ruth's gift disappearing:** Friedman; CG; Kligman. **Humiliating Ruth at Norman party:** James Brooks. **"In a white rage"; "like a broken doll":** Kligman, pp. 168–69. **Jackson slapping her before and Ruth liking it:** Kligman; see also, e.g., Kligman, p. 152; Friedman, p. 235. **"Beat her up"; "real violence":** Terry Liss. **Return to New York:** Kligman, p. 171. Kligman's book is intentionally obscure on dating. But JP was alone for at least a week prior to his death. This means that if she left on a Thursday, as she claimed, it had to be August 2.
Wandering on beach: Ibram Lassaw. **Walking by roadside:** Joe Liss. **Parked in front of houses:** Carone. **Calling Wilcox:** Wilcox. **Calling the Smiths:** Jane Smith. **Dog incident; "like the walking dead":** Carone. **"The dog died":** Q. by Carone. **"Disillusioned with Ruth":** Carone. **Lee's week in the Midi; spurned by Peggy:** LK to JP, from Saint-Rémy-de-Provence, n.d. **"Everything I had done":** PG, p. 288. **Guggenheim's gifts:** She gave away *Galaxy* (OC&T 169, I, pp. 166–67) in 1949; *Watery Paths* (OC&T 171, I, pp. 168–69) in 1950; *Magic Lantern* (OC&T 172, I, p. 170) in 1954; *The Nest* (OC&T 174, I, p. 172); *Reflections of the Big Dipper* (OC&T 175, I, pp. 172–73) in 1950; *Prism* (OC&T 176, I, p. 174) in 1954; *Full Fathom Five* (OC&T 180, I, p. 178) in 1952; and *Phosphorescence* (OC&T 183, I, pp. 182–83) in 1950. She retained only *Enchanted Forest* (OC&T 173, I, p. 171), *Sea Change* (OC&T 177, I, pp. 174–75), and *Alchemy* (OC&T 179, I, p. 177) at the time of JP's death.

Refused to find a room: Weld, p. 387. **Staying with Jenkins:** Jenkins.
Calling Lee's friends: Zogbaum; Cile Lord; Southgate. **Not too late or drunk:** Zogbaum. **Fingernail incident:** Nancy Smith. **Never calling Kligman:** Kligman; Wagstaff; see Kligman, p. 185: Although she compresses the time to two days, Kligman says only that *she* called JP. Carone remembers specifically that he visited JP on a Sunday before his death and Ruth was in New York. That would have to have been Sunday, August 5. In her account, Kligman does not acknowledge being in New York except on the Thursday and Friday immediately before Saturday, August 11. **Walking property:** James Brooks. **"My God":** Q. in DP&G, "Who Was JP?" p. 52. **Potter fence:** Potter, p. 215. **Pile of boulders:** Potter, p. 253. **"You know I'm a painter":** Q. in Kligman, p. 127. **"I'm no good":** Q. in Kligman, p. 129.
"Your case"; "the thing to do"; "I sometimes feel": LRP to JP, Dec. 11, 1927. **Urinating on rocks:** Potter, p. 253. **"In this life":** LRP to JP, Dec. 11, 1927. **Letter in kitchen drawer; Jackson sobbing:** Carone. **"Is it that":** Still to JP, Dec. 1955. **August 9 call:** Kligman; Jane Smith; see also Tony Smith, q. in DP&G, "Who Was JP?" p. 54. **"Sullen"; "lost":** Kligman, p. 185. **Canceling visit with Smith:** Smith, q. in DP&G, "Who Was JP?" p. 54. **Smith's return:** Jane Smith. **"We talked":** Q. in DP&G, "Who Was JP?" p. 54. **"Get into portraits"; "do a lot":** Jane Smith, recalling Tony. **Visit to Stony Hill Farm:** Penny Potter, q. in Potter, p. 237. **Four cases of beer:** Harris, int. by Shorthall, Nov. 9, 1959. **"Drunk and babbling":** Cile Lord. **Trying to sleep:** Friedman, p. 233. **Not seeing Marca-Relli for weeks:** Marca-Relli. **"Now that Jackson":** Marca-Relli; see also Friedman, p. 254. **"God, that's a great"; "life is beautiful":** Q. by Marca-Relli; see similar account in Friedman, p. 253.
Fight over building jack: Potter, p. 238. **"I hated the impression":** Kligman, p. 189. **"Eye-opener":** Cavagnaro, q. in Potter, p. 239. **Kligman crushed by cat's disappearance:** Kligman, p. 190. **"Maybe Blanche":** Kligman, p. 199. **"Don't count":** Q. in Kligman, p. 199. **Edith twenty-five:** "Toll of Ten Lives in Motor Crashes." **Description of Metzger:** Kligman, p. 65. **German Jew who fled Nazis:** Iris Lord. **Manicurist:** Terry Liss. **Receptionist:** Kligman. **Ended relationship; "let your fantasy":** Kligman, p. 187. **"Meeting" Goering:** Kligman, p. 193. **Jackson not interested in Metzger:** Kligman, p. 189. **Dishes in sink:** Cile Lord. **Looking for kitten; Jackson interrogating dogs:** Kligman, p. 190. **Photograph:** In possession of Kligman. **Jackson driving by beach:** Kligman. **Ruth and Edith left alone:** Kligman, p. 192. **Refusing coffee:** Kligman, p. 196. **Kligman wanting to go to party:** Kligman. **Three dollars per person:** CG. **"Maybe it would be fun":** Kligman, p. 197. **"Didn't want to face":** Ossorio, int. by Shorthall, Nov. 9, 1959. **"Lovely scoop neckline":** Kligman, p. 199. **Edith's and Jackson's attire:** Memo from Harry M. Steele, chief, East Hampton Town Police, to John H. Nugent, coroner, Suffolk County, N.Y., Aug. 12, 1956. **Still bickering in car:** Kligman.
"Ruth, he's drunk": Q. in Kligman, p. 200. **"Good evening":** Policeman, q. in Kligman, p. 200, **"Nothing's wrong":** Q. in Kligman, p. 200. **"Pasty"; "Hey, Jackson":** Wilcox. **"I don't feel":** Q. by Wilcox. **Driving to bar:** In her book, Kligman identifies the bar as the Cottage Inn, although she says they did not go inside; Wilcox believes it was Cavagnaro's, because of its convenient location, but Cavagnaro doesn't remember JP coming in that night with Ruth and Edith. If JP fell asleep in the car, however, Cavagnaro might not have recognized the two women alone.

Ossorio introducing Hambro: Ossorio; Ossorio, int. by Shorthall, Nov. 9, 1959. **Maid taking message:** Ossorio. **"Call for help":** Q. in Kligman, p. 200. **"Get her back":** Q. by Kligman. **"He's drunk":** Q. in Kligman, p. 201. **"No, he's not":** Kligman: "She didn't want to get back in the car. I made her." **Edith in back seat:** Kligman. **"Stop the car":** Q. in Kligman, p. 201. **"Edith, stop"; "please, Jackson":** Kligman, p. 201. **Jackson leaning forward:** Joan Ward. **"Expected to lift off":** Kligman. **"Let me out":** Metzger, q. in Kligman, p. 201. **Description of road; Jackson slowing down there:** Wilcox. **High crown in road:** Richard and Allene Talmage, int. by Shorthall, Nov. 9, 1959. **Description of accident:** Official Police Accident Report, East Hampton Town Police, #914, Aug. 11, 1956; Kligman; on-scene witness recollections, q. in Potter, pp. 240-46. **"This is it":** Kligman.
Trajectory: Earl Finch, q. in Potter, p. 244. Finch bases his estimate on the place where JP hit the tree that killed him. "He might have survived if he'd missed it." There is some discrepancy between witnesses on the scene, including Finch, and the official report, which says that JP's body was found only nine feet west of the car. Other witnesses say that the body was far back in the woods and took some time to find. Even Finch, who prepared the official report, says that JP flew fifty feet before hitting the tree; see Potter, p. 244. **Lee hearing about Jackson's death:** Jenkins.

EPILOGUE: GLACIAL ERRATIC

SOURCES

See Chapter 44.

NOTES

Funeral service: "Toll of Ten Lives," Aug. 16, 1956. **Namuth trying to take photo:** Frederick Williams, q. in Potter, pp. 249-50. **Lee refusing to sit with Pollocks:** FLP. **"Where were you":** Q. by Ruth Stein. **"It made me think":** Gina Knee, q. in Potter, p. 258. **Greenberg asked to give eulogy; "the girl Jackson killed":** CG, q. in Potter, p. 253. **Reverend George Nicholson:** Potter, p. 254. **Irrelevant:** Brach; Heller; Resnick. **Kadish wailing:** FLP. **Grave site:** Superintendent Jarvis Wood, q. in Potter, pp. 254-55: LK paid $300 for the plots. **Pallbearers:** Potter, p. 256. **Sande and Kadish near dogs:** Feldman. **Weeping:** FLP. **De Kooning and others lingering:** Resnick. **Potter hauling stone from backyard:** Potter, p. 269. **Little finding new stone:** Little, q. in Potter, p. 269. **Forty-ton rock:** Harry Cullum, q. in Potter, p. 269. **Potter digging rock out of ground:** Potter, pp. 269-70.
Stella's return to Tingley: She left on October 18, 1956 (SMP to Irene Crippen, Jan. 6, 1957) for a trip to see her brother Cameron in Pittsburgh. **"I just had to do":** SMP to Irene Crippen, Jan. 6, 1957. **"Circulatory problems":** Mary Kreuzer to MLP and FLP, Mar. 22, 1958. **Sande dying:** Les McClure to Irene and Harold Crippen, Mar. 4, 1964. For leukemia, see Kadish. Charles says it was lymphoma—cancer of the lymph glands. **Arloie after Sande's death:** SWP. **Lee painting out of *Easter and the Totem*:** CG: "Krasner spent the rest of her career painting out of that picture." **Lee dying; "natural causes":** Ruth Stein.

CREDITS

See page 807 for key to abbreviations.

Pages viii, 534, 620, 622, 650, 666, 668, 709: Hans Namuth; 9, 42, 52, 61, 66, 101, 106, 111, 116, 117, 140 (right), 159, 193, 289, 522, 618, 775: Courtesy JP Papers, AAA, Smithsonian Institution; 11, 16: Courtesy Irene Crippen; 17, 23, 51, 94, 230: Courtesy FLP; 19, 30: Courtesy Clair B. Heyer; 35, 37, 133, 307: Courtesy ACM; 38, 39, 78, 643, 725: Courtesy MJP; 48, 77, 153, 292: Courtesy CCP Papers, AAA, Smithsonian Institution; 56: Courtesy Allan Mori; 60: Authors' collection; 70: Courtesy Evelyn Porter Trowbridge; 74, 76, 98, 569: Courtesy CCP; 75, 84: Gregory White Smith; 82: Courtesy Tim Purdy; 95: Courtesy Evelyn Minsch McGinn; 113: Courtesy Robert Cooter; 115: Courtesy Riverside Polytechnic High School; 124: Courtesy Elizabeth Duncan; 130, 138, 140 (left): Courtesy Krishnamurti Foundation of America; 157: Philip Goldstein (Guston) / Courtesy Karleen Marienthal, Manual Arts High School, Los Angeles; 148: Courtesy Berthe Laxineta; 151: Courtesy Harold Lehman; 154: Courtesy Pomona College, Claremont, CA; 157, 496: Herbert Matter / Courtesy Mercedes Matter and JP Papers, AAA, Smithsonian Institution; 165, 221, 301: Courtesy Pollock-Krasner Foundation, Inc., and Metropolitan Museum of Art, NY; 171, 285, 383, 423: Courtesy Peter A. Juley and Son Collection, National Museum of American Art, Smithsonian Institution; 174, 181 (left): Courtesy Larry A. James; 174, 184: Courtesy Polly Burroughs; 173: Courtesy Kansas City Art Institute and Nelson-Atkins Museum of Art, Kansas City, MO; 187 (left), 282 (right): Courtesy Lyman Field and United Missouri Bank of Kansas City, N.A., Co-Trustees of the Thomas Hart and Rita P. Benton Testamentary Trusts; 187 (right), 191: Courtesy Mr. and Mrs. John W. Mecom, Jr. / photo: Norlene Tips; 189, 190: Courtesy Equitable Life Assurance Society of the U.S.; 208: Courtesy private collection, New York; 209: Courtesy Spencer Museum of Art, University of Kansas, Elizabeth M. Watkins Fund; 210: Alfred Eisenstaedt, *Life* magazine, © Time, Inc.; 221 (right), 252: Courtesy Pollock-Krasner Foundation, Inc. / photo: Zindman/Fremont; 244: Courtesy Jason McCoy; 245: Courtesy Sculptors' Guild Papers, AAA, Smithsonian Institution; 248: Courtesy Alexandra Cromwell; 249: Courtesy Gerald Peters Gallery, Santa Fe, NM; 250: Courtesy Canajoharie Library and Art Gallery, Canajoharie, NY; 251: Courtesy National Museum of American Art, Smithsonian Institution, Washington, DC; 253, 751: Courtesy Robert Miller Gallery, New York; 261: Courtesy Reuben Kadish; 280: Courtesy Albright-Knox Art Gallery, Buffalo, NY, Martha Jackson Collection, 1974; 282 (left): Courtesy Nelson-Atkins Museum of Art, Kansas City, MO, gift of Rita P. Benton; 283: Courtesy Robert P. Miller; 299, 300: Copyright © 1986, Courtesy Trustees of Dartmouth College, Hanover, NH; 304: Courtesy Rebecca Hicks; 316: Courtesy Medical Archives of the New York Hospital–Cornell Medical Center; 323: Courtesy R. A. Ellison / photo: R. A. Ellison; 328: Courtesy Joseph Henderson;

332, 351: Courtesy Maxwell Galleries, Ltd., San Francisco; 335: Courtesy Phyllis and David Adelson, Brookline, MA / photo courtesy Nielsen Gallery, Boston, MA; 338: Collection of Whitney Museum of American Art. Purchase, with funds from the Drawing Committee and the Julia B. Engel Purchase Fund. 85.18; 343: Courtesy Hedda Sterne; 352 (left): Courtesy University Museum, University of Pennsylvania (neg. # 134052); 352 (right): Courtesy Tate Gallery, London; 353: Courtesy Musée Picasso, Paris / © Photo R.M.N.—SPADEM; 362: Courtesy Violet de Laszlo; 368, 369, 370, 549: Courtesy Ruth Stein; 376, 387, 640: Courtesy LK; 378: Courtesy Bettmann Archive; 380: Courtesy Ronald Stein; 392: Ronald Stein / Courtesy Ruth Stein; 394: Courtesy Menil Collection, Houston, TX / photo: Hickey & Robertson, Houston; 419: George Platt Lynes / Courtesy MOMA, New York; 436: Gisele Freund / Courtesy PhotoResearchers, Inc., and Jacqueline Bograd Weld; 440: Berenice Abbott / Courtesy Commerce Graphics Ltd., Inc., and Jacqueline Bograd Weld; 453, 729: Courtesy Musée National d'Art Moderne, Centre National d'Art et de Culture Georges Pompidou, Paris; 457 (left): Reuben Kadish; and 457 (right): Jackson Pollock / Courtesy Reuben Kadish; 456: Courtesy San Francisco Museum of Modern Art, Albert M. Bender Collection, Albert M. Bender Bequest Fund Purchase, 45.1308; 458: Courtesy Metropolitan Museum of Art, New York, Purchase, Rogers, Fletcher and Harris Brisbane Dick Funds and Joseph Pulitzer Bequest, 1982 (1982.20); 487: Courtesy Photography Collection, Harry Ransom Humanities Research Center, University of Texas at Austin; 493: Courtesy Merle Hubbard; 495: Courtesy Mr. and Mrs. Harry W. Anderson, Atherton, CA; 505, 626: Martha Holmes / Courtesy *Life* magazine, © 1949 Time, Inc.; 513: Courtesy Jason McCoy, Inc.; 517: Ronald Stein / Courtesy JP Papers, AAA, Smithsonian Institution; 518: Courtesy Art Institute of Chicago, gift of Mr. and Mrs. Edward Morris through Exchange, 1987.261, copyright © 1989 The Art Institute of Chicago; 519: Rudolph Burckhardt; 525: Courtesy MOMA, New York, bequest of LK; 526: Lost / photo courtesy Maxwell Galleries, Ltd., San Francisco; 527: Courtesy Thomas Ammann Fine Art AG Zurich; 530, 544, 582: Courtesy Roger Wilcox; 537: Courtesy Joslyn Art Museum, Omaha, NE, gift of Peggy Guggenheim; 538: Courtesy Robert P. and Arlene R. Kogod, Washington, DC; 546: Jon Naar, copyright © 1963, 1989; 554: Courtesy Dallas Museum of Art, gift of Mr. and Mrs. Bernard J. Reis; 563: Courtesy Harry Jackson / Copyright Wyoming Foundry Studios, Inc., 1980; 567: Courtesy Nationalmuseum, Moderna Museet, Stockholm; 589: Ben Schultz / Courtesy Peter Blake; 590 (left): Courtesy Peter Getty, New York; 590 (right): Collection of Wellesley College Museum, bequest of Merrill Miller Lake, Class of 1936; 595: © Arnold Newman / Courtesy *Life* magazine, © 1949, 1977 Time, Inc., and Betty Parsons Gallery;

598: © Studio ARAx / Courtesy Ted Dragon; 603: Nina
Leen / Courtesy *Life* magazine, © 1951 Time, Inc.; 614:
Lawrence Larkin / Courtesy JP Papers, AAA, Smithsonian
Institution; 616: Courtesy Kunstammlung Nordrhein-West-
falen, Dusseldorf; 617: Courtesy Metropolitan Museum of Art,
New York, George A. Hearn Fund, 1957 (57.92); 641: Cour-
tesy Museum of Fine Arts, Houston, Sarah Campbell Blaffer
Foundation Funds and museum purchase; 651: Courtesy Na-
tional Gallery of Canada, Ottawa; 665: Courtesy Staatsgalerie,
Stuttgart, West Germany; 669: Courtesy MOMA, New York,
acquired through the Lillie P. Bliss Bequest and the Mr. and
Mrs. David Rockefeller Fund; 671: Hans Namuth / Courtesy
Alfonso Ossorio; 685: Courtesy Sidney Janis; 697: Paul Fee-
ley / Courtesy Helen Wheelwright; 702, 711: Courtesy May
Rosenberg and Patia Rosenberg-Yasin; 717: Courtesy Solo-
mon R. Guggenheim Museum, New York; 718: Selden Rodman; 726: Courtesy Mr. and Mrs. Robert Meyerhoff,
Baltimore; 730: Courtesy Dallas Museum of Art, gift of Algur
H. Meadows and the Meadows Foundation Incorporated; 734:
© Arnold Newman; 757: John Reed / Courtesy Phyllis Reed
and JP Papers, AAA, Smithsonian Institution; 760: Ted Ya-
mashira / Courtesy Adele Callaway; 767: Courtesy B. H.
Friedman; 790: Edith Metzger / Courtesy Ruth Kligman;
795: Susan Wood, © 1984.

COLOR INSERT

Page 1 (top): Courtesy Pollock-Krasner Foundation, Inc., and
Gerald Peters Gallery, Santa Fe, NM; 1 (bottom): Courtesy
Mr. and Mrs. Gerald P. Peters, Santa Fe, N.M.; 2 (top): Cour-
tesy Tate Gallery, London; 2 (bottom): Courtesy MOMA, New
York, bequest of LK; 3 (top), 4 (bottom), 6 (top and bottom), 7
(top), 8 (bottom): Courtesy MOMA, New York; 3 (bottom):
Courtesy Peggy Guggenheim Collection, Venice, and
Solomon R. Guggenheim Foundation, New York /
photo: David Heald; 4 (top): Courtesy Philadelphia Museum
of Art, partial gift of Mrs. H. Gates Lloyd, no. 215, Accession
Number 174-232.1; 5 (top): Courtesy University of Iowa Mu-
seum of Art, gift of Peggy Guggenheim, 195.9.6 / photo:
Randall Tosh; 5 (bottom): Collection Frieder Burda, Baden-
Baden, West Germany; 7 (bottom): Courtesy National Gallery
of Art, Washington, DC, Ailsa Mellon Bruce Fund; 8 (top):
Courtesy Australian National Gallery, Canberra.

**Grateful acknowledgment is made to all those who
granted permission to use previously unpublished materials:** James Brooks; Jeanne Bultman; Stephen J. Campbell
of the United Missouri Bank of Kansas City, n.a., for the Trustees of the Thomas Hart and Rita P. Benton Testamentary
Trusts; Donnelly Lee Casto; Irene Crippen; Whitney Darrow,
Jr.; Michael de Laszlo for Violet de Laszlo; Ted Dragon; Elizabeth Duncan; Clement Greenberg; Ben Heller; Clair B.
Heyer; Rebecca Hicks; Merle Hubbard; Reuben Kadish; Jacob
Kainen; Lillian Kiesler; Carolyn Knute; Lee Krasner; Melvin
P. Lader; Berthe Laxineta; Harold Lehman; Karleen Marien-
thal for Manual Arts High School, Los Angeles; Arloie
McCoy; William McNaught, Archives of American Art,
Smithsonian Institution; Daniel T. Miller, Jr.; Robert Moth-
erwell; John Bernard Myers; Sophia Mumford; Annalee New-
man; Alfonso A. Ossorio; Charles Pollock; Frank Pollock for
himself and for the Estates of Roy and Stella Pollock; Jay
Pollock; William P. Raynor for the Betty Parsons Estate; Patia
M. Rosenberg-Yasin for May Tabak Rosenberg; Patricia Still;
Eugene Victor Thaw for the Pollock-Krasner Foundation,
Inc.; Irving Sandler; Dorothy Seiberling; Jane L. Smith; Ron-
ald Stein; Araks V. Tolegian; Aram Tolegian.

INDEX